HARRAP

PAPERBACK
PORTUGUESE
DICTIONARY

English-Portuguese/Portuguese-English

This edition published in Great Britain 2001
by Chambers Harrap Publishers Ltd
7 Hopetoun Crescent, Edinburgh EH7 4AY

© Havas Éducation Référence 1999
Reprinted 2002

ISBN 0 245 60699 8

HARRAP

PAPERBACK
PORTUGUESE
DICTIONARY

English-Portuguese/Portuguese-English

HARRAP

OS COMPOSTOS EM INGLÊS

Em inglês os compostos são vocábulos com um só significado, mas formados por mais de uma palavra; por exemplo **point of view**, **kiss of life**, **virtual reality** ou **West Indies**. Uma das características deste dicionário é o fato de os compostos terem uma entrada própria e seguirem rigorosamente a ordem alfabética. Assim, **blood poisoning** figura depois de **bloodhound** que por seu lado surge depois de **blood donor**.

ENGLISH COMPOUNDS

A compound is a word or expression which has a single meaning but is made up of more than one word, e.g. **point of view**, **kiss of life**, **virtual reality** and **West Indies**. It is a feature of this dictionary that English compounds appear in the A-Z list in strict alphabetical order. The compound **blood poisoning** will therefore come after **bloodhound** which itself follows **blood donor**.

MARCAS REGISTRADAS

O símbolo ® indica que a palavra em questão é uma marca registrada. Este símbolo, ou a sua eventual ausência, não afeta, no entanto, a situação legal da marca.

TRADEMARKS

Words considered to be trademarks have been designated in this dictionary by the symbol ®. However, neither the presence nor the absence of such designation should be regarded as affecting the legal status of any trademark.

AO LEITOR

Este dicionário é ideal para atender às necessidades do estudante de inglês, seja aprendendo a língua na escola ou em casa, seja em viagens ao exterior.

É um referência prática criada para fornecer respostas claras e precisas para os inúmeros problemas encontrados no estudo da língua inglesa. Com 40 000 palavras e expressões e 55 000 traduções, incluindo abreviaturas e substantivos próprios, o dicionário permite ao usuário entender e apreciar uma grande variedade de textos.

Graças a uma cobertura detalhada do vocabulário básico da língua inglesa e a indicadores de sentido que possibilitam uma tradução acurada, escrever em inglês corretamente e com segurança deixou de ser um problema.

Não hesite em enviar-nos as suas sugestões ou dúvidas, pois elas poderão ser muito úteis e ajudar a tornar este dicionário ainda melhor.

A EDITORA

TO OUR READERS

This dictionary is ideal for all your language needs, from language learning at school and at home to traveling abroad.

This handy reference is designed to provide fast and clear solutions to the various problems encountered when studying present-day Portuguese. With 40,000 references and 55,000 translations, including many common abbreviations and proper names, it enables the user to understand and enjoy a wide range of reading material.

Writing idiomatic Portuguese with confidence is no longer a problem thanks to the dictionary's detailed coverage of essential vocabulary and helpful sense-markers which guide the user to the most appropriate translation.

Send us your comments or queries – you will be helping to make this dictionary an even better book.

THE PUBLISHER

ABREVIATURAS		ABBREVIATIONS
abreviatura	*abrev/abbr*	abbreviation
adjetivo	*adj*	adjective
adjetivo feminino	*adj f*	feminine adjective
adjetivo masculino	*adj m*	masculine adjective
advérbio	*adv*	adverb
inglês americano	*Am*	American English
anatomia	*ANAT*	anatomy
automóvel	*AUT*	automobile, cars
auxiliar	*aux*	auxiliary
português do Brasil	*Br*	Brazilian Portuguese
inglês britânico	*Brit*	British English
comércio	*COM(M)*	commerce, business
comparativo	*comp(ar)*	comparative
informática	*COMPUT*	computers
conjunção	*conj*	conjunction
contínuo	*cont*	continuous
culinária	*CULIN*	culinary, cooking
economia	*ECON*	economics
educação, escola	*EDUC*	school, education
esporte	*ESP*	sport
interjeição	*excl*	exclamation
substantivo feminino	*f*	feminine noun`
familiar	*fam*	informal
figurado	*fig*	figurative
finanças	*FIN*	finance, financial
formal	*fml*	formal
inseparável	*fus*	inseparable

inseparável — indica que o "phrasal verb" (verbo + preposição ou advérbio) não pode ser separado, colocando-se o objeto entre o verbo e a segunda partícula da locução, p. ex. com **look after** diz-se *I looked after him* mas não *I looked him after*

inseparable — shows that a phrasal verb is "fused", i.e. inseparable, e.g. **look after** where the object cannot come between the verb and the particle, e.g. *I looked after him* but not *I looked him after*

geralmente	*gen*	generally
gramática	*GRAM(M)*	grammar
familiar	*inf*	informal
informática	*INFORM*	computers
interjeição	*interj*	exclamation
invariável	*inv*	invariable
jurídico	*JUR*	juridical, legal
substantivo masculino	*m*	masculine noun
matemática	*MAT(H)*	mathematics

VII

medicina	MED	medicine
substantivo masculino e feminino	mf	masculine and feminine noun
substantivo masculino com desinência feminina	m, f	masculine noun with a feminine inflection
termos militares	MIL	military
música	MÚS/MUS	music
substantivo	n	noun
termos náuticos	NÁUT/NAUT	nautical, maritime
numeral	num	numeral
	o.s.	oneself
pejorativo	pej	pejorative
plural	pl	plural
política	POL	politics
português de Portugal	Port	European Portuguese
particípio passado	pp	past participle
preposição	prep	preposition
pronome	pron	pronoun
passado	pt	past tense
marca registrada	®	registered trademark
religião	RELIG	religion
substantivo	s	noun
alguém	sb	somebody
educação, escola	SCH	school, education
inglês escocês	Scot	Scottish English
separável	sep	separable

– indica que o "phrasal verb" (verbo + preposição ou advérbio) pode ser separado, colocando-se o objeto entre o verbo e a segunda partícula da locução, p. ex. com **let in** diz-se *I let her in* — shows that a phrasal verb is separable, e.g. **let in**. where the object can come between the verb and the particle, *I let her in*

singular	sg	singular
algo	sthg	something
sujeito	suj/subj	subject
superlativo	sup(erl)	superlative
termos técnicos	TEC(H)	technology
televisão	TV	television
verbo	v/vb	verb
verbo intransitivo	vi	intransitive verb
verbo impessoal	v impess / v impers	impersonal verb
verbo pronominal	vp	pronominal verb
verbo transitivo	vt	transitive verb
vulgar	vulg	vulgar
equivalente cultural	≃	cultural equivalent

TRANSCRIÇÃO FONÉTICA	PHONETIC TRANSCRIPTION

Vogais portuguesas / English vowels

[a]	pá, amar		[ɪ]	pit, big, rid
[ɛ]	sé, seta, hera		[e]	pet, tend
[c]	ler, mês		[æ]	pat, bag, mad
[i]	ir, sino, nave		[ʌ]	run, cut
[ɔ]	nota, pó		[ɒ]	pot, log
[o]	corvo, avô		[ʊ]	put, full
[u]	azul, tribo		[ə]	mother, suppose
			[i:]	bean, weed
			[ɑ:]	barn, car, laugh
			[ɔ:]	born, lawn
			[u:]	loop, loose
			[ɜ:]	burn, learn, bird

Ditongos portugueses / English diphthongs

[aj]	faixa, mais		[eɪ]	bay, late, great
[ej]	leite, rei		[aɪ]	buy, light, aisle
[ɛj]	hotéis, pastéis		[ɔɪ]	boy, foil
[ɔj]	herói, bóia		[əʊ]	no, road, blow
[oj]	coisa, noite		[aʊ]	now, shout, town
[uj]	azuis, fui		[ɪə]	peer, fierce, idea
[aw]	nau, jaula		[eə]	pair, bear, share
[ɛw]	céu, véu		[ʊə]	poor, sure, tour
[ew]	deus, seu			
[iw]	riu, viu			

Vogais nasais / Nasal vowels

[ã]	maçã, santo
[ẽ]	lençol, sempre
[ĩ]	fim, patim
[õ]	onde, com, honra
[ũ]	jejum, nunca

Ditongos nasais / Nasal diphthongs

[ãj]	cãibra, mãe
[ãw]	betão, cão
[ẽj]	bem, quem
[õj]	cordões, leões

Semivogais / Semi-vowels

sereia, maio	[j]	you, spaniel
luar, quadro, poema	[w]	wet, why, twin

Consoantes		Consonants
beijo, abrir	[b]	bottle, bib
casa, dique	[k]	come, kitchen
dama, prenda	[d]	dog, did
dia, bonde	[dʒ]	jet, fridge
fado, afinal	[f]	fib, physical
grande, agora	[g]	gag, great
gelo, cisne, anjo	[ʒ]	usual, measure
	[h]	how, perhaps
lata, feliz, cola	[l]	little, help
folha, ilha	[ʎ]	
mel, amigo	[m]	metal, comb
novo, mina	[n]	night, dinner
linha, sonho	[ɲ]	
anca, inglês	[ŋ]	sung, parking
pão, gripe	[p]	pop, people
cura, era	[r]	right, carry
rádio, terra	[x]	loch
cima, desse, caça	[s]	seal, peace
noz, bis, caixa, chá	[ʃ]	sheep, machine
tema, lata, porta	[t]	train, tip
tio, infantil	[tʃ]	chain, wretched
	[θ]	think, fifth
	[ð]	this, with
vela, ave	[v]	vine, livid
zelo, brisa	[z]	zip, his

[ʳ] só se pronuncia quando é seguido de uma palavra que começa por vogal.

[ʳ] is pronounced only when followed by a word beginning with a vowel.

O símbolo fonético [(x)] em português indica que o 'r' no final da palavra é quase sempre levemente pronunciado, exceto ao ser seguido por uma vogal, quando então é pronunciado [r].

The symbol [(x)] in Portuguese phonetics indicates that final 'r' is often barely sounded unless it is followed by a word beginning with a vowel, in which case it is pronounced [r].

O símbolo ['] indica a sílaba tônica, onde recai o acento principal; [,] indica a sílaba subtônica, onde recai o acento secundário.

The symbol ['] indicates that the following syllable carries primary stress and [,] that the following syllable carries secondary stress.

No lado português as regras de pronúncia seguidas são as do português falado no Rio de Janeiro, exceto nos verbetes seguidos pela abreviatura Port que correspondem ao português europeu e cuja pronúncia é a de Lisboa.

Portuguese phonetics reflect the language as spoken in Rio de Janeiro, except for entries marked Port, which relate specifically to European Portuguese and where the pronunciation given is that of Lisbon.

Conjugações

Chave: A = presente do indicativo, B = pretérito imperfeito do indicativo, C = pretérito perfeito do indicativo, D = pretérito mais-que-perfeito do indicativo, E = futuro do indicativo, F = condicional, G = presente do subjuntivo, H = futuro do subjuntivo, I = pretérito imperfeito do subjuntivo, J = imperativo, K = gerúndio, L = infinitivo pessoal, M = particípio passado.

ANDAR: A ando, andas, anda, andamos, andais, andam, B andava, andavas, andava, andávamos, andáveis, andavam, C andei, andaste, andou, andamos, andastes, andaram, D andara, andaras, andara, andáramos, andáreis, andaram, E andarei, andarás, andará, andaremos, andareis, andarão, F andaria, andarias, andaria, andaríamos, andaríeis, andariam, G ande, andes, ande, andemos, andeis, andem, H andar, andares, andar, andarmos, andardes, andarem, I andasse, andasses, andasse, andássemos, andásseis, andassem, J anda, ande, andemos, andai, andem, K andando, L andar, andares, andar, andarmos, andardes, andarem, M andado.

chover: A chove, B chovia, C choveu, G chova, H chover, I chovesse, M chovido.

COMER: A como, comes, come, comemos, comeis, comem, B comia, comias, comia, comíamos, comíeis, comiam, C comi, comeste, comeu, comemos, comestes, comeram, D comera, comeras, comera, comêramos, comêreis, comeram, E comerei, comerás, comerá, comeremos, comereis, comerão, F comeria, comerias, comeria, comeríamos, comeríeis, comeriam, G coma, comas, coma, comamos, comais, comam, H comer, comeres, comer, comermos, comerdes, comerem, I comesse, comesses, comesse, comêssemos, comêsseis, comessem, J come, coma, comamos, comei, comam, K comendo, L comer, comeres, comer, comermos, comerdes, comerem, M comido.

conduzir: A conduzo, conduzes, conduz, etc., B conduzia, etc., C conduzi, conduziste, etc., G conduza, etc., I conduzisse, etc., J conduz, conduza, etc., M conduzido.

conhecer: A conheço, conheces, etc., B conhecia, etc., C conheci, conheceste, etc., D conhecera, etc., I conhecesse, conhecesses, etc., J conhece, conheça, etc., M conhecido.

conseguir: A consigo, consegues, consegue, etc., C consegui, conseguiste, etc., D conseguira, conseguiras, etc., E conseguirei, conseguirás, etc., J consegue, consiga, consigamos, consegui, consigam.

dar: A dou, dás, dá, damos, dais, dão, B dava, etc., C dei, deste, deu, demos, destes, deram, D dera, deras, etc., E darei, darás, etc., F daria, etc., G dê, dês, dê, dêmos, deis. dêem, H der, deres, etc., I desse, desses, etc., J dá, dê, dêmos, dai, dêem, K dando, L dar, dares, dar, darmos, dardes, darem, M dado.

dizer: A digo, dizes, diz, dizemos, dizeis, dizem ; B dizia, dizias, etc., C disse, disseste, disse, dissemos, dissestes, disseram, D dissera, disseras, etc., E direi, dirás, dirá, etc., F diria, dirias, etc., G diga, digas, etc., H disser, disseres, disser, dissermos, disserdes, disserem, I dissesse, dissesses. etc., J diz, diga, etc., K dizendo, L dizer, dizeres, dizer, dizermos, dizerdes, dizerem, M dito.

dormir: A durmo, dormes, dorme, dormimos, dormis, dormem, B dormia, dormias, etc., C dormi, dormiste, etc., H dormir, dormires, etc., J dorme, durma, durmamos, dormi, durmam, M dormido.

escrever: A escrevo, escreves, etc., B escrevia, escrevias, etc., C escrevi, escreveste, escreveu, etc., D escrevera, escreveras, etc., I escrevesse, escrevesses, etc., J escreve, escreva, etc., M escrito.

ESTAR: A estou, estás, está, estamos, estais, estão, B estava, estavas, estava, estávamos, estáveis, estavam, C estive, estiveste, esteve, estivemos, estivestes, estiveram, D estivera, estiveras, estivera, estivéramos, estivéreis, estiveram, E estarei, estarás, estará, estaremos, estareis, estarão, F estaria, estarias, estaria, estaríamos, estaríeis, estariam, G esteja, estejas, esteja, estejamos, estejais, estejam, H estiver, estiveres, estiver, estivermos, estiverdes, estiverem, I estivesse, estivesses, estivesse, estivéssemos, estivésseis, estivessem, J está, esteja, estejamos, estai, estejam, K estando, L estar, estares, estar, estarmos, estardes, estarem, M estado.

fazer: A faço, fazes, faz, etc., B fazia, fazias, etc., C fiz, fizeste, fez, fizemos, fizestes, fizeram, D fizera, fizeras, etc., E farei, farás, etc., F faria, farias, etc., G faça, faças, etc.; H fizer, fizeres, etc., I fizesse, fizesses, etc., J faz, faça, façamos, fazei, façam, M feito.

ir: A vou, vais, vai, vamos, ides, vão, B ia, ias, íamos, etc., C fui, foste, foi, fomos, fostes, foram, D fora, foras, fora, fôramos, fôreis, foram, E irei, irás, irá, iremos, ireis, irão, F iria, irias, iríamos, etc., G vá, vás, vá, vamos, vades, vão, H for, fores, for, formos, fordes, forem, I fosse, fosses, fosse, fôssemos, fôsseis, fossem, J vai, vá, vamos, ide, vão, K indo, L ir, ires, ir, irmos, irdes, irem, M ido.

ler: A leio, lês, lê, lemos, ledes, lêem, B lia, lias, etc., C li, leste, leu, etc., G leia, leias, etc., M lido.

nascer: A nasço, nasces, etc., B nascia, etc., C nasci, nasceste, nasceu, etc., D nascera, etc., G nasça, nasças, etc., H nascer, nasceres, etc., I nascesse, etc., M nascido.

negociar: A negoc(e)io, negoc(e)ias, negoc(e)ia, negociamos, negociais, negoc(e)iam, B negociava, etc., C negociei, negociaste, etc., G negoc(e)ie, negoc(e)ies, negoc(e)ie, negociemos, negocieis, negoc(e)iem, J negoc(e)ia, negoc(e)ie, negociemos, negociai, negoc(e)iem, M negociado.

oferecer: A ofereço, ofereces, etc., B oferecia, etc., C ofereci, ofereceste, ofereceu, etc., D oferecera, etc., G ofereça, ofereças, etc., I oferecesse, etc., J oferece, ofereça, ofereçamos, oferecei, ofereçam, M oferecido.

ouvir: A ouço, ouves, ouve, etc., B ouvia, etc., C ouvi, ouviste, ouviu, etc., D ouvira, etc., G ouça, ouças, etc., H ouvir, ouvires, etc., I ouvisse, ouvisses, etc., J ouve, ouça, ouçamos, ouvi, ouçam, M ouvido.

parecer: A pareço, pareces, parece, etc., B parecia, etc., C pareci, pareceste, etc., D parecera, etc., G pareça, pareças, etc., H parecer, pareceres, etc., I parecesse, parecesses, etc., M parecido.

PARTIR: A parto, partes, parte, partimos, partis, partem, **B** partia, partias, partia, partíamos, partíeis, partiam, **C** parti, partiste, partiu, partimos, partistes, partiram, **D** partira, partiras, partira, partíramos, partíreis, partiram, **G** parta, partas, parta, partamos, partais, partam, **H** partir, partires, partir, partirmos, partirdes, partirem, **I** partisse, partisses, partisse, partíssemos, partísseis, partissem, **J** parte, parta, partamos, parti, partam, **K** partindo, **L** partir, partires, partir, partirmos, partirdes, partirem, **M** partido.

passear: A passeio, passeias, passeia, passeamos, passeais, passeiam, **B** passeava, passeavas, etc., **C** passeei, passeaste, etc., **E** passearei, passearás, etc., **G** passeie, passeies, etc., **J** passeia, passeie, passeemos, passeai, passeiem, **M** passeado.

pedir: A peço, pedes, pede, etc., **C** pedi, pediste, pediu, etc., **G** peça, peças, etc., **J** pede, peça, peçamos, pedi, peçam, **M** pedido.

perder: A perco, perdes, perde, perdemos, perdeis, perdem, **C** perdi, perdeste, perdeu, etc., **F** perderia, perderias, etc., **G** perca, percas, perca, etc., **H** perder, perderes, etc., **I** perdesse, perdesses, etc., **J** perde, perca, percamos, perdei, percam, **M** perdido.

poder: A posso, podes, pode, podemos, podeis, podem, **B** podia, podias, etc., **C** pude, pudeste, pôde, pudemos, pudestes, puderam, **G** possa, possamos, etc., **H** puder, puderes, puder, etc., **I** pudesse, pudéssemos, etc.

pôr: A ponho, pões, põe, pomos, pondes, põem, **B** punha, púnhamos, etc., **C** pus, puseste, pôs, pusemos, pusestes, puseram, **D** pusera, puséramos, etc., **E** porei, porás, etc., **F** poria, porias, etc., **G** ponha, ponhas, etc., **H** puser, pusermos, etc., **I** pusesse, puséssemos, etc., **J** põe, ponha, ponhamos, ponde, ponham, **K** pondo, **L** pôr, pores, pôr, pormos, pordes, porem, **M** posto.

querer: A quero, queres, quer, queremos, quereis, querem, **C** quis, quiseste, quis, quisemos, quisestes, quiseram, **D** quisera, quiséramos, etc., **G** queira, queiramos, etc., **H** quiser, quisermos, etc., **I** quisesse, quiséssemos, etc., **J** quer, queira, queiramos, querei, queiram, **K** querendo, **L** querer, quereres, querer, querermos, quererdes, quererem, **M** querido.

rir: A rio, ris, ri, rimos, rides, riem, **B** ria, ríamos, etc., **C** ri, riste, riu, rimos, ristes, riram, **D** rira, ríramos, etc., **G** ria, rias, etc., **H** rir, rires, etc., **I** risse, ríssemos, etc., **J** ri, ria, riamos, ride, riam, **K** rindo, **M** rido.

saber: A sei, sabes, sabe, sabemos, sabeis, sabem, **B** sabia, sabíamos, etc., **C** soube, soubeste, soube, soubemos, soubestes, souberam, **D** soubera, soubéramos, etc., **G** saiba, saibas, saiba, saibamos, saibais, saibam, **H** souber, souberes, etc., **I** soubesse, soubesses, etc., **J** sabe, saiba, saibamos, sabei, saibam, **M** sabido.

sair: A saio, sais, sai, saímos, saís, saem, **B** saía, saías, etc., **C** saí, saíste, saiu, etc., **D** saíra, saíras, etc., **G** saia, saias, saia, saiamos, saiais, saiam, **H** sair, saíres, sair, etc., **I** saísse, saísses, etc., **J** sai, saia, saiamos, saí, saiam, **K** saindo, **M** saído.

SENTAR-SE: A sento-me, sentas-te, senta-se, sentamo-nos, sentais-vos, sentam-se, **B** sentava-me, sentavas-te, sentava-se, sentávamo-nos, sentáveis-vos, sentavam-se, **C** sentei-me, sentaste-te, sentou-se, sentámo-nos, sentastes-vos, sentaram-se, **D** sentara-me, sentaras-te, sentara-se, sentáramo-nos, sentáreis-vos, sentaram-se, **E** sentar-me-ei, sentar-te-ás, sentar-se-á, sentar-nos-emos, sentar-vos-eis, sentar-se-ão, **F** sentar-me-ia, sentar-te-ias, sentar-se-ia, sentar-nos-íamos, sentar-vos-íeis, sentar-se-iam, **G** me sente, te sentes, se sente, nos sentemos, vos senteis, se sentem, **H** me sentar, te sentares, se sentar, nos sentarmos, vos sentardes, se sentarem, **I** me sentasse, te sentasses, se sentasse, nos sentássemos, vos sentásseis, se sentassem, **J** senta-te, sente-se, sentemo-nos, sentai-vos, sentem-se, **K** sentando-se, **L** sentar-me, sentares-te, sentar-se, sentarmo-nos, sentardes-vos, sentarem-se, **M** sentado.

sentir: **A** sinto, sentes, sente, sentimos, sentis, sentem, **B** sentia, sentias, etc., **C** senti, sentiste, sentiu, etc., **D** sentira, etc., **G** sinta, sintas, etc., **I** sentisse, sentisses, etc., **H** sentir, sentires, etc., **J** sente, sinta, sintamos, senti, sintam, **M** sentido.

SER: **A** sou, és, é, somos, sois, são, **B** era, eras, era, éramos, éreis, eram, **C** fui, foste, foi, fomos, fostes, foram, **D** fora, foras, fora, fôramos, fôreis, foram, **F** seria, serias, seria, seríamos, seríeis, seriam, **G** seja, sejas, seja, sejamos, sejais, sejam, **H** for, fores, for, formos, fordes, forem, **I** fosse, fosses, fosse, fôssemos, fôsseis, fossem, **J** sê, seja, sejamos, sede, sejam, **K** sendo, **L** ser, seres, ser, sermos, serdes, serem, **M** sido.

TER: **A** tenho, tens, tem, temos, tendes, têm, **B** tinha, tinhas, tinha, tínhamos, tínheis, tinham, **C** tive, tiveste, teve, tivemos, tivestes, tiveram, **D** tivera, tiveras, tivera, tivéramos, tivéreis, tiveram, **E** terei, terás, terá, teremos, tereis, terão, **F** teria, terias, teria, teríamos, teríeis, teriam, **G** tenha, tenhas, tenha, tenhamos, tenhais, tenham, **H** tiver, tiveres, tiver, tivermos, tiverdes, tiverem, **I** tivesse, tivesses, tivesse, tivéssemos, tivésseis, tivessem, **J** tem, tenha, tenhamos, tende, tenham, **K** tendo, **L** ter, teres, ter, termos, terdes, terem, **M** tido.

trazer: **A** trago, trazes, traz, trazemos, trazeis, trazem, **B** trazia, trazias, etc., **C** trouxe, trouxeste, trouxe, trouxemos, trouxestes, trouxeram, **D** trouxera, trouxeras, etc., **E** trarei, trarás, trará, traremos, trareis, trarão, **F** traria, trarias, etc., **G** traga, tragas, etc., **H** trouxer, trouxeres, etc., **I** trouxesse, trouxesses, etc., **J** traz, traga, tragamos, trazei, tragam, **K** trazendo, **L** trazer, trazeres, trazer, trazermos, trazerdes, trazerem, **M** trazido.

ver: **A** vejo, vês, vê, vemos, vedes, vêem, **B** via, vias, etc., **C** vi, viste, viu, vimos, vistes, viram, **D** vira, viras, etc., **E** verei, verás, etc., **G** veja, vejas, veja, etc., **H** vir, vires, vir, virmos, virdes, virem, **I** visse, visses, visse, etc., **J** vê, veja, vejamos, vede, vejam, **K** vendo, **L** ver, veres, ver, vermos, verdes, verem, **M** visto.

vir: **A** venho, vens, vem, vimos, vindes, vêm, **B** vinha, vinhas, etc., **C** vim, vieste, veio, viemos, viestes, vieram, **D** viera, vieras, etc., **E** virei, virás, etc., **G** venha, venhas, etc., **H** vier, vieres, vier, etc., **I** viesse, viesses, etc., **J** vem, venha, venhamos, vinde, venham, **K** vindo, **L** vir, vires, vir, virmos, virdes, virem, **M** vindo.

viver: **A** vivo, vives, etc., **B** vivia, vivias, etc., **C** vivi, viveste, viveu, etc., **G** viva, vivas, etc., **I** vivesse, vivesses, etc., **J** vive, viva, vivamos, vivei, vivam, **M** vivido.

ENGLISH IRREGULAR VERBS

Infinitive	Past Tense	Past Participle
arise	arose	arisen
awake	awoke	awoken
be	was/were	been
bear	bore	born(e)
beat	beat	beaten
begin	began	begun
bend	bent	bent
bet	bet /betted	bet /betted
bid	bid	bid
bind	bound	bound
bite	bit	bitten
bleed	bled	bled
blow	blew	blown
break	broke	broken
breed	bred	bred
bring	brought	brought
build	built	built
burn	burnt /burned	burnt /burned
burst	burst	burst
buy	bought	bought
can	could	–
cast	cast	cast
catch	caught	caught
choose	chose	chosen
come	came	come
cost	cost	cost
creep	crept	crept
cut	cut	cut
deal	dealt	dealt
dig	dug	dug
do	did	done
draw	drew	drawn
dream	dreamed /dreamt	dreamed /dreamt
drink	drank	drunk
drive	drove	driven
eat	ate	eaten
fall	fell	fallen
feed	fed	fed
feel	felt	felt
fight	fought	fought
find	found	found
fling	flung	flung
fly	flew	flown
forget	forgot	forgotten
freeze	froze	frozen
get	got	got (Am gotten)
give	gave	given
go	went	gone
grind	ground	ground
grow	grew	grown

Infinitive	Past Tense	Past Participle
hang	hung / hanged	hung / hanged
have	had	had
hear	heard	heard
hide	hid	hidden
hit	hit	hit
hold	held	held
hurt	hurt	hurt
keep	kept	kept
kneel	knelt / kneeled	knelt / kneeled
know	knew	known
lay	laid	laid
lead	led	led
lean	leant / leaned	leant / leaned
leap	leapt / leaped	leapt / leaped
learn	learnt / learned	learnt / learned
leave	left	left
lend	lent	lent
let	let	let
lie	lay	lain
light	lit / lighted	lit / lighted
lose	lost	lost
make	made	made
may	might	–
mean	meant	meant
meet	met	met
mow	mowed	mown /mowed
pay	paid	paid
put	put	put
quit	quit / quitted	quit /quitted
read	read	read
rid	rid	rid
ride	rode	ridden
ring	rang	rung
rise	rose	risen
run	ran	run
saw	sawed	sawn
say	said	said
see	saw	seen
seek	sought	sought
sell	sold	sold
send	sent	sent
set	set	set
shake	shook	shaken
shall	should	–
shed	shed	shed
shine	shone	shone
shoot	shot	shot
show	showed	shown
shrink	shrank	shrunk

Infinitive	Past Tense	Past Participle
shut	shut	shut
sing	sang	sung
sink	sank	sunk
sit	sat	sat
sleep	slept	slept
slide	slid	slid
sling	slung	slung
smell	smelt /smelled	smelt /smelled
sow	sowed	sown /sowed
speak	spoke	spoken
speed	sped /speeded	sped /speeded
spell	spelt /spelled	spelt /spelled
spend	spent	spent
spill	spilt /spilled	spilt /spilled
spin	spun	spun
spit	spat	spat
split	split	split
spoil	spoiled /spoilt	spoiled /spoilt
spread	spread	spread
spring	sprang	sprung
stand	stood	stood
steal	stole	stolen
stick	stuck	stuck
sting	stung	stung
stink	stank	stunk
strike	struck	struck /stricken
swear	swore	sworn
sweep	swept	swept
swell	swelled	swollen /swelled
swim	swam	swum
swing	swung	swung
take	took	taken
teach	taught	taught
tear	tore	torn
tell	told	told
think	thought	thought
throw	threw	thrown
tread	trod	trodden
wake	woke /waked	woken /waked
wear	wore	worn
weave	wove /weaved	woven /weaved
weep	wept	wept
win	won	won
wind	wound	wound
wring	wrung	wrung
write	wrote	written

a [a] *artigo definido* → **o** ♦ *prep* **1.** *(introduz um complemento indireto)* to; **mostrar algo a alguém** to show sthg to sb; **diga ao Zé para vir** tell Zé to come; **pede o chapéu ao Paulo** ask Paulo for the hat.
2. *(relativo a direção)* to; **fomos à praia** we went to the beach; **vamos ao cinema** we're going to the cinema; **cheguei a Salvador ontem** I arrived in Salvador yesterday.
3. *(relativo a posição, lugar, distância)*: **é à esquerda/direita** it's on the left/right; **fica a 10 quilômetros** it's 10 kilometres away.
4. *(relativo a quantidade, medida, preço)*: **aos centos/às dezenas** by the hundred/dozen; **a quanto estão as peras?** how much are the pears?; **vender algo a metro** to sell sthg by the metre.
5. *(indica modo, maneira)*: **feito à mão** handmade; **bater à máquina** to type; **sal a gosto** salt to taste.
6. *(relativo a velocidade)*: **dirigir a 60 km/h** to drive at 60 km/h; **ela ia a 100 por hora** she was going at 100 kilometres an hour.
7. *(indica freqüência)*: **três vezes ao dia** three times a day; **estou lá às terças e quintas** I'm there on Tuesdays and Thursdays.
8. *(introduz complemento de tempo)*: **as lojas abrem às 9 horas** the shops open at 9 (o'clock); **chegam daqui a 2 horas** they're arriving in 2 hours' time; **fica a dez minutos daqui** it's ten minutes from here; **à noite** at night.
9. *(indica série)*: **de ... a** from ... to; **façam os exercícios de um a dez** do exercises one to ten.
10. *(seguido de infinitivo para exprimir momento)*: **ele começou a falar** he started speaking; **ele tropeçou ao subir no ônibus** he tripped over as he was getting on the bus.
11. *(seguido de infinitivo indicando duas ações)*: **ela sentou-se a ler** she sat down and started to read.

à [a] = **a + a,** → **a.**

aba ['aba] *f (de chapéu)* brim; *(corte de carne)* side.

abacate [aba'katʃi] *m* avocado.

abacaxi [abaka'ʃi] *m* pineapple.

abadia [aba'dʒia] *f* abbey.

abafado, -da [aba'fadu, -da] *adj (ar)* stuffy; *(tempo)* close.

abafar [aba'fa(x)] *vt (ruído)* to muffle ♦ *vi (sufocar)* to stifle.

abaixar [abaj'ʃa(x)] *vt* to lower.
⌐ abaixar-se *vp* to stoop.

abaixo [a'bajʃu] *adv* down; **jogar ~** *(árvore)* to cut down; **mais ~** further down; **~ de** below; **~ o governo!** down with the government!

abaixo-assinado [a,bajʃuasi'nadu] *(pl* **abaixo-assinados** [a,bajʃuasi'naduʃ]) *m* petition.

abajur [aba'ʒu(x)] *(pl* **-res** [-riʃ]) *m* lampshade.

abalar [aba'la(x)] *vt (estremecer)* to shake.

abalo [a'balu] *m*: **~ (sísmico OU de terra)** earth tremor.

abanar [aba'na(x)] *vt (cabeça)* to shake; *(rabo)* to wag.

abandonado, -da [abãndo'nadu, -da] *adj (lugar)* deserted; *(cão, carro)* abandoned.

abandonar [abãndo'na(x)] *vt* to abandon.

abandono [abãn'donu] *m* abandonment; **ao ~** abandoned; **~ do lar** desertion.

abarcar [abax'ka(x)] *vt* to cover.

abarrotado, -da [abaxo'tadu, -da] *adj* packed.

abarrotar [abaxo'ta(x)] *vi* to be full up ♦ *vt* to pack; **a ~ de** packed with.

abastecer [abaʃte'se(x)] *vt* to supply. ❏ **abastecer-se** *vp* to stock up.

abastecimento [abaʃtesi'mẽntu] *m* supply.

abater [aba'te(x)] *vt* (*baixar*) to reduce; (*avião*) to shoot down; (*árvore*) to fell; (*animal*) to slaughter.

abatimento [abatʃi'mẽntu] *m* (*desconto*) reduction; (*fraqueza*) weakness.

abcesso [ab'sɛsu] *m* abscess.

abdicar [abdʒi'ka(x)] *vi* to abdicate.

abdómen [ab'dɔmɛn] *m* (*Port*) = **abdômen**.

abdômen [ab'domẽ] *m* (*Br*) abdomen.

abdominal [abdomi'naw] (*pl* **-ais** [-ajʃ]) *adj* abdominal. ❏ **abdominais** *mpl*: **fazer abdominais** to do sit-ups.

á-bê-cê [abe'se] *m* abc.

abecedário [abese'darju] *m* alphabet.

abeirar-se [abej'raxsi] : **abeirar-se de** *vp + prep* to draw near to.

abelha [a'beʎa] *f* bee.

abelhudo, -da [abe'ʎudu, -da] *adj* nosy.

aberração [abexa'sãw] (*pl* **-ões** [-õjʃ]) *f* aberration.

aberto, -ta [a'bɛxtu, -ta] *pp* → **abrir** ♦ *adj* open.

abertura [abex'tura] *f* opening; (*MUS*) overture; **"~ fácil"** "easy to open".

abeto [a'betu] *m* fir tree.

ABI *f* (*abrev de Associação Brasileira de Imprensa*) *Brazilian press association which also functions as a political pressure group.*

abismo [a'biʒmu] *m* abyss.

abóbada [a'bɔbada] *f* vault.

abóbora [a'bɔbora] *f* pumpkin.

abóbora-menina [a,bɔborame'nina] (*pl* **abóboras-meninas** [a,bɔboraʒme'ninaʃ]) *f* sweet pumpkin.

abobrinha [abo'briɲa] *f* (*Br*) courgette (*Brit*), zucchini (*Am*).

abolir [abo'li(x)] *vt* to abolish.

abominar [abomi'na(x)] *vt* to loathe.

abono [a'bonu] *m*: **~ de família** (*Port*) child benefit.

abordagem [abox'daʒẽ] (*pl* **-ns** [-ʃ]) *f* (*de tema, situação*) handling, treatment.

abordar [abox'da(x)] *vt* (*pessoa*) to approach; (*assunto*) to broach.

aborígene [abo'riʒeni] *mf* aborigine.

aborrecer [aboxe'se(x)] *vt* (*irritar*) to annoy; (*entediar*) to bore. ❏ **aborrecer-se** *vp* (*irritar-se*) to get annoyed; (*entediar-se*) to get bored.

aborrecido, -da [aboxe'sidu, -da] *adj* (*chato*) tedious; (*zangado*) annoyed.

aborrecimento [aboxesi'mẽntu] *m* (*tédio*) boredom; (*contrariedade*) annoyance.

abortar [abox'ta(x)] *vi* (*MED*) (*espontaneamente*) to have a miscarriage; (*intencionalmente*) to have an abortion.

aborto [a'boxtu] *m* (*MED*) (*espontâneo*) miscarriage; (*intencional*) abortion.

abotoar [abo'twa(x)] *vt* to button (up).

abraçar [abra'sa(x)] *vt* to hug. ❏ **abraçar-se** *vp* to hug each other.

abraço [a'brasu] *m* hug; **um ~** (*em carta, postal*) best wishes.

abrandar [abrãn'da(x)] *vt* (*dor*) to ease ♦ *vi* (*vento*) to drop; (*chuva*) to ease off.

abranger [abrã'ʒe(x)] *vt* to include.

abre-latas [abre'lataʃ] *m inv* (*Port*) tin opener (*Brit*), can opener (*Am*).

abreviação [abrevja'sãw] (*pl* **-ões** [-õjʃ]) *f* abbreviation.

abreviatura [abrevja'tura] *f* abbreviation.

abridor [abri'do(x)] (*pl* **-res** [-riʃ]) *m* (*Br*): **~ de garrafa** bottle opener; **~ de lata** tin opener (*Brit*), can opener (*Am*).

abrigar [abri'ga(x)] *vt* to shelter. ❏ **abrigar-se** *vp* to take cover.

abrigo [a'brigu] *m* shelter; **ao ~ de** under cover of.

abril [a'briw] *m* April, → **setembro**.

abrir [a'bri(x)] *vt & vi* to open; **~ o apetite** to whet one's appetite; **~ a boca** (*bocejar*) to yawn; **~ uma exceção** to make an exception; **~ mão de algo** (*fig*) to forego sthg; **~ os olhos** (*fig*) to open one's eyes. ❏ **abrir-se** *vp*: **~-se com alguém** to confide in sb.

absinto [ab'sĩntu] *m* absinthe.

absolutamente [absolu'ta'mẽntʃi] *adv* absolutely.

absoluto, -ta [abso'lutu, -ta] *adj* absolute.

absolver [absow've(x)] *vt (perdoar)* to absolve; *(JUR)* to acquit.

absorção [absox'sāw] *f* absorption.

absorvente [absox'vēntʃi] *adj* absorbent.

⅃ **absorventes** *mpl*: **~s diários** panty liners.

absorver [absɔr've(x)] *vt* to absorb.

abstémio, -mia [abʃtɛmju, -mja] *m, f (Port)* = **abstêmio**.

abstêmio, -mia [abʃtemju, -mja] *m, f (Br)* teetotaller.

abstracto, -ta [abʃtratu, -ta] *adj (Port)* = **abstrato**.

abstrato, -ta [abʃtratu, -ta] *adj (Br)* abstract.

absurdo, -da [ab suxdu, -da] *adj* absurd ♦ *m* nonsense.

abundância [abūn'dāsja] *f* abundance.

abundante [abūn'dāntʃi] *adj* abundant.

abusado, -da [abu'zadu, -da] *adj (Br: atrevido)* forward.

abusar [abu'za(x)] *vi* to overdo things; **~ de alguém** to abuse sb; **~ da bebida/do tabaco** to drink/smoke too much.

abuso [a'buzu] *m (de álcool, droga)* abuse; *(JUR)* indecent assault.

a.C. *(abrev de antes de Cristo)* BC.

a/c *(abrev de aos cuidados de)* c/o.

acabamento [akaba'mēntu] *m* finish.

acabar [aka ba(x)] *vt* to finish ♦ *vi (tempo, programa, filme)* to finish, to end; *(água, pão, leite)* to run out; **~ com algo** to put an end to sthg; **~ com alguém** *(matar)* to kill sb; **~ de fazer algo** to have just done sthg; **~ bem** to end well; **~ por fazer algo** to end up doing sthg.

⅃ **acabar-se** *vp* to run out; **acabou-se!** that's enough!

acácia [a'kasja] *f* acacia.

academia [akade'mia] *f* academy; **~ de belas-artes** Academy of Fine Arts; **~ de ginástica** gymnasium.

açafrão [asa'frāw] *m* saffron.

acalmar [akaw'ma(x)] *vt* to calm ♦ *vi (vento, dor)* to abate.

⅃ **acalmar-se** *vp* to calm down.

acampamento [akãmpa mēntu] *m* camp.

acampar [akãm'pa(x)] *vi* to camp.

acanhado, -da [aka'ɲadu, -da] *adj* shy.

acanhar-se [aka'ɲaxsi] *vp* to be shy.

ação [a'sāw] *(pl* **-ões** [-ōjʃ]) *f (Br)* action; *(título de crédito)* share; *(de poema, peça teatral)* plot; **entrar em ~** to take action.

acarajé [akara'ʒɛ] *m (CULIN) beancake fried in palm oil and served with a spicy sauce.*

acariciar [akari'sja(x)] *vt* to caress.

acaso [a'kazu] *m* chance, accident; **ao ~** at random; **por ~** by chance OU accident.

acastanhado, -da [akaʃta'ɲadu, -da] *adj* brownish.

acatar [aka'ta(x)] *vt (ordem, lei)* to obey.

acção [a'sāw] *(pl* **-ões** [-ōjʃ]) *f (Port)* = **ação**.

accionar [asju'nar] *vt (Port)* = **acionar**.

accionista [asju'niʃta] *mf (Port)* = **acionista**.

acções → **acção**.

aceder [ase'de(x)] *vi* to consent.

aceitar [asej'ta(x)] *vt* to accept.

aceito, -ta [a'sejtu, -ta] *pp* → **aceitar**.

acelerador [aselera'do(x)] *(pl* **-res** [-riʃ]) *m (AUT)* accelerator *(Brit)*, gas pedal *(Am)*.

acelerar [asele'ra(x)] *vt* to speed up ♦ *vi* to accelerate.

acenar [ase'na(x)] *vi (com braço)* to wave; *(com cabeça)* to nod.

acender [asēn'de(x)] *vt (cigarro, vela, lareira)* to light; *(lâmpada, candeeiro)* to switch OU turn on.

aceno [a'senu] *m (with arm)* gesture; **um ~ de cabeça** a nod.

acento [a'sēntu] *m (sinal gráfico)* accent; *(inflexão)* stress; **~ agudo/grave** acute/grave accent; **~ circunflexo** circumflex.

acepção [asep'sāw] *(pl* **-ões** [-ōjʃ]) *f* sense.

acerca [a'sexka] : **acerca de** *prep* about, concerning.

acerola [ase'rɔla] *f small bitter red fruit commonly used in juice and ice cream.*

acertar [asex'ta(x)] *vt (relógio)* to set ♦ *vi*: **~ em** *(em alvo)* to hit; *(em resposta)* to get right; **~ com** *(com lugar, local)* to find; **acertou!** *(adivinhaste)* you got it right!

acervo [a'sexvu] *m (de museu, fundação)* collection.

aceso, -sa [a'sezu. -za] *pp* → **acender** ◆ *adj (luz, lume)* on; *(discussão)* heated.

acessível [ase'sivew] (*pl* **-eis** [-ejʃ]) *adj* accessible; *(preço)* affordable; *(pessoa)* approachable.

acesso [a'sesu] *m* access; *(de raiva, histeria)* fit; **de fácil** ~ easy to get to.

acessório [ase'sɔrju] *m* accessory.

acetona [ase'tona] *f* nail varnish remover.

achado [a'ʃadu] *m (descoberta)* find; *(pechincha)* bargain.

achar [a'ʃa(x)] *vt* to find; ~ **que** to think (that); **acho que não** I don't think so; **acho que sim** I think so.

acidentado, -da [asidēn'tadu, -da] *adj (terreno)* rough; *(viagem, férias)* eventful ◆ *m, f* injured person.

acidental [asidēn'taw] (*pl* **-ais** [-ajʃ]) *adj* accidental.

acidentalmente [asidēntaw'mēntʃi] *adv* accidentally.

acidente [asi'dēntʃi] *m* accident; *(de terreno)* bump.

acidez [asi'deʒ] *f* acidity.

ácido, -da [asidu, -da] *adj (sabor)* sour ◆ *m* acid; ~ **cítrico/sulfúrico** citric/sulphuric acid.

acima [a'sima] *adv* up; **mais** ~ higher up; ~ **de** above; ~ **de tudo** above all.

acionar [asjo'na(x)] *vt (Br)* to set in motion.

acionista [asjo'niʃta] *mf (Br)* shareholder.

acne ['akni] *f* acne.

aço ['asu] *m* steel; ~ **inoxidável** stainless steel.

acocorar-se [akoko'raxsi] *vp* to squat (down).

ações → **ação**.

acolhimento [akoʎi'mēntu] *m* welcome.

acompanhamento [akōmpaɲa'mēntu] *m (de evolução, situação)* following; *(de prato de carne, peixe)* side dish, side order; *(MUS)* accompaniment.

acompanhante [akōmpa'ɲāntʃi] *mf* companion; *(MUS)* accompanist.

acompanhar [akōmpa'ɲa(x)] *vt* to accompany; *(programa, situação)* to follow.

aconchegador, -ra [akōʃega'do(x). -ra] (*mpl* **-res** [-riʃ]. *fpl* **-s** [-ʃ]) *adj* cosy.

aconselhar [akōse'ʎa(x)] *vt* to advise. ⏌ **aconselhar-se** *vp* to get advice.

aconselhável [akōse'ʎavew] (*pl* **-eis** [-ejʃ]) *adj* advisable; **pouco** ~ inadvisable.

acontecer [akōnte'se(x)] *vi* to happen; **(mas) acontece que ...** but as it happens ...; **aconteça o que** ~ come what may.

acontecimento [akōntesi'mēntu] *m* event.

acordar [akox'da(x)] *vt & vi* to wake up.

acorde [a'kɔxdʒi] *m (MUS)* chord.

acordeão [akox'dʒjãw] (*pl* **-ões** [-õjʃ]) *m* accordion.

acordo [a'koxdu] *m* agreement; *(JUR)* accord; **de** ~**!** all right!; **estar de** ~ **com** to agree with; **de** ~ **com** in accordance with.

acorrentar [akoxēn'ta(x)] *vt* to chain (up).

acostamento [akoʃta'mēntu] *m (Br)* hard shoulder *(Brit)*, shoulder *(Am)*.

acostumado, -da [akoʃtu'madu. -da] *adj*: **estar** ~ **a algo** to be used to sthg.

acostumar-se [akoʃtu'maxsi] *vp*: ~ **com algo** to get used to sthg; ~ **a fazer algo** to get used to doing sthg.

açougue [a'sogi] *m (Br)* butcher's (shop).

açougueiro, -ra [aso'gejru. -ra] *m, f (Br)* butcher.

A.C.P. *(abrev de Automóvel Clube de Portugal)* = AA *(Brit)*, = AAA *(Am)*.

acre ['akri] *adj (sabor)* bitter; *(cheiro)* acrid.

acreditar [akredʒi'ta(x)] *vi* to believe; ~ **em** to believe in.

acrescentar [akresēn'ta(x)] *vt* to add.

acréscimo [a'kresimu] *m* increase.

acrílica [a'krilika] *adj f* → **fibra**.

acrobata [akro'bata] *mf* acrobat.

activo, -va [a'tivu. -va] *adj (Port)* = **ativo**.

acto ['atu] *m (Port)* = **ato**.

actor, -triz [a'tor. 'triʃ] (*mpl* **-res** [-reʃ], *fpl* **-zes** [-zeʃ]) *m, f (Port)* = **ator**.

actual [a'twal] (*pl* **-ais** [-ajʃ]) *adj (Port)* = **atual**.

actuar [a'twar] *vi (Port)* = **atuar**.

açúcar [a'suka(x)] *m* sugar; ~ **preto/branco** brown/white sugar; ~ **em cubos** sugar cubes *(pl)*; ~ **mascavo** muscovado sugar; ~ **em pó** caster sugar.

açucareiro [asuka'rejru] *m* sugar bowl.

acumulação [akumula'sãw] (*pl* **-ões** [-õjʃ]) *f* accumulation.

acumular [akumu'la(x)] *vt* to accumulate.

acupunctura [akupũn'tura] *f* acupuncture.

acusação [akuza'sãw] (*pl* -ões [-õjʃ]) *f* (*denúncia*) accusation; (*queixa*) complaint; (*JUR: declaração*) charge; (*JUR: acusador*) plaintiff.

acusar [aku'za(x)] *vt* to accuse; (*revelar*) to reveal.

A.D. (*abrev de Anno Domini*) AD.

adaptação [adapta'sãw] (*pl* -ões [-õjʃ]) *f* adaptation.

adaptado, -da [adap'tadu, -da] *adj* (*adequado*) appropriate.

adaptador [adapta'do(x)] (*pl* -res [-riʃ]) *m* adaptor.

adaptar [adap'ta(x)] *vt* to adapt.
⎿ **adaptar-se** *vp*: ~-se a to adapt to.

adega [a'dɛga] *f* wine cellar; ~ **cooperativa** wine cellar run by a cooperative.

adepto, -ta [a'dɛptu, -ta] *m, f* supporter.

adequado, -da [ade'kwadu, -da] *adj* appropriate.

adereço [ade'resu] *m* (*em teatro, espetáculo*) prop.

aderente [ade'rẽntʃi] *adj* (*pneu*) nonskid ◆ *mf* (*partidário*) supporter.

aderir [ade'ri(x)] *vi* to stick; ~ **a algo** (*fig: a idéia, partido*) to support sthg.

adesão [ade'zãw] (*pl* -ões [-õjʃ]) *f* (*a idéia, partido*) support.

adesivo, -va [ade'zivu, -va] *adj* adhesive ◆ *m* adhesive tape.

adesões → adesão.

adeus [a'dewʃ] *m* goodbye ◆ *interj* goodbye!; **dizer** ~ to say goodbye.

adiamento [adʒja'mẽntu] *m* postponement.

adiantado, -da [adʒjãn'tadu, -da] *adj* (*no tempo*) ahead of schedule; (*no espaço*) advanced ◆ *adv*: **chegar** ~ to arrive early; **estar** ~ (*relógio*) to be fast; **pagar** ~ to pay in advance.

adiantar [adʒjãn'ta(x)] *vt* (*relógio*) to put forward; (*dinheiro*) to advance; (*trabalho*) to get ahead with ◆ *v impess*: **não adianta gritar** there's no point in shouting.
⎿ **adiantar-se** *vp* (*no espaço*) to get ahead.

adiante [a'dʒjãntʃi] *adv* ahead ◆ *interj* forward!; **mais** ~ further on; **passar** ~ to overlook; **e por aí** ~ and so forth.

adiar [a'dʒja(x)] *vt* to postpone.

adição [adʒi'sãw] (*pl* -ões [-õjʃ]) *f* addition.

adicionar [adʒisjo'na(x)] *vt* (*acrescentar*) to add; (*somar*) to add up.

adições → adição.

adivinha [adʒi'viɲa] *f* riddle.

adivinhar [adʒivi'ɲa(x)] *vt* to guess; (*futuro*) to predict; (*decifrar*) to solve.

adjectivo [adʒɛ'tivu] *m* (*Port*) = **adjetivo**.

adjetivo [adʒɛ'tivu] *m* (*Br*) adjective.

adjunto, -ta [ad'ʒũntu, -ta] *m, f* assistant ◆ *adj* assistant (*antes de s*).

administração [adʒiminiʃtra'sãw] *f* administration; (*os administradores*) management; (*local*) administrative office.

administrador, -ra [adʒiminiʃtra'do(x), -ra] (*mpl* -res [-riʃ], *fpl* -s [-ʃ]) *m, f* administrator.

administrar [adʒiminiʃ'tra(x)] *vt* to administer.

admiração [adʒimira'sãw] *f* (*espanto*) amazement; (*respeito, estima*) admiration.

admirador, -ra [adʒimira'do(x), -ra] (*mpl* -res [-riʃ], *fpl* -s [-ʃ]) *m, f* admirer.

admirar [adʒimi'ra(x)] *vt* (*contemplar*) to admire; (*espantar*) to amaze.
⎿ **admirar-se** *vp* to be surprised.

admirável [adʒimi'ravɛw] (*pl* -eis [-ejʃ]) *adj* (*incrível*) amazing; (*digno de respeito*) admirable.

admissão [adʒimi'sãw] (*pl* -ões [-õjʃ]) *f* admission.

admitir [adʒimi'tʃi(x)] *vt* (*permitir*) to allow; (*deixar entrar*) to admit.

adoçante [ado'sãntʃi] *m* sweetener.

adoção [ado'sãw] (*pl* -ões [-õjʃ]) *f* (*Br*) adoption.

adoçar [ado'sa(x)] *vt* to sweeten.

adoecer [adoe'se(x)] *vi* to fall ill.

adolescência [adole'sẽsja] *f* adolescence.

adolescente [adole'sẽntʃi] *mf* adolescent.

adopção [ado'sãw] (*pl* -ões [-õjʃ]) *f* (*Port*) = **adoção**.

adorar [ado'ra(x)] *vt* to adore, to love.

adorável [ado'ravɛw] (*pl* -eis [-ejʃ]) *adj* adorable.

adormecer [adoxme'se(x)] *vt* to send to sleep ◆ *vi* to fall asleep.

adornar [adox'na(x)] *vt* to adorn.

adotado, -da [ado'tadu, -da] *adj* adopted.

adotar [ado'ta(x)] *vt* to adopt; *(livro)* to choose.

adquirir [adʒiki'ri(x)] *vt* to acquire.

adrenalina [adrena'lina] *f* adrenalin.

adulterar [aduwte'ra(x)] *vt* to adulterate.

adultério [aduw'terju] *m* adultery.

adulto, -ta [a'duwtu, -ta] *adj & m, f* adult.

advérbio [ad'vɛxbju] *m* adverb.

adversário, -ria [adʒivɛx'sarju, -rja] *adj* opposing ◆ *m, f* opponent.

advertência [adʒivɛx'tẽsja] *f* warning.

advogado, -da [adʒivo'gadu, -da] *m, f* lawyer *(Brit)*, attorney *(Am)*.

á-é-i-ó-u [aɛjɔu] *m*: **aprender o ~** *(as vogais)* to learn to spell; *(o essencial de algo)* to learn the basics.

aéreo, -rea [a'ɛrju, -rja] *adj* air *(antes de s)*; *(fig: distraído)* absentminded.

aerobarco [aɛro'baxku] *m (Br)* hovercraft.

aerodinâmico, -ca [aɛrodʒi'namiku, -ka] *adj* aerodynamic.

aeródromo [aɛ'rɔdromu] *m* airfield.

aeromoça [aɛro'mosa] *f (Br)* air hostess.

aeromodelismo [a‚ɛromode'liʒmu] *m* model aeroplane making.

aeronáutica [aɛro'nawtʃika] *f (Br)* airforce.

aeroporto [aɛro'poxtu] *m* airport.

aerossol [aɛro'sɔw] *(pl* -óis [-ɔjʃ]*) m* aerosol.

afagar [afa'ga(x)] *vt* to stroke.

afastado, -da [afaʃ'tadu, -da] *adj (distante)* remote; *(retirado)* isolated.

afastar [afaʃ'ta(x)] *vt (desviar)* to move away; *(apartar)* to separate.

❏ **afastar-se** *vp (desviar-se)* to move away; *(distanciar-se)* to distance o.s.

afável [a'favɛw] *(pl* -eis [-ɛjʃ]*) adj* friendly.

afecto [a'fɛtu] *m (Port)* = **afeto**.

afeição [afej'sãw] *f (afecto)* affection; *(inclinação)* liking.

afetar [afe'ta(x)] *vt* to affect.

afetivo, -va [afe'tʃivu, -va] *adj (pessoa)* affectionate; *(carência, problema, vida)* emotional.

afeto [a'fɛtu] *m (Br)* affection.

afetuoso, -osa [afe'tuozu, -ɔza] *adj* affectionate.

afiadeira [afja'dejra] *f (Port)* pencil sharpener.

afiado, -da [a'fjadu, -da] *adj* sharp.

afiambrado [afjãm'bradu] *m* chopped pork slices *(pl)*.

afiar [a'fja(x)] *vt* to sharpen.

aficionado, -da [afisjo'nadu, -da] *m, f* enthusiast.

afilhado, -da [afi'ʎadu, -da] *m, f* godson *(f* goddaughter).

afim [a'fĩ] *(pl* -ns [-ʃ]*) adj* related ◆ *m (parente)* relative, relation.

afinado, -da [afi'nadu, -da] *adj (instrumento musical)* in tune; *(motor)* tuned.

afinal [afi'naw] *adv*: **~ (de contas)** after all.

afinar [afi'na(x)] *vt (instrumento, motor, travões)* to tune.

afinidade [afini'dadʒi] *f* affinity.

afins → **afim**.

afirmação [afixma'sãw] *(pl* -ões [-õjʃ]*) f* statement.

afirmar [afix'ma(x)] *vt* to state.

afirmativo, -va [afixma'tʃivu, -va] *adj* affirmative.

afixar [afik'sa(x)] *vt (cartaz, aviso)* to put up.

aflição [afli'sãw] *(pl* -ões [-õjʃ]*) f* distress.

afligir [afli'ʒi(x)] *vt* to distress.

❏ **afligir-se** *vp* to distress o.s.; **~-se com** to worry about.

aflito, -ta [a'flitu, -ta] *pp* → **afligir**.

aflorar [aflo'ra(x)] *vt (assunto, tema)* to touch on ◆ *vi* to surface.

afluência [aflu'ẽsja] *f* stream.

afluente [aflu'ẽtʃi] *m* tributary.

afobado, -da [afo'badu, -da] *adj (Br) (apressado)* rushed; *(atrapalhado)* flustered.

afogado, -da [afo'gadu, -da] *adj (pessoa)* drowned; *(motor)* flooded ◆ *m, f* drowned person.

afogador [afoga'do(x)] *(pl* -res [-riʃ]*) m (Br)* choke.

afogamento [afoga'mẽtu] *m* drowning.

afogar [afo'ga(x)] *vt* to drown.

❏ **afogar-se** *vp* to drown.

afónico, -ca [a'fɔniku, -ka] *adj (Port)* = **afônico**.

afônico, -ca [a'foniku, -ka] *adj (Br)*: **estar ~** to have lost one's voice.

afortunado, -da [afoxtu'nadu, -da]

adj lucky, fortunate.

afresco [a'freʃku] *m (Br)* fresco.

África ['afrika] *f:* **a ~ Africa; a ~ do Sul** South Africa.

africano, -na [afri'kanu. -na] *adj & m, f* African.

afro-brasileiro, -ra [afrobrazi'lejru. -ra] *adj* Afro-Brazilian ◆ *m, f* Brazilian person of African extraction.

afronta [a'frõta] *f* insult.

afrouxar [afro'ʃa(x)] *vt (cinto, laço de sapato)* to loosen.

afta ['afta] *f* mouth ulcer.

afugentar [afugẽ'ta(x)] *vt* to drive away.

afundar [afũ'da(x)] *vt* to sink.

⏋ afundar-se *vp* to sink.

agachar-se [aga'ʃaxsi] *vp* to squat.

agarrar [aga'xa(x)] *vt (apanhar, segurar)* to grab; *(alcançar, apanhar no ar)* to catch.

⏋ agarrar-se *vp:* **~-se a** *(segurar-se a)* to grab hold of; *(pegar-se a)* to stick to; *(dedicar-se a)* to get stuck into; **~-se aos livros** *(fam)* to study hard.

agasalhar-se [agaza'ʃaxsi] *vp* to wrap up warm.

agasalho [aga'zaʎu] *m (casaco)* coat; *(pulôver)* jumper.

ágeis → ágil.

agência [a'ʒẽsja] *f* office; **~ bancária** branch *(of a bank);* **~ de câmbio** bureau de change; **~ de correio** *(Br)* post office; **~ funerária** funeral director's; **~ imobiliária** estate agent's *(Brit)*, real estate office *(Am);* **~ de viagens** travel agent's.

agenda [a'ʒẽda] *f (livro)* diary; *(plano de reunião)* agenda.

agente [a'ʒẽtʃi] *mf (de polícia)* policeman *(f* policewoman); *(de vendas)* sales representative; **"~ autorizado"** *authorized agent for the sale of lottery tickets and football coupons;* **~ secreto** secret agent.

ágil ['aʒiw] *(pl* **ágeis** ['aʒejʃ]) *adj* agile.

agilidade [aʒili'dadʒi] *f* agility.

ágio ['aʒju] *m* premium.

agir [a'ʒi(x)] *vi* to act.

agitação [aʒita'sãw] *f* agitation.

agitado, -da [aʒi'tadu. -da] *adj (pessoa)* agitated; *(mar)* rough; *(tempo)* unsettled.

agitar [aʒi'ta(x)] *vt (líquido)* to shake; **"agite antes de abrir"** "shake well before opening".

⏋ agitar-se *vp* to get agitated.

aglomeração [aglomera'sãw] *(pl* **-ões** [-õjʃ]) *f (de pessoas)* crowd; *(de detritos)* pile.

aglomerar [aglome'ra(x)] *vt* to pile up.

agonia [ago'nia] *f (angústia)* agony; *(náusea)* nausea; *(antes da morte)* death throes *(pl).*

agora [a'gɔra] *adv* now; **é ~ ou nunca** it's now or never; **só ~!** at last!; **só ~ é que cheguei** I've only just arrived; **~ mesmo** right now; **~ que** now that; **essa ~!** whatever next!; **por ~** for the time being.

agosto [a'goʃtu] *m (Br)* August, → **setembro.**

agradar [agra'da(x)] *vi:* **~ a alguém** to please sb.

agradável [agra'davɛw] *(pl* **-eis** [-ejʃ]) *adj* pleasant.

agradecer [agrade'se(x)] *vt* to thank ◆ *vi:* **~ a alguém algo, ~ algo a alguém** to thank sb for sthg.

agradecido, -da [agrade'sidu. -da] *adj* grateful; **mal ~** ungrateful; **muito ~!** many thanks!.

agradecimento [agradesi'mẽtu] *m* thanks *(pl).*

agrafador [agrafa'dor] *(pl* **-res** [-reʃ]) *m (Port)* stapler.

agrafo [a'grafu] *m (Port)* staple.

agravamento [agrava'mẽtu] *m* worsening.

agravante [agra'vãtʃi] *adj* aggravating ◆ *f* aggravating circumstance.

agravar [agra'va(x)] *vt* to make worse.

agredir [agre'dʒi(x)] *vt* to attack.

agregado [agre'gadu] *m:* **~ familiar** household.

agressão [agre'sãw] *(pl* **-ões** [-õjʃ]) *f (ataque)* attack.

agressivo, -va [agre'sivu, -va] *adj* aggressive.

agressões → agressão.

agreste [a'grɛʃtʃi] *adj (paisagem)* wild; *(tempo)* stormy.

agrião [agri'ãw] *(pl* **-ões** [-õjʃ]) *m* watercress.

agrícola [a'grikola] *adj* agricultural.

agricultor, -ra [agrikuw'to(x). -ra] *(mpl* **-res** [-riʃ]. *fpl* **-s** [-ʃ]) *m, f* farmer.

agricultura [agrikuw'tura] *f* agriculture.

agridoce [agri'dosi] *adj* sweet-and-sour.

agriões → agrião.

agronomia [agrono'mia] f agronomy.

agrupar [agru'pa(x)] vt to group together.

água ['agwa] f water; ~ **doce/salgada** fresh/salt water; ~ **benta** holy water; ~ **corrente** running water; ~ **destilada** distilled water; ~ **mineral com gás** OU **gaseificada** fizzy OU sparkling mineral water; ~ **mineral sem gás** still mineral water; ~ **potável** drinking water; ~ **sanitária** (Br) household bleach; ~ **tônica** tonic water; **de dar ~ na boca** mouthwatering.

aguaceiro [agwa'sejru] m downpour.

água-de-colônia [,agwad3iko'lonja] f eau de cologne.

aguado, -da [a'gwadu, -da] adj watery.

água-oxigenada [,agw(a)ɔksiʒe'nada] f hydrogen peroxide.

aguardar [agwar'da(x)] vt to wait for.

aguardente [agwax'dẽntʃi] f spirit (Brit), liquor (Am); ~ **de cana** rum; ~ **de pêra** pear brandy; ~ **velha** brandy.

aguarela [agwa'rɛla] f (Port) watercolour.

aguarrás [agwa'xaʃ] f turpentine.

água-viva [,agwa'viva] (pl **águas-vivas** [,agwaʒ'vivaʃ]) f jellyfish.

aguçado, -da [agu'sadu, -da] adj sharp.

aguçar [agu'sa(x)] vt to sharpen.

agudo, -da [a'gudu, -da] adj (dor) sharp; (som, voz) shrill; (doença) acute.

aguentar [agwẽn'tar] vt (Port) = **agüentar**.

agüentar [agwẽn'ta(x)] vt (Br) to stand.

⊔ **agüentar com** v + prep (Br) (peso) to support.

águia ['agja] f eagle.

agulha [a'guʎa] f needle.

agulheta [agu'ʎeta] f nozzle.

aí [a'i] adv there; (então) then; **por ~** (direção) that way; (em lugar indeterminado) over there; **tem alguém por ~ assaltando turistas** someone is going around mugging tourists.

ai [aj] interj ouch!

AIDS [ajdʒs] f (Br) AIDS.

ainda [a'inda] adv still; ~ **agora** only just; ~ **assim** even so; ~ **bem!** thank goodness!; ~ **bem que** thank goodness; ~ **não** not yet; ~ **por cima** to cap

it all; ~ **que** even though.

aipim [aj'pĩ] (pl **-ns** [-ʃ]) m cassava, manioc.

aipo ['ajpu] m celery.

ajeitar [aʒej'ta(x)] vt (cabelo) to tidy up; (gravata, saia) to straighten.

⊐ **ajeitar-se** vp (acomodar-se) to make o.s. comfortable; **~-se com algo** (saber lidar com) to get to grips with sthg.

ajoelhar-se [aʒwe'ʎaxsi] vp to kneel down.

ajuda [a'ʒuda] f help.

ajudante [aʒu'dãntʃi] mf helper.

ajudar [aʒu'da(x)] vt to help.

ajuste [a'ʒuʃtʃi] m: ~ **de contas** revenge.

Al. (abrev de alameda) Ave.

ala ['ala] f (fileira) row; (de edifício) wing.

alambique [alãm'biki] m still.

alameda [ala'meda] f avenue.

alargar [alax'ga(x)] vt (estrada) to widen; (peça de roupa) to let out; (em tempo, influência) to extend; (negócio) to expand ◆ vi (pulôver, luvas, etc) to stretch.

alarido [ala'ridu] m uproar.

alarmante [alax'mãntʃi] adj alarming.

alarme [a'laxmi] m alarm; **falso ~, ~ falso** false alarm.

alastrar [alaʃ'tra(x)] vt to spread.

⊐ **alastrar-se** vp to spread.

alavanca [ala'vãŋka] f lever.

albergue [aw'bexgi] m hostel.

albufeira [awbu'fejra] f lagoon.

álbum ['awbũ] (pl **-ns** [-ʃ]) m album.

alça ['awsa] f (de vestido, combinação, arma) strap; (de bolsa, mala) handle.

alcachofra [awka'ʃofra] f artichoke.

alcançar [awkã'sa(x)] vt to reach; (apanhar) to catch up; (obter) to get; (compreender) to grasp.

alcance [aw'kãsi] m (de mão) reach; (de vista, projéctil) range; **ao ~ de** (de mão) within reach of; (de vista, projéctil) within range of; **fora do ~ de** (de mão) out of reach of; (de vista, projéctil) out of range of.

alçapão [awsa'pãw] (pl **-ões** [-õjʃ]) m trapdoor.

alcaparras [awka'paxaʃ] fpl capers.

alçapões → alçapão.

alcateia [awka'teja] f pack.

alcatifa [awka'tʃifa] *f* carpet.

alcatra [aw'katra] *f* rump.

alcatrão [awka'trãw] *m* tar.

álcool ['awk(w)ɔw] *m (bebidas alcoólicas)* alcohol; *(étano)* ethanol; ~ **etílico** ethyl alcohol.

alcoólatra [aw'kɔlatra] *m, f* alcoholic.

alcoólico, -ca [aw'kwɔliku, -ka] *adj & m, f* alcoholic.

Alcorão [awko'rãw] *m* Koran.

alcunha [aw'kuɲa] *f* nickname.

aldeia [aw'deja] *f* village.

alecrim [ale'krĩ] *m* rosemary.

alegação [alega'sãw] (*pl* **-ões** [-õjʃ]) *f (acusação)* allegation; *(explicação)* explanation; *(JUR: defesa)* stated defence.

alegar [ale'ga(x)] *vt* to state; *(explicar)* to claim.

alegoria [alego'ria] *f* allegory.

alegórico [ale'gɔriku] *adj m* → **carro**.

alegrar [ale'gra(x)] *vt (pessoa)* to cheer up; *(ambiente, casa)* to brighten up; *(festa)* to liven up.

⊐ **alegrar-se** *vp* to cheer up.

alegre [a'legri] *adj (dia, cor)* bright; *(pessoa)* cheerful; *(fig: bêbado)* merry.

alegria [ale'gria] *f* joy.

aleijado, -da [alej'ʒadu, -da] *adj* crippled.

aleijar [alej'ʒa(x)] *vt (Br: mutilar)* to cripple; *(Port: machucar)* to hurt.

além [a'lẽj] *adv* over there ◆ *m*: **o** ~ the hereafter; ~ **disso** besides; **mais** ~ further on.

alemã → **alemão**.

alemães → **alemão**.

Alemanha [ale'maɲa] *f*: **a** ~ Germany.

alemão, -mã [ale'mãw, -mã] (*mpl* **-ães** [-ãjʃ], *fpl* **-s** [-ʃ]) *adj & m, f* German ◆ *m (língua)* German.

além-mar [alẽj'ma(x)] *adv & m* overseas.

alentejano, -na [alẽnte'ʒanu, -na] *adj* of/relating to the Alentejo ◆ *m, f* native/inhabitant of the Alentejo.

alergia [alex'ʒia] *f* allergy; *(fig: a trabalho, estudo)* aversion.

alérgico, -ca [a'lexʒiku, -ka] *adj* allergic.

alerta [a'lexta] *adv* on the alert ◆ *m* alert.

alfa ['awfa] *m* → **comboio**.

alfabético, -ca [awfa'bɛtʃiku, -ka] *adj* alphabetical.

alfabeto [awfa'bɛtu] *m* alphabet.

alface [aw'fasi] *f* lettuce.

alfacinha [awfa'siɲa] *mf (fam)* colloquial term for a native or inhabitant of Lisbon.

alfaiate [awfa'jatʃi] *m* tailor.

alfândega [aw'fãndega] *f* customs *(pl).*

alfazema [awfa'zema] *f* lavender.

alfinete [awfi'netʃi] *m* pin; *(jóia)* brooch; ~ **de gravata** tie pin; ~ **de segurança** safety pin.

alforreca [awfo'xɛka] *f* jellyfish.

alga ['awga] *f* seaweed.

algarismo [awga'riʒmu] *m* numeral.

algazarra [awga'zaxa] *f* racket.

álgebra ['awʒebra] *f* algebra.

algemas [aw'ʒemaʃ] *fpl* handcuffs.

algibeira [awʒi'bejra] *f* pocket.

algo ['awgu] *pron* something.

algodão [awgo'dãw] *m* cotton; ~ **doce** candy floss *(Brit)*, cotton candy *(Am)*; ~ **hidrófilo** cotton wool.

alguém [aw'gẽj] *pron (em afirmações)* somebody, someone; *(em perguntas)* anybody, anyone; **ser** ~ *(ser importante)* to be somebody.

algum, -ma [aw'gũ, -ma] (*mpl* **-ns** [-ʃ], *fpl* **-s** [-ʃ]) *adj (indeterminado)* some; *(em interrogativas, negativas)* any ◆ *pron (indicando pessoa)* somebody; *(indicando coisa)* one; *(em interrogativas: pessoa)* anybody; *(em interrogativas: coisa)* any; ~ **dia** one OU some day; **alguma coisa** something, anything; **alguma vez** sometime; **não há melhora alguma** there's no improvement.

⊐ **alguma** *f (evento, feito)* something.

⊐ **alguns, algumas** *pron pl* some.

algures [aw'guriʃ] *adv* somewhere.

alheio, alheia [a'ʎeju, a'ʎeja] *adj (de outrem)* someone else's; *(desconhecido)* foreign; *(distraído)* distracted; ~ **a** *(sem consciência de)* oblivious to.

alho ['aʎu] *m* garlic; ~ **francês** *(Port)* leek.

alho-poró [aʎupo'rɔ] (*pl* **alhos-porós** [aʎuʃpo'rɔjʃ]) *m (Br)* leek.

alho-porro [aʎu'poxu] (*pl* **alhos-porros** [aʎuʃ'poxuʃ]) *m* wild leek.

ali [a'li] *adv* there; **aqui e** ~ here and there; **até** ~ up until then; **logo** ~ just there; **por** ~ **(algures)** around there (somewhere); **ele foi por** ~ he went that way.

aliado, -da [a'ljadu. -da] *adj* allied ♦ *m*, *f* ally.

aliança [a'ljãsa] *f* alliance; *(anel)* wedding ring.

aliar [a'lja(x)] *vt* to ally.

⊐ aliar-se *vp* to form an alliance.

aliás [a'ljajʃ] *adv (a propósito)* as a matter of fact; *(além disso)* moreover.

álibi ['alibi] *m* alibi.

alicate [ali'katʃi] *m* pliers *(pl)*.

alice [a'lisi] *f (Br)* anchovies *(pl)*.

alicerce [ali'sexsi] *m* foundation.

aliciante [ali'sjãntʃi] *adj* enticing ♦ *m* enticement.

aliciar [ali'sja(x)] *vt* to entice.

alienado, -da [alje'nadu. -da] *adj (pessoa)* alienated; *(bem)* transferred.

alimentação [alimẽnta'sãw] *f (alimentos)* food; *(acto)* feeding; *(dieta alimentar)* diet; *(de máquina)* supply.

alimentar [alimẽn'ta(x)] *(pl -res* [-riʃ]*) adj* food *(antes de s)* ♦ *vt (pessoa, animal)* to feed; *(máquina)* to fuel.

⊐ alimentar-se *vp* to eat.

alimentício, -cia [alimẽn'tʃisju. -sja] *adj* nutritious.

alimento [ali'mẽntu] *m (comida)* food; *(nutrição)* nutriment.

⊐ alimentos *mpl (Port: JUR)* alimony *(sg)*.

alinhado, -da [ali'nadu. -da] *adj (em linha)* aligned; *(pessoa)* elegant.

alinhamento [alina'mẽntu] *m (IN-FORM)* justification.

alinhar [ali'na(x)] *vt (pôr em linha)* to align; *(INFORM: texto)* to justify.

alinhavar [alina'va(x)] *vt* to tack.

alisar [ali'za(x)] *vt* to smooth.

alistar [aliʃ'ta(x)] *vt* to recruit.

⊐ alistar-se *vp (em exército)* to enlist; *(em partido)* to join.

aliviar [ali'vja(x)] *vt (dor)* to relieve; *(peso)* to lighten.

alívio [a'livju] *m* relief; *(de peso)* lightening.

alma ['awma] *f* soul.

almoçar [awmo'sa(x)] *vi* to have lunch ♦ *vt* to have for lunch.

almoço [aw'mosu] *m* lunch.

almofada [awmo'fada] *f (de cama)* pillow; *(de sofá)* cushion; *(de carimbo)* inkpad.

almôndega [aw'mõndega] *f* meatball.

alô [a'lo] *interj (Br)* hello!

alojamento [aloʒa'mẽntu] *m (acto)* housing; *(lugar)* accommodation *(Brit)*,

accommodations *(pl) (Am)*.

alojar [alo'ʒa(x)] *vt* to put up.

⊐ alojar-se *vp* to stay.

alpendre [aw'pẽndri] *m* porch.

alpercata [awpex'kata] *f* sandal.

alperce [aw'pexsi] *m* apricot.

Alpes ['awpiʃ] *mpl*: **os ~** the Alps.

alpinismo [awpi'niʒmu] *m* mountaineering; **fazer ~** to go climbing.

alpinista [awpi'niʃta] *mf* mountaineer.

alta ['awta] *f (de preço, valor)* rise; *(de cidade) geographically higher and generally more wealthy part of a city;* **dar ~ a** *(doente)* to discharge; **ter ~** *(de hospital)* to be discharged.

altar [aw'ta(x)] *(pl -res* [-riʃ]*) m* altar.

alteração [awtera'sãw] *(pl -ões* [-õjʃ]*) f* alteration; **sem ~** unaltered.

alterar [awte'ra(x)] *vt* to alter.

alternar [awtex'na(x)] *vt* to alternate.

alternativa [awtexna'tʃiva] *f* alternative.

altifalante [awtifa'lãnte] *m (Port)* = alto-falante.

altitude [awtʃi'tudʒi] *f* altitude.

altivez [awtʃi'veʒ] *f (orgulho)* pride; *(arrogância)* haughtiness.

altivo, -va [aw'tʃivu. -va] *adj (orgulhoso)* proud; *(arrogante)* haughty.

alto, -ta ['awtu. -ta] *adj* high; *(pessoa, árvore, edifício)* tall; *(som, voz)* loud ♦ *interj* stop! ♦ *m (cume)* top; *(céu)* heaven ♦ *adv (falar, rir)* loud; *(relativo a posição)* high; **alta costura** haute couture; **ao ~** upright; **do ~ de** from the top of; **por ~** *(fig)* superficially; **o mais ~/a mais alta** *(pessoa)* the tallest; *(objeto)* the highest.

alto-falante ['awtofa'lãtʃi] *m (Br)* loudspeaker.

altura [aw'tura] *f (de pessoa, objecto)* height; *(de som)* level; *(altitude)* altitude; *(ocasião, época)* time; *(momento)* moment; **o muro tem um metro de ~** the wall is a metre high; **a certa** OU **dada ~** at a given moment; **nessa ~** at that time; **por ~ de** around; **estar à ~ da situação** to be equal to the task.

alucinação [alusina'sãw] *(pl -ões* [-õjʃ]*) f* hallucination.

alucinante [alusi'nãntʃi] *adj* amazing.

aludir [alu'di(x)] : **aludir a** *v + prep* to allude to.

alugar [alu'ga(x)] *vt (casa)* to rent;

(carro) to hire *(Brit)*, to rent *(Am)*.

❑ **alugar-se** *vpr:* **"aluga-se" "to let"** *(Brit)*, **"for rent"** *(Am)*; **"alugam-se quartos"** "rooms to let".

aluguel [alu'gɛw] *(pl* **-éis** [-'ɛjʃ]) *m (Br) (de carro)* hire *(Brit)*, rental *(Am)*.

aluguer [alu'gɛr] *(pl* **-res** [-reʃ]) *m (Port)* = **aluguel**.

aluir [a'lwi(x)] *vi* to collapse.

alumiar [alu'mja(x)] *vt* to light up.

alumínio [alu'minju] *m* aluminium.

aluno, -na [a'lunu, -na] *m, f (de escola)* pupil; *(de universidade)* student.

alusão [alu'zãw] *(pl* **-ões** [-õjʃ]) *f* allusion; **fazer ~ a** to allude to.

alvejar [awve'ʒa(x)] *vt* to shoot.

alvo ['awvu] *m* target.

alvorada [awvo'rada] *f* dawn.

alvoroço [awvo'rosu] *m (gritaria)* uproar; *(excitação)* commotion.

amabilidade [amabili'dadʒi] *f* kindness.

amaciador [amasja'dor] *(pl* **-res** [-riʃ]) *m (Port) (de cabelo)* conditioner; *(para roupa)* fabric softener.

amaciante [ama'sjãntʃi] *f (Br):* **~ (de roupa)** fabric softener.

amador, -ra [ama'do(x), -ra] *(mpl* **-res** [-riʃ], *fpl* **-s** [-ʃ]) *adj & m, f* amateur.

amadurecer [amadure'se(x)] *vi (fruta)* to ripen; *(pessoa)* to mature; *(fig: idéia)* to develop.

âmago ['amagu] *m* heart.

amainar [amaj'na(x)] *vt (vela)* to lower ♦ *vi (fig: vento, chuva)* to abate..

amaldiçoar [amawdi'swa(x)] *vt* to curse.

amálgama [a'mawgama] *f* amalgam.

amalgamar [amawga'ma(x)] *vt* to amalgamate.

amamentar [amamẽn'ta(x)] *vt* to breastfeed.

amanhã [ama'ɲã] *adv & m* tomorrow; **~ de manhã** tomorrow morning; **~ à noite/tarde** tomorrow evening/afternoon; **depois de ~** the day after tomorrow; **o ~** the future.

amanhecer [amaɲe'se(x)] *m* dawn ♦ *v impess:* **já amanheceu** dawn has broken.

amansar [amã'sa(x)] *vt* to tame.

amante [a'mãntʃi] *mf* lover; **ser ~ de** to be a lover of.

amanteigado, -da [amãntej'gadu, -da] *adj (molho)* buttery; *(queijo)* creamy.

amar [a'ma(x)] *vt* to love.

amarelado, -da [amare'ladu, -da] *adj* yellowish.

amarelinha [amare'liɲa] *f (Br: jogo)* hopscotch.

amarelo, -la [ama'rɛlu, -la] *adj & m* yellow.

amargar [amax'ga(x)] *vi* to taste bitter ♦ *vt (desilusão)* to suffer.

amargo, -ga [a'maxgu, -ga] *adj* bitter; *(fig: vida)* hard.

amarrar [ama'xa(x)] *vt (barco)* to moor; *(pessoa, animal)* to tie up.

amarrotado, -da [amaxo'tadu, -da] *adj (papel)* crumpled; *(roupa)* creased.

amarrotar [amaxo'ta(x)] *vt (papel)* to crumple (up); *(roupa)* to crease.

amassar [ama'sa(x)] *vt (cimento)* to mix; *(pão)* to knead; *(carro)* to smash up.

amável [a'mavew] *(pl* **-eis** [-ejʃ]) *adj* kind.

Amazonas [ama'zonaʃ] *m:* **o ~** the Amazon.

Amazônia [ama'zonja] *f:* **a ~** the Amazon region.

âmbar ['ãmba(x)] *m* amber.

ambição [ãmbi'sãw] *(pl* **-ões** [-õjʃ]) *f* ambition.

ambientador [ãmbjẽnta'dor] *(pl* **-res** [-reʃ]) *m (Port):* **~ do ar** air freshener.

ambiental [ãmbjẽn'taw] *(pl* **-ais** [-ajʃ]) *adj* environmental.

ambiente [ãm'bjẽntʃi] *m (natural)* environment; *(ar)* atmosphere.

ambigüidade [ãmbigwi'dadʒi] *f* ambiguity.

ambíguo, -gua [ãm'bigwu, -gwa] *adj* ambiguous.

âmbito ['ãmbitu] *m* sphere.

ambos, -bas [ãmbuʃ, -baʃ] *adj pl* both ♦ *pron pl* both (of them).

ambrosia [ãmbro'zia] *f* sweet custard pudding made with eggs and milk.

ambulância [ãmbu'lãsja] *f* ambulance.

ambulante [ãmbu'lãntʃi] *adj* travelling.

ambulatório [ãmbula'tɔrju] *m (Br) (de hospital)* outpatients' (department); *(de escola, fábrica)* medical room.

ameaça [ame'asa] *f* threat; **sob ~** under threat.

ameaçar [amea'sa(x)] *vt* to threaten; **ameaça chover** it looks like rain.

amedrontar [amedrõn'ta(x)] *vt* to frighten.

ameixa [a'mejʃa] *f* plum.
amêndoa [a'mẽndwa] *f* almond; **~ amarga** *almond liqueur, served chilled.*
amendoeira [amẽn'dwejra] *f* almond tree.
amendoim [amẽn'dwĩ] (*pl* **-ns** [-ʃ]) *m* peanut; **~ torrado** roasted peanuts *(pl)*.
ameno, -na [a'menu, -na] *adj (temperatura, clima)* mild.
América [a'mɛrika] *f*: **a ~** America; **a ~ Central** Central America; **a ~ Latina** Latin America; **a ~ do Norte** North America; **a ~ do Sul** South America.
americano, -na [ameri'kanu, -na] *adj & m, f* American.
ametista [ame'tiʃta] *f* amethyst.
amianto [a'mjãntu] *m* asbestos.
amido [a'midu] *m* starch; **~ de milho** cornflour *(Brit)*, cornstarch *(Am)*.
amigável [ami'gavew] (*pl* **-eis** [-ejʃ]) *adj* friendly.
amígdalas [a'migdalaʃ] *fpl* tonsils.
amigdalite [amigda'litʃi] *f* tonsillitis.
amigo, -ga [a'migu, -ga] *m, f* friend ♦ *adj* friendly.
amistoso, -osa [amiʃ'tozu, -ɔza] *adj* friendly.
amizade [ami'zadʒi] *f* friendship.
amnésia [am'nɛzja] *f* amnesia.
amnistia [amneʃ'tia] *f (Port)* = **anistia**.
amolação [amola'sãw] (*pl* **-ões** [-õjʃ]) *f (Br: chateação)* nuisance.
amolar [amo'la(x)] *vt (afiar)* to sharpen; *(Br: aborrecer)* to bother.
amolecer [amole'se(x)] *vt* to soften.
amoníaco [amo'niaku] *m* ammonia.
amontoar [amõn'twa(x)] *vt* to pile up; *(dinheiro, riquezas)* to amass.
❏ amontoar-se *vp* to pile up.
amor [a'mo(x)] (*pl* **-res** [-riʃ]) *m* love; **fazer ~** to make love.
amora [a'mɔra] *f (de silva)* blackberry; *(de amoreira)* mulberry.
amordaçar [amoxda'sa(x)] *vt* to gag.
amoroso, -osa [amo'rozu, -ɔza] *adj* affectionate.
amor-perfeito [a,moxpex'fejtu] (*pl* **amores-perfeitos** [a,moriʃpex'fejtuʃ]) *m* pansy.
amor-próprio [a,mox'prɔpriu] *m* self-esteem.
amortecedor [amoxtese'do(x)] (*pl* **-res** [-riʃ]) *m* shock absorber.

amortização [amoxtiza'sãw] (*pl* **-ões** [-õjʃ]) *f* repayment by instalments.
amortizar [amoxti'za(x)] *vt* to repay by instalments.
amostra [a'mɔʃtra] *f* sample; *(prova)* show; **~ grátis** free sample.
amparar [ãmpa'ra(x)] *vt* to support.
amparo [ãm'paru] *m* support.
ampliação [ãmplia'sãw] (*pl* **-ões** [-õjʃ]) *f (de fotografia)* enlargement.
ampliar [ãmpli'a(x)] *vt (fotografia)* to enlarge.
amplificador [ãmplifika'do(x)] (*pl* **-res** [-riʃ]) *m (de som)* amplifier.
amplificar [ãmplifi'ka(x)] *vt (som)* to amplify.
amplitude [ãmpli'tudʒi] *f* extent.
amplo, -pla [ãmplu, -pla] *adj (quarto, cama)* spacious; *(estrada)* wide; *(conhecimento)* extensive.
ampola [ãm'pola] *f* phial.
amputar [ãmpu'ta(x)] *vt* to amputate.
amuado, -da [a'mwadu, -da] *adj* sulky.
amuar [a'mwa(x)] *vi (criança)* to sulk.
anã → anão.
anacronismo [anakro'niʒmu] *m* anachronism.
anagrama [ana'grama] *m* anagram.
analfabeto, -ta [anawfa'bɛtu, -ta] *m, f & adj* illiterate.
analgésico [anaw'ʒɛziku] *m* painkiller.
analisar [anali'za(x)] *vt* to analyse.
análise [a'nalizi] *f* analysis; *(Port: a sangue, urina)* test; **em última ~** in the final analysis.
analista [ana'liʃta] *mf* analyst.
analogia [analo'ʒia] *f* analogy.
ananás [ana'naʃ] (*pl* **-ases** [-azeʃ]) *m* pineapple.
anão, anã [a'nãw, a'nã] (*mpl* **-ões** [-õjʃ], *fpl* **-s** [-ʃ]) *m, f* dwarf.
anarquia [anax'kia] *f* anarchy.
anatomia [anato'mia] *f* anatomy.
anca [ãŋka] *f* hip.
anchovas [ã'ʃovaʃ] *fpl* anchovies.
ancinho [ã'siɲu] *m* rake.
âncora [ãŋkora] *f* anchor.
andaime [ãn'dajmi] *m* scaffold.
andamento [ãnda'mẽntu] *m (velocidade)* speed; *(rumo)* direction; *(MUS)* tempo; **em ~** *(em progresso)* in progress.
andar [ãn'da(x)] (*pl* **-res** [-riʃ]) *vi* to

walk ◆ *vt (distância, tempo)* to walk for ◆ *m (de edifício)* floor; *(maneira de caminhar)* walk; **ele anda um pouco deprimido ultimamente** he has been a bit depressed lately; **gosto de ~ a cavalo** I like horse-riding; **~ de avião** to fly; **~ de bicicleta** to cycle; **~ a pé** to walk; **o ~ de baixo** *(de casa)* downstairs; **o ~ de cima** *(de casa)* upstairs.

Andes [ˈãndiʃ] *mpl:* **os ~** the Andes.

andorinha [ãndoˈriɲa] *f* swallow.

Andorra [ãnˈdoxa] *s* Andorra.

anedota [aneˈdɔta] *f* joke.

anel [aˈnɛw] *(pl* **-éis** *[-ɛjʃ]) m* ring; *(de cabelo)* ringlet; *(de corrente)* link; **~ de noivado** engagement ring.

anemia [aneˈmia] *f* anaemia.

anestesia [anɛʃteˈzia] *f* anaesthetic; **~ geral/local** general/local anaesthetic.

anestesiar [anɛʃteˈzja(x)] *vt* to anaesthetize.

anexar [anɛkˈsa(x)] *vt* to attach; **~ algo a algo** to attach sthg to sthg.

anexo, -xa [aˈnɛksu, -ksa] *adj* attached.

anfiteatro [ãfiˈtʒjatru] *m* amphitheatre; *(sala de aula)* lecture theatre.

angariar [ãŋgaˈrja(x)] *vt (dinheiro)* to raise.

angina [ãˈʒina] *f:* **~ de peito** angina (pectoris).

❏ **anginas** *fpl* tonsillitis *(sg)*.

anglicano, -na [ãŋgliˈkanu, -na] *adj* Anglican.

Angola [ãŋˈgola] *s* Angola.

angolano, -na [ãŋgoˈlanu, -na] *adj & m, f* Angolan.

angra [ˈãŋgra] *f* inlet.

angu [ãŋˈgu] *m* a gruel made with cornflour or cassava.

ângulo [ˈãŋgulu] *m* angle.

angústia [ũŋˈguʃtʒja] *f* anguish.

animação [animaˈsãw] *f (alegria)* liveliness; *(entusiasmo)* enthusiasm; *(movimento)* bustle.

animado, -da [aniˈmadu, -da] *adj (alegre)* lively; *(entusiasmado)* enthusiastic; *(movimentado)* bustling.

animador, -ra [animaˈdo(x), -ra] *(mpl* **-res** *[-riʃ], fpl* **-s** *[-ʃ]) adj (que alegra)* cheering; *(que encoraja)* encouraging.

animal [aniˈmaw] *(pl* **-ais** *[-ajʃ]) m* animal; **~ doméstico** pet; **~ selvagem** wild animal.

animar [aniˈma(x)] *vt (alegrar)* to cheer up.

❏ **animar-se** *vp (alegrar-se)* to cheer up.

ânimo [ˈanimu] *m* courage.

aniquilar [anikiˈla(x)] *vt* to annihilate.

anis [aˈniʃ] *(pl* **-ses** *[-zeʃ]) m (licor)* anisette; *(planta)* aniseed.

anistia [aniʃˈtʃia] *f (Br)* amnesty.

aniversário [anivexˈsarju] *m (de pessoa)* birthday; *(de acontecimento)* anniversary; **feliz ~!** Happy Birthday!

anjo [ˈãʒu] *m* angel.

ano [ˈanu] *m* year; **quantos ~s você tem?** how old are you?; **faço ~s amanhã** it's my birthday tomorrow; **~ bissexto** leap year; **~ letivo** academic year; **Ano Novo** New Year, Hogmanay *(Scot)*; **~ após ~** year after year.

anões → anão.

anoitecer [anojteˈse(x)] *m* dusk, nightfall ◆ *v impess* to get dark.

anomalia [anomaˈlia] *f* anomaly.

anoraque [anoˈraki] *m* anorak.

anorexia [anorɛkˈsia] *f* anorexia.

anormal [anoxˈmaw] *(pl* **-ais** *[-ajʃ]) adj* abnormal; *(idiota)* stupid; *(incomum)* unusual ◆ *m, f (idiota)* moron.

anormalidade [anoxmaliˈdadʒi] *f* abnormality.

anotação [anotaˈsãw] *(pl* **-ões** *[-õjʃ]) f* note.

anotar [anoˈta(x)] *vt* to note down.

ânsia [ˈãsja] *f* anxiety.

ansiar [ãˈsja(x)] : **ansiar por** *v + prep* to long for.

ansiedade [ãsjeˈdadʒi] *f* anxiety.

ansioso, -osa [ãˈsjozu, -ɔza] *adj* anxious.

antebraço [ãntʃiˈbrasu] *m* forearm.

antecedência [ãntɛseˈdẽsja] *f:* **com ~** in advance.

antecedente [ãntɛseˈdẽtʃi] *adj* preceding.

❏ **antecedentes** *mpl (médicos)* records; *(criminais)* record *(sg)*.

antecipação [ãntɛsipaˈsãw] *(pl* **-ões** *[-õjʃ]) f* anticipation.

antecipadamente [ãntɛsipadaˈmẽtʃi] *adv* in advance, beforehand.

antecipar [ãntɛsiˈpa(x)] *vt* to anticipate.

❏ **antecipar-se** *vp* to get there first.

antemão [ãntʃeˈmãw] : **de antemão** *adv* beforehand.

antena [ãnˈtena] *f* aerial; **~ parabólica** satellite dish.

anteontem [ãntʃiˈõntẽ] *adv* the day before yesterday.

antepassado [ãntʃipaˈsadu] *m* ancestor.

anterior [ãnteˈrjo(x)] (*pl* **-res** [-riʃ]) *adj* previous.

antes [ˈãntʃ] *adv* before; *(primeiramente)* first; ~ **assim** (it's) just as well; ~ **de** before; ~ **de mais (nada)** first of all; **o quanto** ~ as soon as possible.

antever [ãnteˈve(x)] *vt* to foresee.

antiaderente [ãntʃiadeˈrẽntʃi] *adj* nonstick.

antibiótico [ãntʃiˈbjɔtʃiku] *m* antibiotic.

anticaspa [ãntʃiˈkaʃpa] *adj inv* anti-dandruff.

anticoncepcional [ãntʃikõsepsjuˈnaw] (*pl* **-ais** [-ajʃ]) *adj* contraceptive.

anticonceptivo [ãntʃikõsepˈtʃivu] *m* contraceptive.

anticongelante [ãntʃikõʒeˈlãntʃi] *m* antifreeze.

anticorpo [ãntʃiˈkoxpu] *m* antibody.

antidepressivo [ãntʃidepreˈsivu] *m* antidepressant.

antídoto [ãnˈtʃidotu] *m* antidote.

antigamente [ãntʃigaˈmẽntʃi] *adv (antes)* formerly; *(no passado)* in the old days.

antigo, -ga [ãnˈtʃigu, -ga] *adj (livro, objeto)* old; *(costume, era)* ancient; *(objeto valioso)* antique.

antiguidade [ãntʃigwiˈdadʒi] *f* antiquity; *(em emprego)* seniority; **a Antiguidade** Antiquity.

⏘ **antiguidades** *fpl* antiques.

antipatia [ãntʃipaˈtʃia] *f* dislike.

antipático, -ca [ãntʃiˈpatʃiku, -ka] *adj* unfriendly.

antipatizar [ãntʃipatʃiˈza(x)] *vi*: ~ **com alguém** to dislike sb.

antiquado, -da [ãntʃiˈkwadu, -da] *adj* old-fashioned.

antiquário [ãntʃiˈkwarju] *m* antique dealer.

anti-séptico, -ca [ãntʃiˈseptʃiku, -ka] *adj* antiseptic.

antologia [ãntoloˈʒia] *f* anthology.

anual [aˈnwaw] (*pl* **-ais** [-ajʃ]) *adj* annual.

anuir [aˈnwi(x)] *vi* to agree.

anulação [anulaˈsãw] (*pl* **-ões** [-õjʃ]) *f* cancellation.

anular [anuˈla(x)] *vt* to cancel ♦ *m* ring finger.

anunciar [anũˈsja(x)] *vt* to announce; *(produto)* to advertise.

anúncio [aˈnũsju] *m (de produto)* advert; *(aviso)* announcement.

ânus [ˈanuʃ] *m* anus.

anzol [ãˈzɔw] (*pl* **-óis** [-ɔjʃ]) *m* fishhook.

ao [aw] = **a** + **o**, → **a**.

aonde [aˈõndʒi] *adv* where; ~ **quer que** ... wherever ....

aos [awʃ] = **a** + **os**, → **a**.

apagado, -da [apaˈgadu, -da] *adj (luz, lume)* out; *(televisão, rádio)* off; *(escrita, desenho)* faint; *(pessoa)* dull.

apagar [apaˈga(x)] *vt (fogo)* to put out; *(televisão, rádio, luz)* to turn OU switch off; *(escrita, desenho)* to rub out.

apaixonado, -da [apajʃoˈnadu, -da] *adj* in love; *(exaltado)* passionate; **estar ~ por** to be in love with.

apaixonante [apajʃoˈnãntʃi] *adj* fascinating.

apaixonar [apajʃoˈna(x)] *vt*: **o futebol apaixona as massas** football thrills the masses.

⏘ **apaixonar-se** *vp* to fall in love; **~-se por** to fall in love with.

apalermado, -da [apalexˈmadu, -da] *adj* silly.

apalpar [apawˈpa(x)] *vt* to touch; ~ **o terreno** *(fig)* to see how the land lies.

apanhar [apaˈɲa(x)] *vt* to catch; *(levantar do chão)* to pick up; ~ **chuva** to get wet; ~ **sol** to sunbathe.

aparador [aparaˈdo(x)] (*pl* **-res** [-riʃ]) *m* sideboard.

apara-lápis [apaˌraˈlapiʃ] *m inv* (Port) pencil sharpener.

aparar [apaˈra(x)] *vt (barba)* to trim; *(sebe, arbusto)* to prune; *(segurar)* to catch; *(lápis)* to sharpen.

aparecer [apareˈse(x)] *vi (surgir)* to appear; *(apresentar-se)* to show up; *(algo perdido)* to turn up.

aparelhagem [apareˈʎaʒẽ] (*pl* **-ns** [-ʃ]) *f*: ~ **(de som)** sound system, stereo.

aparelho [apaˈreʎu] *m* appliance; ~ **digestivo** digestive system; ~ **para os dentes** brace.

aparência [apaˈrẽsja] *f* appearance.

aparentar [aparẽˈta(x)] *vt* to look like; **aparenta ter uns 40 anos** he looks about 40.

aparente [apaˈrẽntʃi] *adj* apparent.

Apart. *abrev* = **apartamento**.

apartado [aparˈtadu] *m* (*Port*) P.O. Box.

apartamento [apaxtaˈmẽntu] *m* flat (*Brit*), apartment (*Am*).

apatia [apaˈtʃia] *f* apathy.

apavorado, -da [apavoˈradu, -da] *adj* terrified.

apear-se [aˈpjaxsi] *vp*: ~ **de** to get off.

apelar [apeˈla(x)] *vi*: ~ **para** to appeal to.

apelido [apeˈlidu] *m* (*Br: alcunha*) nickname; (*Port: nome de família*) surname.

apelo [aˈpelu] *m* appeal; **fazer um ~ a** to appeal to.

apenas [aˈpenaʃ] *adv* only ♦ *conj* as soon as; **quero ~ um copo de água** all I want is a glass of water.

apêndice [aˈpẽndʒisi] *m* appendix.

apendicite [apẽndʒiˈsitʃi] *f* appendicitis.

aperceber-se [apexseˈbexsi] *vp*: ~ **de algo** to realize; ~ **de que** (*verificar*) to realize (that).

aperfeiçoamento [apexfejswaˈmẽntu] *m* improvement.

aperfeiçoar [apexfejˈswa(x)] *vt* to improve.

aperitivo [aperiˈtʃivu] *m* (*vinho*) aperitif; (*tira-gosto*) appetizer.

apertado, -da [apexˈtadu, -da] *adj* tight; (*estrada*) narrow.

apertar [apexˈta(x)] *vt* (*comprimir*) to squeeze; (*botão, interruptor*) to press; (*cinto de segurança*) to fasten; (*parafuso, porca*) to tighten; (*casaco, vestido*) to take in.

aperto [aˈpextu] *m* (*de parafuso*) tightening; (*aglomeração*) crush; (*fig: dificuldade*) tight corner; ~ **de mão** handshake.

apesar [apeˈza(x)] : **apesar de** *prep* despite, in spite of.

apetecer [apeteˈse(x)] *vi*: **apetece-me um bolo** I feel like (having) a cake; **apetece-me sair** I feel like going out.

apetite [apeˈtʃitʃi] *m* appetite; **bom ~!** enjoy your meal!

apetitoso, -osa [apetʃiˈtozu, -ɔza] *adj* appetizing.

apetrecho [apeˈtreʃu] *m* tool; ~**s de pesca** fishing tackle (*sg*).

apimentado, -da [apimẽnˈtadu, -da] *adj* (*com pimenta*) peppery; (*picante*) spicy.

apinhado, -da [apiˈɲadu, -da] *adj*: ~ **de** packed with.

apitar [apiˈta(x)] *vi* (*trem, chaleira*) to whistle; (*árbitro*) to blow the whistle.

apito [aˈpitu] *m* whistle.

aplaudir [aplawˈdi(x)] *vt & vi* to applaud.

aplauso [aˈplawzu] *m* applause.

aplicação [aplikaˈsãw] (*pl* -ões [-õjʃ]) *f* (*em estudo, trabalho*) diligence; (*acessório*) appliqué; (*de dinheiro*) investment.

aplicado, -da [apliˈkadu, -da] *adj* (*aluno*) diligent; (*matemática, lingüística*) applied.

aplicar [apliˈka(x)] *vt* to apply; (*curativo, injeção*) to administer.

apoderar-se [apodeˈraxsi] : **apoderar-se** *vp* + *prep* to take control of.

apodrecer [apodreˈse(x)] *vt & vi* to rot.

apoiar [apoˈja(x)] *vt* to support; ~ **algo em algo** to rest sthg on OU against sthg.

❑ **apoiar-se** *vp* to hold on; ~**-se em** OU **a** to lean on OU against.

apoio [aˈpoju] *m* support.

apólice [aˈpɔlisi] *f*: ~ (**de seguro**) (insurance) policy.

apontador [apõntaˈdo(x)] (*pl* -**res** [-riʃ]) *m* (*Br: de lápis*) pencil sharpener.

apontamento [apõntaˈmẽntu] *m* note.

apontar [apõnˈta(x)] *vt* (*arma*) to aim; (*erro, falha*) to point out; (*tomar nota de*) to note down; (*razões, argumentos*) to put forward ♦ *vi*: ~ **para algo** to point to sthg.

aporrinhação [apoxiɲaˈsãw] (*pl* -ões [-õjʃ]) *f* (*Br: fam. aborrecimento*) annoyance.

após [aˈpɔjʃ] *prep* after ♦ *adv* afterwards.

após-barba [apɔjʒˈbaxba] *adj* (*Br*) → **loção**.

aposentado, -da [apozẽnˈtadu, -da] *adj* (*Br*) retired ♦ *m, f* (*Br*) pensioner.

aposentadoria [apozẽntadoˈria] *f* (*Br*) (*fato*) retirement; (*dinheiro*) pension.

aposento [apoˈzẽntu] *m* room.

aposta [aˈpɔʃta] *f* bet.

apostar [apoʃˈta(x)] *vt* to bet.

apostila [apoʃ'tʃila] f (Br) lecture notes (pl).

apóstrofo [a'pɔʃtrofu] m apostrophe.

aprazível [apra'zivɛw] (pl **-eis** [-ejʃ]) adj pleasant.

apreciação [apresja'sãw] (pl **-ões** [-õjʃ]) f (avaliação) assessment.

apreciar [apre'sja(x)] vt (gostar) to like; (avaliar) to judge, to assess; (paisagem, vista) to admire.

apreender [apriẽn'de(x)] vt (confiscar) to seize; (assimilar) to grasp.

apreensão [apriẽ'sãw] (pl **-ões** [-õjʃ]) f (de bens, produtos) seizure; (de novos conhecimentos) grasp; (preocupação) apprehension.

apreensivo, -va [apriẽ'sivu, -va] adj apprehensive.

aprender [aprẽn'de(x)] vi & vt to learn; ~ **a fazer algo** to learn to do sthg.

aprendiz [aprẽn'dʒiʒ] (pl **-zes** [-ziʃ]) m (de ofício) apprentice; (principiante) beginner.

aprendizagem [aprẽndʒi'zaʒẽ] f learning.

aprendizes → aprendiz.

apresentação [aprezẽnta'sãw] (pl **-ões** [-õjʃ]) f presentation; (aspecto) appearance; **a ~ do programa estará a cargo do Herman José** the programme will be presented by Herman José.

apresentador, -ra [aprezẽnta'do(x), -ra] (mpl **-res** [-riʃ], fpl **-s** [-ʃ]) m, f presenter.

apresentar [aprezẽn'ta(x)] vt (espetáculo) to present; (pessoa) to introduce; (exibir) to show.

❏ **apresentar-se** vp (comparecer) to report; **~-se a alguém** (a desconhecido) to introduce o.s. to sb.

apressado, -da [apre'sadu, -da] adj (pessoa) rushed; (decisão) hasty ♦ adv: **sair/entrar ~** to rush in/out.

apressar-se [apre'saxsi] vp to hurry up.

aprofundar [aprofũn'da(x)] vt (fig: assunto) to study in depth.

aprovação [aprova'sãw] (pl **-ões** [-õjʃ]) f approval; (em exame) pass.

aprovado, -da [apro'vadu, -da] adj: **ser ~** (EDUC) to pass.

aprovar [apru'va(x)] vt to approve; (em exame) to pass.

aproveitador, -ra [aprovejta'do(x), -ra] (mpl **-res** [-riʃ], fpl **-s** [-ʃ]) adj & m, f

(oportunista) opportunist.

aproveitamento [aprovejta'mẽntu] m (uso) use; (EDUC) progress.

❏ **aproveitamentos** mpl leftovers.

aproveitar [aprovej'ta(x)] vt (a ocasião) to take advantage of; (férias) to make the most of; (utilizar) to make use of.

❏ **aproveitar-se** vp: **~-se de** to take advantage of.

aproximadamente [aprosi,mada'mẽntʃi] adv approximately.

aproximado, -da [aprosi'madu, -da] adj approximate.

aproximar [aprosi'ma(x)] vt (objetos) to bring closer; (pessoas) to bring together.

❏ **aproximar-se** vp to come closer; **~-se de** to approach; **aproxima-se uma pessoa/um carro** someone/a car is coming.

aptidão [aptʃi'dãw] (pl **-ões** [-õjʃ]) f aptitude; (vocação) talent.

apto, -ta ['aptu, -ta] adj capable.

Apto. abrev (Br) = **apartamento**.

apunhalar [apuɲa'la(x)] vt to stab.

apuração [apura'sãw] (pl **-ões** [-õjʃ]) f selection.

apurado, -da [apu'radu, -da] adj selected; (sabor) distinctive; (visão, olfato) keen.

apurar [apu'ra(x)] vt (selecionar) to pick; (averiguar) to find out; (sabor) to bring out.

apuro [a'puru] m (dificuldade) fix; **estar em ~s** to be in a fix; **meter-se em ~s** to get into trouble.

aquarela [akwa'rɛla] f (Br) watercolour.

aquário [a'kwarju] m aquarium.

❏ **Aquário** m Aquarius.

aquático, -ca [a'kwatʃiku, -ka] adj aquatic; (ESP) water (antes de s).

aquecedor [akese'do(x)] (pl **-res** [-riʃ]) m heater.

aquecer [ake'se(x)] vt & vi to heat up.

❏ **aquecer-se** vp to warm o.s. up.

aquecimento [akesi'mẽntu] m heating; **~ central** central heating.

aqueduto [ake'dutu] m aqueduct.

àquela ['akɛla] = **a + aquela**, → **aquele.**

aquele, aquela [a'keli, a'kɛla] adj that, those (pl) ♦ pron that (one); **~ ali** that one there; **~ que** (relativo a pessoa) the one who, those who (pl); (relativo *a objeto)* the one which; **peça àquele homem/àquela mulher** ask that man/woman.

àquele ['akeli] = a + **aquele**, → **aquele**.

aqui [a'ki] *adv* here; **até ~** *(relativo a tempo)* up until now; **logo ~** right here; **por ~** this way; **por ~ em algum canto** somewhere around here.

aquilo [a'kilu] *pron* that; **você chama ~ de carro!** you call that a car!

àquilo [a'kilu] = a + **aquilo**, → **aquilo**.

aquisição [akizi'sãw] *(pl* **-ões** [-õjʃ]) *f* acquisition.

ar ['a(x)] *(pl* **ares** [ariʃ]) *m* air; *(brisa)* breeze; **dar ~es de** to pretend to be; **dar-se ~es de importante** to put on airs (and graces); **ir ao/sair do ~** *(em rádio, TV)* to go on/off the air; **ir pelos ~es** *(explodir)* to blow up; **ter ~ de** to look ou seem like; **~ condicionado** air conditioning; **ao ~** *(lançar, atirar)* into the air; **ao ~ livre** in the open air.

árabe ['arabi] *adj & mf* Arab ◆ *m (língua)* Arabic.

aragem [a'raʒẽ] *(pl* **-ns** [-ʃ]) *f* breeze.

arame [a'rami] *m* wire; **~ farpado** barbed wire.

aranha [a'raɲa] *f* spider.

arara [a'rara] *f* cockatoo.

arbitragem [axbi'traʒẽ] *(pl* **-ns** [-ʃ]) *f (de jogo)* refereeing; *(de litígio)* arbitration.

arbitrar [axbi'tra(x)] *vt (jogo)* to referee.

árbitro ['axbitru] *m (de jogo)* referee.

arborizado, -da [axbori'zadu, -da] *adj* wooded.

arbusto [ax'buʃtu] *m* bush.

arca ['axka] *f* trunk.

arcaico, -ca [ax'kajku, -ka] *adj* archaic.

archote [ax'ʃotʃi] *m* torch.

arco ['axku] *m (de edifício, construção)* arch; *(curva)* arc; *(de flechas)* bow; *(brinquedo)* hoop.

arco-íris [ax'kwiriʃ] *(pl* **arcos-íris** [axku'ziriʃ]) *m* rainbow.

ardência [ax'dẽsja] *f (Br) (de pele)* stinging; *(de estômago)* heartburn.

ardente [ax'dẽtʃi] *adj (fig: amor, paixão)* passionate.

arder [ax'de(x)] *vi* to burn; *(pele)* to sting.

ardor [ax'do(x)] *(pl* **-res** [-riʃ]) *m (de*

pele) stinging; **com ~** ardently.

ardósia [ax'dɔzja] *f* slate.

árduo, -dua ['axdwu, -dwa] *adj* arduous.

área ['arja] *f* area; *(fig: campo de ação)* field; **~ de serviço** *(em apartamento)* utility area; **grande ~** *(em futebol)* penalty area.

areal [a'rɛaw] *(pl* **-ais** [-ajʃ]) *m* beach.

areia [a'reja] *f* sand; **~s movediças** quicksand *(sg).*

arejar [are'ʒa(x)] *vt* to air ◆ *vi (fig: sair)* to get some air.

arena [a'rena] *f (de circo)* ring; *(de praça de touros)* bullring.

arenoso, -osa [are'nozu, -ɔza] *adj* sandy.

arenque [a'rẽŋki] *m* herring.

ares → **ar**.

Argentina [axʒẽn'tʃina] *f:* **a ~** Argentina.

argila [ax'ʒila] *f* clay.

argola [ax'gɔla] *f (anel)* ring; *(de porta)* knocker.

argolas *fpl (ESP)* rings; *(brincos)* hoop earrings.

argumentação [axgumẽnta'sãw] *(pl* **-ões** [-õjʃ]) *f* argument.

argumentar [axgumẽn'ta(x)] *vt & vi* to argue.

argumento [axgu'mẽntu] *m* argument; *(de filme)* plot.

ária ['arja] *f* aria.

árido, -da ['aridu, -da] *adj* arid.

Áries ['ariʃ] *m (Br)* Aries.

arma ['axma] *f* weapon; **~ branca** knife; **~ de fogo** firearm.

armação [axma'sãw] *(pl* **-ões** [-õjʃ]) *f* frame; *(de animal)* horns *(pl)*; *(de barco)* rigging; *(de óculos)* frames *(pl).*

armadilha [axma'diʎa] *f* trap.

armado, -da [ax'madu, -da] *adj* armed.

armadura [axma'dura] *f* suit of armour; *(de edifício)* framework.

armamento [axma'mẽntu] *m* armaments *(pl)*; *(de navio)* equipment.

armar [ax'ma(x)] *vt* to arm; *(tenda)* to put up.

armário [ax'marju] *m* cupboard; *(de roupa)* wardrobe.

armazém [axma'zẽ] *(pl* **-ns** [-ʃ]) *m* warehouse; **grande ~** *(loja)* department store.

aro ['aru] *m (de roda)* rim; *(de janela)* frame.

aroma [aˈroma] *m* aroma; *(em iogurte, bebida)* flavour; **com ~ de morango** strawberry flavour.

arpão [axˈpãw] (*pl* -ões [-õjʃ]) *m* harpoon.

arqueologia [axkjoloˈʒia] *f* archeology.

arquibancada [axkibãŋˈkada] *f (Br)* grandstand.

arquipélago [axkiˈpɛlagu] *m* archipelago.

arquitecto, -ta [arkiˈtɛtu, -ta] *m, f (Port)* = **arquiteto**.

arquitectura [arkitɛˈtura] *f (Port)* = **arquitetura**.

arquiteto, -ta [axkiˈtɛtu, -ta] *m, f (Br)* architect.

arquitetura [axkitɛˈtura] *f (Br)* architecture.

arquivo [axˈkivu] *m* archive; *(móvel)* filing cabinet; *(cartório)* registry office; *(Br: INFORM)* file.

arraial [axaˈjaw] (*pl* -ais [-ajʃ]) *m* = fete.

arrancar [axãŋˈka(x)] *vt (árvore, batatas)* to dig up; *(folhas, pêlos)* to pull out; *(dente)* to extract ♦ *vi (partir)* to set off; **~ algo das mãos de alguém** to snatch sthg from sb.

arranha-céus [aˌxaɲaˈsɛwʃ] *m inv* skyscraper.

arranhão [axaˈɲãw] (*pl* -ões [-õjʃ]) *m* scratch.

arranhar [axaˈɲa(x)] *vt* to scratch; *(parede, carro)* to scrape; **~ um pouco de algo** to get by in sthg.

⏝ **arranhar-se** *vp* to scratch o.s.

arranhões → **arranhão**.

arranjar [axãˈʒa(x)] *vt (reparar)* to fix, to repair; *(adquirir)* to get; **~ problemas** to get into trouble.

arranque [aˈxãŋki] *m* → **motor**..

arrasar [axaˈza(x)] *vt* to devastate.

arrastar [axaʃˈta(x)] *vt* to drag (along ou away).

arrecadar [axɛkaˈda(x)] *vt (objeto)* to store away; *(dinheiro)* to collect.

arredondado, -da [axɛdõˈdadu, -da] *adj (forma)* round, rounded; *(fig: valor)* rounded up.

arredondar [axɛdõˈda(x)] *vt (forma)* to make round; *(fig: valor)* to round up.

arredores [axeˈdɔriʃ] *mpl* outskirts.

arrefecer [axefeˈse(x)] *vi (tempo, ar)* to cool down; *(comida)* to get cold; *(fig: entusiasmo)* to cool.

arregaçar [axegaˈsa(x)] *vt (mangas, calças)* to roll up.

arreios [aˈxejuʃ] *mpl (de cavalo)* harness *(sg)*.

arremedar [axemeˈda(x)] *vt (imitar)* to ape.

arremessar [axemeˈsa(x)] *vt (pedra, flecha)* to hurl.

arrendamento [axẽndaˈmẽntu] *m (de casa)* rent.

arrendar [axẽnˈda(x)] *vt (casa)* to rent; **~ uma casa a alguém** to rent (out) a house to sb.

arrendatário, -ria [axẽndaˈtarju, -rja] *m, f (de casa)* tenant.

arrepender-se [axepẽnˈdexsi] *vp:* **~ de (ter feito) algo** to regret (doing) sthg.

arrepiar [axeˈpja(x)] *vt (pêlo, cabelo)* to make stand on end.

⏝ **arrepiar-se** *vp (de frio)* to shiver; *(de medo)* to shudder.

arrepio [axeˈpiu] *m (de frio)* shiver; *(de medo)* shudder.

arriscado, -da [axiʃˈkadu, -da] *adj (perigoso)* risky; *(corajoso)* daring.

arriscar [axiʃˈka(x)] *vt (pôr em risco)* to risk.

⏝ **arriscar-se** *vp* to take a risk.

arrogância [axoˈgãsja] *f (presunção)* arrogance.

arrogante [axoˈgãntʃi] *adj (presumido)* arrogant.

arrombar [axõmˈba(x)] *vt (porta, janela, cofre)* to force (open).

arrotar [axoˈta(x)] *vi* to burp, to belch.

arroto [aˈxotu] *m* burp, belch.

arroz [aˈxoʒ] *m* rice; **~ de forno** baked dish containing rice, chicken and/or prawns, vegetables and olives.

arroz-doce [axoʒˈdosi] *m* rice pudding.

arruaça [aˈxwasa] *f* street riot.

arruaceiro, -ra [axwaˈsejru, -ra] *adj* riotous ♦ *m, f* rioter.

arrumado, -da [axuˈmadu, -da] *adj (casa, secretária, gaveta)* tidy; *(mala)* packed *(fig: resolvido)* sorted (out).

arrumar [axuˈma(x)] *vt (casa, secretária, gaveta)* to tidy up; *(mala)* to pack.

arte [ˈaxtʃi] *f* art; **~s marciais** martial arts; **a sétima ~** cinema *(Brit)*, the movies *(pl) (Am)*.

artéria [ax'tɛrjɐ] *f* artery.

arterial [axte'rjaw] (*pl* **-ais** [-ajʃ]) *adj* → **pressão, tensão.**

artesanato [axteza'natu] *m* craftwork, handicraft.

articulação [axtʃikula'sãw] (*pl* **-ões** [-õjʃ]) *f (de ossos)* joint; *(de palavras)* articulation.

artificial [axtʃifi'sjaw] (*pl* **-ais** [-ajʃ]) *adj* artificial.

artigo [ax'tʃigu] *m* article; *(produto)* item; "**~s a declarar**" "goods to declare"; **~s de primeira necessidade** essential goods.

artista [ax'tʃiʃtɐ] *mf* artist.

artístico, -ca [ax'tʃiʃtʃiku, -ka] *adj* artistic.

artrite [ax'tritʃi] *f* arthritis.

árvore ['axvori] *f* tree.

as [aʃ] → **a.**

ás ['ajʃ] (*pl* **ases** ['azeʃ]) *m* ace; **ser um ~** to be a whizz.

às [ajʃ] = **a + as,** → **a.**

asa ['aza] *f* wing; *(de utensílio)* handle.

asa-delta [aza'dɛwtɐ] (*pl* **asas-delta** [azaʒ'dɛwtɐ]) *f* hang-glider.

ascensor [aʃsẽ'so(x)] (*pl* **-res** [-riʃ]) *m (em prédio)* lift *(Brit)*, elevator *(Am)*; *(em rua, encosta)* funicular.

asco ['aʃku] *m* disgust.

ases → **ás.**

asfalto [aʃ'fawtu] *m* asphalt.

asfixia [aʃfik'sia] *f* asphyxia, suffocation.

Ásia ['azjɐ] *f*: **a ~** Asia.

asiático, -ca [a'zjatʃiku, -ka] *adj & m, f* Asian.

asma ['aʒma] *f* asthma.

asmático, -ca [aʒ'matʃiku, -ka] *adj & m, f* asthmatic.

asneira [aʒ'nejrɐ] *f (tolice)* nonsense; *(obscenidade)* swear word.

asno ['aʒnu] *m* donkey; *(fig: estúpido)* ass.

aspargo [aʃ'paxgu] *m (Br)* asparagus.

aspecto [aʃ'pɛktu] *m* appearance; *(ponto de vista)* aspect.

áspero, -ra ['aʃperu, -ra] *adj* rough; *(voz)* harsh.

aspirador [aʃpira'do(x)] (*pl* **-res** [-riʃ]) *m* vacuum cleaner, Hoover®.

aspirar [aʃpi'ra(x)] *vt* to vacuum, to hoover.

❏ **aspirar a** *v + prep (desejar)* to aspire to.

aspirina® [aʃpi'rinɐ] *f* aspirin; **~ efervescente** soluble aspirin.

asqueroso, -osa [aʃke'rozu, -ɔza] *adj* disgusting, revolting.

assado, -da [a'sadu, -da] *adj & m (CULIN)* roast.

assadura [asa'durɐ] *f (de carne)* roast; *(em bebê)* nappy rash.

assalariado, -da [asala'rjadu, -da] *m, f* (salaried) employee.

assaltante [asaw'tãntʃi] *mf* burglar.

assaltar [asaw'ta(x)] *vt (pessoa)* to mug; *(casa)* to burgle; *(banco)* to rob.

assalto [a'sawtu] *m (a pessoa)* mugging; *(a casa)* burglery; *(a banco)* robbery; *(em boxe)* round; **~ à mão armada** armed robbery.

assar [a'sa(x)] *vt* to roast.

assassinar [asasi'na(x)] *vt* to murder.

assassínio [asa'sinju] *m* murder.

assassino, -na [asa'sinu, -na] *m, f* murderer.

assediar [ase'dʒja(x)] *vt (importunar)* to pester; *(sexualmente)* to harass.

assédio [a'sɛdʒju] *m* harassment; **~ sexual** sexual harassment.

assegurar [asegu'ra(x)] *vt* to assure.

❏ **assegurar-se** *vp*: **~-se de que** to make sure (that).

asseio [a'seju] *m (limpeza)* cleanliness.

assembléia [asẽm'blɛja] *f* assembly; *(reunião)* meeting; **~ geral** annual general meeting; **a Assembléia da República** Portuguese houses of parliament.

assemelhar-se [aseme'ʎaxsi] : **assemelhar-se a** *vp + prep* to look like.

assento [a'sẽntu] *m* seat.

assim [a'si] *adv (do mesmo modo)* like this; *(deste modo)* therefore; **~, sim!** that's better!; **como ~?** I'm sorry?; **~ mesmo** just so; **~, ~ so-so; ~ que** as soon as.

assimilar [asimi'la(x)] *vt* to assimilate.

assinar [asi'na(x)] *vt* to sign; *(revista)* to subscribe to.

assinatura [asina'turɐ] *f* signature; *(de revista)* subscription; *(de trem)* season ticket.

assistência [asiʃ'tẽsjɐ] *f (auxílio)* help; *(público)* audience; **~ médica** medical aid.

assistir [asiʃ'tʃi(x)] *vt (ajudar)* to help.

❏ **assistir a** *v + prep (a espetáculo)* to

attend; *(a programa)* to watch; *(a acidente, acontecimento)* to witness.

assoalho [aˈsoaʎu] *m (Br: de casa)* floor.

assoar [aˈswa(x)] *vt* to blow.
❑ **assoar-se** *vp* to blow one's nose.

assobiar [asoˈbja(x)] *vi* to whistle.

assobio [asoˈbiu] *m* whistle.

associação [asosjaˈsãw] *(pl* -ões [-õjʃ]) *f* association.

assombrado, -da [asõmˈbradu. -da] *adj (fig: casa, local)* haunted.

assombro [aˈsõmbru] *m* amazement.

assunto [aˈsũntu] *m* subject; **~ encerrado!** subject closed!

assustador, -ra [asuʃtaˈdo(x). -ra] *(mpl* -res [-riʃ], *fpl* -s [-ʃ]) *adj* frightening.

assustar [asuʃˈta(x)] *vt* to frighten.
❑ **assustar-se** *vp* to be frightened.

asterisco [aʃteˈriʃku] *m* asterisk.

astral [aʃˈtraw] *(pl* -ais [-ajʃ]) *m (Br: fam: humor)*: **hoje estou com baixo ~** I'm feeling out of sorts today.

astro [ˈaʃtru] *m* star.

astrologia [aʃtroloˈʒia] *f* astrology.

astronauta [aʃtroˈnawta] *mf* astronaut.

astronomia [aʃtronoˈmia] *f* astronomy.

astúcia [aʃˈtusja] *f* astuteness.

atacadista [atakaˈdiʃta] *mf* wholesaler.

atacado [ataˈkadu] *m*: **comprar por ~** to buy wholesale.

atacador [atakaˈdor] *(pl* -res [-reʃ]) *m (Port: de sapatos)* shoelace.

atacante [ataˈkãntʃi] *adj (ESP)* attacking ◆ *mf (ESP)* forward.

atacar [ataˈka(x)] *vt* to attack.

atadura [ataˈdura] *f (Br)* bandage.

atalho [aˈtaʎu] *m* short cut.

ataque [aˈtaki] *m* attack; **~ cardíaco** heart attack.

atar [aˈta(x)] *vt (sapatos)* to lace OU do up; *(saco)* to do up; *(corda, cordão, fio)* to tie.

atarracado, -da [ataxaˈkadu. -da] *adj* stocky.

até [aˈte] *prep (limite no espaço)* as far as; *(limite no tempo)* until ◆ *adv* even; **~ agora** so far; **~ amanhã!** see you tomorrow!; **~ logo!** see you later!; **~ mais!** *(em conversa)* speak to you soon!; **~ que enfim!** at (long) last!; **~ porque** because.

atear [ateˈa(x)] *vt (incendiar)* to set fire to; *(avivar)* to rekindle.

atéia → **ateu.**

ateliê [ateˈlje] *m (Br)* = **atelier.**

atelier [ateˈlje] *m (Port)* studio.

atemorizar [atemoriˈza(x)] *vt* to terrify.

atenção [atẽˈsãw] *(pl* -ões [-õjʃ]) *f* attention; *(cuidado)* care; *(cortesia)* courtesy ◆ *interj* watch OU look out!; **chamar a ~ de alguém para algo** to draw sb's attention to sthg; **prestar ~** to pay attention.

atender [atẽnˈde(x)] *vt (telefone)* to answer; *(em loja)* to serve; *(em hospital)* to see.

atendimento [atẽndʒiˈmẽntu] *m (de telefone)* answering; *(em loja, hospital)* service.

atentado [atẽnˈtadu] *m* attempt *(on sb's life).*

atenuante [ateˈnwãntʃi] *f* extenuating circumstance.

atenuar [ateˈnwa(x)] *vt* to soften.

aterragem [ateˈxaʒẽj] *(pl* -ns [-ʃ]) *f (Port)* = **aterrissagem.**

aterrar [ateˈxar] *vi (Port)* = **aterrissar.**

aterrissagem [atexiˈsaʒẽj] *(pl* -ns [-ʃ]) *f (Br)* landing.

aterrissar [atexiˈsa(x)] *vi (Br)* to land ◆ *vt (aterrorizar)* to terrify.

aterro [aˈtexu] *m* landfill.

aterrorizar [atexoriˈza(x)] *vt* to terrify.

atestado [ateʃˈtadu] *m* certificate; **~ médico** doctor's certificate; **~ de óbito** death certificate.

ateu, atéia [aˈtew. aˈteja] *m, f* atheist.

atiçar [atʃiˈsa(x)] *vt (lume)* to poke.

atingir [atʃĩˈʒi(x)] *vt* to reach; *(ferir, afetar)* to hit; *(objetivo)* to achieve; *(compreender)* to grasp; *(abranger)* to cover.

atirar [atʃiˈra(x)] *vt* to throw ◆ *vi (com arma)* to shoot.

atitude [atʃiˈtudʒi] *f* attitude.

atividade [atʃiviˈdadʒi] *f* activity.

ativo, -va [aˈtʃivu. -va] *adj (Br)* active.

Atlântico [aˈtlãntʃiku] *m*: **o ~** the Atlantic.

atlas [ˈatlaʃ] *m inv* atlas.

atleta [atˈleta] *mf* athlete.

atletismo [atleˈtʃiʒmu] *m* athletics *(sg).*

atmosfera [atmoſˈfɛra] f atmosphere.

ato [ˈatu] m (Br) (acção) action; (de peça de teatro) act.

atômico, -ca [aˈtomiku, -ka] adj atomic.

ator, atriz [aˈto(x), atriʒ] (mpl **-res** [-riʃ], fpl **-zes** [-ziʃ]) m, f (Br) actor (f actress).

atordoado, -da [atoxˈdwadu, -da] adj stunned.

atores → ator.

atormentado, -da [atoxmẽnˈtadu, -da] adj troubled.

atração [atraˈsãw] (pl **-ões** [-õjʃ]) f (Br) attraction; (de pessoa) attractiveness.

atracção [atraˈsãw] (pl **-ões** [-õjʃ]) f (Port) = atração.

atrações → atração.

atractivo, -va [atraˈtivu, -va] adj (Port) = atrativo.

atraente [atraˈẽntʃi] adj attractive.

atraiçoar [atrajˈswa(x)] vt to betray.

❏ **atraiçoar-se** vp to give o.s. away.

atrair [atraˈi(x)] vt to attract.

atrapalhar [atrapaˈʎa(x)] vt (perturbar) to confuse; (dificultar) to get in the way of.

❏ **atrapalhar-se** vp to get all confused.

atrás [aˈtrajʃ] adv (detrás) behind; (para trás) back there; **há dias ~** a few days ago; **~ de** (no espaço) behind; (no tempo) after; **ficar com pé ~** (fig) to be on one's guard.

atrasado, -da [atraˈzadu, -da] adj (pessoa) late; (país, região) backward; **chegar ~** to arrive late; **estar ~** to be late.

atrasar [atraˈza(x)] vi (trem, ônibus) to be delayed ◆ vt (trabalho) to delay; (fig: prejudicar) to hinder.

❏ **atrasar-se** vp to be late.

atraso [aˈtrazu] m delay; (de país) backwardness.

atrativo, -va [atraˈtʃivu, -va] adj (Br) attractive ◆ m (Br) attraction.

através [atraˈvejʃ] : **através de** prep (pelo meio de) through; (por meio de) by.

atravessar [atraveˈsa(x)] vt (rua, rio) to cross; (pôr ao través) to put across; (fig: situação, fase) to go through.

atrelado [atreˈladu] m trailer.

atrever-se [atreˈvexsi] : **atrever-se** vp (ousar) to dare; **~ a fazer algo** to

dare to do sthg.

atrevido, -da [atreˈvidu, -da] adj (malcriado) cheeky; (audaz) daring.

atrevimento [atreviˈmẽntu] m (audácia) daring; **que ~!** what a cheek!

atribuir [atriˈbwi(x)] vt to attribute; (cargo) to give.

atributo [atriˈbutu] m attribute.

átrio [ˈatriu] m (de edifício) hall.

atrito [aˈtritu] m friction.

❏ **atritos** mpl disagreements.

atriz → ator.

atropelamento [atropelaˈmẽntu] m road accident (involving a pedestrian being run over).

atropelar [atropeˈla(x)] vt to run over.

atuação [atwaˈsãw] (pl **-ões** [-õjʃ]) f (procedimento) behaviour; (em espetáculo) acting; (espetáculo) performance.

atual [aˈtwaw] (pl **-ais** [-ajʃ]) adj (Br) (presente) current; (moderno) modern.

atualizar [atwaliˈza(x)] vt (tornar atual) to modernize; (INFORM: ficheiro) to update.

atualmente [atwawˈmẽntʃi] adv currently.

atuar [aˈtwa(x)] vi (Br) to act.

atum [aˈtũ] m tuna.

aturdido, -da [aturˈdʒidu, -da] adj stunned.

audácia [awˈdasja] f audacity.

audição [awdʒiˈsãw] (pl **-ões** [-õjʃ]) f hearing; (de peça musical, concerto) recital.

audiência [awˈdʒjẽsja] f (JUR) hearing.

audiovisual [awdʒjɔviˈzwaw] (pl **-ais** [-ajʃ]) adj audiovisual.

auditório [awdʒiˈtɔrju] m auditorium; (público ouvinte) audience.

auge [ˈawʒi] m peak.

aula [ˈawla] f class, lesson.

aumentar [awmẽnˈta(x)] vt & vi to increase.

aumento [awˈmẽntu] m increase; (de ordenado) rise (Brit), raise (Am).

auréola [awˈrɛwla] f halo.

aurora [awˈrɔra] f dawn; **~ boreal** northern lights (pl).

auscultador [awʃkuwtaˈdo(x)] (pl **-res** [-riʃ]) m receiver.

❏ **auscultadores** mpl headphones.

ausência [awˈzẽsja] f absence.

ausentar-se [awzẽnˈtaxsi] vp: **~ de**

(de país, sala) to leave.
ausente [awˈzẽntʃi] *adj* absent.
Austrália [awʃˈtralja] *f*: **a ~**
Australia.
australiano, -na [awʃtraˈljanu. -na]
adj & m, f Australian.
Áustria [ˈawʃtria] *f*: **a ~** Austria.
austríaco, -ca [awʃˈtriaku. -ka] *adj &*
m, f Austrian.
autenticar [awtẽntʃiˈka(x)] *vt (JUR:*
documento, assinatura) to authenticate.
autêntico, -ca [awˈtẽntʃiku. -ka] *adj*
(verdadeiro) real; *(JUR)* authenticated.
autocarro [awtoˈkaxu] *m* bus; *(entre*
cidades) coach; **apanhar o ~** to catch
the bus.
autoclismo [awtoˈkliʒmu] *m (Port)*
flush; **puxar o ~** to flush the toilet.
autocolante [awtokoˈlãntʃi] *adj* self-
adhesive ♦ *m* sticker.
autodomínio [awtodoˈminju] *m* self-
control.
autódromo [awˈtɔdromu] *m* race
track.
auto-escola [awtɔiʃˈkɔla] *f* driving
school.
auto-estima [awtɔeʃˈtʃima] *f* self-
esteem.
auto-estrada [awtɔʃˈtrada] *f* motorway *(Brit)*, freeway *(Am)*.
autografar [awtografaˈfa(x)] *vt* to autograph.
autógrafo [awˈtɔgrafu] *m* autograph.
autolocadora [awtolokaˈdora] *f (Br)*
car rental.
automático, -ca [awtoˈmatʃiku. -ka]
adj automatic.
automatização [awtomatʃizaˈsãw]
(pl **-ões** [-õjʃ]) *f* automation.
automobilismo [awtomobiˈliʒmu] *m*
motor racing.
automobilista [awtomobiˈliʃta] *mf*
motorist.
automotora [awtomoˈtora] *f* diesel
train.
automóvel [awtoˈmɔvɛw] *(pl* **-eis**
[-ejʃ]) *m* motorcar *(Brit)*, automobile
(Am).
autópsia [awˈtɔpsja] *f (MED)* autopsy.
autor, -ra [awˈto(x). -ra] *(mpl* **-res**
[-riʃ]. *fpl* **-s** [-ʃ]) *m, f* author; *(de idéia)*
originator; *(de brincadeira)* instigator;
(JUR: de crime) perpetrator.
auto-retrato [awtoxeˈtratu] *m* self-
portrait.
autoridade [awtoriˈdadʒi] *f* authority.

autorização [awtorizaˈsãw] *(pl* **-ões**
[-õjʃ]) *f* authorization.
autorizar [awtoriˈza(x)] *vt* to authorize.
auxiliar [awsiˈlja(x)] *(pl* **-res** [-riʃ]) *adj*
auxiliary ♦ *mf* assistant ♦ *vt* to assist.
auxílio [awˈsilju] *m* help.
auxílio-desemprego [awˈsilju-
dʒizẽmˈpregu] *(pl* **auxílios-desemprego**
[awˈsiljuʒdʒizẽmˈpregu]) *m (Br)* unemployment benefit.
Av. *(abrev de avenida)* Ave.
avalanche [avaˈlãʃi] *f* avalanche.
avaliação [avaljaˈsãw] *(pl* **-ões** [-õjʃ])
f assessment; *(JUR)* valuation.
avaliar [avaˈlja(x)] *vt* to assess; *(gas-*
tos) to estimate; *(valor de objeto)* to
value; **a ~ por** judging by.
avançado, -da [avãˈsadu. -da] *adj*
advanced; *(pessoa)* progressive ♦ *m, f*
(ESP) forward ♦ *m (de caravana)*
awning.
avançar [avãˈsa(x)] *vi* to advance.
avarento, -ta [avaˈrẽntu. -ta] *adj*
miserly.
avaria [avaˈria] *f* breakdown.
avariado, -da [avaˈrjadu. -da] *adj* out
of order; *(carro)* broken down.
ave [ˈavi] *f* bird.
aveia [aˈveja] *f* oats *(pl)*.
avelã [aveˈlã] *f* hazelnut.
avenca [aˈvẽŋka] *f* maidenhair fern.
avenida [aveˈnida] *f* avenue.
avental [avẽnˈtaw] *(pl* **-ais** [-ajʃ]) *m*
apron.
aventura [avẽnˈtura] *f* adventure;
(amorosa) affair; **partir para a ~** to set
out on an adventure.
aventureiro, -ra [avẽntuˈrejru. -ra]
m, f adventurer.
averiguação [averigwaˈsãw] *(pl* **-ões**
[-õjʃ]) *f* investigation.
averiguar [averiˈgwa(x)] *vt* to investigate; *(verdade)* to find out.
avesso [aˈvesu] *m (de casaco, saco)*
reverse; *(contrário)* opposite ♦ *adj*: **~ a**
averse to; **pelo ~** inside out.
avestruz [aveʃˈtruʃ] *(pl* **-zes** [-ʒiʃ]) *f*
ostrich.
avião [aˈvjãw] *(pl* **-ões** [-õjʃ]) *m* plane;
"por ~" "by airmail".
ávido, -da [ˈavidu. -da] *adj*: **~ de**
greedy for.
aviões → avião.
avisar [aviˈza(x)] *vt* to warn; *(notificar)*
to inform.

aviso [a'vizu] *m (advertência)* warning; *(sinal, letreiro, notificação)* notice; ~ **de recepção** acknowledgement of receipt.

avistar [aviʃ'ta(x)] *vt* to see.

avô, avó [a'vo, a'vɔ] *m, f* grandfather *(f* grandmother).

avós [a'vɔʃ] *mpl* grandparents.

avulso, -sa [a'vuwsu, -sa] *adj* separate ◆ *adv* separately.

axila [ak'sila] *f* armpit.

azar [a'za(x)] *(pl* **-res** [-riʃ]) *m (falta de sorte)* bad luck; *(acaso)* chance; **estar com** ~ to be out of luck; **por** ~ as luck would have it.

azarado, -da [aza'radu, -da] *m, f* unlucky person.

azares → **azar**.

azedar [aze'da(x)] *vi* to turn sour.

azedo, -da [a'zedu, -da] *adj* sour.

azeite [a'zejtʃi] *m* olive oil.

azeitona [azej'tona] *f* olive; ~**s pretas** black olives; ~**s recheadas** stuffed olives.

azevinho [aze'viɲu] *m* holly.

azinheira [azi'ɲejra] *f* holm oak.

azul [a'zuw] *(pl* **azuis** [a'zujʃ]) *adj & m* blue.

azul-claro, azul-clara [a,zuw-'klaru, a,zuw'klara] *(mpl* **azul-claros** [a,zuw'klaruʃ], *fpl* **azul-claras** [a,zuw-'klaraʃ]) *adj* pale blue.

azulejo [azu'leʒu] *m* glazed tile.

azul-escuro, azul-escura [a,zuweʃ-'kuru, a,zuweʃ'kura] *(mpl* **azul-escuros** [a,zuweʃ'kuruʃ], *fpl* **azul-escuras** [a,zuweʃ-'kuraʃ]) *adj* dark blue.

azul-marinho [a,zuwma'riɲu] *adj inv* navy (blue).

azul-turquesa [a,zuwtux'keza] *adj inv* turquoise.

B

baba ['baba] f dribble.

babá [ba'ba] f (Br) nanny.

babar-se [ba'baxsi] vp to dribble.

baby-sitter [,bejbi'site(x)] f baby-sitter.

bacalhau [baka'ʎaw] m (peixe) cod; (em culinária) salt cod; ~ **assado (na brasa)** barbecued salt cod seasoned with olive oil and garlic, served with roast potatoes; ~ **à Brás** salt cod fried with onions and garlic then mixed with eggs, finely cut chips and olives; ~ **cru desfiado** raw pieces of salt cod seasoned with olive oil and garlic; ~ **à Gomes de Sá** pieces of salt cod, onion and potato baked with olive oil, eggs and olives.

bacia [ba'sia] f basin; (ANAT) pelvis.

baço, -ça ['basu. -sa] adj (metal, espelho) tarnished; (tinta, cor) matt ♦ m (ANAT) spleen.

bacon ['bejkõ] m bacon.

bactéria [bak'tɛrja] f bacterium.

badejo [ba'deʒu] m pollack.

badminton [bad'mĩtõ] m badminton.

bafo [bafu] m breath.

bafômetro [ba'fometru] m (Br) Breathalyser®.

baforada [bafo'rada] f puff.

bagaço [ba'gasu] m (Port) strong spirit similar to brandy.

bagageira [baga'ʒejra] f (Port) (de carro) boot (Brit), trunk (Am); (de ônibus) luggage rack.

bagageiro [baga'ʒejru] m porter.

bagagem [ba'gaʒẽ] (pl -ns [-ʃ]) f luggage (Brit), baggage (Am); **despachar/depositar a ~** to check in/leave one's luggage.

bagatela [baga'tɛla] f trifle.

bago ['bagu] m (de uva) grape; (de trigo) grain.

bagunça [ba'gũsa] f (Br) mess.

Bahia [ba'ia] f (Br) Bahia.

baía [ba'ia] f bay.

❑ **Baía** f (Port) = **Bahia**.

bailado [baj'ladu] m (ballet) ballet; (dança) dance.

bailarino, -na [bajla'rinu, -na] m, f ballet dancer.

baile ['bajli] m ball.

bainha [ba'iɲa] f (de calças, saia, etc) hem; (de espada) scabbard.

bairro ['bajxu] m neighbourhood; (divisão administrativa) district; ~ **de lata** (Port) shanty town.

baixa ['bajʃa] f (em quantidade) decrease; (de preço) reduction; (Br: médica) discharge; (em guerra) casualty.

baixar [baj'ʃa(x)] vt to lower ♦ vi (preço, valor) to come down.

❑ **baixar-se** vp to bend down.

baixo, -xa ['bajʃu. -ʃa] adj low; (pessoa) short; (qualidade) poor; (profundidade) shallow; (fig: desprezível) mean ♦ adv (falar, rir) quietly; (relativo a posição) low ♦ m (instrumento) bass; **o mais ~/a mais baixa** (pessoa) the shortest; (objeto, preço) the lowest; **para ~** down; **por ~ de** under(neath); **estar em ~** (Port: estar abatido) to be out of sorts.

bala ['bala] f bullet; (Br: doce) sweet; **à prova de ~** bullet-proof.

balança [ba'lãsa] f scales (pl).

❑ **Balança** f (Port: signo do zodíaco) Libra.

balançar [balã'sa(x)] vt (balanço) to swing; (barco) to rock ♦ vi (balanço) to swing; (barco) to rock.

balanço [ba'lãsu] m (de criança) swing; (ação) swinging.

balão [ba'lãw] (pl -ões [-õjʃ]) m balloon; (de transporte) hot-air balloon.

balbuciar [bawbu'sja(x)] vt & vi to mumble.

balbúrdia [baw'buxdʒja] f (desordem) shambles (sg); (barulho) racket.

balcão [baw'kãw] (pl -ões [-õjʃ]) m (de bar, loja) counter; (de teatro) circle; (de casa) balcony; ~ **nobre/simples** (Br: de teatro) dress/upper circle.

balde ['bawdʒi] m bucket.

baldeação [bawdʒja'sãw] (pl -ões [-õjʃ]) f (Br) change; **fazer** ~ to change.

balé [ba'lɛ] m (Br) ballet.

baleia [ba'leja] f whale.

baliza [ba'liza] f (ESP) goal.

ballet [ba'lɛ] m (Port) = **balé**.

balneário [baw'njarju] m changing room.

balões → **balão**.

balofo, -fa [ba'lofu, -fa] adj (pessoa) flabby.

baloiço [ba'lojsu] m (Port) swing.

bálsamo ['bawsamu] m balsam, balm; (fig: alívio) comfort.

bambu [bãm'bu] m bamboo.

banal [ba'naw] (pl -ais [-ajʃ]) adj banal.

banana [ba'nana] f banana.

bananada [bana'nada] f dessert made with banana puree.

bananeira [bana'nejra] f banana tree.

banca ['bãŋka] f (Br): ~ **de jornais** newsstand.

bancada [bãŋ'kada] f (de cozinha) worktop; (de trabalho) bench; (Port: de estádio) grandstand.

bancário, -ria [bãŋ'karju, -rja] adj banking (antes de s) ♦ m, f bank clerk.

banco ['bãŋku] m (de cozinha) stool; (de carro) seat; (FIN) bank; (de hospital) casualty (Brit), emergency room (Am); ~ **de areia** sandbank; ~ **de dados** (INFORM) database; ~ **de jardim** (park) bench.

banda ['bãnda] f side; (filarmônica) brass band; (de rock) band; **de** ~ (de lado) sideways; **pôr de** ~ (fig: pessoa) to shun.

bandarilha [bãnda'riʎa] f barbed dart thrust into a bull's back.

bandeira [bãn'dejra] f flag; (em transporte público) destination screen; **dar** ~ (Br: fam) to give the game away.

bandeja [bãn'deʒa] f tray.

bandejão [bãnde'ʒãw] (pl -ões [-õjʃ]) f (Br) canteen meal.

bandido, -da [bãn'dʒidu, -da] m, f bandit.

bando ['bãndu] m (de aves) flock; (de criminosos) gang.

bandolim [bãndo'lĩ] (pl -ns [-ʃ]) m mandolin.

bangaló [bãŋga'lɔ] m (Port) = **bangalô**.

bangalô [bãŋga'lo] m (Br) bungalow.

banha ['baɲa] f: ~ **(de porco)** lard.

banheira [ba'ɲejra] f bathtub.

banheiro [ba'ɲejru] m (Br: quarto de banho) bathroom; (Port: de praia, piscina) lifeguard.

banhista [ba'ɲiʃta] mf bather.

banho ['baɲu] m (em banheira) bath; (em piscina, mar) swim; **tomar** ~ (em banheira) to have a bath; (em chuveiro) to have a shower; (em piscina, mar) to have a swim; **tomar um** ~/~**s de sol** to sunbathe.

banho-maria [,baɲuma'ria] m: **cozinhar algo em** ~ to cook sthg in a bain-marie.

banir [ba'ni(x)] vt (proibir) to ban; (expulsar) to banish.

banjo ['bãʒu] m banjo.

banquete [bãŋ'ketʃi] m banquet.

baptismo [ba'tiʒmu] m (Port) = **batismo**.

baptizado [bati'zadu] m (Port) = **batizado**.

bar [ba(x)] (pl -res [-riʃ]) m bar.

baralhar [bara'ʎa(x)] vt (cartas de jogar) to shuffle; (confundir) to confuse. ❑ **baralhar-se** vp to get confused.

baralho [ba'raʎu] m: ~ **(de cartas)** pack (of cards) (Brit), deck (of cards) (Am).

barão [ba'rãw] (pl -ões [-õjʃ]) m baron.

barata [ba'rata] f cockroach.

barato, -ta [ba'ratu, -ta] adj cheap ♦ adv cheaply ♦ m (Br: fam) fun; **mais** ~ cheaper; **o mais** ~ the cheapest; **foi o maior** ~! (Br) it was great!

barba ['baxba] f beard; **fazer a** ~ to shave.

barbante [bax'bãntʃi] m (Br) string.

barbatana [baxba'tana] f (de peixe) fin; (de nadador) flipper.

barbeador [barbja'do(x)] (pl -res [-riʃ]) m: ~ **(elétrico)** (electric) shaver.

barbear-se [bax'bjaxsi] vp to shave.

barbeiro [bax'bejru] m barber's (shop).

barca ['baxka] f (Br) ferry.

barco ['baxku] m boat; ~ **a motor** speedboat; ~ **a remo** rowing boat; ~ **à**

vela sailing boat.
bares → **bar**.
barman ['baxmãn] (*pl* **-s** [-ʃ]) *m* barman.
barões → **barão**.
baronesa [baro'neza] *f* baroness.
barra ['baxa] *f* bar; *(Br: foz)* rivermouth; *(Br: fam: situação)* situation.
barraca [ba'xaka] *f (de feira)* stall; *(Br: de camping)* tent.
barraco [ba'xaku] *m (Br)* shack.
barragem [ba'xaʒẽ] (*pl* **-ns** [-ʃ]) *f* dam.
barranco [ba'xãŋku] *m* ravine.
barrar [ba'xa(x)] *vt* to bar.
barreira [ba'xejra] *f (de rio, estrada)* embankment; *(ESP)* hurdle; *(fig: obstáculo)* obstacle.
barrento, -ta [ba'xẽntu, -ta] *adj* clayey.
barrete [ba'xetʃi] *m* hat; *(Port: fam: decepção)* flop.
barriga [ba'xiga] *f* belly; **minha ~ está roncando** my stomach's rumbling; **~ da perna** calf; **de ~ para cima/para baixo** face up/down.
barril [ba'xiw] (*pl* **-is** [-iʃ]) *m* barrel.
barro ['baxu] *m* clay.
barroco, -ca [ba'xoku, -ka] *adj & m* baroque.
barulhento, -ta [baru'ʎẽntu, -ta] *adj* noisy.
barulho [ba'ruʎu] *m (ruído)* noise; *(confusão)* commotion; **pouco ~!** quieten down!
base ['bazi] *f* base; *(de maquilhagem)* foundation; *(fundamento)* basis.
basebol [bejze'bɔw] *m* baseball.
básico, -ca ['baziku, -ka] *adj* basic.
basílica [ba'zilika] *f* basilica.
basquete ['baʃketʃi] *m* = **basquetebol**.
basquetebol [baʃketʃi'bɔw] *m* basketball.
basta ['baʃta] *interj* that's enough!
bastante [baʃ'tãntʃi] *adv (muito)* a lot; *(suficiente)* enough ◆ *adj (muito)* a lot of; *(suficiente)* enough; **ele é ~ feio** he is quite ugly.
bastar [baʃ'ta(x)] *vi* to be enough.
bastidores [baʃtʃi'doreʃ] *mpl* wings.
bata ['bata] *f (para senhora)* pinafore; *(para médico)* (white) coat.
batalha [ba'taʎa] *f* battle; **~ naval** *(jogo)* battleships *(sg)*.

batata [ba'tata] *f* potato; **~ doce** sweet potato; **~ palha** *very finely cut chips;* **~s assadas/cozidas** roast/boiled potatoes; **~s fritas** chips *(Brit)*, French fries *(Am)*; **~s fritas (de pacote)** crisps *(Brit)*, chips *(Am)*.
batedeira [bate'dejra] *f:* **~ (eléctrica)** mixer.
bátega ['batega] *f* downpour.
batente [ba'tẽntʃi] *m (meia-porta)* door *(of double doors); (aldraba)* doorknocker.
bate-papo [,batʃi'papu] (*pl* **batepapos** [,batʃi'papuʃ]) *m (Br)* chat.
bater [ba'te(x)] *vt* to beat; *(asas)* to flap; *(roupa)* to scrub ◆ *vi (coração)* to beat; *(porta, janela)* to bang; **ela estava batendo queixo** her teeth were chattering because of the cold; **~ a** *(porta, janela)* to knock at; **~ com algo contra** OU **em algo** to crash sthg into sthg; **~ em** to hit; **~ à máquina** *(Br)* to type; **~ papo** *(Br)* to chat; **~ o pé** *(teimar)* to put one's foot down; **~ com o pé** to stamp one's foot; **~ com a porta** to slam the door; **bateu a bota** *(fam: morrer)* he popped his clogs; **ela não bate bem** she's off her head.
bateria [bate'ria] *f (de carro, motor)* battery; *(MÚS)* drums *(pl)*.
baterista [bate'riʃta] *mf* drummer.
batida [ba'tʃida] *f (Br) (de veículo)* crash; *(de polícia)* raid; *(bebida) blended drink containing "cachaça", sugar and fruit* .
batido [ba'tʃidu] *m (Port)* milkshake.
batismo [ba'tʃiʒmu] *m (Br)* baptism.
batizado [batʃi'zadu] *m (Br)* christening.
batom [ba'tõ] (*pl* **-ns** [-ʃ]) *m* lipstick; **~ para o cieiro** *(Port)* chapstick.
batota [ba'tɔta] *f (Port)* cheating; **fazer ~** to cheat.
batuque [ba'tuki] *m (Br: MÚS)* Afro-Brazilian dance.
baú [ba'u] *m* trunk.
baunilha [baw'niʎa] *f* vanilla.
bazar [ba'za(x)] (*pl* **-res** [-riʃ]) *m* bazaar.
BB *m (abrev de Banco do Brasil)* Bank of Brazil.
BCG *m (clínica)* tuberculosis clinic; *(vacina)* BCG.
bêbado, -da ['bebadu, -da] *adj & m, f* drunk.
bebé [be'bɛ] *m (Port)* = **bebê**.

bebê [be'be] *m (Br)* baby; "**~ a bordo**" "baby on board".

bebedeira [bebe'dejra] *f* drunkenness; **tomar uma ~** to get drunk.

beber [be'be(x)] *vt & vi* to drink.

bebida [be'bida] *f* drink.

beça [bɛsa] **: à beça** *adv (Br: fam)* a lot ◆ *adj (Br: fam)* loads of, a lot of; **o concerto foi bom à ~** the concert was really good.

beco [bɛku] *m* alley; **~ sem saída** dead end.

bege [bɛʒi] *adj inv* beige.

begónia [be'gɔnja] *f (Port)* = **begônia**.

begônia [be'gonja] *f (Br)* begonia.

beija-flor [bejʒa'flo(x)] *(pl* **beija-flores** [bejʒa'floriʃ]*) m* hummingbird.

beijar [bej'ʒa(x)] *vt* to kiss.
❑ **beijar-se** *vp* to kiss.

beijo [bejʒu] *m* kiss.

beira [bejra] *f (de estrada)* side; *(de rio)* bank; *(de precipício)* edge; **à ~ de** *(junto de)* beside; *(fig: no limiar de)* on the verge of.

beira-mar [bejra'ma(x)] *f* seaside; **à ~** by the sea.

beira-rio [bejra'xiu] *f* riverside; **à ~** by the river.

belas-artes [bɛla'zaxtʃiʃ] *fpl* fine arts.

beldade [bew'dadʒi] *f* beauty.

beleza [be'leza] *f* beauty; **que ~!** how wonderful!

belga [bɛwga] *adj & mf* Belgian.

Bélgica [bɛwʒika] *f*: **a ~** Belgium.

beliche [be'liʃi] *m* bunk.

beliscão [beliʃ'kãw] *(pl* **-ões** [-õjʃ]*) m* pinch.

beliscar [beliʃ'ka(x)] *vt* to pinch.

beliscões → **beliscão**.

belo, -la [bɛlu, -la] *adj* beautiful; *(homem)* handsome; *(momento)* wonderful; *(dia, sentimento, livro)* fine.

bem [bej] *adv* **1.** *(de forma satisfatória, correta)* well; **fala ~ inglês** she speaks English well; **fez ~!** you did the right thing!
2. *(exprime opinião favorável)*: **estar ~** *(de saúde)* to be well; *(de aspecto)* to look good; *(relativo a comodidade)* to be comfortable; **cheirar/saber ~** to smell/taste good.
3. *(suficiente)*: **estar ~** to be enough.
4. *(muito)* very; **queria o bife ~ passado** I'd like my steak well-done; **queria uma bebida ~ gelada** I'd like an

ice-cold drink.
5. *(bastante)* quite; **é um carro ~ espaçoso** it's quite a spacious car; **é um lugar ~ bonito** it's quite a pretty spot.
6. *(exatamente)* right; **não é ~ assim** it isn't quite like that; **não é ~ aqui é mais abaixo** it isn't here exactly, it's further down.
7. *(em locuções)*: **eu ~ que lhe avisei** I told you so; **eu ~ que ajudava mas não posso** I'd be glad to help but I can't; **~ como** as well as; **~ feito!** it serves you right!; **está ~!** OK!, all right!; **muito ~!** very good!; **ou ~ ... ou ~ ...** either ...or ...; **você vai ter que ir por ~ ou por mal** you'll have to go whether you like it or not; **se ~ que** although, even though.
◆ *m* **1.** *(o que é bom)* good.
2. *(bem-estar, proveito)* good; **praticar o ~** to do good; **é para o seu ~** it's for your own good.
◆ *adj inv (pej)*: **gente ~** the well-heeled; **menino ~** rich kid.
❑ **bens** *mpl (posses)* property *(sg)*; *(produtos)* goods; **bens imóveis** OU **de raiz** real estate *(sg)*; **bens de consumo** consumer goods.

bem-disposto, -osta [bejdʒiʃ'poʃtu, -ɔʃta] *adj (bem humorado)* good-humoured.

bem-estar [bejʃ'ta(x)] *m* wellbeing.

bem-vindo, -da [bej'vĩndu, -da] *adj* welcome.

bendizer [bẽndʒi'ze(x)] *vt* to praise.

beneficência [benefi'sẽsja] *f* charity.

beneficiar [benefi'sja(x)] *vt* to benefit.

benefício [bene'fisju] *m* benefit.

benéfico, -ca [be'nɛfiku, -ka] *adj* beneficial.

benevolência [benevo'lẽsja] *f* benevolence.

bengala [bẽŋ'gala] *f* walking stick.

bengaleiro [bẽŋga'lejru] *m (em casa de espetáculos)* cloakroom; *(cabide)* coat stand.

benigno, -gna [be'nignu, -gna] *adj* benign.

bens → **bem**.

benzer [bẽ'ze(x)] *vt* to bless.
❑ **benzer-se** *vp* to cross o.s.

berbequim [berbe'kĩ] *(pl* **-ns** [-ʃ]*) m (Port)* drill.

berbigão [bexbi'gãw] *(pl* **-ões** [-õjʃ]*) m* cockle.

berço ['bexsu] *m* cot *(Brit)*, crib *(Am)*.

berlinde [ber'lindɛ] *m (Port)* marble.

beringela [beri'ʒɛla] *f (Port)* = **berinjela**.

berinjela [beri'ʒɛla] *f (Br)* aubergine *(Brit)*, eggplant *(Am)*.

berloque [bex'lɔki] *m* pendant.

bermuda [bex'muda] *f (Br)* Bermuda shorts.

besouro [be'zoru] *m* beetle.

besta ['bɛʃta] *f (cavalgadura)* mount.

besteira [beʃ'tejra] *f (Br) (fam) (asneira)* nonsense; *(insignificância)* trifle.

bestial [beʃ'tjal] *(pl -ais* [-ajʃ]) *adj (Port: fam)* brilliant.

besugo [be'zugu] *m* sea bream.

besuntar [bezũn'ta(x)] *vt* to grease.

betão [be'tãw] *m (Port)* concrete.

beterraba [bete'xaba] *f* beetroot.

betoneira [beto'nejra] *f* cement mixer.

bétula ['bɛtula] *f* birch.

bexiga [be'ʃiga] *f* bladder; **~s doidas** *(fam: varicela)* chickenpox *(sg)*.

bezerro [be'zexu] *m* calf.

BI *m (Port: abrev de Bilhete de Identidade)* ID card.

biberão [bibe'rãw] *(pl -ões* [-õjʃ]) *m (Port)* (baby's) bottle.

Bíblia ['biblia] *f* Bible.

biblioteca [biblio'tɛka] *f* library; **~ itinerante** mobile library.

bibliotecário, -ria [bibljote'karju, -rja] *m, f* librarian.

bica ['bika] *f (de água)* tap; *(Port: café)* espresso; **suar em ~(s)** to drip with sweat.

bicar [bi'ka(x)] *vt & vi* to peck.

bicha ['biʃa] *f (lombriga)* worm; *(Br: pej: homossexual)* queer; *(Port: fila)* queue.

bicho ['biʃu] *m (animal)* animal; *(inseto)* bug.

bicho-da-seda [biʃuda'seda] *(pl* **bichos-da-seda**) [biʃuʃda'seda] *m* silkworm.

bicicleta [besi'klɛta] *f* bicycle.

bico ['biku] *m (de sapato)* toe; *(de ave)* beak; *(de fogão)* burner; *(de seio)* nipple; *(Br: fam: trabalho)* odd job.

bidé [bi'dɛ] *m (Port)* = **bidê**.

bidê [bi'dɛ] *m (Br)* bidet.

bife ['bifi] *m* steak.

bifurcação [bifuxka'sãw] *(pl -ões* [-õjʃ]) *f* fork.

bigode [bi'gɔdʒi] *m* moustache.

bijutaria [biʒuta'ria] *f (Port)* = **bijuteria**.

bijuteria [biʒute'ria] *f (Br)* costume jewellery.

bilha ['biʎa] *f (de água)* (earthenware) pot; *(de gás)* gas bottle.

bilhão [bi'ʎãw] *(pl -ões* [-õjʃ]) *num (Br: mil milhões)* thousand million *(Brit)*, billion *(Am)*; *(Port)* = **bilião**.

bilhar [bi'ʎa(x)] *(pl -res* [-riʃ]) *m (jogo)* billiards *(sg)*; *(mesa)* billiard table; **jogar ~** to play billiards.

bilhete [bi'ʎetʃi] *m* ticket; **~ de ida** *(Port)* single (ticket) *(Brit)*, one-way ticket *(Am)*; **~ de ida e volta** return (ticket) *(Brit)*, round-trip ticket *(Am)*; **~ de identidade** *(Port)* identity card; **~ simples** *(em metrô)* single (ticket).

bilheteira [biʎe'tejra] *f (Port)* = **bilheteria**.

bilheteria [biʎete'ria] *f (Br) (de teatro, cinema)* box office.

bilhões → **bilhão**.

bilião [bi'ljãw] *(pl -ões* [-õjʃ]) *num (Port: milhão de milhões)* billion *(Brit)*, trillion *(Am)*; *(Br)* = **bilhão**.

bilingue [bi'lĩgɛ] *adj (Port)* = **bilíngüe**.

bilíngüe [bi'lĩgwi] *adj (Br)* bilingual.

biliões → **bilião**.

bílis ['biliʃ] *f* bile.

bingo ['bĩgu] *m* bingo.

binóculo [bi'nɔkulu] *m* binoculars *(pl)*.

biografia [bjogra'fia] *f* biography.

biologia [bjolo'ʒia] *f* biology.

biólogo, -ga ['bjɔlogu, -ga] *m, f* biologist.

biombo ['bjõmbu] *m* screen.

biopsia [bjɔp'sia] *f* biopsy.

biqueira [bi'kejra] *f (de sapato)* toe.

biquíni [bi'kini] *m* bikini.

birra ['bixa] *f* tantrum; **fazer ~** to throw a tantrum.

bis [biʃ] *interj* encore!

bisavô, -vó [biza'vo, -vɔ] *m, f* great-grandfather *(f* greatgrandmother).

bisavós [biza'vɔʃ] *mpl* great-grandparents.

biscoito [biʃ'kojtu] *m* biscuit *(Brit)*, cookie *(Am)*.

bisnaga [biʒ'naga] *f (tubo)* tube; *(Br: pão)* French stick.

bisneto, -ta [biʒˈnɛtu, -ta] *m, f* great-grandson (*f* great-granddaughter).
bispo [ˈbiʃpu] *m* bishop.
bissexto [biˈsejʃtu] *adj m* → **ano**.
bisteca [biʃˈtɛka] *f (Br)* steak.
bisturi [biʃtuˈri] *m* scalpel.
bit [ˈbitʃi] *m* bit.
bizarro, -a [biˈzaxu. -a] *adj* bizarre.
blasfemar [blaʃfeˈma(x)] *vi* to blaspheme.
blasfémia [blaʃˈfɛmja] *f (Port)* = **blasfêmia**.
blasfêmia [blaʃˈfemja] *f (Br)* blasphemy.
blazer [ˈblejzɛ(x)] (*pl* **-res** [-riʃ]) *m* blazer.
bloco [ˈblɔku] *m (de folhas)* writing pad; *(de apontamentos, notas)* notepad; *(de apartamentos, concreto)* block.
bloquear [blɔkˈja(x)] *vt* to block.
blusa [ˈbluza] *f* blouse.
blusão [bluˈzãw] (*pl* **-ões** [-õjʃ]) *m* jacket.
boa¹ → **bom**.
boa² [ˈbɔa] *f* boa constrictor.
boas-festas [ˌbɔaʒˈfɛʃtaʃ] *fpl*: **dar as ~ a alguém** to wish sb a Merry Christmas.
boas-vindas [ˌbɔaʒˈvĩdaʃ] *fpl*: **dar as ~ a alguém** to welcome sb.
boate [ˈbwatʃi] *f (Br)* nightclub.
boato [ˈbwatu] *m* rumour.
bobagem [bɔˈbaʒẽ] (*pl* **-ns** [-ʃ]) *f (Br)* nonsense *(sg)*.
bobina [bɔˈbina] *f (de circuito elétrico)* coil; *(de fio, corda)* reel.
bobo, -ba [ˈbobu. -ba] *adj* silly.
boca [ˈbɔka] *f* mouth; *(de rua, túnel)* entrance; *(de fogão)* ring; *(Port: fam: dito provocatório)* gibe.
bocado [bɔˈkadu] *m (de pão, bolo, queijo)* piece.
bocal [bɔˈkaw] (*pl* **-ais** [-ajʃ]) *m (de castiçal)* mouth; *(de instrumento musical)* mouthpiece.
bocejar [bɔseˈʒa(x)] *vi* to yawn.
bochecha [buˈʃeʃa] *f* cheek.
bochechar [bɔʃeˈʃa(x)] *vi* to gargle.
boda [ˈbɔda] *f* wedding; **~s de ouro/prata** golden/silver wedding *(sg)*.
bode [ˈbɔdʒi] *m* billy goat; **~ expiatório** scapegoat.
bofetada [bɔfeˈtada] *f* slap.
boi [ˈbɔj] *m* ox.
bóia [ˈbɔja] *f* float; *(de barco)* life buoy.

boiada [bɔˈjada] *f (Br)* herd of cattle.
boiar [bɔˈja(x)] *vi* to float.
boina [ˈbɔjna] *f* flat cap.
bola [ˈbɔla] *f* ball; *(fam: cabeça)* head; **dar ~ para** (*Br: fam: flertar com*) to flirt with; **não ser certo da ~** (*Br: fam*) to be away with the fairies.
bolacha [bɔˈlaʃa] *f (Port)* biscuit; **~ de água e sal** water biscuit.
bolbo [ˈbowbu] *m* bulb.
boleia [bɔˈleja] *f* lift *(Brit)*, ride *(Am)*; **apanhar ~** to hitch a lift; **dar ~ a alguém** to give sb a lift; **pedir ~** (*Port*) to hitchhike.
boletim [bɔleˈtʃĩ] (*pl* **-ns** [-ʃ]) *m (de notícias)* bulletin; *(revista)* newsletter; *(EDUC)* report; **~ meteorológico** weather forecast.
bolha [ˈboʎa] *f (em pele)* blister; *(em líquido)* bubble.
Bolívia [bɔˈlivja] *f*: **a ~** Bolivia.
bolo [ˈbolu] *m* cake; **~ inglês** fruit cake; **dar o ~ em alguém** to stand sb up.
bolor [bɔˈlo(x)] *m* mould.
bolota [bɔˈlɔta] *f* acorn.
bolsa [ˈbowsa] *f (mala)* bag; *(para dinheiro)* purse; **~ de estudos** student grant; **~ de valores** stock exchange.
bolso [ˈbowsu] *m* pocket.
bom, boa [ˈbõ. ˈboa] (*mpl* **bons** [ˈbõʃ]. *fpl* **boas** [ˈboaʃ]) *adj* good; *(bondoso)* kind, nice; *(são)* well; *(adequado)* suitable; **tudo ~?** (*Br: fam*) how's it going?, how are you doing?
bomba [ˈbõmba] *f (de ar, água)* pump; *(explosivo)* bomb; **~ atômica** atomic bomb; **~ de chocolate** = chocolate éclair; **~ de gasolina** petrol station *(Brit)*, filling station *(Am)*; **levar ~** *(fam)* to fail.
bombardear [bõmbaxˈdʒja(x)] *vt* to bomb.
bombazina [bõmbaˈzina] *f (Port)* corduroy.
bombeiro [bõmˈbejru] *m* firefighter; *(Br: encanador)* plumber; **os ~s (voluntários)** fire brigade *(Brit)*, fire department *(Am)*.
bombo [ˈbõmbu] *m* bass drum.
bombom [bõmˈbõ] (*pl* **-ns** [-ʃ]) *m* chocolate.
bondade [bõˈdadʒi] *f* goodness.
bonde [ˈbõdʒi] *m (Br)* tram *(Brit)*, streetcar *(Am)*; **ir de ~** to take the tram.

bondoso, -osa [bōn'dozu. -ɔza] *adj* kind.

boné [bɔ'nɛ] *m* cap.

boneca [bo'nɛka] *f* doll; ~ **de trapos** rag doll.

boneco [bo'nɛku] *m (brinquedo)* doll; *(desenho)* matchstick figure; ~ **de neve** snowman.

bonito, -ta [bo'nitu. -ta] *adj* pretty; *(homem)* good-looking; *(momento)* wonderful; *(gesto, atitude, sentimento)* kind; *(dia)* nice.

bons → bom.

bónus ['bɔnuʃ] *m inv (Port)* = bônus.

bônus ['bonuʃ] *m inv (Br) (de empresa)* bonus; *(de loja)* voucher.

borboleta [boxbo'leta] *f* butterfly.

borbulha [box'buʎa] *f (em pele)* pimple; *(de suco, água, champanhe)* bubble.

borbulhar [boxbu'ʎa(x)] *vi (líquido)* to bubble.

borda ['bɔxda] *f* edge; *(de estrada, rio)* side; **à ~ d'água** at the water's edge.

bordado, -da [box'dadu. -da] *adj* embroidered ♦ *m* embroidery.

bordar [box'da(x)] *vt & vi* to embroider.

bordel [box'dɛw] *(pl* -éis [-ɛjʃ]) *m* brothel.

bordo ['boxdu] *m (de navio, passeio)* side; **a ~** on board.

borra ['bɔxa] *f (de café)* grounds *(pl)*; *(de vinho)* dregs *(pl)*.

borracha [bo'xaʃa] *f* rubber *(Brit)*, eraser *(Am)*; *(material)* rubber.

borracheiro [boxa'ʃejru] *m (Br) person who repairs and sells tyres at a garage.*

borrão [bo'xãw] *(pl* -ões [-õjʃ]) *m* blot.

borrasca [bo'xaʃka] *f* storm.

borrego [bo'xegu] *m (Port)* lamb.

borrifar [boxi'fa(x)] *vt*: ~ **algo com algo** to sprinkle sthg with sthg.

borrões → borrão.

bosque ['bɔʃki] *m* wood.

bossa ['bɔsa] *f* hump; ~ **nova** Brazilian musical movement from the 1960s.

bota ['bɔta] *f* boot.

botânica [bo'tanika] *f* botany, → botânico.

botânico, -ca [bo'taniku. -ka] *m, f* botanist ♦ *adj m* → jardim.

botão [bo'tãw] *(pl* -ões [-õjʃ]) *m (de vestuário, aparelho)* button; *(de flor)* bud; ~ **de punho** cuff link.

botar [bo'ta(x)] *vt* to put; *(vestir,*

calçar) to put on; *(suj: ave)* to lay; *(defeito)* to find; ~ **algo em dia** to update sthg; ~ **algo fora** to throw sthg away.

bote ['bɔtʃi] *m* boat; ~ **salva-vidas** lifeboat.

botequim [botʃi'kĩ] *(pl* -ns [-ʃ]) *m (Br)* cafe.

botija [bo'tiʒa] *f (Port: de gás)* bottle.

botijão [botʃi'ʒãw] *(pl* -ões [-õjʃ]) *m (Br: de gás)* bottle.

botões → botão.

boutique [bu'tike] *f (Port)* = butique.

boxe ['bɔksi] *m* boxing.

braçadeira [brasa'dejra] *f (para natação)* armband; *(de cano, mangueira)* bracket; *(de cortina)* tie-back.

bracelete [brase'letʃi] *m ou f* bracelet.

braço ['brasu] *m* arm; *(de viola, violino, violoncelo)* neck; *(de rio)* branch; *(de mar)* inlet; **não dar o ~ torcer** not to give in; **meter o ~ em alguém** *(Br: fam)* to hit sb; **de ~ dado** arm in arm.

bradar [bra'da(x)] *vt* to cry out ♦ *vi* to clamour.

braguilha [bra'giʎa] *f* flies *(pl)*.

branco, -ca ['brãŋku. -ka] *adj & m* white ♦ *m, f (pessoa)* white man *(f* white woman); **em ~** *(folha, cheque)* blank.

brandir [brãn'dʒi(x)] *vt* to brandish.

brando, -da ['brãndu. -da] *adj* gentle; **cozinhar em fogo ~** to simmer.

brasa ['braza] *f* ember.

brasão [bra'zãw] *(pl* -ões [-õjʃ]) *m* coat of arms.

Brasil [bra'ziw] *m*: **o ~** Brazil.

brasileiro, -ra [brazi'lejru. -ra] *adj & m, f* Brazilian.

Brasília [bra'zilja] *s* Brasília.

brasões → brasão.

bravio, -via [bra'viu. -'via] *adj* wild.

bravo, -va ['bravu. -va] *adj (valente)* brave; *(selvagem)* wild; *(tempestuoso)* rough; *(Br: fig: furioso)* angry ♦ *interj* bravo!

brejo ['breʒu] *m (Br)* swamp.

breve ['brevi] *adj* short; **em ~** soon; **até ~!** see you soon!

brevemente [.brevi'mẽntʃi] *adv* shortly.

briga ['briga] *f* fight.

brigada [bri'gada] *f (de trânsito)* patrol; *(de trabalhadores)* band.

brilhante [bri'ʎãntʃi] *adj (cabelo, metal)* shiny; *(olhos)* bright; *(fig: exce-*

lente) brilliant ♦ *m* diamond.

brilhar [bri'ʎa(x)] *vi* to shine.

brilho ['briʎu] *m (de cabelo, metal)* shine; *(de olhos, sol)* brightness.

brincadeira [brĩŋka'dejra] *f (jogo)* game; *(gracejo)* joke.

brincalhão, -lhona [brĩŋka'ʎãw. -'ʎona] *(mpl* **-ões** [-õjʃ], *fpl* **-s** [-ʃ]) *adj* playful ♦ *m, f* joker.

brincar [brĩŋ'ka(x)] *vi (criança)* to play; *(gracejar)* to joke.

brinco ['brĩŋku] *m* earring.

brincos-de-princesa [,brĩŋkuʒdʒipri'seza] *mpl* fuchsia *(sg).*

brindar [brĩn'da(x)] *vi (fazer um brinde)* to drink a toast ♦ *vt (presentear);* ~ **alguém com algo** to give sthg as a present to sb; ~ **à saúde de alguém** to drink to sb.

brinde ['brĩndʒi] *m (presente)* present; **fazer um** ~ to propose a toast.

brinquedo [brĩŋ'kedu] *m* toy.

brisa ['briza] *f* breeze.

britânico, -ca [bri'taniku. -ka] *adj* British ♦ *m, f* British person; **os** ~**s** the British.

broca ['brɔka] *f* drill.

broche ['brɔʃi] *m* brooch.

brochura [bro'ʃura] *f* brochure.

brócolis ['brɔkoliʃ] *mpl (Br)* broccoli *(sg).*

brócolos ['brɔkoluʃ] *mpl (Port)* = **brócolis.**

bronca ['brõŋka] *f (fam) (confusão)* fuss; *(Br: repreensão)* telling-off.

bronquite [brõŋ'kitʃi] *f* bronchitis.

bronze ['brõzi] *m* bronze.

bronzeado, -da [brõ'zeadu. -da] *adj* tanned ♦ *m* (sun)tan.

bronzeador [brõzea'do(x)] *(pl* **-res** [-riʃ]) *m* suntan cream OU lotion.

bronzear-se [brõ'zjaxsi] *vp* to get a (sun)tan.

brotar [bro'ta(x)] *vi (água)* to well up; *(flor, planta)* to sprout ♦ *vt (líquido)* to spurt.

bruços ['brusuʃ] *mpl (estilo de natação)* breaststroke *(sg);* **de** ~ *(posição)* face down.

bruma ['bruma] *f* mist.

brusco, -ca ['bruʃku. -ka] *adj (pessoa)* brusque; *(gesto, movimento)* sudden.

brushing ['braʃĩŋ] *m* blow-dry.

brutal [bru'taw] *(pl* **-ais** [-ajʃ]) *adj* brutal.

bruto, -ta ['brutu. -ta] *adj* rough; *(peso)* gross; **à bruta** heavy-handedly; **em** ~ raw.

bruxa ['bruʃa] *f* witch.

bucho ['buʃu] *m (fam: ventre)* gut.

búfalo ['bufalu] *m* buffalo.

bufê [bu'fe] *m (Br) (de sala de jantar)* sideboard; *(de festas)* buffet.

bufete [bu'fetɛ] *m (Port)* = **bufê.**

bugigangas [buʒi'gãŋgaʃ] *fpl* knick-knacks.

bula ['bula] *f (de remédio)* instruction leaflet.

bule ['buli] *m (para chá)* teapot; *(para café)* coffee pot.

Bulgária [buw'garja] *f:* **a** ~ Bulgaria.

búlgaro, -ra ['buwgaru. -ra] *adj & m, f* Bulgarian ♦ *m (língua)* Bulgarian.

bulldozer [buw'dɔzɛ(x)] *(pl* **-res** [-riʃ]) *m* bulldozer.

bunda ['bũnda] *f (Br: fam)* bottom.

buraco [bu'raku] *m* hole.

burla ['burla] *f* fraud.

burlão, -lona [bur'lãw. -lona] *(mpl* **-ões** [-õjʃ], *fpl* **-s** [-ʃ]) *m, f* fraudster.

burocracia [burokra'sia] *f* bureaucracy.

burro, -a ['buxu. -a] *m, f* donkey ♦ *adj (estúpido)* stupid.

busca ['buʃka] *f* search; **em** ~ **de** in search of.

buscar [buʃ'ka(x)] *vt* to search for, to look for; **ir** ~ to pick up.

bússola ['busola] *f* compass.

bustiê [buʃ'tʃie] *m (Br)* boob tube.

busto ['buʃtu] *m* bust.

butique [bu'tʃiki] *f (Br)* boutique.

buzina [bu'zina] *f* horn.

buzinar [buzi'na(x)] *vi* to sound the horn.

búzio ['buzju] *m* conch.

B.V. *abrev* = **Bombeiros Voluntários.**

C

c/ *(abrev de conta de banco)* a/c.

cá ['ka] *adv* here; **venha ~, por favor** come here, please.

C.ª *(abrev de Companhia)* Co.

cabana [ka'bana] *f* hut.

cabeça [ka'besa] *f* head; *(de alho)* bulb; **por ~** per head; **à ~** *(à frente)* at the front; **de ~ para baixo** upside down; **fazer a ~ de alguém** to talk sb round; **não ter pé nem ~** to make no sense; **perder a ~** to lose one's head.

cabeçada [kabe'sada] *f (pancada com a cabeça)* head butt; *(em futebol)* header.

cabeçalho [kabe'saʎu] *m* masthead.

cabeceira [kabe'sejra] *f* head.

cabeçudo, -da [kabe'sudu, -da] *adj (teimoso)* stubborn.

cabedal [kabe'daw] *(pl -ais [-ajʃ]) m* leather.

cabeleira [kabe'lejra] *f (verdadeira)* head of hair; *(postiça)* wig.

cabeleireiro, -ra [kabelej'rejru, -ra] *m, f (profissão)* hairdresser ♦ *m (local)* hairdresser's (salon).

cabelo [ka'belu] *m* hair; **ir cortar o ~** to get one's hair cut.

caber [ka'be(x)] *vi* to fit in.
❑ **caber a** *v + prep:* **~ a alguém fazer algo** to be up to sb to do sthg.

cabide [ka'bidʒi] *m (de chapéu)* hat stand; *(de roupa)* (clothes) hanger.

cabine [ka'bini] *f (telefónica)* telephone box; *(de navio, avião)* cabin; *(de trem)* compartment.

cabisbaixo, -xa [kabiʒ'bajʃu, -ʃa] *adj (fig: triste)* downcast.

cabo [kabu] *m* cable; *(de utensílio)* handle; *(de terra)* cape; *(de exército)* corporal; **até o ~** to the end; **ao ~ de** after; **de ~ a rabo** from beginning to end; **dar ~ de algo** *(fam)* to wreck sthg.

Cabo-Verde [kabu'vexdʒi] *s* Cape Verde.

cabo-verdiano, -na [kabuvex'dʒjanu, -na] *adj* relating to Cape Verde ♦ *m, f* native/inhabitant of Cape Verde.

cabra ['kabra] *f* goat.

cabrito [ka'britu] *m* kid (goat); **~ assado** kid seasoned with garlic, bay leaves, "piripiri" and herbs, baked and served with potatoes.

caça ['kasa] *f (ação)* hunting; *(animal caçado)* game ♦ *m (avião)* fighter plane; **~ submarina** underwater fishing.

caçador, -ra [kasa'do(x), -ra] *(mpl -res [-riʃ], fpl -s [-ʃ]) m, f* hunter.

cação [ka'sãw] *m* dogfish.

caçar [ka'sa(x)] *vt* to hunt.

caçarola [kasa'rɔla] *f (de barro)* earthenware pot; *(panela)* saucepan.

cacau [ka'kaw] *m* cocoa.

cacetada [kase'tada] *f* blow.

cacete [ka'setʃi] *m (pau)* stick; **ela é chata para ~** she's a real bore!

cachaça [ka'ʃasa] *f* white rum.

caché [ka'ʃɛ] *m (Port)* = **cachê**.

cachê [ka'ʃe] *m (Br)* fee.

cachecol [kaʃe'kɔw] *(pl -óis [-ɔjʃ]) m* scarf.

cachimbo [ka'ʃĩmbu] *m* pipe.

cacho ['kaʃu] *m (de uvas, flores)* bunch; *(de cabelo)* lock.

cachorro [ka'ʃoxu] *m (Port: cão pequeno)* puppy; *(Br: qualquer cão)* dog; **~ (quente)** hot dog.

cacifo [ka'sifu] *m (cofre)* safe; *(armário)* locker.

cacto ['katu] *m* cactus.

cada ['kada] *adj (um)* each; *(todos)* every; **~ duas semanas** every two weeks; **~ qual** each one; **~ um/uma** each (one); **um/uma de ~ vez** one at a time; **~ vez mais** more and more; **~**

vez que every time; **aqui é ~ um por si** everyone looks out for themselves here.

cadarço [ka'daxsu] *m (Br)* shoelace.

cadastro [ka'daʃtru] *m* criminal record.

cadáver [ka'davɛ(x)] (*pl* -res [-riʃ]) *m* corpse.

cadê [ka'de] *adv (Br: fam):* ~ ...? where's ...?, where are ...? (*pl*).

cadeado [ka'dʒjadu] *m* padlock.

cadeia [ka'deja] *f (fila)* chain; *(prisão)* prison.

cadeira [ka'dejra] *f (assento)* chair; *(disciplina)* subject; ~ **de rodas** wheelchair.

cadela [ka'dɛla] *f* bitch.

cadência [ka'dẽsja] *f* rhythm.

caderno [ka'dɛrnu] *m* notebook.

caducar [kadu'ka(x)] *vi* to expire.

caduco, -ca [ka'duku, -ka] *adj (pessoa)* senile.

cães → cão.

café [ka'fɛ] *m* coffee; *(local)* cafe; ~ **com leite** white coffee; ~ **da manhã** *(Br)* breakfast; ~ **moído/solúvel** ground/instant coffee.

cafeína [kafe'ina] *f* caffeine.

cafeteira [kafe'tejra] *f* coffee pot.

cafezinho [kafe'ziɲu] *m (Br)* espresso.

cágado ['kagadu] *m* terrapin.

caiar [ka'ja(x)] *vt* to whitewash.

caibo ['kajbu] → **caber.**

cãibra ['kãjmbra] *f* cramp.

caipira [kaj'pira] *adj (Br)* provincial ♦ *mf (Br)* yokel.

caipirinha [kajpi'riɲa] *f cocktail made of "cachaça", lime juice, sugar and crushed ice.*

cair [ka'i(x)] *vi* to fall; *(luz)* to shine; ~ **bem/mal** *(comida)* to go down well/badly; ~ **na realidade** ou **em si** to come to one's senses; **nessa não caio eu!** I won't fall for that!

cais ['kajʃ] *m inv (de rio, mar)* harbour; ~ **de embarque** quay.

caixa ['kajʃa] *f* box; *(seção de banco, loja)* counter; *(em supermercado)* checkout; *(banco)* savings bank; *(segurança social)* social security; *(de arma)* chamber ♦ *mf (profissão)* cashier; ~ **alta/baixa** upper/lower case; ~ **automático** cashpoint; ~ **de mudanças** *(Br)* gearbox; ~ **craniana**

cranium; ~ **de crédito** bank; ~ **do correio** *(em Portugal)* letterbox; *(no Brasil)* postbox; ~ **de fósforos** matchbox; ~ **de pagamento** *(em estacionamento)* cashier's desk; ~ **registadora** cash register; ~ **toráxica** thorax; ~ **de velocidades** *(Port)* gearbox.

caixão [kaj'ʃãw] (*pl* -ões [-õjʃ]) *m* coffin *(Brit)*, casket *(Am)*.

caixeiro [kaj'ʃejru] *m:* ~ **viajante** travelling salesman.

caixilho [kaj'ʃiʎu] *m* frame.

caixões → caixão.

caixote [kaj'ʃɔtʃi] *m* box; ~ **do lixo** *(Port)* bin.

caju [ka'ʒu] *m* cashew nut.

cal ['kaw] *f* lime.

calado, -da [ka'ladu, -da] *adj* quiet; **fique ~!** shut up!, be quiet!

calafrio [kala'friu] *m* shiver.

calamidade [kalami'dadʒi] *f* calamity.

calão [ka'lãw] *m (Port)* slang.

calar-se [ka'laxsi] *vp* to fall silent; **cale-se!** shut up!

calça ['kawsa] *f (Br)* trousers *(pl)*.

calçada [kaw'sada] *f* pavement; *(Port: rua)* cobbled street.

calçadeira [kawsa'dejra] *f* shoehorn.

calçado, -da [kaw'sadu, -da] *adj (rua)* cobbled ♦ *m* footwear.

calcanhar [kawka'ɲa(x)] (*pl* -res [-riʃ]) *m* heel.

calção [kaw'sãw] (*pl* -ões [-õjʃ]) *m (Br)* shorts *(pl)*; ~ **de banho** swimming trunks *(pl)*.

calcar [kaw'ka(x)] *vt (pisar)* to stand on; *(comprimir)* to press down.

calçar [kaw'sa(x)] *vt (sapatos, meias, luvas)* to put on; *(rua, passeio)* to pave; **que número você calça?** what size (shoe) do you take?; **calço 37** I'm a (size) 37.

calcário [kaw'karju] *m* limestone.

calças ['kalsaʃ] *fpl (Port)* = **calça.**

calcinha [kaw'siɲa] *f (Br)* knickers *(pl)*.

cálcio ['kawsju] *m* calcium.

calço ['kawsu] *m* wedge; ~ **de freio** brake pad.

calções [kal'sõjʃ] *mpl (Port)* = **calção.**

calculadora [kawkula'dora] *f* calculator; ~ **de bolso** pocket calculator.

calcular [kawku'la(x)] *vt (número, valor)* to calculate; *(conjecturar)* to reckon.

cálculo ['kawkulu] *m (aritmético, algébrico)* calculation; *(disciplina)* calculus; **pelos meus ~s estaremos lá em uma hora** I reckon we'll be there in an hour.

calda ['kawda] *f* syrup.

caldeira [kaw'dejra] *f* boiler.

caldeirada [kawdej'rada] *f (CULIN)* fish stew cooked in a tomato and herb sauce with potatoes.

caldo ['kawdu] *m (sopa)* broth; *(de carne, sopa, vegetais)* stock; *(Br: suco de fruto, planta)* juice; **~ de cana** *(Br)* thick juice made from sugarcane pulp; **~ verde** spring green soup served with "chouriço", a drop of olive oil and maize bread.

calendário [kalēn'darju] *m* calendar.

calhamaço [kaʎa'masu] *m (fam: livro)* tome.

calhar [ka'ʎa(x)] *vi (vir a propósito)*: **calhou eu estar lá** I happened to be there; **ela calhou de telefonar** she happened to ring; **~ bem/mal** to be convenient/inconvenient; **se ~** *(Port)* perhaps, maybe; **vir a ~** to come at just the right time.

calhau [ka'ʎaw] *m* stone.

calibragem [kali'braʒē] *(pl -ns [-ʃ])* *f*: **~ (dos pneus)** tyre pressure.

calibre [ka'libri] *m* calibre.

cálice ['kalisi] *m (copo)* port OU liqueur glass; *(sagrado)* chalice.

calista [ka'liʃta] *mf* chiropodist *(Brit)*, podiatrist *(Am)*.

calma ['kawma] *f* calm ◆ *interj* take it easy!, calm down!; **ter ~** to keep calm.

calmante [kaw'mãntʃi] *m* tranquillizer ◆ *adj* soothing.

calmo, -ma ['kawmu, -ma] *adj* calm; *(lugar)* quiet.

calo ['kalu] *m* callus; *(de pé)* corn.

caloiro, -ra [ka'lojru, -ra] *m, f* fresher *(Brit)*, freshman *(Am)*.

calor [ka'lo(x)] *m* heat; **estar com ~** to be hot.

caloria [kalo'ria] *f* calorie.

calorífero, -ra [kalo'riferu, -ra] *adj* calorific ◆ *m* heater.

calúnia [ka'lunja] *f* slander.

calvo, -va ['kawvu, -va] *adj* bald.

cama ['kama] *f* bed; **~ de campismo** camp bed; **~ de casal** double bed; **~**

de solteiro single bed; **estar de ~** to be bedridden.

camada [ka'mada] *f* layer; *(de tinta, verniz)* coat; **a ~ do ozônio** the ozone layer.

camaleão [kama'ljãw] *(pl -ões [-õjʃ])* *m* chameleon.

câmara ['kamara] *f*: **~ fotográfica** camera; **~ municipal** *(elementos)* town council; *(Port: edifício)* town hall *(Brit)*, city hall *(Am)*; **~ de vídeo** camcorder; **em ~ lenta** in slow motion.

camarada [kama'rada] *mf (de partido)* comrade; *(fam: forma de tratamento)* mate, pal ◆ *adj (preço)* good.

câmara-de-ar [kamara'dʒia(x)] *(pl câmaras-de-ar* [kamaraʒ'dʒia(x)]*) f* inner tube.

camarão [kama'rãw] *(pl -ões [-õjʃ])* *m* shrimp.

camarata [kama'rata] *f* dormitory.

camarim [kama'rĩ] *(pl -ns [-ʃ])* *m* dressing room.

camarões → camarão.

camarote [kama'rɔtʃi] *m (de navio)* cabin; *(de teatro)* box.

cambalear [kãmba'lja(x)] *vi* to stagger.

cambalhota [kãmba'ʎɔta] *f* somersault; *(trambolhão)* tumble.

câmbio ['kãmbju] *m (troca de valores)* exchange; *(preço de transação)* exchange rate; *(Br: de veículo)* gear lever.

cambraia [kãm'braja] *f* cambric.

camelo [ka'melu] *m* camel.

camelô [kame'lo] *m (Br)* street pedlar.

camião [ka'mjãw] *(pl -ões [-õjʃ])* *m (Port)* = **caminhão**.

caminhada [kami'nada] *f* walk.

caminhão [kami'nãw] *(pl -ões [-õjʃ])* *m (Br)* lorry *(Brit)*, truck *(Am)*.

caminhar [kami'na(x)] *vi* to walk.

caminho [ka'minu] *m* way; *(via)* path; **estou a ~** I'm on my way; **a ~ de** on the way to; **pelo ~** on the way; **cortar ~** to take a short cut.

caminho-de-ferro [ka,minude'fexu] *(pl caminhos-de-ferro* [ka,minuʒde'fexu]*) m (Port)* railway *(Brit)*, railroad *(Am)*.

caminhões → caminhão.

caminhoneiro, -ra [kamino'nejru, -ra] *m, f (Br)* lorry driver *(Brit)*, truck driver *(Am)*.

caminhonete [kamjoˈnɛta] *f (Br)* *(para passageiros)* minibus; *(para mercadorias)* van.

camiões → camião.

camioneta [kamjuˈnɛta] *f (Port)* = caminhonete.

camionista [kamjuˈniʃta] *mf (Port)* = caminhoneiro.

camisa [kaˈmiza] *f* shirt.

camisa-de-forças [ka.mizadʒiˈfoxsaʃ] *(pl* camisas-de-forças [ka.mizaʒdʒiˈfoxsaʃ]) *f* straitjacket.

camiseta [kamiˈzɛta] *f (Br)* T-shirt.

camisinha [kamiˈziɲa] *f (Br: fam: preservativo)* condom.

camisola [kamiˈzɔla] *f (Port: de lã, algodão)* sweater; *(Br: de dormir)* nightdress; **~ de gola alta** *(Port)* polo neck *(Brit)*, turtleneck *(Am)*; **~ interior** *(Port)* vest; **~ de manga curta** *(Port)* T-shirt.

camomila [kamoˈmila] *f* camomile.

campainha [kãmpaˈiɲa] *f* bell.

campanário [kãmpaˈnarju] *m* belfry.

campanha [kãmˈpaɲa] *f* campaign; **~ eleitoral** election campaign; **~ de verão/inverno** summer/winter season.

campeão, -peã [kãmˈpjãw. -pjã] *(mpl* -ões [-õjʃ]. *fpl* -s [-ʃ]) *m, f* champion.

campeonato [kãmpjoˈnatu] *m* championship.

campestre [kãmˈpɛʃtri] *adj* country *(antes de s)*.

camping [kãmˈpĩ] *m (Br)* camping; *(local)* campsite.

campismo [kãmˈpiʒmu] *m* camping.

campista [kãmˈpiʃta] *mf* camper.

campo [ˈkãmpu] *m* country(side); *(de esporte)* pitch; *(terreno)* field; **~ de futebol** football pitch; **~ de golfe** golf course; **~ de jogos** playing field; **~ de squash/ténis** *(Port)* squash/tennis court; **~ de tiro** firing range.

camponês, -esa [ˈkãmpoˈneʃ. -eza] *(mpl* -eses [-eziʃ]. *fpl* -s [-ʃ]) *m, f* peasant.

camuflagem [kamuˈflaʒẽ] *(pl* -ns [-ʃ]) *f* camouflage.

camuflar [kamuˈfla(x)] *vt* to camouflage.

camurça [kaˈmuxsa] *f* suede.

cana [ˈkana] *f (planta)* bamboo; *(material)* cane; *(bengala)* walking stick; *(Br: cana-de-açúcar)* sugarcane; **ir em ~** *(Br: fam)* to be arrested; **~ de pesca** *(Port)* fishing rod.

Canadá [kanaˈda] *m*: **o ~** Canada.

cana-de-açúcar [.kanadʒiaˈsuka(x)] *(pl* canas-de-açúcar [.kanaʒdʒiaˈsuka(x)]) *f* sugarcane.

canadense [kanaˈdẽsi] *adj & mf (Br)* Canadian.

canadiano, -na [kanaˈdjanu. -na] *adj & m, f (Port)* = canadense.

canal [kaˈnaw] *(pl* -ais [-ajʃ]) *m* channel; *(de navegação)* canal; **o Canal da Mancha** the (English) Channel.

canalha [kaˈnaʎa] *f (Port: fam: crianças)* kids *(pl)* ♦ *mf (patife)* good-for-nothing.

canalização [kanalizaˈsãw] *(pl* -ões [-õjʃ]) *f (de água)* plumbing; *(de gás)* piping.

canalizador, -ra [kanalizaˈdor. -ra] *(mpl* -res [-reʃ]. *fpl* -s [-ʃ]) *m, f (Port)* plumber.

canalizar [kanaliˈza(x)] *vt (água, gás)* to lay pipes for; *(fig: esforços, fundos)* to channel.

canapé [kanaˈpɛ] *m* sofa.

canapê [kanaˈpe] *m (Br)* canapé.

canário [kaˈnarju] *m* canary.

canastra [kaˈnaʃtra] *f* large basket.

canção [kãˈsãw] *(pl* -ões [-õjʃ]) *f* song.

cancela [kãˈsɛla] *f (de casa, jardim)* gate; *(de passagem de nível)* barrier.

cancelamento [kãselaˈmẽtu] *m* cancellation.

cancelar [kãseˈla(x)] *vt* to cancel.

câncer [ˈkãse(x)] *(pl* -res [-riʃ]) *m (Br)* cancer.

⊐ Câncer *m (Br)* Cancer.

cancerígeno, -na [kãseˈriʒenu. -na] *adj* carcinogenic.

canções → canção.

cancro [ˈkãŋkru] *m (Port)* = câncer.

candeeiro [kãnˈdjejru] *m (Br: a petróleo)* oil lamp; *(Port: a eletricidade)* lamp.

candelabro [kãndeˈlabru] *m (lustre)* chandelier; *(castiçal)* candelabra.

candidato, -ta [kãndʒiˈdatu. -ta] *m, f*: **~ (a)** candidate (for).

candomblé [kãndõmˈblɛ] *m* Afro-Brazilian religion centred around musical rituals and dance.

caneca [kaˈnɛka] *f* mug; *(medida de cerveja)* half-litre measure of beer.

canela [kaˈnɛla] *f (condimento)* cinnamon; *(de perna)* shin; **esticar a ~** *(fig: morrer)* to kick the bucket.

caneta [kaˈneta] *f* pen; **~ de feltro**

felt-tip (pen); ~ **de tinta permanente** fountain pen.

cangaceiro [kãŋga'sejru] *m (Br)* bandit.

canguru [kãŋgu'ru] *m* kangaroo.

canhão [ka'nãw] *(pl* **-ões** [-õjʃ]*) m (arma)* cannon; *(vale)* canyon.

canhoto, -ota [ka'ɲotu, -ɔta] *adj* left-handed ◆ *m, f* left-handed person.

canibal [kani'baw] *(pl* **-ais** [-ajʃ]*) mf* cannibal.

caniço [ka'nisu] *m* reed.

canil [ka'niw] *(pl* **-is** [-iʃ]*) m* kennel.

caninha [ka'niɲa] *f (Br: cachaça)* rum.

canis → **canil**.

canivete [kani'vetʃi] *m* penknife.

canja ['kãʒa] *f:* ~ **(de galinha)** chicken broth; **é ~!** it's a piece of cake!

cano ['kanu] *m* pipe; *(de arma)* barrel; ~ **de esgoto** drainpipe.

canoa [ka'noa] *f* canoe.

canoagem [ka'nwaʒẽ] *f* canoeing; **fazer** ~ to go canoeing.

cansaço [kã'sasu] *m* tiredness.

cansado, -da [kã'sadu, -da] *adj:* **estar** ~ to be tired.

cansar [kã'sa(x)] *vt* to tire out.

⌐ **cansar-se** *vp* to get tired.

cansativo, -va [kãsa'tʃivu, -va] *adj (fatigante)* tiring; *(maçante)* tedious.

cantar [kãn'ta(x)] *vi & vt* to sing.

cantarolar [kãntaro'la(x)] *vi & vt* to hum.

cantiga [kãn'tʃiga] *f (canção)* ballad.

cantil [kãn'tʃiw] *(pl* **-is** [-iʃ]*) m* flask.

cantina [kãn'tʃina] *f* canteen; *(de instituição de caridade)* soup kitchen.

cantis → **cantil**.

canto ['kãntu] *m* corner; *(forma de cantar)* singing; *(de galo)* crowing; **estou aprendendo** ~ I'm having singing lessons.

cantor, -ra [kãn'to(x), -ra] *(mpl* **-res** [-riʃ]*, fpl* **-s** [-ʃ]*) m, f* singer.

canudo [ka'nudu] *m* tube; *(Br: para bebida)* straw; *(fam: diploma de curso)* degree certificate.

cão ['kãw] *(pl* **cães** ['kãjʃ]*) m* dog; ~ **de guarda** guard dog.

caos ['kawʃ] *m* chaos.

caótico, -ca [ka'ɔtiku, -ka] *adj* chaotic.

capa ['kapa] *f (dossier, pasta)* folder; *(peça de vestuário)* cape; *(de livro, caderno)* cover; ~ **impermeável** rain cape.

capacete [kapa'setʃi] *m (de moto)* crash helmet; *(de proteção)* hard hat.

capacidade [kapasi'dadʒi] *f* capacity; *(fig: talento)* ability.

capar [ka'pa(x)] *vt* to castrate; *(animal de estimação)* to neuter; *(cavalo)* to geld.

capaz [ka'paʃ] *(pl* **-zes** [-ziʃ]*) adj* capable; **ser** ~ **de fazer algo** to be able to do sthg; **é** ~ **de chover** it might rain.

capela [ka'pɛla] *f* chapel.

capitã → **capitão**.

capitães → **capitão**.

capital [kapi'taw] *(pl* **-ais** [-ajʃ]*) f & m* capital.

capitalismo [kapita'liʒmu] *m* capitalism.

capitalista [kapita'liʃta] *adj & mf* capitalist.

capitão, -tã [kapi'tãw, -tã] *(mpl* **-ães** [-ãjʃ]*, fpl* **-s** [-ʃ]*) m, f* captain.

capítulo [ka'pitulu] *m* chapter.

capô [ka'po] *m (de carro)* bonnet *(Brit)*, hood *(Am)*.

capoeira [ka'pwejra] *f* coop; *(prática esportiva)* Brazilian fighting dance.

capota [ka'pɔta] *f (de carro)* bonnet *(Brit)*, hood *(Am)*.

capotar [kapo'ta(x)] *vi* to overturn.

capote [ka'pɔtʃi] *m* overcoat.

cappuccino [kapu'tʃinu] *m* cappuccino.

capricho [ka'priʃu] *m* whim.

Capricórnio [kapri'kɔrnju] *m* Capricorn.

cápsula ['kapsula] *f* capsule.

captar [kap'ta(x)] *vt (água)* to collect; *(sinal, onda)* to receive; *(atenção)* to attract.

capuz [ka'puʃ] *(pl* **-zes** [-ziʃ]*) m* hood.

caqui [ka'ki] *m* khaki.

cara ['kara] *f* face; *(aspecto)* appearance ◆ *m (Br: fam)* guy; ~**s ou coroas?** heads or tails?; ~ **a** ~ face to face; **dar de** ~ **com** *(fig)* to come face to face with; **não vou com a** ~ **dele** I don't like the look of him; **ter** ~ **de poucos amigos** to look like a hard nut.

carabina [kara'bina] *f* rifle.

caracol [kara'kɔw] *(pl* **-óis** [-ɔjʃ]*) m*

(animal) snail; *(de cabelo)* curl.

carácter [kaˈratɐr] *(pl* **caracteres** [karaˈtɛrɨʃ]) *m (Port)* = **caráter**.

característica [karatɨˈriʃʃika] *f* characteristic.

característico, -ca [karatɨˈriʃʃiku, -ka] *adj* characteristic.

carambola [karɐ̃ˈbɔla] *f* star fruit.

caramelo [karaˈmɛlu] *m* toffee.

caranguejo [karɐ̃ˈgɐjʒu] *m* crab.

⌐ **Caranguejo** *m (Port)* Cancer.

caratê [karaˈte] *m (Br)* karate.

caráter [kaˈratɛr(x)] *(pl* **-res** [-riʃ]) *m (Br)* character; *(tipo)* type.

caravana [karaˈvana] *f (Port: viatura)* caravan *(Brit)*, trailer *(Am)*; *(de gente)* caravan.

carbonizado, -da [kaxboniˈzadu, -da] *adj* charred.

carbono [kaxˈbonu] *m* carbon.

carburador [kaxburaˈdo(x)] *(pl* **-res** [-riʃ]) *m* carburettor.

cardápio [kaxˈdapju] *m (Br)* menu.

cardíaco, -ca [kaxˈdʒiaku, -ka] *adj* cardiac.

cardo [ˈkaxdu] *m* thistle.

cardume [kaxˈdumi] *m* shoal.

careca [kaˈrɛka] *adj* bald ◆ *f* bald patch.

carecer [karɨˈse(x)] : **carecer de** *v + prep (ter falta de)* to lack; *(precisar de)* to need.

carência [kaˈrẽsja] *f (falta)* lack; *(necessidade)* need.

careta [kaˈrɛta] *f* grimace; **fazer ~s** to pull faces.

carga [ˈkaxga] *f (de barco, avião)* cargo; *(de trem, caminhão)* freight; *(de pessoa, animal)* load; *(de projétil)* charge; **~ máxima** maximum load.

cargo [ˈkaxgu] *m (função)* post; *(responsabilidade)* responsibility; **deixar a ~ de** to leave in charge of; **estar a ~ de** to be the responsibility of; **ter a ~** to be in charge of.

cariado, -da [kaˈrjadu, -da] *adj* decayed.

caricatura [karikaˈtura] *f* caricature.

carícia [kaˈrisja] *f* caress.

caridade [kariˈdadʒi] *f* charity.

cárie [ˈkari] *f* tooth decay.

caril [kaˈriw] *m* curry powder.

carimbar [karĩˈba(x)] *vt* to stamp.

carimbo [kaˈrĩbu] *m* stamp; *(em carta)* postmark.

carinho [kaˈriɲu] *m* affection.

carinhoso, -osa [kariˈɲozu, -ɔza] *adj* affectionate.

carioca [kaˈrjɔka] *mf (pessoa)* native/inhabitant of Rio de Janeiro ◆ *m (Port: café)* weak espresso; **~ de limão** *(Port)* fresh lemon infusion.

carisma [kaˈriʒma] *m* charisma.

carnal [kaxˈnaw] *(pl* **-ais** [-ajʃ]) *adj* carnal.

Carnaval [kaxnaˈvaw] *m* Carnival.

carne [ˈkaxni] *f (de comer)* meat; *(tecido muscular)* flesh; **~ de carneiro** lamb;; **~ picada** mince *(Brit)*, mincemeat *(Am)*; **~ de porco** pork; **~ de vaca** beef; **em ~ e osso** in the flesh.

carnê [kaxˈne] *m (Br) (caderno)* notebook; *(de pagamentos)* payment book.

carneiro [kaxˈnejru] *m (animal)* sheep; *(reprodutor)* ram; *(carne)* mutton.

⌐ **Carneiro** *m (Port)* Aries.

carniceiro [karniˈsejru] *m (Port)* butcher.

carnudo, -da [kaxˈnudu, -da] *adj (lábios)* full; *(fruto)* fleshy.

caro, -ra [ˈkaru, -ra] *adj (de preço elevado)* expensive, dear; *(querido)* dear.

carochinha [karoˈʃiɲa] *f* → **história**.

caroço [kaˈrosu] *m (de fruto)* stone; *(em corpo)* lump.

carona [kaˈrona] *f (Br)* lift *(Brit)*, ride *(Am)*; **pegar uma ~** to hitch a lift; **dar uma ~ a alguém** to give sb a lift; **pedir ~** to hitchhike.

carpete [kaxˈpɛtʃi] *f* carpet.

carpinteiro [kaxpĩˈtejru] *m* carpenter.

carraça [kaˈxasa] *f* tick.

carrapicho [kaxaˈpiʃu] *m* topknot.

carregado, -da [kaxɨˈgadu, -da] *adj (cor)* dark; *(tempo)* muggy; **estar ~ de** to be loaded down with.

carregador [kaxegaˈdo(x)] *(pl* **-res** [-riʃ]) *m (em estação, hotel)* porter.

carregar [kaxɨˈga(x)] *vt* to load; *(transportar)* to carry; *(pilha, bateria)* to charge ◆ *vi (pesar)* to be heavy; **~ em algo** *(exagerar)* to overdo sthg; *(Port: apertar)* to press sthg.

carreira [kaˈxejra] *f (profissão)* career; *(fileira)* row; *(de transportes coletivos)* route; *(pequena corrida)* race.

carrinha [kaˈxiɲa] *f (Port) (para pas-*

sageiros) minibus; *(para mercadorias)* van.

carrinho [ka'xiɲu] *m*: ~ **de bebê** pushchair *(Brit)*, stroller *(Am)*; ~ **de mão** wheelbarrow; ~ **de supermercado** trolley *(Brit)*, cart *(Am)*.

carro ['kaxu] *m* car; ~ **alegórico** carnival float; ~ **de aluguel** hire car; ~ **de corrida** racing car; ~ **de passeio** *(Br)* saloon (car) *(Brit)*, sedan *(Am)*; ~ **de praça** taxi.

carro-chefe [,kaxuʃ'ʃɛfi] *(pl* **carros-chefes** [,kaxuʃ'ʃɛfiʃ]) *f (Br) (coisa mais importante)* flagship; *(de desfile)* main float.

carroça [ka'xɔsa] *f* cart.

carroçaria [kaxosa'ria] *f* bodywork.

carro-leito [,kaxu'lejtu] *(pl* **carros-leitos** [,kaxuʃ'lejtuʃ]) *f (Br)* sleeping car.

carro-restaurante [,kaxuxeʃtaw'rantʃi] *(pl* **carros-restaurantes** [,kaxuʃxeʃtaw'rantʃiʃ]) *f (Br)* dining car.

carrossel [kaxɔ'sɛw] *(pl* **-éis** [-ɛjʃ]) *m* merry-go-round *(Brit)*, carousel *(Am)*.

carruagem [ka'xwaʒẽ] *(pl* **-ns** [-ʃ]) *f (Port: vagão)* carriage *(Brit)*, car *(Am)*.

carruagem-cama [ka,xwaʒẽ'kama] *(pl* **carruagens-cama** [ka,xwaʒẽʃ'kama]) *f (Port)* sleeping car.

carruagem-restaurante [ka,xwaʒẽxeʃtaw'rãntɛ] *(pl* **carruagens-restaurante** [ka,xwaʒẽʃxeʃtaw'rãntɛ]) *f (Port)* dining car.

carta ['kaxta] *f* letter; *(mapa)* map; *(de baralho)* card; ~ **de apresentação** covering letter; ~ **(de condução)** *(Port)* driving licence *(Brit)*, driver's license *(Am)*; ~ **registada** registered letter.

cartão [kax'tãw] *(pl* **-ões** [-õjʃ]) *m* card; *(papelão)* cardboard; ~ **bancário** bank card; ~ **de crédito** credit card; ~ **de embarque/desembarque** boarding/landing card; ~ **jovem** *young person's discount card*; ~ **multibanco** *(Port)* cashpoint card; ~ **postal** *(Br)* postcard.

cartão-de-visita [kax,tãwdʒivi'zita] *(pl* **cartões-de-visita** [kar,tõjʒdʒivi'zita]) *m* business card.

cartaz [kax'taʃ] *(pl* **-zes** [-ziʃ]) *m* poster.

carteira [kax'tejra] *f (de dinheiro)* wallet; *(mala de senhora)* handbag; *(de sala de aula)* desk; ~ **de identidade** *(Br)*

identity card; ~ **de motorista** *(Br)* driving licence *(Brit)*, driver's license *(Am)*.

carteiro [kax'tejru] *m* postman *(Brit)*, mailman *(Am)*.

cartões → **cartão**.

cartolina [kaxto'lina] *f* card.

cartório [kax'tɔrju] *m* registry office; ~ **notarial** notary's office.

cartucho [kax'tuʃu] *m (para mercadoria)* paper bag; *(munição)* cartridge; *(embrulho)* packet.

caruru [karu'ru] *m* mashed okra or green amaranth leaves with shrimps, fish and palm oil.

carvalho [kax'vaʎu] *m* oak.

carvão [kax'vãw] *m* coal; ~ **de lenha** charcoal.

casa ['kaza] *f* house; *(lar)* home; *(de botão)* buttonhole; **em** ~ at home; **ir para** ~ to go home; ~ **de banho** *(Port)* bathroom; ~ **de câmbio** *(Br)* bureau de change; ~ **de saúde** private hospital; **faça como se estivesse em sua** ~! make yourself at home!

casaco [ka'zaku] *m* jacket; ~ **comprido** coat; ~ **de malha** cardigan.

casado, -da [ka'zadu, -da] *adj* married.

casal [ka'zaw] *(pl* **-ais** [-ajʃ]) *m* couple.

casamento [kaza'mẽntu] *m* marriage; *(cerimônia)* wedding.

casar [ka'za(x)] *vt* to marry ♦ *vi* to get married.

⊔ **casar-se** *vp* to get married.

casca ['kaʃka] *f (de ovo, noz, etc)* shell; *(de laranja, maçã, etc)* peel.

cascalho [kaʃ'kaʎu] *m* rubble.

cascata [kaʃ'kata] *f* waterfall.

cascavel [kaʃka'vɛw] *(pl* **-éis** [-ɛjʃ]) *f* rattlesnake.

casco ['kaʃku] *m (de vinho)* cask; *(de navio)* hull; *(de cavalo, boi, ovelha, etc)* hoof.

caseiro, -ra [ka'zejru, -ra] *adj* homemade; *(pessoa)* home-loving ♦ *m, f* estate worker *(provided with free accommodation for self and family)*.

casino [ka'zinu] *m (Port)* = **cassino**.

caso ['kazu] *m (circunstância)* case; *(acontecimento)* affair ♦ *conj* in case; **no** ~ **de** in the event of; **"em** ~ **de emergência ..."** "in an emergency ..."; **"em** ~ **de incêndio ..."** "in case of fire ..."; **em todo o** ~ in any case;

em último ~ as a last resort; **não fazer** ~ **de algo/alguém** to ignore sthg/sb.

caspa [ˈkaʃpa] f dandruff.

casquilho [kaʃˈkiʎu] m socket.

casquinha [kaʃˈkiɲa] f (de prata, ouro) leaf; (Br: de sorvete) cone.

cassete [kaˈsɛtʃi] f cassette, tape; ~ **(de vídeo)** (video)tape.

cassetete [kaseˈtɛtʃi] m truncheon.

cassino [kaˈsinu] m (Br) casino.

castanha [kaʃˈtaɲa] f (fruto do castanheiro) chestnut; (fruto do cajueiro) cashew nut; **~s assadas** roast chestnuts.

castanheiro [kaʃtaˈɲejru] m chestnut tree.

castanho, -nha [kaʃˈtaɲu. -ɲa] adj brown ◆ m (madeira) chestnut.

castelo [kaʃˈtɛlu] m castle.

castiçal [kaʃtʃiˈsaw] (pl -ais [-ajʃ]) m candlestick.

castidade [kaʃtʃiˈdadʒi] f chastity.

castigar [kaʃtʃiˈga(x)] vt to punish.

castigo [kaʃˈtʃigu] m punishment.

casto, -ta [ˈkaʃtu. -ta] adj chaste.

castor [kaʃˈto(x)] (pl -res [-riʃ]) m beaver.

castrar [kaʃˈtra(x)] vt to castrate.

casual [kaˈzwaw] (pl -ais [-ajʃ]) adj chance (antes de s).

casualidade [kazwaliˈdadʒi] f chance; **por** ~ by chance.

casulo [kaˈzulu] m cocoon.

catacumbas [kataˈkũbaʃ] fpl catacombs.

catálogo [kaˈtalogu] m catalogue.

catamarã [katamaˈrã] m catamaran.

catarata [kataˈrata] f waterfall; (MED) cataract; **as ~s do Iguaçu** the Iguaçu Falls.

catarro [kaˈtaxu] m catarrh.

catástrofe [kaˈtaʃtrofi] f catastrophe.

catatua [kataˈtua] f cockatoo.

cata-vento [kataˈvẽtu] (pl **cata-ventos** [kataˈvẽtuʃ]) m weather vane.

catedral [kateˈdraw] (pl -ais [-ajʃ]) f cathedral.

categoria [kategoˈria] f category; (posição) position; (qualidade) class; **de** ~ first-rate.

cativar [katʃiˈva(x)] vt to captivate.

cativeiro [katʃiˈvejru] m: **em** ~ in captivity.

católico, -ca [kaˈtɔliku. -ka] adj & m, f Catholic.

catorze [kaˈtoxzi] num fourteen, → **seis**.

caução [kawˈsãw] (pl -ões [-õjʃ]) f (JUR) bail; **pagar** ~ to pay bail.

cauda [ˈkawda] f (de animal) tail; (de manto, vestido) train.

caudal [kawˈdaw] (pl -ais [-ajʃ]) m flow.

caule [ˈkawli] m stem.

causa [ˈkawza] f (motivo) reason; (de acidente, doença) cause; (JUR: acção judicial) case; **por** ~ **de** because of.

causar [kawˈza(x)] vt to cause; ~ **danos a** to damage.

cautela [kawˈtɛla] f caution; (de loteria) part-share of a lottery ticket; **ter** ~ **com** to be careful with; **com** ~ cautiously; **à** OU **por** ~ as a safeguard.

cauteloso, -osa [kawteˈlozu. -ɔza] adj cautious.

cavala [kaˈvala] f mackerel.

cavalaria [kavalaˈria] f cavalry.

cavaleiro [kavaˈlejru] m rider; (em tourada) bullfighter on horseback; (medieval) knight.

cavalete [kavaˈlɛtʃi] m easel.

cavalgar [kavawˈga(x)] vi to ride ◆ vt (égua, ginete) to ride; (obstáculo, barreira) to jump.

cavalheiro [kavaˈʎejru] m gentleman.

cavalinho-de-pau [kavaˌliɲudʒiˈpaw] (pl **cavalinhos-de-pau** [kavaˌliɲuʒdʒiˈpaw]) m hobbyhorse.

cavalo [kaˈvalu] m horse.

cavanhaque [kavaˈɲaki] m goatee (beard).

cavaquinho [kavaˈkiɲu] m small four-stringed guitar.

cavar [kaˈva(x)] vt (terra) to dig, (decote) to lower.

cave [ˈkavi] f (de vinho) wine cellar; (Port: de casa) basement.

caveira [kaˈvejra] f skull.

caverna [kaˈvɛxna] f cave.

caviar [kaˈvja(x)] m caviar.

cavidade [kaviˈdadʒi] f cavity.

caxemira [kaʃeˈmira] f cashmere.

caxumba [kaˈʃũba] f (Br) mumps (sg).

c/c (abrev de conta corrente) a/c.

CD m (abrev de compact disc) CD.

CD-i m (abrev de compact disc-

interativo) CDI.

CD-ROM [sede'rɔmi] *m* CD-ROM.

CE *f (abrev de Comunidade Europeia)* EC.

cear ['sja(x)] *vi* to have dinner ♦ *vt* to have for dinner.

cebola [se'bola] *f* onion.

cebolada [sebo'lada] *f fried onion sauce.*

cebolinha [sebo'liɲa] *f (de conserva)* pickled onions *(pl)*; *(Br: erva comestível)* chives *(pl)*.

cebolinho [sebo'liɲu] *m (Port)* chives *(pl)*.

ceder [se'de(x)] *vt (lugar)* to give up; *(objeto)* to lend ♦ *vi (dar-se por vencido)* to give in; *(ponte)* to give way; *(corda, nó)* to slacken; *(chuva)* to ease up; *(vento)* to drop; *"~ a passagem"* "give way".

cedilha [se'diʎa] *f* cedilla. ·

cedo ['sedu] *adv* early; *(depressa)* soon; **muito ~** very early; **desde muito ~** *(desde criança)* from an early age; **mais ~ ou mais tarde** sooner or later.

cedro ['sedru] *m* cedar.

cegar [se'ga(x)] *vt* to blind ♦ *vi* to go blind.

cego, -ga ['sɛgu, -ga] *adj (pessoa)* blind; *(faca)* blunt ♦ *m, f* blind man *(f blind woman)*; **às cegas** blindly.

cegonha [se'goɲa] *f* stork.

ceia ['seja] *f* supper.

cela ['sɛla] *f* cell.

celebração [selebra'sãw] *(pl -ões* [-õjʃ]) *f* celebration.

celebrar [sele'bra(x)] *vt* to celebrate; *(casamento)* to hold; *(contrato)* to sign.

célebre ['sɛlebri] *adj* famous.

celebridade [selebri'dadʒi] *f* celebrity.

celeiro [se'lejru] *m* granary.

celibatário, -ria [seliba'tarju, -rja] *m, f* bachelor *(f single woman).*

celibato [seli'batu] *m* celibacy.

celofane [selo'fani] *m* Cellophane[®].

célula ['sɛlula] *f* cell.

celular [selu'la(x)] *m (Br: telefone)* mobile phone.

cem ['sẽ] *num* one OU a hundred; **~ mil** a hundred thousand, **→ seis**.

cemitério [semi'tɛrju] *m* cemetery.

cena ['sena] *f* scene; *(palco)* stage; **entrar em ~** *(fig)* to come on the

scene; **fazer uma ~** *(fig)* to to make a scene.

cenário [se'narju] *m* scenery; *(de programa televisivo)* set.

cenoura [se'nora] *f* carrot.

censo ['sẽsu] *f* census.

censura [sẽ'sura] *f (crítica)* criticism; *(de Estado, autoridade)* censorship.

centavo [sẽ'tavu] *m old coin equivalent to a tenth of a real.*

centeio [sẽ'teju] *m* rye.

centelha [sẽ'teʎa] *f* spark.

centena [sẽ'tena] *f* hundred; **uma ~ de pessoas** a hundred people.

centenário [sẽte'narju] *m* centenary.

centésimo, -ma [sẽ'tezimu, -ma] *num* hundredth, **→ sexto**.

centígrado [sẽ'tʃigradu] *adj m* **→ grau**.

centímetro [sẽ'tʃimetru] *m* centimetre.

cento ['sẽtu] *m* hundred; **~ e vinte** a hundred and twenty; **por ~** percent.

centopeia [sẽto'peja] *f* centipede.

central [sẽ'traw] *(pl -ais* [-ajʃ]) *adj* central ♦ *f (de instituição, organização)* head office; *(de eletricidade, energia atômica)* power station; **~ elétrica** power station; **~ nuclear** nuclear power station; **~ telefônica** telephone exchange.

centrar [sẽ'tra(x)] *vt (atenção, esforço)* to focus; *(texto, página)* to centre.

centro ['sẽtru] *m* centre; **~ da cidade** city centre; **~ comercial** shopping centre *(Brit)*, shopping mall *(Am)*; **~ de saúde** health clinic.

centroavante [sẽtroa'vãntʃi] *m (Br: em futebol)* centre forward.

CEP *m (Br: abrev de Código de Endereçamento Postal)* postcode *(Brit)*, zip code *(Am)*.

céptico, -ca [sɛ(p)tiku, -ka] *adj (Port)* = cético.

cera ['sera] *f* wax; **~ depilatória** hair-removing OU depilatory wax.

cerâmica [se'ramika] *f (objeto)* piece of pottery; *(atividade)* ceramics *(sg)*.

ceramista [sera'miʃta] *mf* potter.

cerca ['sexka] *f* fence ♦ *adv*: **~ de** about; **há ~ de uma semana** nearly a week ago.

cercar [sex'ka(x)] *vt* to surround.

cereal [se'rjal] *(pl -ais* [-ajʃ]) *m* cereal.

cérebro ['sɛrebru] *m* brain.

cereja [se'reʒa] *f* cherry.

cerimónia [seri'mɔnja] *f (Port)* = **cerimônia**.

cerimônia [seri'monja] *f (Br) (religiosa)* ceremony; *(festa)* party; *(etiqueta)* formality.

cerrado, -da [se'xadu, -da] *adj (nevoeiro)* thick.

certeza [sex'teza] *f* certainty; **dar a ~** to confirm; **ter a ~ de que** to be sure (that); **você pode ter a ~ que vou** I'm definitely going; **com ~** *(sem dúvida)* of course; *(provavelmente)* probably; **com ~!** of course!; **de ~** definitely.

certidão [sexti'dãw] *(pl* **-ões** [-õjʃ]) *f* certificate.

certificado [sextʃifi'kadu] *m* certificate.

certificar-se [sextʃifi'kaxsi] *vp* to check; **~ de algo** to check sthg.

certo, -ta ['sextu, -ta] *adj (exacto)* right; *(infalível)* certain ♦ *adv* correctly; **certas pessoas** certain people; **a conta não bate ~** the bill isn't quite right; **dar ~** to work out; **o ~ é ele não vir** I'm sure he won't come; **ao ~** *(exactamente)* exactly; *(provàvelmente)* probably.

cerveja [sex'veʒa] *f* beer; **~ imperial** draught beer; **~ preta** stout.

cervejaria [sexveʒa'ria] *f* bar.

cervical [sexvi'kaw] *(pl* **-ais** [-ajʃ]) *adj* cervical.

cessar [se'sa(x)] *vi & vt* to cease.

cesta ['seʃta] *f* small basket.

cesto ['seʃtu] *m* basket; **~ de vime** wicker basket.

cético, -ca ['sɛtʃiku, -ka] *adj (Br)* sceptical ♦ *m, f (Br)* sceptic.

cetim [se'tʃi] *m* satin.

céu [sɛw] *m* sky; *(RELIG)* heaven; **a ~ aberto** *(fig: à vista de todos)* in broad daylight.

céu-da-boca ['sɛwda,boka] *m* roof of the mouth.

cevada [se'vada] *f* barley; *(bebida)* barley coffee.

chá ['ʃa] *m* tea; **~ dançante** tea dance; **~ com limão** tea with lemon; **~ de limão** lemon tea.

chacal [ʃa'kaw] *(pl* **-ais** [-ajʃ]) *m* jackal.

chacota [ʃa'kɔta] *f* mockery.

chafariz [ʃafa'riʃ] *(pl* **-zes** [-ziʃ]) *m* fountain.

chafurdar [ʃafux'da(x)] *vi* to wallow.

chaga ['ʃaga] *f* open wound, sore.

chalé [ʃa'lɛ] *m* chalet.

chaleira [ʃa'lejra] *f* kettle.

chama ['ʃama] *f* flame.

chamada [ʃa'mada] *f (de telefone)* call; *(de exame)* sitting; **fazer a ~** *(EDUC)* to call the register; **~ a cobrar** *(no destinatário)* reverse charge call *(Brit)*, collect call *(Am)*; **~ interurbana/local** long-distance/local call.

chamar [ʃa'ma(x)] *vt* to call ♦ *vi (telefone)* to ring.

❏ **chamar-se** *vp* to be called; **como é que você se chama?** what's your name?; **eu me chamo Carlos** my name is Carlos.

chaminé [ʃami'nɛ] *f* chimney; *(de lareira)* chimney-piece; *(de fábrica)* chimney stack.

champanhe [ʃãm'paɲi] *m* champagne.

champô [ʃãm'po] *(Port) m* = **xampu**.

chamuscar [ʃamuʃ'ka(x)] *vt* to singe.

chance [ʃãsi] *f* chance.

chantagear [ʃãnta'ʒja(x)] *vt* to blackmail.

chantagem [ʃãn'taʒẽ] *(pl* **-ns** [-ʃ]) *f* blackmail.

chantilly [ʃãntʃi'li] *m* whipped cream.

chão [ʃãw] *m (solo)* ground; *(pavimento)* floor; **cair no ~** to fall over.

chapa ['ʃapa] *f (Br: matrícula, placa)* numberplate *(Brit)*, license plate *(Am)*; *(Port: carroçaria)* bodywork.

chapéu [ʃa'pɛw] *m* hat; *(de sol, chuva)* umbrella; **ser de tirar o ~** to be superb.

chapéu-de-sol [ʃa,pɛwdʒi'sɔw] *(pl* **chapéus-de-sol** [ʃa,pɛwdʒis'sɔw]) *m* parasol.

charco ['ʃaxku] *m* puddle.

charcutaria [ʃaxkuta'ria] *f* ~ delicatessen.

charme ['ʃaxmi] *m* charm.

charneca [ʃax'neka] *f* moor.

charrete [ʃa'xetʃi] *f* chariot.

charter ['ʃarte(x)] *(pl* **-res** [-riʃ]) *m*: **(voo) ~** charter flight.

charuto [ʃa'rutu] *m* cigar.

chassis [ʃa'si] *m inv* chassis.

chatear [ʃa'tʃja(x)] *vt* to annoy.

chatice [ʃa'tʃisi] *f (fam: tédio)* drag.

chato, -ta ['ʃatu, -ta] *adj (fam: tedioso)*

boring; *(pé)* flat.

chauvinista [ʃoviˈniʃta] *m, f* chauvinist.

chave [ˈʃavi] *f* key.

chave-de-fendas [ˌʃavidʒiˈfẽndaʃ] *(pl* **chaves-de-fendas** [ˌʃavizdʒiˈfẽndaʃ]*) f* screwdriver.

chave-de-ignição [ˌʃavidʒigniˈsãw] *(pl* **chaves-de-ignição** [ˌʃavizdʒigniˈsãw]*) f* ignition key.

chave-inglesa [ˌʃavĩˈgleza] *(pl* **chaves-inglesas** [ˌʃavizĩˈglezaʃ]*) f* monkey wrench.

chaveiro [ʃaˈvejru] *m* keyring.

chávena [ˈʃavena] *f (Port)* cup.

check-in [tʃeˈkini] *(pl* **check-ins** [ʃeˈkineʃ]*) m* check-in; **fazer o ~** to check in.

check-up [tʃeˈkapi] *(pl* **check-ups** [tʃeˈkapiʃ]*) m* check-up.

chefe [ˈʃefi] *mf (de trabalhadores)* boss; *(de partido)* leader; *(de empresa)* head; *(de tribo, organização)* chief.

chefe-de-estação [ˌʃefidʒiestaˈsãw] *(pl* **chefes-de-estação** [ˌʃefizdʒiestaˈsãw]*) mf* stationmaster.

chegada [ʃeˈgada] *f* arrival; **"chegadas"** "arrivals"; **"~s domésticas"** "domestic arrivals"; **"~s internacionais"** "international arrivals".

chegado, -da [ʃeˈgadu, -da] *adj* close.

chegar [ʃeˈga(x)] *vi* to arrive; *(momento, altura, hora)* to come; *(ser suficiente)* to be enough; **~ bem** to arrive safely; **~ ao fim** to come to an end.

❑ **chegar-se** *vp (aproximar-se)* to come closer; *(afastar-se)* to move over; **~-se a** to come closer to.

cheia [ˈʃeja] *f* flood.

cheio, cheia [ˈʃeju, ˈʃeja] *adj* full; **~ de** full of; **estar ~** to have had enough.

cheirar [ʃejˈra(x)] *vt & vi* to smell; **~ bem/mal** to smell good/awful.

cheiro [ˈʃejru] *m* smell.

cheque [ˈʃeki] *m* cheque; *(em xadrez)* check; **~ em branco** blank cheque; **~ sem fundos** OU **sem provisão** uncovered cheque; **~ pré-datado** pre-dated cheque; **~ de viagem** traveller's cheque; **~ visado** authorized cheque.

cheque-mate [ˌʃekiˈmatʃi] *(pl* **cheque-mates** [ˌʃekiˈmatiʃ]*) m* checkmate.

cherne [ˈʃɛxni] *m* grouper.

chiar [ˈʃja(x)] *vi* to squeak; *(porco)* to squeal; *(pneu)* to screech.

chiclete [ʃiˈkletʃi] *m (Br)* chewing gum.

chicória [ʃiˈkɔrja] *f* chicory.

chicote [ʃiˈkɔtʃi] *m* whip.

chifre [ˈʃifri] *m* horn.

Chile [ˈʃili] *m*: **o ~** Chile.

chimarrão [ʃimaˈxãw] *m* unsweetened *maté tea.*

chimpanzé [ˌʃĩpãˈzɛ] *m* chimpanzee.

China [ˈʃina] *f*: **a ~** China.

chinelos [ʃiˈneluʃ] *mpl* flip-flops *(Brit)*, thongs *(Am)*; **~ (de quarto)** slippers.

chinês, -esa [ʃiˈneʃ, -ɛza] *(mpl* **-eses** [-eziʃ]*, fpl* **-s** [-ʃ]*) adj & m, f* Chinese ♦ *m (língua)* Chinese; **isso para mim é ~** it's all double-Dutch to me!

chinó [ʃiˈnɔ] *m* toupee.

chique [ˈʃiki] *adj* chic.

chispe [ˈʃiʃpi] *m* pig's trotter.

chita [ˈʃita] *f* cotton print.

chiu [ˈʃiu] *interj* shush!

chocalhar [ʃokaˈʎa(x)] *vt (líquido)* to shake ♦ *vi (tilintar)* to jingle.

chocalho [ʃoˈkaʎu] *m* bell.

chocante [ʃoˈkãntʃi] *adj* shocking.

chocar [ʃoˈka(x)] *vi (veículos)* to crash; *(galinha)* to brood; ♦ *vt (indignar)* to shock; *(ovos)* to hatch; **~ com** *(pessoa)* to bump into; *(veículo)* to crash into.

chocho, -cha [ˈʃoʃu, -ʃa] *adj (noz)* empty; *(festa)* dull.

chocolate [ʃokoˈlatʃi] *m* chocolate; *(bebida)* chocolate drink; **~ amargo** OU **negro** plain chocolate; **~ branco** white chocolate; **~ de leite** milk chocolate; **~ em pó** cocoa.

chofer [ʃoˈfɛ(x)] *(pl* **-res** [-riʃ]*) m* driver.

chope [ˈʃopi] *m (Br)* draught beer.

choque [ˈʃɔki] *m (colisão)* crash; *(comoção)* shock.

choramingar [ʃoramĩˈga(x)] *vi* to snivel.

chorão, -rona [ʃoˈrãw, -ˈrona] *(mpl* **-ões** [-õjʃ]*, fpl* **-s** [-ʃ]*) adj* tearful ♦ *m (árvore)* weeping willow; *(brinquedo)* baby doll that cries.

chorar [ʃoˈra(x)] *vi & vt (verter lágrimas)* to cry; **~ de rir** to cry with laughter.

chorinho [ʃoˈriɲu] *m (Br: MÚS)* type of melancholy Brazilian music.

choro [ˈʃoru] *m* crying.

chorões → chorão.

choupo [ˈʃopu] *m* poplar.

chouriço [ʃoˈrisu] *m (no Brasil)* black pudding; *(em Portugal)* spiced, smoked pork sausage.

chover [ʃoˈve(x)] *v impess* to rain; ~ a cântaros to pour with rain.

chuchu [ʃuˈʃu] *m* chayote; **pra** ~ *(Br: fam: muito)* loads.

chulé [ʃuˈlɛ] *m (fam)* foot odour.

chulo, -la [ˈʃulu, -la] *adj (Br)* vulgar ♦ *m (Port: fam)* pimp.

chumaço [ʃuˈmasu] *m* shoulder pad.

chumbar [ʃũˈba(x)] *vt (soldar)* to solder; *(atirar em)* to fire at ♦ *vi (Port: fam: reprovar)* to flunk.

chumbo [ˈʃũbu] *m* lead; *(tiro)* gunshot; **a caixa está um ~** the box weighs a ton.

chupa-chupa [ʃupaˈʃupa] *(pl* **chupa-chupas** [ʃupaˈʃupaʃ]) *m (Port)* lollipop.

chupar [ʃuˈpa(x)] *vt* to suck.

chupeta [ʃuˈpeta] *f* dummy *(Brit)*, pacifier *(Am)*.

churrascaria [ʃuxaʃkaˈria] *f* restaurant serving barbecued meat and poultry.

churrasco [ʃuˈxaʃku] *m* barbecue.

churrasquinho [ʃuxaʃˈkiɲu] *m (Br)* kebab.

churro [ˈʃuxu] *m* fried twist of batter covered in sugar.

chutar [ʃuˈta(x)] *vt & vi* to kick.

chuteira [ʃuˈtejra] *f* football boot.

chuva [ˈʃuva] *f* rain.

chuveiro [ʃuˈvejru] *m* shower.

chuviscar [ʃuviʃˈka(x)] *vi* to drizzle.

chuvoso, -osa [ʃuˈvozu, -ɔza] *adj* rainy.

C.ia *(abrev de Companhia)* Co.

ciberespaço [sibereʃˈpasu] *m* cyberspace.

cibernética [sibexˈnetʃika] *f* cybernetics *(sg)*.

cibernético [sibexˈnetʃiku] *adj* m → espaço.

cicatriz [sikaˈtriʃ] *(pl* **-zes** [-ziʃ]) *f* scar.

cicatrizar [sikatriˈza(x)] *vi (ferida)* to heal (up).

cicatrizes → cicatriz.

cicerone [siseˈrɔni] *m* guide.

ciclismo [siˈkliʒmu] *m* cycling; **fazer** ~ to go cycling.

ciclista [siˈkliʃta] *mf* cyclist.

ciclo [ˈsiklu] *m* cycle; *(de conferências)* series.

ciclomotor [siklomoˈto(x)] *(pl* **-es**

[-iʃ]) *m* moped.

ciclone [siˈklɔni] *m* cyclone; *(região de baixas pressões)* depression.

cidadã → cidadão.

cidadania [sidadaˈnia] *f* citizenship.

cidadão, -dã [sidaˈdãw, -dã] *(mpl* **-ãos** [-ãwʃ], *fpl* **-s** [-ʃ]) *m, f* citizen.

cidade [siˈdadʒi] *f* city; ~ **universitária** campus.

cieiro [ˈsjejru] *m (Port) chapping caused by cold, windy weather.*

ciência [ˈsjẽsja] *f* science; ~s **físico-químicas** physical sciences; ~s **naturais** natural sciences.

ciente [ˈsjẽtʃi] *adj* aware; **estar ~ de** to be aware of.

científico, -ca [sjẽˈtʃifiku, -ka] *adj* scientific.

cientista [sjẽˈtʃiʃta] *mf* scientist.

cifra [ˈsifra] *f* sum; *(número)* figure.

cigano, -na [siˈganu, -na] *m, f* gypsy.

cigarra [siˈgaxa] *f* cicada.

cigarreira [sigaˈxejra] *f* cigarette case.

cigarrilha [sigaˈxiʎa] *f* cigarillo.

cigarro [siˈgaxu] *m* cigarette; ~s **com filtro** filter-tipped cigarettes; ~s **sem filtro** untipped cigarettes; ~s **mentolados** menthol cigarettes.

cilada [siˈlada] *f* trap; **caiu na ~** he fell for it.

cilindro [siˈlĩdru] *m* cylinder; *(rolo)* roller; *(de aquecimento de água)* boiler.

cílio [ˈsilju] *m* eyelash.

cima [ˈsima] *f*: **de ~** from above; **de ~ abaixo** from top to bottom; **de ~ de** off; **em ~** above; **em ~ de** on top of; **para ~** up; **para ~ de** over; **por ~ de** over.

cimeira [siˈmejra] *f* summit.

cimentar [simẽˈta(x)] *vt* to cement.

cimento [siˈmẽtu] *m* cement.

cimo [ˈsimu] *m* top.

cinco [ˈsĩku] *num* five, → seis.

cineasta [siˈnjaʃta] *mf* film director.

cinema [siˈnema] *m (local)* cinema *(Brit)*, movie theater *(Am)*; *(arte)* cinema.

cinemateca [sinemaˈtɛka] *f (local)* filmhouse; *(coleção de filmes)* film library.

cinematográfico, -ca [sinematoˈgrafiku, -ka] *adj* film *(antes de s)*.

cine-teatro [sineˈteatru] *m* filmhouse.

cínico, -ca ['siniku, -ka] *adj (hipócrita)* hypocritical.

cinismo [si'niʒmu] *m (hipocrisia)* hypocrisy.

cinquenta [sĩŋ'kwẽnta] *num* fifty, → seis.

cinta ['sĩnta] *f (cintura)* waist; *(faixa de pano)* sash; *(roupa interior)* girdle.

cintilar [sĩntʃi'la(x)] *vi* to twinkle.

cinto ['sĩntu] *m* belt; ~ **de segurança** seatbelt.

cintura [sĩn'tura] *f* waist.

cinturão [sĩntu'rãw] *(mpl* -ões [-õjʃ]) *m (Br)* belt; ~ **industrial** industrial belt; ~ **verde** green belt.

cinza ['sĩza] *f* ash ◆ *adj & m (Br)* grey. ⅃ **cinzas** *fpl (restos mortais)* ashes.

cinzeiro [sĩ'zejru] *m* ashtray.

cinzel [sĩ'zɛw] *(pl* -éis [-ɛjʃ]) *m* chisel.

cinzento, -ta [sĩ'zẽntu, -ta] *adj & m* grey.

cio ['siu] *m*: **estar no ~** *(fêmeas)* to be on heat; *(machos)* to be in rut.

cipreste [si'prɛʃtʃi] *m* cypress.

circo ['sixku] *m* circus.

circuito [six'kwitu] *m* circuit; ~ **elétrico** electric circuit; ~ **turístico** tourist trail.

circulação [sixkula'sãw] *f* circulation; *(de veículos)* traffic.

circular [sixku'la(x)] *(pl* -res [-riʃ]) *vi* to circulate; *(pedestre)* to walk about; *(carro)* to drive ◆ *adj & f* circular.

círculo ['sixkulu] *m* circle; ~ **polar** polar circle.

circunferência [sixkũfe'rẽsja] *f* circumference.

circunflexo [sixkũ'flɛksu] *adj m* → **acento**.

circunstância [sixkũʃ'tãsja] *f* circumstance; **nas ~s** under the circumstances.

círio ['sirju] *m* large candle.

cirurgia [sirux'ʒia] *f* surgery; ~ **plástica** plastic surgery.

cirurgião, -giã [sirux'ʒjãw, -ʒjã] *(mpl* -ões [-õjʃ], *fpl* -s [-ʃ]) *m*, *f* surgeon.

cirúrgico, -ca [si'ruxʒiku, -ka] *adj* surgical.

cirurgiões → **cirurgião**.

cisco ['siʃku] *m* speck.

cisma ['siʒma] *f* fixation.

cisne ['siʒni] *m* swan.

cisterna [siʃ'tɛxna] *f* tank.

cistite [siʃ'tʃitʃi] *f* cystitis.

citação [sita'sãw] *(pl* -ões [-õjʃ]) *f* quotation.

citar [si'ta(x)] *vt* to quote.

cítrico ['sitriku] *adj m* → **ácido**.

citrinos [si'trinuʃ] *mpl* citrus fruit *(sg)*.

ciúme ['sjumi] *m* jealousy; **ter ~s de alguém** to be jealous of sb.

ciumento, -ta [sju'mẽntu, -ta] *adj* jealous.

cívico, -ca ['siviku, -ka] *adj* civic.

civil [si'viw] *(pl* -is [-iʃ]) *adj* civil.

civilização [siviliza'sãw] *(pl* -ões [-õjʃ]) *f* civilization.

civilizar [sivili'za(x)] *vt* to civilize.

civis → **civil**.

cl. *(abrev de centilitro)* cl.

clamar [kla'ma(x)] *vi* to cry out.

clamor [kla'mo(x)] *(pl* -res [-riʃ]) *m* outcry.

clandestino, -na [klãndeʃ'tʃinu, -na] *adj* clandestine ◆ *m*, *f* stowaway.

clara ['klara] *f* white.

clarabóia [klara'bɔja] *f* skylight.

clarão [kla'rãw] *(pl* -ões [-õjʃ]) *m* flash.

clarear [kla'rja(x)] *vi* to brighten up.

clarete [kla'retʃi] *m* rosé.

clareza [kla'reza] *f*: **falar com ~** to speak clearly.

claridade [klari'dadʒi] *f* brightness.

clarinete [klari'netʃi] *m* clarinet.

claro, -ra ['klaru, -ra] *adj (com luz)* bright; *(cor)* light; *(preciso, sincero)* clear ◆ *adv* clearly; ~ **que sim!** of course!; **é ~!** of course!; **passar a noite em ~** to have a sleepless night.

clarões → **clarão**.

classe ['klasi] *f* class; **ter ~** to have class; **de primeira/segunda ~** first/second class; ~ **social** social class; ~ **turística** tourist class.

clássico, -ca ['klasiku, -ka] *adj* classic; *(música)* classical.

classificação [klasifika'sãw] *(pl* -ões [-õjʃ]) *f* results *(pl).*

classificados [klasefi'kaduʃ] *mpl* classified ads.

classificar [klasifi'ka(x)] *vt (EDUC: aluno)* to appraise; *(ordenar)* to classify. ⅃ **classificar-se** *vp (em competição)* to qualify.

claustro ['klawʃtru] *m* cloister.

cláusula ['klawzula] *f* clause.

clave ['klavi] *f* clef; ~ **de sol** treble clef.

clavícula [klaˈvikula] *f* collarbone.

clemência [kleˈmẽsja] *f* clemency.

clero [ˈklɛru] *m* clergy.

cliché [kliˈʃe] *m* (*Port*) = **clichê**.

clichê [kliˈʃe] *m* (*Br*) cliché.

cliente [kliˈẽtʃi] *mf* client.

clientela [kliẽˈtɛla] *f* customers (*pl*).

clima [ˈklima] *m* climate; (*fig: ambiente*) atmosphere.

clímax [ˈklimaks] *m inv* climax; **atingir o ~** to reach a climax.

clínica [ˈklinika] *f* clinic; **~ dentária** dental practice; **~ geral** general practice.

clínico [ˈkliniku] *m* clinician; **~ geral** GP.

clipe [ˈklipi] *m* paper clip.

cloro [ˈklɔru] *m* chlorine.

clube [ˈklubi] *m* club; **~ de futebol/vídeo** football/video club.

cm. (*abrev de centímetro*) cm.

coador [kwaˈdo(x)] (*pl* -**res** [-riʃ]) *m* strainer.

coagir [kwaˈʒi(x)] *vt* to coerce.

coagular [kwaguˈla(x)] *vt & vi* to clot.

coágulo [ˈkwagulu] *m* clot.

coalhar [kwaˈʎa(x)] *vt & vi* to curdle.

coar [ˈkwa(x)] *vt* to strain.

cobaia [koˈbaja] *f* guinea pig.

cobarde [koˈbaxdʒi] *adj & mf* = **covarde**.

coberta [koˈbɛxta] *f* (*de cama*) bedspread; (*de navio*) deck.

coberto, -ta [koˈbɛxtu, -ta] *adj* covered ♦ *m* shelter.

cobertor [kobexˈto(x)] (*pl* -**res** [-riʃ]) *m* blanket.

cobertura [kobexˈtura] *f* (*tecto*) roof; (*Br: apartamento*) penthouse; (*de acontecimento, situação*) coverage; **o cheque foi recusado por falta de ~** the cheque bounced due to lack of funds.

cobiça [koˈbisa] *f* (*avidez*) greed; (*inveja*) envy.

cobiçar [kobiˈsa(x)] *vt* (*ambicionar*) to covet; (*invejar*) to envy.

cobra [ˈkɔbra] *f* snake.

cobrador, -ra [kobraˈdo(x), -ra] (*mpl* -**res** [-riʃ], *fpl* -**s** [-ʃ]) *m*, *f* (*em trem, ônibus*) conductor (*f* conductress); (*de água, luz*) meter reader.

cobrança [koˈbrãsa] *f* (*ação de cobrar*) charging.

cobrar [koˈbra(x)] *vt* to charge; (*imposto, dívida*) to collect.

cobre [ˈkɔbri] *m* copper.

cobrir [koˈbri(x)] *vt* to cover.

cocada [koˈkada] *f* dessert made with dessicated coconut and milk.

coçado, -da [koˈsadu, -da] *adj* worn.

cocaína [kokaˈina] *f* cocaine.

coçar [koˈsa(x)] *vt* to scratch.

❏ **coçar-se** *vp* to scratch o.s.

cóccix [ˈkɔksis] *m* coccyx.

cócegas [ˈkɔsigaʃ] *fpl*: **fazer ~** to tickle; **ter ~** to be ticklish.

coceira [koˈsejra] *f* itch.

cochichar [koʃiˈʃa(x)] *vt & vi* to whisper.

cochilo [koˈʃilu] *m* (*Br*) nap; **tirar um ~** (*Br*) to take a nap.

coco [ˈkoku] *m* coconut.

cócoras [ˈkɔkoraʃ] *fpl*: **pôr-se de ~** to squat.

côdea [ˈkodʒja] *f* crust.

código [ˈkɔdʒigu] *m* code; **~ de barras** bar code; **~ civil** civil law; **~ de trânsito** highway code; **~ postal** postcode.

codorniz [kodoxˈniʃ] (*pl* -**zes** [-ziʃ]) *f* quail.

coelho [ˈkweʎu] *m* rabbit; **~ à caçadora** *rabbit cooked slowly in a white wine, onion and herb sauce which is then thickened with the rabbit's blood.*

coentro [ˈkwẽtru] *m* coriander.

coerência [koeˈrẽsja] *f* coherence.

coerente [koeˈrẽtʃi] *adj* coherent.

cofre [ˈkɔfri] *m* safe.

cofre-forte [ˌkɔfriˈfɔxtʃi] (*pl* **cofres-fortes** [ˌkɔfriʃˈfɔxtʃiʃ]) *m* safe.

cofre-noturno [ˌkɔfrinoˈtuxnu] (*pl* **cofres-noturnos** [ˌkɔfriʒnoˈtuxnuʃ]) *m* night safe.

cogitar [koʒiˈta(x)] *vt* to think (up) ♦ *vi* (*pensar*) to think.

cogumelo [koguˈmɛlu] *m* mushroom.

coice [ˈkojsi] *m* kick; (*de arma*) recoil.

coincidência [koĩsiˈdẽsja] *f* coincidence; **por ~** as it happens.

coincidir [kwĩsiˈdi(x)] *vi* to coincide.

❏ **coincidir com** *v* + *prep* to coincide with; (*opinião*) to agree with.

coisa [ˈkojza] *f* thing; (**deseja**) **mais alguma ~?** would you like anything else?; **não comprei ~ nenhuma** I didn't buy anything, I bought nothing; **alguma ~** something; **~ de** roughly; **a ~ está preta!** things are bleak!; **não ser grande ~** to be nothing special.

coitado, -da [koj'tadu. -da] *adj* poor, unfortunate ♦ *interj* poor thing!

cola ['kɔla] *f* glue.

colaborar [kolabu'ra(x)] *vi* to collaborate.

colapso [ko'lapsu] *m* collapse.

colar [ko'la(x)] *(pl -res* [-riʃ]) *vt* to glue, to stick ♦ *vi* to stick ♦ *m* necklace.

⌐ **colar de** *v* + *prep (Br: fam)* to crib from.

colarinho [kola'riɲu] *m* collar.

colcha ['kowʃa] *f* bedspread.

colchão [kow'ʃãw] *(pl -ões* [-õjʃ]) *m* mattress; **~ de molas/palha** spring/ straw mattress.

colcheia [kow'ʃeja] *f* crotchet *(Brit)*, quarter note *(Am)*.

colchete [kow'ʃetʃi] *m (de vestuário)* hook; *(sinal de pontuação)* square bracket.

colchões → colchão.

coleção [kole'sãw] *(pl -ões* [-õjʃ]) *f (Br)* collection; **fazer ~ de algo** to collect sthg; **~ de selos** stamp collection.

colecção [kule'sãw] *(pl -ões* [-õjʃ]) *f (Port)* = **coleção.**

colecionador, -ra [kolesjona'do(x). -ra] *(mpl -res* [-riʃ]. *fpl -s* [-ʃ]) *m, f* collector.

coleccionar [kulesju'nar] *vt (Port)* = **colecionar.**

colecções → colecção.

colecionar [kolesjo'na(x)] *vt (Br)* to collect.

coleções → coleção.

colectivo, -va [kule'tivu. -va] *adj (Port)* = **coletivo.**

colega [ko'lega] *mf* colleague; **~ de carteira** *person you sit next to at school*; **~ de trabalho** (work) colleague; **~ de turma** classmate.

colégio [ko'lɛʒju] *m* school; **~ interno** boarding school.

coleira [ko'lejra] *f* collar.

cólera ['kɔlera] *f* fury; *(MED)* cholera.

colérico, -ca [ko'lɛriku. -ka] *adj* furious.

colesterol [koleʃte'rɔw] *m* cholesterol.

colete [ko'letʃi] *m* waistcoat; **~ salva- vidas** life jacket.

coletivo, -va [kole'tʃivu. -va] *adj (Br)* *(decisão)* collective; *(reunião)* general; *(transporte)* public.

colheita [ko'ʎejta] *f* harvest.

colher[1] [ko'ʎe(x)] *vt (fruto, vegetal, flo-*

res) to pick; *(cereais)* to harvest.

colher[2] [ko'ʎɛ(x)] *(pl -res* [-riʃ]) *f (uten- sílio)* spoon; *(quantidade)* spoonful; **~ de café** *(utensílio)* coffee spoon; *(quan- tidade)* = half teaspoon; **~ de chá** tea- spoon; **~ de pau** wooden spoon; **~ de sopa** *(utensílio)* soup spoon; *(quanti- dade)* = tablespoon.

colibri [koli'bri] *m* hummingbird.

cólica ['kɔlika] *f* colic.

colidir [koli'dʒi(x)] *vi* to collide; **~ com** to collide with.

coligação [koliga'sãw] *(pl -ões* [-õjʃ]) *f* coalition.

colina [ko'lina] *f* hill.

colisão [koli'zãw] *(pl -ões* [-õjʃ]) *f* col- lision.

collants [ko'lãʃ] *mpl* tights *(Brit)*, panty hose *(sg) (Am)*.

colmeia [kow'meja] *f* beehive.

colo ['kɔlu] *m* lap; **levar uma criança no ~** to carry a child.

colocação [koloka'sãw] *(pl -ões* [-õjʃ]) *f* placing; *(de roda, vidro)* fitting; *(emprego)* post, job.

colocar [kolo'ka(x)] *vt* to place; *(roda, vidro)* to fit; *(cortina)* to put up; *(empre- gar)* to employ; *(problema)* to pose.

Colômbia [ko'lõmbja] *f*: **a ~** Co- lombia.

cólon ['kɔlõ] *m* colon.

colónia [ku'lɔnja] *f (Port)* = **colônia.**

colônia [ko'lonja] *f (Br)* colony; *(per- fume)* cologne; **~ de férias** summer camp.

coloquial [kolo'kjaw] *(pl -ais* [-ajʃ]) *adj* colloquial.

colóquio [ko'lɔkju] *m* conference.

colorante [kolo'rãntʃi] *m* colouring.

colorau [kolo'raw] *m* paprika.

colorido, -da [kolo'ridu. -da] *adj* coloured; *(com muitas cores)* colour- ful.

colorir [kolo'ri(x)] *vt* to colour in.

coluna [ko'luna] *f* column; *(de rádio, hi-fi)* speaker; **~ vertebral** spinal col- umn.

com [kõ] *prep* with; *(indica causa)* because of; **só ~ muito esforço é que ele conseguiu** he only managed it through a lot of hard work; **estar ~ dor de cabeça** to have a headache; **estar ~ fome** to be hungry; **estar ~ pressa** to be in a hurry.

coma ['koma] *m ou f (MED)* coma.

comandante [komãn'dãntʃi] *m (de*

navio, polícia) commander; *(de exército)* major.

comandar [komãn'da(x)] *vt* to command, to be in charge of.

comando [ko'mãndu] *m* command; *(de máquina, sistema)* control; **estar no ~ de algo** to be in charge of sthg.

combate [kõm'batʃi] *m (luta)* fight; *(batalha)* fighting.

combater [kõmba'te(x)] *vi* to fight.

combinação [kõmbina'sãw] *(pl* **-ões** [-õjʃ]*)* f combination; *(acordo)* agreement; *(plano)* arrangement; *(peça de vestuário)* slip.

combinar [kõmbi'na(x)] *vt* to combine; *(planejar)* to plan ◆ *vi (cores, roupas)* to go together; **está combinado!** it's a deal!; **~ com** to go with; **~ algo com alguém** to arrange sthg with sb.

comboio [kõm'boju] *m (Port)* train; **apanhar/perder o ~** to catch/miss the train.

combustível [kõmbuʃ'tʃivew] *(pl* **-eis** [-ejʃ]*)* m fuel.

começar [kome'sa(x)] *vt & vi* to start, to begin; **~ a fazer algo** to start OU begin to do sthg; **~ de/por** to start from/with; **~ por fazer algo** to start by doing sthg; **para ~** to start (with).

começo [ko'mesu] *m* start, beginning.

comédia [ko'mɛdʒja] *f* comedy.

comediante [kome'dʒjãntʃi] *mf* comic actor *(f* actress).

comemorar [komemo'ra(x)] *vt* to commemorate.

comentar [komẽn'ta(x)] *vt (mencionar)* to mention; *(analisar)* to comment on; *(criticar maliciosamente)* to make comments about.

comentário [komẽn'tarju] *m* comment; *(de evento esportivo)* commentary.

comer [ko'me(x)] *(pl* **-res** [-riʃ]*)* vt to eat; *(em xadrez, damas)* to take ◆ *vi (alimentar-se)* to eat ◆ *m (alimento)* food; *(refeição)* meal.

comercial [komex'sjaw] *(pl* **-ais** [-ajʃ]*)* adj commercial.

comercialização [komexsjaliza'sãw] *f* sale.

comercializar [komexsjali'za(x)] *vt* to sell.

comerciante [komex'sjãntʃi] *mf* shopkeeper.

comércio [ko'mɛxsju] *m* commerce; *(lojas)* shops *(pl).*

comeres → comer.

comestível [komeʃ'tʃivew] *(pl* **-eis** [-ejʃ]*)* adj edible.

cometer [kome'te(x)] *vt (delito)* to commit; *(erro)* to make.

comichão [komi'ʃãw] *(pl* **-ões** [-õjʃ]*)* f itch; **fazer ~** to itch.

comício [ko'misju] *m* rally.

cómico, -ca ['kɔmiku. -ka] *adj (Port)* = **cômico.**

cômico, -ca ['komiku. -ka] *adj (Br) (actor)* comic; *(engraçado)* funny, comical.

comida [ko'mida] *f* food; *(refeição)* meal; **~ para bebê** baby food; **~ congelada** frozen food.

comigo [ko'migu] *pron* with me; **estava falando ~ mesmo** I was talking to myself.

comilão, -lona [komi'lãw, -lona] *(mpl* **-ões** [-õjʃ]. *fpl* **-s** [-ʃ]*)* m, f *(fam)* glutton.

cominho [ko'miɲu] *m* cumin.

comissão [komi'sãw] *(pl* **-ões** [-õjʃ]*)* f commission.

comissário [komi'sarju] *m (de polícia)* superintendent; *(de navio)* purser; **~ de bordo** air steward.

comissões → comissão.

comité [komi'te] *m (Port)* = **comitê.**

comitê [komi'te] *m (Br)* committee.

como ['komu] *adv* 1. *(comparativo)* like; **não é ~ o outro** it's not like the other one; **~ quem não quer nada** casually; **~ se nada estivesse acontecendo** as if nothing was going on. 2. *(de que maneira)* how; **~?** *(o que disse)* I'm sorry?, pardon? 3. *(marca intensidade)*: **~ ele é inteligente!** he's so clever!, how clever he is!; **~ é difícil arranjar lugar para estacionar!** it's so difficult to find a parking space!; **~ você se engana!** how wrong you are! ◆ *conj* 1. *(introduz comparação)* like; **é bonita, ~ a mãe** she's pretty, (just) like her mother. 2. *(da forma que)* as; **~ queira!** as you wish!; **seja ~ for** in any case. 3. *(por exemplo)* like, such as; **as cidades grandes ~ São Paulo** big cities like São Paulo 4. *(na qualidade de)* as; **~ mãe fiquei muito preocupada** as a mother I felt very concerned; **~ prêmio ela ganhou um carro** she won a car for a prize. 5. *(visto que)* as, since; **~ estávamos**

atrasados fomos de táxi we took a taxi as we were running late; **~ não atenderam pensamos que não estavam** we thought you weren't in as there was no answer.
6. *(em locuções):* **~ deve ser** *adv (corretamente)* properly.
♦ *adj (próprio)* suitable.

comoção [komoˈsãw] *(pl -ões* [-ˈõjʃ]) *f (emoção)* emotion; *(agitação)* commotion.

cómoda [ˈkɔmuda] *f (Port)* = cômoda.

cômoda [ˈkomoda] *f (Br)* chest of drawers.

comodidade [komodʒiˈdadʒi] *f* comfort.

comodismo [komoˈdʒiʒmu] *m* complacency.

comodista [komoˈdʒiʃta] *mf* complacent person.

cómodo, -da [ˈkɔmudu. -da] *adj (Port)* = cômodo.

cômodo, -da [ˈkomodu. -da] *adj (Br)* comfortable.

comovedor, -ra [komoveˈdo(x). -ra] *(mpl* **-res** [-riʃ]. *fpl* **-s** [-ʃ]) *adj* moving.

comovente [komoˈvẽtʃi] *adj* touching.

comover [komoˈve(x)] *vt* to move.
❏ **comover-se** *vp* to be moved.

comovido, -da [komoˈvidu. -da] *adj* moved.

compacto, -ta [kõˈpaktu. -ta] *adj* compact; *(denso)* thick; *(sólido)* hard ♦ *m (CD)* compact disc, CD; *(Br: disco de vinil)* record.

compaixão [kõpajˈʃãw] *f* compassion.

companheiro, -ra [kõpaˈɲejru. -ra] *m, f (acompanhante)* companion; *(de turma)* classmate; *(em casal)* partner.

companhia [kõpaˈɲia] *f* company; **fazer ~ a alguém** to keep sb company; **~ de aviação** airline; **~ de navegação** shipping line; **~ de seguros** insurance company; **em ~ de alguém** with sb.

comparação [kõparaˈsãw] *(pl -ões* [-ˈõjʃ]) *f* comparison; **não ter ~ com** to bear no comparison with; **em ~ com** in comparison with.

comparar [kõpaˈra(x)] *vt* to compare; **~ algo a** OU **com algo** to compare sthg to OU with sthg.

comparecer [kõpareˈse(x)] *vi* to ap-

pear, to attend; **~ a algo** to attend sthg.

compartilhar [kõpaxtʃiˈʎa(x)] *vt* to share; **~ algo com alguém** to share sthg with sb.

compartimento [kõpaxtʃiˈmẽtu] *m* compartment; *(de casa)* room.

compartir [kõpaxˈtʃi(x)] *vt* to share.

compasso [kõˈpasu] *m* compasses *(pl); (Mús)* time.

compatível [kõpaˈtʃivew] *(pl -eis* [-ejʃ]) *adj* compatible; **~ com** compatible with.

compatriota [kõpatrjˈɔta] *mf* compatriot.

compensação [kõpẽsaˈsãw] *(pl -ões* [-ˈõjʃ]) *f* compensation; *(vantagem)* advantage.

compensar [kõpẽˈsa(x)] *vt* to compensate; *(recompensar)* to make up for; **não compensa o esforço** it isn't worth the effort.

competência [kõpeˈtẽsja] *f* competence; *(responsabilidade)* responsibility.

competente [kõpeˈtẽtʃi] *adj* competent.

competição [kõpetʃiˈsãw] *(pl -ões* [-ˈõjʃ]) *f* competition.

competir [kõpeˈtʃi(x)] *vi* to compete; **~ com** *(rivalizar com)* to compete with.

competitivo, -va [kõpetʃiˈtʃivu. -va] *adj* competitive.

compilar [kõpiˈla(x)] *vt* to compile.

complacente [kõplaˈsẽtʃi] *adj* indulgent.

complementar [kõplemẽˈta(x)] *(pl -res* [-riʃ]) *adj* complementary.

complemento [kõpleˈmẽtu] *m* complement; *(em trem)* supplement.

completamente [kõmpletaˈmẽtʃi] *adv* completely.

completar [kõpleˈta(x)] *vt (preencher)* to fill in; *(terminar)* to complete.

completo, -ta [kõˈpletu. -ta] *adj* completed; *(cheio)* full; *(inteiro)* complete.

complexo, -xa [kõˈpleksu. -ksa] *adj & m* complex.

complicação [kõplikaˈsãw] *(pl -ões* [-ˈõjʃ]) *f* complication.

complicado, -da [kõpliˈkadu. -da] *adj* complicated.

complicar [kõpliˈka(x)] *vt* to complicate.

⊔ complicar-se *vp* to become OU get complicated.

componente [kõmpo'nẽntʃi] *mf* component.

compor [kõm'po(x)] *vt (música, poema)* to compose; *(consertar)* to repair; *(arrumar)* to tidy; *(fazer parte de)* to make up.

⊐ compor-se *vp (arranjar-se)* to tidy o.s. up.

⊐ compor-se de *vp + prep (ser formado por)* to be made up of.

comporta [kõm'pɔxta] *f* sluice gate.

comportamento [kõmpoxta'mẽntu] *m* behaviour.

comportar [kõmpox'ta(x)] *vt (conter em si)* to hold; *(admitir)* to permit.

⊐ comportar-se *vp* to behave.

composição [kõmpozi'sãw] *(pl -ões* [-õjʃ]) *f* composition; *(EDUC)* essay.

compositor, -ra [kõmpozi'to(x), -ra] *(mpl -res* [-riʃ], *fpl -s* [-ʃ]) *m, f (MÚS)* composer.

composto, -osta [kõm'poʃtu, -ɔʃta] *m (GRAM)* compound ◆ *adj:* **ser ~ por** to be composed of.

compostura [kõmpoʃ'tura] *f* composure; *(boa educação)* manners *(pl).*

compota [kõm'pɔta] *f* preserve.

compra ['kõmpra] *f* purchase; **ir às** OU **fazer ~s** to go shopping.

comprar [kõm'pra(x)] *vt* to buy.

compreender [kõmprjẽn'de(x)] *vt* to understand; *(incluir)* to comprise.

compreensão [kõmprjẽ'sãw] *f* understanding.

compreensivo, -va [kõmprjẽ'sivu, -va] *adj* understanding.

compressa [kõm'prɛsa] *f* compress; **~ esterilizada** sterile dressing.

comprido, -da [kõm'pridu, -da] *adj* long; **deitar-se ao ~** to lie down flat.

comprimento [kõmpri'mẽntu] *m* length; **tem 5 metros de ~** it's 5 metres long.

comprimido, -da [kõmpri'midu, -da] *adj* compressed ◆ *m* pill; **~ para dormir** sleeping pill; **~ para a dor** painkiller; **~ para o enjôo** travel sickness pill.

comprimir [kõmpri'mi(x)] *vt (apertar)* to squeeze; *(reduzir de volume)* to compress.

comprometer [kõmprome'te(x)] *vt* to compromise.

⊐ comprometer-se *vp* to compro-

mise o.s.; **~-se a fazer algo** to commit o.s. to doing sthg.

compromisso [kõmpru'misu] *m (obrigação)* commitment; *(acordo)* agreement; **tenho um ~** I've got a prior engagement.

comprovação [kõmprova'sãw] *(pl -ões* [-õjʃ]) *f* proof.

comprovar [kõmpro'va(x)] *vt* to prove.

computador [kõmputa'do(x)] *(pl -res* [-riʃ]) *m* computer; **~ pessoal** personal computer.

comum [ko'mũ] *(pl -ns* [-ʃ]) *adj (frequente)* common; *(vulgar)* ordinary; *(partilhado)* shared.

comunhão [komu'ɲãw] *(pl -ões* [-õjʃ]) *f (RELIG)* Communion; **~ de bens** joint ownership *(in marriage).*

comunicação [komunika'sãw] *(pl -ões* [-õjʃ]) *f* communication; *(comunicado)* announcement.

comunicado [komuni'kadu] *m* communiqué.

comunicar [komuni'ka(x)] *vt* to communicate; *(mensagem)* to pass on ◆ *vi* to communicate; **~ algo a alguém** to inform sb of sthg; **~ com** to communicate with.

comunidade [komuni'dadʒi] *f* community; **a Comunidade Européia** the European Community.

comunismo [komu'niʒmu] *m* communism.

comunista [komu'niʃta] *adj & mf* communist.

comuns → comum.

comutar [komu'ta(x)] *vt (pena)* to commute.

conceber [kõse'be(x)] *vt (filho)* to conceive; *(plano, sistema)* to think up.

conceder [kõse'de(x)] *vt (dar)* to give; *(prêmio, bolsa)* to award.

conceito [kõ'sejtu] *m* concept.

conceituado, -da [kõsej'twadu, -da] *adj* respected.

concelho [kõ'seʎu] *m* = municipality.

concentração [kõsẽntra'sãw] *(pl -ões* [-õjʃ]) *f* concentration; *(de pessoas)* gathering.

concentrado, -da [kõsẽn'tradu, -da] *adj (atento)* intent; *(produto, suco)* concentrated ◆ *m:* **~ de tomate** tomato puree.

concentrar [kõsẽn'tra(x)] *vt (atenção, esforços)* to concentrate; *(reunir)* to bring together.

❏ **concentrar-se** *vp* to concentrate; **~-se em** *(estudo, trabalho)* to concentrate on; *(lugar)* to group together in.

concepção [kõsep'sãw] *(pl -ões* [-õjʃ]) *f* concept; *(de filho)* conception.

concerto [kõ'sextu] *m* concert.

concessão [kõse'sãw] *(pl -ões* [-õjʃ]) *f (de prêmio)* awarding; *(de bolsa)* granting; *(de desconto)* concession.

concessionária [kõsesjo'narja] *f (Br)* licensed dealer; **~ automóvel** car dealer.

concessionário [kõsesju'narju] *m (Port)* = concessionária.

concessões → concessão.

concha ['kõʃa] *f* shell; *(de sopa)* ladle.

conciliação [kõsilja'sãw] *(pl -ões* [-õjʃ]) *f* reconciliation.

conciliar [kõsi'lja(x)] *vt* to reconcile.

concluir [kõŋklu'i(x)] *vt* to conclude; *(acabar)* to finish.

conclusão [kõŋklu'zãw] *(pl -ões* [-õjʃ]) *f* conclusion; **em ~** in conclusion.

concordância [kõŋkox'dãsja] *f* agreement; **em ~ com** in accordance with.

concordar [kõŋkox'da(x)] *vi* to agree; **~ com** to agree with; **~ em fazer algo** to agree to do sthg.

concorrência [kõŋko'xẽsja] *f* competition.

concorrente [kõŋko'xẽtʃi] *adj (equipe)* opposing; *(produto, empresa)* rival ♦ *mf (em concurso, competição)* contestant; *(em disputa)* rival.

concorrer [kõŋko'xe(x)] *vi* to compete; **~ a algo** *(emprego, posição)* to apply for sthg.

concretizar [kõŋkreti'za(x)] *vt* to realize.

concreto, -ta [kõŋ'krɛtu, -ta] *adj & m* concrete.

concurso [kõŋ'kuxsu] *m (de televisão)* game show; *(de rádio)* contest; *(de música, literatura)* competition; *(para emprego)* open competition.

conde ['kõdʒi] *m* count.

condenação [kõdena'sãw] *(pl -ões* [-õjʃ]) *f* condemnation; *(JUR: sentença)* sentence.

condenar [kõde'na(x)] *vt* to condemn; *(JUR: sentenciar)* to sentence.

condensação [kõdẽsa'sãw] *f* condensation.

condensado [kõdẽ'sadu] *adj m* → leite.

condensar [kõdẽ'sa(x)] *vt* to condense.

condescendência [kõdesẽ'dẽsja] *f* compliance.

condescendente [kõdesẽ'dẽtʃi] *adj* compliant.

condescender [kõdesẽn'de(x)] *vi* to agree; **~ em fazer algo** to agree to do sthg.

condessa [kõ'desa] *f* countess.

condição [kõdʒi'sãw] *(pl -ões* [-õjʃ]) *f* condition; *(classe social)* status; **estar em boas/más condições** to be in good/bad condition.

condicionado, -da [kõdʒisjo'nadu, -da] *adj* restricted.

condicional [kõdʒisjo'naw] *m*: **o ~** the conditional.

condicionar [kõdʒisjo'na(x)] *vt* to restrict.

condições → condição.

condimentar [kõdʒimẽn'ta(x)] *vt* to season.

condimento [kõdʒi'mẽntu] *m* seasoning.

condizer [kõdʒi'ze(x)] *vi* to go together; **~ com** to go with.

condolências [kõdo'lẽsjaʃ] *fpl* condolences; **as minhas ~** my condolences.

condomínio [kõdo'minju] *m* maintenance fee.

condómino [kõ'dɔminu] *m (Port)* = condômino.

condômino [kõ'dominu] *m (Br)* proprietor *(in a block of flats).*

condor [kõ'do(x)] *(pl -res* [-riʃ]) *m* condor.

condução [kõdu'sãw] *f (de governo)* running; *(Br: transporte)* transport; *(Port: de veículo)* driving.

conduta [kõ'duta] *f (tubo, cano)* chute; *(comportamento)* behaviour; **~ de gás** gas piping.

condutor, -ra [kõdu'to(x), -ra] *(mpl -res* [-riʃ]. *fpl -s* [-ʃ]) *m, f* driver ♦ *adj* conductive.

conduzir [kõdu'zi(x)] *vt (administrar)* to run; *(Port: dirigir)* to drive ♦ *vi (Port: dirigir)* to drive; **~ a** to lead to.

cone ['kɔni] *m* cone.

conexão [konek'sãw] *(pl -ões* [-õjʃ]) *f* connection.

confecção [kõfɛk'sãw] *(pl -ões* [-õjʃ])

f (de peça de vestuário) making; *(de prato culinário)* preparation.

confeccionar [kõfɛksjoˈna(x)] *vt* to make.

confecções → confecção.

confeitaria [kõfejtaˈria] *f* sweet shop *(Brit)*, candy store *(Am)*.

conferência [kõfeˈrẽsja] *f* conference.

conferir [kõfeˈri(x)] *vt* to check ♦ *vi (estar exato)* to be correct.

confessar [kõfeˈsa(x)] *vt* to confess.

◡ **confessar-se** *vp* to confess.

confessionário [kõfesjoˈnarju] *m* confessional.

confiança [kõfiˈãsa] *f (fé)* trust; *(segurança)* confidence; *(familiaridade)* familiarity; **ter ~ em** to trust; **ser de ~** to be reliable.

confiar [kõfiˈa(x)] *vt:* **~ algo a alguém** *(segredo)* to tell sb sthg in confidence; **~ alguém a alguém** to leave sb in sb's care.

◡ **confiar em** *v + prep (pessoa)* to trust; *(futuro, resultado)* to have faith in.

confidência [kõfiˈdẽsja] *f* confidence.

confidencial [kõfidẽˈsjaw] *(pl* **-ais** [-ajʃ]) *adj* confidential.

confirmação [kõfixmaˈsãw] *(pl* **-ões** [-õjʃ]) *f* confirmation.

confirmar [kõfixˈma(x)] *vt* to confirm.

◡ **confirmar-se** *vp* to come true.

confiscar [kõfiʃˈka(x)] *vt* to confiscate.

confissão [kõfiˈsãw] *(pl* **-ões** [-õjʃ]) *f* confession.

conflito [kõˈflitu] *m* conflict; *(desavença)* argument.

conformar-se [kõfoxˈmaxsi] *vp (resignar-se)* to resign o.s.; **~ com** to resign o.s. to.

conforme [kõˈfoxmi] *conj* as ♦ *prep (dependendo de como)* depending on; *(de acordo com)* according to.

conformidade [kõfoxmiˈdadʒi] *f* conformity; **em ~ com** in accordance with.

confortar [kõfoxˈta(x)] *vt* to comfort.

confortável [kõfoxˈtavew] *(pl* **-eis** [-ejʃ]) *adj* comfortable.

conforto [kõˈfoxtu] *m* comfort.

confraternizar [kõfratexniˈza(x)] *vi* to fraternize; **~ com** to fraternize with.

confrontação [kõfrõntaˈsãw] *(pl* **-ões** [-õjʃ]) *f* confrontation.

confrontar [kõfrõnˈta(x)] *vt* to confront; *(comparar)* to compare.

◡ **confrontar-se** *vp* to come face to face; **~-se com** *(deparar com)* to be confronted with.

confronto [kõˈfrõntu] *m* confrontation; *(comparação)* comparison.

confundir [kõfũnˈdi(x)] *vt (pessoa)* to confuse; *(rua, significado)* to mistake; *(números)* to mix up.

◡ **confundir-se** *vp (enganar-se)* to make a mistake; **~-se com** *(ser muito parecido a)* to be taken for.

confusão [kõfuˈzãw] *(pl* **-ões** [-õjʃ]) *f* confusion; *(tumulto)* commotion; **armar ~** to cause trouble; **fazer ~** to get mixed up.

confuso, -sa [kõˈfuzu, -za] *adj (desordenado)* mixed up; *(obscuro)* confusing; *(confundido)* confused.

confusões → confusão.

congelado, -da [kõʒeˈladu, -da] *adj* frozen.

congelador [kõʒelaˈdo(x)] *(pl* **-res** [-riʃ]) *m (Port)* freezer.

congelar [kõʒeˈla(x)] *vt & vi* to freeze.

congestão [kõʒeʃˈtãw] *(pl* **-ões** [-õjʃ]) *f* congestion.

congestionado, -da [kõʒeʃtʃjoˈnadu, -da] *adj* congested.

congestionamento [kõʒeʃtʃjonaˈmẽntu] *m (de trânsito)* congestion.

congestionar [kõʒeʃtʃjoˈna(x)] *vt (trânsito)* to block.

congestões → congestão.

congratular [kõŋgratuˈla(x)] *vt* to congratulate.

congresso [kõŋˈgresu] *m* congress.

conhaque [koˈɲaki] *m* cognac.

conhecedor, -ra [koɲeseˈdo(x), -ra] *(mpl* **-res** [-riʃ], *fpl* **-s** [-ʃ]) *m, f:* **ser ~ de** to be an authority on.

conhecer [koɲeˈse(x)] *vt* to know; *(ser apresentado a)* to meet; *(reconhecer)* to recognize.

conhecido, -da [koɲeˈsidu, -da] *adj* well-known ♦ *m, f* acquaintance.

conhecimento [koɲesiˈmẽntu] *m* knowledge; *(experiência)* experience; **dar ~ de algo a alguém** to inform sb of sthg; **tomar ~ de algo** to find out about sthg; **é do ~ de todos** it is common knowledge.

⊔ **conhecimentos** *mpl* contacts; *(cultura)* knowledge *(sg)*; **(ele) é uma pessoa com ~s** he is a knowledgeable OU cultured person.

conjugado [kõʒuˈgadu] *m (Br)* studio flat.

cônjuge [ˈkõʒuʒi] *mf* spouse.

conjunção [kõʒũˈsãw] *(pl -ões* [-õjʃ]) *f (GRAM)* conjunction; *(união)* union.

conjuntiva [kõʒũˈtʃiva] *f* conjunctiva.

conjuntivite [kõʒũtʃiˈvitʃi] *f* conjunctivitis.

conjunto [kõˈʒũtu] *m* set; *(de rock)* band; *(de roupa)* outfit.

connosco [koˈnoʃku] *pron (Port)* = conosco.

conosco [koˈnoʃku] *pron (Br)* with us.

conquanto [kõŋˈkwãntu] *conj* even though.

conquista [kõŋˈkiʃta] *f* conquest.

conquistar [kõŋkiʃˈta(x)] *vt* to conquer; *(posição, trabalho)* to get; *(seduzir)* to win over.

consciência [kõʃsjˈesja] *f* conscience; *(conhecimento)* awareness; **ter ~ de algo** to be aware of sthg; **ter a ~ pesada** to have a guilty conscience; **tomar ~ de algo** to become aware of sthg.

consciente [kõʃsjˈẽntʃi] *adj (acordado)* conscious; *(responsável)* aware ♦ *m*: **o ~** the conscious mind.

consecutivo, -va [kõsekuˈtʃivu, -va] *adj* consecutive.

conseguinte [kõseˈgĩntʃi] : **por conseguinte** *adv* consequently.

conseguir [kõseˈgi(x)] *vt* to get; **~ fazer algo** to manage to do sthg.

conselho [kõˈseʎu] *m* piece of advice; *(órgão coletivo)* council; **dar ~s** to give advice; **Conselho de Ministros** Cabinet.

consenso [kõˈsẽsu] *m* consensus.

consentimento [kõsẽntʃiˈmẽntu] *m* consent.

consentir [kõsẽnˈtʃi(x)] *vt* to consent to.

consequência [kõseˈkwẽsja] *pron (Port)* = conseqüência.

conseqüência [kõseˈkwẽsja] *f (Br)* consequence; **em** OU **como ~** as a consequence.

consertar [kõsexˈta(x)] *vt* to repair, to fix.

conserto [kõˈsextu] *m* repair.

conserva [kõˈsɛrva] *f*: **de ~** canned, tinned.

⊐ **conservas** *fpl* tinned OU canned food *(sg)*.

conservação [kõsexvaˈsãw] *f* conservation; *(de alimento)* preservation.

conservar [kõsexˈva(x)] *vt* to preserve.

conservatório [kõsexvaˈtɔrju] *m* conservatoire *(Brit)*, conservatory *(Am)*.

consideração [kõsideraˈsãw] *(pl -ões* [-õjʃ]) *f* consideration; *(crítica)* point; **ter algo em ~** to take sthg into consideration.

considerar [kõsideˈra(x)] *vt* to consider; **~ que** to consider (that).

⊔ **considerar-se** *vp*: **ele considera-se o maior** he thinks he's the best.

considerável [kõsideˈravew] *(pl -eis* [-ejʃ]) *adj* considerable; *(feito, conquista)* significant.

consigo [kõˈsigu] *pron (com ele)* with him; *(com ela)* with her; *(com você)* with you; *(com eles, elas)* with them; *(relativo a coisa, animal)* with it; **ela estava a falar ~ própria** she was talking to herself.

consistência [kõsiʃˈtẽsja] *f* consistency; *(de objeto, madeira)* solidity.

consistente [kõsiʃˈtẽntʃi] *adj (coerente)* consistent; *(espesso)* thick; *(sólido)* solid.

consistir [kõsiʃˈtʃi(x)] : **consistir em** *v* + *prep (ser composto por)* to consist of; *(basear-se em)* to consist in.

consoada [kõˈswada] *f* meal eaten late on Christmas Eve which traditionally consists of boiled salt cod with boiled potatoes, cabbage and boiled eggs.

consoante [kõˈswãntʃi] *f* consonant ♦ *prep (dependendo de)* depending on; *(conforme)* according to.

consolar [kõsoˈla(x)] *vt* to console.

⊔ **consolar-se** *vp* to console o.s.

consomé [kõsɔˈmɛ] *m (Port)* = consomê.

consomê [kõsoˈme] *m (Br)* consommé.

conspícuo, -cua [kõʃˈpikwu, -kwa] *adj* conspicuous.

conspiração [kõʃpiraˈsãw] *(pl -ões* [-õjʃ]) *f* conspiracy.

constante [kõʃˈtãntʃi] *adj* constant.

constar [kõʃˈta(x)] *v impess*: **consta que ...** it is said that ....

contentor

❑ **constar de** v + prep (consistir em) to consist of; (figurar em) to appear in.

constatar [kõʃtaˈta(x)] vt: ~ **que** (notar que) to realize (that).

consternado, -da [kõʃterˈnadu, -da] adj distraught.

constipação [kõʃtʃipaˈsãw] (pl -ões [-õjʃ]) f (Br: prisão de ventre) constipation; (Port: resfriado) cold.

constipado, -da [kõʃtʃiˈpadu, -da] adj: **estar** ~ (Br: ter prisão de ventre) to be constipated; (Port: estar resfriado) to have a cold.

constipar-se [kõʃtʃiˈparsɛ] vp (Port) to catch a cold.

constituição [kõʃtʃitwiˈsãw] (pl -ões [-õjʃ]) f constitution.

constituir [kõʃtʃitwiˈ(x)] vt (formar) to set up; (representar) to constitute.

constranger [kõʃtrãˈʒe(x)] vt (embaraçar) to embarrass; (obrigar) to force.

❑ **constranger-se** vp (embaraçar-se) to be embarrassed.

constrangimento [kõʃtrãʒiˈmẽtu] m (embaraço) embarrassment; (obrigação) constraint.

construção [kõʃtruˈsãw] (pl -ões [-õjʃ]) f construction.

construir [kõʃtruˈi(x)] vt to build; (frase) to construct.

construtivo, -va [kõʃtruˈtivu, -va] adj constructive.

construtor, -ra [kõʃtruˈto(x), -ra] (mpl -es [-iʃ], fpl -s [-ʃ]) m, f builder.

cônsul [ˈkõsuw] (pl -es [-iʃ]) mf consul.

consulado [kõsuˈladu] m consulate.

cônsules → **cônsul**.

consulta [kõˈsuwta] f (com médico) appointment; (de texto, dicionário) consultation.

consultar [kõsuwˈta(x)] vi (médico) to hold a surgery ♦ vt to consult.

consultório [kõsuwˈtɔrju] m (de médico) surgery.

consumidor, -ra [kõsumiˈdo(x), -ra] (mpl -res [-riʃ], fpl -s [-ʃ]) m, f consumer.

consumir [kõsuˈmi(x)] vt & vi to consume.

consumo [kõˈsumu] m consumption.

conta [ˈkõta] f (de restaurante, café, etc) bill; (de banco) account; (de colar) bead; **a** ~**, por favor** could I have the bill, please?; **o jantar é por minha** ~ dinner's on me; **abrir uma** ~ to open an account; **dar-se** ~ **de que** to realize

(that); **fazer de** ~ **que** to pretend (that); **ter em** ~ to take into account; **tomar** ~ **de** to look after; ~ **bancária** bank account; ~ **corrente** current account; ~ **à ordem** deposit account; **vezes sem** ~ countless times.

contabilidade [kõtabeliˈdadʒi] f accountancy; (departamento) accounts department.

contabilista [kõtabeˈliʃta] mf (Port) accountant.

contacto [kõˈta(k)tu] m (Port) = **contato**.

contador [kõtaˈdo(x)] (pl -res [-riʃ]) m (Br: profissional) accountant; (medidor) meter; ~ **de estórias** storyteller.

contagem [kõˈtaʒẽ] (pl -ns [-ʃ]) f (de gasto de água, de luz, etc) meter-reading; (de votos, bilhetes, etc) counting.

contagiar [kõtaˈʒja(x)] vt to infect.

contágio [kõˈtaʒju] m infection, contagion.

contagioso, -osa [kõtaˈʒjozu, -ɔza] adj contagious, infectious.

conta-gotas [ˌkõtaˈgotaʃ] m inv dropper.

contaminação [kõtaminaˈsãw] (pl -ões [-õjʃ]) f contamination.

contaminar [kõtamiˈna(x)] vt to contaminate.

conta-quilómetros [ˌkõtakiˈlɔmetruʃ] m inv (Port) speedometer.

contar [kõˈta(x)] vt to count; (narrar, explicar) to tell ♦ vi (calcular) to count; ~ **algo a alguém** to tell sb sthg; ~ **fazer algo** (tencionar) to expect to do sthg; ~ **com** to count on

contatar [kõtaˈta(x)] vt to contact.

contato [kõˈtatu] m (Br) contact; (de motor) ignition; **entrar em** ~ **com** (contatar) to get in touch with.

contemplar [kõtẽˈpla(x)] vt to contemplate; ~ **alguém com algo** to give sb sthg.

contemporâneo, -nea [kõtẽpoˈranju, -nja] adj & m, f contemporary.

contentamento [kõtẽtaˈmẽtu] m contentment.

contentar [kõtẽˈta(x)] vt to keep happy.

❑ **contentar a** v + prep to please.

❑ **contentar-se com** vp + prep to content o.s. with.

contente [kõˈtẽtʃi] adj happy.

contentor [kõtẽˈto(x)] (pl -es [-iʃ])

m container; ~ **do lixo** large bin.
conter [kõn'te(x)] *vt (ter)* to contain; *(refrear)* to hold back.
⏘ **conter-se** *vp* to restrain o.s.
conterrâneo, -nea [kõnte'xanju. -nja] *m, f* compatriot.
contestação [kõnteʃta'sãw] *(pl -ões [-õjʃ])* *f (resposta)* answer; *(polêmica)* controversy.
contestar [kõnteʃ'ta(x)] *vt (refutar)* to dispute; *(replicar)* to answer.
conteúdo [kõn'tʃudu] *m (de recipiente)* contents *(pl)*; *(de carta, texto)* content.
contexto [kõn'teʃtu] *m* context.
contigo [kõn'tigu] *pron* with you.
continente [kõntʃi'nẽntʃi] *m* continent.
continuação [kõntʃinwa'sãw] *(pl -ões [-õjʃ])* *f* continuation.
continuamente [kõntʃinwa'mẽntʃi] *adv (sem interrupção)* continuously; *(repetidamente)* continually.
continuar [kõntʃi'nwa(x)] *vt* to continue ◆ *vi* to carry on; ~ **a fazer algo** to continue doing sthg; ~ **com algo** to carry on with sthg.
contínuo, -nua [kõn'tʃinwu. -nwa] *adj (sem interrupção)* continuous; *(repetido)* continual ◆ *m, f* caretaker.
conto [kõntu] *m (Port: mil escudos)* thousand escudos; *(história)* story.
contornar [kõntox'na(x)] *vt (edifício, muro, etc)* to go round; *(problema, situação)* to get round.
contra [kõntra] *prep* against ◆ *m*: **pesar** OU **ver os prós e os ~s** to weigh up the pros and the cons.
contra-ataque [kõntra'taki] *m* counterattack.
contrabaixo [kõntra'bajʃu] *m* double bass.
contrabando [kõntra'bãndu] *m (de mercadorias)* smuggling; *(mercadoria)* contraband.
contracepção [ˌkõntrasep'sãw] *f* contraception.
contraceptivo, -va [ˌkõntrasep'tʃivu, -va] *adj & m* contraceptive.
contradição [ˌkõntradʒi'sãw] *(pl -ões [-õjʃ])* *f* contradiction.
contradizer [ˌkõntradʒi'ze(x)] *vt* to contradict.
contrafilé [kõntrafi'lɛ] *m (Br)* rump steak.
contra-indicação [ˌkõntraĩndʒika'sãw] *(pl -ões [-õjʃ])* *f (de medicamento)* contraindication.
contrair [kõntra'i(x)] *vt (doença)* to catch, to contract; *(dívida)* to run up; *(vício, hábito)* to acquire; ~ **matrimônio** to get married.
contramão [kõntra'mãw] *f (de rua, estrada)* the other side of the road; **ir pela ~** to drive on the wrong side of the road.
contrapartida [ˌkõntrapar'tʃida] *f* compensation; **em ~** on the other hand.
contrariar [kõntra'rja(x)] *vt (contradizer)* to contradict; *(aborrecer)* to annoy.
contrariedade [kõntrarje'dadʒi] *f (aborrecimento)* annoyance.
contrário, -ria [kõn'trarju. -rja] *adj (oposto)* opposite; *(adversário)* opposing ◆ *m*: **o ~** the opposite; **ser ~ a algo** to be against sthg; **de ~** otherwise; **pelo ~** (quite) the contrary; **em sentido ~** in the opposite direction.
contra-senso [kõntra'sẽsu] *m (absurdo)* nonsense; *(em tradução)* mistranslation.
contrastar [kõntraʃ'ta(x)] *vt & vi* to contrast; ~ **com** to contrast with.
contraste [kõn'traʃtʃi] *m* contrast; **em ~ com** in contrast with.
contratar [kõntra'ta(x)] *vt* to hire.
contratempo [ˌkõntra'tẽmpu] *m* setback.
contrato [kõn'tratu] *m* contract.
contribuinte [kõntri'bwĩntʃi] *mf* taxpayer.
contribuir [kõntri'bwi(x)] *vi* to contribute; ~ **com algo** to contribute sthg; ~ **para algo** to contribute towards sthg.
controlar [kõntro'la(x)] *vt* to control.
⏘ **controlar-se** *vp* to control o.s.
controle [kõn'troli] *m (Br)* control; ~ **remoto** remote control.
controlo [kõn'trolu] *m (Port)* = **controle.**
controvérsia [kõntro'vɛrsja] *f* controversy.
controverso, -sa [kõntro'vɛrsu. -sa] *adj* controversial.
contudo [kõn'tudu] *conj* however.
contusão [kõntu'zãw] *(pl -ões [-õjʃ])* *f* bruise.
convalescença [kõvaleʃ'sẽsa] *f* convalescence.
convenção [kõvẽ'sãw] *(pl -ões [-õjʃ])*

f convention.

convencer [kõvẽ'se(x)] *vt* to convince; ~ **alguém a fazer algo** to persuade sb to do sthg; ~ **alguém de algo** to convince sb of sthg; ~ **alguém de que** to convince sb (that).

❏ **convencer-se** *vp* to be convinced; **~-se de que** to become convinced (that).

convencido, -da [kõvẽ'sidu. -da] *adj* conceited.

convencional [kõvẽsjo'naw] (*pl* **-ais** [-ajʃ]) *adj* conventional.

convenções → convenção.

conveniente [kõve'njẽntʃi] *adj* convenient.

convento [kõ'vẽntu] *m* convent.

conversa [kõvex'sa] *f* conversation; ~ **fiada** chitchat; **não ir na** ~ not to be taken in.

conversar [kõvex'sa(x)] *vi* to talk; ~ **com** to talk to.

conversível [kõvex'sivew] (*pl* **-eis** [-ejʃ]) *m* (*Br: carro*) convertible.

converter [kõvex'te(x)] *vt* (*transformar*): ~ **algo/alguém em** to convert sthg/sb into.

❏ **converter-se** *vp* to convert; **~-se a** to convert to; **~-se em** to turn into.

convés [kõ'vɛʃ] (*pl* **-eses** [-ɛziʃ]) *m* deck.

convidado, -da [kõvi'dadu. -da] *adj* guest (*antes de s*) ◆ *m*, *f* guest.

convidar [kõvi'da(x)] *vt* to invite.

convir [kõ'vi(x)] *vi* (*ser útil*) to be a good idea; (*ser adequado*) to be suitable; **é de** ~ **que** admittedly.

convite [kõ'vitʃi] *m* invitation.

convivência [kõvi'vẽsja] *f* (*vida em comum*) living together; (*familiaridade*) familiarity.

conviver [kõvi've(x)] : **conviver com** *v* + *prep* (*ter convivência com*) to live with; (*amigos, colegas*) to socialize with.

convívio [kõ'vivju] *m* (*convivência*) contact; (*festa*) social gathering.

convocar [kõvo'ka(x)] *vt* to summon; ~ **alguém para algo** to summon sb to sthg.

convosco [kõ'voʃku] *pron* with you.

convulsão [kõvuw'sãw] (*pl* **-ões** [-õjʃ]) *f* (*física*) convulsion; (*social*) upheaval.

cooperação [kwopera'sãw] (*pl* **-ões** [-õjʃ]) *f* cooperation.

cooperar [kwope'ra(x)] *vi* to cooperate.

cooperativa [kwopera'tiva] *f* cooperative.

coordenar [kworde'na(x)] *vt* to coordinate.

copa ['kɔpa] *f* (*divisão de casa*) pantry; (*de árvore*) top; (*de chapéu*) crown; (*Br: torneio esportivo*) cup.

❏ **copas** *fpl* (*naipe de cartas*) hearts.

cópia ['kɔpja] *f* copy.

copiar [ko'pja(x)] *vt* to copy ◆ *vi* (*Port: em exame, teste*) to cheat.

copo ['kɔpu] *m* glass; **tomar** OU **beber um** ~ to have a drink; **ser um bom** ~ (*fam*) to be able to hold one's drink.

copo-d'água [.kɔpud'agwa] (*pl* **copos-d'água** [.kɔpuʒd'agwa]) *m* (*Port*) reception.

coqueiro [ko'kejru] *m* coconut palm.

coquetel [koke'tɛw] (*pl* **-éis** [-ɛiʃ]) *m* cocktail.

cor[1] ['kɔ(x)] : **de cor** *adv*: **aprender/ saber algo de** ~ to learn/know sthg by heart; **saber algo de** ~ **e salteado** to know sthg backwards.

cor[2] ['ko(x)] (*pl* **-res** [-riʃ]) *f* colour; **mudar de** ~ to change colour; **perder a** ~ to fade; **de** ~ (*pessoa*) coloured.

coração [kora'sãw] (*pl* **-ões** [-õjʃ]) *m* heart; **ter bom** ~ to be kind-hearted.

corado, -da [ko'radu. -da] *adj* (*pessoa*) red, flushed; (*frango, assado, etc*) brown.

coragem [ko'raʒẽ] *f* courage ◆ *interj* chin up!

corais → coral.

corajoso, -osa [kora'ʒozu. ɔza] *adj* courageous.

coral [ko'raw] (*pl* **-ais** [-ajʃ]) *m* coral.

corante [ko'rãntʃi] *m* colouring; **"sem ~s nem conservantes"** "contains no colouring or preservatives".

corar [ko'ra(x)] *vi* to blush ◆ *vt* (*frango, assado, etc*) to brown.

Corcovado [koxko'vadu] *m*: **o** ~ the Corcovado mountain in Rio de Janeiro.

corda ['kɔrda] *f* rope; (*de instrumento musical*) string; (*de relógio, brinquedo*) clockwork; **dar** ~ **a** (*relógio, brinquedo*) to wind up; ~ **de saltar** skipping rope; **~s vocais** vocal cords.

cordão [kor'dãw] (*pl* **-ões** [-õjʃ]) *m* (*Port: de sapatos*) shoelace; (*jóia*) gold chain; ~ **umbilical** umbilical cord.

cordeiro [kor'dejru] *m* lamb.
cordel [kor'dɛw] (*pl* -**éis** [-ɛiʃ]) *m* string.
cor-de-laranja [kordʒila'raʒa] *adj inv* orange.
cor-de-rosa [.kordʒi'xɔza] *adj inv* pink.
cordial [kor'dʒjaw] (*pl* -**ais** [-ajʃ]) *adj* cordial.
cordilheira [kordʒi'ʎejra] *f* mountain range.
cordões → **cordão**.
cores → **cor²**.
coreto [ko'retu] *m* bandstand.
corinto [ko'rĩntu] *m* currant.
córnea ['kɔxnja] *f* cornea.
corneta [kox'neta] *f* cornet.
cornflakes® [kɔxni'flejkiʃ] *mpl* Cornflakes®.
coro ['koru] *m* choir; *(de música)* chorus; **em ~** in unison.
coroa [ko'roa] *f* crown; *(de enterro)* wreath.
corpo ['koxpu] *m* body; *(cadáver)* corpse; **~ de bombeiros** fire brigade.
corporal [koxpo'raw] (*pl* -**ais** [-ajʃ]) *adj* → **odor**.
correção [koxe'sãw] (*pl* -**ões** [-õjʃ]) *f* *(Br)* correctness; *(de exame, teste)* correction.
correcção [kuxɛ'sãw] (*pl* -**ões** [-õjʃ]) *f* *(Port)* = **correção**.
correções → **correção**.
corredor, -ra [koxe'do(x), -ra] (*mpl* -**res** [-riʃ], *fpl* -**s** [-ʃ]) *m, f* runner ♦ *m* *(de casa)* corridor.
correia [ko'xeja] *f* *(tira de couro)* strap; **~ da ventoinha** fan belt.
correio [ko'xeju] *m* post, mail; *(pessoa)* postman (*f* postwoman) *(Brit)*, mailman (*f* mailwoman) *(Am)*; *(local)* post office; **~ azul** *(Port)* fast mail service; – firstclass mail *(Brit)*; **~ eletrônico** e-mail, electronic mail; **~ expresso** express mail; **~ de voz** voice mail; **pelo ~** by post.
corrente [ko'xẽntʃi] *adj* current; *(água)* running ♦ *f* current; *(de bicicleta)* chain; **~ alternada** alternating current; **~ de ar** draught.
correr [ko'xe(x)] *vi* to run; *(tempo)* to pass; *(notícia, rumor)* to go around ♦ *vt* to run; **~ as cortinas** to draw the curtains; **~ com alguém** to get rid of sb; **~ perigo** to be in danger; **fazer algo correndo** to do sthg in a rush.

correspondência [koxeʃpõn'dẽsja] *f* correspondence.
correspondente [koxeʃpõn'dẽntʃi] *adj* corresponding ♦ *mf* correspondent.
corresponder [koxeʃpõn'de(x)] *vi* to correspond; *(retribuir)* to reciprocate; **~ a** to correspond with.
⌐ corresponder-se *vp* *(escrever-se)* to write to each other; **~-se com alguém** to correspond with sb.
corretamente [ko.xɛta'mẽntʃi] *adv* correctly.
correto [ko'xɛtu] *adj* correct.
corretor, -ra [koxe'to(x), -ra] (*mpl* -**res** [-riʃ], *fpl* -**s** [-ʃ]) *m, f* broker ♦ *m*: *(fluido)* correction fluid; **~ de imóveis** estate agent *(Brit)*, real estate agent *(Am)*; **~ da Bolsa** stockbroker.
corrida [ko'xida] *f* *(de velocidade)* race; *(tourada)* bullfight; *(de táxi)* fare; **~ de automóveis** rally; **~ de cavalos** horse race; **~ à Portuguesa** Portuguese bullfight.
corrigir [koxi'ʒi(x)] *vt* to correct.
⌐ corrigir-se *vp* to mend one's ways.
corrimão [koxi'mãw] (*pl* -**s** [-ʃ] ou -**ões** [-õjʃ]) *m* *(de escada)* handrail, banister; *(de varanda)* railing.
corrimento [koxi'mẽntu] *m* *(de vagina)* discharge.
corrimões → **corrimão**.
corroborar [koxobo'ra(x)] *vt* to corroborate.
corromper [koxõm'pe(x)] *vt* to corrupt; *(subornar)* to bribe.
corrupção [koxup'sãw] (*pl* -**ões** [-õjʃ]) *f* corruption; **~ de menores** *(JUR)* corruption of minors.
corrupto, -ta [ko'xuptu, -ta] *adj* corrupt.
cortar [kox'ta(x)] *vt* to cut; *(carne assada)* to carve; *(gás, eletricidade)* to cut off; *(rua, estrada)* to block off ♦ *vi* to be sharp; **~ em algo** to cut back on sthg; **~ relações (com alguém)** to break up (with sb).
⌐ cortar-se *vp* to cut o.s.
corte ['kɔxtʃi] *m* cut; **~ de cabelo** haircut.
cortejo [kox'teʒu] *m* procession; **~ fúnebre** funeral procession.
cortesia [koxte'zia] *f* courtesy.
cortiça [kox'tʃisa] *f* cork.
cortiço [kox'tʃisu] *f* slum tenement.
cortina [kox'tʃina] *f* curtain.

cortinados [koxt∫iʼnadu∫] *mpl* curtains.

coruja [koʼruʒa] *f* owl.

corvina [koxʼvina] *f* black bream.

corvo [ʼkoxvu] *m* crow.

cós [ʼkɔ∫] *m inv* waistband.

coser [koʼze(x)] *vt & vi* to sew.

cosmético [koʒˈmɛt∫iku] *m* cosmetic.

cosmopolita [koʒmopoʼlita] *mf & adj* cosmopolitan.

costa [ʼkɔ∫ta] *f* coast; *(de montanha)* slope; **dar à ~** to wash ashore.

⌐ **costas** *fpl* back *(sg)*.

costela [ko∫ʼtɛla] *f* rib.

costeleta [ko∫teˈleta] *f (de porco, carneiro)* chop; *(de vitela)* cutlet.

costumar [ko∫tuˈma(x)] *vt*: **~ fazer algo** to usually do sthg; **ela costuma chegar na hora** she usually arrives on time ◆ *v impess*: **costuma chover muito** it tends to rain a lot.

costume [ko∫ˈtumi] *m (hábito)* habit; *(uso social)* custom; **como de ~** as usual; **por ~** usually.

costura [ko∫ˈtura] *f (atividade)* sewing; *(de operação cirúrgica)* scar.

costurar [ko∫tuˈra(x)] *vt (roupa)* to sew (up); *(ferida, corte)* to stitch up.

cotação [kotaˈsãw] *(pl -ões* [-õj∫]*) f (de mercadoria, título)* quoted price; **~ bancária** bank rate.

cotidiano [kot∫iˈdjanu] *adj (Br)* daily ◆ *m* everyday life.

cotonetes [kotoˈnɛt∫] *mpl* cotton buds.

cotovelada [kotoveˈlada] *f* poke with the elbow; **dar uma ~ em alguém** to elbow sb.

cotovelo [kotoˈvelu] *m* elbow.

cotovia [kotoˈvia] *f* lark.

coube [ˈkobi] → **caber**.

couchette [koˈ∫et∫i] *f* couchette.

couraça [koˈrasa] *f (de tartaruga, cágado)* shell.

courgette [kurˈʒet∫] *f (Port)* courgette *(Brit)*, zucchini *(Am)*.

couro [ˈkoru] *m* leather; **~ cabeludo** scalp.

couve [ˈkovi] *f* cabbage; **~ lombarda** savoy cabbage; **~ à mineira** *chopped spring greens lightly fried in butter and garlic;* **~ portuguesa** kale; **~ roxa** red cabbage.

couve-de-Bruxelas [kovidʒibruˈ∫ela∫] *(pl* **couves-de-Bruxelas** [koviʒdʒibruˈ∫ela∫]*) f* brussels sprout.

couve-flor [kovɛˈflo(x)] *(pl* **couves-flores** [kovɛˈflore∫]*) f* cauliflower.

couve-galega [kovigaˈlega] *(pl* **couves-galegas** [koviʒgaˈlega∫]*) f* kale.

couvert [koˈvɛ(x)] *m* cover charge.

cova [ˈkɔva] *f* pit; *(sepultura)* grave.

covarde [koˈvaxdʒi] *adj* cowardly ◆ *m* coward.

covardia [kovaxˈdʒia] *f* cowardice.

coveiro [koˈvejru] *m* gravedigger.

coxa [ˈko∫a] *f* thigh; **~ de galinha** chicken rissole.

coxia [koˈ∫ia] *f* aisle.

coxo, -xa [ˈko∫u. -∫a] *adj* lame.

cozer [koˈze(x)] *vt* to boil; *(bolo, torta, empada)* to bake.

cozido, -da [koˈzidu. -da] *adj* boiled; *(bolo, torta, empada)* baked ◆ *m*: **~ (à portuguesa)** *a mixture of boiled meats including chicken, beef, pig's ear, "chouriço", black pudding and vegetables, served with rice.*

cozinha [koˈzipa] *f* kitchen; *(arte)* cookery.

cozinhar [koziˈpa(x)] *vt & vi* to cook.

cozinheiro, -ra [koziˈpejru. -ra] *m, f* cook.

crachá [kraˈ∫a] *m* badge.

crânio [ˈkranju] *m* skull.

craque [ˈkraki] *mf (fam)* expert.

cratera [kraˈtera] *f* crater.

cravar [kraˈva(x)] *vt*: **~ algo em algo** *(unhas)* to dig sthg into sthg; *(dentes, faca)* to sink sthg into sthg; **~ os olhos em** to stare at.

cravinho [kraˈvipu] *m (Port)* clove.

cravo [ˈkravu] *m (flor)* carnation; *(instrumento)* harpsichord; *(Br: em rosto)* blackhead; *(Br: especiaria)* clove; *(Port: verruga)* wart.

creche [ˈkrɛ∫] *f* crèche.

credencial [kredẽsiˈaw] *(pl -ais* [-aj∫]*) f (médica)* letter of referral from a GP to a specialist.

crediário [kreˈdʒjarju] *m (Br)* hire purchase *(Brit)*, installment plan *(Am)*.

crédito [ˈkrɛd∫itu] *m* credit; **comprar/vender a ~** to buy/sell on credit.

credor, -ra [kreˈdo(x). -ra] *(mpl -res* [-ri∫]. *fpl -s* [-∫]*) m, f* creditor.

crédulo, -la [ˈkrɛdulu. -wa] *adj* gullible.

cremar [kreˈma(x)] *vt* to cremate.

crematório [kremaˈtɔrju] *m* crematorium.

creme [ˈkrɛmi] *m* cream; *(licor)* cream

liqueur; ~ **de barba** shaving cream; ~ **hidratante** moisturizer; ~ **de leite** *(Br)* single cream; ~ **de limpeza** cleanser; ~ **de noite** cold cream; ~ **rinse** *(Br)* conditioner.

cremoso, -osa [kre'mozu. -ɔza] *adj* creamy.

crença ['krēsa] *f* belief.

crente ['krēntʃi] *mf* believer.

crepe ['krɛpi] *m* crepe.

crepúsculo [kre'puʃkulu]· *m (de manhã)* daybreak; *(à noite)* twilight.

crer ['kre(x)] *vi* to believe; *(supor)* to suppose ♦ *vt:* ~ **que** *(acreditar)* to believe (that); *(supor)* to suppose (that); **ver para** ~ seeing is believing.

crescente [kre'sēntʃi] *adj* growing ♦ *m (fase da lua)* crescent.

crescer [kre'se(x)] *vi* to grow; *(aumentar)* to rise; *(sobejar)* to be left (over).

crespo, -pa ['kreʃpu. -pa] *adj (cabelo)* very curly; *(rugoso)* rough.

cretino, -na [kre'tinu. -na] *m, f* idiot.

cria ['kria] *f* young.

criado, -da [kri'adu. -da] *m, f* servant.

criador, -ra [kria'do(x). -ra] *(mpl -res* [-riʃ]. *fpl -s* [-ʃ]) *m, f* creator; *(de animais)* breeder.

criança [kri'ãsa] *f* child; ~ **de colo** infant; **quando** ~ as a child; **ser** ~ to be childish.

criar [kri'a(x)] *vt* to create; *(filhos)* to bring up; *(animais)* to raise; ~ **caso** to make trouble.

❑ **criar-se** *vp (produzir-se)* to form; *(pessoa)* to grow up.

criatividade [kriatʃivi'dadʒi] *f* creativity.

criativo, -va [kria'tʃivu. -va] *adj* creative.

criatura [kria'tura] *f* creature.

crime ['krimi] *m* crime.

criminalidade [kriminali'dadʒi] *f* crime.

criminoso, -osa [krimi'nozu. -ɔza] *m, f* criminal.

crina ['krina] *f* mane.

crisântemo [kri'zãntemu] *m* chrysanthemum.

crise ['krizi] *f* crisis; *(em doença)* attack; *(de nervos, histeria)* fit.

crista ['kriʃta] *f (de ave)* crest; *(de montanha)* ridge; **estar na** ~ **da onda** to be all the rage.

cristã → **cristão**.

cristal [kriʃ'taw] *(pl -ais* [-ajʃ]) *m* crystal.

cristaleira [kriʃta'lejra] *f* china cabinet.

cristão, -tã [kriʃ'tãw. -tã] *adj & m, f* Christian.

critério [kri'tɛrju] *m* criterion.

crítica ['kritika] *f (de obra, peça, filme)* review; *(censura)* criticism.

criticar [kriti'ka(x)] *vt (obra)* to review; *(pessoa, atitude)* to criticize.

crivo ['krivu] *m* sieve; *(de regador)* rose.

crocante [krɔ'kãntʃi] *adj* crunchy.

croché [krɔ'ʃɛ] *m (Port)* = **crochê**.

crochê [krɔ'ʃe] *m (Br)* crochet.

crocodilo [krɔko'dilu] *m* crocodile.

cromo ['krɔmu] *m* sticker.

crónica ['krɔnika] *f (Port)* = **crônica**.

crônica ['kronika] *f (Br) (de jornal)* (newspaper) column; *(conto)* short story.

crónico, -ca ['krɔniku. -ka] *adj (Port)* = **crônico**.

crônico, -ca *adj* ['kroniku. -ka] *(Br) (doença)* chronic.

cronológico, -ca [krono'lɔʒiku. -ka] *adj* chronological.

cronometrar [kronome'tra(x)] *vt* to time.

cronómetro [kru'nɔmetru] *m (Port)* = **cronômetro**.

cronômetro [kro'nometru] *m (Br)* stopwatch.

croquete [kro'ketʃi] *m* croquette.

crosta ['krɔʃta] *f (de ferida)* scab; *(da Terra)* crust.

cru, crua ['kru. 'krua] *adj (comida)* raw; *(tecido)* unbleached; *(realidade)* harsh.

crucial [kru'sjaw] *(pl -ais* [-ajʃ]) *adj* crucial.

crucifixo [kruse'fiksu] *m* crucifix.

cruel [kru'ɛw] *(pl -éis* [-ɛiʃ]) *adj* cruel.

cruz ['kruʃ] *(pl -zes* [-ziʃ]) *f* cross; **a Cruz Vermelha** the Red Cross.

cruzamento [kruza'mēntu] *m (em estrada)* crossroads *(sg)*; *(de raças)* crossbreed.

cruzar [kru'za(x)] *vt* to cross; *(braços)* to fold.

❑ **cruzar-se** *vp (interceptar-se)* to cross; **~-se com alguém** to bump into sb.

cruzeiro [kru'zejru] *m* cruise; *(antiga unidade monetária)* cruzeiro.

cu ['ku] *m (vulg)* arse *(Brit)*, ass *(Am)*.

Cuba libre [‚kuba'libri] *f* rum and cola.

cúbico, -ca ['kubiku, -ka] *adj* cubic.

cubículo [ku'bikulu] *m* cubicle.

cubo ['kubu] *m* cube; ~ **de gelo** ice cube.

cuco ['kuku] *m* cuckoo.

cueca ['kwɛka] *f* briefs *(pl)*.

cuidado, -da [kui'dadu, -da] *adj (casa, jardim, etc)* well looked after ♦ *m* care ♦ *interj* (be) careful!; **ter ~** to take care, to be careful; **aos ~s de alguém** care of sb; **com ~** carefully, with care.

cuidar [kui'da(x)] : **cuidar de** *v + prep* to take care of.

❏ **cuidar-se** *vp* to look after o.s.

cujo, -ja ['kuʒu, -ʒa] *pron (de quem)* whose; *(de que)* of which.

culinária [kuli'narja] *f* cookery.

culminar [kuwmi'na(x)] : **culminar em** *v + prep* to culminate in.

culpa ['kuwpa] *f* fault; **ter ~ de algo** to be to blame for sthg; **por ~ de** due to.

culpado, -da [kuw'padu, -da] *adj* guilty.

cultivar [kuwti'va(x)] *vt* to cultivate.

❏ **cultivar-se** *vp* to educate o.s.

culto, -ta ['kuwtu, -ta] *adj* well-educated ♦ *m* cult.

cultura [kuw'tura] *f* culture; *(agrícola)* crop; *(conhecimentos)* knowledge.

cultural [kuwtu'raw] *(pl* **-ais** [-ajʃ]) *adj* cultural.

cume ['kumi] *m* summit.

cúmplice ['kumplisi] *mf* accomplice.

cumplicidade [kumplisi'dadʒi] *f* complicity.

cumprimentar [kumprimẽn'ta(x)] *vt* to greet.

cumprimento [kumpri'mẽntu] *m* greeting.

❏ **cumprimentos** *mpl* regards; **Com os melhores ~s** Yours sincerely; **~s a ...** give my regards to ....

cumprir [kum'pri(x)] *vt (tarefa, ordem, missão)* to carry out; *(promessa)* to keep; *(pena, sentença)* to serve; *(lei)* to obey ♦ *v impess*: **~ a alguém fazer algo** *(caber a)* to be sb's turn to do sthg; *(ser o dever de)* to be sb's responsibility to do sthg.

cúmulo ['kumulu] *m* height; **é o ~!** that's the limit!

cunha ['kuɲa] *f* wedge.

cunhado, -da [ku'ɲadu, -da] *m, f* brother-in-law *(f* sister-in-law).

cunhar [ku'ɲa(x)] *vt (moeda)* to mint.

cupão [ku'pãw] *(pl* **-ões** [-õjʃ]) *m (Port)* = **cupom**.

cupom [ku'põ] *(pl* **-ns** [-ʃ]) *m (Br)* voucher.

cúpula ['kupula] *f* dome.

cura ['kura] *f* cure; *(de queijo, presunto, etc)* curing.

curar [ku'ra(x)] *vt* to cure ♦ *vi (sarar)* to heal.

❏ **curar-se** *vp* to recover.

curativo [kura'tʃivu] *m* dressing.

curinga [ku'rĩga] *m (de jogo de cartas)* joker; *(Br: em futebol)* substitute.

curiosidade [kurjuzi'dadʒi] *f* curiosity.

curioso, -osa [ku'rjozu, -ɔza] *adj* curious ♦ *m, f (bisbilhoteiro)* busybody; *(espectador)* onlooker; *(amador)* amateur.

curral [ku'xaw] *(pl* **-ais** [-ajʃ]) *m* pen.

currículo [ku'xikulu] *m* curriculum vitae, CV.

curso ['kursu] *m* course; *(de universidade)* degree course; *(alunos de um curso)* year; **ter um ~ de algo** *(universitário)* to have a degree in sthg; **~ intensivo** intensive course; **~ superior** (university) degree; **em ~** *(ano, semana, etc)* current; *(em funcionamento)* in operation; *(em andamento)* in progress.

cursor [kux'so(x)] *(pl* **-res** [-riʃ]) *m (INFORM)* cursor.

curtir [kux'ti(x)] *vt (peles, couros)* to tan; *(fam: desfrutar)* to enjoy.

curto, -ta ['kuxtu, -ta] *adj* short; **a ~ prazo** in the short term.

curto-circuito [‚kuxtusix'kwitu] *(pl* **curtos-circuitos** [‚kuxtuʃsix'kwituʃ]) *m* short circuit.

curva ['kuxva] *f (de estrada, caminho, etc)* bend; *(de corpo)* curve.

curvar [kux'va(x)] *vt* to bend; *(cabeça)* to bow.

❏ **curvar-se** *vp (inclinar-se)* to bend over; *(fig: humilhar-se)* to lower o.s.

cuscuz [kuʃ'kuʃ] *m* couscous; *(prato árabe)* couscous served with vegetables and spicy lamb; *(prato brasileiro)* steamed seafood, eggs and peas served on couscous.

cuspir [kuʃˈpi(x)] *vi & vt* to spit.
cuspe [ˈkuʃpi] *m (Br)* spit.
cuspo [ˈkuʃpu] *m (Port)* = **cuspe.**
custa [ˈkuʃta] : **à custa de** *prep* at the expense of.
⌐ **custas** *fpl (JUR)* costs.
custar [kuʃˈta(x)] *vt & vi (valer)* to cost; **custa muito a fazer** it's hard to do; **quanto custa?** how much is it?;

custe o que ~ at all costs, at any cost.
custo [ˈkuʃtu] *m (preço, despesa)* cost; *(fig: dificuldade)* difficulty; **~ de vida** cost of living; **a ~** with difficulty.
cutia [kuˈtʃia] *f* agouti.
cutícula [kuˈtʃikula] *f* cuticle.
c.v. *m (abrev de curriculum vitae)* C.V.
c/v *abrev* = **cave.**

D

da [da] = de + a, → de.

dá ['da] → dar.

dactilografar [da(k)tilografar] vt (Port) = datilografar.

dádiva ['dadiva] f donation.

dado, -da ['dadu, -da] adj (sociável) sociable; (determinado) given ◆ m (de jogar) dice; (de problema, cálculo) factor; (informação) fact; ~ **que** (visto que) given that.

⌐ **dados** mpl (jogo) dice; (INFORM) data (sg); **jogar ~s** to play dice.

daí [da'i] adv = de + aí; (relativo a espaço) from there; (relativo a tempo): ~ **a um mês/um ano/dez minutos** a month/a year/ten minutes later; ~ **em** OU **por diante** from then on; **e ~?** so what?; **sai ~!** get out of there!

dali [da'li] adv = de + ali; (relativo a espaço) from there; (relativo a tempo): ~ **a uma semana/um mês/uma hora** a week/a month/an hour later; ~ **em** OU **por diante** from then on.

daltónico, -ca [dal'toniku, -ka] adj & m, f (Port) = **daltônico**.

daltônico, -ca [daw'toniku, -ka] adj (Br) colour-blind ◆ m, f (Br) colour-blind person.

dama ['dama] f (senhora) lady; (de jogo de damas) draught (Brit), checker (Am); (de baralho de cartas) queen; ~ **de honor** (Port) bridesmaid; ~ **de honra** (Br) bridesmaid.

⌐ **damas** fpl draughts (sg) (Brit), checkers (sg) (Am); **jogar ~s** to play draughts.

damasco [da'maʃku] m apricot.

dança ['dãsa] f dance; ~s **folclóricas** country dancing (sg).

dançar [dã'sa(x)] vi to dance; (oscilar) to sway ◆ vt to dance.

danceteria [dãsete'ria] f (Br) disco.

danificar [danifi'ka(x)] vt to damage.

dano ['danu] m damage.

dantes ['dãtiʃ] adv in the old days.

dão ['dãw] → dar.

Dão ['dãw] m Portuguese wine-producing area.

daquela [da'kela] = de + aquela, → **aquela**.

daquele [da'keli] = de + aquele, → **de**.

daqui [da'ki] adv = de + aqui; (deste lugar) from here; (deste momento): ~ **a um ano/mês** in a year/month; **ele saiu ~ às nove** he left here at nine; ~ **a pouco** in a little while; ~ **em** OU **por diante** from now on.

daquilo [da'kilu] = de + aquilo, → **aquilo**.

dar ['da(x)] vt **1.** (entregar, presentear) to give; ~ **algo a alguém** to give sthg to sb, to give sthg to sb.

2. (produzir) to produce.

3. (causar, provocar) to give; **dá-me sono/pena** it makes me sleepy/sad; **isto vai ~ muito que fazer** this is going to be a lot of work; **só dá problemas** it's nothing but trouble.

4. (filme, programa): **deu no noticiário hoje** it was on the news today.

5. (exprime ação) to give; ~ **um berro** to give a cry; ~ **um pontapé em alguém** to kick sb; ~ **um passeio** to go for a walk.

6. (festa, concerto) to hold; **vão ~ uma festa** they're going to have OU throw a party.

7. (dizer) to say; **ele me deu boa-noite** he said good night to me.

8. (ensinar) to teach; **o que é que você está dando nas suas aulas?** what are you teaching (at the moment)?; **ela dá aula numa escola** she teaches at a school; **gostaria de ~ aulas de Inglês** I would like to teach English.

9. (aprender, estudar) to do; **o que é que estão dando em Inglês?** what are you doing in English (at the moment)?; **estamos dando o verbo "to be"** we're doing the verb "to be".

♦ *vi* 1. *(horas)*: **já deram cinco horas** the clock has struck five.

2. *(condizer)*: **~ com** to go with; **as cores não dão umas com as outras** the colours clash.

3. *(proporcionar)*: **~ de beber a alguém** to give sb something to drink; **~ de comer a alguém** to feed sb.

4. *(em locuções)*: **dá igual** OU **no mesmo** it doesn't matter.

❑ **dar com** *v + prep (encontrar, descobrir)* to meet; **dei com ele no cinema** I met him at the cinema.

❑ **dar em** *v + prep (resultar)*: **a discussão não vai ~ em nada** the discussion will come to nothing.

❑ **dar para** *v + prep (servir para, ser útil para)* to be good for; *(suj: varanda, janela)* to look onto; *(suj: porta)* to lead to; *(ser suficiente para)* to be enough for; *(ser possível)* to be possible; **dá para você fazer isso hoje?** could you do it today?; **dá para ir a pé?** is it within walking distance?; **não vai ~ para eu chegar a horas** I won't be able to get there on time.

❑ **dar por** *v + prep (aperceber-se de)* to notice.

❑ **dar-se** *vp*: **~-se bem/mal com alguém** to get on well/badly with sb; **não me dou bem com condimentos** spices don't agree with me; **deu-se mal com a brincadeira** his plan backfired; **~-se por vencido** to give in.

dardo ['daxdu] *m (arma)* spear; *(ESP)* javelin.

❑ **dardos** *mpl* darts *(sg)*; **jogar ~s** to play darts.

das [daʃ] = de + as, → **Je**.

data ['data] *f* date; **~ de nascimento** date of birth.

datilografar [datʃilografa'fa(x)] *vt (Br)* to type.

datilógrafo, -fa [datʃi'lografu, -fa] *m, f (Br)* typist.

d.C. *(abrev de depois de Cristo)* AD.

de [dʒi] *prep* 1. *(indica posse)* of; **o lápis do Mário** Mário's pencil; **o carro daquele homem** that man's car; **a recepção do hotel** the hotel reception; **a casa é dela** it's her house.

2. *(indica matéria)* (made) of; **um bolo ~ chocolate** a chocolate cake; **um reló-** gio **~ ouro** a gold watch.

3. *(indica conteúdo)* of; **um copo ~ água** a glass of water.

4. *(usado em descrições, determinações)*: **uma camisola ~ manga curta** a short-sleeved T-shirt; **uma nota ~ 50 reais** a 50-real note; **o senhor ~ preto** the man in black.

5. *(indica assunto)* about; **fale da viagem** tell me about the trip; **um livro ~ informática** a book about OU on computers; **um livro ~ geografia** a geography book.

6. *(indica origem)* from; **sou ~ Coimbra** I'm from Coimbra; **os habitantes do bairro** the locals; **um produto do Brasil** a Brazilian product.

7. *(indica tempo)*: **o jornal das nove** the nine o'clock news; **partimos às três da tarde** we left at three in the afternoon; **trabalho das nove às cinco** I work from nine to five.

8. *(indica uso)*: **a sala ~ espera** the waiting room; **uma máquina ~ calcular** a calculator; **a porta ~ entrada** the front door.

9. *(usado em denominações, nomes)* of.

10. *(indica causa, modo)*: **chorar ~ alegria** to cry with joy; **está tudo ~ pernas para o ar** everything is upside down; **morrer ~ frio** to freeze to death; **viajou ~ carro** he travelled by car.

11. *(indica autor)* by; **um filme ~ Cacá Diegues** a film by Cacá Diegues; **o último livro ~ Érico Veríssimo** Érico Veríssimo's latest book.

12. *(introduz um complemento)*: **cheio ~ gente** full of people; **desconfiar ~ alguém** to distrust sb; **difícil ~ esquecer** hard to forget; **gostar ~ algo/alguém** to like sthg/sb.

13. *(em comparações)*: **do que** than; **é mais rápido do que este** it's faster than this one.

14. *(em superlativos)* of; **o melhor ~ todos** the best of all.

15. *(dentre)* of; **uma daquelas cadeiras** one of those chairs; **um dia destes** one of these days; **um desses hotéis serve** any one of those hotels will do.

16. *(indica série)*: **~ dois em dois dias** every two days; **~ quinze em quinze minutos** every fifteen minutes; **~ três em três metros** every three metres.

debaixo [deˈbajʃu] *adv* underneath; ~ de under.

debate [deˈbatʃi] *m* debate.

debater [debaˈte(x)] *vt* to debate.

⏌ **debater-se** *vp* to struggle.

débil [ˈdɛbiw] (*pl* **-beis** [-bejʃ]) *adj* weak ♦ *mf*: ~ **mental** mentally handicapped person.

debitar [debiˈta(x)] *vt* to debit.

débito [ˈdɛbitu] *m* debit; *(de rio)* volume.

debruçar-se [debruˈsaxsi] *vp* to lean over; ~ **sobre algo** *(problema, questão)* to look into sthg.

década [ˈdɛkada] *f* decade; **na ~ de oitenta/noventa** in the 80s/90s.

decadência [dekaˈdẽsja] *f* decadence.

decadente [dekaˈdẽtʃi] *adj* decadent.

decapitar [dekapiˈta(x)] *vt* to behead.

decência [deˈsẽsja] *f* decency.

decente [deˈsẽtʃi] *adj* decent.

decepar [deseˈpa(x)] *vt* to cut off.

decepção [deseˈsãw] (*pl* **-ões** [-õjʃ]) *f* disappointment.

decidido, -da [desiˈdʒidu, -da] *adj* *(pessoa)* determined; *(resolvido)* settled.

decidir [desiˈdʒi(x)] *vt* to decide; ~ **fazer algo** to decide to do sthg.

⏌ **decidir-se** *vp* to make up one's mind; ~**-se a fazer algo** to make up one's mind to do sthg.

decifrar [desiˈfra(x)] *vt* to decipher.

decimal [desiˈmaw] (*pl* **-ais** [-ajʃ]) *adj* decimal.

décimo, -ma [ˈdɛsimu, -ma] *num* tenth ♦ *m* *(em loteria)* tenth share of a lottery ticket, → **sexto**.

decisão [desiˈzãw] (*pl* **-ões** [-õjʃ]) *f* *(resolução)* decision.

declamar [deklaˈma(x)] *vt & vi* to recite.

declaração [deklaraˈsãw] (*pl* **-ões** [-õjʃ]) *f* statement; *(de amor)* declaration; ~ **amigável (de acidente automóvel)** *jointly agreed insurance statement made by drivers after an accident.*

declarar [deklaˈra(x)] *vt* to declare; **"nada a ~"** "nothing to declare".

⏌ **declarar-se** *vp (confessar sentimentos)* to declare one's love; *(manifestar-se)* to express an opinion.

declínio [deˈklinju] *m* decline.

declive [deˈklivi] *m* slope.

decolagem [dekoˈlaʒẽ] *f (Br) (de* avião) takeoff.

decomposição [dekõmpoziˈsãw] (*pl* **-ões** [-õjʃ]) *f* decomposition.

decoração [dekoraˈsãw] (*pl* **-ões** [-õjʃ]) *f* decoration.

decorar [dekoˈra(x)] *vt (ornamentar)* to decorate; *(memorizar)* to memorize.

decorativo, -va [dekoraˈtʃivu, -va] *adj* decorative.

decorrente [dekoˈxẽtʃi] *adj* resulting; ~ **de** resulting from.

decote [deˈkɔtʃi] *m* neckline; ~ **em bico** OU **em V** V-neck; ~ **redondo** round neck.

decrescer [dekreˈse(x)] *vi* to decrease.

decretar [dekreˈta(x)] *vt* to decree.

decreto [deˈkretu] *m* decree.

decreto-lei [deˌkretuˈlej] (*pl* **decretos-lei** [deˌkretuʒˈlej]) *m* *law issued by the Government which overrules any existing legislation.*

decurso [deˈkursu] *m*: **no ~ de** in the course of.

dedal [deˈdaw] (*pl* **-ais** [-ajʃ]) *m* thimble.

dedão [deˈdãw] (*pl* **-ões** [-õjʃ]) *m (Br) (de mão)* thumb; *(de pé)* big toe.

dedicação [dedʒikaˈsãw] (*pl* **-ões** [-õjʃ]) *f* dedication.

dedicar [dedʒiˈka(x)] *vt (livro, música, obra)* to dedicate; *(tempo, atenção, energias)* to devote.

⏌ **dedicar-se a** *vp + prep* to devote o.s. to; **a que se dedica?** what do you do?

dedo [ˈdedu] *m (de mão)* finger; *(de pé)* toe; *(medida)* inch; **levantar o ~** to put one's hand up.

dedões → **dedão**.

dedução [deduˈsãw] (*pl* **-ões** [-õjʃ]) *f* deduction.

deduzir [deduˈzi(x)] *vt (descontar)* to deduct; *(concluir)* to deduce.

defeito [deˈfejtu] *m* defect.

defeituoso, -osa [defejˈtwozu, -ɔza] *adj (produto)* defective.

defender [defẽˈde(x)] *vt* to defend.

⏌ **defender-se** *vp* to defend o.s.; ~**-se de** to defend o.s. against.

defensor, -ra [defẽˈso(x), -ra] (*mpl* **-res** [-riʃ], *fpl* **-s** [-ʃ]) *m, f* defender.

deferimento [deferiˈmẽtu] *m* approval; **"pede ~"** *expression used at the end of any formal letter of request sent to an institution or government office asking them to grant a request.*

defesa [de'feza] *f* defence; *(de tese)* viva voce *(oral exam taken to support one's thesis at university)*.

défice ['dɛfisi] *m* deficit.

deficiência [defi'sjẽsja] *f* deficiency; *(física)* handicap.

deficiente [defi'sjẽntʃi] *adj* deficient ♦ *mf* handicapped person; **~ físico** physically handicapped person; **~ mental** mentally handicapped person; **~ motor** *person with a motor neurone disease.*

definição [defini'sãw] *(pl* **-ões** [-õjʃ]) *f* definition.

definir [defi'ni(x)] *vt (palavra, sentido)* to define; *(estratégia, plano, regras)* to set out.

⃞ **definir-se** *vp* to make one's mind up.

definitivamente [definitʃiva-'mẽtʃi] *adv (para sempre)* for good; *(sem dúvida)* definitely.

definitivo, -va [definiˈtʃivu, -va] *adj (decisão, resposta)* final; *(separação, mudança)* permanent.

deformação [defoxma'sãw] *(pl* **-ões** [-õjʃ]) *f (de corpo)* deformity; *(de forma, realidade)* distortion.

deformar [defox'ma(x)] *vt (corpo)* to deform; *(forma, imagem, realidade)* to distort.

defrontar [defrõ'ta(x)] *vt* to confront.

defronte [deˈfrõtʃi] *adv* opposite; **~ de** opposite.

defumado, -da [defu'madu, -da] *adj* smoked.

defumar [defu'ma(x)] *vt* to smoke.

degelo [de'ʒelu] *m* thaw.

degolar [dego'la(x)] *vt* to behead.

degradante [degra'dãtʃi] *adj* degrading.

degradar [degra'da(x)] *vt* to degrade.

⃞ **degradar-se** *vp (saúde, relações)* to deteriorate; *(humilhar-se)* to demean o.s.

degrau [deˈgraw] *m* step.

degustação [deguʃta'sãw] *f* tasting.

degustar [deguʃ'ta(x)] *vt* to taste.

dei ['dej] → **dar.**

deitar [dej'ta(x)] *vt (estender)* to lay (down); *(em cama)* to put to bed; **~ abaixo** to knock down; **~ fora algo** *(Port: pôr no lixo)* to throw sthg away OU out; **~ fora** *(Port) (verter)* to spill over; *(vomitar)* to throw up.

⃞ **deitar-se** *vp (na cama)* to go to bed; *(no chão)* to lie down.

deixa ['dejʃa] *f* cue.

deixar [dej'ʃa(x)] *vt* leave; *(permitir)* to allow, to let; *(vício, estudos)* to give up ♦ *vi:* **~ de fazer algo** to stop doing sthg; **não ~ de fazer algo** to be sure to do sthg; **deixa que eu acabe isto** let me finish this; **você deixou a cama por fazer** you didn't make the bed; **~ alguém fazer algo** to let sb do sthg; **~ algo para** to leave sthg for; **~ algo de lado** to put sthg aside; **~ algo/alguém em paz** to leave sthg/sb alone; **~ algo/alguém para trás** to leave sthg/sb behind; **~ cair** to drop.

⃞ **deixar-se** *vp:* **~-se levar por** to get carried away with; **deixa de brincadeiras!** stop fooling around!; **ela não se deixou enganar** she wasn't to be fooled; **~ de fazer algo** to stop doing sthg.

dela ['dɛla] = **de + ela,** → **de.**

dele ['deli] = **de + ele,** → **de.**

delegacia [delega'sia] *f (Br)* police station.

delegado, -da [dele'gadu, -da] *m, f (Br: de polícia)* police superintendent *(Brit)*, police captain *(Am)*; *(de turma)* form captain; *(de país, governo, instituição)* delegate.

deleitar [delej'ta(x)] *vt* to delight.

⃞ **deleitar-se com** *vp + prep* to delight in.

delgado, -da [dew'gadu, -da] *adj (pessoa)* slim; *(fio, corda, pau, barra)* thin.

deliberação [delibera'sãw] *(pl* **-ões** [-õjʃ]) *f* decision.

deliberar [delibe'ra(x)] *vt* to decide on ♦ *vi* to deliberate.

delicadeza [delika'deza] *f* delicacy; *(cortesia)* courtesy; *(cuidado)* care.

delícia [de'lisja] *f (sensação)* pleasure; *(manjar)* delicacy; **que ~!** how lovely!

delicioso, -osa [deli'sjozu, -ɔza] *adj* delicious.

delinear [deli'nja(x)] *vt* to outline.

delinquência [delĩ'kwẽsja] *f (Port)* = **delinqüência.**

delinqüência [delĩ'kwẽsja] *f (Br)* delinquency; **~ juvenil** juvenile delinquency.

delinqüente [delĩ'kwẽtʃi] *mf* delinquent.

delirante [deli'rãtʃi] *adj (fig: incrível)* amazing.

delirar [deli'ra(x)] *vi* to be delirious.

delírio [de'lirju] *m* (*MED*) delirium; (*fig: excitação*) excitement.

delito [de'litu] *m* crime.

demais [de'majʃ] *adv* (*com verbos*) too much; (*com adjectivos*) too ♦ *pron:* **os/as ~** the rest; **isto já é ~!** this really is too much!; **ser ~** (*ser o máximo*) to be brilliant.

demasia [dema'zia] : **em demasia** *adv* too much.

demasiado, -da [dema'zjadu, -da] *adj* (*com substantivos singulares*) too much; (*com substantivos plurais*) too many ♦ *adv* (*com verbos*) too much; (*com adjectivos*) too.

demência [de'mẽsja] *f* dementia.

demente [de'mẽntʃi] *adj* insane.

demissão [demi'sãw] (*pl* **-ões** [-õjʃ]) *f* (*involuntária*) dismissal; (*voluntária*) resignation; **pedir ~** to resign.

demitir [demi'tʃi(x)] *vt* to dismiss.

❏ **demitir-se** *vp* to resign.

democracia [demokra'sia] *f* democracy.

democrata [demo'krata] *mf* democrat ♦ *adj* democratic.

democrático, -ca [demo'kratʃiku, -ka] *adj* democratic.

demolição [demoli'sãw] (*pl* **-ões** [-õjʃ]) *f* demolition.

demolir [demo'li(x)] *vt* to demolish.

demónio [de'mɔnju] *m* (*Port*) = **demônio**.

demônio [de'mɔnju] *m* (*Br*) devil.

demonstração [demõʃtra'sãw] (*pl* **-ões** [-õjʃ]) *f* demonstration; (*prova*) display.

demonstrar [demõʃ'tra(x)] *vt* to demonstrate; (*revelar*) to show.

demora [de'mɔra] *f* delay; **sem ~** without delay.

demorado, -da [demo'radu, -da] *adj* (*longo*) lengthy; (*lento*) slow.

demorar [demo'ra(x)] *vi* to take time ♦ *vt* (*tardar*) to take; (*atrasar*) to detain; **vai ~ muito?** will it take long?

❏ **demorar-se** *vp* to take too long; **demorei-me por causa do trânsito** I got held up in the traffic.

dendê [dẽ'de] *m* palm oil.

denegrir [dene'gri(x)] *vt* (*fig: manchar*) to blacken.

dengue ['dẽgi] *f* dengue fever; **~ hemorrágica** chronic dengue fever.

denominação [denomina'sãw] (*pl* **-ões** [-õjʃ]) *f* denomination.

denotar [deno'ta(x)] *vt* to show.

densidade [dẽsi'dadʒi] *f* density.

denso, -sa ['dẽsu, -sa] *adj* dense.

dentada [dẽ'tada] *f* bite.

dentadura [dẽta'dura] *f* (*natural*) teeth (*pl*); (*postiça*) dentures (*pl*).

dente ['dẽntʃi] *m* tooth; (*de elefante, elefante marinho*) tusk; (*de garfo, ancinho*) prong; **~ de alho** clove of garlic; **~ do siso** wisdom tooth; **~s postiços** false teeth.

dentífrico, -ca [dẽ'tʃifriku, -ka] *adj* tooth (*antes de s*) ♦ *m* toothpaste.

dentista [dẽ'tʃiʃta] *mf* dentist.

dentre ['dẽntri] = **de** + **entre**, → **entre**.

dentro ['dẽntru] *adv* (*no interior*) in, inside; **~ de** (*relativo a espaço físico*) in, inside; (*relativo a espaço temporal*) in, within; **~ em pouco** OU **em breve** soon; **aqui ~** in here; **lá ~** inside; **por ~** inside; **por ~ de** on the inside of; **estar por ~ de algo** to be in the know about sthg.

denúncia [de'nũsja] *f* (*revelação*) exposure; (*acusação*) accusation.

denunciar [denũ'sja(x)] *vt* to report.

deparar [depa'ra(x)] : **deparar com** *v* + *prep* (*encontrar*) to come across; (*enfrentar*) to come up against.

❏ **deparar-se** *vp* (*surgir*) to arise.

departamento [departa'mẽntu] *m* department.

dependência [depẽ'dẽsja] *f* (*de casa*) room; (*de vício, droga*) dependency; (*de chefe, pai, mãe*) dependence.

dependente [depẽ'dẽntʃi] *adj* dependent.

depender [depẽ'de(x)] *vi*: **depende ... it depends ....**

❏ **depender de** *v* + *prep* (*de droga, pai, mãe*) to be dependent on; (*de circunstâncias, tempo, dinheiro*) to depend on.

depilar [depi'la(x)] *vt* to remove hair from; (*com cera*) to wax.

depilatório, -ria [depila'tɔrju, -rja] *adj* hair-removing ♦ *m* depilatory.

depoimento [depoj'mẽntu] *m* (*em esquadra*) statement; **prestar ~** to give evidence.

depois [de'pojʃ] *adv* (*relativo a espaço*) after; (*relativo a tempo*) afterwards; **~ se vê!** we'll see!; **e ~?** so?; **a sobremesa fica para ~** we'll leave the dessert for later; **deixar algo para ~** to leave sthg for later; **dias/semanas/anos ~** days/weeks/years later; **~ de amanhã** the day after tomorrow; **~ de** after; **~ que** since; **logo ~** straight afterwards.

depor [de'po(x)] *vi (JUR)* to give evidence ♦ *vt (governo, ministro)* to overthrow.

depositar [depozi'ta(x)] *vt* to pay in; **~ confiança em alguém** to place one's trust in sb.
⏌ **depositar-se** *vp* to settle.

depósito [de'pozitu] *m (em banco)* deposit; *(armazém)* warehouse; *(reservatório)* tank; *(sedimento)* sediment; ; **~ de bagagens** *(Br)* left-luggage office *(Brit)*, baggage room *(Am)*; **~ de gasolina** *(Port: de veículo)* petrol tank.

depravação [deprava'sãw] *(pl -ões* [-õjʃ]) *f* depravity.

depreciação [depresja'sãw] *(pl -ões* [-õjʃ]) *f* depreciation.

depressa [de'presa] *adv* quickly ♦ *interj* hurry up!; **anda ~ com isso!** hurry up with that!

depressão [depre'sãw] *(pl -ões* [-õjʃ]) *f* depression; **~ econômica** (economic) depression.

deprimente [depri'mẽntʃi] *adj* depressing.

deprimir [depri'mi(x)] *vt* to depress.

deputado, -da [depu'tadu, -da] *m, f* deputy.

deriva [de'riva] *f:* **ir à ~** to drift; **estar à ~** to be adrift.

derivar [deri'va(x)] *vi* to drift.
⏌ **derivar de** *v + prep (palavra, termo)* to derive from; *(produto)* to be made from; *(problema)* to stem from.

dermatologista [dermatolo'ʒiʃta] *mf* dermatologist.

derramamento [dexama'mẽntu] *m (de líquido)* spillage; *(de lágrimas, sangue)* shedding.

derramar [dexa'ma(x)] *vt (líquido)* to spill; *(lágrimas, sangue)* to shed; *(farinha, feijão)* to drop.

derrame [de'xami] *m (MED)* hemorrhage.

derrapagem [dexa'paʒẽ] *(pl -ns* [-ʃ]) *f* skid.

derrapar [dexa'pa(x)] *vi* to skid.

derreter [dexe'te(x)] *vt* to melt.
⏌ **derreter-se** *vp* to melt.

derrota [de'xɔta] *f* defeat.

derrotar [dexo'ta(x)] *vt* to defeat.

derrubar [dexu'ba(x)] *vt (objecto, pessoa)* to knock over; *(casa)* to knock down; *(árvore)* to cut down; *(fig: governo, sistema)* to overthrow.

desabafar [dʒizaba'fa(x)] *vi* to get it off one's chest.

desabamento [dʒizaba'mẽntu] *m (de terra, pedras)* landslide; *(de edifício)* collapse.

desabar [dʒiza'ba(x)] *vi* to collapse.

desabitado, -da [dʒizabi'tadu, -da] *adj* unoccupied.

desabotoar [dʒizabo'twa(x)] *vt* to unbutton.

desabrigado, -da [dʒizabri'gadu, -da] *adj (sem casa, lar)* homeless; *(exposto ao tempo)* exposed.

desabrochar [dʒizabro'ʃa(x)] *vi* to open.

desacompanhado, -da [dʒizakõmpa'ɲadu, -da] *adj* unaccompanied.

desaconselhar [dʒizakõse'ʎa(x)] *vt:* **~ algo (a alguém)** to advise (sb) against sthg.

desaconselhável [dʒizakõse'ʎavew] *(pl -eis* [-ejʃ]) *adj* inadvisable.

desacordado, -da [dʒizakor'dadu, -da] *adj* unconscious.

desacostumado, -da [dʒizakoʃtu'madu, -da] *adj* unaccustomed.

desacreditar [dʒizakredi'ta(x)] *vt* to discredit.
⏌ **desacreditar-se** *vp* to be discredited.

desactualizado, -da [dezatwali'zadu, -da] *adj (Port)* = **desatualizado**.

desafinado, -da [dʒizafi'nadu, -da] *adj (instrumento)* out of tune; *(voz)* tuneless.

desafinar [dʒizafi'na(x)] *vi* to be out of tune.

desafio [dʒiza'fiu] *m* challenge; *(Port: de futebol, basquetebol, etc)* match.

desafortunado, -da [dʒizafoxtu'nadu, -da] *adj* unlucky.

desagradar [dʒizagra'da(x)] : **desagradar a** *v + prep* to displease.

desaguar [dʒiza'gwa(x)] *vi:* **~ em** to flow into.

desajeitado, -da [dʒizaʒej'tadu, -da] *adj* clumsy.

desalinhado, -da [dʒizali'ɲadu, -da] *adj* untidy.

desalinho [dʒiza'liɲu] *m (em forma de vestir)* sloppiness; *(desordem)* untidiness; **em ~** in disarray.

desalojar [dʒizaloˈʒa(x)] *vt* to evict.

desamarrar [dʒizamaˈxa(x)] *vt* to untie.

desamparado, -da [dezãmpaˈradu. -da] *adj* abandoned.

desamparar [dʒizãmpaˈra(x)] *vt* to abandon.

desanimado, -da [dʒizaniˈmadu. -da] *adj* down.

desanimar [dʒizaniˈma(x)] *vt* to discourage ◆ *vi* to lose heart.

desânimo [dʒiˈzanimu] *m* dejection.

desanuviar [dʒizanuˈvja(x)] *vt (fig) (cabeça)* to clear; *(espírito)* to lift ◆ *vi (céu)* to clear; *(fig: espairecer)* to unwind.

desaparafusar [dʒizaparafuˈza(x)] *vt* to unscrew.

desaparecer [dʒizapareˈse(x)] *vi* to disappear.

desaparecido, -da [dʒizapareˈsidu. -da] *adj* missing ◆ *m, f* missing person.

desaparecimento [dʒizaparesiˈmẽtu] *m* disappearance.

desapertar [dʒizaperˈta(x)] *vt* to undo.

desapontado, -da [dʒizapõˈtadu. -da] *adj* disappointed.

desapontamento [dʒizapõtaˈmẽtu] *m* disappointment.

desapontar [dʒizapõˈta(x)] *vt* to disappoint.

desarmamento [dʒizaxmaˈmẽtu] *m* disarmament.

desarmar [dʒizaxˈma(x)] *vt* to disarm; *(barraca, cama, estante)* to dismantle.

desarranjado, -da [dʒizaxãˈʒadu. -da] *adj* dishevelled.

desarranjar [dʒizaxãˈʒa(x)] *vt* to mess up.

desarrumado, -da [dʒizaxuˈmadu. -da] *adj* untidy.

desarrumar [dʒizaxuˈma(x)] *vt* to mess up.

desarticulado, -da [dʒizaxtʃikuˈladu. -da] *adj* dislocated.

desassossego [dʒizasoˈsegu] *m* disquiet.

desastrado, -da [dʒizaʃˈtradu. -da] *adj* clumsy.

desastre [dʒiˈzaʃtri] *m (de automóvel)* accident, crash; *(desgraça)* disaster.

desatar [dʒizaˈta(x)] *vt* to untie ◆ *vi:* **~ a fazer algo** to start doing sthg; **~ a**

rir/chorar to burst out laughing/crying.

desatento, -ta [dʒizaˈtẽtu. -ta] *adj* distracted.

desatino [dʒizaˈtinu] *m (fam: chatice)* hassle.

desatualizado, -da [dʒizatwaliˈzadu. -da] *adj (Br) (máquina, livro, sistema)* outdated; *(pessoa)* out of touch.

desavença [dʒizaˈvẽsa] *f* quarrel.

desavergonhado, -da [dʒizavexgoˈɲadu. -da] *adj* cheeky ◆ *m, f* shameless person.

desbaratar [dʒiʒbaraˈta(x)] *vt* to squander.

desbastar [dʒiʒbaʃˈta(x)] *vt (cabelo)* to thin (out).

desbotado, -da [dʒiʒboˈtadu. -da] *adj* faded.

desbotar [dʒiʒboˈta(x)] *vt & vi* to fade.

desbravar [dʒiʒbraˈva(x)] *vt* to clear.

descabido, -da [dʒiʃkaˈbidu. -da] *adj* inappropriate.

descafeinado, -da [dʒiʃkafejˈnadu. -da] *adj* decaffeinated ◆ *m* decaffeinated coffee.

descalçar [dʒiʃkawˈsa(x)] *vt* to take off.

descalço, -ça [dʒiʃˈkawsu. -sa] *pp →* **descalçar** ◆ *adj* barefoot.

descampado, -da [dʒiʃkãmˈpadu. -da] *adj* exposed ◆ *m* open ground.

descansado, -da [dʒiʃkãˈsadu. -da] *adj* carefree; **fique ~!** don't worry!

descansar [dʒiʃkãˈsa(x)] *vi* to rest.

descanso [dʒiʃˈkãsu] *m* rest; *(Br: para prato)* place mat.

descapotável [deʃkapoˈtavɛl] *(pl* **-eis** [-ejʃ]) *adj (Port: carro)* convertible.

descarado, -da [dʒiʃkaˈradu. -da] *adj* cheeky.

descaramento [dʒiʃkaraˈmẽtu] *m* cheek(iness).

descarga [dʒiʃˈkaxga] *f (descarregamento)* unloading; *(de arma)* shot; *(Br: de vaso sanitário)* flush; **dar a ~** *(Br)* to flush the toilet; **~ elétrica** electrical discharge.

descarregar [dʒiʃkaxeˈga(x)] *vt (carga)* to unload; *(arma)* to fire; *(fig: raiva, frustração)* to vent.

◗ **descarregar-se** *vp (bateria, pilha)* to go flat.

descarrilamento [dʒiʃkaxilaˈmẽtu] *m* derailment.

descarrilar [dʒiʃkaxiˈla(x)] *vi* to be derailed.

descartar-se [dʒiʃkaxˈtaxsi] : **descartar-se de** *vp* + *prep* to get rid of.

descartável [dʒiʃkaxˈtavɛw] (*pl* **-eis**) *adj* disposable.

descascar [dʒiʃkaʃˈka(x)] *vt* (*fruta, batatas*) to peel; (*nozes*) to shell.

descendência [desẽˈdẽsja] *f* descendants (*pl*).

descendente [desẽˈdẽtʃi] *mf* descendant.

descender [desẽˈde(x)] : **descender de** *v* + *prep* to descend from.

descentralizar [dʒiʃsẽtraliˈza(x)] *vt* to decentralize.

descer [deˈse(x)] *vt* (*escadas, rua, montanha*) to go/come down; (*estore*) to lower ◆ *vi* (*temperatura, preço*) to go down; ~ (**de**) (*de muro, escada, mesa*) to go/come down (from); (*de cavalo*) to dismount (from); (*de carro*) to get out (of); (*de ônibus, trem*) to get off.

descida [deˈsida] *f* (*de rua, estrada*) slope; (*de avião*) descent; (*de preço, valor*) fall; "**~** **perigosa**" "steep descent".

descoberta [dʒiʃkoˈbɛxta] *f* (*descobrimento*) discovery; (*invento*) invention.

descobrimento [dʒiʃkobriˈmẽtu] *m* discovery.

⊃ **Descobrimentos** *mpl*: **os Descobrimentos** the Discoveries.

descobrir [dʒiʃkoˈbri(x)] *vt* to discover; (*destapar, desvendar*) to uncover.

descolagem [deʃkuˈlaʒẽ] (*pl* **-ns** [-ʃ]) *f* (*Port*) = **decolagem**.

descolar [deʃkuˈlar] *vt* (*selo, fita-cola, adesivo*) to remove.

descoloração [dʒiʃkoloraˈsãw] (*pl* **-ões** [-õjʃ]) *f* discoloration; **fazer uma ~** to have one's hair bleached.

descompor [dʒiʃkõmˈpo(x)] *vt* to reprimand.

descompostura [dʒiʃkõmpoʃˈtura] *f* reprimand; **passar uma ~ a alguém** to give sb a good talking to.

descomunal [dʒiʃkomuˈnaw] (*pl* **-ais** [-ajʃ]) *adj* huge.

desconcentrar [dʒiʃkõsẽˈtra(x)] *vt* to distract.

desconfiar [dʒiʃkõˈfja(x)] *vt*: ~ **que** to suspect (that).

⊿ **desconfiar de** *v* + *prep* (*não ter confiança em*) to distrust; (*suspeitar de*) to suspect.

desconfortável [dʒiʃkõforˈtavɛw] (*pl* **-eis** [-ejʃ]) *adj* uncomfortable.

desconforto [dʒiʃkõˈfortu] *m* discomfort.

descongelar [dʒiʃkõʒeˈla(x)] *vt* to defrost.

desconhecer [dʒiʃkoɲeˈse(x)] *vt*: **desconheço a resposta** I don't know the answer; **desconheço o seu paradeiro** I don't know where he is.

desconhecido, -da [dʒiʃkoɲeˈsidu, -da] *adj* unknown ◆ *m, f* stranger.

desconsolado, -da [dʒiʃkõsoˈladu, -da] *adj* (*triste*) disheartened; (*insípido*) insipid.

descontar [dʒiʃkõˈta(x)] *vt* (*deduzir*) to deduct; (*cheque*) to debit.

descontentamento [dʒiʃkõtẽtaˈmẽtu] *m* discontent.

desconto [dʒiʃˈkõtu] *m* discount.

descontraído, -da [dʒiʃkõtraˈidu, -da] *adj* relaxed.

descontrair [dʒiʃkõtraˈi(x)] *vt* to relax.

⊃ **descontrair-se** *vp* to relax.

descontrolado, -da [dʒiʃkõtroˈladu, -da] *adj* (*pessoa*) hysterical; (*máquina*) out of control.

descontrolar-se [deʃkõtruˈlaxsi] *vp* to lose control.

desconversar [dʒiʃkõvexˈsa(x)] *vi* to change the subject.

descortinar [dʒiʃkoxtʃiˈna(x)] *vt* to discover.

descoser [dʒiʃkoˈze(x)] *vt* to unstitch.

⊿ **descoser-se** *vp* to come apart at the seams.

descrever [dʒiʃkreˈve(x)] *vt* to describe.

descrição [dʒiʃkriˈsãw] (*pl* **-ões** [-õjʃ]) *f* description.

descuidado, -da [dʒiʃkuiˈdadu, -da] *adj* untidy.

descuidar [dʒiʃkuiˈda(x)] *vt* to neglect.

⊿ **descuidar-se** *vp* (*não ter cuidado*) to be careless.

descuido [dʒiʃˈkuidu] *m* (*imprudência*) carelessness.

desculpa [dʒiʃˈkuwpa] *f* excuse; **pedir ~ a alguém por algo** to apologize to sb for sthg.

desculpar [dʒiʃkuwˈpa(x)] *vt* to excuse; **desculpe! machuquei-o?** I'm sorry! did I hurt you?; **desculpe, pode me dizer as horas?** excuse me, do you have the time?

⊐ **desculpar-se** *vp (pedir desculpa)* to apologize; *(justificar-se)* to justify o.s.; **~-se com algo** to use sthg as an excuse.

desde ['deʒdʒi] *prep (relativamente a espaço, variedade)* from; *(relativamente a tempo)* since; **~ aí** since then; **~ que** *(relativo a tempo)* since; *(indica condição)* if.

desdém [deʒ'dẽ] *m* contempt.

desdenhar [deʒde'ɲa(x)] *vt* to scorn ♦ *vi:* **~ de** to scoff at.

desdentado, -da [dʒiʒdẽn'tadu, -da] *adj* toothless.

desdizer [dʒiʒdi'ze(x)] *vt* to contradict.

⊐ **desdizer-se** *vp* to go back on one's word.

desdobrar [dʒiʒdo'bra(x)] *vt (jornal, roupa, tecido)* to unfold; *(subdividir)* to divide up.

desejar [deze'ʒa(x)] *vt* to want; **o que é que você deseja?** what would you like?; **deseja mais alguma coisa?** would you like anything else?; **desejo-lhe boa sorte!** I wish you (good) luck!

desejo [de'zeʒu] *m (vontade)* wish; *(anseio)* desire.

deselegante [dʒizele'gãntʃi] *adj* inelegant.

desembaciar [dʒizẽmba'sja(x)] *vt* to clean.

desembaraçado, -da [dʒizẽmbara'sadu, -da] *adj (desenrascado)* resourceful; *(expedito)* prompt.

desembaraçar [dʒizẽmbara'sa(x)] *vt* to untangle.

⊐ **desembaraçar-se** *vp* to hurry up; **~-se de algo** to rid o.s. of sthg.

desembaraço [dʒizẽmba'rasu] *m* ease.

desembarcar [dʒizẽmbax'ka(x)] *vt (carga)* to unload ♦ *vi* to disembark.

desembarque [dʒizẽm'baxki] *m (de carga)* unloading; *(de passageiros)* disembarkation; **"desembarque"** *(Br: em aeroporto)* "arrivals".

desembocar [dʒizẽmbo'ka(x)] *vi:* **~ em** *(rio)* to flow into; *(rua, caminho)* to lead into.

desembolsar [dʒizẽmbow'sa(x)] *vt (fam: pagar)* to cough up.

desembrulhar [dʒizẽmbru'ʎa(x)] *vt*

to unwrap, to open.

desempatar [dezẽmpa'ta(x)] *vt* to decide (the winner of).

desempenhar [dʒizẽmpe'ɲa(x)] *vt* to carry out; *(papel em peça, filme)* to play.

desempenho [dʒizẽm'peɲu] *m* performance; *(de obrigação)* fulfilment.

desemperrar [dʒizẽmpe'xa(x)] *vt* to loosen.

desempregado, -da [dʒizẽmpre'gadu, -da] *m, f* unemployed person.

desemprego [dʒizẽm'pregu] *m* unemployment; **estar no ~** to be unemployed.

desencadear [dʒizẽŋka'dʒja(x)] *vt* to give rise to.

⊐ **desencadear-se** *v impess (tempestade)* to break.

desencaixar [dʒizẽŋkaj'ʃa(x)] *vt* to dislodge.

⊐ **desencaixar-se** *vp* to come apart.

desencaixotar [dʒizẽŋkajʃu'ta(x)] *vt* to unpack.

desencantar [dʒizẽŋkãn'ta(x)] *vt (fam: achar)* to unearth; *(desiludir)* to disillusion.

desencontrar-se [dʒizẽŋkõn'traxsi] *vp* to miss each other.

desencorajar [dʒizẽŋkora'ʒa(x)] *vt* to discourage.

desencostar [dʒizẽŋkoʃ'ta(x)] *vt* to move away.

⊐ **desencostar-se** *vp:* **~-se de** to move away from.

desenferrujar [dʒizẽfexu'ʒa(x)] *vt* to remove the rust from; *(fig: língua)* to brush up; *(fig: pernas)* to stretch.

desenfreado, -da [dʒizẽfri'adu, -da] *adj* unbridled.

desenganado, -da [dʒizẽŋga'nadu, -da] *adj (doente)* incurable.

desenganar [dʒizẽŋga'na(x)] *vt (doente)* to give no hope of recovery to; *(tirar as ilusões a)* to disillusion.

desengonçado, -da [dʒizẽŋgõ'sadu, -da] *adj (pessoa)* supple; *(objeto)* loose.

desenhar [deze'ɲa(x)] *vt* to draw.

⊐ **desenhar-se** *vp (aparecer)* to appear; *(esboçar-se)* to take shape.

desenho [de'zeɲu] *m* drawing; **~s animados** cartoons.

desenlace [dʒizẽ'lasi] *m (de filme, história)* ending; *(de evento)* outcome.

desenrolar [dʒizẽxo'la(x)] *vt* to unroll.

❐ **desenrolar-se** *vp (ocorrer)* to take place.

desentendido, -da [dʒizēntēn'dʒidu, -da] *adj*: **fazer-se de ~** to feign ignorance.

desenterrar [dʒizēnte'xa(x)] *vt* to dig up.

desentupir [dʒizēntu'pi(x)] *vt* to unblock.

desenvolver [dʒizēvow've(x)] *vt* to develop.

❐ **desenvolver-se** *vp* to develop.

desenvolvido, -da [dʒizēvow'vidu, -da] *adj* developed.

desenvolvimento [dʒizēvowvi'mēntu] *m* development; *(progresso)* progress; *(crescimento)* growth.

desequilibrar-se [dʒizekili'braxsi] *vp* to lose one's balance.

deserto, -ta [de'zɛxtu, -ta] *adj* deserted ◆ *m* desert.

desesperado, -da [dʒizeʃpe'radu, -da] *adj* desperate.

desesperar [dʒizeʃpe'ra(x)] *vt (levar ao desespero)* to drive to despair; *(encolerizar)* to infuriate ◆ *vi* to despair.

desfalecer [dʒiʃfale'se(x)] *vi* to faint.

desfavorável [dʒiʃfavo'ravew] *(pl -eis* [-ejʃ]) *adj* unfavourable.

desfazer [dʒiʃfa'ze(x)] *vt (costura, alinhavo, nó)* to undo; *(dúvida, engano)* to dispel; *(grupo)* to disperse; *(noivado)* to break off; *(contrato)* to dissolve; *(reduzir a polpa)* to mash (up).

❐ **desfazer-se** *vp* to disintegrate; **o vidro desfez-se em mil pedaços** the glass broke into a thousand pieces.

❐ **desfazer-se de** *vp + prep* to get rid of.

desfecho [dʒiʃ'feʃu] *m* outcome.

desfeita [dʒiʃ'fejta] *f* insult.

desfeito, -ta [dʒiʃ'fejtu, -ta] *adj (em polpa)* mashed; *(cama)* unmade; *(puzzle)* in pieces; *(fig: desfigurado)* disfigured; *(acordo, casamento)* broken.

desfiar [dʒiʃ'fja(x)] *vt (bacalhau)* to shred.

❐ **desfiar-se** *vp (tecido, camisola)* to fray.

desfigurar [dʒiʃfigu'ra(x)] *vt (feições de pessoa)* to disfigure; *(fig: verdade)* to distort.

desfiladeiro [dʒiʃfila'dejru] *m* gorge.

desfilar [dʒiʃfi'la(x)] *vi* to parade.

desfile [dʒiʃ'fili] *m* parade; **~ de moda** fashion show.

desforra [dʒiʃ'fɔxa] *f* revenge.

desfrutar [dʒiʃfru'ta(x)] : **desfrutar de** *v + prep (possuir)* to have; *(tirar proveito de)* to enjoy.

desgastante [dʒiʒgaʃ'tāntʃi] *adj* exhausting.

desgastar [dʒiʒgaʃ'ta(x)] *vt (gastar)* to wear away, to erode; *(fig: cansar)* to wear out.

❐ **desgastar-se** *vp (gastar-se)* to wear down.

desgostar [dʒiʒgoʃ'ta(x)] *vt* to upset.

❐ **desgostar a** *v + prep* to displease.

desgosto [dʒiʒ'goʃtu] *m (infelicidade)* misfortune; *(mágoa)* sorrow.

desgraça [dʒiʒ'grasa] *f* misfortune.

desgrenhado, -da [dʒiʒgre'ɲadu, -da] *adj* dishevelled.

desidratação [dezidrata'sāw] *(pl -ões* [-õjʃ]) *f* dehydration.

desidratado, -da [dʒizidra'tadu, -da] *adj* dehydrated.

desidratar [dʒizidra'ta(x)] *vt* to dehydrate.

❐ **desidratar-se** *vp* to become dehydrated.

design [de'zajni] *m* design.

designação [dezigna'sāw] *(pl -ões* [-õjʃ]) *f* designation.

designar [dezig'na(x)] *vt* to designate.

designer [de'zajne(x)] *mf* designer.

desiludir [dʒizilu'di(x)] *vt* to let down.

❐ **desiludir-se com** *vp + prep* to become disillusioned with.

desilusão [dʒizilu'zāw] *(pl -ões* [-õjʃ]) *f* disillusion.

desimpedido, -da [dʒizīmpe'dʒidu, -da] *adj (linha de telefone)* free; *(rua, trânsito)* clear.

desimpedir [dʒizīmpe'dʒi(x)] *vt* to clear.

desinchar [dʒizī'ʃa(x)] *vi* to go down.

desinfetante [dʒizīfe'tāntʃi] *adj & m* disinfectant; **~ para a boca** mouthwash.

desinfectar [dezīfe'tar] *vt (Port)* = **desinfetar**.

desinfetar [dʒizīfe'ta(x)] *vt (Br)* to disinfect.

desinibido, -da [dʒizini'bidu, -da] *adj* uninhibited.

desintegrar-se [dʒizīnte'graxsi] *vp* to disintegrate.

desinteressado, -da [dʒizīntere-

'sadu, -da] *adj* uninterested; *(altruísta)* unselfish.

desinteressar-se [dʒizĩntere'saxsi] : **desinteressar-se de** *vp + prep* to lose interest in.

desinteresse [dʒizĩnte'resi] *m* lack of interest; *(abnegação)* unselfishness.

desistência [dezif'tẽsja] *f* cancellation.

desistir [dezif't∫i(x)] *vi* to give up; ~ **de algo** *(de reserva, vôo)* to cancel sthg; ~ **de fazer algo** *(de fumar, correr, trabalhar)* to give up doing sthg.

desleal [dʒiʒ'ljaw] *(pl -ais* [-ajʃ]) *adj* disloyal.

desleixado, -da [dʒiʒlej'ʃadu, -da] *adj* slovenly.

desleixo [dʒiʒ'lejʃu] *m* carelessness.

desligado, -da [dʒiʒli'gadu, -da] *adj (aparelho)* switched off; *(telefone)* off the hook; *(fam: aéreo)* absent-minded.

desligar [dʒiʒli'ga(x)] *vt (rádio, TV)* to switch off; *(telefone)* to put down.

deslizar [dʒiʒli'za(x)] *vi* to slide.

deslize [dʒiʒ'lizi] *m (fig: lapso)* slip.

deslocado, -da [dʒiʒlo'kadu, -da] *adj* dislocated; *(desambientado)* out of place.

deslocar [dʒiʒlo'ka(x)] *vt* to dislocate; ⊐ **deslocar-se** *vp* to be put out of joint; **~-se para** to go to; **~-se com** to move with; **~-se de** to go from.

deslumbrante [dʒiʒlũm'brãntʃi] *adj* amazing.

deslumbrar [dʒiʒlũm'bra(x)] *vt* to dazzle.

desmaiado, -da [dʒiʒma'jadu, -da] *adj (desfalecido)* unconscious, *(desbotado)* faded.

desmaiar [dʒiʒma'ja(x)] *vi* to faint.

desmaio [dʒiʒ'maju] *m* faint.

desmamar [dʒiʒma'ma(x)] *vt* to wean.

desmancha-prazeres [dʒiʒ,mãʃapra'zerif] *mf inv* killjoy.

desmanchar [dʒiʒmã'ʃa(x)] *vt (desmontar)* to take apart; *(renda, costura)* to undo; *(noivado)* to break (off).
⊐ **desmanchar-se** *vp* to come apart.

desmarcar [dʒiʒmax'ka(x)] *vt (consulta, reserva)* to cancel.

desmedido, -da [dʒiʒme'dʒidu, -da] *adj* excessive.

desmentido [dʒiʒmẽn'tʃidu] *m* denial.

desmentir [dʒiʒmẽn'tʃi(x)] *vt (negar)* to deny; *(contradizer)* to contradict.

desmesurado, -da [dʒiʒmezu'radu, -da] *adj* excessive.

desmontar [dʒiʒmõn'ta(x)] *vt (máquina)* to dismantle; *(construção)* to take down; *(fig: intriga, combinação)* to uncover.

desmoralizar [dʒiʒmorali'za(x)] *vt (desanimar)* to demoralize; *(tirar o bom nome de)* to disparage.

desmoronamento [dʒiʒmorona'mẽntu] *m (de casa)* collapse; *(de terra)* landslide.

desmoronar [dʒiʒmoro'na(x)] *vt* to demolish.
⊃ **desmoronar-se** *vp* to collapse.

desnatado [dʒiʒna'tadu] *adj m* → **leite**.

desnecessário, -ria [dʒiʒnese'sarju, -rja] *adj* unnecessary.

desnível [dʒiʒ'nivew] *(pl -eis* [-ejʃ]) *m (de terreno)* unevenness; *(de valor)* gap.

desobedecer [dʒizobede'se(x)] : **desobedecer a** *v + prep* to disobey.

desobediência [dʒizobe'dʒjẽsja] *f* disobedience.

desobediente [dʒizobe'dʒẽntʃi] *adj* disobedient.

desobstruir [dʒizobftru'i(x)] *vt* to unblock.

desocupado, -da [dʒizoku'padu, -da] *adj* free; *(casa, apartamento)* unoccupied.

desocupar [dʒizoku'pa(x)] *vt* to vacate.

desodorante [dʒizodo'rãtʃi] *adj (Br)* deodorant *(antes de s)* ◆ *m (Br)* deodorant.

desodorizante [dezoduri'zãnte] *adj & m (Port)* = **desodorante**.

desonesto, -ta [dʒizo'neʃtu, -ta] *adj* dishonest.

desordem [dʒi'zoxdẽ] *f* disorder; **em ~** *(quarto, papéis)* untidy.

desorganizado, -da [dʒizoxgani'zadu, -da] *adj* disorganized.

desorientação [dʒizorjẽnta'sãw] *f* disorientation.

desorientado, -da [dʒizorjẽn'tadu, -da] *adj* disorientated.

despachar [dʒiʃpa'ʃa(x)] *vt (bagagem, mercadorias, encomenda)* to send off.
⊐ **despachar-se** *vp (apressar-se)* to hurry (up).

despedida [dʒiʃpe'dʒida] *f* farewell.

despedir [dʒiʃpe'dʒi(x)] *vt* to fire.
⊐ **despedir-se** *vp (dizer adeus)* to say

goodbye; *(demitir-se)* to resign.
despejar [dʒiʃpeˈʒa(x)] *vt (líquido)* to empty (out); *(lixo)* to throw out; *(de casa, apartamento)* to evict.
despejo [dʒiʃˈpeʒu] *m (de casa, apartamento)* eviction.
⊔ **despejos** *mpl (lixo)* rubbish *(sg) (Brit)*, garbage *(sg) (Am)*.
despensa [dʒiʃˈpẽsa] *f* larder.
despenteado, -da [dʒiʃpẽnˈtʒjadu, -da] *adj* dishevelled.
despentear [dʒiʃpẽnˈtʒja(x)] *vt* to mess up.
⊔ **despentear-se** *vp* to mess up one's hair.
despercebido, -da [dʒiʃpexseˈbidu. -da] *adj* unnoticed; **fazer-se de ~** to pretend not to know; **passar ~** to go unnoticed.
desperdiçar [dʒiʃpexdʒiˈsa(x)] *vt* to waste.
desperdício [dʒiʃpexˈdʒisju] *m* waste.
⊔ **desperdícios** *mpl* scraps.
despertador [dʒiʃpextaˈdo(x)] *(pl* **-res** [-riʃ]) *m* alarm clock.
despertar [dʒiʃpexˈta(x)] *vt* to wake up; *(fig: estimular)* to arouse; *(fig: dar origem a)* to give rise to ◆ *vi (acordar)* to wake up.
despesa [dʒiʃˈpeza] *f* expense.
⊔ **despesas** *fpl (de empresa, organismo)* expenses.
despido, -da [dʒiʃˈpidu. -da] *adj* naked.
despir [dʒiʃˈpi(x)] *vt* to undress.
⊔ **despir-se** *vp* to get undressed.
desportista [deʃpurˈtiʃta] *mf (Port)* = esportista.
desportivo, -va [deʃpurˈtivu. -va] *adj (Port)* = esportivo.
desporto [deʃˈportu] *m (Port)* = esporte.
despregar [dʒiʃpreˈga(x)] *vt* to remove.
⊔ **despregar-se** *vp (soltar-se)* to come loose.
desprender [dʒiʃprẽnˈde(x)] *vt* to unfasten.
⊔ **desprender-se** *vp* to come unfastened.
despreocupado, -da [dʒiʃprioku-padu. -da] *adj* carefree.
desprevenido, -da [dʒiʃpreveˈnidu. -da] *adj* unprepared.
desprezar [dʒiʃpreˈza(x)] *vt* to scorn.

desproporcionado, -da [dʒiʃpro-poxsjoˈnadu. -da] *adj* disproportionate.
desqualificar [dʒiʃkwalifiˈka(x)] *vt* to disqualify.
desquitado, -da [dʒiʃkiˈtadu. -da] *adj (Br)* separated.
dessa [ˈdɛsa] = de + essa, → de.
desse [ˈdesi] = de + esse, → de.
desta [ˈdɛʃta] = de + esta, → de.
destacar [dʒiʃtaˈka(x)] *vt (separar)* to detach; *(enfatizar)* to emphasize.
⊔ **destacar-se** *vp (distinguir-se)* to stand out.
destacável [dʒiʃtaˈkavew] *(pl* **-eis** [-ejʃ]) *adj* detachable ◆ *m (de formulário)* tear-off slip; *(de revista, jornal)* supplement.
destapar [dʒiʃtaˈpa(x)] *vt* to uncover.
destaque [dʒiʃˈtaki] *m* prominence; **em ~** in focus.
deste [ˈdeʃtʃi] = de + este, → de.
destemido, -da [deʃteˈmidu. -da] *adj* fearless.
destilada [deʃtʃiˈlada] *adj f* → água.
destilar [deʃtʃiˈla(x)] *vt* to distil.
destinar [deʃtʃiˈna(x)] *vt*: **~ algo para** to earmark sthg for.
⊔ **destinar-se** *vp + prep (ter por fim)* to be aimed at; *(ser endereçado a)* to be addressed to.
destinatário, -ria [deʃtʃinaˈtarju. -rja] *m, f (de carta)* addressee; *(de mensagem)* recipient.
destino [deʃtʃinu] *m (de viagem)* destination; **o ~** *(fado)* destiny; **com ~ a Londres** *(vôo, trem)* to London.
destituir [deʃtʃiˈtwi(x)] *vt (demitir)* to dismiss.
destrancar [dʒiʃtrãnˈka(x)] *vt* to unlock.
destreza [deʃˈtreza] *f (agilidade)* deftness; *(habilidade)* dexterity.
destro, -tra [ˈdeʃtru. -tra] *adj* right-handed; *(ágil)* deft; *(hábil)* skilled.
destroços [dʒiʃˈtrɔsuʃ] *mpl* wreckage *(sg).*
destruição [dʒiʃtruiˈsãw] *f* destruction.
destruir [dʒiʃtruˈi(x)] *vt* to destroy.
desuso [dʒiˈzuzu] *m*: **cair em ~** to fall into disuse.
desvalorização [dʒiʒvalorizaˈsãw] *(pl* **-ões** [-õjʃ]) *f* devaluation.
desvalorizar [dʒiʒvaloriˈza(x)] *vt* to devalue.
⊔ **desvalorizar-se** *vp* to depreciate.

desvantagem [dʒiʒvãn'taʒẽ] (pl -ns [-ʃ]) f disadvantage.

desviar [dʒiʒ'vja(x)] vt to move; (dinheiro) to embezzle; (trânsito) to divert.

❑ **desviar-se** vp to get out of the way; ~-se de algo to move out of the way of sthg.

desvio [dʒiʒ'viu] m (estrada secundária) turn-off; (de caminho) diversion; (de dinheiro) embezzlement.

detalhe [de'taʎi] m detail.

detectar [dete'ta(x)] vt to detect.

detector [dete'to(x)] (pl -res [-riʃ]) m detector; ~ de incêndios smoke alarm; ~ de radiações Geiger counter.

detenção [detẽ'sãw] (pl -ões [-õjʃ]) f detention; (prisão) arrest.

deter [de'te(x)] vt (parar) to stop; (prender) to detain.

❑ **deter-se** vp (parar) to stop; (conter-se) to restrain o.s.

detergente [detex'ʒẽtʃi] m (para louça) washing-up liquid; (para roupa) detergent.

deterioração [deterjora'sãw] f deterioration.

deteriorar [deterjo'ra(x)] vt (danificar) to damage.

❑ **deteriorar-se** vp (estragar-se) to deteriorate.

determinação [determina'sãw] (pl -ões [-õjʃ]) f (força de vontade) determination; (cálculo) calculation; (resolução) decision; (ordem) order.

determinar [determi'na(x)] vt (calcular, decidir) to determine; (ordenar) to order.

detestar [deteʃ'ta(x)] vt to detest.

detrás [de'trajʃ] adv (relativo a espaço) behind; (relativo a tempo) afterwards; ~ de (relativo a tempo) after; (por) ~ de (pela retaguarda de) behind.

detritos [de'trituʃ] mpl debris (sg).

deturpar [detux'pa(x)] vt to distort.

deu ['dew] → dar.

deus, -sa [dewʃ, -za] (pl -ses [-ziʃ], fpl -s [-ʃ]) m, f god (f goddess).

❑ **Deus** m God.

devagar [dʒiva'ga(x)] adv slowly.

dever [de've(x)] (pl -res [-riʃ]) m duty
◆ vt: ~ algo a alguém to owe sb sthg; você deve lavar os dentes todos os dias you should brush your teeth every day; o trem deve estar atrasado the train must be late; ~ cívico civic duty.

❑ **deveres** mpl (trabalho de casa) homework (sg).

devidamente [de,vida'mẽtʃi] adv properly.

devido, -da [de'vidu, -da] adj (correto) proper; ~ a due to.

devolução [devolu'sãw] (pl -ões [-õjʃ]) f (de dinheiro, cheque) refund; (de objeto emprestado, compra) return.

devolver [devow've(x)] vt (dinheiro, cheque) to refund; (objeto emprestado, compra) to return.

devorar [devo'ra(x)] vt to devour.

dez ['dɛʒ] num ten, → seis.

dezanove [deza'nɔve] num (Port) = dezenove.

dezasseis [deza'sejʃ] num (Port) = dezesseis.

dezassete [deza'sete] num (Port) = dezessete.

dezembro [de'zẽbru] m December, → setembro.

dezena [de'zena] f (set of) ten.

dezenove [deze'nɔvi] num (Br) nineteen, → seis.

dezesseis [deze'sejʃ] num (Br) sixteen, → seis.

dezessete [deze'setʃi] num (Br) seventeen, → seis.

dezoito [de'zɔitu] num eighteen, → seis.

DF abrev (Br) = Distrito Federal.

dia ['dʒia] m day; bom ~! good morning!; já é de ~ it's morning already; do ~ of the day; qualquer ~ any day; no ~ seguinte the day after; no ~ vinte on the twentieth; por (cada) ~ per day; todos os ~s every day; um ~ destes one of these days; estar em ~ to be up-to-date; pôr-se em ~ to bring o.s. up-to-date; pôr algo em ~ to update sthg; ~ de anos (Port) birthday; o ~ a ~ daily life; ~ de folga day off; ~ Santo religious holiday; ~ de semana weekday; ~ de Todos-os-Santos All Saints' Day; ~ útil weekday.

diabetes [dʒia'bɛtʃiʃ] m diabetes.

diabético, -ca [dʒia'bɛtʃiku, -ka] adj & m, f diabetic.

diabo [dʒiabu] m devil; porque ~ ...? (fam) why the hell ...?

diafragma [dʒia'fragma] m diaphragm.

diagnóstico [dʒiag'nɔʃtʃiku] m diagnosis.

dialecto [dja'lɛtu] *m (Port)* = **dialeto**.
dialeto [dʒa'lɛtu] *m (Br)* dialect.
dialogar [dʒjalo'ga(x)] *vi* to talk.
diálogo ['dʒjalogu] *m* dialogue.
diamante [dʒja'mãntʃi] *m* diamond.
diâmetro ['dʒjametru] *m* diameter.
diante ['dʒjãntʃi] : **diante de** *prep (relativo a tempo)* before; *(relativo a espaço)* in front of; *(perante)* in the face of.
dianteira [dʒjãn'tejra] *f (frente)* front; *(liderança)* lead.
diapositivo [dʒjapozi'tivu] *m* slide.
diária ['dʒjarja] *f (de pensão, hotel)* daily rate.
diariamente [.dʒjarja'mẽntʃi] *adv* daily, every day.
diário, -ria ['dʒjarju, -rja] *adj* daily ◆ *m* diary.
diarreia [dʒja'xaja] *f (Port)* = **diarréia**.
diarréia [dʒja'xɛja] *f (Br)* diarrhoea.
dica ['dʒika] *f (fam)* hint.
dicionário [dʒisjo'narju] *m* dictionary; ~ **de bolso** pocket dictionary.
didáctico, -ca [di'datiku, -ka] *adj (Port)* = **didático**.
didático, -ca [dʒi'datʃiku, -ka] *adj (Br)* educational.
diesel ['dʒizɛw] *adj inv* diesel.
dieta ['dʒjɛta] *f* diet.
dietético, -ca [dʒjɛ'tɛtʃiku, -ka] *adj (produto)* dietetic.
difamar [dʒifa'ma(x)] *vt (verbalmente)* to slander; *(por escrito)* to libel.
diferença [dʒifɛ'rɛsa] *f* difference.
diferenciar [dʒifɛrẽ'sja(x)] *vt* to differentiate.
diferente [dʒifɛ'rẽntʃi] *adj* different.
difícil [di'fisiw] *(pl* **-ceis** [-sejʃ]) *adj* difficult.
dificuldade [dʒefikuw'dadʒi] *f* difficulty.
dificultar [dʒifikuw'ta(x)] *vt* to make difficult; *(funcionamento, progresso)* to hinder.
difundir [dʒifũn'di(x)] *vt (informação, notícia)* to spread; *(calor, luz)* to give off; *(programa de rádio)* to broadcast.
difusão [dʒifu'zãw] *f (de informação, notícia)* dissemination; *(de luz, calor)* diffusion; *(por televisão, rádio)* broadcasting.
digerir [dʒiʒe'ri(x)] *vt* to digest.
digestão [dʒiʒeʃ'tãw] *f* digestion.
digestivo, -va [dʒiʒeʃ'tʃivu, -va] *adj*

digestive ◆ *m* after-dinner drink.
digital [dʒiʒi'taw] *(pl* **-ais** [-ajʃ]) *adj* digital.
digitalizador [dʒiʒitaliza'do(x)] *(pl* **-res** [-riʃ]) *m* scanner.
digitar [dʒiʒi'ta(x)] *vt* to key in.
dígito ['dʒiʒitu] *m* digit.
dignidade [dʒigni'dadʒi] *f* dignity.
dilatar [dʒila'ta(x)] *vt* to expand; *(prazo)* to extend.
❑ **dilatar-se** *vp* to expand.
dilema [dʒi'lɛma] *m* dilemma.
diluir [dʒi'lwi(x)] *vt* to dilute.
dimensão [dʒimẽ'sãw] *(pl* **-ões** [-õjʃ]) *f* dimension.
diminuir [dʒimi'nwi(x)] *vi (em preço, número, força)* to decrease; *(em volume, quantidade)* to diminish ◆ *vt (reduzir)* to reduce.
diminutivo [dʒiminu'tʃivu] *m* diminutive.
Dinamarca [dʒina'marka] *f:* **a ~** Denmark.
dinamarquês, -esa [dʒinamar'keʃ, -eza] *(mpl* **-eses** [-eziʃ], *fpl* **-s** [-ʃ]) *adj & m* Danish ◆ *m, f* Dane.
dinâmico, -ca [dʒi'namiku, -ka] *adj* dynamic.
dinamismo [dʒina'miʒmu] *m* dynamism.
dinamite [dʒina'mitʃi] *f* dynamite.
dínamo [dʒinamu] *m* dynamo.
dinastia [dʒinaʃ'tʃia] *f* dynasty.
dinheiro [dʒi'nejru] *m* money; **ter ~** to have money; **~ miúdo** loose change; **~ trocado** change.
dinossauro [dʒino'sawru] *m* dinosaur.
dióspiro [dʒjɔʃpiru] *m* sharon fruit.
diploma [dʒi'ploma] *m* diploma.
dique ['dʒiki] *m* dike.
direção [dʒire'sãw] *(pl* **-ões** [-õjʃ]) *f (Br) (endereço)* address; *(de veículo)* steering; *(rumo)* direction; *(de empresa)* management.
direcção [dirɛ'sãw] *(pl* **-ões** [-õjʃ]) *f (Port)* = **direção**.
direções → direção.
directo, -ta [di'rɛtu, -ta] *adj (Port)* = **direto**.
direita [dʒi'rejta] *f:* **a ~** *(mão)* one's right hand; *(lado)* the right hand side; *(em política)* the Right; **conduza pela ~** drive on the right; **siga pela ~** keep right; **à ~ (de)** on the right (of); **virar à ~** to turn right; **ser de ~** *(POL)*

to be right-wing.

direito, -ta [dʒiˈrejtu, -ta] *adj (mão, perna, lado)* right; *(corte, linha)* straight; *(pessoa)* honest; *(justo)* fair ◆ *m (privilégio)* right; *(leis, curso)* law; *(taxa, imposto)* duty ◆ *adv (Br: correctamente)* properly; **ir ~ a** to go straight to; **ir ~ ao assunto** to get straight to the point; **pôr-se ~** to stand up straight; **sempre a ~** straight ahead; **os ~s humanos** human rights; **não há ~!** it's not fair!

direto, -ta [dʒiˈretu, -ta] *adj (Br)* direct; *(transmissão)* live.

diretor, -ra [dʒiˈreto(x), -ra] *(mpl -res* [-riʃ], *fpl -s* [-ʃ]) *m, f (de escola)* head; *(de empresa)* director.

dirigente [dʒiriˈʒẽtʃi] *mf* leader.

dirigir [dʒiriˈʒi(x)] *vt (empresa)* to run; *(filme, peça de teatro)* to direct; *(orquestra)* to conduct; *(projeto, equipe)* to head; *(Br: veículo)* to drive ◆ *vi (Br)* to drive; **~ algo a alguém** to address sthg to sb; **~ algo para algo** to point sthg towards sthg.

❏ **dirigir-se a** *vp + prep (pessoa)* to talk to; *(público, ouvintes)* to address, *(local)* to head for; **"este aviso dirige-se a todos os usuários"** "this is a public announcement".

❏ **dirigir-se para** *vp + prep* to head towards.

dirigível [dʒiriˈʒivɛw] *(pl -eis* [-ejʃ]) *m* airship.

discar [dʒiʃˈka(x)] *vt & vi* to dial.

disciplina [dʒiʃiˈplina] *f* discipline; *(EDUC: cadeira)* subject.

disco-jóquei [dʒiskoˈʒɔkej] *(pl disco-jóqueis* [dʒiskoˈʒɔkejʃ]) *mf* disc jockey.

disco [dʒiʃku] *m* record; *(INFORM)* disk; *(de telefone)* dial; *(em atletismo)* discus; **~ compacto** compact disc; **~ rígido** hard disk; **~ voador** flying saucer; **~s de algodão** cotton wool pads.

discordar [dʒiʃkoxˈda(x)] *vi* to disagree; **~ de alguém em algo** to disagree with sb about sthg.

discórdia [dʒiʃˈkɔrdʒja] *f* dissent; **semear a ~** to sow the seeds of dissent.

discoteca [dʒiʃkoˈtɛka] *f (para dançar)* (night)club; *(loja)* record shop *(Brit)*, record store *(Am)*; *(coleção)* record collection.

discreto, -ta [dʒiʃˈkrɛtu, -ta] *adj (pessoa)* discreet; *(roupa)* sensible.

discriminação [dʒiʃkriminaˈsãw] *f* discrimination.

discriminar [dʒiʃkrimiˈna(x)] *vt* to discriminate against.

discurso [dʒiʃˈkuxsu] *m* speech; **~ direto/indireto** direct/indirect speech.

discussão [dʒiʃkuˈsãw] *(pl -ões* [-õjʃ]) *f (debate)* discussion; *(briga)* argument.

discutir [dʒiʃkuˈti(x)] *vt (idéia, assunto)* to discuss ◆ *vi (brigar)* to argue.

disenteria [dʒizẽteˈria] *f* dysentery.

disfarçar [dʒiʃfaxˈsa(x)] *vt* to disguise ◆ *vi* to pretend.

❏ **disfarçar-se** *vp* to disguise o.s.; **~-se de** to dress up as.

disfarce [dʒiʃˈfaxsi] *m* disguise.

dislexia [dʒizlɛkˈsia] *f* dyslexia.

disléxico, -ca [dʒizˈlɛksiku, -ka] *adj & m, f* dyslexic.

disparador [dʒiʃparaˈdo(x)] *(pl -res* [-riʃ]) *m (de máquina fotográfica)* shutter release.

disparar [dʒiʃpaˈra(x)] *vt (arma, bala)* to shoot ◆ *vi (arma, máquina fotográfica)* to go off.

disparatado, -da [dʒiʃparaˈtadu, -da] *adj* foolish.

disparate [dʒiʃpaˈratʃi] *m* nonsense.

dispensar [dʒiʃpẽˈsa(x)] *vt* to do without; **~ alguém de algo** to excuse sb from sthg; **~ algo a alguém** to lend sthg to sb.

dispersar [dʒiʃpexˈsa(x)] *vt* to scatter ◆ *vi* to disperse.

❏ **dispersar-se** *vp* to disperse.

disperso, -sa [dʒiʃˈpexsu, -sa] *pp* → **dispersar**.

disponível [dʒiʃpoˈnivɛw] *(pl -eis* [-ejʃ]) *adj* available.

dispor [dʒiʃˈpo(x)] *vt (colocar)* to arrange.

❏ **dispor de** *v + prep* to have; *(de posição)* to hold.

❏ **dispor-se a** *vp + prep*: **~-se a fazer algo** to offer to do sthg.

dispositivo [dʒiʃpoziˈtivu] *m* device.

disposto, -osta [dʒiʃˈpoʃtu, -ɔʃta] *adj* ready; **estar ~ a fazer algo** to be prepared to do sthg; **estar bem ~** *(de bom humor)* to be in a good mood.

disputa [dʒiʃˈputa] *f (competição)* competition; *(discussão)* dispute.

disputar [dʒiʃpuˈta(x)] *vt (troféu, lugar)* to compete for.

disquete [dʒiʃˈkɛtʃi] *f* diskette.

dissimular [dʒisimuˈla(x)] *vt (fingir)* to hide; *(encobrir)* to cover up.

dissipar [dʒisi'pa(x)] vt (cheiro, fumo) to get rid of; (mal-entendido, confusão) to clear up.

⏍ **dissipar-se** vp to disappear.

disso ['dʒisu] = de + isso, → isso.

dissolver [dʒisow've(x)] vt to dissolve.

⏍ **dissolver-se** vp to dissolve.

dissuadir [dʒiswa'di(x)] vt to dissuade.

distância [dʒiʃ'tãsja] f distance; **a que ~ fica?** how far (away) is it?; **fica a um quilômetro de ~** it's one kilometre away; **à ~** from a distance.

distanciar [dʒiʃtã'sja(x)] vt (em espaço, tempo) to distance; (pessoas) to drive apart.

⏍ **distanciar-se** vp (em espaço) to move away; (pessoas) to grow apart; **~-se de** (em espaço) to move away from; (em idéias, atitudes, etc) to differ from.

distante [dʒiʃ'tãntʃi] adj distant.

distinção [dʒiʃtʃĩ'sãw] (pl -ões [-õjʃ]) f distinction.

distinguir [dʒiʃtʃĩŋ'gi(x)] vt (ver) to make out; (diferenciar) to distinguish.

⏍ **distinguir-se** vp (diferenciar-se) to differ; (em exame, trabalho, estudos) to excel o.s.

distinto, -ta [dʒiʃ'tʃĩntu, -ta] adj (diferente) different; (ruído, som) distinct; (pessoa) distinguished.

disto [dʒiʃtu] = de + isto, → isto.

distorção [dʒiʃtox'sãw] (pl -ões [-õjʃ]) f distortion.

distração [dʒiʃtra'sãw] (pl -ões [-õjʃ]) f (Br) (falta de atenção) absentmindedness; (esquecimento, diversão) distraction; (descuido) oversight.

distracção [diʃtra'sãw] (pl -ões [-õjʃ]) f (Port) = distração.

distrações → distração.

distraído, -da [dʒiʃtra'idu, -da] adj absent-minded.

distrair [dʒiʃtra'i(x)] vt (entreter) to amuse; (fazer perder atenção) to distract.

⏍ **distrair-se** vp (divertir-se) to enjoy o.s.; (descuidar-se) to get distracted.

distribuição [dʒiʃtribwi'sãw] (pl -ões [-õjʃ]) f (de correspondência postal) delivery; (AUT) timing; (de trabalho, comida) distribution.

distribuidor, -ra [dʒiʃtribwi'do(x), -ra] (mpl -res [-riʃ], fpl -s [-ʃ]) m, f (de produto) distributor ♦ m (AUT) distributor.

distrito [dʒiʃ'tritu] m district; **Distrito Federal** term for Brasilia, home of Brazil's federal government.

distúrbio [dʒiʃ'tuxbju] m disturbance; (Br: MED) disorder.

ditado [dʒi'tadu] m (de texto, frase) dictation; (provérbio) saying.

ditador, -ra [dʒita'do(x), -ra] (mpl -res [-riʃ], fpl -s [-ʃ]) m, f dictator.

ditadura [dʒita'dura] f dictatorship.

ditafone® [dʒikta'foni] m Dictaphone®.

ditar [dʒi'ta(x)] vt to dictate.

dito, -ta [dʒitu, -ta] pp → dizer.

ditongo [dʒi'tõŋgu] m diphthong.

diurno, -na ['dʒjuxnu, -na] adj daytime.

divã [dʒi'vã] m divan.

divagar [dʒiva'ga(x)] vi (afastar-se de assunto) to digress; (devanear) to daydream; (caminhar ao acaso) to wander.

diversão [dʒivex'sãw] (pl -ões [-õjʃ]) f (distração) amusement.

diverso, -sa [dʒi'vexsu, -sa] adj (variado) diverse.

⏍ **diversos, -sas** adj pl (muitos) various.

diversões → diversão.

divertido, -da [dʒivex'tʃidu, -da] adj amusing.

divertimento [dʒivextʃi'mẽntu] m amusement.

divertir [dʒivex'tʃi(x)] vt to amuse.

⏍ **divertir-se** vp to enjoy o.s.

dívida ['dʒivida] f debt.

dividendos [dʒivi'dẽnduʃ] mpl dividends.

dividir [dʒivi'di(x)] vt (repartir) to share out; (separar) to separate; (MAT) to divide ♦ vi (MAT) to divide.

⏍ **dividir-se** vp (separar-se) to split up; (ramificar-se) to divide.

divino, -na [dʒi'vinu, -na] adj divine.

divisão [dʒivi'zãw] (pl -ões [-õjʃ]) f division; (de casa) room.

divisas [dʒi'vizaʃ] fpl (COM) foreign currency (sg).

divisões → divisão.

divorciado, -da [dʒivox'sjadu, -da] adj divorced.

divorciar-se [dʒivox'sjaxsi] vp to get divorced; **~-se de alguém** to divorce sb.

divórcio [dʒi'vɔxsju] m divorce.

divulgar [dʒivuw'ga(x)] vt (informação,

idéia) to disseminate; *(produto, serviço)* to market.

dizer [dʒi'ze(x)] *vt* to say; ~ **algo a alguém** to tell sb sthg; ~ **a alguém que faça algo** to tell sb to do sthg; **como se diz ...?** how do you say ...?

DJ [di'ʒej] *mf (abrev de disc-jóquei)* DJ.

do [du] = **de + o, → o.**

doação [dwa'sãw] *(pl* **-ões** [-õjʃ])* *f* donation.

doar ['dwa(x)] *vt* to donate.

dobra ['dɔbra] *f* fold; *(de calças)* turn-up *(Brit)*, cuff *(Am)*.

dobradiça [dɔbra'disa] *f* hinge.

dobrado, -da [do'bradu, -da] *adj* folded; *(Port: filme, programa de TV)* dubbed.

dobrar [do'bra(x)] *vt (jornal, lençol, roupa)* to fold; *(joelho, costas)* to bend; *(Port: filme, programa de TV)* to dub ♦ *vi (duplicar)* to double; ~ **a esquina** to turn the corner.

⌐ **dobrar-se** *vp (curvar-se)* to bend over.

dobro ['dobru] *m:* **o ~** double.

doca ['dɔka] *f* dock.

doce ['dosi] *adj (bebida, comida)* sweet; *(pessoa)* gentle ♦ *m (sobremesa)* sweet; *(geléia, compota)* jam; ~ **de ovos** egg yolks and sugar blended and cooked, used as a filling in cakes, sweets and pastries.

dóceis → dócil.

docente [do'sẽtʃi] *adj* teaching ♦ *mf* teacher.

dócil ['dɔsiw] *(pl* **-ceis** [-sejʃ])* *adj* docile.

documentação [dokumẽta'sãw] *f (documentos)* papers *(pl).*

documentário [dokumẽ'tarju] *m* documentary.

documento [doku'mẽtu] *m* document.

doçura [do'sura] *f (fig)* gentleness.

doença ['dwẽsa] *f* disease; ~ **venérea** venereal disease.

doente [dwẽtʃi] *adj* ill ♦ *mf* sick person; ~ **mental** psychiatric patient.

doentio, -tia [dwẽtʃiu, -tʃia] *adj (lugar, atmosfera)* unwholesome; *(pessoa)* sickly.

doer ['dwe(x)] *vi* to hurt.

doido, -da ['dojdu, -da] *adj* mad ♦ *m, f* madman *(f* madwoman); **ser ~ por** to be mad about; ~ **varrido** *(fam)* complete nutter.

dois, duas ['dojʃ, 'duaʃ] *num* two; ~ **a ~** in twos, → **seis.**

dólar ['dɔla(x)] *(pl* **-res** [-riʃ])* *m* dollar.

doleiro [do'lejru] *m (Br)* black market money dealer *(usually in US dollars).*

dolorido, -da [dolo'ridu, -da] *adj* sore.

doloroso, -osa [dolo'rozu, -ɔza] *adj* painful.

dom ['dõ] *(pl* **-ns** [-ʃ])* *m* gift.

domador, -ra [doma'do(x), -ra] *(mpl* **-res** [-riʃ], *fpl* **-s** [-ʃ])* *m, f* tamer.

doméstica [do'mɛʃtʃika] *f* housewife.

domesticado, -da [domeʃtʃi'kadu, -da] *adj* tame.

domesticar [domeʃtʃi'ka(x)] *vt* to tame.

doméstico, -ca [do'mɛʃtʃiku, -ka] *adj* domestic.

domicílio [domi'silju] *m* residence.

dominar [domi'na(x)] *vt* to control; *(país)* to rule; *(situação)* to be in control of; *(língua)* to be fluent in; *(incêndio)* to bring under control.

⌐ **dominar-se** *vp (conter-se)* to control o.s.

domingo [do'mĩgu] *m* Sunday, → **sexta-feira.**

domínio [do'minju] *m (controle)* control; *(autoridade)* authority; *(sector, campo)* field: *(território)* domain; *(de língua)* command.

dominó [domi'nɔ] *m (jogo)* dominoes *(sg);* **jogar ~** to play dominoes.

dona ['dona] *f (título)* Mrs; ~ **de casa** housewife, → **dono.**

dono, -na ['donu, -na] *m, f* owner.

dons → dom.

dopar [do'pa(x)] *vt* to drug.

dor ['do(x)] *(pl* **-res** [-riʃ])* *f (física)* pain; *(moral)* grief; ~ **de barriga** stomachache; ~ **de cabeça** headache; ~ **de dente** toothache; ~ **de estômago** stomachache; ~ **de garganta** sore throat; ~ **lombar** backache; ~ **de ouvido** earache; ~**es menstruais** period pains; ~ **de cotovelo** *(fig)* jealousy.

dormente [dor'mẽtʃi] *adj* numb.

dormida [dor'mida] *f* sleep; **dar uma ~** to have a sleep.

dormir [dor'mi(x)] *vi* to sleep ♦ *vt* to sleep (for).

dormitório [dormi'tɔrju] *m* dormitory.

dosagem [du'zaʒãj] (*pl* **-ns** [-ʃ]) *f* dosage.

dose ['dɔzi] *f (de medicamento)* dose; *(de bebida)* measure; *(em restaurante)* portion.

dossiê [do'sje] *m (Br) (de documentação, processo)* file; ~ **(escolar)** folder.

dossier [dɔ'sje] *m (Port)* = **dossiê**.

dotado, -da [do'tadu, -da] *adj (talentoso)* gifted.

dou ['do] → **dar**.

dourado, -da [do'radu, -da] *adj* golden.

doutor, -ra [do'to(x), -ra] (*mpl* **-res** [-riʃ]. *fpl* **-s** [-ʃ]) *m, f (médico, pessoa doutorada)* doctor.

Doutor, -ra [do'to(x), -ra] *m, f* title *attributed to anyone with a university degree.*

doutrina [do'trina] *f* doctrine.

doze ['dozi] *num* twelve, → **seis**.

Dr. *(abrev de Doutor)* Dr.

Dra. *(abrev de Doutora)* Dr.

dragão [dra'gãw] (*pl* **-ões** [-õjʃ]) *m* dragon.

dragar [dra'ga(x)] *vt (rio, lago)* to dredge.

drágea ['draʒja] *f (Br)* tablet.

drageia [dra'ʒaja] *f (Port)* = **drágea**.

dragões → **dragão**.

drama ['drama] *m* drama.

dramatizar [dramatʃi'za(x)] *vt (fig)* to dramatize.

dramaturgo, -ga [drama'turgu, -ga] *m, f* playwright.

drástico, -ca ['draʃtʃiku, -ka] *adj* drastic.

drenar [dre'na(x)] *vt* to drain.

dreno ['drenu] *m (MED)* drainage tube.

driblar [dri'bla(x)] *vi & vt* to dribble.

drinque ['drĩŋki] *m (Br)* drink.

drive ['drajvi] *f (INFORM)* drive.

droga ['drɔga] *f* drug; *(coisa de má qualidade)* rubbish ♦ *interj* blast!

drogado, -da [dro'gadu. -da] *m, f* drug addict.

drogar [dro'ga(x)] *vt* to drug.

⊔ drogar-se *vp* to take drugs.

drogaria [droga'ria] *f* chemist's *(Brit)*, drugstore *(Am)*.

dto. *abrev* = **direito**.

duas → **dois**.

dublar [du'blax] *vt (Br: filme, programa de TV)* to dub.

duche ['duʃe] *m (Port)* shower; **tomar uma** ~ to have a shower.

duende ['dwẽndʒi] *m* goblin.

dum [dũ] = **de** + **um**, → **um**.

duma ['duma] = **de** + **uma**, → **um**.

duna ['duna] *f* dune.

duns [dũʃ] = **de** + **uns**, → **um**.

dupla ['dupla] *f (par)* duo, pair; *(Br: em esporte)* doubles *(sg)*.

dúplex ['dupleks] *m inv* maisonette *(Brit)*, duplex *(Am)*.

duplicado [dupli'kadu] *m* duplicate; **em** ~ in duplicate.

duplicar [dupli'ka(x)] *vt & vi* to double.

duplo, -pla ['duplu. -pla] *adj* double ♦ *m*: **o** ~ double.

duração [dura'sãw] *f (de férias, concerto, curso)* length; *(de produto deteriorável)* shelf life.

duradouro, -ra [dura'doru. -ra] *adj* lasting.

durante [du'rãntʃi] *prep* during; ~ **3 horas** for three hours.

durar [du'ra(x)] *vi* to last.

durex® [du'rɛks] *adj (Br)* → **fita**.

dureza [du'reza] *f (de objeto, substância)* hardness; *(de caráter)* harshness.

durmo ['durmu] → **dormir**.

duro, -ra ['duru. -ra] *adj* hard; *(pão)* stale; *(carne)* tough.

dúvida ['duvida] *f* doubt; **estou em** ~ I'm not sure; **pôr em** ~ to doubt; **sem** ~! absolutely!; **tirar** ~**s** to sort queries out.

duvidoso, -osa [duvi'dozu. -ɔza] *adj* dubious.

duzentos, -tas [du'zẽntuʃ. -taʃ] *num* two hundred, → **seis**.

dúzia ['duzja] *f* dozen; **uma** ~ **de ovos** a dozen eggs; **vender à** ~ to sell by the dozen; **meia** ~ half a dozen.

E

e [i] *conj* and.

é ['ε] → **ser.**

E. *(abrev de Este)* E.

ébano ['ɛbanu] *m* ebony.

ébrio, ébria ['ɛbriu. 'ɛbria] *adj* inebriated.

ebulição [ibuli'sãw] *f (fervura)* boiling.

écharpe [e'ʃarpi] *f* scarf.

eclipse [e'klipsi] *m* eclipse.

eco ['ɛku] *m* echo.

ecoar [e'kwa(x)] *vi* to echo.

ecografia [ekogra'fia] *f* ultrasound.

ecologia [ekolo'ʒia] *f* ecology.

ecológico, -ca [eko'lɔʒiku. -ka] *adj* ecological.

economia [ekono'mia] *f (ciência)* economics *(sg); (de país)* economy; *(poupança)* saving.

⊐ economias *fpl* savings.

económico, -ca [iku'nɔmiku. -ka] *adj (Port)* = **econômico.**

econômico, -ca [eko'nomiku. -ka] *adj (Br) (pessoa)* frugal; *(barato)* cheap; *(carro, motor, dispositivo)* economical; *(situação, crise)* economic.

economista [ekono'miʃta] *mf* economist.

economizar [ekonomi'za(x)] *vt* to save ♦ *vi* to economize.

ecoturismo [ekotu'riʒmu] *m* ecotourism.

ecrã ['ɛkrã] *m* screen.

ECT *f (abrev de Empresa Brasileira de Correios e Telégrafos)* Brazilian postal services.

ECU ['ɛku] *m* ECU.

eczema [ek'zema] *m* eczema.

edição [edʒi'sãw] *(pl* -**ões** [-'õjʃ]) *f (exemplares)* edition; *(publicação)* publishing.

edifício [edʒi'fisju] *m* building.

edifício-garagem [edʒifisjuga'raʒẽ] *(pl* **edifícios-garagens** [edʒifisjuʒga-**'raʒẽ]) *m (Br)* multistorey car park *(Brit)*, multistory parking lot *(Am).*

editar [edʒi'ta(x)] *vt (livro, revista)* to publish; *(disco)* to release; *(programa, matéria)* to edit.

editor, -ra [edʒi'to(x). -ra] *(mpl* -**res** [-riʃ]. *fpl* -**s** [-ʃ]) *m, f (que publica)* publisher; *(que edita)* editor.

editora [edʒi'tora] *f (empresa, estabelecimento)* publishing house, → **editor.**

editores → **editor.**

edredão [edre'dãw] *(pl* -**ões** [-õjʃ]) *m (Port)* = **edredom.**

edredom [edre'dõ] *(pl* -**ns** [-ʃ]) *m (Br)* duvet.

educação [eduka'sãw] *f* education; *(cortesia)* manners *(pl).*

educado, -da [edu'kadu. -da] *adj* polite.

educar [edu'ka(x)] *vt (filhos)* to bring up; *(alunos)* to educate.

efectivo, -va [efe'tivu. -va] *adj (Port)* = **efetivo.**

efectuar [efe'twar] *vt (Port)* = **efetuar.**

efeito [e'fejtu] *m* effect; **com ~** *(realmente)* really, indeed; **sem ~** invalid.

efervescente [iferveʃ'sẽtʃi] *adj* → **aspirina.**

efetivamente [efɾtʃiva'mẽtʃi] *adv* indeed.

efetivo, -va [efe'tʃivu. -va] *adj (Br) (real)* genuine; *(funcionário, empregado)* permanent.

efetuar [efe'twa(x)] *vt (Br) (realizar)* to carry out; *(compra, pagamento, viagem)* to make.

eficácia [efi'kasja] *f (de plano, solução, sistema)* effectiveness; *(de pessoa)* efficiency.

eficaz [efi'kaʃ] *(pl* -**zes** [-ziʃ]) *adj (plano, solução, sistema)* effective; *(pessoa)* efficient.

eficiência [efi'sjèsja] f *(de plano, método, sistema)* effectiveness; *(de pessoa)* efficiency.

eficiente [efi'sjènt∫i] adj *(plano, método, sistema)* effective; *(pessoa)* efficient.

efusivo, -va [efu'zivu. -va] adj effusive.

egoísmo [e'gwiʒmu] m selfishness.

egoísta [e'gwi∫ta] adj selfish ♦ mf selfish person.

égua ['egwa] f mare.

eis ['ej∫] adv here is/are; **~ senão quando** when all of a sudden.

eixo ['ej∫u] m *(de roda)* axle; *(de máquina)* shaft; *(em geometria)* axis.

ejaculação [eʒakula'sãw] *(pl* -ões [-õj∫]) f ejaculation.

ejacular [eʒaku'la(x)] vt & vi to ejaculate.

ela ['ɛla] pron *(pessoa)* she; *(coisa, animal)* it; *(com preposição: pessoa)* her; *(com preposição: coisa)* it; **e ~?** what about her?; **é ~** it's her; **~ mesma** OU **própria** (she) herself.

⌐ elas pron pl they; *(com preposição)* them.

elaboração [elabora'sãw] f *(de plano, sistema)* working out, development; *(de trabalho escrito)* writing.

elaborar [elabo'ra(x)] vt *(trabalho, texto)* to work on; *(plano, lista)* to draw up.

elasticidade [ela∫tisi'dadʒi] f elasticity.

elástico, -ca [e'la∫t∫iku. -ka] adj elastic ♦ m *(material)* elastic; *(para segurar papel)* rubber band.

ele ['eli] pron *(pessoa)* he; *(coisa, animal)* it; *(com preposição: pessoa)* him; *(com preposição: coisa, animal)* it; **e ~?** what about him?; **é ~** it's him; **~ mesmo** OU **próprio** (he) himself.

⌐ eles pron pl they; *(com preposição)* them.

eléctrico, -ca [i'lɛtriku. -ka] adj *(Port)* = **elétrico** ♦ m *(Port)* tram *(Brit)*, streetcar *(Am)*.

electrónica [ilɛ'tronika] f *(Port)* = **eletrônica**.

elefante [ele'fãnt∫i] m elephant.

elegância [ele'gãsja] f elegance; *(de modos)* refinement.

elegante [ele'gãnt∫i] adj *(esbelto)* slim; *(bem vestido)* elegant.

eleger [ele'ʒe(x)] vt *(ministro, presi-* dente, deputado) to elect; *(sistema, método, manual)* to choose.

eleição [elej'sãw] *(pl* -ões [-õj∫]) f *(de ministro, presidente, deputado)* election; *(de sistema, método, manual)* choice.

⌐ eleições fpl elections.

eleito, -ta [e'lejtu. -ta] pp → **eleger** ♦ adj *(presidente, ministro, deputado)* elected.

eleitor, -ra [elej'to(x). -ra] *(mpl* -res [-ri∫], fpl -s [-∫]) m, f voter.

elementar [elemēn'ta(x)] *(pl* -es [-i∫]) adj *(fundamental)* basic; *(primário)* elementary.

elemento [ele'mēntu] m element; *(de equipa, grupo)* member; *(informação)* factor.

⌐ elementos mpl data *(sg)*; **os ~s** the elements.

eletricidade [eletrisi'dadʒi] f electricity.

eletricista [eletri'si∫ta] mf electrician.

elétrico, -ca [e'lɛtriku. -ka] adj *(Br)* electric .

eletrizar [eletri'za(x)] vt *(fig: entusiasmar)* to electrify.

eletrodoméstico [e.letrodo'mɛ∫- t∫iku] m electric household appliance.

eletrônica [ele'tronika] f *(Br)* electronics.

eletrônico, -ca [ele'troniku. -ka] adj electronic.

elevação [eleva'sãw] *(pl* -ões [-õj∫]) f area of high ground.

elevado, -da [ele'vadu. -da] adj high.

elevador [eleva'do(x)] *(pl* -res [-ri∫]) m lift *(Brit)*, elevator *(Am)*.

elevar [ele'va(x)] vt to raise; *(promover)* to elevate.

⌐ elevar-se vp to rise.

eliminar [elemi'na(x)] vt to eliminate.

elite [e'lit∫i] f elite.

elo ['ɛlu] m *(de cadeia)* link; **~ de ligação** *(fig)* link.

elogiar [elo'ʒia(x)] vt to praise.

elogio [elo'ʒiu] m praise.

eloqüência [elo'kwẽsja] f eloquence.

eloquente [ilu'kwẽnte] adj *(Port)* = **eloqüente**.

eloqüente [elo'kwẽnt∫i] adj *(Br)* eloquent.

em [ẽ] prep **1.** *(no interior de)* in; **os papéis estão naquela gaveta** the papers are in that drawer; **vivo no**

norte I live in the north.
2. *(sobre)* on; **coloca uma jarra nesta mesa** put a vase on this table.
3. *(em certo ponto de)* in; **ela está na sala** she's in the living room; **estar ~ casa/no trabalho** to be at home/at work.
4. *(relativo a cidade, país)* in; **~ Londres/Paris** in London/Paris; **~ Portugal/França** in Portugal/France; **no Brasil** in Brazil; **nos Estados Unidos** in the (United) States.
5. *(indica tempo)* in; *(dia)* on; *(época)* at; **faço isso num dia** I can do that in a day; **ela nasceu ~ 1970/num sábado** she was born in 1970/on a Saturday; **vou de férias no Verão/Natal** I'm going on holiday in the summer/at Christmas; **vou lá nas férias** I'm going there during the holidays.
6. *(indica modo)* in; **paguei ~ reais** I paid in reals; **respondi-lhe ~ português** I answered him in Portuguese; **ela gastou tudo em cigarros** she spent it all on cigarettes.
7. *(indica assunto)*: **ele é um perito ~ economia** he's an expert in economics; **nisso de computador, a Carlota é a melhor** when it comes to computers, Carlota is the best; **sou licenciada ~ Letras/Direito** I'm an arts/law graduate.
8. *(indica estado)* in; **~ boas condições** in good condition; **não descer com o trem ~ movimento** passengers should not alight until the train has stopped.
9. *(introduz complemento)*: **a palavra caiu ~ desuso** the word is no longer used; **não acredito nele** I don't believe him; **não penses nele** don't think about him.

emagrecer [emagre'se(x)] *vi* to lose weight.
emancipado, -da [emãsi'padu, -da] *adj* emancipated.
emaranhado, -da [emara'nadu, -da] *adj* tangled.
embaciado, -da [ẽmba'sjadu, -da] *adj* steamed up.
embaciar [ẽmba'sja(x)] *vt* to steam up.
embaixada [ẽmbaj'fada] *f* embassy.
embaixador, -ra [ẽmbajfa'do(x), -ra] *(mpl* -res [-rif], *fpl* -s [-f]) *m, f* ambassador.
embaixatriz [ẽmbajfa'trif] *(pl* -zes [-zif]) *f* ambassadress.

embaixo [ẽm'bajfu] *adv (Br) (em espaço)* downstairs; *(em lista)* at the bottom; **~ de** under(neath).
embalagem [ẽmba'laʒẽ] *(pl* -ns [-f]) *f* packaging; *(pacote)* packet.
embalar [ẽmba'la(x)] *vt (produto)* to package; *(bebê)* to rock.
embaraçar [ẽmbara'sa(x)] *vt (desconcertar)* to embarrass; *(estorvar)* to hinder.
⏋ **embaraçar-se** *vp (atrapalhar-se)* to get flustered.
embaraço [ẽmba'rasu] *m (vergonha)* embarrassment; *(estorvo)* hindrance.
embarcação [ẽmbaxka'sãw] *(pl* -ões [-õjf]) *f* vessel.
embarcar [ẽmbax'ka(x)] *vi* to board; **~ em** *(navio, avião, comboio)* to board; *(aventura, negócio)* to embark on.
embarque [ẽm'baxki] *m* boarding; **zona** OU **local de ~** boarding point.
embebedar-se [ẽmbebe'daxsi] *vp* to get drunk.
embeber [ẽmbe'be(x)] *vt* to soak; **~ algo em algo** to soak sthg in sthg.
embelezar [ẽmbele'za(x)] *vt* to embellish.
emblema [ẽm'blema] *m* emblem.
embora [ẽm'bɔra] *conj* even though ◆ *adv*: **ir(-se) ~** to leave; **vai ~!** go away!
emboscada [ẽmbof'kada] *f* ambush.
embraiagem [ẽmbra'jaʒẽ] *(pl* -ns [-f]) *f (Port)* = **embreagem**.
EMBRATUR [ẽmbra'tu(x)] *f (abrev de Empresa Brasileira de Turismo) Brazilian tourist board.*
embreagem [ẽmbre'aʒẽ] *(pl* -ns [-f]) *f (Br)* clutch.
embriagar-se [ẽmbria'gaxsi] *vp* to get drunk.
embrulhar [ẽmbru'ʎa(x)] *vt* to wrap up; *(misturar)* to muddle up.
embrulho [ẽm'bruʎu] *m* package.
embutido, -da [ẽmbu'tʃidu, -da] *adj* fitted.
emendar [emẽ'da(x)] *vt* to correct.
⏋ **emendar-se** *vp* to mend one's ways.
ementa [e'mẽta] *f (Port)* menu; **~ turística** set menu.
emergência [emex'ʒẽsja] *f* emergency.
emigração [emigra'sãw] *f* emigration.
emigrante [emi'grãtʃi] *mf* emigrant.
emigrar [emi'gra(x)] *vi* to emigrate; **~**

para to emigrate to.
emissão [emi'sãw] (*pl* **-ões** [-õjʃ]) *f (de programa)* broadcast; *(de calor, gases)* emission.
emissor, -ra [emi'so(x), -ra] (*mpl* **-res** [-riʃ], *fpl* **-s** [-ʃ]) *adj* broadcasting ◆ *m (rádio)* transmitter; *(de mensagem)* sender.
emissora [emi'sora] *f (de rádio)* radio station.
emissores → emissor.
emitir [emi'tʃi(x)] *vt (calor, luz, som)* to emit; *(moeda)* to issue; *(programa)* to broadcast.
emoção [emo'sãw] (*pl* **-ões** [-õjʃ]) *f (comoção)* emotion; *(excitação)* excitement.
emoldurar [emowdu'ra(x)] *vt* to frame.
emotivo, -va [emo'tʃivu, -va] *adj* emotional.
empacotar [ẽmpako'ta(x)] *vt* to pack up.
empada [ẽm'pada] *f* pasty; **~ de galinha** chicken pasty.
empadão [ẽmpa'dãw] (*pl* **-ões** [-õjʃ]) *m* pie *(made with mashed potato)*.
empadinha [ẽmpa'dʒiɲa] *f (Br)* pasty; **~ de camarão** prawn pasty; **~ de palmito** palm-heart pasty; **~ de queijo** cheese pasty.
empadões → empadão.
empalhar [ẽmpa'ʎa(x)] *vt* to stuff.
empanturrar [ẽmpãntu'xa(x)] *vt*: **~ alguém com algo** *(fam)* to stuff sb full of sthg.
⊐ **empanturrar-se** *vp (fam)* to stuff o.s.
empatar [ẽmpa'ta(x)] *vi* to draw ◆ *vt (dinheiro)* to tie up; **~ alguém** *(estorvar a)* to get in sb's way.
empate [ẽm'patʃi] *m* draw, tie.
empenado, -da [ẽmpe'nadu, -da] *adj* warped.
empenhar [ẽmpe'ɲa(x)] *vt* to pawn.
⊐ **empenhar-se** *vp (esforçar-se)* to do one's utmost; *(endividar-se)* to get into debt; **~-se em algo** to do one's utmost to do sthg.
empestar [ẽmpeʃ'ta(x)] *vt* to stink out.
empilhar [ẽmpi'ʎa(x)] *vt* to pile up.
empinar [ẽmpi'na(x)] *vt (bicicleta, moto)* to do a wheelie on.
⊐ **empinar-se** *vp (cavalo)* to rear (up); *(bicicleta, moto)* to do a wheelie.

emplastro [ẽm'plaʃtru] *m* plaster.
empobrecer [ẽmpobre'se(x)] *vt (pessoa, país)* to impoverish; *(terreno)* to deplete ◆ *vi (pessoa, país)* to become poor; *(terreno)* to become depleted.
empolgante [ẽmpow'gãntʃi] *adj* gripping.
empreender [ẽmpriẽn'de(x)] *vt (negócio, trabalho)* to start.
empreendimento [ẽmpriẽndʒi'mẽntu] *m (investimento)* venture; *(empenho)* investment.
empregado, -da [ẽmpre'gadu, -da] *m, f (em empresa)* employee; **~ de balcão** sales assistant; **~ de bar** barman *(f* barmaid); **~ (doméstico)** domestic servant; **~ (de mesa)** waiter *(f* waitress).
empregar [ẽmpre'ga(x)] *vt (pessoa, método, técnica)* to employ; *(dinheiro, tempo)* to spend; *(objeto, ferramenta)* to use.
⊐ **empregar-se** *vp (arranjar emprego)* to get a job; *(utilizar-se)* to be used.
emprego [ẽm'pregu] *m (trabalho, ocupação)* job; *(uso)* use; **o ~** *(em geral)* employment.
empregue [ẽm'pregi] *pp* → empregar.
empresa [ẽm'preza] *f* firm.
emprestado, -da [ẽmpreʃ'tadu, -da] *adj* borrowed; **pedir algo ~** to borrow sthg.
emprestar [ẽmpreʃ'ta(x)] *vt*: **~ algo a alguém** to lend sthg to sb.
empréstimo [ẽm'preʃtʃimu] *m* loan.
empunhar [ẽmpu'ɲa(x)] *vt* to hold.
empurrão [ẽmpu'xãw] (*pl* **-ões** [-õjʃ]) *m* shove.
empurrar [ẽmpu'xa(x)] *vt* to push; "empurre" "push".
empurrões → empurrão.
encabeçar [ẽŋkabe'sa(x)] *vt* to head.
encadernação [ẽŋkadexna'sãw] (*pl* **-ões** [-õjʃ]) *f (capa)* cover; *(ato)* binding.
encaixar [ẽŋkaj'ʃa(x)] *vt* to fit; *(fig: meter na cabeça)* to get into one's head.
⊐ **encaixar-se** *vp* to fit in.
encaixe [ẽŋ'kajʃi] *m* slot; **~ do flash** fitting *(for camera flash)*.
encaixotar [ẽŋkajʃo'ta(x)] *vt* to box.
encalhar [ẽŋka'ʎa(x)] *vt & vi* to run aground.
encaminhar [ẽŋkami'ɲa(x)] *vt (aconselhar)* to provide guidance for ou to; **~ algo/alguém para** to refer sthg/sb to.
⊐ **encaminhar-se para** *vp + prep* to head towards.

encanador, -ra [ēŋkana'dox. -ra] (*mpl* **-res** [-riʃ]. *fpl* **-s** [-ʃ]) *m, f (Br)* plumber.

encantador, -ra [ēŋkānta'do(x). -ra] (*mpl* **-res** [-riʃ]. *fpl* **-s** [-ʃ]) *adj* delightful.

encantar [ēŋkān'ta(x)] *vt* to delight.

encaracolado, -da [ēŋkarako'ladu. -da] *adj* curly.

encarar [ēŋka'ra(x)] *vt* to face.

⌐ **encarar com** *v* + *prep* to come face to face with.

encardido, -da [ēŋkar'dʒidu. -da] *adj* grubby.

encarnado, -da [ēŋkar'nadu. -da] *adj* scarlet, red.

encarregado, -da [ēŋkaxe'gadu. -da] *m, f* person in charge; *(de operários)* foreman (*f* forewoman).

encarregar [ēŋkaxe'ga(x)] *vt*: ~ **alguém de fazer algo** to put sb in charge of doing sthg.

encastrado, -da [ēŋkaʃ'tradu. -da] *adj* fitted; *(pedra em jóia)* set.

encenação [ēsena'sāw] (*pl* **-ões** [-õjʃ]) *f (de peça teatral)* staging.

encenar [ēse'na(x)] *vt (peça teatral)* to stage, to put on.

encerar [ēse'ra(x)] *vt* to wax.

encerrado, -da [ēse'xadu. -da] *adj* closed.

encerramento [ēsexa'mēntu] *m (de concerto, espetáculo)* end; *(de loja)* closure.

encerrar [ēse'xa(x)] *vt* to close; *(concerto, espetáculo)* to end.

encharcar [ēʃar'ka(x)] *vt* to soak.

⌐ **encharcar-se** *vp* to get soaked.

enchente [ē'ʃēntʃi] *f* flood.

enchova [ē'ʃova] *f (peixe)* snapper; *(Br: alice)* anchovy.

encoberto, -ta [ēŋko'bɛxtu. -ta] *adj (céu, tempo)* overcast; *(oculto)* hidden.

encolher [ēŋko'ʎe(x)] *vt (ombros)* to shrug; *(pernas)* to bend; *(barriga)* to pull in ◆ *vi* to shrink.

⌐ **encolher-se** *vp* to huddle.

encomenda [ēŋko'mēnda] *f* order; **feito por** ~ made to order; ~ **postal** mail order.

encomendar [ēŋkomēn'da(x)] *vt* to order; ~ **algo a alguém** *(comprar)* to order sthg from sb; *(obra, escultura, pintura)* to commission sthg from sb.

encontrar [ēŋkōn'tra(x)] *vt* to find; *(pessoa por acaso)* to bump into.

⌐ **encontrar-se** *vp (ter encontro)* to meet; *(estar)* to be; ~**-se com alguém** to meet up with sb.

encontro [ēŋ'kōntru] *m (profissional)* appointment; *(amoroso)* date.

encorajar [ēŋkora'ʒa(x)] *vt* to encourage.

encorpado, -da [ēŋkor'padu. -da] *adj (pessoa)* burly; *(vinho)* full-bodied.

encosta [ēŋ'kɔʃta] *f* slope.

encostar [ēŋkoʃ'ta(x)] *vt (carro)* to park; *(porta)* to leave ajar; *(cabeça)* to lay down; ~ **algo em algo** *(mesa, cadeira)* to put sthg against sthg; *(escada, vara)* to lean sthg against sthg.

⌐ **encostar-se** *vp*: ~**-se a** *(parede, carro, poste)* to lean against.

encosto [ēŋ'koʃtu] *m (de assento)* back.

encruzilhada [ēŋkruzi'ʎada] *f* crossroads *(sg)*.

endereço [ēnde'resu] *m* address.

endireitar [ēndirej'ta(x)] *vt* to straighten; *(objeto caído)* to put upright.

⌐ **endireitar-se** *vp (pôr-se direito)* to stand up straight.

endívia [ēn'dʒivja] *f* endive.

endoidecer [ēndojde'se(x)] *vt* to drive mad ◆ *vi* to go mad.

endossar [ēndo'sa(x)] *vt* to endorse.

endurecer [ēndure'se(x)] *vt & vi* to harden.

energia [enex'ʒia] *f* energy; ~ **eólica/nuclear/solar** wind/nuclear/solar power.

enevoado, -da [ene'vwadu. -da] *adj* cloudy.

enfarte [ē'faxtʃi] *m*: ~ **(do miocárdio)** heart attack.

ênfase [ē'fazi] *f* emphasis.

enfatizar [ēfatʃi'za(x)] *vt* to emphasize.

enfeitiçar [ēfejtʃi'sa(x)] *vt* to bewitch.

enfermagem [ēfex'maʒē] *f* nursing.

enfermaria [ēfexma'ria] *f* ward.

enfermeiro, -ra [ēfex'mejru. -ra] *m, f* nurse.

enferrujar [ēfexu'ʒa(x)] *vt & vi* to rust.

enfiar [ē'fja(x)] *vt (calça, mangas, camisola)* to pull ou put on; ~ **algo em algo** to put sthg in sthg.

enfim [ē'fĩ] *adv (finalmente)* at last ◆ *interj* oh well!

enforcar [ẽfoxˈka(x)] *vt* to hang.
⊐ **enforcar-se** *vp* to hang o.s.

enfraquecer [ẽfrakeˈse(x)] *vt & vi* to weaken.

enfrentar [ẽfrẽnˈta(x)] *vt* to confront.

enfurecer [ẽfureˈse(x)] *vt* to infuriate.
⊔ **enfurecer-se** *vp* to get angry.

enganado, -da [ẽgaˈnadu. -da] *adj:* **estar ~** to be wrong; **ser ~** *(ser ludibriado)* to be deceived; *(por cônjuge)* to be cheated on.

enganar [ẽgaˈna(x)] *vt* to deceive; *(cônjuge)* to cheat on.
⊐ **enganar-se** *vp* *(estar errado)* to be wrong; *(errar)* to make a mistake.

engano [ẽˈganu] *m* mistake; **é ~** *(em conversa telefônica)* you've got the wrong number.

engarrafado, -da [ẽgaxaˈfadu. -da] *adj* *(líquido)* bottled; *(trânsito)* blocked.

engarrafamento [ẽgaxafaˈmẽntu] *m* *(de trânsito)* traffic jam; *(de líquido)* bottling.

engasgar-se [ẽgaʒˈgaxsi] *vp* to choke.

engenharia [ẽʒeɲaˈria] *f* engineering.

engenheiro, -ra [ẽʒeˈɲejru. -ra] *m, f* engineer.

engenhoso, -osa [ẽʒeˈɲozu. -ɔza] *adj* ingenious.

engessar [ẽʒeˈsa(x)] *vt* to set in a plaster cast.

englobar [ẽgloˈba(x)] *vt* to encompass.

engodo [ẽˈgodu] *m* bait.

engolir [ẽgoˈli(x)] *vt* to swallow.

engomar [ẽgoˈma(x)] *vt* *(passar a ferro)* to iron; *(com goma)* to starch.

engordar [ẽgorˈda(x)] *vi* *(pessoa)* to put on weight; *(alimento)* to be fattening ♦ *vt* *(animal)* to fatten up.

engordurado, -da [ẽgordu'radu. -da] *adj* greasy.

engraçado, -da [ẽgraˈsadu. -da] *adj* funny.

engravidar [ẽgraviˈda(x)] *vi* to get pregnant ♦ *vt:* **~ alguém** to get sb pregnant.

engraxar [ẽgraˈʃa(x)] *vt* to polish; *(Port: fam: professor, chefe, etc)* to butter up.

engraxate [ẽgraˈʃatʃi] *m (Br)* shoe shiner.

engrenagem [ẽgreˈnaʒẽ] *(pl -ns [-ʃ])* *f* mechanism.

engrossar [ẽgroˈsa(x)] *vt & vi* to thicken.

enguia [ẽ'gia] *f* eel.

enguiçar [ẽgiˈsa(x)] *vi (motor, máquina)* to play up.

enigma [eˈnigma] *m (adivinha)* riddle; *(mistério)* enigma.

enjoado, -da [ẽˈʒwadu. -da] *adj* sick; *(em carro, barco)* travelsick.

enjoar [ẽˈʒwa(x)] *vi* to get travelsick ♦ *vt* to get sick of.

enjoo [ẽˈʒou] *m (Port)* = **enjôo**.

enjôo [ẽˈʒou] *m (Br) (náusea)* sickness; *(em barco, avião, ônibus)* travel sickness.

enlatado, -da [ẽlaˈtadu. -da] *adj (comida)* tinned *(Brit)*, canned *(Am)*; *(cultura, filme)* imported.
⊐ **enlatados** *mpl* tinned foods *(Brit)*, canned foods *(Am)*.

enlouquecer [ẽlokeˈse(x)] *vt* to drive mad ♦ *vi* to go mad.

enorme [eˈnɔrmi] *adj* huge, enormous.

enquanto [ẽˈkwantu] *conj* while; **~ (que)** whereas; **por ~** for the time being.

enraivecer [ẽxajveˈse(x)] *vt* to enrage.

enraivecido, -da [ẽxajveˈsidu. -da] *adj* enraged.

enredo [ẽˈxedu] *m* plot.

enriquecer [ẽxikeˈse(x)] *vt* to make rich; *(melhorar)* to enrich ♦ *vi* to get rich.

enrolar [ẽxoˈla(x)] *vt (papel, tapete, fio)* to roll up; *(cabelo)* to curl; *(cigarro)* to roll; *(fam: enganar)* to take for a ride.

enroscar [ẽxoʃˈka(x)] *vt (tampa)* to screw on; *(parafuso)* to screw in.
⊐ **enroscar-se** *vp (cobra)* to coil up; *(gato, cão)* to curl up; *(emaranhar-se)* to get tangled up.

enrugar [ẽxoˈga(x)] *vt (roupa, papel)* to crease; *(pele)* to wrinkle ♦ *vi (pele)* to wrinkle.

ensaiar [ẽsaˈja(x)] *vt (peça, dança)* to rehearse; *(sistema)* to test.

ensaio [ẽˈsaju] *m (de peça, dança)* rehearsal; *(de sistema)* test; *(texto literário)* essay.

enseada [ẽˈsjada] *f* cove.

ensinamento [ẽsinaˈmẽntu] *m (lição)* teaching; *(preceito)* saying.

ensinar [ẽsiˈna(x)] *vt (em escola, universidade)* to teach; *(caminho, direção)* to show; ~ **alguém a fazer algo** to teach sb how to do sthg; ~ **algo a alguém** *(língua, método)* to teach sb sthg; *(caminho)* to show sb sthg.

ensino [ẽ'sinu] *m (actividade)* teaching; *(método, sistema)* education; ~ **superior** higher education.

ensolarado, -da [ẽsola'radu, -da] *adj* sunny.

ensopado [ẽso'padu] *m* stew.

ensopar [ẽso'pa(x)] *vt* to soak.

❏ **ensopar-se** *vp* to get soaked.

ensurdecedor, -ra [ẽsurdese'do(x), -ra] *(mpl -res* [-rif]*, fpl -s* [-ʃ]*) adj* deafening.

ensurdecer [ẽsurde'se(x)] *vt* to deafen ♦ *vi (ficar surdo)* to go deaf.

entalar [ẽnta'la(x)] *vt (dedo, pé)* to trap; *(peça de roupa)* to tuck in.

entanto [ẽn'tãntu] : **no entanto** *conj* however.

então [ẽn'tãw] *adv* then ♦ *interj* so!; **desde** ~ since then.

enteado, -da [ẽnte'adu, -da] *m, f* stepson *(f* stepdaughter*)*.

entender [ẽntẽn'de(x)] *vt (perceber)* to understand ♦ *vi (compreender)* to understand; **dar a** ~ **que** to give the impression (that); ~ **que** to think (that).

❏ **entender de** *v + prep* to know about.

❏ **entender-se** *vp* to get along; **não me entendo com isto** I can't get the hang of this; ~**-se com alguém** *(chegar a acordo com)* to come to an agreement with sb.

enternecedor, -ra [ẽternese'do(x), -ra] *(mpl -res* [-rif]*, fpl -s* [-ʃ]*) adj* touching.

enternecer [ẽnterne'se(x)] *vt* to touch.

enterrar [ẽnte'xa(x)] *vt* to bury.

❏ **enterrar-se** *vp* to sink.

enterro [ẽn'texu] *m* funeral.

entonação [ẽntona'sãw] *(pl -ões* [-õjʃ]*) f* intonation.

entornar [ẽntor'na(x)] *vt* to spill.

entorse [ẽn'tɔxsi] *f* sprain.

entortar [ẽntor'ta(x)] *vt* to bend.

entrada [ẽn'trada] *f* entrance; *(vestíbulo)* hall; *(prato)* starter; *(bilhete para espetáculo)* ticket; *(de dicionário)* entry; *(pagamento inicial)* down payment, deposit; **como** ~, **o que deseja?** what would you like as a starter?;

"**entrada**" "way in"; "~ **livre**" "free admission"; "~ **proibida**" "no entry".

entranhas [ẽn'traɲaʃ] *fpl* entrails.

entrar [ẽn'tra(x)] *vi* to enter, to go/come in; *(encaixar)* to go in; ~ **com algo** to contribute sthg; ~ **em algo** *(penetrar, ingressar em)* to enter sthg; *(participar em)* to take part in sthg; **entro em férias amanhã** my holidays start tomorrow; **não entremos em discussões** let's not start arguing; ~ **em algo** *(carro)* to get in sthg; *(ônibus, trem)* to get on sthg; *(equipe, grupo)* to join sthg.

entre [ẽntri] *prep* between; *(no meio de muitos)* among(st); *(cerca de)* about; **aqui** ~ **nós** between you and me; ~ **si** amongst themselves.

entreaberto, -ta [ẽntria'bextu, -ta] *adj (janela)* half-open; *(porta)* ajar.

entreajuda [ẽntrea'ʒuda] *f* teamwork.

entrecosto [ẽntre'koʃtu] *m* spare ribs *(pl)*.

entrega [ẽn'trega] *f (de encomenda, mercadoria, carta)* delivery; *(rendição)* surrender; ~ **a domicílio** home delivery.

entregar [ẽntre'ga(x)] *vt:* ~ **algo a alguém** *(dar)* to give sthg to sb; *(encomenda, carta)* to deliver sthg to sb.

❏ **entregar-se** *vp (render-se)* to surrender; ~**-se a** *(abandonar-se a)* to abandon o.s. to; *(dedicar-se a)* to dedicate o.s. to.

entrelinha [ẽntre'liɲa] *f* line space.

entremeado, -da [ẽntri'mjadu, -da] *adj (toucinho)* streaky.

entretanto [ẽntri'tãntu] *adv* meanwhile, in the meantime ♦ *conj (Br: todavia)* however.

entreter [ẽntre'te(x)] *vt* to entertain.

❏ **entreter-se** *vp* to amuse o.s.

entrevado, -da [ẽn'trevadu, -da] *adj* paralysed.

entrevista [ẽntre'viʃta] *f* interview.

entrevistador, -ra [ẽntre'viʃtado(x), -ra] *(mpl -res* [-rif]*, fpl -s* [-ʃ]*) m, f* interviewer.

entristecer [ẽntriʃte'se(x)] *vt* to sadden ♦ *vi* to grow sad.

entroncamento [ẽntrõŋka'mẽntu] *m* junction.

entupido, -da [ẽntu'pidu, -da] *adj* blocked.

entupir [ẽntu'pi(x)] *vt* to block.

❏ **entupir-se** *vp* to become blocked.
entusiasmar [ẽntuzjaʒˈma(x)] *vt* to excite.
❒ **entusiasmar-se** *vp* to get excited.
entusiasmo [ẽntuˈzjaʒmu] *m* enthusiasm.
entusiasta [ẽntuˈzjaʃta] *mf* enthusiast.
enumeração [enumeraˈsãw] (*pl* -ões [-õjʃ]) *f* enumeration.
enumerar [enumeˈra(x)] *vt* to list.
enunciado [enũˈsjadu] *m (de teste, exame)* (exam) paper.
enunciar [enũˈsja(x)] *vt* to express.
envelhecer [ẽveʎeˈse(x)] *vt* to age ◆ *vi* to grow old.
envelope [ẽveˈlɔpi] *m* envelope.
envenenamento [ẽvenenaˈmẽntu] *m* poisoning.
envenenar [ẽveneˈna(x)] *vt* to poison.
❒ **envenenar-se** *vp* to poison o.s.
enveredar [ẽvereˈda(x)] : **enveredar por** *v + prep (fig)* to take up.
envergonhado, -da [ẽvergoˈɲadu, -da] *adj* shy.
envergonhar [ẽvergoˈɲa(x)] *vt* to embarrass.
❏ **envergonhar-se** *vp (ter vergonha)* to be embarrassed.
envernizar [ẽverniˈza(x)] *vt* to varnish.
enviar [ẽˈvja(x)] *vt* to send.
envidraçado, -da [ẽvidraˈsadu, -da] *adj* glazed.
envio [ẽˈviu] *m* sending.
enviuvar [ẽvjuˈva(x)] *vi* to be widowed.
envolver [ẽvowˈve(x)] *vt (incluir)* to involve; *(embrulhar)* to wrap up; *(misturar)* to mix up.
❏ **envolver-se em** *vp + prep (imiscuir-se em)* to get involved in.
enxada [ẽˈʃada] *f* hoe.
enxaguar [ẽʃaˈgwa(x)] *vt* to rinse.
enxame [ẽˈʃami] *m* swarm.
enxaqueca [ẽʃaˈkeka] *f* migraine.
enxergar [ẽʃexˈga(x)] *vt (descortinar)* to see; *(avistar)* to make out.
enxerto [ẽˈʃextu] *m (de planta)* cutting; *(MED: de pele)* graft.
enxofre [ẽˈʃofri] *m* sulphur.
enxotar [ẽʃoˈta(x)] *vt* to chase away.
enxugar [ẽʃuˈga(x)] *vt & vi* to dry.
enxurrada [ẽʃuˈxada] *f* torrent.
enxuto, -ta [ẽˈʃutu, -ta] *adj* dry.

enzima [ẽˈzima] *f* enzyme.
eólica [ɛˈɔlika] *adj f* → **energia**.
epicentro [epiˈsẽntru] *m* epicentre.
epidemia [epideˈmia] *f* epidemic.
epilepsia [epilepˈsia] *f* epilepsy.
epílogo [eˈpilugu] *m* epilogue.
episódio [epiˈzɔdju] *m* episode.
epitáfio [epiˈtafju] *m* epitaph.
época [ˈɛpoka] *f (período)* era, period; *(estação)* season; ~ **alta/baixa** *(de turismo)* high/low season.
equação [ekwaˈsãw] (*pl* -ões [-õjʃ]) *f* equation.
Equador [ekwaˈdo(x)] *m*: **o** ~ Ecuador.
equilibrar [ekiliˈbra(x)] *vt* to balance.
❏ **equilibrar-se** *vp* to balance.
equilíbrio [ekiˈlibriu] *m* balance.
equipa [iˈkipa] *f (Port)* = **equipe**.
equipamento [ekipaˈmẽntu] *m (esportivo)* kit; *(de empresa, fábrica)* equipment.
equipar [ekiˈpa(x)] *vt* to equip.
❏ **equipar-se** *vp* to kit o.s. out.
equiparar [ekipaˈra(x)] *vt* to compare.
❏ **equiparar-se** *vp* to be equal; ~-**se a** to equal.
equipe [eˈkipi] *f (Br)* team.
equitação [ekitaˈsãw] *f* (horse) riding.
equivalente [ekivaˈlẽntʃi] *adj & m* equivalent.
equivocar-se [ekivoˈkaxsi] *vp* to make a mistake.
equívoco [eˈkivoku] *m* mistake.
era¹ [ˈɛra] → **ser**.
era² [ˈɛra] *f* era.
erecto, -ta [iˈrɛktu, -ta] *adj (Port)* = **ereto**.
ereto, -ta [eˈretu, -ta] *adj (Br) (em pé)* upright; *(direito)* erect.
erguer [exˈge(x)] *vt (levantar)* to lift up; *(criar)* to put up.
❏ **erguer-se** *vp* to get up.
eriçado, -da [eriˈsadu, -da] *adj (cabelo, pêlo)* on end.
erigir [eriˈʒi(x)] *vt (monumento)* to erect; *(fundação)* to set up.
erosão [eroˈzãw] *f* erosion.
erótico, -ca [iˈrɔtiku, -ka] *adj* erotic.
erotismo [eroˈtiʒmu] *m* eroticism.
erradicar [exadʒiˈka(x)] *vt* to eradicate.
errado, -da [eˈxadu, -da] *adj* wrong.

errar [e'xa(x)] *vt* to get wrong ◆ *vi* *(enganar-se)* to make a mistake; *(vaguear)* to wander.

erro [ɛxu] *m* mistake.

erróneo, -nea [i'xɔnju, -nja] *adj (Port)* = **errôneo**.

errôneo, -nea [e'xonju, -nja] *adj (Br)* wrong.

erudição [erudʒi'sãw] *f* erudition.

erudito, -ta [eru'dʒitu, -ta] *adj* erudite.

erupção [erup'sãw] *(pl* **-ões** [-õjʃ]) *f (em pele)* rash; *(vulcânica)* eruption.

erva ['ɛxva] *f* grass; **~ daninha** weed.

erva-cidreira [ɛxva'sidrejra] *f* lemon verbena.

erva-doce [ɛxva'dosi] *f* aniseed.

erva-mate [ɛxva'matʃi] *f* maté, *herbal infusion drunk out of a gourd.*

ervanário [ɛxva'narju] *m* herbalist.

ervilha [ɛx'viʎa] *f* pea.

ervilhas-de-cheiro [ɛx,viʎaʒdʒi-'ʃejru] *fpl* sweet peas.

és [ɛʃ] → **ser**.

esbaforido, -da [iʒbafu'ridu, -da] *adj* breathless.

esbanjar [iʒbã'ʒa(x)] *vt (dinheiro)* to squander.

esbarrar [iʒba'xa(x)] *vi*: **~ com** OU **contra** to bump into; **~ em algo** *(chocar com)* to bump into sthg; *(deparar com)* to come up against sthg.

esbelto, -ta [iʒ'bɛwtu, -ta] *adj* slim.

esboço [iʒ'bosu] *m* sketch.

esbofetear [iʒbofe'tʒja(x)] *vt* to slap.

esburacar [iʒbura'ka(x)] *vt* to make holes in.

❑ **esburacar-se** *vp* to fall apart.

escabeche [iʃka'bɛʃi] *m (molho)* sauce *made from olive oil, garlic, onion and herbs, used to preserve cooked fish.*

escada [iʃ'kada] *f (de casa, edifício)* stairs *(pl)*; *(portátil)* ladder; **~ de caracol** spiral staircase; **~ rolante** escalator.

escadote [iʃka'dɔtʃi] *m* stepladder.

escala [iʃ'kala] *f* scale; *(de avião, navio)* stopover *(Brit)*, layover *(Am)*; **fazer ~** *(avião)* to stop over; **em grande ~** on a grand scale.

escalada [iʃka'lada] *f (de conflito)* escalation.

escalão [iʃka'lãw] *(pl* **-ões** [-õjʃ]) *m* grade.

escalar [iʃka'la(x)] *vt (montanha)* to climb.

escaldar [iʃkaw'da(x)] *vt (alimento)* to blanch ◆ *vi (estar muito quente)* to be scalding hot.

❑ **escaldar-se** *vp (queimar-se)* to scald o.s.

escalfado, -da [iʃkaw'fadu, -da] *adj (Port)* poached.

escalfar [iʃkaw'fa(x)] *vt (Port)* to poach.

escalões → **escalão**.

escalope [iʃka'lɔpi] *m* escalope.

escama [iʃ'kama] *f (de peixe)* scale.

escamar [iʃka'ma(x)] *vt (peixe)* to scale.

escandalizar [iʃkãndali'za(x)] *vt* to scandalize.

❑ **escandalizar-se** *vp* to be scandalized.

escândalo [iʃ'kãndalu] *m* scandal; **dar ~** to cause a scene.

escangalhar [iʃkãnga'ʎa(x)] *vt* to ruin.

❑ **escangalhar-se** *vp* to fall apart.

escaninho [iʃka'niɲu] *m* pigeonhole.

escanteio [iʃkãn'teju] *m (Br: em futebol)* corner.

escapar [iʃka'pa(x)] *vi* to escape; **~ de** to escape from.

❑ **escapar-se** *vp (escoar-se)* to leak; *(fugir)* to escape.

escape [iʃ'kapi] *m* exhaust.

escapulir-se [iʃkapu'lixsi] *vp (Port: fugir)* to run away.

escaravelho [iʃkara'veʎu] *m* beetle.

escarlate [eʃkar'latʃi] *adj* scarlet.

escarlatina [iʃkarla'tina] *f* scarlet fever.

escárnio [iʃ'karnju] *m* mockery.

escarpado, -da [iʃkar'padu, -da] *adj* steep.

escarrar [iʃka'xa(x)] *vi* to hawk.

escassez [iʃka'seʒ] *f* scarcity.

escasso, -a [iʃ'kasu, -a] *adj* scarce.

escavação [iʃkava'sãw] *(pl* **-ões** [-õjʃ]) *f* dig, excavation.

escavar [iʃka'va(x)] *vt* to excavate.

esclarecer [iʃklare'se(x)] *vt* to clarify.

esclarecimento [iʃklaresi'mẽntu] *m (informação)* information; *(explicação)* explanation.

escoar [iʃ'kwa(x)] *vt* to drain away.

❑ **escoar-se** *vp* to drain away.

escocês, -esa [iʃko'seʃ, -eza] *(mpl* **-eses** [-eziʃ]. *fpl* **-s** [-ʃ]) *adj* Scottish ◆ *m, f* Scot, Scotsman *(f* Scotswoman);

os escoceses the Scottish, the Scots.
Escócia [iʃˈkɔsja] f: **a ~** Scotland.
escola [iʃˈkɔla] f school; **~ politécnica** college of higher education offering vocational degrees and training for jobs in industry; **~ primária/secundária** primary/secondary school; **~ pública** state school; **~ de samba** group organized to put on dance pageants during Carnival parades.
escolar [iʃkoˈla(x)] (pl **-res** [-riʃ]) adj (livro, equipamento) school (antes de s).
escolha [iʃˈkoʎa] f choice; **você tem vários livros à ~** you have several books to choose from.
escolher [iʃkoˈʎe(x)] vt & vi to choose.
escombros [iʃˈkõmbruʃ] mpl ruins.
esconder [iʃkõˈde(x)] vt to hide.
 ⅎ esconder-se vp to hide.
esconderijo [iʃkõdeˈriʒu] m hideaway, hiding place.
escondidas [iʃkõˈdʒidaʃ] **: às escondidas** adv in secret.
escondido, -da [iʃkõˈdʒidu, -da] adj hidden.
escorar [iʃkɔˈra(x)] vt (edifício, muro) to shore up; (árvore) to prop up.
escorpião [iʃkoxˈpjãw] (pl **-ões** [-õjʃ]) m scorpion.
 ⅎ Escorpião m Scorpio.
escorrega [iʃkoˈxega] m slide.
escorregadio, -dia [iʃkoxegaˈdʒiu, -dʒia] adj slippery.
escorregar [iʃkoxeˈga(x)] vi (involuntariamente) to slip; (deslizar) to slide.
escorrer [iʃkoˈxe(x)] vt to drain ◆ vi (pingar) to drip.
escoteiro, -ra [iʃkoˈtejru, -ra] m, f (Br) (depois dos 11 anos) Scout (f Guide); (entre os 7 e 11 anos) Cub (f Brownie).
escotilha [iʃkoˈtiʎa] f hatch.
escova [iʃˈkova] f brush; **~ de dentes** toothbrush; **~ de unhas** nailbrush.
escovar [iʃkoˈva(x)] vt (cabelo, dentes, roupa) to brush; (cão, gato) to groom.
escravatura [iʃkravaˈtura] f slavery.
escravo, -va [iʃˈkravu, -va] m, f slave.
escrever [iʃkreˈve(x)] vt & vi to write; **~ à máquina** (Port) to type.
 ⅎ escrever-se vp to write to one another; **como é que se escreve ...?** how do you spell ...?
escrevinhar [iʃkreviˈɲa(x)] vt to scribble.

escrita [iʃˈkrita] f (caligrafia) handwriting.
escrito, -ta [iʃˈkritu, -ta] pp → **escrever** ◆ adj written; **por ~** in writing.
escritor, -ra [iʃkriˈto(x), -ra] (mpl **-res** [-riʃ], fpl **-s** [-ʃ]) m, f writer.
escritório [iʃkriˈtɔrju] m (de casa) study; (de advogado, empresa) office.
escritura [iʃkriˈtura] f deed.
escrivaninha [iʃkrivaˈniɲa] f writing desk.
escrúpulo [iʃˈkrupulu] m scruple; **não ter ~s** to have no scruples.
escudo [iʃˈkudu] m (unidade monetária) escudo; (arma) shield.
esculpir [iʃkuwˈpi(x)] vt to sculpt.
escultor, -ra [iʃkuwˈto(x), -ra] (mpl **-res** [-riʃ], fpl **-s** [-ʃ]) m, f sculptor (f sculptress).
escultura [iʃkuwˈtura] f sculpture.
escuras [iʃˈkuraʃ] **: às escuras** adv in the dark; **ficou tudo às ~** everything went dark.
escurecer [iʃkureˈse(x)] vi (céu, noite) to get dark ◆ vt (tinta, água) to darken.
escuridão [iʃkuriˈdãw] f darkness.
escuro, -ra [iʃˈkuru, -ra] adj dark ◆ m darkness.
escutar [iʃkuˈta(x)] vt to listen to ◆ vi to listen.
escuteiro, -ra [iʃkuˈtejru, -ra] m, f (Port) = escoteiro.
esfaquear [iʃfaˈkja(x)] vt to stab.
esfarelar [iʃfareˈla(x)] vt to crumble.
 ⅎ esfarelar-se vp to crumble.
esfarrapado, -da [iʃfaxaˈpadu, -da] adj tattered.
esfera [iʃˈfɛra] f sphere.
esférico, -ca [iʃˈfɛriku, -ka] adj spherical ◆ m (Port: bola de futebol) football.
esferográfica [iʃfɛrɔˈgrafika] f Biro®.
esferovite [iʃfɛrɔˈvitʃi] m polystyrene.
esfoladela [iʃfolaˈdɛla] f graze.
esfolar [iʃfoˈla(x)] vt to skin.
esfomeado, -da [iʃfɔˈmjadu, -da] adj starving.
esforçado, -da [iʃfoxˈsadu, -da] adj hard-working.
esforçar-se [iʃfoxˈsaxsi] vp to work hard.
esfregão [iʃfreˈgãw] (pl **-ões** [-õjʃ]) m (de louça) scourer; (de chão) mop.
esfregar [iʃfreˈga(x)] vt (friccionar) to

rub; *(roupa)* to scrub; *(louça)* to scour.

esfregões → **esfregão**.

esfriar [iʃfriˈa(x)] *vi* to cool (down); *(tempo)* to get cold.

esfuziante [iʃfuˈzjãntʃi] *adj (deslumbrante)* dazzling; *(ruidoso)* buzzing.

esganar [iʒgaˈna(x)] *vt* to strangle.

esganiçado, -da [iʒganiˈsadu, -da] *adj* shrill.

esgotado, -da [iʒgoˈtadu, -da] *adj (produto)* sold out; *(cansado)* exhausted.

esgotamento [iʒgotaˈmẽntu] *m* exhaustion; *(mental, nervoso)* breakdown.

esgotar [iʒgoˈta(x)] *vt* to use up .

❏ **esgotar-se** *vp (produto)* to sell out; *(extenuar-se)* to exhaust o.s.

esgoto [iʒˈgotu] *m (de casa)* drain; *(de rua, cidade)* sewer.

esgrima [iʒˈgrima] *f* fencing; **praticar ~** to fence.

esgueirar-se [iʒgejˈraxsi] *vp* to sneak off.

esguichar [iʒgiˈʃa(x)] *vt & vi* to squirt.

esguicho [iʒˈgiʃu] *m (jato de água)* squirt; *(repuxo)* sprinkler; *(de mangueira)* nozzle.

esguio, -guia [iʒˈgiu, -ˈgia] *adj* slender.

eslavo, -va [iʒˈlavu, -va] *adj* Slavonic ♦ *m, f* Slav.

esmagador, -ra [iʒmagaˈdo(x), -ra] *(mpl -res* [-riʃ]. *fpl -s* [-ʃ]) *adj (vitória, maioria)* overwhelming; *(peso)* crushing.

esmagar [iʒmaˈga(x)] *vt* to crush.

esmalte [iʒˈmawtʃi] *m* enamel; *(de unhas)* nail varnish.

esmeralda [iʒmeˈrawda] *f* emerald.

esmerar-se [iʒmeˈraxsi] *vp* to take great pains.

esmigalhar [iʒmigaˈʎa(x)] *vt (pão, broa, bolo)* to crumble; *(vidro, porcelana)* to shatter.

❏ **esmigalhar-se** *vp (pão, broa, bolo)* to crumble; *(vidro, porcelana)* to shatter.

esmola [iʒˈmɔla] *f*: **pedir ~** to beg.

esmurrar [iʒmuˈxa(x)] *vt (dar murros em)* to punch.

espaçar [iʃpaˈsa(x)] *vt* to space out.

espacial [iʃpaˈsjaw] *(pl -ais* [-ajʃ]) *adj* space *(antes de s).*

espaço [iʃˈpasu] *m* space; **o ~** (outer) space; **há ~ para muitas pessoas**

there's room for lots of people; **~ cibernético** cyberspace.

espaçoso, -osa [iʃpaˈsozu, -ɔza] *adj* spacious.

espada [iʃˈpada] *f* sword.

❏ **espadas** *fpl (naipe de cartas)* spades.

espadarte [iʃpaˈdaxtʃi] *m* garfish.

espaguete [iʃpaˈgetʃi] *m (Br)* spaghetti.

espairecer [iʃpajreˈse(x)] *vi* to relax.

espalhar [iʃpaˈʎa(x)] *vt (dispersar)* to scatter; *(noticia, boato)* to spread.

❏ **espalhar-se** *vp (dispersar-se)* to scatter; *(estatelar-se)* to fall over; *(noticia, boato)* to spread.

espanador [iʃpanaˈdo(x)] *(pl* **-res** [-riʃ]) *m* feather duster.

espancar [iʃpãnˈka(x)] *vt* to beat (up).

Espanha [iʃˈpaɲa] *f*: **a ~** Spain.

espanhol, -la [iʃpaˈɲɔw, -la] *(mpl* **-óis** [-ɔjʃ]. *fpl* **-s** [-ʃ]) *adj & m* Spanish ♦ *m, f (pessoa)* Spaniard; **os espanhóis** the Spanish.

espantalho [iʃpãnˈtaʎu] *m* scarecrow.

espantar [iʃpãnˈta(x)] *vt* to astonish, to astound; *(afugentar)* to scare off; **tome um café para ~ o sono** have a coffee to keep you awake.

❏ **espantar-se** *vp (admirar-se)* to be astonished; *(fugir)* to run off.

espanto [iʃˈpãntu] *m (admiração)* astonishment; *(medo)* fright.

esparadrapo [iʃparaˈdrapu] *m (Br)* (sticking) plaster *(Brit),* Bandaid® *(Am).*

espargo [eʃˈpargu] *m (Port)* asparagus.

esparguete [eʃparˈgete] *m (Port)* = **espaguete**.

espartilho [iʃpaxˈtiʎu] *m* corset.

espasmo [iʃˈpaʒmu] *m* spasm.

espátula [iʃˈpatula] *f* spatula.

especial [iʃpeˈsjaw] *(pl* **-ais** [-ajʃ]) *adj* special; **em ~** especially; **~ para** especially for.

especialidade [iʃpesjaliˈdadʒi] *f* speciality.

especialista [iʃpesjaˈliʃta] *m, f (perito)* expert; *(médico especializado)* specialist ♦ *adj* specialist.

especiarias [iʃpesjaˈriaʃ] *fpl* spices.

espécie [iʃˈpɛsji] *f (tipo)* kind, sort; *(de seres vivos)* species *(sg);* **a ~ humana** the human race; **uma ~ de** a kind ou sort of; **~ em vias de extinção** endangered species.

especificar [iʃpesifiˈka(x)] *vt* to specify.

espécime [iʃˈpɛsimi] *m* specimen.

espectáculo [cʃpɛˈtakulu] *m (Port)* = espetáculo.

espectador, -ra [iʃpɛktaˈdo(x), -ra] *(mpl* **-res** [-riʃ]. *fpl* **-s** [-ʃ]) *m, f (de programa televisivo)* viewer; *(de evento esportivo)* spectator; *(de espetáculo de circo, teatro, etc)* member of the audience.

espectro [iʃˈpɛktru] *m (fantasma)* spectre.

especulação [iʃpɛkulaˈsau] *(pl* **-ões** [-õiʃ]) *f* speculation.

especular [iʃpɛkuˈla(x)] *vi* to speculate; **~ sobre algo** to speculate on ou about sthg.

espelho [iʃˈpɛʎu] *m* mirror; **~ retrovisor** rear-view mirror.

espera [iʃˈpɛra] *f* wait; **estar à ~ de** to be waiting for.

esperança [iʃpɛˈrãsa] *f* hope.

esperar [iʃpɛˈra(x)] *vt (aguardar)* to wait for; *(ter esperança em)* to expect ♦ *vi (aguardar)* to wait; **~ que** to hope (that); **fazer alguém ~** to keep sb waiting; **ir ~ alguém** to meet sb; **como era de ~** as was to be expected.

esperma [iʃˈpɛxma] *m* sperm.

espertalhão, -lhona [iʃpɛxtaˈʎãw, -ˈʎona] *(mpl* **-ões** [-õiʃ]. *fpl* **-s** [-ʃ]) *m, f* smart aleck.

esperteza [iʃpɛxˈteza] *f* cunning.

esperto, -ta [iʃˈpɛxtu, -ta] *adj (astuto)* cunning; *(activo)* lively.

espesso, -a [iʃˈpɛsu, -a] *adj* thick.

espessura [iʃpɛˈsura] *f* thickness.

espetacular [iʃpɛtakuˈla(x)] *(pl* **-es** [-iʃ]) *adj* spectacular.

espetáculo [iʃpɛˈtakulu] *m (Br) (de circo, teatro)* show; **~ de luzes e som** concert and firework display, often the finale of a festival; **~ de variedades** variety show.

espetada [cʃpɛˈtada] *f (Port)* shish kebab; **~ mista** shish kebab with both meat and vegetable pieces.

espetar [iʃpɛˈta(x)] *vt* to pierce.
❏ **espetar-se** *vp* to prick o.s.

espeto [iʃˈpɛtu] *m (de ferro)* spit; *(de pau)* stake.

espevitado, -da [iʃpɛviˈtadu, -da] *adj* lively.

espezinhar [iʃpɛziˈɲa(x)] *vt* to trample on; *(sujar)* to dirty.

espia [iʃˈpia] *f (cabo)* cable, → **espião**.

espião, -pia [iʃˈpjãw, -ˈpia] *(mpl* **-ões**

[-õiʃ]. *fpl* **-s** [-ʃ]) *m, f* spy.

espiar [iʃˈpja(x)] *vt* to spy on.

espiga [iʃˈpiga] *f* ear.

espinafre [iʃpiˈnafri] *m* spinach.

espingarda [iʃpĩˈgarda] *f* shotgun.

espinha [iʃˈpiɲa] *f (de peixe)* bone; *(em pele)* spot; **~ (dorsal)** backbone, spine.

espinho [iʃˈpiɲu] *m (de rosa, silva)* thorn; *(de porco-espinho)* quill.

espiões → **espião**.

espiral [iʃpiˈraw] *(pl* **-ais** [-ajʃ]) *f* spiral; **em ~** spiral.

espírito [iʃˈpiritu] *m* spirit.

espiritual [iʃpiriˈtwaw] *(pl* **-ais** [-ajʃ]) *adj* spiritual.

espirrar [iʃpiˈxa(x)] *vi (dar espirros)* to sneeze; *(esguichar)* to spit.

esplanada [iʃplaˈnada] *f* esplanade.

esplêndido, -da [iʃˈplẽdidu, -da] *adj* splendid.

esplendor [iʃplẽˈdo(x)] *m (luxo)* splendour; *(brilho)* brilliance.

espoleta [iʃpoˈleta] *f* fuse.

esponja [iʃˈpõʒa] *f* sponge; **passar uma ~ sobre o assunto** *(fig: esquecer)* to wipe the slate clean.

espontaneidade [iʃpõtaneiˈdadʒi] *f* spontaneity.

espontâneo, -nea [iʃpõˈtanju, -nja] *adj* spontaneous.

espora [iʃˈpɔra] *f* spur.

esporádico, -ca [iʃpoˈradʒiku, -ka] *adj* sporadic.

esporte [iʃˈpɔxtʃi] *m (Br)* sport.

esportista [iʃpɔxˈtʃiʃta] *mf (Br)* sportsman *(f* sportswoman).

esportivo, -va [iʃpɔxˈtʃivu, -va] *adj (Br)* sports *(antes de s).*

esposo, -sa [iʃˈpozu, -za] *m, f* husband *(f* wife).

espreguiçar-se [iʃpregiˈsaxsi] *vp* to stretch.

espreita [iʃˈprejta] : **à espreita** *adv* on the lookout.

espreitar [iʃprejˈta(x)] *vt* to peep at.

espremedor [iʃpremeˈdo(x)] *(pl* **-res** [-riʃ]) *m (juice)* squeezer.

espremer [iʃpreˈme(x)] *vt* to squeeze.

espuma [iʃˈpuma] *f (de mar)* surf; *(de sabão)* lather; *(de banho)* foam.

espumante [iʃpuˈmãtʃi] *adj* sparkling ♦ *m* sparkling wine.

espumoso, -osa [iʃpuˈmozu, -ɔza]

adj & m = **espumante**.

Esq. *(abrev de esquerdo)* L.

esquadra [eʃˈkwadra] f fleet; *(Port: delegacia)* police station.

esquadro [iʃˈkwadru] m set square.

esquecer [iʃkeˈse(x)] vt to forget.

⏌ **esquecer-se** vp to forget; **~-se algo/de fazer algo** to forget sthg/to do sthg.

esquecido, -da [iʃkeˈsidu, -da] adj absent-minded, forgetful ♦ m, f absent-minded person.

esquecimento [iʃkesiˈmẽntu] m forgetfulness.

esqueleto [iʃkeˈletu] m skeleton.

esquema [iʃˈkema] m *(diagrama)* diagram; *(sistema)* scheme.

esquentador [iʃkẽntaˈdo(x)] *(pl* -res [-riʃ]) m *(de água)* immersion heater; *(aquecedor)* heater.

esquentar [iʃkẽnˈta(x)] vt to heat up.

esquerda [iʃˈkexda] f: **a ~** *(mão)* one's left hand; *(lado)* the left-hand side; *(em política)* the Left; **dirija pela ~** drive on the left; **mantenha ~** keep left; **à ~ (de)** on the left (of); **virar à ~** to turn left; **ser de ~** *(POL)* to be left-wing.

esquerdo, -da [iʃˈkexdu, -da] adj *(mão, perna, lado)* left; *(canhoto)* left-handed.

esqui [iʃˈki] m *(utensílio)* ski; *(esporte)* skiing; **~ aquático** water-skiing.

esquiar [iʃˈkja(x)] vi to ski.

esquilo [iʃˈkilu] m squirrel.

esquina [iʃˈkina] f corner.

esquisito, -ta [iʃkiˈzitu, -ta] adj *(estranho)* strange, weird; *(picuinhas)* fussy.

esquivar-se [iʃkiˈvaxsi] vp to escape; **~ a fazer algo** to get out of doing sthg.

esquivo, -va [iʃˈkivu, -va] adj *(arisco)* shy.

esse, essa [ˈesi, ˈɛsa] adj that, those *(pl)* ♦ pron that (one), those (ones) *(pl)*; **essa é boa!** you must be joking!; **só faltava mais essa!** that's the final straw!

essência [eˈsẽsja] f essence.

essencial [esẽˈsjaw] *(pl* -ais [-ajʃ]) adj essential ♦ m: **o ~** *(o indispensável)* the bare essentials *(pl)*; *(o importante)* the important thing.

esta → este².

está [iʃˈta] → **estar**.

estabelecer [iʃtabeleˈse(x)] vt to establish.

⏌ **estabelecer-se** vp to establish o.s.

estabelecimento [iʃtabelesiˈmẽntu] m *(casa comercial)* business; *(instituição)* establishment; **~ de ensino** school.

estabilidade [iʃtabiliˈdadʒi] f stability.

estabilizador [iʃtabilizaˈdo(x)] *(pl* -res [-riʃ]) m: **~ (de corrente)** stabilizer.

estábulo [iʃˈtabulu] m stable.

estaca [iʃˈtaka] f stake.

estação [iʃtaˈsãw] *(pl* -ões [-õjʃ]) f *(de trem, ônibus)* station; *(do ano, turismo, vendas)* season; **~ de águas** *(Br)* spa; **~ de rádio** radio station.

estacionamento [iʃtasjonaˈmẽntu] m *(acto)* parking; *(lugar)* parking space; **"~ privativo"** "private parking"; **"~ proibido"** "no parking".

estacionar [iʃtasjoˈna(x)] vt & vi to park.

estações → estação.

estada [iʃˈtada] f stay.

estadia [iʃtaˈdʒia] f = **estada**.

estádio [iʃˈtadʒju] m *(de futebol, atletismo)* stadium; *(fase)* phase.

estadista [iʃtaˈdʒiʃta] mf statesman *(f* stateswoman).

estado [iʃˈtadu] m state; **em bom/mau ~** *(objeto)* in good/bad condition; **~ civil** marital status; **~ físico** level of fitness.

⏌ **Estado** m: **o Estado** the State; **os Estados Unidos** the United States.

estalagem [iʃtaˈlaʒẽ] *(pl* -ns [-ʃ]) f inn.

estalar [iʃtaˈla(x)] vi *(porcelana, vidro, osso)* to crack; *(lenha)* to crackle ♦ vt: **~ a língua** to click one's tongue; **~ os dedos** to snap one's fingers.

estalido [iʃtaˈlidu] m *(estalo)* crack; *(crepitação)* crackle.

estalo [iʃˈtalu] m *(ruido)* crack; **me deu um ~** *(fig)* the penny dropped.

estampado, -da [iʃtãmˈpadu, -da] adj printed.

estancar [iʃtãŋˈka(x)] vt *(líquido)* to stop; *(sangue)* to staunch ♦ vi *(sangue)* to stop.

estância [iʃˈtãsja] f *(Br: quinta)* ranch; **~ balneária** bathing resort; **~ de férias** holiday resort; **~ hidromineral** *(Br)* spa; **~ termal** spa.

estanho [iʃˈtaɲu] m tin.

estante [iʃˈtãntʃi] f bookcase.

estão [iʃˈtãw] → **estar**.

estapafúrdio, -dia [iʃtapaˈfurdʒju. -dʒja] *adj (excêntrico)* outrageous; *(esquisito)* peculiar.

estar [iʃˈta(x)] *vi* **1.** *(com lugar)* to be; *(em casa)* to be at home, to be in; **ela estará lá à hora certa** she'll be there on time; **estarei no emprego às dez** I'll be at work at ten; **está? está lá?** *(Port: ao telefone)* hello? hello?
2. *(exprime estado)* to be; **está quebrado** it's out of order; **~ bem/mal de saúde** to be well/unwell; **está muito calor/frio** it's very hot/cold.
3. *(manter-se)* to be; **estive em casa toda a tarde** I was at home all afternoon; **estive esperando uma hora** I waited for an hour; **estive fora três anos** I lived abroad for three years.
4. *(em locuções)*: **está bem** OU **certo!** OK!, all right!
⅃ **estar a** *v + prep (relativo a preço)* to cost, to be; *(Port: seguido de infinitivo)*: **ele está a estudar** he's studying; **o camarão está a 25 reais o quilo** prawns costs OU are 25 reals a kilo.
⅃ **estar de** *v + prep*: **~ de baixa/férias** to be on sick leave/holiday; **~ de saia** to be wearing a skirt; **~ de vigia** to keep watch.
⅃ **estar para** *v + prep*: **~ para fazer algo** to be about to do sthg; **estou para sair** I'm about to go out, I'm just going out; **ele está para chegar** he'll be here any minute now; **não estou para brincadeiras** I'm not in the mood for silly games.
⅃ **estar perante** *v + prep (frente a)* to be facing; **você está perante um gênio** you're in the presence of a genius.
⅃ **estar por** *v + prep (apoiar)* to support; *(por realizar)*: **a cama está por fazer** the bed hasn't been made yet; **a limpeza está por fazer** the cleaning hasn't been done yet.
⅃ **estar sem** *v + prep*: **estou sem tempo** I haven't got the time; **estou sem dinheiro** I haven't got any cash; **ele está sem comer há dois dias** he hasn't eaten for two days.

estardalhaço [iʃtaxdaˈʎasu] *m* racket.

estarrecer [iʃtaxeˈse(x)] *vt* to terrify.

estatal [iʃtaˈtaw] *(pl* **-ais** [-ajʃ]) *adj* state *(antes de s)*.

estático, -ca [iʃˈtatʃiku, -ka] *adj* static.

estátua [iʃˈtatwa] *f* statue.

estatura [iʃtaˈtura] *f* stature.

estatuto [iʃtaˈtutu] *m (regulamento)* statute; *(de pessoa)* status.

este¹ [ˈɛʃtʃi] *m* east; **a** OU **no ~** in the east; **a ~ de** east of.

este², esta [ˈɛʃtʃi. ˈɛʃta] *adj* this, these *(pl)* ◆ *pron* this (one), these (ones) *(pl)*; **~ mês (que vem) vou de férias** I'm going on holiday next month; **não o vi esta semana** I haven't seen him this week.

esteira [iʃˈtejra] *f (de chão)* mat; *(de praia)* beach mat.

estendal [eʃtɛnˈdal] *(pl* **-ais** [-ajʃ]) *m (Port)* washing line.

estender [iʃtɛnˈde(x)] *vt (braços, pernas)* to stretch (out); *(jornal)* to spread out; *(roupa no varal)* to hang out; *(prazo, estadia)* to extend.
⅃ **estender-se** *vp (no espaço)* to stretch out; *(no tempo)* to go on.

estenografia [iʃtenograˈfia] *f* shorthand.

estepe [iʃˈtɛpi] *f* steppes *(pl)*.

estéreis → **estéril**.

estereofónico, -ca [eʃterjoˈfoniku, -ka] *adj (Port)* = **estereofônico**.

estereofônico, -ca [iʃterjoˈfoniku, -ka] *adj (Br)* stereo(phonic).

estéril [iʃˈtɛriw] *(pl* **-reis** [-rejʃ]) *adj* infertile.

esterilizar [iʃteriliˈza(x)] *vt* to sterilize.

estética [iʃˈtɛtika] *f* aesthetics *(sg)*.

estetoscópio [iʃtetoʃˈkɔpju] *m* stethoscope.

esteve [iʃˈtevi] → **estar**.

estiar [iʃˈtʃja(x)] *vi* to stop raining.

estibordo [iʃtʃiˈbɔxdu] *m* starboard.

esticar [iʃtʃiˈka(x)] *vt* to stretch.
⅃ **esticar-se** *vp* to stretch out.

estigma [iʃˈtʃigma] *m* stigma.

estilhaçar [iʃtʃiʎaˈsa(x)] *vt* to shatter.
⅃ **estilhaçar-se** *vp* to shatter.

estilhaço [iʃtʃiˈʎasu] *m* splinter.

estilo [iʃˈtʃilu] *m* style.

estima [iʃˈtʃima] *f* esteem.

estimar [iʃtʃiˈma(x)] *vt* to cherish.

estimativa [iʃtʃimaˈtʃiva] *f* estimate.

estimulante [iʃtʃimuˈlãntʃi] *adj* stimulating ◆ *m* stimulant.

estimular [iʃtʃimuˈla(x)] *vt* to stimulate.

estipular [eʃtʃipuˈla(x)] *vt* to stipulate.

estivador, -ra [iʃtʃiva'do(x). -ra] *(mpl -res* [-riʃ], *fpl* **-s** [-ʃ]) *m, f* docker *(Brit),* stevedore *(Am).*

estive [iʃ'tivi] → **estar.**

estofo [iʃ'tofu] *m* stuffing.

estojo [iʃ'toʒu] *m* set; ~ **(de lápis)** pencil case; ~ **de primeiros-socorros** first-aid kit.

estômago [iʃ'tomagu] *m* stomach.

estontear [iʃtõn'tʃia(x)] *vt* to bewilder.

estore [iʃ'tɔri] *m* blind.

estorninho [iʃtox'niɲu] *m* starling.

estou [iʃ'to] → **estar.**

estourado, -da [iʃto'radu. -da] *adj (fam: cansado)* knackered.

estourar [iʃto'ra(x)] *vt (balão, bola)* to burst; *(fam: dinheiro)* to blow ♦ *vi (balão, bola)* to burst; *(pneu)* to blow out; *(bomba, explosivo)* to explode.

estouro [iʃ'toru] *m (de balão, bola, pneu)* bursting; *(ruído)* bang; **dar o ~** *(fam: zangar-se)* to blow a fuse.

estrábico, -ca [iʃ'trabiku. -ka] *adj* cross-eyed ♦ *m, f* cross-eyed person.

estrabismo [iʃtra'biʒmu] *m* squint.

estrada [iʃ'trada] *f* road; ~ **de via dupla** dual carriageway; ~ **de ferro** *(Br)* railway *(Brit),* railroad *(Am);* ~ **secundária** minor road.

estrado [iʃ'tradu] *m* platform.

estragado, -da [iʃtra'gadu. -da] *adj (leite, comida)* off; *(pão)* stale; *(aparelho, máquina)* out of order.

estragão [iʃtra'gãw] *m* tarragon.

estragar [iʃtra'ga(x)] *vt (aparelho, máquina)* to break; *(desperdiçar)* to waste.

⊃ **estragar-se** *vp (comida, leite)* to go off.

estrangeiro, -ra [iʃtrã'ʒejru. -ra] *adj (cidade, país, língua)* foreign ♦ *m, f (pessoa)* foreigner ♦ *m:* **o** ~ foreign countries *(pl);* **ir para o** ~ to go abroad; **viver no** ~ to live abroad.

estrangular [iʃtrãgu'la(x)] *vt* to strangle.

estranhar [iʃtra'ɲa(x)] *vt* to find odd.

estranho, -nha [iʃ'traɲu. -ɲa] *adj* odd ♦ *m, f* stranger.

estratégia [iʃtra'tɛʒja] *f* strategy.

estrear [iʃtri'a(x)] *vt (roupa, sapatos)* to wear for the first time ♦ *vi (peça teatral)* to open; *(filme)* to premiere.

estreia [eʃ'traja] *f (Port)* = **estréia.**

estréia [iʃ'treja] *f (Br) (de ator):* debut;

(de peça teatral) opening night; *(de filme)* premiere.

estreitar [iʃtrej'ta(x)] *vt (roupa)* to take in ♦ *vi (estrada, caminho)* to narrow.

estreito, -ta [iʃ'trejtu. -ta] *adj* narrow; *(roupa)* tight ♦ *m (canal)* strait.

estrela [iʃ'trela] *f* star; ~ **cadente** shooting star; **ver ~s** *(fig: ter dor violenta)* to see stars.

estremecer [iʃtreme'se(x)] *vt* to shake ♦ *vi (tremer)* to shake; *(assustar-se)* to be shaken.

estria [iʃ'tria] *f (em coxas, quadris, seios)* stretchmark; *(em superfície)* groove.

estribo [iʃ'tribu] *m* stirrup.

estridente [iʃtri'dẽntʃi] *adj* strident.

estrofe [iʃ'trɔfi] *f* stanza.

estrondo [iʃ'trõndu] *m (som)* bang; *(fig: pompa)* ostentation.

estropiar [iʃtro'pja(x)] *vt* to maim.

estrume [iʃ'trumi] *m* manure.

estrutura [iʃtru'tura] *f* structure.

estuário [iʃ'twarju] *m* estuary.

estudante [iʃtu'dãntʃi] *mf* student.

estudar [iʃtu'da(x)] *vt & vi* to study.

estúdio [iʃ'tudʒju] *m* studio; *(apartamento)* studio flat.

estudioso, -osa [iʃtu'dʒjozu. -ɔza] *adj* studious.

estudo [iʃ'tudu] *m* study; **em** ~ under consideration.

estufa [iʃ'tufa] *f (de jardim)* greenhouse; *(de fogão)* plate warmer; *(tipo de fogão)* heater.

estupefação [eʃtupefa'sãw] *f (Br)* astonishment.

estupefacção [iʃtupefa'sãw] *f (Port)* = **estupefação.**

estupefaciente [iʃtupefa'sjẽntʃi] *m* drug.

estupefacto, -ta [eʃtupe'fa(k)tu. -ta] *adj (Port)* = **estupefato.**

estupefato, -ta [iʃtupe'fatu. -ta] *adj (Br)* astounded.

estupendo, -da [iʃtu'pẽndu. -da] *adj (extraordinário)* remarkable; *(ótimo)* great.

estupidez [iʃtupi'deʃ] *f* stupidity.

estúpido, -da [iʃ'tupidu. -da] *m, f* idiot.

estupro [iʃ'tupru] *m* rape.

estuque [iʃ'tuki] *m* plaster.

esvaziar [iʒva'zja(x)] *vt* to empty.

esvoaçar [iʒvwaˈsa(x)] *vi (ave)* to flutter.

etapa [iˈtapa] *f* stage; **fazer algo por ~s** to do sthg by OU in stages.

éter [ˈɛtɛ(x)] *m* ether.

eternidade [etexniˈdadʒi] *f* eternity; **demorar/esperar uma ~** to take/wait ages.

eterno, -na [eˈtexnu, -na] *adj* eternal.

ética [ˈɛtʃika] *f* ethics *(pl)*.

ético, -ca [ˈɛtʃiku, -ka] *adj* ethical.

etílico [eˈtʃiliku] *adj m* **→ álcool**.

etiqueta [etʃiˈketa] *f (rótulo)* label, tag; *(social)* etiquette.

étnico, -ca [ˈɛtniku, -ka] *adj* ethnic.

eu [ˈew] *pron (sujeito)* I; **e ~?** what about me?; **sou ~** it's me; **~ mesmo** OU **próprio** (I) myself.

E.U.A. *mpl (abrev de Estados Unidos da América)* USA.

eucalipto [ewkaˈliptu] *m* eucalyptus.

eufemismo [ewfeˈmiʒmu] *m* euphemism.

euforia [ewfoˈria] *f* euphoria.

Eurocheque® [ewroˈʃeki] *m* Eurocheque®.

Europa [ewˈrɔpa] *f*: **a ~** Europe.

europeu, -péia [ewruˈpew, -peja] *adj & m, f* European.

evacuação [evakwaˈsãw] *(pl* **-ões** [-õjʃ]) *f* evacuation.

evacuar [evaˈkwa(x)] *vt* to evacuate.

evadir-se [evaˈdixsi] *vp* to escape.

Evangelho [evãˈʒeʎu] *m*: **o ~** the Gospel.

evaporar [evapoˈra(x)] *vt* to evaporate.

⌐ **evaporar-se** *vp (líquido)* to evaporate; *(fig: desaparecer)* to vanish.

evasão [evaˈzãw] *(pl* **-ões** [-õjʃ]) *f (de prisão, rotina)* escape; *(evasiva)* evasion.

evasiva [evaˈziva] *f* evasion.

evasivo, -va [evaˈzivu, -va] *adj* evasive.

evasões → evasão.

evento [eˈvẽtu] *m* event.

eventual [evẽˈtwaw] *(pl* **-ais** [-ajʃ]) *adj (possível)* possible.

evidência [eviˈdẽsja] *f* evidence.

evidenciar [evidẽˈsja(x)] *vt* to show.

⌐ **evidenciar-se** *vp* to draw attention to o.s.

evidente [eviˈdẽtʃi] *adj* evident, obvious; **como é ~** obviously.

evitar [eviˈta(x)] *vt* to avoid; **~ que algo aconteça** to avoid sthg happening.

evocar [evoˈka(x)] *vt* to evoke.

evolução [evoluˈsãw] *f* evolution.

evoluir [evoˈlwi(x)] *vi* to evolve.

exacto, -ta [eˈzatu, -ta] *adj (Port)* = **exato**.

exagerar [ezaʒeˈra(x)] *vt* to exaggerate.

exagero [ezaˈʒeru] *m* exaggeration, overstatement; **é um ~!** it's too much!; **sem ~** seriously.

exalar [ezaˈla(x)] *vt* to give off.

exaltado, -da [ezawˈtadu, -da] *adj* exasperated.

exaltar [ezawˈta(x)] *vt (elogiar)* to exalt; *(irritar)* to exasperate.

⌐ **exaltar-se** *vp (irritar-se)* to lose one's temper.

exame [eˈzami] *m (escolar, universitário)* exam; *(médico)* examination; **~ de aptidão física** medical.

examinar [ezamiˈna(x)] *vt* to examine.

exatamente [eˌzataˈmẽtʃi] *adv* exactly ♦ *interj* exactly!

exatidão [ezatʃiˈdãw] *f (precisão)* precision; *(rigor)* accuracy; **com ~** exactly.

exato, -ta [eˈzatu, -ta] *adj (Br) (preciso)* precise; *(rigoroso)* accurate; *(correto)* correct.

exaustão [ezawˈʃtãw] *f* exhaustion.

exausto, -ta [eˈzawʃtu, -ta] *adj* exhausted.

exaustor [ezawˈʃto(x)] *(pl* **-res** [-riʃ]) *m* extractor fan.

exceção [eˌ(ʃ)seˈsãw] *(pl* **-ões** [-õjʃ]) *f (Br)* exception; **à** OU **com a ~ de** except for; **fora de ~** out of the ordinary; **sem ~** without exception.

excedente [eseˈdẽtʃi] *m* surplus; **~s de leite/manteiga** milk/butter mountain *(sg)*.

exceder [eseˈde(x)] *vt* to exceed.

⌐ **exceder-se** *vp (exagerar)* to go too far; *(enfurecer-se)* to lose one's temper; **~-se em** to overdo.

excelente [eseˈlẽtʃi] *adj* excellent.

excelentíssimo, -ma [eseˈlẽtʃisimu, -ma] *superl formal term of address used in correspondence*.

excêntrico, -ca [eˈsẽtriku, -ka] *adj* eccentric.

excepção [eʃseˈsãw] *(pl* **-ões** [-õjʃ]) *f (Port)* = **exceção**.

excepcional [esesju'naw] (*pl -ais* [-ajʃ]) *adj* exceptional.
excepções → excepção.
excepto [e'sɛtu] *prep (Port)* = exceto.
excerto [e'sɛxtu] *m* excerpt.
excessivo, -va [ese'sivu, -va] *adj* excessive.
excesso [e'sɛsu] *m* excess; **em ~** too much; **~ de peso** *(relativo a bagagem)* excess baggage; *(relativo a pessoa)* excess weight; **~ de velocidade** speeding.
exceto [e'sɛtu] *prep (Br)* except, apart from.
excitação [esita'sãw] *f (entusiasmo)* excitement; *(irritação)* agitation.
excitado, -da [esi'tadu, -da] *adj (entusiasmado)* excited; *(irritado)* agitated.
excitante [esi'tãntʃi] *adj* exciting.
exclamação [iʃklama'sãw] (*pl -ões* [-õjʃ]) *f* exclamation.
exclamar [iʃkla'ma(x)] *vi* to exclaim.
excluir [iʃklu'i(x)] *vt* to exclude.
exclusivo, -va [iʃklu'zivu, -va] *adj & m* exclusive; **ter o ~ de** to corner the market in.
excursão [iʃkux'sãw] (*pl -ões* [-õjʃ]) *f (de ônibus)* (coach) trip.
execução [ezeku'sãw] *f (de objeto)* production; *(de trabalho, plano, projeto)* execution; *(de prato culinário)* preparation; **pôr algo em ~** to put sthg into practice.
executar [ezeku'ta(x)] *vt (música, cena teatral)* to perform; *(desenho, pintura)* to produce; *(ordem, plano, trabalho)* to carry out; *(matar)* to execute.
executivo, -va [ezeku'tivu, -va] *m, f* executive.
exemplar [ezẽm'pla(x)] (*pl -es* [-iʃ]) *adj* exemplary ♦ *m (de espécie, raça)* specimen; *(de livro, revista)* copy.
exemplo [e'zẽmplu] *m* example; **por ~** for example; **a título de ~** as an example.
exercer [ezex'se(x)] *vt (profissão)* to practise; *(função)* to fulfil; *(influência)* to exercise ♦ *vi* to practise; **ela exerceu o cargo de presidente vários anos** she was the president for several years.
exercício [ezex'sisju] *m* exercise; *(de profissão, atividade)* practice.
exercitar [ezexsi'ta(x)] *vt* to exercise.
⊐ exercitar-se *vp* to take exercise.
exército [e'zɛxsitu] *m* army.

exibição [ezchi'sãw] (*pl -ões* [-õjʃ]) *f* show; *(de peça teatral, filme)* showing; *(Port: de quadros, esculturas)* exhibition; **em ~** *(peça teatral, filme)* showing.
exibir [ezi'bi(x)] *vt* to show; *(quadro, escultura)* to exhibit.
⊐ exibir-se *vp* to show off.
exigência [ezi'ʒẽsja] *f* demand.
exigir [ezi'ʒi(x)] *vt* to demand.
existência [eziʃ'tẽsja] *f* existence.
existir [eziʃ'ti(x)] *vi* to exist.
êxito ['ezitu] *m* success; **ter ~** to be successful.
Exma. *abrev* = excelentíssima.
Exmo. *abrev* = excelentíssimo.
exorcismo [ezox'siʒmu] *m* exorcism.
exorcista [ezox'siʃta] *mf* exorcist.
exortação [ezoxta'sãw] (*pl -ões* [-õjʃ]) *f* exhortation.
exótico, -ca [e'zɔtʃiku, -ka] *adj* exotic.
expansão [iʃpã'sãw] (*pl -ões* [-õjʃ]) *f (progresso)* expansion; *(alegria)* expansiveness.
expansivo, -va [iʃpã'sivu, -va] *adj* expansive.
expansões → expansão.
expectativa [iʃpɛkta'tʃiva] *f* expectation; **ficar na ~ de** to expect.
expediente [iʃpe'dʒjẽntʃi] *m (de repartição, estabelecimento comercial)* business hours *(pl)*.
expedir [iʃpe'dʒi(x)] *vt* to dispatch.
experiência [iʃpe'rjẽsja] *f (ensaio)* experiment; *(conhecimento)* experience; **com ~** experienced.
experiente [iʃpe'rjẽntʃi] *adj* experienced.
experimentar [iʃperimẽ'ta(x)] *vt (máquina)* to test; *(carro)* to test-drive; *(peça de roupa, calçado)* to try on; *(comida, bebida)* to try; *(sensação, emoção)* to experience.
expirar [iʃpi'ra(x)] *vt* to exhale ♦ *vi (prazo)* to expire.
explicação [iʃplika'sãw] (*pl -ões* [-õjʃ]) *f* explanation; *(aula particular)* private lesson.
explicar [iʃpli'ka(x)] *vt* to explain.
⊐ explicar-se *vp* to explain o.s.
explícito, -ta [iʃ'plisitu, -ta] *adj* explicit.
explodir [iʃplo'di(x)] *vi* to explode.
exploração [iʃplora'sãw] *f (investigação)* exploration; *(abuso)* exploitation.

explorar [iʃploˈra(x)] vt (investigar) to explore; (abusar de) to exploit.

explosão [iʃploˈzãw] (pl -ões [-õjʃ]) f explosion.

expor [iʃˈpo(x)] vt (ideia) to put forward; (situação) to explain; (exibir) to exhibit; (produtos) to display.

❏ **expor-se a** vp + prep to expose o.s. to.

exportação [iʃpoxtaˈsãw] (pl -ões [-õjʃ]) f export.

exportar [iʃpoxˈta(x)] vt to export.

exposição [iʃpoziˈsãw] (pl -ões [-õjʃ]) f (de pintura, fotografia) exhibition; (em fotografia) exposure; (de produtos) display; (narração) account; **em ~** on show.

exposto, -osta [iʃˈpoʃtu, -ɔʃta] adj (em exposição) on show; (produtos) on display.

expressão [iʃpreˈsãw] (pl -ões [-õjʃ]) f expression; **~ escrita** literacy; **~ oral** oral expression.

expressar [iʃpreˈsa(x)] vt to express.

❏ **expressar-se** vp to express o.s.

expressivo, -va [iʃpreˈsivu, -va] adj expressive.

expresso, -a [iʃˈpresu, -a] adj & m express.

expressões → expressão.

exprimir [iʃpriˈmi(x)] vt to express.

❏ **exprimir-se** vp to express o.s.

expropriar [iʃpropriˈa(x)] vt to expropriate.

expulsar [iʃpuwˈsa(x)] vt to expel.

expulso, -sa [iʃˈpuwsu, -sa] pp → expulsar ◆ adj expelled.

extensão [iʃtẽˈsãw] (pl -ões [-õjʃ]) f extension; (dimensão espacial) extent; (dimensão temporal) duration.

extenso, -sa [iʃˈtẽsu, -sa] adj long; (vasto) extensive; **escrever algo por ~** to write sthg out in full.

extensões → extensão.

extenuado, -da [iʃteˈnwadu, -da] adj worn-out.

extenuante [iʃteˈnwãntʃi] adj tiring.

exterior [iʃteˈrjo(x)] (pl -es [-iʃ]) adj outside; (calma, aparência) outward; (Br: política, comércio) foreign ◆ m (parte exterior) exterior; (aparência) outside; **o ~** (Br: o estrangeiro) foreign countries (pl); **para o/no ~** (Br) abroad.

externo, -na [iʃˈtɛxnu, -na] adj external; (Port: política, comércio) foreign.

extinção [iʃtĩˈsãw] f extinction.

extinguir [iʃtĩˈgi(x)] vt (fogo) to extinguish, to put out; (lei, norma) to abolish.

❏ **extinguir-se** vp (apagar-se) to go out; (desaparecer) to become extinct, to die out.

extinto, -ta [iʃˈtĩtu, -ta] pp → extinguir ◆ adj (espécie animal, vegetal) extinct; (fogo) extinguished; (lei, norma) defunct.

extintor [iʃtĩˈto(x)] (pl -es [-iʃ]) m fire extinguisher.

extra [ˈejʃtra] adj extra ◆ m (de automóvel) spare part; (em despesa) extras (pl); (em emprego) perk.

extração [iʃtraˈsãw] (pl -ões [-õjʃ]) f (Br) extraction; (de órgão) removal; (de loteria) draw.

extracção [eʃtraˈsãw] (pl -ões [-õjʃ]) f (Port) = extração.

extrações → extração.

extracto [eʃˈtratu] m (Port) = extrato.

extraditar [iʃtradʒiˈta(x)] vt to extradite.

extrair [iʃtraˈi(x)] vt to extract; (número de loteria) to draw; **~ algo de algo** to extract sthg from sthg.

extraordinário, -ria [iʃtraordʒiˈnarju, -rja] adj extraordinary.

extrato [iʃˈtratu] m (Br) extract; (de conta bancária) statement.

extravagância [iʃtravaˈgãsja] f extravagance.

extraviado, -da [iʃtraˈvjadu, -da] adj lost.

extraviar [iʃtraˈvja(x)] vt to lose.

❏ **extraviar-se** vp to get lost.

extremidade [iʃtremiˈdadʒi] f extremity.

extremo, -ma [iʃˈtremu, -ma] adj (decisão, medida) drastic; (temperatura, condição) extreme ◆ m extreme; **em caso ~** if the worst comes to the worst; **ir de um ~ ao outro** (fig) to go from one extreme to the other; **chegar ao ~** to go to extremes.

extrovertido, -da [iʃtrovexˈtʃidu, -da] adj outgoing.

exuberante [ezubeˈrãntʃi] adj (pessoa) exuberant; (roupa) garish; (vegetação) lush.

exumar [ezuˈma(x)] vt to exhume.

ex-voto [ɛksˈvɔtu] m ex-voto.

F

fábrica ['fabrika] f factory.

fabricante [fabri'kãntʃi] m manufacturer.

fabricar [fabri'ka(x)] vt to make, to manufacture.

fabrico [fa'briku] m manufacture.

fabuloso, -osa [fabu'lozu, -ɔza] adj fabulous.

faca ['faka] f knife.

face ['fasi] f face; **fazer ~ a** to face up to; **em ~** opposite; **em ~ de** in view of; **~ a ~** face to face.

fáceis → fácil.

fachada [fa'ʃada] f facade.

fácil ['fasiw] (pl **-ceis** [-sejʃ]) adj easy.

facilidade [fasili'dadʒi] f (destreza) ease; (aptidão) aptitude; **com ~** with ease.

facilitar [fasili'ta(x)] vt to facilitate; **ele facilitou-nos o uso do seu equipamento** he let us use his equipment.

faço ['fasu] → **fazer.**

facto ['fa(k)tu] m (Port) = **fato.**

factor [fa(k)'tor] (mpl **-res** [-reʃ]) m (Port) = **fator.**

factual [fa'twal] (pl **-ais** [-ajʃ]) adj (Port) = **fatual.**

factura [fa'tura] f (Port) = **fatura.**

faculdade [fakuw'dadʒi] f faculty.

facultativo, -va [fakuwta'tʃivu, -va] adj optional.

fada ['fada] f fairy.

fadiga [fa'dʒiga] f fatigue.

fadista [fa'dʒiʃta] mf "fado" singer.

fado ['fadu] m (destino) destiny, fate; (música) a type of melancholy Portuguese folk song set to music.

fagulha [fa'guʎa] f spark.

faia ['faja] f beech.

faiança [fa'jãsa] f glazed ceramics (pl).

faisão [faj'zãw] (pl **-ões** [-õjʃ]) m pheasant.

faísca [fa'iʃka] f spark.

faisões → faisão.

faixa ['fajʃa] f (em estrada) lane; (para cintura) cummerbund; (ligadura) bandage; **~ (de pedestres)** (Br) pedestrian crossing; **~ de rodagem** lane.

fala ['fala] f (dom de falar) speech; **ser de poucas ~s** to be the silent type.

falador, -deira [fala'do(x), -dejra] (mpl **-res** [-riʃ], fpl **-s** [-ʃ]) adj talkative ♦ m, f chatterbox.

falar [fa'la(x)] vi to talk, to speak ♦ vt (idioma) to speak; **~ com alguém** to speak to sb; **~ de** to talk about; **para a verdade** to tell the truth; **sem ~ em** not to mention; **~ claro** to speak clearly; **~ pelos cotovelos** to talk the hind legs off a donkey; **~ a sério** to be serious.

falcão [faw'kãw] (pl **-ões** [-õjʃ]) m falcon.

falecer [fale'se(x)] vi to pass away.

falecido, -da [fale'sidu, -da] m, f deceased.

falecimento [falesi'mẽntu] m death.

falência [fa'lẽsja] f bankruptcy; **ir à ~** to go bankrupt.

falha ['faʎa] f (lacuna) omission; (em terreno, sistema) fault.

falhar [fa'ʎu(x)] vt to miss ♦ vi (não acertar) to miss; (não funcionar) to fail; **ela falhou na primeira (tentativa)** she failed at her first attempt.

falido, -da [fa'lidu, -da] adj bankrupt.

falir [fa'li(x)] vi to go bankrupt.

falsário, -ria [faw'sarju, -rja] m, f forger.

falsidade [fawsi'dadʒi] f falseness.

falsificar [fawsifi'ka(x)] vt to forge.

falso, -sa ['fawsu, -sa] adj false; (documento, passaporte) forged; (dinheiro) counterfeit; (jóia, pele) fake ♦ adv: **jurar ~** to commit perjury.

falta ['fawta] f fault; *(carência)* lack; *(em futebol)* foul; *(infração)* offence; **este aluno tem muitas ~s** this pupil has a very poor attendance record; **sinto muita ~ de um relógio** I really need a watch; **sentir ~ de** to miss; **ter ~ de algo** to be short of sthg; **à ~ de melhor** for want of anything better; **fazer algo sem ~** to do sthg without fail; **por ~ de** for lack of.

faltar [faw'ta(x)] *vi (não haver)* to be missing; *(estar ausente)* to be absent; **falta muito para as férias** the holidays are a long way off; **falta pouco para o trem chegar** the train will arrive soon; **falta sal na comida** the food needs salt; **faltam 5 km para chegarmos lá** we've got 5 km to go before we get there; **era só o que faltava!** that's all we needed!; **~ às aulas** to play truant; **~ ao trabalho** not to turn up to work.

fama ['fama] f *(reputação)* reputation; *(notoriedade)* fame; **ter ~ de ser bom/mau** *(lugar)* to have a good/bad reputation.

família [fa'milja] f family; **em ~** among friends.

familiar [fami'lja(x)] *(pl* **-es** [-iʃ]) *adj (ambiente, atmosfera)* informal; *(da família)* family *(antes de s)* ◆ *m* relative.

faminto, -ta [fa'mĩntu, -ta] *adj* starving.

famoso, -osa [fa'mozu, -ɔza] *adj* famous.

fanático, -ca [fa'natʃiku, -ka] *adj* fanatical ◆ *m, f* fanatic.

fantasia [fãnta'zia] f *(capricho)* fantasy; *(imaginação)* imagination; *(disfarce)* fancy dress.

fantasiar [fãnta'zja(x)] *vi* to fantasize.

⏉ fantasiar-se *vp* to dress up (in fancy dress); **~-se de** to dress up as.

fantasma [fãn'taʒma] *m* ghost.

fantástico, -ca [fãn'taʃtʃiku, -ka] *adj* fantastic ◆ *interj* fantastic!

fantoche [fãn'tɔʃi] *m* puppet.

farda ['faxda] f uniform.

farei [fa'rej] → **fazer**.

farelo [fa'rɛlu] *m* bran.

faringe [fa'rĩʒi] f pharynx.

farinha [fa'riɲa] f flour; **~ de centeio** rye flour; **~ integral** wholemeal flour; **~ de milho** cornflour *(Brit)*, cornstarch *(Am)*; **~ de rosca** *(Br)* breadcrumbs *(pl)*; **~ de trigo** plain flour.

farmacêutico, -ca [faxma'sewtiku, -ka] *adj* pharmaceutical ◆ *m, f* pharmacist.

farmácia [fax'masja] f *(estabelecimento)* chemist's (shop) *(Brit)*, pharmacy *(Am)*; *(ciência)* pharmacy.

faro ['faru] *m* sense of smell.

farofa [fa'rɔfa] f cassava flour fried with onion, bacon, eggs or olives, often served with "feijoada" in Brazil.

farol [fa'rɔw] *(pl* **-óis** [-ɔjʃ]) *m (de veículo)* headlight; *(torre)* lighthouse; **~ alto** *(Br)* full beam *(Brit)*, high beam *(Am)*; **~ baixo** *(Br)* dipped beam *(Brit)*, low beam *(Am)*.

farpa ['faxpa] f *(de agulha)* hook; *(em tourada)* banderilla; *(em pele)* splinter.

farpado [fax'padu] *adj m* → **arame**.

farra ['faxa] f: **vamos cair na ~!** let's go paint the town red!

farrapo [fa'xapu] *m* rag.

farsa ['faxsa] f farce.

fartar-se [fax'taxsi] *vp (saciar-se)* to stuff o.s.; *(cansar-se)* to get fed up; **~-se de** *(comida)* to stuff o.s. with; *(trabalho, pessoa)* to get fed up with; **me fartei de tanto rir** I laughed my head off

farto, -ta ['faxtu, -ta] *adj (saciado)* full; **estar ~ (de)** *(cansado de)* to be fed up (with).

fartura [fax'tura] f abundance.

fascinante [fasi'nãntʃi] *adj* fascinating.

fascinar [fasi'na(x)] *vt* to fascinate.

fascismo [fa'siʒmu] *m* fascism.

fascista [fa'siʃta] *adj & mf* fascist.

fase ['fazi] f phase.

fastidioso, -osa [faʃtʃi'dʒozu, -ɔza] *adj* tedious.

fatal [fa'taw] *(pl* **-ais** [-ajʃ]) *adj* fatal.

fatalidade [fatali'dadʒi] f misfortune.

fatia [fa'tʃia] f slice.

fatigante [fatʃi'gãntʃi] *adj* exhausting.

fato ['fatu] *m* fact; *(Port: terno)* suit; **ser ~ consumado** to be a fait accompli; **de ~** indeed; **pelo ~ de** because, due to the fact that; **~ de banho** *(Port)* swimsuit.

fato-macaco [fatuma'kaku] *(pl* **fatos-macacos** [fatuʒma'kakuʃ]) *m (Port)* boiler suit *(Brit)*, overall *(Am)*.

fator [fa'to(x)] *(mpl* **-res** [-riʃ]) *m (Br)* factor.

fatual [fa'twaw] *(pl* **-ais** [-ajʃ]) *adj (Br)* factual.

fatura [faˈtura] f (Br) invoice.

fauna [ˈfawna] f fauna.

favas [ˈfavaʃ] fpl broad beans; ~ à **portuguesa** *rich broad bean stew cooked with bacon, "chouriço", onion, garlic, coriander and bay leaves.*

favela [faˈvɛla] f (Br) shantytown, slum.

favor [faˈvo(x)] (pl -res [-riʃ]) m favour; "é ~ **fechar a porta**" "please close the door"; **faça ~ de entrar** do come in; **faz ~** (para chamar a atenção) excuse me; **fazer um ~ a alguém** to do sb a favour; **ser a ~ de** to be in favour of; **faz ~** please; **por ~** please.

favorável [favoˈravɛw] (pl -eis [-ejʃ]) adj favourable; **o resultado nos foi ~** the result was in our favour; **ser ~ a algo** to be in favour of sthg.

favores → favor.

favorito, -ta [favoˈritu, -ta] adj favourite.

fax [ˈfaksi] (pl -es [-iʃ]) m fax; ~ **modem** fax modem; **enviar** OU **mandar um ~** to send a fax.

faz [ˈfaʃ] → fazer.

fazenda [faˈzẽda] f (Br: quinta) ranch; (tecido) cloth.

fazendeiro, -ra [fazẽˈdeiru, -ra] m, f (Br) landowner.

fazer [faˈze(x)] vt **1.** (produzir) to make; ~ **muito barulho** to make a lot of noise; ~ **planos/um vestido** to make plans/a dress; ~ **uma pergunta** to ask a question.
2. (comida) to make.
3. (gerar) to produce; **o chocolate faz borbulhas** chocolate gives you spots.
4. (realizar): **estou fazendo um curso de computadores** I'm doing a computer course; **vamos ~ uma festa** we're having a party.
5. (praticar): **você devia ~ mais exercício** you should exercise more; **faço jogging todas as manhãs** I go jogging every morning.
6. (cama) to make.
7. (transformar) to make; ~ **alguém feliz** to make sb happy.
8. (anos): **faço anos amanhã** it's my birthday tomorrow; **fazemos cinco anos de casados** we've been married (for) five years.
9. (obrigar) to make; ~ **alguém fazer algo** to make sb do sthg; ~ **alguém rir/chorar** to make sb laugh/cry.

10. (cálculo, conta) to do; **faz a conta para ver quanto é** work out the bill to see what it comes to.
♦ vi **1.** (em teatro, cinema): ~ **de** to play (the part of), to be.
2. (aparentar): ~ **como se** to act as if.
3. (causar): ~ **bem/mal a algo** to be good/bad for sthg; ~ **bem/mal a alguém** (suj: coisa) to be good/bad for sb; ~ **mal a alguém** (suj: pessoa) to hurt sb.
4. (obrigar): **faça (com) que ele venha** make him come.
♦ v impess **1.** (Br): **faz frio/calor** it's cold/hot.
2. (tempo): **faz um ano que não o vejo** it's a year since I last saw him; **faz tempo que estou à espera** I've been waiting for a while; **o Sérgio partiu faz três meses** Sérgio left three months ago.
3. (importar): **não faz mal se está quebrado** it doesn't matter if it's broken; **tanto faz** it doesn't matter.
⌐ **fazer-se** vp (preparar-se) to be made; (ser correto): **é assim que se faz** that's the way to do it; **~-se com** (ser preparado com) to be made with.
⌐ **fazer-se de** vp + prep (pretender ser): **ele gosta de ~-se de importante** he likes to act important; **~-se de tolo** to act stupid; **~-se de desentendido** to feign ignorance.

fé [ˈfɛ] f faith; **de boa/má ~** in good/bad faith.

febre [ˈfɛbri] f (MED) fever; **estar com ~** to have a temperature.

febre-do-feno [ˌfɛbriduˈfenu] f hay fever.

fechado, -da [feˈʃadu, -da] adj shut, closed; (torneira) turned off; (luz) switched off; (flor) unopened, (fig: reservado) private; "~ **para balanço**" "closed for stocktaking"; "~ **para férias**" "closed for holidays"; "~ **para obras**" "closed for refurbishment".

fechadura [feʃaˈdura] f lock.

fechar [feˈʃa(x)] vt (porta, janela) to shut, to close; (carro) to lock; (torneira) to turn off; (luz) to switch off; (negócio) to close; (loja, estabelecimento, fábrica) to close down ♦ vi (ferida) to heal; (estabelecimento) to shut, to close; ~ **algo à chave** to lock sthg.
⌐ **fechar-se** vp (encerrar-se) to shut o.s

up OU away; *(calar-se)* to withdraw (into o.s.).

fecho [ˈfɛʃu] *m (de peça de vestuário)* zip *(Brit)*, zipper *(Am)*; *(de porta, janela)* lock; *(de espectáculo, acontecimento)* end; *(de colar, pulseira)* fastener; ~ **éclair** zip *(Brit)*, zipper *(Am)*.

fécula [ˈfɛkula] *f* starch; ~ **de batata** potato starch.

fecundar [fekũnˈda(x)] *vt* to fertilize.

feder [feˈde(x)] *vi* to stink.

federação [federaˈsãw] *(pl -ões* [-õjʃ]) *f* federation.

fedor [feˈdo(x)] *m* stench.

feijão [fejˈʒãw] *(pl -ões* [-õjʃ]) *m* bean.

feijão-fradinho [fejʒãwfraˈdʒiɲu] *(pl* **feijões-fradinhos** [fejʒõjʒfraˈdʒiɲuʃ]) *m* black-eyed bean *(Brit)*, black-eyed pea *(Am)*.

feijão-mulatinho [fejʒãwmulaˈtʃiɲu] *(pl* **feijões-mulatinhos** [fejʒõjʒmulaˈtʃiɲuʃ]) *m* red bean similar to the kidney bean.

feijão-preto [fejʒãwˈpretu] *(pl* **feijões-pretos** [fejʒõjʒˈpretuʃ]) *m* black bean.

feijão-verde [fejʒãwˈvexdʒi] *(pl* **feijões-verdes** [fejʒõjʒˈvexdʒiʃ]) *m* green bean.

feijoada [fejˈʒwada] *f* bean stew; ~ **brasileira** *black bean stew cooked with salt beef and various cuts of pork, served with "farofa", spring greens, rice and an orange;* ~ **à trasmontana** *bean stew cooked with cuts of pork and "chouriço", cabbage, carrot and herbs, served with rice.*

feijões → **feijão.**

feio, feia [ˈfejo, ˈfeja] *adj* ugly; *(atitude, situação)* nasty.

feira [ˈfejra] *f* market; ~ **da ladra** *(Port)* flea market; ~ **livre** *(Br)* street market; ~ **do livro** book fair; **fazer a** ~ to go to the market.

feitiçaria [fejtʃisaˈria] *f* witchcraft.

feiticeira [fejtʃiˈsejra] *f* enchantress.

feiticeiro [fejtʃiˈsejru] *m* wizard.

feitiço [fejˈtʃisu] *m* spell.

feitio [fejˈtʃiu] *m (forma)* shape; *(caráter)* temper; *(de peça de vestuário)* cut; **ter bom** ~ *(pessoa)* to be good-natured.

feito, -ta [ˈfejtu, -ta] *pp* → **fazer** ♦ *adj (adulto)* mature; *(realizado)* finished, done ♦ *m (façanha)* deed; ~ **à mão** handmade; ~ **sob medida** made-to-measure; ~ **de** made of; **dito e** ~ **no** sooner said than done.

feixe [ˈfejʃi] *m (de palha, lenha)* bundle; *(Br: de luz)* beam.

fel [ˈfɛw] *m* bile.

felicidade [felisiˈdadʒi] *f (contentamento)* happiness; *(boa sorte)* luck; ~**s!** all the best!

felicitar [felisiˈta(x)] *vt* to congratulate; ~ **alguém por algo** to congratulate sb on sthg.

felino, -na [feˈlinu, -na] *adj* feline ♦ *m* cat.

feliz [feˈliʒ] *(pl -zes* [-ziʃ]) *adj* happy; *(afortunado)* lucky; *(bem executado)* successful; **Feliz Ano Novo!** Happy New Year!

felizmente [feliʒˈmẽntʃi] *adv* fortunately.

felpudo, -da [fewˈpudu, -da] *adj* fluffy.

feltro [ˈfewtru] *m* felt.

fêmea [ˈfemja] *f* female.

feminino, -na [femiˈninu, -na] *adj & m* feminine.

feminismo [femeˈniʒmu] *m* feminism.

feminista [femiˈniʃta] *mf* feminist.

fenda [ˈfẽnda] *f* crack.

fender [fẽnˈde(x)] *vt* to crack.

⊐ **fender-se** *vp* to crack.

feno [ˈfenu] *m* hay.

fenomenal [fenomeˈnaw] *(pl -ais* [-ajʃ]) *adj* phenomenal.

fenómeno [feˈnɔmenu] *m (Port)* = **fenômeno.**

fenômeno [feˈnomenu] *m (Br)* phenomenon.

fera [ˈfɛra] *f* wild animal.

feriado [feˈrjadu] *m* public holiday; ~ **nacional** public holiday.

férias [ˈfɛrjaʃ] *fpl* holiday *(sg)*; **estar de** OU **em** ~ to be on holiday; **ir de** ~ to go on holiday.

ferida [feˈrida] *f (ferimento)* wound, → **ferido.**

ferido, -da [feˈridu, -da] *adj (em acidente, queda)* injured; *(em combate)* wounded; *(fig: ofendido)* hurt ♦ *m, f:* **houve 20** ~**s** 20 people were injured.

ferimento [feriˈmẽntu] *m (de queda, acidente)* injury; *(de arma)* wound.

ferir [feˈri(x)] *vt* to hurt; *(com arma)* to wound.

⊐ **ferir-se** *vp (em queda, acidente)* to hurt o.s.

fermentar [fexmẽnˈta(x)] *vi* to ferment.

fermento [fexˈmẽntu] *m* yeast.

feroz [fe'rɔʃ] (*pl* **-zes** [-ziʃ]) *adj* fierce.

ferradura [fexa'dura] *f* horseshoe.

ferragens [fe'xaʒãjʃ] *fpl* → **loja**.

ferramenta [fexa'mẽnta] *f (instrumento individual)* tool; *(conjunto de instrumentos)* tools *(pl).*

ferrão [fe'xãw] (*pl* **-ões** [-õjʃ]) *m* sting.

ferreiro [fe'xejru] *m* blacksmith.

ferro ['fɛxu] *m* iron.

ferrões → **ferrão**.

ferrolho [fe'xoʎu] *m* bolt.

ferro-velho [ˌfɛxu'vɛʎu] (*pl* **ferros-velhos** [ˌfɛxuʒ'vɛʎuʃ]) *m* scrapyard.

ferrovia [fexo'via] *f (Br)* train track.

ferrugem [fe'xuʒẽ] *f (de metal)* rust; *(de chaminé)* soot.

ferry-boat [fɛxi'bowt] (*pl* **ferry-boats** [fɛxi'bowts]) *m* ferry.

fértil ['fɛxtiw] (*pl* **-teis** [-tejʃ]) *adj* fertile.

fertilidade [fextʃili'dadʒi] *f* fertility.

fertilizante [fextʃili'zãntʃi] *m* fertilizer.

ferver [fex've(x)] *vt* to boil ◆ *vi (leite, água)* to boil; *(vinho)* to ferment; *(fig: de raiva, indignação)* to seethe.

fervor [fex'vo(x)] *m* fervour.

fervura [fex'vura] *f:* **cozer algo até levantar ~** to bring sthg to the boil.

festa ['fɛʃta] *f* party; **boas ~s!** Merry Christmas and a Happy New Year!; **~s juninas** *Brazilian religious festivals held in June in honour of the Saints;* **~s dos Santos Populares** *Portuguese religious festivals held in June in honour of St John, St Peter and St Anthony.*

☐ **festas** *fpl (carícias)* caresses; **fazer ~s a** *(a pessoa)* to caress; *(a animal)* to stroke.

festejar [feʃte'ʒa(x)] *vt* to celebrate.

festim [feʃ'tʃĩ] (*pl* **-ns** [-ʃ]) *m* party.

festival [feʃtʃi'vaw] (*pl* **-ais** [-ajʃ]) *m (de música, cinema)* festival; *(de canção)* contest.

fétido, -da ['fɛtʃidu, -da] *adj* fetid.

feto ['fɛtu] *m (planta)* fern; *(embrião)* foetus.

fevereiro [feve'rejru] *m (Br)* February, → **setembro**.

fez ['fɛʒ] → **fazer**.

fezes ['fɛziʃ] *fpl* faeces.

fiação [fja'sãw] (*pl* **-ões** [-õjʃ]) *f (fábrica)* textile mill.

fiambre ['fjãmbri] *m* ham.

fiar ['fja(x)] *vt (linho, lã)* to spin ◆ *vi (vender a crédito)* to sell on credit.

☐ **fiar-se em** *vp + prep* to trust.

fiasco ['fjaʃku] *m* fiasco.

fibra ['fibra] *f* fibre; *(fig: coragem)* courage; **~ (acrílica)** acrylic.

ficar [fi'ka(x)] *vi* to be; *(permanecer)* to stay; *(restar)* to be left (over); *(rico, gordo)* to get; **ele ficou todo corado** he went bright red; **essa roupa não lhe fica bem** those clothes don't suit you; **fiquei trabalhando até tarde** I worked late; **~ bem** to look good; **~ mal** not to look good; **~ com algo** to take sthg; **~ de fazer algo** to promise to do sthg; **~ em primeiro lugar** to come first; **~ por** *(custar)* to come to; **~ sem algo** to be left without sthg.

ficção [fik'sãw] *f* fiction.

ficha ['fiʃa] *f (dentária, médica)* records *(pl)*; *(EDUC: teste)* test; *(formulário)* form; *(Port: elétrica)* plug; **~ dupla/tripla** *(Port)* double/triple socket adaptor.

fichário [fi'ʃarju] *m (caixa)* index card holder; *(fichas)* index cards *(pl).*

fictício, -cia [fik'tʃisju, -sja] *adj* fictional.

fidelidade [fideli'dadʒi] *f* fidelity; **~ (conjugal)** faithfulness (to one's partner).

fiel ['fjɛw] (*pl* **-éis** [-ɛiʃ]) *adj* faithful ◆ *m* believer.

fígado ['figadu] *m* liver.

figa ['figaʃ] *fpl:* **fazer ~** = to cross one's fingers.

figo ['figu] *m* fig; **~s secos** dried figs.

figueira [fi'gejra] *f* fig tree.

figura [fi'gura] *f* figure; **fazer boa/má ~** to come across well/badly.

figurante [figu'rãntʃi] *mf* extra.

figurar [figu'ra(x)] *:* **figurar em** *v + prep* to appear in.

figurino [figu'rinu] *m (de moda)* fashion plate.

fila ['fila] *f* queue (*Brit*), line (*Am*); **em ~ (indiana)** in line.

filarmónica [filar'monika] *f (Port)* = **filarmônica.**

filarmônica [filax'monika] *f (Br)* philharmonic (orchestra).

filatelia [filate'lia] *f* stamp collecting, philately.

filé [fi'lɛ] *m (Br)* fillet.

fileira [fi'lejra] *f* row.

filete [fi'lete] *m (Port)* fillet; **~s (de pescada)** hake fillets.

filho, -lha [ˈfiʎu, -ʎa] *m, f* son (*f* daughter); **os nossos ~s** our children; **~ da puta** (*vulg*) bastard (*Brit*), son of a bitch (*Am*).

filhote [fiˈʎɔtʃi] *m* (*de cadela*) puppy; (*de raposa, urso, etc*) cub; **a mãe olhava pelos ~s** the mother looked after her young.

filial [fiˈljaw] (*pl* -ais [-ajʃ]) *f* branch.

filigrana [filiˈgrana] *f* filigree.

filmadora [fiwmaˈdɔra] *f* (*Br*): **~ (de vídeo)** video camera.

filmar [fiwˈma(x)] *vt* to film, to shoot.

filme [ˈfiwmi] *m* (*de cinema*) film (*Brit*), movie (*Am*); (*de máquina fotográfica*) film.

filosofia [filozoˈfia] *f* philosophy.

filósofo, -fa [fiˈlɔzofu, -fa] *m, f* philosopher.

filtrar [fiwˈtra(x)] *vt* to filter.

filtro [ˈfiwtru] *m* filter.

fim [fĩ] (*pl* -ns [-ʃ]) *m* end; (*objetivo*) aim; **ter por ~ fazer algo** to aim to do sthg; **ter um ~ em vista** to have an end in mind; **o ~ do mundo** (*lugar distante*) the back of beyond; (*desgraça total*) the end of the world; **a ~ de** in order to; **no ~** in the end; **ao ~ e ao cabo** at the end of the day; **estar a ~ de** (*Br*) to fancy.

fim-de-semana [ˌfĩdʒiseˈmana] (*pl* **fins-de-semana** [ˌfĩʒdʒiseˈmana]) *m* weekend.

Finados [fiˈnaduʃ] *mpl*: **os ~** All Souls' Day (*sg*).

final [fiˈnaw] (*pl* -ais [-ajʃ]) *adj & f* (*último*) final ◆ *m* end.

finalidade [finaliˈdadʒi] *f* (*objetivo*) aim, purpose; (*de máquina*) application.

finalista [finaˈliʃta] *mf* (*em competição*) finalist; (*de curso*) finalyear student.

finanças [fiˈnãsaʃ] *fpl* finances.

fingir [fĩˈʒi(x)] *vt* to pretend.

finlandês, -esa [fĩlãˈdeʃ, -eza] (*mpl* -eses [-eziʃ], *fpl* -s [-ʃ]) *adj & m* Finnish ◆ *m, f* Finn.

Finlândia [fĩˈlãdʒja] *f*: **a ~** Finland.

fino, -na [ˈfinu, -na] *adj* (*fio, cabelo*) fine; (*roupa*) smart; (*hotel, restaurante*) exclusive; (*pessoa*) refined; (*bebida*) fortified; (*Br: fam: bom*): **ele é gente fina** he's a good sort.

fins → fim.

fio [ˈfiu] *m* (*de matéria têxtil*) thread; (*elétrico*) wire; (*de líquido*) trickle; **~ dental** dental floss; **~s de ovos** sweet

threads of egg yolk and sugar poured over cakes, puddings and pastries; **perder o ~ à meada** to lose one's thread.

firma [ˈfixma] *f* (*Br: empresa*) firm.

firme [ˈfixmi] *adj* firm.

firmeza [fixˈmeza] *f* (*solidez*) firmness; (*estabilidade*) stability; (*fig: perseverança*) resolve.

fiscal [fiʃˈkaw] (*pl* -ais [-ajʃ]) *adj* fiscal ◆ *mf* (*tax*) inspector.

fisco [ˈfiʃku] *m* (*instituição*) ≈ the Inland Revenue (*Brit*), ~ the Internal Revenue (*Am*).

física [ˈfizika] *f* (*ciência*) physics (*sg*), → físico.

físico, -ca [ˈfiziku, -ka] *adj* physical ◆ *m* (*de pessoa*) physique ◆ *m, f* (*profissão*) physicist.

fisionomia [fizjonoˈmia] *f* features (*pl*).

fisioterapia [ˌfizjɔteraˈpia] *f* physiotherapy.

fita [ˈfita] *f* (*de tecido*) ribbon; (*fingimento*) pretence; (*filme*) film; **~ adesiva** (*Port*) adhesive tape; **~ (de cabelo)** hairband; **~ durex®** (*Br*) ~ Sellotape® (*Brit*), ~ Scotch tape® (*Am*); **~ isoladora** (*Port*) insulating tape; **~ (para máquina de escrever)** typewriter ribbon; **~ métrica** tape measure; **~ de vídeo** (*Br*) video cassette OU tape; **fazer ~** (*fingir*) to put on an act.

fita-cola [ˌfitaˈkola] *f inv* (*Port*) Sellotape® (*Brit*), Scotch tape® (*Am*).

fitar [fiˈta(x)] *vt* to stare at.

fivela [fiˈvɛla] *f* buckle.

fixador [fiksaˈdo(x)] (*pl* -res [-riʃ]) *m* (*de cabelo*) hairspray; (*em fotografia, desenho*) fixative.

fixar [fikˈsa(x)] *vt* to fix; (*aprender de cor*) to memorize.

⌐ fixar-se *vp* (*estabelecer-se*) to establish o.s.

fixo, -xa [ˈfiksu, -ksa] *pp* → fixar ◆ *adj* fixed; (*cor*) fast.

fiz [fiʒ] → fazer.

flamengo [flaˈmẽŋgu] *adj m* → queijo.

flamingo [flaˈmĩŋgu] *m* flamingo.

flanco [ˈflãŋku] *m* flank.

flanela [flaˈnɛla] *f* flannel.

flash [ˈflaʃi] *m* flash.

flauta [ˈflawta] *f* flute; **~ de bisel** recorder; **~ de pã** panpipes (*pl*).

flecha [ˈflɛʃa] *f* arrow.

fleuma [ˈflewma] *f* phlegm.

flexível [flɛkˈsivew] (*pl* -eis [-ejʃ]) *adj* flexible.

flippers ['flipɛrs] *mpl* pinball *(sg)*; **jogar ~** to play pinball.

floco ['flɔku] *m (de pêlo, lã)* fluff *(Brit)*, fuzz *(Am)*; **~ de neve** snowflake; **~s de aveia** porridge *(sg)*; **~s de milho** cornflakes.

flor ['flɔ(x)] *(pl -res* [-riʃ]*) f* flower; **em ~** in bloom; **ter os nervos à ~ da pele** to be highly strung; **estar na ~ da idade** to be in one's prime.

floresta [flo'rɛʃta] *f* forest.

florido, -da [flo'ridu, -da] *adj (árvore, campo, jardim)* full of flowers; *(tecido, papel)* flowery.

florista [flo'riʃta] *mf* florist ◆ *f* florist's (shop).

fluência [flu'ẽsja] *f* fluency.

fluentemente [fluˌẽntʃi'mẽntʃi] *adv* fluently.

fluido, -da [flu'idu, -da] *adj* fluid ◆ *m (líquido)* fluid; *(fam: força misteriosa)* vibes *(pl)*.

fluminense [flumi'nẽsi] *adj* of/relating to Rio de Janeiro State.

flúor ['fluɔ(x)] *m* fluoride.

fluorescente [flureʃ'sẽntʃi] *adj* fluorescent.

flutuante [flu'twãntʃi] *adj (objeto)* floating; *(preço, inflação, temperatura)* fluctuating.

flutuar [flu'twa(x)] *vi* to float.

fluvial [flu'vjaw] *(pl -ais* [-ajʃ]*) adj* river *(antes de s)*.

fluxo ['fluksu] *m* flow.

fobia [fo'bia] *f* phobia.

focinho [fo'siɲu] *m* snout.

foco ['fɔku] *m (de luz, lâmpada)* beam; *(de atenção)* focus; *(de doença)* centre.

fofo, -fa ['fofu, -fa] *adj* soft; *(bolo)* light.

fofoca [fo'fɔka] *f (Br: mexerico)* piece of gossip.

fogão [fo'gãw] *(pl -ões* [-õjʃ]*) m* cooker *(Brit)*, stove *(Am)*.

foge ['fɔʒi] → **fugir**.

fogem ['fɔʒẽ] → **fugir**.

fogo ['fogu] *(pl* **fogos** ['fɔguʒ]*) m* fire; **~ posto** arson.

fogo-de-artifício [ˌfogudʒiaxtʃiˈfisju] *(pl* **fogos-de-artifício** [ˌfoguʒdʒiaxtʃiˈfisju]*) m (foguetes)* fireworks *(pl)*; *(espectáculo)* firework display.

fogões → **fogão**.

fogueira [fo'gejra] *f* fire.

foguetão [foge'tãw] *(pl -ões* [-õjʃ]*) m* rocket.

foguete [fo'getʃi] *m* rocket.

foguetões → **foguetão**.

foi ['foj] → **ser, ir**.

foice ['fojsi] *f (pequena)* sickle; *(grande)* scythe.

folclore [fow'klɔri] *m (música)* folk music; *(dança)* folk-dancing.

folclórico, -ca [fow'klɔriku, -ka] *adj (música, dança)* folk *(antes de s)*; *(fig: berrante)* garish.

fôlego ['folegu] *m* breath; **tomar ~** to get one's breath back.

folga ['fowga] *f (de trabalho)* day off; *(espaço livre)* gap; **estar de ~** to be on one's day off.

folha ['foʎa] *f (de planta, árvore)* leaf; *(de jornal, livro, revista)* page; **~ de alumínio** tinfoil; **~ de cálculo** spreadsheet; **~ (de papel)** sheet of paper; **~ lisa/quadriculada** plain/squared paper; **~ pautada** lined paper.

folha-de-flandres [ˌfoʎadʒiˈflãndriʃ] *(pl* **folhas-de-flandres** [ˌfoʎaʒdʒiˈflãndriʃ]*) f* corrugated iron.

folhado, -da [fo'ʎadu, -da] *adj (massa)* puff *(antes de s)*; *(bolo)* made with puff pastry ◆ *m (CULIN)* pastry.

folhagem [fo'ʎaʒẽ] *f* foliage.

folhear [fo'ʎja(x)] *vt* to leaf through.

folheto [fo'ʎetu] *m* leaflet.

folia [fo'lia] *f* revelry.

folião, -liona [fo'ljãw, -ljona] *(mpl -ões* [-õjʃ]*, fpl -s* [-ʃ]*), m, f* reveller.

fome ['fɔmi] *f* hunger; **estar com** ou **ter ~** to be hungry; **passar ~** to go hungry.

fone ['fɔni] *m (Br: de telefone)* receiver, handset.

fonética [fo'nɛtʃika] *f* phonetics *(sg)*.

fonte ['fõntʃi] *f (chafariz)* fountain; *(de cabeça)* temple; *(fig: de texto, trabalho, informação)* source.

fora ['fɔra] *adv (no exterior)* out; *(no estrangeiro)* abroad ◆ *prep* apart from ◆ *interj* get out!; **~ de série** extraordinary; **"~ de serviço"** "out of order"; **estar/ficar ~ de si** to be beside o.s.; **ficar de ~** not to join in; **~ de mão** *(dirigir)* on the wrong side of the road; **lá ~** *(no estrangeiro)* abroad; *(no exterior)* outside; **por esse país ~** throughout the country; **dar um ~ em alguém** *(Br)* to chuck sb.

foram [fo'rãw] → **ser, ir**.

força ['foxsa] *f (energia)* strength; *(mi-*

litar, policial) force; ~ **de vontade** will power; **as ~s armadas** the armed forces; **à** ~ by force; **por** ~ by force; **não cheguei a horas por razões de ~ maior** I didn't arrive on time for reasons beyond my control.

forçar [fox'sa(x)] *vt* to force.

forjar [fox'ʒa(x)] *vt* to forge.

forma[1] ['fɔxma] *f* shape; *(maneira)* way; **de** ~ **que** therefore; **de qualquer** ~ anyway; **em** ~ **de** in the shape of; **em** ~ **de estrela** star-shaped; **estar em** ~ to be in shape.

forma[2] ['fɔrma] *f (Port)* = **fôrma**.

fôrma ['fɔxma] *f (Br) (de bolos)* cake tin; *(de sapato)* shoe tree.

formação [foxma'sãw] *(pl* **-ões** [-õjʃ]*)* *f* formation; *(treino)* training.

formal [fox'maw] *(pl* **-ais** [-ajʃ]*)* *adj* formal.

formalidade [foxmali'dadʒi] *f* formality.

formar [fox'ma(x)] *vt* to form; *(educar)* to train.

⸋ **formar-se** *vp (terminar curso universitário)* to graduate.

formatar [foxma'ta(x)] *vt* to format.

formidável [foxmi'davew] *(pl* **-eis** [-ejʃ]*)* *adj* fantastic.

formiga [fox'miga] *f* ant.

formoso, -osa [fox'mozu, -ɔza] *adj* beautiful; *(homem)* handsome.

fórmula ['fɔxmula] *f* formula; **Fórmula 1** Formula 1.

formular [foxmu'la(x)] *vt (palavra, frase)* to formulate; *(desejo)* to express.

formulário [foxmu'larju] *m* form.

fornecedor, -ra [foxnese'do(x), -ra] *(mpl* **-res** [-riʃ], *fpl* **-s** [-ʃ]*)* *m, f (de estabelecimento)* supplier; *(fam: de droga)* dealer.

fornecer [foxne'se(x)] *vt* to supply; ~ **alguém com algo** to supply sb with sthg.

⸋ **fornecer-se** *vp* to stock up.

fornecimento [foxnesi'mẽtu] *m* supply.

forno ['fornu] *m* oven.

forquilha [fox'kiʎa] *f* fork *(Brit)*, pitchfork *(Am)*.

forrar [fo'xa(x)] *vt* to line; *(livro)* to cover.

forró [fo'xɔ] *m (Br)* party.

fortalecer [foxtale'se(x)] *vt* to strengthen.

fortaleza [foxta'leza] *f* fortress.

forte ['fɔxtʃi] *adj* strong; *(calor, dor)* intense; *(chuva)* heavy; *(voz, som)* loud; *(comida)* filling; *(golpe, choque)* hefty; *(bebida)* stiff ♦ *m* fort; **essa é ~!** pull the other one!

fortuna [fox'tuna] *f* fortune.

fósforo ['fɔʃforu] *m (de acender)* match.

fossa ['fɔsa] *f* septic tank; **estar na ~** *(fig: deprimido)* to be down in the dumps.

fóssil ['fɔsiw] *(pl* **-eis** [-ejʃ]*)* *m* fossil.

fosso ['fosu] *m* moat.

foste ['foʃtʃi]→ **ser, ir**.

foto ['fɔtu] *f* photo.

fotocópia [foto'kɔpja] *f* photocopy.

fotografar [fotogra'fa(x)] *vt* to photograph.

fotografia [fotogra'fia] *f (arte)* photography; *(objeto)* photograph; ~ **para passaporte** passport photo.

fotógrafo, -fa [fo'tɔgrafu, -fa] *m, f* photographer.

fotómetro [fo'tɔmetru] *m* light meter.

foz ['fɔʃ] *f* river mouth.

fração [fra'sãw] *(pl* **-ões** [-õjʃ]*)* *f (Br)* fraction.

fracasso [fra'kasu] *m* failure.

fracção [fra'sãw] *(pl* **-ões** [-õjʃ]*)* *f (Port)* = **fração**.

fraco, -ca [fraku, -ka] *adj* weak; *(dor)* slight; *(chuva, vento)* light; *(voz, som)* faint; *(qualidade)* poor; **ter um ~ por alguém** *(fig: paixão)* to have a crush on sb.

frações → **fração**.

fractura [fra'tura] *f (Port)* = **fratura**.

frade ['fradʒi] *m* friar.

frágil ['fraʒiw] *(pl* **-geis** [-ʒejʃ]*)* *adj* fragile.

fragmento [frag'mẽtu] *m* fragment; *(de obra literária, manuscrito)* extract.

fragrância [fra'grãsja] *f* fragrance.

fralda ['frawda] *f* nappy *(Brit)*, diaper *(Am)*; ~**s descartáveis** disposable nappies.

framboesa [frãm'bweza] *f* raspberry.

França ['frãsa] *f:* **a ~** France.

francamente [frãka'mẽtʃi] *adv* frankly ♦ *interj* honestly!

francês, -esa [frã'seʃ, -eza] *(mpl* **-eses** [-eziʃ], *fpl* **-s** [-ʃ]*)* *adj & m* French ♦ *m, f (pessoa)* Frenchman *(f* Frenchwoman); **os franceses** the French.

franco, -ca ['frãku, -ka] *adj* frank; **para ser ~ ...** to be quite honest ....

frango ['frãŋgu] *m* chicken; *(em futebol)* sitter; ~ **assado** roast chicken; ~ **churrasco** barbecued chicken in a spicy sauce; ~ **na púcara** chicken stewed with tomatoes, onions, smoked ham, garlic, port, brandy, white wine and raisins.

franja ['frãʒa] *f (de toalha, cortina, sofá)* fringe; *(de cabelo)* fringe (Brit), bangs *(pl) (Am).*

franqueza [frãŋ'keza] *f* frankness; **com** ~ frankly.

franquia [frãŋ'kia] *f (COM)* franchise; *(selo postal)* postage; *(isenção)* exemption.

franzino, -na [frã'zinu, -na] *adj* frail.

fraqueza [fra'keza] *f* weakness; *(fome)* hunger; *(cansaço)* exhaustion.

frasco ['frafku] *m* jar.

frase ['frazi] *f* sentence.

fratura [fra'tura] *f (Br)* fracture.

fraude ['frawdʒi] *f* fraud.

frear [fre'a(x)] *vi (Br)* to brake.

freguês, -esa [fre'gef, -eza] *(mpl* **-eses** [-ezif], *fpl* **-s** [-ʃ]) *m, f* customer.

freio ['fraju] *m (de veículo)* brake; *(de cavalo)* bit.

freixo ['frejʃu] *m* ash.

frenético, -ca [fre'nɛtfiku, -ka] *adj* frenetic.

frente ['frẽtʃi] *f* front; **olha-me de** ~! look me in the face!; **dar de** ~ **com** *(encontrar)* to bump into; **fazer** ~ **a** to stand up to, to confront; **ir para a** ~ **com** to go ahead with; ~ **fria/quente** cold/warm front; **à** ~ ahead; **à** ~ **de** *(na dianteira de)* in front of; *(chegar, ir, partir)* ahead of; **em** ~ *(defronte)* opposite; **em** ~ **de,** ~ **a** opposite; ~ **a** ~ face to face.

froquência [fre'kwesja] *f (Port)* = **freqüência.**

freqüência [fre'kwẽsja] *f (Br)* frequency; **com** ~ frequently.

freqüentar [frekwẽn'ta(x)] *vt (casa de alguém)* to visit frequently; *(curso)* to attend; *(local)* to frequent.

freqüentemente [frekwẽtʃi'mẽtʃi] *adv* frequently.

frescão [fref'kãw] *(pl* **-ões** [-õjʃ]) *m (Br: ônibus)* air-conditioned coach.

fresco, -ca ['frefku, -ka] *adj* fresh; *(tempo, bebida, roupa)* cool; *(muito exigente)* fussy; *(fam:efeminado)* camp ♦ *m (Port: pintura)* fresco.

frescobol [fref'kobɔw] *m (Br)* racquetball *(played at the beach).*

frescões → **frescão.**

frescura [fref'kura] *f* freshness; *(em relação a temperatura)* coolness.

fressura [fre'sura] *f* offal.

frete ['frɛtʃi] *m (de ônibus)* fee *(for hire of both bus and driver)*; *(de táxi)* fare.

frevo ['frevu] *m* Brazilian carnival dance.

fricção [frik'sãw] *(pl* **-ões** [-õjʃ]) *f (esfregação)* rubbing; *(atrito)* friction.

frieira [fri'ejra] *f* chilblain.

frieza [fri'eza] *f* coldness.

frigideira [friʒi'dejra] *f* frying pan.

frigorífico [frigo'rifiku] *m* fridge.

frio, fria ['friu, 'fria] *adj* & *m* cold; **está** ~ it's cold; **estar com** ou **ter** ~ to be cold; **estava um** ~ **de rachar** *(fam)* it was absolutely freezing.

⌐ **frios** *mpl (Br: CULIN)* cold meats.

frisar [fri'za(x)] *vt (cabelo)* to curl; *(fig: enfatizar)* to highlight.

fritar [fri'ta(x)] *vt (em pouco óleo)* to fry; *(em muito óleo)* to deep-fry.

frito, -ta ['fritu, -ta] *adj* fried; **estar** ~ *(fam)* to be done for.

fritura [fri'tura] *f (alimento frito)* fried food.

frízer ['frizɛx] *(pl* **-res** [-rif]) *m (Br) (de geladeira)* freezer; *(congelador)* deep freeze.

fronha ['frona] *f* pillowcase.

fronte ['frõtʃi] *f (testa)* forehead.

fronteira [frõn'tejra] *f* border; **além** ~s abroad.

frota ['frɔta] *f* fleet.

frustrado, -da [fruf'tradu, -da] *adj* frustrated.

frustrante [fruf'trãtʃi] *adj* frustrating.

fruta ['fruta] *f* fruit; ~ **em calda** fruit in syrup; ~ **da época** fruit in season.

fruta-do-conde [frutadu'kõdʒi] *(pl* **frutas-do-conde** [frutaʒdu'kõdʒi]) *f* custard apple.

frutaria [fruta'ria] *f* fruit shop.

fruto ['frutu] *m* fruit; ~**s secos** dried fruits.

tubá [fu'ba] *m* cornmeal.

fuga ['fuga] *f (de gás, água)* leak; *(evasão)* escape; **pôr-se em** ~ to run away; **em** ~ on the run.

fugir [fu'ʒi(x)] *vi* to run away; ~ **a** ou **de** to run away from.

fugitivo, -va [fuʒi'tʃivu, -va] *adj* fleeting ♦ *m, f* fugitive.

fui ['fuĩ] → **ser, ir**.

fulano, -na [fu'lanu, -na] *m, f* what's-his-name (*f* what's-her-name); **era um ~ qualquer** it was just some guy.

fuligem [fu'liʒɛ] *f* soot.

fulo, -la ['fulu, -la] *adj* furious; **~ da vida** fuming.

fumaça [fu'masa] *f* smoke.

fumador, -ra [fuma'dor, -ra] (*mpl* -es [-eʃ], *fpl* -s [-ʃ]) *m, f* (Port) smoker.

fumante [fu'mãntʃi] *mf* (Br) smoker.

fumar [fu'ma(x)] *vt & vi* to smoke.

fumo ['fumu] *m* smoke.

função [fũ'sãw] (*pl* -ões [-õjʃ]) *f* (*de pessoa*) role; (*de máquina*) function; **exercer a ~ de** to act as; **~ pública** civil service.

funcho ['fũʃu] *m* fennel.

funcionamento [fũsjona'mẽntu] *m* operation; **em ~** in operation; **tenho o motor em ~** I've got the engine running.

funcionar [fũsjo'na(x)] *vi* (*máquina*) to work; (*estabelecimento*) to be open.

funcionário, -ria [fũsjo'narju, -rja] *m, f* employee; **~ público** civil servant.

funções → **função**.

fundação [fũnda'sãw] (*pl* -ões [-õjʃ]) *f* foundation.

fundamental [fũndamẽn'taw] (*pl* -ais [-ajʃ]) *adj* fundamental.

fundamento [fũnda'mẽntu] *m* (*motivo*) grounds (*pl*); (*justificação*) basis; **sem ~** unfounded.

fundar [fũn'da(x)] *vt* to found; **~ algo em algo** (*basear*) to base sthg on sthg.

fundido, -da [fũn'dʒidu, -da] *adj* (*metal*) molten; (*queijo*) melted.

fundir [fũn'dʒi(x)] *vt* to melt.

⊐ **fundir-se** *vp* to melt.

fundo, -da ['fũndu, -da] *adj* deep ♦ *m* (*de rio, piscina, poço*) bottom; (*em economia*) fund; **ir ao ~ da questão** to get to the bottom of the matter; **sem ~** bottomless.

fúnebre ['funɛbri] *adj* (fig: *lúgubre*) funereal.

funeral [fune'raw] (*pl* -ais [-ajʃ]) *m* funeral.

fungo ['fũŋgu] *m* fungus.

funil [fu'niw] (*pl* -is [-iʃ]) *m* funnel.

furacão [fura'kãw] (*pl* -ões [-õjʃ]) *m* hurricane.

furadeira [fura'dejra] *f* (Br) drill.

furado, -da [fu'radu, -da] *adj* (*pneu*) flat; (*orelha*) pierced.

furador [fura'do(x)] (*pl* -res [-riʃ]) *m* hole punch.

furar [fu'ra(x)] *vt* (*folha*) to punch holes in; (*saco*) to make a hole in; (*pneu*) to puncture; (*orelha*) to pierce; (*fig: fila*) to jump.

furgão [fux'gãw] (*pl* -ões [-õjʃ]) *m* (*veículo*) van.

fúria ['furja] *f* fury.

furnas ['fuxnaʃ] *fpl* hot OU thermal springs.

furo ['furu] *m* (*em pneu*) puncture; (*em saco, orelha*) hole.

furtar [fux'ta(x)] *vt* to steal.

⊐ **furtar-se a** *vp* + *prep* to avoid.

furúnculo [fu'rũŋkulu] *m* boil.

fusão [fu'zãw] (*pl* -ões [-õjʃ]) *f* fusion; (*de empresas*) merger.

fusível [fu'zivɛw] (*pl* -eis [-ejʃ]) *m* fuse.

fuso ['fuzu] *m*: **~ horário** time zone.

fusões → **fusão**.

futebol [futʃi'bɔw] *m* football (Brit), soccer (Am).

fútil ['futʃiw] (*pl* -teis [-tejʃ]) *adj* (frivolo) frivolous; (*insignificante*) trivial; (vão) futile.

futilidade [futʃili'dadʒi] *f* (frivolidade) frivolity; (*coisa inútil*) triviality; (*inutilidade*) futility.

futuro, -ra [fu'turu, -ra] *adj & m* future; **o ~** (GRAM) the future (tense); **de ~** in future; **no ~** in the future; **para o ~** for the future; **ter ~** to have a future.

fuzil [fu'ziw] (*pl* -is [-iʃ]) *m* rifle.

fuzileiro [fuzi'lejru] *m* fusilier.

fuzis → **fuzil**.

G

gabar [ga'ba(x)] *vt* to praise.
⌐ **gabar-se** *vp* to boast; ~-se de algo
to boast about sthg.

gabardine [gabax'dʒini] *f* raincoat.

gabinete [gabi'netʃi] *m* (compartimento) booth; (escritório) office.

gado ['gadu] *m* cattle.

gaélico [ga'ɛliku] *m* Gaelic.

gafanhoto [gafa'ɲotu] *m* grasshopper.

gafe ['gafi] *f* gaffe.

gagueira [ga'gejra] *f (Br)* stammer.

gaguejar [gage'ʒa(x)] *vi* to stutter, to
stammer.

gaguez [ga'geʃ] *f (Port)* = gagueira.

galato, -ta [ga'jatu, -ta] *adj (Br)*
funny.

gaio ['gaju] *m* jay.

gaiola [ga'jɔla] *f* cage.

gaita ['gajta] *f* pipe ♦ *interj* damn!

gaita-de-foles [.gajtadʒi'fɔliʃ] *(pl*
gaitas-de-foles [.gajtaʒdʒi'fɔliʃ]) *f* bagpipes *(pl)*.

gaivota [gaj'vɔta] *f* seagull.

gajo, -ja ['gaʒu, -ʒa] *m, f (Port: fam)*
guy *(f girl)*.

gala ['gala] *f* gala.

galão [ga'lãw] *(pl* **-ões** [-õjʃ]) *m (bebida)* tall glass of milky coffee; *(medida)*
gallon.

galáxia [ga'laksja] *f* galaxy.

galera [ga'lɛra] *f (Br: fam: turma)* gang.

galeria [gale'ria] *f* gallery; *(corredor,
ala)* corridor; *(local para compras)*
arcade; ~ de arte art gallery.

galês, -esa [ga'leʃ, -eza] *(mpl* **-eses**
[-eziʃ]. *fpl* **-s** [-ʃ]) *adj & m* Welsh ♦ *m, f*
Welshman *(f* Welshwoman); os galeses the Welsh.

galeto [ga'letu] *m (Br)* poussin *(Brit)*,
spring chicken *(Am)*.

galgo ['gawgu] *m* greyhound.

galho ['gaʎu] *m (de árvore)* branch;

(de veado) antler.

galinha [ga'liɲa] *f* hen.

galinheiro [gali'ɲejru] *m* henhouse.

galo ['galu] *m* rooster, cock; *(fam: na
testa)* bump.

galochas [ga'lɔʃaʃ] *fpl* wellington
boots *(Brit)*, rubber boots *(Am)*.

galões → galão.

galopar [galo'pa(x)] *vi* to gallop.

gama ['gama] *f* range.

gambas ['gãbaʃ] *fpl (Port)* king
prawns.

gamela [ga'mɛla] *f* trough.

gamo ['gamu] *m* fallow deer.

gana ['gana] *f (fam) (ódio)* hatred; ter
~s de to feel like; ter ~s a alguém to
hate sb.

ganância [ga'nãsja] *f* greed.

ganancioso, -osa [ganã'sjozu, -ɔza]
adj greedy.

gancho ['gãʃu] *m (peça curva)* hook;
(Port: de cabelo) hairgrip *(Brit)*, bobby
pin *(Am)*.

ganga ['gãga] *f (Port)* denim.

gangorra [gã'goxa] *f (Br)* seesaw.

gangrena [gã'grena] *f* gangrene.

gangue ['gãgi] *f (Br: fam: turma)*
gang.

ganhar [ga'ɲa(x)] *vt* to win; *(dinheiro,
respeito)* to earn; *(peso)* to put on;
(velocidade) to pick up ♦ *vi (vencer)* to
win; ~ de alguém to beat sb; ~ com
algo to benefit from sthg; ~ a vida OU
o pão to earn a living

ganho ['gaɲu] *m* gain.

ganir [ga'ni(x)] *vi* to whine.

ganso ['gãsu] *m* goose.

garagem [ga'raʒẽ] *(pl* **-ns** [-ʃ]) *f*
garage.

garanhão [gara'ɲãw] *(pl* **-ões** [-õjʃ]) *m*
stallion.

garantia [garã'tʃia] *f* guarantee.

garantir [garã'tʃi(x)] *vt* to vouch for;

~ que to guarantee (that); **eu garanto que está certo** I can assure you that it's correct.

garça ['gaxsa] f heron.

garçom [gax'sõ] (pl -ns [-ʃ]) m (Br) waiter.

garçon [gar'sõ] m (Port) = **garçom**.

garçonete [garso'netʃi] f (Br) waitress.

garçons → **garçom**.

gare ['gari] f platform.

garfo ['gaxfu] m (utensílio) fork; (de bicicleta) forks (pl); **ser um bom ~** to enjoy one's food.

gargalhada [gaxga'ʎada] f shriek of laughter; **dar uma ~** to laugh; **desatar às ~s** to burst out laughing.

gargalo [gax'galu] m neck (of a bottle).

garganta [gax'gãnta] f throat.

gargarejar [gaxgare'ʒa(x)] vi to gargle.

gari [ga'ri] m (Br) road sweeper.

garoto, -ta [ga'rotu, -ta] m, f (miúdo) boy (f girl), kid; (Br: namorado) boyfriend (f girlfriend) ♦ m (in Port: bebida) espresso coffee with a drop of milk.

garoupa [ga'ropa] f grouper.

garra ['gaxa] f (de animal) claw; (fig: talento, genica) flair; **ter ~** (talento) to show great talent.

garrafa [ga'xafa] f bottle; **~ térmica** Thermos® (flask).

garrafão [gaxa'fãw] (pl -ões [-õjʃ]) m (utensílio) flagon; (em estrada) bottleneck.

garrote [ga'xɔtʃi] m (MED) tourniquet.

garupa [ga'rupa] f (de cavalo) hindquarters (pl).

gás ['gajʃ] (pl gases ['gaziʃ]) m gas; **~ butano** butane (gas); **~ lacrimogêneo** tear gas.

⌐ gases mpl (intestinais) wind (sg).

gaseificada [gazeifi'kada] adj → **água**.

gases → **gás**.

gasóleo [ga'zɔlju] m diesel (oil).

gasolina [gazo'lina] f petrol (Brit), gas (Am); **~ sem chumbo** unleaded petrol; **~ normal/super** two-star/four-star petrol.

gasosa [ga'zɔza] f soda.

gastar [gaʃ'ta(x)] vt to use; (desperdiçar) to waste; (sola de sapato) to wear down; **~ tempo/dinheiro** (usar) to spend time/money; (desperdiçar) to

waste time/money.

⌐ gastar-se vp (consumir-se) to be used; (desperdiçar-se) to be wasted; (desgastar-se) to wear down.

gasto, -ta ['gaʃtu, -ta] pp → **gastar** ♦ adj (dinheiro) spent; (água, eletricidade) used; (usado) worn ♦ m expense.

gástrico, -ca ['gaʃtriku, -ka] adj gastric.

gastrite [gaʃ'tritʃi] f gastritis.

gastrónomo, -ma [gaʃ'trɔnumu, -ma] m, f (Port) = **gastrônomo**.

gastrônomo, -ma [gaʃ'tronomu, -ma] m, f (Br) gourmet.

gatilho [ga'tʃiʎu] m trigger.

gatinhar [gatʃi'ɲa(x)] vi to crawl.

gato, -ta ['gatu, -ta] m, f cat; (Br: fam: homem, mulher bonita) dish (f babe).

gatuno, -na [ga'tunu, -na] m, f thief.

gaveta [ga'veta] f drawer.

gaze ['gazi] f gauze.

gazela [ga'zɛla] f gazelle.

gazeta [ga'zeta] f gazette; **fazer ~** (fam) to play truant (Brit), to play hooky (Am).

geada ['ʒjada] f frost.

geladeira [ʒela'deira] f (Br) fridge.

gelado, -da [ʒe'ladu, -da] adj frozen ♦ m (Port) ice cream.

gelar [ʒe'la(x)] vt & vi to freeze.

gelataria [ʒelata'ria] f (Port) ice-cream parlour.

gelatina [ʒela'tʃina] f (de animal) gelatine; (de frutas) jelly (Brit), Jello® (Am).

geleia [ʒe'laja] f (Port) = **geléia**.

geléia [ʒe'lɛja] f (Br) jam (Brit), jelly (Am).

gelo ['ʒelu] m ice; **quebrar o ~** (fig) to break the ice.

gema ['ʒema] f yolk; **da ~** (genuíno) real.

gémeo, -mea ['ʒɛmju, -mja] adj & m, f (Port) = **gêmeo**.

gêmeo, -mea ['ʒemju, -mja] adj (Br) twin ♦ m, f: **os ~s** the twins; **o meu irmão ~** my twin brother.

⌐ Gêmeos m inv (Br) Gemini (sg).

gemer [ʒe'me(x)] vi to groan.

gemido [ʒe'midu] m groan.

gene ['ʒeni] m gene.

general [ʒene'raw] (pl -ais [-ajʃ]) m general.

generalizar [ʒenerali'za(x)] vt to make widespread ♦ vi to generalize.

⌐ **generalizar-se** *vp* to become wide-spread.

género ['ʒɛnɛru] *m (Port)* = gênero.

gênero ['ʒeneru] *m (Br) (tipo)* kind, type; *(espécie)* genus; *(GRAM)* gender; *(em literatura, pintura)* genre; **o ~ humano** the human race.

⌐ **gêneros** *mpl (Br) (mercadoria)* goods; **~s alimentícios** foodstuffs.

generosidade [ʒɛnɛrozi'dadʒi] *f* generosity.

generoso, -osa [ʒɛnɛ'rozu, ɔza] *adj* generous; *(vinho)* full-bodied.

genética [ʒɛ'nɛtʃika] *f* genetics *(sg)*.

gengibre [ʒẽ'ʒibri] *m* ginger.

gengiva [ʒẽ'ʒiva] *f* gum.

genial [ʒe'njaw] *(pl* -ais [-ajʃ]) *adj* brilliant.

génio ['ʒɛnju] *m (Port)* = gênio.

gênio ['ʒenju] *m (Br) (pessoa)* genius; *(irascibilidade)* temper; **ter mau ~** to have a short temper.

genital [ʒeni'taw] *(pl* -ais [-ajʃ]) *adj* genital.

genro ['ʒɛxu] *m* son-in-law.

gente ['ʒẽtʃi] *f (pessoas)* people *(pl)*; *(fam: família)* family; **a ~** *(nós)* we; *(com preposição)* us; **toda a ~** everyone.

⌐ **gentes** *fpl*: **as ~s** the peoples.

gentil [ʒẽtʃiw] *(pl* -is [-iʃ]) *adj (amável)* kind; *(bem-educado)* polite.

genuíno, -na [ʒe'nwinu, -na] *adj* genuine.

geografia [ʒjogra'fia] *f* geography.

geologia [ʒjolo'ʒia] *f* geology.

geometria [ʒjome'tria] *f* geometry; **~ descritiva** *subject studied at secondary school by those wanting to go into architecture or engineering.*

geração [ʒɛra'sãw] *(pl* -ões [-õjʃ]) *f* generation.

gerador [ʒɛra'do(x)] *(pl* -res [-riʃ]) *m* generator.

geral [ʒe'raw] *(pl* -ais [-ajʃ]) *adj* general ♦ *f (em teatro)* cheapest seats at the theatre; **de um modo ~** generally speaking; **em ~** generally; **no ~** in general.

geralmente [ʒeraw'mẽtʃi] *adv* generally.

gerânio [ʒe'ranju] *m* geranium.

gerar [ʒe'ra(x)] *vt* to create.

⌐ **gerar-se** *vp* to form.

gerência [ʒe'rẽsja] *f* management.

gerente [ʒe'rẽtʃi] *mf* manager *(f* manageress).

gerir [ʒe'ri(x)] *vt* to manage.

germe ['ʒɛxmi] *m* germ.

gesso ['ʒesu] *m (MED)* plaster cast.

gesticular [ʒeʃtʃiku'la(x)] *vi* to gesticulate.

gesto ['ʒeʃtu] *m* gesture.

gibi [ʒi'bi] *m (Br: revista)* comic.

gigante [ʒi'gãtʃi] *adj & m* giant.

gilete [ʒi'lɛte] *f (Port)* razor.

gim [ʒi] *(pl* -ns [-ʃ]) *m* gin; **um ~ tônico** a gin and tonic.

ginásio [ʒi'nazju] *m* gym.

ginasta [ʒi'naʃta] *mf* gymnast.

ginástica [ʒi'naʃtʃika] *f* gymnastics *(sg)*; **fazer ~** to exercise.

gincana [ʒiŋ'kana] *f fun obstacle race or rally held during local festivals.*

ginecologia [ʒinekolo'ʒia] *f* gynaecology.

ginecologista [ʒinɛkulu'ʒiʃta] *mf* gynaecologist.

ginja ['ʒiʒa] *f* morello cherry.

gins → gim.

gira-discos [ʒira'diʃkuʃ] *m inv (Port)* record player.

girafa [ʒi'rafa] *f* giraffe.

girar [ʒi'ra(x)] *vi & vt* to turn.

girassol [ʒira'sɔw] *(pl* -óis [-ɔjʃ]) *m* sunflower.

gíria ['ʒirja] *f (calão)* slang; *(médica, académica)* jargon.

giro, -ra ['ʒiru, -ra] *adj (Port: fam: bonito)* good-looking ♦ *m (passeio)* stroll; *(de polícia)* beat; *(de vigilante)* rounds *(pl)*; **dar um ~** to go for a stroll.

giz ['ʒiʃ] *m* chalk.

glacial [gla'sjaw] *(pl* -ais [-ajʃ]) *adj (frio)* freezing; *(área)* glacial; *(fig: olhar, ambiente)* frosty.

gladíolo [gla'dʒiolu] *m* gladiolus.

glândula ['glãdula] *f* gland.

glaucoma [glaw'koma] *m* glaucoma.

glicerina [glise'rina] *f* glycerine.

global [glo'baw] *(pl* -ais [-ajʃ]) *adj* global.

globo ['globu] *m* globe; *(de lâmpada)* lampshade.

glóbulo ['globulu] *m* corpuscle.

glória ['glɔrja] *f* glory.

glossário [glo'sarju] *m* glossary.

glutão, -tona [glu'tãw, -tona] *(mpl* -ões [-õjʃ], *fpl* -s [-ʃ]) *m, f* glutton.

Goa ['goa] *s* Goa.

goela ['gwɛla] *f* gullet.

goiaba [go'jaba] *f* guava.

goiabada [goja'bada] *f* guava jelly.

gol ['gow] (*pl* **goles** ['gɔliʃ]) *m (Br)* goal.

gola ['gɔla] *f* collar.

gole ['gɔli] *m (pequeno)* sip; *(grande)* swig.

goleiro [go'lejru] *m (Br)* goalkeeper.

goles → **gol**.

golfe ['gowfi] *m* golf.

golfinho [gow'fiɲu] *m* dolphin.

golfo ['gowfu] *m* gulf.

golo ['golu] *m (Port)* = **gol**.

golpe ['gɔwpi] *m* cut; *(pancada, choque)* blow; **~ de Estado** coup (d'état); **~ de mestre** masterstroke.

goma ['goma] *f* starch.

gomo ['gomu] *m* segment.

gôndola ['gõndula] *f* gondola.

gongo ['gõŋgu] *m* gong.

gordo, -da ['gordu, -da] *adj (pessoa, animal)* fat; *(leite)* full-fat; *(alimento)* fatty; *(substância)* oily.

gordura [gox'dura] *f (substância)* fat.

gorduroso, -osa [goxdu'rozu, -ɔza] *adj* greasy.

gorila [go'rila] *m* gorilla.

gorjeta [gox'ʒeta] *f* tip.

gorro ['goxu] *m* woolly hat.

gostar [guʃ'ta(x)] : **gostar de** *v + prep* to like; **~ de fazer algo** to like doing sthg.

gosto ['goʃtu] *m* taste; **com todo o ~!** with pleasure!; **dá ~ ver** it's a joy to behold; **faço ~ em ...** it gives me great pleasure to ...; **ter ~ de** *(Br: saber a)* to taste like; **tomar o ~ a algo** to take a liking to sthg; **bom/mau ~** good/bad taste; **~ não se discute** there's no accounting for taste.

gota ['gota] *f (pingo)* drop; *(MED)* gout; **~ a ~** drop by drop.

goteira [go'tejra] *f (cano)* gutter; *(fenda)* leak.

gotejar [gote'ʒa(x)] *vi* to drip.

governo [go'vexnu] *m* government; **~ civil** = local government office.

gozar [go'za(x)] *vt* to enjoy ◆ *vi (fam: brincar)* to joke; **~ com** *(fam: troçar de)* to make fun of; **~ de** *(desfrutar de)* to enjoy.

gr. *(abrev de grama)* g.

Grã-Bretanha [grãmbre'taɲa] *f*: **a ~** Great Britain.

graça ['grasa] *f (gracejo)* joke; *(humor)* humour; *(elegância)* grace; *(atração)* charm; **achar ~ em alguém/algo** to find sb/sthg amusing; **ter ~** to be funny; **~s a** thanks to; **de ~** free (of charge);

sem ~ *(desconcertado)* embarrassed.

gracejar [grase'ʒa(x)] *vi* to joke.

gracejo [gra'seʒu] *m (piada)* joke; *(galanteio)* flirtatious remark.

gracioso, -osa [gra'sjozu, -ɔza] *adj* graceful.

grade ['gradʒi] *f (vedação)* bars (*pl*); *(Port: de cerveja, Coca-Cola®)* crate.

⌐ grades *fpl (fam: cadeia)* jail; **estar atrás das ~s** to be behind bars.

graduação [gradwa'sãw] (*pl* **-ões** [-õjʃ]) *f* graduation; *(de bebida)* alcohol content.

graduado, -da [gra'dwadu, -da] *adj* graduated ◆ *m, f* graduate.

gradual [gra'dwaw] (*pl* **-ais** [-ajʃ]) *adj* gradual.

graduar-se [gra'dwaxsi] *vp* to graduate.

grafia [gra'fia] *f (maneira de escrever)* handwriting; *(ortografia)* spelling.

gráfico ['grafiku] *m* graph.

gralha ['graʎa] *f (ave)* magpie; *(erro tipográfico)* typo.

grama¹ ['grama] *m* gram.

grama² ['grama] *f (Br: relva)* grass.

gramado [gra'madu] *m (Br) (terreno)* lawn; *(de campo de futebol)* pitch.

gramar [gra'ma(x)] *vt (Port: fam: gostar de)* to like; *(fam: aguentar)* to stand.

gramática [gra'matʃika] *f* grammar.

gramofone [gramo'fɔni] *m* gramophone.

grampeador [grãmpja'dox] (*pl* **-res** [-riʃ]) *m (Br)* stapler.

grampear [grãm'pja(x)] *vt (Br) (folhas, papéis)* to staple; *(telefone)* to tap.

grampo ['grãmpu] *m (Br) (de cabelo)* hairgrip *(Brit)*, bobby pin *(Am)*; *(para grampeador)* staple; *(em ligação telefônica)* tap.

granada [gra'nada] *f* grenade.

grande ['grãndʒi] *adj* big; *(em altura)* tall; *(em comprimento)* long; *(em importância)* great; *(em gravidade)* serious; **~ penalidade** *(em futebol)* penalty.

granito [gra'nitu] *m* granite.

granizo [gra'nizu] *m* hailstones (*pl*), hail.

granulado, -da [granu'ladu, -da] *adj* granulated.

grão ['grãw] *m* grain; *(de café)* bean; *(grão-de-bico)* chickpeas (*pl*).

grão-de-bico [grãwdʒi'biku] *m* chickpeas (*pl*).

grasnar [graʒ'na(x)] *vi (corvo)* to caw;

(pato) to quack; *(ganso)* to honk.

gratidão [gratʃiˈdãw] f gratitude.

gratificação [gratʃifikaˈsãw] *(pl* **-ões** [-õjʃ]) f *(gorjeta)* tip; *(remuneração)* payment.

gratificante [gratʃifiˈkãntʃi] *adj* gratifying.

gratificar [gratʃifiˈka(x)] *vt (dar gorjeta a)* to tip; *(recompensar)* to reward.

gratinado, -da [gratʃiˈnadu, -da] *adj* au gratin.

gratinar [gratʃiˈna(x)] *vi*: **pôr algo para ~** to cook sthg au gratin.

grátis [ˈgratʃiʃ] *adv & adj inv* free.

grato, -ta [ˈgratu, -ta] *adj* grateful.

grau [ˈgraw] m degree; **~s centígrados** degrees centigrade; **primeiro/segundo ~** *(Br)* primary/secondary school.

gravação [gravaˈsãw] *(pl* **-ões** [-õjʃ]) f recording.

gravador [gravaˈdo(x)] *(pl* **-res** [-riʃ]) m tape recorder.

gravar [graˈva(x)] *vt (música, conversa)* to record; *(em metal, jóia)* to engrave.

gravata [graˈvata] f tie.

grave [ˈgravi] *adj (sério)* serious; *(voz)* deep; *(tom)* low; *(GRAM: acento)* grave.

grávida [ˈgravida] *adj* f pregnant.

gravidade [graviˈdadʒi] f gravity.

gravidez [graviˈdeʒ] f pregnancy.

gravura [graˈvura] f *(imagem)* picture.

graxa [ˈgraʃa] f shoe polish.

Grécia [ˈgrɛsja] f: **a ~** Greece.

grego, -ga [ˈgregu, -ga] *adj & m, f* Greek ♦ m *(língua)* Greek.

grelha [ˈgreʎa] f grill; **bife na ~** grilled steak.

grelhado, -da [greˈʎadu, -da] *adj* grilled ♦ m grilled dish; **~ misto** mixed grill.

grelhador [greʎaˈdo(x)] *(pl* **-res** [-riʃ]) m barbecue; *(de fogão)* grill.

grelhar [greˈʎa(x)] *vt* to grill.

grená [greˈna] *adj* dark red.

greta [ˈgreta] f crack.

gretado, -da [greˈtadu, -da] *adj* chapped, cracked.

greve [ˈgrɛvi] f strike; **fazer ~** to go on strike; **em ~** on strike; **~ de fome** hunger strike.

grilo [ˈgrilu] m cricket.

grinalda [griˈnawda] f *(em funeral)* wreath; *(para cabelo)* garland.

gripe [ˈgripi] f flu; **estar com ~** to have the flu.

grisalho, -lha [griˈzaʎu, -ʎa] *adj* grey.

gritar [griˈta(x)] *vi & vt* to shout; **~ com alguém** to shout at sb.

grito [ˈgritu] m shout; **de ~s** *(Port: fam: hilariante)* hilarious.

groselha [groˈzeʎa] f redcurrant.

grosseiro, -ra [groˈsejru, -ra] *adj* crude; *(tecido)* coarse.

grosso, grossa [ˈgrosu, ˈgrɔsa] *adj* thick; *(Br: mal educado)* rude; *(voz)* deep; *(Port: fam: embriagado)* sloshed.

grotesco, -ca [groˈteʃku, -ka] *adj* grotesque.

grua [ˈgrua] f crane.

grunhido [gruˈɲidu] m grunt.

grunhir [gruˈɲi(x)] *vi* to grunt.

grupo [ˈgrupu] m group; **em ~** as a group; **~ de risco** risk group; **~ sanguíneo** blood group.

gruta [ˈgruta] f cave.

guache [ˈgwaʃi] m gouache.

guaraná [gwaraˈna] m *fizzy drink made from guarana seeds;* **~ em pó** powdered guarana seeds.

guarda [ˈgwaxda] mf *(polícia)* policeman *(f* policewoman*)* ♦ f *(vigilância)* guard.

guarda-chuva [ˌgwaxdaˈʃuva] *(pl* **guarda-chuvas** [ˌgwardaˈʃuvaʃ]) m umbrella.

guarda-costas [ˌgwaxdaˈkɔʃtaʃ] mf *inv* bodyguard.

guarda-fatos [ˌgwardaˈfatuʃ] m *inv (Port)* wardrobe.

guarda-fiscal [ˌgwardafiʃˈkal] *(pl* **guardas-fiscais** [ˌgwardaʃfiʃˈkajʃ]) mf *(Port)* customs and excise officer.

guarda-florestal [ˌgwaxdaflores-ˈtaw] *(pl* **guardas-florestais** [ˌgwaxdaʃfloresˈtajʃ]) mf forest ranger.

guarda-jóias [ˌgwardaˈʒɔjaʃ] m *inv (Port)* jewellery box.

guarda-lamas [ˌgwardaˈlamaʃ] m *inv (Port)* mudguard.

guarda-louça [ˌgwaxdaˈlosa] *(pl* **guarda-louças** [ˌgwardaˈlosaʃ]) m cupboard.

guardanapo [ˌgwaxdaˈnapu] m napkin; **~s de papel** paper napkins.

guarda-noturno [ˌgwaxdanoˈtuxnu] *(pl* **guardas-noturnos** [ˌgwaxdaʒnoˈtuxnuʃ]) m night-watchman.

guardar [gwaxˈda(x)] *vt (vigiar)* to look after; *(arrecadar)* to put away; *(reservar)* to keep.

guarda-redes [gwarda'xedeʃ] *m inv* (*Port*) goalkeeper.

guarda-roupa [gwaxda'xopa] (*pl* **guarda-roupas** [gwaxda'xopaʃ]) *m* wardrobe.

guarda-sol [gwaxda'sɔw] (*pl* **guarda-sóis** [gwaxda'sɔjʃ]) *m* parasol.

guarda-vassouras [gwardava'soraʃ] *m inv* (*Port*) skirting board (*Brit*), baseboard (*Am*).

guarda-vestidos [gwardaveʃ'tiduʃ] *m inv* (*Port*) wardrobe.

guarnecido, -da [gwaxne'sidu, -da] *adj*: ~ **com** garnished with.

guarnição [gwaxni'sãw] (*pl* **-ões** [-õjʃ]) *f* garnish.

Guatemala [gwate'mala] *f*: **a ~** Guatemala.

gude ['gudʒi] *m* (*Br*) marbles (*sg*).

guelra ['gɛwxa] *f* gill.

guerra ['gɛxa] *f* war; **fazer ~ a** to wage war against OU on; **estar em pé de ~** to be at war.

guia ['gia] *mf* (*profissão*) guide ◆ *m* (*livro, folheto*) guide; ~ **intérprete** tour guide (*fluent in foreign languages*); ~ **turístico** tourist guide.

guiador [gja'dor] (*pl* **-res** [-reʃ]) *m* (*Port*) = **guidom**.

guiar ['gja(x)] *vt* to guide; (*automóvel, ônibus*) to drive ◆ *vi* (*dirigir*) to drive.

guiché [gi'ʃɛ] *m* (*Port*) = **guichê**.

guichê [gi'ʃɛ] *m* (*Br*) counter.

guidom [gi'dõ] (*pl* **-ns** [-ʃ]) *m* (*Br*) (*de automóvel*) steering wheel; (*de bicicleta*) handlebars (*pl*).

guilhotina [giʎo'tʃina] *f* guillotine.

guincho ['gĩʃu] *m* (*som*) squeal; (*máquina*) winch.

guindaste [gĩ'daʃtʃi] *m* crane.

Guiné-Bissau [gi,nɛbi'saw] *f*: **a ~** Guinea-Bissau.

guineense [gi'njẽsi] *adj & mf* Guinean.

guisado, -da [gi'zadu, -da] *adj* stewed ◆ *m* stew.

guisar [gi'za(x)] *vt* (*CULIN*) to stew.

guitarra [gi'taxa] *f* guitar.

guitarrista [gita'xiʃta] *mf* guitarist.

guizo ['gizu] *m* bell.

gula ['gula] *f* gluttony.

guloseima [gulo'zejma] *f* sweet (*Brit*), candy (*Am*).

guloso, -osa [gu'lozu, -ɔza] *adj* greedy ◆ *m, f* glutton; **ser ~** to have a sweet tooth.

gume ['gumi] *m* (cutting) edge.

guri, -ria [gu'ri, -'ria] *m, f* (*Br*) kid.

H

h. *(abrev de hora)* h, hr.

há [a] → haver.

hábil ['abiw] *(pl* -beis [-bejʃ]) *adj (capaz)* skilful; *(astuto)* clever.

habilidade [abili'dadʒi] *f (capacidade)* ability; *(argúcia)* cleverness; *(talento)* skill.

⊐ **habilidades** *fpl (malabarismos)* juggling *(sg)*.

habilitação [abilita'sãw] *f* competence.

⊔ **habilitações** *fpl* qualifications.

habitação [abita'sãw] *(pl* -ões [-õjʃ]) *f* residence.

habitante [abi'tãntʃi] *mf (de bairro)* resident; *(de país, região)* inhabitant.

habitar [abi'ta(x)] *vt* to live in ◆ *vi* to live; **~ em** to live in.

hábito ['abitu] *m* habit; **como é ~** as usual; **ter o ~ de fazer algo** to have a habit of doing sthg; **por ~** as a rule.

habitual [abi'twaw] *(pl* -ais [-ajʃ]) *adj (rotineiro)* regular; *(freqüente)* common.

habitualmente [abitwaw'mẽntʃi] *adv* usually.

habituar [abi'twa(x)] *vt*: **~ alguém a algo/a fazer algo** to accustom sb to sthg/to doing sthg.

⊐ **habituar-se** *vp*: **~-se a** to get used to.

hálito ['alitu] *m* breath; **mau ~** bad breath.

hall [ɔw] *m (de casa)* hall; *(de teatro, hotel)* foyer; **~ (da entrada)** (entrance) hall.

haltere [aw'tɛri] *m* dumbbell.

halterofilia [awterofi'lia] *f* weight-lifting.

hambúrguer [ãm'buxgɛ(x)] *(pl* -es [-iʃ]) *m* hamburger.

hangar [ãŋ'ga(x)] *(pl* -res [-riʃ]) *m* hangar.

hardware [ax'dwɛri] *m* hardware.

harmonia [axmo'nia] *f* harmony.

harmónica [ar'mɔnika] *f (Port)* = **harmônica**.

harmônica [ax'monika] *f (Br)* harmonica.

harpa ['axpa] *f* harp.

haste ['aʃtʃi] *f (de bandeira)* pole; *(de árvore)* branch.

haver [a've(x)] *v impess* **1.** *(existir, estar, ter lugar)*: **há** there is, there are *(pl)*; **havia** there was, there were *(pl)*; **há um café muito bom ao fim da rua** there's a very good cafe at the end of the street; **não há nada aqui** there's nothing here; **não há correio amanhã** there's no post tomorrow.

2. *(exprime tempo)*: **estou esperando há dez minutos** I've been waiting for ten minutes; **há séculos que não vou lá** I haven't been there for ages; **há três dias que não o vejo** I haven't seen him for three days.

3. *(exprime obrigação)*: **há que esperar três dias** you'll have to wait for three days.

4. *(em locuções)*: **haja o que houver** come what may; **não há de quê!** don't mention it!

◆ *v aux (em tempos compostos)* to have; **ele havia chegado há pouco** he had just arrived; **como não havia comido estava com fome** I was hungry as I hadn't eaten; **havíamos reservado com antecedência** we'd booked in advance.

⊔ **haver de** *v + prep (dever)* to have; *(exprime intenção)*: **hei-de conseguir** *(Port)* I'll make it; **hei de ir** *(Br)* I'll go.

⊔ **haver-se com** *vp + prep*: **~-se com alguém** *(prestar contas a)* to answer to sb.

⊔ **haveres** *mpl (pertences)* belongings; *(bens)* assets.

haxixe [a'ʃiʃi] *m* hashish.

hectare [ɛk'tari] *m* hectare.
hélice ['ɛlisi] *f* propeller.
helicóptero [eli'kɔpteru] *m* helicopter.
hélio ['ɛlju] *m* helium.
hematoma [ema'toma] *m* large bruise.
hemofílico, -ca [emo'filiku. -ka] *m, f* hemophiliac.
hemorragia [emoxa'ʒia] *f* hemorrhage; ~ **cerebral** brain hemorrhage; ~ **nasal** nosebleed.
hemorróidas [emo'xɔidaʃ] *fpl* piles, hemorrhoids.
hepatite [epa'tʃitʃi] *f* hepatitis.
hera ['ɛra] *f* ivy.
herança [e'rãsa] *f* inheritance.
herbicida [exbi'sida] *m* herbicide.
herdar [ex'da(x)] *vt* to inherit.
herdeiro, -ra [ex'dejru. -ra] *m, f* heir (*f* heiress).
hermético, -ca [ex'metʃiku. -ka] *adj* airtight.
hérnia ['ɛxnja] *f* hernia.
herói [e'rɔi] *m* hero.
heroína [e'rwina] *f* (*pessoa*) heroine; (*estupefaciente*) heroin.
hesitação [ezita'sãw] (*pl* -ões [-õjʃ]) *f* hesitation.
hesitar [ezi'ta(x)] *vi* to hesitate.
heterossexual [eterosɛk'swaw] (*pl* -ais [-ajʃ]) *adj & mf* heterosexual.
hibernar [ibex'na(x)] *vi* to hibernate.
híbrido, -da ['ibridu. -da] *adj* hybrid.
hidratante [idra'tãtʃi] *adj* moisturizing.
hidroavião [idroa'vjãw] (*pl* -ões [-õjʃ]) *m* seaplane.
hidrófilo [i'drɔfilu] *adj m* → **algodão**.
hidrogénio [idro'ʒenju] *m* (*Port*) = **hidrogênio**.
hidrogênio [idro'ʒenju] *m* (*Br*) hydrogen.
hierarquia [jerar'kia] *f* hierarchy.
hífen ['ifɛn] (*pl* -es [-iʃ]) *m* hyphen.
hifenização [ifeniza'sãw] *f* hyphenation.
hi-fi [aj'faj] *m* hi-fi.
higiene [i'ʒjeni] *f* hygiene.
hilariante [ila'rjãtʃi] *adj* hilarious.
hino [inu] *m* (*de país*) anthem; (*de igreja*) hymn.
hipermercado [ipexmex'kadu] *m* hypermarket.
hipertensão [ipextẽ'sãw] *f* high blood pressure.

hípico, -ca ['ipiku. -ka] *adj* (*centro*) riding (*antes de s*); (*concurso*) showjumping (*antes de s*).
hipismo [i'piʒmu] *m* (*equitação*) horse riding; (*competição*) show jumping.
hipnotismo [ipnɔtʃiʒmu] *m* hypnotism.
hipocondríaco, -ca [ipokõ'driaku. -ka] *m, f* hypochondriac.
hipocrisia [ipokre'zia] *f* hypocrisy.
hipócrita [i'pɔkrita] *mf* hypocrite.
hipódromo [i'pɔdrumu] *m* racecourse.
hipopótamo [ipo'pɔtamu] *m* hippopotamus.
hipoteca [ipo'tɛka] *f* mortgage.
hipótese [i'pɔtezi] *f* (*suposição*) hypothesis; (*possibilidade*) chance; **em ~ alguma** on no account; **na melhor das ~s** at best; **na pior das ~s** at worst.
histeria [iʃte'ria] *f* hysteria.
histérico, -ca [iʃtɛriku. -ka] *adj* hysterical.
história [iʃ'tɔrja] *f* (*de país, mundo, época*) history; (*narrativa*) story; ~ **da Arte** history of art; ~ **da carochinha** fairy tale; ~**s em quadrinhos** comic strips.
hobby ['ɔbi] (*pl* **hobbies** ['ɔbiʃ]) *m* hobby.
hoje ['oʒi] *adv* today; ~ **em dia** nowadays; **queria o jornal de ~** I would like today's paper; **de ~ a oito/quinze dias** a week/a fortnight today; **de ~ em diante** from now on; **por ~ é só** that's all for today.
Holanda [o'lãda] *f*: **a ~** Holland.
holandês, -esa [olã'deʃ. -eza] (*mpl* -eses [-eziʃ], *fpl* -s [-ʃ]) *adj* Dutch ◆ *m, f* Dutchman (*f* Dutchwoman); **os holandeses** the Dutch.
holofote [olo'fɔtʃi] *m* floodlight.
homem ['ɔmẽ] (*pl* -ns [-ʃ]) *m* man; **"homens"** "gentlemen".
homenagear [omena'ʒja(x)] *vt* to pay tribute to.
homenagem [ome'naʒẽ] (*pl* -ns [-ʃ]) *f* tribute.
homens → **homem**.
homicida [omi'sida] *mf* murderer.
homicídio [omi'sidju] *m* murder; ~ **involuntário** manslaughter.
homossexual [omosɛk'swaw] (*pl* -ais [-ajʃ]) *mf* homosexual.
honestidade [oneʃtʃi'dadʒi] *f* honesty.

honesto, -ta [oˈnɛʃtu, -ta] *adj* honest.
honorário [onoˈrarju] *adj* honorary.
⊔ **honorários** *mpl* fees.
honra [ˈõxa] *f* honour; **ter a ~ de fazer algo** to have the honour of doing sthg; **em ~ de** in honour of.
honrado, -da [õˈxadu, -da] *adj* honest.
honrar [õˈxa(x)] *vt (dívida)* to honour.
⊐ **honrar-se de** *vp + prep* to be proud of.
honroso, -osa [õˈxozu, -ɔza] *adj* honourable.
hóquei [ˈɔkej] *m (ESP)* hockey (Brit), field hockey (Am); **~ sobre gelo** ice hockey; **~ em patins** roller hockey.
hora [ˈɔra] *f (período de tempo)* hour; *(momento determinado)* time; **que ~s são?** what time is it?; **são cinco ~s** it's five o'clock; **a que ~s é ...?** what time is ...?; **é ~ de partir** it's time to leave; **esta na ~ do almoço** it's time for lunch; **na ~ H** in the nick of time; **~ de ponta** (Port) rush hour; **~ extraordinárias** overtime *(sg)*; **~s vagas** free OU spare time *(sg)*; **de ~ em ~** every hour; **na ~** on time; **~s e ~s** for hours; **chegar a ~s** to arrive on time; **chegar em cima da ~** to arrive just in time; **à última ~** at the last minute.
horário [oˈrarju] *m (de trem, ônibus, escola)* timetable; *(de estabelecimento)* opening hours *(pl)*; **~ de atendimento** OU **funcionamento** opening hours *(pl)*; **~ nobre** prime time.
horizontal [orizõˈtaw] *(pl* -ais [-ajʃ]*) adj* horizontal.
horizonte [oriˈzõtʃi] *m* horizon.
horóscopo [oˈrɔʃkopu] *m* horoscope, stars *(pl)*.
horrendo, -da [oˈxẽdu, -da] *adj (feio)* hideous; *(chocante)* horrific.
horripilante [oxipiˈlãtʃi] *adj* horrifying.
horrível [oˈxivɛw] *(pl* -eis [-ɛjʃ]*) adj* horrible.
horror [oˈxo(x)] *(pl* -res [-riʃ]*) m* horror; **que ~!** how awful!; **ter ~ a algo** to have a horror of sthg; **um ~ de** *(fam)* a vast number of; **dizer ~es de alguém** to say horrible things about sb.
horta [ˈɔxta] *f* vegetable garden.
hortaliça [oxtaˈlisa] *f* greens *(pl)*.
hortelã [oxteˈlã] *f* mint.
hortelã-pimenta [oxtɛˌlãpiˈmẽta] *f* peppermint.
hortênsia [oxˈtẽsja] *f* hydrangea.

horticultor, -ra [oxtʃikuwˈto(x), -ra] *(mpl* -res [-riʃ]*, fpl* -s [-ʃ]*) m, f* market gardener (Brit), truck farmer (Am).
hortigranjeiros [oxtʃigrãˈʒeiruʃ] *mpl (Br)* vegetables.
hospedagem [oʃpeˈdaʒẽ] *f* accommodation.
hospedar [oʃpeˈda(x)] *vt* to put up.
⊐ **hospedar-se** *vp*: **~-se em** to stay at.
hóspede [ˈɔʃpedʒi] *mf* guest.
hospedeira [oʃpeˈdejra] *f (Port)*: **~ (de bordo)** air hostess.
hospício [oʃˈpisju] *m* home.
hospital [oʃpiˈtaw] *(pl* -ais [-ajʃ]*) m* hospital.
hospitaleiro, -ra [oʃpitaˈlejru, -ra] *adj* hospitable.
hospitalidade [oʃpitaliˈdadʒi] *f* hospitality.
hostil [oʃˈtiw] *(pl* -is [-iʃ]*) adj (gente, ar, comportamento)* hostile; *(vento, frio)* biting.
hotel [oˈtɛw] *(pl* -éis [-ɛiʃ]*) m* hotel.
houve [ˈovi] → **haver**.
hovercraft [ovexˈkraft] *m* hovercraft.
humanidade [umaniˈdadʒi] *f* humanity.
⊔ **humanidades** *fpl* humanities.
humanitário, -ria [umaniˈtarju, -rja] *adj* humanitarian.
humano, -na [uˈmanu, -na] *adj* human; *(compassivo)* humane ◆ *m* human (being).
humidade [umiˈdadɛ] *f (Port)* = **umidade.**
húmido, -da [ˈumidu, -da] *adj (Port)* = **úmido.**
humildade [umiwˈdadʒi] *f* humility.
humilde [uˈmiwdʒi] *adj (pobre)* poor; *(modesto)* humble.
humilhação [umiʎaˈsãw] *(pl* -ões [-õiʃ]*) f* humiliation.
humilhante [umiˈʎãtʃi] *adj* humiliating.
humilhar [umiˈʎa(x)] *vt* to humiliate.
⊐ **humilhar-se** *vp* to humble o.s.
humor [uˈmo(x)] *m* humour; **estar de bom/mau ~** to be in a good/bad mood.
humorista [umoˈriʃta] *mf* comedian *(f* comedienne).
húngaro, -ra [ˈũŋgaru, -ra] *adj & m, f* Hungarian ◆ *m (língua)* Hungarian.
Hungria [ũŋˈgria] *f*: **a ~** Hungary.
hurra [ˈuxa] *interj* hurrah!

I

ia ['ia] → **ir**.

iate ['jatʃi] *m* yacht.

ibérico, -ca [i'bɛriku, -ka] *adj* Iberian.

ibero-americano, -na [i,bɛrwa-meri'kanu, -na] *adj & m, f* Latin American.

içar [i'sa(x)] *vt* to hoist.

ICM/S *m* (Br: abrev de Imposto sobre a circulação de Mercadorias e Serviços) = VAT *(Brit)*, = sales tax *(Am)*.

ícone ['ikɔni] *m* icon.

icterícia [ikte'risja] *f* jaundice.

ida ['ida] *f (partida)* departure; *(jornada)* outward journey.

idade [i'dadʒi] *f* age; **de ~** elderly; **de meia ~** middle-aged; **oito anos de ~** eight years of age.

ideal [i'dʒjaw] *(pl* **-ais** [-ajʃ]) *adj & m* ideal.

idealista [idʒja'liʃta] *adj* idealistic ♦ *mf* idealist.

ideia [i'daja] *f (Port)* = **idéia**.

idéia [i'dʒɛja] *f (Br)* idea; **que ~!** you must be joking!; **mudar de ~** to change one's mind; **não fazer ~** not to have a clue.

idêntico, -ca [i'dʒentʃiku, -ka] *adj* identical.

identidade [idʒentʃi'dadʒi] *f* identity.

identificação [idʒentʃifika'sãw] *f* identification.

identificar [idʒentʃifi'ka(x)] *vt* to identify.

⊐ identificar-se *vp* to identify o.s.

ideologia [idʒjolo'ʒia] *f* ideology.

idílico, -ca [i'dʒiliku, -ka] *adj* idyllic.

idioma [i'dʒjoma] *m* language.

idiota [i'dʒjɔta] *adj* idiotic ♦ *mf* idiot.

ídolo [idulu] *m* idol.

idóneo, -nea [i'dɔnju, -nja] *adj (Port)* = **idôneo**.

idôneo, -nea [i'dɔnju, -nja] *adj (Br)* reliable.

idoso, -osa [i'dozu, -ɔza] *adj* elderly ♦ *m, f* old man *(f* old woman*)*; **os ~s** the elderly.

Iemanjá [jemã'ʒa] *f goddess of the sea in Afro-Brazilian religion.*

igarapé [igara'pɛ] *m (Br)* narrow river.

ignição [igni'sãw] *f* ignition.

ignorado, -da [igno'radu, -da] *adj* unknown.

ignorância [igno'rãsja] *f* ignorance.

ignorante [igno'rãntʃi] *mf* ignoramus.

ignorar [igno'ra(x)] *vt*: **~ algo** not to know sthg; **~ alguém** to ignore sb.

igreja [i'greʒa] *f* church.

igual [i'gwaw] *(pl* **-ais** [-ajʃ]) *adj* the same; *(parecido)* similar ♦ *m (pessoa)* equal; *(sinal)* equals sign; **os dois são iguais** they are (both) the same; **ser ~ a** to be the same as; **12 e 12 ~ a 24** 12 and 12 equals **ou** is 24; **sem ~** unrivalled.

igualar [igwa'la(x)] *vt* to make equal.

⊐ igualar-se *vp*: **~-se a alguém** to be sb's equal; **~-se a algo** to be comparable with sthg.

igualdade [igwaw'dadʒi] *f* equality.

igualmente [igwaw'mentʃi] *adv* equally ♦ *interj* likewise!

ilegal [ile'gaw] *(pl* **-ais** [-ajʃ]) *adj* illegal.

ilegalidade [ilegali'dadʒi] *f* crime.

ilegítimo, -ma [ile'ʒitʃimu, -ma] *adj (filho)* illegitimate; *(ato)* illegal.

ilegível [ile'ʒivew] *(pl* **-eis** [-ejʃ]) *adj* illegible.

ileso, -sa [i'lezu, -za] *adj* unharmed.

ilha ['iʎa] *f* island.

ilícito, -ta [i'lisitu, -ta] *adj* illicit.

ilimitado, -da [ilimi'tadu, -da] *adj* unlimited.

Ilma. abrev = **Ilustríssima.**

Ilmo. abrev = **Ilustríssimo.**

ilógico, -ca [iˈlɔʒiku. -ka] adj illogical.

iludir [iluˈdi(x)] vt to deceive.

⏷ **iludir-se** vp to delude o.s.

iluminação [iluminaˈsãw] f lighting.

iluminado, -da [ilumiˈnadu. -da] adj illuminated, lit up.

iluminar [ilumiˈna(x)] vt to illuminate, to light up.

ilusão [iluˈzãw] (pl -ões [-õjʃ]) f illusion; **não ter ilusões** to have no illusions; **perder as ilusões** to become disillusioned; ~ **ótica** optical illusion.

ilustração [iluʃtraˈsãw] (pl -ões [-õjʃ]) f illustration.

ilustrado, -da [iluʃˈtradu. -da] adj illustrated.

ilustrar [iluʃˈtra(x)] vt (exemplificar) to illustrate.

ilustre [iˈluʃtri] adj illustrious.

ilustríssimo, -ma [iluʃˈtrisimu. -ma] superl (em carta) very formal term of address used in correspondence.

imã [iˈmã] m (Br) magnet.

imaculado, -da [imakuˈladu. -da] adj immaculate.

imagem [iˈmaʒẽ] (pl -ns [-ʃ]) f picture; (pessoal) image.

imaginação [imaʒinaˈsãw] f imagination.

imaginar [imaʒiˈna(x)] vt (inventar) to think up; (supor) to imagine.

⏷ **imaginar-se** vp: **ele se imagina um Adônis** he thinks he's God's gift to women.

imaginativo, -va [imaʒinaˈtʃivu. -va] adj imaginative.

iman [ˈiman] (pl -es [-eʃ]) m (Port) = **imã.**

imaturo, -ra [imaˈturu. -ra] adj immature.

imbatível [ĩbaˈtʃivεw] (pl -eis [-ejʃ]) adj unbeatable.

imbecil [ĩbeˈsiw] (pl -is [-iʃ]) adj stupid ◆ mf idiot.

imediações [imedʒjaˈsõjʃ] fpl surrounding area (sg); **nas ~ de** in the vicinity of.

imediatamente [imeˌdʒjataˈmẽtʃi] adv immediately.

imediato, -ta [imeˈdʒjatu. -ta] adj immediate; **de ~** immediately.

imenso, -sa [iˈmẽsu. -sa] adj huge ◆ adv a lot; **está um calor ~** it's boiling (hot); **está um frio ~** it's freezing (cold).

imergir [imexˈʒi(x)] vt (mergulhar) to immerse.

imigração [imigraˈsãw] f immigration.

imigrante [imiˈgrãtʃi] mf immigrant.

imigrar [imiˈgra(x)] vi to immigrate.

iminente [imiˈnẽtʃi] adj imminent.

imitação [imitaˈsãw] (pl -ões [-õjʃ]) f (de produto) imitation; (de pessoa) impersonation.

imitar [imiˈta(x)] vt (produto) to copy; (comportamento) to imitate; (pessoa) to impersonate.

imobiliária [imobiˈljarja] f estate agent's (Brit), realtor's (Am).

imobilizar [imobiliˈza(x)] vt to immobilize.

⏌ **imobilizar-se** vp to come to a standstill.

imoral [imoˈraw] (pl -ais [-ajʃ]) adj immoral.

imóvel [iˈmɔvεw] (pl -eis [-ejʃ]) adj motionless ◆ m (prédio) building; (valor imóvel) property.

impaciência [ĩpaˈsjesja] f impatience.

impaciente [ĩpaˈsjẽtʃi] adj impatient.

impacto [ĩˈpaktu] m impact.

ímpar [ˈĩpa(x)] (pl -res [-riʃ]) adj (número) odd; (objeto) unique; (ação) unequalled.

imparcial [ĩpaxˈsjaw] (pl -ais [-ajʃ]) adj impartial.

ímpares → **ímpar.**

impasse [ĩˈpasi] m impasse.

impecável [ĩpeˈkavεw] (pl -eis [-ejʃ]) adj (trabalho, roupa, limpeza) impeccable; (fam: pessoa) great.

impedido, -da [ĩpeˈdʒidu. -da] adj (caminho, estrada) blocked; (linha) engaged (Brit), busy (Am).

impedimento [ĩpedʒiˈmẽtu] m obstacle.

impedir [ĩpeˈdʒi(x)] vt (trânsito, circulação) to block; ~ **alguém de fazer algo** to prevent sb from doing sthg.

impelir [ĩpeˈli(x)] vt to push.

impenetrável [ĩpeneˈtravεw] (pl -eis [-ejʃ]) adj impenetrable.

impensável [ĩpẽˈsavεw] (pl -eis [-ejʃ]) adj unthinkable.

imperador [ĩperaˈdo(x)] (pl -res [-riʃ]) m emperor.

imperativo, -va [ĩperaˈtʃivu. -va]

adj & m imperative.

imperatriz [ĩmpera'triʃ] (*pl* **-zes** [-zeʃ]) *f* empress.

imperdoável [ĩmpex'dwavew] (*pl* **-eis** [-ejʃ]) *adj* unforgivable.

imperfeição [ĩmpexfej'sãw] (*pl* **-ões** [-õjʃ]) *f (defeito)* defect.

imperfeito, -ta [ĩmpex'fejtu, -ta] *adj* faulty ◆ *m (GRAM)* imperfect.

imperial [ĩmpe'rjaw] (*pl* **-ais** [-ajʃ]) *f (Port: copo de cerveja)* glass of draught beer.

impermeável [ĩmpex'mjavew] (*pl* **-eis** [-ejʃ]) *m* thin anorak ◆ *adj* waterproof.

impertinente [ĩmpextʃi'nẽntʃi] *adj* impertinent.

imperturbável [ĩmpextux'bavew] (*pl* **-eis** [-ejʃ]) *adj* serene.

impessoal [ĩmpe'swaw] (*pl* **-ais** [-ajʃ]) *adj* impersonal.

impetuoso, -osa [ĩmpe'twozu, -ɔza] *adj* impetuous.

impiedade [ĩmpje'dadʒi] *f* irreverence.

implacável [ĩmpla'kavew] (*pl* **-eis** [-ejʃ]) *adj* ruthless; *(vento, chuva, frio)* relentless.

implantação [ĩmplãnta'sãw] *f* introduction.

implementar [ĩmplemẽn'ta(x)] *vt* to implement.

implicar [ĩmpli'ka(x)] *vt (envolver)* to implicate; *(acarretar)* to involve.

❏ **implicar com** *v* + *prep* to have a go at.

implícito, -ta [ĩm'plisitu, -ta] *adj* implicit.

implorar [ĩmplo'ra(x)] *vt* to implore.

imponente [ĩmpo'nẽntʃi] *adj (grandioso)* imposing; *(altivo)* arrogant.

impopular [ĩmpopu'la(x)] (*pl* **-es** [-iʃ]) *adj* unpopular.

impor [ĩm'po(x)] *vt (respeito, silêncio)* to command; *(ordem)* to impose; **~ algo a alguém** to impose sthg on sb.

❏ **impor-se** *vp* to command respect.

importação [ĩmpoxta'sãw] (*pl* **-ões** [-õjʃ]) *f* import.

importado, -da [ĩmpox'tadu, -da] *adj* imported.

importância [ĩmpox'tãsja] *f (valor)* importance; *(quantia monetária)* amount.

importante [ĩmpox'tãntʃi] *adj* important ◆ *m*: **o ~ é ...** the important thing is ....

importar [ĩmpox'ta(x)] *vt (mercadoria, produto, idéia)* to import ◆ *vi (ter importância)* to matter.

❏ **importar-se** *vp (fazer caso)* to mind; **você se importa de fechar a porta?** would you mind closing the door?

imposição [ĩmpozi'sãw] (*pl* **-ões** [-õjʃ]) *f* condition.

impossibilitar [ĩmposibili'ta(x)] *vt* to prevent.

impossível [ĩmpo'sivew] (*pl* **-eis** [-ejʃ]) *adj & m* impossible ◆ *m*: **querer o ~** to ask the impossible.

imposto [ĩm'poʃtu] *m* tax; **~ de renda** *(Br)* income tax; **~ sobre o rendimento** *(Port)* income tax; **~ sobre o valor acrescentado** *(Port)* value added tax *(Brit)*, sales tax *(Am)*.

impostor, -ra [ĩmpoʃ'to(x), -ra] (*mpl* **-res** [-riʃ], *fpl* **-s** [-ʃ]) *m, f* impostor.

impotente [ĩmpo'tẽntʃi] *adj* impotent.

impraticável [ĩmpratʃi'kavew] (*pl* **-eis** [-ejʃ]) *adj (estrada, caminho)* impassable.

impreciso, -sa [ĩmpre'sizu, -za] *adj* vague.

impregnar [ĩmpreg'na(x)] *vt* to impregnate.

❏ **impregnar-se de** *vp* + *prep* to become impregnated with.

imprensa [ĩm'prẽsa] *f* press.

imprescindível [ĩmpreʃsĩn'dʒivew] (*pl* **-eis** [-ejʃ]) *adj* indispensable.

impressão [ĩmpre'sãw] (*pl* **-ões** [-õjʃ]) *f (sensação)* impression; *(de jornal, livro)* printing; **ter a ~ de que** to get the impression (that); **tenho a ~ que vai chover** I think it's going to rain; **~ digital** fingerprint; **causar boa ~** to make a good impression.

impressionante [ĩmpresju'nãntʃi] *adj (incrível)* amazing; *(comovente)* moving.

impressionar [ĩmpresju'na(x)] *vt (causar admiração a)* to amaze; *(comover)* to move.

impresso, -a [ĩm'presu, -a] *adj* printed ◆ *m* form.

impressões → impressão.

impressora [ĩmpre'sora] *f* printer.

imprestável [ĩmpreʃ'tavew] (*pl* **-eis** [-ejʃ]) *adj (não prestativo)* unhelpful; *(inútil)* useless.

imprevisível [ĩmprevi'zivew] (*pl* **-eis**

[-ejʃ]) *adj* unpredictable.

imprevisto, -ta [ĩmpreˈviʃtu, -ta] *adj* unexpected ♦ *m* unexpected event.

imprimir [ĩmpriˈmi(x)] *vt* to print.

impróprio, -pria [ĩmˈprɔpriu, -pria] *adj*: ~ **para** unsuitable for; ~ **para consumo** unfit for human consumption.

improvável [ĩmproˈvavew] (*pl* **-eis** [-ejʃ]) *adj* unlikely.

improvisar [ĩmproviˈza(x)] *vt & vi* to improvise.

improviso [ĩmproˈvizu] *m* improvisation; **de** ~ impromptu; **fazer um discurso de** ~ to make an impromptu speech.

imprudente [ĩpruˈdẽntʃi] *adj* rash.

impulsionar [ĩmpuwsjuˈna(x)] *vt* to push forward.

impulsivo, -va [ĩmpuwˈsivu, -va] *adj* impulsive.

impulso [ĩmˈpuwsu] *m* (*incitamento*) impulse; (*de ligação telefônica*) unit.

impune [ĩmˈpuni] *adj* unpunished.

impureza [ĩmpuˈreza] *f* impurity.

impuro, -ra [ĩmˈpuru, -ra] *adj* impure.

imundície [imũnˈdʒisji] *f* (*sujeira*) dirt; (*lixo*) rubbish.

imune [iˈmuni] *adj* (*isento*): ~ **a** immune to.

inábil [iˈnabiw] (*pl* **-beis** [-bejʃ]) *adj* incompetent.

inabitado, -da [inabiˈtadu, -da] *adj* uninhabited.

inacabado, -da [inakaˈbadu, -da] *adj* unfinished.

inaceitável [inasejˈtavew] (*pl* **-eis** [-ejʃ]) *adj* unacceptable.

inacessível [inaseˈsivew] (*pl* **-eis** [-ejʃ]) *adj* inaccessible.

inacreditável [inakredʒiˈtavew] (*pl* **-eis** [-ejʃ]) *adj* unbelievable.

inactividade [inatɛviˈdade] *f* (*Port*) = **inatividade**.

inadequado, -da [inadeˈkwadu, -da] *adj* inadequate.

inadiável [inaˈdjavew] (*pl* **-eis** [-ejʃ]) *adj* (*encontro, reunião, problema*) pressing.

inadvertido, -da [inadverˈtʃidu, -da] *adj* unnoticed.

inalador [inalaˈdo(x)] (*pl* **-res** [-riʃ]) *m* inhaler.

inalar [inaˈla(x)] *vt* to inhale.

inalcançável [inawkãˈsavew] (*pl* **-eis** [-ejʃ]) *adj* unattainable.

inanimado, -da [inaniˈmadu, -da] *adj* inanimate.

inaptidão [inaptʃiˈdãw] *f* unsuitability.

inapto, -pta [iˈnaptu, -pta] *adj* unsuitable.

inarticulado, -da [inaxtʃikuˈladu, -da] *adj* inarticulate.

inatingível [inatʃĩˈʒivew] (*pl* **-eis** [-ejʃ]) *adj* unattainable.

inatividade [inatʃiviˈdadʒi] *f* (*Br*) inactivity; **na** ~ (*pessoa*) out of work.

inativo, -va [inaˈtʃivu, -va] *adj* inactive; (*pessoa*) out of work.

inato, -ta [iˈnatu, -ta] *adj* innate.

inauguração [inawguraˈsãw] (*pl* **-ões** [-õjʃ]) *f* inauguration.

inaugurar [inawguˈra(x)] *vt* to inaugurate.

incansável [ĩkãˈsavew] (*pl* **-eis** [-ejʃ]) *adj* tireless.

incapacidade [ĩkapasiˈdadʒi] *f* inability.

incapaz [ĩkaˈpaʃ] (*pl* **-zes** [-ziʃ]) *adj* incapable.

incendiar [ĩsẽnˈdʒja(x)] *vt* to set fire to.

⏴ **incendiar-se** *vp* to catch fire.

incêndio [ĩˈsẽndʒju] *m* fire.

incenso [ĩˈsẽsu] *m* incense.

incentivar [ĩsẽntʃiˈva(x)] *vt* to motivate.

incentivo [ĩsẽnˈtʃivu] *m* incentive.

incerteza [ĩsexˈteza] *f* doubt, uncertainty; **ficar na** ~ to be left in doubt.

incerto, -ta [ĩˈsextu, -ta] *adj* uncertain.

incesto [ĩˈseʃtu] *m* incest.

inchação [ĩʃaˈsãw] (*pl* **-ões** [-õjʃ]) *m* (*Br*) swelling.

inchaço [ĩˈʃasu] *m* swelling

inchado, -da [ĩˈʃadu, -da] *adj* (*entumescido*) swollen; (*fig: envaidecido*) puffed up (with pride).

inchar [ĩˈʃa(x)] *vi* to swell.

incidência [ĩsiˈdẽsja] *f* incidence.

incidente [ĩsiˈdẽntʃi] *m* incident.

incineração [ĩsineraˈsãw] (*pl* **-ões** [-õjʃ]) *f* incineration.

incisivo, -va [ĩsiˈzivu, -va] *adj* (*fig: penetrante*) incisive ♦ *m* (*dente*) incisor.

incitar [ĩsiˈta(x)] *vt* to incite.

inclemente [ĩkleˈmẽntʃi] *adj* merciless.

inclinação [ĩklinaˈsãw] (*pl* **-ões**

[-õjʃ]) f inclination.
inclinado, -da [ĩŋkliˈnadu, -da] adj slanting.
inclinar [ĩŋkliˈna(x)] vt to tilt.
❑ **inclinar-se** vp to lean.
incluir [ĩŋkluˈi(x)] vt to include; (inserir) to enclose.
inclusive [ĩŋkluˈzive] adv even; **de 11 a 20, ~** from 11 to 20 inclusive.
incoerente [ĩŋkweˈrẽntʃi] adj incoherent.
incógnita [ĩŋˈkɔgnita] f enigma, mystery.
incógnito, -ta [ĩˈkɔgnitu, -ta] adj unknown.
incolor [ĩŋkoˈlo(x)] (pl -res [-riʃ]) adj colourless.
incomodar [ĩŋkomoˈda(x)] vt to bother; "favor não ~" "do not disturb".
❑ **incomodar-se** vp to bother; **você se incomoda se eu fumar?** do you mind if I smoke?
incómodo, -da [ĩŋˈkɔmudu, -da] adj & m (Port) = **incômodo**.
incômodo, -da [ĩŋˈkomudu, -da] adj (Br) uncomfortable ◆ m (Br) nuisance; (menstruação) period.
incomparável [ĩŋkõmpaˈravew] (pl -eis [-ejʃ]) adj incomparable.
incompatível [ĩŋkõmpaˈtʃivew] (pl -eis [-ejʃ]) adj incompatible.
incompetente [ĩŋkõmpeˈtẽntʃi] adj & mf incompetent.
incompleto, -ta [ĩŋkõmˈpletu, -ta] adj unfinished.
incomum [ĩŋkoˈmũ] (pl -ns [-ʃ]) adj uncommon.
incomunicável [ĩŋkomuniˈkavew] (pl -eis [-ejʃ]) adj (isolado) isolated; (bens) non-transferable.
incomuns → **incomun**.
inconcebível [ĩŋkõseˈbivew] (pl -eis [-ejʃ]) adj inconceivable.
incondicional [ĩŋkõndʒisjoˈnaw] (pl -ais [-ajʃ]) adj unconditional.
inconformado, -da [ĩŋkõfoxˈmadu, -da] adj unresigned.
inconfundível [ĩŋkõfũˈdʒivew] (pl -eis [-ejʃ]) adj unmistakable.
inconsciência [ĩŋkõʃˈsjẽsja] f thoughtlessness.
inconsciente [ĩŋkõʃˈsjẽntʃi] adj (MED) unconscious; (irresponsável) thoughtless ◆ m unconscious.
incontestável [ĩŋkõnteʃˈtavew] (pl -eis [-ejʃ]) adj indisputable.

inconveniência [ĩŋkõveˈnjẽsja] f inconvenience.
inconveniente [ĩŋkõveˈnjẽntʃi] adj (pessoa) tactless; (assunto) awkward ◆ m (problema) problem; (desvantagem) disadvantage.
incorporar [ĩŋkoxpoˈra(x)] vt to incorporate.
incorrecto, -ta [ĩŋkuˈxɛtu, -ta] adj (Port) = **incorreto**.
incorreto, -ta [ĩŋkoˈxɛtu, -ta] adj (Br) (errado) incorrect; (malcriado) rude.
incorrigível [ĩŋkoxiˈʒivew] (pl -eis [-ejʃ]) adj incorrigible.
incrédulo, -la [ĩŋˈkredulu, -la] adj incredulous.
incrível [ĩŋˈkrivew] (pl -eis [-ejʃ]) adj incredible.
incubadora [ĩŋkubaˈdora] f incubator.
inculto, -ta [ĩŋˈkuwtu, -ta] adj (pessoa) uneducated; (terreno) uncultivated.
incumbir [ĩŋkũmˈbi(x)] vt to put in charge; **~ alguém de fazer algo** to ask sb to do sthg.
❑ **incumbir a** v + prep: **~ a alguém fazer algo** to be sb's turn to do sthg.
❑ **incumbir-se de** vp + prep: **~-se de fazer algo** to take it upon o.s. to do sthg.
incurável [ĩŋkuˈravew] (pl -eis [-ejʃ]) adj incurable.
indagar [ĩndaˈga(x)] vi to inquire.
indecente [ĩndeˈsẽntʃi] adj indecent.
indecisão [ĩndesiˈzãw] (pl -ões [-õjʃ]) f indecision, indecisiveness.
indeciso, -sa [ĩndeˈsizu, -za] adj (futuro, situação) uncertain; (pessoa) indecisive; **estar ~** to be undecided.
indecisões → **indecisão**.
indecoroso, -osa [ĩndekuˈrozo, -ɔza] adj improper.
indefeso, -sa [ĩndeˈfezu, -za] adj defenceless.
indefinido, -da [ĩndefiˈnidu, -da] adj indefinite.
indelicado, -da [ĩndeliˈkadu, -da] adj offhand.
indemnizar [ĩndemniˈzar] vt (Port) = **indenizar**.
indenização [ĩndenizaˈsãw] (pl -ões [-õjʃ]) f compensation.
indenizar [ĩndeniˈza(x)] vt (Br) to compensate.
independência [ĩndepẽnˈdẽsja] f

independence.

independente [ĩdepèn'dẽntʃi] *adj* independent.

independentemente [ĩdepèn,dẽntʃi'mẽntʃi] : **independentemente de** *prep* independently of.

indescritível [indeʃkri'tʃivew] (*pl* -eis [-ejʃ]) *adj* indescribable.

indesejável [ĩndeze'ʒavew] (*pl* -eis [-ejʃ]) *adj* undesirable.

indestrutível [ĩndeʃtru'tʃivew] (*pl* -eis [-ejʃ]) *adj* indestructible; *(fig: argumento)* watertight.

indeterminado, -da [ĩndetexmi'nadu, -da] *adj* indeterminate.

indevido, -da [ĩnde'vidu, -da] *adj* inappropriate.

Índia ['ĩndʒja] *f:* **a ~** India.

indiano, -na [ĩn'dʒjanu, -na] *adj & m, f* Indian.

indicação [ĩndʒika'sãw] (*pl* -ões [-õjʃ]) *f (de caminho, direção)* directions *(pl); (sinal)* mark; *(instrução)* indication.

indicador [ĩndʒika'do(x)] (*pl* -res [-riʃ]) *m (dedo)* index finger; *(de temperatura, velocímetro)* indicator.

indicar [ĩndʒi'ka(x)] *vt* to show.

indicativo, -va [ĩndʒika'tʃivu, -va] *adj* indicative ◆ *m (de telefone)* dialling code *(Brit)*, area code *(Am); (GRAM)* indicative.

índice ['ĩndʒisi] *m (em livro)* index; *(nível)* rate; **~ de inflação** inflation rate.

indiferença [ĩndʒife'resa] *f* indifference.

indiferente [ĩndʒife'rẽntʃi] *adj* indifferent; **para mim é ~** I don't care.

indígena [ĩn'dʒiʒena] *adj & mf (nativo)* native; *(índio)* Indian.

indigestão [ĩndʒiʒeʃ'tãw] *f* indigestion.

indigesto, -ta [ĩndʒi'ʒeʃtu, -ta] *adj* indigestible.

indignação [ĩndʒigna'sãw] (*pl* -ões [-õjʃ]) *f* indignation.

indigno, -gna [ĩn'dʒignu, -gna] *adj (pessoa)* unworthy; *(situação)* degrading.

índio, -dia ['ĩndʒju, -dja] *adj & m, f* Indian.

indirecto, -ta [ĩndi'retu, -ta] *adj (Port)* = **indireto**.

indireta [ĩndʒi'reta] *f (fig: comentário)* dig.

indireto, -ta [ĩndʒi'retu, -ta] *adj (Br)* indirect.

indisciplinado, -da [ĩndʒiʃsipli'nadu, -da] *adj* undisciplined.

indiscreto, -ta [ĩndʒiʃ'kretu, -ta] *adj* indiscreet.

indiscutível [ĩndʒiʃku'tʃivew] (*pl* -eis [-ejʃ]) *adj* indisputable.

indispensável [ĩndʒiʃpẽ'savew] (*pl* -eis [-ejʃ]) *adj* indispensable ◆ *m:* **o ~** the bare essentials *(pl).*

indisposição [ĩndʒiʃpozi'sãw] (*pl* -ões [-õjʃ]) *f* stomach upset.

indisposto, -osta [ĩndʒiʃ'poʃtu, -ɔʃta] *adj* unwell.

indistinto, -ta [ĩndʒiʃ'tʃĩntu, -ta] *adj (pouco visível)* vague; *(forma, som)* faint.

individual [ĩndʒivi'dwaw] (*pl* -ais [-ajʃ]) *adj* individual; *(quarto, tarefa)* single; *(mesa)* for one.

indivíduo [ĩnde'vidwu] *m* individual; *(fam: homem)* guy.

índole ['ĩndoli] *f* nature.

indolor [ĩndo'lo(x)] (*pl* -res [-riʃ]) *adj* painless.

Indonésia [ĩndo'nezja] *f:* **a ~** Indonesia.

indulgência [ĩnduw'ʒesja] *f* leniency.

indulgente [ĩnduw'ʒẽntʃi] *adj* lenient.

indumentária [ĩndumẽn'tarja] *f (traje)* costume; *(pej: farrapo)* rag.

indústria [ĩn'duʃtrja] *f* industry.

induzir [ĩndu'zi(x)] *vt:* **~ alguém a fazer algo** to persuade sb to do sthg; **~ alguém em erro** to mislead sb.

inédito, -ta [i'nedʒitu, -ta] *adj (livro)* unpublished; *(original)* unique; *(acontecimento)* unprecedented.

ineficaz [inefi'kaʃ] (*pl* -zes [-ziʃ]) *adj* ineffective.

inegável [ine'gavew] (*pl* -eis [-ejʃ]) *adj* undeniable.

inércia [i'nexsja] *f* inertia.

inerte [i'nextʃi] *adj* inert.

inesgotável [inezgo'tavew] (*pl* -eis [-ejʃ]) *adj* inexhaustible.

inesperado, -da [ineʃpe'radu, -da] *adj* unexpected.

inesquecível [ineʃke'sivew] (*pl* -eis [-ejʃ]) *adj* unforgettable.

inestimável [ineʃtʃi'mavew] (*pl* -eis [-ejʃ]) *adj* invaluable; **de valor ~** priceless.

inevitável [inevi'tavew] (*pl* -eis [-ejʃ]) *adj* inevitable.

inexequível [ineze'kwivew] (*pl* -eis [-ejʃ]) *adj* impracticable.

inexistência [inezif'tẽsja] f: ~ de lack of.

inexperiência [inefpe'rjẽsja] f inexperience.

inexperiente [inefpe'rjẽntʃi] adj inexperienced; (fig: inocente) innocent.

infalível [ĩfa'livew] (pl -eis [-ejʃ]) adj (método, sistema, plano) infallible; (inevitável) certain.

infâmia [ĩ'famja] f slander.

infância [ĩ'fãsja] f childhood.

infantário [ĩfãn'tarju] m (Port) nursery school.

infantil [ĩfãn'tiw] (pl -is [-iʃ]) adj (literatura, programa) children's (antes de s); (pej: imaturo) childish.

infecção [ĩfɛ'sãw] (pl -ões [-õjʃ]) f (MED) infection.

infeccioso, -osa [ĩfɛ'sjozu, -ɔza] adj infectious.

infecções → infecção.

infectado, -da [ĩfɛ'tadu, -da] adj infected.

infectar [ĩfɛ'ta(x)] vi to get infected ◆ vt to infect.

infelicidade [ĩfelisi'dadʒi] f (tristeza) unhappiness; (desgraça) misfortune; **mas que ~!** what a shame!; **tive a ~ de ...** I had the misfortune of ....

infeliz [ĩfe'liʒ] (pl -zes [-ziʃ]) adj (acontecimento, notícia) sad; (comentário, resposta) inappropriate ◆ mf wretch; **ser ~** to be unhappy.

infelizmente [ĩfeliʒ'mẽntʃi] adv unfortunately.

inferior [ĩfe'rjo(x)] (pl -res [-riʃ]) adj lower; (em valor, qualidade) inferior; **andar ~** downstairs.

inferno [ĩ'fɛxnu] m: **o Inferno** Hell; **isto é um ~!** what a nightmare!; **vá para o ~!** (fam) go to hell!

infertilidade [ĩfextʃili'dadʒi] f infertility.

infestar [ĩfeʃ'ta(x)] vt to infest.

infiel [ĩ'fjew] (pl -éis [-ɛjʃ]) adj (marido, esposa) unfaithful; (amigo) disloyal.

infiltrar-se [ĩfiw'traxsi] vp (água, chuva) to seep in.

ínfimo, -ma [ĩfimu, -ma] adj minute; (fig: sem importância) pointless.

infindável [ĩfĩ'davew] (pl -eis [-ejʃ]) adj endless.

infinidade [ĩfini'dadʒi] f infinity.

infinitivo [ĩfini'tʃivu] m: **o ~** (GRAM) the infinitive.

infinito, -ta [ĩfi'nitu, -ta] adj & m infinite.

inflação [ĩfla'sãw] f inflation.

inflamação [ĩflama'sãw] (pl -ões [-õjʃ]) f inflammation.

inflamado, -da [ĩfla'madu, -da] adj inflamed.

inflamar [ĩfla'ma(x)] vt (incendiar) to set on fire, to set alight; (fig: entusiasmar) to inflame.

inflamável [ĩfla'mavew] (pl -eis [-ejʃ]) adj inflammable (Brit), flammable (Am).

inflexível [ĩflɛk'sivew] (pl -eis [-ejʃ]) adj inflexible; (fig: implacável, rigoroso) unbending.

influência [ĩflu'ẽsja] f influence; **ter ~** to be influential.

influente [ĩflu'ẽntʃi] adj influential.

influir [ĩflu'i(x)] : **influir em** v + prep to influence.

informação [ĩfoxma'sãw] (pl -ões [-õjʃ]) f information; (notícia) news (sg); **ele não me deu informação nenhuma** he didn't give me any information. ⌐ **informações** fpl (serviço telefônico) directory enquiries (Brit), directory assistance (sg) (Am); **"informações"** "enquiries".

informal [ĩfox'maw] (pl -ais [-ajʃ]) adj informal.

informalidade [ĩfoxmali'dadʒi] f informality.

informar [ĩfox'ma(x)] vt to inform; **~ alguém de ou sobre algo** to inform sb of sthg. ⌐ **informar-se** vp to find out.

informática [ĩfox'matʃika] f information technology, computing.

informativo, -va [ĩfoxma'tʃivu, -va] adj informative.

informatizar [ĩfurmatʃi'za(x)] vt to computerize.

infortúnio [ĩfox'tunju] m misfortune.

infração [ĩfra'sãw] (pl -ões [-õjʃ]) f (Br) (de lei) offence; (de norma, regra) breach.

infracção [ĩfra'sãw] (pl -ões [-õjʃ]) f (Port) = infração.

infrações → infração.

infractor, -ra [ĩfra'tor, -ra] (mpl -res [-reʃ]. fpl -s [-ʃ]) m, f (Port) = infrator.

infrator, -ra [ĩfra'to(x), -ra] (mpl -res [-riʃ]. fpl -s [-ʃ]) m, f (Br) offender.

infravermelho, -lha [ĩfravex'meʎu.

-ʎa] *adj* infrared.

infringir [ĩfrĩ'ʒi(x)] *vt* to infringe.

infrutífero, -ra [ĩfruˈtʃiferu, -ra] *adj* fruitless.

infundado, -da [ĩfũnˈdadu, -da] *adj* unfounded.

ingenuidade [ĩʒenwiˈdadʒi] *f* ingenuity.

ingénuo, -nua [ĩˈʒɛnwu, -nwa] *adj & m, f (Port)* = ingênuo.

ingênuo, -nua [ĩˈʒenwu, -nwa] *adj (Br)* naive ♦ *m, f (Br)* naive person.

ingerir [ĩʒeˈri(x)] *vt* to ingest.

Inglaterra [ĩŋglaˈtexa] *f:* **a ~** England.

inglês, -esa [ĩŋˈgleʃ, -eza] *(mpl* -eses [-eziʃ], *fpl* -s [-ʃ]) *adj & m* English ♦ *m, f (pessoa)* Englishman *(f* Englishwoman); **os ingleses** the English; **para ~ ver** for show.

ingratidão [ĩŋgratʃiˈdãw] *f* ingratitude.

ingrato, -ta [ĩŋˈgratu, -ta] *adj (pessoa)* ungrateful; *(trabalho)* thankless.

ingrediente [ĩŋgreˈdjẽntʃi] *m* ingredient.

íngreme [ĩŋgremi] *adj* steep.

ingresso [ĩŋˈgresu] *m (em curso, universidade, partido)* enrolment; *(bilhete de cinema, teatro, etc)* ticket.

inhame [iˈɲami] *m* yam.

inibição [inibiˈsãw] *(pl* -ões [-õjʃ]) *f* inhibition.

inibido, -da [iniˈbidu, -da] *adj* inhibited.

inicial [iniˈsjaw] *(pl* -ais [-ajʃ]) *adj & f* initial.

iniciar [iniˈsja(x)] *vt* to start, to begin.

⅃ **iniciar-se** *vp* to start.

iniciativa [inisjaˈtʃiva] *f* initiative; **ter ~** to show initiative.

início [iˈnisju] *m* start, beginning; **no ~** at first; **desde o ~** from the start.

inimigo, -ga [iniˈmigu, -ga] *adj* enemy *(antes de s)* ♦ *m, f* enemy.

ininterruptamente [inĩnteˌxuptaˈmẽntʃi] *adv* continuously.

injeção [ĩʒeˈsãw] *(pl* -ões [-õjʃ]) *f (Br)* injection.

injecção [ĩʒeˈsãw] *(pl* -ões [-õjʃ]) *f (Port)* = injeção.

injeções → injeção.

injetar [ĩʒeˈtar] *vt (Port)* = injetar.

injetar [ĩʒeˈta(x)] *vt (Br)* to inject.

⅃ **injetar-se** *vp (Br) (fam: drogar-se)* to be on drugs.

injúria [ĩˈʒurja] *f* insult.

injuriar [ĩʒuˈrja(x)] *vt* to insult.

injustiça [ĩʒuʃˈtʃisa] *f* injustice.

injusto, -ta [ĩˈʒuʃtu, -ta] *adj* unfair.

inocência [inoˈsẽsja] *f* innocence.

inocentar [inosẽnˈta(x)] *vt:* **~ alguém (de algo)** *(JUR)* to clear sb (of sthg).

inocente [inoˈsẽntʃi] *adj* innocent; **ser** OU **estar ~** to be innocent.

inoculação [inɔkulaˈsãw] *(pl* -ões [-õjʃ]) *f* inoculation.

inócuo, -cua [iˈnɔkwu, -kwa] *adj* innocuous.

inofensivo, -va [inofẽˈsivu, -va] *adj* harmless.

inoportuno, -na [inopoxˈtunu, -na] *adj (pessoa)* tactless; *(comentário, momento)* inopportune.

inovação [inovaˈsãw] *(pl* -ões [-õjʃ]) *f* innovation.

inox [iˈnoksi] *m* stainless steel.

inoxidável [inoksiˈdavew] *(pl* -eis [-ejʃ]) *adj (aço)* stainless; *(material)* rustproof.

inquérito [ĩŋˈkɛritu] *m (sondagem)* opinion poll, survey; *(de polícia, comissão)* investigation.

inquietação [ĩŋkjetaˈsãw] *f (agitação)* restlessness; *(preocupação)* worry.

inquietante [ĩŋkjeˈtãntʃi] *adj* worrying, disturbing.

inquilino, -na [ĩŋkiˈlinu, -na] *m, f* tenant.

insaciável [ĩsaˈsjavew] *(pl* -eis [-ejʃ]) *adj* insatiable.

insalubre [ĩsaˈlubri] *adj (comida, bebida)* unhealthy; *(local)* insalubrious.

insanidade [ĩsaniˈdadʒi] *f* insanity.

insatisfação [ĩsatʃiʃfaˈsãw] *(pl* -ões [-õjʃ]) *f* dissatisfaction.

insatisfatório, -ria [ĩsatʃiʃfaˈtɔrju, -rja] *adj* unsatisfactory.

insatisfeito, -ta [ĩsatʃiʃˈfejtu, -ta] *adj* dissatisfied.

inscrever [ĩʃkreˈve(x)] *vt* to enrol; **~ alguém em algo** to enrol sb on OU for sthg.

⅃ **inscrever-se** *vp:* **~-se em algo** to enrol on OU for sthg.

inscrição [ĩʃkriˈsãw] *(pl* -ões [-õjʃ]) *f (em pedra)* inscription; *(em curso, cadeira)* enrolment.

inseticida [ĩsetʃiˈsida] *m* insecticide.

insecto [ĩˈsetu] *m (Port)* = inseto.

insegurança [ĩseguˈrãsa] *f* insecurity.

inseguro, -ra [ĩseˈguru, -ra] *adj (área,

rua) unsafe; *(pessoa)* insecure.

inseminação [ĩsemina'sãw] *(pl -ões* [-õjʃ]) *f:* ~ **artificial** artificial insemination.

insensato, -ta [ĩsĕ'satu, -ta] *adj (decisão, comportamento)* foolish.

insensibilidade [ĩsĕsibili'dadʒi] *f* insensitivity.

insensível [ĩsĕ'sivew] *(pl -eis* [-ejʃ]) *adj* insensitive.

inseparável [ĩsepa'ravew] *(pl -eis* [-ejʃ]) *adj* inseparable.

inserir [ĩse'ri(x)] *vt (colocar)* to insert; *(INFORM: dados)* to enter.

❐ **inserir-se em** *vp + prep (fazer parte de)* to be part of.

inseto [ĩ'setu] *m (Br)* insect.

insidioso, -osa [ĩsi'dʒjozu, -ɔza] *adj* insidious.

insígnia [ĩ'signja] *f* insignia.

insignificante [ĩsignifi'kãntʃi] *adj* insignificant.

insincero, -ra [ĩsĩ'seru, -ra] *adj* insincere.

insinuar [ĩsi'nwa(x)] *vt* to insinuate.

insípido, -da [ĩ'sipidu, -da] *adj* insipid.

insistência [ĩsiʃ'tẽsja] *f* insistence.

insistente [ĩsiʃ'tẽntʃi] *adj* insistent.

insistir [ĩsiʃ'ti(x)] *vi* to insist; **eu estou sempre insistindo com ela para ter cuidado** I'm always telling her to be careful; ~ **em fazer algo** to insist on doing sthg.

insociável [ĩso'sjavew] *(pl -eis* [-ejʃ]) *adj* unsociable.

insolação [ĩsola'sãw] *(pl -ões* [-õjʃ]) *f* sunstroke.

insolente [ĩso'lẽntʃi] *adj* insolent ♦ *mf* insolent person.

insólito, -ta [ĩ'sɔlitu, -ta] *adj* unusual.

insónia [ĩ'sɔnja] *f (Port)* = **insônia**.

insônia [ĩ'sõnja] *f (Br)* insomnia.

insosso, -a [ĩ'sosu, -a] *adj* bland; *(fig: pouco interessante)* insipid.

inspeção [ĩʃpe'sãw] *(pl -ões* [-õjʃ]) *f (Br)* inspection.

inspecção [ĩʃpe'sãw] *(pl -ões* [-õjʃ]) *f (Port)* = **inspeção**.

inspeccionar [ĩʃpesjo'nar] *vt (Port)* = **inspecionar**.

inspecções → **inspecção**.

inspecionar [ĩʃpesjo'na(x)] *vt (Br)* to inspect.

inspeções → **inspeção**.

inspector, -ra [ĩʃpe'tor, -ra] *(mpl -res* [-reʃ], *fpl -s* [-ʃ]) *m, f (Port)* = **inspetor**.

inspetor, -ra [ĩʃpe'to(x), -ra] *(mpl -res* [-riʃ], *fpl -s* [-ʃ]) *m, f (Br)* inspector.

inspiração [ĩʃpira'sãw] *(pl -ões* [-õjʃ]) *f* inspiration.

inspirador, -ra [ĩʃpira'do(x), -ra] *(mpl -res* [-riʃ], *fpl -s* [-ʃ]) *adj* inspiring.

inspirar [ĩʃpi'ra(x)] *vt (respirar)* to breathe in; *(fig: sugerir)* to inspire.

instabilidade [ĩʃtabili'dadʒi] *f* instability.

instalação [ĩʃtala'sãw] *(pl -ões* [-õjʃ]) *f* installation; ~ **elétrica** wiring.

❐ **instalações** *fpl* facilities.

instalar [ĩʃta'la(x)] *vt* to install.

❐ **instalar-se** *vp (em casa, local)* to move in; *(em cadeira)* to make o.s. comfortable.

instantâneo, -nea [ĩʃtãn'tanju, -nja] *adj* instantaneous ♦ *m* snapshot.

instante [ĩʃ'tãntʃi] *m* moment; **um ~!** just a minute!; **dentro de ~s** shortly; **de um ~ para o outro** suddenly; **nesse ~** at that moment; **num ~** in a second; **faço isso num ~** it'll only take me a minute; **por ~s** for a moment; **a qualquer ~** at any moment; **a todo o ~** all the time.

instintivo, -va [ĩʃtʃĩn'tʃivu, -va] *adj* instinctive.

instinto [ĩʃ'tʃĩntu] *m* instinct.

instituição [ĩʃtʃitwi'sãw] *(pl -ões* [-õjʃ]) *f* institution.

instituto [ĩʃtʃi'tutu] *m* institute; ~ **de beleza** beauty salon; ~ **de línguas** language school.

instrução [ĩʃtru'sãw] *(pl -ões* [-õjʃ]) *f (indicação)* instruction; *(educação)* education.

instruir [ĩʃtru'i(x)] *vt* to instruct.

instrumental [ĩʃtrumẽn'taw] *(pl -ais* [-ajʃ]) *adj* instrumental.

instrumento [ĩʃtru'mẽntu] *m (ferramenta)* tool; *(musical)* instrument.

instrutivo, -va [ĩʃtru'tʃivu, -va] *adj* instructive.

instrutor, -ra [ĩʃtru'to(x), -ra] *(mpl -res* [-riʃ], *fpl -s* [-ʃ]) *m, f (professor)* instructor; *(de direção)* driving instructor.

insubordinação [ĩsuboxdʒina'sãw] *(pl -ões* [-õjʃ]) *f (mau comportamento)* disobedience; *(rebelião)* insubordination.

insubstituível [ĩsubʃtʃi'twivew] *(pl*

-eis [-ejʃ] *adj* irreplaceable.

insucesso [ĩsu'sesu] *m* failure; **o ~ escolar** underperforming at school.

insuficiência [ĩsufi'sjẽsjɐ] *f (falta, carência)* lack; *(incapacidade)* failure; **~ cardíaca** heart failure.

insuficiente [ĩsufi'sjẽntʃi] *adj* insufficient ◆ *m (EDUC: nota)* fail.

insuflável [ĩsu'flavew] *(pl* **-eis** [-ejʃ]) *adj* inflatable; *(boneca)* blow-up.

insulina [ĩsu'lina] *f* insulin.

insultar [ĩsuw'ta(x)] *vt* to insult.

insuperável [ĩsupe'ravew] *(pl* **-eis** [-ejʃ]) *adj* insurmountable.

insuportável [ĩsupox'tavew] *(pl* **-eis** [-ejʃ]) *adj* unbearable.

intacto, -ta [ĩ'ta(k)tu, -ta] *adj (Port)* = intato.

intato, -ta [ĩ'tatu, -ta] *adj (Br)* intact.

íntegra ['ĩtegra] *f*: **na ~** in full.

integral [ĩte'graw] *(pl* **-ais** [-ajʃ]) *adj* whole.

integrar [ĩte'gra(x)] *vt* to include.

⊐ **integrar-se** *vp* to become integrated.

integridade [ĩtegri'dadʒi] *f* integrity.

íntegro, -gra ['ĩtegru, -gra] *adj* honest

inteiramente [ĩ,tejra'mẽntʃi] *adv* entirely.

inteirar-se [ĩtej'raxsi] : **inteirar-se de** *vp* + *prep* to find out about.

inteiro, -ra [ĩ'tejru, -ra] *adj (todo)* whole; *(não partido)* intact.

intelectual [ĩtele'twaw] *(pl* **-ais** [-ajʃ]) *adj & mf* intellectual.

inteligência [ĩteli'ʒẽsjɐ] *f* intelligence.

inteligente [ĩteli'ʒẽntʃi] *adj* intelligent.

intenção [ĩtẽ'sãw] *(pl* **-ões** [-õjʃ]) *f* intention; **ter ~ de fazer algo** to intend to do sthg; **sem ~** unintentionally; **com** OU **na melhor das intenções** with the best of intentions; **ter segundas intenções** to have an ulterior motive.

intensidade [ĩtẽsi'dadʒi] *f* intensity.

intensivo, -va [ĩtẽ'sivu, -va] *adj* intensive.

intenso, -sa [ĩ'tẽsu, -sa] *adj* intense; *(chuva)* heavy; *(trabalho)* hard; *(vento)* high.

interactivo, -va [ĩtera'tivu, -va] *adj*

(Port) = **interativo**.

interativo, -va [ĩtera'tʃivu, -va] *adj (Br)* interactive.

intercâmbio [ĩter'kãmbju] *m* exchange.

interceder [ĩtexse'de(x)] *vi*: **~ por alguém** to intercede on behalf of sb.

interceptar [ĩtexsep'ta(x)] *vt* to intercept.

interdição [ĩtexdʒi'sãw] *(pl* **-ões** [-õjʃ]) *f (proibição)* ban; *(encerramento)* closure.

interditar [ĩtexdʒi'ta(x)] *vt* to *(proibir)* ban; *(encerrar)* to close; **interditaram a rua** they closed off the road.

interessado, -da [ĩtere'sadu, -da] *adj* interested.

interessante [ĩtere'sãntʃi] *adj* interesting.

interessar [ĩtere'sa(x)] *vi* to be of interest; **a religião não me interessa** religion doesn't interest me; **não me interessa!** I don't care!

⊐ **interessar-se por** *vp* + *prep* to be interested in; **só agora é que ele se interessou pelo caso** he's only recently taken an interest in the affair.

interesse [ĩte'resi] *m* interest; *(importância)* significance; *(proveito próprio)* self-interest; **no ~ de** in the interests of; **por ~** out of self-interest; **sem ~** of no interest.

interface [ĩtex'fasi] *f* interface.

interferência [ĩtexfe'rẽsjɐ] *f* interference.

⊐ **interferências** *fpl (em imagem, rádio)* interference *(sg)*

interferir [ĩtexfe'ri(x)] : **interferir em** *v* + *prep* to interfere in.

interfone [ĩtex'fɔni] *m* intercom.

interior [ĩte'rjo(x)] *(pl* **-res** [-riʃ]) *adj (quarto, porta)* inner ◆ *m (de área, caixa)* inside; *(de casa, país)* interior.

interjeição [ĩtexʒej'sãw] *(pl* **-ões** [-õjʃ]) *f* interjection.

interlocutor, -ra [ĩtexloku'to(x), -ra] *(mpl* **-res** [-riʃ], *fpl* **-s** [-ʃ]) *m, f* speaker.

interlúdio [ĩtex'ludʒju] *m* interlude.

intermediário, -ria [ĩtexme'dʒjarju, -rja] *m, f* intermediary.

intermédio [ĩter'medju] *m*: **por ~ de** through.

interminável [ĩtexmi'navew] *(pl* **-eis** [-ejʃ]) *adj* endless.

intermitente [ĩntɛxmi'tẽntʃi] *adj* intermittent.

internacional [ĩntɛxnasju'naw] (*pl* -ais [-ajʃ]) *adj* international.

internar [ĩntɛx'na(x)] *vt* (*MED*) to admit.

internato [ĩntɛx'natu] *m* boarding school.

Internet [ĩntɛx'nɛtʃi] *f*: **a ~** the Internet.

interno, -na [ĩn'tɛxnu, -na] *adj* internal; (*colégio*) boarding (*antes de s*).

interpretação [ĩntɛxpreta'sãw] (*pl* -ões [-õjʃ]) *f* (*de texto, mensagem*) interpretation; (*de papel, canção*) performance; (*tradução*) interpreting.

interpretar [ĩntɛxpre'ta(x)] *vt* (*texto, mensagem*) to interpret; (*papel*) to play; (*música*) to perform.

intérprete [ĩn'tɛxpretʃi] *mf* performer; (*tradutor*) interpreter.

interrogação [ĩntɛxoga'sãw] (*pl* -ões [-õjʃ]) *f* (*pergunta*) question; (*interrogatório*) interrogation.

interrogar [ĩntɛxu'ga(x)] *vt* (*perguntar a*) to question; (*em tribunal*) to cross-examine.

interrupção [ĩntɛxup'sãw] (*pl* -ões [-õjʃ]) *f* interruption; **sem ~** without interruption.

interruptor [ĩntɛxup'to(x)] (*pl* -res [-riʃ]) *m* switch.

interurbano, -na [ĩntɛxux'banu, -na] *adj* (*telefonema*) long-distance.

intervalo [ĩntɛx'valu] *m* (*de programa, aula*) break; (*de espetáculo*) interval.

intervenção [ĩntɛxvẽ'sãw] (*pl* -ões [-õjʃ]) *f* (*ação*) intervention; (*discurso*) speech; **~ cirúrgica** operation.

intervir [ĩntɛx'vi(x)] *vi* (*participar*) to participate; (*interferir*) to intervene; **~ em** (*participar em*) to participate in; (*interferir em*) to intervene in.

intestino [ĩntɛʃ'tʃinu] *m* intestine; **~ delgado/grosso** small/large intestine.

intimar [ĩntʃi'ma(x)] *vt* (*JUR*) to summon; **~ alguém a fazer algo** to order sb to do sthg.

intimidação [ĩntʃimida'sãw] (*pl* -ões [-õjʃ]) *f* intimidation.

intimidade [ĩntʃimi'dadʒi] *f* (*proximidade*) intimacy; (*privacidade*) privacy.

intimidar [ĩntʃimi'da(x)] *vt* to intimidate.

⌐ **intimidar-se** *vp* to be intimidated.

íntimo, -ma ['ĩntʃimu, -ma] *adj* (*pessoa*) close; (*sentimentos*) intimate; (*objetos*) personal ◆ *m*: **no ~** deep down; **ser ~ de alguém** to be close to sb.

intolerância [ĩntole'rãsja] *f* intolerance.

intolerante [ĩntole'rãntʃi] *adj* (*pessoa*) intolerant; (*lei, atitude*) rigid.

intoxicação [ĩntoksika'sãw] (*pl* -ões [-õjʃ]) *f* poisoning; **~ alimentar** food poisoning.

intransigente [ĩntrãzi'ʒẽntʃi] *adj* intransigent.

intransitável [ĩntrãzi'tavew] (*pl* -eis [-ejʃ]) *adj* impassable.

intransitivo [ĩntrãzi'tʃivu] *adj* *m* → **verbo**.

intransponível [ĩntrãʃpo'nivew] (*pl* -eis [-ejʃ]) *adj* (*rio, obstáculo*) impassable; (*problema*) insurmountable.

intratável [ĩntra'tavew] (*pl* -eis [-ejʃ]) *adj* (*pessoa*) difficult.

intravenoso, -osa [ĩntrave'nozu, -ɔza] *adj* intravenous.

intrépido, -da [ĩn'trɛpidu, -da] *adj* intrepid.

intriga [ĩn'triga] *f* (*de livro, história*) plot; (*bisbilhotice*) piece of gossip.

intrigante [ĩntri'gãntʃi] *adj* (*curioso*) intriguing; (*bisbilhoteiro*) gossipy.

introdução [ĩntrodu'sãw] (*pl* -ões [-õjʃ]) *f* introduction; (*inserção*) insertion.

introduzir [ĩntrodu'zi(x)] *vt* (*inserir*) to insert.

intrometer-se [ĩntrome'texsi] *vp* to interfere; **~ em** to meddle in.

intrometido, -da [ĩntrome'tʃidu, -da] *adj* meddling.

intromissão [ĩntromi'sãw] (*pl* -ões [-õjʃ]) *f* interference, meddling.

introvertido, -da [ĩntrovex'tʃidu, -da] *adj* introverted.

intruso, -sa [ĩn'truzu, -za] *m, f* intruder.

intuição [ĩntwi'sãw] (*pl* -ões [-õjʃ]) *f* intuition; **por ~** intuitively.

intuito [ĩn'twitu] *m* aim; **com o ~ de fazer algo** with the aim of doing sthg.

inumano, -na [inu'manu, -na] *adj* inhuman.

inúmeros, -ras [i'numeruʃ, -raʃ] *adj pl* countless.

inundação [inũnda'sãw] (*pl* -ões [-õjʃ]) *f* flood.

inundar [inũn'da(x)] *vt* to flood.

inútil [i'nutʃiw] (*pl* -teis [-tejʃ]) *adj*

(desnecessário) useless; *(vão)* pointless.

inutilmente [i,nutʃiw'mẽntʃi] *adv* in vain.

invadir [iva'di(x)] *vt* to invade.

invalidez [ĩvali'deʒ] *f* disability.

inválido, -da [ĩ'validu, -da] *adj (pessoa)* disabled ◆ *m, f* disabled person.

invariável [iva'rjavɛw] *(pl -eis* [-ejʃ]) *adj* invariable.

invasão [iva'zãw] *(pl -ões* [-õjʃ]) *f* invasion.

inveja [ĩ've3a] *f* envy; **ter ~ de alguém** to envy sb.

invejar [ĩve'3a(x)] *vt* to envy.

invejoso, -osa [ĩve'3ozu, -ɔza] *adj* envious.

invenção [ĩvẽ'sãw] *(pl -ões* [-õjʃ]) *f* invention.

inventar [ĩvẽ'ta(x)] *vt (criar)* to invent; *(fig: mentir)* to make up.

inventário [ĩvẽ'tarju] *m* inventory.

inventor, -ra [ĩvẽ'to(x), -ra] *(mpl -res* [-riʃ], *fpl -s* [-ʃ]) *m, f* inventor.

inverno [ĩ'vɛxnu] *m* winter; **no ~** in the winter.

inverosímil [ĩveru'zimil] *(pl -meis* [mejʃ]) *adj (Port)* = **inverossímil**.

inverossímil [ĩvero'simiw] *(pl -meis* [-mejʃ]) *(Br)* unlikely, improbable.

inversão [ĩvex'sãw] *(pl -ões* [-õjʃ]) *f* inversion; **fazer a ~ de marcha** to go into reverse.

inverso, -sa [ĩ'vɛxsu, -sa] *adj* opposite ◆ *m*: **o ~** the opposite.

inversões → inversão.

inverter [ĩvex'te(x)] *vt (ordem, posição)* to invert; *(sentido, marcha)* to reverse.

invés [ĩ'vɛʃ] *m*: **ao ~ de** instead of.

investida [ĩveʃ'tʃida] *f (ataque)* attack; *(tentativa)* attempt.

investigação [ĩveʃtʃiga'sãw] *(pl -ões* [-õjʃ]) *f (policial)* investigation; *(científica)* research.

investigar [ĩveʃtʃiga(x)] *vt (acontecimento, crime)* to investigate; *(cientificamente)* to research.

investimento [ĩveʃtʃi'mẽntu] *m* investment.

investir [ĩveʃtʃi(x)] *vt* to invest ◆ *vi*: **~ (em algo)** to invest (in sthg).

inviável [ĩ'vjavɛw] *(pl -eis* [-ejʃ]) *adj* impracticable.

invisível [ĩve'zivew] *(pl -eis* [-ejʃ]) *adj* invisible.

invocar [ĩvo'ka(x)] *vt* to invoke.

invólucro [ĩ'vɔlukru] *m* wrapping.

involuntário, -ria [ĩvolũ'tarju, -rja] *adj* involuntary.

iodo ['jodu] *m* iodine.

ioga ['jɔga] *m ou f* yoga.

iogurte [ju'guxtʃi] *m* yoghurt.

iô-iô [jo'jo] *(pl iô-iôs* [jo'joʃ]) *m* yoyo.

ipê [i'pe] *m type of Brazilian tree*.

ir [i'(x)] *vi* 1. *(deslocar-se)* to go; **fomos de ônibus** we went by bus; **iremos a pé** we'll go on foot, we'll walk; **vamos?** shall we go?

2. *(assistir, frequentar)* to go; **ele nunca vai às reuniões** he never goes to the meetings; **você não vai à aula?** aren't you going to your class?; **vou ao cinema muitas vezes** I go to the cinema a lot.

3. *(estender-se)* to go; **o caminho vai até ao lago** the path goes to the lake.

4. *(desenrolar-se)* to go; **isto não vai nada bem** this isn't going at all well; **como vai você?** how are you?; **como vão as coisas?** how's things?; **os negócios vão mal** business is bad.

5. *(exprime duração gradual)*: **~ fazendo algo** to carry on doing sthg; **eu vou andando** I'll carry on; **va tentando!** keep trying!

6. *(seguido de infinitivo)*: **vou falar com ele** I'll speak to him; **você vai gostar** you'll like it; **não vou fazer nada** I'm not going to do anything.

7. *(seguido de gerúndio)*: **ia caindo** I almost fell; **ia morrendo** I nearly died.

8. *(em locuções)*: **~ ter (a desembocar)** to lead to; **~ ter com (encontrar)** to meet. **⌐ ir de** *v + prep (ir disfarçado)* to go as; *(partir)*: **vou de férias amanhã** I'm going on holiday tomorrow.

⌐ ir por *v + prep (auto-estrada, escadas)* to take; **~ pela esquerda/direita** to go left/right; **~ pelo jardim** to go through the garden.

⌐ ir-se *vp (partir)* to go; **ele já se foi** he's already left; **~-se embora** to leave.

ira ['ira] *f* rage.

irascível [iraʃ'sivew] *(pl -eis* [-ejʃ]) *adj* irascible.

íris ['iriʃ] *f inv* iris.

Irlanda [ix'lãnda] *f*: **a ~** Ireland, Eire; **a ~ do Norte** Northern Ireland.

irlandês, -esa [ixlãn'deʃ, -eza] *(mpl -eses* [-eziʃ], *fpl -s* [-ʃ]) *adj & m* Irish ◆ *m, f (pessoa)* Irishman *(f* Irishwoman); **os irlandeses** the Irish.

irmã [ix'mã] f *(freira)* nun, → **irmão**.

irmão, -mã [ix'mãw, -mã] m, f brother (f sister).

ironia [iro'nia] f irony.

irra ['ixa] *interj* damn!

irracional [ixasjo'naw] *(pl* -ais [-ajʃ]) *adj* irrational.

irradiação [ixadʒja'sãw] *(pl* -ões [-õjʃ]) f irradiation.

irradiar [ixa'dʒja(x)] *vt (luz)* to radiate.

irreal [i'xjaw] *(pl* -ais [-ajʃ]) *adj* unreal.

irreconciliável [ixekõsi'ljavew] *(pl* -eis [-ejʃ]) *adj* irreconcilable.

irreconhecível [ixekoɲe'sivew] *(pl* -eis [-ejʃ]) *adj* unrecognizable.

irrecuperável [ixekupe'ravew] *(pl* -eis [-ejʃ]) *adj (perdido)* irretrievable; *(estragado)* irreparable; *(doente, viciado)* incurable.

irregular [ixegu'la(x)] *(pl* -es [-iʃ]) *adj* irregular; *(superfície)* uneven.

irrelevante [ixele'vãntʃi] *adj* irrelevant.

irremediável [ixeme'dʒjavew] *(pl* -eis [-ejʃ]) *adj* irremediable.

irreprimível [ixepri'mivew] *(pl* -eis [-ejʃ]) *adj* irrepressible.

irrequieto, -ta [ixe'kjetu, -ta] *adj (criança)* boisterous.

irresistível [ixeziʃ'tʃivew] *(pl* -eis [-ejʃ]) *adj* irresistible; *(apetite, vontade)* overwhelming.

irresponsável [ixeʃpõ'savew] *(pl* -eis [-ejʃ]) *adj* irresponsible.

irrigação [ixiga'sãw] *(pl* -ões [-õjʃ]) f irrigation.

irrisório, -ria [ixi'zɔrju, -rja] *adj* derisory.

irritação [ixita'sãw] *(pl* -ões [-õjʃ]) f irritation; **~ de pele** OU **cutânea** (skin) rash.

irritante [ixi'tãntʃi] *adj* irritating.

irritar [ixi'ta(x)] *vt* to irritate.

❏ **irritar-se** *vp* to get irritated.

isca ['iʃka] f *(para pesca)* bait.

isenção [izẽ'sãw] *(pl* -ões [-õjʃ]) f exemption.

isento, -ta [i'zẽntu, -ta] *adj* exempt; **~ de** exempt from.

isolado, -da [izo'ladu, -da] *adj (lugar)* remote; *(pessoa, objeto)* isolated.

isolamento [izola'mẽntu] m *(solidão)* isolation; *(de janela, cabo)* insulation.

isolar [izo'la(x)] *vt (pessoa)* to isolate; *(janela, cabo)* to insulate.

isopor® [izo'pox] m *(Br)* polystyrene.

isqueiro [iʃ'kejru] m *(de cigarro)* lighter; *(de fogão a gás)* ignition button.

isso ['isu] *pron* that ◆ *interj* that's it!; **como vai ~?** how's it going?; **foi por ~ que ele não veio** that's why he didn't come; **é por ~ mesmo que eu não vou!** that is exactly why I'm not going!; **~ não!** no way!; **não gosto disso** I don't like that; **não mexa nisso!** leave that alone!; **nem por ~** not really; **para ~** (in order) to do that.

istmo [iʃt'ʃimu] m isthmus.

isto ['iʃtu] *pron* this; **disto eu não quero** I don't want any of this; **escreva nisto** write on this; **~ é** *(quer dizer)* that is (to say); **~ é que é vida!** this is the life!

Itália [i'talja] f: **a ~** Italy.

italiana [ita'ljana] f *very strong espresso*, → **italiano**.

italiano, -na [ita'ljanu, -na] *adj & m, f* Italian ◆ m *(língua)* Italian.

itálico [i'taliku] m italic type, italics *(pl)*; **em ~** in italics.

itinerário [itʃine'rarju] m itinerary; **~ turístico** tourist route OU trail.

iúca ['juka] f yucca.

IVA ['iva] m *(Port: abrev de Imposto sobre o Valor Acrescentado)* VAT *(Brit)*, sales tax *(Am)*.

J

já ['ʒa] *adv (agora)* now; *(de seguida)* right away, at once; **até ~!** see you soon!; **é para ~!** coming up!; **~ acabei** I've already finished; **~ que estamos aqui, podíamos ir ao cinema** since we're here, we might as well go to the cinema; **você ~ esteve em Salvador?** have you ever been to Salvador?; **você ~ foi a Salvador?** have you been to Salvador yet?; **~ não sei o que fazer** I don't know what else I can do; **desde ~** in advance; **~ era** it's past it; **~ que** since.

jabuti [ʒabu'tʃi] *m* giant tortoise.

jabuticaba [ʒabutʃi'kaba] *f* dark red Brazilian berry with sweet white flesh.

jacarandá [ʒakarän'da] *m* jacaranda *(South American tree valued for its wood).*

jacaré [ʒaka'rɛ] *m* crocodile.

jacinto [ʒa'sĩntu] *m* hyacinth.

jacto [ʒatu] *m (Port)* = jato.

Jacuzzi® [ʒaku'zi] *m* Jacuzzi®.

jade ['ʒadʒi] *m* jade.

jaguar [ʒa'gwa(x)] *(pl -res* [-riʃ]) *m* jaguar.

jamais [ʒu'majʃ] *adv* never; **o livro mais interessante que ~ li** the most interesting book I've ever read.

janeiro [ʒa'nejru] *m* January, → setembro.

janela [ʒa'nɛla] *f* window.

jangada [ʒãŋ'gada] *f* raft.

jantar [ʒãn'ta(x)] *(pl -res* [-riʃ]) *m* dinner ◆ *vi* to have dinner ◆ *vt* to have for dinner.

jante ['ʒãntʃi] *f* (wheel) rim.

Japão [ʒa'pãw] *m*: **o ~** Japan.

japonês, -esa [ʒapo'neʃ, -eza] *(mpl -eses* [-eziʃ], *fpl -s* [-ʃ]) *adj & m, f* Japanese ◆ *m (língua)* Japanese.

jaqueta [ʒa'keta] *f* jacket.

jararaca [ʒara'raka] *f* extremely ven-

omous viper-like snake found in South America.

jardim [ʒax'dʒĩ] *(pl -ns* [-ʃ]) *m (de casa)* garden; *(público)* park; **~ botânico** botanical gardens *(pl)*; **~ de infância** kindergarten; **~ zoológico** zoo.

jardim-escola [ʒa,dʒiʃ'kɔla] *(pl jardins-escolas* [ʒar,dʒiʒ'kɔlaʃ]) *m (Port)* kindergarten.

jardineiras [ʒaxdʒi'nejraʃ] *fpl (calças)* dungarees *(Brit)*, overalls *(Am)*.

jardineiro, -ra [ʒaxdʒi'nejru, -ra] *m, f* gardener.

jardins → jardim

jarra [ʒaxa] *f (para flores)* vase; *(para vinho)* carafe.

jarrão [ʒa'xãw] *(pl -ões* [-õjʃ]) *m* (large) vase.

jarro [ʒaxu] *m (para bebida)* jug; *(flor)* arum lily.

jarrões → jarrão.

jasmim [ʒaʒ'mĩ] *(pl -ns* [-ʃ]) *m* jasmine.

jato [ʒatu] *m (Br)* jet.

jaula [ʒawla] *f* cage.

javali [ʒava'li] *m* wild boar.

jazer [ʒa'ze(x)] *vi* to lie.

jazigo [ʒa'zigu] *m* tomb.

jazz ['dʒazi] *m* jazz.

jeans ['dʒiniʃ] *m inv (Br)* jeans *(pl)* ◆ *mpl (Port)* jeans.

jeito ['ʒejtu] *m (modo)* way; *(comportamento)* manner; **não tem ~!** *(Br)* it's hopeless!; **com ~** carefully; **dar um ~ em algo** *(tornozelo, pulso)* to sprain sthg; *(reparar)* to fix sthg; **ficar sem ~** *(Br)* to feel embarrassed; **ter falta de ~ para algo** to be bad at sthg; **ter ~ para algo** to be good at sthg; **tomar ~** *(Br)* to learn one's lesson; **de ~ nenhum!** no way!

jejum [ʒe'ʒũ] *(pl -ns* [-ʃ]) *m* fast; **em ~** on an empty stomach.

jesuíta [ʒe'zwita] *m (RELIG)* Jesuit.

jet ski [dʒɛt'ski] *m* jet-skiing.

jibóia [ʒi'bɔja] *f* boa constrictor.

jipe [ʒipi] *m* Jeep®.

joalharia [ʒwaʎaˈria] *f (Port)* = **joalheria**.

joalheria [ʒwaʎeˈria] *f (Br) (loja)* jeweller's (shop); *(jóias)* jewellery.

joanete [ʒwaˈnetʃi] *m* bunion.

joaninha [ʒwaˈniɲa] *f* ladybird *(Brit)*, ladybug *(Am)*.

joelheira [ʒweˈʎeira] *f* knee pad.

joelho [ʒweˈʎu] *m* knee; **de ~s** on one's knees.

jogada [ʒoˈgada] *f (lance de jogo)* go, turn; *(em xadrez)* move; *(em futebol, basquete)* shot.

jogar [ʒoˈga(x)] *vi* to play; *(em jogo de azar)* to gamble ♦ *vt* to play; *(apostar)* to bet; *(atirar)* to throw; **~ bola** to play ball; **~ às cartas** to play cards; **~ fora** *(Br)* to throw away OU out.

❏ **jogar-se a** *vp + prep (pessoa)* to lunge at; **ele jogou-se no chão** he threw himself to the floor.

jogo [ʒogu] *(pl* **jogos** [ʒoguʃ]) *m (de ténis, xadrez)* game; *(de futebol, rúgbi)* match; *(conjunto)* set; *(jogos de azar)* gambling; **~ do bicho** *(unlicensed)* lottery in which every group of numbers is represented by an animal; **~ do galo** *(Port)* noughts and crosses *(sg)*; **~s de vídeo** video games; **os Jogos Olímpicos** the Olympics.

jogo-da-velha [ʒoguˈdaˈveʎa] *(pl* **jogos-da-velha** [ʒoguʒdaˈveʎa]) *m (Br)* noughts and crosses *(sg)*.

jóia [ʒɔja] *f (brincos, anel)* jewel; *(pagamento)* membership fee.

jóquei [ʒɔkei] *m* jockey.

jornada [ʒoxˈnada] *f (caminhada)* journey; **~ de trabalho** working day.

jornal [ʒoxˈnaw] *(pl* **-ais** [-ajʃ]) *m* newspaper.

jornaleiro, -ra [ʒoxnaˈlejru, -ra] *m, f (Br)* newsagent ♦ *m (Br)* newsagent's (shop).

jornalista [ʒoxnaˈliʃta] *mf* journalist.

jorrar [ʒoˈxa(x)] *vi* to gush.

jovem [ʒɔvẽ] *(pl* **-ns** [-ʃ]) *adj* young ♦ *mf* young man *(f* young woman).

jovial [ʒoˈvjaw] *(pl* **-ais** [-ajʃ]) *adj* jolly.

joystick [dʒɔiʃtʃiki] *m* joystick.

juba [ʒuba] *f* mane.

judaico, -ca [ʒuˈdajku, -ka] *adj* Jewish.

judeu, -dia [ʒuˈdew, -dʃia] *m, f* Jew.

judicial [ʒudʃiˈsjaw] *(pl* **-ais** [-ajʃ]) *adj* legal; **o poder ~** the judiciary.

judiciária [ʒudiˈsjarja] *f (Port) (polícia)* police; *(local)* police station.

judo [ʒudu] *m (Port)* = **judô**.

judô [ʒuˈdo] *m (Br)* judo.

Jugoslávia [ʒugoʒˈlavja] *f (Port)*: **a ~** Yugoslavia.

juiz, juíza [ʒwiʃ, ʒwiza] *(mpl* **-zes** [-zeʃ], *fpl* **-s** [-ʃ]) *m, f* judge; **~ de linha** *(Port: em futebol)* linesman.

juízo [ʒwizu] *m (parecer)* opinion ♦ *interj* behave yourself!; **perder o ~** to lose one's mind; **ter ~** to be sensible.

jujuba [ʒuˈʒuba] *f (bala)* jelly bean.

julgamento [ʒuwgaˈmẽtu] *m (acto)* judgement; *(audiência)* trial.

julgar [ʒuwˈga(x)] *vt (JUR)* to judge; *(achar, opinar)* to think ♦ *vi (JUR)* to pass sentence.

❏ **julgar-se** *vp*: **ele julga-se o maior** he thinks he's the best.

julho [ʒuʎu] *m* July, → **setembro**.

jumento [ʒuˈmẽtu] *m* donkey.

junco [ʒũku] *m* reed, rush.

junho [ʒuɲu] *m* June, → **setembro**.

júnior [ʒunjɔ(x)] *(pl* **juniores** [ʒuˈnjɔriʃ]) *adj* youngest ♦ *mf (ESP)* junior.

junta [ʒũta] *f* joint; *(POL)* junta.

juntamente [ʒũtaˈmẽtʃi] : **juntamente com** *prep* together with.

juntar [ʒũˈta(x)] *vt (reunir)* to gather together; *(dinheiro)* to save; *(adicionar)* to add; **~ o útil ao agradável** to mix business with pleasure.

❏ **juntar-se** *vp (reunir-se)* to gather round; *(encontrar-se)* to meet; *(amigar-se)* to move in together.

junto, -ta [ʒũtu, -ta] *pp* → **juntar** ♦ *adj* together ♦ *adv*: **~ de** OU **a** by; **~ com** along with.

jura [ʒura] *f* vow.

juramento [ʒuraˈmẽtu] *m* oath.

jurar [ʒuˈra(x)] *vt & vi* to swear.

júri [ʒuri] *m* jury.

jurídico, -ca [ʒuˈridʒiku, -ka] *adj* legal.

juros [ʒuruʃ] *mpl* interest *(sg)*.

justeza [ʒuʃˈteza] *f (precisão)* precision; *(imparcialidade)* fairness.

justiça [ʒuʃˈtʃisa] f justice; *(organismo)* judiciary.

justificação [ʒuʃtʃifikaˈsãw] *(pl -ões* [-õjʃ]) f *(razão)* justification; *(escrita)* statement.

justificar [ʒuʃtʃifiˈka(x)] vt to justify. ⏘ **justificar-se** vp to justify o.s.

justificativa [ʒuʃtʃifikaˈtiva] f justification.

justo, -ta [ˈʒuʃtu, -ta] adj *(exato)* precise; *(imparcial)* fair; *(cingido)* fitted.

juvenil [ʒuveˈniw] *(pl -is* [-iʃ]) adj *(moda, centro, literatura)* for teenagers; *(delinqüente, comportamento)* juvenile.

juventude [ʒuvẽˈtudʒi] f *(época)* youth; *(jovens)* young people *(pl)*.

K

karaokê [karaoˈke] *m* karaoke.
karaté [karaˈte] *m (Port)* = **caratê**.
kart [ˈkaxtʃi] *m* go-kart.
karting [ˈkaxtʃiŋ] *m* go-karting.
ketchup [kɛˈtʃupi] *m* ketchup.
kg *(abrev de quilograma)* kg.
kit [ˈkitʃi] *m* kit.

kitchenette [kitʃiˈnɛtʃi] *f* kitchenette.
kiwi [ˈkiwi] *m* kiwi fruit.
km *(abrev de quilômetro)* km.
km/h *(abrev de quilômetro por hora)*
km/h.
KO [kɛˈɔ] *(abrev de knock-out)* KO.

L

lá [la] *adv* there; **quero ~ saber!** what do I care!; **sei ~!** how should I know!; **vá ~!** go on!; **para ~ de** beyond.

lã [lã] *f* wool.

-la [la] *pron (pessoa)* her; *(coisa)* it; *(você)* you.

labareda [laba'reda] *f* flame.

lábio ['labju] *m* lip.

labirinto [labi'rĩntu] *m* labyrinth.

laboratório [labora'tɔrju] *m* laboratory.

laca ['laka] *f (Port)* hairspray.

laço ['lasu] *m* bow; *(de parentesco, amizade)* bond.

lacónico, -ca [la'kɔniku, -ka] *adj (Port)* = **lacônico**.

lacônico, -ca [la'koniku, -ka] *adj (Br)* laconic.

lacrar [la'kra(x)] *vt* to seal *(with sealing wax)*.

lacrimogénio [lakrimɔ'ʒɛnju] *adj m (Port)* = **lacrimogênio**.

lacrimogêneo [lakrimɔ'ʒenju] *adj m (Br)* → **gás**.

lácteo, -tea ['laktju, -tja] *adj (produto)* dairy *(antes de s)*.

lacticínios [lati'sinjuʃ] *mpl (Port)* = **laticínios**.

lacuna [la'kuna] *f (espaço vazio)* gap; *(esquecimento)* oversight.

ladeira [la'dejra] *f* slope.

lado ['ladu] *m* side; *(lugar)* place; **gosto de me deitar de ~** I like to sleep on my side; **deixar** OU **pôr de ~** to set aside; **o ~ fraco** weak point; **o vizinho do ~** the next-door neighbour; **ao ~ de** next to, beside; **~ a ~** side by side; **de ~ a ~** from one end to the other; **de um ~ para o outro** back and forth; **por todo o ~** OU **todos os ~s** all over the place; **por um ~ ... por outro ~ ...** on the one hand ... on the other hand ....

ladrão, ladra [la'drãw, 'ladra] *(mpl -ões* [-õjʃ], *fpl -s* [-ʃ]) *m, f* thief.

ladrilho [la'driʎu] *m* floor tile.

ladrões → **ladrão**.

lagarta [la'gaxta] *f (bicho)* caterpillar.

lagartixa [lagax'tʃiʃa] *f* gecko.

lagarto [la'gaxtu] *m* lizard.

lago ['lagu] *m (natural)* lake; *(de jardim)* pond.

lagoa [la'goa] *f* lake.

lagosta [la'goʃta] *f* lobster.

lagostim [lagoʃ'tʃĩ] *(pl -ns* [-ʃ]) *m* langoustine.

lágrima ['lagrima] *f* tear.

laje ['laʒi] *f (de pavimento)* paving stone; *(de construção)* slab.

lama ['lama] *f* mud.

lamacento, -ta [lama'sẽntu, -ta] *adj* muddy.

lambada [lãm'bada] *m (dança)* lambada.

lamber [lãm'be(x)] *vt* to lick; **~ tudo** *(fam)* to lick the plate clean.

⌐ **lamber-se** *vp (cão)* to lick o.s.; *(gato)* to wash o.s.

lamentar [lamẽn'ta(x)] *vt* to lament.

⌐ **lamentar-se** *vp* to moan.

lamentável [lamẽn'tavεw] *(pl -eis* [-ejʃ]) *adj* regrettable.

lâmina ['lamina] *f* blade; **~ de barbear** razor blade.

lâmpada ['lãmpada] *f (light)* bulb.

lampião [lãm'pjãw] *(pl -ões* [-õjʃ]) *m* lantern.

lampreia [lãm'preja] *f* lamprey.

lança ['lãsa] *f* lance, spear.

lançar [lã'sa(x)] *vt (lança, bola, dardo)* to throw; *(novo filme, disco)* to release; *(campanha, livro, produto)* to launch.

⌐ **lançar-se** *vp*: **~-se a** to launch o.s. at; **~-se sobre** to throw o.s. on.

lance ['lãsi] *m (em licitação)* bid; *(ESP: jogada)* shot; *(Br: fam: fato)* fact; **~ de**

escada flight of stairs.
lancha ['lãʃa] f launch.
lanchar [lã'ʃa(x)] vi to have tea.
lanche ['lãʃi] m tea (light afternoon meal).
lanchonete [lãʃo'nɛtʃi] f (Br) snack bar.
lancinante [lãsi'nãntʃi] adj (dor) shooting; (grito) piercing.
lanço ['lãsu] m (Port) (em licitação) bid; ~ de escadas flight of stairs.
lânguido, -da ['lãŋgidu, -da] adj languid.
lantejoula [lãnte'ʒola] f sequin.
lanterna [lãn'tɛxna] f lantern; ~ de bolso torch (Brit), flashlight (Am).
lapela [la'pɛla] f lapel.
lápide ['lapidʒi] f (em monumento, estátua) memorial stone; (em túmulo) tombstone.
lápis ['lapiʃ] m inv pencil; ~ de cor coloured pencil; ~ de cera wax crayon; ~ para os olhos eyeliner.
lapiseira [lapi'zejra] f (em Portugal) ballpoint pen; (no Brasil) propelling pencil.
lapso ['lapsu] m (de tempo) period; (esquecimento) slip; **por** ~ by mistake.
laquê [la'ke] m (Br) hairspray.
lar ['la(x)] (pl -res [-riʃ]) m home; ~ (de idosos) old people's home.
laranja [la'rãʒa] f orange.
laranjada [larã'ʒada] f (Port) orangeade; (Br) orange juice.
laranjeira [larã'ʒejra] f orange tree.
lareira [la'rejra] f fireplace.
lares → lar.
largada [lax'gada] f start.
largar [lax'ga(x)] vt (soltar) to let go; (libertar) to set free; (deixar cair) to drop; (velas) to unfurl; (abandonar) to leave.
largo, -ga ['laxgu, -ga] adj (caminho, estrada, cama) wide; (roupa) loose ◆ m (praça) square; **tem 3 metros de** ~ it's 3 metres wide; **ao** ~ at a distance.
largura [lax'gura] f width.
laringe [la'rĩʒi] f larynx.
larva ['laxva] f larva.
-las [laʃ] pron pl (elas) them; (vocês) you.
lasanha [la'zaɲa] f lasagne.
lasca ['laʃka] f (de madeira) splinter; (de pedra) chip.
laser ['lejzɛ(x)] (pl -res [-riʃ]) m laser.

lástima ['laʃtʃima] f (pena) shame; (miséria) misery.
lastimável [laʃtʃi'mavɛw] (pl -eis [-ɛjʃ]) adj (acontecimento) regrettable; (erro) unfortunate; (situação, estado) deplorable.
lata ['lata] f tin; (de bebida) can; ~ (de conserva) tin (Brit), can (Am); ~ de lixo (Br) litter bin (Brit), trashcan (Am).
latão [la'tãw] (pl -ões [-õjʃ]) m (metal) brass; (vasilha) large can.
latejar [late'ʒa(x)] vi to throb.
latente [la'tẽntʃi] adj latent.
lateral [late'raw] (pl -ais [-ajʃ]) adj lateral.
laticínios [latʃi'sinjuʃ] mpl (Br) dairy products.
latido [la'tʃidu] m barking.
latifúndio [latʃi'fũndʒju] m large rural estate.
latim [la'tʃĩ] m Latin.
latino, -na [la'tʃinu, -na] adj Latin.
latino-americano, -na [la'tʃinwameri'kanu, -na] adj & m, f Latin American.
latir [la'tʃi(x)] vi to bark.
latitude [latʃi'tudʒi] f latitude.
latões → latão.
lava ['lava] f lava.
lavabo [la'vabu] m (pia) washbasin; (banheiro) toilet (Brit), restroom (Am).
lavagem [la'vaʒẽ] (pl -ns [-ʃ]) f washing; ~ **automática** automatic car wash; ~ **cerebral** brainwashing; ~ **a seco** dry-cleaning.
lavanda [la'vãnda] f lavender.
lavandaria [lavãnda'ria] f (Port) = lavanderia.
lavanderia [lavãnde'ria] f (Br) (loja, local) laundry; ~ **automática** launderette; ~ **a seco** dry cleaner's (shop).
lavar [la'va(x)] vt to wash; ~ **os dentes** to clean OU brush one's teeth; ~ **a louça** to wash the dishes; ~ **a roupa** to do the washing.
⌐ lavar-se vp to have a wash.
lavável [la'vavɛw] (pl -eis [-ɛjʃ]) adj washable.
lavrador, -ra [lavra'do(x), -ra] (mpl -res [-riʃ], fpl -s [-ʃ]) m, f farm labourer.
laxante [la'ʃãntʃi] adj & m laxative.
lazer [la'ze(x)] m: **horas** OU **ou momentos de** ~ spare OU free time; **centro de** ~ leisure centre.
Lda (Port: abrev de limitada) Ltd.
lê ['le] → ler.

leal [le'aw] (*pl* -**ais** [-ajʃ]) *adj* loyal.

leão [le'ãw] (*pl* -**ões** [-õjʃ]) *m* lion.

❑ **Leão** *m* Leo.

lebre ['lɛbri] *f* hare; **comer gato por ~** to be ripped off.

leccionar [lɛsju'nar] *vt & vi (Port)* = lecionar.

lecionar [lesjo'na(x)] *vt & vi (Br)* to teach.

lectivo, -va [lɛ'tivu, -va] *adj (Port)* = letivo.

lêem ['leẽ] → **ler.**

legal [le'gaw] (*pl* -**ais** [-ajʃ]) *adj (segundo a Lei)* legal; *(Br: fam)* great.

legalidade [legali'dadʒi] *f* legality.

legalizar [legali'za(x)] *vt (actividade)* to legalize; *(documento, assinatura)* to authenticate.

legenda [le'ʒẽda] *f (em mapa)* key; *(em fotografia)* caption; *(mito)* legend.

❑ **legendas** *fpl (em cinema, televisão)* subtitles.

legislação [leʒizla'sãw] *f* legislation.

legitimar [leʒitʃi'ma(x)] *vt* to legitimize; *(documento, assinatura)* to authenticate.

legítimo, -ma [le'ʒitʃimu, -ma] *adj* legitimate; *(autêntico)* genuine.

legível [le'ʒivew] (*pl* -**eis** [-ejʃ]) *adj* legible.

légua ['lɛgwa] *f* league; **ficar a ~s de distância** to be miles away.

legumes [le'gumeʃ] *mpl* vegetables.

lei ['lej] *f* law; **fazer tudo pela ~ do menor esforço** to do everything with the least possible effort; **segundo a ~** according to the law.

leilão [lej'lãw] (*pl* -**ões** [-õjʃ]) *m* auction.

leio ['leju] → **ler.**

leitão [lej'tãw] (*pl* -**ões** [-õjʃ]) *m* suckling pig.

leitaria [lejta'ria] *f (Port)* = leiteria.

leite ['lejtʃi] *m* milk; **~ gordo/meio-gordo/magro** *(Port)* full-fat/semi-skimmed/skimmed milk; **~ pasteurizado/ultrapasteurizado** pasteurized/UHT milk; **~ integral/desnatado** *(Br)* full-fat/skimmed milk; **~ achocolatado** chocolate milk; **~ de côco** coconut milk; **~ condensado** condensed milk; **~ creme** crème brûlée; **~ em pó** powdered milk.

leite-de-onça [lejtʃi'dʒõsa] *m (Br)* milk mixed with "cachaça".

leiteiro, -ra [lej'tejru, -ra] *m, f* milkman (*f* milkwoman).

leiteria [lejte'ria] *f (Br)* dairy.

leito ['lejtu] *m* bed.

leitões → **leitão.**

leitor, -ra [lej'to(x), -ra] (*mpl* -**res** [-riʃ], *fpl* -**s** [-ʃ]) *m, f* reader; *(Port: professor assistente)* language assistant ◆ *m (de cassetes, CD)* player; **~ de cassetes** cassette player; **~ de CD** CD player; **~ de vídeo** video(recorder) *(Brit)*, VCR *(Am).*

leitura [lej'tura] *f* reading.

lema ['lema] *m* motto.

lembrança [lẽ'brãsa] *f* memory; *(prenda)* memento; **dê-lhe ~s** send him/her my regards.

lembrar [lẽ'bra(x)] *vt (recordar)* to remember; *(assemelhar-se a)* to look like; **~ algo a alguém** to remind sb of sthg; **~ alguém de fazer algo** to remind sb to do sthg.

❑ **lembrar-se** *vp* to remember; **~-se de** to remember; **~-se de fazer algo** to remember to do sthg.

leme ['lemi] *m (posição)* helm; *(objeto)* rudder.

lenço ['lẽsu] *m* handkerchief; **~ da cabeça** headscarf; **~ de papel** tissue; **~ (do pescoço)** scarf.

lençol [lẽ'sɔw] (*pl* -**óis** [-ɔjʃ]) *m* sheet; **~ de água** water table.

lenha ['leɲa] *f* firewood.

lente ['lẽtʃi] *f* lens; **~s de contato** contact lenses.

lentidão [lẽtʃi'dãw] *f*: **com ~** slowly.

lentilha [lẽ'tʃiʎa] *f* lentil.

lento, -ta ['lẽtu, -ta] *adj* slow.

leoa [le'oa] *f* lioness.

leões → **leão.**

leopardo [ljo'paxdu] *m* leopard.

lepra ['lɛpra] *f* leprosy.

leque ['lɛki] *m* fan.

ler ['le(x)] *vt & vi* to read.

lesão [le'zãw] (*pl* -**ões** [-õjʃ]) *f (ferida, contusão)* injury; *(prejuízo)* harm.

lesar [le'za(x)] *vt (ferir)* to injure; *(prejudicar)* to harm.

lésbica ['lɛʒbika] *f* lesbian.

lesma ['leʒma] *f* slug; *(fig: pessoa lenta)* slowcoach *(Brit)*, slowpoke *(Am).*

lesões → **lesão.**

leste ['lɛʃtʃi] *m* east; **os países de ~** Eastern European countries; **a OU no ~** in the east; **a ~ de** east of; **estar a ~**

de algo *(fam)* not to have a clue about sthg.

letal [le'taw] *(pl* **-ais** [-ajʃ]) *adj* lethal.

letivo, -va [le'tʃivu, -va] *adj (Br) (ano)* academic, school *(antes de s).*

letra ['letra] *f (do alfabeto)* letter; *(maneira de escrever)* handwriting; *(título de crédito)* bill; **~ maiúscula** capital letters *(pl);* **~ de imprensa** block capitals *(pl);* **~ de fôrma** *(Br)* block capitals *(pl).*

⊔ **letras** *fpl (área de estudo)* arts.

letreiro [le'trejru] *m* sign.

leu ['lew] → **ler.**

léu ['lɛu] *m*: **ao ~** uncovered.

leucemia [lewse'mia] *f* leukaemia.

levantamento [levãnta'mẽntu] *m* survey; **~ de peso** weightlifting.

levantar [levãn'ta(x)] *vt (erguer)* to raise, to lift; **~ dinheiro** to raise money; **~ a mesa** to clear the table; **~ vôo** to take off.

⊔ **levantar-se** *vp (de cama)* to get up; *(de cadeira, chão)* to stand up.

levar [le'va(x)] *vt* to take; *(carregar)* to carry; *(induzir)* to lead; *(filme)* to show; *(fam: porrada, bofetada)* to get; **este recipiente leva cinco litros** this container holds five litres; **~ alguém a fazer algo** to make sb do sthg; **~ a cabo algo** to carry sthg out; **~ a mal algo** to take sthg the wrong way; **deixar-se ~** to get taken for a ride.

leve ['lɛvi] *adj* light.

leviandade [levjãn'dadʒi] *f* rashness.

leviano, -na [le'vjanu, -na] *adj* rash.

léxico ['lɛksiku] *m* lexicon.

lha [ʎa] = **lhe + a,** → **lhe.**

lhe [ʎi] *pron (ele)* (to) him; *(ela)* (to) her; *(você)* (to) you; **já ~ dei a chave do quarto** I've already given him/her/you the key to the room; **aquele livro ali, ela deu-lhe como presente** that book there, she gave it to him/her/you as a present.

lhes [ʎeʃ] *pron pl (eles, elas)* (to) them; *(vocês)* (to) you.

lho [ʎu] = **lhe + o, lhes + o,** → **lhe.**

li ['li] → **ler.**

libélula [li'bɛlula] *f* dragonfly.

liberação [libera'sãw] *f* liberation.

liberal [libe'raw] *(pl* **-ais** [-ajʃ]) *adj & mf* liberal.

liberalização [liberaliza'sãw] *f* deregulation.

liberar [libe'ra(x)] *vt (pessoa)* to free, to liberate; *(comércio, consumo)* to deregulate.

liberdade [libex'dadʒi] *f* freedom; **pôr em ~** to set free; **tomar a ~ de fazer algo** to take the liberty of doing sthg.

libertar [libex'ta(x)] *vt* to set free.

liberto, -ta [li'bextu, -ta] *pp* → **libertar.**

libra ['libra] *f* pound.

⊔ **Libra** *f (Br: signo do Zodíaco)* Libra.

lição [li'sãw] *(pl* **-ões** [-õjʃ]) *f* lesson; **dar uma ~ a alguém** to teach sb a lesson; **que isso lhe sirva de ~!** let that be a lesson to you!

licença [li'sẽsa] *f (autorização)* permission; *(de veículo)* registration document; *(de arma)* licence; **com ~** excuse me; **~ de maternidade** *(para mãe)* maternity leave; *(para pai)* paternity leave.

licenciado, -da [lisẽ'sjadu, -da] *m, f* graduate.

licenciatura [lisẽsja'tura] *f* degree.

liceu [li'sew] *m* = secondary school *(Brit)*, = high school *(Am).*

lições → **lição.**

licor [li'ko(x)] *(pl* **-res** [-riʃ]) *m* liqueur.

lidar [li'da(x)] : **lidar com** *v + prep* to deal with.

líder ['lide(x)] *(pl* **-res** [-riʃ]) *mf* leader.

lido, -da ['lidu, -da] *pp* → **ler.**

liga ['liga] *f (associação)* league; *(de meias)* garter.

ligação [liga'sãw] *(pl* **-ões** [-õjʃ]) *f (de amor, amizade)* relationship; *(telefônica)* connection.

ligado, -da [li'gadu, -da] *adj (luz, televisão)* (switched OU turned) on.

ligadura [liga'dura] *f* bandage.

ligamento [liga'mẽntu] *m* ligament.

ligar [li'ga(x)] *vt (luz, televisão)* to switch OU turn on; *(em tomada)* to plug in ♦ *vi (telefonar)* to call; **~ para** *(telefonar para)* to call; *(dar atenção a)* to take notice of.

ligeiro, -ra [li'ʒejru, -ra] *light; (ferimento)* slight.

lilás [li'laʃ] *(pl* **-ases** [-aziʃ]) *m & adj* lilac.

lima ['lima] *f (Port)* file.

limão [li'mãw] *(pl* **-ões** [-õjʃ]) *m (Br)* lime; *(Port)* lemon.

limão-galego [li,mãwga'legu] *(pl* **limões-galegos** [li,mõjʒga'leguʃ]) *m (Br)* lemon.

limiar [limja(x)] *m* threshold; **no ~ de algo** on the threshold of sthg.

limitação [limita'sãw] (*pl* **-ões** [-õjʃ]) *f (de direitos, movimentos)* restriction; *(de terreno)* boundary.

⊐ **limitações** *fpl (intelectuais)* limitations.

limitar [limi'ta(x)] *vt* to limit.

⊐ **limitar-se** a *vp + prep* to limit o.s. to.

limite [li'mitʃi] *m* limit; *(de terreno)* boundary; **~ de velocidade** speed limit; **sem ~s** limitless; **passar dos ~s** *(fig)* to overstep the mark.

limo [limu] *m* slime.

limoeiro [li'mwejru] *m* lemon tree.

limões → **limão**.

limonada [limo'nada] *f* lemonade.

limpador [limpa'do(x)] (*pl* **-res** [-riʃ]) *m (Br)*: **~ de pára-brisas** windscreen wiper *(Brit)*, windshield wiper *(Am)*.

limpa-pára-brisas [ˌlĩmpapara'brizaʃ] *m inv (Port)* windscreen wiper *(Brit)*, windshield wiper *(Am)*.

limpar [lĩm'pa(x)] *vt* to clean; *(pratos)* to dry; *(boca)* to wipe; *(mãos)* to wash; *(fam: roubar)* to clean out; **~ o pó** to do the dusting.

limpa-vidros [ˌlĩmpa'vidruʃ] *m inv (instrumento)* window wiper; *(detergente)* window-cleaning fluid.

limpeza [lĩm'peza] *f (ação)* cleaning; *(asseio)* cleanliness.

limpo, -pa [lĩmpu, -pa] *pp* → **limpar** ◆ *adj (sem sujeira)* clean; *(céu)* clear; **estar OU ficar ~** *(fam)* to be broke; **tirar algo a ~** to clear sthg up.

limusine [limu'zini] *f* limousine.

lince [lĩsi] *m* lynx.

lindo, -da [lĩndu, -da] *adj* beautiful.

lingerie [lãʒe'xi] *f* lingerie.

lingote [lĩŋ'gotʃi] *m* ingot.

língua [lĩŋgwa] *f (ANAT)* tongue; *(idioma)* language; **bater com a ~ nos dentes** *(fam: denunciar)* to grass; **dobrar a ~** to watch one's language; **morder a ~** to bite one's tongue; **ter algo na ponta da ~** to have sthg on the tip of one's tongue.

linguado [lĩŋ'gwadu] *m* sole.

linguagem [lĩŋ'gwaʒẽ] (*pl* **-ns** [-ʃ]) *f* language.

linguarudo, -da [lĩŋgwa'rudu, -da] *adj* gossipy.

línguas-de-gato [ˌlĩŋgwaʒdʒi'gatu] *fpl* small, thin sweet biscuits.

lingueta [lĩŋ'gweta] *f* catch.

linguiça [lĩŋ'gwisa] *f* long, thin, spicy dry sausage made with lean pork and seasoned with paprika.

linha [lĩɲa] *f* line; *(de coser)* thread; **~ jovem** teenage range; **manter a ~** to keep trim; **~ férrea** *(Port)* (train) tracks *(pl)*; **em ~** in a line.

linho [lĩɲu] *m* linen.

linóleo [li'nɔlju] *m* linoleum.

liquidação [likida'sãw] (*pl* **-ões** [-õjʃ]) *f (de dívida)* settlement; **~ total** clearance OU closing-down sale.

liquidar [liki'da(x)] *vt (dívida)* to pay off; *(matar)* to liquidate; *(mercadorias)* to sell off.

liquidificador [likwidʒifika'do(x)] (*pl* **-res** [-riʃ]) *m (Br)* liquidizer, blender.

liquidificadora [likidifika'dora] *f (Port)* = **liquidificador**.

líquido, -da [likidu, -da] *adj (substância)* liquid; *(COM)* net ◆ *m* liquid.

lírio [lirju] *m* lily.

Lisboa [liʒ'boa] *s* Lisbon.

lisboeta [liʒ'bweta] *adj* of/relating to Lisbon ◆ *mf* native/inhabitant of Lisbon.

liso, -sa [lizu, -za] *adj (superfície)* flat; *(cabelo)* straight; *(folha)* plain; **estar OU ficar ~** *(fam: sem dinheiro)* to be skint.

lista [liʃta] *f* list; *(menu)* menu; **~ de preços** price list; **~ telefônica** telephone directory; **~ de vinhos** wine list.

listra [liʃtra] *f* stripe.

literal [lite'raw] (*pl* **-ais** [-ajʃ]) *adj* literal.

literário, -ria [lite'rarju, -rja] *adj* literary.

literatura [litera'tura] *f* literature; **~ de cordel** *popular literature from the northeast of Brazil.*

litígio [li'tʃiʒju] *m* litigation.

litogravura [litogra'vura] *f* lithography.

litoral [lito'raw] (*pl* **-ais** [-ajʃ]) *adj* coastal ◆ *m*: **o ~** the coast.

litro [litru] *m* litre.

lívido, -da [lividu, -da] *adj* pallid.

livrar [li'vra(x)] : **livrar-se de** *vp + prep* to get rid of.

livraria [livra'ria] *f* bookshop *(Brit)*, book store *(Am)*.

livre [livri] *adj* free; **"livre"** *(em táxi)* "for hire"; *(em W.C.)* "vacant".

livro [livru] *m* book; **~ de bolso**

pocket-size paperback; ~ **de capa dura** hardback.

lixa ['liʃa] *f* sandpaper; *(para unhas)* nail file.

lixeira [li'ʃejra] *f (em prédio)* rubbish chute; *(local)* rubbish dump *(Brit)*, garbage dump *(Am)*.

lixívia [le'ʃivja] *f (Port)* bleach.

lixo ['liʃu] *m* rubbish *(Brit)*, garbage *(Am)*.

-lo [lu] *pron (pessoa)* him; *(coisa)* it; *(você)* you.

L.º *(abrev)* = **largo**.

lobo ['lobu] *m* wolf.

lóbulo ['lɔbulu] *m (de orelha)* earlobe.

local [lo'kaw] *(pl* **-ais** [-ajʃ]) *m* place ◆ *adj* local.

localidade [lokali'dadʒi] *f* town.

localização [lokaliza'sãw] *(pl* **-ões** [-õjʃ]) *f* location.

loção [lo'sãw] *(pl* **-ões** [-õjʃ]) *f* lotion; ~ **para após a barba** aftershave; ~ **capilar** hair lotion.

locatario, -ria [loka'tarju, -rja] *m, f* tenant.

loções → **loção**.

locomotiva [lokomo'tʃiva] *f* locomotive.

locução [loku'sãw] *(pl* **-ões** [-õjʃ]) *f (de filme, programa)* narration; *(GRAM)* phrase.

locutor, -ra [loku'to(x), -ra] *(mpl* **-res** [-riʃ], *fpl* **-s** [-ʃ]) *m, f (de rádio, televisão)* announcer.

lodo ['lodu] *m* mud.

lógica ['lɔʒika] *f* logic.

logo ['lɔgu] *adv* immediately; **mais** ~ later; ~ **de seguida** immediately; ~ **que** as soon as; ~ **agora que** now (that).

logotipo [logo'tʃipu] *m* logo.

loja ['lɔʒa] *f* shop *(Brit)*, store *(Am)*; ~ **de artigos esportivos** sports shop; ~ **de artigos fotográficos** camera shop; ~ **de brinquedos** toyshop; ~ **de bugigangas** junk shop; ~ **de ferragens** hardware shop; ~ **de lembranças** souvenir shop; ~ **de produtos dietéticos** health-food shop.

lombada [lõm'bada] *f* spine.

lombinho [lõm'biɲu] *m* tenderloin *(of pork)*.

lombo ['lõmbu] *m* loin; ~ **assado** roast loin of pork marinated in dry white wine and paprika, then smeared with lard or covered in bacon before cooking.

lombriga [lõm'briga] *f* roundworm.

lona ['lona] *f* canvas.

Londres ['lõndriʃ] *s* London.

londrino, -na ['lõn'drinu, -na] *adj* of/relating to London.

longa-metragem [ˌlõŋgame'traʒẽ] *(pl* **longas-metragens** [ˌlõŋgaʒme'traʒẽʃ]) *f* feature film.

longe ['lõʒi] *adv* far; ~ **disso!** on the contrary!; **ao** ~ in the distance; **de** ~ *(fig)* by far; **ir** ~ **demais** to go too far.

longitude [lõʒi'tudʒi] *f* longitude.

longo, -ga ['lõŋgu, -ga] *adj* long; **ao** ~ **de** along; **ao** ~ **dos anos** over time.

lontra ['lõntra] *f* otter.

-los ['luʃ] *pron pl (eles)* them; *(vocês)* you.

losango [lo'zãŋgu] *m* lozenge.

lotação [lota'sãw] *(pl* **-ões** [-õjʃ]) *f (de cinema, teatro)* capacity; "~ **esgotada**" "sold out".

lotaria [luta'ria] *f (Port)* = **loteria**.

lote ['lɔtʃi] *m (de terreno)* plot; *(de prédios)* street number.

loteria [lote'ria] *f (Br)* lottery; ~ **esportiva** = football pools *(pl) (Brit)*, soccer sweepstakes *(pl) (Am)*.

loto ['lotu] *m (jogo)* lotto.

louça ['losa] *f* china; *(pratos, xícaras, pires, etc)* crockery.

louco, -ca ['loku, -ka] *adj* mad, crazy ◆ *m, f* lunatic; **estar** OU **ficar** ~ **de alegria** to be over the moon; **ser** ~ **por** to be crazy about.

loucura [lo'kura] *f* madness.

louro, -ra ['loru, -ra] *adj* blond ◆ *m (condimento)* bay leaf.

louva-a-deus [ˌlova'dewʃ] *m inv* praying mantis.

louvar [lo'va(x)] *vt* to praise.

louvável [lo'vavew] *(pl* **-eis** [-ejʃ]) *adj* praiseworthy.

LP *m (abrev de long-play)* LP.

Ltda *(Br: abrev de limitada)* Ltd.

L.te *(abrev de lote)* ~ No. *(Brit)*, = # *(Am)*.

lua ['lua] *f* moon; **estar de** ~ to be in a mood; **viver no mundo da** ~ to have one's head in the clouds.

lua-de-mel [ˌluadʒi'mew] *(pl* **luas-de-mel** [ˌluaʒdʒi'mew]) *f* honeymoon.

luar ['lwa(x)] *m* moonlight.

lubrificante [lubrifi'kãntʃi] *m* lubricant.

lubrificar [lubrifi'ka(x)] *vt* to lubricate.

lucidez [lusi'deʃ] f clarity.
lúcido, -da ['lusidu, -da] adj lucid.
lúcio ['lusju] m pike.
lucrar [lu'kra(x)] vi to profit; ~ **com** to profit from.
lucrativo, -va [lukra'tʃivu, -va] adj lucrative.
lucro ['lukru] m profit.
lúdico, -ca ['ludʒiku, -ka] adj play (antes de s).
lugar [lu'ga(x)] (pl -res [-riʃ]) m place; **em primeiro ~** (em esporte) in first place; (antes) first; **ter ~** (ocorrer) to take place; **em ~ de** instead of; **dar o ~ a alguém** to give one's seat to sb; **tomar o ~ de alguém** to take sb's place.
lugar-comum [lu,gaxku'mũ] (pl **lugares-comuns** [lu,gariʃku'mũʃ]) m cliché.
lugares → lugar.
lúgubre ['lugubri] adj gloomy.
lula [lula] f squid; **~s grelhadas** grilled squid served with a butter, lemon and parsley sauce.
lume ['lumi] m (fogueira) fire; (Port: chama) flame.
luminária [lumi'narja] f (Br) lamp; **~ de mesa** table lamp; **~ de pé** standard lamp (Brit), floor lamp (Am).
luminosidade [luminozi'dadʒi] f brightness.

luminoso, -osa [lumi'nozu, -ɔza] adj bright; (fig: idéia, solução) brilliant.
lunar [lu'na(x)] (pl -res [-riʃ]) adj lunar.
lunático, -ca [lu'natʃiku, -ka] m, f lunatic.
luneta [lu'neta] f (Br: telescópio) telescope.
lupa ['lupa] f magnifying glass.
lustre ['luʃtri] m shine; (luminária) chandelier; **dar o ~ em algo** to polish sthg.
lustro ['luʃtru] m shine.
luta ['luta] f fight.
lutar [lu'ta(x)] vi to fight; **~ contra/por** to fight against/for.
luto ['lutu] m mourning; **estar de ~** to be in mourning.
luva ['luva] f glove.
Luxemburgo [luʃẽm'buxgu] m: **o ~** Luxembourg.
luxo ['luʃu] m luxury; **de ~** luxury (antes de s).
luxuoso, -osa [lu'ʃwozu, -ɔza] adj luxurious.
luxúria [lu'ʃurja] f lust.
luxuriante [luʃu'rjãntʃi] adj luxuriant.
luz ['luʃ] (pl -zes [-ʒiʃ]) f light; **dar à ~ (um menino)** to give birth (to a baby boy); **~ do sol** sunlight.
luzir [lu'zi(x)] vi to glow.
lycra® ['likra] f Lycra®.

M

ma [ma] = me + a, → **me**.

má → **mau**.

maca ['maka] f stretcher.

maçã [ma'sã] f apple; ~ **assada** baked apple.

macabro, -bra [ma'kabru, -bra] adj macabre.

macacão [maka'kãw] (pl **-ões** [-õjʃ]) m (roupa) jumpsuit; (protetor) boiler suit (Brit), overall (Am).

macaco, -ca [ma'kaku, -ka] m, f monkey ♦ m (AUT) jack.

macacões → **macacão**.

maçã-de-adão [ma,sãdʒja'dãw] (pl **maçãs-de-adão** [ma,sãʒdʒja'dãw]) f Adam's apple.

maçador, -ra [masa'dor, -ra] (mpl **-res** [-rcʃ], fpl **-s** [-ʃ]) adj (Port) boring.

maçaneta [masa'neta] f knob.

maçante [ma'sãntʃi] adj (Br) boring.

maçapão [masa'pãw] m marzipan.

maçarico [masariku] m blowtorch.

maçaroca [masa'rɔka] f corncob.

macarrão [maka'xãw] m (Br: massa) pasta; (Port: tipo de massa) macaroni.

Macau [ma'kaw] s Macao.

macedônia [mase'donja] f mixed vegetables (pl); ~ **(de frutas)** fruit salad.

macete [ma'setʃi] m mallet.

machado [ma'ʃadu] m axe.

machismo [ma'ʃiʒmu] m male chauvinism.

machista [ma'ʃiʃta] adj chauvinistic ♦ m male chauvinist.

macho ['maʃu] adj m (animal) male; (homem) virile ♦ m (animal) male.

machucado, -da [maʃu'kadu, -da] adj (Br: ferido) hurt.

machucar [maʃu'kax] vt (Br) to hurt. ❏ **machucar-se** vp (Br) to hurt o.s.

maciço, -ça [ma'sisu, -sa] adj solid.

macieira [ma'sjejra] f apple tree.

macio, -cia [ma'siu, -'sia] adj soft.

maço ['masu] m mallet; ~ **(de cigarros)** packet (of cigarettes); ~ **de folhas** block of paper.

macumba [ma'kũmba] f voodoo.

madeira [ma'dejra] f wood.

Madeira [ma'dejra] m (vinho) Madeira ♦ f: **a** ~ Madeira.

madeixa [ma'dejʃa] f (de cabelo) lock.

madrasta [ma'draʃta] f stepmother.

madrepérola [,madre'pɛrola] f mother-of-pearl.

madressilva [,madre'siwva] f honeysuckle.

madrinha [ma'driɲa] f (de baptismo) godmother.

madrugada [madru'gada] f (amanhecer) dawn; (noite) early morning; **de ~** (fig: muito cedo) at the crack of dawn.

madrugar [madru'ga(x)] vi to get up very early.

maduro, -ra [ma'duru, -ra] adj mature; (fruto) ripe.

mãe ['mãj] f mother.

maestro [ma'cʃtru] m conductor.

magia [ma'ʒia] f magic.

mágico, -ca ['maʒiku, -ka] adj magical ♦ m, f magician.

magistrado, -da [maʒiʃ'tradu, -da] m, f magistrate.

magnético, -ca [mag'nctʃiku, -ka] adj magnetic.

magnífico, -ca [mag'nifiku, -ka] adj magnificent.

magnitude [magni'tudʒi] f magnitude.

magnólia [mag'nɔlja] f magnolia.

mago, -ga ['magu, -ga] m, f wizard (f witch).

mágoa ['magwa] f sorrow.

magoado, -da [ma'gwadu, -da] adj hurt.

magoar [ma'gwa(x)] vt to hurt.

⌐ **magoar-se** *vp* to hurt o.s.
magro, -gra [ˈmagru, -gra] *adj* thin.
maio [ˈmaju] *m* May, → **setembro**.
maiô [maˈjo] *m* (Br) (de ginástica) leotard; (de banho) swimsuit.
maionese [majoˈnɛzi] *f* mayonnaise.
maior [maˈjɔ(x)] (pl -res [-riʃ]) *adj* (em tamanho) bigger; (em número) higher; (em quantidade, importância) greater ♦ *mf*: **o/a** ~ (em tamanho) the biggest; (em número) the highest; (em quantidade, importância) the greatest; **ser** ~ **de idade** to be an adult; **a** ~ **parte de** most of.
maioria [majoˈria] *f* majority.
maioridade [majoriˈdaʒi] *f* adulthood.
mais [majʃ] *adv* 1. (em comparações) more; **a Ana é** ~ **alta/inteligente** Ana is taller/ more intelligent; ~ **do que** more than; ~ ... **do que** ... more ... than ...; **é** ~ **alta do que eu** she's taller than me; **bebeu um copo a** ~! he's had one too many!; **deram-me dinheiro a** ~ they gave me too much money.
2. (como superlativo): **o/a** ~ ... the most ...; **o** ~ **engraçado/ inteligente** the funniest/most intelligent.
3. (indica adição) any more; **não necessito de** ~ **trabalho** I don't need any more work; **não necessito de** ~ **ninguém** I don't need anyone else.
4. (indica intensidade): **que dia** ~ **feliz!** what a great day!; **que casa** ~ **feia!** what a horrible house!
5. (indica preferência): **vale** ~ **a pena ficar em casa** it would be better to stay at home; **gosto** ~ **de comida chinesa** I prefer Chinese food.
6. (em locuções): **de** ~ **a** ~ (ainda por cima) what's more; ~ **ou menos** more or less; **por** ~ **que se esforce** however hard he tries, **sem** ~ **nem menos** for no apparent reason; **uma vez** ~, ~ **uma vez** once OU yet again.
♦ *adj inv* 1. (em comparações) more; **eles têm** ~ **dinheiro** they have more money; **está** ~ **calor hoje** it's hotter today; ~ ... **do que** more ... than.
2. (como superlativo) (the) most; **a pessoa que** ~ **discos vendeu** the person who sold (the) most records; **os que** ~ **dinheiro têm** those who have (the) most money.
3. (indica adição) more; ~ **água, por favor** I'd like some more water,

please; ~ **alguma coisa?** anything else?; **tenho** ~ **três dias de férias** I've got another three days' holiday left.
♦ *conj* and; **eu** ~ **o Luís vamos** Luís and I are going; **quero uma sopa** ~ **pão com manteiga** I'd like some soup and some bread and butter.
♦ *prep* (indica soma) plus; **dois** ~ **dois são quatro** two plus two is four.
maitre [ˈmɛtre] *m* (Br) head waiter.
major [maˈʒɔ(x)] (pl -res [-riʃ]) *m* major.
mal [maw] (pl -les [-liʃ]) *m* (doença) illness; (dano) harm ♦ *adv* (erradamente) wrong ♦ *conj* (assim que) as soon as; **o** ~ **evil**; ~ **cheguei, telefonei logo** I phoned the minute I arrived; **estar** ~ (de saúde) to be ill; **cheirar** ~ to smell; **não faz** ~ it doesn't matter; **ouço/vejo** ~ I can't hear/see very well; **passar** ~ (ter enjôo) to feel sick.
mala [ˈmala] *f* (de mão, roupa) bag; (do carro) boot (Brit), trunk (Am); ~ **frigorífica** cool box; ~ **de viagem** suitcase; **fazer as** ~s to pack.
malabarismo [malabaˈriʒmu] *m* juggling; **fazer** ~s to juggle.
malabarista [malabaˈriʃta] *mf* juggler.
mal-acabado, -da [ˌmawakaˈbadu, -da] *adj* (Br) badly finished.
malagueta [malaˈgeta] *f* chilli (pepper).
malandro, -dra [maˈlãndru, -dra] *adj* (preguiçoso) lazy; (matreiro) crafty ♦ *m, f* (patife) rogue.
malária [maˈlarja] *f* malaria.
malcriado, -da [mawkriˈadu, -da] *adj* rude.
maldade [mawˈdadʒi] *f* evil.
maldição [mawdiˈsãw] (pl -ões [-õjʃ]) *f* curse.
maldito, -ta [mawˈdʒitu, -ta] *adj* damned.
maldizer [mawdʒiˈze(x)] *vt* (amaldiçoar) to curse; (falar mal de) to speak ill of.
maldoso, -osa [mawˈdozu, -ɔza] *adj* evil.
mal-educado, -da [maleduˈkadu, -da] *adj* rude.
malefício [maleˈfisju] *m* hazard.
mal-entendido [ˌmalĩntẽnˈdʒidu] (pl **mal-entendidos** [ˌmalĩntẽnˈdiduʃ]) *m* misunderstanding.
males → **mal**.

mal-estar [maleʃ'ta(x)] (pl **mal-estares** [maleʃ'tareʃ]) m (dor física) discomfort; (inquietude) uneasiness.

maleta [ma'leta] f travel bag.

malfeitor, -ra [mawfej'to(x), -ra] (mpl **-res** [-riʃ]. fpl **-s** [-ʃ]) m, f criminal.

malha ['maʎa] f (tecido) wool; (em rede) mesh; (Br: de ginástica) leotard; **fazer ~** (Port) to knit.

malhado, -da [ma'ʎadu, -da] adj (animal) mottled.

malhar [ma'ʎa(x)] vt to thresh ♦ vi (fam: fazer ginástica) to work out.

mal-humorado, -da [malumo'radu, -da] adj bad-tempered.

malícia [ma'lisja] f malice.

maligno, -gna [ma'lignu, -gna] adj malignant.

malmequer [mawme'ke(x)] (pl **-es** [-iʃ]) m marigold.

mal-passado, -da [mawpa'sadu, -da] adj (bife) rare.

malta ['mawta] f (fam) gang.

maltratar [mawtra'ta(x)] vt (bater em) to ill-treat; (descuidar, estragar) to damage.

maluco, -ca [ma'luku, -ka] adj crazy ♦ m, f lunatic.

malvadez [mawva'deʃ] f wickedness.

malvado, -da [maw'vadu, -da] adj wicked.

mama ['mama] f breast.

mamadeira [mama'deira] f (Br) baby's bottle.

mamão [ma'mãw] (pl **-ões** [-õjʃ]) m papaya, pawpaw.

mamar [ma'ma(x)] vi to be breastfed; **dar de ~ a** (amamentar) to breast-feed; (com mamadeira) to bottle-feed.

mamífero [ma'miferu] m mammal.

mamilo [ma'milu] m nipple.

maminha [ma'miɲa] f (Br) very tender rump steak.

mamões → mamão.

manada [ma'nada] f herd.

mancar [mãŋ'ka(x)] vi to limp.

mancha ['mãʃa] f (em animal, pele) mark, spot; (nódoa) stain.

Mancha ['mãʃa] f: **o canal da ~** the English Channel.

manchar [mã'ʃa(x)] vt to stain.

manchete [mã'ʃetʃi] f (Br: de jornal) headline.

manco, -ca ['mãŋku, -ka] adj lame.

mandar [mãn'da(x)] vi to be in charge

♦ vt: ~ **alguém fazer algo** to tell sb to do sthg; ~ **fazer algo** to have sthg done; ~ **alguém passear** (fam) to send sb packing; ~ **vir** (encomendar) to send for; ~ **alguém à merda** (vulg) to tell sb to piss off; ~ **em** to be in charge of; **ele gosta de ~ nos outros** he likes to boss everyone about OU around.

mandioca [mãn'dʒjɔka] f cassava, manioc; **(farinha de) ~** cassava (flour).

maneira [ma'nejra] f way; **de uma ~ geral** as a rule; **temos de fazer tudo à ~ dele** we have to do everything his way; **de ~ alguma** OU **nenhuma!** certainly not!; **de ~ que** so (that); **de qualquer ~** (de todo jeito) anyway; (em desordem) any old how; **desta ~** in this way; **de toda a ~** anyway; **de tal ~ ... que ...** so ... that ...; **de uma ~ ou de outra** one way or another.

⊐ **maneiras** fpl: **ter ~s** to have good manners; **não ter ~s** to have bad manners.

manejar [mane'ʒa(x)] vt (carro) to drive; (barco) to sail.

manejável [mane'ʒavɛw] (pl **-eis** [-ejʃ]) adj manageable.

manequim [mane'kĩ] (pl **-ns** [-ʃ]) m (em vitrine) dummy ♦ mf (pessoa) model.

maneta [ma'neta] adj one-handed; (sem braço) one-armed.

manga ['mãŋga] f (de peça de vestuário) sleeve; (fruto) mango; **em ~s de camisa** in shirtsleeves.

mangueira [mãŋ'gejra] f (para regar, lavar) hose; (árvore) mango tree.

manha ['maɲa] f: **ter ~** to be sharp; **fazer ~** to put on an act.

manhã [ma'ɲã] f morning; **de ~** in the morning; **duas da ~** two in the morning; **ontem de ~** yesterday morning.

mania [ma'nia] f (obsessão) obsession; (hábito) habit.

manicómio [mani'kɔmju] m (Port) = **manicômio**.

manicômio [mani'komju] m (Br) asylum.

manicura [mani'kura] f = **manicure**.

manicure [mani'kuri] f manicure.

manifestação [manifeʃta'sãw] (pl **-ões** [-õjʃ]) f (expressão) expression; (POL) demonstration.

manifestar [manifeʃ'ta(x)] vt (afeto, fúria, etc) to express.

⊐ **manifestar-se** vp (protestar) to

demonstrate.

manipular [manipu'la(x)] *vt (máquina)* to handle; *(fig: influenciar)* to manipulate.

manivela [mani'vɛla] *f* crank.

manjericão [mãʒeri'kãw] *m* basil.

manobra [ma'nɔbra] *f (de carro)* manoeuvre; *(de trem)* shunting.

mansão [mã'sãw] *(pl* -ões [-õjʃ]*) f* mansion.

mansidão [mãsi'dãw] *f (de pessoa)* gentleness; *(de animal)* tameness.

manso, -sa [ˈmãsu, -sa] *adj (animal)* tame; *(mar)* calm.

mansões → **mansão**.

manta [ˈmãnta] *f* blanket.

manteiga [mãn'tejga] *f* butter; ~ **de cacau** cocoa butter.

manteigueira [mãntej'gejra] *f* butter dish.

manter [mãn'te(x)] *vt* to keep; *(família)* to support; *(relação)* to have; ~ **a palavra** to keep one's word.

⌐ **manter-se** *vp* to stay, to remain; ~-**se em forma** to keep fit.

manual [ma'nwaw] *(pl* -ais [-ajʃ]*) adj* manual ♦ *m* manual, guide; ~ **(escolar)** textbook.

manuscrito, -ta [manuʃ'kritu, -ta] *adj* hand-written ♦ *m* manuscript.

manusear [manu'zea(x)] *vt (livro)* to handle; *(objeto, ferramenta)* to use.

manutenção [manutẽ'sãw] *f* maintenance.

mão [ˈmãw] *f (ANAT)* hand; *(de estrada)* side; **apertar a ~** to shake hands; **dar a ~ a alguém** to hold sb's hand; *(fig: ajudar)* to help sb out; **de ~s dadas** hand in hand; **à ~** *(lavar, escrever)* by hand; **dar uma ~ a alguém** to give OU lend sb a hand; **estar à ~** to be handy; **ter algo à ~** to have sthg to hand.

mão-de-obra [mãw'dʒiɔbra] *f* workforce.

mapa [ˈmapa] *m* map; ~ **das estradas** road map.

mapa-múndi [ˌmapaˈmũndʒi] *(pl* mapas-múndi [ˌmapaʒˈmũndʒi]*) m* world map.

maquete [ma'kɛtʃi] *f* model.

maquiagem [maki'aʒãj] *(pl* -ns [-ʃ]*) f* make-up.

maquiar [ma'kjax] *vt (Br)* to make up.

⌐ **maquiar-se** *vp (Br)* to put one's make-up on.

maquilhar [maki'ʎa(x)] *vt (Port)* = maquiar.

máquina [ˈmakina] *f* machine; ~ **de barbear** shaver; ~ **de costura** sewing machine; ~ **de escrever** typewriter; ~ **de filmar** film camera; ~ **fotográfica** camera; ~ **de lavar** *(para roupa)* washing machine; *(para louça)* dishwasher; ~ **de secar** tumble-dryer.

maquinaria [makina'ria] *f* machinery.

mar [ˈma(x)] *(pl* -res [-riʃ]*) m* sea; ~ **alto, alto** ~ high seas *(pl)*; **por** ~ by sea.

maracujá [maraku'ʒa] *m* passion fruit.

maravilha [mara'viʎa] *f* wonder; **que** ~! how wonderful!; **correr às mil** ~**s** to be a great success; **dizer** ~**s de** to rave about; **fazer** ~**s** to do wonders.

maravilhoso, -osa [maravi'ʎozu, -ɔza] *adj* wonderful.

marca [ˈmaxka] *f* mark; *(de carro, roupa)* make, brand; ~ **registrada** trademark; **de** ~ *(roupa)* designer *(antes de s)*.

marcação [maxka'sãw] *(pl* -ões [-õjʃ]*) f* booking; **a** ~ **de consultas realiza-se entre as nove e as dez** appointments must be made between nine and ten.

marcar [max'ka(x)] *vt (assinalar, indicar)* to mark; *(lugar)* to book; *(número)* to dial; *(ESP)* to score; ~ **encontro com alguém** to arrange to meet sb; ~ **uma consulta/hora** to make an appointment.

marcha [ˈmaxʃa] *f (desfile)* march; *(ritmo)* pace; ~**s populares** *colourful processions during local festivals*; ~ **à ré** *(Br)* reverse.

marcha-atrás [ˌmaxʃa'trajʃ] *f inv (Port: de carro)* reverse; **fazer** ~ to reverse.

marchar [max'ʃa(x)] *vi* to march.

marcial [max'sjaw] *(pl* -ais [-ajʃ]*) adj* martial.

marco [ˈmaxku] *m (em estrada, caminho)* landmark; *(moeda)* mark; ~ **do correio** *(Port)* postbox.

março [ˈmarsu] *m* March, → **setembro**.

maré [ma'rɛ] *f* tide; **estar de boa** ~ to be in good spirits.

maré-alta [maˌrɛ'awta] *(pl* marés-altas [maˌrɛ'zawtaʃ]*) f* high tide.

maré-baixa [maˌrɛ'bajʃa] *(pl* marés-

baixas [marɛʒ'bajʃaʃ]) *f* low tide.
maremoto [mare'motu] *m* tidal wave.
mares → mar.
marfim [max'fĩ] *m* ivory.
margarida [maxga'rida] *f* daisy.
margarina [maxga'rina] *f* margarine.
margem ['maxʒẽ] (*pl* **-ns** [-ʃ]) *f (de rio)* bank; *(em texto, livro, documento)* margin; **à ~ da sociedade** on the fringe of society; **pôr à ~** *(fig: ignorar)* to leave out; **pôr-se à ~** not to take part.
marginal [maxʒi'naw] (*pl* **-ais** [-ajʃ]) *adj* marginal ♦ *mf* criminal.
marido [ma'ridu] *m* husband.
marimbondo [marĩm'bõndu] *m (Br)* wasp.
marina [ma'rina] *f* marina.
marinada [mari'nada] *f* marinade.
marinha [ma'riɲa] *f* navy.
marinheiro, -ra [mari'ɲejru, -ra] *m, f* sailor.
marionete [marjo'netʃi] *f* puppet.
mariposa [mari'poza] *f (ESP)* butterfly; *(inseto)* moth.
marisco [ma'riʃku] *m* shellfish.
marítimo, -ma [ma'ritʃimu, -ma] *adj* sea *(antes de s)*.
marketing ['marketʃĩŋ] *m* marketing.
marmelada [maxme'lada] *f* quince jelly.
marmeleiro [maxme'lejru] *m* quince tree.
marmelo [max'mɛlu] *m* quince.
mármore ['maxmori] *m* marble.
marquise [max'kizi] *f* conservatory.
Marrocos [ma'xɔkuʃ] *s* Morocco.
marrom [ma'xõ] (*pl* **-ns** [-ʃ]) *adj (Br)* brown.
martelar [maxte'la(x)] *vt* to hammer in.
martelo [max'tɛlu] *m* hammer.
mártir ['maxti(x)] (*pl* **-res** [-riʃ]) *mf* martyr.
mas¹ [maʃ] = me + as, → me.
mas² [ma(j)ʃ] *conj* but ♦ *m*: **nem ~ nem meio ~!** no buts!
mascar [maʃ'ka(x)] *vt* to chew.
máscara ['maʃkara] *f* mask.
mascarar-se [maʃka'raxsi] *vp* to dress up.
mascavo [maʃ'kavu] *adj m* → açúcar.
mascote [maʃ'kɔtʃi] *f* mascot.
masculino, -na [maʃku'linu, -na] *adj* masculine; *(sexo)* male.

masoquista [mazu'kiʃta] *adj* masochistic ♦ *mf* masochist.
massa ['masa] *f (espaguete, lasanha)* pasta; *(de pão)* dough; *(de bolo)* mix; **~ folhada** *(Port)* puff pastry; **~ folheada** *(Br)* puff pastry; **em ~** *(fig: em grande número)* en masse.
massacre [ma'sakri] *m* massacre.
massagear [masa'ʒea(x)] *vt (Br)* to massage.
massagem [ma'saʒẽ] (*pl* **-ns** [-ʃ]) *f* massage.
massagista [masa'ʒiʃta] *mf* masseur *(f* masseuse).
massajar [masa'ʒar] *vt (Port)* = massagear.
mastigar [maʃtʃi'ga(x)] *vt* to chew.
mastro ['maʃtru] *m (NÁUT)* mast; *(de bandeira)* pole.
masturbar-se [maʃtux'baxsi] *vp* to masturbate.
mata ['mata] *f (bosque)* wood; *(Br: floresta)* forest.
mata-borrão [,matabo'xãw] (*pl* **mata-borrões** [,matabo'xõjʃ]) *m* blotting paper.
matadouro [mata'doru] *m* slaughterhouse.
matar [ma'ta(x)] *vt* to kill; *(fome)* to stay; *(sede)* to quench; **~ aula** *(Br)* to skip class; **~ o tempo** to pass the time. ⌐ **matar-se** *vp (suicidar-se)* to kill o.s.; **~-se de fazer algo** to kill o.s. doing sthg.
mata-ratos [,mata'xatuʃ] *m inv* rat poison.
mate ['matʃi] *adj (sem brilho)* matt; ♦ *m (Br: planta, infusão)* maté, *herbal infusion drunk out of a gourd*.
matemática [mate'matʃika] *f* mathematics *(sg)*.
matéria [ma'tɛrja] *f (substância)* matter; *(EDUC)* subject; *(material)* material; **em ~ de** on the subject of.
material [mate'rjaw] (*pl* **-ais** [-ajʃ]) *adj (bens)* material ♦ *m* materials *(pl)*; **~ escolar** school materials *(pl)*.
matéria-prima [ma,tɛrja'prima] (*pl* **matérias-primas** [ma,tɛrjaʃ'primaʃ]) *f* raw material.
maternidade [matexni'dadʒi] *f (hospital)* maternity hospital.
matinê [matʃi'ne] *f (Br)* matinée.
matinée [mati'ne] *f (Port)* = matinê.
matizado, -da [matʃi'zadu, -da] *adj* speckled.

mato ['matu] *m* (*Br: bosque*) wood; (*tipo de vegetação*) bush.

matrícula [ma'trikula] *f* (*de carro*) numberplate (*Brit*), license plate (*Am*); (*em escola, universidade*) matriculation.

matrimónio [matri'mɔnju] *m* (*Port*) (*casamento*) = **matrimônio**.

matrimônio [matri'monju] *m* (*Br*) marriage.

matriz [ma'triʃ] (*pl* -**zes** [-ziʃ]) *f* (*de foto, tipografia*) original; (*igreja*) mother church; (*COM: sede*) head office.

maturidade [maturi'dadʒi] *f* maturity.

matuto, -ta [ma'tutu, -ta] *adj* (*Br: provinciano*) provincial.

mau, má ['maw, ma] *adj* bad; **nada ~**! not bad at all!

mausoléu [mawzo'lɛu] *m* mausoleum.

maus-tratos [mawʃ'tratuʃ] *mpl* abuse (*sg*).

maxilar [maksi'la(x)] (*pl* -**res** [-riʃ]) *m* jaw.

máximo, -ma ['masimu, -ma] maximum; (*temperatura, nota*) highest ♦ *m*: **o ~** the most; **faz o ~ que você puder** do your best; **no ~** at most; **ao ~** to the full.

◆ **máximos** *mpl* (*Port*) full beam headlights (*Brit*), high beams (*Am*).

me [mi] *pron* (*complemento direto*) me; (*complemento indireto*) (to) me; (*reflexo*) myself; **eu nunca ~ engano** I'm never wrong; **eu ~ machuquei** I hurt myself; **você já ~ contou essa história** you've already told me that story; **vou-~ embora** (*Port*) I'm going.

meados ['mjaduʃ] *mpl*: **em ~ de** in the middle of.

mecânica [me'kanika] *f* mechanics (*sg*), → **mecânico**.

mecânico, -ca [me'kaniku, -ka] *adj* mechanical ♦ *m, f* mechanic.

mecanismo [meka'niʒmu] *m* mechanism.

mecha ['mɛʃa] *f* (*de vela*) wick; (*de cabelo*) tuft; **fazer ~ no cabelo** to have one's hair highlighted.

meço ['mɛsu] → **medir**.

medalha [me'daʎa] *f* medal.

média ['mɛdʒa] *f* average; **à ~ de** at an average of; **em ~** on average; **ter ~ de** (*EDUC*) to average.

mediano, -na [me'dʒjanu, -na] *adj* (*médio*) medium; (*sofrível*) average.

mediante [me'dʒjãntʃi] *prep* by means of, through; **irei ~ certas condições** I'll go on certain conditions.

medicação [medʒika'sãw] (*pl* -**ões** [-õjʃ]) *f* medication.

medicamento [medʒika'mẽntu] *m* medicine.

medicina [medʒi'sina] *f* medicine.

médico, -ca ['mɛdʒiku, -ka] *m, f* doctor; **~ de clínica geral** GP, general practitioner.

medida [me'dʒida] *f* (*grandeza, quantidade*) measurement; (*precaução, decisão*) measure; **feito sob ~** made to measure; **ficar na ~** to be a perfect fit; **em certa ~** to a certain extent; **na ~ do possível** as far as possible; **à ~ que** as; **tomar ~s** to take steps OU measures.

medieval [medʒje'vaw] (*pl* -**ais** [-ajʃ]) *adj* medieval.

médio, -dia ['mɛdʒju, -dja] *adj* (*tamanho*) medium; (*qualidade*) average ♦ *m* (*dedo*) middle finger; (*EDUC: nota*) pass.

◆ **médios** *mpl* (*Port*) dipped headlights (*Brit*), low beams (*Am*).

mediocre [me'dʒjukri] *adj* mediocre.

medir [me'dʒi(x)] *vt* to measure; **quanto (é que) você mede?** how tall are you?; **eu meço 1,70 m** I'm 5 foot 7 inches.

meditar [medʒi'ta(x)] *vi* to meditate; **~ sobre algo** to think sthg over.

Mediterrâneo [medʒite'xanju] *m*: **o (mar) ~** the Mediterranean (Sea).

medo ['medu] *m* fear; **ter ~** to be frightened; **ter ~ de** to be afraid of; **você pode ir sem ~ porque não é perigoso** don't be afraid to go as it isn't dangerous.

medonho, -nha [me'doɲu, -ɲa] *adj* (*feio*) hideous.

medroso, -osa [me'drozu, -ɔza] *adj* frightened.

medula [me'dula] *f* (*bone*) marrow.

medusa [me'duza] *f* jellyfish.

megabyte [mega'bajtʃi] *m* megabyte.

meia ['meja] *f* (*Br: em número*) six; **~ de leite** white coffee.

meia-calça [,meja'kawsa] (*pl* **meias-calças** [,meaʃ'kawsaʃ]) *f* tights (*pl*) (*Brit*), pantyhose (*Am*).

meia-hora [,meja'ɔra] (*pl* **meias-horas** [,meja'zɔraʃ]) *f* half an hour.

meia-idade [,mejej'dadʒi] f middle age; **de ~** middle-aged.
meia-noite [,meja'nojtʃi] f midnight.
meias ['mejaʃ] fpl socks; **~ de lycra** Lycra® tights.
meias-medidas [,mejaʒme'dʒidaʃ] fpl: **não estar com ~** not to be content with half measures.
meias-palavras [,mejaʃpa'lavraʃ] fpl: **não ser de ~** not to mince one's words.
meigo, -ga ['mejgu, -ga] adj sweet.
meio, meia ['meju, 'meja] adj half ♦ m (modo, recurso) way; (social) circles (pl); **meia pensão** half board; **~ ambiente** environment; **~ bilhete** half-fare; **a meia voz** under one's breath; **no ~ de** (duas coisas) between; (rua, mesa, multidão) in the middle of.
meio-dia [,meju'dʒia] m midday, noon.
meio-quilo [,meju'kilu] (pl **meios-quilos** [,mejuʃ'kiluʃ]) m half a kilo.
meio-seco [,meju'seku] adj m (vinho) medium dry.
mel ['mɛw] m honey.
melaço [me'lasu] m molasses (pl).
melado, -da [me'ladu, -da] adj (Br: pegajoso) sticky.
melancia [melã'sia] f watermelon.
melancolia [melãŋko'lia] f melancholy.
melancólico, -ca [melãŋ'kɔliku, -ka] adj melancholy.
melão [me'lãw] (pl **-ões** [-õjʃ]) m melon.
melga ['mɛlga] f (Port) (insecto) midge; (fam: pessoa chata) pest.
melhor [me'ʎɔ(x)] (pl **-res** [-riʃ]) adj & adv better ♦ m: **o/a ~** (pessoa, coisa) the best one; **o ~ a fazer é ...** the best thing to do is ...; **o ~ é não ir** it would be best not to go; **ou ~** or rather; **tanto ~!** all the better!; **estar ~** (de saúde) to feel better; **ser do ~ que há** to be the best there is; **cada vez ~** better and better.
melhorar [meʎo'ra(x)] vt to improve ♦ vi to get better, to improve.
melhores → melhor.
melindrar [melĩn'dra(x)] vt to hurt.
melindroso, -osa [melĩn'drozu, -ɔza] adj (pessoa) touchy; (assunto, questão, problema) delicate.
melodia [melo'dʒia] f tune.

melodrama [melo'drama] m melodrama.
melodramático, -ca [melodra'matʃiku, -ka] adj melodramatic.
melões → melão.
melro ['mɛwxu] m blackbird.
membro ['mẽmbru] m (perna, braço) limb; (de clube, associação) member.
memorando [memo'rãndu] m memorandum, memo.
memória [me'mɔrja] f memory; **de ~** off by heart.
memorizar [memori'za(x)] vt to memorize.
mencionar [mẽsjo'na(x)] vt to mention.
mendigar [mẽndʒi'ga(x)] vi to beg.
mendigo, -ga [mẽn'dʒigu, -ga] m, f beggar.
meningite [menĩ'ʒitʃi] f meningitis.
menino, -na [me'ninu, -na] m, f boy (f girl).
menopausa [meno'pawza] f menopause.
menor [me'nɔ(x)] (pl **-res** [-riʃ]) adj (em tamanho) smaller; (em número) lower; (em importância) minor; (mínimo) least ♦ mf minor; **não faço a ~ idéia** I haven't got a clue; **o/a ~** the least; (em tamanho) the smallest; **ser ~ de idade** to be underage.
menos ['menuʃ] adv 1. (em comparações) less; **a Ana é ~ inteligente** Ana is less intelligent, Ana isn't as intelligent; **~ do que** less than; **~ ... do que** less ... than; **tenho ~ trabalho do que ele** I have less work than him; **tenho um livro a ~** I'm one book short; **deram-me 5 reais a ~** they gave me 5 reals too little.
2. (como superlativo): **o/a ~ ...** the least ...; **o ~ caro/interessante** the cheapest/least interesting.
3. (Port: com as horas): **são dez ~ um quarto** it's a quarter to ten.
4. (em locuções): **a ~ que** unless; **ao ~, pelo ~** at least; **isso é o de ~** that's the least of it; **pouco ~ de** just under.
♦ adj inv 1. (em comparações) less, fewer (pl); **como ~ carne** I eat less meat; **eles têm ~ posses** they've got fewer possessions; **está ~ frio do que ontem** it's not as cold as it was yesterday; **~ ... do que** less ... than, fewer ... than (pl).
2. (como superlativo) (the) least, (the)

fewest *(pl)*; **as que ~ bolos comeram** those who ate (the) fewest cakes; **os que ~ dinheiro têm** those who have (the) least money.

♦ *prep* **1.** *(exceto)* except (for); **todos gostaram ~ ele** they all liked it except (for) him; **tudo ~ isso** anything but that.

2. *(indica subtração)* minus; **três ~ dois é igual a um** three minus two equals one.

menosprezar [menuʃpre'za(x)] *vt* to underrate.

mensageiro, -ra [mẽsa'ʒejru, -ra] *m, f* messenger.

mensagem [mẽsa'ʒẽ] *(pl* **-ns** [-ʃ]*) f* message.

mensal [mẽ'saw] *(pl* **-ais** [-ajʃ]*) adj* monthly.

mensalmente [mẽsaw'mẽntʃi] *adv* monthly.

menstruação [mẽʃtrua'sãw] *f* menstruation.

mentalidade [mẽntali'dadʒi] *f* mentality.

mente ['mẽntʃi] *f* mind; **ter em ~ fazer algo** to plan to do sthg.

mentir [mẽn'ti(x)] *vi* to lie.

mentira [mẽn'tira] *f* lie ♦ *interj* rubbish!; **parece ~!** I can't believe it!

mentiroso, -osa [mẽntʃi'rozu, -ɔza] *m, f* liar.

mentol [mẽn'tɔw] *m* menthol.

menu [me'nu] *m* menu.

mercado [mex'kadu] *m* market; **~ municipal** (town) market; **~ negro** black market.

❑ **Mercado** *m*: **o Mercado Único** the Single European Market.

mercadoria [mexkado'ria] *f* goods *(pl)*.

mercearia [mexsja'ria] *f* grocer's (shop).

MERCOSUL [mexko'suw] *m* South American economic community comprising Argentina, Brasil, Paraguay and Uruguay.

mercúrio [mex'kurju] *m* mercury.

mercurocromo [mexkuro'kromu] *m* Mercurochrome® *(antibacterial lotion)*.

merecer [mere'se(x)] *vt* to deserve.

merecido, -da [mere'sidu, -da] *adj* deserved.

merenda [me'rẽda] *f (lanche)* tea *(light afternoon meal)*; *(em excursão)* picnic.

merengue [me'rẽgi] *m* meringue.

mergulhador, -ra [merguʎa'do(x),

-ra] *(mpl* **-res** [-riʃ], *fpl* **-s** [-ʃ]*) m, f* diver.

mergulhar [mergu'ʎa(x)] *vi* to dive ♦ *vt*: **~ algo em algo** to dip sthg in sthg.

mergulho [mex'guʎu] *m* dive; **dar um ~** to dive.

meridiano [meri'dʒjanu] *m* meridian.

meridional [meridʒjo'naw] *(pl* **-ais** [-ajʃ]*) adj* southern.

mérito ['mɛritu] *m* merit; **por ~ próprio** on one's own merits.

mês [meʃ] *(pl* **meses** ['mezeʃ]*) m* month; **todo ~** every month; **(de) ~ a ~** every month; **por ~** a OU per month.

mesa ['meza] *f* table; **estar na ~** to be at the table.

mesada [me'zada] *f* monthly allowance.

mesa-de-cabeceira [,mezadʒikabe-'sejra] *(pl* **mesas-de-cabeceira** [,meza-dʒikabe'sejra]*) f* bedside table.

mescla ['meʃkla] *f* mixture.

mesclar [meʃ'kla(x)] *vt* to mix.

meses → mês.

meseta [me'zeta] *f* plateau.

mesmo, -ma ['meʒmu, -ma] *adj* same ♦ *adv (até)* even; *(exatamente)* exactly; *(para enfatizar)* really ♦ *pron*: **o ~/a mesma** the same; **eu ~** I myself; **comprou-o para ele ~/ela mesma** he/she bought it for himself/herself; **isso ~!** that's it!; **~ assim** even so; **~ que** OU **se** even if; **nem ~** not even; **o ~ que** the same thing as; **valer o ~ que** to cost the same as; **só ~** only.

mesquinho, -nha [meʃ'kiɲu, -ɲa] *adj* mean.

mesquita [meʃ'kita] *f* mosque.

mestiço, -ça [meʃ'tʃisu, -sa] *adj* of mixed race ♦ *m, f* person of mixed race.

mestre ['mɛʃtri] *m* master.

mestre-de-cerimônias [,mɛʃtredʒi-seri'monjaʃ] *(pl* **mestres-de-cerimônias** [,mɛʃtriʒdʒiseri'monjaʃ]*) m* master of ceremonies; *(em festa)* host.

mestre-sala [,mɛʃtri'sala] *(pl* **mestres-sala** [,mɛʃtriʃ'sala]*) m (Br: em desfile)* principal figure on a carnival float.

meta ['mɛta] *f (em corrida)* finishing line; *(objetivo)* goal.

metabolismo [metabo'liʒmu] *m* metabolism.

metade [me'tadʒi] *f* half; **~ do preço** half-price; **fazer as coisas pela ~** to do things half-heartedly; **fazer algo na ~ do tempo** to do sthg in half the time.

metáfora [me'tafora] *f* metaphor.

metal [mɛˈtaw] (*pl* **-ais** [-ajʃ]) *m* metal.
metálico, -ca [mɛˈtaliku, -ka] *adj (objecto)* metal; *(som)* metallic.
metalurgia [mɛtaluxˈʒia] *f* metallurgy.
meteorito [metjuˈritu] *m* meteorite.
meteoro [mɛˈtjoru] *m* meteor.
meteorologia [mɛteorolɔˈʒia] *f (ciência)* meteorology; *(em televisão)* weather report.
meter [meˈte(x)] *vt* to put; ~ algo/alguém em algo to put sthg/sb in sthg; ~ **medo** to be frightening; ~ **medo em alguém** to frighten sb.
⅃ **meter-se** *vp* to get involved; ~-se **em algo** to get involved in sthg; ~-se **na vida dos outros** to poke one's nose into other people's business; ~-se **onde não é chamado** to stick one's oar in; ~-se **com alguém** to have a go at sb.
meticuloso, -osa [mɛtʃikuˈlozu, -ɔza] *adj* meticulous.
metódico, -ca [mɛˈtɔdʃiku, -ka] *adj* methodical.
método [mɛtodu] *m* method; **com** ~ methodically; **sem** ~ haphazardly.
metralhadora [metraʎaˈdora] *f* machine gun.
métrico, -ca [ˈmɛtriku, -ka] *adj* metric.
metro [ˈmɛtru] *m (medida)* metre; *(fita métrica)* tape measure; *(Port: abrev de metropolitano)* = **metrô**.
metrô [meˈtro] *m (Br) (abrev de metropolitano)* underground *(Brit)*, subway *(Am)*.
metropolitano [metropoliˈtanu] *m* underground *(Brit)*, subway *(Am)*.
meu, minha [ˈmew, ˈmiɲa] *adj* my ♦ *pron*: **o** ~/**a minha** mine; **um amigo** ~ a friend of mine; **os** ~**s** *(a minha família)* my family.
mexer [meˈʃe(x)] *vt (corpo)* to move; *(CULIN)* to stir ♦ *vi (mover-se)* to move; ~ **em algo** to touch sthg.
⅃ **mexer-se** *vp (despachar-se)* to hurry up; *(mover-se)* to move; **mexa-se!** get a move on!
mexerica [meʃeˈrika] *f (Br)* tangerine.
mexerico [meʃeˈriku] *m* gossip.
México [ˈmɛʃiku] *m*: **o** ~ Mexico.
mexido, -da [meˈʃidu, -da] *adj* lively.
mexilhão [meʃiˈʎãw] (*pl* **-ões** [-õjʃ]) *m* mussel.
mg *(abrev de miligrama)* mg.

miar [ˈmja(x)] *vi* to miaow.
micróbio [miˈkrɔbju] *m* germ.
microfone [mikroˈfɔni] *m* microphone.
microondas [mikroˈõndaʃ] *m inv* microwave.
microscópio [mikroʃˈkɔpju] *m* microscope.
migalha [miˈgaʎa] *f* crumb.
migração [migraˈsãw] (*pl* **-ões** [-õjʃ]) *f* migration.
mijar [miˈʒa(x)] *vi (vulg)* to piss.
mil [ˈmiw] *num* a OU one thousand; **três** ~ three thousand; ~ **novecentos e noventa e sete** nineteen ninety-seven; → **seis**.
milagre [miˈlagri] *m* miracle.
milénio [miˈlɛnju] *m (Port)* = **milênio**.
milênio [miˈlenju] *m (Br)* millennium.
mil-folhas [miwˈfoʎaʃ] *m inv* millefeuille *(Brit)*, napoleon *(Am)*.
milha [ˈmiʎa] *f* mile.
milhão [miˈʎãw] (*pl* **-ões** [-õjʃ]) *num* million; **um** ~ **de pessoas** OU **indivíduos** a million people, → **seis**.
milhar [miˈʎa(x)] (*pl* **-res** [-riʃ]) *num* thousand, → **seis**.
milho [ˈmiʎu] *m* maize *(Brit)*, corn *(Am)*; ~ **doce** sweetcorn.
milhões → **milhão**.
miligrama [miliˈgrama] *m* milligram.
mililitro [miliˈlitru] *m* millilitre.
milímetro [miˈlimetru] *m* millimetre.
milionário, -ria [miljoˈnarju, -rja] *m, f* millionaire *(f* millionairess).
militante [miliˈtãntʃi] *mf* militant.
mim [ˈmi] *pron (com preposição: complemento indireto)* me; *(com preposição: reflexo)* myself; **a** ~, **você não engana** you don't fool me; **comprei-o para** ~ *(mesmo* OU **próprio)** I bought it for myself.
mimado, -da [miˈmadu, -da] *adj* spoilt.
mimar [miˈma(x)] *vt (criança)* to spoil; *(por gestos)* to mimic.
mímica [ˈmimika] *f* mime.
mimo [ˈmimu] *m* cuddle; **dar** ~**s a alguém** to spoil sb; **ser um** ~ to be great.
mina [ˈmina] *f (de carvão, ouro)* mine.
mindinho [mĩnˈdʒiɲu] *m* little finger.
mineiro, -ra [miˈnejru, -ra] *m, f* miner.

mineral [mine'raw] (*pl* **-ais** [-ajʃ]) *m* mineral.
minério [mi'nɛrju] *m* ore.
minha → **meu.**
minhoca [mi'ɲɔka] *f* earthworm.
miniatura [minja'tura] *f* miniature; **em ~** in miniature.
mini-mercado [,minimex'kadu] *m* corner shop.
mínimo, -ma ['minimu, -ma] *adj* minimum ◆ *m*: **o ~** the minimum; **não faço a mínima idéia!** I haven't got a clue!; **no ~** at least.
mini-saia [,mini'saja] *f (Port)* = **minissaia.**
minissaia [,mini'saja] *f (Br)* miniskirt.
ministério [miniʃ'tɛrju] *m* ministry.
ministro, -tra [mi'niʃtru, -tra] *m, f* minister.
minoria [mino'ria] *f* minority; **estar em ~** to be in the minority.
minúscula [mi'nuʃkula] *f* small letter; **em ~s** in small letters.
minúsculo, -la [mi'nuʃkulu, -la] *adj (muito pequeno)* minuscule, tiny; *(letra)* small.
minuto [mi'nutu] *m* minute; **só um ~!** hang on a minute!; **contar os ~s** to count the minutes; **dentro de poucos ~s** in a few minutes; **em poucos ~s** in no time at all.
miolo ['mjolu] *m (de pão, bolo) soft part of bread or cake.*
⌐ **miolos** *mpl* brains.
míope ['mjupi] *adj* shortsighted.
miopia [mju'pia] *f* shortsightedness.
miosótis [mjo'zɔtʃiʃ] *m inv* forget-me-not.
miradouro [mira'doru] *m* viewpoint.
miragem [mi'raʒẽ] (*pl* **-ns** [-ʃ]) *f* mirage.
mirar [mi'ra(x)] *vt (observar)* to look at.
⌐ **mirar-se** *vp*: **~-se em algo** to look at o.s. in sthg.
miscelânea [miʃse'lanja] *f (mistura)* mixture; *(fig: confusão)* jumble.
miserável [mize'ravɛw] (*pl* **-eis** [-ejʃ]) *adj (pobre)* poverty-stricken; *(desgraçado)* unfortunate.
miséria [mi'zɛrja] *f (pobreza)* poverty; *(desgraça)* misery; *(sordidez)* squalor; *(pouca quantidade)* pittance.
misericórdia [mizeri'kɔrdja] *f* mercy; **pedir ~** to ask for mercy.
missa ['misa] *f* mass.
missão [mi'sãw] (*pl* **-ões** [-õjʃ]) *f* mission.
míssil ['misiw] (*pl* **-eis** [-ejʃ]) *m* missile.
missionário, -ria [misjo'narju, -rja] *m, f* missionary.
missões → **missão.**
mistério [miʃ'tɛrju] *m* mystery.
misterioso, -osa [miʃte'rjozu, -ɔza] *adj* mysterious.
misto, -ta ['miʃtu, -ta] *adj* mixed ◆ *m (CULIN)*: **~ quente** *toasted sandwich filled with cheese and ham.*
mistura [miʃ'tura] *f* mixture.
misturar [miʃtu'ra(x)] *vt* to mix; *(fig: confundir)* to mix up.
mito ['mitu] *m* myth.
miúdo, -da ['mjudu, -da] *adj* small ◆ *m, f* kid.
⌐ **miúdos** *mpl*: **~s de galinha** giblets; **trocar algo em ~s** to explain sthg.
ml *(abrev de mililitro)* ml.
mm *(abrev de milímetro)* mm.
mo [mu] = **me + o,** → **me.**
mobília [mo'bilja] *f* furniture.
mobiliário [mobi'ljarju] *m* furnishings *(pl)*.
moçambicano, -na [mosãmbi'kanu, -na] *adj* of/relating to Mozambique ◆ *m, f* native/inhabitant of Mozambique.
Moçambique [mosãm'biki] *s* Mozambique.
mocassim [moka'sĩ] (*pl* **-ns** [-ʃ]) *mpl* mocassin.
mochila [mo'ʃila] *f* rucksack.
mocidade [mosi'dadʒi] *f* youth.
moço, -ça ['mosu, -sa] *adj* young ◆ *m, f* boy (*f* girl); **~ de recados** errand boy.
mocotó [moko'tɔ] *m (Br)* shank.
moda ['mɔda] *f* fashion; **à ~ de** in the style of; **estar fora de ~** to be out of fashion, **estar na ~** to be in fashion, to be fashionable; **sair de ~** to go out of fashion.
modalidade [modali'dadʒi] *f (de esporte)* discipline; *(de pagamento)* method.
modelo [mo'delu] *m* model; *(de roupa)* design; **servir de ~** to serve as an example; **tomar por ~** to take as an example.
modem ['mɔdem] *m* modem.
moderado, -da [mode'radu, -da] *adj* moderate.
moderar [mode'ra(x)] *vt (restringir)* to moderate; *(reunião, debate)* to chair.

modernizar [modexni'za(x)] *vt* to modernize.

moderno, -na [mo'dexnu. -na] *adj* modern.

modéstia [mo'dɛʃtʃa] *f* modesty; ~ à **parte** modesty aside.

modesto, -ta [mo'dɛʃtu, -ta] *adj* modest.

modificar [modʒifi'ka(x)] *vt* to modify.

❑ **modificar-se** *vp* to change.

modo ['mɔdu] *m* way; *(GRAM)* mood; ~ **de usar** instructions *(pl)*; **com bons** ~s politely; **com maus** ~s impolitely; **de certo** ~ in some ways; **de** ~ **nenhum!** no way!; **de** ~ **que** so (that); **de qualquer** ~ anyway; **de tal** ~ **que** so much that.

módulo ['mɔdulu] *m* *(EDUC)* module; *(Port: de ônibus, elétrico)* ticket.

moeda ['mwɛda] *f* *(de metal)* coin; *(em geral)* currency; ~ **estrangeira** foreign currency.

moer ['mwe(x)] *vt* to grind.

mofo ['mofu] *m* mould.

mogno ['mɔgnu] *m* mahogany.

moído, -da ['mwidu. -da] *adj* *(café, pimenta)* ground; **estar** ~ *(fam: estar cansado)* to be done in; **ter o corpo** ~ to be all aches and pains.

moinho ['mwiɲu] *m* mill; ~ **de café** coffee grinder; ~ **de vento** windmill.

mola ['mɔla] *f* *(em colchão, sofá)* spring; *(Port: de abotoar)* press stud *(Brit)*, snap fastener *(Am)*; ~ **de roupa** clothes peg *(Brit)*, clothes pin *(Am)*.

molar [mo'la(x)] *(pl* **-res** [-riʃ]) *m* molar.

moldar [mow'da(x)] *vt* to mould.

moldura [mow'dura] *f* frame.

mole ['mɔli] *adj* soft; *(pessoa)* docile.

molécula [mu'lɛkula] *f* molecule.

molestar [moleʃ'ta(x)] *vt* *(maltratar)* to hurt; *(aborrecer)* to annoy.

molhar [mo'ʎa(x)] *vt* to wet.

❑ **molhar-se** *vp* to get wet.

molheira [mo'ʎejra] *f* gravy boat.

molho¹ ['moʎu] *m* sauce; ~ **de tomate** tomato sauce; **pôr de** ~ to soak.

molho² ['mɔʎu] *m* *(de lenha)* stack; *(de palha, erva)* bundle; ~ **de chaves** bunch of keys.

molinete [moli'netʃi] *m* *(de cana de pesca)* reel.

momentaneamente [momẽn.tanja-'mẽntʃi] *adv* momentarily.

momento [mo'mẽntu] *m* moment; **um** ~! just a moment!; **a qualquer** ~ any minute now; **até o** ~ (up) until now; **de/neste** ~ at the moment; **dentro de** ~s shortly; **de um** ~ **para o outro** any time now; **em dado** ~ at any given moment; **por** ~s for a second.

monarca [mo'naxka] *mf* monarch.

monarquia [monax'kia] *f* monarchy.

monge ['mõʒi] *m* monk.

monitor, -ra [moni'to(x), -ra] *(mpl* **-res** [-riʃ], *fpl* **-s** [-ʃ]) *m, f* *(em colônia de férias)* activities coordinator ◆ *m* *(de televisão)* (television) screen; *(de computador)* monitor, VDU.

monopólio [mono'pɔlju] *m* monopoly.

monossílabo [mono'silabu] *m* monosyllable.

monotonia [monoto'nia] *f* monotony.

monótono, -na [mo'nɔtonu, -na] *adj* *(pessoa)* tedious; *(vida, trabalho)* monotonous.

monstro ['mõʃtru] *m* monster.

montagem [mõn'taʒẽ] *(pl* **-ns** [-ʃ]) *f* *(de máquina)* assembly; *(de esquema)* drawing up; *(de fotografia)* montage; *(de filme)* editing.

montanha [mõn'taɲa] *f* mountain.

montanha-russa [mõn.taɲa'rusa] *(pl* **montanhas-russas** [mõn.taɲaʃ'rusaʃ]) *f* roller coaster.

montanhismo [mõnta'niʒmu] *m* mountaineering.

montanhoso, -osa [mõnta'ɲozu. -ɔza] *adj* mountainous.

montante [mõn'tãntʃi] *m* total.

montar [mõn'ta(x)] *vt* *(barraca)* to put up; *(acampamento)* to set up; *(máquina)* to assemble; *(filme)* to edit ◆ *vi* *(fazer hipismo)* to ride; ~ **a cavalo** to ride (a horse).

monte ['mõntʃi] *m* *(montanha)* mountain; **comida aos** ~s loads of food; **um** ~ **de, ~s de** *(fam)* loads ou masses of; **a** ~ piled up.

montra ['mõntra] *f* *(Port)* (window) display.

monumental [monumẽn'taw] *(pl* **-ais** [-ajʃ]) *adj* *(enorme)* monumental; *(grandioso)* magnificent.

monumento [monu'mẽntu] *m* monument; ~ **comemorativo** memorial.

moqueca [mo'kɛka] *f* stew *made of*

fish, seafood and eggs, seasoned with parsley, coriander, lemon, onion, coconut milk, palm oil and peppercorns.

morada [mu'rada] *f (Port)* address.

moradia [mora'dia] *f* house.

morador, -ra [mora'do(x), -ra] *(mpl -res* [-rif], *fpl* **-s** [-ʃ]) *m, f* resident.

moral [mo'raw] *(pl -ais* [-ajʃ]) *adj* moral ◆ *f (social)* morals *(pl); (conclusão)* moral ◆ *m (ânimo, disposição)* morale.

morango [mo'rãŋgu] *m* strawberry.

morar [mo'ra(x)] *vi* to live.

mórbido, -da ['mɔxbidu, -da] *adj* morbid.

morcego [mox'segu] *m* bat.

mordaça [mox'dasa] *f (em pessoa)* gag; *(em animal)* muzzle.

morder [mox'de(x)] *vt* to bite.

mordida [mox'dida] *f* bite.

mordomo [mox'domu] *m* butler.

moreno, -na [mo'renu, -na] *adj (tez, pele)* dark; *(de sol)* tanned.

morfina [mox'fina] *f* morphine.

moribundo, -da [mori'bũndu, -da] *adj* dying.

morno, morna ['moxnu, 'morna] *adj* lukewarm.

morrer [mo'xe(x)] *vi* to die; *(fogo, luz)* to die down; *(Br: motor)* to stall; **estou morrendo de fome** I'm starving: **~ de vontade de fazer algo** to be dying to do sthg.

morro ['moxu] *m (monte)* hill; *(Br: favela)* slum.

mortadela [moxta'dela] *f* Mortadella, *large pork sausage served cold in thin slices.*

mortal [mox'taw] *(pl -ais* [-ajʃ]) *adj (pessoa, animal)* mortal; *(acidente, ferida)* fatal; *(doença)* terminal ◆ *mf* mortal.

mortalha [mox'taʎa] *f (de cadáver)* shroud.

mortalidade [moxtali'dadʒi] *f* mortality; **~ infantil** infant mortality.

morte ['moxtʃi] *f (natural)* death; *(homicídio)* murder; **estar pensando na ~ da bezerra** to have a good wallow; **ser de ~** *(fam: cômico)* to be hysterical.

mortífero, -ra [mox'tʃiferu, -ra] *adj* lethal.

morto, morta ['moxtu, 'morta] *pp* → **matar** ◆ *adj* dead ◆ *m, f* dead person; **estar ~** to be dead; **estar ~ para fazer algo** to be dying to do sthg; **estar ~ de**

cansaço/fome to be exhausted/starving; **ser ~** to be killed.

mos [moʃ] = **me** + **os**, → **me**.

mosaico [mo'zajku] *m* mosaic.

mosca ['moʃka] *f* fly; **acertar na ~** to hit the nail on the head.

moscatel [moʃka'tεw] *(pl -éis* [-εiʃ]) *m* Muscatel, *sweet white liqueur wine.*

mosquiteiro [moʃki'tejru] *m* mosquito net.

mosquito [moʃ'kitu] *m* mosquito.

mostarda [moʃ'taxda] *f* mustard.

mosteiro [moʃ'tejru] *m* monastery.

mostrador [moʃtra'do(x)] *(pl -es* [-iʃ]) *m (de relógio)* face; *(de velocímetro)* dial.

mostrar [moʃ'tra(x)] *vt* to show; **~ algo a alguém** to show sthg to sb, to show sb sthg; **~ interesse em** to show an interest in.

mostruário [moʃtru'arju] *m* showcase.

mota ['mɔta] *f (Port)* = **moto**.

mote ['mɔtʃi] *m* motto.

motel [mo'tεw] *(pl -éis* [-εiʃ]) *m* motel.

motim [mo'tʃĩ] *(pl -ns* [-ʃ]) *m* uprising.

motivar [motʃi'va(x)] *vt (causar)* to cause; *(aluno)* to motivate.

motivo [mo'tʃivu] *m* motive; **por ~ de** due to; **sem ~s** for no reason.

moto ['mɔtu] *f* motorbike.

motocicleta [ˌmotosi'kleta] *f* moped.

motocross [moto'krɔsi] *m* motocross.

motor [mo'to(x)] *(pl -res* [-riʃ]) *m* engine, motor; **~ de arranque** starter motor.

motorista [moto'riʃta] *mf* driver.

motoserra [moto'sεxa] *f* chain saw.

mourisco, -ca [mo'riʃku, -ka] *adj* Moorish.

Mouros ['moruʃ] *mpl:* **os ~** the Moors.

mousse [muse] *f (Port)* = **musse**.

movediça [move'dʒisa] *adj f* → **areia**.

móvel ['mɔvεw] *(pl -eis* [-εjʃ]) *adj* mobile ◆ *m* piece of furniture.
⊐ **móveis** *mpl* furniture *(sg).*

mover [mo've(x)] *vt* to move; *(campanha)* to instigate.
⊐ **mover-se** *vp* to move.

movimentado, -da [movimẽn'tadu, -da] *adj (rua, local)* busy.

movimento [movi'mẽntu] *m* movement; *(em rua, estabelecimento)* activity;

em ~ in motion.
MPB f (Br: abrev de Música Popular Brasileira) generic name for Brazilian popular music.
muco ['muku] m mucus.
mudança [mu'dãsa] f (modificação) change; (de casa) move; (de veículo) gear.
mudar [mu'da(x)] vt (alterar) to change; (de posição) to move ♦ vi (alterar-se) to change.
❏ **mudar de** v + prep to change; (de casa) to move; ~ **de idéia** to change one's mind; ~ **de roupa** to change (one's clothes).
❏ **mudar-se** vp to move (house); ~**-se para** to move to.
mudez [mu'deʒ] f muteness.
mudo, -da ['mudu, -da] adj (pessoa) dumb; (cinema) silent; **ficar** ~ (fig) to be lost for words.
muito, -ta ['mũĩntu, -ta] adj a lot of ♦ pron a lot ♦ adv (com verbo) a lot; (com adjetivo) very; **já não tenho** ~ **tempo** I don't have much time left; **há** ~ **tempo** a long time ago; **tenho** ~ **sono** I'm really tired; ~ **bem!** very good!; ~ **antes** long before; ~ **pior** much ou far worse; **quando** ~ at the most; **querer** ~ **a alguém** to care about sb a great deal; **não ganho** ~ I don't earn much.
mula ['mula] f mule.
mulato, -ta [mu'latu, -ta] adj & m, f mulatto.
muleta [mu'leta] f crutch.
mulher [mu'ʎɛ(x)] (pl -res [-riʃ]) f woman; (esposa) wife.
multa ['muwta] f fine; **levar uma** ~ to get a fine.
multar [muw'ta(x)] vt to fine.
multidão [muwti'dãw] (pl -ões [-õjʃ]) f (de pessoas) crowd; (de coisas) host.
multinacional [,muwtʃinaʒju'naw] (pl -ais [-ajʃ]) f multinational.
multiplicar [muwtʃipli'ka(x)] vt & vi to multiply; ~ **por** to multiply by.
❏ **multiplicar-se** vp (reproduzir-se) to multiply.
múltiplo, -pla ['muwtʃiplu, -pla] adj & m multiple.
múmia ['mumja] f mummy.
mundial [mũn'dʒjaw] (pl -ais [-ajʃ]) adj world (antes de s) ♦ m (de futebol) World Cup; (de atletismo, etc) World Championships (pl).

mundo ['mũndu] m world; **o outro** ~ the hereafter; **não é nada do outro** ~ it's nothing out of the ordinary; **por nada deste** ~ for the world; **vai ser o fim do** ~ all hell will break loose; **todo (o)** ~ (Br) everyone, everybody; **viver no** ~ **da lua** to live in a world of one's own.
munição [muni'sãw] (pl -ões [-õjʃ]) f ammunition.
municipal [munisi'paw] (pl -ais [-ajʃ]) adj town (antes de s), municipal.
município [muni'sipju] m (cidade) town; (organismo) town council.
munições → munição.
munir [mu'ni(x)] vt: ~ **alguém de algo** to supply sb with sthg.
❏ **munir-se de** vp + prep to arm o.s. with.
mural [mu'raw] (pl -ais [-ajʃ]) m mural.
muralha [mu'raʎa] f wall; (fortaleza) ramparts (pl).
murchar [mux'ʃa(x)] vi to wilt.
murcho, -cha ['muxʃu, -ʃa] adj (flor, planta) wilted; (fig: sem animação) listless.
murmurar [muxmu'ra(x)] vt to murmur.
murmúrio [mux'murju] m murmur.
muro ['muru] m wall.
murro ['muxu] m punch; **dar um** ~ **em alguém** to punch sb; **dar um** ~ **em algo** to thump sthg.
murta ['muxta] f myrtle.
musa ['muza] f muse.
musculação [muʃkula'sãw] f body building.
músculo ['muʃkulu] m muscle.
musculoso, -osa [muʃku'lozu, -ɔza] adj muscular.
museu [mu'zew] m museum; ~ **de arte moderna** modern art gallery.
musgo ['muʒgu] m moss.
música ['muzika] f music; ~ **clássica/folclórica** classical/folk music; ~ **de câmara** chamber music; ~ **pop** pop music; ~ **sinfônica** orchestral music; **dançar conforme a** ~ (fig) to play along.
músico ['muziku] m musician.
musse ['musi] f (Br) mousse; ~ **de chocolate** chocolate mousse.
mútuo, -tua ['mutwu, -twa] adj mutual; **de** ~ **acordo** by mutual agreement.

N

N *(abrev de Norte)* N.
na [na] = **em + a**, → **em**.
-na [na] *pron (pessoa)* her; *(coisa)* it; *(você)* you.
nabo ['nabu] *m (planta)* turnip.
nação [na'sãw] (*pl* **-ões** [-õjʃ]) *f* nation.
nacional [nasjo'naw] (*pl* **-ais** [-ajʃ]) *adj* national.
nacionalidade [nasjonali'dadʒi] *f* nationality.
nacionalismo [nasjona'liʒmu] *m* nationalism.
nações → **nação**.
nada ['nada] *pron (coisa nenhuma)* nothing; *(em negativas)* anything ◆ *adv*: **não gosto ~ disto** I don't like it at all; **não dei por ~** I didn't notice a thing; **de ~!** don't mention it!; **~ de novo** nothing new; **ou tudo ou ~** all or nothing; **antes de mais ~** first of all; **é uma coisa de ~** it's nothing (at all); **não prestar** OU **servir para ~** to be no help at all, to be useless; **não serve de ~ resmungar** there's no point moaning.
nadador, -ra [nada'do(x), -ra] (*mpl* **-res** [-riʃ], *fpl* **-s** [-ʃ]) *m, f* swimmer; **~ salvador** lifeguard.
nadar [na'da(x)] *vi* to swim; **~ em** *(fig: ter muito de)* to be swimming in.
nádegas ['nadegaʃ] *fpl* buttocks.
naipe ['najpi] *m* suit.
namorado, -da [namo'radu, -da] *m, f* boyfriend (*f* girlfriend).
não [nãw] *adv (em respostas)* no; *(em negativas)* not; **ainda ~ o vi** I still haven't seen him; **~ é aqui, pois ~?** it isn't here, is it?; **~ tem mais ingressos** there aren't any tickets left; **~ é?** isn't it?; **pelo sim, pelo ~** just in case.
não-fumador, -ra [nãwfuma'dor, -ra] (*mpl* **-res** [-reʃ], *fpl* **-s** [-ʃ]) *m, f (Port)* = **não-fumante**.
não-fumante [ˌnãwfu'mãntʃi] *mf (Br)* non-smoker.
napa ['napa] *f* leatherette.
naquela [na'kɛla] = **em + aquela**, → **em**.
naquele [na'keli] = **em + aquele**, → **em**.
naquilo [na'kilu] = **em + aquilo**, → **em**.
narciso [nax'sizu] *m* narcissus.
narcótico [nax'kɔtʃiku] *m* narcotic.
narina [na'rina] *f* nostril.
nariz [na'riʃ] (*pl* **-zes** [-ziʃ]) *m* nose; **meter o ~ em tudo** to be a busybody; **torcer o ~ (para algo)** *(fig)* to turn one's nose up (at sthg).
narração [naxa'sãw] (*pl* **-ões** [-õjʃ]) *f (ato)* narration; *(conto, história)* narrative.
narrar [na'xa(x)] *vt* to narrate.
narrativa [naxa'tʃiva] *f* narrative.
nas [naʃ] = **em + as**, → **em**.
-nas [naʃ] *pron pl (elas)* them; *(vocês)* you.
nascença [naʃ'sẽsa] *f* birth; **de ~** *(problema, defeito)* congenital.
nascente [naʃ'sẽntʃi] *f (de rio)* source; *(de água)* spring.
nascer [naʃ'se(x)] *vi (pessoa, animal)* to be born; *(planta)* to sprout; *(sol)* to rise ◆ *m (de sol)* sunrise; *(de lua)* moonrise; **~ para ser algo** to be born to be sthg.
nascimento [naʃsi'mẽntu] *m* birth.
nata ['nata] *f* cream.
❑ **natas** *fpl (Port: para bater)* whipping cream *(sg)*.
natação [nata'sãw] *f* swimming.
natal [na'taw] (*pl* **-ais** [-ajʃ]) *adj (aldeia, cidade)* home *(antes de s)*.
❑ **Natal** *m* Christmas; **Feliz Natal!** Merry Christmas!
nativo, -va [na'tʃivu, -va] *adj & m, f* native.

NATO [ˈnatu] f NATO.

natural [natuˈraw] (pl **-ais** [-ajʃ]) adj natural; **ao ~** (fruta) fresh; **como é ~** as is only natural; **é ~ que** it's understandable (that); **ser ~ de** to be from.

naturalidade [naturaliˈdadʒi] f (origem) birthplace; (simplicidade) naturalness.

naturalmente [naturawˈmẽntʃi] adv naturally ◆ interj naturally!, of course!

natureza [natuˈreza] f nature; **da mesma ~** of the same kind; **~ morta** still life; **por ~** by nature.

⊐ Natureza f: **a Natureza** Nature.

nau [ˈnaw] f ship.

naufragar [nawfraˈga(x)] vi to be wrecked.

naufrágio [nawˈfraʒju] m shipwreck.

náusea [ˈnawzea] f nausea; **dar ~s a alguém** to make sb feel sick.

náutico, -ca [ˈnawtʃiku, -ka] adj (atividade) water (antes de s); (clube) sailing (antes de s).

navalha [naˈvaʎa] f penknife.

nave [ˈnavi] f (de igreja) nave; **~ espacial** spaceship.

navegação [navegaˈsãw] f navigation.

navegar [naveˈga(x)] vi to sail; **~ na Internet** to surf the Net.

navio [naˈviu] m ship.

NB (abrev de Note Bem) NB.

NE (abrev de Nordeste) NE.

neblina [neˈblina] f mist.

necessário, -ria [neseˈsarju, -rja] adj necessary ◆ m: **o ~** the bare necessities (pl); **quando ~** when necessary; **se ~** if necessary; **é ~ passaporte** you need your passport.

necessidade [nesesiˈdadʒi] f (carência) necessity, need; **de primeira ~** essential; **sem ~** needlessly; **ter ~ de fazer algo** to need to do sthg; **fazer uma ~** (fam) to relieve o.s.

necessitar [nesesiˈta(x)] vt to need.

⊐ necessitar de v + prep to need; **~ de fazer algo** to need to do sthg.

necrotério [nekroˈterju] m morgue.

néctar [ˈnɛkta(x)] (pl **-res** [-riʃ]) m nectar.

neerlandês, -esa [nexlãˈdeʃ, -eza] (mpl **-eses** [-ezifʃ], fpl **-s** [-ʃ]) adj & m Dutch ◆ m, f (pessoa) Dutchman (f Dutchwoman); **os neerlandeses** the Dutch.

nefasto, -ta [neˈfaʃtu, -ta] adj (acontecimento) terrible; (atmosfera) bad.

negar [neˈga(x)] vt to deny.

⊐ negar-se vp: **~-se algo** to deny o.s. sthg; **~-se a fazer algo** to refuse to do sthg.

negativa [negaˈtiva] f (Port) (EDUC) fail; **ter ~** to fail.

negativo, -va [negaˈtʃivu. -va] adj negative; (saldo bancário) overdrawn; (temperatura) minus ◆ m (de filme, fotografia) negative.

negligência [negliˈʒẽsja] f negligence.

negligente [negliˈʒẽntʃi] adj negligent.

negociação [negosjaˈsãw] (pl **-ões** [-õjʃ]) f negotiation.

negociar [negoˈsja(x)] vt (acordo, preço) to negotiate ◆ vi (COM) to do business.

negócio [neˈgɔsju] m business; (transação) deal; **fazer ~s com alguém** to do business with sb; **~ da China** easy money; **~s escusos** shady deals.

negro, -gra [ˈnegru, -gra] adj black; (céu) dark; (raça) negro; (fig: difícil) bleak ◆ m, f black man (f black woman).

nela [ˈnela] = em + ela, → em.

nele [ˈneli] = em + ele, → em.

nem [nẽ] adv not even ◆ conj: **não gosto ~ de cerveja ~ de vinho** I don't like either beer or wine; **não gosto ~ de um ~ de outro** I don't like either of them; **~ por isso** not really; **~ que** even if; **~ sempre** not always; **~ tudo** not everything; **~ ... ~** neither ... nor; **~ um ~ outro** neither one nor the other; **~ pensar!** (fam) don't even think of it!

nenhum, -ma [neˈɲũ, -ma] (mpl **-ns** [-ʃ], fpl **-s** [-ʃ]) adj no ◆ pron none; **não comprei livros nenhuns** I didn't buy any books; **não quero nenhuma bebida** I don't want a drink; **não tive problema ~** I didn't have any problems; **~ professor é perfeito** no teacher is perfect; **~ de** none of, not one of; **~ dos dois** neither of them.

neozelandês, -esa [neozelãˈdeʃ. -eza] (mpl **-eses** [-ezifʃ], fpl **-s** [-ʃ]) adj of/relating to New Zealand ◆ m, f native/inhabitant of New Zealand.

nervo [ˈnexvu] nerve; (em carne) sinew.

⊐ nervos mpl (fam) nerves.

nervosismo [nεxvo'ziʒmu] *m* nerves *(pl)*.

nêspera ['nɛʃpεra] *f* loquat, *plum-like yellow fruit*.

nessa ['nɛsa] = em + essa, → em.

nesse ['nɛsi] = em + esse, → em.

nesta ['nɛʃta] = em + esta, → em.

neste ['nɛʃtʃi] = em + este, → em.

neto, -ta ['nεtu. -ta] *m, f* grandson (*f* granddaughter).

neurose [new'rɔzi] *f* neurosis.

neutralidade [newtrali'dadʒi] *f* neutrality.

neutralizar [newtrali'za(x)] *vt* to neutralize.

neutro, -tra ['newtru. -tra] *adj* neutral; *(GRAM)* neuter.

nevar [ne'va(x)] *v impess* to snow; **está nevando** it's snowing.

neve ['nεvi] *f* snow.

névoa ['nεvwa] *f* mist.

nevoeiro [ne'vwejru] *m* fog.

Nicarágua [nika'ragwa] *f*: **a ~** Nicaragua.

nicotina [niko'tʃina] *f* nicotine.

ninguém [nĩŋ'gaj] *pron* nobody, no one; *(em negativas)* anyone, anybody; **não tem ~ (em casa)** there's nobody in; **não vi ~** I didn't see anyone.

ninho ['niɲu] *m* nest; *(fig: lar)* home.

níquel ['nikεw] *(pl -eis* [-εjʃ]) *m* nickel.

nissei [ni'sej] *mf* (Br) Brazilian of Japanese parentage.

nisso ['nisu] = em + isso, → em.

nisto ['niʃtu] = em + isto, → em.

nitidez [nitʃi'deʒ] *f* clarity.

nítido, -da ['nitʃidu. -da] *adj* clear.

nitrato [ni'tratu] *m* nitrate; **~ de prata** silver nitrate *(for the treatment of warts and corns)*.

nível ['nivεw] *(pl -eis* [-εjʃ]) *m* level; *(qualidade)* quality; **ao ~ de** in terms of; **~ de vida** standard of living.

no [nu] = em + o, → em.

nó ['nɔ] *m* knot; *(em dedo)* knuckle; **dar um ~** to tie a knot; **dar o ~** *(casar-se)* to tie the knot.

nº *(abrev de número)* no.

-no [nu] *pron (pessoa)* him; *(coisa)* it; *(você)* you.

NO *(abrev de Noroeste)* NW.

nobre ['nɔbri] *adj* noble.

noção [no'sãw] *(pl -ões* [-õjʃ]) *f* notion.

nocivo, -va [no'sivu. -va] *adj (produto)* noxious; *(alimento)* unwholesome.

noções → noção.

noturno, -na [no'turnu. -na] *adj* (Port) = noturno.

nódoa ['nɔdwa] *f (em roupa, toalha)* stain; *(em reputação)* blemish; **~ negra** (Port) bruise.

nogueira [no'gejra] *f* walnut tree.

noite ['nojtʃi] *f* night; *(fim da tarde)* evening; **boa ~!** good night!; **à ~** at night; **esta ~** *(mais tarde)* tonight; *(ao fim da tarde)* this evening; **dia e ~** night and day; **por ~** a OU per night; **da ~ para o dia** overnight.

noivado [noj'vadu] *m* engagement.

noivo, -va ['nojvu. -va] *m, f* fiancé (*f* fiancée); **estar ~ de alguém** to be engaged to sb.

⌐ noivos *mpl* bride and groom; **eles estão ~s** they are engaged.

nojento, -ta [no'ʒẽntu. -ta] *adj* disgusting.

nojo ['noʒu] *m* disgust, revulsion; **dar ~** to be disgusting; **ter** OU **sentir ~ de** to be disgusted by.

nome ['nomi] *m* name; *(GRAM)* noun; **~ de batismo** Christian name; **~ completo** full name; **~ próprio, primeiro ~** first name; **em ~ de** on behalf of.

nomeação [nomja'sãw] *(pl -ões* [-õjʃ]) *f (para prêmio)* nomination; *(para cargo)* appointment.

nomeadamente [no,mjada'mẽntʃi] *adv* namely.

nomear [no'mja(x)] *vt (mencionar nome de)* to name; *(para prêmio)* to nominate; *(para cargo)* to appoint.

nonagésimo, -ma [nona'ʒεzimu. -ma] *num* ninetieth, → sexto.

nono, -na ['nonu. -na] *num* ninth, → sexto.

nora ['nɔra] *f (familiar)* daughter-in-law; *(para água)* waterwheel.

nordeste [nɔx'dεʃtʃi] *m* northeast; **no ~** in the northeast.

norma ['nɔxma] *f (padrão)* standard; *(regra)* rule; **por ~** as a rule.

normal [nɔx'maw] *(pl -ais* [-ajʃ]) *adj* normal.

normalmente [nɔxmaw'mẽntʃi] *adv* normally.

noroeste [nɔrwεʃtʃi] *m* northwest; **no ~** in the northwest.

norte ['nɔxtʃi] *adj (vento, direção)* northerly ♦ *m* north; **a** OU **no ~** in the north; **ao ~ de** north of.

norte-americano, -na [nɔxtʒiameri'kanu, -na] *adj & m, f* (North) American.

Noruega [no'rwɛga] *f:* a ~ Norway.

norueguês, -esa [norwe'geʃ, -eza] (*mpl* **-eses** [-eziʃ], *fpl* **-s** [-ʃ]) *adj & m, f* Norwegian ◆ *m (língua)* Norwegian.

nos¹ [noʃ] = **em** + **os**, → **em**.

nos² [noʃ] *pron pl (complemento direto)* us; *(complemento indireto)* (to) us; *(reflexo)* ourselves; *(recíproco)* each other, one another; ; **ela ~ falou** she told us; **nós nos machucamos** we hurt ourselves; **não ~ deixem!** don't leave us!; **nunca ~ enganamos** we're never wrong; **~ beijamos** we kissed (each other); **odiamo-~** we hate each other; **vamo-~ embora** (*Port*) we're going.

nós ['nɔʃ] *pron pl (sujeito)* we; *(complemento)* us; **e ~?** what about us?; **somos ~** it's us; **~ mesmos** OU **próprios** we ourselves.

-nos [noʃ] *pron pl (eles)* them; *(vocês)* you, → **nos²**.

nosso, -a ['nɔsu, -a] *adj* our ◆ *pron:* **o ~/a nossa** ours; **um amigo ~** a friend of ours; **os ~s** *(a nossa família)* our family.

nostalgia [noʃtaw'ʒia] *f* nostalgia.

nostálgico, -ca [noʃtaw'ʒiku, -ka] *adj* nostalgic.

nota ['nɔta] *f* note; *(classificação)* mark; **tomar ~ de algo** to make a note of sthg.

notário, -ria [no'tarju, -rja] *m, f* notary (public).

notável [no'tavɛw] (*pl* **-eis** [-ejʃ]) *adj (ilustre)* distinguished; *(extraordinário)* outstanding.

notebook ['notʃibuki] *m (INFORM)* notebook.

notícia [no'tʃisja] *f* piece of news. ↲ **notícias** *fpl (noticiário)* news *(sg)*.

noticiário [notʃi'sjarju] *m* news bulletin, newscast.

notificar [notʃifi'ka(x)] *vt* to notify.

notório, -ria [no'tɔrju, -rja] *adj* wellknown.

noturno, -na [no'tuxnu, -na] *adj (Br) (atividade)* night *(antes de s)*; *(aula)* evening *(antes de s)*; *(pessoa, animal)* nocturnal.

nova ['nɔva] *f* piece of news; **ter boas ~s** to have some good news.

Nova Iorque [,nɔva'jɔxki] *s* New York.

novamente [,nɔva'mēntʃi] *adv* again.

novato, -ta [no'vatu, -ta] *m, f* beginner.

Nova Zelândia [,nɔvaze'lãndja] *f:* a ~ New Zealand.

nove ['nɔvi] *num* nine, → **seis**.

novecentos, -tas [nɔve'sẽntuʃ, -taʃ] *num* nine hundred, → **seis**.

novela [no'vɛla] *f (livro)* novella; *(Br: em televisão)* soap opera.

novelo [no'vɛlu] *m* ball.

novembro [no'vẽmbru] *m* November, → **setembro**.

noventa [no'vẽta] *num* ninety, → **seis**.

novidade [novi'dadʒi] *f (notícia)* piece of news; *(em vestuário)* latest fashion; *(novo disco)* new release; **há ~s?** any news?; **~ editorial** latest publication.

novilho [no'viʎu] *m (animal)* bullock (2-3 *years old)*; *(carne)* beef.

novo, nova ['novu, 'nɔva] *adj* new; *(jovem)* young; **~ em folha** brand new.

noz ['nɔʃ] (*pl* **-zes** [-ziʃ]) *f* walnut.

noz-moscada [,nɔʒmoʃ'kada] *f* nutmeg.

nu, nua ['nu, 'nua] *adj* naked; **~ em pêlo** stark naked.

nublado, -da [nu'bladu, -da] *adj* cloudy.

nuca ['nuka] *f* nape (of the neck).

nuclear [nukle'a(x)] (*pl* **-res** [-riʃ]) *adj* nuclear.

núcleo ['nukliu] *m* nucleus.

nudez [nu'deʒ] *f* nudity.

nudista [nu'dʒiʃta] *mf* nudist.

nulo, -la ['nulu, -la] *adj (sem efeito, valor)* null and void; *(incapaz)* useless; *(nenhum)* nonexistent.

num [nũ] = **em** + **um**, → **em**.

numa ['numa] = **em** + **uma**, → **em**.

numeral [nume'raw] (*pl* **-ais** [-ajʃ]) *m* numeral.

numerar [nume'ra(x)] *vt* to number.

numerário [nume'rarju] *m* cash.

número ['numeru] *m* number; *(de sapatos, peça de vestuário)* size; *(de revista)* issue; **~ de código** PIN number; **~ de contribuinte** = National Insurance number *(Brit)*, = social security number *(Am)*; **~ de passaporte** passport number; **~ de telefone** telephone number.

numeroso, -osa [nume'rozu, -ɔza] *adj (família, grupo)* large; *(vantagens, ocasiões)* numerous.

numismática [numiʒ'matʃika] *f*

numismatics *(sg)*.

nunca ['nũŋka] *adv* never; **mais do que** ~ more than ever; ~ **mais** never again; ~ **se sabe** you never know; ~ **na vida** never ever.

nuns [nũʃ] = em + uns, → em.

núpcias ['nupsjaʃ] *fpl* marriage *(sg)*.

nutrição [nutri·sãw] *f* nutrition.

nutrir [nuˈtri(x)] *vt (fig: acalentar)* to nurture; ~ **uma paixão por alguém** to carry a torch for sb.

nutritivo, -va [nutriˈtʃivu, -va] *adj* nutritious.

nuvem ['nuvẽ] *(pl* **-ns** [-ʃ]) *f* cloud.

N.W. *(abrev de Noroeste)* NW.

o, a [u. a] (*mpl* **os** [uʃ]. *fpl* **as** [aʃ]) *artigo definido* **1.** *(com substantivo genérico)* the; **a casa** the house; **o hotel** the hotel; **os alunos** the students.
2. *(com substantivo abstrato):* **a vida** life; **o amor** love; **os nervos** nerves.
3. *(com adjetivo substantivado):* **o melhor/pior** the best/worst; **vou fazer o possível** I'll do what I can.
4. *(com nomes geográficos):* **a Inglaterra** England; **o Amazonas** the Amazon; **o Brasil** Brazil; **os Estados Unidos** the United States; **os Pirineus** the Pyrenees.
5. *(indicando posse):* **quebrei o nariz** I broke my nose; **estou com os pés frios** my feet are cold.
6. *(com nome de pessoa):* **o Hernani** Hernani; **a Helena** Helena; **o Sr. Mendes** Mr Mendes.
7. *(por cada)* a, per; **3 reais a dúzia** 3 reals a dozen.
8. *(com datas)* the; **o dois de Abril** the second of April, April the second.
♦ *pron* **1.** *(pessoa)* him (*f* her), them (*pl*); **eu a deixei ali** I left her there; **ela o amava muito** she loved him very much; **não os vi** I didn't see them.
2. *(você, vocês)* you; **prazer em conhecê-los, meus senhores** pleased to meet you, gentlemen.
3. *(coisa)* it, them (*pl*); **onde estão os papéis? não consigo achá-los** where are the papers? I can't find them.
4. *(em locuções):* **o/a da esquerda** the one on the left; **os que desejarem vir terão de pagar** those who wish to come will have to pay; **o que (é que) ...?** what ...?; **o que (é que) está acontecendo** what's going on? ; **era o que eu pensava** it's just as I thought; **o quê?** what?
oásis [ɔaziʃ] *m inv* oasis.
ob. *(abrev de observação)* = NB.

oba [oba] *interj (Br) (de surpresa)* wow!; *(saudação)* hi!
obedecer [obedeˈse(x)] *vi* to do as one is told, to obey; **~ a** to obey.
obediente [obeˈdʒjẽntʃi] *adj* obedient.
obesidade [obeziˈdadʒi] *f* obesity.
obeso, -sa [oˈbezu. -za] *adj* obese.
óbito [ˈɔbitu] *m* death.
obituário [obiˈtwarju] *m* obituary.
objeção [obʒeˈsãw] (*pl* **-ões** [-õjʃ]) *f* (*Br*) objection.
objecção [obʒeˈsãw] (*pl* **-ões** [-õjʃ]) *f* (*Port*) = objeção.
objecto [obˈʒɛtu] *m* (*Port*) = objeto.
objector [obʒeˈtor] (*pl* **-res** [-reʃ]) *m* (*Port*): **~ de consciência** conscientious objector.
objetiva [obʒeˈtʃiva] *f (de máquina fotográfica)* lens.
objetivo, -va [obʒeˈtʃivu. -va] *adj & m* objective.
objeto [obˈʒɛtu] *m* (*Br*) object.
oboé [oˈbwɛ] *m* oboe.
obra [ˈɔbra] *f* work; *(construção)* building site; **~ de arte** work of art; **~ de caridade** *(instituição)* charity.
⊐ **obras** *fpl (reparações)* repairs; **"em obras"** "closed for refurbishment".
obra-prima [ˌɔbraˈprima] (*pl* **obras-primas** [ˌɔbraʃˈprimaʃ]) *f* masterpiece.
obrigação [obrigaˈsãw] (*pl* **-ões** [-õjʃ]) *f* obligation; *(título de crédito)* bond.
obrigado, -da [obriˈgadu. -da] *interj* thank you!; **muito ~!** thank you very much!
obrigar [obriˈga(x)] *vt:* **~ alguém a fazer algo** to force sb to do sthg.
obrigatório, -ria [obrigaˈtɔrju. -rja] *adj* compulsory.
obs. *abrev* = **observações**.
obsceno, -na [obʃˈsenu. -na] *adj* obscene.

observação [obsɛxva'sãw] (*pl* -ões [-õjʃ]) *f* observation; *(de lei, regra)* observance.

⨽ **observações** *fpl* *(em formulário)* remarks.

observador, -ra [obsɛxva'do(x), -ra] (*mpl* -res [-riʃ], *fpl* -s [-ʃ]) *m, f* observer.

observar [obsɛx'va(x)] *vt* to observe; *(dizer)* to remark.

observatório [obsɛxva'tɔrju] *m* observatory.

obsessão [obse'sãw] (*pl* -ões [-õjʃ]) *f* obsession.

obsoleto, -ta [obso'lɛtu, -ta] *adj* obsolete.

obstáculo [obʃ'takulu] *m* obstacle.

obstetra [obʃ'tɛtra] *mf* obstetrician.

obstinado, -da [obʃtʃi'nadu, -da] *adj* obstinate.

obstrução [obʃtru'sãw] (*pl* -ões [-õjʃ]) *f* obstruction.

obter [ob'te(x)] *vt* to get.

obturação [obtura'sãw] (*pl* -ões [-õjʃ]) *f (de dente)* filling.

obturador [obtura'do(x)] (*pl* -res [-riʃ]) *m (de máquina fotográfica)* shutter.

óbvio, -via ['ɔbvju, -vja] *adj* obvious; **como é ~** obviously.

ocasião [oka'zjãw] (*pl* -ões [-õjʃ]) *f (momento determinado)* occasion; *(oportunidade)* opportunity; **nessa ~** at the time; **por ~ de** during.

Oceania [o'sjanja] *f:* **a ~** Oceania.

oceano [o'sjanu] *m* ocean.

ocidental [osidẽn'taw] (*pl* -ais [-ajʃ]) *adj* western.

⨽ **ocidentais** *mpl:* **os ocidentais** Westerners.

ocidente [osi'dẽntʃi] *m* west.

⨽ **Ocidente** *m:* **o Ocidente** the West.

ócio ['ɔsju] *m* leisure.

oco, oca ['oku, 'oka] *adj* hollow.

ocorrência [oko'xẽsja] *f (incidente)* incident; *(frequência)* occurrence.

ocorrer [oko'xe(x)] *vi* to happen.

octogésimo, -ma [okto'ʒɛzimu, -ma] *num* eightieth, → **sexto**.

oculista [oku'liʃta] *mf (médico)* optometrist; *(vendedor)* optician.

óculos ['ɔkuluʃ] *mpl* glasses; **~ escuros** sunglasses.

ocultar [okuw'ta(x)] *vt* to hide.

⨽ **ocultar-se** *vp* to hide.

oculto, -ta [o'kuwtu, -ta] *pp* → **ocultar**.

ocupação [okupa'sãw] (*pl* -ões [-õjʃ]) *f* occupation.

ocupado, -da [oku'padu, -da] *adj (casa)* occupied; *(lugar, assento)* taken; *(pessoa)* busy; **"ocupado"** "engaged".

ocupar [oku'pa(x)] *vt* to take up; *(casa)* to live in; *(tempo)* to occupy.

⨽ **ocupar-se** *vp* to keep o.s. busy; **~-se a fazer algo** to spend one's time doing sthg; **~-se de** to see to.

odiar [o'dʒja(x)] *vt* to hate.

ódio ['ɔdʒju] *m* hatred.

odor [o'do(x)] (*pl* -res [-riʃ]) *m* odour; **~ corporal** body odour.

oeste ['wɛʃtʃi] *m* west; **a ou no ~** in the west; **a ~ de** to the west of.

ofegante [ofe'gãntʃi] *adj* breathless.

ofegar [ofe'ga(x)] *vi* to pant.

ofender [ofẽn'de(x)] *vt* to offend.

⨽ **ofender-se** *vp* to take offence; **~-se com algo** to take offence at sthg.

oferecer [ofere'se(x)] *vt* to offer; *(dar)* to give; **~ algo a alguém** *(presente, ajuda, lugar)* to give sb sthg; *(emprego)* to offer sb sthg.

⨽ **oferecer-se** *vp:* **~-se para fazer algo** to offer to do sthg.

oferta [o'fɛxta] *f (presente)* gift; *(de emprego)* offer; *(COM)* supply.

oficial [ofi'sjaw] (*pl* -ais [-ajʃ]) *adj* official ◆ *mf (em marinha, exército)* officer.

oficina [ofi'sina] *f* garage.

ofício [o'fisju] *m (profissão)* trade; *(carta)* official letter.

oftalmologista [ɔftawmolo'ʒiʃta] *mf* ophthalmologist.

ofuscar [ofuʃ'ka(x)] *vt* to dazzle.

oi ['oj] *interj (Br)* hi!

oitavo, -va [oj'tavu, -va] *num* eighth, → **sexto**.

oitenta [oj'tẽnta] *num* eighty, → **seis**.

oito ['ojtu] *num* eight; **nem ~ nem oitenta!** there's no need to exaggerate!, → **seis**.

oitocentos, -tas [ojto'sẽntuʃ, -taʃ] *num* eight hundred, → **seis**.

OK [ɔ'kej] *interj* OK!

olá [ɔ'la] *interj* hello!

olaria [ola'ria] *f* pottery.

oleado [o'ljadu] *m* oil cloth; *(vestimenta)* oilskins *(pl)*.

óleo ['ɔlju] *m* oil; **~ de cozinha** (cooking) oil; **~ de bronzear** suntan oil; **~ de girassol/soja** sunflower/soya oil; **~ vegetal** vegetable oil.

oleoduto [ɔljɔˈdutu] *m* pipeline *(for oil)*.

oleoso, -osa [oˈljozu. -ɔza] *adj* greasy.

olfacto [olˈfatu] *m (Port)* = **olfato**.

olfato [owˈfatu] *m (Br)* sense of smell.

olhadela [oʎaˈdɛla] *f* glance; **dar uma ~ em algo** to have a quick look at sthg.

olhar [oˈʎa(x)] (*pl* **-res** [-riʃ]) *vt* to look at ◆ *vi* to look ◆ *m* look; **~ para** to look at; **~ por** to look after.

olheiras [oˈʎejraʃ] *fpl*: **ter ~** to have dark rings under one's eyes.

olho [ˈoʎu] (*pl* **olhos** [ˈɔʎuʃ]) *m* eye; **~ mágico** peephole; **a ~ nu** with the naked eye; **a ~s vistos** visibly; **aos ~s de** in the eyes of; **custar os ~s da cara** to cost an arm and a leg; **não pregar ~** not to sleep a wink; **ver com bons/maus ~s** to approve/disapprove of.

olho-de-sogra [ˌoʎudʒiˈsogra] (*pl* **olhos-de-sogra** [ˌoʎuʃdʒiˈsogra]) *m cake made with dates and coconut*.

olímpico, -ca [oˈlĩmpiku. -ka] *adj* Olympic.

oliveira [oliˈvejra] *f* olive tree.

ombro [ˈõmbru] *m* shoulder; **encolher os ~s** to shrug one's shoulders.

omelete [omeˈlɛtʃi] *f* omelette.

omissão [omiˈsãw] (*pl* **-ões** [-õjʃ]) *f* omission.

omitir [omiˈti(x)] *vt* to omit.

omnipotente [ˌɔmnipoˈtẽntʃi] *adj* omnipotent.

omoplata [omoˈplata] *f* shoulder-blade.

onça [ˈõsa] *f (animal)* jaguar; *(medida)* ounce.

onda [ˈõnda] *f* wave; **~ média/longa/curta** medium/long/short wave; **fazer ~** *(fam: criar problemas)* to make waves; **ir na ~** *(deixar-se enganar)* to fall for it.

onde [ˈõndʒi] *adv* where; **por ~ vamos?** which way are we going?

ondulado, -da [õnduˈladu. -da] *adj (cabelo)* wavy; *(superfície)* rippled.

oneroso, -osa [oneˈrozu. -ɔza] *adj* expensive.

ONG *f (abrev de Organização Não Governamental)* NGO.

ônibus [ˈonibuʃ] *m inv (Br)* bus.

ónix [ˈɔniks] *m* onyx.

ontem [ˈõntẽ] *adv* yesterday; **~ de manhã/à tarde** yesterday morning/afternoon; **~ à noite** last night.

ONU [ˈɔnu] *f (abrev de Organização das Nações Unidas)* UN.

onze [ˈõzi] *num* eleven, → **seis**.

opaco, -ca [oˈpaku. -ka] *adj* opaque.

opala [oˈpala] *f* opal.

opção [opˈsãw] (*pl* **-ões** [-õjʃ]) *f* option.

ópera [ˈɔpera] *f* opera.

operação [operaˈsãw] (*pl* **-ões** [-õjʃ]) *f* operation; *(comercial)* transaction.

operador, -ra [operaˈdo(x). -ra] (*mpl* **-res** [-riʃ], *fpl* **-s** [-ʃ]) *m, f*: **~ de computadores** computer operator.

operar [opeˈra(x)] *vi (MED)* to operate ◆ *vt (MED)* to operate on.

❏ **operar-se** *vp (realizar-se)* to take place.

operário, -ria [opeˈrarju. -rja] *m, f* worker.

opereta [opeˈreta] *f* operetta.

opinar [opiˈna(x)] *vt* to think ◆ *vi* to give one's opinion.

opinião [opiˈnjãw] (*pl* **-ões** [-õjʃ]) *f* opinion; **na minha ~** in my opinion; **na ~ dele** in his opinion; **ser da ~ que** to be of the opinion that; **a ~ pública** public opinion.

ópio [ˈɔpju] *m* opium.

oponente [opoˈnẽntʃi] *mf* opponent.

opor-se [oˈpoxsi] *vp* to object; **~ a** to oppose.

oportunidade [opoxtuniˈdadʒi] *f* opportunity.

oportuno, -na [opoxˈtunu. -na] *adj* opportune.

oposição [opoziˈsãw] *f* opposition; *(diferença)* contrast; **a ~** *(POL)* the Opposition.

oposto, -osta [oˈpoʃtu. -ɔʃta] *adj* opposite ◆ *m*: **o ~** the opposite; **~ a** opposite.

opressão [opreˈsãw] (*pl* **-ões** [-õjʃ]) *f* oppression.

opressivo, -va [opreˈsivu. -va] *adj* oppressive.

opressões → opressão.

oprimir [opriˈmi(x)] *vt* to oppress.

optar [opˈta(x)] *vi* to choose; **~ por algo** to opt for sthg; **~ por fazer algo** to opt to do sthg, to choose to do sthg.

optimismo [otiˈmiʒmu] *m (Port)* = **otimismo**.

óptimo, -ma ['ɔtimu. -ma] *adj (Port)* = **ótimo**.

ora ['ɔra] *interj* come on! ♦ *conj* well ♦ *adv*: **por ~** for now; **~ essa!** well, well!; **~ ..., ~ ...** one minute ..., the next ....

oração [ora'sãw] *(pl -ões* [-õjʃ]) *f (prece)* prayer; *(frase)* clause.

orador, -ra [ora'do(x). -ra] *(mpl -res* [-riʃ]. *fpl -s* [-ʃ]) *m, f* (public) speaker.

oral [o'raw] *(pl -ais* [-ajʃ]) *adj & f* oral.

orangotango [orãŋgo'tãŋgu] *m* orangutang.

orar [o'ra(x)] *vi (discursar)* to give a speech; *(rezar)* to pray.

órbita [ˈɔxbita] *f (de olho)* socket; *(de planeta)* orbit; *(fig: de ação, influência)* sphere.

orçamento [oxsa'mẽntu] *m (de Estado, empresa)* budget; *(para trabalho, serviço)* estimate.

ordem ['ɔxdẽ] *(pl -ns* [-ʃ]) *f* order; **até segunda ~** until further notice; **de primeira ~** first-rate; **de tal ~ que** such that; **pôr algo em ~** to tidy sthg up; **por ~** in order; **por ~ de alguém** on the orders of sb; **sempre às ordens!** don't mention it!

ordenado [oxde'nadu] *m* wage.

ordenhar [oxde'ɲa(x)] *vt* to milk.

ordens → ordem.

ordinário, -ria [oxdʒi'narju. -rja] *adj (grosseiro)* crude.

orégano [o'reganu] *m (Br)* oregano.

orégão [o'rɛgãw] *m (Port)* = **orégano**.

orelha [o'reʎa] *f (ANAT)* ear; *(de calçado)* tongue.

orfanato [oxfa'natu] *m* orphanage.

órfão, -fã ['ɔxfãw. -fã] *m, f* orphan.

orfeão [ox'feãw] *(pl -ões* [-õjʃ]) *m* choral society.

orgânico, -ca [ox'ganiku. -ka] *adj* organic.

organismo [oxga'niʒmu] *m* body.

organização [oxganiza'sãw] *(pl -ões* [-õjʃ]) *f* organization.

órgão ['ɔxgãw] *m* organ; *(de empresa)* body; **~s sexuais** OU **genitais** sexual organs, genitals.

orgasmo [ox'gaʒmu] *m* orgasm.

orgia [ox'ʒia] *f* orgy.

orgulhar-se [oxgu'ʎaxsi] **: orgulhar-se de** *vp + prep* to be proud of.

orgulho [ox'guʎu] *m* pride.

orientação [orjẽnta'sãw] *(pl -ões* [-õjʃ]) *f* direction; **~ escolar** careers

advice *(at school)*; **~ profissional** careers advice.

oriental [orjẽn'taw] *(pl -ais* [-ajʃ]) *adj (do este)* eastern; *(do Extremo Oriente)* oriental.

❑ **orientais** *mpl*: **os orientais** the Orientals.

orientar [orjẽn'ta(x)] *vt (guiar)* to direct; *(aconselhar)* to advise.

❑ **orientar-se por** *vp + prep* to follow.

oriente [o'rjẽntʃi] *m* east.

❑ **Oriente** *m*: **o Oriente** the Orient.

orifício [ori'fisju] *m* orifice.

origem [o'riʒẽ] *(pl -ns* [-ʃ]) *f* origin.

original [oriʒi'naw] *(pl -ais* [-ajʃ]) *adj & m* original.

originar [oriʒi'na(x)] *vt* to cause.

❑ **originar-se** *vp* to arise.

oriundo, -da [o'rjũndu. -da] *adj*: **~ de** from.

orixá [ori'ʃa] *mf (Br)* god or goddess of any of the Afro-Brazilian religions.

ornamentar [oxnamẽn'ta(x)] *vt* to decorate.

ornamento [oxna'mẽntu] *m* ornament.

ornitologia [oxnitolo'ʒia] *f* ornithology.

orquestra [ox'kɛʃtra] *f* orchestra.

orquídea [ox'kidʒia] *f* orchid.

ortografia [oxtogra'fia] *f* spelling.

ortopedia [oxtope'dʒia] *f* orthopaedics *(sg)*.

ortopédico, -ca [oxtp'pedʒiku. -ka] *adj* orthopaedic.

ortopedista [oxtope'dʒiʃta] *mf* orthopaedic surgeon.

orvalho [ox'vaʎu] *m* dew.

os → o.

oscilação [oʃsila'sãw] *(pl -ões* [-õjʃ]) *f (balanço)* swinging; *(variação)* fluctuation.

oscilar [oʃsi'la(x)] *vi (balançar)* to swing; *(variar)* to fluctuate; **~ entre** to fluctuate between.

osso ['osu] *(pl ossos* ['ɔsuʃ]) *m* bone.

ostensivamente [oʃtẽˌsiva'mẽntʃi] *adv* ostentatiously.

ostensivo, -va [oʃtẽ'sivu. -va] *adj (provocatório)* blatant; *(exibicionista)* ostentatious.

ostentar [oʃtẽn'ta(x)] *vt* to show off.

ostra ['oʃtra] *f* oyster.

OTAN [o'tã] *f (abrev de Organização do Tratado do Atlântico Norte)* = **NATO**.

otimismo [otʃiˈmiʒmu] *m (Br)* optimism.

ótimo, -ma [ˈɔtʃimu, -ma] *adj (Br)* great ♦ *interj (Br)* great!, excellent!

otorrinolaringologista [ˌoto-
ˌxinolaˌrĩŋɡoloˈʒiʃta] *mf* ear, nose and throat specialist.

ou [o] *conj* or; ~ ... ~ either ... or.

ouço [ˈosu] → **ouvir**.

ouriço [oˈrisu] *m (de castanheiro)* shell.

ouriço-cacheiro [oˌrisukaˈʃejru] *(pl* **ouriços-cacheiros** [oˌrisuʃkaˈʃejruʃ]) *m* hedgehog.

ouriço-do-mar [oˌrisuduˈma(x)] *(pl* **ouriços-do-mar** [oˌrisuʒduˈma(x)]) *m* sea urchin.

ourives [oˈriviʃ] *mf inv* jeweller.

ourivesaria [orivezaˈria] *f* jeweller's (shop).

ouro [ˈoru] gold; ~ **de lei** *19.25-carat gold*.

⌐ ouros *mpl (naipe de cartas)* diamonds.

Ouro Preto [ˌoruˈpretu] *s* Ouro Preto.

ousadia [ozaˈdʒia] *f* audacity.

ousar [oˈza(x)] *vt* to dare to.

outdoor [awtˈdɔr] *m (propaganda)* outdoor advertising; *(cartaz)* hoarding *(Brit)*, billboard *(Am)*.

outono [oˈtonu] *m* autumn *(Brit)*, fall *(Am)*.

outro, -tra [ˈotru, -tra] *adj* another *(sg)*, other *(pl)* ♦ *pron (outra coisa)* another *(sg)*, others *(pl)*; *(outra pessoa)* someone else; **o ~/a outra** the other (one); **os ~s** the others; ~ **copo** another glass; **~s dois copos** another two

glasses; ~ **dia** another day; **no ~ dia** *(no dia seguinte)* the next day; *(relativo a dia passado)* the other day; **um ou ~** one or the other; **um após o ~** one after the other.

outubro [oˈtubru] *m* October, → **setembro**.

ouve [ˈovi] → **ouvir**.

ouvido [oˈvidu] *m (ANAT)* ear; *(audição)* hearing; **dar ~s a alguém** to listen to sb; **ser todo ~s** to be all ears; **ter bom ~** to have good hearing; **tocar de ~** to play by ear.

ouvinte [oˈvĩtʃi] *mf* listener.

ouvir [oˈvi(x)] *vt & vi* to hear; **você está ouvindo?** are you listening?; **estar ouvindo algo/alguém** to be listening to sthg/sb.

ovação [ovaˈsãw] *(pl* **-ões** [-õjʃ]) *f* ovation.

oval [oˈvaw] *(pl* **-ais** [-ajʃ]) *adj* oval.

ovário [oˈvarju] *m* ovary.

ovelha [oˈveʎa] *f* sheep; *(fêmea)* ewe; ~ **negra** black sheep.

OVNI [ˈɔvni] *m (abrev de Objeto Voador Não Identificado)* UFO.

ovo [ˈovu] *(pl* **ovos** [ˈɔvuʃ]) *m* egg; ~ **cozido/escalfado** boiled/poached egg; ~ **estrelado** fried egg; **~s mexidos** scrambled eggs; **~s de Páscoa** Easter eggs.

óvulo [ˈɔvulu] *m* ovum.

oxigénio [ɔksiˈʒenju] *m (Port)* = **oxigênio**.

oxigênio [oksiˈʒenju] *m (Br)* oxygen.

ozônio [oˈzonju] *m (Br)* ozone.

ozono [oˈzonu] *m (Port)* = **ozônio**.

P

p. *(abrev de página)* p.

P. *(abrev de Praça)* = Sq.

pá ['pa] *f (utensílio)* spade ♦ *m (Port: fam: forma de tratamento)* mate *(Brit)*, man *(Am)*.

pacato, -ta [pa'katu, -ta] *adj* easygoing.

paciência [pa'sjēsja] *f* patience; **perder a ~** to lose one's patience; **ter ~** to be patient.

paciente [pa'sjēntʃi] *adj & mf* patient.

pacífico, -ca [pa'sifiku, -ka] *adj* peaceful.
⊐ **Pacífico** *m*: **o Pacífico** the Pacific.

pacifista [pasi'fiʃta] *mf* pacifist.

paçoca [pa'sɔka] *f (prato) a dish made with fresh or dried meat, cooked and minced, then fried and mixed with cornflour or cassava; (doce) dessert made from ground peanuts, milk, eggs and sugar.*

pacote [pa'kɔtʃi] *m* packet; *(em turismo)* package; **~ de açúcar** *(pequeno)* packet of sugar.

padaria [pada'ria] *f* bakery.

padecer [pade'se(x)] : **padecer de** *v + prep* to suffer from.

padeiro, -ra [pa'dejru, -ra] *m, f* baker.

padrão [pa'drãw] *(pl -ões* [-õjʃ]) *m (de produto)* model; *(de tecido)* pattern; **~ de vida** standard of living.

padrasto [pa'draʃtu] *m* stepfather.

padre ['padri] *m* priest.

padrinho [pa'driɲu] *m* godfather.

padrões → **padrão**.

pães → **pão**.

pág. *(abrev de página)* p.

pagamento [paga'mēntu] *m* payment; **~ em dinheiro** OU **numerário** cash payment; **~ a prestações** hire purchase *(Brit)*, installment plan *(Am)*.

pagar [pa'ga(x)] *vt* to pay; *(estudos)* to pay for; *(fig: consequências)* to suffer ♦ *vi*: **~ por** *(sofrer consequências por)* to pay for; **~ algo a alguém** to pay sb sthg; **quanto você pagou pelo bilhete?** how much did you pay for the ticket? **~ à vista** to pay cash up front.

página ['paʒina] *f* page; **as Páginas Amarelas** the Yellow Pages[®].

pago, -ga ['pagu, -ga] *pp* → **pagar**.

pagode [pa'gɔdʒi] *m (fam: farra)* fun.

págs. *(abrev de páginas)* pp.

pai ['paj] *m* father.

pai-de-santo [pajdʒi'sãntu] *(pl pais-de-santo* [pajʒdʒi'sãntu]) *m "candomblé" or "umbanda" priest.*

painel [paj'nɛw] *(pl -éis* [-ɛjʃ]) *m* panel; *(de veículo)* dashboard; **~ solar** solar panel.

paio ['paju] *m very lean "chouriço".*

pais ['pajʃ] *mpl (progenitores)* parents.

país [pa'iʃ] *(pl -ses* [-ziʃ]) *m* country.

paisagem [paj'zaʒãj] *(pl -ns* [-ʃ]) *f (vista)* view; *(pintura)* landscape.

País de Gales [pa,iʒdʒi'galiʃ] *m*: **o ~** Wales.

países → **país**.

paixão [paj'ʃãw] *(pl -ões* [-õjʃ]) *f* passion.

pajé [pa'ʒɛ] *m (Br)* witch doctor.

palacete [pala'setʃi] *m* small palace.

palácio [pa'lasju] *m* palace; **Palácio da Justiça** Law Courts *(pl)*.

paladar [pala'da(x)] *(pl -res* [-riʃ]) *m* taste.

palafita [pala'fita] *f* house on stilts.

palavra [pa'lavra] *f* word ♦ *interj* honest!; **dar a ~ a alguém** to give sb the opportunity to speak.

palavrão [pala'vrãw] *(pl -ões* [-õjʃ]) *m* swearword.

palavras-cruzadas [pa,lavraʃkru-'zadaʃ] *fpl* crossword (puzzle) *(sg)*.

palavrões → **palavrão**.

palco ['pawku] *m* stage.
palerma [pa'lɛxma] *mf* fool.
palestra [pa'lɛʃtra] *f* lecture.
paleta [pa'leta] *f* palette.
paletó [pale'tɔ] *m* jacket.
palha ['paʎa] *f* straw.
palhaço [pa'ʎasu] *m* clown.
palhinha [pa'ʎiɲa] *f* straw.
pálido, -da ['palidu, -da] *adj* pale.
paliteiro [pali'tejru] *m* toothpick
holder.
palito [pa'litu] *m (para dentes)* toothpick; ~ **de fósforo** matchstick; **ser um**
~ *(fig: pessoa)* to be as thin as a rake.
palma ['pawma] *f* palm.
⊐ **palmas** *fpl* clapping *(sg)*; **bater ~s** to
clap; **uma salva de ~s** a round of
applause.
palmeira [paw'mejra] *f* palm tree.
palmito [paw'mitu] *m* palm heart.
palmo ['pawmu] *m* (hand) span; ~ **a** ~
inch by inch.
PALOP *mpl (abrev de Países Africanos
de Língua Oficial Portuguesa):* **os** ~
acronym for African countries where
Portuguese is an official language.
palpável [paw'pavɛw] *(pl* -**eis** [-ɛjʃ])
adj tangible.
pálpebra ['pawpebra] *f* eyelid.
palpitação [pawpita'sãw] *(pl* -**ões**
[-õjʃ]) *f* beating.
palpitar [pawpi'ta(x)] *vi* to beat.
palpite [paw'pitʃi] *m* tip; *(suposição)*
hunch.
paludismo [palu'dʒizmu] *m* malaria.
pamonha [pa'moɲa] *f cake made from
maize, coconut milk, butter, cinnamon,
sweet herbs and sugar, and baked
wrapped in banana skin.*
Panamá [pana'ma] *m:* **o** ~ Panama.
pancada [pãŋ'kada] *f (com pau, mão)*
blow; *(choque)* knock; *(de relógio)*
stroke; **dar** ~ **em alguém** to beat sb
up; ~ **d'água** sudden downpour; **ser** ~
(fam) to be crazy.
pâncreas ['pãŋkrjaʃ] *m inv* pancreas.
panda ['pãnda] *m* panda.
pandeiro [pãn'dejru] *m* tambourine.
pandemónio [pãnde'mɔnju] *m (Port)*
= **pandemônio**.
pandemônio [pãnde'monju] *m (Br)*
pandemonium.
pane ['pani] *f* breakdown.
panela [pa'nɛla] *f* pot; ~ **de pressão**
pressure cooker.

panfleto [pã'fletu] *m* pamphlet.
pânico ['paniku] *m* panic; **entrar em** ~
to panic.
pano ['panu] *m (tecido)* cloth; *(em
teatro)* curtain; ~ **de fundo** backdrop.
panorama [pano'rama] *m* panorama.
panqueca [pãŋ'kɛka] *f* pancake.
pantanal [pãnta'naw] *(pl* -**ais** [-ajʃ]) *m*
swampland.
⊐ **Pantanal** *m:* **o Pantanal** the
Pantanal.
pântano ['pãntanu] *m* swamp.
pantera [pãn'tɛra] *f* panther.
pantomima [pãnto'mima] *f* mime,
dumb show.
pantufas [pãn'tufaʃ] *fpl* slippers.
pão ['pãw] *(pl* **pães** ['pãjʃ]) *m* bread; ~
de centeio rye bread; ~ **de fôrma** loaf;
~ **francês** roll; ~ **integral** wholemeal
bread; ~ **de leite** *small sweet bread
glazed with egg yolk before baking;* ~
ralado *(Port)* breadcrumbs *(pl);* ~ **de
segunda** crusty white loaf; **o Pão de
Açúcar** Sugar Loaf Mountain; **comer o**
~ **que o diabo amassou** *(fig)* to have a
rough time of it.
pão-de-ló [ˌpãwdʒi'lɔ] *(pl* **pães-de-ló**
[ˌpãjʒdʒi'lɔ]) *m* sponge cake.
papa ['papa] *f (para bebê)* baby food
◆ *m* pope; *(fig: ás)* ace.
papagaio [papa'gaju] *m (ave)* parrot;
(brinquedo) kite.
papeira [pa'pejra] *f (Port)* mumps
(sg).
papel [pa'pɛw] *(pl* -**éis** [-ɛjʃ]) *m* paper;
~ **A4** A4 paper; ~ **de alumínio** tinfoil;
~ **de carta** writing paper; ~ **de
embrulho** wrapping paper; ~ **higiênico**
toilet paper; ~ **de máquina** typing
paper; ~ **de parede** wallpaper; ~
químico *(Port)* carbon paper; ~ **recicla-
do** recycled paper; ~ **vegetal** *(de cozinha)* greaseproof paper; *(de desenho)*
tracing paper.
papelão [pape'lãw] *m* cardboard.
papelaria [papela'ria] *f* stationer's
(shop).
papel-carbono [paˌpɛukax'bonu] *m
(Br)* carbon paper.
papo ['papu] *m (de ave)* crop; *(Br: conversa)* chat; **levar** OU **bater um** ~ *(Br:
fam)* to (have a) chat; ~**s de anjo** *small
pastries made of syrup, jam, eggs and cinnamon, dusted with sugar on serving.*
papo-furado [ˌpapufu'radu] *m (Br:
fam)* nonsense.

papoila [pa'pojla] f = **papoula**.

papo-seco [ˌpapu'seku] (pl **papos-secos** [ˌpapuʃ'sekuʃ]) m roll.

papoula [pa'pola] f poppy.

paquerar [pake'ra(x)] vt (Br: fam) to flirt with, to chat up ◆ vi (Br: fam) to flirt.

paquete [pa'ketʃi] m (navio) (steam-powered) ocean liner.

par ['pa(x)] (pl **-res** [-riʃ]) adj (número) even ◆ m pair; (casal) couple; **estar a ~ de algo** to be up to date on sthg; **~es masculinos/femininos/mistos** (Port: em tênis) men's/women's/mixed doubles; **a ~** side by side; **aos ~es** in pairs.

para ['para] prep 1. (exprime finalidade, destinação) for; **um telefonema ~ o senhor** a phone call for you; **queria algo ~ comer** I would like something to eat; **~ que serve isto?** what's this for?
2. (indica motivo, objetivo) (in order) to; **cheguei mais cedo ~ arranjar lugar** I arrived early (in order) to get a place; **era só ~ lhe agradar** I only wanted to please you.
3. (indica direção) towards; **apontou ~ cima/baixo** he pointed upwards/downwards; **olhei ~ ela** I looked at her; **seguiu ~ o aeroporto** he headed for the airport; **vá ~ casa!** go home!
4. (relativo a tempo) for; **quero isso pronto ~ amanhã** I want it done for tomorrow; **estará pronto ~ a semana/o ano** it'll be ready next week/year; **são quinze ~ as três** it's a quarter to three (Brit), it's a quarter of three (Am).
5. (em comparações): **é caro demais ~ as minhas posses** it's too expensive for my budget; **~ o que come, está magro** he's thin, considering how much he eats.
6. (relativo a opinião, sentimento): **~ mim** as far as I'm concerned.
7. (exprime a iminência): **estar ~ fazer algo** to be about to do sthg; **o ônibus está ~ sair** the bus is about to leave; **ele está ~ chegar** he'll be here any minute now.
8. (em locuções): **~ mais de** well over; **~ que** so that; **é ~ já!** coming up!

parabéns [para'bẽʃ] mpl congratulations ◆ interj (em geral) congratulations!; (por aniversário) happy birthday!; **dar os ~ a alguém** (em geral) to

congratulate sb; (por aniversário) to wish sb a happy birthday; **você está de ~** you're to be congratulated.

parabólica [para'bɔlika] f satellite dish.

pára-brisas [ˌpara'brizaʃ] m inv windscreen (Brit), windshield (Am).

pára-choques [ˌpara'ʃɔkiʃ] m inv bumper.

parada [pa'rada] f (de jogo) bet, stake; (militar) parade; **~ (de ônibus)** (Br) (bus) stop.

paradeiro [para'dejru] m where-abouts (pl).

parado, -da [pa'radu, -da] adj (pessoa, animal) motionless; (carro) stationary; (máquina) switched off; (sem vida) dull.

paradoxo [para'dɔksu] m paradox.

parafina [para'fina] f paraffin.

parafrasear [parafra'zja(x)] vt to paraphrase.

parafuso [para'fuzu] m screw.

paragem [pa'raʒẽ] (pl **-ns** [-ʃ]) f stop, halt; **~ (de autocarro)** (Port) (bus) stop.

parágrafo [pa'ragrafu] m paragraph.

Paraguai [para'gwaj] m: **o ~** Paraguay.

paraíso [para'izu] m paradise.

pára-lamas [ˌpara'lamaʃ] m inv mud-guard (Brit), fender (Am).

paralelo, -la [para'lɛlu, -la] adj & m parallel; **sem ~** unparalleled.

paralisar [parali'za(x)] vt to paralyse.

paralisia [parali'zia] f paralysis.

paralítico, -ca [para'litiku, -ka] m, f paralytic.

paranóico, -ca [para'nɔiku, -ka] m, f (fam) nutter ◆ adj paranoid.

parapeito [para'pejtu] m window-sill.

pára-quedas [ˌpara'kedaʃ] m inv parachute.

pára-quedista [ˌparake'diʃta] mf parachutist.

parar [pa'ra(x)] vt & vi to stop; **"pare, escute, olhe"** "stop, look and listen"; **ir ~ em** to end up in; **~ de fazer algo** to stop doing sthg; **sem ~** non-stop.

pára-raios [ˌpara'xajuʃ] m inv light-ning conductor (Brit), lightning rod (Am).

parasita [para'zita] m parasite.

parceiro, -ra [pax'sejru, -ra] m, f partner.

parcela [pax'sɛla] f (de soma) item; (fragmento) fragment, bit.

parceria [paxse'ria] f partnership.

parcial [par'sjaw] (pl **-ais** [-ajʃ]) adj (não completo) partial; (faccioso) biased.

parcómetro [par'kɔmetru] m (Port) = **parquímetro**.

pardal [pax'daw] (pl **-ais** [-ajʃ]) m house sparrow.

pardo, -da ['paxdu. -da] adj dark grey.

parecer [pare'se(x)] vi to look ◆ m opinion ◆ v impess: **parece que vai chover** it looks like rain, it looks as if it's going to rain; **parece-me que sim** I think so; **ao que parece** by the look of things; **que lhe parece?** what do you think?

❑ **parecer-se** vp to look alike; **~-se com alguém** to look like sb.

parecido, -da [pare'sidu. -da] adj similar; **são muito ~s** they are very alike.

paredão [pare'dãw] (pl **-ões** [-õjʃ]) m thick wall.

parede [pa'redʒi] f wall; **morar ~s meias com** to live next door to.

paredões → **paredão**.

parente, -ta [pa'rẽntʃi. -ta] m, f relative; **~ próximo** close relative.

parêntese [pa'rẽntezi] m (sinal) bracket; (frase) parenthesis; **entre ~s** in brackets.

pares → **par**.

pargo ['paxgu] m sea bream.

parir [pa'ri(x)] vt to give birth to ◆ vi to give birth.

parlamento [paxla'mẽntu] m parliament.

paróquia [pa'rɔkja] f parish.

parque ['paxki] m park; **~ de campismo** (Port) campsite (Brit), campground (Am); **~ de diversões** amusement park; **~ de estacionamento** car park (Brit), parking lot (Am); **~ industrial** industrial estate; **~ infantil** (Port) playground; **~ nacional** national park; **~ natural** nature reserve.

parquímetro [pax'kimetru] m parking meter.

parte ['paxtʃi] f part; (fração) bit; (JUR) party; **dar ~ de** (informar) to report; **fazer ~ de** to be part of; **tomar ~ de** to take part in; **em outra ~** somewhere else; **por toda a ~** everywhere; **da ~ de** on behalf of; **de ~ a ~** mutual; **em ~** in part.

parteira [pax'tejra] f midwife.

participação [paxtʃisipa'sãw] (pl **-ões** [-õjʃ]) f participation; (comunicado) announcement; (em negócio) involvement; (a polícia, autoridade) report.

participante [paxtʃisi'pãntʃi] mf participant.

participar [paxtʃisi'pa(x)] vi to participate ◆ vt: **~ algo a alguém** (informar) to inform sb of sthg; (comunicar) to report sthg to sb; **~ de algo** to take part in sthg.

particípio [paxtʃi'sipju] m participle; **~ passado/presente** past/present participle.

particular [paxtʃiku'la(x)] (pl **-res** [-riʃ]) adj (individual) particular; (privado) private, privately owned.

partida [pax'tʃida] f (saída) departure; (em esporte) match; **estar de ~** to be about to leave; **à ~** at the beginning.

partidário, -ria [partʃi'darju. -rja] m, f supporter.

partido, -da [pax'tʃidu. -da] adj broken ◆ m: **~** (político) (political) party.

partilhar [paxtʃi'ʎa(x)] vt to share.

partir [pax'tʃi(x)] vt to break ◆ vi (ir embora) to leave, to depart; **ele partiu para o estrangeiro** he went abroad; **~ de** (lugar) to leave; **a ~ de** from; **a ~ de agora** from now on.

❑ **partir-se** vp (quebrar-se) to break.

parto ['paxtu] m birth.

parvo, -va ['paxvu. -va] m, f idiot.

Páscoa ['paʃkwa] f Easter; **~ feliz!** Happy Easter!

pasmado, -da [paʒ'madu. -da] adj dumbstruck.

passa ['pasa] f (fruto) raisin.

passadeira [pasa'dejra] f (Port: para peões) pedestrian crossing.

passado, -da [pa'sadu. -da] adj (no passado) past; (anterior) last ◆ m past; **mal ~** (CULIN: bife, carne) rare; **bem ~** (CULIN: bife, carne) well-done.

passageiro, -ra [pasa'ʒejru. -ra] m, f passenger ◆ adj passing.

passagem [pa'saʒẽ] (pl **-ns** [-ʃ]) f passage; (bilhete) ticket; **~ de ano** New Year, Hogmanay (Scot); **~ de ida** (Br) single (ticket) (Brit), one-way ticket (Am); **~ de ida e volta** (Br) return (ticket) (Brit), round-trip ticket (Am); **~ de nível** level crossing; **~ subterrânea** subway (Brit), underpass (Am).

passaporte [pasa'pɔrtʃi] m passport.

passar [pa'sa(x)] *vt* 1. *(deslizar, filtrar)*: ~ **algo por algo** to pass sthg through sthg; **ela passou a mão pelo cabelo** she ran her hand through her hair; **passou o creme bronzeador nos braços** he put suntan cream on his arms; ~ **por água** to rinse.
2. *(chegar, fazer chegar)* to pass; **pode me passar o sal?** would you pass me the salt?
3. *(a ferro)*: ~ **algo (a ferro)**, ~ **(a ferro) algo** to iron sthg; **você já passou a roupa (a ferro)?** have you done the ironing yet?
4. *(contagiar)* to pass on.
5. *(mudar)*: ~ **algo para** to move sthg to.
6. *(ultrapassar)* to pass.
7. *(tempo)* to spend; **passei um ano em Portugal** I spent a year in Portugal.
8. *(exame)* to pass.
9. *(fronteira)* to cross.
10. *(vídeo, disco)* to put on.
11. *(em televisão, cinema)* to show.
12. *(admitir)*: **deixar** ~ **algo** to let sthg pass.
♦ *vi* 1. *(ir, circular)* to go; **o (ônibus) 7 não passa por aqui** the number 7 doesn't come this way.
2. *(revisor, ônibus)*: **já passou o (ônibus) 7/o revisor?** has the number 7/the ticket inspector been?
3. *(tempo)* to go by; **já passa das dez horas** it's past ten o'clock; **o tempo passa muito depressa** time flies.
4. *(terminar)* to be over; **o verão já passou** summer's over; **a dor já passou** the pain's gone.
5. *(a nível diferente)* to go up; **ele passou para o segundo ano** he went up into second year; **passa para primeira (velocidade)** go into first (gear); **quero ~ para um nível mais alto** I want to move up to a more advanced level.
6. *(mudar de ação, tema)*: ~ **a** to move on to.
7. *(em locuções)*: **como você tem passado?** *(de saúde)* how have you been?; ~ **bem** *(tempo, férias)* to enjoy; **passe bem!** good day to you!; ~ **mal** *(de saúde)* to feel ill; **não** ~ **de** to be no more than; ~ **(bem) sem** to be fine without; **não** ~ **sem** never to be without; **o que passou, passou** let bygones be bygones.

⊐ **passar por** *v + prep (ser considerado*

como) to pass as OU for; *(fig: atravessar)* to go through; **fazer-se** ~ **por** to pass o.s. off as.
⊐ **passar-se** *vp (acontecer)* to happen; **o que é que se passa?** what's going on?.
passarela [pasa'rɛla] *f (Br: de rua, estrada)* pedestrian crossing; *(para desfile de moda)* catwalk.
pássaro [pasaru] *m* bird.
passatempo [ˌpasa'tẽmpu] *m* hobby, pastime.
passe ['pasi] *m (de ônibus)* (bus) pass; *(de trem)* season ticket.
passear [pa'sja(x)] *vt (cão)* to walk
♦ *vi* to go for a walk.
passeata [pa'sjata] *f (passeio)* stroll; *(Br: marcha de protesto)* demonstration.
passeio [pa'saju] *m (em rua)* pavement *(Brit)*, sidewalk *(Am)*; *(caminhada)* walk.
passional [pasjo'naw] *(pl* -**ais** [-ajʃ]*) adj* passionate.
passista [pa'siʃta] *mf (Br)* skilled samba dancer, especially one who dances in Carnival parades in Brazil.
passível [pa'sivɛw] *(pl* -**eis** [-ejʃ]*) adj*: ~ **de** liable to.
passivo, -va [pa'sivu, -va] *adj* passive
♦ *m (COM)* liabilities *(pl)*.
passo ['pasu] *m (movimento)* step; *(modo de andar)* walk; *(ritmo)* pace; **dar o primeiro** ~ to make the first move; **a dois** ~**s (de)** round the corner (from); **ao** ~ **que** whilst; ~ **a** ~ step by step.
pasta ['paʃta] *f* briefcase; *(de escola)* satchel; *(para papéis)* folder; *(de ministro)* portfolio; *(massa)* paste; ~ **dentífrica** OU **de dentes** toothpaste.
pastar [paʃ'ta(x)] *vi* to graze.
pastel [paʃ'tɛw] *(pl* -**éis** [-ɛjʃ]*) m* pie; *(em pintura)* pastel; *(Port: bolo)* cake; ~ **de bacalhau** small cod fishcake; ~ **de carne** = sausage roll; ~ **de galinha** chicken pasty.
pastelaria [paʃtela'ria] *f (local)* patisserie; *(comida)* pastries *(pl)*.
pasteurizado, -da [paʃtewri'zadu, -da] *adj* pasteurized.
pastilha [paʃ'tiʎa] *f (doce)* pastille; *(medicamento)* tablet, pill; ~ **(elástica)** *(Port)* (chewing) gum; ~ **para a garganta** throat lozenge; ~ **para a tosse** cough sweet.
pasto ['paʃtu] *m* pasture.
pastor, -ra [paʃ'to(x), -ra] *(mpl* -**res** [-riʃ], *fpl* -**s** [-ʃ]*) m, f* shepherd *(f* shep-

herdess) ♦ *m* minister.

pata ['pata] *f (perna de animal)* leg; *(pé de gato, cão)* paw; *(pé de cavalo, cabra)* hoof.

patamar [pata'ma(x)] *(pl -res* [-riʃ]) *m* landing.

paté [pa'te] *m (Port)* = **patê**.

patê [pa'te] *m (Br)* pâté.

patente [pa'tẽtʃi] *adj (visível)* obvious ♦ *f (de máquina, invento)* patent; *(de militar)* rank.

paternal [patex'naw] *(pl -ais* [-ajʃ]) *adj (afetuoso)* fatherly.

pateta [pa'teta] *mf* twit.

patético, -ca [pa'tɛtʃiku, -ka] *adj* pathetic.

patife [pa'tʃifi] *m* scoundrel.

patim [pa'tʃĩ] *(pl -ns* [-ʃ]) *m (de rodas)* roller skate; *(de gelo)* ice skate.

patinação [patʃina'sãw] *f (Br)* skating; ~ **artística** figure skating; ~ **no gelo** ice skating.

patinagem [patʃi'naʒẽ] *f (Port)* = **patinação**.

patinar [patʃi'na(x)] *vi (com patins)* to skate; *(veículo)* to spin.

patins → **patim**.

pátio ['patʃiu] *m* patio.

pato ['patu] *m* duck.

patologia [patolo'ʒia] *f* pathology.

patológico, -ca [pato'lɔʒiku, -ka] *adj* pathological.

patrão, -troa [pa'trãw, -'troa] *(mpl -ões* [-õjʃ], *fpl -s* [-ʃ]) *m, f* boss.

pátria ['patria] *f* native country.

património [patri'mɔnju] *m (Port)* = **patrimônio**.

patrimônio [patri'monju] *m (Br) (de empresa, fundação)* assets *(pl)*; *(herança)* inheritance; ~ **nacional** national heritage.

patriota [patri'ɔta] *mf* patriot.

patroa → **patrão**.

patrocinador, -ra [patrosina'do(x), -ra] *(mpl -res* [-riʃ], *fpl -s* [-ʃ]) *m, f* sponsor.

patrocinar [patrosi'na(x)] *vt* to sponsor.

patrões → **patrão**.

patrulha [pa'truʎa] *f* patrol.

pau ['paw] *m* stick.

⨽ **paus** *mpl (naipe de cartas)* clubs.

paulista [paw'liʃta] *mf* native/inhabitant of São Paulo.

pausa ['pawza] *f (intervalo)* break;

(silêncio) pause.

pauta ['pawta] *f (de alunos)* register; *(de música)* stave.

pavão [pa'vãw] *(pl -ões* [-õjʃ]) *m* peacock.

pavê [pa've] *m* liqueur-soaked sponge fingers set in layers with a sweet filling made from melted chocolate, egg yolks and butter.

pavilhão [pavi'ʎãw] *(pl -ões* [-õjʃ]) *m* pavilion; ~ **esportivo** sports pavilion.

pavimentar [pavimẽ'ta(x)] *vt* to pave.

pavimento [pavi'mẽtu] *m (de estrada, rua)* road surface; *(andar de edifício)* floor.

pavões → **pavão**.

pavor [pa'vo(x)] *m* terror; **ter ~ de** to be terrified of.

paz ['paʃ] *(pl -zes* [-ziʃ]) *f* peace; **deixar algo/alguém em ~** to leave sthg/sb in peace; **fazer as ~es** to make (it) up; **que descanse em ~** (may he/she) rest in peace.

PC *m (abrev de Personal Computer)* PC.

Pça. *(abrev de praça)* Sq.

pé ['pɛ] *m* foot; *(de planta)* stem, stalk; *(em vinho)* dregs *(pl)*; **andar na ponta dos ~s** to walk on tiptoe; **pôr-se de ~** to stand up; **ter ~** *(em água)* to be able to stand; **não ter ~** *(em água)* not to be able to touch the bottom; **a ~** on foot; **ao ~ de** near; **em ~** de ~ standing (up); **em ~ de igualdade** on an equal footing.

peão [pjãw] *(pl -ões* [-õjʃ]) *m (Port: indivíduo a pé)* pedestrian; *(em xadrez)* pawn.

peça ['pɛsa] *f* piece; *(divisão de casa)* room; ~ **(de teatro)** play.

pecado [pe'kadu] *m* sin.

pechincha [pe'ʃiʃa] *f* bargain.

peço ['pɛsu] → **pedir**.

peculiar [peku'lja(x)] *(pl -es* [-iʃ]) *adj* peculiar.

pedaço [pe'dasu] *m* piece; *(de tempo)* while; **andamos um bom ~** we walked a good part of the way; **estou aqui há ~** I've been here for a while; **estar caindo aos ~s** to be falling to bits.

pedágio [pe'daʒju] *m (Br)* toll.

pedal [pe'daw] *(pl -ais* [-ajʃ]) *m* pedal.

pede ['pɛdʒi] → **pedir**.

pé-de-cabra [pɛde'kabra] *(pl pés-de-cabra* [pɛʒde'kabra]) *m* crowbar.

pé-de-moleque [ˌpɛdʒimoˈlɛki] (pl **pés-de-moleque** [ˌpɛdʒimoˈlɛki]) m hard peanut nougat.

pedestal [pedeˈʃtaw] (pl -ais [-ajʃ]) m pedestal.

pedestre [peˈdɛʃtri] adj (zona, faixa) pedestrian (antes de s) ◆ m (Br: indivíduo a pé) pedestrian.

pediatra [peˈdʒjatra] mf paediatrician.

pediatria [pedʒjaˈtria] f paediatrics (sg).

pedido [peˈdʒidu] m request; (em restaurante) order; **a ~ de alguém** at sb's request.

pedinte [peˈdʒĩtʃi] mf beggar.

pedir [peˈdʒi(x)] vt (em restaurante, bar) to order; (preço) to ask ◆ vi (mendigar) to beg; **~ algo a alguém** to ask sb for sthg; **~ a alguém que faça algo** to ask sb to do sthg; **~ algo emprestado a alguém** to borrow sthg from sb.

pedra [ˈpedra] f stone; (lápide) tombstone; (granizo) hailstone; (de isqueiro) flint; (de dominó) domino; **~ (preciosa)** precious stone, gem.

pedra-pomes [ˌpedraˈpomiʃ] (pl **pedras-pomes** [ˌpedraʃˈpomiʃ]) f pumice stone.

pedra-sabão [ˌpedrasaˈbãw] (pl **pedras-sabão** [ˌpedraʃsaˈbãw]) f (Br) soapstone.

pedreiro [peˈdrejru] m bricklayer.

pega [ˈpega] f (ave) magpie.

pegada [peˈgada] f footprint.

pegado, -da [peˈgadu, -da] adj (colado) stuck; (contíguo) adjoining.

pegajoso, -osa [pegaˈʒozu, -ɔza] adj sticky.

pegar [peˈga(x)] vt to catch; (hábito, vício, mania) to pick up ◆ vi (motor) to start; (idéia, moda) to catch on; (planta) to take; **peguei uma gripe** I got the flu; **~ em algo** to pick sthg up; **~ fogo em algo** to set fire to sthg; **~ no sono** to fall asleep.

❏ **pegar-se** vp (agarrar-se) to stick; (brigar) to come to blows.

peito [ˈpejtu] m (seio) breast; (parte do tronco) chest; (de camisa, blusa) front.

peitoril [pejtoˈriw] (pl -is [-iʃ]) m windowsill.

peixaria [pejʃaˈria] f fishmonger's (shop).

peixe [ˈpejʃi] m fish; **~ congelado** frozen fish.

❏ **Peixes** m inv (signo do Zodíaco) Pisces.

peixe-agulha [ˌpejʃaˈguʎa] m garfish.

peixe-espada [ˌpejʃeʃˈpada] m scabbard fish.

peixe-vermelho [ˌpejʃevexˈmeʎu] m carp.

pejorativo, -va [peʒoraˈtʃivu, -va] adj pejorative.

pela [ˈpela] = **por + a**, → **por**.

pelado, -da [peˈladu, -da] adj (cabeça) shorn; (Br: fam: nu) starkers; (Port: fruta) peeled.

pele [ˈpɛli] f skin; (couro) leather.

pelica [peˈlika] f kid (leather).

pelicano [peliˈkanu] m pelican.

película [peˈlikula] f film; **~ aderente** Clingfilm® (Brit), plastic wrap (Am).

pelo [ˈpelu] = **por + o**, → **por**.

pêlo [ˈpelu] m (de animal) fur; (de pessoa) hair.

Pelourinho [peloˈriɲu] m: **o ~ (de Salvador)** the Pelourinho district in Salvador.

peluche [peˈluʃe] m (Port) = **pelúcia**.

pelúcia [peˈlusja] f plush.

peludo, -da [peˈludu, -da] adj hairy.

pélvis [ˈpɛwviʃ] m ou f inv pelvis.

pena [ˈpena] f (de ave) feather; (de escrever) quill; (dó) pity; (castigo) sentence; **que ~!** what a shame!; **cumprir ~** to serve a prison term; **dar ~** to be a shame; **ter ~ de alguém** to feel sorry for sb; **tenho ~ de não poder ir** I'm sorry (that) I can't go; **valer a ~** to be worth one's while; **~ capital** capital punishment; **~ de morte** death penalty.

penalidade [penaliˈdadʒi] f penalty.

pênalti [peˈnawtʃi] m (Br) penalty.

penalty [peˈnalti] m (Port) = **pênalti**.

pendente [pẽˈdẽtʃi] adj pending ◆ m pendant.

pendurar [pẽduˈra(x)] vt to hang; **~ algo em algo** to hang sthg on sthg.

❏ **pendurar-se em** vp + prep to hang from.

penedo [peˈnedu] m boulder.

peneira [peˈnejra] f sieve.

penetrante [peneˈtrãtʃi] adj penetrating.

penetrar [peneˈtra(x)] : **penetrar em** v + prep (entrar em) to go into.

penhasco [peˈɲaʃku] m cliff.

penicilina [penisiˈlina] f penicillin.

penico [pe'niku] *m* chamber pot; *(para crianças)* potty.
península [pe'nĩsula] *f* peninsula.
pénis ['penis] *m inv (Port)* = **pênis**.
pênis ['penis] *m inv (Br)* penis.
penitência [peni'tẽsja] *f* penance.
penitenciária [penitẽ'sjarja] *f* prison.
penoso, -osa [pe'nozu, .ɔza] *adj* hard.
pensamento [pẽsa'mẽntu] *m (espírito)* mind; *(reflexão)* thought.
pensão [pẽ'sãw] *(pl* **-ões** [-õjʃ]) *f (hospedaria)* guesthouse; *(de invalidez, velhice)* pension; ~ **alimentícia** *(Br)* alimony, maintenance; ~ **completa** full board; ~ **residencial** – bed and breakfast.
pensar [pẽ'sa(x)] *vi (raciocinar)* to think; *(refletir)* to have a think ♦ *vt (tencionar)* to intend; ~ **em** to think about; ~ **que** to think (that); **nem** ~! no way!
pensionista [pẽsjo'niʃta] *mf (aposentado)* pensioner.
penso ['pẽsu] *m (Port)* dressing; ~ **higiénico** sanitary towel; ~ **rápido** (sticking) plaster *(Brit)*, Bandaid™ *(Am)*.
pensões → **pensão**.
pente ['pẽntʃi] *m* comb.
penteado [pẽn'tʃjadu] *m* hairstyle.
Pentecostes [pẽntʃi'kɔʃtʃiʃ] *m (católico)* Whit Sunday; *(judeu)* Pentecost.
penugem [pe'nuʒẽ] *f* down.
penúltimo, -ma [pe'nuwtʃimu, .ma] *adj* penultimate.
penumbra [pe'nũmbra] *f* semi-darkness, half-light.
penúria [pe'nurja] *f* penury.
peões → **peão**.
pepino [pe'pinu] *m* cucumber.
pequeno, -na [pe'kenu, .na] *adj* small, little; *(em comprimento)* short.
pequeno-almoço [pe,kenuaľmosu] *(pl* **pequenos-almoços** [pe,kenuzaľmɔsuʃ]) *m (Port)* breakfast.
pêra ['pera] *(pl* **peras** ['peraʃ]) *f (fruto)* pear; *(barba)* goatee (beard); ~ **abacate** avocado.
perante [pe'rãntʃi] *prep* in the presence of; **estou ~ um grande problema** I've come up against a big problem.
perceber [pexse'be(x)] *vt (entender)* to understand; *(aperceber-se)* to realize.
❏ **perceber de** *v* + *prep* to know about.

percentagem [pexsẽn'taʒẽ] *(pl* **-ns** [-ʃ]) *f* percentage.
percevejo [pexse'veʒu] *m* bug; *(Br: tacha)* drawing pin *(Brit)*, thumbstack *(Am)*.
perco ['pexku] → **perder**.
percorrer [pexko'xe(x)] *vt (caminho, distância)* to travel; *(país)* to travel through; *(cidade, ruas)* to go round; ~ **algo com os olhos** OU **com a vista** to skim through sthg.
percurso [pex'kuxsu] *m* route.
percussão [pexku'sãw] *f* percussion.
perda ['pexda] *f* loss; *(desperdício)* waste.
perdão [pex'dãw] *m* pardon ♦ *interj* sorry!; ~? pardon?; **pedir ~** to ask (for) forgiveness.
perde ['pexdʒi] → **perder**.
perder [pex'de(x)] *vt* to lose; *(tempo)* to waste; *(trem, ônibus)* to miss ♦ *vi* to lose; ~ **a cabeça** to lose one's head; ~ **os sentidos** to pass out; ~ **alguém de vista** to lose sight of sb.
◡ **perder-se** *vp* to get lost.
perdição [pexdʒi'sãw] *f* downfall.
perdido, -da [pex'dʒidu, .da] *adj* lost; **"achados e ~s "** "lost property" *(Brit)*, "lost and found" *(Am)*; **ser ~ por** *(fam)* to be mad about.
perdiz [pex'dʒiʃ] *(pl* **-zes** [-ziʃ]) *f* partridge.
perdoar [pex'dwa(x)] *vt* to forgive.
perdurar [pexdu'ra(x)] *vi* to endure.
perecível [pere'sivew] *(pl* **-eis** [-ejʃ]) *adj* perishable.
peregrinação [peregrina'sãw] *(pl* **-ões** [-õjʃ]) *f* pilgrimage.
peregrino, -na [pere'grinu, .na] *m, f* pilgrim.
pereira [pe'rejra] *f* pear tree.
peremptório, -ria [perẽmp'tɔrju, .rja] *adj* peremptory.
perene [pe'reni] *adj* perennial.
perfeição [pexfej'sãw] *f* perfection.
perfeitamente [pex,fejta'mẽntʃi] *adv* perfectly ♦ *interj* exactly!
perfeito, -ta [pex'fejtu, .ta] *adj* perfect.
pérfido, -da ['pexfidu, .da] *adj* malicious.
perfil [pex'fiw] *(pl* **-is** [-iʃ]) *m* profile; **de ~** in profile.
perfumaria [pexfuma'ria] *f* perfumery.
perfume [pex'fumi] *m* perfume.

perfurar [pɛxfuˈra(x)] *vt* to perforate, to make a hole in.

pergaminho [pɛxgaˈmiɲu] *m* parchment.

pergunta [pɛxˈgũnta] *f* question.

perguntar [pɛxgũnˈta(x)] *vt* to ask ◆ *vi*: ~ **por alguém** to ask after sb; ~ **sobre algo** to ask about sthg; ~ **algo a alguém** to ask sb sthg.

periferia [perifeˈria] *f* outskirts *(pl)*.

perigo [peˈrigu] *m* danger; **"~ de incêndio"** "danger – fire risk"; **"~ de morte"** "danger of death"; **"~ – queda de materiais"** "danger – falling masonry".

perigoso, -osa [periˈgozu, -ɔza] *adj* dangerous.

perímetro [peˈrimetru] *m* perimeter.

periódico, -ca [peˈrjɔdiku, -ka] *adj* periodic.

período [peˈriodu] *m* period; *(de ano escolar)* term *(Brit)*, semester *(Am)*.

periquito [periˈkitu] *m* budgerigar.

perito, -ta [peˈritu, -ta] *m, f & adj* expert; **ser ~ em algo** to be an expert in sthg.

permanecer [pexmaneˈse(x)] *vi* to stay, to remain.

⸣ **permanecer em** *v + prep* to stay at.

⸣ **permanecer por** *v + prep* to remain; **o problema permanece por resolver** the problem remains to be solved.

permanência [pexmaˈnẽsja] *f (estada)* stay; *(de problema, situação)* persistence.

permanente [pexmaˈnẽntʃi] *adj (emprego)* permanent; *(situação)* ongoing; *(dor, ruído)* continuous ◆ *f (penteado)* perm.

permissão [pexmiˈsãw] *f* permission; **pedir ~ para fazer algo** to ask permission to do sthg.

permitir [pexmiˈti(x)] *vt* to allow.

perna [ˈpexna] *f* leg; *(de letra)* descender.

pernil [pexˈniw] *(pl* -**is** [-iʃ]*)* *m* haunch.

pernilongo [pexniˈlõŋgu] *m (Port: ave)* avocet; *(Br: mosquito)* mosquito.

pernis → pernil.

pérola [ˈpɛrola] *f* pearl.

perpendicular [pexpẽndʒikuˈla(x)] *(pl* -**res** [-riʃ]*)* *adj & f* perpendicular.

perpetrar [pexpeˈtra(x)] *vt* to perpetrate.

perpetuar [pexpeˈtwa(x)] *vt* to immortalize.

⸣ **perpetuar-se** *vp (eternizar-se)* to last forever; *(prolongar-se)* to last.

perplexidade [pexplɛksiˈdadʒi] *f* perplexity.

perplexo, -xa [pexˈplɛksu, -ksa] *adj* perplexed.

perseguição [pexsegiˈsãw] *(pl* -**ões** [-õjʃ]*)* *f (de pessoa, criminoso)* pursuit; *(assédio)* persecution.

perseguir [pexseˈgi(x)] *vt (seguir)* to follow; *(assediar)* to persecute.

perseverante [pexseveˈrãntʃi] *adj* persevering.

perseverar [pexseveˈra(x)] *vi* to persevere.

persiana [pexˈsjana] *f* blind.

persistente [pexsisˈtẽntʃi] *adj* persistent.

personagem [pexsoˈnaʒẽ] *(pl* -**ns** [-ʃ]*)* *m* ou *f* character.

personalidade [pexsonaliˈdadʒi] *f* personality.

perspectiva [pexʃpeˈtʃiva] *f* perspective.

perspicácia [pexʃpiˈkasja] *f* shrewdness.

perspicaz [pexʃpiˈkaʃ] *(pl* -**zes** [-ziʃ]*)* *adj* shrewd.

persuadir [pexswaˈdi(x)] *vt*: ~ **alguém de algo** to persuade sb of sthg; ~ **alguém a fazer algo** to persuade sb to do sthg.

⸣ **persuadir-se** *vp* to convince o.s.

persuasão [pexswaˈzãw] *f* persuasion.

persuasivo, -va [pexswaˈzivu, -va] *adj* persuasive.

pertencente [pextẽˈsẽntʃi] *adj*: ~ **a** *(que pertence a)* belonging to; *(relativo a)* relating to.

pertencer [pextẽˈse(x)] *vi* to belong; ~ **a** to belong to; ~ **a alguém fazer algo** to be sb's responsibility to do sthg.

perto [ˈpextu] *adj* nearby ◆ *adv* near, close; ~ **de** *(relativo a tempo, quantidade)* around; *(relativo a espaço)* near; **ao** ou **de ~** close up.

perturbar [pextuxˈba(x)] *vt* to disturb.

peru [peˈru] *m* turkey.

Peru [peˈru] *m*: **o ~** Peru.

peruca [peˈruka] *f* wig.

perverso, -sa [pexˈvexsu, -sa] *adj (malvado)* wicked.

perverter [pɛxver'te(x)] *vt* to corrupt.

pervertido, -da [pɛxvex'tʃidu, -da] *adj* perverted.

pesadelo [peza'delu] *m* nightmare.

pesado, -da [pe'zadu, -da] *adj* heavy.

pêsames ['pezamiʃ] *mpl* condolences; **os meus ~** my condolences.

pesar [pe'za(x)] *vt* to weigh; *(fig: conseqüências)* to weigh (up) ♦ *vi (ser pesado)* to be heavy; *(influir)* to carry weight.

pesca ['peʃka] *f* fishing; **~ com linha** angling.

pescada [peʃ'kada] *f* hake.

pescadinha [peʃka'dʒiɲa] *f* whiting.

pescador, -ra [peʃka'do(x), -ra] *(mpl* **-res** [-riʃ]. *fpl* **-s** [-ʃ]) *m, f* fisherman *(f* fisherwoman).

pescar [peʃ'ka(x)] *vt* to fish for ♦ *vi* to go fishing, to fish.

pescoço [peʃ'kosu] *m* neck.

peso ['pezu] *m* weight; **~ bruto/líquido** gross/net weight.

pesquisa [peʃ'kiza] *f* research.

pêssego ['pesegu] *m* peach.

pessegueiro [pese'gejru] *m* peach tree.

pessimista [pesi'miʃta] *mf* pessimist.

péssimo, -ma [pesimu, -ma] *adj* horrendous, awful.

pessoa [pe'soa] *f* person; **quatro ~s** four people; **em ~** in person.

pessoal [pe'swaw] *(pl* **-ais** [-ajʃ]) *adj (individual)* personal; *(vida)* private ♦ *m* staff.

pestana [peʃ'tana] *f* eyelash; **queimar as ~s** *(fig: estudar muito)* to hit the books.

pestanejar [peʃtane'ʒa(x)] *vi* to blink.

peste ['pɛʃtʃi] *f* plague.

pesticida [peʃtʃi'sida] *m* pesticide.

pétala ['pɛtala] *f* petal.

peteca [pe'tɛka] *f (Br: de badminton)* shuttlecock.

petição [petʃi'sãw] *(pl* **-ões** [-õjʃ]) *f* petition.

petinga [pe'tʃiŋga] *f* whitebait.

petiscar [petʃiʃ'ka(x)] *vt (provar)* to taste ♦ *vi (comer)* to nibble, to pick; **quem não arrisca não petisca** nothing ventured, nothing gained.

petisco [pe'tʃiʃku] *m (iguaria)* delicacy; *(tira-gosto)* snack.

petit-pois [petʃi'pwa] *mpl (Brit)* petit-pois.

petrificar [petrifi'ka(x)] *vt* to petrify.

petroleiro [petro'lejru] *m* oil tanker.

petróleo [pe'trɔlju] *m (rocha sedimentar)* petroleum; *(combustível)* oil.

petulância [petu'lãsja] *f (insolência)* impudence; *(vaidade)* arrogance.

petulante [petu'lãntʃi] *adj (insolente)* impudent; *(vaidoso)* arrogant.

pia ['pia] *f* sink; **~ batismal** font.

piada ['pjada] *f (anedota)* joke; *(dito espirituoso)* wisecrack.

pianista [pja'niʃta] *mf* pianist.

piano ['pjanu] *m* piano.

pião ['pjãw] *(pl* **-ões** [-õjʃ]) *m (brinquedo)* spinning top; *(com carro)* handbrake turn.

piar ['pja(x)] *vi* to chirp.

picada [pi'kada] *f (de ave)* peck; *(de inseto)* bite.

picadinho [pika'dʒiɲu] *m (Br)* minced meat stew.

picado, -da [pi'kadu, -da] *adj (carne)* minced *(Brit)*, ground *(Am)*; *(cebola, salsa)* chopped; *(furado)* pierced ♦ *m (ensopado)* minced meat stew.

picanha [pi'kaɲa] *f (Br)* tenderest part of rump steak, often served at the end of a "rodízio".

picante [pi'kãntʃi] *adj (apimentado)* spicy; *(fig: malicioso)* saucy.

pica-pau [,pika'paw] *(pl* **pica-paus** [,pika'pawʃ]) *m* woodpecker.

picar [pi'ka(x)] *vt (com alfinete, agulha)* to prick; *(carne)* to mince *(Brit)*, to grind *(Am)*; *(cebola, salsa)* to chop ♦ *vi (peixe)* to bite.

⅃ **picar-se** *vp (ferir-se)* to prick o.s.

picareta [pika'reta] *f* pick ♦ *mf (mau caráter)* crook.

picles ['pikleʃ] *mpl (Br)* pickles.

pico ['piku] *m (montanha)* peak; *(espinho)* thorn.

picolé [piko'lɛ] *m (Br)* ice lolly *(Brit)*, Popsicle® *(Am)*.

picotado, -da [piko'tadu, -da] *adj* perforated ♦ *m* perforated edge.

piedade [pje'dadʒi] *f* pity; **ter ~ de alguém** to take pity on sb.

pifar [pi'fa(x)] *vi* to break; *(carro)* to break down; *(plano, projeto)* to fall through.

pigmento [pig'mẽntu] *m* pigment.

pijama [pi'ʒama] *m* pyjamas *(pl)*.

pikles ['pikleʃ] *mpl (Port)* = **picles**.

pilantra [pi'lãntra] *mf* crook.

pilar [pi'la(x)] *(pl* **-res** [-riʃ]) *m* pillar.

pilha [ˈpiʎa] *f* battery; *(de papel, livros, etc)* pile; **uma ~ de nervos** a bundle of nerves; **~s de** *(fam)* heaps of.

pilhar [piˈʎa(x)] *vt (saquear)* to pillage; *(roubar)* to steal.

pilotar [piloˈta(x)] *vt* to pilot.

piloto [piˈlotu] *m (de avião)* pilot; *(de automóvel)* driver.

pílula [ˈpilula] *f* pill; **tomar a ~** to be on the pill.

pimenta [piˈmẽnta] *f* pepper *(seasoning)*.

pimenta-do-reino [pi,mẽntaduˈxeinu] *f* (white) pepper.

pimentão [pimẽnˈtãw] *(pl* **-ões** [-ˈõjʃ]) *m (Br)* pepper *(vegetable)*.

pimentão-doce [pimẽntãwˈdosi] *m* paprika.

pimento [piˈmẽntu] *m (Port)* = **pimentão**.

pin [ˈpin] *m* badge.

pinça [ˈpĩsa] *f* tweezers *(pl)*.

píncaro [ˈpĩŋkaru] *m (de montanha)* summit.

pincel [pĩˈsɛw] *(pl* **-éis** [-ɛiʃ]) *m* brush.

pinga [ˈpĩŋga] *f (gota)* drop; *(fam: aguardente)* booze.

pingar [pĩŋˈga(x)] *vi* to drip.

pingente [pĩˈʒẽntʃi] *m (de colar)* pendant; *(brinco)* pendant earring.

pingue-pongue [ˌpĩŋgeˈpõŋgi] *m* Ping-pong®, table tennis.

pinguim [pĩŋˈgwĩ] *(pl* **-ns** [-ʃ]) *m (Port)* = **pingüim**.

pingüim [pĩŋˈgwĩ] *(pl* **-ns** [-ʃ]) *m (Br)* penguin.

pinhal [piˈɲaw] *(pl* **-ais** [-ajʃ]) *m* pinewood.

pinhão [piˈɲãw] *(pl* **-ões** [-ˈõjʃ]) *m* pine kernel *ou* nut.

pinheiro [piˈɲeiru] *m* pine tree.

pinho [ˈpiɲu] *m* pine.

pinhões → pinhão.

pinta [ˈpĩnta] *f (mancha)* spot; *(fam: aparência)* look; **ter ~ de** *(fam)* to look like.

pintado, -da [pĩnˈtadu, -da] *adj (colorido)* coloured; **"~ de fresco"** "wet paint"; **"~ à mão"** "hand-painted".

pintar [pĩnˈta(x)] *vt (quadro, parede)* to paint; *(olhos)* to put make up on; *(cabelo)* to dye; *(desenho, boneco)* to colour in ◆ *vi (artista, pintor)* to paint; *(Br: fam: pessoa)* to turn up; *(Br: fam: problema)* to crop up; *(Br: fam: oportunidade)* to come up; **~ os lábios** to put lipstick on.

⅃ pintar-se *vp* to wear make-up.

pintarroxo [pĩntaˈxoʃu] *m* linnet.

pintassilgo [pĩntaˈsiwgu] *m* goldfinch.

pinto [ˈpĩntu] *m (pintainho)* chick.

pintor, -ra [pĩnˈto(x), -ra] *(mpl* **-es** [-iʃ]. *fpl* **-s** [-ʃ]) *m, f* painter.

pintura [pĩnˈtura] *f* painting.

piões → pião.

piolho [ˈpjoʎu] *m* louse.

pionés [pjoˈnɛʃ] *(pl* **-eses** [-ɛzeʃ]) *m (Port)* drawing pin *(Brit)*, thumbtack *(Am)*.

pior [ˈpjɔ(x)] *(pl* **-res** [-riʃ]) *adj & adv* worse ◆ *m:* **o/a ~** *(pessoa, coisa)* the worst one; **está cada vez ~** it's getting worse and worse; **ser do ~ que há** *(fam)* to be the pits.

piorar [pjoˈra(x)] *vi* to get worse ◆ *vt (situação)* to worsen.

piores → pior.

pipa [ˈpipa] *f (de vinho)* cask; *(Br: papagaio de papel)* kite.

pipoca [piˈpɔka] *f* popcorn.

pipoqueiro, -ra [pipoˈkeiru. -ra] *m, f (Br)* popcorn seller.

piquenique [pikeˈniki] *m* picnic.

pirâmide [piˈramidʒi] *f* pyramid.

piranha [piˈraɲa] *f* piranha.

pirão [piˈrãw] *m* cassava-flour porridge, eaten as a side dish.

pirata [piˈrata] *m* pirate.

pires [ˈpiriʃ] *m inv* saucer.

pírex® [ˈpirɛkʃ] *m* Pyrex®.

pirilampo [piriˈlãmpu] *m* firefly.

Pirineus [piriˈnewʃ] *mpl:* **os ~** the Pyrenees.

piripiri [piriˈpiri] *m (malagueta)* chilli (pepper); *(molho)* = Tabasco® sauce.

pirueta [piˈrweta] *f* pirouette.

pisar [piˈza(x)] *vt (com pé)* to step on; *(contundir)* to bruise.

pisca-pisca [ˌpiʃkaˈpiʃka] *m* indicator.

piscar [piʃˈka(x)] *vt (olho)* to wink; *(olhos)* to blink ◆ *vi (luz)* to flicker.

piscina [piʃˈsina] *f* swimming pool; **~ ao ar livre** open-air swimming pool; **~ coberta** covered *ou* indoor swimming pool.

pisco [ˈpiʃku] *m* robin.

piso [ˈpizu] *m* floor; **~ escorregadio/irregular** slippery/uneven surface.

pista [ˈpiʃta] *f (indício)* clue; *(de corridas)* racetrack; *(de aviação)* runway; *(de*

dança) dancefloor; *(de circo)* ring; ~ **de
rodagem** *(Br)* carriageway.

pistácio [piʃˈtasju] *m* pistachio.

pistão [piʃˈtãw] *(pl* -ões [-õjʃ]) *m* piston.

pistola [piʃˈtɔla] *f* pistol.

pitada [piˈtada] *f* pinch.

pitanga [piˈtãŋga] *f variety of cherry*.

pitoresco, -ca [pitoˈreʃku, -ka] *adj*
picturesque.

pivete [piˈvetʃi] *m (Br: criança aban-
donada)* street child; *(Port: mau cheiro)*
stink.

pizza [ˈpiza] *f* pizza.

pizzaria [pizaˈria] *f* pizzeria.

placa [ˈplaka] *f (de madeira, plástico)*
sheet; *(de metal)* plate; *(de fogão)* hob;
(em porta) plaque; *(em estrada)* sign;
(dentadura) set of) false teeth.

plágio [ˈplaʒju] *m* plagiarism.

planador [planaˈdo(x)] *(pl* -res [-riʃ])
m glider.

planalto [plaˈnawtu] *m* plateau.

planear [plaˈnjar] *vt (Port)* = plane-
jar.

planejamento [planeʒaˈmẽtu] *m*
planning; ~ **familiar** family planning.

planejar [planeˈʒa(x)] *vt (Br)* to plan;
~ **fazer algo** to plan to do sthg.

planeta [plaˈneta] *m* planet.

planetário [planeˈtarju] *m* planetar-
ium.

planície [plaˈnisji] *f* plain.

plano, -na [ˈplanu, -na] *adj* flat ♦ *m*
plan.

planta [ˈplãta] *f (vegetal)* plant; *(de
pé)* sole; *(de cidade, casa)* plan.

plantão [plãˈtãw] *(pl* -ões [-õjʃ]) *m
(turno)* shift; **estar de ~** to be on duty.

plantar [plãˈta(x)] *vt* to plant.

plástica [ˈplaʃtʃika] *f* plastic surgery.

plasticina [plaʃtʃiˈsina] *f (Port)* = plas-
tilina.

plástico [ˈplaʃtʃiku] *m* plastic.

plastilina [plaʃtʃiˈlina] *f (Br)*
Plasticine⁽ᴿ⁾.

plataforma [plataˈfɔxma] *f* platform.

plátano [ˈplatanu] *m* plane (tree).

plateia [plaˈtaja] *f (Port)* = platéia.

platéia [plaˈtɛja] *f (Br) (local)* stalls
(pl); *(público)* audience.

platina [plaˈtʃina] *f* platinum.

platinados [platʃiˈnaduʃ] *mpl* points.

plausível [plawˈzivew] *(pl* -eis [-ejʃ])
adj plausible.

plebiscito [plebiˈsitu] *m (Br)* referendum.

plenamente [ˌplenaˈmẽtʃi] *adv*
totally.

pleno, -na [ˈplenu, -na] *adj* total; ~ **de**
full of; **em ~ dia** in broad daylight; **em
~ inverno** in the middle of winter.

plural [pluˈraw] *(pl* -ais [-ajʃ]) *m* plural.

plutónio [pluˈtɔnju] *m (Port)* =
plutônio.

plutônio [pluˈtonju] *m (Br)* pluto-
nium.

pneu [ˈpnew] *m* tyre; ~ **sobressalente**
spare tyre.

pneumonia [pnewmoˈnia] *f* pneumonia.

pó [ˈpɔ] *m (poeira)* dust; *(substância
pulverizada)* powder; ~ **de talco** talcum powder; **limpar o ~** to do the
dusting.

pobre [ˈpɔbri] *adj* poor ♦ *mf (pedinte)*
beggar.

pobreza [poˈbreza] *f* poverty.

poça [ˈpɔsa] *f* pool.

poção [poˈsãw] *(pl* -ões [-õjʃ]) *f*
potion.

pocilga [poˈsiwga] *f* pigsty.

poço [ˈposu] *m (de água, petróleo)* well;
(buraco) pit.

poções → poção.

podar [poˈda(x)] *vt* to prune.

pode [ˈpɔdʒi] → poder.

pôde [ˈpodʒi] → poder.

pó-de-arroz [ˌpɔdʒjaˈxoʃ] *m* face
powder.

poder [poˈde(x)] *(pl* -res [-riʃ]) *m* **1.**
(político, influência) power; **estar no ~**
to be in power; ~ **de compra** purchas-
ing power; **não tenho ~es nenhuns**
I'm powerless to help.

2. *(possessão)* possession; **estar em ~
de alguém** to be in sb's hands; **ter em
seu ~ algo** to have sthg in one's possession.

♦ *v aux* **1.** *(ser capaz de):* ~ **fazer algo**
to be able to do sthg; **posso fazê-lo** I
can do it; **posso ajudar?** can I help?;
você podia tê-lo feito antes you could
have done it beforehand; **não posso
mais!** *(em relação a cansaço)* I've had
enough!; *(em relação a comida)* I'm full
up!

2. *(estar autorizado para):* ~ **fazer algo**
to be allowed to do sthg; **posso fumar?**
may I smoke?; **você não pode esta-**

cionar aqui you can't park here; **não pude sair ontem** I wasn't allowed (to go) out yesterday.
3. *(ser capaz moralmente)* can; **não podemos magoá-lo** we can't hurt him.
4. *(exprime possibilidade):* **você podia ter vindo de ônibus** you could have come by bus; **cuidado que você pode se machucar!** be careful, you might hurt yourself!
5. *(exprime indignação, queixa):* **não pode ser!** this is outrageous!; **você podia nos ter avisado!** you could have warned us!; **pudera!** no wonder!
♦ *v impess (ser possível):* **pode não ser verdade** it might not be true; **pode acontecer a qualquer um** it could happen to anyone.
⌐ poder com *v + prep (suportar)* to be able to stand; *(rival, adversário)* to be able to handle; *(peso)* to be able to carry; **você não pode com tanto peso** you can't carry all that; **não posso com ele** I can't stand him.

poderoso, -osa [pode'rozu, -ɔza] *adj* powerful.
podre [pɔdri] *adj* rotten.
põe [põi] → **pôr**.
poeira [pwejra] *f* dust.
poema [pwema] *m* poem.
poesia [pwi'zia] *f (gênero literário)* poetry; *(poema)* poem.
poeta [pwɛta] *m* poet.
poetisa [pwɛt'fiza] *f (female)* poet.
pois [pojf] *conj (porque)* because; *(então)* then ♦ *interj* right!; ~ **sim!** certainly!, of course!; ~ **não? em que posso ajudá-lo?** can I help you?; ~ **bem** now then, right then.
polaco [pu'laku] *adj & m (Port)* Polish ♦ *m, f (Port)* Pole.
polegar [pole'ga(x)] *(pl -res [-rif]) m* thumb.
polémica [pu'lɛmika] *f (Port)* = **polêmica**.
polêmica [po'lemika] *f (Br)* controversy.
pólen [pɔlɛn] *m* pollen.
polícia [po'lisja] *f* police ♦ *mf* policeman *(f* policewoman*);* ~ **militar** military police; ~ **rodoviária** traffic police.
policial [poli'sjaw] *(pl -ais [-ajf]) mf (Br)* policeman *(f* policewoman*).*
polido, -da [po'lidu, -da] *adj (lustroso)* polished; *(liso)* smooth.
polir [po'li(x)] *vt (dar lustre em)* to pol-

ish; *(alisar)* to smooth out; *(fig: educar)* to educate.
politécnica [poli'tɛknika] *adj f* → **escola**.
política [po'litfika] *f (arte de governar)* politics *(sg); (de governo, partido)* policy; ~ **externa** foreign policy; ~ **exterior** foreign policy.
político, -ca [po'litfiku, -ka] *m, f* politician ♦ *adj* political.
pólo [pɔlu] *m* pole; *(esporte)* polo; ~ **aquático** water polo.
polonês, -esa [polo'nef, -eza] *(mpl -eses [-ezif], fpl -s [-f]) adj & m (Br)* Polish ♦ *m, f (Br)* Pole.
Polónia [pu'lɔnja] *f (Port)* = **Polônia**.
Polônia [po'lonja] *f (Br)* Poland.
polpa [powpa] *f* pulp.
poltrona [pow'trona] *f* armchair.
poluição [polwi'sãw] *f* pollution.
poluído, -da [po'lwidu, -da] *adj* polluted.
poluir [po'lwi(x)] *vt* to pollute.
polvo [powvu] *m* octopus.
pólvora [powvora] *f* gunpowder.
pomada [po'mada] *f* ointment; ~ **anti-séptica** antiseptic ointment.
pomar [po'ma(x)] *(pl -res [-rif]) m* orchard.
pombo, -ba [pombu, -ba] *m, f* pigeon; **pomba da paz** white dove.
pomo-de-adão [pomodʒia'dãw] *(pl pomos-de-adão* [pomozdʒia'dãw]) *m* Adam's apple.
pomposo, -osa [põm'pozu, -ɔza] *adj* pompous.
ponderação [põndera'sãw] *f* thought, consideration.
ponderado, -da [põnde'radu, -da] *adj* prudent.
ponderar [põnde'ra(x)] *vt* to consider.
pónei [ponej] *m (Port)* = **pônei**.
pônei [ponej] *m (Br)* pony.
ponho [ponu] → **pôr**.
ponta [põnta] *f (de lápis)* point; *(de vara, linha, cigarro)* end; *(de superfície)* edge; *(de dedo, língua, nariz)* tip; **tenho a palavra na ~ da língua** I've got it on the tip of my tongue; **de ~ a ~** from one end to the other.
pontada [põn'tada] *f* stitch.
pontapé [põnta'pɛ] *m* kick; ~ **livre** free kick; ~ **de saída** kickoff.
pontaria [põnta'ria] *f*: **fazer ~** to take aim; **ter ~** to be a good shot.
ponte [põntfi] *f* bridge.

ponteiro [põn'tejru] *m (de relógio)* hand.

pontiagudo, -da [põntʃja'gudu, -da] *adj* pointed.

ponto ['põntu] *m* point; *(de costura, ferimento, tricot)* stitch; *(marca)* dot; *(sinal ortográfico)* full stop *(Brit)*, period *(Am); (Br: parada)* stop; *(lugar)* place; *(Port: teste, exame)* test; **às 9 em ~** at 9 on the dot; **estar a ~ de fazer algo** to be on the point of doing sthg; **até certo ~** up to a point; **dois ~s** colon; **~ cardeal** compass point; **~ de encontro** meeting point; **~ de exclamação** exclamation mark; **~ final** full stop *(Brit)*, period *(Am)*; **~ de interrogação** question mark; **~ morto** *(em veículo)* neutral; **~ de ônibus** bus stop; **~ de partida** starting point; **~ de táxi** taxi rank; **~ e vírgula** semicolon; **~ de vista** point of view.

pontuação [põntwa'sãw] *(pl* -ões [-õjʃ]) *f (em gramática)* punctuation; *(em competição)* score.

pontual [põn'twaw] *(pl* -ais [-ajʃ]) *adj* punctual.

pontuar [põn'twa(x)] *vt (texto)* to punctuate.

popa ['popa] *f* stern.

popelina [pope'lina] *f* poplin.

população [popula'sãw] *f* population.

popular [popu'la(x)] *(pl* -res [-riʃ]) *adj* popular; *(música, arte)* folk.

póquer ['pɔkɛr] *m (Port)* = **pôquer**.

pôquer ['pokɛ(x)] *m (Br)* poker.

por [po(x)] *prep* **1.** *(indica causa)* because of, due to; **foi ~ sua causa** it was your fault; **~ falta de fundos** due to lack of funds; **~ hábito** through force of habit.
2. *(indica objetivo)* for; **lutar ~ algo** to fight for sthg.
3. *(indica meio, modo, agente)* by; **foi escrito pela Cristina** it was written by Cristina; **~ correio/fax** by post/fax; **~ escrito** in writing; **~ avião** air mail.
4. *(relativo a tempo)* for; **partiu ~ duas semanas** he went away for two weeks.
5. *(relativo a lugar)* through; **entramos no Brasil ~ Paraguay** we crossed into Brazil via Paraguay; **está ~ aí** it's round there somewhere; **~ onde você vai?** which way are you going?; **vamos ~ aqui** we're going this way.

6. *(relativo a troca, preço)* for; **paguei apenas 20 reais ~ este casaco** I only paid 20 reals for this jacket; **troquei o carro velho ~ um novo** I exchanged my old car for a new one.
7. *(indica distribuição)* per; **25 ~ cento** 25 per cent; **são 100 reais ~ dia/mês** it's 100 reals per day/month.
8. *(em locuções):* **~ que** why; **~ que (é que)** ...? why ...?; **~ mim tudo bem!** that's fine by me!

pôr ['po(x)] *vt* to put; *(vestir, calçar)* to put on; *(problema, dúvida, questão)* to raise; *(defeitos)* to find; *(suj: ave)* to lay; *(depositar dinheiro)* to pay in ♦ *vi (galinhas)* to lay (eggs) ♦ *m:* **o ~ do sol** sunset; **~ algo em algo** to put sthg in/on sthg; **~ algo em funcionamento** to start sthg up; **~ algo mais baixo/alto** *(música, som)* to turn sthg down/up; **~ a mesa** to set OU lay the table.

⊔ pôr-se *vp (nervoso, contente)* to become; *(sol)* to set; **~-se a fazer algo** to begin to do sthg; **~-se de pé** to stand up.

porca ['pɔxka] *f (peça)* nut; *(animal)* sow.

porção [pox'sãw] *(pl* -ões [-õjʃ]) *f* portion, helping.

porcaria [poxka'ria] *f* rubbish; *(sujeira)* mess; *(pus)* pus; **isto é uma ~** this is rubbish; **(que) ~!** damn!

porcelana [poxse'lana] *f* porcelain.

porco ['poxku] *m (animal)* pig; *(carne)* pork.

porções → porção.

porco-espinho [poxkuiʃ'piɲu] *(pl* **porcos-espinhos** [pɔrkuziʃ'piɲuʃ]) *m* porcupine.

porém [po'rẽj] *conj* however.

pormenor [poxme'nɔ(x)] *(pl* -es [-iʃ]) *m* detail; **em ~** in detail.

pornografia [poxnogra'fia] *f* pornography.

poro ['pɔru] *m* pore.

porque ['poxki] *conj* because ♦ *adv (Port)* why.

porquê [pox'ke] *adv (Port)* why ♦ *m:* **o ~ de** the reason for.

porquinho-da-índia [pox,kiɲuda-'ĩndʒja] *(pl* **porquinhos-da-índia** [pox,kiɲuʒda'ĩndʒja]) *m* guinea pig.

porra ['poxa] *interj (vulg)* bloody hell!

porta ['pɔxta] *f* door; **~ automática** automatic door; **~ corrediça** sliding door; **~ giratória** revolving door.

porta-aviões [ˌpɔxtaˈvjõiʃ] *m inv* aircraft carrier.

porta-bagagem [ˌpɔxtabaˈgaʒẽ] (*pl* **porta-bagagens** [ˌpɔxtabaˈgaʒẽʃ]) *m (em carro)* boot *(Brit)*, trunk *(Am)*; *(em ônibus)* luggage hold; *(em trem)* luggage rack.

porta-bandeira [ˌpɔxtabãnˈdejra] (*pl* **porta-bandeiras** [ˌpɔxtabãnˈdejraʃ]) *mf* standard-bearer.

porta-chaves [ˌpɔxtaˈʃaviʃ] *m inv (Port)* key ring.

portador, -ra [pɔxtaˈdo(x), -ra] (*mpl* **-res** [-riʃ], *fpl* **-s** [-ʃ]) *m, f (de doença, vírus)* carrier; *(FIN)* bearer; **ao ~** *(cheque, ação, obrigação)* to the bearer.

portagem [puɾˈtaʒẽj] (*pl* **-ns** [-ʃ]) *f (Port)* toll.

porta-jóias [ˌpɔxtaˈʒɔjaʃ] *m inv* jewellery box.

porta-lápis [ˌpɔxtaˈlapiʃ] *m inv* pencil case.

porta-luvas [ˌpɔxtaˈluvaʃ] *m inv* glove compartment.

porta-moedas [ˌpɔxtaˈmwedaʃ] *m inv* purse.

portanto [pɔxˈtãntu] *conj* so, therefore.

portão [pɔxˈtãw] (*pl* **-ões** [-õjʃ]) *m* gate.

portaria [pɔxtaˈria] *f (de edifício)* main entrance; *(documento)* decree.

portátil [pɔxˈtatʃiw] (*pl* **-eis** [-ejʃ]) *adj (telefone)* portable; *(computador)* laptop.

porta-voz [ˌpɔxtaˈvɔjʃ] (*pl* **porta-vozes** [ˌpɔxtaˈvɔziʃ]) *mf* spokesman (*f* spokeswoman).

porte [ˈpɔxtʃi] *m (postura)* posture; *(em caminhão)* haulage; *(em avião, navio, trem)* freight; **"~ pago"** "postage paid".

porteiro, -ra [pɔxˈtejru, -ra] *m, f* porter.

pórtico [ˈpɔxtʃiku] *m* portico.

porto [ˈpɔxtu] *m* port.

portões → **portão**.

Portugal [pɔxtuˈgal] *s* Portugal.

português, -esa [pɔxtuˈgeʃ, -eza] (*mpl* **-eses** [-eziʃ], *fpl* **-s** [-ʃ]) *adj & m, f* Portuguese ◆ *m (língua)* Portuguese; **à portuguesa** in the Portuguese way.

porventura [pɔxvẽnˈtura] *adv* by any chance.

pôs [pojʃ] → **pôr**.

posar [poˈza(x)] *vi* to pose.

posição [poziˈsãw] (*pl* **-ões** [-õjʃ]) *f* position; *(moral, política)* stance.

positivo, -va [poziˈtʃivu, -va] *adj* positive; *(valor, saldo)* in the black, in credit ◆ *m (de fotografia)* print.

posologia [pozoloˈʒia] *f* dosage.

posse [ˈpɔsi] *f* possession; **estar em ~ de** to be in possession of.

❑ **posses** *fpl*: **ter ~s** to be wealthy.

possessão [poseˈsãw] (*pl* **-ões** [-õjʃ]) *f (posse)* possession, ownership; *(domínio)* control.

possessivo, -va [poseˈsivu, -va] *adj* possessive.

possessões → **possessão**.

possibilidade [posibiliˈdadʒi] *f* possibility.

possibilitar [posibiliˈta(x)] *vt* to make possible.

possível [poˈsivew] (*pl* **-eis** [-ejʃ]) *adj* possible ◆ *m*: **fazer o ~ (para fazer algo)** to do one's best (to do sthg); **não é ~!** *(exprime incredulidade)* it's incredible!; **logo que ~** as soon as possible; **o mais cedo ~** as soon as possible; **o máximo ~** as much as possible; **se ~** if possible.

posso [ˈpɔsu] → **poder**.

possuir [poˈswi(x)] *vt (carro, casa)* to own; *(desfrutar de)* to have.

postal [poʃˈtaw] (*pl* **-ais** [-ajʃ]) *m* postcard; **~ ilustrado** picture postcard.

posta-restante [ˌpɔʃtaxeʃˈtãntʃi] (*pl* **postas-restantes** [ˌpɔʃtaʒxeʃˈtãntiʃ]) *f* poste restante.

poste [ˈpɔʃtʃi] *m* pole; **~ (de alta tensão)** pylon; **~ (de iluminação)** lamppost.

poster [ˈpɔʃtɛɾ] (*pl* **-res** [-reʃ]) *m (Port)* = **pôster**.

pôster [ˈpɔʃte(x)] (*pl* **-res** [-riʃ]) *m (Br)* poster.

posteridade [poʃteriˈdadʒi] *f* posterity

posterior [poʃteˈrjo(x)] (*pl* **-res** [-riʃ]) *adj (em tempo, ordem)* subsequent; *(em espaço)* back, rear.

posteriormente [puʃterjorˈmẽntʃi] *adv* subsequently.

postiço, -ça [poʃˈtʃisu, -sa] *adj* false.

postigo [poʃˈtʃigu] *m* hatch.

posto [ˈpoʃtu] *m (em emprego)* position; *(de polícia, bombeiros)* station; **~ de gasolina** petrol station *(Brit)*, filling station *(Am)*; **~ médico** *(Port: em escola)* first-aid room; **~ de saúde** clinic; **"~ de venda autorizado"** *sign indicating* *that bus tickets can be bought.*

póstumo, -ma ['pɔʃtumu, -ma] *adj* posthumous.

postura [poʃ'tura] *f* posture.

potável [po'tavɛw] *adj* → **água**.

pote ['pɔtʃi] *m* jar.

potência [pu'tẽsja] *f* power.

potencial [potẽ'sjaw] (*pl* **-ais** [-ajʃ]) *adj & m* potential.

potente [po'tẽtʃi] *adj* powerful.

potro ['potru] *m* colt.

pouco, -ca ['poku, -ka] *adj & pron (no singular)* little, not much; *(no plural)* few, not many ◆ *adv (relativo a tempo)* not long; *(relativo a quantidade)* not much; *(com adjetivo)* not very ◆ *m*: **um ~** a little, a bit; **ele come ~** he doesn't eat much; **ele é ~ inteligente/amável** he isn't very bright/friendly; **falta ~ para chegarmos lá** it won't be long before we get there; **falta ~ para o verão** it's almost summer(time); **um ~ de** a bit of; **um ~ mais de** a bit more; **custar ~** *(ser barato)* to be cheap; **ficar a ~s passos de** to be near; **daí a ~** shortly afterwards; **daqui a ~** in a little while; **há ~** a short while ago; **~ a ~** little by little; **por ~** nearly; **fazer ~ de** to make fun of.

poupa ['popa] *f* quiff.

poupança [po'pãsa] *f* saving.

⊔ poupanças *fpl* savings.

poupar [po'pa(x)] *vt* to save ◆ *vi* to save up.

pouquinho [po'kiɲu] *m*: **só um ~** just a little; **um ~ de** a little.

pousada [po'zada] *f building of artistic or historic interest which has been converted into a luxury hotel*; **~ da juventude** *(Port)* youth hostel.

pousar [po'za(x)] *vt* to put down ◆ *vi (ave)* to perch; *(avião)* to land.

povo ['povu] *m* people *(pl)*.

povoação [povwa'sãw] (*pl* **-ões** [-õjʃ]) *f* village.

povoar [po'vwa(x)] *vt* to populate.

p.p. *(abrev de páginas)* pp.

PR *abrev* = **Presidente da República**, → **presidente**.

praça ['prasa] *f (largo)* square; *(mercado)* market(place); **~ de táxis** *(Port)* taxi rank; **~ de touros** bullring.

prado ['pradu] *m* meadow.

praga ['praga] *f* plague; *(palavrão, maldição)* curse.

pragmático, -ca [prag'matʃiku, -ka] *adj* pragmatic.

praia ['praja] *f* beach; **~ para nudistas** nudist beach.

prancha ['prãʃa] *f* board; **~ de saltos** diving board; **~ de surf** surfboard.

pranto ['prãtu] *m* wailing.

prata ['prata] *f* silver; **(feito) de ~** (made of) silver.

prateado, -da [pra'tʃjadu, -da] *adj* silver(y).

prateleira [prate'lejra] *f* shelf.

prática ['pratʃika] *f (experiência)* experience; *(de esporte)* playing; **na ~** in practice; **pôr algo em ~** to put sthg into practice; **ter ~** to have experience.

praticante [pratʃi'kãtʃi] *adj* practising ◆ *mf*: **~ de esporte** sportsman (*f* sportswoman).

praticar [pratʃi'ka(x)] *vt* to practise; *(esporte)* to play.

praticável [pratʃi'kavɛw] (*pl* **-eis** [-ejʃ]) *adj (ação)* feasible; *(estrada)* passable.

prático, -ca ['pratʃiku, -ka] *adj* practical.

prato ['pratu] *m (louça)* plate; *(refeição)* dish; **~ fundo** soup bowl; **~ da casa** speciality of the house; **~ do dia** dish of the day; **~ raso** dinner plate; **~ de sopa** *(utensílio)* soup plate; *(comida)* bowl of soup; **pôr tudo em ~s limpos** *(fam)* to make a clean breast of it.

⊔ pratos *mpl (MÚS)* cymbals.

praxe ['praʃi] *f (costume)* custom; **ser de ~** to be the norm.

prazer [pra'ze(x)] (*pl* **-res** [-riʃ]) *m* pleasure; **muito ~!** pleased to meet you!; **~ em conhecê-lo!** pleased to meet you!; **o ~ é (todo) meu!** the pleasure is all mine!; **ela faz tudo a seu bel ~** she does as she pleases; **com ~** with pleasure; **por ~** for pleasure.

prazo ['prazu] *m* period; **~ de validade** expiry date; **a curto/longo/médio ~** in the short/long/medium term.

pré-aviso [prɛa'vizu] (*pl* **pré-avisos** [prɛa'vizuʃ]) *m* advance warning, prior notice.

precário, -ria [prɛ'karju, -rja] *adj* precarious.

precaução [prekaw'sãw] (*pl* **-ões** [-õjʃ]) *f* precaution; **por ~** as a precaution.

precaver-se [preka'vexsi] *vp* to take

precautions; ~ **contra** to take precautions against.
precavido, -da [prɛkaˈvidu, -da] adj prudent; **vim** ~ I've come prepared.
prece [ˈprɛsi] f prayer.
precedência [preseˈdẽsja] f precedence; **ter** ~ **sobre** to take precedence over.
preceder [preseˈde(x)] vt to precede.
precioso, -osa [preˈsjozu, -ɔza] adj precious.
precipício [presiˈpisju] m precipice.
precipitação [presipitaˈsãw] (pl -ões [-õjʃ]) f (pressa) haste; (chuva) rainfall.
precipitar-se [presepiˈtaxsi] vp (pessoa) to act rashly; (acontecimentos) to gain momentum.
precisamente [presizaˈmẽtʃi] adv precisely.
precisão [presiˈzãw] f accuracy; **com** ~ accurately.
precisar [presiˈza(x)] vt (especificar) to specify.
⃝ **precisar de** v + prep to need; ~ **de fazer algo** to need to do sthg.
preciso, -sa [preˈsizu, -za] adj accurate, precise; **é** ~ **ter calma** keep calm; **é** ~ **passaporte** you need your passport.
preço [ˈpresu] m price; ~ **de ocasião** special offer; ~ **reduzido** reduced price; ~ **de liquidação** sale price.
precoce [preˈkɔsi] adj (criança) precocious; (decisão) hasty.
preconcebido, -da [prɛkõseˈbidu, -da] adj preconceived.
preconceito [prɛkõˈsejtu] m prejudice.
precursor, -ra [prekuxˈso(x), -ra] (mpl -res [-riʃ], fpl -s [-ʃ]) m, f forerunner.
predador, -ra [predaˈdo(x), -ra] (mpl -es [-iʃ], fpl -s [-ʃ]) adj predatory.
predecessor, -ra [predeseˈso(x), -ra] (mpl -res [-riʃ], fpl -s [-ʃ]) m, f predecessor.
predileção [predʒileˈsãw] (pl -ões [-õjʃ]) f (Br) preference; **ter** ~ **por** to prefer.
predilecção [prediˈleˈsãw] (pl -ões [-õjʃ]) f (Port) = **predileção**.
predileções → **predileção**.
predilecto, -ta [prediˈlɛtu, -ta] adj (Port) = **predileto**.
predileto, -ta [predʒiˈlɛtu, -ta] adj (Br) favourite.

prédio [ˈprɛdʒju] m building; ~ **de apartamentos** block of flats (Brit), apartment building (Am).
predominante [predumiˈnãtʃi] adj predominant.
predominar [predomiˈna(x)] vi to predominate.
preencher [priẽˈʃe(x)] vt to fill in.
pré-fabricado, -da [prɛfabriˈkadu, -da] adj prefabricated.
prefácio [preˈfasju] m preface.
prefeito, -ta [preˈfejtu, -ta] m, f (Br) mayor.
prefeitura [prefejˈtura] f (Br) town hall (Brit), city hall (Am).
preferência [prefeˈrẽsja] f preference; **dar** ~ **a** to give preference to; **ter** ~ **por** to prefer, to have a preference for; **de** ~ preferably.
preferido, -da [prefeˈridu, -da] adj favourite.
preferir [prefeˈri(x)] vt to prefer; ~ **fazer algo** to prefer doing sthg; **eu preferia que viajássemos de dia** I would prefer to travel by day.
prefixo [preˈfiksu] m prefix.
prega [ˈprɛga] f pleat.
pregar¹ [preˈga(x)] vt (prego) to hammer in; (botões) to sew on.
pregar² [preˈga(x)] vt (sermão) to preach.
prego [ˈprɛgu] m nail; (Br: fam: casa de penhor) pawn shop.
preguiça [preˈgisa] f laziness.
pré-histórico, -ca [prɛiʃˈtɔriku, -ka] adj prehistoric.
prejudicar [preʒudʒiˈka(x)] vt (pessoa) to harm; (carreira, relação, saúde) to damage.
prejudicial [preʒudʒiˈsjaw] (pl -ais [-ajʃ]) adj: ~ **para** damaging to.
prejuízo [preˈʒwizu] m (dano) damage; (em negócio) loss; **em** ~ **de** to the detriment of; **sem** ~ **de** without detriment to.
prematuro, -ra [premaˈturu, -ra] adj premature.
premiado, -da [preˈmjadu, -da] adj prizewinning.
premiar [preˈmja(x)] vt to award a prize to; (recompensar) to reward.
prémio [ˈprɛmju] m (Port) = **prêmio**.
prêmio [ˈprẽmju] m (Br) (em concurso, competição) prize; (recompensa) reward; (em seguros) premium; **grande** ~ (em Fórmula 1) grand prix.

premonição [premoni'sãw] (*pl* -ões [-õjʃ]) *f* premonition.

pré-natal [ˌprɛna'taw] *adj* (*pl* -ais) *(roupa, vestuário)* maternity *(antes de s)*.

prenda ['prẽda] *f* present, gift.

prendado, -da [prẽ'dadu, -da] *adj* gifted.

prender [prẽ'de(x)] *vt* to tie up; *(pessoa)* to arrest.

❏ **prender-se** *vp* to get stuck.

prenome [pre'nome] *m* first name, Christian name.

prenunciar [prenũ'sja(x)] *vt* (*predizer*) to foretell.

preocupação [preokupa'sãw] (*pl* -ões [-õjʃ]) *f* worry.

preocupado, -da [prioku'padu, -da] *adj* worried.

preocupar [preoku'pa(x)] *vt* to worry.

❏ **preocupar-se** *vp* to worry; **~-se com** to worry about.

pré-pagamento [ˌprɛpaga'mẽtu] *m* prepayment.

preparação [prepara'sãw] (*pl* -ões [-õjʃ]) *f* preparation.

preparado, -da [prepa'radu, -da] *adj* ready ◆ *m* preparation.

preparar [prepa'ra(x)] *vt* to prepare.

❏ **preparar-se** *vp* to get ready; **~-se para algo** to get ready for sthg.

preposição [prepozi'sãw] (*pl* -ões [-õjʃ]) *f* preposition.

prepotente [prepo'tẽtʃi] *adj* domineering.

presença [pre'zẽsa] *f* presence; **na ~ de** in the presence of; **~ de espírito** presence of mind.

presenciar [prezẽ'sja(x)] *vt* to witness.

presente [pre'zẽtʃi] *adj & m* present; **o ~ (do indicativo)** the present tense.

preservação [prezexva'sãw] (*pl* -ões [-õjʃ]) *f* (*de costumes, língua*) preservation; *(de natureza)* conservation.

preservar [prezex'va(x)] *vt* to preserve.

preservativo [prezexva't ʃivu] *m* condom.

presidência [prezi'dẽsja] *f* presidency.

presidente [prezi'dẽtʃi] *mf* (*de país, organização*) president; *(de empresa, associação)* chairman (*f* chairwoman) *(Brit)*, president *(Am)*; **Presidente da Câmara** *(Port)* mayor; **Presidente da**

República President of the Republic.

presidir [prezi'dʒi(x)] *vi*: **~ a algo** to chair sthg.

presilha [pre'ziʎa] *f* (belt) loop.

preso, -sa ['prezu, -za] *pp* → **prender** ◆ *adj* tied up; *(capturado)* imprisoned; *(que não se move)* stuck ◆ *m, f (prisioneiro)* prisoner.

pressa ['prɛsa] *f* hurry; **estar com** OU **ter ~** to be in a hurry OU rush; **estar sem ~** not to be in a hurry OU rush; **às ~s** quickly, hurriedly.

presságio [pre'saʒju] *m* premonition.

pressão [pre'sãw] (*pl* -ões [-õjʃ]) *f* pressure; **~ (arterial) alta/baixa** *(Br: MED)* high/low blood pressure; **~ atmosférica** atmospheric pressure; **~ dos pneus** tyre pressure; **estar sob ~** *(pessoa)* to be under pressure.

pressentimento [presẽtʃi'mẽtu] *m* feeling.

pressentir [presẽt'ʃi(x)] *vt*: **~ que** to have a feeling (that).

pressionar [presjo'na(x)] *vt* (*botão*) to press; *(pessoa)* to pressurize.

pressões → **pressão**.

pressupor [presu'po(x)] *vt* to presuppose.

prestação [presta'sãw] (*pl* -ões [-õjʃ]) *f* (*de serviço*) provision; *(de pagamento)* instalment; **pagar a prestações** to pay in instalments.

prestar [pres'ta(x)] *vt* (*ajuda*) to give; *(serviço)* to provide; *(contas)* to render; *(atenção)* to pay ◆ *vi* (*ser útil*) to be useful; **isso presta para alguma coisa?** is that any good?; **não ~** to be no good; **não ~ para nada** to be totally useless; **~ um serviço a alguém** to do sthg for sb.

❏ **prestar-se a** *vp + prep* (*ser adequado para*) to be suitable for; *(estar disposto a)* to leave o.s. open to.

prestativo, -va [presta'tʃivu, -va] *adj* helpful.

prestes ['prestʃiʃ] *adj inv*: **estar ~ a fazer algo** to be just about to do sthg.

prestidigitador, -ra [prestʃidʒiʒita-'do(x), -ra] (*mpl* -res [-riʃ], *fpl* -s [-ʃ]) *m, f* conjurer.

prestígio [prestʃiʒju] *m* prestige.

presumir [prezu'mi(x)] *vt* to presume.

presunçoso, -osa [prezũ'sozu, -ɔza] *adj* (*pessoa*) conceited; *(discurso, artigo)* pretentious.

presunto [pre'zũtu] *m* ham.

prêt-a-porter [prɛtapoxte] *m inv*
(Br) ready-to-wear clothes *(pl)*.
pretender [pretẽ'de(x)] *vt (querer)* to
want; *(afirmar)* to claim; ~ **fazer algo**
to intend to do sthg.
pretensão [pretẽ'sãw] *(pl* **-ões** [-õjʃ])
f (desejo) wish, aspiration.
⅃ **pretensões** *fpl (vaidade)* pretentiousness *(sg);* **ter pretensões** to be
pretentious.
pretérito [pre'teritu] *m (GRAM)*
preterite, past tense; ~ **perfeito (sim**
ples) simple past (tense); ~ **imperfeito**
(simples) imperfect (tense).
pretexto [pre'tejʃtu] *m* excuse; **sob ~**
algum under no circumstances; **a** OU
sob o ~ de on OU under the pretext of.
preto, -ta [pretu, -ta] *adj & m, f*
black; **pôr o ~ no branco** to set the
record straight.
prevalecer [prevale'se(x)] *vi* to prevail.
prevenção [prevẽ'sãw] *(pl* **-ões** [-õjʃ])
f (de doença, acidente) prevention;
(aviso) warning; **estar de ~** to be on
guard; ~ **rodoviária** road safety and
accident prevention; **por ~** as a precaution.
prevenido, -da [preve'nidu, -da] *adj*
cautious; **estar ~** to be prepared.
prevenir [preve'ni(x)] *vt (avisar)* to
warn; *(evitar)* to prevent; ~ **alguém de**
algo to warn sb of sthg.
preventivo, -va [prevẽ'tʃivu, -va]
adj preventive.
prever [pre've(x)] *vt* to foresee;
(tempo) to forecast.
previamente [prevja'mẽtʃi] *adv*
beforehand.
prévio, -via ['prevju, -vja] *adj* prior.
previsão [previ'zãw] *(pl* **-ões** [-õjʃ]) *f*
forecast; ~ **do tempo** weather forecast.
previsível [previ'zivew] *(pl* **-eis** [-ejʃ])
adj foreseeable.
previsões → previsão.
previsto, -ta [pre'viʃtu, -ta] *adj*
expected; **como ~** as expected.
prezado, -da [pre'zadu, -da] *adj*
(querido) dear; **Prezado ...** *(fml: em*
carta) Dear ....
primária [pri'marja] *f (EDUC)* primary
school.
primário, -ria [pri'marju, -rja] *adj*
(básico) basic; *(EDUC)* primary.
primavera [prima'vera] *f (estação)*

spring; *(flor)* primrose.
primeira [pri'mejra] *f (em veículo)* first
(gear), → **primeiro**.
primeiro, -ra [pri'mejru, -ra] *adj, adv*
& num first ◆ *m, f:* **o ~/a primeira da**
turma top of the class; **à primeira**
vista at first sight; **de primeira** first-
class; **em ~ lugar** firstly, first; **primeira**
classe *(EDUC)* primary one *(Brit),* first
grade *(Am);* **~s socorros** *(MED)* first aid
(sg); ~ **de tudo** *(antes de mais)* first of
all, → **sexto**.
primeiro-ministro, primeira-
ministra [pri,mejrumi'niʃtru, pri,mejra-
mi'niʃtra] *(mpl* **primeiros-ministros**
[pri,mejruʒmi'niʃtruʃ]. *fpl* **primeiras-**
ministras [pri,mejraʒmi'niʃtraʃ]) *m, f*
prime minister.
primitivo, -va [primi'tʃivu, -va] *adj*
primitive.
primo, -ma ['primu, -ma] *m, f* cousin.
primogénito, -ta [primo'ʒenitu, -ta]
m, f (Port) = **primogênito**.
primogênito, -ta [primo'ʒenitu, -ta]
m, f (Br) firstborn.
princesa [prĩ'seza] *f* princess.
principal [prĩsi'paw] *(pl* **-ais** [-ajʃ]) *adj*
main.
principalmente [prĩsipaw'mẽtʃi]
adv mainly, especially.
príncipe ['prĩsipi] *m* prince.
principiante [prĩse'pjãtʃi] *mf*
beginner.
principiar [prĩsi'pja(x)] *vt & vi* to
start, to begin.
princípio [prĩ'sipju] *m* beginning;
(moral) principle; **partir do ~ que ...** to
work on the basis that ...; **a ~** to start
with; **desde o ~** from the beginning;
em ~ in principle; **por ~** on principle.
prioridade [priori'dadʒi] *f* priority; ~
de passagem *(AUT)* right of way.
prisão [pri'zãw] *(pl* **-ões** [-õjʃ]) *f (ato)*
imprisonment; *(local)* prison; ~ **de**
ventre constipation.
privação [priva'sãw] *(pl* **-ões** [-õjʃ]) *f*
loss.
⅃ **privações** *fpl* misery *(sg),* hardship
(sg).
privacidade [privasi'dadʒi] *f* privacy.
privações → privação.
privada [pri'vada] *f (Br)* toilet.
privado, -da [pri'vadu, -da] *adj* private.
privar [pri'va(x)] *vt:* ~ **alguém de algo**
to deprive sb of sthg.

⌐ **privar-se de** *vp* + *prep* to go without.

privativo, -va [privaˈtʃivu, -va] *adj* private.

privilegiado, -da [priviliˈʒjadu, -da] *adj (pessoa)* privileged; *(local)* exceptional.

privilegiar [priviliˈʒja(x)] *vt* to favour.

privilégio [priviˈleʒju] *m* privilege.

proa [ˈproa] *f* prow.

probabilidade [probabiliˈdadʒi] *f* probability.

problema [proˈblema] *m* problem; **ter ~s com** to have problems with.

procedente [proseˈdẽntʃi] *adj:* **~ de** *(ônibus, trem, avião)* from.

proceder [proseˈde(x)] *vi (agir)* to proceed, to act; **~ com** to proceed with.

processador [prosesaˈdo(x)] *(pl* **-es** [-iʃ]) *m:* **~ de texto** word processor.

processamento [prosesaˈmẽntu] *m* processing.

processar [proseˈsa(x)] *vt (JUR: pessoa, empresa)* to prosecute; *(JUR: por danos pessoais, materiais)* to sue; *(INFORM: dados, texto)* to process.

processo [proˈsɛsu] *m (sistema)* process; *(JUR)* (law)suit.

procissão [prosiˈsãw] *(pl* **-ões** [-õjʃ]) *f* procession.

proclamar [proklaˈma(x)] *vt* to proclaim.

procura [proˈkura] *f (busca)* search; *(COM)* demand; **andar à ~ de** to be looking for.

procurador, -ra [prokuraˈdo(x), -ra] *(mpl* **-res** [-riʃ], *fpl* **-s** [-ʃ]) *m, f* proxy; **~ da República** = Public Prosecutor.

procurar [prokuˈra(x)] *vt* to look for; **~ fazer algo** to try to do sthg.

prodígio [proˈdʒiʒju] *m* prodigy.

produção [produˈsãw] *(pl* **-ões** [-õjʃ]) *f* production.

produtividade [produtʃiviˈdadʒi] *f* productivity.

produtivo, -va [produˈtʃivu, -va] *adj (que produz)* productive; *(lucrativo)* profitable.

produto [proˈdutu] *m* product; **~ alimentar** foodstuff; **~ de limpeza** cleaning product; **~ natural** natural product.

produtor, -ra [produˈto(x), -ra] *(mpl* **-res** [-riʃ], *fpl* **-s** [-ʃ]) *m, f* producer.

produzir [produˈzi(x)] *vt* to produce.

proeminente [proimiˈnẽntʃi] *adj (saliente)* protruding; *(importante)* prominent.

proeza [proˈeza] *f* deed.

profanar [profaˈna(x)] *vt (igreja, cemitério)* to desecrate; *(memória)* to be disrespectful about.

profecia [profeˈsia] *f* prophecy.

proferir [profeˈri(x)] *vt (discurso)* to give; *(palavra)* to utter; *(insulto)* to hurl; *(desejo)* to make; *(sentença)* to pronounce.

professor, -ra [profeˈso(x), -ra] *(mpl* **-res** [-riʃ], *fpl* **-s** [-ʃ]) *m, f* teacher.

profeta [proˈfɛta] *m* prophet.

profetisa [profeˈtʃiza] *f* prophetess.

profiláctico, -ca [profiˈlatiku, -ka] *adj (Port)* = profilático.

profilático, -ca [profiˈlatʃiku, -ka] *adj (Br)* prophylactic.

profissão [profiˈsãw] *(pl* **-ões** [-õjʃ]) *f* profession.

profissional [profisjoˈnaw] *(pl* **-ais** [-ajʃ]) *adj & mf* professional.

profissões → profissão.

profundidade [profũndʒiˈdadʒi] *f* depth; **tem três metros de ~** it's three metres deep.

profundo, -da [proˈfũndu, -da] *adj* deep; *(idéia, argumento, sentimento)* profound.

prognóstico [progˈnɔʃtʃiku] *m (MED)* prognosis; *(de tempo)* forecast.

programa [proˈgrama] *m* programme; *(EDUC)* syllabus, curriculum; *(INFORM)* program.

programação [programaˈsãw] *(pl* **-ões** [-õjʃ]) *f (em televisão, rádio)* programmes *(pl)*; *(INFORM)* programming.

progredir [progreˈdi(x)] *vi* to make progress; *(doença)* to progress; **~ em** to make progress in.

progresso [proˈgrɛsu] *m* progress; **fazer ~s** to make progress.

proibição [proibiˈsãw] *(pl* **-ões** [-õjʃ]) *f* ban.

proibido, -da [proiˈbidu, -da] *adj* prohibited; **"proibida a entrada"** "no entry"; **"~ afixar anúncios"** "stick no bills"; **"~ estacionar"** "no parking"; **"~ fumar"** "no smoking"; **"~ para menores de 18"** "adults only".

proibir [proiˈbi(x)] *vt (consumo)* to forbid; *(acontecimento, publicação)* to ban; **~ alguém de fazer algo** to forbid sb to do sthg.

projeção [proʒeˈsãw] (*pl* -ões [-õjʃ]) *f* (*Br*) projection.

projecção [pruʒeˈsãw] (*pl* -ões [-õjʃ]) *f* (*Port*) = **projeção**.

projeções → **projeção**.

projéctil [pruʒeˈtil] (*pl* -teis [-tejʃ]) *m* (*Port*) = **projétil**.

projecto [pruʒetu] *m* (*Port*) = **projeto**.

projector [pruʒeˈtor] (*pl* -res [-reʃ]) *m* (*Port*) = **projetor**.

projétil [proʒeˈtʃiw] (*pl* -teis [-teiʃ]) *m* (*Br*) projectile.

projeto [proʒetu] *m* (*Br*) project, plan.

projetor [proʒeˈto(x)] (*pl* -res [-riʃ]) *m* (*Br*) projector; (*de luz*) spotlight.

proliferar [prolifeˈra(x)] *vi* to proliferate.

prólogo [ˈprɔlogu] *m* prologue.

prolongado, -da [prolõˈgadu, -da] *adj* extended.

prolongar [prolõˈga(x)] *vt* (*prazo*) to extend; (*férias, estada*) to prolong.

❑ **prolongar-se** *vp* (*demorar-se*) to last.

promessa [proˈmɛsa] *f* promise.

prometer [prɔmeˈte(x)] *vt* to promise; ~ **algo a alguém** to promise sb sthg; ~ **fazer algo** to promise to do sthg; ~ **que** to promise (that).

promíscuo, -cua [proˈmiʃkwu, -kwa] *adj* promiscuous.

promissor, -ra [promiˈso(x), -ra] (*mpl* -res [-riʃ]. *fpl* -s [-ʃ]) *adj* promising.

promoção [promoˈsãw] (*pl* -ões [-õjʃ]) *f* promotion; **em** ~ on special offer.

promontório [promõˈtɔrju] *m* headland.

promover [promoˈve(x)] *vt* to promote.

pronome [proˈnomi] *m* (*GRAM*) pronoun.

pronto, -ta [ˈprõtu, -ta] *adj* (*preparado*) ready; (*resposta*) prompt ♦ *interj* that's that!; **estar** ~ to be ready; **estar** ~ **para fazer algo** to be willing to do sthg; **estar** ~ **para fazer algo** to be ready to do sthg.

pronto-a-vestir [ˌprõtwaveʃˈtʃi(x)] *m inv* (*vestuário*) ready-to-wear clothes (*pl*); (*loja*) clothes shop.

pronto-socorro [prõtusoˈkoxu] *m* (*veículo*) ambulance.

pronúncia [proˈnũsja] *f* (*pronunciação*) pronunciation; (*sotaque*) accent.

pronunciar [pronũˈsja(x)] *vt* (*palavra, frase*) to pronounce; (*discurso*) to give.

❑ **pronunciar-se** *vp* (*palavra*) to be pronounced; (*exprimir opinião*) to express one's opinion.

propaganda [propaˈgãda] *f* (*de produto*) advertising; (*POL*) propaganda.

propensão [propẽˈsãw] (*pl* -ões [-õjʃ]) *f* propensity.

propina [proˈpina] *f* (*gorjeta*) tip.

propor [proˈpo(x)] *vt* (*sugerir*) to propose; (*negócio*) to offer.

proporção [proporˈsãw] (*pl* -ões [-õjʃ]) *f* proportion; **em** ~ in proportion.

❑ **proporções** *fpl* (*dimensões*) measurements.

proporcional [proporsjoˈnaw] (*pl* -ais [-ajʃ]) *adj* proportional; ~ **a** proportional to.

proporções → **proporção**.

propósito [proˈpɔzitu] *m* purpose; **a** ~, **quando e que você vai de férias?** by the way, when are you going on holiday?; **com o** ~ **de** with the intention of; **de** ~ on purpose.

❑ **propósitos** *mpl* (*maneiras*) manners.

propriedade [propriˈedadʒi] *f* property; "~ **privada**" "private property".

proprietário, -ria [propriˈetarju, -rja] *m, f* owner.

próprio, -pria [ˈprɔpriu, -pria] *adj* (*carro, casa*) own; (*adequado*) suitable; (*característico*) particular ♦ *m, f:* **é o** ~/a **própria** (*em conversa telefônica*) speaking; ~ **para** suitable for; ~ **para consumo** fit for human consumption; **eu** ~ I myself; **o** ~ **presidente** the president himself.

prosa [ˈprɔza] *f* prose.

prospecto [proʃˈpɛ(k)tu] *m* leaflet.

prosperar [proʃpeˈra(x)] *vi* to prosper.

prosperidade [proʃperiˈdadʒi] *f* prosperity.

prosseguir [proseˈgi(x)] *vt* (*estudos, investigações*) to continue ♦ *vi* (*continuar*) to proceed, to carry on; **se** ~ **com este tipo de comportamento, será despedido** if you continue to behave in this way, you will be fired.

prostituta [proʃtʃiˈtuta] *f* prostitute.

protagonista [protagoˈniʃta] *mf* protagonist.

proteção [proteˈsãw] (*pl* -ões [-õjʃ]) *f* (*Br*) protection.

protecção [prute'sãw] (*pl* -ões [-õjʃ]) *f (Port)* = proteção.

proteções → proteção.

protector, -ra [prute'tor, -ra] (*mpl* -res [-reʃ]. *fpl* -s [-ʃ]) *adj & m, f (Port)* = protetor.

proteger [prote'ʒe(x)] *vt* to protect.

proteína [prote'ina] *f* protein.

prótese [prɔtɛzi] *f (MED)* prosthesis; ~ **dentária** dental prosthesis.

protestante [proteʃ'tãntʃi] *adj & mf (RELIG)* Protestant.

protestar [proteʃ'ta(x)] *vi* to protest; ~ **contra** to protest against.

protesto [pro'tɛʃtu] *m* protest.

protetor, -ra [prote'to(x), -ra] (*mpl* -res [-riʃ]. *fpl* -s [-ʃ]) *m, f (Br)* protector ◆ *adj* protective; ~ **(solar)** sunscreen.

protocolo [proto'kɔlu] *m (em audiência)* transcription; *(regras)* protocol.

protuberância [protube'rãsja] *f* protuberance.

prova ['prɔva] *f* proof; *(ESP)* event; *(teste)* exam; **à ~ d'água** waterproof; **à ~ de fogo** fireproof; **à ~ de óleo** oil-resistant; **dar ~s de** to show; **pôr à ~** to put to the test; **prestar ~s** *(fazer exames)* to take exams.

provar [pro'va(x)] *vt (fato)* to prove; *(comida)* to try; *(roupa)* to try on.

provável [pro'vavɛw] (*pl* -eis [-ejʃ]) *adj* probable; **pouco ~** unlikely.

proveito [pro'vejtu] *m* benefit; **bom ~!** enjoy your meal!; **em ~ de** for the benefit of; **tirar ~ de algo** to benefit from sthg.

proveniente [prove'njẽntʃi] *adj*: ~ **de** (coming) from.

provérbio [pro'vɛrbju] *m* proverb.

prover-se [pro'vexsi] : **prover-se de** *vp* + *prep (abastecer-se de)* to provide o.s. with; *(munir-se de)* to equip o.s. with.

proveta [pro'vɛta] *f* test tube.

providência [provi'dẽsja] *f* measure; **tomar ~s** to take measures.

providenciar [providẽ'sja(x)] *vt* to arrange (for) ◆ *vi*: ~ **(para) que** to make sure (that).

província [pro'vĩsja] *f* province.

provisório, -ria [provi'zɔrju, -rja] *adj* temporary.

provocador, -ra [provoka'do(x), -ra] (*mpl* -res [-riʃ]. *fpl* -s [-ʃ]) *adj* provocative.

provocante [provo'kãntʃi] *adj* provocative.

provocar [provo'ka(x)] *vt (causar)* to cause; *(irritar)* to provoke.

provolone [provo'loni] *m* hard cheese made from cow's milk.

proximidade [prosimi'dadʒi] *f* proximity.

 ⌐ **proximidades** *fpl (arredores)* neighbourhood *(sg)*.

próximo, -ma ['prɔsimu, -ma] *adj (em espaço, tempo)* near; *(seguinte)* next; *(íntimo)* close ◆ *pron*: **o ~/a próxima** the next one; **quem é o ~?** who's next?; **até a próxima!** see you!; ~ **de** near (to); **nos ~s dias/meses** in the next few days/months.

prudência [pru'dẽsja] *f* care, caution.

prudente [pru'dẽntʃi] *adj* careful, cautious.

prurido [pru'ridu] *m* itch.

P.S. *(abrev de Post Scriptum)* PS.

pseudónimo [psew'dɔnimu] *m (Port)* = pseudônimo.

pseudônimo [psew'donimu] *m (Br)* pseudonym.

psicanálise [psika'nalizi] *f* psychoanalysis.

psicanalista [psikana'liʃta] *mf* psychoanalyst.

psicologia [psikolo'ʒia] *f* psychology.

psicológico, -ca [psiko'lɔʒiku, -ka] *adj* psychological.

psicólogo, -ga [psi'kɔlogu, -ga] *m, f* psychologist.

psiquiatra [psi'kjatra] *mf* psychiatrist.

puberdade [puber'dadʒi] *f* puberty.

publicação [publika'sãw] (*pl* -ões [-õjʃ]) *f* publication.

publicar [publi'ka(x)] *vt* to publish.

publicidade [publisi'dadʒi] *f (atividade, curso)* advertising; *(anúncio)* ad(vert); *(divulgação, difusão)* publicity.

público, -ca ['publiku, -ka] *adj (jardim, via)* public; *(escola)* state *(antes de s)*; *(empresa)* state-owned ◆ *m (de espetáculo)* audience; **o ~ em geral** the general public; **tornar ~ algo** to make sthg public; **em ~** in public.

pude ['pudʒi] → poder.

pudim [pu'dʒĩ] (*pl* -ns [-ʃ]) *m* pudding; ~ **flan** crème caramel; ~ **de leite** custard *(sg)*.

puf ['pufɛ] *interj (de enfado)* pah!; *(de cansaço)* phew!

pugilismo [puʒi'liʒmu] *m* boxing.

puído, -da ['pwidu. -da] *adj* worn.
pular [pu'la(x)] *vi* to jump ◆ *vt* to jump over.
pulga ['puwga] *f* flea; **estar com a ~ atrás da orelha** *(fig: estar suspeitoso)* to think something is up.
pulmão [puw'mãw] *(pl* **-ões** [-õjʃ]) *m* lung.
pulo ['pulu] *m* jump; **dar um ~ até** to pop over to; **dar ~s** to jump up and down; **num ~** in a flash.
pulôver [pu'love(x)] *(pl* **-res** [-riʃ]) *m* pullover.
pulsação [puwsa'sãw] *(pl* **-ões** [-õjʃ]) *f* beat.
pulseira [puw'sejra] *f* bracelet.
pulso ['puwsu] *m* wrist; *(pulsação)* pulse; **medir** OU **tirar o ~ de alguém** to take sb's pulse.
pulverizar [puwveri'za(x)] *vt (com líquido)* to spray; *(reduzir a pó)* to pulverize.
punha ['puɲa] → **poder.**
punhado [pu'ɲadu] *m*: **um ~ de** a handful of.
punhal [pu'ɲaw] *(pl* **-ais** [-ajʃ]) *m* dagger.
punho ['puɲu] *m (mão fechada)* fist; *(pulso)* wrist; *(de casaco, camisa, blusa)* cuff; *(de a ma, faca)* hilt.
punição [puni'sãw] *(pl* **-ões** [-õjʃ]) *f* punishment.
punir [pu'ni(x)] *vt* to punish.

pupila [pu'pila] *f* pupil.
puré [pu're] *m (Port)* = **purê.**
purê [pu're] *m (Br)* puree; **~ (de batata)** mashed potatoes *(pl).*
pureza [pu'reza] *f* purity.
purgante [pux'gãntʃi] *m* purgative.
purificador, -ra [purifika'do(x), -ra] *(mpl* **-res** [-riʃ], *fpl* **-s** [-ʃ]) *adj* purifying ◆ *m*: **~ do ar** air freshener.
purificar [purifi'ka(x)] *vt (sangue)* to purify; *(ar)* to freshen.
puritano, -na [puri'tanu, -na] *adj* puritanical.
puro, -ra ['puru, -ra] *adj* pure; **pura lã** pure wool; **a pura verdade** the plain truth; **pura e simplesmente** simply.
puro-sangue [.puru'sãngi] *m inv* thoroughbred.
púrpura ['puxpura] *f* purple.
pus¹ ['puʃ] → **pôr.**
pus² ['puʃ] *m* pus.
puta ['puta] *f (vulg)* whore.
puxador [puʃa'do(x)] *(pl* **-res** [-riʃ]) *m* handle.
puxão [pu'ʃãw] *(pl* **-ões** [-õjʃ]) *m* tug.
puxar [pu'ʃa(x)] *vt (cabelo, cordel)* to pull; *(banco, cadeira)* to pull up; **"puxar","puxe"** *(aviso em porta)* "pull"; **~ o autoclismo** *(Port)* to flush the toilet; **~ o saco de alguém** *(Br: fam)* to suck up to sb.
puxões → **puxão.**

Q

q.b. *(abrev de quanto baste)* as required.

Q.I. *m (abrev de quociente de inteligência)* IQ.

quadra [ˈkwadra] *f (em poesia)* quatrain; ~ **de tênis/squash** *(Br)* tennis/squash court.

quadrado, -da [kwaˈdradu, -da] *adj & m* square.

quadragésimo, -ma [kwadraˈʒɛzimu, -ma] *num* fortieth, → **sexto.**

quadril [kwaˈdriw] *(pl* -is [-iʃ]) *m* hip.

quadro [ˈkwadru] *m* picture; *(em sala de aula)* board; *(pintura)* painting.

quadro-negro [ˌkwadruˈnegru] *(pl* **quadros-negros** [ˌkwadruʒˈnegruʃ]) *m (Br)* blackboard.

quaisquer → **qualquer.**

qual [kwaw] *(pl* -ais [-ajʃ]) *adj* which ◆ *conj (fml: como)* like ◆ *interj (Br)* what! ◆ *pron (em interrogativa)* what; *(especificando)* which (one); o/a ~ *(sujeito: pessoa)* who; *(complemento: pessoa)* whom; *(sujeito, complemento: coisa)* which; **cada** ~ everyone; ~ **deles ...?** which one (of them) ...?; ~ **nada** OU **quê!** what!

qualidade [kwaliˈdadʒi] *f* quality; *(espécie)* type; **na** ~ **de** in the capacity of.

qualificação [kwalifikaˈsãw] *(pl* -ões [-õjʃ]) *f* qualification.

qualificado, -da [kwalifiˈkadu, -da] *adj* qualified.

qualquer [kwawˈkɛ(x)] *(pl* **quaisquer** [kwajʃˈkɛ(x)]) *adj & pron* any; **está por aqui em** ~ **lugar** it's (around) here somewhere; ~ **um deles** any of them; ~ **um dos dois** either of them; ~ **um** OU **pessoa** anyone, anybody; **a** ~ **momento** at any time.

quando [ˈkwãndu] *adv* when ◆ *conj* when; *(ao passo que)* while, whilst; **de** ~ **em** ~ from time to time; **desde** ~

how long; ~ **mais não seja** at least; ~ **muito** at (the) most; ~ **quer que** whenever.

quantia [kwãnˈtʃia] *f* amount, sum.

quantidade [kwãntʃiˈdadʒi] *f* amount, quantity; **em** ~ in large quantities.

quanto, -ta [ˈkwãntu, -ta] *adj* **1.** *(em interrogativas: singular)* how much; *(em interrogativas: plural)* how many; ~ **tempo temos?** how much time have we got?; ~ **tempo temos de esperar?** how long do we have to wait?; **quantas vezes você já esteve aqui?** how many times have you been here? **2.** *(em exclamações)* what a lot of; ~ **dinheiro!** what a lot of money!; ~**s erros!** what a lot of mistakes! **3.** *(em locuções):* **uns** ~**s/umas quantas** some; **umas quantas pessoas** a few people. ◆ *pron* **1.** *(em interrogativas: singular)* how much; *(em interrogativas: plural)* how many; ~ **você quer?** how much do you want?; ~**s você quer?** how many do you want?; ~ **custam?** how much do they cost? **2.** *(relativo a pessoas):* **todos** ~**s** everyone who *(sg)*; **agradeceu a todos** ~**s o ajudaram** he thanked everyone who helped him. **3.** *(tudo o que)* everything, all; **coma** ~/~**s você quiser** eat as much/as many as you like; **tudo** ~ **disse é verdade** everything he said is true. **4.** *(compara quantidades):* ~ **mais se tem, mais se quer** the more you have, the more you want. **5.** *(em locuções):* **não há espaço para um,** ~ **mais para dois** there's hardly enough room for one, let alone two; ~ **a as regards;** ~ **antes** as soon as possible; ~ **mais não seja** at the very least; ~ **mais melhor** the more the merrier;

uns ~s/umas quantas some.

quarenta [kwaˈrẽnta] *num* forty, → seis.

quarentena [kwarẽnˈtena] *f* quarantine.

Quaresma [kwaˈrɛʒma] *f* Lent.

quarta [ˈkwarta] *f (em veículo)* fourth (gear), → quarto.

quarta-feira [ˌkwaxtaˈfejra] (*pl* **quartas-feiras** [ˌkwaxtaʃˈfejraʃ]) *f* Wednesday, → sexta-feira.

quarteirão [kwaxtejˈrãw] (*pl* -ões [-õjʃ]) *m (área)* block.

quartel [kwaxˈtɛw] (*pl* -éis [-ɛiʃ]) *m (MIL)* barracks (*pl*).

quarteto [kwaxˈtetu] *m* quartet.

quarto, -ta [ˈkwaxtu, -ta] *num* fourth ♦ *m (divisão de casa)* room; *(parte)* quarter; "~ para alugar" "room to let"; ~ **de banho** *(Port)* bathroom; ~ **de casal** double room; ~ **com duas camas** twin room; ~ **de hora** quarter of an hour, → sexto.

quartzo [ˈkwaxtsu] *m* quartz.

quase [ˈkwazi] *adv* almost, nearly; ~ **que caí** I almost fell over; ~ **nada** almost nothing, hardly anything; ~ **nunca** hardly ever; ~ ~ very nearly; ~ **sempre** nearly always.

quatro [ˈkwatru] *num* four, → seis.

quatrocentos, -tas [kwatroˈsẽntuʃ, -taʃ] *num* four hundred, → seis.

que [ki] *adj inv* 1. *(em interrogativas)* what, which; ~ **livros você quer?** which books do you want?; ~ **dia é hoje?** what day is it today?; ~ **horas são?** what time is it?
2. *(em exclamações)*: **mas ~ belo dia!** what a beautiful day!; ~ **fome!** I'm starving!; ~ **maravilha!** how wonderful!
♦ *pron* 1. *(em interrogativas)* what; ~ **é isso?** what's that?; **o ~ você quer?** what do you want?; **o ~ você vai comer?** what are you going to have (to eat)?
2. *(uso relativo: sujeito)* who; *(coisa)* which, that; **o homem ~ está correndo** the man who's running; **a guerra ~ começou em 1939** the war which OU that started in 1939.
3. *(uso relativo: complemento)* whom, that; *(coisa)* which, that; **o bolo ~ comi era ótimo** the cake (that) I had was great; **o homem ~ conheci** the man (that) I met.

♦ *conj* 1. *(com complemento direto)* that; **disse-me ~ ia de férias** he told me (that) he was going on holiday.
2. *(em comparações)*: **(do)** ~ than; **é mais caro (do)** ~ **o outro** it's more expensive than the other.
3. *(exprime causa)*: **leva o guarda-chuva ~ está chovendo** take an umbrella as it's raining; **vai depressa ~ você está atrasado** you're late, so you'd better hurry.
4. *(exprime consequência)* that; **pediu-me tanto ~ acabei por lhe dar** he asked me for it so persistently that I ended up giving it to him.
5. *(exprime tempo)*: **há horas ~ estou à espera** I've been waiting for hours; **há muito ~ lá não vou** I haven't been there for ages.
6. *(indica desejo)* that; **espero ~ você se divirta** I hope (that) you have a good time; **quero ~ você o faça** I want you to do it; ~ **você seja feliz!** all the best!
7. *(em locuções)*: ~ **nem** like; **chorou ~ nem um bebê** he cried like a baby.

quê [ke] *interj* what! ♦ *pron (interrogativo)* what ♦ *m*: **um** ~ (a certain) something; **um** ~ **de** a touch of; **não tem de** ~! not at all!, don't mention it!; **sem** ~ **nem para** ~ *(sem motivos)* for no apparent reason.

quebra-cabeças [ˌkɛbrakaˈbesaʃ] *m inv (passatempo)* puzzle; *(fig: problema)* headache.

quebrado, -da [kɛˈbradu, -da] *adj (partido)* broken; *(Br: enguiçado)* broken down.

quebra-mar [ˌkɛbraˈma(x)] (*pl* **quebra-mares** [ˌkɛbraˈmariʃ]) *m* breakwater.

quebra-nozes [ˌkɛbraˈnɔziʃ] *m inv* nutcracker.

quebrar [keˈbra(x)] *vt* to break; *(Br: avariar)* to break down; "~ **em caso de emergência**" "in case of emergency break glass"; ~ **a cara** *(Br: fig)* to come a cropper.
❏ **quebrar-se** *vp* to break.

queda [ˈkɛda] *f* fall; **ter** ~ **para** *(fig: vocação)* to have a flair for.

queijada [kejˈʒada] *f* cake made from eggs, milk, cheese, sugar and flour.

queijo [ˈkejʒu] *m* cheese; ~ **curado** cured cheese; ~ **de cabra** goat's cheese; ~ **flamengo** ≃ Edam; ~ **fresco** fresh goat's cheese; ~ **de ovelha** hard *cheese made from ewe's milk;* ~ **prato** *soft cheese made from ewe's milk;* ~ **ralado** grated cheese.

queijo-de-minas [ˌkejʒudʒiˈminaʃ] *m soft, mild, white cheese.*

queimado, -da [kejˈmadu. -da] *adj* burnt; *(pelo sol)* sunburnt.

queimadura [kejmaˈdura] *f* burn; ~ **de sol** sunburn.

queimar [kejˈma(x)] *vt* to burn. ˈ **queimar-se** *vp* to burn o.s.; *(com sol)* to get sunburnt.

queima-roupa [ˌkejmaˈxopa] *f*: **à** ~ *(disparar)* point-blank; *(tiro)* at point-blank range.

queixa [ˈkejʃa] *f (lamentação)* moan; *(em polícia)* complaint; **apresentar** ~ *(em polícia)* to register a complaint; **fazer** ~ **de alguém** to complain about sb.

queixar-se [kejˈʃaxsi] *vp* to moan; ~ **a alguém (de algo)** to complain to sb (about sthg); ~ **de** to complain about.

queixo [ˈkejʃu] *m* chin; **tinha tanto frio que estava batendo** ~ he was so cold that his teeth were chattering.

queixoso, -osa [kejˈʃozu. -ɔza] *m, f (JUR)* plaintiff.

quem [kẽj] *pron (interrogativo: sujeito)* who; *(interrogativo: complemento)* who, whom; *(indefinido)* whoever; ~ **diria!** who would have thought it!; ~ **é?** *(na porta)* who's there?; ~ **fala?** *(no telefone)* who's speaking?; ~ **me dera ser rico!** if only I were rich!; ~ **quer que** whoever; **seja** ~ **for** no matter who it is.

quentão [kẽˈtãw] *m alcoholic drink made with "cachaça", ginger and sugar, served hot.*

quente [ˈkẽtʃi] *adj* hot; *(roupa)* warm; *(Br: fam: informação, fonte)* reliable.

quer [kɛ(x)] *conj*: ~ ... ~ whether ... or; **quem** ~ **que seja** whoever; **onde** ~ **que seja** wherever; **o que** ~ **que seja** whatever.

querer [keˈre(x)] *vt* to want; **como quiser!** as you wish!; **por favor, queria ... excuse me, I'd like ...; **sem** ~ *(sem intenção)* unintentionally, by accident; ~ **muito a alguém** *(amar)* to love sb; ~ **bem a alguém** to care about sb; **não** ~ **mal a alguém** to wish sb no ill; ~ **dizer** *(significar)* to mean. ˈ **querer-se** *vp*: **eles se querem muito**

they're very much in love.

querido, -da [keˈridu. -da] *adj* dear.

querosene [kerɔˈzeni] *m* kerosene.

questão [keʃˈtãw] *(pl* **-ões** [- õjʃ]) *f* question; *(discussão)* quarrel; **há** ~ **de dez minutos** about ten minutes ago; **fazer** ~ **(de fazer algo)** to insist (on doing sthg); **pôr algo em** ~ to question sthg; **ser** ~ **de** to be a matter of; **em** ~ in question.

quiabo [ˈkjabu] *m* okra.

quibe [ˈkibi] *m Arabic dish made with mince and wholemeal flour, seasoned with mint and different spices.*

quiçá [kiˈsa] *adv* maybe.

quieto, -ta [ˈkjɛtu. -ta] *adj (parado, imóvel)* still; *(calado, calmo)* quiet.

quietude [kjeˈtudʒi] *f* tranquillity.

quilate [kiˈlatʃi] *m* carat.

quilo [ˈkilu] *m* kilo; **o** ~ **a** OU per kilo.

quilometragem [kilomeˈtraʒẽ] *(pl* **-ns** [-ʃ]) *f* ~ mileage, *distance travelled in kilometres.*

quilómetro [kiˈlɔmetru] *m (Port)* = **quilômetro.**

quilômetro [kiˈlometru] *m (Br)* kilometre.

química [ˈkimika] *f* chemistry, → **químico.**

químico, -ca [ˈkimiku. -ka] *m, f* chemist.

quindim [kĩˈdʒĩ] *(pl* **-ns** [-ʃ]) *m dessert made with egg yolks, sugar and coconut.*

quinhão [kiˈɲãw] *(pl* **-ões** [-õjʃ]) *m* share.

quinhentos, -tas [kiˈɲẽtuʃ. -taʃ] *num* five hundred, → **seis.**

quinhões → **quinhão.**

quinquagésimo, -ma [kwĩkwaˈʒɛzimu. -ma] *num* fiftieth, → **sexto.**

quinquilharias [kĩkiʎaˈriaʃ] *fpl* junk *(sg).*

quinta [ˈkĩta] *f* farm, → **quinto.**

quinta-feira [ˌkĩtaˈfejra] *(pl* **quintas-feiras** [ˌkĩtaʃˈfejraʃ]) *f* Thursday, → **sexta-feira.**

quintal [kĩˈtaw] *(pl* **-ais** [-ajʃ]) *m (terreno)* back garden; *(medida)* unit of weight equivalent to 60 kilos.

quinteto [kĩˈtetu] *m* quintet.

quinto, -ta [ˈkĩtu. -ta] *num* fifth, → **sexto.**

quinze [ˈkĩzi] *num* fifteen; ~ **dias** a fortnight.

quinzena [kĩˈzena] *f* fortnight.

quiosque [ˈkjɔʃki] *m* kiosk.
quis [ˈkiʃ] → **querer**.
quisto [ˈkiʃtu] *m* cyst.
quitanda [kiˈtãnda] *f (Br: loja)* grocer's (shop).
quites [ˈkitiʃ] *adj inv*: **estar ~ (com**

alguém) to be quits (with sb).
quociente [kwɔˈsjẽntʃi] *m* quotient.
quota [ˈkwɔta] *f (parte)* quota; *(de clube)* membership fee.
quotidiano, -na [kutʃiˈdjanu, -na] *adj* daily ◆ *m* everyday life.

R

R. *(abrev de rua)* Rd.

R$ *(abrev de real)* R$.

rã ['xã] *f* frog.

rabanada [xaba'nada] *f* French toast.

rabanete [xaba'netʃi] *m* radish.

rabicho [xa'biʃu] *m* ponytail.

rabino, -na [xa'binu, -na] *adj (criança)* naughty ♦ *m (sacerdote)* rabbi.

rabiscar [xabiʃ'ka(x)] *vi & vt* to scribble.

rabisco [xa'biʃku] *m* scrawl.

rabo ['xabu] *m (de ave, animal)* tail; *(Br: vulg: ânus)* arse; *(Port: fam: nádegas)* bum.

rabugento, -ta [xabu'ʒẽntu, -ta] *adj* grumpy.

raça ['xasa] *f* race; *(animal)* breed; **de ~** *(cão, gato)* pedigree; *(cavalo)* thoroughbred.

ração [xa'sãw] *(pl* -ões [-õjʃ]) *f (de animal)* feed; *(em prisão, tropa)* food, rations *(pl).*

rachadura [xaʃa'dura] *f* crack.

rachar [xa'ʃa(x)] *vt (lenha)* to chop; *(conta)* to split ♦ *vi (abrir fenda)* to crack.

raciocínio [xasjo'sinju] *m* reasoning.

racional [xasjo'naw] *(pl* -ais [-ajʃ]) *adj* rational.

racismo [xa'siʒmu] *m* racism.

rações → **ração**.

radar [xa'da(x)] *(pl* -res [-riʃ]) *m* radar.

radiação [xadʒja'sãw] *(pl* -ões [-õjʃ]) *f* radiation.

radiador [xadʒja'do(x)] *(pl* -res [-riʃ]) *m* radiator.

radiante [xa'dʒjãntʃi] *adj* radiant.

radical [xadʒi'kaw] *(pl* -ais [-ajʃ]) *adj* radical.

rádio ['xadʒju] *m (telefonia)* radio ♦ *f (emissora)* radio station.

radioactivo, -va [ˌxadʒjua'tivu, -va] *adj (Port)* = **radioativo**.

radioativo, -va [ˌxadʒjoa'tʃivu, -va] *adj (Br)* radioactive.

rádio-despertador [ˌxadʒjodeʃpexta'do(x)] *(pl* **rádio-despertadores** [ˌxadʒjodeʃpexta'doriʃ]) *m* radio alarm.

radiografia [ˌxadʒjogra'fia] *f* X-ray.

radiotáxi [ˌxadʒjo'taksi] *m* minicab.

ráfia ['xafja] *f* raffia.

rafting ['xaftĩŋ] *m* rafting.

râguebi ['xagbi] *m (Port)* = **rúgbi**.

raia ['xaja] *f* skate.

rainha [xa'ina] *f* queen.

raio ['xaju] *m* ray; *(de roda)* spoke; *(relâmpago)* flash of lightning; **~s X** X-rays.

raiva ['xajva] *f (doença)* rabies *(sg);* *(fúria)* rage; **ter ~ de alguém** to hate sb.

raivoso, -osa [xaj'vozu, -ɔza] *adj (pessoa)* furious; *(animal)* rabid.

raiz [xa'iʃ] *(pl* -zes [-ziʃ]) *f* root.

rajada [xa'ʒada] *f (de vento)* blast, gust.

ralador [xala'do(x)] *(pl* -res [-riʃ]) *m* grater.

ralar [xa'la(x)] *vt (alimentos)* to grate; *(joelho, cotovelo)* to graze.

⊐ ralar-se *vp (fig: preocupar-se)* to worry; **não se rale com isso** don't worry about that.

ralhar [xa'ʎa(x)] *vi:* **~ com alguém** *(repreender)* to tell sb off.

rali [xa'li] *m* rally.

ralo, -la ['xalu, -la] *adj (cabelo)* thin; *(café)* weak; *(sopa)* watery ♦ *m* drain.

rama ['xama] *f* foliage.

ramificar [xamifi'ka(x)] *vt (negócio)* to expand.

⊐ ramificar-se *vp (negócio)* to branch out.

raminho [xa'minu] *m (de salsa, coentro, etc)* sprig.

ramo ['xamu] *m* branch; **mudar de ~** to change career.

rampa ['xãmpa] f *(plataforma)* ramp; *(rua, ladeira)* steep incline.

rancho ['xãʃu] m *(de pessoas)* group; *(fam: refeição)* meal.

ranço ['xãsu] m: **ter ~** *(manteiga, azeite)* to be rancid; *(queijo, carne)* to be off.

rancor [xãŋ'ko(x)] m resentment.

rancoroso, -osa [xãŋko'rozu, -ɔza] adj resentful.

rançoso, -osa [xã'sozu, -ɔza] adj *(manteiga, azeite)* rancid; *(queijo, carne)* off.

ranhura [xa'ɲura] f *(em madeira, parede)* groove; *(em telefone público)* slot.

rapar [xa'pa(x)] vt *(raspar)* to scrape; *(cabelo, pernas)* to shave; *(barba)* to shave off; *(fam: roubar)* to steal.

rapariga [xapa'riga] f *(Port)* girl.

rapaz [xa'paʒ] *(pl* **-zes** [-ziʃ]*)* m boy.

rapé [xa'pɛ] m snuff.

rapidez [xapi'deʒ] f speed.

rápido, -da ['xapidu, -da] adj fast; *(breve)* quick ♦ m *(trem)* express (train); *(em rio)* rapids *(pl)* ♦ adv quickly.

raposa [xa'poza] f fox.

rapsódia [xap'sɔdja] f rhapsody.

raptar [xap'ta(x)] vt to abduct, to kidnap.

rapto ['xaptu] m abduction, kidnapping.

raquete [xa'kɛtʃi] f racket.

raquítico, -ca [xa'kitʃiku, -ka] adj *(fig: subdesenvolvido)* underdeveloped.

raramente [,xara'mẽtʃi] adv rarely.

rarefeito, -ta [xare'fejtu, -ta] adj rarefied.

raridade [xari'dadʒi] f rarity.

raro, -ra ['xaru, -ra] adj rare; *(pouco espesso)* thin; **raras vezes** rarely.

rascunhar [xaʃku'ɲa(x)] vt to draft.

rascunho [xaʃ'kuɲu] m draft.

rasgado, -da [xaʒ'gadu, -da] adj *(tecido, folha)* torn; *(sorriso)* broad.

rasgão [xaʒ'gãw] *(pl* **-ões** [-õjʃ]*)* m *(em tecido, folha)* tear; *(em pele)* cut.

rasgar [xaʒ'ga(x)] vt to tear.

⌐ **rasgar-se** vp to tear.

rasgões → **rasgão**.

raso, -sa ['xazu, -za] adj *(nivelado)* flat; *(de pouca profundidade)* shallow; *(salto)* low.

raspa ['xaʃpa] f *(de limão, laranja)* grated zest.

raspar [xaʃ'pa(x)] vt *(pele de limão, laranja)* to grate.

rasteira [xaʃ'tejra] f: **passar uma ~ em alguém** to trip sb up.

rasteiro, -ra [xaʃ'tejru, -ra] adj *(vegetação)* low-lying.

rastejante [xaʃte'ʒãntʃi] adj *(planta, vegetação)* trailing; *(animal)* crawling.

rastejar [xaʃte'ʒa(x)] vi to crawl.

rasto ['xaʃtu] m *(Port)* = **rastro**.

rastro ['xaʃtru] m *(Br)* trace.

ratazana [xata'zana] f rat.

rato ['xatu] m mouse.

ravina [xa'vina] f ravine.

razão [xa'zãw] *(pl* **-ões** [-õjʃ]*)* f reason; **dar ~ a alguém** to admit that sb is right; **ter ~** to be right; **este comportamento não tem ~ de ser** there's no reason for this kind of behaviour; **com ~** rightly so; **sem ~** for no reason.

r/c *(Port: abrev de* **rés-do-chão**) ground floor *(Brit)*, first floor *(Am)*.

ré [xɛ] f *(de navio)* stern, → **réu**.

reabastecer [xjabaʃte'se(x)] vt to restock; *(avião, carro)* to refuel.

⌐ **reabastecer-se** vp to restock.

reação [xea'sãw] *(pl* **-ões** [-õjʃ]*)* f *(Br)* reaction.

reacção [xja'sãw] *(pl* **-ões** [-õjʃ]*)* f *(Port)* = **reação**.

reaccionário, -ria [xjasju'narju, -rja] adj *(Port)* = **reacionário**.

reacções → **reacção**.

reacionário, -ria [xeasjo'narju, -rja] adj *(Br)* reactionary.

reações → **reação**.

reagir [xea'ʒi(x)] vi: **~ (a algo)** *(provocação, ideia)* to react (to sthg); *(a medicamento, tratamento)* to respond (to sthg).

real ['xeaw] *(pl* **-ais** [-ajʃ]*)* adj *(verdadeiro)* real; *(relativo a rei, realeza)* royal ♦ m *(moeda)* real, Brazilian currency.

realçar [xeaw'sa(x)] vt *(cor, traço)* to accentuate; *(fato, idéia)* to emphasize.

realejo [xea'leʒu] m barrel organ.

realeza [xea'leza] f royalty.

realidade [xeali'dadʒi] f reality; **na ~** in fact; **~ virtual** virtual reality.

realista [xea'liʃta] mf realist.

realização [xealiza'sãw] *(pl* **-ões** [-õjʃ]*)* f *(de tarefa, trabalho)* carrying out; *(de projeto, plano)* implementation; *(de sonho, desejo)* fulfilment, realization; *(de dinheiro)* realization; *(de* *filme)* production.

realizador, -ra [xealiza'do(x), -ra] *(mpl -res* [-riʃ]. *fpl -s* [-ʃ]) *m, f (de filme)* director.

realizar [xeali'za(x)] *vt (tarefa, trabalho)* to carry out; *(projeto, plano)* to implement; *(sonho, desejo)* to fulfil, to realize; *(dinheiro)* to realize; *(filme)* to direct.

⊐ **realizar-se** *vp (espetáculo)* to be performed; *(sonho, desejo)* to be fulfilled, to come true.

realmente [xeaw'mẽntʃi] *adv (efetivamente)* actually.

reanimar [xeani'ma(x)] *vt (MED) (depois de parada cardíaca)* to resuscitate; *(depois de desmaio)* to revive.

reatar [xea'ta(x)] *vt (conversação)* to resume; *(amizade)* to rekindle.

reaver [xea've(x)] *vt (recuperar)* to recover.

reavivar [xeavi'va(x)] *vt (memória)* to refresh; *(chama)* to rekindle.

rebaixar [xebaj'ʃa(x)] *vt (teto, preço)* to lower; *(pessoa)* to humiliate.

⊐ **rebaixar-se** *vp* to lower o.s.

rebanho [xe'baɲu] *m* flock.

rebelde [xe'bɛwdʒi] *mf* rebel.

rebentar [xebẽn'ta(x)] *vi (balão, pneu)* to burst; *(bomba)* to explode; *(lâmpada)* to blow ◆ *vt (balão, pneu)* to burst; *(bomba)* to let off; **~ com algo** to destroy sthg.

rebocador [xeboka'do(x)] *(pl -res* [-riʃ]) *m (navio)* tug(boat).

rebocar [xebo'ka(x)] *vt* to tow.

rebolar [xebo'la(x)] *vi* to sway.

rebuçado [xebu'sadu] *m (Port)* sweet *(Brit),* candy *(Am).*

rebuliço [xebu'lisu] *m* commotion.

recado [xe'kadu] *m* message; **dar um ~ a alguém** to give sb a message; **deixar ~** to leave a message.

recaída [xeka'ida] *f* relapse; **ter uma ~** to have a relapse.

recair [xeka'i(x)] *vi:* **~ sobre** to fall upon.

recanto [xe'kãntu] *m* corner.

recapitular [xekapitu'la(x)] *vt* to sum up.

recatado, -da [xeka'tadu, -da] *adj (púdico)* modest; *(discreto)* discreet.

recauchutar [xekawʃu'ta(x)] *vt* to retread.

recear [xe'sja(x)] *vt* to fear.

receber [xese'be(x)] *vt* to receive;

(bofetada, pontapé) to get; *(dar as boas-vindas a)* to welcome; *(pessoas)* to entertain ◆ *vi (ter visitas)* to entertain.

receio [xe'saju] *m* fear.

receita [xe'sejta] *f (de médico)* prescription; *(culinária)* recipe; *(de Estado, empresa)* revenue.

receitar [xesej'ta(x)] *vt* to prescribe.

recém-casado, -da [xe,sɛka'zadu, -da] *m, f* newly-wed.

recém-chegado, -da [xe,sɛʃe'gadu, -da] *adj* recently arrived.

recém-nascido, -da [xe,sɛnaʃ'sidu, -da] *adj* newborn ◆ *m, f* newborn baby.

recente [xe'sẽntʃi] *adj* recent.

receoso, -osa [xe'sjozu, -ɔza] *adj* fearful; **estar ~ de** to be apprehensive about.

recepção [xese'sãw] *(pl -ões* [-õjʃ]) *f* reception; *(de mensagem, carta)* receipt.

recepcionista [xesɛsjo'niʃta] *mf* receptionist.

recepções → recepção.

receptivo, -va [xese'tʃivu, -va] *adj* receptive; **mostrar-se ~ a** to be receptive to.

receptor [xese'to(x)] *(pl -res* [-riʃ]) *m (de mensagem)* recipient; *(televisão, rádio)* receiver.

recessão [xese'sãw] *(pl -ões* [-õjʃ]) *f* recession.

recheado, -da [xe'ʃjadu, -da] *adj (bolo, bombom)* filled; *(peru, vegetal)* stuffed.

rechear [xe'ʃja(x)] *vt (bolo)* to fill; *(peru)* to stuff.

recheio [xe'ʃeju] *m (de bolo, bombom)* filling; *(de peru, vegetal)* stuffing.

rechonchudo, -da [xeʃõ'ʃudu, -da] *adj* chubby.

recibo [xe'sibu] *m* receipt.

reciclagem [xesi'klaʒẽ] *f* recycling.

reciclar [xesi'kla(x)] *vt* to recycle.

reciclável [xesi'klavew] *(pl -eis* [-ejʃ]) *adj* recyclable.

recife [xe'sifi] *m* reef.

recinto [xe'sĩntu] *m (espaço delimitado)* enclosure; *(à volta de edifício)* grounds *(pl).*

recipiente [xesi'pjẽntʃi] *m* container.

recíproco, -ca [xe'siproku, -ka] *adj* reciprocal.

recital [xesi'taw] *(pl -ais* [-ajʃ]) *m* recital.

recitar [xesi'ta(x)] *vt & vi* to recite.

reclamação [xeklama'sãw] (*pl* -ões [-õjʃ]) *f* complaint; **livro de reclamações** complaints book.

reclamar [xekla'ma(x)] *vi* to complain.

reclame [xɛ'klami] *m* advertisement.

recobrar [xeko'bra(x)] *vt* to resume.

recolher [xeko'ʎe(x)] *vt* to collect; *(passageiros)* to pick up; *(frutos, legumes)* to pick.

recolhimento [xekoʎi'mẽntu] *m (coleta)* collection; *(retiro)* retreat.

recomeçar [xekome'sa(x)] *vt* to begin again.

recomendação [xekomẽnda'sãw] (*pl* -ões [-õjʃ]) *f* recommendation.

⊔ **recomendações** *fpl (cumprimentos)* (kind) regards.

recomendar [xekomẽn'da(x)] *vt* to recommend.

recomendável [xekomẽn'davɛw] (*pl* -eis [-ejʃ]) *adj* advisable; **pouco ~** *(lugar)* unsafe.

recompensa [xekõm'pẽsa] *f* reward.

recompor [xekõm'po(x)] *vt* to rearrange.

⊔ **recompor-se** *vp (de susto)* to compose o.s.; *(de doença)* to recover.

reconciliação [xekõsilja'sãw] (*pl* -ões [-õjʃ]) *f* reconciliation.

reconhecer [xekoɲe'se(x)] *vt* to recognize; *(erro, culpa)* to acknowledge; *(documento, assinatura)* to witness.

reconhecimento [xekoɲesi'mẽntu] *m* recognition; *(de erro, culpa)* acknowledgement; *(de documento, assinatura)* witnessing.

reconstituir [xekõʃtʃitwi(x)] *vt* to reconstruct.

recordação [xekorda'sãw] (*pl* -ões [-õjʃ]) *f (memória)* memory; *(presente)* keepsake, souvenir.

recordar [xekor'da(x)] *vt* to remember.

⊔ **recordar-se** *vp* to remember; **~-se de** to remember.

recorrer [xeko'xe(x)] *vi (JUR)* to appeal; **~ a** to resort to.

recortar [xekor'ta(x)] *vt* to cut out.

recreio [xe'kreju] *m (tempo)* break; *(local)* playground.

recriar [xekri'a(x)] *vt* to recreate.

recriminar [xekrimi'na(x)] *vt* to reproach.

recruta [xe'kruta] *m* recruit ◆ *f* first three months of military service.

recta ['xɛta] *f (Port)* = **reta**.

rectângulo [xɛ'tãŋgulu] *m (Port)* = **retângulo**.

recto, -ta ['xɛtu, -ta] *adj (Port)* = **reto**.

recuar [xe'kwa(x)] *vt (veículo)* to back, to reverse ◆ *vi (em espaço)* to move back; *(em tempo)* to go back.

recuperação [xekupera'sãw] *f* recovery; *(de objeto, edifício antigo)* restoration.

recuperar [xekupe'ra(x)] *vt (algo perdido)* to recover; *(objeto, edifício antigo)* to restore.

⊐ **recuperar-se** *vp (de choque, doença)* to recover.

recurso [xe'kuxsu] *m (JUR)* appeal; *(meio)* resort; **em último ~** as a last resort.

⊐ **recursos** *mpl (bens)* resources.

recusa [xe'kuza] *f* refusal.

redactor, -ra [xeda'tor, -ra] (*mpl* -res [-reʃ], *fpl* -s [-ʃ]) *m, f (Port)* = **redator**.

redator, -ra [xeda'to(x), -ra] (*mpl* -res [-riʃ], *fpl* -s [-ʃ]) *m, f (Br) (de jornal)* editor.

rede ['xedʒi] *f (de pesca)* net; *(de vedação)* netting; *(de cabelo)* hairnet; *(para dormir)* hammock; *(de vias de comunicação)* network; *(de água, luz, gás)* mains (*pl*).

rédea ['xedʒa] *f* rein.

redigir [xedʒi'ʒi(x)] *vt* to write.

redobrar [xedo'bra(x)] *vt* to double.

redondamente [xe,dõnda'mẽntʃi] *adv (enganar-se)* utterly.

redondo, -da [xe'dõndu, -da] *adj* round.

redor [xe'do(x)] *m*: **em** OU **ao ~ (de)** around, about.

redução [xedu'sãw] (*pl* -ões [-õjʃ]) *f* reduction.

redundância [xedũn'dãsja] *f* tautology.

reduzido, -da [xedu'zidu, -da] *adj* reduced.

reduzir [xedu'zi(x)] *vt* to reduce.

reembolsar [xjẽmbow'sa(x)] *vt* to refund.

reembolso [xjẽm'bowsu] *m* refund.

reencontro [xjẽŋ'kõntru] *m* reunion.

refazer [xefa'ze(x)] *vt* rebuild.

⊔ **refazer-se** *vp* to recover.

refeição [xefej'sãw] (*pl* -ões [-õjʃ]) *f* meal; **nas refeições** at mealtimes; **~ ligeira** snack.

refeitório [xefejˈtɔrju] *m* refectory, canteen.

refém [xeˈfẽ] (*pl* **-ns** [-ʃ]) *mf* hostage.

referência [xefeˈrẽsja] *f* reference; **fazer ~ a** to refer to.

⊐ referências *fpl (para emprego)* references.

referendo [xefeˈrẽndu] *m* referendum.

referente [xefeˈrẽntʃi] *adj*: **~ a** relating to.

referir [xefeˈri(x)] *vt* to mention.

⊐ referir-se a *vp + prep* to refer to; **no que se refere a** as regards.

refinado, -da [xefiˈnadu, -da] *adj* refined.

refinaria [xefinaˈria] *f* refinery.

reflectir [xefleˈtir] *vt & vi (Port)* = **refletir**.

reflector [xefleˈtor] (*pl* **-res** [-riʃ]) *m (Port)* = **refletor**.

refletir [xefleˈtʃi(x)] *vt & vi (Br)* to reflect; **~ sobre algo** to reflect on sthg.

⊐ refletir-se em *vp + prep (Br)* to be reflected in.

refletor [xefleˈto(x)] (*pl* **-res** [-riʃ]) *m (Br)* reflector.

reflexão [xeflekˈsãw] (*pl* **-ões** [-õjʃ]) *f* reflection.

reflexo [xeˈfleksu] *m* reflection; *(reação)* reflex (action).

reflexões → reflexão.

refogado, -da [xefoˈgadu, -da] *adj (carne, peixe)* stewed; *(cebola)* fried ◆ *m (molho)* fried garlic and onion; *(ensopado)* stew.

refogar [xefoˈga(x)] *vt* to stew.

reforçado, -da [xeforˈsadu, -da] *adj (esforço, energia)* redoubled; *(objeto, substância)* reinforced.

reforçar [xeforˈsa(x)] *vt (idéia, argumento)* to back up; *(objeto, substância)* to reinforce.

reforma [xeˈfɔrma] *f (de sistema)* reform; *(de casa, edifício)* refurbishment; *(de pessoa)* retirement.

reformado, -da [xefoxˈmadu, -da] *m, f (pensionista)* pensioner.

refractário, -ria [xefraˈtarju, -rja] *adj (Port)* = **refratário**.

refrão [xeˈfrãw] (*pl* **-ões** [-õjʃ]) *m* chorus.

refratário, -ria [xefraˈtarju, -rja] *adj (Br) (ladrilho, vidro)* heat-resistant; *(utensílio)* ovenproof.

refrear [xefriˈa(x)] *vt* to contain.

⊐ refrear-se *vp* to contain o.s.

refrescante [xefreʃˈkãntʃi] *adj* refreshing.

refrescar [xefreʃˈka(x)] *vt (suj: bebida, ar)* to refresh; *(cabeça)* to clear.

⊐ refrescar-se *vp* to cool down.

refresco [xeˈfreʃku] *m* soft drink.

refrigerante [xefriʒeˈrãntʃi] *m* soft drink.

refrões → refrão.

refugiado, -da [xefuˈʒjadu, -da] *m, f* refugee.

refugiar-se [xefuˈʒjaxsi] *vp (asilar-se)* to take refuge; *(abrigar-se)* to take shelter; *(esconder-se)* to hide.

refúgio [xeˈfuʒju] *m* refuge.

refugo [xeˈfugu] *m* refuse.

refutar [xefuˈta(x)] *vt* to refute.

rega [ˈxega] *f (de plantas)* watering; *(de terra)* irrigation.

regaço [xeˈgasu] *m* lap.

regador [xegaˈdo(x)] (*pl* **-res** [-riʃ]) *m* watering can.

regalias [xegaˈliaʃ] *fpl (em emprego)* perks.

regar [xeˈga(x)] *vt (plantas)* to water; *(terra)* to irrigate; *(prato, comida)* to season.

regata [xeˈgata] *f* regatta.

regenerar-se [xeʒeneˈraxsi] *vp* to mend one's ways.

reger [xeˈʒe(x)] *vt (orquestra, banda)* to conduct.

região [xeˈʒjãw] (*pl* **-ões** [-õjʃ]) *f* region; **~ demarcada** *classification guaranteeing the source of a wine, its method of production and grape variety*.

regime [xeˈʒimi] *m (político)* regime; *(dieta)* diet.

regiões → região.

regional [xeʒjoˈnaw] (*pl* **-ais** [-ajʃ]) *adj* regional.

registado, -da [xeʒiʃˈtadu, -da] *adj (Port)* = **registrado**.

registar [xeʒiʃˈtar] *vt (Port)* = **registrar**.

registo [xeˈʒiʃtu] *m (Port)* = **registro**.

registrado, -da [xeʒiʃˈtradu, -da] *adj (Br)* registered.

registrar [xeʒiʃˈtra(x)] *vt (Br)* to register; *(acontecimento, mudança)* to record.

registro [xeˈʒiʃtru] *m (Br)* register; *(repartição)* registry office; *(de correio)* registration; **Registro Civil** registry office; **Registro Predial** registry *(for all* *matters relating to the buying and selling of property).*

regra [ˈxɛgra] *f* rule; **não fugir à ~** to be no exception; **(como) ~ geral** as a rule; **por ~** as a rule.

regressar [xɛgreˈsa(x)] *vi* to return; **~ a** to return to.

regresso [xeˈgresu] *m* return; **estar de ~** to be back.

régua [ˈxɛgwa] *f* ruler.

regulamento [xegulaˈmẽntu] *m* regulations *(pl).*

regular [xeguˈla(x)] *(pl* **-res** [-riʃ]) *adj* regular; *(tamanho, qualidade)* standard; *(uniforme)* even; *(vôo)* scheduled ◆ *vt (regulamentar)* to regulate; *(mecanismo)* to adjust.

rei [xej] *m* king.

reinado [xejˈnadu] *m* reign.

reinar [xejˈna(x)] *vi* to reign.

Reino Unido [xejnuˈnidu] *m*: **o ~** the United Kingdom.

reivindicação [xejvĩndʒikaˈsãw] *(pl* **-ões** [-õjʃ]) *f* claim.

reivindicar [xejvĩndiˈka(x)] *vt* to claim.

rejeição [xeʒejˈsãw] *(pl* **-ões** [-õjʃ]) *f* rejection.

rejeitar [xeʒejˈta(x)] *vt* to reject.

relação [xelaˈsãw] *(pl* **-ões** [-õjʃ]) *f* relation; *(entre pessoas, países)* relationship; **com ou em ~ a** in relation to. ⏌ **relações** *fpl (relacionamento)* relations; *(ato sexual)*: **ter relações com alguém** to sleep with sb; **relações públicas** public relations.

relâmpago [xeˈlãmpagu] *m* flash of lightning.

relatar [xelaˈta(x)] *vt (jogo de futebol)* to commentate on; *(acontecimento)* to relate.

relativo, -va [xelaˈtʃivu, -va] *adj* relative; **~ a** relating to.

relatório [xelaˈtɔrju] *m* report.

relaxado, -da [xelaˈʃadu, -da] *adj* relaxed.

relaxante [xelaˈʃãntʃi] *adj* relaxing ◆ *m (medicamento)* tranquillizer.

relaxar [xelaˈʃa(x)] *vt* to relax. ⏌ **relaxar-se** *vp* to relax.

relembrar [xelẽmˈbra(x)] *vt* to recall.

relevo [xeˈlevu] *m* relief; **dar ~ a** to highlight.

religião [xeliˈʒjãw] *(pl* **-ões** [-õjʃ]) *f* religion.

relíquia [xeˈlikja] *f* relic.

relógio [xeˈlɔʒju] *m (de parede, mesa)* clock; *(de pulso)* watch; **~ de cuco** cuckoo clock; **~ de sol** sundial.

relojoaria [xeloʒwaˈria] *f* watchmaker's (shop).

relutância [xeloˈtãsja] *f* reluctance.

reluzente [xeluˈzẽntʃi] *adj* gleaming.

relva [ˈxɛlva] *f (Port)* grass.

relvado [xɛlˈvaduj] *m (Port) (relva)* lawn; *(campo de futebol)* football pitch.

remar [xeˈma(x)] *vi* to row.

rematar [xemaˈta(x)] *vt (concluir)* to finish.

remediar [xemeˈdʒja(x)] *vt* to remedy.

remédio [xeˈmɛdʒju] *m* remedy; **não tem ~** *(fig)* it can't be helped.

remendar [xemẽnˈda(x)] *vt* to mend.

remendo [xeˈmẽndu] *m* patch.

remessa [xeˈmɛsa] *f (de produtos)* shipment, consignment; *(de dinheiro)* remittance.

remetente [xemeˈtẽntʃi] *mf* sender.

remeter [xemeˈte(x)] *vt* to send.

remexer [xemeˈʃe(x)] *vt* to rummage through.

remo [ˈxemu] *m (longo)* oar; *(curto)* paddle.

remoção [xemoˈsãw] *(pl* **-ões** [-õjʃ]) *f* removal.

remorso [xeˈmɔxsu] *m* remorse.

remoto [xeˈmɔtu] *adj* remote.

remover [xemoˈve(x)] *vt* to remove.

remuneração [xemuneraˈsãw] *(pl* **-ões** [-õjʃ]) *f* remuneration.

renascer [xenaʃˈse(x)] *vi* to be born again.

Renascimento [xenaʃsiˈmẽntu] *m*: **o ~** the Renaissance.

renda [ˈxẽnda] *f (Br: rendimento)* income; *(de vestido, blusa)* lace trim; *(Port: de casa, apartamento)* rent; **imposto de ~** income tax; **~ nacional** gross national product; **famílias de baixa ~** low-income families.

renegar [xeneˈga(x)] *vt* to reject.

renovação [xenovaˈsãw] *(pl* **-ões** [-õjʃ]) *f (de contrato, amizade)* renewal; *(de edifício)* renovation.

renovar [xenoˈva(x)] *vt* to renew; *(consertar)* to renovate; *(substituir)* to replace.

rentabilidade [xẽntabiliˈdadʒi] *f* profitability.

rentável [xẽnˈtavɛw] *(pl* **-eis** [-ejʃ]) *adj* profitable.

renúncia [xeˈnũsja] f renunciation.

renunciar [xenũˈsja(x)] vt to renounce.

reparação [xeparaˈsãw] (pl -ões [-õjʃ]) f (conserto) repair.

reparar [xepaˈra(x)] vt (consertar) to repair; (restaurar) to restore; ~ que to notice (that).

⎦ **reparar em** v + prep (notar) to notice.

repartição [xepaxtʃiˈsãw] (pl -ões [-õjʃ]) f (partilha) division; (distribuição) distribution; (local) department; ~ pública government office.

repartir [xepaxtˈʃi(x)] vt (partilhar) to divide; (distribuir) to distribute; ~ algo com alguém to share sthg with sb; ~ algo em algo to split sthg up into sthg.

repelente [xepeˈlẽntʃi] adj repellent ◆ m: ~ (de insetos) insect repellent.

repente [xeˈpẽntʃi] m outburst; de ~ suddenly.

repentino, -na [xepẽnˈtʃinu, -na] adj sudden.

repercussão [xepexkuˈsãw] (pl -ões [-õjʃ]) f (impacto) response; (consequência) repercussion.

repertório [xepexˈtɔrju] m repertoire.

repetição [xepetʃiˈsãw] (pl -ões [-õjʃ]) f repetition.

repetidamente [xepetʃidaˈmẽntʃi] adv repeatedly.

repetido, -da [xepeˈtʃidu, -da] adj repeated.

repetir [xepeˈtʃi(x)] vt to repeat; (prato, refeição) to have seconds of.

⎦ **repetir-se** vp to happen again.

replay [xiˈplej] m action replay.

replicar [xepliˈka(x)] vt: ~ que to reply that.

repolho [xeˈpoʎu] m cabbage.

repor [xeˈpo(x)] vt (dinheiro) to replace; ~ algo no lugar to put sthg back (where it belongs); ~ a verdade to set the record straight.

reportagem [xepoxˈtaʒẽ] (pl -ns [-ʃ]) f (em rádio, televisão) report; (em jornal, revista) article.

repórter [xeˈpɔxtɛ(x)] (pl -res [-riʃ]) mf reporter.

repousar [xepoˈza(x)] vt & vi to rest.

repreender [xepriẽnˈde(x)] vt to rebuke.

represa [xeˈpreza] f weir.

represália [xepreˈzalja] f reprisal.

representação [xeprezẽntaˈsãw] (pl -ões [-õjʃ]) f performance; (imagem) representation.

representante [xeprezẽnˈtãntʃi] mf representative; ~ oficial authorized agent.

representar [xepreˈzẽnˈta(x)] vt to represent; (cena) to perform; (papel) to play; (pôr em cena) to put on; (significar) to mean ◆ vi (ator) to act.

repressão [xepreˈsãw] (pl -ões [-õjʃ]) f suppression.

reprimir [xepriˈmi(x)] vt to suppress.

reprise [xeˈprizi] f revival.

reprodução [xeproduˈsãw] (pl -ões [-õjʃ]) f reproduction.

reproduzir [xeproduˈzi(x)] vt (evento) to reenact; (quadro, escultura) to reproduce.

⎦ **reproduzir-se** vp to reproduce.

reprovar [xeproˈva(x)] vt (atitude, comportamento) to disapprove of; (lei, projeto) to reject; (ano escolar, exame) to fail.

réptil [ˈxeptiw] (pl -teis [-tejʃ]) m reptile.

república [xeˈpublika] f (sistema político) republic; (de estudantes) student house, fraternity (Am); a República Brasileira the Brazilian Republic.

repudiar [xepuˈdʒja(x)] vt to repudiate.

repugnância [xepugˈnãsja] f repugnance.

repugnante [xepugˈnãntʃi] adj repugnant.

repulsa [xeˈpuwsa] f repulsion.

repulsivo, -va [xepuwˈsivu, -va] adj repulsive.

reputação [xeputaˈsãw] (pl -ões [-õjʃ]) f (fama) reputation; (importância social) standing.

requeijão [xekejˈʒãw] (pl -ões [-õjʃ]) m = cottage cheese.

requerer [xekeˈre(x)] vt (precisar de) to require; (por requerimento) to request.

requerimento [xekeriˈmẽntu] m request form.

requintado, -da [xekĩnˈtadu, -da] adj exquisite.

requinte [xeˈkĩntʃi] m style.

requisito [xekiˈzitu] m requirement.

⎦ **requisitos** mpl (dotes) attributes.

rescindir [xeʃsĩnˈdi(x)] vt (contrato) to break.

resto

rés-do-chão [xɛʒdu'ʃãw] *m (Port)* inv ground floor *(Brit)*, first floor *(Am)*.
resenha [xe'zaɲa] *f (televisiva, de rádio)* listings *(pl)*.
reserva [xe'zɛxva] *f* reservation; *(de alimentos, provisões)* reserves *(pl)*; *(de animais, plantas, vinho)* reserve; ~ **de caça** game reserve; ~ **natural** nature reserve.
reservado, -da [xezex'vadu. -da] *adj* reserved; *(íntimo)* secluded.
reservar [xezex'va(x)] *vt (quarto, lugar, bilhete)* to book; *(guardar)* to set aside.
resfriado [xeʃfri'adu] *m (Br)* cold.
resgate [xeʒ'gatʃi] *m* ransom.
resguardar [xeʒgwax'da(x)] *vt* to protect.
❑ **resguardar-se** *vp*: ~-**se de** to protect o.s. from.
residência [xezi'dẽsja] *f* residence; *(académica)* hall of residence.
residir [xezi'dʒi(x)] : **residir em** *v + prep* to reside in.
resíduo [xe'zidwu] *m* residue.
resignação [xezigna'sãw] *f* resignation.
resignar-se [xezig'naxsi] *vp* to resign o.s.
resina [xe'zina] *f* resin.
resistência [xeziʃ'tẽsja] *f (de pessoa)* stamina; *(de material, parede)* strength; *(de aquecedor elétrico)* resistor.
resistente [xeziʃ'tẽntʃi] *adj* resistant.
resistir [xeziʃ'tʃi(x)] *vi* to resist; ~ **a algo** *(ataque, doença)* to resist sthg; *(suportar)* to withstand sthg.
resmungar [xeʒmũŋ'ga(x)] *vt* to mutter ◆ *vi* to grumble.
resolução [xezolu'sãw] *(pl* -ões [-õjʃ]*) f* resolution; *(firmeza, coragem)* resolve.
resolver [xezow've(x)] *vt* to solve; ~ **fazer algo** to decide to do sthg.
❑ **resolver-se** *vp* to make up one's mind.
respectivo, -va [xeʃpɛ'tivu. -va] *adj* respective.
respeitar [xeʃpej'ta(x)] *vt* to respect.
❑ **respeitar a** *v + prep*: **no que respeita a** as regards.
respeitável [xeʃpej'tavew] *(pl* -eis [-ejʃ]*) adj* respectable; *(fig: grande)* considerable.
respeito [xeʃ'pejtu] *m* respect; **dizer ~ a** to concern; **ter ~ por** to have respect for; **a ~ de, com ~ a**

with respect to.
respiração [xeʃpira'sãw] *f* breathing.
respirar [xeʃpi'ra(x)] *vt & vi* to breathe.
resplandecente [xeʃplãnde'sẽntʃi] *adj* dazzling.
responder [xeʃpõn'de(x)] *vt* to answer ◆ *vi (dar resposta)* to answer; *(replicar)* to answer back; *(ir a tribunal)* to appear (in court); *(reagir)* to respond; ~ **a** *(carta, pergunta)* to answer.
❑ **responder por** *v + prep* to answer for.
responsabilidade [xeʃpõsabili'dadʒi] *f* responsibility.
responsabilizar [xeʃpõsabili'za(x)] *vt*: ~ **alguém/algo por algo** to hold sb/sthg responsible for sthg.
❑ **responsabilizar-se** *vp*: ~-**se por** to take responsibility for.
responsável [xeʃpõ'savew] *(pl* -eis [-ejʃ]*) adj* responsible ◆ *mf* person in charge; ~ **por** responsible for.
resposta [xeʃ'pɔʃta] *f* answer; *(a carta)* reply; *(reação)* response.
resquício [xeʃ'kisju] *m* vestige.
ressabiado, -da [xesa'bjadu. -da] *adj (desconfiado)* cautious; *(ressentido)* resentful.
ressaca [xe'saku] *f* hangover.
ressaltar [xesaw'ta(x)] *vt* to highlight ◆ *vi* to stand out.
ressentimento [xesẽntʃi'mẽntu] *m* resentment.
ressentir-se [xesẽn'tixsi] *vp* to take offence; ~ **de algo** *(sentir o efeito de)* to feel the effects of sthg.
ressurgimento [xesuxʒi'mẽntu] *m* resurgence.
ressuscitar [xesusi'ta(x)] *vt* to resurrect ◆ *vi* to be resurrected.
restabelecer [xeʃtabele'se(x)] *vt* to reinstate.
❑ **restabelecer-se** *vp* to recover.
restar [xeʃ'ta(x)] *vi* to be left.
restauração [xeʃtawra'sãw] *(pl* -ões [-õjʃ]*) f (de edifício)* restoration; *(de forças, energia)* recovery.
restaurante [xeʃtaw'rãntʃi] *m* restaurant; ~ **panorâmico** *restaurant offering panoramic views over an area.*
restaurar [xeʃtaw'ra(x)] *vt* to restore.
restinga [xeʃ'tʃĩŋga] *f* sandbank.
restituir [xeʃtʃi'twi(x)] *vt* to return.
resto ['xeʃtu] *m (sobra)* rest; *(MAT)* remainder.

⅃ **restos** *mpl (sobras)* leftovers; **~s mortais** remains.

resultado [xezuw'tadu] *m* result; *(em exame, teste, competição)* results *(pl)*.

resultar [xezuw'ta(x)] *vi* to work; **~ de algo** to result from sthg; **~ em algo** to result in sthg.

resumir [xezu'mi(x)] *vt* to summarize.

⅃ **resumir-se a** *vp + prep* to come down to.

resumo [xe'zumu] *m* summary; **em ~** in short.

reta ['xeta] *f (Br) (linha)* straight line; *(em estrada)* straight stretch of road.

retaguarda [,xeta'gwarda] *f* rear; **na ~** at the rear.

retalho [xe'taʎu] *m (de fazenda)* remnant; **a ~** *(Port: vender, comprar)* retail.

retaliação [xetalja'saw] *(pl -ões* [-õjʃ]) *f* retaliation.

retaliar [xeta'lja(x)] *vt & vi* to retaliate.

retângulo [xe'tãngulu] *m (Br)* rectangle.

retardar [xetax'da(x)] *vt* to delay.

reter [xe'te(x)] *vt (parar)* to stop; *(impulso, lágrimas, ira)* to hold back; *(deter)* to detain; *(em memória)* to retain.

reticente [xetʃi'sẽntʃi] *adj* reticent.

retina [xe'tʃina] *f* retina.

retirada [xetʃi'rada] *f* retreat.

retirar [xetʃi'ra(x)] *vt (remover)* to remove; *(afirmação)* to withdraw.

⅃ **retirar-se** *vp (recolher-se)* to retire; **~-se de algo** to withdraw from sthg; **ela retirou-se da sala** she left the room.

reto, -ta [xetu, -ta] *adj & m (Br) (linha, estrada)* straight; *(justo)* upright ◆ *m (ANAT)* rectum.

retorcido, -da [xetox'sidu, -da] *adj* wrought.

retórica [xe'tɔrika] *f* rhetoric.

retornar [xetox'na(x)] *vi* to return; **~ a** to return to.

retraído, -da [xetra'idu, -da] *adj* retiring.

retrato [xe'tratu] *m* portrait; *(fotografia)* photograph.

retribuir [xetri'bwi(x)] *vt* to return.

retroceder [xetrose'de(x)] *vi* to go back.

retrógrado, -da [xe'trɔgradu, -da] *adj* retrograde.

retrovisor [xetrovi'zo(x)] *(pl -es* [-iʃ]) *m* rearview mirror.

réu, ré ['xɛu, 'xɛ] *m, f* accused.

reumatismo [xewma'tʃiʒmu] *m* rheumatism.

reunião [xju'njãw] *(pl -ões* [-õjʃ]) *f* meeting.

reunir [xju'ni(x)] *vt (pessoas, objetos)* to bring together; *(provas)* to gather.

⅃ **reunir-se** *vp (encontrar-se)* to meet.

réveillon [xeve'jõ] *m* New Year's Eve dinner and party.

revelação [xevela'saw] *(pl -ões* [-õjʃ]) *f* revelation; *(de fotografia)* development.

revelar [xeve'la(x)] *vt (segredo, notícia)* to reveal; *(fotografia)* to develop; *(interesse, talento)* to show.

⅃ **revelar-se** *vp (manifestar-se)* to prove to be.

revendedor, -ra [xevẽnde'do(x), -ra] *(mpl -res* [-riʃ], *fpl -s* [-ʃ]) *m, f* retailer.

rever [xe've(x)] *vt (pessoa)* to see again; *(texto, trabalho)* to revise.

reverso [xe'vɛrsu] *m* back.

revés [xe'vɛʃ] *(pl -eses* [-ɛziʃ]) *m* setback; **ao ~** the wrong way round.

revestir [xeveʃtʃi(x)] *vt* to cover.

revezar-se [xeve'zaxsi] *vp* to take turns.

revirado, -da [xevi'radu, -da] *adj (gola, pontas)* turned-up; *(olhos)* rolling; *(casa, gaveta)* untidy.

reviravolta [xe,vira'vowta] *f* spin; *(fig: em situação)* U-turn.

revisão [xevi'zãw] *(pl -ões* [-õjʃ]) *f (de lei)* review; *(de texto, prova tipográfica)* proofreading; *(de máquina, carro)* service; *(de matéria, aula)* revision *(Brit)*, review *(Am)*.

revisor, -ra [xevi'zo(x), -ra] *(mpl -res* [-riʃ], *fpl -s* [-ʃ]) *m, f (em transporte público)* ticket inspector; *(de texto, provas tipográficas)* proofreader.

revista [xe'viʃta] *f (publicação)* magazine; *(peça teatral)* revue; *(inspeção)* review; **~ em quadrinhos** *(Br)* comic.

revolta [xe'vowta] *f (rebelião)* revolt; *(indignação)* outrage.

revoltar-se [xevow'taxsi] *vp (sublevar-se)* to revolt; *(indignar-se)* to be outraged; **~-se com algo** to be revolted by sthg.

revolução [xevolu'saw] *(pl -ões* [-õjʃ]) *f* revolution.

revolver [xevow've(x)] *vt (papéis, lixo)*

to rummage through; *(terra)* to dig over.

revólver [xɛˈvɔwvɛ(x)] *(pl* **-es** [-iʃ]) *m* revolver.

rezar [xɛˈza(x)] *vi (orar)* to pray ◆ *vt (missa, oração)* to say.

ri [ˈxi] → **rir**.

riacho [ˈxjaʃu] *m* brook.

ribeira [xiˈbejra] *f* stream.

ribeirão [xibejˈrãw] *(pl* **-ões** [-õjʃ]) *m* stream.

ribeirinho, -nha [xibejˈriɲu. -ɲa] *adj* river *(antes de s)*.

ribeirões → **ribeirão**.

rico, -ca [ˈxiku. -ka] *adj* rich; **~ em** rich in.

ricota [xiˈkɔta] *f* ricotta cheese.

ridicularizar [xidʒikulariˈza(x)] *vt* to ridicule.

ridículo, -la [xiˈdʒikulu. -la] *adj* ridiculous; *(insignificante)* laughable ◆ *m* absurdity.

rido [ˈxidu] → **rir**.

rifa [ˈxifa] *f (sorteio)* raffle; *(bilhete)* raffle ticket.

rigidez [xiʒiˈdeʒ] *f (de músculos, ossos)* stiffness; *(de caráter, costumes)* inflexibility.

rigor [xiˈgo(x)] *(pl* **-res** [-riʃ]) *m* rigour; *(de frio, calor, caráter)* severity.

rijo, -ja [ˈxiʒu. -ʒa] *adj* tough; *(pão, queijo, fruto)* hard; *(pessoa)* hardy.

rim [xĩ] *(pl* **-ns** [-ʃ]) *m* kidney.
❏ **rins** *mpl (parte do corpo)* lower back *(sg)*.

rima [ˈxima] *f (de verso)* rhyme.
❏ **rimas** *fpl (versos)* verses.

rímel® [ˈximɛw] *(pl* **-eis** [-ɛjʃ]) *m* mascara.

ringue [ˈxĩgi] *m (boxing)* ring.

rinoceronte [xinoseˈrõntʃi] *m* rhinoceros.

rinque [ˈxĩki] *m* rink.

rins → **rim**.

rio¹ [ˈxju] → **rir**.

rio² [ˈxju] *m* river; **~ abaixo** downstream; **~ acima** upstream.

Rio de Janeiro [xiudʒiʒaˈnejru] *m*: **o ~** Rio de Janeiro.

riqueza [xiˈkeza] *f (de país, pessoa, região)* wealth; *(de solo, cores, idéias)* richness.

rir [ˈxi(x)] *vi* to laugh; **desatar a ~** to burst out laughing; **morrer de ~** to laugh one's head off.

ris [ˈxiʃ] → **rir**.

risada [xiˈzada] *f* laugh.

risca [ˈxiʃka] *f* stripe; **de ~s** striped.

riscar [xiʃˈka(x)] *vt (frase)* to cross out; *(folha)* to scribble on; *(parede, carro, móvel)* to scratch.

risco [ˈxiʃku] *m (traço)* mark; *(linha)* line; *(em cabelo)* parting *(Brit)*, part *(Am)*; *(perigo)* risk; **correr o ~ de** to run the risk of; **pôr em ~** to put at risk; **~ ao meio/ao lado** *(relativo a cabelo)* middle/side parting.

riso [ˈxizu] *m* laugh; **~ amarelo** grimace.

risoto [xiˈzotu] *m* risotto.

ríspido, -da [ˈxiʃpidu. -da] *adj* stern.

rissol [xiˈsɔl] *(pl* **-óis** [-ɔjʃ]) *m (Port)* = **rissole**.

rissole [xiˈsɔli] *m (Br)* small semicircular fried cake with a fish or meat filling coated in breadcrumbs.

ritmo [ˈxitʒimu] *m (de movimento, andamento)* pace; *(em música)* rhythm; *(do coração)* beat.

ritual [xiˈtwaw] *(pl* **-ais** [-ajʃ]) *m* ritual.

riu [ˈxiu] → **rir**.

rival [xiˈvaw] *(pl* **-ais** [-ajʃ]) *mf* rival.

rivalidade [xivaliˈdadʒi] *f* rivalry.

robalo [roˈbalu] *m* sea bass.

robertos [roˈbɛrtuʃ] *mpl (Port)* puppets.

robô [rɔˈbo] *m* robot.

robusto, -ta [xoˈbuʃtu. -ta] *adj* robust.

roça [ˈxɔsa] *f (Br: zona rural)* countryside.

rocambole [xokãmˈbɔli] *m (Br)* roulade.

roçar [xoˈsa(x)] *vt* to brush.

rocha [ˈxɔʃa] *f* rock.

rochedo [xoˈʃedu] *m* crag.

rock [ˈxɔki] *m* rock (music).

roda [ˈxɔda] *f (de carro, bicicleta)* wheel; *(de saia, vestido)* flare; *(de pessoas)* circle, ring.

rodada [xoˈdada] *f* round.

rodagem [xoˈdaʒẽ] *f* → **faixa**.

rodapé [xodaˈpɛ] *f* skirting board; **nota de ~** footnote.

rodar [xoˈda(x)] *vt (fazer girar)* to turn; *(rapidamente)* to spin; *(filme)* to shoot ◆ *vi (girar)* to turn; *(rapidamente)* to spin.

rodear [xoˈdea(x)] *vt* to surround.

❑ **rodear-se de** *vp* + *prep* to surround o.s. with.

rodela [xoˈdɛla] *f* slice.

rodízio [xoˈdʒizju] *m* restaurant.

rododendro [xodoˈdẽndru] *m* rhododendron.

rodopiar [xodoˈpja(x)] *vi* to whirl (around).

rodovia [xodoˈvia] *f (Br)* motorway *(Brit)*, expressway *(Am)*; ~ **com pedágio** toll motorway *(Brit)*, turnpike *(Am)*.

rodoviária [xodoˈvjarja] *f (local)* bus station.

roer [ˈxwe(x)] *vt (rato)* to gnaw (at); *(cão)* chew.

rola [ˈxola] *f* turtle dove.

rolar [xoˈla(x)] *vi* to roll.

roleta [xoˈleta] *f* roulette; ~ **russa** Russian roulette.

rolha [ˈxoʎa] *f (de borracha, plástico)* stopper; ~ **de cortiça** cork.

rolo [ˈxolu] *m* roller; *(fotográfico)* roll (of film); ~ **de pastel** rolling pin.

romã [xoˈmã] *f* pomegranate.

romance [xoˈmãsi] *m* romance; *(gênero)* novel; *(sentimental)* romantic novel; ~ **cor-de-rosa** = Mills and Boon; ~ **policial** detective novel.

romântico, -ca [xoˈmãntʃiku, -ka] *adj* romantic.

romaria [xomaˈria] *f popular religious festival combining a religious ceremony and dancing, eating etc.*

romper [xõmˈpe(x)] *vt (corda, cabo)* to snap; *(contrato)* to break ♦ *vi (namorados, noivos)* to split up; ~ **com** to split up with.

❑ **romper-se** *vp (rasgar-se)* to tear.

ronda [ˈxõnda] *f (de polícia)* beat; *(de guarda-noturno)* rounds *(pl)*; **fazer a ~** to do the rounds.

rosa [ˈxɔza] *f* rose; **um mar de ~s** a bed of roses.

rosário [xoˈzarju] *m* rosary.

rosbife [xoʒˈbifi] *m* roast beef.

rosca [ˈxoʃka] *f (de garrafa, tampa, parafuso)* thread; *(CULIN: pão)* ring-shaped loaf of bread; *(biscoito para bebê)* rusk.

rosé [xɔˈzɛ] *m* rosé.

roseira [xoˈzejra] *f* rosebush.

rosnar [xoʒˈna(x)] *vi* to growl.

rosto [ˈxoʃtu] *m* face.

rota [ˈxɔta] *f (de navio)* course; *(de avião)* route.

rotativo, -va [xutaˈtʃivu, -va] *adj* rotary.

roteiro [xoˈtejru] *m* route.

rotina [xoˈtʃina] *f* routine.

roto, -ta [ˈxotu, -ta] *pp* → **romper** ♦ *adj (roupa)* torn.

rótula [ˈxɔtula] *f* kneecap.

rotular [xotuˈla(x)] *vt* to label.

rótulo [ˈxɔtulu] *m* label.

rotunda [xoˈtũnda] *f (Port)* roundabout *(Brit)*, traffic circle *(Am)*.

roubar [xoˈba(x)] *vt & vi* to steal; ~ **algo de alguém** to steal sthg from sb; **fui roubado** I've been robbed.

roubo [ˈxobu] *m (ato)* robbery, theft; *(coisa roubada)* stolen item; *(fig: preço exagerado)* daylight robbery.

rouco, -ca [ˈxoku, -ka] *adj* hoarse.

roupa [ˈxopa] *f (vestuário)* clothes *(pl)*; *(de cama)* bed linen.

roupão [xoˈpãw] *(pl* **-ões** [-õjʃ]*)* dressing gown *(Brit)*, bathrobe *(Am)*.

rouxinol [xoʃiˈnɔw] *(pl* **-óis** [-ɔjʃ]*)* m nightingale.

roxo, -xa [ˈxoʃu, -ʃa] *adj* violet.

rua [ˈxua] *f* street ♦ *interj* get out!; ~ **abaixo/acima** down/up the street.

rubéola [xuˈbɛula] *f* German measles *(sg)*.

rubi [xuˈbi] *m* ruby.

rubor [xuˈbo(x)] *(pl* **-res** [-riʃ]*)* m blush.

ruborizar-se [xuboriˈzaxsi] *vp* to blush, to go red.

rubrica [xuˈbrika] *f* signature.

ruço, -ça [ˈxusu, -sa] *adj (grisalho)* grey.

rúcola [ˈxukola] *f* rocket.

rude [ˈxudʒi] *adj* coarse.

ruela [ˈxwela] *f* back street.

ruga [ˈxuga] *f (em pele)* wrinkle; *(em tecido)* crease.

rúgbi [ˈxugbi] *m (Br)* rugby.

rugido [xuˈʒidu] *m* roar.

rugir [xuˈʒi(x)] *vi* to roar.

ruído [xwidu] *m* noise.

ruim [xuˈĩ] *(pl* **-ns** [-ʃ]*)* adj bad.

ruínas [xwinaʃ] *fpl* ruins.

ruins → **ruim**.

ruivo, -va [ˈxuivu, -va] *adj (cabelo)* red ♦ *m, f* redhead.

rum [ˈxũ] *m* rum.

rumar [xuˈma(x)] : **rumar a** *v* + *prep* to steer towards.

rumba [ˈxũmba] *f* rumba.

rumo [ˈxumu] *m* direction.

rumor [xuˈmo(x)] (*pl* **-res** [-riʃ]) *m* rumour.

ruptura [xupˈtura] *f (de relação, contrato)* breaking-off; *(de ligamento)* rupture.

rural [xuˈraw] (*pl* **-ais** [-ajʃ]) *adj* rural.

rush [ˈxaʃ] *m (Br)* rush hour.

Rússia [ˈxusja] *f*: **a ~** Russia.

russo, -a [ˈxusu, -sa] *adj & m, f* Russian ◆ *m (língua)* Russian.

rústico, -ca [ˈxuʃtʃiku, -ka] *adj* rustic.

S

S.A. *(abrev de Sociedade Anônima)* = plc *(Brit)*, = Ltd *(Brit)*, = Inc *(Am)*.

sábado ['sabadu] *m* Saturday, → **sexta-feira**.

sabão [sa'bãw] *(pl* **-ões** [-õjʃ]) *m* soap; **~ em pó** soap powder; **levar um ~** *(fam)* to be told off; **passar um ~ em alguém** *(fam)* to tell sb off.

sabedoria [sabedo'ria] *f* wisdom.

saber [sa'be(x)] *vt* to know ◆ *vi (Port: ter sabor)* to taste ◆ *m* knowledge; **ele não sabe nada sobre computadores** he doesn't know a thing about computers; **não quero ~!** I don't want to know!; **~ fazer algo** to know how to do sthg; **sei falar inglês** I can speak English; **fazer ~ que** to make it known (that); **sem ~** unwittingly, unknowingly; **~ de** to know about; **vir** OR **ficar a ~ de algo** to find out about sthg.

sabiá [sa'bja] *f* thrush.

sabões → **sabão**.

sabonete [sabo'netʃi] *m* (bar of) soap.

saboneteira [sabone'tejra] *f* soap dish.

sabor [sa'bo(x)] *(pl* **-res** [-riʃ]) *m (gosto)* taste; *(aroma)* flavour.

saborear [sabo'rja(x)] *vt (provar)* to taste; *(comer devagar)* to savour; *(fig: sol, férias, descanso)* to enjoy.

sabores → **sabor**.

sabotagem [sabo'taʒẽ] *(pl* **-ns** [-ʃ]) *f* sabotage.

sabotar [sabo'ta(x)] *vt* to sabotage.

sabugueiro [sabu'gejru] *m* elder.

saca ['saka] *f* bag.

sacar [sa'ka(x)] *vt (Br: fam: compreender)* to understand.

sacarina [saka'rina] *f* saccharin.

saca-rolhas [,saka'xoʎaʃ] *m inv* corkscrew.

sacarose [saka'rɔzi] *f* sucrose.

sacerdote [sasex'dɔtʃi] *m* priest.

sacho ['saʃu] *m* hoe.

saciar [sa'sja(x)] *vt (fome)* to satisfy; *(sede)* to quench.

⊔ **saciar-se** *vp* to be satisfied.

saco ['saku] *m (pequeno)* bag; *(grande)* sack; **~ de água quente** hot-water bottle; **~ de dormir** sleeping bag; **~ de lixo** bin bag *(Brit)*, garbage bag *(Am)*; **~ de plástico** plastic bag; **~ de viagem** travel bag; **eu não tenho ~ de ir lá** *(fam)* I can't be bothered to go; **puxar o ~ de alguém** *(fam)* to suck up to somebody; **ser um ~** *(fam)* to be a pain.

saco-cama [,saku'kama] *(pl* **sacos-cama** [,sakuʃ'kama]) *m* sleeping bag.

sacola [sa'kɔla] *f* bag.

sacramento [sakra'mẽtu] *m* sacrament.

⊔ **sacramentos** *mpl* last rites.

sacrificar [sakrifi'ka(x)] *vt* to sacrifice.

⊔ **sacrificar-se** *vp*: **~-se por alguém** to make sacrifices for sb.

sacrilégio [sakri'lɛʒju] *m* sacrilege.

sacristia [sakriʃ'tʃia] *f* sacristy.

sacro, -cra ['sakru, -kra] *adj* sacred.

sacudir [saku'dʒi(x)] *vt* to shake.

sádico, -ca ['sadʒiku, -ka] *adj* sadistic ◆ *m, f* sadist.

sadio, -dia [sa'dʒiu, -'dia] *adj* healthy.

saem ['sajẽ] → **sair**.

safio [sa'fiu] *m (small)* conger eel.

safira [sa'fira] *f* sapphire.

Sagitário [saʒi'tarju] *m* Sagittarius.

sagrado, -da [sa'gradu, -da] *adj* holy, sacred.

saguão [sa'gwãw] *(pl* **-ões** [-õjʃ]) *m* courtyard.

sai ['saj] → **sair**.

saí [sa'i] → **sair**.

saia ['saja] *f* skirt.

saia-calça [ˌsajaˈkawsa] (pl **saias-calça** [ˌsajaʃˈkawsa]) f culottes (pl).

saída [saˈida] f exit, way out; (de ônibus, trem) departure; (de problema, situação) way out; "~ de emergência" "emergency exit"; **dar uma** ~ to pop out; **estar de** ~ to be on one's way out; **ter** ~ (produto) to sell well.

saio [ˈsaju] → **sair**.

sair [saˈi(x)] vi to go/come out; (partir) to go, to leave; (separar-se) to come off; (ser publicado) to come out; **sai daí!** come out of there!; ~ **a** (custar) to work out as.

⎣ **sair-se** vp: **~-se bem/mal** to come off well/badly.

sais → **sal**.

saiu [saˈiu] → **sair**.

sal [ˈsaw] (pl **sais** [ˈsajʃ]) m salt; **sem** ~ unsalted; ~ **comum** OU **marinho** sea salt; ~ **refinado** table salt; **sais de banho** bath salts; **sais de cheirar** smelling salts; **sais de fruta** liver salts.

sala [ˈsala] f room; ~ **de aula** classroom; ~ **de espera** waiting room; ~ **(de estar)** living OU sitting room; ~ **de jantar** dining room; ~ **de jogos** amusement arcade.

salada [saˈlada] f salad; ~ **de alface** green salad (of lettuce only); ~ **de feijão frade** black-eye bean salad with onion, parsley, garlic and egg; ~ **de frutas** fruit salad; ~ **mista** mixed salad; ~ **russa** Russian salad; ~ **de tomate** tomato salad.

saladeira [salaˈdejra] f salad bowl.

salamandra [salaˈmãndra] f salamander.

salame [saˈlami] m salami.

salão [saˈlãw] (pl **-ões** [-ˈõjʃ]) m hall; (exposição coletiva) exhibition; ~ **de beleza** beauty salon; ~ **de chá** tea room; ~ **de festas** reception room.

salário [saˈlarju] m salary; ~ **mínimo** minimum wage.

salário-família [saˌlarjufaˈmilja] (pl **salários-família** [saˌlarjuʃfaˈmilja]) m (Br) family allowance.

saldar [sawˈda(x)] vt (conta) to settle; (dívida) to pay off; (mercadorias) to sell off at a reduced price.

saldo [ˈsawdu] m (de conta bancária) balance; **em** ~ (Port: mercadorias) on sale.

salgadinhos [sawgaˈdʒiɲuʃ] mpl savoury snacks.

salgado, -da [sawˈgadu, -da] adj (comida) salty; (bacalhau, água) salt (antes de s).

salgueiro [sawˈgejru] m willow.

salientar [saljẽˈta(x)] vt to point out.

⎣ **salientar-se** vp (evidenciar-se) to excel o.s.

saliente [saˈljẽtʃi] adj protruding.

saliva [saˈliva] f saliva.

salmão [sawˈmãw] m salmon; ~ **defumado** smoked salmon.

salmonela [sawmoˈnɛla] f salmonella.

salmonete [sawmoˈnetʃi] m red mullet.

salmoura [sawˈmora] f brine.

salões → **salão**.

salpicão [sawpiˈkãw] (pl **-ões** [-ˈõjʃ]) m (enchido) paprika salami; (prato) chicken and smoked ham salad with carrot, peppers and onion.

salpicar [sawpiˈka(x)] vt to sprinkle; (sujar com pingos) to splash, to spatter.

salpicões → **salpicão**.

salsa [ˈsawsa] f parsley.

salsicha [sawˈsiʃa] f sausage.

saltar [sawˈta(x)] vt to jump over ♦ vi (dar saltos) to jump; (ir pelo ar) to fly off; ~ **à vista** OU **aos olhos** to be as plain as day.

salteado, -da [sawˈteadu, -da] adj (entremeado) alternating.

salto [ˈsawtu] m jump; (de calçado) heel; **de** ~ **alto** high-heeled; ~ **em altura** high jump; ~ **baixo** OU **raso** (de calçado) flat OU low heel; ~ **em comprimento** long jump; ~ **mortal** somersault; ~ **à vara** (Port) pole vault.

salutar [saluˈta(x)] (pl **-res** [-riʃ]) adj healthy.

salva [ˈsawva] f (planta) sage; (bandeja) salver; ~ **de palmas** round of applause.

salvação [sawvaˈsãw] f salvation; (remédio) cure; **não haver** ~ to be beyond repair.

salvaguardar [ˌsawvagwaxˈda(x)] vt to safeguard.

salvamento [sawvaˈmẽtu] m rescue.

salvar [sawˈva(x)] vt to save; ~ **as aparências** to keep up appearances.

⎣ **salvar-se** vp to escape.

salva-vidas [ˌsawvaˈvidaʃ] m inv lifeboat.

salvo, -va [ˈsawvu, -va] pp → **salvar** ♦ adj safe ♦ prep except; **estar a** ~ to be safe; **pôr-se a** ~ to escape; ~ **erro**

unless I'm mistaken; ~ **se** unless.

samba ['sãmba] *m* samba.

samba-canção [ˌsãmbakãˈsãw] (*pl* **sambas-canções** [ˌsãmbaʃkãˈsõiʃ]) *m* slower style of samba with romantic lyrics; *(Br: fam: cueca)* boxer shorts *(pl)*.

sambar [sãmˈba(x)] *vi* to dance to samba.

sambista [sãmˈbiʃta] *mf (dançarino)* samba dancer.

sambódromo [sãmˈbɔdromu] *m* place where samba is rehearsed and danced.

sanatório [sanaˈtɔrju] *m* sanatorium.

sanção [sãˈsãw] (*pl* **-ões** [-õjʃ]) *f* sanction.

sandálias [sãnˈdaljaʃ] *fpl* sandals.

sandes [ˈsãndeʃ] *f inv (Port)* = **sanduíche**.

sanduíche [sãnˈdwiʃi] *m (Br)* sandwich; ~ **misto** ham and cheese sandwich ♦ *f (Port)* sandwich.

sanfona [sãˈfona] *f (Br: acordeão)* accordion.

sangrar [sãŋˈgra(x)] *vi* to bleed.

sangria [sãŋˈgria] *f* sangria.

sangue [ˈsãŋgi] *m* blood; **exame de ~** blood test.

sangue-frio [ˌsãŋgiˈfriu] *m (presença de espírito)* presence of mind.

sanguessuga [ˌsãŋgeˈsuga] *f* leech.

sanguíneo [sãŋˈg(w)inju] *adj m* → **vaso**.

sanidade [saniˈdadʒi] *f (mental)* sanity.

sanita [saˈnita] *f (Port)* toilet bowl.

sanitários [saniˈtarjuʃ] *mpl* toilets.

Santo, -ta [ˈsãntu, -ta] *m, f* Saint; **o ~ Padre** the Holy Father.

santuário [sãnˈtwarju] *m* sanctuary, shrine.

são[1] [sãw] → **ser**.

são[2], **sã** [sãw, sã] *adj (saudável)* healthy; *(fruto)* unblemished; **~ e salvo** safe and sound.

São [sãw] *m* = **Santo**.

São Paulo [sãwˈpawlu] *s* São Paulo.

sapataria [sapataˈria] *f* shoe shop.

sapateado [sapaˈtʒjadu] *m* tap dancing.

sapateiro, -ra [sapaˈtejru, -ra] *m, f* cobbler.

sapatilhas [sapaˈtiʎaʃ] *fpl (Port: de ténis, etc)* trainers *(Brit)*, sneakers *(Am)*; *(Br: de bailarinos)* ballet shoes.

sapato [saˈpatu] *m* shoe; **~s de salto**

alto high-heeled shoes.

sapé [saˈpɛ] *m (Br)* type of Brazilian grass commonly used for thatching huts.

sapo [ˈsapu] *m* toad.

saquinho [saˈkiɲu] *m*: **~ de chá** tea bag.

sarampo [saˈrãmpu] *m* measles *(sg)*.

sarapatel [sarapaˈtɛw] (*pl* **-éis** [-ɛiʃ]) *m* pork stew with liver and kidneys, tomatoes, nuts, apple and raisins.

sarar [saˈra(x)] *vi & vt (cicatrizar)* to heal.

sarcasmo [saxˈkaʒmu] *m* sarcasm.

sarda [ˈsaxda] *f* freckle.

sardinha [saxˈdʒiɲa] *f (peixe)* sardine; **~s assadas** grilled sardines.

sargento [saxˈʒẽntu] *m* sergeant.

sarjeta [saxˈʒeta] *f* gutter.

SARL *(Port: abrev de Sociedade Anónima de Responsabilidade Limitada)* ~ plc, ≈ Ltd *(Brit)*, ~ Inc *(Am)*.

sarro [ˈsaxu] *m (em vinho)* sediment; *(em dentes)* tartar.

satélite [saˈtɛlitʃi] *m* satellite.

sátira [ˈsatʃira] *f* satire.

satisfação [satʃiʃfaˈsãw] (*pl* **-ões** [-õjʃ]) *f* satisfaction; **não ter que dar satisfações a ninguém** not to have to answer to anyone; **pedir satisfações a alguém** to demand an explanation from sb.

satisfatório, -ria [satʃiʃfaˈtɔrju, -rja] *adj* satisfactory.

satisfazer [satʃiʃfaˈze(x)] *vt (agradar a)* to satisfy; *(cumprir)* to meet ♦ *vi (ser suficiente)* to be satisfactory.

❑ satisfazer-se *vp*: **~-se com** to content o.s. with.

satisfeito, -ta [satʃiʃˈfejtu, -ta] *adj* satisfied; **dar-se por ~ (com)** to be satisfied (with).

saudação [sawdaˈsãw] (*pl* **-ões** [-õjʃ]) *f* greeting.

saudade [sawˈdadʒi] *f* nostalgia; **ter ~s de** to miss; **ela deixou muitas ~s** everyone misses her; **matar ~s** *(de lugar)* to revisit old haunts; *(de pessoa)* to look up old friends; **sinto muitas ~s de Bahia** I miss Bahia so much.

saudar [sawˈda(x)] *vt* to greet.

saudável [sawˈdavɛw] (*pl* **-eis** [-ejʃ]) *adj* healthy.

saúde [saˈudʒi] *f* health ♦ *interj* cheers!

sauna [ˈsawna] *f* sauna.

saveiro [saˈvejru] *m* narrow, flat-

*bottomed fishing boat with the prow high-
er than the stern.*

saxofone [saksɔ'fɔni] *m* saxophone.

scanner ['skanɛ(x)] (*pl* **-res** [-riʃ]) *m*
scanner.

scooter ['skutɛ(x)] (*pl* **-res** [-riʃ]) *f*
scooter.

se [si] *pron* **1.** *(reflexo: pessoa)* himself
(*f* herself), themselves (*pl*); *(você, vocês)*
yourself, yourselves (*pl*); *(impessoal)*
oneself; **lavar-~** to wash (oneself);
eles ~ perderam they got lost; **vocês ~
perderam** you got lost. **2.** *(reflexo: coisa, animal)* itself, themselves (*pl*); **o vidro partiu-~** the glass
broke. **3.** *(recíproco)* each other; **escrevem-~
regularmente** they write to each other
regularly; **não ~ cruzam** *(fam)* they
can't stand each other. **4.** *(com sujeito indeterminado)*: **"aluga-~
quarto"** "room for rent"; **"vende-~"**
"for sale"; **come-~ bem aqui** the food
is very good here.
♦ *conj* **1.** *(indica condição)* if; **~ tiver
tempo, escrevo** I'll write if I have time.
2. *(indica causa)* if; **~ você está com
fome, come alguma coisa** if you're
hungry, have something to eat. **3.** *(indica comparação)* if; **~ um é feio, o
outro ainda é pior** if you think he's
ugly, you should see the other one. **4.** *(em interrogativas)*: **que tal ~ fôssemos ao cinema?** how about going to
the cinema?; **e ~ ela não vier?** what if
she doesn't come? **5.** *(exprime desejo)* if; **~ pelo menos
tivesse dinheiro!** if only I had the
money! **6.** *(em interrogativa indireta)* if,
whether; **avisem-me ~ quiserem ir**
let me know if you'd like to go;
perguntei-lhe ~ gostou I asked him if
he liked it. **7.** *(em locuções)*: **~ bem que** even
though, although.

sé [sɛ] *f* cathedral; **~ catedral** cathedral.

sebe [sɛbi] *f* fence; **~ viva** hedge.

sebento, -ta [se'bẽntu, -ta] *adj*
grimy.

sebo ['sebu] *m* suet.

seca ['sɛka] *f* drought.

secador [seka'do(x)] (*pl* **-res** [-riʃ]) *m*
hairdryer.

seção [se'sãw] (*pl* **-ões** [-õjʃ]) *f* (*Br*)

department; **~ de achados e perdidos**
lost property office *(Brit)*, lost-and-
found office *(Am)*.

secar [se'ka(x)] *vt* to dry ♦ *vi (planta,
árvore)* to wither; *(rio, poço, lago)* to dry
up; *(roupa, cabelo)* to dry.

secção [sɛk'sãw] (*pl* **-ões** [-õjʃ]) *f* (*Port*)
= **seção**.

seco, -ca ['seku, -ka] *pp* → **secar** ♦ *adj*
dry; *(carne, peixe, fruto)* dried; *(fig: rispi-
do)* curt.

secretaria [sekreta'ria] *f (de escola,
repartição pública)* secretary's office; **~
de Estado** government department.

secretária [sekre'tarja] *f (móvel)*
desk; **~ eletrônica** *(Br)* answering
machine, → **secretário**.

secretário, -ria [sekre'tarju, -rja] *m,
f* secretary; **Secretário de Estado**
Secretary of State.

secreto, -ta [se'krɛtu, -ta] *adj* secret.

sectário, -ria [sɛk'tarju, -rja] *adj* sec-
tarian.

sector [sɛ'tor] (*pl* **-res** [-riʃ]) *m* (*Port*) =
setor.

secular [seku'la(x)] (*pl* **-res** [-riʃ]) *adj*
ancient.

século ['sɛkulu] *m* century.

secundário, -ria [sekũn'darju, -rja]
adj secondary; *(estrada)* minor.

seda ['seda] *f* silk.

sedativo [seda'tʃivu] *m* sedative.

sede[1] ['sɛdʒi] *f (de empresa, organização)* headquarters (*pl*).

sede[2] ['sedʒi] *f* thirst; **ter ~** to be
thirsty; **ter ~ de** to thirst after; **matar
a ~** to quench one's thirst.

sedimento [sedʒi'mẽntu] *m* sediment.

sedoso, -osa [se'dozu, -ɔza] *adj* silky.

sedução [sedu'sãw] (*pl* **-ões** [-õjʃ]) *f*
seduction.

sedutor, -ra [sedu'to(x), -ra] (*mpl* **-res**
[-riʃ]. *fpl* **-s** [-ʃ]) *adj* seductive.

seduzir [sedu'zi(x)] *vt* to seduce.

segmento [seg'mẽntu] *m* segment.

segredo [se'gredu] *m* secret; *(reserva)*
secrecy.

segregar [segre'ga(x)] *vt (pôr de lado)*
to segregate; *(secreção)* to secrete.
⊐ **segregar-se** *vp (isolar-se)* to cut o.s.
off.

seguida [se'gida] *f*: **em** OU **de ~**
immediately.

seguidamente [se,gida'mẽntʃi] *adv
(sem interrupção)* continuously; *(de*

seguida) straight afterwards.

seguido, -da [se'gidu. -da] *adj (contínuo)* continuous; **o manual ~ este ano é ...** the textbook we're using this year is ...; **dias/anos ~s** days/years on end; **~ de** followed by.

seguinte [se'gĩtʃi] *adj* following ◆ *mf*: **o/a ~** the next one; **o dia/mês ~** the following day/ month.

seguir [se'gi(x)] *vt* to follow; *(perseguir)* to chase; *(carreira, profissão)* to pursue ◆ *vi (continuar)* to go on, to carry on; **~ com algo** to continue with sthg; **~ para** to travel on to; **~ por** to travel on OU along; **a ~** afterwards; **a ~ a** after.

segunda [se'gũda] *f (de veículo)* second (gear), → **segundo**.

segunda-feira [se.gũda'fejra] *(pl* **segundas-feiras** [se.gũdaʃ'fejraʃ]) *f* Monday, → **sexta-feira**.

segundo, -da [se'gũdu. -da] *num & m* second ◆ *prep* according to ◆ *adv* secondly; **em segunda mão** second-hand, → **sexto**.

seguramente [se.gura'mẽtʃi] *adv* surely.

segurança [segu'rãsa] *f* security; *(sem perigo)* safety; *(confiança)* confidence; *(certeza)* certainty; **a Segurança Social** Social Security; **com ~** *(agir, afirmar)* confidently; **em ~** in safety.

segurar [segu'ra(x)] *vt (agarrar)* to hold on to.

seguro, -ra [se'guru. -ra] *adj* safe; *(firme, preso)* secure; *(mesa, cadeira)* steady; *(garantido)* guaranteed ◆ *m (de carro, casa, vida)* insurance; **estar ~** *(estar a salvo)* to be safe; *(ter certeza)* to be certain OU sure; **pôr no ~** to insure; **ser ~ de si** to be self-assured; **~ de doença** *(Port)* health insurance; **~ de responsabilidade civil** third-party insurance; **~ contra terceiros** third-party insurance; **~ contra todos os riscos** fully comprehensive insurance; **~ de viagem** travel insurance; **~ de vida** life insurance.

seguro-saúde [se.gurusa'udʒi] *(pl* **seguros-saúde** [se.guruʃsa'udʒi]) *m (Br)* health insurance.

sei ['sej] → **saber**.

seio ['saju] *m* breast.

seis ['sejʃ] *adj num* six ◆ *m* six; *(dia)* sixth ◆ *mpl (temperatura)* six (degrees) ◆ *fpl:* **às ~** at six (o'clock); **(são) ~**

horas (it's) six o'clock; **ele tem ~ anos** he's six years old; **eles eram ~** there were six of them; **~ de janeiro** the sixth of January; **página ~** page six; **trinta e ~** thirty-six; **o ~ de copas** the six of hearts; **estão ~ graus centígrados** it's six degrees centigrade; **de ~ em ~ semanas/horas** every six weeks/hours; **empataram ~ a ~** *(em partida)* they drew six-all; **~ a zero** *(em partida)* six-nil.

seiscentos, -tas [sejʃ'sẽtuʃ. -taʃ] *num* six hundred, → **seis**.

seita ['sejta] *f* sect.

seiva ['sejva] *f* sap.

seixo ['sejʃu] *m* pebble.

sela ['sela] *f* saddle.

selar [se'la(x)] *vt (cavalo, égua)* to saddle; *(carta, subscrito)* to stamp; *(documento oficial, pacto)* to seal.

seleção [sele'sãw] *f (Br) (escolha)* selection; *(equipe nacional)* team.

selecção [sele'sãw] *f (Port)* = **seleção**.

seleccionar [selesju'nar] *vt (Port)* = **selecionar**.

selecionar [selesjo'na(x)] *vt (Br)* to select.

selecto, -ta [se'letu. -ta] *adj (Port)* = **seleto**.

seleto, -ta [se'letu. -ta] *adj (Br)* exclusive.

self-service [sewf'sexvisi] *(pl* **self-services** [sewf'sexviseʃ]) *m* self-service *cafe or restaurant.*

selim [se'lĩ] *(pl* **-ns** [-ʃ]) *m (de bicicleta)* saddle.

selo ['selu] *m* stamp; **~ de garantia** *(em produto)* tamper-proof seal.

selva ['sewva] *f* jungle.

selvagem [sew'vaʒẽ] *(pl* **-ns** [-ʃ]) *adj* wild ◆ *mf (pessoa)* savage.

sem [sẽ] *prep* without; **estou ~ fazer nada há muito tempo** I haven't done anything for ages; **ele saiu ~ que eu notasse** he left without me noticing; **estar ~ água/gasolina** to be out of water/petrol; **~ mais nem menos** for no reason whatsoever; **~ data** undated.

sem-abrigo [sẽa'brigu] *mf inv* homeless person; **os ~** the homeless.

semáforos [se'maforuʃ] *mpl* traffic lights.

semana [se'mana] *f* week; **~ a ~** week by week; **por ~** a OU per week; **a Semana Santa** Holy Week.

semanada [sema'nada] *f* pocket money.

semanal [sema'naw] (*pl* **-ais** [-ajʃ]) *adj* weekly.

semblante [sẽm'blãntʃi] *m* face.

semear [se'mja(x)] *vt* (*trigo, batatas, etc*) to sow; (*ódio, discórdia*) to spread.

semelhança [seme'ʎãsa] *f* resemblance; **à ~ de** like.

semelhante [seme'ʎãntʃi] *adj* similar; **~ a** like, similar to.

sémen [semɛn] *m* (*Port*) = **sêmen**.

sêmen [semɛn] *m* (*Br*) semen.

semente [se'mẽntʃi] *f* seed.

semestral [semeʃ'traw] (*pl* **-ais** [-ajʃ]) *adj* half-yearly, six-monthly.

semestre [se'mɛʃtri] *m* period of six months.

seminário [semi'narju] *m* (*grupo de estudos*) seminar; (*para eclesiásticos*) seminary.

sêmola ['semola] *f* semolina.

semolina [semo'lina] *f* semolina.

sempre ['sẽmpri] *adv* always; **o mesmo de ~** the usual; **como ~** as usual; **para ~** forever; **~ que** whenever.

sem-vergonha [sãjvex'goɲa] *mf inv* rogue.

sena ['sena] *f in cards, the sixth of any suit.*

senado [se'nadu] *m* senate.

senão [se'nãw] *conj* otherwise.

senha ['seɲa] *f* (*sinal*) sign; (*palavra de acesso*) password; **~ de saída** ticket given at a venue to allow you to come and go without paying the entrance fee again.

senhor, -ra [se'ɲo(x), -ra] (*mpl* **-res** [-riʃ], *fpl* **-s** [-ʃ]) *m, f* (*em geral*) man (*f* woman); (*formalmente*) gentleman (*f* lady); (*antes de nome*) Mr (*f* Mrs, Ms); (*ao dirigir a palavra*) Sir (*f* Madam); **"senhoras"** "ladies"; **Caro** OU **Exmo. Senhor** (*em carta*) Dear Sir; **Cara** OU **Exma. Senhora** (*em carta*) Dear Madam; **bom dia meus senhores/minhas senhoras!** good morning (gentlemen/ladies)!

senhorio, -ria [seɲo'riu, -ria] *m, f* landlord (*f* landlady).

senil [se'niw] (*pl* **-is** [-iʃ]) *adj* senile.

sensação [sẽsa'sãw] (*pl* **-ões** [-õjʃ]) *f* sensation, feeling; (*intuição*) feeling; **causar ~** to cause a sensation.

sensacional [sẽsasjo'naw] (*pl* **-ais** [-ajʃ]) *adj* sensational.

sensações → sensação.

sensato, -ta [sẽ'satu, -ta] *adj* sensible.

sensível [sẽ'sivew] (*pl* **-eis** [-ejʃ]) *adj* sensitive.

senso ['sẽsu] *m* sense; **ter bom ~** to be sensible; **ter ~ prático** to be practical; **~ comum** common sense.

sensual [sẽ'swaw] (*pl* **-ais** [-ajʃ]) *adj* sensual.

sentado, -da [sẽ'tadu, -da] *adj* seated; **estar ~** to be sitting down.

sentar-se [sẽn'taxsi] *vp* to sit down.

sentença [sẽn'tẽsa] *f* sentence.

sentido, -da [sẽn'tʃidu, -da] *adj* (*melindrado*) touchy ◆ *m* sense; (*significado*) meaning; (*direção*) direction; **fazer ~** to make sense; **em certo ~** to a certain extent; **ir em ~ proibido** (*Port*) to go the wrong way up a one-way street; **(rua de) ~ único** one-way street.

sentimental [sẽntʃimẽn'taw] (*pl* **-ais** [-ajʃ]) *adj* sentimental.

sentimento [sẽntʃi'mẽntu] *m* feeling; **os meus ~s** my deepest sympathy.

sentinela [sẽntʃi'nɛla] *mf* guard; **estar de ~** to be on guard duty.

sentir [sẽn'tʃi(x)] *vt* to feel; **sinto muito!** I'm terribly sorry!; **~ falta de** to miss; **~ vontade de fazer algo** to feel like doing sthg.

❏ **sentir-se** *vp* to feel.

separação [separa'sãw] (*pl* **-ões** [-õjʃ]) *f* separation.

separado, -da [sepa'radu, -da] *adj* (*independente*) separate; (*cônjuges*) separated; **em ~** separately.

separar [sepa'ra(x)] *vt* (*dividir*) to separate; (*reservar*) to put aside.

❏ **separar-se** *vt* to separate.

septuagésimo, -ma [septwa'ʒɛzimu, -ma] *num* seventieth, → **sexto**.

sepultar [sepuw'ta(x)] *vt* to bury.

sepultura [sepuw'tura] *f* grave.

sequência [se'kwẽsja] *f* (*Port*) = **seqüência**.

seqüência [se'kwẽsja] *f* (*Br*) sequence.

sequer [se'kɛ(x)] *adv*: **nem ~** not even; **ele nem ~ falou comigo** he didn't even speak to me.

seqüestrador, -ra [sekweʃtra'do(x), -ra] (*mpl* **-res** [-riʃ], *fpl* **-s** [-ʃ]) *m, f* kidnapper.

sequestrar [sekeʃ'trar] *vt* (*Port*) = **seqüestrar**.

seqüestrar [sekweʃˈtra(x)] *vt (Br)* to kidnap, to abduct.

seqüestro [seˈkweʃtru] *m* kidnapping, abduction.

sequóia [seˈkwɔja] *f* sequoia.

ser [ˈse(x)] (*pl* **-res** [-riʃ]) *m (criatura)* being; **~ humano** human being.

◆ *vi* 1. *(para descrever)* to be; **é demasiado longo** it's too long; **são bonitos** they're lovely; **sou médico** I'm a doctor.

2. *(para designar lugar, origem)* to be; **ele é do Brasil** he's from Brazil; **é em São Paulo** it's in São Paulo; **sou brasileira** I'm Brazilian.

3. *(custar)* to be; **quanto é? – são 100 reais** how much is it? – (it's) 100 reals.

4. *(com data, dia, hora)* to be; **hoje é sexta** it's Friday today; **que horas são?** what time is it?; **são seis horas** it's six o'clock.

5. *(exprime possessão)* to be; **é do Ricardo** it's Ricardo's; **este carro é seu?** is this car yours?; **os livros eram meus** the books were mine.

6. *(em locuções)*: **a não ~ que** unless; **que foi?** what's wrong?; **ou seja** in other words; **será que ele vem?** do you think he's coming?

◆ *v aux (forma a voz passiva)* to be; **foi visto na saída do cinema** he was seen on his way out of the cinema.

◆ *v impess* 1. *(exprime tempo)* to be; **é de dia/noite** it's daytime/ night; **é tarde/cedo** it's late/early.

2. *(com adjetivo)* to be; **é difícil dizer** it's difficult to say; **é fácil de ver** it's easy to see.

⏺ **ser** *de v + prep (matéria)* to be made of; *(ser adepto de)* to be a supporter of; **eles são do Flamengo** they're Flamengo supporters.

serão [seˈrãw] (*pl* **-ões** [-õjʃ]) *m (reunião)* get-together; *(noite)* evening; **fazer ~** to stay up late.

sereia [seˈreja] *f (de navio, farol)* siren; *(ser lendário)* mermaid.

serenar [sereˈna(x)] *vt (acalmar)* to calm ◆ *vi (acalmar-se)* to calm down; *(tempo)* to clear up.

serenata [sereˈnata] *f* serenade.

seres → **ser**.

seresta [seˈrɛʃta] *f (Br)* = **serenata**.

seriado [seˈrjadu] *m (Br)* (TV) series *(sg)*.

série [ˈsɛrji] *f* series *(sg)*; *(de bilhetes de metro)* book; **uma ~ de** a series of.

seriedade [serjeˈdadʒi] *f* seriousness; *(honestidade)* honesty.

seringa [seˈrĩŋga] *f* syringe.

seringueira [serĩŋˈgejra] *f* rubber plant.

sério, -ria [ˈsɛrju, -rja] *adj* serious; *(honrado)* honest ◆ *adv*: **a ~?** seriously?; **levar** OU **tomar a ~** to take seriously.

sermão [sexˈmãw] (*pl* **-ões** [-õjʃ]) *m* sermon.

serões → **serão**.

seronegativo, -va [sɛroneɡaˈtivu, -va] *adj (Port)* = **soronegativo**.

seropositivo, -va [sɛropuziˈtivu, -va] *adj (Port)* = **soropositivo**.

serpente [sexˈpẽtʃi] *f* serpent.

serpentina [sexpẽˈtʃina] *f* streamer.

serra [ˈsɛxa] *f (instrumento)* saw; *(em geografia)* mountain range.

serralheiro [sexaˈʎejru] *m* locksmith.

serrar [seˈxa(x)] *vt* to saw.

sertanejo, -ja [sextaˈneʒu, -ʒa] *adj* of/relating to the "sertão".

sertão [sexˈtãw] *m* remote, arid lands in the interior of northeastern Brazil.

servente [sexˈvẽtʃi] *m (de pedreiro)* (bricklayer's) mate.

serventia [sexvẽˈtʃia] *f (préstimo)* use; *(de casa, edifício, terreno)* access road OU path.

serviço [sexˈvisu] *m* service; *(trabalho)* work; **"fora de ~"** "out of service"; **"~ incluído"** "service included"; **~ cívico** social service.

servil [sexˈviw] (*pl* **-is** [-iʃ]) *adj* servile.

servir [sexˈvi(x)] *vt* to serve ◆ *vi (criado, empregado)* to serve; *(ser útil)* to be useful; *(roupa, calçado)* to fit; **em que posso servi-lo?** how may I help you?; **~ de algo** to serve as sthg.

⏺ **servir-se** *vp (de bebida, comida)* to help o.s.; **~-se de** *(fazer uso de)* to make use of.

servis → **servil**.

sessão [seˈsãw] (*pl* **-ões** [-õjʃ]) *f (de filme)* showing; *(em televisão)* broadcast; *(de debate político, científico)* meeting; *(em tribunal)* session.

sessenta [seˈsẽta] *num* sixty, → **seis**.

sessões → **sessão**.

sesta [ˈsɛʃta] *f* afternoon nap.

seta [ˈsɛta] *f* arrow.

sete [sɛtʃi] *num* seven, → **seis**.

setecentos, -tas [sɛtɛ'sɛntuʃ, -taʃ] *num* seven hundred, → **seis**.

setembro [sɛ'tɛmbru] *m* September; **durante o mês de ~** during (the month of) September; **em ~** in September; **em meados de ~** in the middle of September, in mid-September; **este mês de ~** *(passado)* last September; *(futuro)* this (coming) September; **o passado/próximo mês de ~** last/next September; **no princípio/final de ~** at the beginning/end of September; **o primeiro de ~** the first of September.

setenta [sɛ'tɛnta] *num* seventy, → **seis**.

sétimo, -ma [sɛtʃimu, -ma] *num* seventh, → **sexto**.

setor [sɛ'to(x)] *(pl -res* [-riʃ]) *m (Br) (ramo)* sector; *(seção)* section.

seu, sua [sew, 'sua] *adj* 1. *(dele)* his; *(dela)* her; *(de você, vocês)* your; *(deles, delas)* their; **ela trouxe o ~ carro** she brought her car; **onde estacionou a sua moto?** where did you park your motorbike?
2. *(de coisa, animal: singular)* its; *(de coisa, animal: plural)* their; **o cachorro foi para a o seu canil** the dog went into his OR its kennel.
◆ *pron:* **o ~/a sua** *(dele)* his; *(dela)* hers; *(deles, delas)* theirs; *(de coisa, animal: singular)* its; *(de coisa, animal: plural)* their; **um amigo ~** a friend of his/hers etc.; **os ~s** *(a família de cada um)* his/her etc. family.
◆ *m, f* 1. *(pej: forma de tratamento)* you; **~ estúpido!** you idiot!; **~s irresponsáveis!** you fools!
2. *(com malícia)* you; **~ capeta!** you little rascal!; **sua danadinha!** you little so-and-so!

severidade [sɛveri'dadʒi] *f* severity.

severo, -ra [sɛ'vɛru, -ra] *adj (inflexível)* strict; *(grave)* severe.

sexagésimo, -ma [sɛksa'ʒɛzimu, -ma] *num* sixtieth, → **sexto**.

sexo ['sɛksu] *m* sex; *(órgão reprodutor)* genitals *(pl)*.

sexta-feira [sɛjʃta'fejra] *(pl* **sextas-feiras** [sɛjʃtaʃ'fejraʃ]) *f* Friday; **às sextas-feiras** on Fridays; **até ~** until Friday; **ela vem ~** she's coming on Friday; **esta ~** *(passada)* last Friday; *(próxima)* next Friday; **hoje é ~** today

is Friday; **todas as sextas-feiras** every Friday; **~ de manhã/à tarde/à noite** Friday morning/afternoon/night; **12 de Junho** Friday 12 June; **~ passada/próxima** last/next Friday; **~ que vem** next Friday; **Sexta-feira Santa** Good Friday.

sexto, -ta [sɛjʃtu, -ta] *adj num* sixth ◆ *m (número)* sixth ◆ *m, f:* **o ~/a sexta** *(pessoa, coisa)* the sixth; **chegar em ~** to come sixth; **capítulo ~** chapter six; **em ~ lugar** in sixth place; **no ~ dia** on the sixth day; **a sexta parte** *(relativo a quantidade)* a sixth; *(de espetáculo, filme)* part six.

sexual [sɛk'swaw] *(pl -ais* [-ajʃ]) *adj* sexual.

sexualidade [sɛkswali'dadʒi] *f* sexuality.

sexy ['sɛksi] *adj* sexy.

shopping ['ʃɔpiŋ] *m* shopping centre *(Brit)*, shopping mall *(Am)*.

short ['ʃɔxtʃi] *m (Br: calção)* shorts *(pl)*.

show ['ʃow] *m* show.

si ['si] *pron* 1. *(complemento indireto: pessoa)* him *(f* her), them *(pl)*; *(você, vocês)* you; **ele disse que a chamada não era para ~** he said the call wasn't for him.
2. *(complemento indireto: coisa, animal)* it, them *(pl)*.
3. *(reflexo: pessoa)* himself *(f* herself), themselves *(pl)*; *(você, vocês)* yourself, yourselves *(pl)*; **comprou-o para ~ (mesmo** OU **próprio)** he bought it for himself; **é para ~ (mesmo** OU **próprio)?** is it for yourself?; **elas sabem tomar conta de ~ (mesmas** OU **próprias)** they know how to look after themselves; **ela é cheia de ~** *(fam)* she's full of herself.
4. *(reflexo: coisa, animal)* itself, themselves *(pl)*; **o livro, em ~, não é caro** the book itself is not expensive.
5. *(impessoal)* oneself; **é sinal de egoísmo só pensar em ~** it's a sign of selfishness to think only of oneself; **cada um por ~** each man for himself.

SIDA ['sida] *f (Port)* AIDS.

siderurgia [sidɛrur'ʒia] *f* iron and steel industry.

sido ['sidu] → **ser**.

sidra ['sidra] *f* cider.

sífilis ['sifiliʃ] *f* syphilis.

sigilo [si'ʒilu] *m* secrecy.

sigla ['sigla] f acronym.

significado [signifi'kadu] m meaning.

significar [signifi'ka(x)] vt to mean.

significativo, -va [signifika'tʃivu, -va] adj significant.

signo ['signu] m sign.

sigo ['sigu] → **seguir**.

sílaba ['silaba] f syllable.

silenciar [silẽ'sja(x)] vt to silence.

silêncio [si'lẽsju] m silence ◆ interj silence!

silencioso, -osa [silẽ'sjozu, -ɔza] adj silent, quiet.

silhueta [si'ʎweta] f silhouette.

silicone [sili'kɔni] m silicone.

silva ['siwva] f bramble.

silvestre [siw'vɛʃtri] adj wild.

sim ['sĩ] adv yes; **penso que ~** I think so; **pelo ~ pelo não** just in case.

símbolo ['sĩmbolu] m symbol.

simetria [sime'tria] f symmetry.

similar [simi'la(x)] (pl **-res** [-riʃ]) adj similar.

simpatia [sĩmpa'tʃia] f (carinho) affection; (cordialidade) friendliness.

simpático, -ca [sĩm'patʃiku, -ka] adj nice; (amigável) friendly.

simpatizante [sĩmpatʃi'zãntʃi] mf sympathizer.

simpatizar [sĩmpatʃi'za(x)] : **simpatizar com** v + prep to like.

simples ['sĩmpleʃ] adj inv simple; (bebida) straight; (em pele) mole; (de nascimento) birthmark; (dinheiro) deposit; **estou aqui há uma hora e nem ~ dele** I've been here for an hour and there's been no sign of him; **dar ~ de si** to

show up; **dar sinais de cansaço** to show signs of fatigue; **em ~ de** as a mark ou sign of; **~ de alarme** alarm; **~ de interrompido** ou **de ocupado** engaged tone.

sinalização [sinaliza'sãw] f road signs (pl).

sinceridade [sĩseri'dadʒi] f sincerity.

sincero, -ra [sĩ'sɛru, -ra] adj sincere.

sindicato [sĩndʒi'katu] m trade union.

síndico ['sĩndʒiku] m (Br) person chosen by other residents to organize the maintenance of an apartment block.

síndrome ['sĩdromi] f syndrome.

sinfonia [sĩfo'nia] f symphony.

sinfônica [sĩ'fonika] adj f → **música**.

singelo, -la [sĩ'ʒɛlu, -la] adj simple.

single [sĩ'geɫ] m (Port) single.

singular [sĩgu'la(x)] (pl **-res** [-riʃ]) adj (único) unique; (extraordinário) strange; (GRAM) singular ◆ m (GRAM) singular; **~es homens/mulheres** (Port: em ténis) men's/ women's singles.

sino ['sinu] m bell.

sinónimo [si'nɔnimu] m (Port) = **sinônimo**.

sinônimo [si'nonimu] m (Br) synonym.

sintaxe [sĩ'tasi] f syntax.

síntese ['sĩtezi] f (resumo) summary.

sintético, -ca [sĩ'tɛtiku, -ka] adj (artificial) synthetic; (resumido) concise.

sintoma [sĩ'toma] m symptom.

sintonizar [sĩntoni'za(x)] vt (rádio) to tune; (estação de rádio) to tune in to.

sinuca [si'nuka] f (Br) snooker.

sinuoso, -osa [si'nwozu, -ɔza] adj (curva, caminho) winding.

sirene [si'rɛni] f siren.

siri [si'ri] m crab.

sirvo ['sixvu] → **servir**.

sísmico [si'ʒmiku] adj m → **abalo**.

siso ['sizu] m (common) sense; **dente de ~** wisdom tooth.

sistema [siʃ'tema] m system; **~ métrico** metric system; **~ nervoso** nervous system; **Sistemas Digitais** (disciplina) computer studies; **por ~** systematically.

sistemático, -ca [siʃte'matʃiku, -ka] adj systematic.

sisudo, -da [si'zudu, -da] adj serious.

sítio ['sitʃju] m (lugar) place; (espaço) room, space; (Br: chácara) small-holding.

situação [sitwa'sãw] (*pl* **-ões** [-õjʃ]) *f* (*localização*) position; (*circunstâncias*) situation; (*estado, condição*) condition.

situado, -da [si'twadu, -da] *adj*: **bem/mal** ~ well/badly situated; ~ **em** situated in; **está** ~ **ao norte de Brasília** it is situated to the north of Brasília.

situar [si'twa(x)] *vt* (*colocar*) to place; (*localizar*) to locate.

⮡ **situar-se** *vp* (*localizar-se*) to be located.

s/l *abrev* = **sobreloja**.

slide [s'lajdʒi] *m* slide.

slip ['slip] *m* (*Port: cueca*) underpants (*pl*).

slogan ['slogãn] *m* slogan.

smoking ['smokĩŋ] *m* dinner jacket (*Brit*), tuxedo (*Am*).

snack-bar [snɛk'ba(x)] (*pl* **snack-bares** [snɛk'barɛʃ]) *m* snack bar.

snooker ['snuker] *m* (*Port*) snooker.

só ['sɔ] *adj* (*sem companhia*) alone; (*solitário*) lonely ◆ *adv* (*apenas*) only; **é** ~ **pedir!** all you need to do is ask!; **um** ~ **minuto do teu tempo** just a minute of your time; **a** ~**s** alone; **não** ~ ... **como também** not only ... but also; ~ **que** only.

SO (*abrev de Sudoeste*) SW.

soalho [s'waʎu] *m* wooden floor.

soar ['swa(x)] *vi & vt* to sound; **soaram as 10 horas** the clock struck 10; ~ **bem** to sound right; ~ **mal** not to sound right.

sob ['sobi] *prep* under.

sobe ['sɔbi] → **subir**.

soberania [sobera'nia] *f* sovereignty.

soberano, -na [sobe'ranu, -na] *adj* sovereign.

soberbo, -ba [su'bexbu, -ba] *adj* (*suntuoso*) superb; (*arrogante*) arrogant.

sobrado [so'bradu] *m* wooden floor.

sobrancelha [sobrã'seʎa] *f* eyebrow.

sobrar [so'bra(x)] *vi* to be left over.

sobre ['sobri] *prep* (*em cima de*) on (top of); (*por cima de*) over; (*acerca de*) about.

sobreaviso [sobrea'vizu] *m*: **estar** OU **ficar de** ~ to be on the alert.

sobrecarga [sobre'kaxga] *f* overload.

sobrecarregar [sobrekaxe'ga(x)] *vt*: ~ **alguém com algo** to overload sb with sthg.

sobreloja [sobre'lɔʒa] *f* mezzanine.

sobremesa [sobre'meza] *f* dessert.

sobrenatural [sobrenatu'raw] (*pl*

-ais [-ajʃ]) *adj* supernatural.

sobrenome [sobri'nomi] *m* (*Br*) surname.

sobrepor [sobre'po(x)] *vt*: ~ **algo a algo** to put sthg on top of sthg.

⮡ **sobrepor-se** *vp* (*problema, trabalho*) to take precedence.

sobrescrito [sobreʃ'kritu] *m* envelope.

sobressair [sobresa'i(x)] *vi* to stand out.

sobressaltar [sobresaw'ta(x)] *vt* to startle.

⮡ **sobressaltar-se** *vp* to be startled.

sobressalto [sobre'sawtu] *m* (*susto*) fright; (*inquietação*) anxiety.

sobretaxa [sobre'taʃa] *f* surcharge.

sobretudo [sobre'tudu] *m* overcoat ◆ *adv* especially, above all.

sobrevivência [sobrevi'vẽsja] *f* survival.

sobrevivente [sobrevi'vẽntʃi] *mf* survivor.

sobreviver [sobrevi've(x)] *vi* to survive.

sobriedade [sobrie'dadʒi] *f* sobriety.

sobrinho, -nha [so'briɲu, -ɲa] *m, f* nephew (*f* niece).

sóbrio, -bria ['sɔbriu, -bria] *adj* sober.

social [so'sjaw] (*pl* **-ais** [-ajʃ]) *adj* social.

socialismo [sosja'liʒmu] *m* socialism.

socialista [sosja'liʃta] *adj & mf* socialist.

sociedade [sosje'dadʒi] *f* society; (*comercial*) partnership.

sócio, -cia ['sɔsju, -sja] *m, f* partner.

sociologia [sosjolo'ʒia] *f* sociology.

sociólogo, -ga [so'sjɔlogu, -ga] *m, f* sociologist.

soco ['soku] *m* (*em pessoa*) punch; (*em mesa*) thump.

socorrer [soko'xe(x)] *vt* to help.

⮡ **socorrer-se de** *vp* + *prep* to resort to, to have recourse to.

socorro [so'koxu] *m* help ◆ *interj* help!; **pedir** ~ to ask for help.

soda ['sɔda] *f* (*bicarbonato*) bicarbonate of soda; (*bebida*) soda water.

sofá [so'fa] *m* sofa; ~ **cama** sofa bed.

sofisticado, -da [sofiʃtʃi'kadu, -da] *adj* sophisticated.

sofrer [so'fre(x)] *vt* to have ◆ *vi* to suffer.

sofrimento [sofri'mẽntu] *m* suffering.

software [sof'tweri] *m* software.

sogro, sogra ['sogru, 'sɔgra] *m, f* father-in-law (*f* mother-in-law).

soirée [swa're] *f* soirée.

sóis → sol.

soja ['sɔʒa] *f* soya.

sol ['sɔw] (*pl* **sóis** ['sɔjʃ]) *m* sun.

sola ['sɔla] *f* sole.

solar [so'la(x)] (*pl* **-res** [-riʃ]) *adj* solar ◆ *m* manor(house).

soldado [sow'dadu] *m* soldier.

soleira [so'lejra] *f* threshold.

solene [so'lɛni] *adj* solemn.

soletrar [sole'tra(x)] *vt* to spell.

solicitar [solisi'ta(x)] *vt* to request.

solícito, -ta [so'lisitu, -ta] *adj* solicitous.

solidão [soli'dãw] *f* solitude.

solidariedade [solidarje'dadʒi] *f* solidarity.

solidário, -ria [soli'darju, -rja] *adj* sharing; **ser ~ com** (*causa, idéia*) to support; (*pessoa*) to stand by.

sólido, -da ['sɔlidu, -da] *adj* solid; (*investimento, negócio*) sound.

solista [so'liʃta] *mf* soloist.

solitário, -ria [soli'tarju, -rja] *adj* (*local*) lonely; (*pessoa*) solitary ◆ *m* (*jóia*) solitaire.

solo ['sɔlu] *m* (*chão*) floor; (*superfície terrestre*) ground; (*terreno arável*) land, soil; (*MÚS*) solo.

soltar [sow'ta(x)] *vt* (*desprender*) to release; (*desatar*) to untie; (*grito, preso*) to let out.

❑ soltar-se *vp* (*desprender-se*) to come loose; (*desatar-se*) to come undone.

solteiro, -ra [sow'tejru, -ra] *adj* single.

solto, -ta ['sowtu, -ta] *pp* → soltar ◆ *adj* (*livre*) loose; (*sozinho*) separate.

solução [solu'sãw] (*pl* **-ões** [-õjʃ]) *f* solution.

soluçar [solu'sa(x)] *vi* (*ter soluços*) to hiccup; (*chorar*) to sob.

solucionar [solusjo'na(x)] *vt* to solve.

soluço [su'lusu] *m* (*contração*) hiccup; (*choro*) sob.

soluções → solução.

solúvel [so'luvew] (*pl* **-eis** [-ejʃ]) *adj* soluble.

som ['sõ] (*pl* **-ns** [-ʃ]) *m* sound; **ao ~ de** to the sound of; **~ estereofônico** stereo sound.

soma ['soma] *f* sum.

somar [so'ma(x)] *vt* to add up.

sombra ['sõmbra] *f* (*escuridão*) shade; (*de corpo*) shadow; (*cosmético*) eye shadow; **à OU na ~** in the shade; **sem ~ de dúvida** beyond a shadow of a doubt.

sombrio, -bria [sõm'briu, -'bria] *adj* (*escuro*) dark; (*melancólico*) sombre; (*lúgubre*) gloomy.

somente [so'mẽntʃi] *adv* only.

sonâmbulo, -la [so'nãmbulu, -la] *m, f* sleepwalker.

sonda ['sõnda] *f* (*MED*) probe; **~ espacial** space probe.

sondagem [sõn'daʒẽ] (*pl* **-ns** [-ʃ]) *f* (*opinion*) poll.

soneca [so'nɛka] *f* nap; **tirar uma ~** to have a nap.

soneto [so'nɛtu] *m* sonnet.

sonhador, -ra [soɲa'do(x), -ra] (*mpl* **-res** [-riʃ], *fpl* **-s** [-ʃ]) *m, f* dreamer.

sonhar [so'ɲa(x)] *vi* to dream; **~ acordado** to daydream; **~ com** to dream about.

sonho ['soɲu] *m* dream; (*Br: CULIN*) doughnut; **de ~** dream (*antes de s*).

sonífero [so'niferu] *m* sleeping pill.

sono ['sonu] *m* sleep; **estou morto de ~** I'm falling asleep; **pegar no ~** to get to sleep; **ter ~** to be sleepy; **~ pesado** deep sleep.

sonolento, -ta [sono'lẽntu, -ta] *adj* sleepy.

sonoro, -ra [so'nɔru, -ra] *adj* sound (*antes de s*).

sons → som.

sonso, -sa ['sõsu, -sa] *adj* two-faced.

sopa ['sopa] *f* soup; **~ de hortaliça/legumes** cabbage/vegetable soup; **~ de marisco** soup made with prawns, onion and tomato; **ser ~** (*fam: ser fácil*) to be a piece of cake.

soporífero [sopo'riferu] *m* sleeping pill.

soprar [so'pra(x)] *vt* (*vela, lume*) to blow out; (*pó*) to blow off; (*resposta*) to whisper ◆ *vi* to blow.

sórdido, -da ['sɔrdʒidu, -da] *adj* squalid.

soro ['soru] *m* (*MED*) serum; (*de leite*) whey; **~ fisiológico** saline solution.

soronegativo, -va [soronega'tʃivu, -va] *adj* (*Br*) HIV-negative.

soropositivo, -va [soropozi'tʃivu,

-va] *adj (Br)* HIV-positive.

sorridente [soxi'dẽntʃi] *adj (cara, face)* smiling; *(pessoa)* cheerful.

sorrir [so'xi(x)] *vi* to smile.

sorriso [so'xizu] *m* smile.

sorte [ˈsɔxtʃi] *f* luck; *(destino)* fate; **boa ~!** good luck!; **tire um cartão/ número à ~** pick a card/ number; **para dar ~** for (good) luck; **estar com ~** to be in luck; **ter ~** to be lucky; **tirar a ~** to draw lots; **a ~ grande** the jackpot; **com ~** *(pessoa)* lucky; **por ~** luckily.

sortear [sox'tea(x)] *vt* to raffle.

sorteio [sox'teju] *m* raffle.

sortido, -da [sox'tʃidu, -da] *adj* assorted ◆ *m* assortment.

sortudo, -da [sox'tudu, -da] *m, f (fam)* lucky person.

sorvete [sox'vetʃi] *m (Br)* ice cream.

sorveteria [soxvete'ria] *f (Br)* ice-cream parlour.

SOS *m (abrev de Save our Souls)* SOS.

sossegado, -da [sose'gadu, -da] *adj* quiet.

sossego [so'segu] *m* peace.

sótão [ˈsɔtãw] *m* attic.

sotaque [so'taki] *m* accent.

sotavento [sɔta'vẽntu] *m* leeward.

soterrar [sote'xa(x)] *vt* to bury.

sou [ˈso] → **ser.**

soube [ˈsobi] → **saber.**

soufflé [suˈfle] *m (Port)* = **suflê.**

soutien [su'tjã] *m (Port)* = **sutiã.**

sova [ˈsɔva] *f* beating.

sovaco [so'vaku] *m* armpit.

sovina [so'vina] *adj* miserly.

sozinho, -nha [sɔ'ziɲu, -ɲa] *adj* alone; **fiz tudo ~** I did it all by myself; **falar/rir ~** to talk/laugh to o.s.

spray [ˈsprej] *m* spray.

squash [ˈskwaʃ] *m* squash.

Sr. *(abrev de senhor)* Mr.

Sra. *(abrev de senhora)* Mrs, Ms.

stand [ˈʃtãde] *(pl* **-des** [-diʃ]) *m (Port) (de automóveis)* (car) dealer; *(em feira de amostras)* stand.

stock [ˈʃtɔke] *m (Port)* stock.

stress [ˈstrεs] *m* stress.

sua → **seu.**

suar [ˈswa(x)] *vi* to sweat.

suástica [ˈswaʃtʃika] *f* swastika.

suave [ˈswavi] *adj* soft; *(brisa, curva)* gentle; *(sabor)* delicate; *(vinho)* smooth; *(cheiro)* subtle; *(dor)* slight.

suavidade [swavi'dadʒi] *f* softness; *(de brisa, curva)* gentleness; *(de sabor)* delicacy; *(de vinho)* smoothness; *(de cheiro)* subtlety.

suavizar [swavi'za(x)] *vt (cheiro, sabor)* to tone down; *(dor)* to ease ◆ *vi (chuva)* to ease; *(vento)* to drop.

subalimentação [subalimẽnta'sãw] *f* undernourishment.

subalimentado, -da [subalimẽn-'tadu, -da] *adj* undernourished.

subalterno, -na [subaw'tεxnu, -na] *m, f & adj (subordinado)* subordinate.

subalugar [subalu'ga(x)] *vt* to sublet.

subconsciente [subkõʃ'sjẽntʃi] *m* subconscious.

subdesenvolvido, -da [subde-zẽvow'vidu, -da] *adj* underdeveloped.

subdesenvolvimento [subde-zẽvowvi'mẽntu] *m* underdevelopment.

súbdito, -ta [ˈsubditu, -ta] *m, f (Port)* = **súdito.**

subentendido, -da [subẽntẽn'dʒidu, -da] *adj* implied.

subida [su'bida] *f (ladeira)* slope; *(de preços)* increase; *(de montanha, escadas)* climb.

subir [su'bi(x)] *vt (escadas, rua, encosta)* to go up; *(montanha, rochedo)* to climb; *(malas, bagagem)* to take up; *(preços, salários)* to increase; *(estore, persiana)* to raise ◆ *vi (ir para cima)* to go up; **~ a** to climb; **~ de posto** *(em emprego)* to be promoted; **~ em** *(Br: em ônibus, avião, etc)* to get on; *(Port: em Lisboa, Porto, etc)* to get on at; **~ para** *(Port)* to get on; **~ por** to go up.

súbito, -ta [ˈsubitu, -ta] *adj* sudden; **de ~** suddenly.

subjectivo, -va [subʒε'tivu, -va] *adj (Port)* = **subjetivo.**

subjetivo, -va [subʒε'tʃivu, -va] *adj (Br)* subjective.

subjugar [subʒu'ga(x)] *vt* to overcome.

❏ **subjugar-se a** *vp + prep* to give in to.

subjuntivo [subʒõn'tʃivu] *m (Br)* subjunctive.

sublime [su'blimi] *adj* sublime.

sublinhar [subli'ɲa(x)] *vt* to underline; *(com entoação)* to stress.

submarino [subma'rinu] *m* submarine.

submergir [submex'ʒi(x)] *vt (imergir)* to submerge; *(inundar)* to flood.

submeter [subme'te(x)] *vt:* ~ algo/alguém a algo to submit sthg/sb to sthg.

◻ **submeter-se a** *vp + prep* to submit to.

submisso, -a [sub'misu, -a] *adj* submissive.

subnutrido, -da [subnu'tridu, -da] *adj* undernourished.

subornar [subox'na(x)] *vt* to bribe.

subsídio [sub'sidju] *m* subsidy.

subsistência [subsif'tēsja] *f (sustento)* subsistence; *(permanência)* continued existence.

subsistir [subsif'ti(x)] *vi (persistir)* to remain; *(sobreviver)* to subsist.

subsolo [sub'sɔlu] *m* subsoil.

substância [subf'tāsja] *f* substance.

substantivo [subftān'ʒivu] *m* noun.

substituir [subftfi'twi(x)] *vt* to substitute; ~ a manteiga por margarina substitute margarine for butter.

substituto, -ta [subftfi'tutu, -ta] *m, f* replacement.

subterrâneo, -nea [subte'xanju, -nja] *adj* underground.

subtil [sub'til] *(pl -is* [-if]*) adj (Port)* = sutil.

subtrair [subtra'i(x)] *vt* to subtract.

suburbano, -na [subux'banu, -na] *adj* suburban.

subúrbio [su'buxbju] *m* suburb.

subversivo, -va [subvex'sivu, -va] *adj* subversive.

sucata [su'kata] *f* scrap.

sucção [suk'sãw] *f* suction.

suceder [suse'de(x)] *vi* to happen.

◻ **suceder a** *v + prep (em cargo)* to succeed; *(vir depois)* to follow.

◻ **suceder-se** *vp* to happen.

sucedido, -da [suse'ʒidu, -da] *m* occurrence ◆ *adj:* ser bem/mal ~ to be successful/unsuccessful.

sucessão [suse'sãw] *(pl -ões* [-õjf]*) f* succession.

sucessivo, -va [suse'sivu, -va] *adj* successive.

sucesso [su'sɛsu] *m* success; fazer ~ to be successful.

sucessões → sucessão.

sucinto, -ta [su'sĩtu, -ta] *adj* succinct.

suco [suku] *m (Br)* juice.

suculento, -ta [suku'lẽtu, -ta] *adj* succulent.

sucumbir [sukũm'bi(x)] *vi (desmoronar)* to crumble; *(morrer)* to die; ~ a to succumb to.

sucursal [sukux'saw] *(pl -ais* [-ajf]*) f (de banco, empresa)* branch.

sudeste [su'dɛftfi] *m* southeast; no ~ in the southeast.

súdito, -ta ['sudʒitu, -ta] *m, f (Br)* subject.

sudoeste [su'dwɛftfi] *m* southwest; no ~ in the southwest.

Suécia ['swɛsja] *f:* a ~ Sweden.

sueco, -ca ['swɛku, -ka] *adj & m* Swedish ◆ *m, f* Swede.

suéter ['swɛte(x)] *(pl -res* [-rif]*) m ou f (Br)* sweater.

suficiente [sufi'sjẽtfi] *adj* enough ◆ *m (EDUC)* pass.

sufixo [su'fiksu] *m* suffix.

suflé [su'fle] *m (Port)* = suflê.

suflê [su'fle] *m (Br)* soufflé.

sufocante [sufo'kãtfi] *adj* oppressive.

sufocar [sufo'ka(x)] *vt & vi* to suffocate.

sugar [su'ga(x)] *vt* to suck.

sugerir [suʒe'ri(x)] *vt* to suggest.

sugestão [suʒef'tãw] *(pl -ões* [-õjf]*) f* suggestion.

sugestivo, -va [suʒef'tfivu, -va] *adj* suggestive.

sugestões → sugestão.

Suíça ['swisa] *f:* a ~ Switzerland.

suíças ['swisaf] *fpl* sideboards *(Brit)*, sideburns *(Am)*.

suicidar-se [swisi'daxsi] *vp* to commit suicide.

suicídio [swi'sidʒju] *m* suicide.

suíço, -ça ['swisu, -sa] *adj & m, f* Swiss.

suíte ['switfi] *f (Br)* suite.

sujar [su'ʒa(x)] *vt* to dirty.

◻ **sujar-se** *vp* to get dirty.

sujeitar [suʒej'ta(x)] *vt:* ~ algo/ alguém a algo to subject sthg/sb to sthg.

◻ **sujeitar-se a** *vp + prep (submeter-se a)* to conform to; ela teve que ~-se a todo tipo de humilhação she was subjected to ritual humiliation.

sujeito, -ta [su'ʒejtu, -ta] *m, f (fam: homem, mulher)* guy *(f girl)* ◆ *m (GRAM)* subject ◆ *adj:* ~ a subject to.

sujo, -ja ['suʒu. -ʒa] *adj* dirty.

sul ['suw] *m* south; **ao** OU **no ~** in the south; **ao ~ de** (to the) south of.

suma ['suma] *f*: **em ~** in short.

sumário, -ria [su'marju. -rja] *adj (explicação)* brief; *(ordem, execução)* summary ◆ *m (resumo)* summary.

sumo ['sumu] *m (Port)* juice; **~ de frutas** fruit juice.

Sumol® [su'mɔw] *(pl* **-óis** [-ɔjʃ]*) f*: **~ (de laranja)** orangeade.

sundae ['sândei] *m (Br)* (ice cream) sundae.

sunga ['sũŋga] *f (Br)* swimming trunks *(pl)*.

suor ['swɔ(x)] *(pl* **-res** [-riʃ]*) m* sweat; **sentir ~es frios** to break out in a cold sweat.

superar [supe'ra(x)] *vt* to overcome.

superficial [supexfi'sjaw] *(pl* **-ais** [-ajʃ]*) adj* superficial.

superfície [supex'fisji] *f* surface; *(área)* area; **na ~** on the surface.

supérfluo, -flua [su'pexflu. -fla] *adj* superfluous.

superior [supe'rjo(x)] *(pl* **-res** [-riʃ]*) adj* higher; *(em espaço)* top; *(em valor, quantidade)* greater ◆ *m* superior; **andar ~** top floor; **mostrar-se ~** to give o.s. airs (and graces).

superioridade [superjori'dadʒi] *f* superiority.

superlativo [supexla'tʃivu] *m* superlative.

superlotado, -da [supexlo'tadu. -da] *adj* packed.

supermercado [supexmex'kadu] *m* supermarket.

superstição [supexʃtʃi'sãw] *(pl* **-ões** [-õjʃ]*) f* superstition.

supersticioso, -osa [supexʃtʃi'sjozu. -ɔza] *adj* superstitious.

superstições → superstição.

supervisão [supexvi'zãw] *f* supervision.

supervisionar [supexvizjo'na(x)] *vt* to supervise.

suplemento [suple'mêntu] *m (de jornal, revista)* (colour) supplement.

suplente [su'plêntʃi] *adj (peça)* spare; *(pessoa)* substitute ◆ *mf (ESP)* substitute.

súplica ['suplika] *f* plea.

suplicar [supli'ka(x)] *vt* to plead; **~ a alguém que faça algo** to beg sb to do sthg.

suplício [su'plisju] *m* torture.

supor [su'po(x)] *vt* to presume.

❏ **supor-se** *vp*: **supõe-se que ela tenha morrido** she is presumed dead.

suportar [supox'ta(x)] *vt (peso, carga)* to support; *(pessoa)* to stand; *(dor, desgosto)* to bear.

suporte [su'pɔxtʃi] *m* support.

suposição [supozi'sãw] *(pl* **-ões** [-õjʃ]*) f* supposition.

supositório [supozi'tɔrju] *m* suppository.

suposto, -osta [su'poʃtu. -ɔʃta] *adj (hipotético)* supposed; *(alegado)* alleged; *(falso)* false ◆ *m* assumption.

supremo, -ma [su'premu. -ma] *adj* supreme.

❏ **Supremo** *m*: **o Supremo (Tribunal de Justiça)** the Supreme Court.

supressão [supre'sãw] *(pl* **-ões** [-õjʃ]*) f (de palavra, frase)* deletion; *(de projeto, empregos)* axing.

suprimir [supri'mi(x)] *vt (palavra, frase)* to delete; *(emprego, projeto)* to axe.

surdez [sux'deʒ] *f* deafness.

surdina [sux'dʒina] *f*: **em ~** in a whisper.

surdo, -da [suxdu. -da] *adj* deaf ◆ *m, f* deaf person; **fazer-se ~** to turn a deaf ear.

surf ['saxfe] *m (Port)* = **surfe**.

surfe ['suxfi] *m (Br)* surfing; **fazer ~** to go surfing.

surfista [sux'fiʃta] *mf* surfer.

surgir [sux'ʒi(x)] *vi (aparecer)* to appear; *(problema, complicação)* to arise

surpreendente [surpriên'dêntʃi] *adj* surprising.

surpreender [surpriên'de(x)] *vt* to surprise.

❏ **surpreender-se** *vp* to be surprised.

surpresa [sur'preza] *f* surprise; **fazer uma ~ a alguém** to give sb a surprise; **de ~** by surprise.

surpreso, -sa [sur'prezu. -za] *adj* surprised.

surto ['suxtu] *m (de doença)* outbreak.

susceptível [suʃse'tivel] *(pl* **-eis** [-ejʃ]*) adj (Port)* = **suscetível**.

suscetível [suʃse'tʃivew] *(pl* **-eis** [-ejʃ]*) adj (Br)* sensitive; **~ a** liable to.

suscitar [suʃsi'ta(x)] *vt* to provoke; *(interesse)* to arouse; *(dificuldades,* *problemas)* to cause.

suspeita [suʃˈpejta] *f* suspicion; **lançar ~s sobre alguém** to cast aspersions on sb, → **suspeito**.

suspeito, -ta [suʃˈpejtu, -ta] *adj* suspicious ◆ *m, f* suspect.

suspender [suʃpẽnˈde(x)] *vt* to suspend.

suspensão [suʃpẽˈsãw] *(pl* **-ões** [-õjʃ]) *f* suspension.

suspense [suʃˈpẽsi] *m* suspense.

suspensões → **suspensão**.

suspensórios [suʃpẽˈsɔrjuʃ] *mpl* braces *(Brit)*, suspenders *(Am)*.

suspirar [suʃpiˈra(x)] *vi* to sigh; **~ por** to long for.

suspiro [suʃˈpiru] *m* sigh; *(doce)* egg whites beaten with sugar used as a pie topping.

sussurrar [susuˈxa(x)] *vi & vt* to whisper.

sussurro [suˈsuxu] *m* whisper.

sustentar [suʃtẽnˈta(x)] *vt* to support; *(afirmar)* to maintain.

suster [suʃˈte(x)] *vt (segurar)* to sustain; *(respiração)* to hold.

susto [suʃtu] *m* fright, shock; **tomar um ~** to get a fright; **pregar** OU **dar um ~ em alguém** to give sb a fright.

sutiã [suˈtʃjã] *m (Br)* bra, brassiere *(Am)*.

sutil [suˈtʃiw] *(pl* **-is** [-iʃ]) *adj (Br)* subtle.

SW *(abrev de Sudoeste)* SW.

T

ta [ta] = te + a, → te.

tabacaria [tabaka'ria] f tobacconist's (shop).

tabaco [ta'baku] m (cigarros) cigarettes (pl); (para cachimbo, enrolar) tobacco.

tabela [ta'bɛla] f (de horários) timetable; (de preços) price list.

taberna [ta'bɛxna] f cheap country-style pub.

tablete [ta'blɛtʃi] m ou f: ~ de chocolate bar of chocolate.

tabu [ta'bu] adj & m taboo.

tábua [tabwa] f board; ~ de passar a ferro (Port) ironing board; ~ de passar roupa (Br) ironing board.

tabuleiro [tabu'lejru] m (para comida) tray; (de damas, xadrez) board; (de ponte) roadway.

tabuleta [tabu'leta] f sign.

tac ['taki] m (abrev de tomografia axial computorizada) CAT scan.

taça ['tasa] f cup; (para comida, doces) bowl; (de champanhe) glass.

tacada [ta'kada] f (em golfe) stroke; (em bilhar) shot.

tacho ['taʃu] m saucepan.

taco ['taku] m (de golfe) club; (de bilhar) cue; (de chão) parquet block.

táctica ['tatika] f (Port) = tática.

táctico, -ca ['tatiku, -ka] adj (Port) = tático.

tacto ['tatu] m (Port) = tato.

tagarela [taga'rɛla] adj talkative ♦ mf chatterbox.

tainha [ta'iɲa] f mullet.

tal ['taw] (pl tais ['tajʃ]) adj such ♦ pron: o/a ~ the one; nunca ouvi falar de ~ coisa/pessoa I've never heard of such a thing/person; livros, tais como estes, são úteis books, such as these, are useful; um ~ senhor some man; na cidade ~ in such-and-such a town; que ~ um passeio? how about a walk?; que ~? how was it?; ~ e qual just like; como ~ so; para ~ for that; ~ como just as.

tala ['tala] f (MED) splint.

talão [ta'lãw] (pl -ões [-õjʃ]) m (de recibo, bilhete) stub; ~ de cheques (Br) cheque book.

talco ['tawku] m talc.

talento [ta'lẽtu] m talent.

talhar [ta'ʎa(x)] vt to cut; (madeira) to carve.

⅃ talhar-se vp (leite) to curdle.

talharim [taʎa'rĩ] m tagliatelle.

talher [ta'ʎɛ(x)] (pl -res [-riʃ]) m (set of) cutlery.

talho ['taʎu] m (Port: açougue) butcher's (shop).

talo ['talu] m (de flor, legume) stem.

talões → talão.

talvez [taw'veʒ] adv perhaps, maybe; ~ sim, ~ não maybe, maybe not.

tamancos [ta'mãŋkuʃ] mpl clogs.

tamanho, -nha [ta'maɲu, -ɲa] m (grandeza) size ♦ adj (tão grande): fiz ~ esforço I made such an effort; qual é o ~ do quarto? how big is the room?

tamanho-família [ta,maɲufa'milja] adj inv (Br: embalagem) family (antes de s).

tâmara ['tamara] f date.

tamarindo [tama'rĩndu] m tamarind.

também [tãm'bẽ] adv also; eu ~ me too; ele ~ não fez nada he didn't do anything either; ~ quero ir I want to go too; ela ~ vem she's coming as well; ele ~ se chama Luís he's also called Luís.

tambor [tãm'bo(x)] (pl -res [-riʃ]) m drum.

tamboril [tãmbo'riw] (pl -is [-iʃ]) m (peixe) monkfish; (MÚS) small drum.

tamborim [tãmbo'rĩ] (pl -ns [-ʃ])

m tambourine.

tamboris → **tamboril**.

Tâmisa ['tamiza] *m*: **o ~** the Thames.

tampa ['tãmpa] *f* lid.

tampão [tãm'pãw] (*pl* **-ões** [-õjʃ]) *m* tampon.

tampo ['tãmpu] *m* (*de mesa*) top; (*de privada*) lid.

tampões → **tampão**.

tampouco ['tãmpoku] *adv* neither.

tanga ['tãga] *f* tanga.

tangerina [tãʒe'rina] *f* tangerine.

tanque ['tãki] *m* tank.

tanto, -ta ['tãntu, -ta] *adj*
1. (*exprime grande quantidade*) so much, so many (*pl*); **~ dinheiro** so much money; **tanta gente** so many people; **tantas flores** so many flowers; **esperei ~ tempo** I waited for so long; **~ ... que** so much ...that.
2. (*indica quantidade indeterminada*) so much, so many (*pl*); **de ~s em ~s dias** every so many days; **são mil e ~s reais** one thousand and something reals.
3. (*em comparações*): **~ ... como** as much ... as, as many ... as (*pl*); **bebi ~ vinho quanto você** I drank as much wine as you; **têm tanta sorte quanto você** they're as lucky as you.
♦ *adv* 1. (*exprime grande quantidade*) so much; **lhe quero ~** I love you so much; **não quero ~ assim** I don't want as much as that.
2. (*em locuções*): **de ~ falar perdi a voz** I lost my voice from talking so much; **~ faz!** it doesn't matter!; **~ melhor** so much the better; **~ pior** too bad; **~ quanto** as far as; **um ~ a** little; **é um ~ caro** it's a bit expensive; **~ um como o outro** both of them; **um ~ quanto** slightly; **~ que** (*pela simples razão que*) so much so that.
♦ *pron* 1. (*indica grande quantidade*) so much, so many (*pl*); **tenho ~!** I've got so much!; **ele não comprou ~s** he didn't buy that many.
2. (*indica igual quantidade*) as much, as many (*pl*); **havia muita gente ali, aqui não era tanta** there were a lot of people over there, but not as many over here.
3. (*indica quantidade indeterminada*) so much, so many (*pl*); **lá para as tantas ele foi embora** he left quite late; **põe uns ~s aqui uns ~s ali** put some over here and some over there; **leva ~s**

quantos você quiser take as many as you want.
4. (*em comparações*): **~ quanto** as much as; **sabe ~ quanto eu do assunto** he knows as much as I do about the affair; **comi ~ quanto o Arnaldo** I ate as much as Arnaldo.
5. (*em locuções*): **às tantas** (*de repente*) all of a sudden; **às tantas da noite** late at night; **não é caso para ~** there's no need to make such a fuss.

tão [tãw] *adv* so; **~ ... como** as ... as; **~ ... que** so ... (that).

TAP ['tapi] *f* (*abrev de Transportes Aéreos Portugueses*) TAP (*Portuguese national airline*).

tapa ['tapa] *m* (*Br: bofetada*) slap.

tapar [ta'pa(x)] *vt* (*com cobertor, lençol*) to cover up; (*garrafa, frasco, panela*) to put the lid on; (*caixa*) to close; (*boca, ouvidos*) to cover; (*nariz*) to hold.

tapeçaria [tapesa'ria] *f* tapestry.

tapete [ta'petʃi] *m* (*grande*) carpet; (*médio*) rug; (*pequeno*) mat; **~ rolante** conveyor belt.

tardar [tax'da(x)] *vi* to take a long time; **ele não tardará a chegar** he won't be long; **~ a** OU **em fazer algo** to take a long time to do sthg; **o mais ~** at the latest.

tarde ['taxdʒi] *f* (*até às seis*) afternoon; (*depois das seis*) evening ♦ *adv* late; **boa ~!** good afternoon/evening!; **à ~** in the afternoon/evening; **já é ~** it's too late; **mais ~** later; **nunca é ~ demais** it's never too late.

tardio, -dia [tax'dʒiu, -'dia] *adj* late.

tarefa [ta'rɛfa] *f* task.

tarifa [ta'rifa] *f* (*preço, taxa*) charge; (*em transportes*) fare; (*lista de preços*) price list.

tartaruga [taxta'ruga] *f* (*terrestre*) turtle; (*aquática*) tortoise.

tas [taʃ] = **te** + **as**, → **te**.

tática [tatʃika] *f* (*Br*) tactic.

tático, -ca [tatʃiku, -ka] *adj* (*Br*) tactical.

tato ['tatu] *m* (*Br*) (*sentido*) touch; (*fig: cuidado, habilidade*) tact; **ter ~** (*fig*) to be tactful.

tatuagem [ta'twaʒẽ] (*pl* **-ns** [-ʃ]) *f* tattoo.

tauromaquia [tawroma'kia] *f* bullfighting.

taxa ['taʃa] *f* (*imposto*) tax; (*percentagem*) rate; **~ de câmbio/juros**

exchange/interest rate.

tax-free [taks'fri] *adj inv* tax-free.

táxi ['taksi] *m* taxi.

taxímetro [tak'simetru] *m* taximeter.

tchau ['tʃaw] *interj* bye!

te [tʃi] *pron (complemento direto)* you; *(complemento indireto)* (to) you; *(reflexo)* yourself; **magoaste-~?** *(Port)* did you hurt yourself?; **vais-~ embora?** *(Port)* are you going?.

tear ['tea(x)] *(pl -res* [-riʃ]) *m* loom; **~ manual** hand loom.

teatral [tea'traw] *(pl -ais* [-ajʃ]) *adj (do teatro)* theatre *(antes de s)*; *(pessoa, comportamento)* theatrical.

teatro ['teatru] *m* theatre; **~ de fantoches** puppet show; **~ de variedades** variety *(Brit)*, vaudeville *(Am)*.

tecelagem [tese'laʒẽ] *(pl -ns* [-ʃ]) *f (local)* textile factory; *(oficio)* weaving.

tecer [te'se(x)] *vt (tapete, tecido)* to weave; *(suj: aranha)* to spin.

tecido [te'sidu] *m (pano)* fabric, cloth; *(ANAT)* tissue.

tecla ['tekla] *f* key.

teclado [te'kladu] *m* keyboard.

técnica ['teknika] *f* technique, → **técnico**.

técnico, -ca ['tekniku, -ka] *adj* technical ◆ *m, f (pessoa)* technician.

tecnologia [teknolo'ʒia] *f* technology; **~ da informação** information technology *(sg)*.

tecnológico, -ca [teknu'lɔʒiku, -ka] *adj* technological.

tecto ['tetu] *m (Port)* = **teto**.

tédio ['tɛdʒiu] *m* boredom.

teia ['teja] *f* web.

teimar [tej'ma(x)] *vi* to insist; **~ em** to insist on.

teimosia [tejmo'zia] *f* stubbornness.

teimoso, -osa [tej'mozu, -ɔza] *adj* stubborn.

teixo ['tejʃu] *m* yew (tree).

tel. *(abrev de telefone)* tel.

tela ['tɛla] *f* canvas; *(tecido)* fabric.

telecomandado, -da [telekomãn'dadu, -da] *adj* remote-controlled ◆ *m* remote control.

teleférico [tele'feriku] *m* cable car.

telefonar [telefo'na(x)] *vi* to (tele)phone; **~ para alguém** to (tele)phone sb.

telefone [tele'fɔni] *m* (tele)phone; **~ público** public payphone.

telefonema [telefo'nema] *m* (tele)phone call; **dar um ~** to make a (tele)phone call.

telefónico, -ca [tele'fɔniku, -ka] *adj (Port)* = **telefônico**.

telefônico, -ca [tele'foniku, -ka] *adj (Br)* (tele)phone *(antes de s)*.

telefonista [telefo'niʃta] *mf* switchboard operator.

telegrafar [telegra'fa(x)] *vt* to cable.

telegrama [tele'grama] *m* telegram; **~ fonado** *(Br)* Telemessage®.

telejornal [teleʒox'naw] *(pl -ais* [-ajʃ]) *m* news *(on TV)* *(sg)* .

telemóvel [tele'mɔvew] *(pl -eis* [-ejʃ]) *m (Port: telefone)* mobile phone.

telenovela [teleno'vela] *f* soap opera.

teleobjectiva [teleobʒe'tiva] *f (Port)* = **teleobjetiva**.

teleobjetiva [teleobʒe'tʃiva] *f (Br)* telephoto lens.

telepatia [telepa'tʃia] *f* telepathy.

telescópio [teleʃ'kɔpju] *m* telescope.

telesqui [teleʃ'ki] *m* ski lift.

televisão [televi'zãw] *(pl -ões* [-õjʃ]) *f* television, TV; **~ a cores** colour television; **~ preto e branco** black-and-white television; **~ por cabo/satélite** cable/satellite television.

televisor [televi'zo(x)] *(pl -res* [-riʃ]) *m* television (set).

telex [te'lɛks] *(pl -es* [-iʃ]) *m* telex.

telha ['teʎa] *f (roof)* tile.

telhado [te'ʎadu] *m* roof.

tem [tẽ] → **ter**.

têm ['tajẽ] → **ter**.

tema ['tema] *m* subject.

temer [te'me(x)] *vt* to be afraid of, to fear; **~ que** to fear (that).

temido, -da [te'midu, -da] *adj* feared.

temível [te'mivew] *(pl -eis* [-ejʃ]) *adj* frightening.

temor [te'mo(x)] *(pl -res* [-riʃ]) *m* fear.

temperado, -da [tẽmpe'radu, -da] *adj (comida)* seasoned; *(clima)* temperate.

temperamento [tẽmpera'mẽntu] *m* temperament.

temperar [tẽmpe'ra(x)] *vt* to season.

temperatura [tẽmpera'tura] *f* temperature.

tempero [tẽm'peru] *m* seasoning.

tempestade [tẽmpeʃ'tadʒi] *f* storm; **uma ~ num copo de água** a storm in a teacup.

templo [ˈtẽmplu] *m* temple.

tempo [ˈtẽmpu] *m (horas, minutos, segundos)* time; *(meteorológico)* weather; *(GRAM)* tense; **chegar a ~ de algo** to arrive in time for sthg; **chegar a ~ de fazer algo** to arrive in time to do sthg; **ganhar ~** to save time; **não ter ~ para algo** not to have time for sthg; **não ter ~ para fazer algo** not to have time to do sthg; **passar o ~ a fazer algo** to spend one's time doing sthg; **poupar ~** to save time; **recuperar o ~ perdido** to make up for lost time; **ser ~ de** to be time to; **em ~ integral** full-time; **~ livre** free time *(sg)*; **antes do ~** prematurely; **ao mesmo ~** at the same time; **dentro de pouco ~** in a little while; **no meu ~** in my day; **naquele ~** in those days; **de ~s a ~s** from time to time; **nos últimos ~s** lately; **por algum ~** for a while; **por ~ indefinido** OU **indeterminado** indefinitely.

têmpora [ˈtẽmpora] *f* temple.

temporada [tẽmpoˈrada] *f* season; **passar uma ~ no estrangeiro/na praia** to spend some time abroad/at the beach.

temporal [tẽmpoˈraw] *(pl* **-ais** [-ajʃ]*)* *m* storm.

temporário, -ria [tẽmpuˈrarju, -rja] *adj* temporary.

tencionar [tẽsjoˈna(x)] *vt:* **~ fazer algo** to intend to do sthg.

tenda [ˈtẽda] *f (para acampar)* tent; *(em mercado)* stall; *(quitanda)* greengrocer's (shop).

tendão [tẽˈdãw] *(pl* **-ões** [-õjʃ]*)* *m* tendon.

tendência [tẽˈdẽsja] *f* tendency; **ter ~ para** to tend to.

tendões → **tendão**.

tenente [teˈnẽtʃi] *mf* lieutenant.

tenho [ˈtaɲu] → **ter**.

ténis [ˈtɛniʃ] *m inv (Port) (ESP)* tennis ◆ *mpl (Port) (sapatos)* trainers *(Brit)*, sneakers *(Am)*.

tênis [ˈteniʃ] *m inv (Br) (ESP)* tennis; *(sapatos)* trainers *(pl) (Brit)*, sneakers *(pl)(Am)*; **~ de mesa** table tennis.

tenro, -ra [ˈtẽxu, -xa] *adj* tender; **de tenra idade** young.

tensão [tẽˈsãw] *(pl* **-ões** [-õjʃ]*)* *f (nervosismo)* tension; *(elétrica)* voltage; **~ arterial alta/baixa** high/low blood pressure.

tenso, -sa [ˈtẽsu, -sa] *adj* tense.

tensões → **tensão**.

tentação [tẽtaˈsãw] *(pl* **-ões** [-õjʃ]*)* *f* temptation.

tentáculo [tẽˈtakulu] *m* tentacle.

tentador, -ra [tẽtaˈdo(x), -ra] *(mpl* **-res** [-riʃ]*, fpl* **-s** [-ʃ]*)* *adj* tempting.

tentar [tẽˈta(x)] *vt (seduzir)* to tempt ◆ *vi (experimentar)* to try; **~ fazer algo** to try to do sthg.

tentativa [tẽtaˈtiva] *f* attempt; **à primeira ~** on one's first attempt OU go; **na ~ de fazer algo** in an attempt to do sthg.

ténue [ˈtɛnwe] *adj (Port)* = **tênue**.

tênue [ˈtenwi] *adj (Br)* faint; *(sabor)* mild.

teologia [tjoloˈʒia] *f* theology.

teor [teoˈ(x)] *m* tenor; *(de álcool, gordura)* content.

teoria [teoˈria] *f* theory; **em ~** in theory.

teoricamente [ˌtjorikaˈmẽtʃi] *adv* theoretically.

tépido, -da [ˈtɛpidu, -da] *adj* tepid.

ter [te(x)] *vt* **1.** *(possuir)* to have; **a casa tem dois quartos** the house has two bedrooms; **ela tem os olhos verdes** she has green eyes; **tenho muito dinheiro** I have a lot of money; **~ saúde/juízo** to be healthy/sensible.
2. *(indica medida, idade)* to be; **a sala tem quatro metros de largura** the room is four metres wide; **que idade você tem?** how old are you?; **tenho dez anos** I'm ten (years old).
3. *(dor, doença)* to have (got); **~ febre** to have a temperature; **~ varicela/sarampo** to have chickenpox/measles; **tenho dor de dentes/cabeça** I've got toothache/a headache.
4. *(sentir)* **~ medo** to be frightened; **tenho frio/calor** I'm cold/hot; **tenho sede/fome** I'm thirsty/hungry.
5. *(exprime sentimento):* **~ amor/ódio a alguém** to love/hate sb; **~ carinho por alguém** to care about sb; **~ afeição por alguém** to be fond of sb.
6. *(conter)* to hold; **esta garrafa tem um litro** this bottle holds one litre; **esta caixa tem apenas três bolos** this box only has three cakes in it.
7. *(discussão, problema)* to have; **eles têm muitos problemas econômicos** they have a lot of money problems; **tivemos uma grande discussão** we had a big argument.

8. *(para desejar)* to have; **tenha umas boas férias!** have a good holiday!; **tenham um bom dia!** have a nice day!
9. *(ter de ir a)* to have; **não tenho aula hoje** I don't have school today; **tenho um encontro** I've got a date; **ele tinha uma reunião, mas não foi** he had a meeting, but he didn't go to it.
10. *(dar à luz)* to have; **ela teve uma menina** she had a baby girl.
♦ *v aux* **1.** *(haver)*: **eles tinham quebrado o vidro** they had broken the window; **tinha alugado a casa** she had rented the house; **tinha chovido e a estrada estava molhada** it had been raining and the road was wet.
2. *(exprime obrigação)*: **~ de fazer algo** to have to do sthg; **temos de estar lá às oito** we have to be there at eight; **tenho muito que fazer** I have a lot to do.

terapeuta [tera'pewta] *mf* therapist.
terapêutico, -ca [tera'petʃiku, -ka] *adj* therapeutic.
terapia [tera'pia] *f* therapy.
terça-feira [texsa'fejra] *(pl* **terças-feiras** [texsaʃ'fejraʃ]*)* *f* Tuesday; **Terça-feira de Carnaval** Shrove Tuesday *(Brit)*, Mardi Gras *(Am)*, → **sexta-feira**.
terceira [tex'sejra] *f (de veículo)* third (gear).
terceiro, -ra [tex'sejru, -ra] *num* third; **a terceira idade** old age, → **sexto**.
terço [texsu] *m (parte)* third; *(rosário)* rosary; **rezar o ~** to say the rosary.
terebintina [terebĩn'tʃina] *f* turpentine, turps *(sg)*.
termas [texmaʃ] *fpl* hot OU thermal baths, spa *(sg)*.
térmico, -ca [tex'miku, -ka] *adj* thermal; **garrafa térmica** Thermos® (flask).
terminal [texmi'naw] *(pl* **-ais** [-ajʃ]*)* *adj* terminal ♦ *m (INFORM)* terminal; **~ rodoviário/ferroviário** coach/rail terminus; **~ aéreo** airport terminal.
terminar [texmi'na(x)] *vt* to finish ♦ *vi* to end; **~ em algo** to end in sthg; **~ por fazer algo** to end up doing sthg.
termo [texmu] *m* term; *(limite, fim)* end, conclusion; *(Port: recipiente)* Thermos® (flask); **pôr ~ a algo** to put an end to sthg.
termómetro [ter'mɔmetru] *m (Port)*

= **termómetro**.
termômetro [ter'mometru] *m (Br)* thermometer.
termostato [texmɔʃ'tatu] *m* thermostat.
terno, -na [texnu, -na] *adj* tender.
ternura [tex'nura] *f* tenderness.
terra [texa] *f (chão)* ground; *(substância)* earth; *(terreno)* land; *(pátria)* homeland; *(solo)* soil; *(localidade)* place; **a Terra** Earth; **~ natal** homeland, country of origin; **por ~** *(viajar)* by land; **~ a ~** down-to-earth; **cair por ~** *(fig: plano, negócio)* to fall through.
terraço [te'xasu] *m* terrace.
terramoto [texa'mɔtu] *m (Port)* = **terremoto**.
terremoto [texe'mɔtu] *m (Br)* earthquake.
terreiro [te'xejru] *m* square.
terreno, -na [te'xenu, -na] *adj* earthly ♦ *m* plot (of land).
térreo, -ea [texju, -ja] *adj (andar, piso)* ground *(antes de s)*.
terrestre [te'xɛʃtri] *adj (de planeta)* terrestrial; *(da terra)* land *(antes de s)* ♦ *mf* earthling.
terrina [te'xina] *f* tureen.
território [texi'tɔrju] *m* territory.
terrível [te'xivew] *(pl* **-eis** [-ɛjʃ]*)* *adj* terrible.
terror [te'xo(x)] *(pl* **-res** [-riʃ]*)* *m* terror.
tese [tɛzi] *f* thesis.
tesoura [te'zora] *f* scissors *(pl)*; **~ de unha** nail scissors.
tesouro [te'zoru] *m* treasure.
testa [tɛʃta] *f* forehead.
testamento [teʃta'mẽntu] *m* will.
testar [teʃ'ta(x)] *vt* to test, to try out.
teste [tɛʃtʃi] *m* test; **~ de alcoolemia** *(Port)* Breathalyser® test; **~ de dosagem alcoólica** *(Br)* Breathalyser® test.
testemunha [teʃte'muɲa] *f* witness; **~ ocular** eyewitness.
testemunho [teʃte'muɲu] *m (JUR)* testimony; *(ESP)* baton *(in relay race)*.
testículos [teʃ'tʃikuluʃ] *m* testicles.
tétano [tɛtanu] *m* tetanus.
teto [tɛtu] *m (Br)* ceiling.
tétrico, -ca [tɛtriku, -ka] *adj* gloomy.
teu, tua [tew, 'tua] *adj* your ♦ *pron*: **o ~/a tua** yours; **um amigo ~** a friend of

yours; **os ~s** *(a tua família)* your family.

teve ['tevi] → **ter**.

têxtil ['tejʃtʃiw] *(pl* **-teis** [-tejʃ]) *m* textile.

texto ['tejʃtu] *m (de livro)* text; *(de peça teatral)* script.

textura [tejʃtura] *f* texture.

texugo [tɛ'ʃugu] *m* badger.

tez ['teʃ] *f* complexion.

ti ['tʃi] *pron (com preposição: complemento indireto)* you; *(com preposição: reflexo)* yourself; **compraste-o para ~ (mesmo OU próprio)?** did you buy it for yourself?

tigela [tʃi'ʒɛla] *f* bowl; **de meia ~** *(fig: de pouco valor)* second-rate.

tigre ['tʃigri] *m* tiger.

tijolo [tʃi'ʒolu] *m* brick.

til ['tiw] *m* tilde.

tília ['tʃilja] *f* lime blossom.

time ['tʃimi] *m (Br)* team.

timidez [tʃimi'deʃ] *f* shyness.

tímido, -da ['tʃimidu, -da] *adj* shy.

timoneiro [tʃimo'nejru] *m (em barco)* helmsman; *(em expedição)* guide.

Timor [tʃi'mo(x)] *s* Timor.

tímpano ['tʃĩpanu] *m (ANAT)* eardrum; *(MÚS)* kettledrum.

tina ['tʃina] *f* tub.

tingido, -da [tʃĩ'ʒidu, -da] *adj* dyed.

tingir [tʃĩ'ʒi(x)] *vt* to dye.

tinha ['tʃina] → **ter**.

tinir [tʃi'ni(x)] *vi* to ring.

tinta ['tʃĩta] *f (para escrever)* ink; *(para pintar)* paint; *(para tingir)* dye.

tinteiro [tʃĩ'tejru] *m* inkwell.

tinto ['tʃĩtu] *adj m* → **vinho**.

tintura [tʃĩ'tura] *f*: **~ de iodo** tincture of iodine.

tinturaria [tʃĩtura'ria] *f (local)* dry cleaner's (shop).

tio, tia ['tʃiu, 'tʃia] *m, f* uncle *(f* aunt).

típico, -ca ['tʃipiku, -ka] *adj (comida, bebida, costume)* traditional; **ser ~ de** to be typical of.

tipo, -pa ['tʃipu, -pa] *m* type ◆ *m, f (Port: fam: pessoa)* guy *(f* girl).

tipografia [tʃipogra'fia] *f (local)* printing works *(pl).*

tíquete-refeição [tʃi,ketʃixefei'sãw] *(pl* **tíquetes-refeição** [tʃi,ketʃiʒxefei-'sãw]) *m (Br)* luncheon voucher.

tiracolo [tʃira'kɔlu] *m*: **a ~** across the shoulder.

tiragem [tʃi'raʒẽ] *(pl* **-ns** [-ʃ]) *f (de jornal, revista)* circulation; *(livro)* print run.

tira-manchas [tʃira'mãʃaʃ] *m inv (Br)* stain remover.

tirania [tʃira'nia] *f* tyranny.

tira-nódoas [tʃira'nɔdwaʃ] *m inv (Port)* = **tira-manchas**.

tirar [tʃi'ra(x)] *vt* to take; *(remover)* to take off; **~ algo de alguém** *(roubar)* to steal sthg from sb; **~ algo à sorte** to pick sthg at random; **~ a mesa** *(Br)* to clear the table.

tirinhas [tʃi'rinaʃ] *fpl* strips; **às** OU **em ~** in strips.

tiritar [tʃiri'ta(x)] *vi* to shiver.

tiro ['tʃiru] *m* shot; **~ ao alvo** target shooting.

tiroteio [tʃiro'teju] *m (tiros)* shooting; *(troca de disparos)* shoot-out.

título ['tʃitulu] *m* title; *(documento)* bond.

tive ['tʃivi] → **ter**.

to [tu] = **te** + **o**, → **te**.

toalete [twa'letʃi] *m (Br) (banheiro)* toilet; *(roupa)* clothes *(pl)* ◆ *f*: **fazer a ~ *(Br)*** to have a wash.

toalha ['twaʎa] *f* towel; **~ de banho** bath towel; **~ de mesa** tablecloth.

tobogã [tɔbɔ'gã] *m* toboggan.

toca-discos [tɔka'dʒiskuʃ] *m inv (Br)* record player.

toca-fitas [tɔka'fitaʃ] *m inv (Br)* cassette player.

tocar [tɔ'ka(x)] *vt (instrumento)* to play ◆ *vi* to touch; *(campainha, sino, telefone)* to ring; *(MÚS)* to play; **~ em** *(em pessoa, objeto)* to touch; *(em assunto)* to touch on; **~ na campainha** to ring the bell.

❏ **tocar a** *v + prep*: **toca a ele pedir uma explicação** it's up to him to ask for an explanation; **no que me toca** as far as I'm concerned.

tocha ['tɔʃa] *f* torch.

todavia [toda'via] *adv* still ◆ *conj* but, however.

todo, -da ['todu, -da] *adj* all; **toda a gente** *(Port)* everyone, everybody; **~ o dia/mês** all day/month; **~ (o) mundo** *(Br)* everyone, everybody; **todas as coisas** everything *(sg);* **~s os dias/meses** every day/month; **~s nós** all of us; **em toda a parte** everywhere; **ao ~** altogether, in total; **de ~** completely; **no ~** all in all.

❏ **todos, -das** *pron pl (pessoas)* everyone *(sg)*, everybody *(sg)*; *(coisas)* all; **quero ~s** I want them all, I want all of them.

Todos-os-Santos [‚toduzuʃˈsãntuʃ] *s* → **dia**.

toldo [ˈtowdu] *m* awning.

tolerância [toleˈrãsja] *f* tolerance.

tolerar [toleˈra(x)] *vt* to tolerate.

tolice [toˈlisi] *f (coisa sem valor)* trifle; *(asneira)* stupid thing.

tolo, -la [ˈtolu, -la] *adj* silly.

tom [ˈtõ] *(pl* **-ns** [-ʃ]) *m* tone; *(de cor)* shade; **em ~ de graça** in jest; **ser de bom ~** to be the done thing.

tomada [toˈmada] *f (elétrica)* socket; *(de lugar, edifício)* seizure; **~ de posse** *(de governo, presidente)* investiture.

tomar [toˈma(x)] *vt* to take; *(bebida)* to have; *(lugar, edifício)* to seize; **toma!** here you are!; **vamos ~ um café!** let's go for a coffee!; **~ ar** to get some air; **~ o café da manhã** to have breakfast; **~ posse** *(de cargo político)* to take office.

tomara [toˈmara] *interj* if only!

tomate [toˈmatʃi] *m* tomato.

tombar [tõmˈba(x)] *vt* to knock over ◆ *vi* to fall.

tombo [ˈtõmbu] *m* tumble; **levar um ~** to fall over.

tomilho [toˈmiʎu] *m* thyme.

tonalidade [tonaliˈdadʒi] *f (de som)* key; *(de cor)* shade.

tonel [toˈnɛw] *(pl* **-éis** [-ɛiʃ]) *m (para vinho)* vat.

tonelada [toneˈlada] *f* tonne.

tónica [ˈtɔnika] *f (Port)* = **tônica**.

tônica [ˈtonika] *f (Br):* **pôr a ~ em** to put emphasis on .

tónico, -ca [ˈtɔniku, -ka] *adj & m (Port)*= **tônico**.

tônico, -ca [ˈtoniku, -ka] *adj (Br)* tonic; *(fortificante)* invigorating ◆ *m (Br) (medicamento)* tonic.

tons → **tom**.

tonto, -ta [ˈtõntu, -ta] *adj (com tonturas)* dizzy; *(tolo)* silly.

tontura [tõnˈtura] *f* dizziness.

topázio [toˈpazju] *m* topaz.

tópico [ˈtɔpiku] *m* topic.

topless [ˈtɔples] *adj* topless; **fazer ~** to go topless.

topo [ˈtopu] *m* top.

toque [ˈtɔki] *m (contato)* touch; *(som)* chime, chiming; *(de campainha)* ring.

toranja [toˈrãʒa] *f* grapefruit.

tórax [ˈtɔraks] *m* thorax.

torcedor, -ra [toxseˈdo(x), -ra] *(mpl* **-res** [-riʃ], *fpl* **-s** [-ʃ]) *m, f (Br: ESP)* supporter, fan.

torcer [toxˈse(x)] *vt* to twist; *(espremer)* to wring out; **~ o nariz para algo** to turn one's nose up at sthg.

⌐ **torcer por** *v + prep (apoiar)* to support.

⌐ **torcer-se** *vp (de riso, dor)* to double up.

torcicolo [toxsiˈkɔlu] *m:* **ter um ~** to have a crick in one's neck.

torcida [toxˈsida] *f (pavio)* wick; *(Br: de futebol)* supporters *(pl).*

torcido, -da [toxˈsidu, -da] *adj* twisted.

tordo [ˈtoxdu] *m* thrush.

tormenta [toxˈmẽnta] *f* storm.

tormento [toxˈmẽntu] *m* torment.

tornado [toxˈnadu] *m* tornado.

tornar [toxˈna(x)] *vt* to make; **~ algo em algo** to turn sthg into sthg.

⌐ **tornar** *a v + prep:* **~ a fazer algo** to do sthg again.

⌐ **tornar-se** *vp* to become.

torneio [toxˈneju] *m* tournament.

torneira [toxˈnejra] *f* tap, faucet *(Am).*

torno [ˈtoxnu] *m:* **em ~ de** around.

tornozelo [toxnoˈzelu] *m* ankle.

torpedo [toxˈpedu] *m* torpedo.

torrada [toˈxada] *f (a slice of)* toast.

torradeira [toxaˈdejra] *f* toaster.

torrão [toˈxãw] *(pl* **-ões** [-õiʃ]) *m (de terra)* clod; **~ de açúcar** sugar lump.

torrar [toˈxa(x)] *vt* to toast.

torre [ˈtoxi] *f (construção)* tower; *(em xadrez)* rook, castle.

torrente [toˈxẽntʃi] *f* torrent.

torresmos [toˈxeʒmuʃ] *mpl cubes of pork marinated in white wine and herbs, then fried and served with boiled potatoes.*

tórrido, -da [ˈtɔxidu, -da] *adj* torrid.

torrões → **torrão**.

torta [ˈtɔrta] *f (Port)* swiss roll.

torto, torta [ˈtoxtu, ˈtɔrta] *adj* bent; **a ~ e a direito** left, right and centre.

tortura [toxˈtura] *f* torture.

tos [tuʃ] = **te** + **os**, → **te**.

tosse [ˈtɔsi] *f* cough; **~ convulsa** whooping cough.

tossir [toˈsi(x)] *vi* to cough.

tosta [ˈtɔʃta] *f (Port)* toasted sandwich.

tostado, -da [toʃˈtadu. -da] *adj (pão)* toasted; *(frango) cooked till golden brown.*

tostão [toʃˈtāw] *(pl -ões* [-ōjʃ]) *m* = copper *(Brit),* = dime *(Am);* **não valer um ~ furado** not to be worth a penny.

total [toˈtaw] *(pl -ais* [-ajʃ]) *adj & m* total; **no ~** in all.

totalidade [tutaliˈdadʒi] *f* whole; **a ~ dos meus alunos** all (of) my students; **na ~** *(no total)* in total; *(totalmente)* completely.

totalmente [totawˈmēntʃi] *adv* totally.

touca [ˈtoka] *f* cap; **~ de banho** *(em piscina)* swimming cap; *(em duche)* shower cap.

toucador [tokaˈdo(x)] *(pl -res* [-riʃ]) *m* dressing table.

toucinho [toˈsiɲu] *m* streaky bacon; **~ defumado** smoked streaky bacon.

toucinho-do-céu [toˌsiɲuduˈsɛu] *(pl toucinhos-do-céu* [toˌsiɲuʒduˈsɛu]) *m pudding made with ground almonds, egg yolks, butter and sugar and covered in caramel.*

toupeira [toˈpejra] *f* mole.

tourada [toˈrada] *f* bullfight.

toureiro [toˈrejru] *m* bullfighter.

touro [ˈtoru] *m* bull.

⊐ **Touro** *m* Taurus.

tóxico, -ca [ˈtɔksiku. -ka] *adj* toxic, poisonous.

Tr. *abrev* = **travessa.**

trabalhador, -ra [trabaʎaˈdo(x). -ra] *(mpl -res* [-riʃ], *fpl -s* [-ʃ]) *adj* hardworking ♦ *m, f* worker.

trabalhar [trabaˈʎa(x)] *vi & vt* to work.

trabalho [traˈbaʎu] *m* work; **~ de casa** *(EDUC)* homework; **~ de parto** labour; **~s manuais** arts and crafts *(subject studied at middle school).*

traça [ˈtrasa] *f* moth.

tração [traˈsāw] *f (Br)* traction.

traçar [traˈsa(x)] *vt (linha, desenho)* to draw; *(plano)* to draw up.

tracção [traˈsāw] *f (Port)* = **tração.**

traço [ˈtrasu] *m (risco)* line; *(vestigio)* trace; *(de rosto, personalidade)* feature.

tractor [traˈtor] *(pl -es* [-eʃ]) *m (Port)* = **trator.**

tradição [tradʒiˈsāw] *(pl -ões* [-ōjʃ]) *f* tradition.

tradicional [tradʒisjoˈnaw] *(pl -ais* [-ajʃ]) *adj* traditional.

tradições → **tradição.**

tradução [traduˈsāw] *(pl -ões* [-ōjʃ]) *f* translation.

tradutor, -ra [traduˈto(x). -ra] *(mpl -res* [-riʃ], *fpl -s* [-ʃ]) *m, f* translator.

traduzir [traduˈzi(x)] *vt & vi* to translate.

tráfego [ˈtrafegu] *m* traffic.

traficante [trafiˈkāntʃi] *mf* trafficker.

traficar [trafiˈka(x)] *vt* to traffic in.

tráfico [ˈtrafiku] *m* traffic.

tragédia [traˈʒɛdʒia] *f* tragedy.

trágico, -ca [ˈtraʒiku. -ka] *adj* tragic.

trago [ˈtragu] →** **trazer.**

traição [trajˈsāw] *(pl -ões* [-ōjʃ]) *f (de amigo, companheiro)* betrayal; *(de país)* treason; **à ~** treacherously.

traidor, -ra [trajˈdo(x). -ra] *(mpl -res* [-riʃ], *fpl -s* [-ʃ]) *m, f* traitor.

traineira [trajˈnejra] *f* trawler.

traje [ˈtraʒi] *m* clothes *(pl);* **~ de noite** evening gown; **~ típico** traditional costume OU dress; **~s menores** underwear *(sg).*

trajecto [traˈʒɛtu] *m (Port)* = **trajeto.**

trajectória [traʒeˈtɔrja] *f (Port)* = **trajetória.**

trajeto [traˈʒɛtu] *m (Br) (caminho)* route; *(viagem)* journey, trip.

trajetória [traʒeˈtɔrja] *f (Br)* trajectory.

tralha [ˈtraʎa] *f (fam)* junk, stuff.

trama [ˈtrama] *f (de fios)* weft; *(de livro, filme)* plot.

tramar [traˈma(x)] *vt:* **~ algo** *(fam: conspirar)* to plot sthg.

trâmite [ˈtramitʃi] *m* procedure; **os ~s legais** legal procedures.

trampolim [trāmpoˈli] *(pl -ns* [-ʃ]) *m* springboard.

tranca [ˈtrāka] *f* bar.

trança [ˈtrāsa] *f* plait *(Brit),* braid *(Am).*

trancar [trāˈka(x)] *vt* to bar.

tranquilidade [trākwiliˈdade] *f (Port)* = **tranqüilidade.**

tranqüilidade [trākwiliˈdadʒi] *f (Br)* peace, tranquillity.

tranqüilizante [trākwiliˈzāntʃi] *adj* reassuring ♦ *m* tranquillizer.

tranqüilo, -la [trāˈkwilu. -la] *adj* calm; *(local)* peaceful.

transação [trāzaˈsāw] *(pl -ões* [-ōjʃ]) *f (Br)* transaction.

transacção [trāzaˈsāw] *(pl -ões* [-ōjʃ])

f (Port) = transação.
transações → transação.
transar [trãˈza(x)] *vt (Br: fam: combinar)* to arrange ♦ *vi:* ~ **com alguém** *(Br: fam)* to have it off with sb.
transatlântico, -ca [trãzatˈlãntʃiku, -ka] *adj* transatlantic ♦ *m* (ocean) liner.
transbordar [trãʒboxˈda(x)] *vi* to overflow; **a** ~ overflowing.
transbordo [trãʒˈboxdu] *m* transfer; **fazer** ~ to transfer.
transe [ˈtrãzi] *m* trance.
transeunte [trãˈzeũntʃi] *mf* passerby.
transferência [trãʃfeˈrẽsja] *f* transfer.
transferir [trãʃfeˈri(x)] *vt* to transfer.
transformador [trãʃfoxmaˈdo(x)] *(pl* -res [-riʃ]) *m* transformer.
transformar [trãʃfoxˈma(x)] *vt* to transform.
transfusão [trãʃfuˈzãw] *(pl* -ões [-õjʃ]) *f:* ~ **de sangue** blood transfusion.
transgredir [trãʒgreˈdi(x)] *vt (lei)* to break, to violate; *(direito)* to infringe.
transgressão [trãʒgreˈsãw] *(pl* -ões [-õjʃ]) *f (de lei)* violation; *(de direito)* infringement.
transição [trãziˈsãw] *(pl* -ões [-õjʃ]) *f* transition.
transístor [trãˈziʃtɔ(x)] *(pl* -res [-iʃ]) *m* transistor.
transitar [trãziˈta(x)] *vi* to circulate; ~ **para** to move on to; ~ **(de ano)** to go up a year.
transitivo, -va [trãziˈtʃivu, -va] *adj (GRAM)* transitive.
trânsito [ˈtrãzitu] *m* traffic; "~ **congestionado"** "heavy traffic ahead"; "~ **proibido"** "no entry" *(for vehicular traffic)*; "~ **nos dois sentidos"** "two-way traffic".
transmissão [trãʒmiˈsãw] *(pl* -ões [-õjʃ]) *f (de rádio, televisão)* broadcast, transmission; *(de mensagem)* passing on; *(de doença, genes)* transmission.
transmitir [trãʒmiˈtʃi(x)] *vt (suj: rádio, televisão)* to broadcast, *(mensagem)* to pass on; *(doença, genes)* to transmit ♦ *vi (rádio, televisão)* to broadcast, to transmit.
transparência [trãʃpaˈrẽsja] *f* transparency.
transparente [trãʃpaˈrẽntʃi] *adj* transparent; *(água)* clear; *(roupa, tecido)* see-through.

transpiração [trãʃpiraˈsãw] *f* perspiration.
transpirar [trãʃpiˈra(x)] *vi* to perspire.
transplantar [trãʃplãnˈta(x)] *vt* to transplant.
transplante [trãʃˈplãntʃi] *m (de planta, árvore)* transplanting; *(de órgão)* transplant.
transportar [trãʃpoxˈta(x)] *vt* to carry; *(suj: veículo)* to transport.
transporte [trãʃˈpɔxtʃi] *m* transport; ~ **coletivo** public transport; ~**s públicos** public transport *(sg)*.
transtornar [trãʃtoxˈna(x)] *vt (pessoa)* to upset; *(reunião, rotina)* to disrupt.
transtorno [trãʃˈtoxnu] *m* disruption; **causar** ~ to cause disruption.
trapalhão, -lhona [trapaˈʎãw, -ʎona] *(mpl* -ões [-õjʃ], *fpl* -s [-ʃ]) *m, f* bungler.
trapézio [traˈpɛzju] *m* trapeze.
trapezista [trapeˈziʃta] *mf* trapeze artist.
trapo [ˈtrapu] *m* rag.
trarei [traˈrej] → trazer.
trás [ˈtrajʃ] *interj* bang! ♦ *prep & adv:* **deixar para** ~ to leave behind; **por** ~ **de** behind; **de** ~ from behind; **para** ~ back(wards).
traseira [traˈzejra] *f (de carro)* rear *(sg)*.
traseiro, -ra [traˈzejru, -ra] *adj (parte, assento)* back *(antes de s)* ♦ *m* backside.
tratado, -da [traˈtadu, -da] *adj* treated; *(assunto)* sorted out ♦ *m (acordo)* treaty; *(ensaio)* treatise.
tratamento [trataˈmẽntu] *m* treatment; *(INFORM)* processing.
tratar [traˈta(x)] *vt* to treat; ~ **alguém bem/mal** to treat sb well/badly.
⊐ **tratar de** *v + prep* to deal with.
⊐ **tratar-se de** *vp + prep:* **trata-se de um erro** it's a mistake; **de quem se trata?** who is it?
trator [traˈto(x)] *(pl* -res [-riʃ]) *m (Br)* tractor.
trauma [ˈtrawma] *m* trauma.
Trav. *(abrev)* = **travessa**.
travão [traˈvãw] *(pl* -ões [-õjʃ]) *m (Port)* brake; ~ **de mão** handbrake.
travar [traˈva(x)] *vt (combate, luta)* to wage ♦ *vi (Port)* to brake; ~ **conhecimento com alguém** to meet sb.
trave [ˈtravi] *f* beam; *(em futebol)* crossbar.

travessa [tra'vesa] f (rua) lane; (peça de louça) platter; (para cabelo) (decorative) comb.

travessão [trave'sãw] (pl -ões [-õjʃ]) m (para cabelo) (decorative) comb; (sinal gráfico) dash.

travesseiro [trave'sejru] m pillow.

travessia [trave'sia] f crossing.

travesso, -a [tra'vesu, -a] adj naughty.

travessões → travessão.

travões → travão.

traz ['trajʃ] → trazer.

trazer [tra'ze(x)] vt to bring; (vestir) to wear; (problemas) to cause; (consequências) to have.

trégua ['trɛgwa] f (descanso) break; (em conflito) truce.

treinador, -ra [trejna'do(x), -ra] (mpl -res [-riʃ], fpl -s [-ʃ]) m, f trainer.

treinar [trej'na(x)] vt to train.
⏷ **treinar-se** vp to train.

treino ['trejnu] m training.

trela ['trɛla] f (para cão) lead.

trem [trẽ] (pl -ns [-ʃ]) m (Br) train; ~ de aterrissagem (de avião) landing gear; ~ de prata luxury train which runs between Rio de Janeiro and São Paulo; de ~ by train; pegar o ~ to catch the train.

tremendo, -da [tre'mẽndu, -da] adj tremendous; (horrível) terrible.

tremer [tre'me(x)] vi to tremble; ~ de frio to shiver with cold.

tremor [tre'mo(x)] (pl -res [-riʃ]) m (de frio) shivering; (de medo) trembling; ~ de terra earthquake.

trémulo, -la ['tremulu, -la] adj (Port) = trêmulo.

trêmulo, -la ['tremulu, -la] adj (Br) (mãos, pernas) trembling; (luz) flickering; (voz) quivering.

trenó [tre'nɔ] m sledge.

trens → trem.

trepadeira [trepa'dejra] f (planta) climber; (roseira) rambler.

trepar [tre'pa(x)] vt & vi to climb; ~ em to climb up.

três [trejʃ] num three, → seis.

trespassar [trespa'sa(x)] vt (loja, estabelecimento) to transfer; (transgredir) to violate.

trevas ['trevaʃ] fpl darkness (sg).

trevo ['trevu] m (planta) clover; (símbolo da Irlanda) shamrock.

treze ['trezi] num thirteen, → seis.

trezentos, -tas [tre'zẽntuʃ, -taʃ] num three hundred, → seis.

triângulo [tri'ãŋgulu] m triangle.

tribo ['tribu] f tribe.

tribuna [tri'buna] f (de estádio) grandstand.

tribunal [tribu'naw] (pl -ais [-ajʃ]) m court.

triciclo [tri'siklu] m tricycle.

tricô [tri'ko] m knitting.

tricotar [triko'ta(x)] vt to knit.

trigésimo, -ma [tri'ʒezimu, -ma] num thirtieth, → sexto.

trigo ['trigu] m wheat.

trilha ['triʎa] f path; ~ sonora (Br) soundtrack.

trilho ['triʎu] m (carril) rail; (caminho) path.

trimestral [trimeʃ'traw] (pl -ais [-ajʃ]) adj quarterly.

trimestre [tri'meʃtri] m quarter.

trincar [triŋ'ka(x)] vt to bite.

trincheira [trĩ'ʃejra] f (escavação) trench.

trinco [triŋku] m latch; **fechar a porta com ~** to leave the door on the latch.

trinta ['trĩnta] num thirty, → seis.

trio ['triu] m trio; ~ elétrico (Br) float on which a show is held and music played during carnival.

tripa ['tripa] f (intestino) gut.
⏷ **tripas** fpl (dobrada) tripe (sg).

tripé [tri'pɛ] m (de máquina fotográfica, telescópio) tripod; (banco) stool.

triplicar [tripli'ka(x)] vt to triple.

tripulação [tripula'sãw] (pl -ões [-õjʃ]) f crew.

tripular [tripu'la(x)] vt to man.

triste ['triʃtʃi] adj (pessoa) unhappy, sad; (local) gloomy.

tristeza [triʃ'teza] f (de pessoa) sadness; (local) gloominess; **que ~!** what a shame!

triunfar [triũ'fa(x)] vi to win.

triunfo [tri'ũfu] m triumph.

trivial [tri'vjaw] (pl -ais [-ajʃ]) adj trivial.

triz [triʃ] m (fam: momento) second; **por um ~** by the skin of one's teeth.

troca ['trɔka] f exchange, swap; **dar algo em ~ de algo** to give sthg in exchange for sthg.

troça ['trɔsa] f: **fazer ~ de** to make fun of.

trocado, -da [tro'kadu, -da] adj mixed-up.

⌐**trocados** *mpl* loose change *(sg)*.

trocar [tro'ka(x)] *vt* to change; *(idéias)* to exchange; *(confundir)* to mix up.

⌐ **trocar de** *v + prep* to change.

◻ **trocar-se** *vp* to get changed.

troco [troku] *m* change; *(fig: resposta)* retort; **dar o ~** *(responder)* to reply in kind; **a ~ de** in exchange for.

troço [trosu] *m (fam) (coisa)* thing; *(tralha)* junk; **ter um ~** *(fam: passar mal)* to be taken ill.

troféu [tro'feu] *m* trophy.

tromba [trõmba] *f (de elefante)* trunk; *(de chuva)* downpour.

trombeta [trõm'beta] *f* trumpet.

trombone [trõm'bɔni] *m*: **~ (de varas)** trombone.

trompa [trõmpa] *f* horn.

trompete [trõm'petʃi] *m* trumpet.

tronco [trõŋku] *m* trunk.

trono [tronu] *m* throne.

tropa [trɔpa] *f* army.

tropeçar [trope'sa(x)] *vi* to trip; **~ em algo** to trip over sthg.

tropical [tropi'kaw] *(pl* -ais [-ajʃ]) *adj* tropical.

trópico [trɔpiku] *m* tropic.

trotar [tro'ta(x)] *vi* to trot.

trotinete [trotʃi'netʃi] *f (de criança)* scooter; *(pequeno trator)* (motorized) cultivator.

trouxa [troʃa] *f* bundle.

trouxas-de-ovos [trosaʒ'dʒiovuʃ] *fpl* dessert consisting of small bundles of *"doce de ovos"*.

trouxe [trosi] → **trazer**.

trovão [tro'vãw] *(pl* -ões [-õjʃ]) *m* clap of thunder.

trovejar [trove'ʒa(x)] *v impess* to thunder.

trovoada [tro'vwada] *f (ruído)* thunder; *(tempestade)* thunderstorm.

trovões → **trovão**.

trucidar [trusi'da(x)] *vt* to slaughter.

trufas [trufaʃ] *fpl* truffles.

trunfo [trũfu] *m* trump.

truque [truki] *m* trick.

trusses [truseʃ] *mpl (Port)* (men's) briefs.

truta [truta] *f* trout.

T-shirt [tʃi'fartʃi] *f* T-shirt.

tu [tu] *pron (Port)* you; **e ~?** what about you?; **és ~?!** is that you?!; **~ mesmo** ou **próprio** you yourself.

tua → **teu**.

tuba [tuba] *f* tuba.

tubarão [tuba'rãw] *(pl* -ões [-õjʃ]) *m* shark.

tuberculose [tubexku'lɔzi] *f* tuberculosis.

tubo [tubu] *m* tube; **~ de ensaio** test tube; **~ de escape** *(Port)* exhaust (pipe) *(Brit)*, tail pipe *(Am)*.

tudo [tudu] *pron inv* everything; **por ~ e por nada** over the slightest thing; **dar ~ por ~** to give one's all.

tulipa [tu'lipa] *f (Br) (planta)* tulip; *(copo)* tall beer glass.

túlipa [tulipa] *f (Port) (planta)* tulip; *(quebra-luz)* (tulip-shaped) lampshade.

tumba [tũmba] *f* tomb.

tumor [tu'mo(x)] *(pl* -res [-riʃ]) *m* tumour; **~ maligno/benigno** malignant/benign tumour.

túmulo [tumulu] *m* tomb.

tumulto [tu'muwtu] *m (alvoroço)* commotion, ruckus; *(revolta)* uproar.

tuna [tuna] *f*: **~ (académica)** group of student minstrels.

túnel [tunɛw] *(pl* -eis [-ejʃ]) *m* tunnel.

túnica [tunika] *f* tunic.

turbina [tux'bina] *f* turbine.

turbulência [turbu'lẽsia] *f* turbulence.

turco, -ca [turku, -ka] *adj* Turkish ◆ *m, f (pessoa)* Turk ◆ *m (língua)* Turkish; *(tecido)* towelling.

turfe [tuxfi] *m (Br) (hipódromo)* racecourse; *(hipismo)* horse racing.

turismo [tu'riʒmu] *m* tourism.

turista [tu'rifta] *mf* tourist.

turístico, -ca [tu'riftfiku, -ka] *adj* tourist *(antes de s)*.

turma [tuxma] *f (em escola)* class; *(Br: fam: amigos)* gang.

turné [turnɛ] *f (Port)* = **turnê**.

turnê [tuxnɛ] *f (Br)* tour.

turno [tuxnu] *m* shift; **por seu ~** in turn; **por ~s** in shifts.

turquesa [tux'keza] *f* turquoise.

Turquia [txr'kia] *f*: **a ~** Turkey.

tutano [tu'tanu] *m* marrow.

tutela [tu'tɛla] *f* guardianship.

tutor, -ra [tu'to(x), -ra] *(mpl* -res [-riʃ], *fpl* -s [-ʃ]) *m, f* guardian.

tutu [tutu] *m*: **~ à mineira** bean stew with cassava flour, salted pork and bacon.

TV *f (abrev de televisão)* TV.

tweed [twidʒi] *m* tweed.

U

UE f (abrev de União Européia) EU.

UEM f (abrev de União Econômica e Monetária) EMU.

uísque [ˈwiski] m whisky.

uivar [uiˈva(x)] vi to howl.

úlcera [ˈuwsera] f ulcer.

ulmeiro [uwˈmejru] m elm.

ultimamente [ˌuwtʃimaˈmẽntʃi] adv lately.

ultimato [uwtʃiˈmatu] m ultimatum.

último, -ma [ˈuwtʃimu, -ma] adj last; (mais recente, novo) latest; (mais alto) top; (mais baixo) bottom ◆ m, f: **o ~/a última** (em ordem, fila) the last one; **a última** (novidade) the latest; **por ~** lastly.

ultraleve [ˌuwtraˈlɛvi] m microlight.

ultramar [ˌuwtraˈma(x)] m overseas.

ultramarino, -na [ˌuwtramaˈrinu, -na] adj overseas.

ultrapassado, -da [ˌuwtrapaˈsadu, -da] adj outdated.

ultrapassagem [ˌuwtrapaˈsaʒẽ] (pl **-ns** [-ʃ]) f overtaking.

ultrapassar [ˌuwtrapaˈsa(x)] vt to overtake.

ultravioleta [ˌuwtravjoˈleta] adj ultraviolet.

um, uma [ũ, ˈuma] (mpl **uns** [ũʃ], fpl **umas** [ˈumaʃ]) artigo indefinido a, an (antes de vogal ou "h" mudo); **~ homem** a man; **uma casa** a house; **uma mulher** a woman; **uma hora** an hour; **uma maçã** an apple.
◆ adj **1.** (exprime quantidade, data indefinida) one, some (pl); **comprei uns livros** I bought some books; **~ dia voltarei** I'll be back one day; **vou umas semanas de férias** I'm going on holiday for a few weeks.
2. (para indicar quantidades) one; **trinta e ~ dias** thirty-one days; **~ litro/metro/quilo** a litre/metre/kilo.

3. (aproximadamente) about, around; **esperei uns dez minutos** I waited for about ten minutes; **estavam lá umas cinquenta pessoas** there were about fifty people there.
4. (para enfatizar): **está ~ frio/calor** it's so cold/hot; **estou com uma sede** I'm so thirsty; **foi ~ daqueles dias!** it was one of those days!
◆ pron (indefinido) one, some (pl) **me dê ~** give me one; **pede mais uma** ask for another one; **só não gosto dum/duma** there's only one (of them) I don't like; **~ deles** one of them; **~ a ~, ~ por ~** one by one.
◆ num one, → seis.

umbanda [ũmˈbãnda] f Afro-Brazilian cult religion.

umbigo [ũmˈbigu] m navel.

umbral [ũmˈbraw] (pl **-ais** [-ajʃ]) m doorway.

umidade [umiˈdadʒi] f (Br) humidity.

úmido, -da [ˈumidu, -da] adj (Br) (tempo) humid; (superfície, tecido) damp.

unanimidade [unanemiˈdadʒi] f: **por ~** unanimously.

UNE f (Br: abrev de União Nacional de Estudantes) Brazilian students' union, ~ NUS (Brit).

Unesco [uˈnɛʃku] f UNESCO.

unha [ˈuɲa] f nail; **fazer as ~s** to do one's nails.

união [uˈnjãw] (pl **-ões** [-õjʃ]) f union; (entre amigos, colegas) unity; **a União Européia** the European Union.

unicamente [unikaˈmẽntʃi] adv only.

único, -ca [ˈuniku, -ka] adj (preço) fixed; (um só) only; (incomparável) unique ◆ m, f: **o ~/a única** the only one; **tamanho ~** one size.

unidade [uniˈdadʒi] f unit; (conformidade, uniformidade) unity; (união) union.

unido, -da [u'nidu, -da] *adj* united; **eles são muito ~s** they're very close.

unificar [unifi'ka(x)] *vt* to unite.

uniforme [uni'fɔxmi] *adj & m* uniform.

uniões → **união**.

unir [u'ni(x)] *vt* to join; *(pessoas, países)* to unite; *(anexar)* to attach. ❏ **unir-se** *vp* to join forces; **~-se contra** to join forces against.

unissex [uni'sɛks] *adj inv (Br)* unisex.

unissexo [uni'sɛksu] *adj inv (Port)* = **unissex**.

unitário, -ria [uni'tarju, -rja] *adj* unitarian.

universal [univex'saw] *(pl* **-ais** [-ajʃ]) *adj* universal.

universidade [univexsi'dadʒi] *f* university.

universo [uni'vɛxsu] *m* universe.

uns → **um**.

untar [ūn'ta(x)] *vt* to grease.

urânio [u'ranju] *m* uranium.

urbano, -na [ux'banu, -na] *adj* urban.

urgência [ux'ʒẽsja] *f* urgency, **com ~** urgently. ❏ **Urgências** *fpl* accident and emergency *(sg)(Brit)*, emergency room *(sg)(Am)*.

urgente [ux'ʒẽtʃi] *adj* urgent.

urgentemente [ux,ʒẽtʃi'mẽtʃi] *adv* urgently.

urina [u'rina] *f* urine.

urinol [uri'nɔw] *(pl* **-óis** [-ɔjʃ]) *m* urinal.

urna ['uxna] *f (de voto)* ballot box.

urrar [u'xa(x)] *vi* to roar.

urso ['uxsu] *m* bear; **~ pardo** grizzly (bear); **~ de pelúcia** teddy bear; **~ polar** polar bear.

urticária [uxtʃi'karja] *f* hives *(pl)*.

urtiga [ux'tʃiga] *f* (stinging) nettle.

Uruguai [uru'gwaj] *m*: **o ~** Uruguay.

urze ['uxzi] *f* heather.

usado, -da [u'zadu, -da] *adj* used; *(gasto)* worn.

usar [u'za(x)] *vt (utilizar)* to use; *(vestir, calçar)* to wear. ❏ **usar de** *v + prep* to use. ❏ **usar-se** *vp* to be used; **agora usa-se muito o marrom** brown is very popular at the moment.

usina [u'zina] *f (Br)* factory; **~ de açúcar** sugar refinery; **~ hidroelétrica** hydroelectric power station; **~ nuclear** nuclear power plant.

uso ['uzu] *m (utilização)* use; *(costume)* custom; **"para ~ externo"** "for external use only"; **fazer ~ de** to make use of; **para ~ próprio** for personal use.

usual [u'zwaw] *(pl* **-ais** [-ajʃ]) *adj* common.

usufruir [uzufru'i(x)] : **usufruir de** *v + prep (possuir)* to enjoy; *(tirar proveito de)* to make the most of.

usurpar [uzux'pa(x)] *vt* to usurp.

úteis → **útil**.

utensílio [utẽ'silju] *m* utensil.

utente [u'tẽte] *mf (Port)* user.

útero ['utɛru] *m* womb.

útil [u'tʃiw] *(pl* **úteis** [u'tɛjʃ]) *adj* useful.

utilidade [utʃili'dadʒi] *f (qualidade)* usefulness; *(proveito)* use; **isto não tem ~ nenhuma** this is useless.

utilização [utʃiliza'sãw] *(pl* **-ões** [-õjʃ]) *f* use.

utilizar [utʃili'za(x)] *vt (empregar)* to use; *(tirar proveito de)* to make use of.

utopia [uto'pia] *f* utopia.

U.V. *(abrev de ultra violeta)* UV.

uva ['uva] *f* grape.

V

V. *(abrev de vide)* v.

vá ['va] → **ir**.

vã → **vão²**.

vaca ['vaka] *f (animal)* cow; *(carne)* beef.

vacilar [vasi'la(x)] *vi (hesitar)* to waver.

vacina [va'sina] *f* vaccine.

vacinação [vasina'sãw] *f* vaccination.

vácuo ['vakwu] *m* vacuum.

vadio, -dia [va'dʒiu, -'dʒia] *adj (cão)* stray; *(pessoa)* idle.

vaga ['vaga] *f (em emprego)* vacancy; *(onda)* wave.

vagabundo, -da [vaga'būndu, -da] *m, f* tramp.

vaga-lume [ˌvaga'lumi] *(pl* **vaga-lumes** [ˌvaga'lumeʃ]) *m* glow-worm.

vagão [va'gãw] *(pl* **-ões** [-õjʃ]) *m (de mercadorias)* wagon; *(Br: de passageiros)* carriage.

vagão-cama [vagãw'kama] *(pl* **vagões-cama** [vagõjʃ'kama]) *m (Port)* = **vagão-leito**.

vagão-leito [vagãw'lejtu] *(pl* **vagões-leito** [vagõjʒ'leitu]) *m (Br)* sleeping car.

vagão-restaurante [vaˌgãwxeʃtaw'rãntʃi] *(pl* **vagões-restaurante** [vaˌgõjʃxeʃtaw'rãntʃi]) *m* buffet car.

vagar [va'ga(x)] *vi (ficar livre)* to be vacant ♦ *m:* **ter ~ (para)** to have time (for).

vagaroso, -osa [vaga'rozu, -ɔza] *adj* slow.

vagem ['vaʒẽ] *(pl* **-ns** [-ʃ]) *f* pod.

⊐ **vagens** *fpl (feijão-verde)* green beans.

vagina [va'ʒina] *f* vagina.

vago, -ga ['vagu, -ga] *adj (lugar)* free; *(casa)* empty; *(indefinido)* vague.

vagões → **vagão**.

vai ['vaj] → **ir**.

vaidade [vaj'dadʒi] *f* vanity.

vaidoso, -osa [vaj'dozu, -ɔza] *adj* vain.

vais ['vajʃ] → **ir**.

vaivém [vaj'vẽ] *(pl* **-ns** [-ʃ]) *m (movimento)* to-ing and fro-ing, comings and goings *(pl)*.

vala ['vala] *f* ditch; **~ comum** *(sepultura)* common grave.

vale¹ ['vali] → **valer**.

vale² ['vali] *m (planície)* valley; **~ postal** postal order.

valente [va'lẽntʃi] *adj (corajoso)* brave; *(forte)* strong.

valer [va'le(x)] *vt (ter o valor de)* to be worth ♦ *vi (ter validade)* to count; **vale mais ...** it's better to ...; **a ~** *(de verdade)* for real; **para ~** for real.

⊐ **valer-se de** *vp + prep* to make use of.

valeta [va'leta] *f* ditch.

valete [va'letʃi] *m* jack.

valeu [va'lew] → **valer**.

valho ['vaʎu] → **valer**.

validação [valida'sãw] *f* validation.

validade [vali'dadʒi] *f* validity.

validar [vali'da(x)] *vt* to validate.

válido, -da ['validu, -da] *adj* valid; **~ até ...** *(produto)* best before ..., use by ...; *(documento)* expiry date ....

valioso, -osa [va'ljozu, -ɔza] *adj* valuable.

valor [va'lo(x)] *(pl* **-res** [-riʃ]) *m (de objeto)* value; *(em exame, teste)* point, mark; *(de pessoa)* worth; **dar ~ a** to value.

⊐ **valores** *mpl (bens, ações, etc)* securities; *(de pessoa, sociedade)* values.

valsa ['vawsa] *f* waltz.

válvula ['vawvula] *f* valve; **~ de segurança** safety valve.

vampiro [vãm'piru] *m* vampire.

vandalismo [vãnda'liʒmu] *m* vandalism.

vândalo, -la ['vãndalu, -la] *m*, *f* vandal.

vangloriar-se [vãnglo'rjaxsi] *vp* to boast; ~ **de** to boast about.

vanguarda [vãn'gwaxda] *f* avant-garde; **esta na** ~ **de** to be in the forefront of.

vantagem [vãn'taʒẽ] (*pl* **-ns** [-ʃ]) *f* advantage; **tirar** ~ **de algo** to take advantage of sthg.

vantajoso, -osa [vãnta'ʒozu, -ɔza] *adj* advantageous.

vão¹ ['vãw] → **ir**.

vão², vã ['vãw, 'vã] *adj* useless ◆ *m*: ~ **das escadas** stairwell; ~ **da porta** doorway; **em** ~ in vain.

vapor [va'po(x)] (*pl* **-res** [-riʃ]) *m* (*de líquido*) steam; (*gás*) vapour.

vaporizador [vaporiza'do(x)] (*pl* **-res** [-riʃ]) *m* atomizer.

vara ['vara] *f* rod; ~ **de pescar** (*Br*) fishing rod.

varal [va'raw] (*pl* **-ais** [-ajʃ]) *m* (*Br: de roupa*) washing line.

varanda [va'rãnda] *f* verandah.

varejeira [vare'ʒejra] *f* bluebottle.

varejo [va'reʒu] *m* (*Br: venda*) retail.

variação [varja'sãw] (*pl* **-ões** [-õjʃ]) *f* variation.

variado, -da [va'rjadu, -da] *adj* varied.

variar [va'rja(x)] *vt* to vary ◆ *vi* to be different; **para** ~ for a change.

varicela [vari'sɛla] *f* chickenpox.

variedade [varje'dadʒi] *f* variety.

varinha [va'riɲa] *f*: ~ **de condão** magic wand; ~ **mágica** (*Port: eletrodoméstico*) hand blender.

varíola [va'rjɔla] *f* smallpox.

vários, -rias [va'rjuʃ, -rjaʃ] *adj pl* several.

variz [va'riʃ] (*pl* **-zes** [-ziʃ]) *f* varicose vein.

varredor, -ra [vaxe'do(x), -ra] (*mpl* **-res** [-riʃ], *fpl* **-s** [-ʃ]) *m*, *f* (*de rua*) road sweeper.

varrer [va'xe(x)] *vt* to sweep; ~ **algo da memória** to blank sthg out of one's mind.

vascular [vaʃku'la(x)] (*pl* **-es** [-iʃ]) *adj* vascular.

vasculhar [vaʃku'ʎa(x)] *vt* (*remexer*) to rummage through; (*investigar*) to probe into.

vaselina® [vaze'lina] *f* Vaseline®.

vasilha [va'ziʎa] *f* barrel.

vaso ['vazu] *m* (*para plantas*) vase; (*Br:* jarra) large jug; (*ANAT*) vessel; ~ **sangüíneo** blood vessel; ~ **sanitário** (*Br*) toilet bowl.

vassoura [va'sora] *f* broom.

vasto, -ta ['vaʃtu, -ta] *adj* vast.

vatapá [vata'pa] *m* Bahian dish made with fish or chicken and coconut milk, shrimps, bread, nuts and palm oil.

Vaticano [vatʃi'kanu] *m*: **o** ~ the Vatican.

vazio, -zia [va'ziu, -'zia] *adj* empty ◆ *m* void; ~ **de** devoid of.

Vd. (*abrev de vide*) V.

vê ['ve] → **ver**.

veado ['vjadu] *m* (*animal*) deer; (*carne*) venison.

vedação [veda'sãw] (*pl* **-ões** [-õjʃ]) *f* fence.

vedado, -da [ve'dadu, -da] *adj* (*edifício, local*) enclosed; (*recipiente*) sealed; (*interdito*) prohibited.

vedar [ve'da(x)] *vt* (*local, edifício*) to enclose; (*recipiente, buraco*) to seal; (*acesso, passagem*) to block.

vêem ['veẽ] → **ver**.

vegetação [veʒeta'sãw] *f* vegetation.

vegetal [veʒe'taw] (*pl* **-ais** [-ajʃ]) *m* vegetable.

vegetariano, -na [veʒeta'rjanu, -na] *adj & m*, *f* vegetarian.

veia ['veja] *f* vein.

veículo [ve'ikulu] *m* vehicle; "~ **longo**" "long vehicle".

veio ['veju] → **ver**.

vejo ['veʒu] → **ver**.

vela ['vɛla] *f* (*de barco*) sail; (*de iluminação*) candle; (*de motor*) spark plug.

veleiro [ve'lejru] *m* sailing ship, tall ship.

velejar [vele'ʒa(x)] *vi* to sail.

velhice [ve'ʎisi] *f* old age.

velho, -lha ['vɛʎu, -ʎa] *adj* old ◆ *m*, *f* old man (*f* old woman).

velocidade [velosi'dadʒi] *f* speed.

velocímetro [velo'simetru] *m* speedometer.

velocípede [velo'sipedʒi] *m*: ~ **com motor** moped.

velório [ve'lɔrju] *m* wake.

veloz [ve'lɔʃ] (*pl* **-zes** [-ziʃ]) *adj* fast.

veludo [ve'ludu] *m* velvet.

vem ['vãj] → **vir**.

vêm [vajãj] → **vir**.

vencedor, -ra [vẽse'do(x), -ra] (*mpl*

-res [-riʃ], *fpl* **-s** [-ʃ]) *m, f* winner ◆ *adj* winning.

vencer [vẽ'se(x)] *vt (adversário)* to beat; *(corrida, competição)* to win; *(fig: obstáculo, timidez, problema)* to overcome ◆ *vi (em competição)* to win; *(prazo de pagamento)* to expire; **deixar-se ~ por** *(cansaço, tristeza)* to give in to.

vencido, -da [vẽ'sidu, -da] *adj* defeated, beaten; **dar-se por ~** to accept defeat.

vencimento [vẽsi'mẽntu] *m (ordenado)* salary; *(de prazo de pagamento)* due date.

venda ['vẽnda] *f (de mercadorias)* sale; *(mercearia)* grocer's (shop); *(para olhos)* blindfold; **pôr à ~** to put on sale; **~ por atacado** wholesale; **~ pelo correio** mail order; **~ pelo telefone** telesales *(pl)*; **~ a varejo** retail.

vendaval [vẽnda'vaw] *(pl* **-ais** [-ajʃ]) *m* gale.

vendedor, -ra [vẽnde'do(x), -ra] *(mpl* **-res** [-riʃ], *fpl* **-s** [-ʃ]) *m, f* seller; **~ de jornais** *(Port)* newsvendor.

vender [vẽn'de(x)] *vt* to sell; **~ a prestações** to sell on hire purchase *(Brit)*, to sell by the installment plan *(Am)*; **~ a vista** to sell for cash.

⌐ **vender-se** *vp:* **"vende-se"** "for sale".

veneno [ve'nenu] *m* poison.

venenoso, -osa [vene'nozu, -ɔza] *adj* poisonous.

venéreo, -rea [ve'nɛrju, -rja] *adj* venereal.

venezianas [vene'zjanaʃ] *fpl* blinds.

Venezuela [vene'zwɛla] *f:* **a ~** Venezuela.

venho ['vaɲu] → **vir**.

vénia ['venja] *f (Port)* = **vênia**.

vênia ['venja] *f (Br) (permissão)* consent; *(reverência)* bow.

vens ['vãjʃ] → **vir**.

ventania [vẽnta'nia] *f* gale.

ventilação [vẽntʃila'sãw] *f* ventilation.

ventilador [vẽntʃila'do(x)] *(pl* **-res** [-riʃ]) *m* (extractor) fan.

ventilar [vẽntʃi'la(x)] *vt* to ventilate.

vento ['vẽntu] *m* wind; **está muito ~** it's very windy.

ventoinha [vẽn'twiɲa] *f* fan.

ventre ['vẽntri] *m* belly.

ventrículo [vẽn'trikulu] *m* ventricle.

ventríloquo, -qua [vẽn'triloku, -ka] *m, f* ventriloquist.

ver ['ve(x)] *vt* to see; *(televisão, filme)* to watch; *(perceber)* to notice; *(examinar)* to look at ◆ *vi* to see ◆ *m:* **a meu ~** in my opinion; **deixar alguém ~ algo** to let sb see sthg; **fazer ~ a alguém que ...** to show sb that ...; **não tenho nada a ~ com isso** it's nothing to do with me.

veracidade [verasi'dadʒi] *f* truthfulness.

veranista [vera'niʃta] *mf* (summer) holidaymaker *(Brit)*, (summer) vacationer *(Am)*.

verão [ve'rãw] *(pl* **-ões** [-õjʃ]) *m* Summer.

verba ['vexba] *f* budget.

verbal [vex'baw] *(pl* **-ais** [-ajʃ]) *adj* verbal.

verbo ['vexbu] *m* verb; **~ intransitivo/transitivo** intransitive/transitive verb.

verdade [vex'dadʒi] *f* truth; **dizer a ~** to tell the truth; **a ~ é que ...** the truth is (that) ...; **na ~** actually; **de ~** real.

verdadeiro, -ra [vexda'dejru, -ra] *adj (verídico)* true; *(genuíno)* real.

verde [vex'dʒi] *adj (de cor verde)* green; *(fruta)* unripe ◆ *m (cor)* green.

verdura [vex'dura] *f* greens *(pl)*.

vereda [ve'reda] *f* path.

veredicto [vere'dʒiktu] *m* verdict.

verga ['vexga] *f (pau fino)* stick; *(para fazer cestos)* wicker.

vergonha [vex'goɲa] *f (timidez)* bashfulness; *(desonra)* shame; **ter ~ to be** shy; **ter ~ de alguém** to be ashamed of sb; **não ter ~ na cara** to be shameless.

verificação [verifika'sãw] *(pl* **-ões** [-õjʃ]) *f* checking.

verificar [verifi'ka(x)] *vt* to check.

⌐ **verificar-se** *vp (acontecer)* to take place.

verme ['vexmi] *m* worm; *(larva)* maggot.

vermelho, -lha [vex'meʎu, -ʎa] *adj & m* red.

vermute [vex'mutʃi] *m* vermouth.

verniz [vex'niʃ] *(pl* **-zes** [-ziʃ]) *m* varnish.

verões → **verão**.

verosímil [veru'zimil] *(pl* **-meis** [-mejʃ]) *adj (Port)* = **verossímil**.

verossímil [vero'simiw] *(pl* **-meis** [-meiʃ]) *adj (Br)* probable.

verruga [ve'xuga] *f* wart; *(em pé)* verruca.

versão [vɛxˈsãw] (*pl* **-ões** [-õjʃ]) *f* version.

versátil [vɛxˈsatʃiw] (*pl* **-teis** [-tejʃ]) *adj* versatile.

verso [ˈvɛxsu] *m* (*de poema*) verse; (*de folha de papel*) other side (*of a page*).

versões → **versão**.

vértebra [ˈvɛxtebra] *f* vertebra.

vertical [vɛxtʃiˈkaw] (*pl* **-ais** [-ajʃ]) *adj* & *f* vertical; **na** ~ upright, vertically.

vértice [ˈvɛxtʃisi] *m* vertex.

vertigem [vɛxˈtʃiʒẽ] (*pl* **-ns** [-ʃ]) *f*: **estou com vertigens** I feel dizzy.

vesgo, -ga [ˈveʒgu, -ga] *adj* cross-eyed.

vesícula [veˈzikula] *f*: ~ **(biliar)** gall bladder.

vespa [ˈvɛʃpa] *f* (*inseto*) wasp; (*motociclo*) scooter.

véspera [ˈvɛʃpera] *f* day before; **na** ~ the day before; **em** ~**s de** on the eve of.

vestiário [vɛʃtʃiˈarju] *m* cloakroom.

vestibular [vɛʃtʃibuˈlax] *m* (*Br*) exam taken at the end of secondary school in Brazil.

vestíbulo [vɛʃˈtʃibulu] *m* foyer.

vestido, -da [vɛʃˈtʃidu, -da] *adj*: ~ **de** dressed in ♦ *m* dress.

vestígio [vɛʃˈtʃiʒju] *m* trace.

vestir [vɛʃˈtʃi(x)] *vt* to dress.

❏ **vestir-se** *vp* to get dressed; ~**-se de** (*disfarçar-se*) to dress up as; (*de azul, negro, etc*) to dress in, to wear.

vestuário [vɛʃtwarju] *m* clothes (*pl*).

veterano, -na [veteˈranu, -na] *m, f* veteran.

veterinário, -ria [veteriˈnarju, -rja] *m, f* vet.

véu [ˈvɛu] *m* veil.

V. Exª (*abrev de Vossa Excelência*) *very formal term of address used in correspondence.*

vexame [veˈʃami] *m* (*escândalo*) scandal; (*humilhação*) humiliation.

vez [ˈveʃ] (*pl* **-zes** [-ziʃ]) *f* time; (*turno*) turn; **alguma** ~ **hei-de conseguir** I'll do it one day; **já lá foste alguma** ~? have you ever been there?; **perder a** ~ (*em fila*) to lose one's place; **à** ~ (*individualmente*) in turn; **de uma só** ~ in one go; **de** ~ once and for all; **de** ~ **em quando** occasionally; **mais de uma** ~ more than once; **na** OU **em** ~ **de** instead of; **outra** ~ again; **uma** ~ once; **às** ~**es** sometimes; **duas** ~**es** twice; **muitas** ~**es** often; **por** ~**es** sometimes;

poucas ~**es** rarely; **era uma** ~ ... once upon a time there was ....

vi [ˈvi] → **ver**.

via [ˈvia] *f* (*estrada, caminho*) route; (*meio*) way; (*documento*) copy *of an official document*; **por** ~ **aérea** by airmail; **por** ~ **de** by means of; **por** ~ **das dúvidas** just in case; **por** ~ **nasal** nasally; **por** ~ **oral** orally; **segunda** ~ (*de documento*) replacement; ~ **pública** public thoroughfare; ~ **rápida** (*em autoestrada*) fast lane; (*estrada*) urban clearway (*Brit*), expressway (*Am*); ~ **verde** (*em portagem, ponte*) lane in which one can drive through a toll without stopping, by means of an electronic device which debits the driver's account automatically; **a Via Láctea** the Milky Way.

viaduto [viaˈdutu] *m* viaduct.

via-férrea [ˌviaˈfɛxja] (*pl* **vias-férreas** [ˌviaʃˈfɛxjaʃ]) *f* (*Port*) railway (*Brit*), railroad (*Am*).

viagem [ˈvjaʒẽ] (*pl* **-ns** [-ʃ]) *f* (*trajeto*) journey; (*excursão*) trip; (*de barco*) voyage; **ir de** ~ to go away; **boa** ~! have a good trip!; ~ **de negócios** business trip.

viajante [vjaˈʒãntʃi] *mf* traveller.

viajar [vjuˈʒa(x)] *vi* to travel; ~ **de** to travel by; ~ **por** (*por país, continente*) to travel through OU across; (*por terra, mar, ar*) to travel by.

viatura [vjaˈtura] *f* vehicle.

viável [ˈvjavɛw] (*pl* **-eis** [-ejʃ]) *adj* (*transitável*) passable; (*exequível*) feasible.

víbora [ˈvibora] *f* viper.

vibração [vibraˈsãw] (*pl* **-ões** [-õjʃ]) *f* vibration.

vibrar [viˈbra(x)] *vi* to vibrate; **ela vibrou de alegria** she was thrilled.

viciado, -da [viˈsjadu, -da] *adj*: **ser** ~ **em algo** to be addicted to sthg.

viciar [viˈsja(x)] *vt* (*informação*) to distort; (*documento*) to falsify; (*corromper*) to corrupt.

❏ **viciar-se** *vp*: ~**-se em** to become addicted to.

vício [ˈvisju] *m* (*de droga, bebida*) addiction; (*defeito*) vice; (*mau hábito*) bad habit.

vida [ˈvida] *f* life; **ganhar a** ~ to earn a living; **perder a** ~ to lose one's life; **tirar a** ~ **de alguém** to take sb's life.

videira [viˈdejra] *f* grapevine.

vídeo [ˈvidʒju] *m* video.

videocassete [ˌvidʒjuka'sɛtɛ] *f (Port)* videotape.

videoclipe [ˌvidʒjo'klipi] *m (pop)* (pop) video.

videoclube [ˌvidʒjo'klubi] *m* video shop.

videodisco [ˌvidʒjo'diʃku] *m* video-disc.

videogame [ˌvidʒjo'gejmi] *m* video-game.

videogravador [ˌvidʒjograva'do(x)] *(pl* **-res** [-riʃ]) *m* videorecorder *(Brit)*, VCR *(Am)*.

vidraça [vi'drasa] *f* windowpane.

vidrão [vi'drãw] *(pl* **-ões** [-õjʃ]) *m (Port)* bottle bank *(Brit)*.

vidro [ˈvidru] *m* glass; *(vidraça)* pane (of glass); *(de carro)* window.

vidrões → **vidrão**.

viela [ˈvjɛla] *f* alley.

vieste [vi'ɛʃtʃi] → **vir**.

viga [ˈviga] *f* beam.

vigário [vi'garju] *m* vicar.

vigésimo, -ma [vi'ʒɛzimu, -ma] *num* twentieth, → **sexto**.

vigia [vi'ʒia] *f (vigilância)* watch; *(janela)* porthole ♦ *mf (guarda)* guard.

vigilância [viʒi'lãsja] *f* vigilance.

vigor [vi'go(x)] *m* vigour; **em ~** *(lei, norma)* in force.

vil [ˈviw] *(pl* **vis** [ˈviʃ]) *adj* despicable.

vila [ˈvila] *f (povoação)* village; *(habitação)* villa.

vilarejo [vila'reʒu] *m* small village.

vim [ˈvĩ] → **vir**.

vime [ˈvimi] *m* wicker.

vinagre [vi'nagri] *m* vinegar.

vinagreta [vina'greta] *f* vinaigrette.

vinco [ˈvĩŋku] *m* crease.

vinda [ˈvĩnda] *f* return.

vindima [vĩn'dʒima] *f* grape harvest.

vindo, -da [ˈvĩndu, -da] *pp* → **vir**.

vingança [vĩŋ'gãsa] *f* revenge.

vingar [vĩŋ'ga(x)] *vt (desforrar-se de)* to avenge ♦ *vi (planta)* to take.

◻ **vingar-se** *vp (desforrar-se)* to take revenge; **~-se de alguém** to take revenge on sb.

vingativo, -va [vĩŋga'tʃivu, -va] *adj* vengeful.

vinha¹ [ˈvĩɲa] → **vir**.

vinha² [ˈvĩɲa] *f* vineyard.

vinha-d'alhos [ˌvĩɲa'daʎuʃ] *f* meat marinade made of garlic, wine or vinegar and bayleaves.

vinheta [vi'ɲɛta] *f (selo)* charity sticker.

vinho [ˈvĩɲu] *m* wine; **~ branco/tinto** white/red wine; **~ da casa** house wine; **~ espumante** OU **espumoso** sparkling wine; **~ de mesa** table wine; **~ moscatel** Muscatel; **~ do Porto** port; **~ rosé** rosé wine; **~ verde** *light, slightly sparkling, young wine.*

vinicultor, -ra [ˌvinikuw'to(x), -ra] *(mpl* **-res** [-riʃ], *fpl* **-s** [-ʃ]) *m, f* wine producer.

vinil [vi'niw] *m* vinyl.

vintage [vĩn'tage] *m* vintage wine.

vinte [ˈvĩntʃi] *num* twenty, → **seis**.

viola [ˈvjɔla] *f* guitar.

violação [vjola'sãw] *(pl* **-ões** [-õjʃ]) *f (de direito, norma)* violation; *(estupro)* rape; *(de segredo)* disclosure.

violão [vjo'lãw] *(pl* **-ões** [-õjʃ]) *m* guitar.

violar [vjo'la(x)] *vt (direito, norma)* to violate; *(pessoa)* to rape; *(segredo)* to disclose, to reveal.

violência [vjo'lẽsja] *f* violence.

violento, -ta [vjo'lẽntu, -ta] *adj* violent.

violeta [vjo'leta] *adj inv & f* violet.

violino [vjo'linu] *m* violin.

violões → **violão**.

violoncelo [vjolõ'sɛlu] *m* cello.

vir [ˈvi(x)] *vi* **1.** *(apresentar-se)* to come; **veio ver-me** he came to see me; **venho visitá-lo amanhã** I'll come and see you tomorrow.

2. *(chegar)* to arrive; **(ele) veio atrasado/adiantado** he arrived late/early; **ela veio no ônibus das onze** she came on the eleven o'clock bus.

3. *(a seguir no tempo)* to come; **a semana/o ano que vem** next week/year.

4. *(estar)* to be; **vem escrito em português** it's written in Portuguese; **vinha embalado** it came in a packet.

5. *(regressar)* to come back; **eles vêm de férias amanhã** they're coming back from holiday tomorrow; **hoje, venho mais tarde** I'll be back later today.

6. *(surgir)* to come; **o carro veio não sei de onde** the car came out of nowhere; **veio-me uma idéia** I've got an idea.

7. *(provir):* **~ de** to come from; **venho agora mesmo de lá** I've just come from there; **~ de fazer algo** to have just been doing sthg.

8. *(em locuções):* **~ a ser** to become;

235

que vem a ser isto? what's the meaning of this?; **~ abaixo** *(edifício, construção)* to collapse; **~ ao mundo** *(nascer)* to come into the world, to be born; **~ a saber (de algo)** to find out (about sthg); **~ sobre** *(arremeter contra)* to lunge at; **~ a tempo de algo** to arrive in time for sthg; **~ a tempo de fazer algo** to arrive in time to do sthg.

virado, -da [viˈradu, -da] *adj (invertido)* upside down; *(tombado)* overturned; *(voltado)* turned up ♦ *m:* **~ à Paulista** bean stew served with smoked sausage, fried eggs and pork chops; **~ para** facing.

vira-lata [ˌviraˈlata] *(pl* **vira-latas** [ˌviraˈlataʃ]) *m (Br) (cão vadio)* stray dog; *(mistura de raças)* mongrel.

virar [viˈra(x)] *vt* to turn; *(carro, camião)* to turn around; *(entornar, derrubar)* to knock over; *(Br: transformar-se em)* to turn into ♦ *vi (mudar de direção)* to change direction; *(Br: mudar)* to change; **~ à direita/esquerda** to turn right/left.

❏ **virar-se** *vp (voltar-se)* to turn over; **~-se contra alguém** to turn against sb; **~-se para** to turn towards.

virgem [ˈvirʒẽ] *(pl* **-ns** [-ʃ]) *mf* virgin ♦ *adj* virgin; *(cassete)* blank.

❏ **Virgem** *f (signo do Zodíaco)* Virgo.

vírgula [ˈvirgula] *f* comma.

viril [viˈriw] *(pl* **-is** [-iʃ]) *adj* virile.

virilha [viˈriʎa] *f* groin.

víris → viril.

virose [viˈrɔzi] *f* viral infection.

virtual [virˈtwaw] *(pl* **-ais** [-ajʃ]) *adj* virtual.

virtude [virˈtudʒi] *f* virtue; **em ~ de** due to.

vírus [ˈviruʃ] *m inv* virus.

vis → vil.

visão [viˈzãw] *(pl* **-ões** [-õjʃ]) *f* vision; *(capacidade de ver)* sight.

visar [viˈza(x)] *vt (com arma)* to take aim at; *(documento)* to endorse; **~ fazer algo** *(ter em vista)* to aim to do sthg.

vísceras [ˈviʃseraʃ] *fpl* innards, internal organs.

viscoso, -osa [viʃˈkozu, -ɔza] *adj* viscous.

viseira [viˈzejra] *f (de boné, capacete)* peak.

visibilidade [viziblidadʒi] *f* visibility.

visita [viˈzita] *f* visit; *(de médico)* house call; **fazer uma ~ a alguém** to

pay sb a visit.

visitante [viziˈtãntʃi] *mf* visitor.

visitar [viziˈta(x)] *vt* to visit.

visível [viˈzivew] *(pl* **-eis** [-ejʃ]) *adj* visible.

vislumbrar [viʒlũmˈbra(x)] *vt* to make out.

visões → visão.

visor [viˈzo(x)] *(pl* **-res** [-riʃ]) *m (de máquina fotográfica)* viewfinder; *(de computador)* screen.

vista [ˈviʃta] *f (visão)* sight; *(olho)* eye; *(panorama)* view; **até à ~!** see you!; **dar nas ~s** to stand out; **ter algo em ~** to have sthg in view; **ter algo em ~** to have one's eye on sthg.

visto, -ta [ˈviʃtu, -ta] *pp → ver* ♦ *adj* well-known ♦ *m (em documento)* stamp; *(documento)* visa; **bem ~!** well spotted!; **nunca ~!** incredible!; **pelo ~** by the look of things; **~ que** since.

vistoso, -osa [viʃˈtozu, -ɔza] *adj* eye-catching.

visual [viˈzwaw] *(pl* **-ais** [-ajʃ]) *adj* visual.

vital [viˈtaw] *(pl* **-ais** [-ajʃ]) *adj* vital.

vitamina [vitaˈmina] *f* vitamin.

vitela [viˈtela] *f (animal)* calf; *(carne)* veal.

vítima [ˈvitʃima] *f (de acusação, ataque)* victim; *(morto em guerra, acidente)* casualty.

vitória [viˈtɔrja] *f* victory.

vitória-régia [viˌtɔrjaˈxeʒja] *(pl* **vitórias-régias** [viˌtɔrjaʒˈxeʒjaʃ]) *f* water lily.

vitral [viˈtraw] *(pl* **-ais** [-ajʃ]) *m* stained-glass window.

vitrina [viˈtrina] *f* (shop) window.

viu [ˈviu] *→ ver.*

viúvo, -va [ˈvjuvu, -va] *m, f* widower *(f* widow).

vivacidade [vivasiˈdadʒi] *f* vivacity.

viveiro [viˈvejru] *m (de plantas)* nursery; *(de trutas)* farm.

vivência [viˈvẽsja] *f (experiência de vida)* experience.

vivenda [viˈvẽda] *f* detached house.

viver [viˈve(x)] *vi (ter vida)* to be alive; *(habitar)* to live ♦ *vt (momento, situação)* to experience; **~ com alguém** to live with sb; **~ de algo** to live off sthg; **~ em** to live in.

víveres [ˈvivereʃ] *mpl* supplies.

vivo, -va [ˈvivu, -va] *adj (com vida)* alive; *(perspicaz)* sharp; *(cor, luz)* bright; *(travesso)* cheeky; **ao** ~ live.

vizinhança [vizi'nãsa] *f (vizinhos)* neighbours *(pl)*; *(arredores)* neighbourhood.

vizinho, -nha [vi'ziɲu, -ɲa] *m, f* neighbour ♦ *adj (país, região)* neighbouring; *(casa)* next; **é o meu ~ do lado** he's my next-door neighbour.

voar ['vwa(x)] *vi* to fly.

vocabulário [vokabu'larju] *m* vocabulary.

vocação [voka'sãw] *(pl* -ões [-õjʃ]) *f* vocation; **ter ~ para** to have a vocation for.

vocalista [voka'liʃta] *mf* lead singer.

você [vo'se] *pron* you; **e ~?** what about you?; **é ~?!** is that you?!; **~ mesmo** OU **próprio** you yourself.

⊐ **vocês** *pron pl* you; **~s mesmos** OU **próprios** you yourselves.

voga ['vɔga] *f:* **estar em ~** to be fashionable.

vogal [vo'gaw] *(pl* -ais [-ajʃ]) *f (letra)* vowel ♦ *mf (de junta, júri, assembléia)* member.

volante [vo'lãntʃi] *m (de veículo)* steering wheel.

volátil [vo'latʃiw] *(pl* -teis [-tejʃ]) *adj* volatile.

vôlei ['vɔlei] *m (Br)* volleyball.

voleibol [.vɔlej'bɔw] *m* = **vôlei**.

volta ['vɔwta] *f (regresso)* return; *(movimento)* turn; *(mudança)* change; *(passeio)* walk; *(em corrida)* lap; *(em competição)* round; **dá duas ~s à chave** turn the key twice; **dar uma ~** to go for a walk OU wander; **dar uma ~ de carro** to go for a drive; **dar a ~ em algo** *(tornear)* to go round sthg; **estar de ~** *(estar de regresso)* to be back; **~ e meia** *(fig)* every now and then; **em toda a ~ de** all the way round; **à ~ de** *(cerca de)* roughly, around; **por ~ de** around.

voltagem [vow'taʒẽ] *f* voltage.

voltar [vow'ta(x)] *vt* to turn over; *(cabeça, olhos, costas)* to turn; *(objeto de dentro para fora)* to turn inside out ♦ *vi (regressar)* to come back; *(ir de novo)* to go back; **~ a fazer algo** to do sthg again; **~ atrás** to go back; **~ para** to return to; **~ atrás na palavra** to go back on one's word; **~ a si** to come round.

⊐ **voltar-se** *vp (virar-se)* to turn round;

~-se para to turn towards.

volume [vo'lumi] *m* volume; *(embrulho)* parcel.

voluntário, -ria [volũn'tarju, -rja] *m, f* volunteer.

volúpia [vo'lupja] *f* voluptuousness.

vomitado [vomi'tadu] *m* vomit.

vomitar [vomi'ta(x)] *vt & vi* to vomit.

vómito ['vɔmitu] *m (Port)* = **vômito**.

vômito ['vomitu] *m (Br)* vomit; **ter ânsias de ~** to feel sick.

vontade [võn'tadʒi] *f (desejo)* wish; *(determinação)* willpower; **pôr-se à ~** to make o.s. comfortable; **ter ~ de fazer algo** to feel like doing sthg; **fazer as ~s de alguém** to pander to sb; **com ~ ou sem ela, você tem que ir** you'll have to go whether you like it or not; **contra a ~ de alguém** against sb's will; **de livre ~** of one's own free will.

voo ['vou] *m (Port)* = **vôo**.

vôo ['vou] *m (Br)* flight; **~ charter** OU **fretado** charter flight; **~ direto** direct flight; **~ doméstico** domestic flight; **~ livre** hang-gliding.

voraz [vo'raʃ] *(pl* -zes [-ziʃ]) *adj* voracious.

vos [vuʃ] *pron pl (complemento direto)* you; *(complemento indireto)* (to) you; *(fml: reflexo)* yourselves; *(fml: recíproco)* each other, one another; **ela chamou-~** *(Port)* she called you; **ele deu-~ isto** *(Port)* he gave this to you, he gave you this.

vós [vɔʃ] *pron (sujeito, complemento direto)* you; *(complemento indireto)* (to) you; **~ mesmos** OU **próprios** you yourselves.

vosso, -a ['vɔsu, -a] *adj* your ♦ *pron:* **o ~/a vossa** yours; **um amigo ~** a friend of yours; **os ~s** *(a vossa família)* your family.

votação [vota'sãw] *(pl* -ões [-õjʃ]) *f* vote.

votar [vo'ta(x)] *vi* to vote; **~ em alguém** to vote for sb.

voto ['vɔtu] *m* vote.

⊐ **votos** *mpl:* **fazer ~s que** to hope (that); **~s de felicidade** *(em carta)* best wishes.

vou [vo] → **ir**.

voz [vɔʃ] *(pl* -zes [-ziʃ]) *f* voice; **ter ~**

ativa em algo to have a say in sthg; em ~ **alta** aloud, out loud; em ~ **baixa** softly.

vulcão [vuwˈkãw] (*pl* **-ões** [-õjʃ]) *m* volcano.

vulgar [vuwˈga(x)] (*pl* **-res** [-riʃ]) *adj* common; *(grosseiro)* vulgar.

vulgaridade [vuwgariˈdadʒi] *f (banalidade)* banality; *(grosseria)* vulgarity.

vulnerável [vuwnɛˈravɛw] (*pl* **-eis** [-ɛjʃ]) *adj* vulnerable.

vulto [ˈvuwtu] *m* figure.

walkie-talkie [ˌwɔkiˈtɔki] (*pl* **walkie-talkies** [ˌwɔkiˈtɔkiʃ]) *m* walkie-talkie.
WC *m* (*abrev de water closet*) WC.
windsurf [wĩndˈsarf] *m* (*Port*) = **windsurfe**.

windsurfe [wĩndˈsuxfi] *m* (*Br*) windsurfing; **fazer ~** to go windsurfing.
windsurfista [wĩndsuxˈfiʃta] *mf* windsurfer.

xadrez [ʃaˈdreʃ] *m* (*jogo*) chess; (*fam: cadeia*) clink; **de ~** (*tecido, saia*) checked.
xale [ˈʃali] *m* shawl.
xampu [ʃãmˈpu] *m* (*Br*) shampoo.
xarope [ʃaˈɾɔpi] *m* syrup; **~ para a tosse** cough syrup OU mixture.
xenofobia [ʃenofoˈbia] *f* xenophobia.
xenófobo, -ba [ʃeˈnɔfobu, -ba] *m, f* xenophobe.
xeque-mate [ʃɛkeˈmatʃi] (*pl* **xeque-mates** [ʃɛkeˈmatʃeʃ]) *m* checkmate.
xerez [ʃeˈreʃ] *m* sherry.

xerocar [ʃeroˈkax] *vt* (*Br*) to photocopy.
xerox® [ʃerɔks] *m inv* (*Br*) (*fotocópia*) photocopy; (*máquina*) photocopier.
xícara [ˈʃikara] *f* cup.
xilofone [ʃiloˈfoni] *m* xylophone.
xilografia [ʃilograˈfia] *f* wood engraving.
xingar [ʃĩˈgax] *vt* (*Br: insultar*) to swear at.
xinxim [ʃĩˈʃĩ] (*pl* **-ns** [-ʃ]) *m chicken or meat stew with prawns, palm oil, peanuts and ground cashew nuts.*
xisto [ˈʃiʃtu] *m* shale.

Z

zagueiro [za'geiru] *m (Br: em futebol)* defence.

Zaire ['zajri] *m*: **o ~** Zaire.

zangado, -da [zãŋ'gadu, -da] *adj* angry.

zangão ['zãŋgãw] *(pl -ões [-õjʃ]) m* drone.

zangar [zãŋ'ga(x)] *vt (irritar)* to annoy. ◔ **zangar-se** *vp (brigar)* to have a row; *(irritar-se)* to get angry.

zangões → **zângão**.

zaragatoa [zaraga'toa] *f* swab.

zarpar [zax'pa(x)] *vi* to set sail.

zebra ['zebra] *f* zebra.

zelador, -ra [zela'do(x), -ra] *(pl -res [-riʃ], fpl -s [-ʃ]) m, f (Br: de edifício)* porter.

zelar [ze'la(x)] : **zelar por** *v + prep* to look after.

zelo ['zelu] *m* care.

zeloso, -osa [ze'lozu, -ɔza] *adj* careful.

zero ['zeru] *num* zero, nought; *(em futebol)* nil; *(em tênis)* love; **partir do ~** to start from scratch; **ser um ~ à esquerda** *(fam)* to be hopeless; **abaixo de ~** below zero, → **seis**.

ziguezague [zig'zagi] *m* zigzag; **andar aos ~s** to zigzag.

zinco ['zĩŋku] *m* zinc.

zíper ['zipe(x)] *(pl -res [-riʃ]) m (Br)* zip *(Brit)*, zipper *(Am)*.

Zodíaco [zo'dʒiaku] *m* zodiac.

zoeira ['z wejra] *f* buzzing.

zombar [zõm'ba(x)] *vi* to jeer; **~ de** to make fun of.

zona ['zona] *f (de país, globo)* area; *(de corpo)* part; *(MED)* shingles *(sg)*; **~ comercial** shopping area; **~ pedestre** pedestrian precinct.

zonzo, -za ['zõzu, -za] *adj* dazed.

zoo ['zu] *m (Port)* = **zôo**.

zôo ['zou] *m (Br)* zoo.

zoologia [zolo'ʒia] *f* zoology.

zoológico [zo'lɔʒiku] *adj m* → **jardim**.

zumbido [zũm'bidu] *m* buzzing.

zumbir [zũm'bi(x)] *vi* to buzz.

zunir [zu'ni(x)] *vi (vento)* to whistle; *(abelha)* to buzz.

zunzum [zũ'zũ] *(pl -ns [-ʃ]) m (fig: boato)* rumour.

zurrar [zu'xa(x)] *vi* to bray.

a [stressed eı, unstressed ə] indefinite article **1.** (referring to indefinite thing, person) um (uma); **a friend** um amigo (uma amiga); **a restaurant** um restaurante; **an apple** uma maçã; **she's a doctor** ela é médica.
2. (instead of the number one): **a hundred and twenty pounds** cento e vinte libras; **a month ago** há um mês; **a thousand** mil; **four and a half** quatro e meio.
3. (in prices, ratios): **three times a year** três vezes ao ano; **£2 a kilo** 2 libras o quilo.

AA n (Brit: abbr of Automobile Association) = TCB (Br), = ACP (Port).

aback [ə'bæk] adv: **to be taken ~** ficar surpreendido(-da).

abandon [ə'bændən] vt abandonar.

abattoir [æbətwɑːr] n matadouro m.

abbey [æbı] n abadia f.

abbreviation [ə,briːvı'eıʃn] n abreviatura f.

abdicate [æbdıkeıt] vi abdicar ♦ vt (responsibility) abdicar de.

abdomen [æbdəmən] n abdómen m.

abduct [əb'dʌkt] vt seqüestrar.

aberration [æbə'reıʃn] n aberração f.

abeyance [ə'beıəns] n (fml): **to fall into ~** (custom) cair em desuso; **to be in ~** (law) não estar em vigor.

abhor [əb'hɔːr] vt abominar.

abide [ə'baıd] vt: **I can't ~ him** não o suporto.

◻ abide by vt fus (rule, law) acatar.

ability [ə'bılətı] n (capability) capacidade f; (skill) habilidade f.

abject [æbdʒekt] adj (poverty) extremo(-ma); (person, apology) humilde.

ablaze [ə'bleız] adj (on fire) em chamas.

able [eıbl] adj competente; **to be ~ to do sthg** poder fazer algo.

abnormal [æb'nɔːml] adj anormal.

aboard [ə'bɔːd] adv a bordo ♦ prep (ship, plane) a bordo de; (train, bus) em.

abode [ə'bəʊd] n (fml) residência f.

abolish [ə'bɒlıʃ] vt abolir.

abolition [æbə'lıʃn] n abolição f.

aborigine [æbə'rıdʒənı] n aborígene mf (da Austrália).

abort [ə'bɔːt] vt (give up) cancelar.

abortion [ə'bɔːʃn] n aborto m; **to have an ~** fazer um aborto, abortar.

abortive [ə'bɔːtıv] adj fracassado(-da).

about [ə'baʊt] adv **1.** (approximately) cerca de; **~ 50** cerca de 50, **at ~ six o'clock** por volta das seis horas.
2. (referring to place) por aí; **to run ~** correr de um lado para o outro; **to walk ~** caminhar por aí.
3. (on the point of): **to be ~ to do sthg** estar prestes a fazer algo.
♦ prep **1.** (concerning) sobre, acerca de; **a book ~ Scotland** um livro sobre a Escócia **what's it ~?** é sobre o quê?; **what ~ a drink?** que tal uma bebida?
2. (referring to place) por; **there are lots of hotels ~ the town** existem muitos hotéis por toda a cidade.

above [ə'bʌv] prep (higher than) por cima de; (more than) mais de ♦ adv (higher) de cima; **children aged ten and ~** crianças com mais de dez anos; **~ all** acima de tudo; **~ average** acima da média.

abrasive [ə'breısıv] adj (product) abrasivo(-va); (person, manner) brusco(-ca).

abreast [ə'brest] *adv* lado a lado; **to keep ~ of sthg** manter-se ao corrente de algo.

abridged [ə'brɪdʒd] *adj* resumido (-da).

abroad [ə'brɔːd] *adv (be, live, work)* no estrangeiro; *(go, move)* para o estrangeiro.

abrupt [ə'brʌpt] *adj* brusco(-ca).

abscess ['æbses] *n* abcesso *m*.

abscond [əb'skɒnd] *vi* fugir.

abseil ['æbseɪl] *vi*: **to ~ down sthg** descer algo por uma corda.

absence ['æbsəns] *n* ausência *f*.

absent ['æbsənt] *adj* ausente.

absentee [,æbsən'tiː] *n* absentista *mf*.

absent-minded [-'maɪndɪd] *adj* distraído(-da).

absolute ['æbsəluːt] *adj* absoluto(-ta).

absolutely [*adv* 'æbsəluːtlɪ, *excl* ,æbsə'luːtlɪ] *adv* absolutamente ◆ *excl* sem dúvida!

absorb [əb'sɔːb] *vt* absorver.

absorbed [əb'sɔːbd] *adj*: **to be ~ in sthg** estar absorvido(-da) em algo.

absorbent [əb'sɔːbənt] *adj* absorvente.

absorption [əb'sɔːpʃn] *n* absorção *f*.

abstain [əb'steɪn] *vi*: **to ~ (from)** abster-se (de).

abstention [əb'stenʃn] *n* abstenção *f*.

abstract ['æbstrækt] *adj* abstrato(-ta) ◆ *n (summary)* resumo *m*.

absurd [əb'sɜːd] *adj* absurdo(-da).

ABTA ['æbtə] *n* associação britânica de agências de viagens.

abundant [ə'bʌndənt] *adj* abundante.

abuse [*n* ə'bjuːs, *vb* ə'bjuːz] *n (insults)* insultos *mpl*; *(wrong use, maltreatment)* abuso *m* ◆ *vt (insult)* insultar; *(use wrongly)* abusar de; *(maltreat)* maltratar.

abusive [ə'bjuːsɪv] *adj* ofensivo(-va).

abysmal [ə'bɪzml] *adj* péssimo(-ma).

AC *(abbr of alternating current)* CA.

academic [,ækə'demɪk] *adj (educational)* acadêmico(-ca) ◆ *n* professor *m* universitário (professora *f* universitária).

academy [ə'kædəmɪ] *n* academia *f*.

accelerate [ək'seləreɪt] *vi* acelerar.

acceleration [ək,selə'reɪʃn] *n* aceleração *f*.

accelerator [ək'seləreɪtəʳ] *n* acelerador *m*.

accent ['æksent] *n (way of speaking)* pronúncia *f*, sotaque *m*; *(mark in writing)* acento *m*.

accept [ək'sept] *vt* aceitar; *(blame, responsibility)* assumir.

acceptable [ək'septəbl] *adj* aceitável.

acceptance [ək'septəns] *n* aceitação *f*.

access ['ækses] *n* acesso *m*.

accessible [ək'sesəbl] *adj* acessível.

accessories [ək'sesərɪz] *npl* acessórios *mpl*.

access road *n* estrada *f* de acesso.

accident ['æksɪdənt] *n* acidente *m*; **by ~** por acaso.

accidental [,æksɪ'dentl] *adj* acidental.

accidentally [,æksɪ'dentəlɪ] *adv (unintentionally)* acidentalmente; *(by chance)* por acaso.

accident insurance *n* seguro *m* contra acidentes.

accident-prone *adj* propenso(-sa) a acidentes.

acclaim [ə'kleɪm] *n* reconhecimento *m*, aclamação *f* ◆ *vt* aplaudir, aclamar.

acclimatize [ə'klaɪmətaɪz] *vi* aclimatar-se.

accommodate [ə'kɒmədeɪt] *vt* alojar.

accommodating [ə'kɒmədeɪtɪŋ] *adj* prestativo(-va).

accommodation [ə,kɒmə'deɪʃn] *n* alojamento *m*.

accommodations [ə,kɒmə'deɪʃnz] *npl (Am)* = **accommodation**.

accompany [ə'kʌmpənɪ] *vt* acompanhar.

accomplice [ə'kʌmplɪs] *n* cúmplice *mf*.

accomplish [ə'kʌmplɪʃ] *vt* conseguir, realizar.

accomplishment [ə'kʌmplɪʃmənt] *n (achievement, finishing)* cumprimento *m*; *(feat, deed)* feito *m*.

❏ **accomplishments** *npl (skills)* aptidões *fpl*.

accord [ə'kɔːd] *n*: **of one's own ~** por iniciativa própria.

accordance [ə'kɔːdəns] *n*: **in ~ with** de acordo com, conforme.

according [ə'kɔːdɪŋ] : **according to** *prep (as stated by)* segundo; *(depending on)* conforme.

accordingly [ə'kɔːdɪŋlɪ] *adv (appropriately)* de forma adequada; *(consequently)* por conseguinte.

accordion [ə'kɔːdɪən] *n* acordeão *m*.

accost [ə'kɒst] *vt* abordar.

account [ə'kaʊnt] *n* *(at bank, shop)* conta *f*; *(report)* relato *m*; **to take into ~** levar em consideração; **on no ~** de modo algum OR nenhum; **on ~ of** devido a.

⊐ account for *vt fus (explain)* justificar; *(constitute)* representar.

accountable [ə'kaʊntəbl] *adj*: **~ for** responsável por.

accountancy [ə'kaʊntənsɪ] *n* contabilidade *f*.

accountant [ə'kaʊntənt] *n* contador *m* (-ra *f*) *(Br)*, contabilista *mf* *(Port)*.

account number *n* número *m* de conta.

accumulate [ə'kjuːmjʊleɪt] *vt* acumular.

accuracy ['ækjʊrəsɪ] *n* *(of description, report)* exatidão *f*; *(of work, figures)* precisão *f*.

accurate ['ækjʊrət] *adj* *(description, report)* exato(-ta); *(work, figures)* preciso(-sa).

accurately ['ækjʊrətlɪ] *adv* *(describe, report)* com exatidão; *(type, measure)* com precisão.

accusation [ækjuː'zeɪʃn] *n* acusação *f*.

accuse [ə'kjuːz] *vt*: **to ~ sb of sthg** acusar alguém de algo.

accused [ə'kjuːzd] *n*: **the ~** o réu (a ré).

accustomed [ə'kʌstəmd] *adj*: **to be ~ to sthg/to doing sthg** estar acostumado(-da) a algo/a fazer algo.

ace [eɪs] *n* *(card)* ás *m*.

ache [eɪk] *vi* doer ◆ *n* dor *f*; **my leg ~s** minha perna está doendo.

achieve [ə'tʃiːv] *vt* conseguir.

achievement [ə'tʃiːvmənt] *n* *(accomplishment)* feito *m*.

Achilles' tendon [ə'kɪliːz-] *n* tendão *m* de Aquiles.

acid ['æsɪd] *adj* ácido(-da) ◆ *n* ácido *m*.

acid rain *n* chuva *f* ácida.

acknowledge [ək'nɒlɪdʒ] *vt* *(accept)* reconhecer; *(letter)* acusar a recepção de.

acne ['æknɪ] *n* acne *f*.

acorn ['eɪkɔːn] *n* bolota *f*.

acoustic [ə'kuːstɪk] *adj* acústico(-ca).

acquaintance [ə'kweɪntəns] *n* *(person)* conhecido *m* (-da *f*).

acquire [ə'kwaɪə'] *vt* adquirir.

acquisitive [ə'kwɪzɪtɪv] *adj* consumidor(-ra).

acquit [ə'kwɪt] *vt*: **to ~ sb of sthg** *(JUR)* absolver alguém de algo; **to ~ o.s. well/badly** *(perform)* sair-se bem/mal.

acquittal [ə'kwɪtl] *n* *(JUR)* absolvição *f*.

acre ['eɪkə'] *n* = 4046,9 m², = meio hectare *m*.

acrid ['ækrɪd] *adj* *(taste, smell)* acre.

acrimonious [ækrɪ'məʊnjəs] *adj* *(words)* azedo(-da); *(quarrel, conflict)* acrimonioso(-osa).

acrobat ['ækrəbæt] *n* acrobata *mf*.

across [ə'krɒs] *prep* *(to other side of)* para o outro lado de; *(from one side to the other of)* de um lado para o outro de; *(on other side of)* do outro lado de ◆ *adv* *(to other side)* para o outro lado; **to walk/drive ~ sthg** atravessar algo (a pé/de carro); **it's 10 miles ~** tem 10 milhas de largura; **~ from** em frente de.

acrylic [ə'krɪlɪk] *n* fibra *f* acrílica.

act [ækt] *vi* atuar; *(in play, film)* representar ◆ *n* ato *m*; *(POL)* lei *f*; *(performance)* atuação *f*, número *m*; **to ~ as** *(serve as)* servir de; **to ~ like** portar-se como.

acting ['æktɪŋ] *adj* substituto(-ta), interino(-na) ◆ *n* *(in play, film)* desempenho *m*; **I enjoy ~** gosto de representar.

action ['ækʃn] *n* ação *f*; *(MIL)* combate *m*; **to take ~** agir; **to put sthg into ~** pôr algo em ação; **out of ~** *(machine)* avariado; *(person)* fora de ação.

action replay *n* repetição *f* (em câmara lenta) da jogada.

activate ['æktɪveɪt] *vt* ativar.

active ['æktɪv] *adj* ativo(-va).

actively ['æktɪvlɪ] *adv* *(seek, promote)* ativamente; *(encourage, discourage)* energeticamente.

activity [æk'tɪvətɪ] *n* atividade *f*.

⊐ activities *npl* *(leisure events)* atividades *fpl* *(recreativas)*.

activity holiday *n* férias organizadas para crianças incluindo, entre outras, atividades desportivas.

act of God *n* catástrofe *f* natural.

actor ['æktə'] *n* ator *m*.

actress ['æktrɪs] *n* atriz *f*.

actual ['æktʃʊəl] *adj* *(real)* verdadeiro(-ra), real; *(for emphasis)* próprio (-pria).

actually ['æktʃʊəlɪ] *adv* na verdade.

acumen [ˈækjumen] *n*: **business ~** jeito *m* para os negócios.

acupuncture [ˈækjupʌŋktʃəʳ] *n* acupuntura *f*.

acute [əˈkjuːt] *adj* agudo(-da).

ad [æd] *n* (*inf*) anúncio *m*.

AD (*abbr of Anno Domini*) d.C.

adamant [ˈædəmənt] *adj*: **to be ~** ser inflexível; **she was ~ that she wouldn't come** ela estava decidida a não vir.

Adam's apple [ˈædəmz-] *n* pomo-de-adão *m*.

adapt [əˈdæpt] *vt* adaptar ◆ *vi* adaptar-se.

adaptable [əˈdæptəbl] *adj* versátil.

adapter [əˈdæptəʳ] *n* (*for foreign plug*) adaptador *m*; (*for several plugs*) benjamin *m* (*Br*), ficha *f* tripla (*Port*).

add [æd] *vt* (*put, say in addition*) acrescentar; (*numbers, prices*) somar, adicionar.

❏ **add up** *vt sep* somar, adicionar.

❏ **add up to** *vt fus* (*total*) ser ao todo.

adder [ˈædəʳ] *n* víbora *f*.

addict [ˈædɪkt] *n* viciado *m* (-da *f*).

addicted [əˈdɪktɪd] *adj*: **to be ~ to sthg** ser viciado(-da) em algo.

addiction [əˈdɪkʃn] *n* vício *m*, dependência *f*.

addictive [əˈdɪktɪv] *adj* (*drug*) que causa dependência; (*exercise, food, TV*) que vicia.

addition [əˈdɪʃn] *n* adição *f*; **in ~** além disso; **in ~ to** além de.

additional [əˈdɪʃənl] *adj* adicional.

additive [ˈædɪtɪv] *n* aditivo *m*.

address [əˈdrɛs] *n* (*on letter*) , endereço *m*, direcção *f* (*Port*) ◆ *vt* (*speak to*) dirigir-se a; (*letter*) dirigir, endereçar.

address book *n* caderno *m* de endereços.

addressee [ˌædrɛˈsiː] *n* destinatário *m* (-ria *f*).

adenoids [ˈædɪnɔɪdz] *npl* adenóides *fpl*.

adept [əˈdept] *adj*: **to be ~** (**at sthg/at doing sthg**) ser especialista (em algo/em fazer algo).

adequate [ˈædɪkwət] *adj* (*sufficient*) suficiente; (*satisfactory*) aceitável.

adhere [ədˈhɪəʳ] *vi*: **to ~ to** (*stick to*) aderir a; (*obey*) respeitar.

adhesive [ədˈhiːsɪv] *adj* adesivo(-va) ◆ *n* cola *f*.

adhesive tape *n* fita *f* adesiva.

adjacent [əˈdʒeɪsənt] *adj* adjacente.

adjective [ˈædʒɪktɪv] *n* adjetivo *m*.

adjoining [əˈdʒɔɪnɪŋ] *adj* contíguo (-gua).

adjourn [əˈdʒɜːn] *vt* (*decision*) adiar; (*meeting*) interromper; (*session*) suspender ◆ *vi* suspender a sessão.

adjudicate [əˈdʒuːdɪkeɪt] *vt* julgar ◆ *vi* julgar, avaliar; **to ~ on sthg** emitir juízo OR sentença sobre algo.

adjust [əˈdʒʌst] *vt* ajustar ◆ *vi*: **to ~ to** adaptar-se a.

adjustable [əˈdʒʌstəbl] *adj* ajustável.

adjustment [əˈdʒʌstmənt] *n* (*to machine*) ajustamento *m*; (*settling in*) adaptação *f*.

ad lib [ˌædˈlɪb] *adj* improvisado(-da) ◆ *adv* (*freely*) livremente ◆ *n* improviso *m*.

❏ **ad-lib** *vi* improvisar.

administration [ədˌmɪnɪˈstreɪʃn] *n* administração *f*.

administrative [ədˈmɪnɪstrətɪv] *adj* administrativo(-va).

administrator [ədˈmɪnɪstreɪtəʳ] *n* administrador *m* (-ra *f*).

admirable [ˈædmərəbl] *adj* admirável.

admiral [ˈædmərəl] *n* almirante *m*.

admiration [ˌædməˈreɪʃn] *n* admiração *f*.

admire [ədˈmaɪəʳ] *vt* admirar.

admirer [ədˈmaɪərəʳ] *n* admirador *m* (-ra *f*).

admission [ədˈmɪʃn] *n* entrada *f*.

admission charge *n* entrada *f*.

admit [ədˈmɪt] *vt* admitir ◆ *vi*: **to ~ to sthg** admitir algo; **"~s one"** (*on ticket*) "válido para uma pessoa".

admittance [ədˈmɪtəns] *n* admissão *f*; **"no ~"** "entrada proibida".

admittedly [ədˈmɪtɪdlɪ] *adv* de fato.

admonish [ədˈmɒnɪʃ] *vt* repreender.

ad nauseam [ˌædˈnɔːzɪæm] *adv* até não poder mais.

ado [əˈduː] *n*: **without further** OR **more ~** sem mais cerimônias OR demora.

adolescence [ˌædəˈlesns] *n* adolescência *f*.

adolescent [ˌædəˈlesnt] *n* adolescente *mf*.

adopt [əˈdɒpt] *vt* adotar.

adopted [əˈdɒptɪd] *adj* adotivo(-va).

adoption [əˈdɒpʃn] *n* adoção *f*.

adorable [əˈdɔːrəbl] *adj* adorável.

adore [əˈdɔːʳ] *vt* adorar.

adorn [əˈdɔːn] *vt* enfeitar.

adrenalin [ə'drɛnəlin] *n* adrenalina *f*.

Adriatic [ɛıdrı'ætık] *n*: **the ~ Sea** o mar Egeu.

adrift [ə'drıft] *adj (boat)* à deriva ♦ *adv*: **to go ~** *(fig: go wrong)* dar errado.

adult [ˈædʌlt] *n* adulto *m* (**-ta** *f*) ♦ *adj (entertainment, films)* para adultos; *(animal)* adulto(-ta).

adult education *n* ensino *m* para adultos.

adultery [ə'dʌltərı] *n* adultério *m*.

advance [əd'vɑːns] *n (money)* adiantamento *m*; *(movement)* avanço *m* ♦ *adj (warning)* prévio(-via); *(payment)* adiantado(-da) ♦ *vt (lend)* adiantar; *(bring forward)* avançar ♦ *vi (move forward)* avançar; *(improve)* progredir.

advance booking *n* reserva *f* antecipada.

advanced [əd'vɑːnst] *adj (student, level)* avançado(-da).

advantage [əd'vɑːntıdʒ] *n (benefit)* vantagem *f*; **to take ~ of** *(opportunity, offer)* aproveitar; *(person)* aproveitar-se de.

advent [ˈædvənt] *n (arrival)* aparecimento *m*.

❏ **Advent** *n (RELIG)* Advento *m*.

adventure [əd'vɛntʃər] *n* aventura *f*.

adventurous [əd'vɛntʃərəs] *adj* aventureiro(-ra).

adverb [ˈædvɜːb] *n* advérbio *m*.

adverse [ˈædvɜːs] *adj* adverso(-sa).

advert [ˈædvɜːt] = **advertisement**.

advertise [ˈædvətaız] *vt (product, event)* anunciar.

advertisement [əd'vɜːtısmənt] *n* anúncio *m*.

advertising [ˈædvətaızıŋ] *n* publicidade *f*.

advice [əd'vaıs] *n* conselhos *mpl*; **a piece of ~** um conselho.

advisable [əd'vaızəbl] *adj* aconselhável.

advise [əd'vaız] *vt* aconselhar; **to ~ sb to do sthg** aconselhar alguém a fazer algo; **to ~ sb against doing sthg** desaconselhar alguém a fazer algo.

adviser [əd'vaızər] *n (Brit)* conselheiro *m* (**-ra** *f*).

advisor [əd'vaızər] *(Am)* = **adviser**.

advisory [əd'vaızərı] *adj* consultivo (-va).

advocate [*n* ˈædvəkət, *vb* ˈædvəkeıt] *n (JUR)* advogado *m* (**-da** *f*) ♦ *vt* advogar.

Aegean [iː'dʒiːən] *n*: **the ~ (Sea)** o mar Egeu.

aerial [ˈɛərıəl] *n* antena *f*.

aerobics [ɛə'rəubıks] *n* aeróbica *f*.

aerodynamic [ɛərəudaı'næmık] *adj* aerodinâmico(-ca).

aeroplane [ˈɛərəpleın] *n* avião *m*.

aerosol [ˈɛərəsɒl] *n* aerossol *m*.

aesthetic [iːs'θɛtık] *adj* estético(-ca).

affable [ˈæfəbl] *adj* afável.

affair [ə'fɛər] *n (event)* acontecimento *m*; *(love affair)* caso *m*; *(matter)* questão *f*.

affect [ə'fɛkt] *vt (influence)* afetar.

affection [ə'fɛkʃn] *n* afeto *m*.

affectionate [ə'fɛkʃnət] *adj* afetuoso(-osa).

affirm [ə'fɜːm] *vt (declare)* afirmar; *(confirm)* confirmar, ratificar.

afflict [ə'flıkt] *vt* assolar; **to be ~ed with sthg** padecer de algo.

affluence [ˈæfluəns] *n* riqueza *f*.

affluent [ˈæfluənt] *adj* rico(-ca).

afford [ə'fɔːd] *vt*: **to be able to ~ sthg** *(holiday, new coat)* poder pagar algo; **I can't ~ it** não tenho dinheiro (que chegue); **I can't ~ the time** não tenho tempo.

affordable [ə'fɔːdəbl] *adj* acessível.

affront [ə'frʌnt] *n* afronta *f*, insulto *m* ♦ *vt* insultar.

afloat [ə'fləut] *adj* a flutuando *(Br)*, a flutuar *(Port)*.

afraid [ə'freıd] *adj* assustado(-da); **to be ~ of** ter medo de; **I'm ~ so/not** receio que sim/não.

afresh [ə'frɛʃ] *adv* de novo.

Africa [ˈæfrıkə] *n* África *f*.

African [ˈæfrıkən] *adj* africano(na) ♦ *n* africano *m* (**-na** *f*).

aft [ɑːft] *adv* na popa.

after [ˈɑːftər] *prep* depois de ♦ *conj* depois de que ♦ *adv* depois, **a quarter ~ ten** *(Am)* dez e um quarto; **to be ~ sb/sthg** *(in search of)* estar atrás de alguém/algo; **~ all** afinal de contas.

❏ **afters** *npl (Brit: inf)* sobremesa *f*.

aftercare [ˈɑːftəkɛər] *n* assistência *f* médica pós-internamento.

aftereffects [ˈɑːftərıˌfɛkts] *npl* efeitos *mpl* secundários.

afterlife [ˈɑːftəlaıf] *n*: **the ~** a outra vida, a vida no outro mundo.

aftermath [ˈɑːftəmæθ] *n (consequences)* consequências *fpl*; *(time)*: **in the ~ of** no período depois de.

afternoon [ɑːftəˈnuːn] n tarde f; **good ~!** boa tarde!

afternoon tea n = lanche m.

aftershave [ˈɑːftəʃeɪv] n loção f para após a barba, after-shave m.

aftersun [ˈɑːftəsʌn] n creme m hidratante (para depois do sol).

afterthought [ˈɑːftəθɔːt] n idéia f OR reflexão f posterior.

afterwards [ˈɑːftəwədz] adv depois, a seguir.

again [əˈgen] adv outra vez; **~ and ~** várias vezes; **never ~** nunca mais.

against [əˈgenst] prep contra; **to lean ~ sthg** apoiar-se em algo; **~ the law** contra a lei.

age [eɪdʒ] n idade f; (old age) velhice f; **under ~** menor de idade; **I haven't seen him for ~s** (inf) há séculos que não o vejo.

aged [eɪdʒd] adj: **~ eight** com oito anos (de idade).

age group n grupo m etário.

age limit n limite m de idade.

agency [ˈeɪdʒənsɪ] n agência f.

agenda [əˈdʒendə] n agenda f.

agent [ˈeɪdʒənt] n agente mf.

aggravate [ˈægrəveɪt] vt (make worse) agravar; (annoy) irritar.

aggregate [ˈægrɪgət] adj total, global ♦ n (total) total m, conjunto m.

aggression [əˈgreʃn] n agressividade f.

aggressive [əˈgresɪv] adj agressivo (-va).

aggrieved [əˈgriːvd] adj ofendido (-da).

aghast [əˈgɑːst] adj horrorizado(-da); **~ at sthg** horrorizado com algo.

agile [Brit ˈædʒaɪl, Am ˈædʒəl] adj ágil.

agility [əˈdʒɪlɪtɪ] n agilidade f.

agitated [ˈædʒɪteɪtɪd] adj agitado (-da).

AGM abbr (Brit) = annual general meeting.

agnostic [ægˈnɒstɪk] adj agnóstico (-ca) ♦ n agnóstico m (-ca f).

ago [əˈgəʊ] adv: **a month ~** há um mês atrás; **how long ~?** há quanto tempo?

agog [əˈgɒg] adj ansioso(-osa); **to be all ~ (with)** estar todo excitado(-da) (com).

agonizing [ˈægənaɪzɪŋ] adj (delay) angustiante; (pain) dilacerante.

agony [ˈægənɪ] n agonia f.

agony aunt n (Brit: inf) conselheira f sentimental.

agree [əˈgriː] vi concordar; **tomato soup doesn't ~ with me** não me dou bem com sopa de tomate; **to ~ to sthg** concordar com algo; **to ~ to do sthg** aceitar fazer algo.

❏ **agree on** vt fus (time, price) chegar a um acordo sobre.

agreeable [əˈgrɪəbl] adj (pleasant) agradável; (willing): **to be ~ to sthg** concordar com algo; **to be ~ to do sthg** concordar em fazer algo.

agreed [əˈgriːd] adj combinado(-da).

agreement [əˈgriːmənt] n acordo m; **in ~ with** de acordo com.

agricultural [ægrɪˈkʌltʃərəl] adj agrícola.

agriculture [ˈægrɪkʌltʃəˈ] n agricultura f.

aground [əˈgraʊnd] adv: **to run ~** encalhar.

ahead [əˈhed] adv (in front) à frente; (forwards) em frente; **the months ~** os próximos meses; **to be ~** (winning) estar à frente; **~ of** (in front of) à frente de; **~ of schedule** adiantado(-da); **they're four points ~** levam quatro pontos de vantagem.

aid [eɪd] n ajuda f ♦ vt ajudar; **in ~ of** em benefício de; **with the ~ of** com a ajuda de.

AIDS [eɪdz] n AIDS f (Br), SIDA f (Port).

ailment [ˈeɪlmənt] n (fml) mal m.

aim [eɪm] n (purpose) objetivo m ♦ vt (gun, camera, hose) apontar ♦ vi: **to ~ (at)** apontar (para); **to ~ to do sthg** ter como objetivo fazer algo.

aimless [ˈeɪmlɪs] adj (person) sem objetivos; (task, existence) sem sentido.

ain't [eɪnt] (inf) = am not, are not, is not, has not, have not.

air [eəˈ] n ar m ♦ vt (room) arejar ♦ adj aéreo(-rea); **by ~** por avião.

air bag n (AUT) air bag m.

airbase [ˈeəbeɪs] n base f aérea.

airbed [ˈeəbed] n colchão m de ar.

airborne [ˈeəbɔːn] adj em vôo.

air-conditioned [-kənˈdɪʃnd] adj climatizado(-da).

air-conditioning [-kənˈdɪʃnɪŋ] n ar m condicionado.

aircraft [ˈeəkrɑːft] (pl inv) n avião m.

aircraft carrier [-ˌkærɪəˈ] n porta-aviões m inv.

airfield [ˈeəfiːld] n aeródromo m.

airforce ['eɔfɔːs] *n* aeronáutica *f (Br)*, força *f* aérea *(Port)*.

air freshener [-ˌfreʃnəʳ] *n* purificador *m* do ambiente OR do ar.

airgun ['ɔɡʌn] *n* pistola *f* de ar comprimido.

airhostess ['eɔˌhəʊstɪs] *n* aeromoça *f (Br)*, hospedeira *f (Port)*.

airing cupboard ['eɔrɪŋ-] *n* armário onde se encontra o cilindro de aquecimento de água, usado para secar roupa.

airletter ['eɔˌletəʳ] *n* aerograma *m*.

airline ['eɔlaɪn] *n* companhia *f* aérea.

airliner ['eɔˌlaɪnəʳ] *n* avião *m* de passageiros.

airlock ['eɔlɒk] *n (in tube, pipe)* bolsa *f* de ar; *(airtight chamber)* câmara *f* OR caixa *f* de ar.

airmail ['eɔmeɪl] *n* correio *m* aéreo; **by ~** por avião.

airplane ['eɔpleɪn] *n (Am)* avião *m*.

airport ['eɔpɔːt] *n* aeroporto *m*.

air raid *n* ataque *m* aéreo.

air rifle *n* espingarda *f* de ar comprimido.

airsick ['eɔsɪk] *adj* enjoado(-da) *(em avião)*.

airspace ['eɔspeɪs] *n* espaço *m* aéreo.

air steward *n* comissário *m* de bordo.

air stewardess *n* aeromoça *f (Br)*, hospedeira *f (Port)*.

airstrip ['eɔstrɪp] *n* pista *f* de aterrissagem *(Br)*, pista *f* de aterragem *(Port)*.

air terminal *n* terminal *m* aéreo.

airtight [eɔtaɪt] *adj* hermético(-ca).

air traffic control *n (people)* pessoal *m* da torre de controle.

air traffic controller *n* controlador *m* aéreo (controladora *f* aérea).

airy ['eɔrɪ] *adj* arejado(-da).

aisle [aɪl] *n* corredor *m*; *(in church)* nave *f*.

aisle seat *n* lugar *m* do lado do corredor.

ajar [ɔ'dʒɔːʳ] *adj* entreaberto(-ta).

aka *(abbr of also known as)* também conhecido(-da) como.

alacrity [ɔ'lækrətɪ] *n* prontidão *f*.

alarm [ɔ'lɑːm] *n* alarme *m* ◆ *vt* alarmar.

alarm clock *n* despertador *m*.

alarmed [ɔ'lɑːmd] *adj (person)* assustado(-da); *(door, car)* provido(-da) de alarme.

alarming [ɔ'lɑːmɪŋ] *adj* alarmante.

alas [ɔ'læs] *excl* ai!

Albania [æl'beɪnjɔ] *n* Albânia *f*.

Albanian [æl'beɪnjɔn] *adj* albanês (-esa) ◆ *n (person)* albanês *m* (-esa *f*); *(language)* albanês *m*.

albeit [ɔːl'biːɪt] *conj* se bem que.

Albert Hall [ˈælbɔt-] *n*: **the ~** o Albert Hall.

album [ˈælbɔm] *n* álbum *m*.

alcohol [ˈælkɔhɒl] *n* álcool *m*.

alcohol-free *adj* sem álcool.

alcoholic [ˌælkɔˈhɒlɪk] *adj* alcoólico (-ca) ◆ *n* alcoólatra *mf (Br)*, alcoólico *m* (-ca *f*) *(Port)*.

alcoholism [ˈælkɔhɒlɪzm] *n* alcoolismo *m*.

alcove [ˈælkɔʊv] *n* alcova *f*.

alderman [ˈɔːldɔmɔn] *(pl* **-men** [-mɔn]) *n* = vereador *m* (-ra *f*), = magistrado *m* (-da *f*) local.

ale [eɪl] *n* cerveja escura com alto teor alcoólico.

alert [ɔ'lɜːt] *adj* atento(-ta) ◆ *vt* alertar.

A level *n (Brit)* = vestibular *m (Br)*, = exame *m* final do 12º ano *(Port)*.

algebra [ˈældʒɪbrɔ] *n* álgebra *f*.

Algeria [æl'dʒɪɔrɪɔ] *n* Argélia *f*.

alias [ˈeɪlɪɔs] *adv* também conhecido (-da) como.

alibi [ˈælɪbaɪ] *n* álibi *m*.

alien [ˈeɪlɪɔn] *n (foreigner)* estrangeiro *m* (-ra *f*); *(from outer space)* extraterrestre *mf*.

alienate [ˈeɪljɔneɪt] *vt (friend, family)* alienar, ganhar a antipatia de.

alight [ɔ'laɪt] *adj* em chamas ◆ *vi (fml: from train, bus)*: **to ~ (from)** apear-se (de).

align [ɔ'laɪn] *vt* alinhar.

alike [ɔ'laɪk] *adj* parecidos(-das) ◆ *adv* da mesma maneira, **to look ~** ser parecidos. parecer-se.

alimony [ˈælɪmɔnɪ] *n* pensão *f* alimentícia *(Br)*, alimentos *mpl (Port)*.

alive [ɔ'laɪv] *adj* vivo(-va).

alkali [ˈælkɔlaɪ] *n* álcali *m*.

all [ɔːl] *adj* 1. *(with singular noun)* todo(-da); **~ the money** o dinheiro todo; **~ the time** sempre; **we were out ~ day** estivemos fora o dia inteiro. 2. *(with plural noun)* todos(-das); **~ the houses** todas as casas; **~ trains stop at Tonbridge** todos os trens param em Tonbridge.

♦ *adv* 1. *(completely)* completamente; ~ **alone** completamente só.
2. *(in scores)*: **it's two ~** estão empatados dois a dois.
3. *(in phrases)*: ~ **but empty** quase vazio(-zia); ~ **over** *adj (finished)* terminado(-da) ♦ *prep* por todo(-da).
♦ *pron* 1. *(everything)* todo *m* (-da *f*); **is that ~?** *(in shop)* é só isso?; **the best of** ~ o melhor de todos.
2. *(everybody)* todos, toda a gente; ~ **of us went** fomos todos.
3. *(in phrases)*: **can I help you at ~** posso ajudar em alguma coisa?; **in ~** *(in total)* ao todo; **in ~ it was a great success** resumindo, foi um grande êxito.

Allah [ˈælə] *n* Alá *m*.

all-around *(Am)* = **all-round**.

allay [əˈleɪ] *vt (fears, doubts)* dissipar; *(anger)* apaziguar.

allegation [ˌælɪˈgeɪʃn] *n* alegação *f*.

allege [əˈledʒ] *vt* alegar.

allegedly [əˈledʒɪdlɪ] *adv* supostamente.

allergic [əˈlɜːdʒɪk] *adj*: **to be ~ to** ser alérgico(-ca) a.

allergy [ˈælədʒɪ] *n* alergia *f*.

alleviate [əˈliːvɪeɪt] *vt* aliviar.

alley [ˈælɪ] *n (narrow street)* ruela *f*.

alliance [əˈlaɪəns] *n (agreement)* aliança *f*.

alligator [ˈælɪgeɪtər] *n* caimão *m*.

all-in *adj (Brit: inclusive)* com tudo incluído.

all-night *adj (bar, petrol station)* aberto(-ta) toda a noite.

allocate [ˈæləkeɪt] *vt* atribuir.

allotment [əˈlɒtmənt] *n (Brit: for vegetables)* parcela de terreno municipal alugado para o cultivo de legumes e flores.

all-out *adj (effort)* máximo(-ma); *(war)* total.

allow [əˈlaʊ] *vt (permit)* permitir; *(time, money)* contar com; **to ~ sb to do sthg** deixar alguém fazer algo; **to be ~ed to do sthg** poder fazer algo.
❑ **allow for** *vt fus* contar com.

allowance [əˈlaʊəns] *n (state benefit)* subsídio *m*; *(for expenses)* ajudas *fpl* de custo; *(Am: pocket money)* mesada *f*.

alloy [ˈælɔɪ] *n* liga *f* (de metal).

all right *adv (satisfactorily)* bem; *(yes, okay)* está bem ♦ *adj*: **is it ~ if I smoke?** posso fumar?; **I thought the film was ~** não achei o filme nada de especial; **is**

everything ~? está tudo bem?

all-round *adj (Brit) (versatile)* multifacetado(-da).

all-time *adj* de todos os tempos.

allusion [əˈluːʒn] *n* alusão *f*.

ally [ˈælaɪ] *n* aliado *m* (-da *f*).

almighty [ɔːlˈmaɪtɪ] *adj (inf: enormous)* tremendo(-da).

almond [ˈɑːmənd] *n* amêndoa *f*.

almost [ˈɔːlməʊst] *adv* quase.

alone [əˈləʊn] *adj & adv* sozinho (-nha); **the decision is yours ~** a decisão é só sua; **to leave sb ~** deixar alguém em paz; **to leave sthg ~** parar de mexer em algo.

along [əˈlɒŋ] *prep (towards one end of)* por; *(alongside)* ao longo de ♦ *adv*: **to walk ~** caminhar; **to bring sthg ~** trazer algo; **all ~** desde o princípio; ~ **with** (junto) com.

alongside [əˌlɒŋˈsaɪd] *prep* ao lado de.

aloof [əˈluːf] *adj* distante.

aloud [əˈlaʊd] *adv* em voz alta.

alphabet [ˈælfəbet] *n* alfabeto *m*.

alphabetical [ˌælfəˈbetɪkl] *adj* alfabético(-ca).

Alps [ælps] *npl*: **the ~** os Alpes.

already [ɔːlˈredɪ] *adv* já.

alright [ˌɔːlˈraɪt] = **all right**.

Alsatian [ælˈseɪʃn] *n (dog)* pastor *m* alemão.

also [ˈɔːlsəʊ] *adv* também.

altar [ˈɔːltər] *n* altar *m*.

alter [ˈɔːltər] *vt* alterar.

alteration [ˌɔːltəˈreɪʃn] *n* alteração *f*.

alternate [*Brit* ɔːlˈtɜːnət, *Am* ˈɔːltərnət] *adj* alternado(-da).

alternating current [ˈɔːltəneɪtɪŋ-] *n* corrente *f* alterna OR alternada.

alternative [ɔːlˈtɜːnətɪv] *adj* alternativo(-va) ♦ *n* alternativa *f*.

alternatively [ɔːlˈtɜːnətɪvlɪ] *adv* em OR como alternativa.

alternative medicine *n* medicina *f* alternativa.

alternator [ˈɔːltəneɪtər] *n* alternador *m*.

although [ɔːlˈðəʊ] *conj* embora, contudo.

altitude [ˈæltɪtjuːd] *n* altitude *f*.

alto [ˈæltəʊ] *(pl* -s*)* *n (female voice)* contralto *m*.

altogether [ˌɔːltəˈgeðər] *adv (completely)* completamente; *(in total)* ao todo, no total.

aluminium [ˌæljuˈmɪnɪəm] *n (Brit)* alumínio *m.*

aluminum [əˈluːmɪnəm] *(Am)* = **aluminium.**

always [ˈɔːlweɪz] *adv* sempre.

a.m. *(abbr of ante meridiem)*: **at 2 ~ às** duas da manhã.

am [æm] → **be.**

amalgamate [əˈmælgəˌmeɪt] *vt* fundir, unir ♦ *vi* fundir-se, unir-se.

amass [əˈmæs] *vt* juntar, acumular.

amateur [ˈæmətəʳ] *n* amador *m* (-ra *f*).

amaze [əˈmeɪz] *vt* surpreender.

amazed [əˈmeɪzd] *adj* espantado(-da), surpreso(-sa).

amazement [əˈmeɪzmənt] *n* espanto *m*, surpresa *f.*

amazing [əˈmeɪzɪŋ] *adj* espantoso (-osa), surpreendente.

Amazon [ˈæməzɪn] *n (river)*: **the ~ o** Amazonas.

ambassador [æmˈbæsədəʳ] *n* embaixador *m* (-ra *f*).

amber [ˈæmbəʳ] *adj (traffic lights)* amarelo(-la); *(jewellery)* âmbar.

ambiguous [æmˈbɪɡjuəs] *adj* ambíguo(-gua).

ambition [æmˈbɪʃn] *n* ambição *f.*

ambitious [æmˈbɪʃəs] *adj* ambicioso(-osa).

ambulance [ˈæmbjuləns] *n* ambulância *f.*

ambush [ˈæmbuʃ] *n* emboscada *f.*

amenable [əˈmiːnəbl] *adj*: **~ (to sthg)** favorável (a algo).

amendment [əˈmendmənt] *n (to text)* correção *f; (to law)* modificação *f.*

amenities [əˈmiːnətɪz] *npl* comodidades *fpl.*

America [əˈmerɪkə] *n* América *f.*

American [əˈmerɪkən] *adj* americano (-na) ♦ *n (person)* americano *m* (-na *f*).

amiable [ˈeɪmɪəbl] *adj* amável.

amicable [ˈæmɪkəbl] *adj* amigável.

amiss [əˈmɪs] *adj* errado(-da) ♦ *adv*: **to take sthg ~** levar algo a mal.

ammonia [əˈməunjə] *n* amoníaco *m.*

ammunition [ˌæmjuˈnɪʃn] *n* munições *fpl.*

amnesia [æmˈniːzɪə] *n* amnésia *f.*

amnesty [ˈæmnəstɪ] *n* anistia *f.*

amok [əˈmɒk] *adv*: **to run ~** ser tomado(-da) por uma crise de loucura furiosa.

among(st) [əˈmʌŋ(st)] *prep* entre.

amoral [ˌeɪˈmɒrəl] *adj (person, behaviour)* amoral.

amount [əˈmaunt] *n (quantity)* quantidade *f; (sum)* quantia *f*, montante *m.*

❏ **amount to** *vt fus (total)* atingir a quantia de.

amp [æmp] *n* ampere *m*; **a 13-~ plug** uma tomada de 13 amperes.

amphibious [æmˈfɪbɪəs] *adj* anfíbio (-bia).

ample [ˈæmpl] *adj* bastante.

amplifier [ˈæmplɪfaɪəʳ] *n* amplificador *m.*

amputate [ˈæmpjuteɪt] *vt* amputar.

Amtrak [ˈæmtræk] *n organismo regulador das ferrovias nos E.U.A.*

amuck [əˈmʌk] = **amok.**

amuse [əˈmjuːz] *vt (make laugh)* divertir; *(entertain)* entreter.

amused [əˈmjuːzd] *adj*: **to be ~ at OR by sthg** *(entertained, delighted)* achar piada OR graça de algo; **to keep o.s. ~** *(occupied)* entreter-se.

amusement [əˈmjuːzmənt] *n* diversão *f*; divertimento *m.*

❏ **amusements** *npl* diversões *fpl.*

amusement arcade *n* sala *f* de jogos.

amusement park *n* parque *m* de diversões.

amusing [əˈmjuːzɪŋ] *adj* divertido (-da).

an [stressed æn, unstressed ən] → **a.**

anaemic [əˈniːmɪk] *adj (Brit) (person)* anêmico(-ca).

anaesthetic [ˌænɪsˈθetɪk] *n (Brit)* anestesia *f.*

analgesic [ˌænælˈdʒiːsɪk] *n* analgésico *m.*

analogy [əˈnælədʒɪ] *n* analogia *f*; **by ~** por analogia.

analyse [ˈænəlaɪz] *vt (Brit)* analisar.

analysis [əˈnæləsɪs] *(pl* **-lyses** [-ləsiːz]*)* *n* análise *f.*

analyst [ˈænəlɪst] *n* analista *mf.*

analytic(al) [ˌænəˈlɪtɪk(l)] *adj* analítico(-ca).

analyze [ˈænəlaɪz] *(Am)* = **analyse.**

anarchist [ˈænəkɪst] *n* anarquista *mf.*

anarchy [ˈænəkɪ] *n* anarquia *f.*

anathema [əˈnæθəmə] *n*: **the concept is ~ to** me para mim, a idéia é inadmissível.

anatomy [ə'nætəmɪ] n anatomia f.
ANC n (abbr of African National Congress) ANC m.
ancestor [ˈænsestəʳ] n antepassado m (-da f).
anchor [ˈæŋkəʳ] n âncora f.
anchovy [ˈæntʃəvɪ] n anchova f.
ancient [ˈeɪnʃənt] adj antigo(-ga).
ancillary [ænˈsɪlərɪ] adj auxiliar.
and [strong form ænd, weak form ənd, ən] conj e; ~ you? e você?; a hundred ~ one cento e um; more ~ more cada vez mais; to go ~ see ir ver.
Andes [ˈændiːz] npl: the ~ os Andes.
Andorra [ænˈdɔːrə] n Andorra s.
anecdote [ˈænɪkdəʊt] n episódio m (cômico).
anemic [əˈniːmɪk] (Am) = anaemic.
anesthetic [ænɪsˈθetɪk] (Am) = anaesthetic.
anew [əˈnjuː] adv de novo.
angel [ˈeɪndʒl] n anjo m.
anger [ˈæŋgəʳ] n raiva f, ira f.
angina [ænˈdʒaɪnə] n angina f de peito.
angle [ˈæŋgl] n ângulo m; at an ~ torto (torta).
angler [ˈæŋgləʳ] n pescador m (-ra f) (de vara).
Anglican [ˈæŋglɪkən] adj anglicano (-na) ♦ n anglicano m (-na f).
angling [ˈæŋglɪŋ] n pesca f (de vara).
Angola [æŋˈgəʊlə] n Angola s.
Angolan [æŋˈgəʊlən] adj angolano(-na) ♦ n angolano m (-na f).
angry [ˈæŋgrɪ] adj (person) zangado (-da); (words) de raiva; to get ~ (with sb) zangar-se (com alguém).
anguish [ˈæŋgwɪʃ] n angústia f.
animal [ˈænɪml] n animal m.
animate [ˈænɪmət] adj animado(-da), vivo(-va).
animated [ˈænɪmeɪtɪd] adj animado (-da).
aniseed [ˈænɪsiːd] n erva-doce f, anis m.
ankle [ˈæŋkl] n tornozelo m.
annex [ˈæneks] n (building) anexo m.
annihilate [əˈnaɪəleɪt] vt aniquilar.
anniversary [ænɪˈvɜːsərɪ] n aniversário m.
announce [əˈnaʊns] vt anunciar.
announcement [əˈnaʊnsmənt] n (on TV, radio) anúncio m; (official) comunicação f.
announcer [əˈnaʊnsəʳ] n (on TV) apresentador m (-ra f); (on radio)

locutor m (-ra f).
annoy [əˈnɔɪ] vt aborrecer, irritar.
annoyance [əˈnɔɪəns] n irritação f.
annoyed [əˈnɔɪd] adj aborrecido(-da), irritado(-da); to get ~ (with) aborrecer-se (com), irritar-se (com).
annoying [əˈnɔɪɪŋ] adj irritante.
annual [ˈænjʊəl] adj anual.
annual general meeting n assembléia f geral (anual).
annul [əˈnʌl] vt anular.
annum [ˈænəm] n: per ~ por ano.
anomaly [əˈnɒməlɪ] n anomalia f.
anonymous [əˈnɒnɪməs] adj anônimo(-ma).
anorak [ˈænəræk] n anoraque m.
anorexia (nervosa) [ænəˈreksɪə (nɜːˈvəʊsə)] n anorexia f (nervosa).
another [əˈnʌðəʳ] adj outro(-tra) ♦ pron outro m (-tra f); in ~ two weeks dentro de (mais) duas semanas; ~ one outro(-tra); one ~ um ao outro (uma à outra); to talk to one ~ falar um com o outro; they love one ~ eles se amam (um ao outro); one after ~ um após o outro.
answer [ˈɑːnsəʳ] n resposta f ♦ vt responder a ♦ vi responder; to ~ the door abrir a porta; to ~ the phone atender o telefone.
❏ **answer back** vi replicar.
answering machine [ˈɑːnsərɪŋ-] = answerphone.
answerphone [ˈɑːnsəfəʊn] n secretária f eletrônica (Br), atendedor m de chamadas (Port).
ant [ænt] n formiga f.
antagonism [ænˈtægənɪzm] n antagonismo m.
antagonize [ænˈtægənaɪz] vt antagonizar.
Antarctic [ænˈtɑːktɪk] n: the ~ o Antártico.
antelope [ˈæntɪləʊp] (pl inv OR -s) n antílope m.
antenatal clinic [æntɪˈneɪtl-] n serviço m de consultas pré-natais.
antenna [ænˈtenə] n (Am: aerial) antena f.
anthem [ˈænθəm] n hino m.
anthology [ænˈθɒlədʒɪ] n antologia f.
antibiotics [æntɪbaɪˈɒtɪks] npl antibióticos mpl.
antibody [ˈæntɪbɒdɪ] n anticorpo m.
anticipate [ænˈtɪsɪpeɪt] vt (expect) esperar; (guess correctly) prever.

anticipation [æn,tɪsɪˈpeɪʃn] *n* antecipação *f*; **in ~ of** antecipando.

anticlimax [ˌæntɪˈklaɪmæks] *n* anticlímax *m inv*.

anticlockwise [ˌæntɪˈklɒkwaɪz] *adv* (*Brit*) no sentido contrário ao dos ponteiros do relógio.

antics [ˈæntɪks] *npl* (*of children, animals*) brincadeiras *fpl*.

anticyclone [ˌæntɪˈsaɪkləʊn] *n* anticiclone *m*.

antidepressant [ˌæntɪdəˈpresnt] *n* antidepressivo *m*.

antidote [ˈæntɪdəʊt] *n* antídoto *m*.

antifreeze [ˈæntɪfriːz] *n* anticongelante *m*.

antihistamine [ˌæntɪˈhɪstəmɪn] *n* anti-histamínico *m*.

antiperspirant [ˌæntɪˈpɜːspərənt] *n* desodorizante *m*.

antiquarian bookshop [ˌæntɪˈkweərɪən-] *n* sebo *m* (*Br*), alfarrabista *m* (*Port*).

antique [ænˈtiːk] *n* antiguidade *f*.

antique shop *n* loja *f* de antiguidades.

antiseptic [ˌæntɪˈseptɪk] *n* antiséptico *m*.

antisocial [ˌæntɪˈsəʊʃl] *adj* anti-social.

antlers [ˈæntləz] *npl* chifres *mpl*.

anxiety [æŋˈzaɪətɪ] *n* ansiedade *f*.

anxious [ˈæŋkʃəs] *adj* ansioso(-osa).

any [ˈenɪ] *adj* **1.** (*in questions*) algum (-ma); **have you got ~ money?** você tem dinheiro?; **have you got ~ postcards?** você tem postais?; **have you got ~ rooms?** você tem algum quarto livre? **2.** (*in negatives*) nenhum(-ma); **I haven't got ~ money** não tenho dinheiro (nenhum); **we don't have ~ rooms** não temos quartos livres. **3.** (*no matter which*) qualquer; **take ~ books you like** leve os livros que quiser; **take ~ one you like** leve aquele que quiser.
♦ *pron* **1.** (*in questions*) algum *m* (-ma *f*); **I'm looking for a hotel – are there ~ nearby?** estou procurando um hotel – há algum aqui perto? **2.** (*in negatives*) nenhum *m* (-ma *f*); **I don't want ~ (of it)** não quero (nada); **I don't want ~ (of them)** não quero nenhum (deles). **3.** (*no matter which one*) qualquer um (qualquer uma); **you can sit at ~ of the tables** podem sentar-se em qualquer uma das mesas.

♦ *adv* **1.** (*in questions*): **~ other questions?** mais alguma pergunta?; **can you drive ~ faster?** vôce pode ir mais depressa?; **is that ~ better?** está melhor assim? **2.** (*in negatives*): **he's not ~ better** ele não está nada melhor; **we can't wait ~ longer** não podemos esperar mais; **we can't afford ~ more** não temos possibilidades para mais.

anybody [ˈenɪbɒdɪ] = **anyone**.

anyhow [ˈenɪhaʊ] *adv* (*carelessly*) de qualquer maneira; (*in any case*) em qualquer caso; (*in spite of that*) de qualquer modo.

anyone [ˈenɪwʌn] *pron* (*any person*) qualquer um (qualquer uma); (*in questions*) alguém; (*in negatives*) ninguém; **I don't like ~** não gosto de ninguém.

anything [ˈenɪθɪŋ] *pron* (*no matter what*) qualquer coisa; (*in questions*) alguma coisa; (*in negatives*) nada; **she didn't say ~** ela não disse nada.

anyway [ˈenɪweɪ] *adv* de qualquer forma OR modo.

anywhere [ˈenɪweəʳ] *adv* (*no matter where*) em/a qualquer lugar; (*in questions*) em/a algum lugar; (*in negatives*) em/a lugar nenhum; **I can't find it ~** não o encontro em lugar nenhum; **sit ~ you like** sente-se onde quiser; **we can go ~** podemos ir a qualquer lugar.

apart [əˈpɑːt] *adv* separado(-da); **to come ~** separar-se; **~ from** (*except for*) exceto, salvo; (*as well as*) para além de.

apartheid [əˈpɑːtheɪt] *n* apartheid *m*.

apartment [əˈpɑːtmənt] *n* (*Am*) apartamento *m*.

apathetic [ˌæpəˈθetɪk] *adj* apático(-ca).

apathy [ˈæpəθɪ] *n* apatia *f*.

ape [eɪp] *n* macaco *m*.

aperitif [əˌperəˈtiːf] *n* aperitivo *m*.

aperture [ˈæpətjʊəʳ] *n* (*of camera*) abertura *f*.

APEX [ˈeɪpeks] *n* (*plane ticket*) bilhete *m* APEX; (*Brit: train ticket*) bilhete de preço reduzido não transmissível que se adquire com duas semanas de antecedência.

apiece [əˈpiːs] *adv*: **they cost £50 ~** custam 50 libras cada um.

apologetic [əˌpɒləˈdʒetɪk] *adj* cheio (cheia) de desculpas.

apologize [əˈpɒlədʒaɪz] *vi*: **to ~** (**to sb for sthg**) pedir desculpa (a alguém por algo).

apology [əˈpɒlədʒɪ] *n* desculpa *f*.

apostle [ə'pɒsl] *n* apóstolo *m*.
apostrophe [ə'pɒstrəfi] *n* apóstrofo *m*.
appal [ə'pɔ:l] *vt (Brit)* horrorizar.
appall [ə'pɔ:l] *(Am)* = appal.
appalling [ə'pɔ:lɪŋ] *adj* horrível, terrível.
apparatus [,æpə'reɪtəs] *n* aparelho *m*.
apparent [ə'pærənt] *adj* aparente.
apparently [ə'pærəntlɪ] *adv* aparentemente.
appeal [ə'pi:l] *n (JUR)* apelação *f*, recurso *m*; *(fundraising campaign)* campanha *f* de coleta de fundos ◆ *vi (JUR)* apelar, recorrer para; **to ~ to sb (for sthg)** apelar a alguém (para algo); **it doesn't ~ to me** não me atrai.
appealing [ə'pi:lɪŋ] *adj* atrativo(-va), sedutor(-ra).
appear [ə'pɪəʳ] *vi* aparecer; *(seem)* parecer; *(before court)* comparecer; **it ~s that** parece que.
appearance [ə'pɪərəns] *n (arrival)* chegada *f*; *(look)* aparência *f*, aspecto *m*.
appease [ə'pi:z] *vt* aplacar, acalmar.
appendices [ə'pendɪsi:z] *pl* → **appendix**.
appendicitis [ə,pendɪ'saɪtɪs] *n* apendicite *f*.
appendix [ə'pendɪks] *(pl* **-dices***) n* apêndice *m*.
appetite [æpɪtaɪt] *n* apetite *m*.
appetizer [æpɪtaɪzəʳ] *n* aperitivo *m*.
appetizing [æpɪtaɪzɪŋ] *adj* apetitoso(-osa).
applaud [ə'plɔ:d] *vt & vi* aplaudir.
applause [ə'plɔ:z] *n* palmas *fpl*.
apple [æpl] *n* maçã *f*.
apple charlotte [-'ʃɑ:lət] *n* pudim de maçã e pão ralado, cozido numa forma forrada e depois coberta com fatias de pão.
apple crumble *n* sobremesa de maçã cozida coberta com uma mistura arenosa de farinha, manteiga e açúcar, cozida no forno.
apple juice *n* suco *m* de maçã.
apple pie *n* torta *f* de maçã.
apple sauce *n* purê *m* de maçã *(servido como acompanhamento de carne de porco)*.
apple tart *n* torta *f* de maçã.
apple tree *n* macieira *f*.
apple turnover [-'tɜ:n,əʊvəʳ] *n* folheado *m* de maçã.
appliance [ə'plaɪəns] *n* aparelho *m*;

electrical/domestic ~ eletrodoméstico *m*.
applicable [ə'plɪkəbl] *adj:* **to be ~ (to)** ser aplicável (a); **if ~** se aplicável.
applicant [æplɪkənt] *n* candidato *m* (-ta *f*).
application [,æplɪ'keɪʃn] *n (for job, membership)* candidatura *f*.
application form *n* formulário *m* de candidatura.
apply [ə'plaɪ] *vt* aplicar ◆ *vi:* **to ~ (to sb for sthg)** *(make request)* requerer (algo a alguém); **to ~ (to sb)** *(be applicable)* ser aplicável (a alguém).
appoint [ə'pɔɪnt] *vt (to job, position)* nomear; **to ~ sb to sthg** nomear alguém para algo; **to ~ sb as sthg** nomear alguém algo.
appointment [ə'pɔɪntmənt] *n (with hairdresser, businessman)* hora *f* marcada; *(with doctor)* consulta *f*; **to have/make an ~ (with)** ter/marcar um encontro (com); **by ~** com hora marcada.
apportion [ə'pɔ:ʃn] *vt (money)* dividir; *(blame)* atribuir.
appraisal [ə'preɪzl] *n* análise *f*, avaliação *f*.
appreciable [ə'pri:ʃəbl] *adj* apreciável.
appreciate [ə'pri:ʃɪeɪt] *vt (be grateful for)* agradecer; *(understand)* compreender; *(like, admire)* apreciar.
appreciation [ə,pri:ʃɪ'eɪʃn] *n (gratitude)* gratidão *f*, apreço *m*; *(understanding)* compreensão *f*; *(liking)* satisfação *f*.
appreciative [ə'pri:ʃjətɪv] *adj (person)* agradecido(-da); *(remark, gesture)* de agradecimento; *(audience)* satisfeito(-ta).
apprehensive [,æprɪ'hensɪv] *adj* apreensivo(-va).
apprentice [ə'prentɪs] *n* aprendiz *m* (-za *f*).
apprenticeship [ə'prentɪsʃɪp] *n* aprendizagem *f*.
approach [ə'prəʊtʃ] *n (road)* acesso *m*; *(to problem, situation)* abordagem *f* ◆ *vt (come nearer to)* aproximar-se de; *(problem, situation)* abordar ◆ *vi* aproximar-se.
approachable [ə'prəʊtʃəbl] *adj* acessível.
appropriate [ə'prəʊprɪət] *adj* apropriado(-da).

approval [əˈpruːvl] *n (favourable opinion)* aprovação *f*; *(permission)* autorização *f*.

approve [əˈpruːv] *vt*: **to ~ of sb/sthg** ver com bons olhos alguém/algo.

approximate [əˈprɒksɪmət] *adj* aproximado(-da).

approximately [əˈprɒksɪmətli] *adv* aproximadamente.

Apr. *abbr* = **April**.

apricot [ˈeɪprɪkɒt] *n* alperce *m*, damasco *m*.

April [ˈeɪprəl] *n* Abril *m*, → **September**.

April Fools' Day *n* ≃ 1° de abril *(Br)*, Dia *m* das mentiras *(Port)*.

apron [ˈeɪprən] *n* avental *m* (de cozinha).

apt [æpt] *adj (appropriate)* apropriado(-da); **to be ~ to do sthg** ser propenso a fazer algo.

aptitude [ˈæptɪtjuːd] *n* aptidão *f*; **to have an ~ for sthg** ter jeito para algo.

aquarium [əˈkweərɪəm] *(pl* **-riums** OR **-ria** [-rɪə]) *n* aquário *m*.

Aquarius [əˈkweərɪəs] *n* Aquário *m*.

aqueduct [ˈækwɪdʌkt] *n* aqueduto *m*.

Arab [ˈærəb] *adj* árabe ◆ *n (person)* árabe *mf*.

Arabic [ˈærəbɪk] *adj* árabe ◆ *n (language)* árabe *m*.

Arabic numeral *n* número *m* arábico.

arable [ˈærəbl] *adj (land)* arável; *(farm, crops)* agrícola.

arbitrary [ˈuːbɪtrərɪ] *adj* arbitrário (-ria).

arbitration [ˌuːbɪˈtreɪʃn] *n* arbitragem *f*; **to go to ~** recorrer a arbitragem.

arc [uːk] *n* arco *m*.

arcade [uːˈkeɪd] *n (for shopping)* galeria *f*; *(of video games)* sala *f* de jogos.

arch [uːtʃ] *n* arco *m*.

archaeologist [ˌuːkɪˈɒlədʒɪst] *n* arqueólogo *m* (-ga *f*).

archaeology [ˌuːkɪˈɒlədʒɪ] *n* arqueologia *f*.

archaic [uːˈkeɪɪk] *adj* arcaico(-ca).

archbishop [ˌuːtʃˈbɪʃəp] *n* arcebispo *m*.

archeology [ˌuːkɪˈɒlədʒɪ] *etc* = **archaeology** *etc*.

archery [ˈuːtʃərɪ] *n* tiro *m* com arco e flechas.

archetypal [ˌuːkɪˈtaɪpl] *adj* típico (-ca).

archipelago [ˌuːkɪˈpeləgəʊ] *(pl* **-s** OR **-es**) *n* arquipélago *m*.

architect [ˈuːkɪtekt] *n* arquiteto *m* (-ta *f*).

architecture [ˈuːkɪtektʃəʳ] *n* arquitetura *f*.

Arctic [ˈuːktɪk] *n*: **the ~** o Ártico.

ardent [ˈuːdənt] *adj* ardente.

arduous [ˈuːdjʊəs] *adj* árduo(-dua).

are [weak form əʳ, strong form uːʳ] → **be**.

area [ˈeərɪə] *n* área *f*.

area code *n (Am)* prefixo *m* (telefônico) *(Br)*, indicativo *m* (telefónico) *(Port)*.

arena [əˈriːnə] *n (at circus)* arena *f*; *(sportsground)* estádio *m*.

aren't [uːnt] = **are not**.

Argentina [ˌuːdʒənˈtiːnə] *n* Argentina *f*.

arguably [ˈuːgjʊəblɪ] *adv* possivelmente.

argue [ˈuːgjuː] *vi*: **to ~ (with sb about sthg)** discutir (com alguém acerca de algo) ◆ *vt*: **to ~ (that)** argumentar que.

argument [ˈuːgjʊmənt] *n (quarrel)* discussão *f*; *(reason)* argumento *m*.

argumentative [ˌuːgjʊˈmentətɪv] *adj (person)* propenso (-sa) a discutir.

arid [ˈærɪd] *adj* árido(-da).

Aries [ˈeərɪːz] *n* Áries *m (Br)*, Carneiro *m (Port)*.

arise [əˈraɪz] *(pt* **arose**, *pp* **arisen** [əˈrɪzn]) *vi*: **to ~ (from)** surgir (de).

aristocracy [ˌærɪˈstɒkrəsɪ] *n* aristocracia *f*.

aristocrat [*Brit* ˈærɪstəkræt, *Am* əˈrɪstəkræt] *n* aristócrata *mf*.

arithmetic [əˈrɪθmətɪk] *n* aritmética *f*.

arm [uːm] *n* braço *m*; *(of garment)* manga *f*

armaments [ˈuːməmənts] *npl* armamento *m*.

armbands [ˈuːmbændz] *npl (for swimming)* braçadeiras *fpl*.

armchair [ˈuːmtʃeəʳ] *n* poltrona *f*.

armed [uːmd] *adj* armado(-da).

armed forces *npl*: **the ~** as forças armadas.

armhole [ˈuːmhəʊl] *n* manga *f*.

armor [ˈuːməʳ] *(Am)* = **armour**.

armour [ˈuːməʳ] *n (Brit)* armadura *f*.

armoured car [ˈuːməd-] *n (Brit)* *n* carro *m* blindado.

armpit ['ɑ:mpɪt] *n* axila *f*, sovaco *m*.
armrest ['ɑ:mrest] *n* braço *m (de cadeira, sofá)*.
arms [ɑ:mz] *npl (weapons)* armas *fpl*.
army ['ɑ:mɪ] *n* exército *m*.
A-road *n (Brit)* = estrada *f* nacional.
aroma [ə'rəumə] *n* aroma *m*.
aromatic [ˌærəʊ'mætɪk] *adj* aromático(-ca).
arose [ə'rəʊz] *pt* → **arise**.
around [ə'raʊnd] *adv (about, round)* por aí; *(present)* por aí/aqui ◆ *prep (surrounding)* em redor de, à volta de; *(to the other side of)* para o outro lado de; *(near)* perto de; *(all over)* por todo (-da); *(approximately)* cerca de; ~ **here** *(in the area)* por aqui; **to turn** ~ virar-se; **to look** ~ *(turn head)* olhar em volta; *(in shop, city)* dar uma olhada.
arouse [ə'raʊz] *vt (suspicion)* levantar; *(fear)* provocar; *(interest)* suscitar.
arrange [ə'reɪndʒ] *vt (books)* arrumar; *(flowers)* arranjar; *(meeting, event)* organizar; **to ~ to do sthg (with sb)** combinar fazer algo (com alguém).
arrangement [ə'reɪndʒmənt] *n (agreement)* combinação *f*; *(layout)* disposição *f*; **by ~** *(tour, service)* com data e hora marcada; **to make ~s (to do sthg)** fazer os preparativos (para fazer algo).
array [ə'reɪ] *n (of objects, people)* variedade *f*.
arrears [ə'rɪəz] *npl (money owed)* atrasos *mpl (Br)*, retroactivos *mpl (Port)*; **to be in ~** *(late)* estar atrasado; **I'm paid monthly in ~** eu sou pago sempre no fim do mês (de trabalho).
arrest [ə'rest] *n* detenção *f*, prisão *f* ◆ *vt* prender; **under ~** sob prisão, preso.
arrival [ə'raɪvl] *n* chegada *f*; **on ~** à chegada; **new ~** *(person)* recém-chegado *m (-da f)*.
arrive [ə'raɪv] *vi* chegar; **to ~ at** chegar a.
arrogant ['ærəgənt] *adj* arrogante.
arrow ['ærəʊ] *n (for shooting)* flecha *f*; *(sign)* seta *f*.
arsenic ['ɑ:snɪk] *n* arsênico *m*.
arson ['ɑ:sn] *n* fogo *m* posto.
art [ɑ:t] *n* arte *f*.
❏ **arts** *npl (humanities)* letras *fpl*; **the ~s** *(fine arts)* as belas-artes.
artefact ['ɑ:tɪfækt] *n* artefato *m*.
artery ['ɑ:tərɪ] *n* artéria *f*.
art gallery *n (commercial)* galeria *f*

de arte; *(public)* museu *m* de arte.
arthritis [ɑ:'θraɪtɪs] *n* artrite *f*.
artichoke ['ɑ:tɪtʃəʊk] *n* alcachofra *f*.
article ['ɑ:tɪkl] *n* artigo *m*.
articulate [ɑ:'tɪkjʊlət] *adj* eloquente.
articulated lorry [ɑ:'tɪkjʊleɪtɪd-] *n (Brit)* jamanta *f (Br)*, camião *m* articulado *(Port)*.
artificial [ˌɑ:tɪ'fɪʃl] *adj* artificial.
artillery [ɑ:'tɪlərɪ] *n (guns)* artilharia *f*.
artist ['ɑ:tɪst] *n (painter)* pintor *m (-ra f)*; *(performer)* artista *mf*.
artistic [ɑ:'tɪstɪk] *adj* artístico(-ca).
arts centre *n* centro *m* cultural.
arty ['ɑ:tɪ] *adj (pej)* com pretensões artísticas.
as [unstressed əz, stressed æz] *adv (in comparisons)*: ~ ... ~ tão ... como; **he's ~ tall ~ I am** ele é tão alto quanto eu; **twice as big** ~ duas vezes maior do que; ~ **many** ~ tantos quantos (tantas quantas); ~ **much** ~ tanto quanto.
◆ *conj* **1.** *(referring to time)* quando; ~ **the plane was coming in to land** quando o avião ia aterrissar.
2. *(referring to manner)* como; **do ~ you like** faz como você quiser; ~ **expected** ... *(tal)* como era de esperar ....
3. *(introducing a statement)* como; ~ **you know** ... como você sabe ....
4. *(because)* porque, como.
5. *(in phrases)*: ~ **for** quanto a; ~ **from** a partir de; ~ **if** como se.
◆ *prep (referring to function, job)* como; **I work** ~ **a teacher** sou professora.
asap *(abbr of as soon as possible)* assim que possível.
ascent [ə'sent] *n (climb)* subida *f*.
ascertain [ˌæsə'teɪn] *vt* confirmar.
ascribe [ə'skraɪb] *vt*: **to ~ sthg to** atribuir algo a.
ash [æʃ] *n (from cigarette, fire)* cinza *f*; *(tree)* freixo *m*.
ashamed [ə'ʃeɪmd] *adj* envergonhado(-da); **to be ~ of** ter vergonha de; **to be ~ to do sthg** ter vergonha de fazer algo.
ashore [ə'ʃɔ:ʳ] *adv* em terra; **to go ~** desembarcar.
ashtray ['æʃtreɪ] *n* cinzeiro *m*.
Ash Wednesday *n* Quarta-feira *f* de Cinzas.
Asia [*Brit* 'eɪʃə, *Am* 'eɪʒə] *n* Ásia *f*.
Asian [*Brit* 'eɪʃn, *Am* 'eɪʒn] *adj* asiático(-ca) ◆ *n* asiático *m (-ca f)*.
aside [ə'saɪd] *adv (to one side)* para o

lado; **to move** ~ afastar-se.

ask [uːsk] vt *(person)* perguntar a; *(request)* pedir; *(invite)* convidar ♦ vi: **to ~ about sthg** *(enquire)* informar-se sobre algo; **to ~ sb about sthg** perguntar a alguém sobre algo; **to ~ sb sthg** perguntar algo a alguém; **to ~ sb to do sthg** pedir a alguém que faça algo; **to ~ sb for sthg** pedir algo a alguém; **to ~ a question** fazer uma pergunta.
⹂ **ask for** vt fus *(ask to talk to)* perguntar por; *(request)* pedir.

askance [əˈskæns] adv: **to look ~ at** olhar desaprovadoramente para.

asking price [ˈuːskɪŋ-] n preço m (pedido).

asleep [əˈsliːp] adj adormecido(-da); **to fall ~** adormecer.

asparagus [əˈspærəgəs] n aspargos *(Br)*, espargos mpl *(Port)*.

asparagus tips npl pontas fpl de aspargos.

aspect [ˈæspekt] n aspecto m.

aspiration [æspəˈreɪʃn] n aspiração f.

aspire [əˈspaɪəʳ] vi: **to ~ to** aspirar a.

aspirin [ˈæsprɪn] n aspirina f.

ass [æs] n *(animal)* asno m.

assailant [əˈseɪlənt] n agressor m (-ra f).

assassinate [əˈsæsɪneɪt] vt assasinar.

assassination [əˌsæsɪˈneɪʃn] n assassínio m, assassinato m.

assault [əˈsɔːlt] n agressão f ♦ vt agredir.

assemble [əˈsembl] vt *(bookcase, model)* montar ♦ vi reunir-se.

assembly [əˈsemblɪ] n *(at school)* reunião regular de alunos e professores.

assembly hall n *(at school)* sala f de reuniões.

assembly line n linha f de montagem.

assembly point n *(at airport, in shopping centre)* ponto m de encontro.

assent [əˈsent] n *(agreement)* aprovação f ♦ vi: **to ~ to sthg** aprovar algo.

assert [əˈsɜːt] vt *(fact, innocence)* afirmar; *(authority)* impor; **to ~ o.s.** impor-se.

assertive [əˈsɜːtɪv] adj firme.

assess [əˈses] vt avaliar.

assessment [əˈsesmənt] n avaliação f.

asset [ˈæset] n *(valuable person, thing)* elemento m valioso.
⹂ **assets** npl bens mpl.

assign [əˈsaɪn] vt: **to ~ sthg to sb** *(give)* ceder algo a alguém; **to ~ sb to**

sthg *(designate)* nomear alguém para algo.

assignment [əˈsaɪnmənt] n *(task)* tarefa f; *(SCH)* trabalho m.

assimilate [əˈsɪmɪleɪt] vt *(learn)* assimilar; *(integrate)*: **to ~ sb (into sthg)** integrar alguém (em algo).

assist [əˈsɪst] vt ajudar.

assistance [əˈsɪstəns] n ajuda f; **to be of ~ (to sb)** ajudar (alguém).

assistant [əˈsɪstənt] n assistente mf, ajudante mf.

associate [n əˈsəʊʃɪət, vb əˈsəʊʃɪeɪt] n *(colleague)* colega mf; *(partner)* sócio m (-cia f) ♦ vt: **to ~ sb/sthg with** associar alguém/algo com OR a; **to be ~d with** *(attitude, person)* estar associado a.

association [əˌsəʊsɪˈeɪʃn] n associação f.

assorted [əˈsɔːtɪd] adj variado(-da).

assortment [əˈsɔːtmənt] n sortimento m *(Br)*, sortido m *(Port)*.

assume [əˈsjuːm] vt *(suppose)* supor; *(control, responsibility)* assumir.

assumption [əˈsʌmpʃn] n *(supposition)* suposição f.

assurance [əˈʃʊərəns] n *(promise)* garantia f; *(insurance)* seguro m.

assure [əˈʃʊəʳ] vt assegurar; **to ~ sb (that)** ... assegurar a alguém que ....

assured [əˈʃʊəd] adj *(confident)* seguro(-ra).

asterisk [ˈæstərɪsk] n asterisco m.

astern [əˈstɜːn] adv na popa.

asthma [ˈæsmə] n asma f.

asthmatic [æsˈmætɪk] adj asmático (-ca).

astonish [əˈstɒnɪʃ] vt surpreender.

astonished [əˈstɒnɪʃt] adj espantado(-da), surpreso(-sa).

astonishing [əˈstɒnɪʃɪŋ] adj espantoso(-osa), surpreendente.

astonishment [əˈstɒnɪʃmənt] n espanto m, surpresa f.

astound [əˈstaʊnd] vt surpreender.

astray [əˈstreɪ] adv: **to go ~** extraviar-se.

astrology [əˈstrɒlədʒɪ] n astrologia f.

astronaut [ˈæstrənɔːt] n astronauta mf.

astronomical [æstrəˈnɒmɪkl] adj *(inf: very large)* astronômico(-ca).

astronomy [əˈstrɒnəmɪ] n astronomia f.

astute [əˈstjuːt] adj astuto(-ta).

asylum [əˈsaɪləm] n *(POL)* asilo m;

(mental hospital) manicômio *m*.
at [unstressed ət, stressed æt] *prep* **1.**
(indicating place, position) em; ~ **home**
em casa; ~ **the hotel** no hotel; ~ **my
mother's** na casa da minha mãe; ~
school na escola.
2. *(indicating direction)* para; **he threw a
plate** ~ **the wall** ele atirou um prato
na parede; **to look** ~ olhar para.
3. *(indicating time)*: ~ **nine o'clock** às
nove horas; ~ **night** à noite; ~
Christmas no Natal.
4. *(indicating rate, level, speed)* a; **it
works out** ~ **£5 each** sai a 5 libras cada
um; ~ **60 km/h** a 60 km/h.
5. *(indicating activity)* a; **to be** ~ **lunch**
estar almoçando; **to be good/bad** ~
sthg ser bom/mau em algo.
6. *(indicating cause)* com.
ate [Brit et, Am eit] *pt* → **eat**.
atheist ['eiθiist] *n* ateu *m* (atéia *f*).
athlete ['æθliːt] *n* atleta *mf*.
athletics [æθ'letiks] *n* atletismo *m*.
Atlantic [ət'læntik] *n*: **the** ~ **(Ocean)**
o (oceano) Atlântico.
atlas ['ætləs] *n* atlas *m inv*.
atmosphere ['ætməsfiə'] *n* atmosfera *f*.
atom ['ætəm] *n* átomo *m*.
atom bomb *n* bomba *f* atômica.
atomic [ə'tɒmik] *adj* atômico(-ca).
atomic bomb = **atom bomb**.
atomizer ['ætəmaizə'] *n* atomizador
m, vaporizador *m*.
atone [ə'təun] *vi*: **to** ~ **for sthg** expiar
algo.
A to Z *n (map)* mapa *m* da cidade.
atrocious [ə'trəuʃəs] *adj* atroz.
atrocity [ə'trɒsəti] *n* atrocidade *f*.
attach [ə'tætʃ] *vt* juntar; **to** ~ **sthg to
sthg** juntar algo a algo.
attaché case [ə'tæʃei-] *n* pasta *f* (de
executivo).
attachment [ə'tætʃmənt] *n (device)*
acessório *m*.
attack [ə'tæk] *n* ataque *m* ◆ *vt* atacar.
attacker [ə'tækə'] *n* agressor *m* (-ra
f).
attain [ə'tein] *vt (fml)* alcançar.
attainment [ə'teinmənt] *n (of happiness, objective)* conquista *f*; *(skill)* aquisição *f*.
attempt [ə'tempt] *n* tentativa *f* ◆ *vt*
tentar; **to** ~ **to do sthg** tentar fazer algo.
attend [ə'tend] *vt (meeting, Mass)*

assistir a; *(school)* frequentar.
❑ **attend to** *vt fus (deal with)* atender a.
attendance [ə'tendəns] *n (people at
concert, match)* assistência *f*; *(at school)*
frequência *f*.
attendant [ə'tendənt] *n* empregado
m (-da *f*).
attention [ə'tenʃn] *n* atenção *f*; **to
pay** ~ **(to)** prestar atenção (a).
attentive [ə'tentiv] *adj (paying attention)* atento(-ta); *(politely helpful)* atencioso(-osa).
attic ['ætik] *n* sótão *m*.
attitude ['ætitjuːd] *n* atitude *f*.
attorney [ə'tɜːni] *n (Am)* advogado *m*
(-da *f*).
attract [ə'trækt] *vt* atrair; *(attention)*
chamar.
attraction [ə'trækʃn] *n* atração *f*;
(attractive feature) atrativo *m*.
attractive [ə'træktiv] *adj* atraente.
attribute [ə'tribjuːt] *vt*: **to** ~ **sthg to**
atribuir algo a.
attrition [ə'triʃn] *n* desgaste *m*.
aubergine ['əubəʒiːn] *n (Brit)* beringela *f*.
auburn ['ɔːbən] *adj* castanho-avermelhado(-da).
auction ['ɔːkʃn] *n* leilão *m*.
auctioneer [ɔːkʃə'niə'] *n* leiloeiro *m*
(-ra *f*).
audible ['ɔːdəbl] *adj* audível.
audience ['ɔːdiəns] *n* público *m*,
audiência *f*.
audio ['ɔːdiəu] *adj* áudio *(inv)*.
audio-visual *adj* audiovisual.
audit ['ɔːdit] *n* verificação *f* (oficial) de
contas ◆ *vt* verificar.
audition [ɔː'diʃn] *n* audição *f*.
auditor ['ɔːditə'] *n (of accounts)* técnico *m* (-ca *f*) de contas.
auditorium [ɔːdi'tɔːriəm] *n* auditório
m.
Aug. *abbr* = **August**.
augur ['ɔːgə'] *vi*: **to** ~ **well/badly** ser
bom/mau sinal.
August ['ɔːgəst] *n* Agosto *m*, →
September.
Auld Lang Syne [ɔːldlæŋ'sain] *n* cantiga tradicional escocesa cantada à meia-noite da véspera de Ano Novo cujo título
significa "os bons tempos de outrora".
aunt [ɑːnt] *n* tia *f*.
au pair [əu'peə'] *n* au pair *mf*.
aural ['ɔːrəl] *adj* auditivo(-va).

auspices [ˈɔːspɪsɪz] *npl*: **under the ~ of** sob os auspícios de.

auspicious [ɔːˈspɪʃəs] *adj* promissor (-ra).

austere [ɒˈstɪər] *adj* austero(-ra).

austerity [ɒˈsterətɪ] *n* austeridade *f*.

Australia [ɒˈstreɪlɪə] *n* Austrália *f*.

Australian [ɒˈstreɪlɪən] *adj* australiano(-na) ♦ *n* australiano *m* (-na *f*).

Austria [ˈɒstrɪə] *n* Áustria *f*.

Austrian [ˈɒstrɪən] *adj* austríaco(-ca) ♦ *n* austríaco *m* (-ca *f*).

authentic [ɔːˈθentɪk] *adj* autêntico (-ca).

author [ˈɔːθər] *n* (*of book, article*) autor *m* (-ra *f*); (*by profession*) escritor *m* (-ra *f*).

authoritarian [ɔːˌθɒrɪˈteərɪən] *adj* autoritário(-ria).

authoritative [ɔːˈθɒrɪtətɪv] *adj* (*person, voice*) autoritário(-ria); (*report*) autorizado(-da).

authority [ɔːˈθɒrətɪ] *n* autoridade *f*; **the authorities** as autoridades.

authorization [ˌɔːθəraɪˈzeɪʃn] *n* autorização *f*.

authorize [ˈɔːθəraɪz] *vt* autorizar; **to ~ sb to do sthg** autorizar alguém a fazer algo.

autistic [ɔːˈtɪstɪk] *adj* autista.

autobiography [ˌɔːtəbaɪˈɒgrəfɪ] *n* autobiografia *f*.

autocratic [ˌɔːtəˈkrætɪk] *adj* autocrático(-ca).

autograph [ˈɔːtəgrɑːf] *n* autógrafo *m*.

automatic [ˌɔːtəˈmætɪk] *adj* automático(-ca); (*fine*) imediato(-ta) ♦ *n* (*car*) carro *m* automático OR com direção assistida.

automatically [ˌɔːtəˈmætɪklɪ] *adv* automaticamente.

automobile [ˈɔːtəməbiːl] *n* (*Am*) automóvel *m*.

autonomy [ɔːˈtɒnəmɪ] *n* autonomia *f*.

autopsy [ˈɔːtɒpsɪ] *n* autópsia *f*.

autumn [ˈɔːtəm] *n* Outono *m*; **in (the) ~** no Outono.

auxiliary (verb) [ɔːgˈzɪljərɪ-] *n* verbo *m* auxiliar.

avail [əˈveɪl] *n*: **to no ~** em vão.

available [əˈveɪləbl] *adj* disponível.

avalanche [ˈævəlɑːnʃ] *n* avalanche *f*.

avarice [ˈævərɪs] *n* avareza *f*.

Ave. (*abbr of avenue*) Av.

avenge [əˈvendʒ] *vt* vingar, vingar-se de.

avenue [ˈævənjuː] *n* avenida *f*.

average [ˈævərɪdʒ] *adj* médio(-dia) ♦ *n* média *f*; **on ~** em média.

aversion [əˈvɜːʃn] *n* aversão *f*.

avert [əˈvɜːt] *vt* (*problem, accident*) evitar; (*eyes, glance*) desviar.

aviation [ˌeɪvɪˈeɪʃn] *n* aviação *f*.

avid [ˈævɪd] *adj* ávido(-da).

avocado [ˌævəˈkɑːdəʊ] (*pl* -s OR -es) *n*: **~ (pear)** pêra *f* abacate.

avoid [əˈvɔɪd] *vt* evitar; **to ~ doing sthg** evitar fazer algo.

await [əˈweɪt] *vt* esperar, aguardar.

awake [əˈweɪk] (*pt* awoke, *pp* awoken) *adj* acordado(-da) ♦ *vi* acordar.

award [əˈwɔːd] *n* (*prize*) prêmio *m* ♦ *vt*: **to ~ sb sthg** (*prize*) atribuir algo a alguém; (*damages, compensation*) adjudicar algo a alguém.

aware [əˈweər] *adj* consciente; **to be ~ of** estar consciente de.

awareness [əˈweənɪs] *n* consciência *f*.

awash [əˈwɒʃ] *adj*: **~ (with)** (*fig: with letters, tourists*) inundado(-da) de.

away [əˈweɪ] *adv* (*go*) embora; (*look, turn*) para outro lado; **to be ~** (*not at home, in office*) não estar; **it's 10 miles ~ (from here)** fica a 10 milhas (daqui); **it's two weeks ~** é daqui a duas semanas; **to go ~ on holiday** ir de férias; **to put sthg ~** guardar algo; **to take sthg ~ (from sb)** tirar algo (de alguém); **to walk/drive ~** afastar-se; **far ~** longe.

awe [ɔː] *n* respeito *m* (*acompanhado de receio*); **to be in ~ of sb** estar impressionado com alguém.

awesome [ˈɔːsəm] *adj* incrível.

awful [ˈɔːfəl] *adj* (*very bad*) horrível; (*very great*) imenso(-sa); **I feel ~** estou me sentindo muito mal; **how ~!** que horror!

awfully [ˈɔːflɪ] *adv* (*very*) muitíssimo.

awkward [ˈɔːkwəd] *adj* (*position*) incômodo(-da); (*shape, size*) pouco prático(-ca); (*situation, question, task*) embaraçoso(-osa); (*movement*) desajeitado(-da); (*time*) inoportuno(na).

awning [ˈɔːnɪŋ] *n* toldo *m*.

awoke [əˈwəʊk] *pt* → awake.

awoken [əˈwəʊkən] *pp* → awake.

awry [əˈraɪ] *adj* torto (torta) ♦ *adv*: **to go ~** dar errado.

axe [æks] *n* machado *m*.

axis [ˈæksɪs] (*pl* axes [ˈæksiːz]) *n* eixo *m*.

axle [ˈæksl] *n* eixo *m*.

Azores [əˈzɔːz] *npl*: **the ~** os Açores.

B

BA *abbr* = **Bachelor of Arts**.
babble ['bæbl] *vi (person)* tagarelar.
baby ['beɪbɪ] *n* bebê *m*; **to have a ~** ter um bebê; **~ sweetcorn** mini-milho *m*.
baby carriage *n (Am)* carrinho *m* de bebê.
baby food *n* comida *f* de bebê.
baby-sit *vi* tomar conta de crianças.
baby-sitter [-'sɪtər] *n* baby-sitter *f*.
baby wipe *n* toalhita *f* para bebê.
bachelor ['bætʃələr] *n* homem *m* solteiro.
Bachelor of Arts *n* = *(titular de uma) licenciatura em letras.*
Bachelor of Science *n* = *(titular de uma) licenciatura em ciências.*
back [bæk] *adv (towards the back)* para trás ♦ *n* costas *fpl; (of car)* parte *f* de trás; *(of room)* fundo *m* ♦ *adj (seat, wheels)* traseiro(-ra) ♦ *vi (car, driver)* recuar ♦ *vt (support)* apoiar; **to call ~** *(telephone)* voltar a telefonar; **to give sthg ~** devolver algo; **to stand ~** afastar-se; **to write ~** responder (a carta); **at the ~ of** na traseira de; **in ~ of** *(Am)* na traseira de; **~ to front** de trás para a frente.
⟂ **back up** *vt sep (support)* apoiar ♦ *vi (car, driver)* dar marcha à ré.
backache ['bækeɪk] *n* dor *f* nas costas.
backbencher [,bæk'bentʃər] *n (Brit: POL)* deputado do governo ou oposição sem cargo.
backbone ['bækbəʊn] *n* coluna *f* vertebral.
backcloth ['bækklɒθ] *n (Brit)* = **backdrop**.
backdate [,bæk'deɪt] *vt*: **a pay rise ~d to June** um aumento de salário com efeito retroativo desde junho.
back door *n* porta *f* traseira.

backdrop ['bækdrɒp] *n* pano *m* de fundo.
backfire [,bæk'faɪər] *vi (car)* dar estouros.
backgammon [,bæk'gæmən] *n* gamão *m*.
background ['bækgraʊnd] *n* cenário *m; (of person)* background *m*.
backhand ['bækhænd] *n* esquerda *f*.
backing ['bækɪŋ] *n (support)* apoio *m; (lining)* reforço *m*.
backlash ['bæklæʃ] *n (reaction)* contra-ataque *m*, reação *f* violenta.
backlog ['bæklɒg] *n* acumulação *f*.
back number *n* número *m* atrasado.
backpack ['bækpæk] *n* mochila *f*.
backpacker ['bækpækər] *n* turista com orçamento reduzido que viaja de mochila e saco de dormir nas costas.
back pay *n* salário *m* em atraso.
back seat *n* banco *m* traseiro.
backside [,bæk'saɪd] *n (inf)* traseiro *m*.
backstage [,bæk'steɪdʒ] *adv (be, stay)* nos bastidores; *(go)* para os bastidores.
back street *n* ruela *f*.
backstroke ['bækstrəʊk] *n* costas *fpl (em natação).*
backup ['bækʌp] *adj (plan, team)* de reserva ♦ *n (support)* apoio *m*.
backward ['bækwəd] *adj (look, movement)* para trás; *(person, country)* atrasado(-da).
backwards ['bækwədz] *adv (move, look)* para trás; *(the wrong way round)* ao contrário.
backyard [,bæk'jɑːd] *n (Brit)* quintal *m*.
bacon ['beɪkən] *n* bacon *m*, toucinho *m*; **~ and eggs** bacon frito e ovos estrelados.
bacteria [bæk'tɪərɪə] *npl* bactérias *fpl*.

bad [bæd] (compar **worse**, superl **worst**) adj mau (má); (serious) grave; (poor, weak) fraco(-ca); (rotten, off) estragado(-da); **to have a ~ back/leg** ter um problema nas costas/na perna; **don't eat that – it's ~ for you** não come isso que vai lhe fazer mal; **not ~** nada mau (má).

badge [bædʒ] n crachá m.

badger [ˈbædʒəʳ] n texugo m.

badly [ˈbædlɪ] (compar **worse**, superl **worst**) adv (poorly) mal; (seriously) gravemente; (very much) imenso.

badly-off adj (poor) pobre, com problemas econômicos.

badly paid [-peɪd] adj mal pago(-ga).

bad-mannered [-ˈmænəd] adj mal-educado(-da).

badminton [ˈbædmɪntən] n badminton m.

bad-tempered [-ˈtempəd] adj com mau gênio.

baffle [ˈbæfl] vt desorientar, confundir.

bag [bæg] n (of paper, plastic) saco m, saca f; (handbag) bolsa f; (suitcase) mala f; **a ~ of crisps** um pacote de batatas fritas.

bagel [ˈbeɪgəl] n pequeno pão em forma de anel.

baggage [ˈbægɪdʒ] n bagagem f.

baggage allowance n peso m limite (de bagagem).

baggage reclaim n recolhimento m de bagagem.

baggage trolley n carrinho m.

baggy [ˈbægɪ] adj largo(-ga).

bagpipes [ˈbægpaɪps] npl gaita-de-foles f.

Bahamas [bəˈhuːməz] npl: **the ~** as Baamas.

bail [beɪl] n fiança f.

bailiff [ˈbeɪlɪf] n oficial mf de justiça.

bait [beɪt] n isca f.

bake [beɪk] vt (cake, souffle) cozer (em forno); (potatoes) assar ♦ n (CULIN) gratinado m.

baked [beɪkt] adj (cake, souffle) cozido(-da); (potatoes) assado(-da).

baked Alaska [-əˈlæskə] n sobremesa de bolo e sorvete coberto de merengue, que se assa no forno durante breves minutos.

baked beans npl feijão m cozido com molho de tomate.

baked potato n batata f assada com casca.

baker [ˈbeɪkəʳ] n padeiro m (-ra f); **~'s** (shop) padaria f.

bakery [ˈbeɪkərɪ] n padaria f.

Bakewell tart [ˈbeɪkwel-] n torta de massa esfarelada recheada com geléia, coberta com uma mistura de ovos, manteiga, açúcar e amêndoas raladas.

baking [ˈbeɪkɪŋ] n (process) cozimento m.

balaclava (helmet) [bæləˈklɑːvə-] n (Brit) passa-montanhas m inv.

balance [ˈbæləns] n (of person) equilíbrio m; (of bank account) saldo m; (remainder) resto m ♦ vt (object) equilibrar.

balanced diet [ˈbælənst-] n dieta f equilibrada.

balcony [ˈbælkənɪ] n (of house) varanda f; (of theatre) balcão m.

bald [bɔːld] adj calvo(-va), careca.

bale [beɪl] n fardo m.

Balkans [ˈbɔːlkənz] npl: **the ~** os Balcãs.

Balkan States [ˈbɔːlkən-] = **Balkans**.

ball [bɔːl] n bola f; (of wool, string) novelo m; (dance) baile m; **on the ~** (fig) a par de tudo.

ballad [ˈbæləd] n balada f.

ballast [ˈbæləst] n lastro m.

ball bearing n rolamento m de esferas.

ball boy n apanha-bolas m inv.

ballerina [ˌbæləˈriːnə] n bailarina f.

ballet [ˈbæleɪ] n bailado m, ballet m, balé m.

ballet dancer n bailarino m (-na f).

ball game n (Am: baseball match) jogo m de basebol; (inf: situation): **this is a whole new ~** isto já é outra história.

balloon [bəˈluːn] n (at party etc) balão m, bola f de soprar.

ballot [ˈbælət] n votação f.

ballpoint pen [ˈbɔːlpɔɪnt-] n esferográfica f.

ballroom [ˈbɔːlrʊm] n salão m de baile.

ballroom dancing n dança f de salão.

balsa(wood) [ˈbɔːlsə(wʊd)] n balsa f.

Baltic [ˈbɔːltɪk] adj báltico(-ca) ♦ n: **the ~ (Sea)** o (mar) Báltico.

Baltic Republic n: **the ~s** as Repúblicas Bálticas.

bamboo [bæmˈbuː] n bambú m.

bamboo shoots npl brotos mpl de bambú.

bamboozle [bæm'buːzl] *vt (inf)* enrolar, passar a perna em.

ban [bæn] *n* proibição *f* ◆ *vt* proibir; **to ~ sb from doing sthg** proibir alguém de fazer algo.

banana [bə'nuːnə] *n* banana *f*.

banana split *n* banana split *m*, *banana cortada ao meio com sorvete, creme e calda de chocolate.*

band [bænd] *n (musical group)* banda *f*; *(strip of paper)* tira *f* de papel; *(rubber)* elástico *m*.

bandage ['bændɪdʒ] *n* atadura *f (Br)*, ligadura *f (Port)* ◆ *vt* ligar.

Band-Aid® ['bændeɪd] *n* esparadrapo *m (Br)*, penso *m* rápido *(Port)*.

B and B *abbr* = **bed and breakfast**.

bandit ['bændɪt] *n* bandido *m* (-da *f*).

bandstand ['bændstænd] *n* coreto *m*.

bandy ['bændɪ] *adj* com as pernas tortas.

⏘ **bandy about** *vt sep* usar a torto e a direito.

bandy-legged [-,legd] *adj* = **bandy**.

bang [bæŋ] *n (loud noise)* estrondo *m* ◆ *vt (hit loudly)* bater em; *(shut loudly, injure)* bater com.

banger ['bæŋər] *n (Brit: inf: sausage)* salsicha *f*; **~s and mash** salsichas com puré de batata.

bangle ['bæŋgl] *n* pulseira *f*.

bangs [bæŋz] *npl (Am)* franja *f*.

banish ['bænɪʃ] *vt* banir.

banister ['bænɪstər] *n* corrimão *m*.

banjo ['bændʒəʊ] *(pl* **-s** OR **-es)** *n* banjo *m*.

bank [bæŋk] *n (for money)* banco *m*; *(of river, lake)* margem *f*; *(slope)* monte *m* (pequeno).

bank account *n* conta *f* bancária.

bank book *n* caderneta *f* bancária.

bank charges *npl* encargos *mpl* bancários *(Br)*, comissões *fpl* bancárias *(Port)*.

bank clerk *n* bancário *m* (-ria *f*) *(Br)*, empregado *m* bancário (empregada *f* bancária) *(Port)*.

bank draft *n* saque *m* bancário *(Br)*, transferência *f* bancária *(Port)*.

banker ['bæŋkər] *n* banqueiro *m* (-ra *f*).

banker's card *n* cartão bancário que é necessário apresentar, como garantia, sempre que se paga por cheque.

bank holiday *n (Brit)* feriado *m*.

bank manager *n* diretor *m* (-ra *f*) de banco.

bank note *n* nota *f* (de banco).

bankrupt ['bæŋkrʌpt] *adj* falido(-da).

bankruptcy ['bæŋkrəptsɪ] *n* falência *f*.

bank statement *n* extrato *m* de conta.

banner ['bænər] *n* cartaz *m*.

bannister ['bænɪstər] = **banister**.

banquet ['bæŋkwɪt] *n (formal dinner)* banquete *m*; *(at Indian restaurant etc)* menu *m* fixo *(para várias pessoas)*.

banter ['bæntər] *n* piadas *fpl*.

bap [bæp] *n (Brit)* pãozinho *m* redondo *(Br)*, papo-seco *m (Port)*.

baptism ['bæptɪzm] *n* batismo *m*.

Baptist ['bæptɪst] *n* batista *mf*.

baptize [*Brit* bæp'taɪz, *Am* 'bæptaɪz] *vt* batizar.

bar [buːr] *n (pub, in hotel)* bar *m*; *(counter in pub)* balcão *m*; *(of metal, soap)* barra *f*; *(of wood)* tranca *f*; *(of chocolate)* barra *f (Br)*, tablete *m* ou *f (Port)* ◆ *vt (obstruct)* bloquear.

barbaric [buː'bærɪk] *adj* bárbaro(-ra).

barbecue ['buːbɪkjuː] *n (apparatus)* churrasqueira *f (Br)*, grelhador *m (Port)*; *(event)* churrasco *m* ◆ *vt* assar (na churrasqueira) *(Br)*, assar (no churrasco) *(Port)*.

barbecue sauce *n* molho *m* para churrasco.

barbed wire [buːbd-] *n* arame *m* farpado.

barber ['buːbər] *n* barbeiro *m*; **~'s** *(shop)* barbearia *f*.

barbiturate [buː'bɪtjʊrət] *n* barbitúrio *m*.

bar code *n* código *m* de barras.

bare [beər] *adj (feet)* descalço(-ça); *(head)* descoberto(-ta); *(arms, legs)* ao léu; *(room, cupboard)* vazio(-zia); **the ~ minimum** o mínimo dos mínimos.

bareback ['beəbæk] *adv* em pêlo, sem arreios.

barefaced ['beəfeɪst] *adj* descarado (-da).

barefoot [,beə'fut] *adv* descalço(-ça).

barely ['beəlɪ] *adv* mal.

bargain ['buːgɪn] *n (agreement)* acordo *m*; *(cheap buy)* pechincha *f* ◆ *vi (haggle)* regatear.

⏘ **bargain for** *vt fus* contar com, esperar.

bargain basement *n* seção *f* de saldos.

barge [bɑːdʒ] n barca f.
◻ **barge in** vi: **to ~ in on sb** interromper alguém.
baritone ['bærɪtəʊn] n barítono m.
bark [bɑːk] n (of tree) casca f ◆ vi latir.
barley ['bɑːlɪ] n cevada f.
barley sugar n (Brit) = bala f (Br), rebuçado m (Port).
barley water n (Brit) refrigerante feito com água e grãos de cevada, açúcar e aromas de fruta.
barmaid ['bɑːmeɪd] n garçonete f (Br), empregada f de bar (Port).
barman ['bɑːmən] (pl **-men** [-mən]) n barman m.
bar meal n comida ligeira e rápida servida em bares.
barn [bɑːn] n celeiro m.
barometer [bəˈrɒmɪtəʳ] n barômetro m.
baron ['bærən] n barão m.
baroness ['bærənɪs] n baronesa f.
baroque [bəˈrɒk] adj barroco(-ca).
barracks ['bærəks] npl quartel m.
barrage ['bærɑːʒ] n (of questions, criticism) chuva f, avalanche f.
barrel ['bærəl] n (of beer, wine, oil) barril m; (of gun) cano m.
barren ['bærən] adj (land, soil) estéril.
barricade [ˌbærɪˈkeɪd] n barricada f.
barrier ['bærɪəʳ] n barreira f.
barring ['bɑːrɪŋ] prep: **~ accidents** excepto se houver acidentes.
barrister ['bærɪstəʳ] n (Brit) advogado m (-da f) (de tribunais superiores).
barrow ['bærəʊ] n (market stall) carro m de mão (para venda de produtos nas feiras).
bartender ['bɑːtendəʳ] n (Am) garçon m (Br), empregado m (-da f) de bar (Port).
barter ['bɑːtəʳ] vi negociar.
base [beɪs] n base f ◆ vt: **to ~ sthg on** basear algo em; **to be ~d in** (located) estar sediado em.
baseball ['beɪsbɔːl] n basebol m.
baseball cap n boné m de basebol.
basement ['beɪsmənt] n (in house) porão m (Br), cave f (Port).
bases ['beɪsiːz] pl → **basis**.
bash [bæʃ] vt (inf) bater com.
bashful ['bæʃfʊl] adj acanhado(-da), tímido(-da).
basic ['beɪsɪk] adj (fundamental) bási-

co(-ca); (accommodation, meal) simples (inv) ◆ npl: **the ~s** os princípios básicos.
basically ['beɪsɪklɪ] adv no fundo.
basil ['bæzl] n manjericão m.
basin ['beɪsn] n (washbasin) pia f, lavatório m (Port); (bowl) tigela f, taça f.
basis ['beɪsɪs] (pl **bases**) n base f; **on a weekly ~** semanalmente; **on the ~ of** tendo em conta.
bask [bɑːsk] vi (sunbathe): **to ~ in the sun** torrar no sol, apanhar sol.
basket ['bɑːskɪt] n cesto m, cesta f.
basketball ['bɑːskɪtbɔːl] n (game) basquetebol m.
basmati rice [bəzˈmætɪ-] n arroz fino e aromático usado em muitos pratos indianos.
bass[1] [beɪs] n (singer) baixo m.
bass[2] [bæs] n (fish) robalo m.
bass drum [beɪs-] n bombo m.
bass (guitar) [beɪs-] n baixo m.
bassoon [bəˈsuːn] n fagote m.
bastard ['bɑːstəd] n (vulg) filho-da-puta m (filha da-puta f), cabrão m (-brona f) (Port).
bastion ['bæstɪən] n (fig) bastião m, baluarte m.
bat [bæt] n (in cricket, baseball) pá f; (in table tennis) raquete f; (animal) morcego m.
batch [bætʃ] n lote m.
bath [bɑːθ] n banho m ◆ vt dar banho em; **to have a ~** tomar banho.
◻ **baths** npl (Brit: public swimming pool) piscina f municipal.
bathe [beɪð] vi tomar banho.
bathing ['beɪðɪŋ] n (Brit) banho m.
bathing cap n touca f de banho.
bathing costume n traje m de banho (Br), fato m de banho (Port).
bathrobe ['bɑːθrəʊb] n roupão m.
bathroom ['bɑːθrʊm] n banheiro m (Br), casa f de banho (Port).
bathroom cabinet n armário m de banheiro.
bath towel n toalha f de banho.
bathtub ['bɑːθtʌb] n banheira f.
baton ['bætən] n (of conductor) batuta f; (truncheon) cassetete m.
batsman ['bætsmən] (pl **-men** [-mən]) n (in cricket) batedor m.
batter ['bætəʳ] n (CULIN) massa mole para panquecas e frituras, polme m (Port) ◆ vt (wife, child) espancar.

battered ['bætəd] *adj (CULIN)* frito em massa mole.

battery ['bætəri] *n (for radio, torch etc)* pilha *f; (for car)* bateria *f.*

battery charger [-.tʃɑːdʒəʳ] *n* aparelho *m* para recarregar pilhas/baterias.

battle ['bætl] *n (in war)* batalha *f; (struggle)* luta *f.*

battlefield ['bætlfiːld] *n* campo *m* de batalha.

battlements ['bætlmənts] *npl* ameias *fpl.*

battleship ['bætlʃɪp] *n* navio *m* de guerra.

bauble ['bɔːbl] *n* buginganga *f.*

bawl [bɔːl] *vt (shout)* bradar ♦ *vi* berrar.

bay [beɪ] *n (on coast)* baía *f; (for parking)* lugar *m* para estacionamento.

bay leaf *n* folha *f* de louro.

bay window *n* janela *f* saliente.

bazaar [bəˈzɑːʳ] *n* bazar *m.*

B & B *abbr* = **bed and breakfast.**

BBC *(abbr of British Broadcasting Corporation)* BBC *f, empresa estatal britânica de radiodifusão.*

BC *(abbr of before Christ)* a.C.

be [biː] *(pt* was, were, *pp* been) *vi* 1. *(exist)* ser; **there is/are** há; **are there any shops near here?** há lojas perto daqui?
2. *(describing quality, permanent condition)* ser; **he's a doctor** ele é médico; **I'm British** sou britânico; **the hotel is near the airport** o hotel é OR fica perto do aeroporto.
3. *(describing state, temporary condition)* estar; **will you ~ in the office tomorrow?** você vai estar no escritório amanhã?; **I'll ~ there at six o'clock** estarei lá às seis horas; **I'm hot/cold** estou com calor/frio, tenho calor/frio.
4. *(referring to movement)*: **has the postman been?** o correio já passou?; **have you ever been to Ireland?** você já esteve na Irlanda?; **I'll ~ there in ten minutes** estarei lá em dez minutos.
5. *(occur)* ser; **the final is in June** a final é em junho.
6. *(referring to health)* estar; **how are you?** como vai você?; **I'm fine** estou bem; **she's ill** ela está doente.
7. *(referring to age)*: **how old are you?** que idade você tem?; **I'm 14 (years old)** tenho 14 anos.

8. *(referring to cost)* ser; **how much is it?** quanto é?; **it's £10** são 10 libras.
9. *(referring to time, dates)* ser; **what time is it?** que horas são?; **it's ten o'clock** são dez horas.
10. *(referring to measurement)* ter; **I'm 60 kilos** tenho 60 quilos; **he is 6 feet tall** ele tem 2 metros de altura; **it's 10 metres wide/long** tem 10 metros de largura/comprimento.
11. *(referring to weather)* estar; **it's hot/cold** está calor/frio; **it's windy/sunny** está ventando/sol; **it's going to be nice today** vai fazer bom tempo hoje.
♦ *aux vb* 1. *(forming continuous tense)* estar; **I'm learning French** estou aprendendo francês *(Br)*, estou a aprender francês *(Port)*; **we've been visiting the museum** tivemos visitando o museu *(Br)*, andámos a visitar o museu *(Port)*.
2. *(forming passive)* ser; **she was given a rise** ela foi aumentada; **the flight was delayed** o vôo atrasou; **there are no tables to ~ had** não há mesas vagas.
3. *(with infinitive to express order)*: **you are not to leave until I say so** você só pode sair quando eu disser; **new arrivals are to wait in reception** os recém-chegados têm que esperar na recepção; **all rooms are to ~ vacated by 10 a.m.** todos os quartos têm que ser desocupados antes das 10 horas da manhã.
4. *(with infinitive to express future tense)*: **the race is to start at noon** a corrida começará ao meio-dia.
5. *(in tag questions)*: **he's very tall, isn't he?** ele é muito alto, não é?; **it's cold, isn't it?** está frio, não está?

beach [biːtʃ] *n* praia *f.*

beacon ['biːkən] *n (warning fire)* fogueira *f* (de aviso); *(lighthouse)* farol *m; (radio beacon)* radiofarol *m.*

bead [biːd] *n* conta *f.*

beagle ['biːgl] *n* bigle *m.*

beak [biːk] *n* bico *m.*

beaker ['biːkəʳ] *n* copo *m.*

beam [biːm] *n (of light)* raio *m; (of wood)* trave *f; (of concrete)* viga *f* ♦ *vi (smile)* sorrir alegremente.

bean [biːn] *n (haricot)* feijão *m; (pod)* feijão *m* verde; *(of coffee)* grão *m.*

beanbag ['biːnbæg] *n* espécie de pufe mole estofado com esferovite.

bean curd [-kɜːd] *n* pasta de soja em

23

23 **began**

cubos muito usada na cozinha chinesa e vegetariana.

beansprouts ['biːnspraʊts] *npl* brotos *mpl* de feijão.

bear [beəʳ] (*pt* bore, *pp* borne) *n (animal)* urso *m* ◆ *vt* suportar, aguentar; **to ~ left/right** virar à esquerda/direita.

bearable ['beərəbl] *adj* suportável.

beard [bɪəd] *n* barba *f*.

bearer ['beərəʳ] *n (of cheque, passport)* portador *m* (-ra *f*).

bearing ['beərɪŋ] *n (relevance)* relevância *f*; **to get one's ~s** orientar-se.

beast [biːst] *n (animal)* animal *m*.

beastly ['biːstlɪ] *adj* horrível.

beat [biːt] (*pt* beat, *pp* beaten ['biːtn]) *n (of heart, pulse)* pulsação *f*; *(MUS)* ritmo *m* ◆ *vt (defeat)* derrotar, vencer; *(hit)* bater em, agredir; *(eggs, cream)* bater.

❏ **beat down** *vi (sun)* bater; *(rain)* cair ◆ *vt sep*: **I ~ him down to £15** consegui que ele baixasse o preço para 15 libras.

❏ **beat up** *vt sep* espancar.

beating ['biːtɪŋ] *n (hitting)* surra *f*, espancamento *m*; *(defeat)* derrota *f*.

beautiful ['bjuːtɪful] *adj (attractive)* lindo(-da); *(very good)* magnífico(-ca).

beautifully ['bjuːtəflɪ] *adv* lindamente.

beauty ['bjuːtɪ] *n* beleza *f*.

beauty parlour [-ˈpaːləʳ] *n* instituto *m* de beleza.

beauty salon = beauty parlour.

beauty spot *n (place)* local *m* de excepcional beleza.

beaver ['biːvəʳ] *n* castor *m*.

became [bɪˈkeɪm] *pt* → become.

because [bɪˈkɒz] *conj* porque; **~ of** por causa de.

beckon ['bekən] *vi*: **to ~ (to)** acenar (a).

become [bɪˈkʌm] (*pt* became, *pp* become) *vi* tornar-se; **what became of him?** que foi feito dele?

bed [bed] *n (for sleeping in)* cama *f*; *(of river)* leito *m*; *(of sea)* fundo *m*; *(CULIN)* base *f*, camada *f*; *(in garden)* canteiro *m*; **in ~** na cama; **to get out of ~** levantar-se (da cama); **to go to ~** ir para a cama; **to go to ~ with sb** ir para a cama com alguém; **to make the ~** fazer a cama.

bed and breakfast *n (Brit)* casa privada onde se oferece dormida e café da manhã a preços acessíveis.

bedclothes ['bedkləʊðz] *npl* roupa *f* de cama.

bedding ['bedɪŋ] *n* roupa *f* de cama.

bed linen *n* lençóis *mpl* (e fronhas).

bedraggled [bɪˈdrægld] *adj* molhado e sujo (molhada e suja).

bedridden ['bedrɪdn] *adj* acamado (-da).

bedroom ['bedrʊm] *n* quarto *m*.

bedside ['bedsaɪd] *n* cabeceira *f* (de cama).

bedside table ['bedsaɪd-] *n* mesinha *f* de cabeceira.

bedsit ['bedsɪt] *n (Brit)* quarto alugado com pia e área para cozinhar.

bedspread ['bedspred] *n* colcha *f*.

bedtime ['bedtaɪm] *n* hora *f* de dormir.

bee [biː] *n* abelha *f*.

beech [biːtʃ] *n* faia *f*.

beef [biːf] *n* carne *f* de vaca; **~ Wellington** *lombo de vaca envolto em massa folhada e servido em fatias*.

beefburger ['biːfˌbɜːgəʳ] *n* hambúrger *m*.

Beefeater ['biːfˌiːtəʳ] *n* alabardeiro *m* (da Torre de Londres).

beefsteak ['biːfsteɪk] *n* bife *m*.

beehive ['biːhaɪv] *n* colméia *f*.

been [biːn] *pp* → be.

beer [bɪəʳ] *n* cerveja *f*; **to have a couple of ~s** beber OR tomar umas cervejas.

beer garden *n* bar *m* ao ar livre *(Br)*, esplanada *f (Port)*.

beer mat *n* descanso *m* para copos.

beet [biːt] *n (sugar beet)* beterraba *m*.

beetle ['biːtl] *n* escaravelho *m*.

beetroot ['biːtruːt] *n* beterraba *f*.

before [bɪˈfɔːʳ] *adv* antes ◆ *prep* antes de; *(fml: in front of)* em frente de ◆ *conj* antes de; **~ you leave** antes de partir; **the day ~** o dia anterior; **the week ~ last** há duas semanas.

beforehand [bɪˈfɔːhænd] *adv* de antemão.

befriend [bɪˈfrend] *vt* fazer amizade com.

beg [beg] *vi* pedir ◆ *vt*: **to ~ sb to do sthg** implorar a alguém que faça algo; **to ~ for sthg** *(for money, food)* pedir algo.

began [bɪˈgæn] *pt* → begin.

beggar [begɔ'] *n* mendigo *m* (-ga *f*).

begin [bɪ'gɪn] (*pt* began, *pp* begun) *vt* & *vi* começar; **to ~ doing** OR **to do sthg** começar a fazer algo; **to ~ by doing sthg** começar por fazer algo; **to ~ with** (*firstly*) para começar.

beginner [bɪ'gɪnə'] *n* principiante *mf*.

beginning [bɪ'gɪnɪŋ] *n* começo *m*.

begrudge [bɪ'grʌdʒ] *vt*: **to ~ sb sthg** (*envy*) enviar algo a alguém; **to ~ doing sthg** (*do unwillingly*) detestar fazer algo.

begun [bɪ'gʌn] *pp* → begin.

behalf [bɪ'hɑːf] *n*: **on ~ of** em nome de.

behave [bɪ'heɪv] *vi* comportar-se; **to ~ (o.s.)** (*be good*) comportar-se.

behavior [bɪ'heɪvjər] (*Am*) = behaviour.

behaviour [bɪ'heɪvjə'] *n* comportamento *m*.

behead [bɪ'hed] *vt* decapitar.

behind [bɪ'haɪnd] *adv* (*at the back*) atrás ♦ *prep* (*at the back of*) atrás de ♦ *n* (*inf*) traseiro *m*; **to be ~ sb** (*supporting*) apoiar alguém; **to be ~ (schedule)** estar atrasado; **to leave sthg ~** esquecer-se de algo; **to stay ~** ficar para trás.

beige [beɪʒ] *adj* bege (*inv*).

being [ˈbiːɪŋ] *n* ser *m*; **to come into ~** nascer.

belated [bɪ'leɪtɪd] *adj* tardio(-dia).

belch [beltʃ] *vi* arrotar.

Belgian [ˈbeldʒən] *adj* belga ♦ *n* belga *mf*.

Belgian waffle *n* (*Am*) = waffle *m* (*Br*), = talassa *f* (*Port*).

Belgium [ˈbeldʒəm] *n* Bélgica *f*.

Belgrade [ˌbel'greɪd] *n* Belgrado *s*.

belief [bɪ'liːf] *n* (*faith*) crença *f*; (*opinion*) opinião *f*.

believe [bɪ'liːv] *vt* (*person, story*) acreditar em; (*think*) achar ♦ *vi*: **to ~ in** (*God, human rights*) crer em; **to ~ in doing sthg** acreditar em fazer algo.

believer [bɪ'liːvə'] *n* crente *mf*.

bell [bel] *n* (*of phone, door*) campainha *f*; (*of church*) sino *m*.

bellboy [ˈbelbɔɪ] *n* bói *m* (*Br*), paquete *m* (*em hotel, clube*) (*Port*).

belligerent [bɪ'lɪdʒərənt] *adj* (*aggressive*) belicoso(-osa), beligerante.

bellow [ˈbeləʊ] *vi* (*person*) gritar; (*bull, cow*) mugir.

bellows [ˈbeləʊz] *n* fole *m*.

belly [ˈbeli] *n* (*inf*) barriga *f*.

bellyache [ˈbelieɪk] *n* dor *f* de barriga.

belly button *n* (*inf*) umbigo *m*.

belong [bɪ'lɒŋ] *vi* (*be in right place*) pertencer; **to ~ to** pertencer a.

belongings [bɪ'lɒŋɪŋz] *npl* pertences *mpl*.

beloved [bɪ'lʌvd] *adj* adorado(-da).

below [bɪ'ləʊ] *adv* em baixo; (*downstairs*) de baixo ♦ *prep* abaixo de; **children ~ the age of ten** crianças com menos de dez anos.

belt [belt] *n* (*for clothes*) cinto *m*; (*TECH*) correia *f*.

beltway [ˈbeltweɪ] *n* (*Am*) circunvalação *f*.

bemused [bɪ'mjuːzd] *adj* confuso (-sa), perplexo(-xa).

bench [bentʃ] *n* banco *m*.

bend [bend] (*pt* & *pp* bent) *n* curva *f* ♦ *vt* dobrar ♦ *vi* (*road, river, pipe*) fazer uma curva.

❑ **bend down** *vi* dobrar-se.

❑ **bend over** *vi* inclinar-se.

beneath [bɪ'niːθ] *adv* debaixo ♦ *prep* (*under*) debaixo de, sob.

benefactor [ˈbenɪfæktə'] *n* benfeitor *m* (-ra *f*).

beneficial [ˌbenɪ'fɪʃl] *adj* benéfico (-ca).

benefit [ˈbenɪfɪt] *n* (*advantage*) benefício *m*; (*money*) subsídio *m* ♦ *vt* beneficiar ♦ *vi*: **to ~ (from)** beneficiar-se (de); **for the ~ of** em benefício de.

Benelux [ˈbenɪlʌks] *n* Benelux *m*.

benevolent [bɪ'nevələnt] *adj* benevolente.

benign [bɪ'naɪn] *adj* (*MED*) benigno (-gna).

bent [bent] *pt* & *pp* → bend.

bequeath [bɪ'kwiːð] *vt* (*money, property*) legar, deixar em testamento.

bereaved [bɪ'riːvd] *adj* (*family*) enlutado(-da).

beret [ˈbereɪ] *n* gorro *m*.

berk [bɜːk] *n* (*Brit: inf*) idiota *mf*, anta *f*.

Berlin [bɜː'lɪn] *n* Berlim *s*.

Bermuda shorts [bəˈmjuːdə-] *npl* bermudas *fpl*.

Bern [bɜːn] *n* Berna *s*.

berry [ˈberi] *n* baga *f*.

berserk [bəˈzɜːk] *adj*: **to go ~** ficar fora de si.

berth [bɜːθ] *n* (*for ship*) ancoradouro

m; (in ship) beliche *m; (in train)* couchette *f.*

beside [bɪˈsaɪd] *prep (next to)* junto a; **to be ~ the point** não ter nada a ver.

besides [bɪˈsaɪdz] *adv* além disso ◆ *prep* além de.

besiege [bɪˈsiːdʒ] *vt (town, fortress)* cercar.

besotted [bɪˈsɒtɪd] *adj* completamente apaixonado(-da); **to be ~ with sb** estar apaixonado por alguém.

best [best] *adj* melhor ◆ *n:* **the ~** o/a melhor; **a pint of ~** *(beer)* = uma caneca de cerveja escura; **to make the ~ of sthg** aproveitar o mais possível algo; **to do one's ~** fazer o melhor possível; **the ~ thing to do is ...** o melhor é ...; **"~ before ..."** "consumir de preferência antes de ..."; **at ~** quanto muito; **all the ~!** felicidades!; *(in letter)* um abraço!; **I like this one ~** gosto mais deste; **she played ~** ela jogou melhor.

best man *n* padrinho *m (de casamento).*

best-seller [-ˈselər] *n (book)* best-seller *m.*

bet [bet] *(pt & pp bet) n* aposta *f* ◆ *vt (gamble)* apostar ◆ *vi:* **to ~ (on)** apostar (em); **I ~ (that) you can't do it** aposto que você não consegue.

betray [bɪˈtreɪ] *vt* trair.

betrayal [bɪˈtreɪəl] *n* traição *f.*

better [ˈbetər] *adj & adv* melhor; **you had ~ ...** é melhor ...; **to get ~** melhorar.

better off *adj (financially)* melhor de vida, *(in a better situation)* melhor.

betting [ˈbetɪŋ] *n* apostas *fpl.*

betting shop *n (Brit)* casa *f* de apostas.

between [bɪˈtwiːn] *prep* entre; **in ~** *prep* entre ◆ *adv (space)* no meio; **"closed ~ 1 and 2"** "fechado entre a uma e as duas"; **what happened in ~?** o que aconteceu nesse entremeio?

beverage [ˈbevərɪdʒ] *n (fml)* bebida *f.*

beware [bɪˈweər] *vi:* **to ~ of** ter cuidado com; **"~ of the dog"** "cuidado com o cachorro".

bewildered [bɪˈwɪldəd] *adj* perplexo(-xa).

beyond [bɪˈjɒnd] *prep (on far side of)* do outro lado de; *(further than)* para além de ◆ *adv* mais além; **~ reach** fora do alcance; **to be ~ doubt** ser sem

sombra de dúvida.

bias [ˈbaɪəs] *n (prejudice)* preconceito *m; (tendency)* tendência *f.*

biased [ˈbaɪəst] *adj* parcial.

bib [bɪb] *n (for baby)* babador *m (Br),* bibe *m (Port).*

bible [ˈbaɪbl] *n* bíblia *f.*

bicarbonate of soda [baɪˈkɑːbənət-] *n* bicarbonato *m* de soda.

biceps [ˈbaɪseps] *n* bíceps *m inv.*

bicker [ˈbɪkər] *vi* discutir.

bicycle [ˈbaɪsɪkl] *n* bicicleta *f.*

bicycle path *n* pista *f* para ciclistas.

bicycle pump *n* bomba *f* (de bicicleta).

bid [bɪd] *(pt & pp bid) n (at auction)* lanço *m; (attempt)* tentativa *f* ◆ *vt (money)* oferecer ◆ *vi:* **to ~ (for)** licitar (para).

bidet [ˈbiːdeɪ] *n* bidê *m.*

bifocals [baɪˈfəʊklz] *npl* óculos *mpl* bifocais.

big [bɪg] *adj* grande; **my ~ brother** o meu irmão mais velho; **how ~ is it?** de que tamanho é?

Big Dipper [-ˈdɪpər] *n (Brit: rollercoaster)* montanha *f* russa; *(Am: constellation):* **the ~** a Ursa Maior.

bigheaded [ˌbɪgˈhedɪd] *adj (inf)* convencido(-da).

bigot [ˈbɪgət] *n* preconceituoso *m* (-osa *f).*

big toe *n* dedão *m* (do pé).

big top *n (tent)* tenda *f* de circo.

big wheel *n (Brit: at fairground)* roda *f* gigante.

bike [baɪk] *n (inf) (bicycle)* bicicleta *f; (motorcycle)* moto *f.*

biking [ˈbaɪkɪŋ] *n:* **to go ~** andar de bicicleta.

bikini [bɪˈkiːnɪ] *n* biquíni *m.*

bikini bottom *n* calça *f* de biquíni *(Br),* cuecas *fpl* de bikini *(Port).*

bikini top *n* sutiã *m* de biquíni *(Br),* soutien *m* de bikini *(Port).*

bilingual [baɪˈlɪŋgwəl] *adj* bilíngüe.

bill [bɪl] *n (for meal, electricity, hotel)* conta *f; (Am: bank note)* nota *f; (at cinema, theatre)* programa *m; (POL)* projeto *m* de lei; **can I have the ~ please?** a conta, por favor.

billboard [ˈbɪlbɔːd] *n* quadro *m* de anúncios *(Br),* placar *m* (publicitário) *(Port).*

billfold [ˈbɪlfəʊld] *n (Am)* carteira *f (de bolso).*

billiards [ˈbɪljədz] n bilhar m.

billion [ˈbɪljən] n (thousand million) bilhão m (Br), mil milhões (Port); (Brit: million million) trilhão m (Br), bilhão (Port).

Bill of Rights n: the ~ os dez primeiros direitos e liberdades do cidadão americano que constam da constituição dos Estados Unidos.

bimbo [ˈbɪmbəʊ] (pl -s OR -es) n (inf: pej) pessoa jovem e bonita mas pouco inteligente.

bin [bɪn] n caixote m do lixo; (for bread, flour) caixa f; (on plane) compartimento m para a bagagem.

bind [baɪnd] (pt & pp **bound**) vt (tie up) atar.

binder [ˈbaɪndəʳ] n (cover) capa f de argolas, dossiẹr m.

binding [ˈbaɪndɪŋ] n (of book) encadernação f; (for ski) peças fpl de fixação (dos esquis).

bingo [ˈbɪŋgəʊ] n bingo m.

binoculars [bɪˈnɒkjʊləʳ] npl binóculo m.

biodegradable [ˌbaɪəʊdɪˈgreɪdəbl] adj biodegradável.

biography [baɪˈɒgrəfɪ] n biografia f.

biological [ˌbaɪəˈlɒdʒɪkl] adj biológico (-ca).

biology [baɪˈɒlədʒɪ] n biologia f.

birch [bɜːtʃ] n vidoeiro m.

bird [bɜːd] n (small) pássaro m; (large) ave f; (Brit: inf: woman) garota (Br), gaja f (Port).

birdie [ˈbɜːdɪ] n (bird) passarinho m; (in golf) birdie m.

bird-watching [-ˌwɒtʃɪŋ] n: I like ~ eu gosto de observar pássaros.

Biro® [ˈbaɪərəʊ] n esferográfica f.

birth [bɜːθ] n nascimento m; by ~ de nascimento; to give ~ to dar à luz.

birth certificate n certidão f de nascimento.

birth control n contracepção f.

birthday [ˈbɜːθdeɪ] n aniversário m; happy ~! feliz aniversário!

birthday card n cartão m de aniversário.

birthday party n festa f de aniversário OR de anos.

birthmark [ˈbɜːθmɑːk] n sinal m (de nascença).

birthplace [ˈbɜːθpleɪs] n local m de nascimento.

biscuit [ˈbɪskɪt] n (Brit) biscoito m

(Br), bolacha f (Port); (Am: scone) bolo ou pão de massa não levedada que se come com geléia ou algo salgado.

bisect [baɪˈsekt] vt (in geometry) bissectar; (subj: road, corridor) ˌvˌdir em dois.

bishop [ˈbɪʃəp] n bispo m.

bison [ˈbaɪsn] n bisonte m.

bistro [ˈbiːstrəʊ] (pl -s) n bar-restaurante m.

bit [bɪt] pt → **bite** ♦ n (piece) pedaço m, bocado m; (of drill) broca f; (of bridle) freio m; a ~ um pouco; a ~ of money um pouco de dinheiro; to do a ~ of walking andar um pouco; not a ~ nem um pouco; ~ by ~ pouco a pouco.

bitch [bɪtʃ] n cadela f.

bitchy [ˈbɪtʃɪ] adj (inf) maldoso(-osa), venenoso(-osa).

bite [baɪt] (pt bit, pp bitten) n (when eating) dentada f; (from insect) picada f; (from snake) mordedura f ♦ vt morder; (subj: insect) picar; to have a ~ to eat mordiscar algo.

biting [ˈbaɪtɪŋ] adj (very cold) penetrante; (caustic) mordaz.

bitter [ˈbɪtəʳ] adj amargo(-ga); (cold, wind) glacial; (argument, conflict) violento(-ta) ♦ n (Brit: beer) tipo de cerveja amarga.

bitter lemon n limonada f (amarga).

bitterness [ˈbɪtənɪs] n (of taste, food) amargor m; (of weather, wind) rigor m; (of person) rancor m, amargura f; (of argument, conflict) violência f.

bizarre [bɪˈzɑːʳ] adj estranho(-nha).

black [blæk] adj preto(-ta); (coffee, tea) sem leite, preto(-ta); (humour) negro (-gra) ♦ n (colour) preto m, negro m; (person) negro m (-gra f).

❑ **black out** vi desmaiar, perder os sentidos.

black and white adj a preto e branco.

blackberry [ˈblækbrɪ] n amora f silvestre.

blackbird [ˈblækbɜːd] n melro m.

blackboard [ˈblækbɔːd] n quadro m (negro).

black cherry n cereja f preta.

blackcurrant [ˌblækˈkʌrənt] n groselha f preta.

blacken [ˈblækn] vt (make dark) enfuscar ♦ vi (sky) escurecer.

black eye *n* olho *m* roxo.
Black Forest gâteau *n bolo de chocolate em camadas com creme e cerejas ou compota de cerejas.*
blackhead ['blækhed] *n* cravo *m (Br)*, ponto *m* negro *(Port)*.
black ice *n* gelo *m (transparente no solo).*
blackmail ['blækmeɪl] *n* chantagem *f* ◆ *vt* chantagear.
blackout ['blækaʊt] *n (power cut)* corte *m* de energia.
black pepper *n* pimenta *f* preta.
black pudding *n (Brit)* = chouriço *m (Br)*, morcela *f (Port)*.
Black Sea *n*: the ~ o Mar Negro.
black sheep *n (fig)* ovelha *f* negra.
blacksmith ['blæksmɪθ] *n* ferreiro *m*.
bladder ['blædər] *n* bexiga *f*.
blade [bleɪd] *n (of knife, saw)* lâmina *f*; *(of propeller, oar)* pá *f*, *(of grass)* pedaço *m*.
blame [bleɪm] *n* culpa *f* ◆ *vt* culpar; **to ~ sb for sthg** culpar alguém de algo; **to ~ sthg on sb** pôr a culpa de algo em alguém.
bland [blænd] *adj (food)* insosso(-a).
blank [blæŋk] *adj (space, page, cassette)* em branco; *(expression)* confuso(-sa) ◆ *n (empty space)* espaço *m* em branco.
blank cheque *n* cheque *m* em branco.
blanket ['blæŋkɪt] *n* cobertor *m*.
blasphemy ['blæsfəmɪ] *n* blasfêmia *f*.
blast [blɑːst] *n (explosion)* explosão *f*; *(of air, wind)* rajada *f* ◆ *excl (inf)* raios!; **at full ~** no máximo.
blasted ['blɑːstɪd] *adj (inf: for emphasis)* maldito(-ta).
blatant ['bleɪtənt] *adj (discrimination, lie)* puro(-ra); *(disobedience)* ostensivo(-va).
blaze [bleɪz] *n (fire)* incêndio *m* ◆ *vi (fire)* arder; *(sun, light)* brilhar intensamente.
blazer ['bleɪzər] *n* blazer *m*.
bleach [bliːtʃ] *n* água *f* sanitária *(Br)*, lixívia *f (Port)* ◆ *vt (clothes)* branquear; *(hair)* descolorar.
bleached [bliːtʃt] *adj (hair)* oxigenado(-da); *(jeans)* debotado(-da).
bleachers ['bliːtʃərz] *npl (Am: SPORT)* arquibancada *f* descoberta.
bleak [bliːk] *adj (weather)* escuro(-ra); *(day, city)* sombrio(-bria).

bleary-eyed [blɪərɪ'aɪd] *adj* com os olhos inchados.
bleat [bliːt] *n (of sheep, goat)* balido *m* ◆ *vi (sheep, goat)* balir; *(fig: complain)* lamuriar-se.
bleed [bliːd] *(pt & pp* **bled** [bled]*) vi* sangrar.
blemish ['blemɪʃ] *n (flaw)* defeito *m*, falha *f*; *(pimple, scar)* marca *f*; *(fig: on name, reputation)* mancha *f*.
blend [blend] *n (of coffee, whisky)* mistura *f* ◆ *vt* misturar.
blender ['blendər] *n* liquidificador *m*.
bless [bles] *vt* abençoar; ~ **you!** *(said after sneeze)* saúde!
blessing ['blesɪŋ] *n* bênção *f*.
blew [bluː] *pt* → **blow**.
blimey ['blaɪmɪ] *excl (Brit: inf)* nossa!
blind [blaɪnd] *adj* cego(-ga) ◆ *n (for window)* persiana *f* ◆ *npl*: **the ~** os cegos.
blind alley *n* beco *m* sem saída.
blind corner *n* curva *f* sem visibilidade.
blindfold ['blaɪndfəʊld] *n* venda *f* ◆ *vt* vendar os olhos de.
blind spot *n (AUT)* ponto *m* cego.
blink [blɪŋk] *vi* piscar os olhos.
blinkers ['blɪŋkəz] *npl (Brit)* antolhos *mpl*.
bliss [blɪs] *n* felicidade *f* absoluta.
blister ['blɪstər] *n* bolha *f* (d'água).
blizzard ['blɪzəd] *n* tempestade *f* de neve.
bloated ['bləʊtɪd] *adj* inchado(-da).
blob [blɒb] *n* gota *f*.
block [blɒk] *n* bloco *m*; *(Am: in town, city)* quarteirão *m* ◆ *vt* obstruir; **to have a ~ed (up) nose** estar com o nariz entupido.
⌐ block up *vt sep* entupir.
blockage ['blɒkɪdʒ] *n* obstrução *f*.
blockbuster [blɒkbʌstər] *n (inf: book)* best-seller *m*; *(film)* sucesso *m* de bilheteira.
block capitals *npl* letra *f* maiúscula OR de imprensa.
block letters *npl* letra *f* maiúscula OR de imprensa.
block of flats *n* bloco *m* de apartamentos, prédio *m*.
bloke [bləʊk] *n (Brit: inf)* cara *m (Br)*, tipo *m (Port)*.
blond [blɒnd] *adj* louro(-ra) ◆ *n* louro *m*.

blonde [blɒnd] *adj* louro(-ra) ♦ *n* loura *f*.

blood [blʌd] *n* sangue *m*.

blood donor *n* doador *m* (-ra *f*) de sangue.

blood group *n* grupo *m* sangüíneo.

bloodhound ['blʌdhaʊnd] *n* sabujo *m*, cão *m* de caça.

blood poisoning *n* septicemia *f*.

blood pressure *n* pressão *f* arterial *(Br)*, tensão *f* arterial *(Port)*; **to have high/low ~** ter a pressão (arterial) alta/baixa.

bloodshed ['blʌdʃed] *n* derramamento *m* de sangue, carnificina *f*.

bloodshot ['blʌdʃɒt] *adj* injetado (-da) de sangue.

blood test *n* exame *m* de sangue.

bloodthirsty ['blʌd,θɜːstɪ] *adj* sedento(-ta) de sangue.

blood transfusion *n* transfusão *f* de sangue.

bloody [blʌdɪ] *adj (hands, handkerchief)* ensangüentado(-da); *(Brit: vulg: damn)* maldito(-ta) ♦ *adv (Brit: vulg):* **you ~ idiot!** seu idiota!

bloody mary [-'meərɪ] *n* vodka com suco de tomate e especiarias.

bloom [bluːm] *n* flor *f* ♦ *vi* florir; **in ~** em flor.

blossom ['blɒsəm] *n* flor *f*.

blot [blɒt] *n* borrão *m*.

blotch [blɒtʃ] *n* mancha *f*.

blotting paper ['blɒtɪŋ-] *n* papel *m* mata-borrão.

blouse [blaʊz] *n* blusa *f*.

blow [bləʊ] *(pt* **blew**, *pp* **blown**) *vt (subj: wind)* fazer voar; *(whistle, trumpet)* soprar em; *(bubbles)* fazer ♦ *vi* soprar; *(fuse)* queimar, rebentar ♦ *n (hit)* golpe *m*; **to ~ one's nose** assoar-se, assoar o nariz.

❏ **blow up** *vt sep (cause to explode)* explodir; *(inflate)* encher ♦ *vi (explode)* explodir; *(storm)* cair.

blow-dry *n* brushing *m* ♦ *vt* secar *(com secador)*.

blowlamp ['bləʊlæmp] *n (Brit)* maçarico *m*.

blown [bləʊn] *pp* → **blow**.

blowout ['bləʊaʊt] *n (of tyre):* **they had a ~ on the motorway** o pneu furou quando estavam na auto-estrada.

blowtorch ['bləʊtɔːtʃ] = **blow lamp**.

BLT *n* sanduíche de bacon grelhado, alface e tomate.

blubber ['blʌbəʳ] *n (of whale)* gordura *f* de baleia ♦ *vi (pej: weep)* choramingar.

blue [bluː] *adj* azul; *(film)* pornográfico(-ca) ♦ *n* azul *m*.

❏ **blues** *n (MUS)* blues *m inv*.

bluebell ['bluːbel] *n* campainha-azul *f*, bom-dia *m*.

blueberry ['bluːbərɪ] *n* arando *m*, uva-do-monte *f*.

bluebottle ['bluː,bɒtl] *n* mosca *f* varejeira.

blue cheese *n* queijo *m* azul.

blue jeans *npl (Am)* jeans *m inv (Br)*, calças *fpl* de ganga *(Port)*.

blueprint ['bluːprɪnt] *n (plan, programme)* plano *m*, projecto *m*.

bluff [blʌf] *n (cliff)* penhasco *m* ♦ *vi* blefar *(Br)*, fazer bluff *(Port)*.

blunder ['blʌndəʳ] *n* asneira *f*.

blunt [blʌnt] *adj (knife)* cego(-ga); *(pencil)* por afiar; *(fig: person)* franco(-ca).

blurb [blɜːb] *n (inf)* texto publicitário que aparece normalmente na contracapa de um livro.

blurred [blɜːd] *adj* desfocado(-da).

blurt [blɜːt] **: blurt out** *vt sep* deixar escapar.

blush [blʌʃ] *vi* corar.

blusher ['blʌʃəʳ] *n* blush *m*.

blustery ['blʌstərɪ] *adj* tempestuoso (-osa).

BMX *(abbr of bicycle motorcross)* BMX *f*.

BO *abbr* = **body odour**.

boar [bɔːʳ] *n (male pig)* porco *m*; *(wild pig)* javali *m*.

board [bɔːd] *n (plank)* tábua *f*; *(for surfing, diving)* prancha *f*; *(notice board)* quadro *m*; *(for games)* tabuleiro *m*; *(blackboard)* quadro *m (negro)*; *(of company)* direção *f*; *(hardboard)* madeira *f* compensada *(Br)*, contraplacado *m (Port)* ♦ *vt (plane, ship)* embarcar em; **~ and lodging** dormida e refeições; **full ~** pensão completa; **half ~** meia pensão; **on ~** *adv* a bordo ♦ *prep (plane, ship)* a bordo de; *(bus)* em.

boarder ['bɔːdəʳ] *n (lodger)* pensionista *mf*; *(at school)* aluno *m* interno (aluna *f* interna).

board game *n* jogo *m* de tabuleiro.

boarding ['bɔːdɪŋ] *n* embarque *m*.

boarding card *n* cartão *m* de embarque.

boardinghouse [ˈbɔːdɪŋhaʊs, pl -haʊzɪz] n pensão f.
boarding school n colégio m interno.
board of directors n direção f.
boast [bəʊst] vi: **to ~ (about sthg)** gabar-se (de algo).
boastful [ˈbəʊstfʊl] adj convencido(-da).
boat [bəʊt] n barco m; **by ~** de barco.
boater [ˈbəʊtəʳ] n (hat) chapéu m de palha.
boat train n (Brit) trem m (Br), comboio m (Port) (de ligação com um barco, ferryboat).
bob [bɒb] n (hairstyle) corte m direito.
bobbin [ˈbɒbɪn] n bobina f, carreto m.
bobby [ˈbɒbɪ] n (Brit: inf: policeman) guarda m, policial m (Br), polícia m (Port).
bobby pin n (Am) grampo m de cabelo (em forma de U).
bobsleigh [ˈbɒbsleɪ] n trenó m, bobsleigh m.
body [ˈbɒdɪ] n corpo m; (of car) carroceria f; (organization) organismo m; (of wine) maturação f.
body building n musculação f, culturismo m (Port).
bodyguard [ˈbɒdɪɡɑːd] n guarda-costas mf.
body odour n odor m corporal.
bodywork [ˈbɒdɪwɜːk] n carroceria f.
bog [bɒɡ] n zona f pantanosa.
bogged down [ˌbɒɡd-] adj: **~ in sthg** (in mud, snow) enterrado(-da) em algo; **don't get ~ in too many details** não entre em demasiados detalhes.
bogus [ˈbəʊɡəs] adj falso(-sa).
boil [bɔɪl] vt (water) ferver; (kettle) pôr para ferver; (food) cozer ◆ vi ferver ◆ n (on skin) furúnculo m.
boiled egg [bɔɪld-] n ovo m cozido.
boiled potatoes [bɔɪld-] npl batatas fpl cozidas.
boiler [ˈbɔɪləʳ] n esquentador m (da água).
boiler suit n (Brit) macacão m (Br), fato-macaco m (Port).
boiling (hot) [ˈbɔɪlɪŋ-] adj (inf) (person) morto(morta) de calor; (weather) abrazador(-ra); (water) fervendo.
boiling point [ˈbɔɪlɪŋ-] n ponto m de ebulição; **to reach ~** ferver.
boisterous [ˈbɔɪstərəs] adj (child,

behaviour) irrequieto(-ta).
bold [bəʊld] adj (brave) audaz.
bollard [ˈbɒlɑːd] n (Brit: on road) poste m.
bolt [bəʊlt] n (on door, window) ferrolho m; (screw) parafuso m (com porca) ◆ vt (door, window) fechar com ferrolho.
bomb [bɒm] n bomba f ◆ vt bombardear.
bombard [bɒmˈbɑːd] vt bombardear.
bomb disposal squad n equipe f (de desmontamento) de explosivos.
bomber [ˈbɒməʳ] n (plane) bombardeiro m.
bombing [ˈbɒmɪŋ] n bombardeio m.
bomb scare n ameaça f de bomba.
bomb shelter n abrigo m (antiaéreo).
bond [bɒnd] n (tie, connection) laço m.
bone [bəʊn] n (of person, animal) osso m; (of fish) espinha f.
boned [bəʊnd] adj (chicken) desossado(-da); (fish) sem espinhas.
bone-dry adj completamente seco(-ca).
bone-idle adj preguiçoso(-osa), malandro(-dra).
boneless [ˈbəʊnləs] adj (chicken, pork) desossado(-da).
bonfire [ˈbɒnfaɪəʳ] n fogueira f.
Bonfire Night n (Brit) 5 de novembro, celebrado com fogueiras e fogo de artifício.
Bonn [bɒn] n Bonn.
bonnet [ˈbɒnɪt] n (Brit: of car) capota f.
bonny [ˈbɒnɪ] adj (Scot) bonito(-ta).
bonus [ˈbəʊnəs] (pl -es) n bônus m inv.
bony [ˈbəʊnɪ] adj (chicken) cheio(-cheia) de ossos; (fish) cheio (cheia) de espinhas.
boo [buː] vi vaiar.
booby trap [ˈbuːbɪ] n (bomb) (bomba) armadilha f; (prank) peça f (Br), partida f (Port).
boogie [ˈbuːɡɪ] vi (inf) sacudir o esqueleto.
book [bʊk] n livro m; (for writing in) caderno m; (of stamps, matches) carteira f; (of tickets) caderneta f ◆ vt (reserve) reservar.
❑ **book in** vi (at hotel) preencher o registro.
bookable [ˈbʊkəbl] adj (seats, flight) reservável.

bookcase ['bukkeɪs] *n* estante *f* (para livros).

booking ['bukɪŋ] *n (reservation)* reserva *f*.

booking office *n* bilheteira *f*.

bookkeeping ['buk,ki:pɪŋ] *n* contabilidade *f*.

booklet ['buklɪt] *n* folheto *m*.

bookmaker's ['buk,meɪkəz] *n* casa *f* de apostas.

bookmark ['bukmɑ:k] *n* marcador *m* de livros.

bookshelf ['bukʃelf] *(pl* -shelves [-ʃelvz]) *n (shelf)* prateleira *f* (para livros); *(bookcase)* estante *f* (para livros).

bookshop ['bukʃɒp] *n* livraria *f*.

bookstall ['bukstɔ:l] *n* quiosque *m* de venda de livros.

bookstore ['bukstɔ:ʳ] = bookshop.

book token *n* espécie de vale para comprar livros.

boom [bu:m] *n (sudden growth)* boom *m* ♦ *vi (voice, guns)* ribombar.

boost [bu:st] *vt* aumentar; *(spirits, morale)* levantar.

booster ['bu:stəʳ] *n (injection)* reforço *m* de vacina.

boot [bu:t] *n (shoe)* bota *f; (Brit: of car)* porta-malas *m* (Br), porta-bagagem *m* (Port).

booth [bu:ð] *n (for telephone)* cabine *f; (at fairground)* barraca *f*.

booty ['bu:tɪ] *n* saque *m*, despojos *mpl*.

booze [bu:z] *n (inf)* álcool *m* ♦ *vi (inf)* beber, encher a cara.

bop [bɒp] *n (inf: dance)*: **to have a ~** sacudir o esqueleto.

border ['bɔ:dəʳ] *n (of country)* fronteira *f; (edge)* borda *f;* **the Borders** região de Escócia que faz fronteira com a Inglaterra.

borderline ['bɔ:dəlaɪn] *n (fig: uncertain division)* fronteira *f* ♦ *adj:* **a ~ case** um caso duvidoso, uma situação indecisa.

bore [bɔ:ʳ] *pt →* bear ♦ *n (inf)* seca *f* ♦ *vt (person)* entediar, aborrecer; *(hole)* fazer.

bored [bɔ:d] *adj* entediado(-da).

boredom ['bɔ:dəm] *n* tédio *m*.

boring ['bɔ:rɪŋ] *adj* maçante *(Br)*, aborrecido(-da) *(Port)*.

born [bɔ:n] *adj:* **to be ~** nascer.

borne [bɔ:n] *pp →* bear.

borough ['bʌrə] *n* município *m*.

borrow ['bɒrəu] *vt:* **to ~ sthg (from sb)** pedir algo emprestado (a alguém).

Bosnia ['bɒznɪə] *n* Bósnia *f*.

Bosnia-Herzegovina [-,heətsəgə-'vi:nə] *n* Bósnia-Herzegovina *f*.

Bosnian ['bɒznɪən] *adj* bósnio(-nia) ♦ *n* bósnio *m* (-nia *f*).

bosom ['buzəm] *n* peito *m*.

boss [bɒs] *n* chefe *mf*.

❏ **boss around** *vt sep* dar ordens a.

bossy ['bɒsɪ] *adj* mandão(-dona).

botanical garden [bə'tænɪkl-] *n* jardim *m* botânico.

botch [bɒtʃ] : **botch up** *vt sep (inf: plan)* dar cabo de; **they really ~ed it up** fizeram um belo serviço!

both [bəuθ] *adj* ambos(-bas) ♦ *pron* ambos *mpl* (-bas *fpl*) ♦ *adv:* **he speaks ~ French and German** ele fala francês e alemão; **~ of them** ambos(-bas), os dois (as duas); **~ of us** nós dois (nós duas).

bother ['bɒðəʳ] *vt (worry)* preocupar; *(annoy, pester)* incomodar ♦ *vi* preocupar-se ♦ *n (trouble)* incômodo *m*, amolação *f;* **I can't be ~ed** não posso me dar ao trabalho; **it's no ~!** não incomoda nada.

bottle ['bɒtl] *n* garrafa *f; (for baby)* mamadeira *f* (Br), biberão *m* (Port); *(of shampoo, medicine)* frasco *m*.

bottle bank *n* ponto *m* de descarte de vidros para reciclagem *(Br)*, vidrão *m* (Port).

bottled ['bɒtld] *adj* engarrafado(-da); **~ beer** cerveja *f* de garrafa; **~ water** água *f* mineral (engarrafada).

bottleneck ['bɒtlnek] *n (in traffic)* engarrafamento *m*.

bottle opener [-,əupnəʳ] *n* abridor *m* de garrafas, saca-rolhas *m inv*.

bottom ['bɒtəm] *adj (lowest)* de baixo; *(last, worst)* último(-ma) ♦ *n* fundo *m; (of hill)* base *f; (buttocks)* traseiro *m* ♦ *adv:* **I came ~ in the exam** tirei a nota mais baixa do exame.

bough [bau] *n* ramo *m*.

bought [bɔ:t] *pt & pp →* buy.

boulder ['bəuldəʳ] *n* pedregulho *m*.

bounce [bauns] *vi (rebound)* pinchar; *(jump)* saltar; **his cheque ~d** ele passou um cheque sem fundos.

bouncer ['baunsəʳ] *n (inf)* segurança *m*, gorila *m*.

bouncy castle *n* castelo de ar para as crianças pularem em cima dele.

bound [baʊnd] *pt & pp* → **bind** ♦ *vi*
correr aos pulos ♦ *adj*: **he's ~ to get it
wrong** o mais certo é ele enganar-se;
it's ~ to rain vai chover na certa; **it's
out of ~s** é zona proibida; **to be ~ for**
(plane, train) (ir) com destino a.

boundary ['baʊndrɪ] *n* fronteira *f*.

bouquet [buːˈkeɪ] *n (of flowers)* ramo
m; *(of wine)* aroma *m*, bouquet *m*.

bourbon ['bɜːbən] *n* bourbon *m*.

bout [baʊt] *n (of illness)* ataque *m*; *(of
activity)* período *m*.

boutique [buːˈtiːk] *n* boutique *f*.

bow¹ [baʊ] *n (of head)* reverência *f*; *(of
ship)* proa *f* ♦ *vi (bend head)* inclinar a
cabeça.

bow² [bəʊ] *n (knot)* laço *m*; *(weapon,
MUS)* arco *m*.

bowels ['baʊəlz] *npl (ANAT)* intestinos
mpl.

bowl [bəʊl] *n* taça *f*, tigela *f*; *(for washing up)* bacia *f*; *(of toilet)* vaso *m (Br)*,
sanita *f (Port)*.

❑ **bowls** *npl* jogo de gramado que consiste em arremessar bolas grandes o mais
perto possível de uma bola pequena.

bow-legged ['bəʊlegɪd] *adj* com as
pernas tortas.

bowler ['bəʊləʳ] *n (in cricket)* lançador
m (-ra f); **~ (hat)** chapéu-coco *m*.

bowling ['bəʊlɪŋ] *n*: **to go ~** ir jogar
boliche *(Br)*, ir jogar bowling *(Port)*.

bowling alley *n* lugar onde se joga
bowling.

bowling green *n* gramado *m (Br)*,
relvado *m (Port)* (para jogar "bowls").

bow tie [bəʊ-] *n* laço *m*.

box [bɒks] *n* caixa *f*; *(on form)* quadrado *m*; *(in theatre)* camarote *m* ♦ *vi* jogar
boxe; **a ~ of chocolates** uma caixa de
bombons.

boxer ['bɒksəʳ] *n* pugilista *m*, lutador
m de boxe.

boxer shorts *npl* boxers *mpl*.

boxing ['bɒksɪŋ] *n* boxe *m*.

Boxing Day *n* o dia 26 de dezembro.

boxing gloves *npl* luvas *fpl* de boxe.

boxing ring *n* ringue *m* de boxe.

box office *n* bilheteira *f*.

boxroom ['bɒksrʊm] *n (Brit)* quarto *m*
pequeno.

boy [bɔɪ] *n* rapaz *m* ♦ *excl (inf)*: **(oh) ~!**
que bom!

boycott ['bɔɪkɒt] *vt* boicotar.

boyfriend ['bɔɪfrend] *n* namorado *m*.

boyish ['bɔɪʃ] *adj (man)* juvenil.

boy scout *n* escoteiro *m*.

BR *abbr* = **British Rail**.

bra [brɑː] *n* sutiã *m (Br)*, soutien *m
(Port)*.

brace [breɪs] *n (for teeth)* aparelho *m*
(para os dentes).

❑ **braces** *npl (Brit)* suspensórios *mpl*.

bracelet ['breɪslɪt] *n* pulseira *f*.

bracken ['brækn] *n* samambaia *f (Br)*,
feto *m (Port)*.

bracket ['brækɪt] *n (written symbol)*
parêntese *m*; *(support)* suporte *m*.

brag [bræg] *vi* gabar-se; **to ~ about**
sthg gabar-se de algo.

braid [breɪd] *n (hairstyle)* trança *f*; *(on
clothes)* galão *m*.

brain [breɪn] *n* cérebro *m*.

brainchild ['breɪntʃaɪld] *n* invenção *f*,
idéia *f*.

brainwash ['breɪnwɒʃ] *vt* fazer uma
lavagem cerebral em.

brainwave ['breɪnweɪv] *n* idéia *f*
genial OR brilhante.

brainy ['breɪnɪ] *adj (inf)* esperto(-ta),
she's really ~ ela é um crânio.

braised [breɪzd] *adj* estufado(-da).

brake [breɪk] *n* freio *m (Br)*, travão *m
(Port)* ♦ *vi* frear *(Br)*, travar *(Port)*.

brake block *n* calço *m* do freio.

brake fluid *n* líquido *m* para os
freios.

brake light *n* luz *f* de freio.

brake pad *n* patilha *f* OR calço *m* do
travão.

brake pedal *n* pedal *m* do freio.

bramble ['bræmbl] *n (bush)* silva *f*.

bran [bræn] *n* farelo *m*.

branch [brɑːntʃ] *n (of tree, subject)*
ramo *m*; *(of bank)* agência *f*; *(of company)* sucursal *f*, filial *f*.

❑ **branch off** *vi* ramificar-se.

branch line *n* ramal *m*.

brand [brænd] *n* marca *f* ♦ *vt*: **to ~ sb
(as)** rotular alguém (de).

brandish ['brændɪʃ] *vt (weapon)* brandir, empunhar; *(letter etc)* agitar.

brand-new *adj* novo (nova) em
folha.

brandy ['brændɪ] *n* conhaque *m*.

brash [bræʃ] *adj (pej)* insolente.

brass [brɑːs] *n* latão *m*.

brass band *n* banda *f* de música.

brasserie ['bræsərɪ] *n* = snack-bar *m*.

brassiere [*Brit* 'bræsɪəʳ, *Am* brəˈzɪr] *n*
sutiã *m (Br)*, soutien *m (Port)*.

brat [bræt] *n (inf)* criança *f* mimada.
bravado [brə'vɑːdəʊ] *n* bravata *f*.
brave [breɪv] *adj* valente.
bravery ['breɪvərɪ] *n* valentia *f*.
bravo [,brɑː'vəʊ] *excl* bravo!
brawl [brɔːl] *n* rixa *f*.
brawn [brɔːn] *n (muscle)* músculos *mpl*, força *f* física; *(Brit: meat)* carne *de porco, normalmente da cabeça, enlatada semelhante a paté.*
bray [breɪ] *vi (donkey)* zurrar.
brazen ['breɪzn] *adj* descarado(-da).
brazier ['breɪzjər] *n* braseira *f*.
Brazil [brə'zɪl] *n* Brasil *m*.
Brazilian [brə'zɪljən] *adj* brasileiro (-ra) ♦ *n* brasileiro *m* (-ra *f*).
brazil nut *n* castanha-do-pará *f*.
breach [briːtʃ] *vt (contract)* quebrar; *(confidence)* abusar de.
bread [bred] *n* pão *m*; ~ **and butter** pão com manteiga.
bread bin *n (Brit)* caixa *f* para pão.
breadboard ['bredbɔːd] *n* tábua *f* para cortar pão.
bread box *(Am)* = **bread bin**.
breadcrumbs ['bredkrʌmz] *npl* farinha *f* de rosca *(Br)*, pão *m* ralado *(Port)*.
breaded ['bredɪd] *adj* panado(-da), à milanesa.
bread knife *n* faca *f* do pão.
bread roll *n* pãozinho *m (Br)*, carcaça *f (Port)*.
breadth [bretθ] *n* largura *f*.
break [breɪk] *(pt* **broke**, *pp* **broken)** *n (interruption)* interrupção *f*; *(in line)* corte *m*; *(rest, pause)* pausa *f*; *(SCH: playtime)* recreio *m* ♦ *vt (damage)* partir, quebrar; *(disobey)* ir contra; *(fail to fulfil)* quebrar; *(a record)* bater; *(news)* dar; *(journey)* interromper ♦ *vi (become damaged)* partir, quebrar; *(dawn)* romper; *(voice)* mudar; **without a** ~ sem parar; **a lucky** ~ um golpe de sorte; **to** ~ **one's leg** quebrar a perna.
❏ **break down** *vi (car, machine)* enguiçar ♦ *vt sep (door, barrier)* derrubar.
❏ **break in** *vi* entrar à força.
❏ **break off** *vt (detach)* partir; *(holiday)* interromper ♦ *vi (stop suddenly)* parar.
❏ **break out** *vi (fire)* começar; *(war)* estourar; *(panic)* instaurar-se; **to** ~ **out in a rash** ganhar alergia.
❏ **break up** *vi (with spouse, partner)* separar-se; *(meeting, marriage)* terminar; *(school, pupils)* terminar as aulas.

breakage ['breɪkɪdʒ] *n* danos *mpl*.
breakdown ['breɪkdaʊn] *n (of car)* enguiço *m*, avaria *f*; *(in communications, negotiation)* ruptura *f*; *(mental)* esgotamento *m*.
breakdown truck *n* reboque *m (Br)*, pronto-socorro *m (Port)*.
breakfast ['brekfəst] *n* café *m* da manhã *(Br)*, pequeno-almoço *m (Port)*; **to have** ~ tomar o café da manhã; **to have sthg for** ~ comer algo no café da manhã.
breakfast cereal *n* cereal *m* (para o café da manhã).
breakfast television *n (Brit)* programação *f* matinal *(na televisão)*.
break-in *n* assalto *m*.
breakneck ['breɪknek] *adj*: **at** ~ **speed** a toda a velocidade, a uma velocidade vertiginosa.
breakthrough ['breɪkθruː] *n* avanço *m*.
breakup ['breɪkʌp] *n (of relationship)* dissolução *f*.
breakwater ['breɪk,wɔːtər] *n* quebramar *m*.
breast [brest] *n* peito *m*.
breastbone ['brestbəʊn] *n* esterno *m*.
breast-feed *vt* amamentar.
breaststroke ['breststrəʊk] *n* nado *m* de peito *(Br)*, bruços *mpl (Port)*.
breath [breθ] *n* hálito *m*; **out of** ~ sem fôlego; **to go for a** ~ **of fresh air** sair para respirar ar fresco; **to take a deep** ~ respirar fundo.
Breathalyser® ['breθəlaɪzər] *n (Brit)*: **I was given a** ~ **test** tive que soprar no bafômetro *m (Br)* OR balão *m (Port)*.
Breathalyzer® ['breθəlaɪzər] *(Am)* = **Breathalyser®**.
breathe [briːð] *vi* respirar.
❏ **breathe in** *vi* inspirar.
❏ **breathe out** *vi* expirar.
breather ['briːðər] *n (inf)* pausa *f* (para tomar fôlego).
breathing ['briːðɪŋ] *n* respiração *f*.
breathless ['breθlɪs] *adj* sem fôlego.
breathtaking ['breθ,teɪkɪŋ] *adj* incrível.
breed [briːd] *(pt & pp* **bred** [bred]) *n (of animal)* raça *f*; *(of plant)* espécie *f* ♦ *vt* criar ♦ *vi* reproduzir-se.
breeze [briːz] *n* brisa *f*.
breezy ['briːzɪ] *adj (weather, day)* ventoso(-osa).
brevity ['brevɪtɪ] *n* brevidade *f*.
brew [bruː] *vt (beer)* fabricar; *(tea, cof-*

fee) preparar ♦ *vi (tea, coffee)* repousar; **has the tea/coffee ~ed yet?** já está pronto o chá/café?

brewer ['bruːəʳ] *n* fabricante *m* de cerveja.

brewery ['brʊərɪ] *n* fábrica *f* de cerveja.

bribe [braɪb] *n* suborno *m* ♦ *vt* subornar.

bribery ['braɪbərɪ] *n* suborno *m*.

bric-a-brac ['brɪkəbræk] *n* bricabraque *m*.

brick [brɪk] *n* tijolo *m*.

bricklayer ['brɪkˌleɪəʳ] *n* pedreiro *m*.

brickwork ['brɪkwɜːk] *n* alvenaria *f (de tijolo).*

bridal ['braɪdl] *adj (dress)* de noiva; *(suite)* nupcial.

bride [braɪd] *n* noiva *f*.

bridegroom ['braɪdgrʊm] *n* noivo *m*.

bridesmaid ['braɪdzmeɪd] *n* dama de honra *(Br)*, dama *f* de honor *(Port)*.

bridge [brɪdʒ] *n* ponte *f; (card game)* bridge *m*.

bridle ['braɪdl] *n* cabeçada *f*.

bridle path *n* pista *f* para cavaleiros.

brief [briːf] *adj* breve ♦ *vt* informar; **in ~** em resumo.

❏ **briefs** *npl (for men)* cueca *f (Br)*, cuecas *fpl (Port); (for women)* calcinha *f (Br)*, cuecas *fpl (Port)*.

briefcase ['briːfkeɪs] *n* pasta *f (para papéis, livros).*

briefing ['briːfɪŋ] *n* briefing *m*, instruções *fpl*.

briefly ['briːflɪ] *adv (for a short time)* por alguns momentos; *(in few words)* em poucas palavras.

brigade [brɪ'geɪd] *n* brigada *f*.

brigadier [ˌbrɪgə'dɪəʳ] *n* brigadeiro *m*.

bright [braɪt] *adj (light, sun, idea)* brilhante; *(room)* claro(-ra); *(colour)* vivo (-va); *(clever)* esperto(-ta); *(lively, cheerful)* alegre; *(smile)* radiante.

brighten ['braɪtn] *vi (become lighter)* clarear, desanuviar; *(become more cheerful)* alegrar-se.

❏ **brighten up** *vt sep* alegrar ♦ *vi (become more cheerful)* alegrar-se; *(weather)* melhorar.

brilliance ['brɪljəns] *n (of idea, person)* gênio *m; (of colour, light, sunshine)* brilho *m; (inf: of performance, goal)* brilhantismo *m*.

brilliant ['brɪljənt] *adj (light, sunshine)* brilhante; *(colour)* vivo(-va); *(idea, person)* genial; *(inf: wonderful)* fantástico (-ca).

Brillo pad® ['brɪləʊ-] *n* = esponja *f* Bombril® *(Br)*, esfregão *m.* Bravo® *(Port)*.

brim [brɪm] *n (of hat)* aba *f;* **it's full to the ~** está cheio até à borda.

brine [braɪn] *n* salmoura *f*.

bring [brɪŋ] *(pt & pp* **brought)** *vt* trazer.

❏ **bring along** *vt sep* trazer.

❏ **bring back** *vt sep (return)* devolver; *(shopping, gift)* trazer.

❏ **bring in** *vt sep (introduce)* introduzir; *(earn)* ganhar.

❏ **bring out** *vt sep (put on sale)* pôr a venda.

❏ **bring up** *vt sep (child)* criar; *(subject)* mencionar; *(food)* vomitar.

brink [brɪŋk] *n:* **on the ~ of** à beira de.

brisk [brɪsk] *adj (quick)* rápido(-da); *(efficient)* desembaraçado(-da); *(wind)* forte.

bristle ['brɪsl] *n (of brush)* cerda *f; (on chin)* pêlo *m*.

Britain ['brɪtn] *n* Grã-Bretanha *f*.

British ['brɪtɪʃ] *adj* britânico(-ca) ♦ *npl:* **the ~** os britânicos.

British Isles *npl:* **the ~** as Ilhas Británicas.

British Rail *n companhia ferroviária británica agora privatizada.*

British Telecom [-'telɪkɒm] *n companhia británica de telecomunicações.*

Briton ['brɪtn] *n* britânico *m* (-ca *f)*.

brittle ['brɪtl] *adj* quebradiço(-ça).

broach [brəʊtʃ] *vt (subject)* abordar.

broad [brɔːd] *adj (wide)* largo(-ga); *(wide-ranging)* amplo(-pla); *(description, outline)* geral; *(accent)* forte.

B road *n (Brit)* estrada *f* secundária.

broad bean *n* fava *f*.

broadcast ['brɔːdkɑːst] *(pt & pp* **broadcast)** *n* transmissão *f* ♦ *vt* transmitir.

broaden ['brɔːdn] *vt* alargar ♦ *vi (river, road)* alargar.

broadly ['brɔːdlɪ] *adv* em geral; **~ speaking** em termos gerais.

broadminded [ˌbrɔːd'maɪndɪd] *adj* aberto(-ta).

broccoli ['brɒkəlɪ] *n* brócolis *mpl (Br)*, bróckolos *mpl (Port)*.

brochure ['brəʊʃəʳ] *n* folheto *m*.

broiled [brɔɪld] *adj (Am)* grelhado(-da).
broke [brəʊk] *pt* → **break** ◆ *adj (inf)* teso(-sa).
broken ['brəʊkn] *pp* → **break** ◆ *adj (window, leg, glass)* partido(-da); *(machine)* com defeito *(Br)*, avariado (-da) *(Port)*; *(English, Portuguese)* incorreto(-ta).
brolly ['brɒlɪ] *n (Brit: inf)* guarda-chuva *m.*
bronchitis [brɒŋ'kaɪtɪs] *n* bronquite *f.*
bronze [brɒnz] *n* bronze *m.*
brooch [brəʊtʃ] *n* broche *m.*
brood [bruːd] *n (of animals)* ninhada *f* ◆ *vi:* to ~ **(over** OR **about sthg)** cismar (com algo).
brook [brʊk] *n* riacho *m.*
broom [bruːm] *n* vassoura *f.*
broomstick ['bruːmstɪk] *n* cabo *m* de vassoura.
broth [brɒθ] *n* sopa consistente de verduras, com carne ou peixe.
brothel ['brɒθl] *n* bordel *m.*
brother ['brʌðə*r*] *n* irmão *m.*
brother-in-law *n* cunhado *m.*
brought [brɔːt] *pt & pp* → **bring.**
brow [braʊ] *n (forehead)* testa *f; (eyebrow)* sobrancelha *f.*
brown [braʊn] *adj* marrom *(Br)*, castanho(-nha) *(Port); (skin)* moreno(-na); *(tanned)* bronzeado(-da) ◆ *n* marrom *m (Br)*, castanho *m (Port).*
brown bread *n* pão *m* integral.
brownie ['braʊnɪ] *n (CULIN)* biscoito de chocolate e nozes.
Brownie ['braʊnɪ] *n* fadinha *f (entre os sete e os dez anos).*
brown paper *n* papel *m* pardo OR de embrulho.
brown rice *n* arroz *m* integral.
brown sauce *n (Brit)* molho picante escuro servido especialmente com batatas fritas.
brown sugar *n* açúcar *m* mascavo.
browse [braʊz] *vi (in shop)* dar uma olhada; to ~ **through** *(book, paper)* passar os olhos em.
browser ['braʊzə*r*] *n:* "~s welcome" "entrada livre".
bruise [bruːz] *n* nódoa *f* negra, equimose *f.*
brunch [brʌntʃ] *n* café da manhã reforçado que se toma muito tarde e que serve de almoço.
brunette [bruː'net] *n* morena *f.*
brunt [brʌnt] *n:* to bear OR take the

~ **of** sthg agüentar o pior/a maior parte de algo.
brush [brʌʃ] *n (for hair, teeth)* escova *f; (for painting)* pincel *m* ◆ *vt (floor)* varrer; *(clothes)* escovar; *(move with hand)* sacudir; to ~ **one's hair** escovar o cabelo; to ~ **one's teeth** escovar os dentes.
brusque [bruːsk] *adj* brusco(-ca).
Brussels ['brʌslz] *n* Bruxelas *s.*
brussels sprouts *npl* couves-de-Bruxelas *fpl.*
brutal ['bruːtl] *adj* brutal.
brute [bruːt] *n (bully)* bruto *m (-ta f).*
BSc *abbr* = **Bachelor of Science.**
BSE *n (abbr of bovine spongiform encephalopathy)* BSE *f*, encefalopatia *f* espongiforme bovina.
BT *abbr* = **British Telecom.**
bubble ['bʌbl] *n* bolha *f; (of soap)* bola *f* de sabão; *(in fizzy drink)* borbulha *f.*
bubble bath *n* espuma *f* de banho.
bubble gum *n* chiclete *m (Br)*, pastilha *f* elástica *(Port).*
bubbly ['bʌblɪ] *n (inf)* espumante *m.*
Bucharest [ˌbuːkə'rest] *n* Bucareste *s.*
buck [bʌk] *n (Am: inf: dollar)* dólar *m; (male animal)* macho *m.*
bucket ['bʌkɪt] *n* balde *m.*
Buckingham Palace ['bʌkɪŋəm-] *n* Palácio *m* de Buckingham.
buckle ['bʌkl] *n* fivela *f* ◆ *vt (fasten)* apertar *(com fivela)* ◆ *vi (warp)* contrair-se.
buck's fizz [ˌbʌks'fɪz] *n* bebida preparada com champanhe e suco de laranja.
bud [bʌd] *n (flower)* botão *m; (leaf)* rebento *m* ◆ *vi (flower)* florescer; *(leaf)* brotar.
Budapest [ˌbjuːdə'pest] *n* Budapeste *s.*
Buddhism ['bʊdɪzm] *n* budismo *m.*
Buddhist ['bʊdɪst] *n* budista *mf.*
budding ['bʌdɪŋ] *adj (aspiring)* potencial.
buddy ['bʌdɪ] *n (inf)* amigo *m (-ga f).*
budge [bʌdʒ] *vi* mexer-se.
budgerigar ['bʌdʒərɪgɑː*r*] *n* periquito *m.*
budget ['bʌdʒɪt] *adj (holiday, travel)* econômico(-ca) ◆ *n* orçamento *m;* the **Budget** *(Brit)* o orçamento do Estado. ❏ **budget for** *vt fus:* to ~ **for sthg** prever as despesas de algo.
budgie ['bʌdʒɪ] *n (inf)* periquito *m.*

buff [bʌf] *n (inf)* fanático *m* (-ca *f*).
buffalo ['bʌfələʊ] (*pl* **-s** OR **-es**) *n* búfalo *m*.
buffalo wings *npl (Am)* asas de frango fritas servidas com um molho picante.
buffer ['bʌfəʳ] *n (on train)* párachoque *m*.
buffet [*Brit* 'bʊfeɪ, *Am* bə'feɪ] *n* bufê *m (Br)*, bufete *m (Port)*.
buffet car *n* vagão-restaurante *m (Br)*, carruagem-restaurante *f (Port)*.
bug [bʌg] *n (insect)* bicho *m; (inf: mild illness)* vírus *m inv* ♦ *vt (inf: annoy)* chatear.
buggy ['bʌgɪ] *n* carrinho *m* de bebê.
bugle ['bjuːgl] *n* corneta *f*.
build [bɪld] (*pt & pp* **built**) *n* constituição *f* física ♦ *vt* construir.
⏺ **build up** *vt sep (strength, speed)* ganhar ♦ *vi* acumular-se.
builder ['bɪldəʳ] *n* constructor *m* (-ra *f*) (civil).
building ['bɪldɪŋ] *n* edifício *m*.
building site *n* canteiro *m* de obras.
building society *n (Brit)* sociedade financeira de crédito imobiliário.
buildup ['bɪldʌp] *n (increase)* aumento *m* (gradual).
built [bɪlt] *pt & pp* → **build**.
built-in *adj* incorporado(-da).
built-up area *n* zona *f* urbanizada.
bulb [bʌlb] *n (for lamp)* lâmpada *f* eléctrica; *(of plant)* bulbo *m*.
Bulgaria [bʌlˈɡeərɪə] *n* Bulgária *f*.
Bulgarian [bʌlˈɡeərɪən] *adj* búlgaro (-ra) ♦ *n (person)* búlgaro *m* (-ra *f*); *(language)* búlgaro *m*.
bulge [bʌldʒ] *vi* fazer volume.
bulk [bʌlk] *n*: **the ~ of** a maior parte de; **in ~** a granel, em grandes quantidades.
bulky ['bʌlkɪ] *adj* volumoso(-osa).
bull [bʊl] *n* touro *m*.
bulldog ['bʊldɒg] *n* buldogue *m*.
bulldozer ['bʊldəʊzəʳ] *n* bulldôzer *m*.
bullet ['bʊlɪt] *n* bala *f*.
bulletin ['bʊlɪtɪn] *n* boletim *m*.
bullet-proof *adj* à prova de bala.
bullfight ['bʊlfaɪt] *n* corrida *f* de touros, tourada *f*.
bullfighter ['bʊlfaɪtəʳ] *n* toureiro *m* (-ra *f*).
bullfighting ['bʊlfaɪtɪŋ] *n* tourada *f*, corridas *fpl* de touros.
bullion ['bʊljən] *n* lingotes *mpl*.

bullock ['bʊlək] *n* boi *m*, novilho *m* castrado.
bullring ['bʊlrɪŋ] *n* praça *f* de touros.
bull's-eye *n* centro *m* (do alvo).
bully ['bʊlɪ] *n* brigão *m* (-gona *f*) ♦ *vt* abusar de, intimidar.
bum [bʌm] *n (inf: bottom)* traseiro *m; (Am: inf: tramp)* vagabundo *m* (-da *f*).
bum bag *n (Brit)* carteira *f* (de cintura).
bumblebee ['bʌmblbiː] *n* abelhão *m*.
bump [bʌmp] *n (on surface)* elevação *f; (on leg)* inchaço *m; (on head)* galo *m; (sound, minor accident)* pancada *f* ♦ *vt (head, leg)* bater com.
⏺ **bump into** *vt fus (hit)* chocar com; *(meet)* encontrar-se com.
bumper ['bʌmpəʳ] *n (on car)* párachoques *m inv; (Am: on train)* párachoque *m*.
bumpy ['bʌmpɪ] *adj* acidentado(-da); **the flight was ~** durante o voo sentiuse um pouco de turbulência.
bun [bʌn] *n (cake)* pão *m* doce *(pequeno); (bread roll)* pãozinho *m (Br)*, carcaça *f (Port); (hairstyle)* coque *m*.
bunch [bʌntʃ] *n (of people)* grupo *m; (of flowers)* ramo *m; (of grapes, bananas)* cacho *m; (of keys)* molho *m*.
bundle ['bʌndl] *n (of clothes)* trouxa *f; (of notes, papers)* maço *m*.
bung [bʌŋ] *n* tampo *m*.
bungalow ['bʌŋgələʊ] *n* bangalô *m*.
bungle ['bʌŋgl] *vt* arruinar, estragar.
bunion ['bʌnjən] *n* joanete *m*.
bunk [bʌŋk] *n (bed)* beliche *m*.
bunk bed *n* beliche *m*.
bunker ['bʌŋkəʳ] *n (shelter)* abrigo *m; (for coal)* paiol *m* de carvão; *(in golf)* bunker *m*.
bunny ['bʌnɪ] *n* coelhinho *m*.
bunting ['bʌntɪŋ] *n (flags)* galhardetes *mpl*.
buoy [*Brit* bɔɪ, *Am* 'buːɪ] *n* bóia *f* (de sinalização).
buoyant ['bɔɪənt] *adj (that floats)* flutuante.
BUPA ['buːpə] *n* companhia seguradora britânica de seguros médicos privados.
burden ['bɜːdn] *n* carga *f*.
bureau ['bjʊərəʊ] (*pl* **-s** OR **-x**) *n (office, branch)* escritório *m*, centro *m; (Brit: desk)* escrivaninha *f; (Am: chest of drawers)* cômoda *f*.
bureaucracy [bjʊəˈrɒkrəsɪ] *n* burocracia *f*.

bureau de change [ˌbjʊərəʊdə-
ˈʃɒndʒ] *n* agência *f* de câmbio.
bureaux [ˌbjʊərəʊz] *pl* → **bureau**.
burger [ˈbɜːgəʳ] *n (hamburger)* hambúrger *m; (made with nuts, vegetables
etc)* hambúrger (vegetariano).
burglar [ˈbɜːgləʳ] *n* assaltante *mf*.
burglar alarm *n* alarme *m* (anti-
roubo).
burglarize [ˈbɜːgləraɪz] *(Am)* = burgle.
burglary [ˈbɜːglərɪ] *n* assalto *m*.
burgle [ˈbɜːgl] *vt* assaltar.
burial [ˈberɪəl] *n* enterro *m*.
burly [ˈbɜːlɪ] *adj* troncudo(-da), bem
constituído(-da).
Burma [ˈbɜːmə] *n* Burma *s*.
burn [bɜːn] *(pt & pp burnt OR burn-
ed) n* queimadura *f* ◆ *vt* queimar ◆ *vi
(be on fire)* arder.
❏ **burn down** *vt sep* incendiar ◆ *vi*
arder.
burner [ˈbɜːnəʳ] *n (on gas cooker)* bico
m, boca *f; (on electric cooker)* placa *f*.
burning (hot) [ˈbɜːnɪŋ-] *adj* muito
quente, escaldante.
Burns' Night [bɜːnz-] *n* 25 de janeiro, aniversário do nascimento do poeta
escocês Robert Burns.
burnt [bɜːnt] *pt & pp* → **burn**.
burp [bɜːp] *vi (inf)* arrotar.
burrow [ˈbʌrəʊ] *n* toca *f*.
bursar [ˈbɜːsəʳ] *n* tesoureiro *m* (-ra *f*).
bursary [ˈbɜːsərɪ] *n (Brit: scholarship,
grant)* bolsa *f* (de estudos).
burst [bɜːst] *(pt & pp burst) n (of gunfire, applause)* salva *f* ◆ *vt & vi* rebentar; **he ~ into the room** ele irrompeu
pelo quarto adentro; **to ~ into tears**
desatar a chorar; **to ~ open** *(door)*
abrir-se de repente.
bursting [ˈbɜːstɪŋ] *adj (full)* cheio(-a);
~ with sthg *(excitement, pride)* vibran-
do com algo; **to be ~ to do sthg**
(eager) estar doido(-da) para fazer
algo.
bury [ˈberɪ] *vt* enterrar.
bus [bʌs] *n* ônibus *m (Br)*, autocarro *m
(Port);* **by ~** de ônibus.
bus conductor [-ˌkəndʌktəʳ] *n*
cobrador *m* (-ra *f*) (de ônibus).
bus driver *n* motorista *mf* (de ônibus).
bush [bʊʃ] *n* arbusto *m*.
bushy [ˈbʊʃɪ] *adj (eyebrows, beard)*
cerrado(-da); *(tail)* peludo(-da).

business [ˈbɪznɪs] *n (commerce, trade)*
negócios *mpl; (shop, firm)* negócio *m;
(things to do, affair)* assunto *m;* **let's get
down to ~** passemos ao que interessa;
mind your own ~! meta-se na sua
vida!; **"~ as usual"** "aberto como de
costume".
business card *n* cartão-de-visita *m*.
business class *n* classe *f* executiva.
business hours *npl (of shops)* horário *m* de funcionamento; *(of offices)*
horário de atendimento.
businesslike [ˈbɪznɪslaɪk] *adj* profissional.
businessman [ˈbɪznɪsmæn] *(pl* -men
[-men]) *n* homem *m* de negócios.
business studies *npl* = práticas *fpl*
administrativas.
business trip *n* viagem *f* de negócios.
businesswoman [ˈbɪznɪsˌwʊmən] *(pl*
-women [-wɪmɪn]) *n* mulher *f* de negócios.
busker [ˈbʌskəʳ] *n (Brit)* músico *m* (-ca
f) de rua.
bus lane *n* faixa *f* para ônibus.
bus pass *n* passe *m* de ônibus.
bus shelter *n* abrigo *m (de parada de
ônibus).*
bus station *n* (estação) rodoviária *f*.
bus stop *n* parada *f* de ônibus *(Br)*,
paragem *f* de autocarro *(Port)*.
bust [bʌst] *n (of woman)* busto *m*
◆ *adj:* **to go ~** *(inf)* falir.
bustle [ˈbʌsl] *n* alvoroço *m,* animação
f.
bus tour *n* excursão *f (de ônibus ou
camionete).*
busy [ˈbɪzɪ] *adj* ocupado(-da); *(street,
office)* movimentado(-da); **to be ~
doing sthg** estar ocupado fazendo
algo.
busybody [ˈbɪzɪˌbɒdɪ] *n (pej)* mexeri-
queiro *m* (-ra *f*), abelhudo *m* (-da *f*).
busy signal *n (Am)* sinal *m* de ocupado.
but [bʌt] *conj* mas ◆ *prep* menos;
you've been nothing ~ trouble você só
tem me dado trabalho; **the last ~ one**
o penúltimo (a penúltima); **~ for** se
não fosse.
butcher [ˈbʊtʃəʳ] *n* carniceiro *m* (-ra
f); **~'s** *(shop)* açougue *m (Br)*, talho *m
(Port)*.
butler [ˈbʌtləʳ] *n* mordomo *m*.
butt [bʌt] *n (of rifle)* coronha *f; (of*

cigarette, cigar) ponta *f*.

butter ['bʌtəʳ] *n* manteiga *f* ◆ *vt* untar com manteiga.

butter bean *n* feijão *m* branco.

buttercup ['bʌtəkʌp] *n* botão-de-ouro *m*, ranúnculo *m*.

butter dish *n* manteigueira *f*.

butterfly ['bʌtəflaɪ] *n* borboleta *f*; *(swimming stroke)* nado *m* borboleta *(Br)*, mariposa *f (Port)*.

butterscotch ['bʌtəskɒtʃ] *n* espécie de caramelo duro feito com manteiga.

buttocks ['bʌtəks] *npl* nádegas *fpl*.

button ['bʌtn] *n* botão *m*; *(Am: badge)* crachá *m*.

buttonhole ['bʌtnhəʊl] *n (hole)* casa *f* (de botão).

button mushroom *n* cogumelo *m* pequeno.

buttress ['bʌtrɪs] *n* contraforte *m*.

buy [baɪ] *(pt & pp* **bought)** *vt* comprar ◆ *n:* **a good** ~ uma boa compra; **to** ~ **sthg for sb, to** ~ **sb sthg** comprar algo para OR de alguém.

buyer ['baɪəʳ] *n (purchaser)* comprador *m* (-ra *f*).

buzz [bʌz] *vi* zumbir ◆ *n (inf: phone call):* **to give sb a** ~ dar uma ligada para alguém.

buzzer ['bʌzəʳ] *n* campainha *f*.

buzzword ['bʌzwɜːd] *n (inf)* modismo *m*.

by [baɪ] *prep* **1.** *(expressing cause, agent)* por; **he's worried** ~ **her absence** está preocupado com a sua ausência; **he was hit** ~ **a car** ele foi atropelado por um carro; **a book** ~ **Irvine Welsh** um livro de Irvine Welsh; **funded** ~ **the government** financiado pelo governo.

2. *(expressing method, means):* ~ **car/bus/plane** de carro/ônibus/avião; ~ **phone/post** pelo telefone/correio; **to pay** ~ **credit card/cheque** pagar com cartão de crédito/cheque; **to win** ~ **cheating** ganhar trapaceando.

3. *(near to, beside)* junto a; ~ **the sea** à beira-mar, junto ao mar.

4. *(past)* por; **a car went** ~ **the house** um carro passou pela casa.

5. *(via)* por; **exit** ~ **the door on the left** sair pela porta do lado esquerdo.

6. *(with time):* **be there** ~ **nine** esteja lá às nove horas; ~ **day** de dia; **it should be ready** ~ **now** já deve estar pronto.

7. *(expressing quantity)* a; **sold** ~ **the dozen** vende-se à dúzia; **prices fell** ~ **20%** os preços baixaram 20%; **we charge** ~ **the hour** cobramos por hora.

8. *(expressing meaning)* com; **what do you mean** ~ **that?** que quer dizer com isso?

9. *(in division, multiplication)* por; **two metres** ~ **five** dois metros por cinco.

10. *(according to)* segundo; ~ **law** segundo a lei; **it's fine** ~ **me** por mim tudo bem.

11. *(expressing gradual process)* a; **one** ~ **one** um a um; **day** ~ **day** dia a dia.

12. *(in phrases):* ~ **mistake** por engano; ~ **oneself** sozinho; ~ **profession** por profissão.

◆ *adv (past):* **to go/drive** ~ passar.

bye(-bye) [baɪ(baɪ)] *excl (inf)* tchau!

bypass ['baɪpɑːs] *n (road)* contorno *m (Br)*, circunvalação *f (Port)*.

by-product *n (product)* subproduto *m*, derivado *m*; *(fig: consequence)* consequência *f*.

bystander ['baɪstændəʳ] *n* espectador *m* (-ra *f*).

C

C (*abbr of Celsius, centigrade*) C.
cab [kæb] *n (taxi)* táxi *m; (of lorry)* cabine *f*.
cabaret [ˈkæbəreɪ] *n* cabaré *m*.
cabbage [ˈkæbɪdʒ] *n* couve *f*.
cabin [ˈkæbɪn] *n (on ship)* camarote *m; (of plane)* cabine *f; (wooden house)* cabana *f*.
cabin crew *n* pessoal *m* de bordo, tripulação *f*.
cabinet [ˈkæbɪnɪt] *n (cupboard)* armário *m; (POL)* conselho *m* de ministros.
cable [ˈkeɪbl] *n* cabo *m*.
cable car *n* teleférico *m*.
cable television *n* televisão *f* a cabo.
cackle [ˈkækl] *vi* cacarejar.
cactus [ˈkæktəs] *(pl* **-tuses** OR **-ti** [-taɪ]) *n* cacto *m*.
cadet [kəˈdet] *n (in police)* cadete *m*.
cadge [kædʒ] *vt (Brit: inf):* **to ~ sthg (off** OR **from sb)** filar algo (de alguém) *(Br)*, cravar algo (a alguém) *(Port)*.
caesarean (section) [sɪˈzeərɪən-] *n (Brit)* cesariana *f*.
Caesar salad [ˈsiːzə-] *n* salada de alface com anchovas, queijo parmesão e cubos de pão torrado ou frito.
cafe [ˈkæfeɪ] *n* café *m*.
cafeteria [ˌkæfɪˈtɪərɪə] *n* cantina *f*.
cafetière [ˌkæfˈtjeər] *n* cafeteira *f (de êmbolo)*.
caffeine [ˈkæfiːn] *n* cafeína *f*.
cage [keɪdʒ] *n* gaiola *f*.
cagey [ˈkeɪdʒɪ] *adj (inf)* reservado (-da).
cagoule [kəˈguːl] *n (Brit)* casaco *m* impermeável *(fino e com capuz)*.
cajole [kəˈdʒəʊl] *vt:* **to ~ sb into doing sthg** induzir alguém a fazer algo.
Cajun [ˈkeɪdʒən] *adj* relativo à comunidade Cajun, de origem francesa, residente na Luisiana.

cake [keɪk] *n* bolo *m; (of soap)* barra *f*.
caked [keɪkt] *adj:* **~ with mud** coberto(-ta) de lama seca.
calcium [ˈkælsɪəm] *n* cálcio *m*.
calculate [ˈkælkjʊleɪt] *vt* calcular.
calculating [ˈkælkjʊleɪtɪŋ] *adj* calculista.
calculation [ˌkælkjʊˈleɪʃn] *n* cálculo *m*.
calculator [ˈkælkjʊleɪtər] *n* calculadora *f*.
calendar [ˈkælɪndər] *n* calendário *m*.
calf [kɑːf] *(pl* **calves**) *n (of cow)* bezerro *m* (-a *f*), vitelo *m* (-la *f*); *(part of leg)* barriga *f* da perna.
caliber [ˈkælɪbər] *(Am)* = **calibre**.
calibre [ˈkælɪbər] *n* calibre *m*.
California [ˌkælɪˈfɔːnjə] *n* Califórnia *f*.
calipers [ˈkælɪpəz] *(Am)* = **callipers**.
call [kɔːl] *n (visit)* visita *f; (phone call, at airport)* chamada *f; (of bird)* grito *m* ◆ *vt* chamar; *(say loudly)* chamar por; *(telephone)* ligar para; *(meeting, election, strike)* convocar; *(flight)* anunciar ◆ *vi (telephone)* telefonar, ligar; *(visit):* **he ~ed to see you** ele passou aqui para lhe ver; **could I have a ~ at eight o'clock, please?** por favor, pode chamar-me às oito?; **on ~** *(nurse, doctor)* de plantão; **to pay sb a ~** visitar alguém; **to be ~ed** chamar-se; **what is he ~ed?** como é que ele se chama?; **this train ~s at ...** este trem pára em ...; **who's ~ing?** é da parte de quem?
❑ **call back** *vt sep* voltar a telefonar a ◆ *vi (phone again)* voltar a telefonar; *(visit again):* **I'll ~ back later** passo aqui mais tarde.
❑ **call for** *vt fus (come to fetch)* ir buscar; *(demand, require)* exigir.
❑ **call on** *vt fus (visit)* ir visitar; **to ~ on sb to do sthg** pedir a alguém para fazer algo.
❑ **call out** *vt sep (name, winner)* anun-

ciar; *(doctor, fire brigade)* chamar ◆ *vi* gritar.

❏ **call up** *vt sep* *(MIL)* chamar, mobilizar; *(telephone)* telefonar para, ligar para.

call box *n* cabine f telefônica.

caller ['kɔːləʳ] *n (visitor)* visita f; *(on phone)* pessoa f que chama.

call-in *n (Am: on radio, TV) programa em que o público participa por telefone.*

calling ['kɔːlɪŋ] *n (profession, trade)* profissão f; *(vocation, urge)* vocação f.

calling card *n (Am)* cartão-de-visita *m.*

callipers ['kælɪpəz] *npl (Brit) (MATH)* compasso *m; (MED)* aparelho *m* ortopédico *(para as pernas).*

callous ['kæləs] *adj (unkind)* insensível.

callus ['kæləs] *n* calo *m.*

calm [kɑːm] *adj* calmo(-ma) ◆ *vt* acalmar.

❏ **calm down** *vt sep* acalmar ◆ *vi* acalmar-se.

Calor gas® [ˈkɑːlə-] *n* gás *m* butano.

calorie ['kælərɪ] *n* caloria f.

calves [kɑːvz] *pl → calf.*

Cambodia [kæmˈbəʊdjə] *n* Camboja *m.*

camcorder ['kæmˌkɔːdəʳ] *n* máquina f de filmar (vídeos).

came [keɪm] *pt → come.*

camel ['kæml] *n* camelo *m.*

camembert ['kæməmbeəʳ] *n* camembert *m.*

cameo ['kæmɪəʊ] *(pl -s) n (piece of jewellery)* camafeu *m; (in acting)* curta aparição f *(de um ator famoso); (in writing)* boa descrição f.

camera ['kæmərə] *n (for photographs)* máquina f OR câmara f fotográfica; *(for filming)* máquina OR câmara de filmar.

cameraman ['kæmərəmæn] *(pl -men* [-men]) *n* operador *m* de câmara, cameraman *m.*

camera shop *n* loja f de artigos fotográficos.

Cameroon [ˌkæməˈruːn] *n* Camarões *mpl.*

camisole ['kæmɪsəʊl] *n* camisola f interior.

camouflage ['kæməflɑːʒ] *n* camuflagem f ◆ *vt* camuflar.

camp [kæmp] *n (for holidaymakers)* colônia f de férias; *(for soldiers)* acampamento *m; (for prisoners)* campo ◆ *vi* acampar.

campaign [kæmˈpeɪn] *n* campanha f ◆ *vi:* **to ~ (for/against)** fazer campanha (a favor de/contra).

camp bed *n* cama f de campanha.

camper ['kæmpəʳ] *n (person)* campista *mf; (van)* trailer *m (Br),* caravana f, roulotte f *(motorizada) (Port).*

campground ['kæmpgraʊnd] *n (Am)* camping *m,* acampamento *m (Br).*

camping ['kæmpɪŋ] *n:* **to go ~** acampar.

camping stove *n* fogareiro *m* (de campismo).

campsite ['kæmpsaɪt] *n* camping *m.*

campus ['kæmpəs] *(pl -es) n* cidade f universitária.

can¹ [kæn] *n* lata f.

can² [weak form kən, strong form kæn] *(pt & conditional* **could**) *aux vb* **1.** *(be able to)* poder; **~ you help me?** podia ajudar-me?; **I ~ see the mountains** posso ver as montanhas.
2. *(know how to)* saber; **~ you drive?** você sabe conduzir?; **I ~ speak Portuguese** eu sei falar português.
3. *(be allowed to)* poder; **you can't smoke here** você não pode fumar aqui.
4. *(in polite requests)* poder; **~ you tell me the time?** podia me dizer as horas?; **~ I speak to the manager?** posso falar com o gerente?
5. *(expressing occasional occurrence)* poder; **it ~ get cold at night** às vezes à noite a temperatura baixa bastante.
6. *(expressing possibility)* poder; **they could be lost** eles podem estar perdidos.

Canada ['kænədə] *n* Canadá *m.*

Canadian [kəˈneɪdɪən] *adj & n* canadense *mf (Br),* canadiano *m* (-na f) *(Port).*

canal [kəˈnæl] *n* canal *m.*

canapé ['kænəpeɪ] *n* canapé *m.*

canary [kəˈneərɪ] *n* canário *m.*

cancel ['kænsl] *vt* cancelar.

cancellation [ˌkænsəˈleɪʃn] *n* cancelamento *m.*

cancer ['kænsəʳ] *n* câncer *m (Br),* cancro *m (Port).*

Cancer ['kænsəʳ] *n* Câncer *m (Br),* Caranguejo *m (Port).*

candelabra [ˌkændɪˈlɑːbrə] *n* candelabro *m.*

candid ['kændɪd] *adj* cândido(-da).

candidate ['kændɪdət] *n* candidato *m* (-ta *f*).

candle ['kændl] *n* vela *f*.

candlelight ['kændllaɪt] *n* luz *f* de vela.

candlelit dinner ['kændllɪt-] *n* jantar *m* à luz de vela.

candlestick ['kændlstɪk] *n* castiçal *m*.

candor ['kændər] *(Am)* = candour.

candour ['kændər] *n (Brit)* candura *f*, candor *m*.

candy ['kændɪ] *n (Am) (confectionery)* guloseimas *fpl; (sweet)* bala *f (Br)*, rebuçado *m (Port)*.

candyfloss ['kændɪflɒs] *n (Brit)* algodão *m* doce.

cane [keɪn] *n (for walking)* bengala *f; (for punishment)* palha *f; (for furniture, baskets)* verga *f*.

canine ['keɪnaɪn] *adj* canino(-na) ◆ *n*: ~ **(tooth)** (dente) canino *m*.

canister ['kænɪstər] *n (for tea)* caixa *f* (para o chá); *(for gas)* lata *f*.

cannabis ['kænəbɪs] *n* maconha *f (Br)*, haxixe *m (Port)*.

canned [kænd] *adj (food, drink)* enlatado(-da).

cannibal ['kænɪbl] *n* canibal *mf*.

cannon ['kænən] *n* canhão *m*.

cannonball ['kænənbɔːl] *n* bala *f* de canhão.

cannot ['kænɒt] = can not.

canny ['kænɪ] *adj (shrewd)* astuto(-ta).

canoe [kə'nuː] *n* canoa *f*.

canoeing [kə'nuːɪŋ] *n* canoagem *f*.

can opener *n* abridor *m* de latas *(Br)*, abre-latas *m inv (Port)*.

canopy ['kænəpɪ] *n (over bed etc)* dossel *m*.

can't [kɑːnt] = cannot.

cantaloup(e) ['kæntəluːp] *n* meloa *f*.

cantankerous [kæn'tæŋkərəs] *adj* intratável.

canteen [kæn'tiːn] *n* cantina *f*.

canter ['kæntər] *n* meio galope *m* ◆ *vi* ir a meio galope.

canvas ['kænvəs] *n (for tent, bag)* lona *f*.

canvass ['kænvəs] *vt (voters)* pedir o voto de; *(investigate)* sondar.

canyon ['kænjən] *n* desfiladeiro *m*.

cap [kæp] *n (hat)* boné *m; (of pen, bottle)* tampa *f; (contraceptive)* diafragma *m*.

capability [ˌkeɪpə'bɪlətɪ] *n* capacidade *f*.

capable ['keɪpəbl] *adj* capaz; **to be ~ of doing sthg** ser capaz de fazer algo.

capacity [kə'pæsɪtɪ] *n* capacidade *f*.

cape [keɪp] *n (of land)* cabo *m; (cloak)* capa *f*.

capers ['keɪpəz] *npl* alcaparras *fpl*.

Cape Verde [-'vɜːd] *n*: **the ~ Islands** as Ilhas de Cabo Verde.

capital ['kæpɪtl] *n (of country)* capital *f; (money)* capital *m; (letter)* maiúscula *f*.

capitalism ['kæpɪtəlɪzm] *n* capitalismo *m*.

capitalist ['kæpɪtəlɪst] *adj* capitalista ◆ *n* capitalista *mf*.

capital punishment *n* pena *f* de morte.

Capitol Hill ['kæpɪtl-] *n* o Capitólio, *sede do Congresso americano, em Washington*.

capitulate [kə'pɪtjʊleɪt] *vi*: **to ~ to sthg** capitular perante algo.

cappuccino [ˌkæpʊ'tʃiːnəʊ] *(pl -s)* *n* cappuccino *m*.

Capricorn ['kæprɪkɔːn] *n* Capricórnio *m*.

capsicum ['kæpsɪkəm] *n* pimentão *m (Br)*, pimento *m (Port)*.

capsize [kæp'saɪz] *vi* virar-se.

capsule ['kæpsjuːl] *n* cápsula *f*.

captain ['kæptɪn] *n* capitão *m* (-tã *f*); *(of plane, ship)* comandante *mf*.

caption ['kæpʃn] *n* legenda *f*.

captivate ['kæptɪveɪt] *vt* cativar.

captive ['kæptɪv] *n* cativo *m* (-va *f*) ◆ *adj (imprisoned)* cativo(-va); *(audience, market)* seguro(-ra).

captor ['kæptər] *n* captor *m* (-ra *f*).

capture ['kæptʃər] *vt (person, animal)* capturar; *(town, castle)* tomar.

car [kɑːr] *n (motorcar)* carro *m*, automóvel *m; (railway wagon)* vagão *m (Br)*, carruagem *f (Port)*.

carafe [kə'ræf] *n* garrafa *f (de boca larga para servir vinho ou água)*.

caramel ['kærəmel] *n (sweet)* caramelo *m; (burnt sugar)* calda *f* caramelada *(Br)*, caramelo líquido *(Port)*.

carat ['kærət] *n* quilate *m;* **24-~ gold** ouro de 24 quilates.

caravan ['kærəvæn] *n (Brit)* trailer *m (Br)*, caravana *f (Port)*.

caravanning ['kærəvænɪŋ] *n (Brit)*: **to go ~** passar férias num trailer.

caravan site *n (Brit)* camping *m* para trailers *(Br)*, parque *m* de campis-

mo para caravanas *(Port)*.
carbohydrate [ˌkuːbəʊˈhaɪdreɪt] *n (in foods)* hidrato *m* de carbono.
carbon [ˈkuːbən] *n* carbono *m*.
carbonated [ˈkuːbəneɪtɪd] *adj* com gás, gaseificado(-da).
carbon copy *n* cópia *f* feita com papel químico.
carbon dioxide [-daɪˈɒksaɪd] *n* dióxido *m* de carbono.
carbon monoxide [-mɒˈnɒksaɪd] *n* monóxido *m* de carbono.
car boot sale *n (Brit)* mercado de objetos usados, cuja venda se faz diretamente do porta-malas dos carros.
carburetor [ˌkuːbəˈretər] *(Am)* = **carburettor**.
carburettor [ˌkuːbəˈretəʳ] *n (Brit)* carburador *m*.
carcass [ˈkuːkəs] *n* carcaça *f*.
car crash *n* acidente *m* de carro.
card [kuːd] *n* cartão *m*; *(postcard)* postal *m*; *(playing card)* carta *f*; *(cardboard)* cartolina *f*, papelão *m*.
⌐ cards *npl (game)* cartas *fpl*.
cardboard [ˈkuːdbɔːd] *n* cartolina *f*, papelão *m*.
cardboard box *n* caixa *f* de papelão.
car deck *n* convés *m* para veículos.
cardiac arrest [ˌkuːdɪæk-] *n* parada *f* cardíaca *(Br)*, paragem *f* cardíaca *(Port)*.
cardigan [ˈkuːdɪgən] *n* casaco *m* de malha.
cardinal [ˈkuːdɪnl] *adj* capital ♦ *n (RELIG)* cardeal *m*.
card index *n (Brit)* fichário *m (Br)*, ficheiro *m (Port)*.
care [keəʳ] *n (attention)* cuidado *m*; *(treatment)* cuidados *mpl* ♦ *vi (mind)* importar-se; **to take ~ of** tomar conta de; **to take ~ not to do sthg** ter cuidado para não fazer algo; **take ~!** *(goodbye)* expressão de afeto utilizada frequentemente em despedidas; **with ~** com cuidado; **would you ~ to …?** *(fml)* você se importaria de …?; **to ~ about** *(think important)* preocupar-se com; *(person)* querer bem a.
career [kəˈrɪəʳ] *n* carreira *f*.
careers adviser [kəˈrɪəz-] *n* orientador *m* (-ra *f*) profissional.
carefree [ˈkeəfriː] *adj* despreocupado(-da).
careful [ˈkeəfʊl] *adj* cuidadoso(-osa); **be ~!** cuidado!

carefully [ˈkeəflɪ] *adv* cuidadosamente.
careless [ˈkeələs] *adj* descuidado(-da).
caress [kəˈres] *n* carícia *f* ♦ *vt* acariciar.
caretaker [ˈkeəˌteɪkəʳ] *n (Brit)* porteiro *m* (-ra *f*).
car ferry *n* barco *m (de travessia que transporta carros)*.
cargo [ˈkuːgəʊ] *(pl* **-es** OR **-s***) n* carga *f*, carregamento *m*.
car hire *n (Brit)* aluguel *m* de carros OR automóveis.
Caribbean [Brit ˌkærɪˈbiːən, Am kəˈrɪbɪən] *n*: **the ~** *(area)* as Caraíbas.
caring [ˈkeərɪŋ] *adj* atencioso(-osa), solícito(-ta).
carnage [ˈkuːnɪdʒ] *n* carnificina *f*.
carnation [kuːˈneɪʃn] *n* cravo *m*.
carnival [ˈkuːnɪvl] *n* carnaval *m*.
carnivorous [kuːˈnɪvərəs] *adj* carnívoro(-ra).
carol [ˈkærəl] *n*: **(Christmas) ~** cântico *m* de Natal.
carousel [ˌkærəˈsel] *n (for luggage)* esteira *f* rolante *(Br)*, tapete *m* rolante *(Port)*; *(Am: merry-go-round)* carrossel *m*.
carp [kuːp] *n* carpa *f*.
car park *n (Brit)* estacionamento *m*.
carpenter [ˈkuːpəntəʳ] *n* carpinteiro *m* (-ra *f*).
carpentry [ˈkuːpəntrɪ] *n* carpintaria *f*.
carpet [ˈkuːpɪt] *n (fitted)* carpete *f (Br)*, alcatifa *f (Port)*; *(not fitted)* tapete *m*.
car phone *n* telefone *m* de carro.
car rental *n (Am)* aluguel *m* de carros OR automóveis.
carriage [ˈkærɪdʒ] *n (Brit: of train)* carruagem *f*; *(horse-drawn)* coche *m*.
carriageway [ˈkærɪdʒweɪ] *n (Brit)* pista *f (Br)*, carril *m (Port)*.
carrier (bag) [ˈkærɪə-] *n* saco *m (de papel ou plástico)*.
carrot [ˈkærət] *n* cenoura *f*.
carrot cake *n* bolo *m* de cenoura.
carry [ˈkærɪ] *vt (bear)* carregar, levar; *(transport)* transportar, levar; *(disease)* transmitir; *(cash, passport, map)* ter (consigo); *(support)* agüentar com ♦ *vi (voice, sound)* ouvir-se.
⌐ carry on *vi (continue)* continuar ♦ *vt fus (continue)* continuar; *(conduct)* reali-

zar; **to ~ on doing sthg** continuar a fazer algo.
❏ **carry out** vt sep (perform) levar a cabo; (fulfil) cumprir.

carrycot ['kærɪkɒt] n (Brit) moisés m inv (Br), alcofa m de bebé (Port).

carryout ['kærɪaʊt] n (Am & Scot) comida f para levar.

carsick ['kuːsɪk] adj enjoado(-da) (em carro).

cart [kuːt] n (for transport) carroça f; (Am: in supermarket) carro m das compras; (inf: video game cartridge) cassete f.

carton ['kuːtn] n pacote m.

cartoon [kuːˈtuːn] n (drawing) desenho m, caricatura f; (film) desenho animado.

cartridge ['kuːtrɪdʒ] n (for gun) cartucho m; (for pen) recarga f.

cartwheel ['kuːtwiːl] n (movement) cambalhota f lateral.

carve [kuːv] vt (wood, stone) esculpir; (meat) cortar.

carvery ['kuːvərɪ] n restaurante onde se servem churrascos cortados diante dos fregueses.

carving ['kuːvɪŋ] n (wooden) talha f; (stone) gravura f.

car wash n lavagem f automática.

case [keɪs] n (Brit: suitcase) mala f; (container) caixa f; (instance, patient) caso m; (JUR: trial) causa f; **in any ~** de qualquer modo; **in ~ of** em caso de; **(just) in ~** caso; **in that ~** nesse caso.

cash [kæʃ] n dinheiro m ◆ vt: **to ~ a cheque** descontar um cheque (Br), levantar um cheque (Port); **to pay ~** pagar em dinheiro.

cash and carry n cash-and-carry m, armazém m de venda a granel.

cash box n cofre m.

cash card n = (cartão) multibanco m.

cash desk n caixa f.

cash dispenser [-ˌdɪˈspensər] n caixa m automático, multibanco m.

cashew (nut) ['kæʃuː-] n caju m, castanha f de caju.

cashier [kæˈʃɪər] n caixa mf.

cash machine = cash dispenser.

cashmere [kæʃˈmɪər] n caxemira f.

cashpoint ['kæʃpɔɪnt] n (Brit) caixa m automático, multibanco m.

cash register n caixa f registadora.

casing ['keɪsɪŋ] n revestimento m.

casino [kəˈsiːnəʊ] (pl -s) n casino m.

cask [kuːsk] n casco m, barril m.

cask-conditioned [-kənˈdɪʃnd] adj fermentado(-da) no barril.

casket ['kuːskɪt] n (for jewels) guarda-jóias m inv.

casserole ['kæsərəʊl] n (stew) ensopado m de forno; **~ (dish)** panela f de ir ao forno.

cassette [kæˈset] n cassete f.

cassette player n toca-fitas m inv (Br), leitor m de cassetes (Port).

cassette recorder n gravador m.

cast [kuːst] (pt & pp cast) n (actors) elenco m; (for broken bone) gesso m ◆ vt (shadow, light, look) lançar; **to ~ doubt on** pôr em dúvida; **to ~ one's vote** votar.
❏ **cast off** vi (boat, ship) zarpar.

castaway ['kuːstəweɪ] n náufrago m (-ga f).

caster ['kuːstər] n (wheel) rodízio m.

caster sugar n (Brit) açúcar m branco (muito fino).

cast iron n ferro m fundido.

castle ['kuːsl] n (building) castelo m; (in chess) torre f.

castor oil ['kuːstər-] n óleo m de rícino.

castrate [kæˈstreɪt] vt castrar.

casual ['kæʒʊəl] adj (relaxed) despreocupado(-da); (manner, clothes) informal; **~ work** trabalho m temporário.

casually ['kæʒʊəlɪ] adv (in a relaxed manner) despreocupadamente; (address, dress) informalmente.

casualty ['kæʒjʊəltɪ] n vítima mf; **~ (ward)** pronto-socorro m (Br), urgências fpl (Port).

cat [kæt] n gato m.

catalog ['kætəlɒg] (Am) = **catalogue**.

catalogue ['kætəlɒg] n catálogo m.

catalyst ['kætəlɪst] n catalisador m.

catalytic converter [ˌkætəlɪtɪkkənˈvɜːtər] n conversor m catalítico (Br), vaso m catalítico (Port).

catapult ['kætəpʌlt] n catapulta f.

cataract ['kætərækt] n (in eye) catarata f.

catarrh [kəˈtuːr] n catarro m.

catastrophe [kəˈtæstrəfɪ] n catástrofe f.

catch [kætʃ] (pt & pp caught) vt apanhar; (attention, imagination) despertar ◆ vi (become hooked) ficar preso ◆ n (of window, door) trinco m; (snag) truque m.

❏ **catch up** *vt sep* alcançar ◆ *vi*: **to ~ up (with)** alcançar.

catching [ˈkætʃɪŋ] *adj (inf)* contagioso(-osa).

catchment area [ˈkætʃmənt-] *n* zona servida por uma escola ou hospital.

catchphrase [ˈkætʃfreɪz] *n* slogan *m*.

catchy [ˈkætʃɪ] *adj* fácil de lembrar.

categorically [ˌkætɪˈgɒrɪklɪ] *adv* categoricamente.

category [ˈkætəgərɪ] *n* categoria *f*.

cater [ˈkeɪtəʳ] **: cater for** *vt fus (Brit) (needs, tastes)* satisfazer; *(anticipate)* contar com.

caterer [ˈkeɪtərəʳ] *n* fornecedor *m* (-ra *f*) *(de serviço de bufê)*.

catering [ˈkeɪtərɪŋ] *n (at wedding etc)* serviço *m* de bufê; *(trade)* = hotelaria *f*.

caterpillar [ˈkætəpɪləʳ] *n* lagarta *f*.

cathedral [kəˈθiːdrəl] *n* catedral *f*.

Catholic [ˈkæθlɪk] *adj* católico(-ca) ◆ *n* católico *m* (-ca *f*).

Catseyes® [ˈkætsaɪz] *npl (Brit)* refletores *mpl (em estrada).*

cattle [ˈkætl] *npl* gado *m*.

cattle grid *n* mata-burro *m* *(ponte de traves espaçadas, destinada a impedir a passagem de animais).*

catwalk [ˈkætwɔːk] *n* passarela *f*.

caught [kɔːt] *pt & pp* → **catch**.

cauliflower [ˈkɒlɪflaʊəʳ] *n* couve-flor *f*.

cauliflower cheese *n* gratinado de couve-flor com molho branco e queijo ralado.

cause [kɔːz] *n* causa *f*; *(justification)* razão *f* ◆ *vt* caˈusar; **to ~ sb to do sthg** fazer (com) que alguém faça algo.

causeway [ˈkɔːzweɪ] *n* calçada *f (sobre água ou zona pantanosa).*

caustic [ˈkɔːstɪk] *adj (chemical)* corrosivo(-va), cáustico(-ca); *(comment)* mordaz.

caustic soda [ˌkɔːstɪk-] *n* soda *f* cáustica.

caution [ˈkɔːʃn] *n (care)* cautela *f*; *(warning)* aviso *m*.

cautious [ˈkɔːʃəs] *adj* cauteloso (-osa).

cavalry [ˈkævlrɪ] *n (on horseback)* cavalaria *f*.

cave [keɪv] *n* gruta *f*.

❏ **cave in** *vi (roof, ceiling)* desabar.

caveman [ˈkeɪvmæn] *(pl -men* [-men]*)* *n* homem *m* das cavernas.

caviar(e) [ˈkævɪɑːʳ] *n* caviar *m*.

cavity [ˈkævətɪ] *n (in tooth)* cavidade *f*.

CB *abrev* = **Citizens' Band**.

cc *n (abbr of cubic centimetre)* cm³.

CD *n (abbr of compact disc)* CD *m*.

CDI *n (abbr of compact disc interactive)* CDI *m*.

CD player *n* som *m* CD *(Br)*, leitor *m* de CDs *(Port)*.

CD-ROM [ˌsiːdiːˈrɒm] *n (abbr of compact disc read only memory)* CD-ROM *m*.

CDW *n (abbr of collision damage waiver)* = franquia *f*, = seguro *m* contra choque, colisão, capotagem, incêndio.

cease [siːs] *vt & vi (fml)* cessar.

ceasefire [ˈsiːsfaɪəʳ] *n* cessar-fogo *m*.

cedar (tree) [ˈsiːdəʳ-] *n* cedro *m*.

ceilidh [ˈkeɪlɪ] *n* festa ou baile tradicional escocês ou irlandês.

ceiling [ˈsiːlɪŋ] *n* teto *m*.

celebrate [ˈselɪbreɪt] *vt & vi (victory, birthday)* celebrar.

celebration [ˌselɪˈbreɪʃn] *n (event)* celebração *f*.

❏ **celebrations** *npl (festivities)* comemorações *fpl*.

celebrity [sɪˈlebrətɪ] *n (person)* celebridade *f*.

celeriac [sɪˈlerɪæk] *n* aipo-rábano *m*.

celery [ˈselərɪ] *n* aipo *m*.

celibate [ˈselɪbət] *adj* celibatário(-ria).

cell [sel] *n (of plant, body)* célula *f*; *(in prison)* cela *f*.

cellar [ˈseləʳ] *n* cave *f*.

cello [ˈtʃeləʊ] *(pl -s)* *n* violoncelo *m*.

Cellophane® [ˈseləfeɪn] *n* celofane *m*.

Celsius [ˈselsɪəs] *adj* centígrado(-da).

Celt [kelt] *n* celta *mf*.

Celtic [ˈkeltɪk] *adj* celta.

cement [sɪˈment] *n* cimento *m*.

cement mixer *n* betoneira *f*.

cemetery [ˈsemɪtrɪ] *n* cemitério *m*.

censor [ˈsensəʳ] *n* censor *m* (-ra *f*) ◆ *vt* censurar.

censorship [ˈsensəʃɪp] *n* censura *f*.

census [ˈsensəs] *n (population survey)* censo *m*.

cent [sent] *n (Am)* cêntimo *m*.

centenary [senˈtiːnərɪ] *n (Brit)* centenário *m*.

centennial [senˈtenjəl] *(Am)* = **centenary**.

center [ˈsentəʳ] *(Am)* = **centre**.

centigrade [ˈsentɪgreɪd] *adj* centígrado(-da).

centilitre ['sɛntɪ.liːtəʳ] n centilitro m.

centimetre ['sɛntɪ.miːtəʳ] n centímetro m.

centipede ['sɛntɪpiːd] n centopeia f.

central ['sɛntrəl] adj central.

Central America n América f Central.

central heating n aquecimento m central.

central locking [-'lɒkɪŋ] n fechadura f centralizada.

central reservation n (Brit) canteiro m central (Br), faixa f separadora central (Port) (em auto-estrada).

centre ['sɛntəʳ] n (Brit) centro m ♦ adj (Brit) central; **the ~ of attention** o centro das atenções.

century ['sɛntʃʊrɪ] n século m.

ceramic [sɪ'ræmɪk] adj de louça OR barro.

❑ **ceramics** npl cerâmica f.

cereal ['sɪərɪəl] n cereal m.

ceremony ['sɛrɪmənɪ] n cerimônia f.

certain ['sɜːtn] adj certo(-ta); **she's ~ to be late** o mais certo é ela chegar atrasada; **to be ~ of sthg** ter a certeza de algo; **to make ~ (that)** assegurar-se de que.

certainly ['sɜːtnlɪ] adv (without doubt) sem dúvida; (of course) com certeza; **~ not!** de modo nenhum!; **I ~ do** com certeza que sim.

certainty ['sɜːtntɪ] n certeza f.

certificate [sə'tɪfɪkət] n (of studies, medical) certificado m; (of birth) certidão f.

certified mail ['sɜːtɪfaɪd-] n (Am) correio m registrado.

certify ['sɜːtɪfaɪ] vt (declare true) comprovar.

cervical smear [sə'vaɪkl-] n exame m de lâmina, esfregaço m cervical.

cervix ['sɜːvɪks] (pl **-ixes** OR **-ices** [-ɪsiːz]) n (of uterus) cérvix m, colo m (do útero).

cesarean (section) [sɪ'zɛərɪən-] (Am) = **caesarean (section)**.

CFC n (abbr of chlorofluorocarbon) CFC m.

chaffinch ['tʃæfɪntʃ] n tentilhão m.

chain [tʃeɪn] n (of metal) corrente f; (of shops, mountains) cadeia f ♦ vt: **to ~ sthg to sthg** prender algo a algo (com corrente).

chain saw n serra f de cadeia (Br),

motoserra f (Port).

chain-smoke vi fumar um cigarro atrás do outro OR cigarro atrás de cigarro.

chain store n loja pertencente a uma cadeia.

chair [tʃeəʳ] n cadeira f.

chair lift n teleférico m (de cadeira).

chairman ['tʃeəmən] (pl **-men** [-mən]) n presidente m.

chairperson ['tʃeə.pɜːsn] (pl **-s**) n presidente mf.

chairwoman ['tʃeə.wʊmən] (pl **-women** [-.wɪmɪn]) n presidente f.

chalet ['ʃæleɪ] n chalé m.

chalk [tʃɔːk] n giz m; **a piece of ~** um pedaço de giz.

chalkboard ['tʃɔːkbɔːd] n (Am) quadro m.

challenge ['tʃælɪndʒ] n desafio m ♦ vt (question) questionar; **to ~ sb (to sthg)** (to fight, competition) desafiar alguém (para algo).

challenging ['tʃælɪndʒɪŋ] adj (task, job) estimulante.

chamber ['tʃeɪmbəʳ] n (room) câmara f.

chambermaid ['tʃeɪmbəmeɪd] n camareira f (Br), empregada f de quarto (Port).

chameleon [kə'miːljən] n camaleão m.

champagne [.ʃæm'peɪn] n champanhe m.

champion ['tʃæmpjən] n campeão m (-peã f).

championship ['tʃæmpjənʃɪp] n campeonato m.

chance [tʃɑːns] n chance f ♦ vt: **to ~ it** (inf) arriscar; **to take a ~** arriscar-se; **by ~** por acaso; **on the off ~** por se acaso.

chancellor ['tʃɑːnsələʳ] n (of country) chanceler m; (of university) reitor m (-ra f).

Chancellor of the Exchequer [.tʃɑːnsələrəvðəɪks'tʃekəʳ] n (Brit) = ministro m (-tra f) da Fazenda (Br), = ministro m (-tra f) das Finanças (Port).

chandelier [.ʃændə'lɪəʳ] n candelabro m, lustre m.

change [tʃeɪndʒ] n (alteration) mudança f; (money received back) troco m; (coins) dinheiro m trocado ♦ vt mudar; (exchange) trocar; (clothes, bedding) mudar de, trocar de ♦ vi mudar; (change clothes) trocar-se, mudar de roupa; **a ~ of clothes** uma muda de roupa; **do you have ~ for a pound?** você pode trocar uma libra?; **for a ~** para variar; **to get ~d** trocar-se, mudar de roupa; **to ~ money** trocar dinheiro; **to ~ a nappy** mudar uma fralda; **to ~ a wheel** mudar uma roda; **to ~ trains/planes** mudar de trem/avião; **all ~!** *(on train)* mudança de trem!

changeable [ˈtʃeɪndʒəbl] *adj (weather)* variável.

change machine *n* máquina automática para trocar dinheiro.

changeover [ˈtʃeɪndʒˌəʊvəʳ] *n:* **~ (to)** mudança *f* (para), passagem *f* (a).

changing room [ˈtʃeɪndʒɪŋ-] *n* vestiário *m*.

channel [ˈtʃænl] *n* canal *m*; **the (English) Channel** o Canal da Mancha.

Channel Islands *npl:* **the ~** as Ilhas do Canal da Mancha.

Channel Tunnel *n:* **the ~** o túnel do Canal da Mancha, o Eurotúnel.

chant [tʃɑːnt] *vt* entoar.

chaos [ˈkeɪɒs] *n* caos *m*.

chaotic [keɪˈɒtɪk] *adj* caótico(-ca).

chap [tʃæp] *n (Brit: inf)* sujeito *m*.

chapatti [tʃəˈpætɪ] *n* pequeno pão não fermentado de origem indiana.

chapel [ˈtʃæpl] *n* capela *f*.

chaplain [ˈtʃæplɪn] *n* capelão *m*.

chapped [tʃæpt] *adj* gretado(-da).

chapter [ˈtʃæptəʳ] *n* capítulo *m*.

character [ˈkærəktəʳ] *n* carácter *m*; *(in film, book, play)* personagem *m ou f*; *(inf: person, individual)* tipo *m*.

characteristic [ˌkærəktəˈrɪstɪk] *adj* característico(-ca) ♦ *n* característica *f*.

characterize [ˈkærəktəraɪz] *vt* caracterizar.

charade [ʃəˈrɑːd] *n* charada *f*.

❏ **charades** *n* charadas *fpl.*

charcoal [ˈtʃɑːkəʊl] *n (for barbecue)* carvão *m* (de lenha).

charge [tʃɑːdʒ] *n (price)* preço *m*, custo *m*; *(JUR)* acusação *f* ♦ *vt (money, customer)* cobrar; *(JUR)* acusar; *(battery)* carregar ♦ *vi (ask money)* cobrar; *(rush)* investir; **to be in ~ (of)** estar encarregado (de); **to take ~ (of)** encarregar-se (de); **free of ~** grátis; **there is no ~ for service** o serviço é grátis.

charge card *n* cartão de crédito que permite fazer compras num estabelecimento e pagar posteriormente.

char-grilled [ˈtʃɑːgrɪld] *adj* assado (-da) na brasa.

chariot [ˈtʃærɪət] *n* charrete *f*.

charisma [kəˈrɪzmə] *n* carisma *m*.

charity [ˈtʃærɪtɪ] *n (organization)* caridade *f*; **to give to ~** contribuir para obras de caridade.

charity shop *n* loja de objetos usados cujas vendas se destinam a causas beneficentes.

charm [tʃɑːm] *n (attractiveness)* charme *m* ♦ *vt* encantar.

charming [ˈtʃɑːmɪŋ] *adj* encantador (-ra).

chart [tʃɑːt] *n (diagram)* gráfico *m*; **the ~s** as paradas de sucesso *(Br)*, os tops de vendas (de discos) *(Port)*.

charter [ˈtʃɑːtəʳ] *n (document)* carta *f* ♦ *vt (plane, boat)* fretar.

chartered accountant [ˈtʃɑːtəd-] *n* perito-contador *m*, perita-contadora *f (Br)*, técnico *m* (-ca *f*) de contas *(Port)*.

charter flight *n* vôo *m* charter.

chase [tʃeɪs] *n* perseguição *f* ♦ *vt* perseguir.

chasm [ˈkæzm] *n (deep crack)* fenda *f* profunda, abismo *m*.

chassis [ˈʃæsɪ] *(pl inv* [-sɪz]) *n (of vehicle)* chassis *m inv*.

chat [tʃæt] *n* conversa *f* ♦ *vi* conversar; **to have a ~ (with)** conversar (com).

❏ **chat up** *vt sep (Brit: inf)* paquerar *(Br)*, engatar *(Port)*.

chat show *n (Brit)* programa *m* de variedades, talk-show *m*.

chatter [ˈtʃætəʳ] *n (of person)* tagarelice *f* ♦ *vi (person)* tagarelar; **her teeth were ~ing** ela estava tiritando.

chatterbox [ˈtʃætəbɒks] *n (inf)* tagarela *mf*.

chatty [ˈtʃætɪ] *adj (letter)* informal, *(person)* tagarela.

chauffeur [ˈʃəʊfəʳ] *n* motorista *mf*.

chauvinist [ˈʃəʊvɪnɪst] *n (sexist)* sexista *mf*; *(nationalist)* chauvinista *mf*; **male ~** machista *m*.

cheap [tʃiːp] *adj* barato(-ta).

cheap day return *n (Brit)* bilhete de ida e volta mais barato, comprado no próprio dia e que só pode ser usado depois das 9.30.

cheaply [ˈtʃiːplɪ] *adv* barato.

cheat [tʃiːt] *n (person)* trapaceiro *m* (-ra *f*) *(Br)*, batoteiro *m* (-ra *f*) *(Port)*; *(thing)* trapaça *f (Br)*, batota *f (Port)*

◆ *vi* trapacear *(Br)*, fazer batota *(Port)*
◆ *vt*: **to ~ sb (out of sthg)** roubar algo de alguém.

check [tʃek] *n (inspection)* inspecção *f*; *(Am: bill)* conta *f*; *(Am: tick)* sinal *m* de visto; *(Am)* = **cheque** ◆ *vt* verificar ◆ *vi* informar-se; **~ for any mistakes** verifique se há erros.

❑ **check in** *vt sep (luggage)* fazer o check-in de ◆ *vi (at hotel)* registrar-se; *(at airport)* fazer o check-in.
❑ **check off** *vt sep* verificar *(em lista)*.
❑ **check out** *vi* deixar o hotel.
❑ **check up** *vi*: **to ~ up (on)** informar-se (sobre).

checked [tʃekt] *adj* quadriculado, de xadrez.
checkers [tʃekəz] *n (Am)* damas *fpl.*
check-in desk *n* (balcão para o) check-in *m*.
checkmate [tʃekmeɪt] *n* xeque-mate *m*.
checkout [tʃekaʊt] *n* caixa *f*.
checkpoint [tʃekpɔɪnt] *n* controle *m*.
checkroom [tʃekrʊm] *n (Am)* vestiário *m (Br)*, bengaleiro *m (Port)*.
checkup [tʃekʌp] *n* exame *m* médico geral, check-up *m*.
cheddar (cheese) *n* (queijo) cheddar *m*, queijo de vaca duro mas macio, amarelo ou alaranjado.
cheek [tʃiːk] *n (of face)* bochecha *f*; **what a ~!** que descaramento!
cheekbone [tʃiːkbəʊn] *n* malar *m*, maçã *f* do rosto.
cheeky [tʃiːkɪ] *adj* descarado(-da), atrevido(-da).
cheer [tʃɪər] *n* aclamação *f* ◆ *vi* aclamar.
cheerful [tʃɪəfʊl] *adj* alegre.
cheerio [tʃɪərɪˈəʊ] *excl (Brit: inf)* tchau!
cheers [tʃɪəz] *excl (when drinking)* saúde!; *(Brit: inf: thank you)* obrigado!
cheese [tʃiːz] *n* queijo *m*.
cheeseboard [tʃiːzbɔːd] *n* tábua *f* de queijos, *queijos diversos e boiscoitos servidos normalmente no final de uma refeição.*
cheeseburger [tʃiːzˌbɜːgər] *n* hambúrger *m* de queijo, cheeseburger *m*.
cheesecake [tʃiːzkeɪk] *n* torta de queijo, creme e açúcar com uma base de biscoitos triturados e guarnecida com fruta em pedaços.
cheetah [tʃiːtə] *n* chita *m*, leopardo *m*.

chef [ʃef] *n* chefe *m* (de cozinha).
chef's special *n* especialidade *f* da casa.
chemical [ˈkemɪkl] *adj* químico(-ca) ◆ *n* substância *f* química.
chemist [ˈkemɪst] *n (Brit: pharmacist)* farmacêutico *m* (-ca *f*); *(scientist)* químico *m* (-ca *f*); **~'s** *(Brit: shop)* farmácia *f*.
chemistry [ˈkemɪstrɪ] *n* química *f*.
cheque [tʃek] *n (Brit)* cheque *m*; **to pay by ~** pagar com cheque.
chequebook [tʃekbʊk] *n* talão *m* de cheques *(Br)*, livro *m* de cheques *(Port)*.
cheque card *n* cartão *f* bancário *(que serve de garantia para cheques).*
cherish [tʃerɪʃ] *vt (hope, memory)* acalentar; *(privilege, right)* valorizar; *(person, thing)* estimar.
cherry [tʃerɪ] *n* cereja *f*.
chess [tʃes] *n* xadrez *m*.
chessboard [tʃesbɔːd] *n* tabuleiro *m* de xadrez.
chessman [tʃesmæn] *(pl -men* [-men]*)* *n* pedra *f* OR peça *f* (de xadrez).
chest [tʃest] *n (of body)* peito *m*; *(box)* arca *f*.
chestnut [tʃesnʌt] *n* castanha *f* ◆ *adj (colour)* marrom *(Br)*, castanho(-nha) *(Port)*.
chest of drawers *n* cômoda *f*.
chew [tʃuː] *vt* mastigar ◆ *n (sweet)* goma *f*.
chewing gum [tʃuːɪŋ-] *n* chiclete *m (Br)*, pastilha *f* elástica *(Port)*.
chic [ʃiːk] *adj* chique.
chicken [tʃɪkɪn] *n* galinha *f*, frango *m*.
chicken breast *n* peito *m* de galinha.
chicken Kiev [-ˈkiːev] *n* empanado de frango com recheio de manteiga, alho e ervas aromáticas.
chickenpox [tʃɪkɪnpɒks] *n* catapora *f (Br)*, varicela *f (Port)*.
chickpea [tʃɪkpiː] *n* grão-de-bico *m*.
chicory [tʃɪkərɪ] *n* chicória *f*.
chief [tʃiːf] *adj (highest-ranking)* chefe; *(main)* principal ◆ *n* chefe *m* (-fa *f*).
chiefly [tʃiːflɪ] *adv (mainly)* principalmente; *(especially)* sobretudo.
chilblain [tʃɪlbleɪn] *n* frieira *f*.
child [tʃaɪld] *(pl* children*)* *n (young boy, girl)* criança *f*; *(son, daughter)* filho *m* (-lha *f*).

child abuse *n* maus-tratos *mpl* infantis.

child benefit *n* (Brit) ≃ salário-família *m* (Br), ≃ abono *m* de família (Port).

childbirth ['tʃaɪldbɜːθ] *n* parto *m*.

childhood ['tʃaɪldhʊd] *n* infância *f*.

childish ['tʃaɪldɪʃ] *adj* (pej) infantil.

childlike ['tʃaɪldlaɪk] *adj* infantil.

childminder ['tʃaɪldˌmaɪndəʳ] *n* (Brit) pessoa que toma conta de crianças em sua própria casa, ama *f* (Port).

children ['tʃɪldrən] *pl* → child.

children's home *n* lar *m* para crianças.

childrenswear ['tʃɪldrənzweəʳ] *n* roupa *f* para crianças.

child seat *n* banco *m* para crianças.

Chile ['tʃɪlɪ] *n* Chile *m*.

chill [tʃɪl] *n* (illness) resfriado *m* ◆ *vt* gelar; **there's a ~ in the air** o tempo está frio.

chilled [tʃɪld] *adj* fresco(-ca); **"serve ~"** "sirva fresco".

chilli ['tʃɪlɪ] (pl -ies) *n* (vegetable) pimenta *f* OR pimentão *m* picante (Br), piripiri *m* (Port); (dish) = chilli con carne.

chilli con carne ['tʃɪlɪkɒnkuːnɪ] *n* ensopado de carne de vaca picada com feijão e pimentão picante.

chilling ['tʃɪlɪŋ] *adj* (frightening) de fazer gelar o sangue nas veias.

chilly ['tʃɪlɪ] *adj* frio (fria).

chime [tʃaɪm] *n* (of bell, clock) toque *m* ◆ *vi* (bell, clock) tocar.

chimney ['tʃɪmnɪ] *n* chaminé *f*.

chimneypot ['tʃɪmnɪpɒt] *n* chaminé *f*.

chimneysweep ['tʃɪmnɪswiːp] *n* limpa-chaminés *m inv*.

chimpanzee [ˌtʃɪmpənˈziː] *n* chimpanzé *m*.

chin [tʃɪn] *n* queixo *m*.

china ['tʃaɪnə] *n* (material) porcelana *f*.

China ['tʃaɪnə] *n* China *f*.

Chinese [ˌtʃaɪˈniːz] *adj* chinês(-esa) ◆ *n* (language) chinês *m* ◆ *npl*: **the ~** os chineses; **a ~ restaurant** um restaurante chinês.

Chinese leaves *npl* (Brit) couve *f* chinesa.

chip [tʃɪp] *n* (small piece, mark) lasca *f*; (counter) ficha *f*; (COMPUT) chip *m* ◆ *vt* lascar.

❏ **chips** *npl* (Brit: French fries) batatas

fpl fritas (em palitos); (Am: crisps) batatas fritas (de pacote).

chip shop *n* (Brit) loja onde se vende batatas fritas e filés de peixe para levar.

chiropodist [kɪˈrɒpədɪst] *n* pedicuro *m* (-ra *f*).

chirp [tʃɜːp] *vi* (bird) chilrear.

chisel ['tʃɪzl] *n* formão *m*.

chitchat ['tʃɪtʃæt] *n* (inf) conversa *f* fiada.

chives [tʃaɪvz] *npl* cebolinha *f* (Br), cebolinho *m* (Port).

chlorine ['klɔːriːn] *n* cloro *m*.

choc-ice ['tʃɒkaɪs] *n* (Brit) tipo de sorvete em forma de bloco, coberto com chocolate.

chocolate ['tʃɒkələt] *n* (food, drink) chocolate *m*; (sweet) bombom *m* ◆ *adj* de chocolate.

chocolate biscuit *n* biscoito *m* de chocolate.

choice [tʃɔɪs] *n* escolha *f* ◆ *adj* de primeira qualidade; **with the dressing of your ~** com o tempero a gosto.

choir ['kwaɪəʳ] *n* coro *m*.

choirboy ['kwaɪəbɔɪ] *n* menino *m* de coro.

choke [tʃəʊk] *vt* sufocar ◆ *vi* (on fishbone etc) engasgar-se; (to death) sufocar ◆ *n* (AUT): **to pull out the ~** fechar o afogador.

cholera ['kɒlərə] *n* cólera *f*.

choose [tʃuːz] (pt chose, pp chosen) *vt & vi* escolher; **to ~ to do sthg** decidir fazer algo.

choos(e)y ['tʃuːzɪ] *adj* exigente.

chop [tʃɒp] *n* (of meat) costeleta *f* ◆ *vt* cortar.

❏ **chop down** *vt sep* abater.

❏ **chop up** *vt sep* picar.

chopper ['tʃɒpəʳ] *n* (inf: helicopter) helicóptero *m*.

chopping board ['tʃɒpɪŋ-] *n* tábua *f* de cozinha.

choppy ['tʃɒpɪ] *adj* encrespado(-da).

chopsticks ['tʃɒpstɪks] *npl* pauzinhos *mpl* chineses.

chop suey [ˌtʃɒpˈsuːɪ] *n* chop suey *m*, prato chinês de brotos de soja, legumes, arroz e carne de porco ou galinha com molho de soja.

chord [kɔːd] *n* acorde *m*.

chore [tʃɔːʳ] *n* tarefa *f*.

chorus ['kɔːrəs] *n* (part of song) refrão *m*; (group of singers, dancers) coro *m*.

chose [tʃəʊz] *pt* → choose.
chosen ['tʃəʊzn] *pp* → choose.
choux pastry [ʃuː-] *n* massa *f* fina.
chowder ['tʃaʊdər] *n* sopa espessa de peixe ou marisco.
chow mein [tʃaʊ'meɪn] *n* chau-min *m*, massa de talharim frita com vegetais, carne ou marisco.
Christ [kraɪst] *n* Cristo *m*.
christen ['krɪsn] *vt (baby)* batizar.
christening ['krɪsnɪŋ] *n* batizado *m*.
Christian ['krɪstʃən] *adj* cristão(-tã) ◆ *n* cristão *m* (-tã *f*).
Christianity [krɪstɪ'ænətɪ] *n* cristianismo *m*.
Christian name *n* nome *m* (de batismo).
Christmas ['krɪsməs] *n* Natal *m*; **Happy ~!** Feliz Natal!, Boas Festas!
Christmas card *n* cartão *m* de Natal.
Christmas carol [-'kærəl] *n* cântico *m* de Natal.
Christmas Day *n* dia *m* de Natal.
Christmas Eve *n* véspera *f* de Natal, noite *f* de Natal.
Christmas pudding *n* sobremesa natalícia feita com frutas cristalizadas, nozes e sebo, servida quente depois de flambada com conhaque.
Christmas tree *n* árvore *f* de Natal.
chrome [krəʊm] *n* cromo *m (Br)*, crómio *m (Port)*.
chronic ['krɒnɪk] *adj (long-lasting)* crônico(-ca); *(habitual)* inveterado(-da).
chronological [krɒnə'lɒdʒɪkl] *adj* cronológico(-ca).
chrysanthemum [krɪ'sænθəməm] *n* crisântemo *m*.
chubby ['tʃʌbɪ] *adj* rechonchudo (-da).
chuck [tʃʌk] *vt (inf) (throw)* atirar; *(boyfriend, girlfriend)* deixar.
❏ **chuck away** *vt sep* jogar fora.
chuckle ['tʃʌkl] *vi* rir *(baixinho)*.
chum [tʃʌm] *n (inf)* amigão *m* (-gona *f*).
chunk [tʃʌŋk] *n* pedaço *m (grande)*.
church [tʃɜːtʃ] *n* igreja *f*; **to go to ~** freqüentar a igreja.
churchyard ['tʃɜːtʃjɑːd] *n* cemitério *m*.
churn [tʃɜːn] *n (for making butter)* batedeira *f* para fazer manteiga; *(for transporting milk)* lata *f* para o leite.

chute [ʃuːt] *n* rampa *f (Br)*, conduta *f (Port)*.
chutney ['tʃʌtnɪ] *n* molho picante agridoce feito com verduras ou frutas em conserva e outros temperos.
cider ['saɪdər] *n* sidra *f*.
cigar [sɪ'gɑːr] *n* charuto *m*.
cigarette [sɪgə'ret] *n* cigarro *m*.
cigarette lighter *n* isqueiro *m*.
Cinderella [sɪndə'relə] *n* Cinderela *f*, Gata-Borralheira *f*.
cinema ['sɪnəmə] *n* cinema *m*.
cinnamon ['sɪnəmən] *n* canela *f*.
circle ['sɜːkl] *n (shape, ring) n* círculo *m; (in theatre)* balcão *m* ◆ *vt (draw circle around)* sublinhar em volta; *(move round)* dar voltas em torno de ◆ *vi (plane)* dar voltas.
circuit ['sɜːkɪt] *n (track)* circuito *m; (lap)* volta *f*.
circular ['sɜːkjʊlər] *adj* circular ◆ *n* circular *f*.
circulate ['sɜːkjʊleɪt] *vi* circular.
circulation [sɜːkjʊ'leɪʃn] *n (of blood)* circulação *f*; *(of newspaper, magazine)* tiragem *f*.
circumcision [sɜːkəm'sɪʒn] *n* circuncisão *f*.
circumference [sə'kʌmfərəns] *n* circunferência *f*.
circumstances ['sɜːkəmstənsɪz] *npl* circunstâncias *fpl*; **in OR under the ~** dadas as circunstâncias.
circus ['sɜːkəs] *n* circo *m*.
CIS *n (abbr of Commonwealth Independent States)* CEI *f*.
cistern ['sɪstən] *n (of toilet)* cisterna *f*.
citizen ['sɪtɪzn] *n (of country)* cidadão *m* (-dã *f*); *(of town)* habitante *mf*.
Citizens' Band *n* faixa *f* do cidadão.
citrus fruit ['sɪtrəs-] *n* citrino *m*.
city ['sɪtɪ] *n* cidade *f*; **the City** a City *(centro financeiro londrino)*.
city centre *n* centro *m* (da cidade).
city hall *n (Am)* = prefeitura *f (Br)*, câmara *f* municipal *(Port)*, paços *mpl* do concelho *(Port)*.
civil ['sɪvl] *adj (involving ordinary citizens)* civil; *(polite)* educado(-da), cortês.
civilian [sɪ'vɪljən] *n* civil *mf*.
civilization [sɪvɪlaɪ'zeɪʃn] *n* civilização *f*.
civilized ['sɪvɪlaɪzd] *adj* civilizado (-da).

civil rights [.sıvl-] *npl* direitos *mpl* civis.

civil servant [.sıvl-] *n* funcionário *m* público (funcionária *f* pública).

civil service [.sıvl-] *n* administração *f* pública.

civil war [.sıvl-] *n* guerra *f* civil.

cl *(abbr of centilitre)* cl.

claim [kleım] *n* (assertion) afirmação *f*; (demand) reivindicação *f*; (for insurance) reclamação *f* ◆ *vt* (allege) afirmar; (demand) reclamar; (credit, responsibility) reivindicar ◆ *vi* (on insurance) reclamar uma indemnização.

claimant ['kleımənt] *n* (of benefit) reclamante *mf*.

claim form *n* impresso *m* de reclamação.

clam [klæm] *n* molusco *m* (Br), amêijoa *f* (Port).

clamber ['klæmbəʳ] *vi* trepar.

clamp [klæmp] *n* (for car) garras *fpl*, imobilizador *m* ◆ *vt* (car) imobilizar.

clan [klæn] *n* clã *m*.

clandestine [klæn'destın] *adj* clandestino(-na).

clap [klæp] *vi* aplaudir.

clapping ['klæpıŋ] *n* palmas *fpl*.

claret ['klærət] *n* clarete *m* (Br), bordéus *m* (Port).

clarify ['klærıfaı] *vt* (explain, expand on) esclarecer, clarificar.

clarinet [klærə'net] *n* clarinete *m*.

clarity ['klærıtı] *n* (of explanation) clareza *f*.

clash [klæʃ] *n* (noise) estrondo *m*; (confrontation) confrontação *f* ◆ *vi* (colours) destoar; (event, date) coincidir.

clasp [klɑːsp] *n* (fastener) fecho *m* ◆ *vt* agarrar (com força).

class [klɑːs] *n* (group of pupils, students) turma *f*; (teaching period) aula *f*; (type, social group) classe *f* ◆ *vt*: **to ~ sb/sthg (as)** classificar alguém/algo (de).

classic ['klæsık] *adj* clássico(-ca) ◆ *n* clássico *m*.

classical ['klæsıkl] *adj* clássico(-ca).

classical music *n* música *f* clássica.

classification [klæsıfı'keıʃn] *n* classificação *f*.

classified ads [klæsıfaıd-] *npl* classificados *mpl*.

classify ['klæsıfaı] *vt* classificar.

classmate ['klɑːsmeıt] *n* colega *mf* de turma.

classroom ['klɑːsrom] *n* sala *f* (de aula).

classy ['klɑːsı] *adj* (inf) de classe.

clause [klɔːz] *n* (in legal document) cláusula *f*; (GRAMM) proposição *f*, oração *f*.

claustrophobic [klɔːstrəˈfəubık] *adj* (person) *adj* claustrofóbico(-ca).

claw [klɔː] *n* (of bird, cat, dog) garra *f*; (of crab, lobster) pinça *f*.

clay [kleı] *n* barro *m*, argila *f*.

clean [kliːn] *adj* limpo(-pa); (page) em branco; (sheets, clothes) lavado(-da) ◆ *vt* limpar; **to ~ one's teeth** escovar os dentes.

cleaner ['kliːnəʳ] *n* (person) faxineiro *m* (-ra *f*) (Br), empregado *m* (-da *f*) de limpeza (Port); (substance) produto *m* de limpeza.

cleaning ['kliːnıŋ] *n* limpeza *f*.

cleanse [klenz] *vt* limpar.

cleanser ['klenzəʳ] *n* (for skin) creme *m* de limpeza.

clean-shaven [-ˈʃeıvn] *adj* sem barba nem bigode.

clear [klıəʳ] *adj* claro(-ra); (unobstructed) livre; (sky) limpo(-pa) ◆ *vt* (area, road) desempedir; (pond) limpar; (jump over) saltar; (declare not guilty) absolver; (authorize) aprovar; (cheque) creditar ◆ *vi* (weather) melhorar; (fog) levantar; **the cheque will ~ in three days' time** o dinheiro estará disponível daqui a três dias; **to be ~ (about sthg)** compreender (algo); **to be ~ of sthg** (not touching) não tocar em algo; **to ~ one's throat** limpar a garganta; **to ~ the table** tirar a mesa.

◆ **clear up** *vt sep* (room, toys) arrumar; (problem, confusion) clarificar ◆ *vi* (weather) melhorar; (tidy up) arrumar.

clearance ['klıərəns] *n* autorização *f*; (free distance) espaço *m* livre.

clear-cut *adj* (issue, plan) bem definido(-da); (division) nítido(-da).

clearing ['klıərıŋ] *n* clareira *f*.

clearly ['klıəlı] *adv* claramente; (obviously) evidentemente.

clearway ['klıəweı] *n* (Brit) estrada onde é proibido estacionar.

cleavage ['kliːvıdʒ] *n* (between breasts) colo *m*.

clef [klef] *n* clave *f*.

clementine ['kleməntaın] *n* clementina *f*.

clench [klentʃ] *vt* (fist, teeth) cerrar.

clergy ['klɜːdʒı] *npl*: **the ~** o clero.

clergyman [ˈklɜːdʒɪmən] (*pl* -men [-mən]) *n* clérigo *m*.

clerical [ˈklerɪkl] *adj* (*in office*) de escritório.

clerk [*Brit* klɑːk. *Am* klɜːrk] *n* (*in office*) empregado *m* (-da *f*) de escritório; (*Am: in shop*) empregado *m* (-da *f*).

clever [ˈklevəʳ] *adj* (*person*) esperto (-ta); (*idea, device*) engenhoso(-osa).

click [klɪk] *n* estalido *m* ♦ *vi* (*make sound*) dar um estalido.

client [ˈklaɪənt] *n* cliente *mf*.

cliff [klɪf] *n* rochedo *m*.

climate [ˈklaɪmɪt] *n* clima *m*.

climax [ˈklaɪmæks] *n* clímax *m inv*.

climb [klaɪm] *vt* (*tree, ladder*) subir em; (*mountain*) escalar ♦ *vi* subir.

❏ **climb down** *vt fus* (*tree, ladder*) descer de; (*mountain*) descer ♦ *vi* descer.

❏ **climb up** *vt fus* (*tree, ladder*) subir em; (*mountain*) escalar.

climber [ˈklaɪməʳ] *n* (*person*) alpinista *mf*.

climbing [ˈklaɪmɪŋ] *n* alpinismo *m*; to go ~ fazer alpinismo.

climbing frame *n* (*Brit*) barras de metal para as crianças treparem.

cling [klɪŋ] (*pt & pp* clung) *vi*: to ~ to (*hold tightly*) agarrar-se a; (*subj: clothes*) colar-se a.

clingfilm [ˈklɪŋfɪlm] *n* (*Brit*) película *f* aderente.

clinic [ˈklɪnɪk] *n* clínica *f*.

clip [klɪp] *n* clip *m* ♦ *vt* (*fasten*) segurar (com clip); (*cut*) cortar; (*ticket*) furar, validar.

clipboard [ˈklɪpbɔːd] *n* clipboard *m*, prancheta *f* com mola (*para segurar papéis*).

clippers [ˈklɪpəz] *npl* (*for hair*) máquina *f* de cortar cabelo; (*for nails*) alicate *m* de unhas (*Br*), corta-unhas *m inv* (*Port*); (*for plants, hedges*) tesoura *f* de aparar OR podar.

clipping [ˈklɪpɪŋ] *n* (*newspaper cutting*) recorte *m* de jornal.

cloak [kləʊk] *n* capa *f*.

cloakroom [ˈkləʊkrʊm] *n* (*for coats*) vestiário *m* (*Br*), bengaleiro *m* (*Port*); (*Brit: toilet*) banheiro *m* (*Br*), lavabos *mpl* (*Port*).

clock [klɒk] *n* relógio *m*; (*mileometer*) velocímetro *m* (*Br*), conta-quilómetros *m inv* (*Port*); round the ~ noite e dia.

clockwise [ˈklɒkwaɪz] *adv* no sentido dos ponteiros do relógio.

clockwork [ˈklɒkwɜːk] *adj* de corda.

clog [klɒg] *n* tamanco *m* ♦ *vt* entupir.

close¹ [kləʊs] *adj* (*near*) junto(-ta); (*relation, friend, contact*) íntimo(-ma); (*link, resemblance*) grande; (*examination*) detalhado(-da); (*race, contest*) renhido(-da) ♦ *adv* perto; ~ by perto; ~ to (*near*) perto de; ~ to tears/laughter a ponto de chorar/rir; ~ to despair nos limites do desespero.

close² [kləʊz] *vt* fechar ♦ *vi* (*door, jar, eyes*) fechar-se; (*shop, office*) fechar; (*deadline, offer, meeting*) terminar.

❏ **close down** *vt sep & vi* fechar (definitivamente).

closed [kləʊzd] *adj* fechado(-da).

closely [ˈkləʊslɪ] *adv* (*related*) intimamente; (*follow, examine*) de perto.

closet [ˈklɒzɪt] *n* (*Am: cupboard*) armário *m*.

close-up [ˈkləʊs-] *n* primeiro plano *m*.

closing time [ˈkləʊzɪŋ-] *n* horário *m* de encerramento.

closure [ˈkləʊʒəʳ] *n* (*of business, company*) encerramento *m*; (*of road, railway line*) bloqueio *m* (*Br*), corte *m* (*Port*).

clot [klɒt] *n* (*of blood*) coágulo *m*.

cloth [klɒθ] *n* (*fabric*) tecido *m*; (*piece of cloth*) pano *m*.

clothes [kləʊðz] *npl* roupa *f*.

clothesline [ˈkləʊðzlaɪn] *n* varal *m* (*Br*), estendal *m* (*Port*).

clothes peg *n* (*Brit*) pregador *m* de roupa (*Br*), mola *f* (para a roupa) (*Port*).

clothespin [ˈkləʊðzpɪn] (*Am*) = clothes peg.

clothes shop *n* loja *f* de vestuário.

clothing [ˈkləʊðɪŋ] *n* roupa *f*.

clotted cream [klɒtɪd-] *n* creme coalhado típico da Cornualha.

cloud [klaʊd] *n* nuvem *f*.

cloudy [ˈklaʊdɪ] *adj* (*sky, day*) nublado(-da); (*liquid*) turvo(-va).

clove [kləʊv] *n* (*of garlic*) dente *m*.

❏ **cloves** *npl* (*spice*) cravo *m* (*Br*), cravinho *m* (*Port*).

clover [ˈkləʊvəʳ] *n* trevo *m*.

clown [klaʊn] *n* palhaço *m*.

club [klʌb] *n* (*organization*) clube *m*; (*nightclub*) discoteca *f*, boate *f*; (*stick*) moca *f*.

❏ **clubs** *npl* (*in cards*) paus *mpl*.

clubbing [ˈklʌbɪŋ] *n*: to go ~ (*inf*) ir à discoteca.

club class *n* = navigator class *f*.

club sandwich *n (Am)* sanduíche *f* (com três ou mais fatias de pão).
club soda *n (Am)* soda *f*.
cluck [klʌk] *vi (hen)* cacarejar.
clue [kluː] *n* pista *f*; **I haven't got a ~** não faço a mínima idéia.
clumsy [ˈklʌmzɪ] *adj (person)* desajeitado(-da).
clung [klʌŋ] *pt & pp* → **cling**.
cluster [ˈklʌstə^r] *n* cacho *m* ◆ *vi (people)* juntar-se, agrupar-se.
clutch [klʌtʃ] *n* embreagem *f* ◆ *vt* apertar.
clutter [ˈklʌtə^r] *n* desordem *f* ◆ *vt* encher.
cm *(abbr of centimetre)* cm.
c/o *(abbr of care of)* a/c.
Co. *(abbr of company)* C.ª.
coach [kəʊtʃ] *n (bus)* ônibus *m (Br)*, autocarro *m (Port); (of train)* vagão *m (Br)*, carruagem *f (Port); (SPORT)* treinador *m* (-ra *f*).
coach party *n (Brit)* grupo *m* de excursionistas.
coach station *n* rodoviária *f*.
coach trip *n (Brit)* excursão *f* (de ônibus).
coal [kəʊl] *n* carvão *m*.
coalition [ˌkəʊəˈlɪʃn] *n (POL)* coligação *f*.
coal mine *n* mina *f* de carvão.
coarse [kɔːs] *adj (rough)* áspero(-ra); *(vulgar)* ordinário(-ria).
coast [kəʊst] *n* costa *f*.
coastal [ˈkəʊstl] *adj* costeiro(-ra).
coaster [ˈkəʊstə^r] *n (for glass)* base *f* para copos.
coastguard [ˈkəʊstɡɑːd] *n (person)* guarda *m* costeiro; *(organization)* guarda *f* costeira.
coastline [ˈkəʊstlaɪn] *n* litoral *m*.
coat [kəʊt] *n (garment)* casaco *m; (of animal)* pêlo *m* ◆ *vt*: **to ~ sthg (with)** cobrir algo (com).
coat hanger *n* cabide *m*.
coating [ˈkəʊtɪŋ] *n (on surface)* revestimento *m; (on food)* camada *f*; **with a ~ of breadcrumbs** à milanesa.
coat of arms *n* brasão *m*.
coax [kəʊks] *vt*: **to ~ sb (to do** OR **into doing sthg)** convencer alguém (a fazer algo).
cobbled street [ˈkɒbld-] *n* calçada *f*, rua calçada com pedras arredondadas.
cobbler [ˈkɒblə^r] *n* sapateiro *m* (-ra *f*).

cobbles [ˈkɒblz] *npl* pedras *fpl* da calçada, *pedras arredondadas para calçamento*.
cobweb [ˈkɒbweb] *n* teia *f* de aranha.
Coca-Cola® [ˌkəʊkəˈkəʊlə] *n* Coca-Cola® *f*.
cocaine [kəʊˈkeɪn] *n* cocaína *f*.
cock [kɒk] *n (male chicken)* galo *m*.
cock-a-leekie [ˌkɒkəˈliːkɪ] *n* caldo de galinha com alho-poró, cenoura e grãos de cevada.
cockerel [ˈkɒkrəl] *n* galo *m* jovem.
cockles [ˈkɒklz] *npl* berbigão *m*.
Cockney [ˈkɒknɪ] *(pl* **-s)** *n (person)* londrino *m* (-na *f*) *(dos bairros populares do leste de Londres); (dialect, accent)* dialeto ou pronúncia do leste de Londres.
cockpit [ˈkɒkpɪt] *n* cabine *f*.
cockroach [ˈkɒkrəʊtʃ] *n* barata *f*.
cocktail [ˈkɒkteɪl] *n* coquetel *m*.
cocktail party *n* coquetel *m*.
cock-up *n (Brit: vulg)* asneira *f*; **to make a ~ (of sthg)** fazer uma merda (de algo).
cocoa [ˈkəʊkəʊ] *n* cacau *m*.
coconut [ˈkəʊkənʌt] *n* coco *m*.
cod [kɒd] *(pl inv)* *n* bacalhau *m*.
code [kəʊd] *n (system)* código *m; (dialling code)* indicativo *m*.
cod-liver oil *n* óleo *m* de fígado de bacalhau.
coeducational [ˌkəʊedjuːˈkeɪʃənl] *adj* misto(-ta).
coffee [ˈkɒfɪ] *n* café *m*; **black ~** café; **white ~** = café *m* com leite *(Br)*, = meia *f* de leite *(Port)*; **ground/instant ~** café moído/instantâneo.
coffee bar *n (Brit)* café *m*.
coffee break *n* intervalo *m* para o café, hora *f* da bica *(Port)*.
coffee morning *n (Brit)* reunião *matinal, normalmente com fins beneficentes, em que se serve café*.
coffeepot [ˈkɒfɪpɒt] *n* bule *m* para o café.
coffee shop *n (cafe)* café *m; (in shops, airports)* cafeteria *f*.
coffee table *n* mesa *f* pequena e baixa.
coffin [ˈkɒfɪn] *n* caixão *m*.
cog (wheel) [kɒɡ-] *n* roda *f* dentada.
coherent [kəʊˈhɪərənt] *adj (logical)* coerente.
coil [kɔɪl] *n (of rope)* rolo *m; (Brit: contraceptive)* DIU *m* ◆ *vt* enrolar.

coin [kɔɪn] *n* moeda *f*.
coinbox [ˈkɔɪnbɒks] *n (Brit)* telefone *m* público (de moedas).
coincide [ˌkəʊɪnˈsaɪd] *vi:* **to ~ (with)** coincidir (com).
coincidence [kəʊˈɪnsɪdəns] *n* coincidência *f*.
coincidental [kəʊˌɪnsɪˈdentl] *adj:* **any similarity is purely ~** qualquer semelhança é pura coincidência.
coke [kəʊk] *n (fuel)* coque *m*; *(inf: cocaine)* coca *f*.
Coke® [kəʊk] *n* Coca-Cola® *f*.
colander [ˈkʌləndəʳ] *n* coador *m (Br)*, escorregador *m (Port)*.
cold [kəʊld] *adj* frio (fria) ◆ *n (illness)* resfriado *m (Br)*, constipação *f (Port)*; *(low temperature)* frio *m*; **to get ~** arrefecer; **to catch (a) ~** resfriar-se *(Br)*, apanhar uma constipação *(Port)*.
cold-blooded *adj (person)* insensível, sem dó nem piedade; *(killing)* a sangue-frio.
cold cuts *(Am)* = **cold meats**.
cold meats *npl* frios *mpl (Br)*, carnes *fpl* frias *(Port)*.
cold sore *n* herpes *f* labial.
coleslaw [ˈkəʊlslɔː] *n* salada de couve, cenoura e cebola picadas com maionese.
colic [ˈkɒlɪk] *n* cólica *f*.
collaborate [kəˈlæbəreɪt] *vi* colaborar.
collapse [kəˈlæps] *vi (building, tent)* cair; *(from exhaustion, illness)* ter um colapso.
collar [ˈkɒləʳ] *n (of coat, blouse)* gola *f*; *(of shirt)* colarinho *m*; *(of dog, cat)* coleira *f*.
collarbone [ˈkɒləbəʊn] *n* clavícula *f*.
colleague [ˈkɒliːɡ] *n* colega *mf*.
collect [kəˈlekt] *vt (gather)* colher; *(as a hobby)* colecionar; *(go and get)* ir buscar; *(money)* cobrar ◆ *vi (dust, leaves)* acumular-se; *(crowd)* juntar-se ◆ *adv (Am):* **to call (sb) ~** fazer uma chamada a cobrar (para o destinatário).
collection [kəˈlekʃn] *n* coleção *f*; *(money)* cobrança *f*; *(of mail)* coleta *f (Br)*, tiragem *f (Port)*.
collector [kəˈlektəʳ] *n (as a hobby)* colecionador *m (-ra f)*.
college [ˈkɒlɪdʒ] *n (school)* colégio *m*; *(Brit: of university)* organismo independente, formado por estudantes e professores, em que se dividem certas

universidades britânicas; *(Am: university)* universidade *f*.
collide [kəˈlaɪd] *vi:* **to ~ (with)** chocar (com).
collie [ˈkɒlɪ] *n* collie *m*.
colliery [ˈkɒljərɪ] *n* mina *f* de carvão.
collision [kəˈlɪʒn] *n* colisão *f*.
colloquial [kəˈləʊkwɪəl] *adj* familiar, coloquial.
cologne [kəˈləʊn] *n* água-de-colônia *f*.
colon [ˈkəʊlən] *n (GRAMM)* dois pontos *mpl*.
colonel [ˈkɜːnl] *n* coronel *m*.
colonial [kəˈləʊnjəl] *adj (rule, power)* colonial.
colonize [ˈkɒlənaɪz] *vt (subj: people)* colonizar.
colony [ˈkɒlənɪ] *n* colônia *f*.
color [ˈkʌlər] *(Am)* = **colour**.
colossal [kəˈlɒsl] *adj* colossal.
colour [ˈkʌləʳ] *n* cor *f* ◆ *adj (photograph, film)* a cores ◆ *vt (hair)* pintar; *(food)* colorir.
❑ **colour in** *vt sep* colorir.
colour-blind *adj* daltónico(-ca).
coloured [ˈkʌləd] *adj (having colour)* colorido(-da); *(person)* de cor; **brightly ~** de cores vivas.
colourful [ˈkʌləful] *adj (picture, garden, scenery)* colorido(-da); *(fig: person, place)* animado(-da).
colouring [ˈkʌlərɪŋ] *n (of food)* corante *m*; *(complexion)* tez *f*.
colouring book *n* livro *m* de colorir.
colour supplement *n* suplemento *m* a cores.
colour television *n* televisão *f* a cores.
colt [kəʊlt] *n* potro *m*.
column [ˈkɒləm] *n* coluna *f*.
coma [ˈkəʊmə] *n* coma *m* ou *f*.
comb [kəʊm] *n* pente *m* ◆ *vt:* **to ~ one's hair** pentear o cabelo.
combat [ˈkɒmbæt] *n* combate *m* ◆ *vt* combater.
combination [ˌkɒmbɪˈneɪʃn] *n* combinação *f*.
combine [kəmˈbaɪn] *vt:* **to ~ sthg (with)** combinar algo (com).
combine harvester [ˈkɒmbaɪnˈhɑːvɪstəʳ] *n* máquina *f* de ceifar e debulhar.
come [kʌm] *(pt* **came**, *pp* **come**) *vi* 1. *(move)* vir; **we came by taxi** nós viemos

de táxi; ~ **and see!** venha ver!; ~ **here!** venha cá!

2. *(arrive)* chegar; **to ~ home** voltar para casa; **they still haven't ~** eles ainda não chegaram; **"coming soon"** "brevemente".

3. *(in order)* vir; **to ~ first/last** *(in sequence)* vir primeiro/no fim; *(in competition)* chegar primeiro/em último *(lugar)*.

4. *(reach):* **to ~ up/down to** chegar a.

5. *(become):* **to ~ loose/undone** desapertar-se; **to ~ true** realizar-se.

6. *(be sold)* vir; **they ~ in packs of six** vêm em pacotes de seis.

❏ **come across** *vt fus* encontrar.

❏ **come along** *vi (progress)* desenvolver-se; *(arrive)* aparecer; ~ **along!** *(as encouragement)* anda!; *(hurry up)* anda logo!

❏ **come apart** *vi* desfazer-se.

❏ **come back** *vi* regressar.

❏ **come down** *vi (price)* baixar.

❏ **come down with** *vt fus (illness)* apanhar.

❏ **come from** *vt fus* vir de.

❏ **come in** *vi (enter)* entrar; *(arrive)* chegar; *(tide)* subir; ~ **in!** entre!

❏ **come off** *vi (button, top)* cair; *(succeed)* resultar.

❏ **come on** *vi (progress)* progredir; ~ **on!** vamos lá!

❏ **come out** *vi* sair; *(sun, moon)* aparecer.

❏ **come over** *vi (visit):* **I'll ~ over tonight** passo por aí hoje à noite.

❏ **come round** *vi (regain consciousness)* voltar a si; **why don't you ~ round tomorrow?** por que você não passa aqui amanhã?

❏ **come to** *vt fus (subj: bill)* ser ao todo.

❏ **come up** *vi (go upstairs)* subir; *(be mentioned, happen)* surgir; *(sun, moon)* aparecer.

❏ **come up with** *vt fus (idea)* arranjar.

comeback ['kʌmbæk] *n (return)* regresso *m*; **to make a ~** *(fashion)* voltar à moda; *(actor etc)* voltar ao palco.

comedian [kə'miːdjən] *n* cómico *m* (-ca *f*).

comedy ['kɒmədɪ] *n (TV programme, film, play)* comédia *f*; *(humour)* humor *m*.

comet ['kɒmɪt] *n* cometa *m*.

comfort ['kʌmfət] *n* conforto *m*; *(consolation)* consolo *m* ◆ *vt* consolar.

comfortable ['kʌmftəbl] *adj* confortável; *(fig: confident)* à vontade; *(financially)* bem de vida; **to be ~** *(after operation)* estar bem.

comfortably ['kʌmftəblɪ] *adv (sit, live)* confortavelmente; *(sleep)* bem ◆ *adj (win)* à vontade.

comic ['kɒmɪk] *adj* cómico(-ca) ◆ *n (person)* cómico *m* (-ca *f*); *(magazine)* histórias *fpl* em quadrinhos *(Br)*, livro *m* de banda desenhada *(Port)*.

comical ['kɒmɪkl] *adj* cómico(-ca).

comic strip *n* história *f* em quadrinhos *(Br)*, banda *f* desenhada *(Port)*.

coming ['kʌmɪŋ] *adj (future)* próximo(-ma), que vem ◆ *n*: ~**s and goings** idas e vindas *fpl*.

comma ['kɒmə] *n* vírgula *f*.

command [kə'mɑːnd] *n (order)* ordem *f*; *(mastery)* domínio *m* ◆ *vt (order)* ordenar; *(be in charge of)* comandar.

commander [kə'mɑːndəʳ] *n* comandante *m*.

commando [kə'mɑːndəʊ] *(pl* -s OR -es*) n (unit)* unidade *f* de comandos; *(soldier)* comando *m*.

commemorate [kə'meməreɪt] *vt* comemorar.

commemoration [kə,memə'reɪʃn] *n*: **in ~ of** em honra de.

commence [kə'mens] *vi (fml)* começar.

commend [kə'mend] *vt (praise):* **to ~ sb (on** OR **for sthg)** elogiar alguém (por algo).

comment ['kɒment] *n* comentário *m* ◆ *vi* comentar.

commentary ['kɒməntrɪ] *n (of event)* relato *m*; *(of football, rugby match)* comentário *m*.

commentator ['kɒmənteɪtəʳ] *n (on TV, radio)* comentarista *mf (Br)*, comentador *m* (-ra *f*) *(Port)*.

commerce ['kɒmɜːs] *n* comércio *m*.

commercial [kə'mɜːʃl] *adj* comercial ◆ *n* anúncio *m* *(em televisão, rádio)*.

commercial break *n* intervalo *m (para a publicidade)*.

commiserate [kə'mɪzəreɪt] *vi:* **to ~ (with sb)** compadecer-se (de alguém).

commission [kə'mɪʃn] *n* comissão *f*.

commit [kə'mɪt] *vt (crime, sin)* cometer; **to ~ o.s. (to sthg)** comprometer-se (a algo); **to ~ suicide** suicidar-se.

commitment [kə'mɪtmənt] *n (dedication)* empenho *m*; *(responsibility)* obrigação *f*, compromisso *m*.

committee [kə'mıtı] *n* comitê *m*, comissão *f*.

commodity [kə'mɒdətı] *n* produto *m*.

common ['kɒmən] *adj* comum; *(pej: vulgar)* vulgar ◆ *n (Brit: land)* gramado *m* público *(Br)*, relvado *m* público *(Port)*; **in ~** em comum.

commonly ['kɒmənlı] *adv (generally)* geralmente.

Common Market *n* Mercado *m* Comum.

commonplace ['kɒmənpleıs] *adj* comum.

common room *n (for teachers)* sala *f* dos professores; *(for students)* sala de convívio.

common sense *n* senso *m* comum.

Commonwealth ['kɒmənwelθ] *n*: **the ~** o Commonwealth.

commotion [kə'məʊʃn] *n* comoção *f*, agitação *f*.

communal ['kɒmjunl] *adj (bathroom, kitchen)* comum.

communicate [kə'mju:nıkeıt] *vi*: **to ~ (with)** comunicar (com).

communication [kə,mju:nı'keıʃn] *n* comunicação *f*.

communication cord *n (Brit)* alarme *m (em trem ou metrô)*.

communion [kə'mju:njən] *n (RELIG)* comunhão *f*.

communism ['kɒmjunısm] *n* comunismo *m*.

communist ['kɒmjunıst] *n* comunista *mf*.

community [kə'mju:nətı] *n* comunidade *f*.

community centre *n* centro *m* social.

commute [kə'mju:t] *vi deslocar-se diariamente de casa para o local de trabalho (em outra localidade)*.

commuter [kə'mju:tə'] *n pessoa que se desloca diariamente de casa para o local de trabalho (em outra localidade)*.

compact [*adj* kəm'pækt, *n* 'kɒmpækt] *adj* compacto(-ta) ◆ *n (for make-up)* caixa *f* de pó-de-arroz; *(Am: car)* carro *m* pequeno.

compact disc [,kɒmpækt-] *n* CD *m*, disco *m* compacto.

compact disc player *n* leitor *m* de CDs.

companion [kəm'pænjən] *n* compa-

nheiro *m* (-ra *f*).

company ['kʌmpənı] *n* companhia *f*; **to keep sb ~** fazer companhia a alguém.

company car *n* carro *m* da empresa.

comparable ['kɒmprəbl] *adj* comparável; **~ to** OR **with** comparável a.

comparative [kəm'pærətıv] *adj (relative)* relativo(-va); *(GRAMM)* comparativo(-va).

comparatively [kəm'pærətıvlı] *adv* comparativamente.

compare [kəm'peə'] *vt*: **to ~ sthg (with)** comparar algo (com); **~d with** comparado com.

comparison [kəm'pærısn] *n* comparação *f*; **in ~ with** em comparação com.

compartment [kəm'pɑ:tmənt] *n* compartimento *m*.

compass ['kʌmpəs] *n (magnetic)* bússola *f*; **a pair of ~es** um compasso.

compassion [kəm'pæʃn] *n* compaixão *f*.

compassionate [kəm'pæʃənət] *adj* compassivo(-va).

compatible [kəm'pætəbl] *adj* compatível.

compel [kəm'pel] *vt (force)* obrigar; **to ~ sb to do sthg** obrigar alguém a fazer algo.

compensate ['kɒmpenseıt] *vt* compensar ◆ *vi*: **to ~ (for sthg)** compensar (algo); **to ~ sb for sthg** compensar alguém por algo.

compensation [,kɒmpen'seıʃn] *n* compensação *f*.

compete [kəm'pi:t] *vi (take part)* participar; **to ~ with sb for sthg** competir com alguém por algo.

competent ['kɒmpıtənt] *adj* competente.

competition [,kɒmpı'tıʃn] *n* competição *f*; **the ~** *(rivals)* a concorrência.

competitive [kəm'petətıv] *adj* competitivo(-va).

competitor [kəm'petıtə'] *n (in race, contest)* participante *mf*; *(COMM, in game, show)* concorrente *mf*.

compile [kəm'paıl] *vt* compilar.

complacency [kəm'pleısnsı] *n* complacência *f*, auto-satisfação *f*.

complain [kəm'pleın] *vi*: **to ~ (about)** queixar-se (de).

complaint [kəm'pleınt] *n (statement)*

queixa *f; (illness)* problema *m*.
complement ['kɒmplɪ‚ment] *vt* complementar.
complementary [‚kɒmplɪ'mentərɪ] *adj* complementar.
complete [kəm'pliːt] *adj* completo (-ta); *(finished)* concluído(-da) ◆ *vt (finish)* concluir; *(a form)* preencher; *(make whole)* completar; ~ **with** completo com.
completely [kəm'pliːtlɪ] *adv* completamente.
completion [kəm'pliːʃn] *n* conclusão *f*.
complex ['kɒmpleks] *adj* complexo (-xa) ◆ *n* complexo *m*.
complexion [kəm'plekʃn] *n (of skin)* tez *f*.
complicate ['kɒmplɪkeɪt] *vt* complicar.
complicated ['kɒmplɪkeɪtɪd] *adj* complicado(-da).
complication [‚kɒmplɪ'keɪʃn] *n* complicação *f*.
compliment [*n* 'kɒmplɪmənt, *vb* 'kɒmplɪment] *n* elogio *m* ◆ *vt* elogiar.
complimentary [‚kɒmplɪ'mentərɪ] *adj (seat, ticket)* gratuito(-ta); *(words, person)* lisonjeiro(-ra).
comply [kəm'plaɪ] *vi*: **to ~ with** sthg *(law, standards)* cumprir algo; *(request)* respeitar algo.
component [kəm'pəʊnənt] *n* componente *mf*.
compose [kəm'pəʊz] *vt (music)* compor; *(letter, poem)* escrever; **to be ~d of** ser composto de.
composed [kəm'pəʊzd] *adj* calmo (-ma).
composer [kəm'pəʊzəʳ] *n* compositor *m* (-ra *f*).
composition [‚kɒmpə'zɪʃn] *n* composição *f*.
compost [*Brit* 'kɒmpɒst, *Am* 'kɒmpəʊst] *n* estrume *m*.
compound ['kɒmpaʊnd] *n (substance)* composto *m*; *(word)* palavra *f* composta.
comprehend [‚kɒmprɪ'hend] *vt (understand)* compreender.
comprehension [‚kɒmprɪ'henʃn] *n* compreensão *f*.
comprehensive [‚kɒmprɪ'hensɪv] *adj* completo(-ta).
comprehensive (school) *n (Brit)* = escola *f* secundária.

compressed air [kəm'prest-] *n* ar *m* comprimido.
comprise [kəm'praɪz] *vt* ser constituído(-da) por.
compromise ['kɒmprəmaɪz] *n* compromisso *m*.
compulsive [kəm'pʌlsɪv] *adj (behaviour, gambler, liar)* compulsivo(-va).
compulsory [kəm'pʌlsərɪ] *adj* obrigatório(-ria).
computer [kəm'pjuːtəʳ] *n* computador *m*.
computer game *n* jogo *m* de computador.
computerized [kəm'pjuːtəraɪzd] *adj* computadorizado(-da).
computer operator *n* operador *m* (-ra *f*) de computador.
computer programmer [-'prəʊgræməʳ] *n* programador *m* (-ra *f*) de computador.
computing [kəm'pjuːtɪŋ] *n* informática *f*.
comrade ['kɒmreɪd] *n* camarada *mf*.
con [kɒn] *n (inf: trick)* truque *m*; **all mod ~s** com todas as comodidades.
concave [kɒn'keɪv] *adj* côncavo(-va).
conceal [kən'siːl] *vt* esconder.
concede [kən'siːd] *vt (admit)* admitir, reconhecer ◆ *vi* ceder.
conceited [kən'siːtɪd] *adj (pej)* convencido(-da).
conceive [kən'siːv] *vt* conceber.
concentrate ['kɒnsəntreɪt] *vi* concentrar-se ◆ *vt*: **to be ~d** *(in one place)* estar concentrado; **to ~ on** sthg concentrar-se em algo.
concentrated ['kɒnsəntreɪtɪd] *adj* concentrado(-da)
concentration [‚kɒnsən'treɪʃn] *n* concentração *f*.
concentration camp *n* campo *m* de concentração.
concept ['kɒnsept] *n* conceito *m*.
concern [kən'sɜːn] *n (worry)* preocupação *f; (matter of interest)* assunto *m*; *(COMM)* negócio *m* ◆ *vt (be about)* ser sobre; *(worry)* preocupar; *(involve)* dizer respeito a; **to be ~ed about** estar preocupado com; **to be ~ed with** tratar de; **to ~ o.s. with** sthg preocupar-se com algo; **as far as I'm ~ed** no que me diz respeito; **it's no ~ of mine** isso não me diz respeito, não é da minha conta.
concerned [kən'sɜːnd] *adj (worried)*

preocupado(-da).

concerning [kən'sɜːnɪŋ] *prep* acerca de.

concert [ˈkɒnsət] *n* concerto *m*.

concert hall *n* sala *f* de concertos.

concertina [ˌkɒnsəˈtiːnə] *n* concertina *f*.

concession [kənˈseʃn] *n* (*reduced price*) desconto *m*.

concise [kənˈsaɪs] *adj* conciso(-sa).

conclude [kənˈkluːd] *vt* concluir ♦ *vi* (*fml: end*) terminar.

conclusion [kənˈkluːʒn] *n* (*decision*) conclusão *f*; (*end*) fim *m*.

conclusive [kənˈkluːsɪv] *adj* concludente, decisivo(-va).

concoction [kənˈkɒkʃn] *n* (*mixture, drink*) mistura *f*.

concourse [ˈkɒŋkɔːs] *n* (*hall*) saguão *m* (*Br*), vestíbulo *m* (*Port*).

concrete [ˈkɒŋkriːt] *adj* (*building, path*) de concreto; (*idea, plan*) concreto(-ta) ♦ *n* concreto *m* (*Br*), betão *m* (*Port*).

concussion [kənˈkʌʃn] *n* traumatismo *m* craniano.

condemn [kənˈdem] *vt* condenar; **to ~ sb to sthg** (*JUR*) condenar alguém a algo.

condensation [ˌkɒndenˈseɪʃn] *n* condensação *f*.

condensed milk [kənˈdenst-] *n* leite *m* condensado.

condescending [ˌkɒndɪˈsendɪŋ] *adj* condescendente.

condition [kənˈdɪʃn] *n* (*state*) estado *m*; (*proviso*) condição *f*; **a heart/liver ~** problemas de coração/fígado; **to be out of ~** não estar em forma; **on ~ that** com a condição de.

⊐ **conditions** *npl* (*circumstances*) condições *fpl*.

conditional [kənˈdɪʃənl] *n* (*GRAMM*) condicional *m*.

conditioner [kənˈdɪʃnər] *n* amaciador *m*.

condo [ˈkɒndəʊ] (*Am: inf*) = **condominium**.

condolences [kənˈdəʊlənsɪz] *npl* condolências *fpl*.

condom [ˈkɒndəm] *n* preservativo *m*.

condominium [ˌkɒndəˈmɪnɪəm] *n* (*Am*) condomínio *m*.

condone [kənˈdəʊn] *vt* defender.

conducive [kənˈdjuːsɪv] *adj*: **~ to** ideal para.

conduct [*vb* kənˈdʌkt, *n* ˈkɒndʌkt] *vt* (*investigation, business*) levar a cabo; (*MUS*) reger ♦ *n* (*fml: behaviour*) conduta *f*; **to ~ o.s.** (*fml*) comportar-se.

conductor [kənˈdʌktər] *n* (*MUS*) maestro *m*; (*on bus*) cobrador *m* (-ra *f*); (*Am: on train*) revisor *m* (-ra *f*).

cone [kəʊn] *n* cone *m*; (*for ice cream*) casquinha *f* (*Br*), cone (*Port*).

confectioner's [kənˈfekʃnəz] *n* (*shop*) confeitaria *f*.

confectionery [kənˈfekʃnərɪ] *n* confeitaria *f*.

confer [kənˈfɜːr] *vi* consultar ♦ *vt* (*fml*): **to ~ sthg on sb** conferir algo com alguém.

conference [ˈkɒnfərəns] *n* conferência *f*.

confess [kənˈfes] *vi*: **to ~ (to sthg)** confessar (algo).

confession [kənˈfeʃn] *n* confissão *f*.

confetti [kənˈfetɪ] *n* confetti *mpl*, papelinhos *mpl* (*Port*).

confide [kənˈfaɪd] *vi*: **to ~ in sb** confiar em alguém.

confidence [ˈkɒnfɪdəns] *n* confiança *f*; **to have ~ in** ter confiança em.

confident [ˈkɒnfɪdənt] *adj* (*self-assured*) seguro(-ra) de si; (*certain*) seguro(-ra).

confidential [ˌkɒnfɪˈdenʃl] *adj* confidencial.

confined [kənˈfaɪnd] *adj* restrito(-ta).

confinement [kənˈfaɪnmənt] *n* reclusão *f*.

confirm [kənˈfɜːm] *vt* confirmar.

confirmation [ˌkɒnfəˈmeɪʃn] *n* confirmação *f*; (*RELIG*) crisma *m*.

confiscate [ˈkɒnfɪskeɪt] *vt* confiscar.

conflict [*n* ˈkɒnflɪkt, *vb* kənˈflɪkt] *n* conflito *m* ♦ *vi*: **to ~ (with)** estar em desacordo (com).

conform [kənˈfɔːm] *vi*: **to ~ (to)** obedecer (a).

confront [kənˈfrʌnt] *vt* confrontar.

confrontation [ˌkɒnfrʌnˈteɪʃn] *n* confrontação *f*.

confuse [kənˈfjuːz] *vt* confundir; **to ~ sthg with sthg** confundir algo com algo.

confused [kənˈfjuːzd] *adj* confuso (-sa).

confusing [kənˈfjuːzɪŋ] *adj* confuso (-sa).

confusion [kənˈfjuːʒn] *n* confusão *f*.

congested [kənˈdʒestɪd] *adj* (*street*)

congestionado(-da).

congestion [kən'dʒestʃn] *n (traffic)* congestionamento *m*.

congratulate [kən'grætʃʊleɪt] *vt*: to ~ sb (on sthg) felicitar alguém (por algo).

congratulations [kən‚grætʃʊ'leɪʃənz] *excl* parabéns!

congregate ['kɒŋgrɪgeɪt] *vi* juntar-se.

congregation [‚kɒŋgrɪ'geɪʃn] *n* congregação *f*.

Congress ['kɒŋgres] *n (Am)* Congresso *m*.

congressman ['kɒŋgresmən] *(pl* -men [-mən]) *n (Am: POL)* congressista *m*.

conifer ['kɒnɪfəʳ] *n* conífera *f*.

conjugation [‚kɒndʒʊ'geɪʃn] *n (GRAMM)* conjugação *f*.

conjunction [kən'dʒʌŋkʃn] *n (GRAMM)* conjunção *f*.

conjunctivitis [kən‚dʒʌŋktɪ'vaɪtɪs] *n* conjuntivite *f*.

conjurer ['kʌndʒərəʳ] *n* prestidigitador *m* (-ra *f*).

conker ['kɒŋkəʳ] *n (Brit)* castanha-da-Índia *f*.

conman ['kɒnmæn] *(pl* -men [-men]) *n* vigarista *mf*, burlão *m (Port)*.

connect [kə'nekt] *vt* ligar ♦ *vi*: to ~ with *(train, plane)* fazer conexão com; to ~ sthg with sthg *(associate)* ligar algo com algo.

connected [kə'nektɪd] *adj* relacionado(-da); ~ with relacionado com.

connecting flight [kə'nektɪŋ-] *n* vôo *m* de conexão.

connection [kə'nekʃn] *n* ligação *f*; a bad ~ *(on phone)* uma ligação ruim; a loose ~ *(in machine)* um fio solto; in ~ with em relação a.

connoisseur [‚kɒnə'sɜːʳ] *n* conhecedor *m* (-ra *f*).

conquer ['kɒŋkəʳ] *vt* conquistar.

conquest ['kɒŋkwest] *n* conquista *f*.

conscience ['kɒnʃəns] *n* consciência *f*.

conscientious [‚kɒnʃɪ'enʃəs] *adj* consciencioso(-osa).

conscious ['kɒnʃəs] *adj (awake)* consciente; *(deliberate)* deliberado(-da); to be ~ of estar consciente de.

consciousness ['kɒnʃəsnɪs] *n* consciência *f*.

conscript ['kɒnskrɪpt] *n (MIL)* recruta *mf*.

consecutive [kən'sekjʊtɪv] *adj* consecutivo(-va).

consent [kən'sent] *n* consentimento *m*.

consequence ['kɒnsɪkwəns] *n (result)* conseqüência *f*.

consequently ['kɒnsɪkwəntlɪ] *adv* conseqüentemente.

conservation [‚kɒnsə'veɪʃn] *n* conservação *f*.

conservative [kən'sɜːvətɪv] *adj* conservador(-ra).

❏ **Conservative** *adj* conservador(-ra) ♦ *n* conservador *m* (-ra *f*).

conservatory [kən'sɜːvətrɪ] *n* jardim-de-inverno *m (Br)*, marquise *f (Port)*.

conserve [*n* kən'sɜːv, *vb* kən'sɜːv] *n* compota *f* ♦ *vt* preservar.

consider [kən'sɪdəʳ] *vt* considerar; to ~ doing sthg pensar em fazer algo.

considerable [kən'sɪdrəbl] *adj* considerável.

considerably [kən'sɪdrəblɪ] *adv* consideravelmente.

considerate [kən'sɪdərət] *adj (person)* gentil; that's very ~ of you que gentileza de sua parte.

consideration [kən‚sɪdə'reɪʃn] *n* consideração *f*; to take sthg into ~ ter algo em consideração.

considering [kən'sɪdərɪŋ] *prep* tendo em conta.

consist [kən'sɪst] : **consist in** *vt fus* consistir em.

❏ **consist of** *vt fus* consistir em.

consistency [kən'sɪstənsɪ] *n* consistência *f*.

consistent [kən'sɪstənt] *adj* consistente.

consolation [‚kɒnsə'leɪʃn] *n* consolação *f*.

console ['kɒnsəʊl] *n* consola *f*.

consonant ['kɒnsənənt] *n* consoante *f*.

conspicuous [kən'spɪkjʊəs] *adj* que dá nas vistas.

conspiracy [kən'spɪrəsɪ] *n* conspiração *f*.

constable ['kʌnstəbl] *n (Brit)* policial *mf (Br)*, polícia *mf (Port)*.

constant ['kɒnstənt] *adj* constante.

constantly ['kɒnstəntlɪ] *adv* constantemente.

constipated ['kɒnstɪpeɪtɪd] *adj*: to be ~ ter prisão de ventre.

constipation [ˌkɒnstɪ'peɪʃn] *n* prisão *f* de ventre, constipação *f (Br)*.

constituency [kən'stɪtjuənsɪ] *n* círculo *m* eleitoral.

constitute ['kɒnstɪtjuːt] *vt (represent)* constituir.

constitution [ˌkɒnstɪ'tjuːʃn] *n (health)* constituição *f* física.

constraint [kən'streɪnt] *n (restriction)* restrição *f*; ~ **on** sthg restrição a algo.

construct [kən'strʌkt] *vt* construir.

construction [kən'strʌkʃn] *n* construção *f*; **under** ~ em construção.

constructive [kən'strʌktɪv] *adj* construtivo(-va).

consul ['kɒnsəl] *n* cônsul *mf*.

consulate ['kɒnsjulət] *n* consulado *m*.

consult [kən'sʌlt] *vt* consultar.

consultant [kən'sʌltənt] *n (Brit: doctor)* médico *m* (-ca *f*) especialista.

consulting room [kən'sʌltɪŋ-] *n* consultório *m*, sala *f* de consultas.

consume [kən'sjuːm] *vt* consumir.

consumer [kən'sjuːmə'] *n* consumidor *m* (-ra *f*).

consumption [kən'sʌmpʃn] *n (use)* consumo *m*.

contact ['kɒntækt] *n* contato *m* ◆ *vt* contatar; **in** ~ **with** em contato com.

contact lens *n* lente *f* de contato.

contagious [kən'teɪdʒəs] *adj* contagioso(-osa).

contain [kən'teɪn] *vt* conter.

container [kən'teɪnə'] *n (bowl etc)* recipiente *m*; *(for cargo)* container *m (Br)*, contentor *m (Port)*.

contaminate [kən'tæmɪneɪt] *vt* contaminar.

contemplate ['kɒntempleɪt] *vt (consider)* contemplar.

contemporary [kən'tempərərɪ] *adj* contemporâneo(-nea) ◆ *n* contemporâneo *m* (-nea *f*).

contempt [kən'tempt] *n (scorn)* desprezo *m*; ~ **for** desprezo por.

contend [kən'tend] : **contend with** *vt fus* enfrentar.

contender [kən'tendə'] *n* candidato *m* (-ta *f*).

content [*adj* kən'tent, *n* 'kɒntent] *adj* satisfeito(-ta) ◆ *n (of vitamins, fibre)* quantidade *f*; *(of alcohol, fat)* teor *m*. ⊐ **contents** *npl (things inside)* conteúdo *m*; *(at beginning of book)* índice *m*.

contented [kən'tentɪd] *adj* contente, satisfeito(-ta).

contest [*n* 'kɒntest, *vb* kən'test] *n (competition)* concurso *m*; *(struggle)* luta *f* ◆ *vt (election, seat)* candidatar-se a; *(decision, will)* contestar.

contestant [kən'testənt] *n (in quiz show)* concorrente *mf*; *(in race)* participante *mf*.

context ['kɒntekst] *n* contexto *m*.

continent ['kɒntɪnənt] *n* continente *m*; **the Continent** *(Brit)* a Europa Continental.

continental [ˌkɒntɪ'nentl] *adj (Brit: European)* da Europa Continental.

continental breakfast *n* típico café da manhã composto por café, pão ou croissants, manteiga e geléia.

continental quilt *n (Brit)* edredom *m (Br)*, edredão *m (Port)*.

continual [kən'tɪnjuəl] *adj* contínuo (-nua).

continually [kən'tɪnjuəlɪ] *adv* continuamente.

continue [kən'tɪnjuː] *vt & vi* continuar; **to** ~ **doing** sthg continuar a fazer algo; **to** ~ **with** sthg continuar com algo.

continuous [kən'tɪnjuəs] *adj* contínuo(-nua).

continuously [kən'tɪnjuəslɪ] *adv* continuamente.

contortion [kən'tɔːʃn] *n (position)* contorção *f*.

contour ['kɒntuə'] *n* contorno *m*.

contraband ['kɒntrəbænd] *adj* de contrabando ◆ *n* contrabando *m*.

contraception [ˌkɒntrə'sepʃn] *n* contracepção *f*.

contraceptive [ˌkɒntrə'septɪv] *n* anticoncepcional *m*.

contract [*n* 'kɒntrækt, *vb* kən'trækt] *n* contrato *m* ◆ *vt (fml: illness)* contrair.

contraction [kən'trækʃn] *n (reduction in size, length)* contração *f*.

contradict [ˌkɒntrə'dɪkt] *vt* contradizer.

contradiction [ˌkɒntrə'dɪkʃn] *n* contradição *f*.

contraflow ['kɒntrəfləʊ] *n (Brit)* estreitamento e/ou inversão do sentido normal de uma pista devido a obras ou acidente, garrafão *m (Port)*.

contraption [kən'træpʃn] *n* geringonça *f*.

contrary ['kɒntrərɪ] *n*: **on the** ~ pelo cohtrário.

contrast [*n* 'kɒntrɑːst, *vb* kən'trɑːst] *n*

contraste *m* ♦ *vt* contrastar; **in ~ to** ao contrário de.

contribute [kən'trɪbjuːt] *vt (help, money)* contribuir com ♦ *vi:* **to ~ to** contribuir para.

contribution [ˌkɒntrɪ'bjuːʃn] *n* contribuição *f*.

contributor [kən'trɪbjʊtəʳ] *n (to magazine, newspaper)* colaborador *m* (-ra *f*).

contrive [kən'traɪv] *vt (fml: manage):* **to ~ to do sthg** conseguir fazer algo.

contrived [kən'traɪvd] *adj (plot, ending)* inverosímil; *(reaction)* forçado (-da).

control [kən'trəʊl] *n* controle *m* ♦ *vt* controlar; **to be in ~** controlar a situação; **out of ~** fora de controle; **under ~** sob controle.
⌐ **controls** *npl (of TV, video)* controle *m (Br)*, telecomando *m (Port); (of plane)* comandos *mpl*.

controller [kən'trəʊləʳ] *n (of TV, radio)* diretor *m* (-ra *f*); **financial ~** administrador *m* (-ra *f*).

control panel *n* painel *m* de controle.

control tower *n* torre *f* de controle.

controversial [ˌkɒntrə'vɜːʃl] *adj* controverso(-sa).

controversy [ˈkɒntrəvɜːsɪ, *Brit* kən'trɒvəsɪ] *n* controvérsia *f*.

convalesce [ˌkɒnvə'les] *vi* convalescer.

convenience [kən'viːnjəns] *n* conveniência *f*; **at your ~** quando (lhe) for possível.

convenience store *n (Am)* ≈ minimercado *m (muitas vezes aberto 24 horas por dia)*.

convenient [kən'viːnjənt] *adj* conveniente.

convent [ˈkɒnvənt] *n* convento *m*.

conventional [kən'venʃənl] *adj* convencional.

converge [kən'vɜːdʒ] *vi* convergir; **to ~ on** convergir em.

conversation [ˌkɒnvə'seɪʃn] *n* conversa *f*.

conversion [kən'vɜːʃn] *n* conversão *f*.

convert [kən'vɜːt] *vt* converter; **to ~ sthg into** converter algo em.

converted [kən'vɜːtɪd] *adj (barn, loft)* convertido(-da).

convertible [kən'vɜːtəbl] *n* conversí-

vel *m (Br)*, carro *m* descapotável *(Port)*.

convex [kɒn'veks] *adj* convexo(-xa).

convey [kən'veɪ] *vt (fml: transport)* transportar; *(idea, impression)* transmitir.

conveyer belt [kən'veɪəʳ-] *n (in airport)* esteira *f* rolante *(Br)*, tapete *m* rolante *(Port); (in factory)* correia *f* transportadora.

conveyor belt [kən'veɪəʳ-] *(Am)* = **conveyer belt**.

convict [*n* 'kɒnvɪkt, *vb* kən'vɪkt] *n* preso *m* (-sa *f*) ♦ *vt:* **to ~ sb (of)** condenar alguém (por).

conviction [kən'vɪkʃn] *n* convicção *f*; *(JUR)* condenação *f*.

convince [kən'vɪns] *vt:* **to ~ sb (of sthg)** convencer alguém (de algo); **to ~ sb to do sthg** convencer alguém a fazer algo.

convincing [kən'vɪnsɪŋ] *adj (person, argument)* convincente; *(victory, win)* esmagador(-ra).

convoy [ˈkɒnvɔɪ] *n* comboio *m*.

convulsion [kən'vʌlʃn] *n (MED)* convulsão *f*.

coo [kuː] *vi (bird)* arrulhar.

cook [kʊk] *n* cozinheiro *m* (-ra *f*) ♦ *vt (meal)* preparar; *(food)* cozinhar ♦ *vi (person)* cozinhar; *(food)* cozer.

cookbook [ˈkʊkbʊk] = **cookery book**.

cooker [ˈkʊkəʳ] *n* fogão *m*.

cookery [ˈkʊkərɪ] *n* culinária *f*.

cookery book *n* livro *m* de culinária OR cozinha.

cookie [ˈkʊkɪ] *n (Am)* biscoito *m (Br)*, bolacha *f (Port)*.

cooking [ˈkʊkɪŋ] *n (activity)* culinária *f*; *(food)* cozinha *f*.

cooking apple *n* maçã *f* para cozer.

cooking oil *n* óleo *m* de cozinhar.

cool [kuːl] *adj (temperature)* fresco (-ca); *(calm)* calmo(-ma); *(unfriendly)* frio (fria); *(inf: great)* genial *(Br)*, bestial *(Port)* ♦ *vt* arrefecer.
⌐ **cool down** *vi (become colder)* arrefecer; *(become calmer)* acalmar-se.

cool box *n (Brit)* mala *f* frigorífica.

cooler [ˈkuːləʳ] *(Am)* = **cool box**.

coop [kuːp] *n* capoeira *f*.
⌐ **coop up** *vt sep (inf)* enfiar.

cooperate [kəʊ'ɒpəreɪt] *vi* cooperar.

cooperation [kəʊˌɒpə'reɪʃn] *n* cooperação *f*.

cooperative [kəʊ'ɒpərətɪv] *adj*

(helpful) cooperante.

coordinate [kəʊˈɔːdɪneɪt] *vt* coordenar.

coordinates [kəʊˈɔːdɪnəts] *npl (clothes)* conjuntos *mpl*.

coordination [kəʊˌɔːdɪˈneɪʃn] *n* coordenação *f*.

cop [kɒp] *n (inf: policeman)* policial *mf (Br)*, polícia *mf (Port)*.

cope [kəʊp] *vi*: **to ~ with** *(problem, situation)* lidar com; *(work)* aguentar.

Copenhagen [ˌkəʊpənˈheɪgən] *n* Copenhague *s*.

copilot [ˈkəʊˌpaɪlət] *n* co-piloto *mf*.

copper [ˈkɒpəʳ] *n* cobre *m*; *(Brit: inf: coin)* = tostão *m*, moedas de cobre no valor de um ou dois pence.

copy [ˈkɒpɪ] *n* cópia *f*; *(of newspaper, book)* exemplar *m* ♦ *vt* copiar.

copyright [ˈkɒpɪraɪt] *n* direitos *mpl* autorais.

coral [ˈkɒrəl] *n* coral *m*.

cord [kɔːd] *n (string)* cordão *m*; *(wire)* fio *m*.

cord(uroy) [ˈkɔːd(ərɔɪ)] *n* veludo *m* cotelê *(Br)*, bombazina *f (Port)*.

core [kɔːʳ] *n (of fruit)* caroço *m*.

coriander [ˌkɒrɪˈændəʳ] *n* coentro *m*.

cork [kɔːk] *n (in bottle)* rolha *f*.

corkscrew [ˈkɔːkskruː] *n* saca-rolhas *m inv*.

corn [kɔːn] *n (Brit: crop)* cereal *m*; *(Am: maize)* milho *m*; *(on foot)* calo *m*.

corned beef [ˌkɔːnd-] *n* carne *f* de vaca enlatada.

corner [ˈkɔːnəʳ] *n* canto *m*; *(bend in road)* curva *f*; **it's just around the ~** fica ali mesmo ao virar a esquina.

corner shop *n (Brit)* mercearia *f*, quitanda *f (Br)*, mini-mercado *m (Port)*.

cornet [ˈkɔːnɪt] *n (Brit: ice-cream cone)* casquinha *f (Br)*, cone *m (Port)*.

cornflakes [ˈkɔːnfleɪks] *npl* Cornflakes® *mpl*, flocos *mpl* de milho.

corn-on-the-cob [-kɒb] *n* espiga de milho cozida, servida com manteiga.

Cornwall [ˈkɔːnwɔːl] *n* Cornualha *f*.

coronation [ˌkɒrəˈneɪʃn] *n* coroação *f*.

corporal [ˈkɔːpərəl] *n* cabo *m*.

corporal punishment *n* castigos *mpl* corporais.

corporation [ˌkɔːpəˈreɪʃn] *n (council)* conselho *m* municipal; *(large company)* corporação *f*, companhia *f*.

corpse [kɔːps] *n* cadáver *m*.

correct [kəˈrekt] *adj* correto(-ta) ♦ *vt* corrigir.

correction [kəˈrekʃn] *n* correção *f*.

correspond [ˌkɒrɪˈspɒnd] *vi*: **to ~ (to)** *(match)* corresponder (a); **to ~ (with)** *(exchange letters)* corresponder-se (com).

correspondence [ˌkɒrɪˈspɒndəns] *n* correspondência *f*.

correspondent [ˌkɒrɪˈspɒndənt] *n* correspondente *mf*.

corresponding [ˌkɒrɪˈspɒndɪŋ] *adj* correspondente.

corridor [ˈkɒrɪdɔːʳ] *n* corredor *m*.

corrosion [kəˈrəʊʒn] *n* corrosão *f*.

corrugated iron [ˈkɒrəgeɪtɪd-] *n* ferro *m* corrugado *(Br)*, folha-de-flandres *f (Port)*.

corrupt [kəˈrʌpt] *adj* corrupto(-ta).

corruption [kəˈrʌpʃn] *n* corrupção *f*.

corset [ˈkɔːsɪt] *n* espartilho *m*.

cosmetics [kɒzˈmetɪks] *npl* cosméticos *mpl*.

cosmopolitan [ˌkɒzməˈpɒlɪtn] *adj* cosmopolita.

cost [kɒst] *(pt & pp* **cost)** *n* custo *m* ♦ *vt* custar; **how much does it ~?** quanto custa?

co-star [ˈkəʊ-] *n* co-protagonista *mf*.

costly [ˈkɒstlɪ] *adj (expensive)* caro (-ra).

costume [ˈkɒstjuːm] *n (of actor)* roupa *f (Br)*, fato *m (Port)*; *(of country, region)* traje *m*.

cosy [ˈkəʊzɪ] *adj (Brit: room, house)* aconchegante.

cot [kɒt] *n (Brit: for baby)* berço *m*; *(Am: camp bed)* cama *f* de campismo.

cottage [ˈkɒtɪdʒ] *n* casa *f* de campo.

cottage cheese *n* = requeijão *m*.

cottage pie *n (Brit)* empadão *m (de carne de vaca picada)*.

cotton [ˈkɒtn] *adj (dress, shirt)* de algodão ♦ *n (cloth)* algodão *m*; *(thread)* linha *f (de coser)*.

cotton candy *n (Am)* algodão *m* doce.

cotton wool *n* algodão *m* (hidrófilo).

couch [kaʊtʃ] *n (sofa)* sofá *m*; *(at doctor's)* cama *f*.

couchette [kuːˈʃet] *n* couchette *f*.

cough [kɒf] *n* tosse *f* ♦ *vi* tossir; **to have a ~** estar com tosse.

cough mixture *n* xarope *m* para a tosse.

cough sweet *n (Brit)* pastilha *f* para a tosse.

cough syrup = cough mixture.

could [kʊd] *pt* → can.

couldn't [ˈkʊdnt] = could not.

could've [ˈkʊdəv] = could have.

council [ˈkaʊnsl] *n (Brit: of town)* prefeitura *f (Br)*, câmara *f (Port)*; *(Brit: of county)* = governo *m* civil; *(organization)* conselho *m*.

council estate *n* conjunto *m* residencial *(Br)*, bairro *m* de habitação social *(Port)* *(pertencente ao Estado)*.

council house *n (Brit)* casa *f* popular *(Br)*, habitação *f* social *(Port)*, casa pertencente ao Estado alugada a baixo preço.

councillor [ˈkaʊnsələʳ] *n (Brit: of town, county)* ~ vereador *m* (-ra *f*).

council tax *n (Brit)* imposto local pago à prefeitura, relativo aos serviços de saneamento, água, transportes, etc, por esta fornecidos.

counsellor [ˈkaʊnsələʳ] *n (Brit)* conselheiro *m* (-ra *f*).

counselor [ˈkaʊnsələʳ] *(Am)* = counsellor

count [kaʊnt] *vt & vi* contar ◆ *n (nobleman)* conde *m*.

◡ **count on** *vt fus* contar com.

countdown [ˈkaʊntdaʊn] *n* contagem *f* decrescente.

counter [ˈkaʊntəʳ] *n (in shop, bank)* balcão *m*; *(in board game)* ficha *f*.

counteract [ˌkaʊntərˈækt] *vt* compensar, contrabalançar.

counterattack [ˌkaʊntərəˈtæk] *n* contra-ataque *m*.

counterclockwise [ˌkaʊntəˈklɒkwaɪz] *adv (Am)* no sentido contrário ao dos ponteiros do relógio.

counterfeit [ˈkaʊntəfɪt] *adj* falso(-sa) ◆ *vt* falsificar, forjar.

counterfoil [ˈkaʊntəfɔɪl] *n* talão *m*.

counterpart [ˈkaʊntəpɑːt] *n* homólogo *m* (-ga *f*).

countess [ˈkaʊntɪs] *n* condessa *f*.

countless [ˈkaʊntlɪs] *adj* inúmeros (-ras).

country [ˈkʌntrɪ] *n* país *m*; *(countryside)* campo *m* ◆ *adj* do campo.

country and western *n* música *f* country.

country dancing *n* dança *f* folclórica.

country house *n* = casa *f* de campo *(Br)*, = solar *m (Port)*.

countryman [ˈkʌntrɪmən] *(pl -men* [-mən]) *n* compatriota *m*.

country road *n* estrada *f* rural.

countryside [ˈkʌntrɪsaɪd] *n* campo *m*.

county [ˈkaʊntɪ] *n (in Britain)* condado *m*; *(in US)* divisão administrativa de um estado, nos EUA.

county council *n (Brit)* organismo que administra um condado, ~ conselho *m* distrital.

coup [kuː] *n*: ~ **(d'état)** golpe *m* de Estado.

couple [ˈkʌpl] *n* casal *m*; **a** ~ **(of)** *(two)* dois (duas); *(a few)* dois ou três (duas ou três).

coupon [ˈkuːpɒn] *n* cupom *m (Br)*, cupão *m (Port)*.

courage [ˈkʌrɪdʒ] *n* coragem *f*.

courgette [kɔːˈʒet] *n (Brit)* abobrinha *f (Br)*, courgette *f (Port)*.

courier [ˈkʊrɪəʳ] *n (for holidaymakers)* guia *mf*; *(for delivering letters, packages)* mensageiro *m* (-ra *f*).

course [kɔːs] *n* curso *m*; *(of meal)* prato *m*; *(of treatment, injections)* tratamento *m*; *(of ship, plane)* rota *f*; *(for golf)* campo *m*; **of** ~ *(certainly)* com certeza, claro; *(evidently)* claro; **of** ~ **not** claro que não; **in the** ~ **of** no decurso de.

coursework [ˈkɔːswɜːk] *n* trabalho *m* realizado durante o curso.

court [kɔːt] *n (JUR: building, room)* tribunal *m*; *(SPORT)* quadra *f (Br)*, campo *m (Port)*; *(of king, queen)* corte *f*.

courteous [ˈkɜːtjəs] *adj* cortês.

courtesy [ˈkɜːtɪsɪ] *n (polite behaviour)* cortesia *f*; **(by)** ~ **of** com a autorização de.

courtesy coach [ˈkɜːtɪsɪ-] *n* ônibus *m* gratuito *(de aeroporto, hotel, etc)*.

courthouse [ˈkɔːthaʊs, *pl* -haʊzɪz] *n (Am)* tribunal *m*.

court shoes *npl* sapatos *mpl* (simples) de salto alto.

courtyard [ˈkɔːtjɑːd] *n* pátio *m*.

cousin [ˈkʌzn] *n* primo *m* (-ma *f*).

cove [kəʊv] *n* enseada *f*.

cover [ˈkʌvəʳ] *n* cobertura *f*; *(lid)* tampa *f*; *(of book, magazine)* capa *f*; *(blanket)* coberta *f* ◆ *vt* cobrir; *(travel)* percorrer; *(apply to)* abranger; **to take** ~ abrigar-se; **to be ~ed in** estar coberto de; **to** ~ **sthg with sthg** cobrir algo com algo.

◡ **cover up** *vt sep (put cover on)* cobrir; *(facts, truth)* encobrir.

coverage [ˈkʌvərɪdʒ] *n* (*of news*) cobertura *f* (jornalística).

cover charge *n* couvert *m*.

covering [ˈkʌvərɪŋ] *n* (*for floor etc*) revestimento *m*; (*of dust, snow etc*) camada *f*.

covering letter *n* (*Brit*) carta *f* de apresentação.

cover letter (*Am*) = **covering letter**.

cover note *n* (*Brit*) apólice *f* de seguro provisória.

cow [kaʊ] *n* (*animal*) vaca *f*.

coward [ˈkaʊəd] *n* covarde *mf*.

cowardly [ˈkaʊədlɪ] *adj* covarde.

cowboy [ˈkaʊbɔɪ] *n* cow-boy *m*, vaqueiro *m* (*Br*).

cower [ˈkaʊəʳ] *vi* encolher-se.

crab [kræb] *n* caranguejo *m*.

crack [kræk] *n* (*in cup, glass, wood*) rachadura *f*; (*gap*) fenda *f* ◆ *vt* (*cup, glass, wood*) rachar; (*nut, egg*) partir; (*inf: joke*) contar; (*whip*) estalar ◆ *vi* rachar.

cracker [ˈkrækəʳ] *n* (*biscuit*) bolacha *f* de água e sal; (*for Christmas*) tubo de papel com uma pequena surpresa, típico do Natal, que produz um estalo ao ser aberto.

cradle [ˈkreɪdl] *n* berço *m*.

craft [krɑːft] *n* (*skill, trade*) ofício *m*; (*boat: pl inv*) embarcação *f*.

craftsman [ˈkrɑːftsmən] (*pl* -men [-mən]) *n* artesão *m*.

craftsmanship [ˈkrɑːftsmənʃɪp] *n* habilidade *f*, arte *f*.

crafty [ˈkrɑːftɪ] *adj* astuto(-ta).

crag [kræg] *n* penhasco *m*, rochedo *m* escarpado.

cram [kræm] *vt*: **to ~ sthg into** enfiar algo em; **to be crammed with** estar a abarrotar de.

cramp [kræmp] *n* cãibra *f*; **stomach ~s** dores *fpl* de estômago (*fortes*).

cranberry [ˈkrænbərɪ] *n* arando *m*.

cranberry sauce *n* molho de arandos normalmente servido com peru assado.

crane [kreɪn] *n* (*machine*) guindaste *m*.

crap [kræp] *n* (*vulg*) merda *f* ◆ *adj* (*vulg*): **the film was ~** o filme era uma porcaria.

crash [kræʃ] *n* (*accident*) colisão *f*; (*noise*) estrondo *m* ◆ *vt* (*car*) bater com ◆ *vi* (*car, plane, train*) colidir.

◙ **crash into** *vt fus* (*wall*) bater contra.

crash helmet *n* capacete *m* (de proteção).

crash landing *n* aterrissagem *f* forçada (*Br*), aterragem *f* forçada (*Port*).

crass [kræs] *adj* grosseiro(-ra); **a ~ mistake** um erro crasso.

crate [kreɪt] *n* grade *f* (*para transporte de fruta, garrafas, etc*).

crater [ˈkreɪtəʳ] *n* cratera *f*.

crave [kreɪv] *vt* desejar (intensamente).

crawl [krɔːl] *vi* (*baby, person*) engatinhar (*Br*), gatinhar (*Port*); (*insect*) rastejar; (*traffic*) arrastar-se ◆ *n* (*swimming stroke*) crawl *m*.

crawler lane [ˈkrɔːləʳ-] *n* (*Brit*) faixa *f* para veículos lentos.

crayfish [ˈkreɪfɪʃ] (*pl inv*) *n* camarão-de-água-doce *m*.

crayon [ˈkreɪɒn] *n* lápis *m* de cera OR giz.

craze [kreɪz] *n* moda *f*.

crazy [ˈkreɪzɪ] *adj* maluco(-ca), louco (ca); **to be ~ about** ser louco por.

crazy golf *n* mini-golfe *m*.

creak [kriːk] *vi* (*door, floorboards*) ranger; (*hinge*) chiar.

cream [kriːm] *n* (*food*) creme *m* (*Br*), natas *fpl* (*Port*); (*for face*) creme *m*; (*for burns*) pomada *f* ◆ *adj* (*in colour*) creme (*inv*).

cream cake *n* (*Brit*) bolo *m* recheado com creme.

cream cheese *n* queijo-creme *m*, queijo *m* para barrar.

cream cracker *n* (*Brit*) biscoito *m* de água e sal.

cream sherry *n* xerez *m* doce.

cream tea *n* (*Brit*) lanche composto por chá e "scones" recheados com creme e doce.

creamy [ˈkriːmɪ] *adj* cremoso(-osa).

crease [kriːs] *n* vinco *m*.

creased [kriːst] *adj* vincado(-da), engelhado(-da) (*Port*).

create [kriːˈeɪt] *vt* (*make*) criar; (*impression*) causar; (*interest*) provocar.

creation [kriːˈeɪʃn] *n* criação *f*.

creative [kriːˈeɪtɪv] *adj* criativo(-va).

creature [ˈkriːtʃəʳ] *n* criatura *f*.

crèche [kreʃ] *n* (*Brit*) creche *f*.

credentials [krɪˈdenʃlz] *npl* (*papers*) identificação *f*, documentos *mpl*; (*fig: qualifications*) capacidades *fpl*; (*references*) credenciais *fpl*.

credibility [ˌkredəˈbɪlətɪ] *n* credibilidade *f*.

credit [ˈkredɪt] *n (praise)* mérito *m*; *(money)* crédito *m*; *(at school, university)* cadeira terminada com nota positiva; **to be in ~** estar com saldo positivo.
⌐ **credits** *npl (of film)* créditos *mpl*.

credit card *n* cartão *m* de crédito; **to pay by ~** pagar com cartão de crédito; **"all major ~s accepted"** = "aceita-se cartão de crédito".

creed [kriːd] *n* credo *m*.

creek [kriːk] *n (inlet)* angra *f*; *(Am: river)* riacho *m*.

creep [kriːp] *(pt & pp* **crept)** *vi (crawl)* arrastar-se ♦ *n (inf: groveller)* puxa-saco *mf (Br)*, graxista *mf (Port)*.

creepy-crawly [ˌkriːpɪˈkrɔːlɪ] *n (inf)* bicho *m*.

cremate [krɪˈmeɪt] *vt* cremar.

cremation [krɪˈmeɪʃn] *n* cremação *f*.

crematorium [ˌkremәˈtɔːrɪəm] *n* crematório *m*.

crepe [kreɪp] *n (thin pancake)* crepe *m*.

crepe paper *n* papel-crepe *m*.

crept [krept] *pt & pp* → **creep**.

crescent [ˈkresnt] *n (shape)* meia-lua *f*; *(street)* rua *f* semi-circular.

cress [kres] *n* agrião *m (muito pequeno)*.

crest [krest] *n (of bird, hill)* crista *f*; *(on coat of arms)* brasão *m*.

crevice [ˈkrevɪs] *n* fenda *f*.

crew [kruː] *n (of ship, plane)* tripulação *f*.

crew cut *n* corte *m* à escovinha OR à máquina zero.

crew neck *n* gola *f* redonda.

crib [krɪb] *n (Am: cot)* berço *m*.

cricket [ˈkrɪkɪt] *n (game)* críquete *m*; *(insect)* grilo *m*.

crime [kraɪm] *n* crime *m*.

criminal [ˈkrɪmɪnl] *adj (behaviour, offence)* criminoso(-osa); *(inf: disgraceful)* vergonhoso(-osa) ♦ *n* criminoso *m* (-osa *f*).

crimson [ˈkrɪmzn] *adj (in colour)* carmesim *(inv)* ♦ *n* carmesim *m*.

cringe [krɪndʒ] *vi (out of fear)* encolher-se; **to ~ (at sthg)** *(inf: with embarrassment)* não saber onde se meter *(perante algo)*.

cripple [ˈkrɪpl] *n* aleijado *m* (-da *f*) ♦ *vt* tornar inválido(-da).

crisis [ˈkraɪsɪs] *(pl* **crises** [ˈkraɪsiːz]) *n* crise *f*.

crisp [krɪsp] *adj* estaladiço(-ça).
⌐ **crisps** *npl (Brit)* batatas *fpl* fritas *(de pacote)*.

crispy [ˈkrɪspɪ] *adj* estaladiço(-ça).

crisscross [ˈkrɪskrɒs] *adj* entrecruzado(-da).

criterion [kraɪˈtɪərɪən] *(pl* **-rions** OR **-ria** [-rɪə]) *n* critério *m*.

critic [ˈkrɪtɪk] *n (reviewer)* crítico *m* (-ca *f*).

critical [ˈkrɪtɪkl] *adj* crítico(-ca); *(serious)* grave; *(disparaging)* severo(-ra).

critically [ˈkrɪtɪklɪ] *adv (seriously)* gravemente; *(crucially)* extremamente; *(analytically)* de forma crítica; *(disparagingly)* severamente.

criticism [ˈkrɪtɪsɪzm] *n* crítica *f*; **I hate ~** detesto críticas.

criticize [ˈkrɪtɪsaɪz] *vt* criticar.

croak [krəʊk] *vi (animal)* grasnar.

Croat [ˈkrəʊæt] *adj* croata ♦ *n (person)* croata *mf*; *(language)* croata *m*.

Croatia [krəʊˈeɪʃə] *n* Croácia *f*.

Croatian [krəʊˈeɪʃn] = **Croat**.

crochet [ˈkrəʊʃeɪ] *n* croché *m*, malha *f*.

crockery [ˈkrɒkərɪ] *n* louça *f*.

crocodile [ˈkrɒkədaɪl] *n* crocodilo *m*.

crocus [ˈkrəʊkəs] *(pl* **-es)** *n* crocus *m inv*.

crook [krʊk] *n (criminal)* vigarista *mf*.

crooked [ˈkrʊkɪd] *adj (bent, twisted)* torto (torta).

crop [krɒp] *n (kind of plant)* cultura *f*, *(harvest)* colheita *f*.
⌐ **crop up** *vi* surgir.

cross [krɒs] *adj* zangado(-da) ♦ *n* cruz *f*; *(mixture)* cruzamento *m* ♦ *vt (road, river, ocean)* atravessar; *(arms, legs)* cruzar; *(Brit: cheque)* barrar ♦ *vi (intersect)* cruzar-se.
⌐ **cross out** *vt sep* riscar.
⌐ **cross over** *vt fus (road)* atravessar.

crossbar [ˈkrɒsbɑː] *n* barra *f* transversal.

cross-Channel ferry *n* barco que faz a travessia do Canal da Mancha.

cross-country (running) *n* corrida *f* pelo campo *(Br)*, corta-mato *m (Port)*.

cross-eyed [-aɪd] *adj* vesgo(-ga).

crossing [ˈkrɒsɪŋ] *n (on road)* faixa *f* para pedestres *(Br)*, passadeira *f (para peões) (Port)*; *(sea journey)* travessia *f*.

crossroads [ˈkrɒsrəʊdz] *(pl inv)* *n* cruzamento *m*.

crosswalk [ˈkrɒswɔːk] *n (Am)* faixa *f* para pedestres *(Br)*, passadeira *f (para peões) (Port)*.

crossword (puzzle) [ˈkrɒswɜːd-] *n* palavras *fpl* cruzadas.

crotch [krɒtʃ] *n* entrepernas *m*.

crouch [kraʊtʃ] *vi* agachar-se.

crouton [ˈkruːtɒn] *n* pedaço de pão torrado ou frito, usado como guarnição em sopas.

crow [krəʊ] *n* corvo *m*.

crowbar [ˈkrəʊbɑːʳ] *n* alavanca *f*, pé-de-cabra *m*.

crowd [kraʊd] *n* multidão *f*; (at match) público *m*.

crowded [ˈkraʊdɪd] *adj* cheio (cheia) (de gente).

crown [kraʊn] *n* coroa *f*; (of head) alto *m* (da cabeça).

Crown Jewels *npl* jóias da coroa britânica.

crucial [ˈkruːʃl] *adj* crucial.

crucifix [ˈkruːsɪfɪks] *n* crucifixo *m*.

crude [kruːd] *adj* grosseiro(-ra).

cruel [krʊəl] *adj* cruel.

cruelty [ˈkrʊəltɪ] *n* crueldade *f*.

cruet (set) [ˈkruːɪt-] *n* galheteiro *m*.

cruise [kruːz] *n* cruzeiro *m* ◆ *vi* (plane) voar; (ship) navegar; (car) rodar.

cruiser [ˈkruːzəʳ] *n* (pleasure boat) cruzeiro *m*.

crumb [krʌm] *n* migalha *f*.

crumble [ˈkrʌmbl] *n* sobremesa feita com fruta cozida coberta com uma massa esfarelada de farinha, açúcar e manteiga ◆ *vi* (building, cliff) desmoronar-se; (cheese) esmigalhar-se.

crumpet [ˈkrʌmpɪt] *n* espécie de crepe pequeno que se come quente com manteiga ou geléia.

crumple [ˈkrʌmpl] *vt* (dress, suit) engelhar; (letter) amarrotar.

crunch [krʌntʃ] *vt* (with teeth) trincar OR mastigar (fazendo ruído).

crunchy [ˈkrʌntʃɪ] *adj* crocante.

crusade [kruːˈseɪd] *n* (war) cruzada *f*.

crush [krʌʃ] *n* (drink) sumo *m* (de fruta) ◆ *vt* esmagar; (ice) partir.

crust [krʌst] *n* (of bread) casca *f* (Br), côdea *f* (Port); (of pie) crosta *f*.

crusty [ˈkrʌstɪ] *adj* estaladiço(-ça).

crutch [krʌtʃ] *n* (stick) muleta *f*; (between legs) = **crotch**.

cry [kraɪ] *n* grito *m* ◆ *vi* (weep) chorar; (shout) gritar.

⊔ **cry out** *vi* gritar.

crystal [ˈkrɪstl] *n* cristal *m*.

crystal clear *adj* (motive, meaning) claro(-ra) como a água.

cub [kʌb] *n* (animal) cria *f*.

Cub [kʌb] *n* escoteiro entre os 8 e os 11 anos.

cubbyhole [ˈkʌbɪhəʊl] *n* cubículo *m*.

cube [kjuːb] *n* cubo *m*.

cubicle [ˈkjuːbɪkl] *n* cubículo *m*.

Cub Scout = **Cub**.

cuckoo [ˈkʊkuː] *n* cuco *m*.

cuckoo clock *n* relógio *m* de cuco.

cucumber [ˈkjuːkʌmbəʳ] *n* pepino *m*.

cuddle [ˈkʌdl] *n* abraço *m*.

cuddly toy [ˈkʌdlɪ-] *n* boneco *m* de pelúcia.

cue [kjuː] *n* (in snooker, pool) taco *m*.

cuff [kʌf] *n* (of sleeve) punho *m*; (Am: of trousers) dobra *f*.

cuff links *npl* botões *mpl* de punho.

cuisine [kwɪˈziːn] *n* cozinha *f*.

cul-de-sac [ˈkʌldəsæk] *n* beco *m* sem saída.

culmination [ˌkʌlmɪˈneɪʃn] *n* culminação *f*.

culottes [kjuːˈlɒts] *npl* saia-calça *f*.

culprit [ˈkʌlprɪt] *n* culpado *m* (-da *f*).

cult [kʌlt] *n* culto *m* ◆ *adj* de culto.

cultivate [ˈkʌltɪveɪt] *vt* cultivar.

cultivated [ˈkʌltɪveɪtɪd] *adj* (person) culto(-ta).

cultural [ˈkʌltʃərəl] *adj* cultural.

culture [ˈkʌltʃəʳ] *n* cultura *f*.

cultured [ˈkʌltʃəd] *adj* culto(-ta).

cumbersome [ˈkʌmbəsəm] *adj* pesado(-da).

cumin [ˈkjuːmɪn] *n* cominho *m*.

cunning [ˈkʌnɪŋ] *adj* esperto(-ta).

cup [kʌp] *n* xícara *f* (Br), chávena *f* (Port); (trophy, competition) taça *f*; (of bra) taça *f* (Br), copa *f* (Port).

cupboard [ˈkʌbəd] *n* armário *m*.

curate [ˈkjʊərət] *n* cura *m*.

curator [kjʊəˈreɪtəʳ] *n* conservador *m* (-ra *f*) (de museu, biblioteca).

curb [kɜːb] *n* (Am) = **kerb**.

curd cheese [kɜːd-] *n* ~ requeijão *m*.

curdle [ˈkɜːdl] *vi* coalhar.

cure [kjʊəʳ] *n* (for illness) cura *f* ◆ *vt* curar.

curfew [ˈkɜːfjuː] *n* toque *f* de recolher.

curiosity [ˌkjʊərɪˈɒsɪtɪ] *n* curiosidade *f*.

curious [ˈkjʊərɪəs] *adj* curioso(-osa).

curl [kɜːl] *n* (of hair) caracol *m* ◆ *vt* (hair) encaracolar.

curler [ˈkɜːləʳ] *n* rolo *m*.

curling tongs [ˈkɜːlɪŋ-] *npl* ferro *m* de frisar OR encaracolar (o cabelo).

curly [ˈkɜːlɪ] *adj* encaracolado(-da).

currant ['kʌrənt] *n* corinto *m*.
currency ['kʌrənsɪ] *n (money)* moeda *f*.
current ['kʌrənt] *adj* actual ◆ *n* corrente *f*.
current account *n (Brit)* conta *f* corrente *(Br)*, conta *f* à ordem *(Port)*.
current affairs *npl* temas *mpl* da atualidade.
currently ['kʌrəntlɪ] *adv* atualmente.
curriculum [kə'rɪkjələm] *n* programa *m* (de estudos).
curriculum vitae [-'viːtaɪ] *n (Brit)* curriculum *m* vitae.
curried ['kʌrɪd] *adj* com caril.
curry ['kʌrɪ] *n* caril *m*.
curse [kɜːs] *vi* praguejar.
cursor ['kɜːsəʳ] *n* cursor *m*.
curt [kɜːt] *adj* seco(-ca).
curtail [kɜː'teɪl] *vt (cut short)* encurtar, abreviar.
curtain ['kɜːtn] *n* cortina *f*.
curts(e)y ['kɜːtsɪ] *n* vênia *f (de mulher)* ◆ *vi* fazer uma vênia.
curve [kɜːv] *n* curva *f* ◆ *vi* descrever uma curva.
curved [kɜːvd] *adj* curvo(-va).
cushion ['kʊʃn] *n* almofada *f*.
custard ['kʌstəd] *n creme à base de farinha, leite e açúcar para acompanhar doces ou fruta cozida*.
custody ['kʌstədɪ] *n* custódia *f*; **in ~** *(JUR)* sob custódia.
custom ['kʌstəm] *n (tradition)* costume *m*; **"thank you for your ~"** "obrigada pela sua visita".
customary ['kʌstəmrɪ] *adj* habitual.
customer ['kʌstəməʳ] *n (of shop)* cliente *mf*.
customer services *n (department)* serviço *m* de assistência a clientes.
customize ['kʌstəmaɪz] *vt* personalizar.
customs ['kʌstəmz] *n* alfândega *f*; **to go through ~** passar pela alfândega.
customs duty *n* impostos *mpl* alfandegários *(Br)*, direitos *mpl* alfandegários *(Port)*.
customs officer *n* inspetor *m* (-ora *f*) alfandegário *(Br)*, empregado *m* alfandegário (empregada *f* alfandegária *(Port)*.
cut [kʌt] *(pt & pp* cut) *n* corte *m* ◆ *vt* cortar; *(reduce)* reduzir, cortar em ◆ *vi (knife, scissors)* cortar; **~ and blow-dry** corte e brushing; **to ~ o.s.** cortar-se; **to ~ the grass** cortar a grama *(Br)*, cortar a relva *(Port)*; **to ~ sthg open** abrir algo.

❑ **cut back** *vi*: **to ~ back on sthg** cortar em algo.
❑ **cut down** *vt sep (tree)* abater.
❑ **cut down on** *vt fus* cortar em.
❑ **cut off** *vt sep* cortar; **I've been ~ off** *(on phone)* a ligação caiu; **to be ~ off** *(isolated)* estar isolado.
❑ **cut out** *vt sep (newspaper article, photo)* recortar ◆ *vi (engine)* morrer; **to ~ out fatty foods** cortar as gorduras; **~ it out!** *(inf)* pára com isso!
❑ **cut up** *vt sep* cortar.
cute [kjuːt] *adj* bonitinho(-nha) *(Br)*, giro(-ra) *(Port)*.
cut-glass *adj* de vidro biselado.
cutlery ['kʌtlərɪ] *n* talheres *mpl*.
cutlet ['kʌtlɪt] *n (of meat)* costeleta *f*; *(of nuts, vegetables)* costeleta vegetariana.
cut-price *adj* a preço reduzido.
cutting ['kʌtɪŋ] *n (from newspaper)* recorte *m*.
CV *n (Brit: abbr of* curriculum vitae) c.v. *m*.
cwt *abbr* = **hundredweight**.
cyberspace ['saɪbəspeɪs] *n* ciberespaço *m*.
cycle ['saɪkl] *n (bicycle)* bicicleta *f*; *(series)* ciclo *m* ◆ *vi* andar de bicicleta.
cycle hire *n* aluguel *m* de bicicletas.
cycle lane *n* faixa *f* para ciclistas.
cycle path *n* pista *f* para ciclistas.
cycling ['saɪklɪŋ] *n* ciclismo *m*; **to go ~** ir andar de bicicleta.
cycling shorts *npl* calções *mpl* de ciclista.
cyclist ['saɪklɪst] *n* ciclista *mf*.
cylinder ['sɪlɪndəʳ] *n (container)* bujão *m (Br)*, botija *f (Port)*; *(in engine)* cilindro *m*.
cymbals ['sɪmblz] *npl* pratos *npl*.
cynic ['sɪnɪk] *n* pessoa que não tem fé nas pessoas nem nas suas intenções.
cynical ['sɪnɪkl] *adj* céptico(-ca) *(em relação às pessoas e às suas intenções)*.
cynicism ['sɪnɪsɪzm] *n* falta de fé nas pessoas e nas suas intenções.
Cypriot ['sɪprɪət] *adj* cipriota ◆ *n* cipriota *mf*.
Cyprus ['saɪprəs] *n* Chipre *f*.
cyst [sɪst] *n* quisto *m*.
czar [zɑː] *n* czar *m*.
Czech [tʃek] *adj* tcheco(-ca) ◆ *n (person)* tcheco *m* (-ca *f*); *(language)* tcheco *m*.
Czechoslovakia [ˌtʃekəslə'vækɪə] *n* Tchecoslováquia *f*.
Czech Republic *n*: **the ~** a República Tcheca.

D

dab [dæb] vt (ointment, cream) aplicar levemente.

dachshund ['dækshund] n (cão) salsicha m.

dad [dæd] n (inf) papá m.

daddy ['dædɪ] n (inf) papá m.

daddy longlegs [-'lɒŋlegz] (pl inv) n pernilongo m (Br), melga f (Port).

daffodil ['dæfədɪl] n narciso m.

daft [dɑːft] adj (Brit: inf) parvo(-va).

dagger ['dægəʳ] n punhal m.

daily ['deɪlɪ] adj diário(-ria) ◆ adv diariamente ◆ n: a ~ (newspaper) um jornal diário.

dainty ['deɪntɪ] adj delicado(-da), fino(-na).

dairy ['deərɪ] n (on farm) vacaria f; (shop) leitaria f.

dairy product n lacticínio m, produto m lácteo (Port).

daisy ['deɪzɪ] n margarida f.

dale [deɪl] n vale m.

dam [dæm] n barragem f.

damage ['dæmɪdʒ] n dano m ◆ vt (house, car) danificar; (back, leg) machucar; (fig: reputation, chances) arruinar.

damn [dæm] excl (inf) droga! ◆ adj (inf) maldito(-ta); **I don't give a ~** não estou nem aí.

damned [dæmd] adv (inf) muito ◆ adj (inf) maldito(-ta); **well, I'll be ~!** nossa!

damp [dæmp] adj úmido(-da) ◆ n umidade f.

dampen ['dæmpən] vt (make wet) umedecer.

damson ['dæmzn] n ameixa f pequena, abrunho m (Port).

dance [dɑːns] n dança f; (social event) baile m ◆ vi dançar; **to have a ~** dançar.

dance floor n pista f de dança.

dancer ['dɑːnsəʳ] n bailarino m (-na f).

dancing ['dɑːnsɪŋ] n dança f; **to go ~** ir dançar.

dandelion ['dændɪlaɪən] n dente-de-leão m.

dandruff ['dændrʌf] n caspa f.

Dane [deɪn] n dinamarquês m (-esa f).

danger ['deɪndʒəʳ] n perigo m; **in ~** em perigo.

dangerous ['deɪndʒərəs] adj perigoso(-osa).

dangle ['dæŋgl] vt & vi balançar.

Danish ['deɪnɪʃ] adj dinamarquês(-esa) ◆ n (language) dinamarquês m.

Danish pastry n bolo de massa folhada recheado com passas, ou qualquer outra fruta.

dank [dæŋk] adj úmido e frio (úmida e fria).

dappled ['dæpld] adj (animal) malhado(-da).

dare [deəʳ] vt: **to ~ to do sthg** ousar fazer algo, atrever-se a fazer algo; **to ~ sb to do sthg** desafiar alguém a fazer algo; **how ~ you!** como se atreve!

daredevil ['deə,devl] n temerário m (-ria f).

daring ['deərɪŋ] adj corajoso(-osa).

dark [dɑːk] adj escuro(-ra); (person, skin) moreno(-na) ◆ n: **after ~** depois do anoitecer; **the ~** o escuro.

dark chocolate n chocolate m amargo OR negro.

darken ['dɑːkn] vi escurecer.

dark glasses npl óculos mpl escuros.

darkness ['dɑːknɪs] n escuridão f.

darkroom ['dɑːkrum] n câmara f escura.

darling ['dɑːlɪŋ] n (term of affection) querido m (-da f).

dart [dɑːt] n dardo m.

⌐ **darts** *n (game)* dardos *mpl*.

dartboard ['dɑːtbɔːd] *n* alvo *m (para jogo de dardos)*.

dash [dæʃ] *n (of liquid)* gota *f; (in writing)* travessão *m ◆ vi* precipitar-se.

dashboard ['dæʃbɔːd] *n* painel *m (Br)*, tablier *m (Port)*.

dashing ['dæʃɪŋ] *adj* fogoso(-osa).

data ['deɪtə] *n* dados *mpl*.

database ['deɪtəbeɪs] *n* banco *m* de base *(Br)*, base *f* de dados *(Port)*.

data processing [-'prəʊsesɪŋ] *n* processamento *m* de dados.

date [deɪt] *n (day)* data *f; (meeting)* encontro *m*, compromisso *m; (Am: person)* namorado *m* (-da *f); (fruit)* tâmara *f ◆ vt (cheque, letter)* datar; *(person)* sair com *◆ vi (become unfashionable)* cair de moda; **what's the ~?** que dia é hoje?; **to have a ~ with sb** ter um encontro OR compromisso com alguém.

dated ['deɪtɪd] *adj* antiquado(-da).

date of birth *n* data *f* de nascimento.

daughter ['dɔːtər] *n* filha *f*.

daughter-in-law *n* nora *f*.

daunting ['dɔːntɪŋ] *adj* assustador(-ra).

dawdle ['dɔːdl] *vi* empatar (tempo).

dawn [dɔːn] *n* amanhecer *m*, madrugada *f*.

day [deɪ] *n* dia *m*; **what ~ is it today?** que dia é hoje?; **what a lovely ~!** que lindo dia!; **to have a ~ off** ter um dia de folga; **to have a ~ out** passar o dia fora; **by ~** de dia; **the ~ after tomorrow** depois de amanhã; **the ~ before** a véspera, o dia anterior; **the ~ before yesterday** anteontem; **the following ~** o dia seguinte; **have a nice ~!** tenha um bom dia!

daybreak ['deɪbreɪk] *n* aurora *f*; **at ~** ao romper da aurora, de madrugada.

daydream ['deɪdriːm] *vi* sonhar acordado.

daylight ['deɪlaɪt] *n* luz *f* do dia.

day return *n (Brit)* bilhete de ida e volta válido por um dia.

dayshift ['deɪʃɪft] *n* turno *m* de dia.

daytime ['deɪtaɪm] *n* dia *m*.

day-to-day *adj (everyday)* quotidiano(-na).

day trip *n* excursão *f*.

daze [deɪz] *vt* aturdir *◆ n*: **in a ~** aturdido(-da).

dazzle ['dæzl] *vt* deslumbrar.

DC *(abbr of direct current)* CC.

deactivate [diːˈæktɪˌveɪt] *vt* desactivar.

dead [ded] *adj* morto (morta); *(not lively)* sem vida, morto (morta); *(telephone line)* cortado(-da); *(battery)* gasto(-ta) *◆ adv (precisely)* mesmo; *(inf: very)* muito; **it's ~ ahead** é mesmo em frente; **" ~ slow"** "dirija devagar".

deaden ['dedn] *vt (noise)* diminuir; *(feeling)* abrandar.

dead end *n (street)* beco *m* sem saída.

dead heat *n* empate *m*.

deadline ['dedlaɪn] *n* prazo *m*.

deadlock ['dedlɒk] *n* impasse *m*.

deadly ['dedlɪ] *adj* mortal; *(aim, accuracy)* infalível *◆ adv* extremamente; **it was ~ boring** foi muito chato.

deaf [def] *adj* surdo(-da) *◆ npl*: **the ~** os surdos.

deaf-and-dumb *adj* surdo-mudo (surda-muda).

deafen ['defn] *vt* ensurdecer.

deaf-mute *adj* surdo-mudo(surda-muda) *◆ n* surdo-mudo *m* (surda-muda *f*).

deafness ['defnɪs] *n* surdez *f*.

deal [diːl] *(pt & pp* **dealt**) *n (agreement)* acordo *m ◆ vt (cards)* dar; **a good/bad ~** um bom/mau negócio; **a great ~ of** muito; **it's a ~!** está combinado!

⌐ **deal in** *vt fus* negociar.

⌐ **deal with** *vt fus (handle)* lidar com; *(be about)* tratar de.

dealer ['diːlər] *n (COMM)* comerciante *mf*, negociante *mf; (in drugs)* fornecedor *m* (-ra *f*).

dealing ['diːlɪŋ] *n* comércio *m*.

⌐ **dealings** *npl (business)* negociações *fpl*.

dealt [delt] *pt & pp →* **deal**.

dean [diːn] *n (of university)* reitor *m* (-ra *f); (of church, cathedral)* decano *m*, deão *m*.

dear [dɪər] *adj (loved)* querido(-da); *(expensive)* caro(-ra) *◆ n*: **my ~** meu querido (minha querida); **Dear Sir** Caro senhor; **Dear Madam** Cara senhora; **Dear John** Querido John; **oh ~!** meu Deus!

death [deθ] *n* morte *f*.

death penalty *n* pena *f* de morte.

debate [dɪˈbeɪt] *n* debate *m ◆ vt*

(wonder) considerar.

debit ['dɛbɪt] *n* débito *m* ♦ *vt (account)* debitar em.

debris ['dɛɪbriː] *n (of building)* escombros *mpl; (of aeroplane)* restos *mpl*.

debt [dɛt] *n (money owed)* dívida *f*; **to be in ~** ter dívidas.

debut ['deɪbjuː] *n* estréia *f*.

Dec. *(abbr of December)* dez.

decade ['dɛkeɪd] *n* década *f*.

decadence ['dɛkədəns] *n* decadência *f*.

decadent ['dɛkədənt] *adj* decadente.

decaff ['diːkæf] *n (inf)* descafeinado *m*.

decaffeinated [dɪ'kæfɪneɪtɪd] *adj* descafeinado(-da).

decanter [dɪ'kæntəʳ] *n* garrafa *f* para licores.

decathlon [dɪ'kæθlɒn] *n* decatlo *m*.

decay [dɪ'keɪ] *n (of building)* deterioração *f; (of wood)* apodrecimento *m; (of tooth)* cárie *f* ♦ *vi (rot)* apodrecer.

deceased [dɪ'siːst] *(pl inv) adj (fml)* falecido(-da) ♦ *n*: **the ~** o falecido (a falecida).

deceit [dɪ'siːt] *n* engano *m*.

deceitful [dɪ'siːtfʊl] *adj* enganador(-ra).

deceive [dɪ'siːv] *vt* enganar.

decelerate [ˌdiː'sɛləreɪt] *vi* abrandar.

December [dɪ'sɛmbəʳ] *n* dezembro, → September.

decent ['diːsnt] *adj* decente; *(kind)* simpático(-ca).

deception [dɪ'sɛpʃn] *n* decepção *f*.

deceptive [dɪ'sɛptɪv] *adj* enganador(-ra).

decide [dɪ'saɪd] *vt (choose)* decidir ♦ *vi* tomar uma decisão; **to ~ to do sthg** decidir fazer algo.

❏ **decide on** *vt fus* decidir-se por.

decidedly [dɪ'saɪdɪdlɪ] *adv* decididamente.

deciduous [dɪ'sɪdjʊəs] *adj* decíduo (-dua).

decimal ['dɛsɪml] *adj* decimal.

decimal point *n* vírgula *f*.

decipher [dɪ'saɪfəʳ] *vt* decifrar.

decision [dɪ'sɪʒn] *n* decisão *f*; **to make a ~** tomar uma decisão.

decisive [dɪ'saɪsɪv] *adj (person)* decidido(-da); *(event, factor)* decisivo(-va).

deck [dɛk] *n (of bus)* andar *m; (of ship)* convés *m; (of cards)* baralho *m*.

deckchair ['dɛktʃeəʳ] *n* espreguiçadeira *f*.

declaration [ˌdɛklə'reɪʃn] *n* declaração *f*.

declare [dɪ'kleəʳ] *vt* declarar; **to ~ that** declarar que; **"goods to ~"** "artigos a declarar"; **"nothing to ~"** "nada a declarar".

decline [dɪ'klaɪn] *n* declínio *m* ♦ *vi (get worse)* declinar; *(refuse)* recusar.

decompose [ˌdiːkəm'pəʊz] *vi* decompor-se.

decorate ['dɛkəreɪt] *vt* decorar.

decoration [ˌdɛkə'reɪʃn] *n (wallpaper, paint, furniture)* decoração *f; (decorative object)* adorno *m*.

decorator ['dɛkəreɪtəʳ] *n* decorador *m* (-ra *f*).

decoy ['diːkɔɪ] *n* chamariz *m*.

decrease [*n* 'diːkriːs, *vb* diː'kriːs] *n* diminuição *f* ♦ *vi* diminuir.

decree [dɪ'kriː] *n (order, decision)* decreto *m; (Am: judgment)* sentença *f* ♦ *vt* decretar; **to ~ that** decretar que.

decrepit [dɪ'krepɪt] *adj* decrépito(-ta).

dedicate ['dɛdɪkeɪt] *vt* dedicar.

dedicated ['dɛdɪkeɪtɪd] *adj (committed)* dedicado(-da).

dedication [ˌdɛdɪ'keɪʃn] *n* dedicação *f*.

deduce [dɪ'djuːs] *vt* deduzir.

deduct [dɪ'dʌkt] *vt* deduzir.

deduction [dɪ'dʌkʃn] *n* dedução *f*.

deed [diːd] *n (action)* ação *f*, ato *m*.

deep [diːp] *adj* profundo(-da); *(colour)* intenso(-sa); *(sound, voice)* grave ♦ *adv* fundo; **the pool is two metres ~** a piscina tem dois metros de profundidade; **to take a ~ breath** respirar fundo.

deep end *n (of swimming pool)* parte *f* funda.

deep freeze *n* freezer *m* (Br), congelador *m* (Port).

deep-fried [-'fraɪd] *adj* frito(-ta).

deep-pan *adj* de massa grossa.

deer [dɪəʳ] *(pl inv) n* veado *m*.

defeat [dɪ'fiːt] *n* derrota *f* ♦ *vt (team, army, government)* derrotar.

defect ['diːfekt] *n* defeito *m*.

defective [dɪ'fektɪv] *adj* defeituoso(-osa).

defence [dɪ'fens] *n (Brit)* defesa *f*.

defenceless [dɪ'fenslɪs] *adj* indefeso(-sa).

defend [dɪ'fend] *vt* defender.

defender [dɪˈfendər] *n (SPORT)* defesa *mf*.

defense [dɪˈfens] *(Am)* = **defence**.

defensive [dɪˈfensɪv] *adj* defensivo (-va).

defiant [dɪˈfaɪənt] *adj* provocador (-ra).

deficiency [dɪˈfɪʃnsɪ] *n (lack)* deficiência *f*.

deficient [dɪˈfɪʃnt] *adj (inadequate)* deficiente; ~ **in sthg** deficiente em algo.

deficit [ˈdefɪsɪt] *n* déficit *m (Br)*, défice *m (Port)*.

define [dɪˈfaɪn] *vt* definir.

definite [ˈdefɪnɪt] *adj (answer, decision)* definitivo(-va); *(person)* seguro (-ra); *(improvement)* nítido(-da).

definite article *n* artigo *m* definido.

definitely [ˈdefɪnɪtlɪ] *adv (certainly)* sem dúvida (alguma); **I'll ~ go** irei de certeza.

definition [ˌdefɪˈnɪʃn] *n (of word)* definição *f*.

deflate [dɪˈfleɪt] *vt (tyre)* esvaziar.

deflect [dɪˈflekt] *vt (ball)* desviar.

defogger [ˌdiːˈfɒgər] *n (Am)* desembaciador *m*.

deformed [dɪˈfɔːmd] *adj* deformado(-da).

defrost [ˌdiːˈfrɒst] *vt (food, fridge)* descongelar; *(Am: demist)* desembaciar.

defy [dɪˈfaɪ] *vt* desafiar; **to ~ sb to do sthg** desafiar alguém a fazer algo.

degrading [dɪˈgreɪdɪŋ] *adj* degradante.

degree [dɪˈgriː] *n (unit of measurement)* grau *m*; *(qualification)* ~ licenciatura *f*; **a ~ of difficulty** uma certa dificuldade; **to have a ~ in sthg** ter uma licenciatura em algo.

dehydrated [ˌdiːhaɪˈdreɪtɪd] *adj* desidratado(-da).

de-ice [ˌdiːˈaɪs] *vt* descongelar.

de-icer [ˌdiːˈaɪsər] *n* produto *m* descongelante.

deity [ˈdiːɪtɪ] *n* divindade *f*.

dejected [dɪˈdʒektɪd] *adj* abatido (-da).

delay [dɪˈleɪ] *n* atraso *m* ♦ *vt* atrasar ♦ *vi* atrasar-se; **without ~** sem demora.

delayed [dɪˈleɪd] *adj (train, flight)* atrasado(-da).

delegate [*n* ˈdelɪgət, *vb* ˈdelɪgeɪt] *n*

delegado *m* (-da *f*) ♦ *vt (person)* delegar.

delete [dɪˈliːt] *vt* suprimir.

deli [ˈdelɪ] *abbr (inf)* = **delicatessen**.

deliberate [dɪˈlɪbərət] *adj (intentional)* deliberado(-da).

deliberately [dɪˈlɪbərətlɪ] *adv (intentionally)* deliberadamente.

delicacy [ˈdelɪkəsɪ] *n (food)* iguaria *f*.

delicate [ˈdelɪkət] *adj* delicado(-da); *(object, china)* frágil; *(taste, smell)* suave.

delicatessen [ˌdelɪkəˈtesn] *n* = charcutaria *f*.

delicious [dɪˈlɪʃəs] *adj* delicioso(-osa).

delight [dɪˈlaɪt] *n (feeling)* prazer *m* ♦ *vt* encantar; **to take (a) ~ in doing sthg** ter prazer em fazer algo.

delighted [dɪˈlaɪtɪd] *adj* encantado (-da).

delightful [dɪˈlaɪtfʊl] *adj* encantador(-ra).

delirious [dɪˈlɪrɪəs] *adj* delirante.

deliver [dɪˈlɪvər] *vt (goods)* entregar; *(letters, newspaper)* distribuir; *(lecture)* dar; *(baby)* fazer o parto de; *(speech)* fazer.

delivery [dɪˈlɪvərɪ] *n (of goods)* entrega *f*; *(of letters)* distribuição *f*; *(birth)* parto *m*.

delude [dɪˈluːd] *vt* enganar.

delusion [dɪˈluːʒn] *n* ilusão *f*.

de luxe [dəˈlʌks] *adj* de luxo.

delve [delv] *vi*: **to ~ into** OR **inside sthg** *(bag, cupboard)* procurar dentro de algo.

demand [dɪˈmɑːnd] *n* exigência *f*; *(claim)* reivindicação *f*; *(COMM)* procura *f* ♦ *vt* exigir; **I ~ to speak to the manager** quero falar com o gerente; **in ~** solicitado.

demanding [dɪˈmɑːndɪŋ] *adj* exigente.

demeanor [dɪˈmiːnər] *(Am)* = **demeanour**.

demeanour [dɪˈmiːnər] *n (Brit) (fml)* comportamento *m*.

demerara sugar [ˌdeməˈreərə-] *n* açúcar *m* mascavo.

demist [ˌdiːˈmɪst] *vt (Brit)* desembaciar.

demister [ˌdiːˈmɪstər] *n (Brit)* desembaciador *m*.

demo [ˈdeməʊ] *(pl -s) abbr (inf)* = **demonstration**.

democracy [dɪˈmɒkrəsɪ] *n* democracia *f*.

Democrat [ˈdeməkræt] *n (Am)* democrata *mf*.

democratic [dema'krætɪk] *adj* democrático(-ca).

demolish [dɪ'mɒlɪʃ] *vt* *(building)* demolir.

demonstrate ['demənstreɪt] *vt* *(prove)* demonstrar; *(machine, appliance)* mostrar como funciona ♦ *vi* manifestar-se.

demonstration [demən'streɪʃn] *n* *(protest)* passeata *f (Br)*, manifestação *f; (of machine, emotions)* demonstração *f*.

demonstrator ['demənstreɪtəʳ] *n* *(protester)* manifestante *mf; (of machine, product)* demonstrador *m* (-ra *f*).

demoralized [dɪ'mɒrəlaɪzd] *adj* desmoralizado(-da).

den [den] *n* toca *f*.

denial [dɪ'naɪəl] *n* desmentido *m*.

denim ['denɪm] *n* brim *m (Br)*, ganga *f (Port)*.

❏ **denims** *npl* jeans *m inv (Br)*, calças *fpl* de ganga *(Port)*.

denim jacket *n* casaco *m* jeans.

Denmark ['denmɑːk] *n* Dinamarca *f*.

denounce [dɪ'naʊns] *vt* denunciar.

dense [dens] *adj* denso(-sa).

density ['densətɪ] *n* densidade *f*.

dent [dent] *n* mossa *f*, amolgadura *f*.

dental ['dentl] *adj* dentário.

dental floss [-flɒs] *n* fio *m* dental.

dental surgeon *n* cirurgião-dentista *mf*.

dental surgery *n* *(place)* clínica *f* dentária.

dentist ['dentɪst] *n* dentista *mf*; **to go to the ~'s** ir ao dentista.

dentures ['dentʃəz] *npl* dentadura *f* postiça.

deny [dɪ'naɪ] *vt* negar.

deodorant [diː'əʊdərənt] *n* deodorante *m (Br)*, desodorizante *m (Port)*.

depart [dɪ'pɑːt] *vi* partir.

department [dɪ'pɑːtmənt] *n* departamento *m; (of government)* = ministério *m; (of shop)* seção *f*.

department store *n* loja *f* de departamentos *(Br)*, grande-armazém *m (Port)*.

departure [dɪ'pɑːtʃəʳ] *n* partida *f*; **"~s"** *(at airport)* "partidas".

departure lounge *n* sala *f* de embarque.

depend [dɪ'pend] *vi*: **it ~s** depende.

❏ **depend on** *vt fus* *(be decided by)* depender de; *(rely on)* confiar em; **~ing**

on dependendo de.

dependable [dɪ'pendəbl] *adj* de confiança, fiável.

dependent [dɪ'pendənt] *adj* *(addicted)* dependente; **~ on** dependente de.

deplorable [dɪ'plɔːrəbl] *adj* deplorável.

deploy [dɪ'plɔɪ] *vt* mobilizar.

deport [dɪ'pɔːt] *vt* deportar.

deposit [dɪ'pɒzɪt] *n* depósito *m; (part-payment)* entrada *f* ♦ *vt* *(put down)* colocar; *(money in bank)* depositar.

deposit account *n* *(Brit)* conta *f* a prazo.

depot ['diːpəʊ] *n* *(Am: for buses, trains)* terminal *m*.

depress [dɪ'pres] *vt* *(person)* deprimir.

depressed [dɪ'prest] *adj* deprimido(-da).

depressing [dɪ'presɪŋ] *adj* deprimente.

depression [dɪ'preʃn] *n* depressão *f*.

deprivation [deprɪ'veɪʃn] *n* privação *f*.

deprive [dɪ'praɪv] *vt*: **to ~ sb of sthg** privar alguém de algo.

depth [depθ] *n* profundidade *f*; **to be out of one's ~** *(when swimming)* não ter pé; *(fig: unable to cope)* não estar à altura; **~ of field** *(in photography)* profundidade de campo; **in ~** a fundo.

deputy ['depjʊtɪ] *adj* adjunto(-ta).

derail [dɪ'reɪl] *vt* *(train)* fazer descarrilhar.

derailleur [dɪ'reɪljəʳ] *n* cremalheira *f*.

derailment [dɪ'reɪlmənt] *n* descarrilhamento *m*.

derby [*Brit* 'dɑːbɪ, *Am* 'dɜːbɪ] *n* *(sports event)* competição *f* (local); *(Am: hat)* chapéu *m* de coco.

derelict ['derəlɪkt] *adj* abandonado(-da).

deride [dɪ'raɪd] *vt* ridicularizar.

derisory [də'raɪzərɪ] *adj* *(amount, fine)* irrisório(-ria); *(laughter, smile)* sardônico(-ca).

derivative [dɪ'rɪvətɪv] *n* derivado *m*.

derogatory [dɪ'rɒgətrɪ] *adj* depreciativo(-va).

derv [dɜːv] *n* *(Brit)* gasóleo *m*.

descend [dɪ'send] *vt & vi* descer.

descendant [dɪ'sendənt] *n* descendente *mf*.

descent [dɪ'sent] *n* descida *f*.

describe [dɪ'skraɪb] *vt* descrever.

description [dɪˈskrɪpʃn] *n* descrição *f*.

desert [*n* ˈdezət, *vb* dɪˈzɜːt] *n* deserto *m* ♦ *vt* abandonar.

deserted [dɪˈzɜːtɪd] *adj* deserto(-ta).

deserter [dɪˈzɜːtər] *n* desertor *m* (-ra *f*).

desert island [ˈdezət-] *n* ilha *f* deserta.

deserve [dɪˈzɜːv] *vt* merecer.

deserving [dɪˈzɜːvɪŋ] *adj* merecedor(-ra).

design [dɪˈzaɪn] *n* desenho *m*; (*art*) design *m* ♦ *vt* desenhar; **to be ~ed for** ser concebido para.

designate [ˈdezɪgneɪt] *vt* (*appoint*) designar.

designer [dɪˈzaɪnər] *n* (*of clothes, sunglasses*) estilista *mf*; (*of product*) designer *mf* ♦ *adj* (*clothes, sunglasses*) de marca.

desirable [dɪˈzaɪərəbl] *adj* desejável.

desire [dɪˈzaɪər] *n* desejo *m* ♦ *vt* desejar; **it leaves a lot to be ~d** deixa muito a desejar.

desk [desk] *n* (*in home, office*) secretária *f*; (*in school*) carteira *f*; (*at airport, station*) balcão *m*; (*at hotel*) recepção *f*.

desktop publishing [ˈdesktɒp-] *n* desktop *m* publishing, editoração *f* eletrônica (*Br*), edição *f* assistida por computador (*Port*).

desolate [ˈdesələt] *adj* (*place*) solitário(-ria), desértico(-ca); (*person*) desolado(-da).

despair [dɪˈspeər] *n* desespero *m*.

despatch [dɪˈspætʃ] = dispatch.

desperate [ˈdespərət] *adj* desesperado(-da); **to be ~ for sthg** precisar de algo desesperadamente.

desperately [ˈdespərətlɪ] *adv* (*want, need, love*) desesperadamente; (*ill*) gravemente; (*poor, unhappy, shy*) muito, terrivelmente.

desperation [ˌdespəˈreɪʃn] *n* desespero *m*; **in ~** desesperado.

despicable [dɪˈspɪkəbl] *adj* desprezível.

despise [dɪˈspaɪz] *vt* desprezar.

despite [dɪˈspaɪt] *prep* apesar de.

dessert [dɪˈzɜːt] *n* sobremesa *f*.

dessertspoon [dɪˈzɜːtspuːn] *n* (*spoon*) colher *f* de sobremesa; (*spoonful*) = colher *f* de sopa.

destination [ˌdestɪˈneɪʃn] *n* destino *m*.

destined [ˈdestɪnd] *adj*: **to be ~ for sthg/to do sthg** (*intended*) estar destinado(-da) a algo/a fazer algo; **~ for** (*place*) com destino a.

destiny [ˈdestɪnɪ] *n* destino *m*.

destitute [ˈdestɪtjuːt] *adj* indigente.

destroy [dɪˈstrɔɪ] *vt* destruir.

destruction [dɪˈstrʌkʃn] *n* destruição *f*.

detach [dɪˈtætʃ] *vt* separar.

detached house [dɪˈtætʃt-] *n* casa *f* (isolada) (*Br*), vivenda *f* (*Port*).

detail [ˈdiːteɪl] *n* pormenor *m*, detalhe *m*; **in ~** em pormenor.
⊃ **details** *npl* (*facts*) informações *fpl*.

detailed [ˈdiːteɪld] *adj* pormenorizado(-da), detalhado(-da).

detain [dɪˈteɪn] *vt* (*in hospital*) manter; (*delay, in custody*) deter, reter.

detect [dɪˈtekt] *vt* detectar.

detective [dɪˈtektɪv] *n* detetive *m*; **a ~ story** uma história policial.

detention [dɪˈtenʃn] *n* (*SCH*) castigo *que consiste em ficar na escola depois das aulas terem terminado.*

deter [dɪˈtɜːr] (*vt* dissuadir, desencorajar; **to ~ sb from doing sthg** dissuadir alguém de fazer algo.

detergent [dɪˈtɜːdʒənt] *n* detergente *m*.

deteriorate [dɪˈtɪərɪəreɪt] *vi* deteriorar.

determination [dɪˌtɜːmɪˈneɪʃn] *n* (*quality*) determinação *f*.

determine [dɪˈtɜːmɪn] *vt* determinar.

determined [dɪˈtɜːmɪnd] *adj* decidido(-da); **to be ~ to do sthg** estar decidido a fazer algo.

deterrent [dɪˈterənt] *n* meio *m* de dissuasão.

detest [dɪˈtest] *vt* detestar.

detonate [ˈdetəneɪt] *vt* fazer detonar ♦ *vi* detonar.

detour [ˈdiːtʊər] *n* desvio *m*.

detract [dɪˈtrækt] *vi*: **to ~ from** (*quality, enjoyment*) diminuir, minorar; (*achievement*) menosprezar.

detrain [diːˈtreɪn] *vi* (*fml*) desembarcar (de trem).

detrimental [ˌdetrɪˈmentl] *adj* prejudicial.

deuce [djuːs] *excl* (*in tennis*) quarenta igual!

devastate [ˈdevəsteɪt] *vt* arrasar.

devastating [ˈdevəsteɪtɪŋ] *adj* (*news, experience, storm*) devastador(-ra);

(remark, argument) arrasador(-ra); *(person, charm, beauty)* irresistível.

develop [dɪ'veləp] *vt (idea, company, land)* desenvolver; *(film)* revelar; *(machine, method)* elaborar; *(illness, habit)* contrair; *(interest)* revelar ◆ *vi (evolve)* desenvolver-se.

developing country [dɪ'veləpɪŋ-] *n* país *m* em vias de desenvolvimento.

development [dɪ'veləpmənt] *n* desenvolvimento *m*; **a housing ~** um conjunto habitacional *(Br)*, uma urbanização *(Port)*.

deviate ['di:vɪeɪt] *vi:* **to ~ from sthg** afastar-se de algo.

device [dɪ'vaɪs] *n* aparelho *m*, dispositivo *m*.

devil ['devl] *n* diabo *m*; **what the ~ ...?** *(inf)* que diabo ...?

devious ['di:vjəs] *adj (person, means)* desonesto(-ta).

devise [dɪ'vaɪz] *vt* conceber.

devolution [ˌdi:və'lu:ʃn] *n (POL)* descentralização *f.*

devote [dɪ'vəʊt] *vt:* **to ~ sthg to sthg** consagrar OR dedicar algo a algo.

devoted [dɪ'vəʊtɪd] *adj* dedicado(-da).

devotion [dɪ'vəʊʃn] *n* devoção *f.*

devour [dɪ'vaʊəʳ] *vt* devorar.

devout [dɪ'vaʊt] *adj* devoto(-ta).

dew [dju:] *n* orvalho *m.*

diabetes [ˌdaɪə'bi:ti:z] *n* diabetes *m.*

diabetic [ˌdaɪə'betɪk] *adj (person)* diabético(-ca); *(chocolate)* para diabéticos ◆ *n* diabético *m* (-ca *f*).

diagnosis [ˌdaɪəg'nəʊsɪs] *(pl* -oses [-əʊsi:z]) *n* diagnóstico *m.*

diagonal [daɪ'ægənl] *adj* diagonal.

diagram ['daɪəgræm] *n* diagrama *m.*

dial ['daɪəl] *n (of clock, radio)* mostrador *m; (of telephone)* disco *m* ◆ *vt* discar *(Br)*, marcar *(Port).*

dialect ['daɪəlekt] *n* dialeto *m.*

dialling code ['daɪəlɪŋ-] *n (Brit)* código *m* de discagem *(Br)*, indicativo *m (Port).*

dialling tone ['daɪəlɪŋ-] *n (Brit)* sinal *m* de discar *(Br)*, sinal de linha *(Port).*

dialog ['daɪəlɒg] *(Am)* = **dialogue.**

dialogue ['daɪəlɒg] *n (Brit)* diálogo *m.*

dial tone *(Am)* = **dialling tone.**

diameter [daɪ'æmɪtəʳ] *n* diâmetro *m.*

diamond ['daɪəmənd] *n (gem)* diamante *m.*

❏ **diamonds** *npl (in cards)* ouros *mpl.*

diaper ['daɪpəʳ] *n (Am)* fralda *f.*

diarrhoea [ˌdaɪə'rɪə] *n* diarréia *f.*

diary ['daɪərɪ] *n (for appointments)* agenda *f; (journal)* diário *m.*

dice [daɪs] *(pl inv)* *n* dado *m.*

diced [daɪst] *adj (food)* cortado(-da) em cubos.

dictate [dɪk'teɪt] *vt* ditar.

dictation [dɪk'teɪʃn] *n* ditado *m.*

dictator [dɪk'teɪtəʳ] *n* ditador *m* (-ra *f*).

dictatorship [dɪk'teɪtəʃɪp] *n* ditadura *f.*

dictionary ['dɪkʃənrɪ] *n* dicionário *m.*

did [dɪd] *pt* → **do.**

didn't ['dɪdnt] = **did not.**

die [daɪ] *(pt & pp* died, *cont* dying) *vi* morrer; **to be dying for sthg** *(inf)* estar doido por algo; **to be dying to do sthg** *(inf)* estar doido por fazer algo.

❏ **die away** *vi* desvanecer-se.

❏ **die out** *vi* desaparecer.

diesel ['di:zl] *n (fuel)* diesel *m (Br)*, gasóleo *m (Port); (car)* carro *m* diesel *(Br)*, carro *m* a gasóleo *(Port).*

diet ['daɪət] *n* dieta *f* ◆ *vi* fazer dieta ◆ *adj* de baixa caloria.

diet Coke® *n* Coca-Cola® *f* light.

differ ['dɪfəʳ] *vi (disagree)* discordar; **to ~ (from)** *(be dissimilar)* ser diferente (de).

difference ['dɪfrəns] *n* diferença *f*; **it makes no ~** é igual, não faz diferença; **a ~ of opinion** uma divergência.

different ['dɪfrənt] *adj* diferente; **to be ~ (from)** ser diferente (de).

differently ['dɪfrəntlɪ] *adv* de outra forma.

difficult ['dɪfɪkəlt] *adj* difícil.

difficulty ['dɪfɪkəltɪ] *n* dificuldade *f.*

dig [dɪg] *(pt & pp* dug) *vt & vi* cavar.

❏ **dig out** *vt sep (rescue)* salvar; *(find)* desenterrar.

❏ **dig up** *vt sep (from ground)* desenterrar.

digest [dɪ'dʒest] *vt* digerir.

digestion [dɪ'dʒestʃn] *n* digestão *f.*

digestive (biscuit) [dɪ'dʒestɪv-] *n (Brit)* biscoito *m* integral.

digit ['dɪdʒɪt] *n (figure)* dígito *m; (finger, toe)* dedo *m.*

digital ['dɪdʒɪtl] *adj* digital.

dignified ['dɪgnɪfaɪd] *adj* digno(-gna).

dignity ['dɪgnətɪ] *n* dignidade *f.*

digress [dar'gres] *vi* afastar-se do tema; **to ~ from sthg** afastar-se de algo.

digs [dɪgz] *npl* (*Brit: inf*) quarto *m* alugado.

dike [daɪk] *n* dique *m*.

dilapidated [dɪ'læpɪdeɪtɪd] *adj* degradado(-da).

dilemma [dɪ'lemə] *n* dilema *m*.

diligent ['dɪlɪdʒənt] *adj* diligente.

dill [dɪl] *n* endro *m*.

dilute [daɪ'luːt] *vt* diluir.

dim [dɪm] *adj* (*light*) fraco(-ca); (*room*) escuro(-ra); (*memory*) vago(-ga); (*inf: stupid*) burro(-a) ◆ *vt* (*light*) diminuir, baixar.

dime [daɪm] *n* (*Am*) *moeda de dez centavos.*

dimensions [dɪ'menʃnz] *npl* (*measurements*) dimensões *fpl*; (*extent*) dimensão *f*.

diminish [dɪ'mɪnɪʃ] *vt & vi* diminuir.

diminutive [dɪ'mɪnjutɪv] *adj* (*fml*) minúsculo(-la) ◆ *n* (*GRAMM*) diminutivo *m*.

dimple ['dɪmpl] *n* covinha *f* (*no rosto*).

din [dɪn] *n* barulho *m*.

dine [daɪn] *vi* jantar.

❏ **dine out** *vi* jantar fora.

diner ['daɪnər] *n* (*Am: restaurant*) *restaurante à beira da estrada que serve refeições a preços baixos*; (*person*) cliente *mf* (*em restaurante*).

dinghy ['dɪŋgɪ] *n* (*with sail*) barco *m* à vela; (*with oars*) barco a remos.

dingy ['dɪndʒɪ] *adj* miserável.

dining car ['daɪnɪŋ-] *n* vagão-restaurante *m* (*Br*), carruagem-restaurante *f* (*Port*).

dining hall ['daɪnɪŋ-] *n* refeitório *m*, cantina *f*.

dining room ['daɪnɪŋ-] *n* sala *f* de jantar.

dinner ['dɪnər] *n* (*at lunchtime*) almoço *m*; (*in evening*) jantar *m*; **to have ~** (*at lunchtime*) almoçar; (*in evening*) jantar.

dinner jacket *n* smoking *m*.

dinner party *n* jantar *m*.

dinner set *n* serviço *m* de jantar.

dinner suit *n* smoking *m*.

dinnertime ['dɪnətaɪm] *n* (*at lunchtime*) hora *f* do almoço; (*in evening*) hora do jantar.

dinosaur ['daɪnəsɔːr] *n* dinossauro *m*.

dip [dɪp] *n* (*in road, land*) depressão *f*; (*food*) molho *m* (*que se serve com legumes crus e salgadinhos*) ◆ *vt* (*into liquid*) mergulhar ◆ *vi* (*road, land*) descer; **to have a ~** (*swim*) dar um mergulho; **to ~ one's headlights** (*Brit*) desligar os faróis, baixar as luzes.

diploma [dɪ'pləumə] *n* diploma *m*.

diplomat ['dɪpləmæt] *n* diplomata *mf*.

diplomatic [,dɪplə'mætɪk] *adj* diplomático(-ca).

dipstick ['dɪpstɪk] *n* vareta *f* (*para medir o óleo do carro*).

direct [dɪ'rekt] *adj* direto(-ta) ◆ *adv* diretamente ◆ *vt* dirigir; (*film, TV programme*) realizar; (*play*) encenar; **can you ~ me to the railway station?** podia me mostrar o caminho para a estação?

direct current *n* corrente *f* contínua.

direction [dɪ'rekʃn] *n* (*of movement*) direção *f*.

❏ **directions** *npl* (*instructions*) instruções *fpl*; **to ask for ~s** pedir indicações.

directly [dɪ'rektlɪ] *adv* (*exactly*) exatamente; (*soon*) diretamente.

director [dɪ'rektər] *n* diretor *m* (-ra *f*); (*of film, TV programme*) realizador *m* (-ra *f*); (*of play*) encenador *m* (-ra *f*).

directory [dɪ'rektərɪ] *n* lista *f* telefônica.

directory enquiries *n* (*Brit*) informações *fpl*.

dirt [dɜːt] *n* sujeira *f*; (*earth*) terra *f*.

dirty [dɜːtɪ] *adj* sujo(-ja); (*joke*) porco (porca).

disability [,dɪsə'bɪlətɪ] *n* deficiência *f*.

disabled [dɪs'eɪbld] *adj* deficiente ◆ *npl*: **the ~** os deficientes; **"~ toilet"** "banheiro para deficientes".

disadvantage [,dɪsəd'vɑːntɪdʒ] *n* desvantagem *f*, inconveniente *m*.

disagree [,dɪsə'griː] *vi* (*people*) não estar de acordo; **to ~ with sb (about)** não concordar com alguém (sobre); **those mussels ~d with me** os mexilhões me fizeram mal.

disagreeable [,dɪsə'griːəbl] *adj* desagradável.

disagreement [,dɪsə'griːmənt] *n* (*argument*) discussão *f*; (*dissimilarity*) diferença *f*.

disallow [,dɪsə'lau] *vt* (*appeal, claim*) rejeitar; (*goal*) anular.

disappear [,dɪsə'pɪər] *vi* desaparecer.

disappearance [,dɪsə'pɪərəns] *n*

desaparecimento *m*.
disappoint [ˌdɪsəˈpɔɪnt] *vt* desiludir.
disappointed [ˌdɪsəˈpɔɪntɪd] *adj* desiludido(-da).
disappointing [ˌdɪsəˈpɔɪntɪŋ] *adj* decepcionante.
disappointment [ˌdɪsəˈpɔɪntmənt] *n* decepção *f*, desapontamento *m*.
disapproval [ˌdɪsəˈpruːvl] *n* desaprovação *f*.
disapprove [ˌdɪsəˈpruːv] *vi*: **to ~ of** não aprovar.
disarmament [dɪsˈɑːməmənt] *n* desarmamento *m*.
disarray [ˌdɪsəˈreɪ] *n*: **in ~** *(clothes, room)* em desordem; *(government, party)* em polvorosa.
disaster [dɪˈzɑːstəʳ] *n* desastre *m*.
disastrous [dɪˈzɑːstrəs] *adj* desastroso(-osa).
disbelief [ˌdɪsbɪˈliːf] *n*: **in** OR **with ~** com incredulidade.
disc [dɪsk] *n (Brit)* disco *m*; *(CD)* CD *m*; **to slip a ~** deslocar uma vértebra.
discard [dɪsˈkɑːd] *vt* desfazer-se de.
discern [dɪˈsɜːn] *vt* discernir, distinguir.
discerning [dɪˈsɜːnɪŋ] *adj (person, taste)* exigente; *(eye)* perspicaz.
discharge [dɪsˈtʃɑːdʒ] *vt (prisoner)* libertar; *(patient)* dar alta a; *(soldier)* dispensar; *(liquid)* despejar; *(smoke, gas)* emitir.
disciple [dɪˈsaɪpl] *n* discíplo *m*.
discipline [ˈdɪsɪplɪn] *n* disciplina *f*.
disc jockey *n* discotecário *m* (-ria *f*) *(Br)*, disc-jóquei *mf*.
disclose [dɪsˈkləʊz] *vt* revelar, divulgar.
disco [ˈdɪskəʊ] *(pl -s)* *n (place)* discoteca *f*; *(event)* baile *m*.
discoloured [dɪsˈkʌləd] *adj* descolorado(-da).
discomfort [dɪsˈkʌmfət] *n* desconforto *m*.
disconcert [ˌdɪskənˈsɜːt] *vt* desconcertar.
disconnect [ˌdɪskəˈnekt] *vt* desligar; *(telephone, gas supply)* cortar.
discontinued [ˌdɪskənˈtɪnjuːd] *adj (product)* que já não se fabrica.
discotheque [ˈdɪskəʊtek] *n (place)* discoteca *f*.
discount [ˈdɪskaʊnt] *n* desconto *m*.
discourage [dɪsˈkʌrɪdʒ] *vt* desencorajar; **to ~ sb from doing sthg**

desencorajar alguém de fazer algo.
discover [dɪsˈkʌvəʳ] *vt* descobrir.
discovery [dɪsˈkʌvərɪ] *n* descoberta *f*.
discreet [dɪsˈkriːt] *adj* discreto(-ta).
discrepancy [dɪsˈkrepənsɪ] *n* discrepância *f*.
discretion [dɪsˈkreʃn] *n (tact)* discrição *f*; *(judgment)* discernimento *m*; **at the ~ of** ao critério de.
discriminate [dɪsˈkrɪmɪneɪt] *vi*: **to ~ against sb** discriminar contra alguém.
discriminating [dɪsˈkrɪmɪneɪtɪŋ] *adj (person, audience)* entendido(-da); *(taste)* refinado(-da).
discrimination [dɪˌskrɪmɪˈneɪʃn] *n* discriminação *f*.
discus [ˈdɪskəs] *(pl -es)* *n* disco *m*.
discuss [dɪsˈkʌs] *vt* discutir.
discussion [dɪsˈkʌʃn] *n* discussão *f*.
disdain [dɪsˈdeɪn] *n* desdém *m*; **~ for** desdém por.
disease [dɪˈziːz] *n* doença *f*.
disembark [ˌdɪsɪmˈbɑːk] *vi* desembarcar.
disgrace [dɪsˈgreɪs] *n* vergonha *f*; **it's a ~!** é uma vergonha!
disgraceful [dɪsˈgreɪsfʊl] *adj* vergonhoso(-osa).
disguise [dɪsˈgaɪz] *n* disfarce *m* ♦ *vt* disfarçar; **in ~** disfarçado.
disgust [dɪsˈgʌst] *n* repugnância *f*, nojo *m* ♦ *vt* enojar, repugnar.
disgusting [dɪsˈgʌstɪŋ] *adj* nojento(-ta).
dish [dɪʃ] *n* prato *m*; **to do the ~es** lavar a louça; **"~ of the day"** "prato do dia".
⊔ **dish up** *vt sep* servir.
dishcloth [ˈdɪʃklɒθ] *n* pano *m* de prato.
disheveled [dɪˈʃevəld] *(Am)* = **dishevelled**.
dishevelled [dɪˈʃevəld] *adj (Brit) (hair)* despenteado(-da); *(person)* desarrumado(-da).
dishonest [dɪsˈɒnɪst] *adj* desonesto(-ta).
dish towel *n (Am)* pano *m* de prato.
dishwasher [ˈdɪʃˌwɒʃəʳ] *n (machine)* máquina *f* de lavar a louça.
disillusioned [ˌdɪsɪˈluːʒnd] *adj* desiludido(-da); **~ with** desiludido com.
disinclined [ˌdɪsɪnˈklaɪnd] *adj*: **to be ~ to do sthg** estar pouco disposto(-osta) a fazer algo.
disinfect [ˌdɪsɪnˈfekt] *vt* desinfectar.

disinfectant [ˌdɪsɪnˈfektənt] n desinfectante m.

disintegrate [dɪsˈɪntɪgreɪt] vi desintegrar-se.

disinterested [ˌdɪsˈɪntrəstɪd] adj (impartial) desinteressado(-da); **to be ~ in** (inf: uninterested) mostrar-se desinteressado por.

disk [dɪsk] n (Am) = **disc**; (COMPUT) disco m; (floppy) disquete f.

disk drive n leitor m de disquetes.

diskette [dɪsˈket] n disquete f.

dislike [dɪsˈlaɪk] n aversão f ◆ vt não gostar de; **to take a ~ to** não simpatizar com.

dislocate [ˈdɪsləkeɪt] vt deslocar.

dismal [ˈdɪzml] adj (weather, place) deprimente; (terrible) péssimo(-ma).

dismantle [dɪsˈmæntl] vt desmontar.

dismay [dɪsˈmeɪ] n consternação f.

dismiss [dɪsˈmɪs] vt (not consider) rejeitar; (from job) despedir; (from classroom) dispensar.

dismissal [dɪsˈmɪsl] n (from job) demissão f, despedida f (Br), despedimento m (Port).

disobedience [ˌdɪsəˈbiːdjəns] n desobediência f.

disobedient [ˌdɪsəˈbiːdjənt] adj desobediente.

disobey [ˌdɪsəˈbeɪ] vt desobedecer.

disorder [dɪsˈɔːdəʳ] n (confusion) desordem f; (violence) distúrbios mpl; (illness) problema m; (mental illness) distúrbio m.

disorderly [dɪsˈɔːdəlɪ] adj (untidy) desordenado(-da); (unruly) turbulento (-ta).

disorganized [dɪsˈɔːɡənaɪzd] adj desorganizado(-da).

disorientated adj (Brit) desorientado(-da).

disoriented (Am) = **disorientated**.

disown [dɪsˈəʊn] vt repudiar.

disparaging [dɪsˈpærɪdʒɪŋ] adj depreciativo(-va).

dispatch [dɪsˈpætʃ] vt enviar.

dispense [dɪsˈpens] : **dispense with** vt fus prescindir de, passar sem.

dispenser [dɪsˈpensəʳ] n (device) máquina f distribuidora.

dispensing chemist [dɪsˈpensɪŋ-] n (Brit: shop) farmácia f.

disperse [dɪsˈpɜːs] vt dispersar ◆ vi dispersar-se.

display [dɪsˈpleɪ] n (of goods) expo-

sição f; (public event) espetáculo m; (readout) visualização f ◆ vt (goods) expor; (feeling, quality) demonstrar; (information) afixar; **on ~** exposto.

displeased [dɪsˈpliːzd] adj descontente.

disposable [dɪsˈpəʊzəbl] adj descartável.

disposal [dɪsˈpəʊzl] n (removal) remoção f; **at sb's ~** à disposição de alguém.

disposed [dɪsˈpəʊzd] adj: **to be ~ to do sthg** (willing) estar disposto(-osta) a fazer algo; **to be well ~ to sthg** (friendly) ser favorável a algo.

disprove [dɪsˈpruːv] (pp -d OR **disproven**) vt refutar.

dispute [dɪsˈpjuːt] n (argument) discussão f; (industrial) conflito m ◆ vt discutir.

disqualify [ˌdɪsˈkwɒlɪfaɪ] vt desqualificar; **to be disqualified from driving** (Brit) ter a carteira apreendida.

disregard [ˌdɪsrɪˈɡɑːd] vt ignorar.

disreputable [dɪsˈrepjʊtəbl] adj pouco respeitável.

disrupt [dɪsˈrʌpt] vt perturbar, transtornar.

disruption [dɪsˈrʌpʃn] n transtorno m.

dissatisfaction [ˈdɪsˌsætɪsˈfækʃn] n descontentamento m.

dissatisfied [ˌdɪsˈsætɪsfaɪd] adj insatisfeito(-ta).

dissect [dɪˈsekt] vt dissecar.

dissent [dɪˈsent] n (disagreement) discordância f ◆ vi: **to ~ from sthg** não concordar com algo.

dissimilar [dɪˈsɪmɪləʳ] adj diferente; **~ to** diferente de.

dissolve [dɪˈzɒlv] vt dissolver ◆ vi dissolver-se.

dissuade [dɪˈsweɪd] vt: **to ~ sb from doing sthg** dissuadir alguém de fazer algo.

distance [ˈdɪstəns] n distância f; **from a ~** de longe; **in the ~** ao longe.

distant [ˈdɪstənt] adj distante.

distil [dɪsˈtɪl] vt (Brit) (liquid) destilar; (fig: information) extrair.

distill [dɪsˈtɪl] (Am) = **distil**.

distilled water [dɪsˈtɪld-] n água f destilada.

distillery [dɪsˈtɪlərɪ] n destilaria f.

distinct [dɪsˈtɪŋkt] adj distinto(-ta).

distinction [dɪsˈtɪŋkʃn] n distinção f.

distinctive [dɪˈstɪŋktɪv] *adj* caracte-rístico(-ca).

distinguish [dɪˈstɪŋgwɪʃ] *vt* distin-guir; **to ~ sthg from sthg** distinguir algo de algo.

distinguished [dɪˈstɪŋgwɪʃt] *adj* dis-tinto(-ta).

distorted [dɪˈstɔːtɪd] *adj* distorcido (-da).

distract [dɪˈstrækt] *vt* distrair.

distraction [dɪˈstrækʃn] *n* distração *f*.

distraught [dɪˈstrɔːt] *adj* cons-ternado(-da).

distress [dɪˈstres] *n* (*pain*) sofrimento *m*, dor *f*; (*anxiety*) angústia *f*.

distressing [dɪˈstresɪŋ] *adj* angustian-te.

distribute [dɪˈstrɪbjuːt] *vt* distribuir.

distribution [ˌdɪstrɪˈbjuːʃn] *n* distri-buição *f*.

distributor [dɪˈstrɪbjʊtəʳ] *n* (*COMM*) distribuidor *m* (-ra *f*); (*AUT*) distribui-dor *m*.

district [ˈdɪstrɪkt] *n* (*region*) = distrito *m*; (*of town*) – bairro *m*, – freguesia *f* (*Port*).

district attorney *n* (*Am*) = Procurador *m* (-ra *f*) da República.

district council *n* (*Brit*) = junta *f* distrital (*Br*), junta *f* de freguesia (*Port*).

distrust [dɪsˈtrʌst] *n* desconfiança *f* ♦ *vt* desconfiar de, não confiar em.

disturb [dɪˈstɜːb] *vt* (*interrupt*) inco-modar; (*worry*) preocupar; (*move*) mexer em; **"do not ~"** "favor não incomodar".

disturbance [dɪˈstɜːbəns] *n* (*violence*) distúrbio *m*.

ditch [dɪtʃ] *n* fosso *m*.

dither [ˈdɪðəʳ] *vi* hesitar.

ditto [ˈdɪtəʊ] *adv* idem.

divan [dɪˈvæn] *n* divã *m*.

dive [daɪv] (*pt Am* **-d** OR **dove**, *pt Brit* **-d**) *n* (*of swimmer*) mergulho *m* ♦ *vi* mergulhar; (*bird, plane*) descer em vôo picado; (*rush*) lançar-se.

diver [ˈdaɪvəʳ] *n* mergulhador *m* (-ra *f*).

diverge [daɪˈvɜːdʒ] *vi* divergir; **to ~ from sthg** divergir de algo.

diversion [daɪˈvɜːʃn] *n* (*of traffic*) des-vio *m*; (*amusement*) diversão *f*.

diversity [daɪˈvɜːsətɪ] *n* diversidade *f*.

divert [daɪˈvɜːt] *vt* desviar.

divide [dɪˈvaɪd] *vt* dividir.

❏ **divide up** *vt sep* dividir.

dividend [ˈdɪvɪdend] *n* (*profit*) divi-dendo *m*.

divine [dɪˈvaɪn] *adj* divino(-na).

diving [ˈdaɪvɪŋ] *n* mergulho *m*; **to go ~** ir mergulhar.

divingboard [ˈdaɪvɪŋbɔːd] *n* trampo-lim *m*, prancha *f* de saltos (*Port*).

division [dɪˈvɪʒn] *n* divisão *f*; (*COMM*) departamento *m*.

divorce [dɪˈvɔːs] *n* divórcio *m* ♦ *vt* divorciar-se de.

divorced [dɪˈvɔːst] *adj* divorciado (-da).

divorcee [dɪvɔːˈsiː] *n* divorciado *m* (-da *f*).

DIY *abbr* = **do-it-yourself**.

dizzy [ˈdɪzɪ] *adj* tonto(-ta).

DJ *n* (*abbr of disc jockey*) DJ.

DNA *n* (*abbr of deoxyribonucleic acid*) ADN *m*.

do [duː] (*pt* **did**, *pp* **done**, *pl* **dos**) *aux vb* **1.** (*in negatives*): **don't ~ that!** não faça isso!; **she didn't see it** ela não o viu.

2. (*in questions*): **~ you like it?** gosta você?; **how ~ you do it?** como é que se faz?

3. (*referring to previous verb*): **~ you smoke? – yes, I ~/no, I don't** você fuma? – sim/não; **I eat more than you ~** eu como mais do que você; **no, I didn't!** não é verdade!; **so ~ I** eu tam-bém.

4. (*in question tags*): **so, you like Scotland, ~ you?** então você gosta da Escócia?; **the train leaves at five o'clock, doesn't it?** o trem sai às cinco, não é (verdade)?

5. (*for emphasis*): **I ~ like this bedroom** eu realmente gosto deste quarto; **~ come in!** faça o favor de entrar!

♦ *vt* **1.** (*perform*) fazer; **to ~ one's homework** fazer o dever de casa; **what is she doing?** o que é que ela está fazendo?; **what can I ~ for you?** em que posso ajudá-lo?

2. (*clean, brush etc*): **to ~ one's hair** pentear-se; **to ~ one's make-up** maquilhar-se; **to ~ one's teeth** esco-var os dentes.

3. (*cause*) fazer; **to ~ damage** fazer estragos; **to ~ sb good** fazer bem a alguém.

4. (*have as job*): **what do you ~?** o que você faz?

5. (*provide, offer*) fazer; **we ~ pizzas for**

under £4 vendemos pizzas por menos de 4 libras.
6. *(study)* estudar.
7. *(subj: vehicle)* ir a; **the car was ~ing 50 mph** o carro ia a 80 km/h.
8. *(inf: visit)* visitar; **we're doing Scotland next week** para a semana vamos visitar a Escócia.
♦ *vi* **1.** *(behave, act)* fazer; **~ as I say** faça como eu lhe digo.
2. *(progress, get on)*: **he did badly/well in his exam** ele foi mal/bem no exame; **how did you ~?** como é que foi?
3. *(be sufficient)* chegar; **will £5 ~?** 5 libras chega?
4. *(in phrases)*: **how do you ~?** *(greeting)* como vai?; **how are you ~ing?** como é que vão as coisas?; **what has that got to ~ with it?** o que é que isso tem a ver?
♦ *n (party)* festa *f*; **~s and don'ts** o que fazer e não fazer.
❏ **do out of** *vt sep (inf)*: **he did us out of £10** ele nos levou 10 libras a mais.
❏ **do up** *vt sep (coat, shirt)* abotoar; *(shoes, laces)* apertar, atar; *(zip)* fechar; *(decorate)* renovar; *(wrap up)* embrulhar.
❏ **do with** *vt fus (need)*: **I could ~ with a drink** eu bem que beberia alguma coisa.
❏ **do without** *vt fus* passar sem.
Doberman ['dəʊbəmən] *n (pl -s) n*: ~ **(pinscher)** doberman *m*.
docile [*Brit* 'dəʊsaɪl, *Am* 'dɒsəl] *adj* dócil.
dock [dɒk] *n (for ships)* doca *f*; *(JUR)* banco *m* dos réus ♦ *vi* atracar.
docker ['dɒkə*r*] *n* estivador *m* (-ra *f*).
docklands ['dɒkləndz] *npl (Brit)* docas *fpl*.
dockyard ['dɒkjɑːd] *n* estaleiro *m*.
doctor ['dɒktə*r*] *n (of medicine)* médico *m* (-ca *f*), doutor *m* (-ra *f*), *(academic)* doutor *m* (-ra *f*); **to go to the ~'s** ir ao médico.
doctrine ['dɒktrɪn] *n* doutrina *f*.
document ['dɒkjʊmənt] *n* documento *m*.
documentary [dɒkjʊ'mentərɪ] *n* documentário *m*.
dodge [dɒdʒ] *vt (question, responsibility, issue)* fugir a, esquivar-se a; *(missile, car)* evitar ♦ *vi* desviar-se.
Dodgems® ['dɒdʒəmz] *npl (Brit)* carrinhos *mpl* de choque.

dodgy ['dɒdʒɪ] *adj (Brit) (inf) (plan, car)* pouco confiável; *(health)* instável.
doe [dəʊ] *n (female deer)* corça *f*; *(female rabbit)* coelha *f*.
does [*weak form* dəz, *strong form* dʌz] → **do.**
doesn't ['dʌznt] = **does not.**
dog [dɒg] *n* cachorro *m (Br)*, cão *m (Port)*.
dog food *n* comida *f* para cachorros.
doggy bag ['dɒgɪ-] *n* saco que em alguns restaurantes é fornecido aos clientes para levarem o que sobrou da refeição.
do-it-yourself *n* sistema *m* faça-você-mesmo *(Br)*, bricolage *f (Port)*.
dole [dəʊl] *n (inf)*: **to be on the ~** *(Brit)* estar desempregado.
doll [dɒl] *n* boneca *f*.
dollar ['dɒlə*r*] *n* dólar *m*.
dolphin ['dɒlfɪn] *n* golfinho *m*.
dome [dəʊm] *n* abóbada *f*.
domestic [də'mestɪk] *adj* doméstico(-ca); *(of country)* nacional.
domestic appliance *n* eletrodoméstico *m*.
domestic flight *n* vôo *m* doméstico.
domestic science *n* economia *f* doméstica, *disciplina opcional na escola*.
dominant ['dɒmɪnənt] *adj* dominante.
dominate ['dɒmɪneɪt] *vt* dominar.
domineering [dɒmɪ'nɪərɪŋ] *adj* autoritário(-ria), dominador(-ra).
dominoes ['dɒmɪnəʊz] *n* dominó *m*.
donate [də'neɪt] *vt* doar.
donation [də'neɪʃn] *n* doação *f*.
done [dʌn] *pp* → **do** ♦ *adj* pronto(-ta).
donkey ['dɒŋkɪ] *n* burro *m*.
donor ['dəʊnə*r*] *n* doador *m* (-ra *f*).
don't [dəʊnt] = **do not.**
doomed [duːmd] *adj* condenado (da), **to be ~ to** estar condenado a.
door [dɔː*r*] *n* porta *f*.
doorbell ['dɔːbel] *n* campainha *f*.
doorknob ['dɔːnɒb] *n* maçaneta *f*.
doorman ['dɔːmən] *(pl -men)* *n* porteiro *m*.
doormat ['dɔːmæt] *n* tapete *m*, capacho *m*.
doormen ['dɔːmən] *pl* → **doorman.**
doorstep ['dɔːstep] *n* degrau *m*; *(Brit: piece of bread)* fatia de pão bem grossa.
doorway ['dɔːweɪ] *n* entrada *f*.

dope [dəʊp] n (inf) (any illegal drug) droga f; (marijuana) erva f, maconha f.

dormitory ['dɔːmətrɪ] n dormitório m.

Dormobile® ['dɔːməbiːl] n trailer m motorizado (Br), caravana f OR roulote f (motorizada) (Port).

dosage ['dəʊsɪdʒ] n dose f.

dose [dəʊs] n (amount) dose f; (of illness) camada f.

dot [dɒt] n ponto m; **on the ~** (fig) em ponto.

dotted line ['dɒtɪd-] n pontilhado m.

double ['dʌbl] adj duplo(-pla) ◆ n (twice the amount) o dobro; (alcohol) dose f dupla ◆ vt & vi duplicar ◆ adv: it's ~ the size tem o dobro do tamanho; to bend sthg ~ dobrar algo ao meio; a ~ whisky um whisky duplo; ~ three, four, two três, três, quatro, dois; ~"r" dois erres.
❑ **doubles** n (in tennis) dupla f (Br), pares mpl (Port).

double bass [-beɪs] n contrabaixo m.

double bed n cama f de casal.

double-breasted [-'brestɪd] adj trespassado(-da).

double-check vt & vi verificar duas vezes.

double chin n papada f.

double cream n (Brit) creme m de leite (Br), natas fpl espessas (Port).

double-cross vt trair.

double-decker (bus) [-'dekə-] n ônibus m de dois andares.

double doors npl porta f dupla.

double-dutch n (Brit): that's ~ to me isso para mim é chinês.

double-glazing [-'gleɪzɪŋ] n vidros mpl duplos.

double room n quarto m de casal.

doubt [daʊt] n dúvida f ◆ vt duvidar de; **I ~ it** duvido; **I ~ she'll be there** duvido que ela esteja lá; **in ~** (person) em dúvida; (outcome) incerto; **no ~** sem dúvida.

doubtful ['daʊtfʊl] adj (uncertain) improvável; **it's ~ that ...** (unlikely) é pouco provável que ....

doubtless ['daʊtlɪs] adv sem dúvida.

dough [dəʊ] n massa f.

doughnut ['dəʊnʌt] n (without hole) = bola f de Berlim; (with hole) Donut® m.

dove¹ [dʌv] n (bird) pomba f.

dove² [dəʊv] pt (Am) → dive.

Dover ['dəʊvə-] n Dover.

Dover sole n linguado de ótima qualidade proveniente do Canal da Mancha.

down [daʊn] adv 1. (towards the bottom) para baixo; **~ here/there** aqui/ali em baixo; **to fall ~** cair; **to go ~** descer.
2. (along): **I'm going ~ to the shops** vou até a loja.
3. (downstairs): **I'll come ~ later** vou descer mais tarde.
4. (southwards) para baixo; **we're going ~ to London** vamos até Londres.
5. (in writing): **to write sthg ~** anotar algo.
6. (in phrases): **to go ~ with** (illness) adoecer com.
◆ prep 1. (towards the bottom of): **they ran ~ the hill** eles correram pelo monte abaixo.
2. (along): **I was walking ~ the street** ia andando pela rua.
◆ adj (inf: depressed) deprimido(-da).
◆ n (feathers) penugem f.
❑ **downs** npl (Brit) colinas fpl.

down-and-out n mendigo m (-ga f).

downfall ['daʊnfɔːl] n queda f, ruína f.

downhearted [daʊn'hɑːtɪd] adj desanimado(-da).

downhill [daʊn'hɪl] adv: **to go ~** (walk, run, ski) descer.

Downing Street ['daʊnɪŋ-] n Downing Street.

down payment n entrada f, sinal m.

downpour ['daʊnpɔː-] n aguaceiro m.

downright ['daʊnraɪt] adj (lie) puro(-ra); (fool) completo(-ta) ◆ adv extremamente.

downstairs [daʊn'steəz] adj do andar de baixo ◆ adv no andar de baixo; **to come** OR **go ~** descer.

downstream [daʊn'striːm] adv rio abaixo.

down-to-earth adj prático(-ca).

downtown [daʊn'taʊn] adj (hotel) central; (train, bus) do centro ◆ adv (live) no centro; (go) ao centro; **~ New York** o centro de Nova Iorque.

down under adv (Brit: inf: to or in Australia) para a/na Austrália.

downward ['daʊnwəd] adj descendente.

downwards ['daʊnwədz] adv para baixo.

dowry ['daʊərɪ] n dote m.

doz. *abbr* = **dozen**.

doze [dəʊz] *vi* dormitar, cochilar.

dozen ['dʌzn] *n* dúzia *f*; **a ~ eggs** uma dúzia de ovos.

Dr *(abbr of Doctor)* Dr. *m* (Dra. *f*).

drab [dræb] *adj* sem graça.

draft [drɑːft] *n* *(early version)* rascunho *m*; *(money order)* ordem *f* de pagamento; *(Am)* = **draught**.

drag [dræg] *vt* *(pull along)* arrastar ♦ *vi* *(along ground)* arrastar-se; **what a ~!** *(inf)* que chatice!

⌐ **drag on** *vi* arrastar-se.

dragon ['drægən] *n* dragão *m*.

dragonfly ['drægnflaɪ] *n* libélula *f*.

drain [dreɪn] *n* *(pipe)* esgoto *m* ♦ *vt* *(tank, radiator)* esvaziar ♦ *vi* *(vegetables, washing-up)* escorrer.

draining board ['dreɪnɪŋ-] *n* escorredor *m* de louça.

drainpipe ['dreɪnpaɪp] *n* cano *m* de esgoto *(Br)*, caleira *f* *(Port)*.

dram [dræm] *n* *(of whisky)* trago *m*.

drama ['drɑːmə] *n* *(play)* peça *f* de teatro; *(art)* teatro *m*; *(excitement)* drama *m*.

dramatic [drə'mætɪk] *adj* dramático(-ca).

dramatist ['dræmətɪst] *n* dramaturgo *m* (-ga *f*).

drank [dræŋk] *pt* → **drink**.

drapes [dreɪps] *npl* *(Am)* cortinas *fpl*, reposteiros *mpl*.

drastic ['dræstɪk] *adj* drástico(-ca).

drastically ['dræstɪklɪ] *adv* drasticamente.

draught [drɑːft] *n* *(Brit)* *(of air)* corrente *f* de ar.

draught beer *n* chope *m* *(Br)*, imperial *f* *(Port)*, fino *m* *(Port)*.

draughtboard ['drɑːftbɔːd] *n* *(Brit)* tabuleiro *m* de (jogo de) damas.

draughts [drɑːfts] *n* *(Brit)* damas *fpl*.

draughty ['drɑːftɪ] *adj* cheio (cheia) de correntes de ar.

draw [drɔː] *(pt* **drew**, *pp* **drawn**) *vt* *(with pen, pencil)* desenhar; *(line)* traçar; *(pull)* puxar; *(attract)* atrair; *(comparison)* estabelecer; *(conclusion)* chegar a ♦ *vi* *(with pen, pencil)* desenhar; *(SPORT)* empatar ♦ *n* *(SPORT: result)* empate *m*; *(lottery)* sorteio *m*; **to ~ the curtains** *(open)* abrir as cortinas; *(close)* fechar as cortinas.

⌐ **draw out** *vt sep* *(money)* levantar.

⌐ **draw up** *vt sep* *(list, contract)* redigir;

(plan) elaborar ♦ *vi* *(car, bus)* parar.

drawback ['drɔːbæk] *n* inconveniente *m*.

drawbridge ['drɔːbrɪdʒ] *n* ponte *f* levadiça.

drawer [drɔːr] *n* gaveta *f*.

drawing ['drɔːɪŋ] *n* desenho *m*.

drawing board *n* prancheta *f* de desenho.

drawing pin *n* *(Brit)* percevejo *m* *(Br)*, pionés *m* *(Port)*.

drawing room *n* sala *f* de estar.

drawl [drɔːl] *n* forma lenta e pouco clara de falar, alongando as vogais.

drawn [drɔːn] *pp* → **draw**.

dread [dred] *n* pavor *m* ♦ *vt* *(exam)* temer; **to ~ doing sthg** temer fazer algo.

dreadful ['dredfʊl] *adj* terrível.

dreadfully ['dredfʊlɪ] *adv* *(badly)* extremamente mal; *(extremely)* extremamente.

dream [driːm] *n* sonho *m* ♦ *vt* sonhar ♦ *vi*: **to ~ (of)** sonhar (com); **a ~ house** uma casa de sonho.

dreary ['drɪərɪ] *adj* *(day, weather)* sombrio(-bria); *(job, work)* monótono(-na); *(person)* enfadonho(-nha).

dregs [dregz] *npl* *(of tea, coffee)* borra *f*.

drench [drentʃ] *vt* encharcar, ensopar; **to be ~ed in/with sthg** estar encharcado em algo.

dress [dres] *n* *(for woman, girl)* vestido *m*; *(clothes)* roupa *f*, fato *m* *(Port)* ♦ *vt* *(person, baby)* vestir; *(wound)* ligar; *(salad)* temperar ♦ *vi* vestir-se; **to be ~ed in** estar vestido de; **to get ~ed** vestir-se.

⌐ **dress up** *vi* *(in costume)* disfarçar-se; *(in best clothes)* vestir-se elegantemente.

dress circle *n* balcão *m* nobre *(Br)*, primeiro balcão *m* *(Port)*.

dresser ['dresər] *n* *(Brit: for crockery)* aparador *m*; *(Am: chest of drawers)* cômoda *f*.

dressing ['dresɪŋ] *n* *(for salad)* tempero *m*; *(for wound)* curativo *m* *(Br)*, penso *m* *(Port)*.

dressing gown *n* robe *m*, roupão *m*.

dressing room *n* camarim *m*.

dressing table *n* toucador *m*.

dressmaker ['dres,meɪkər] *n* costureiro *m* (-ra *f*).

dress rehearsal *n* ensaio *m* geral.

drew [druː] *pt* → **draw**.

dribble ['drɪbl] *vi* *(liquid)* pingar; *(baby)* babar-se.

dried [draɪd] *adj (herbs, fruit, flowers)* seco(-ca); *(milk, eggs)* em pó.

drier ['draɪəʳ] = **dryer**.

drift [drɪft] *n (of snow)* monte *m* ◆ *vi (in wind)* ser levado pelo vento; *(in water)* ser levado pela água, derivar.

drill [drɪl] *n (electric tool)* furadeira *f (Br)*, berbequim *m (Port)*; *(manual tool, of dentist)* broca *f* ◆ *vt (hole)* furar.

drink [drɪŋk] *(pt* **drank**, *pp* **drunk)** *n (of water, tea etc)* bebida *f*; *(alcoholic)* copo *m*, bebida ◆ *vt & vi* beber; **would you like a ~?** quer beber OR tomar algo?; **to have a ~** *(alcoholic)* beber OR tomar um copo.

drinkable ['drɪŋkəbl] *adj (safe to drink)* potável; *(wine)* razoável.

drink-driving *n (Brit)* ato de dirigir sob a influência de álcool.

drinking water ['drɪŋkɪŋ-] *n* água *f* potável.

drip [drɪp] *n (drop)* gota *f*; *(MED)* aparelho *m* de soro ◆ *vi* pingar.

drip-dry *adj* que não necessita ser passado a ferro.

dripping (wet) ['drɪpɪŋ-] *adj* encharcado(-da).

drive [draɪv] *(pt* **drove**, *pp* **driven)** *n (journey)* viagem *f*; *(in front of house)* acesso *m*, caminho *m* ◆ *vt (car, bus, train)* dirigir *(Br)*, conduzir *(Port)*; *(take in car)* levar (em carro) ◆ *vi (drive car)* dirigir *(Br)*, conduzir *(Port)*; *(travel in car)* ir de carro; **to go for a ~** ir dar um passeio de carro; **it's driven by electricity** funciona a electricidade; **to ~ sb to do sthg** levar alguém a fazer algo; **to ~ sb mad** deixar alguém louco.

drivel ['drɪvl] *n* disparates *mpl*.

driven ['drɪvn] *pp* → **drive**.

driver ['draɪvəʳ] *n (of car, taxi)* motorista *mf*; *(of bus)* condutor *m* (-ra *f*); *(of train)* maquinista *mf*.

driver's license *(Am)* = **driving licence**.

driveshaft ['draɪvʃɑːft] *n* eixo *m* motor, transmissão *f*.

driveway ['draɪvweɪ] *n* acesso *m*, caminho *m*.

driving ['draɪvɪŋ] *n* direção *f (Br)*, condução *f (Port)*.

driving instructor *n* instrutor *m* (-ra *f*) de auto-escola.

driving lesson *n* aula *f* de direção

(Br), aula *f* de condução *(Port)*.

driving licence *n (Brit)* carteira *f* de motorista *(Br)*, carta *f* de condução *(Port)*.

driving school *n* auto-escola *f (Br)*, escola *f* de condução *(Port)*.

driving test *n* exame *m* de direção *(Br)*, exame *m* de condução *(Port)*.

drizzle ['drɪzl] *n* chuvisco *m*.

drone [drəun] *n (sound of insect)* zumbido *m*; *(of plane, voices)* ruído *m*.

drop [drɒp] *n* gota *f*, pingo *m*; *(distance down)* descida *f*; *(decrease)* queda *f* ◆ *vt (let fall by accident)* deixar cair; *(let fall on purpose)* jogar; *(reduce)* baixar; *(from vehicle)* deixar; *(omit)* omitir ◆ *vi (fall)* cair; *(decrease)* baixar; **to ~ a hint that** dar a entender que; **to ~ sb a line** escrever uma palavrinha a alguém.
  ❏ **drop in** *vi (inf)*: **to ~ in on sb** passar por casa de alguém.
  ❏ **drop off** *vt sep (from vehicle)* deixar ◆ *vi (fall asleep)* adormecer; *(fall off)* cair.
  ❏ **drop out** *vi (of college)* abandonar os estudos; *(of race)* desistir.

dropout ['drɒpaut] *n (from society)* marginal *mf*; *(from university)* pessoa *f* que abandona os estudos.

droppings ['drɒpɪŋz] *npl* excrementos *mpl* (de animal).

drought [draut] *n* seca *f*.

drove [drəuv] *pt* → **drive**.

drown [draun] *vi* afogar-se.

drowsy ['drauzɪ] *adj* sonolento(-ta).

drug [drʌg] *n* droga *f* ◆ *vt* drogar.

drug abuse *n* consumo *m* de drogas, toxicodependência *f*.

drug addict *n* drogado *m* (-da *f*), toxicômano *m* (-na *f*).

druggist ['drʌgɪst] *n (Am)* farmacêutico *m* (-ca *f*).

drugstore ['drʌgstɔːʳ] *n (Am)* farmácia *f*.

drum [drʌm] *n (MUS)* tambor *m*; *(container)* barril *m*; **to play the ~s** tocar bateria.

drummer ['drʌməʳ] *n* baterista *mf*.

drumstick ['drʌmstɪk] *n (of chicken)* perna *f*.

drunk [drʌŋk] *pp* → **drink** ◆ *adj* bêbado(-da) ◆ *n* bêbado *m* (-da *f*); **to get ~** embebedar-se.

drunk-driving *(Am)* = **drink-driving**.

drunken ['drʌŋkn] *adj (person)* bêbado(-da); *(party, talk)* de bêbados.

dry [draɪ] *adj* seco(-ca) ◆ *vt (hands, washing-up)* limpar, secar; *(clothes)* secar ◆ *vi* secar; **to ~ o.s.** limpar-se; **to ~ one's hair** secar o cabelo.

❑ **dry up** *vi (become dry)* secar; *(dry the dishes)* limpar.

dry-clean *vt* limpar a seco.

dry cleaner's *n* lavanderia *f*.

dryer ['draɪə'] *n (for clothes)* máquina *f* de secar; *(for hair)* secador *m*.

dry-roasted peanuts [-'rəʊstɪd] *npl* amendoins *mpl* torrados.

dry ski slope *n* pista *f* de ski artificial.

DSS *n (Brit)* ministério britânico da Segurança Social.

DTP *abbr* = desktop publishing.

dual ['dju:əl] *adj* duplo(-pla).

dual carriageway *n (Brit)* via *f* dupla *(Br)*, via *f* rápida *(Port)*.

dubbed [dʌbd] *adj (film)* dublado (-da) *(Br)*, dobrado(-da) *(Port)*.

dubious ['dju:bjəs] *adj (suspect)* duvidoso(-osa).

Dublin ['dʌblɪn] *n* Dublim *s*.

duchess ['dʌtʃɪs] *n* duquesa *f*

duck [dʌk] *n* pato *m* ◆ *vi* abaixar-se.

duckling ['dʌklɪŋ] *n (animal)* patinho *m*; *(food)* pato *m*.

dud [dʌd] *adj (coin, note)* falso(-sa); *(cheque)* sem fundos *(Br)*, careca *(Port)*; *(machine, video, idea)* inútil; *(bomb, shell, bullet)* que não rebentou.

due [dju:] *adj (owed)* devido(-da); *(to be paid)* a pagar; **the train is ~ at eight o'clock** a chegada do trem está prevista para as oito; **in ~ course** no tempo devido; **~ to** devido a.

duel ['dju:əl] *n* duelo *m*.

duet [dju:'et] *n* dueto *m*.

duffel bag ['dʌfl-] *n* saco *m* tipo marinheiro.

duffel coat ['dʌfl-] *n* casaco *m (grosso de inverno com capuz)*.

dug [dʌg] *pt & pp* → **dig**.

duke [dju:k] *n* duque *m*.

dull [dʌl] *adj (boring)* chato(-ta), aborrecido(-da); *(not bright)* baço(-ça); *(weather)* cinzento (-ta); *(pain)* incômodo(-da).

duly ['dju:lɪ] *adv (properly)* devidamente; *(as expected)* como era de se esperar.

dumb [dʌm] *adj (inf: stupid)* estúpido(-da); *(unable to speak)* mudo (-da).

dumbfound [dʌm'faʊnd] *vt* deixar estupefato(-ta); **to be ~ed** ficar estupefato.

dummy ['dʌmɪ] *n (Brit: for baby)* chupeta *f*; *(for clothes)* manequim *m*.

dump [dʌmp] *n (for rubbish)* lixeira *f*; *(inf: place)* espelunca *f* ◆ *vt (drop carelessly)* deixar cair; *(get rid of)* desfazer-se de.

dumper (truck) ['dʌmpə'-] *n (Brit)* caminhão *m* basculante *(Br)*, camião *m* basculante *(Port)*.

dumpling ['dʌmplɪŋ] *n* bolinho *m* de massa cozido e servido com ensopados.

dump truck *(Am)* = **dumper (truck)**.

dunce [dʌns] *n* burro *m* (-a *f*).

dune [dju:n] *n* duna *f*.

dung [dʌŋ] *n* excremento *m*, bosta *f*.

dungarees [,dʌŋgə'ri:z] *npl (Brit: for work)* macacão *m (Br)*, fato-macaco *m (Port)*; *(fashion item)* jardineiras *fpl*; *(Am: jeans)* jeans *m inv (Br)*, calças *fpl* de ganga *(Port)*.

dungeon ['dʌndʒən] *n* masmorra *f*.

duo ['dju:əʊ] *n* duo *m*.

duplicate ['dju:plɪkət] *n* duplicado *m*.

duration [dju'reɪʃn] *n* duração *f*; **for the ~ of** durante.

during ['djʊərɪŋ] *prep* durante.

dusk [dʌsk] *n* crepúsculo *m*.

dust [dʌst] *n (in building)* pó *m*; *(on ground)* pó, poeira *f* ◆ *vt (furniture, object)* tirar o pó de.

dustbin ['dʌstbɪn] *n (Brit)* lata *f* de lixo *(Br)*, caixote *m* do lixo *(Port)*.

dustcart ['dʌstkɑ:t] *n (Brit)* caminhão *m* do lixo *(Br)*, camião *m* do lixo *(Port)*.

duster ['dʌstə'] *n* pano *m* de pó.

dustman ['dʌstmən] *(pl* **-men** [-mən]*)* *n (Brit)* lixeiro *m (Br)*, gari *m (Br)*, homem *m* do lixo *(Port)*.

dustpan ['dʌstpæn] *n* pá *f* de lixo.

dusty ['dʌstɪ] *adj (road)* poeirento(-ta); *(room, air)* cheio (cheia) de pó.

Dutch [dʌtʃ] *adj* holandês(-esa) ◆ *n (language)* neerlandês *m*, holandês *m* ◆ *npl*: **the ~** os holandeses.

Dutchman ['dʌtʃmən] *(pl* **-men** [-mən]*)* *n* holandês *m*.

Dutchwoman ['dʌtʃ,wʊmən] *(pl* **-women** [-,wɪmɪn]*)* *n* holandesa *f*.

duty ['dju:tɪ] *n (moral obligation)* dever *m*; *(tax)* taxa *f*; **to be on ~** estar de plantão; **to be off ~** estar de folga.

❑ **duties** *npl (job)* funções *fpl*.

duty chemist's *n* farmácia *f* de plantão.

duty-free *adj* livre de impostos ♦ *n (article)* artigo *m* isento de impostos alfandegários.

duty-free shop *n* duty-free shop *m*, loja *f* franca *(Port)*.

duvet ['du:veɪ] *n* edredom *m (Br)*, edredão *m (Port)*.

duvet cover *n (Brit)* capa *f* de edredom.

dwarf [dwɔ:f] *(pl* **dwarves** [dwɔ:vz]) *n* anão *m* (anã *f*).

dwelling ['dwelɪŋ] *n (fml)* moradia *f.*

dye [daɪ] *n* tinta *f* (para tingir) ♦ *vt* tingir.

dying ['daɪɪŋ] *cont* → **die**.

dyke [daɪk] = **dike**.

dynamic [daɪ'næmɪk] *adj* dinâmico(-ca).

dynamite ['daɪnəmaɪt] *n* dinamite *f.*

dynamo ['daɪnəməʊ] *(pl* **-s)** *n* dínamo *m.*

dynasty [*Brit* 'dɪnəstɪ, *Am* 'daɪnəstɪ] *n* dinastia *f.*

dyslexic [dɪs'leksɪk] *adj* disléxico(-ca).

E

E (abbr of east) E.

E111 n E111 m, impresso necessário para obter assistência médica nos outros países da União Européia.

each [i:tʃ] adj & pron cada; ~ **one** cada um (cada uma); ~ **of them** cada um deles (cada uma delas); ~ **other** um ao outro; **they fought** ~ **other** lutaram um contra o outro; **we know** ~ **other** nós nos conhecemos; **one** ~ um a cada um; **one of** ~ um de cada.

eager [ˈiːgəʳ] adj (pupil) entusiasta; (expression) de entusiasmo; **to be** ~ **to do sthg** estar ansioso por fazer algo; ~ **to please** doido para agradar.

eagle [ˈiːgl] n águia f.

ear [ɪəʳ] n orelha f; (of corn) espiga f.

earache [ˈɪəreɪk] n dor f de ouvidos; **I've got** ~ estou com dor de ouvidos.

eardrum [ˈɪədrʌm] n tímpano m.

earl [ɜːl] n conde m.

earlier [ˈɜːlɪəʳ] adj anterior ♦ adv antes; ~ **on** antes.

earlobe [ˈɪələʊb] n lóbulo m da orelha.

early [ˈɜːlɪ] adj (before usual or arranged time) antecipado(-da) ♦ adv cedo; **I need to catch an** ~ **train** preciso pegar um trem que passa mais cedo; **it arrived an hour** ~ chegou uma hora mais cedo; ~ **last year** no início do ano passado, **in the** ~ **morning** de madrugada; **at the earliest** o mais cedo possível, no mínimo; ~ **on** cedo; **to have an** ~ **night** deitar-se cedo.

earn [ɜːn] vt ganhar; **to** ~ **a living** ganhar a vida.

earnest [ˈɜːnɪst] adj sério(-ria); **to begin in** ~ começar a sério.

earnings [ˈɜːnɪŋz] npl rendimentos mpl.

earphones [ˈɪəfəʊnz] npl fones mpl de ouvido (Br), auscultadores mpl (Port).

earplugs [ˈɪəplʌgz] npl tampões mpl auriculares OR para os ouvidos.

earrings [ˈɪərɪŋz] npl brincos mpl.

earshot [ˈɪəʃɒt] n: **within** ~ ao alcance do ouvido; **out of** ~ fora do alcance do ouvido.

earth [ɜːθ] n terra f; (Brit: electrical connection) fio m terra ♦ vt (Brit: appliance) ligar à terra; **how on** ~ ...? como diabo ...?

earthenware [ˈɜːθnweəʳ] adj de barro.

earthquake [ˈɜːθkweɪk] n terremoto m.

earthworm [ˈɜːθwɜːm] n minhoca f.

earwig [ˈɪəwɪg] n lacrainha f (Br), bicha-cadela f (Port).

ease [iːz] n facilidade f ♦ vt (pain, tension) aliviar; (problem) minorar; **at** ~ à vontade; **with** ~ com facilidade, facilmente.

⌐ ease off vi diminuir.

easel [ˈiːzl] n cavalete m.

easily [ˈiːzɪlɪ] adv (without difficulty) facilmente; (by far) de longe.

east [iːst] n leste m, este m ♦ adj leste, este ♦ adv (be situated) a leste; (fly, walk) para este, para leste; **in the** ~ **of England** no leste da Inglaterra; **the East** (Asia) o Oriente.

eastbound [ˈiːstbaʊnd] adj em direção a leste OR ao este.

East End n: **the** ~ o leste de Londres.

Easter [ˈiːstəʳ] n Páscoa f.

Easter egg n ovo m de Páscoa.

easterly [ˈiːstəlɪ] adj (wind) de leste; **in an** ~ **direction** em direção ao leste OR este; **the most** ~ **point** o ponto mais a leste OR este.

eastern [ˈiːstən] adj de leste, do este.

⌐ Eastern adj (Asian) oriental.

Eastern Europe n Europa f de Leste.

eastward ['i:stwəd] *adj:* **in an ~ direction** em direção ao leste OR este.

eastwards ['i:stwədz] *adv* em direção ao leste OR este, para leste OR este.

easy ['i:zɪ] *adj* fácil; **to take it ~** *(relax)* levar as coisas com calma; **take it ~!** *(be calm)* tenha calma!

easy chair *n* poltrona *f*, cadeirão *m*.

easygoing [,i:zɪ'gəʊɪŋ] *adj* descontraído(-da).

eat [i:t] *(pt* **ate**, *pp* **eaten** ['i:tn]) *vt & vi* comer.

❑ **eat out** *vi* comer fora.

eating apple ['i:tɪŋ-] *n* maçã *f* (para comer).

eaves ['i:vz] *npl* beirais *mpl*.

ebony ['ebənɪ] *n* ébano *m*.

EC *n* (*abbr of* European Community) CE *f*.

eccentric [ɪk'sentrɪk] *adj* excêntrico(-ca).

echo ['ekəʊ] *(pl* **-es**) *n* eco *m* ♦ *vi* ecoar.

eclipse [ɪ'klɪps] *n* eclipse *m*.

ecological [,i:kə'lɒdʒɪkl] *adj* ecológico(-ca).

ecology [ɪ'kɒlədʒɪ] *n* ecologia *f*.

economic [,i:kə'nɒmɪk] *adj* econômico(-ca).

❑ **economics** *n* economia *f*.

economical [,i:kə'nɒmɪkl] *adj* econômico(-ca).

economize [ɪ'kɒnəmaɪz] *vi* economizar.

economy [ɪ'kɒnəmɪ] *n* economia *f*.

economy class *n* classe *f* turística.

economy size *adj* de tamanho econômico.

ecotourism [i:kəʊ'tʊərɪzm] *n* ecoturismo *m*.

ecstasy ['ekstəsɪ] *n* (great joy) êxtase *m*; *(drug)* ecstasy *f*.

ecstatic [ek'stætɪk] *adj* extasiado (-da).

ECU ['ekju:] *n* ECU *m*.

eczema ['eksɪmə] *n* eczema *m*.

edge [edʒ] *n* (border) beira *f*; (of table, coin, plate) borda *f*; (of knife) fio *m*, gume *m*.

edible ['edɪbl] *adj* comestível.

Edinburgh ['edɪnbrə] *n* Edimburgo *s*.

Edinburgh Festival *n*: **the ~** o Festival de Edimburgo.

edit ['edɪt] *vt* (text) corrigir, revisar; (newspaper, magazine) dirigir; (film, programme) montar.

edition [ɪ'dɪʃn] *n* edição *f*.

editor ['edɪtəʳ] *n* (of text) editor *m* (-ra *f*); (of newspaper, magazine) diretor *m* (-ra *f*); (of film, TV programme) técnico *m* (-ca *f*) de montagem.

editorial [,edɪ'tɔ:rɪəl] *n* editorial *m*.

educate ['edʒʊkeɪt] *vt* educar.

education [,edʒʊ'keɪʃn] *n* educação *f*.

educational [,edʒʊ'keɪʃənl] *adj* (establishment, policy) educacional; (toy, experience) didático(-ca).

eel [i:l] *n* enguia *f*.

eerie ['ɪərɪ] *adj* sinistro(-tra), arrepiante.

effect [ɪ'fekt] *n* efeito *m*; **to put sthg into ~** pôr em prática; **to take ~** (medicine) fazer efeito; (law) entrar em vigor.

effective [ɪ'fektɪv] *adj* (successful) eficaz; (law, system) em vigor.

effectively [ɪ'fektɪvlɪ] *adv* (successfully) eficazmente, com eficácia; (in fact) com efeito.

effeminate [ɪ'femɪnət] *adj* efeminado(-da).

efficiency [ɪ'fɪʃənsɪ] *n* (of person) eficiência *f*; (of factory) economia *f*.

efficient [ɪ'fɪʃənt] *adj* (person) eficiente; (factory) econômico(-ca).

effluent ['efluənt] *n* águas *fpl* residuais, esgotos *mpl*.

effort ['efət] *n* esforço *m*; **to make an ~ to do sthg** fazer um esforço para fazer algo; **it's not worth the ~** não vale a pena o esforço.

effortless ['efətlɪs] *adj* (easy) fácil; (natural) natural.

e.g. *adv* e.g., p. ex.

egg [eg] *n* ovo *m*.

egg cup *n* oveiro *m*, pequeno suporte para ovos quentes.

egg mayonnaise *n* recheio para sanduíches composto por ovo cozido e maionese.

eggplant ['egplɑ:nt] *n* (Am) beringela *f*.

eggshell ['egʃel] *n* casca *f* de ovo.

egg white *n* clara *f* de ovo.

egg yolk *n* gema *f* de ovo.

ego ['i:gəʊ] *(pl* **-s**) *n* ego *m*, amor *m* próprio.

egoistic [,i:gəʊ'ɪstɪk] *adj* egoísta.

egotistic(al) [,i:gə'tɪstɪk(l)] *adj* egotista.

Egypt ['i:dʒɪpt] *n* Egipto *m*.

Egyptian [ɪ'dʒɪpʃn] *adj* egípcio(-cia)

♦ *n* egípcio *m* (-cia *f*).
eiderdown ['aɪdədaʊn] *n* edredom *m*
(Br), edredão *m (Port)*.
eight [eɪt] *num* oito, → **six**.
eighteen [,eɪ'tiːn] *num* dezoito, →
six.
eighteenth [,eɪ'tiːnθ] *num* décimo
oitavo (décima oitava), → **sixth**.
eighth [eɪtθ] *num* oitavo(-va), →
sixth.
eightieth ['eɪtɪɪθ] *num* octogésimo
(-ma), → **sixth**.
eighty ['eɪtɪ] *num* oitenta, → **six**.
Eire ['eərə] *n* República *f* da Irlanda.
Eisteddfod [aɪ'stedfəd] *n* festival cultural galês.
either ['aɪðəʳ, 'iːðəʳ] *adj*: ~ **book will
do** qualquer um dos livros serve
♦ *pron*: **I'll take ~ (of them)** levo qualquer um (dos dois); **I don't like ~ (of
them)** não gosto de nenhum (deles)
♦ *adv*: **I can't ~** também não posso; **~
... or** ou ... ou; **I don't speak ~ Portuguese or English** não falo nem português nem inglês; **on ~ side** dos dois
lados.
eject [ɪ'dʒekt] *vt (cassette)* tirar.
elaborate [ɪ'læbrət] *adj* elaborado
(-da), complicado(-da).
elapse [ɪ'læps] *vi* decorrer.
elastic [ɪ'læstɪk] *n* elástico *m*.
elasticated [ɪ'læstɪkeɪtɪd] *adj* elásti-
co(-ca).
elastic band *n (Brit)* elástico *m*.
elbow ['elbəʊ] *n* cotovelo *m*.
elder ['eldəʳ] *adj* mais velho(-lha).
elderly ['eldəlɪ] *adj* idoso(-osa) ♦ *npl*:
the ~ os idosos.
eldest ['eldɪst] *adj* mais velho(-lha).
elect [ɪ'lekt] *vt* eleger; **to ~ to do sthg**
(fml: choose) escolher fazer algo.
election [ɪ'lekʃn] *n* eleição *f*.
electioneering [ɪ,lekʃə'nɪərɪŋ] *n* propaganda *f* eleitoral.
electorate [ɪ'lektərət] *n*: **the ~** o elei-
torado.
electric [ɪ'lektrɪk] *adj* elétrico(-ca).
electrical [ɪ'lektrɪkl] *adj* elétrico(-ca).
electrical goods *npl* eletro-
domésticos *mpl*.
electric blanket *n* cobertor *m* elétrico.
electric cooker *n* fogão *m* elétrico.
electric drill *n* furadeira *f* elétrica
(Br), berbequim *m* (eléctrico) *(Port)*.

electric fence *n* vedação *f* eletrifi-
cada.
electric fire *n* radiador *m* OR aquecedor *m* elétrico.
electrician [ɪlek'trɪʃn] *n* electricista *mf*.
electricity [ɪlek'trɪsətɪ] *n* eletricidade *f*.
electric shock *n* choque *m* elétrico.
electrocute [ɪ'lektrəkjuːt] *vt* eletro-
cutar.
electronic [ɪlek'trɒnɪk] *adj* ele-
trônico(-ca).
electronic mail *n* correio *m* eletrônico.
elegant ['elɪgənt] *adj* elegante.
element ['elɪmənt] *n* elemento *m*; *(of
fire, kettle)* resistência *f*; **the ~s**
(weather) os elementos.
elementary [,elɪ'mentərɪ] *adj* elementar.
elementary school *n (Am)* escola *f*
primária.
elephant ['elɪfənt] *n* elefante *m*.
elevator ['elɪveɪtəʳ] *n (Am)* elevador *m*.
eleven [ɪ'levn] *num* onze, → **six**.
elevenses [ɪ'levnzɪz] *n (Brit)* refeição
leve por volta das onze da manhã.
eleventh [ɪ'levnθ] *num* décimo primeiro (décima primeira), → **sixth**.
eligible ['elɪdʒəbl] *adj (qualified, suitable)* apto(-ta); *(bachelor)* elegível.
eliminate [ɪ'lɪmɪneɪt] *vt* eliminar.
elitist [ɪ'liːtɪst] *adj* elitista ♦ *n* elitista
mf.
Elizabethan [ɪ,lɪzə'biːθn] *adj* isabeli-
no(-na) *(segunda metade do séc. XVI)*.
elk [elk] *(pl inv* OR **-s)** *n* alce *m*.
elm [elm] *n* ulmeiro *m*, olmo *m*.
eloquent ['eləkwənt] *adj* eloqüente.
else [els] *adv*: **I don't want anything ~**
não quero mais nada; **anything ~?**
mais alguma coisa?; **everyone ~** os
outros todos (as outras todas); **nobody
~** mais ninguém; **nothing ~** mais
nada; **somebody ~** mais alguém;
something ~ outra coisa; **somewhere
~** outro lugar; **what ~?** que mais?; **who
~?** quem mais?; **or ~** ou então, senão.
elsewhere [els'weəʳ] *adv (be, search)*
noutro lugar, *(with verbs of motion)* para
outro lado.
elude [ɪ'luːd] *vt (police, pursuers)* elu-
dir; *(subj: fact, idea, name)* escapar a.
elusive [ɪ'luːsɪv] *adj (success, quality)*
difícil de alcançar; *(person, animal)* difícil de encontrar.

e-mail *n (abbr of electronic mail)* e-mail *m*.

emancipate [ɪ'mænsɪpeɪt] *vt:* **to ~ sb from sthg** libertar alguém de algo.

embankment [ɪm'bæŋkmənt] *n (next to river)* margem *f; (next to road, railway)* barreira *f*.

embark [ɪm'bɑːk] *vi (board ship)* embarcar.

embarkation card [,embɑː'keɪʃn-] *n* cartão *m* de embarque.

embarrass [ɪm'bærəs] *vt* envergonhar.

embarrassed [ɪm'bærəst] *adj* envergonhado(-da).

embarrassing [ɪm'bærəsɪŋ] *adj* embaraçoso(-osa).

embarrassment [ɪm'bærəsmənt] *n* vergonha *f*.

embassy ['embəsɪ] *n* embaixada *f*.

embers ['embəz] *npl* brasas *fpl*.

emblem ['embləm] *n* emblema *m*.

embossed [ɪm'bɒst] *adj (paper)* timbrado(-da); *(wallpaper)* em relevo; *(leather)* gravado(-da); *(design, lettering):* **~ (on sthg)** gravado (em algo).

embrace [ɪm'breɪs] *vt* abraçar.

embroidered [ɪm'brɔɪdəd] *adj* bordado(-da).

embroidery [ɪm'brɔɪdərɪ] *n* bordado *m*.

embryo ['embrɪəʊ] *(pl -s)* *n* embrião *m*.

emerald ['emərəld] *n* esmeralda *f*.

emerge [ɪ'mɜːdʒ] *vi (from place)* emergir, sair; *(fact, truth)* vir à tona.

emergency [ɪ'mɜːdʒənsɪ] *n* emergência *f* ◆ *adj* de emergência; **in an ~** em caso de emergência.

emergency exit *n* saída *f* de emergência.

emergency landing *n* aterissagem *f* de emergência.

emergency services *npl* serviços *mpl* de emergência.

emery board ['emərɪ-] *n* lixa *f* (para as unhas).

emigrant ['emɪɡrənt] *n* emigrante *mf*.

emigrate ['emɪɡreɪt] *vi* emigrar.

eminent ['emɪnənt] *adj* eminente.

emission [ɪ'mɪʃn] *n* emissão *f*.

emit [ɪ'mɪt] *vt* emitir.

emotion [ɪ'məʊʃn] *n* emoção *f*.

emotional [ɪ'məʊʃənl] *adj (situation, scene)* comovente; *(person)* emotivo(-va).

emperor ['empərər] *n* imperador *m*.

emphasis ['emfəsɪs] *(pl -ases [-əsiːz])* *n* ênfase *f*.

emphasize ['emfəsaɪz] *vt* enfatizar, sublinhar.

emphatically [ɪm'fætɪklɪ] *adv (say, state)* enfaticamente; *(agree)* plenamente; *(disagree)* em absoluto.

empire ['empaɪər] *n* império *m*.

employ [ɪm'plɔɪ] *vt* empregar.

employed [ɪm'plɔɪd] *adj* empregado(-da).

employee [ɪm'plɔɪiː] *n* empregado *m* (-da *f*).

employer [ɪm'plɔɪər] *n* patrão *m* (-troa *f*).

employment [ɪm'plɔɪmənt] *n* emprego *m*.

employment agency *n* agência *f* de emprego.

empress ['emprɪs] *n* imperatriz *f*.

empty ['emptɪ] *adj (containing nothing)* vazio(-zia); *(threat, promise)* vão (vã) ◆ *vt* esvaziar.

empty-handed [-'hændɪd] *adv* de mãos vazias OR a abanar.

EMU *n* UEM *f*.

emulate ['emjʊleɪt] *vt* emular.

emulsion (paint) [ɪ'mʌlʃn-] *n* tinta *f* de emulsão.

enable [ɪ'neɪbl] *vt:* **to ~ sb to do sthg** permitir a alguém fazer algo.

enamel [ɪ'næml] *n* esmalte *m*.

enchanted [ɪn'tʃɑːntɪd] *adj:* **~ by** OR **with sthg** encantado(-da) com algo.

enchanting [ɪn'tʃɑːntɪŋ] *adj* encantador(-ra).

encircle [ɪn'sɜːkl] *vt* rodear.

enclose [ɪn'kləʊz] *vt (surround)* rodear; *(with letter)* juntar.

enclosed [ɪn'kləʊzd] *adj (space)* vedado(-da).

enclosure [ɪn'kləʊʒər] *n (place)* recinto *m*.

encore ['ɒŋkɔːr] *n* bis *m* ◆ *excl* bis!

encounter [ɪn'kaʊntər] *vt* encontrar.

encourage [ɪn'kʌrɪdʒ] *vt* encorajar; **to ~ sb to do sthg** encorajar alguém a fazer algo.

encouragement [ɪn'kʌrɪdʒmənt] *n* encorajamento *m*.

encyclopedia [ɪn,saɪklə'piːdjə] *n* enciclopédia *f*.

end [end] *n* fim *m; (furthest point)* extremo *m; (of string, finger)* ponta *f*

♦ *vt* acabar, terminar; *(war, practice)* acabar com ♦ *vi* acabar, terminar; **to come to an ~** chegar ao fim; **to put an ~ to sthg** acabar com algo; **for days on ~** durante dias e dias OR dias a fio; **in the ~** no fim; **to make ~s meet** conseguir que o dinheiro chegue ao fim do mês.

❑ **end up** *vi* acabar; **to ~ up doing sthg** acabar por fazer algo.

endanger [ɪnˈdeɪndʒəʳ] *vt* pôr em risco OR perigo.

endangered species [ɪnˈdeɪndʒəd-] *n* espécie *f* em vias de extinção.

endearing [ɪnˈdɪərɪŋ] *adj* cativante.

ending [ˈendɪŋ] *n (of story, film, book)* fim *m*, final *m*; *(GRAMM)* terminação *f*.

endive [ˈendaɪv] *n* endívia *f*.

endless [ˈendlɪs] *adj* infinito(-ta), sem fim.

endorsement [ɪnˈdɔːsmənt] *n (of driving licence)* multa anotada na carteira de motorista.

endurance [ɪnˈdjuərəns] *n* resistência *f*.

endure [ɪnˈdjuəʳ] *vt* suportar.

endways [ˈendweɪz] *adv (Brit) (not sideways)* ao comprido; *(with ends touching)* ponta com ponta, extremidade com extremidade.

endwise [ˈendwaɪz] *(Am)* = **endways**.

enemy [ˈenɪmɪ] *n* inimigo *m* (-ga *f*).

energetic [ˌenəˈdʒetɪk] *adj* energético(-ca), ativo(-va).

energy [ˈenədʒɪ] *n* energia *f*.

enforce [ɪnˈfɔːs] *vt (law)* aplicar, fazer cumprir.

engaged [ɪnˈgeɪdʒd] *adj (to be married)* noivo(-va); *(Brit: phone)* ocupado(-da) *(Br)*, impedido(-da) *(Port)*; *(toilet)* ocupado(-da); **to get ~** ficar noivo.

engaged tone *n (Brit)* sinal *m* de ocupado *(Br)*, sinal de impedido *(Port)*.

engagement [ɪnˈgeɪdʒmənt] *n (to marry)* noivado *m*; *(appointment)* compromisso *m*, encontro *m*.

engagement ring *n* anel *m* de noivado.

engine [ˈendʒɪn] *n (of vehicle)* motor *m*; *(of train)* máquina *f*.

engine driver *n (Brit)* maquinista *mf*.

engineer [ˌendʒɪˈnɪəʳ] *n (of roads, machinery)* engenheiro *m* (-ra *f*); *(to do repairs)* técnico *m* (-ca *f*).

engineering [ˌendʒɪˈnɪərɪŋ] *n* engenharia *f*.

engineering works *npl (on railway line)* trabalhos *mpl* na linha.

England [ˈɪŋglənd] *n* Inglaterra *f*.

English [ˈɪŋglɪʃ] *adj* inglês(-esa) ♦ *n (language)* inglês *m* ♦ *npl*: **the ~** os ingleses.

English breakfast *n* café da manhã tradicional composto por ovos e bacon fritos, salsichas e torradas, acompanhado de café ou chá.

English Channel *n*: **the ~** o Canal da Mancha.

Englishman [ˈɪŋglɪʃmən] *(pl* **-men** [-mən]) *n* inglês *m*.

Englishwoman [ˈɪŋglɪʃˌwumən] *(pl* **-women** [-ˌwɪmɪn]) *n* inglesa *f*.

engrave [ɪnˈgreɪv] *vt* gravar.

engraving [ɪnˈgreɪvɪŋ] *n* gravura *f*.

engrossed [ɪnˈgrəust] *adj*: **to be ~ in sthg** estar absorto(-ta) em algo.

enhance [ɪnˈhɑːns] *vt (value)* aumentar; *(reputation, chances)* melhorar; *(beauty)* realçar.

enjoy [ɪnˈdʒɔɪ] *vt* gostar de; **to ~ doing sthg** gostar de fazer algo; **to ~ o.s.** divertir-se; **~ your meal!** bom apetite!

enjoyable [ɪnˈdʒɔɪəbl] *adj* agradável.

enjoyment [ɪnˈdʒɔɪmənt] *n* prazer *m*.

enlarge [ɪnˈlɑːdʒ] *vt (photograph, building)* ampliar; *(scope)* alargar.

❑ **enlarge on** *vt fus* desenvolver, alargar-se sobre.

enlargement [ɪnˈlɑːdʒmənt] *n (of photo)* ampliação *f*.

enlightened [ɪnˈlaɪtnd] *adj* esclarecido(-da).

enormity [ɪˈnɔːmətɪ] *n* enormidade *f*.

enormous [ɪˈnɔːməs] *adj* enorme.

enough [ɪˈnʌf] *adj* suficiente ♦ *pron* o suficiente ♦ *adv* suficientemente; **~ time** tempo suficiente; **is that ~?** chega?, **it's not big ~** não é suficientemente grande; **I've had ~ of your cheek!** estou farto do seu atrevimento!

enquire [ɪnˈkwaɪəʳ] *vi* informar-se.

enquiry [ɪnˈkwaɪərɪ] *n (question)* pergunta *f*; *(investigation)* inquérito *m*, investigação *f*; **"Enquiries"** "Informações".

enquiry desk *n* (balcão *m* de) informações *fpl*.

enraged [ɪnˈreɪdʒd] *adj* enraivecido(-da).

enrol [ɪnˈrəul] *vi (Brit)* matricular-se.

enroll [ɪnˈrəul] *(Am)* = **enrol**.

ensue [ɪnˈsjuː] *vi (fml)* surgir, acontecer.

en suite bathroom [ɒnˈswiːt] *n* banheiro *m* privativo.

ensure [ɪnˈʃʊəʳ] *vt* assegurar, garantir.

entail [ɪnˈteɪl] *vt (involve)* implicar.

enter [ˈentəʳ] *vt* entrar em; *(college, army)* entrar para; *(competition)* inscrever-se em; *(on form)* escrever ♦ *vi* entrar; *(in competition)* inscrever-se.

enterprise [ˈentəpraɪz] *n (business)* empresa *f*.

enterprising [ˈentəpraɪzɪŋ] *adj* empreendedor(-ra).

entertain [ˌentəˈteɪn] *vt (amuse)* entreter.

entertainer [ˌentəˈteɪnəʳ] *n* artista *mf* (de variedades).

entertaining [ˌentəˈteɪnɪŋ] *adj* divertido(-da).

entertainment [ˌentəˈteɪnmənt] *n (amusement)* divertimento *m*; *(show)* espetáculo *m*.

enthusiasm [ɪnˈθjuːzɪæzm] *n* entusiasmo *m*.

enthusiast [ɪnˈθjuːzɪæst] *n* entusiasta *mf*.

enthusiastic [ɪnˌθjuːzɪˈæstɪk] *adj* entusiástico(-ca).

entice [ɪnˈtaɪs] *vt* seduzir; **to ~ sb into** sthg atrair alguém para algo.

entire [ɪnˈtaɪəʳ] *adj* inteiro(-ra).

entirely [ɪnˈtaɪəlɪ] *adv* completamente.

entirety [ɪnˈtaɪərətɪ] *n*: **in its ~** na totalidade.

entitle [ɪnˈtaɪtl] *vt*: **to ~ sb to sthg** dar a alguém o direito a algo; **to ~ sb to do sthg** dar o direito a alguém de fazer algo.

entitled [ɪnˈtaɪtld] *adj*: **to be ~ to sthg** ter direito a algo; **to be ~ to do sthg** ter o direito de fazer algo.

entrance [ˈentrəns] *n* entrada *f*.

entrance examination *n* exame *m* de admissão.

entrance fee *n* entrada *f*.

entrant [ˈentrənt] *n (in competition)* participante *mf*.

entrepreneur [ˌɒntrəprəˈnɜːʳ] *n* empresário *m* (-ria *f*).

entry [ˈentrɪ] *n* entrada *f*; *(in competition)* inscrição *f*, candidatura *f*; **"no ~"** *(sign on door)* "entrada proibida"; *(road sign)* "acesso proibido".

entry form *n* impresso *m* OR folha *f* de inscrição.

entry phone *n* interfone *m*.

envelope [ˈenvələʊp] *n* envelope *m*.

envious [ˈenvɪəs] *adj* invejoso(-osa).

environment [ɪnˈvaɪərənmənt] *n* meio *m*; **the ~** o meio ambiente.

environmental [ɪnˌvaɪərənˈmentl] *adj* ambiental.

environmentally friendly [ɪnˌvaɪərənˈmentəlɪ-] *adj* amigo(-ga) do ambiente.

envy [ˈenvɪ] *vt* invejar.

epic [ˈepɪk] *n* epopéia *f*.

epidemic [ˌepɪˈdemɪk] *n* epidemia *f*.

epileptic [ˌepɪˈleptɪk] *adj* epiléptico(-ca).

episode [ˈepɪsəʊd] *n* episódio *m*.

equal [ˈiːkwəl] *adj* igual ♦ *vt* igualar; **to be ~ to** *(number)* ser igual a.

equality [ɪˈkwɒlətɪ] *n* igualdade *f*.

equalize [ˈiːkwəlaɪz] *vi* igualar.

equalizer [ˈiːkwəlaɪzəʳ] *n* gol *m* de empate *(Br)*, golo *m* da igualdade *(Port)*.

equally [ˈiːkwəlɪ] *adv (bad, good, matched)* igualmente; *(pay, treat)* de forma igual, da mesma forma; *(share)* por igual; *(at the same time)* ao mesmo tempo.

equal opportunities *npl* igualdade *f* de oportunidades.

equation [ɪˈkweɪʒn] *n* equação *f*.

equator [ɪˈkweɪtəʳ] *n*: **the ~** o equador.

equilibrium [ˌiːkwɪˈlɪbrɪəm] *n* equilíbrio *m*.

equip [ɪˈkwɪp] *vt*: **to ~ sb/sthg with** equipar alguém/algo com.

equipment [ɪˈkwɪpmənt] *n* equipamento *m*.

equipped [ɪˈkwɪpt] *adj*: **to be ~ with** estar equipado(-da) com.

equivalent [ɪˈkwɪvələnt] *adj* equivalente ♦ *n* equivalente *m*.

ER *n (Am: abbr of emergency room)* Urgências *fpl*.

era [ˈɪərə] *n* era *f*.

eradicate [ɪˈrædɪkeɪt] *vt* erradicar.

erase [ɪˈreɪz] *vt (letter, word)* apagar.

eraser [ɪˈreɪzəʳ] *n* borracha *f* (de apagar).

erect [ɪˈrekt] *adj* erecto(-ta) ♦ *vt (tent)* montar; *(monument)* erigir.

ERM *n* mecanismo de câmbio do SME.

ermine [ˈɜːmɪn] *n* arminho *m*.

erosion [ɪˈrəʊʒn] *n (of soil, rock)* erosão *f*.

erotic [ɪˈrɒtɪk] *adj* erótico(-ca).

errand [ˈerənd] *n* recado *m*.

erratic [ɪˈrætɪk] *adj* irregular.

error ['erəʳ] *n* erro *m*.

erupt [ɪ'rʌpt] *vi (volcano)* entrar em erupção; *(violence, war)* estourar.

eruption [ɪ'rʌpʃn] *n (of volcano)* erupção *f*; *(of war)* deflagração *f*.

escalator ['eskəleɪtəʳ] *n* escadas *fpl* rolantes.

escalope ['eskəlɒp] *n* escalope *m*.

escape [ɪ'skeɪp] *n* fuga *f* ◆ *vi:* to ~ **(from)** *(from prison, danger)* fugir (de); *(leak)* escapar (de).

escapism [ɪ'skeɪpɪzm] *n* evasão *f* (à realidade).

escort [*n* 'eskɔːt, *vb* ɪ'skɔːt] *n (guard)* escolta *f* ◆ *vt* escoltar.

Eskimo ['eskɪməʊ] *(pl inv* OR **-s)** *n (person)* esquimó *mf*.

espadrilles ['espədrɪlz] *npl* alpercatas *fpl*.

especially [ɪ'speʃəlɪ] *adv (in particular)* sobretudo; *(on purpose)* especialmente; *(very)* particularmente.

esplanade [,esplə'neɪd] *n* passeio *m*, avenida *f* à beira-mar.

espresso [ɪ'spresəʊ] *(pl* **-s)** *n* café *m*.

esquire [ɪ'skwaɪəʳ] *n*: **D. Lowis,** ~ Ex.ᵐᵒ Sr. D. Lowis.

essay ['eseɪ] *n (at school)* redação *f*, composição *f*; *(at university)* trabalho *m* escrito.

essence ['esns] *n* essência *f*; **in** ~ no fundo.

essential [ɪ'senʃl] *adj* essencial.
⏚ **essentials** *npl*: **the** ~**s** o essencial; **the bare** ~**s** o mínimo indispensável.

essentially [ɪ'senʃəlɪ] *adv* essencialmente.

establish [ɪ'stæblɪʃ] *vt* estabelecer.

establishment [ɪ'stæblɪʃmənt] *n (business)* estabelecimento *m*.

estate [ɪ'steɪt] *n (land in country)* propriedade *f*; *(for housing)* conjunto *m* habitacional *(Br)*, urbanização *f (Port)*; *(Brit: car)* = **estate car.**

estate agency *n (Brit)* agência *f* imobiliária.

estate agent *n (Brit)* agente *m* imobiliário (agente *f* imobiliária).

estate car *n (Brit)* perua *f (Br)*, carrinha *f (Port)*.

esteem [ɪ'stiːm] *vt* admirar, estimar ◆ *n* consideração *f*, estima *f*.

esthetic [iːsˈθetɪk] *(Am)* = **aesthetic.**

estimate [*n* 'estɪmət, *vb* 'estɪmeɪt] *n (guess)* estimativa *f*; *(from builder, plumber)* orçamento *m* ◆ *vt* calcular.

Estonia [e'stəʊnjə] *n* Estônia *f*.

estuary ['estjʊərɪ] *n* estuário *m*.

etc. *(abbr of etcetera)* etc.

eternal [ɪ'tɜːnl] *adj (everlasting)* eterno(-na); *(fig: perpetual, continual)* contínuo(-nua).

Ethiopia [iːˈθɪəʊpjə] *n* Etiópia *f*.

ethnic minority ['eθnɪk-] *n* minoria *f* étnica.

etiquette ['etɪket] *n* etiqueta *f*.

EU *n (abbr of European Union)* UE *f*.

euphemism ['juːfəmɪzm] *n* eufemismo *m*.

Eurocheque ['jʊərəʊˌtʃek] *n* Eurocheque *m*.

Europe ['jʊərəp] *n* Europa *f*.

European [,jʊərə'pɪən] *adj* europeu(-péia) ◆ *n* europeu *m* (-péia *f*).

European Community *n* Comunidade *f* Européia.

European Parliament *n*: **the** ~ o Parlamento Europeu.

euthanasia [,juːθə'neɪzjə] *n* eutanásia *f*.

evacuate [ɪ'vækjʊeɪt] *vt* evacuar.

evade [ɪ'veɪd] *vt (person)* evitar; *(issue, responsibility)* fugir a.

evaluate [ɪ'væljʊeɪt] *vt* avaliar.

evaporate [ɪ'væpəreɪt] *vi* evaporar.

evaporated milk [ɪ'væpəreɪtɪd-] *n* leite *m* evaporado.

eve [iːv] *n*: **on the** ~ **of** na véspera de.

even ['iːvn] *adj (level)* plano(-na); *(equal)* igual; *(number)* par ◆ *adv (emphasizing surprise)* mesmo; *(in comparisons)* ainda; **to break** ~ funcionar sem lucros nem prejuízos; ~ **so** mesmo assim; ~ **though** ainda que; **not** ~ nem mesmo OR sequer.

evening ['iːvnɪŋ] *n (from 5 p.m. until 8 p.m.)* fim *m* da tarde; *(from 8 p.m. onwards)* noite *f*; *(event)* serão *m*, noite *f*; **good** ~! boa tarde!, boa noite!; **in the** ~ ao fim da tarde, à noite.

evening classes *npl* aulas *fpl* à noite.

evening dress *n (formal clothes)* traje *m* de cerimônia; *(woman's garment)* vestido *m* de noite.

evening meal *n* jantar *m*, refeição *f* da noite.

event [ɪ'vent] *n (occurrence)* acontecimento *m*; *(SPORT)* prova *f*; **in the** ~ **of** *(fml)* em caso de.

eventful [ɪ'ventfʊl] *adj* movimentado(-da), fértil em acontecimentos.

eventual [ɪ'ventʃʊəl] *adj* final.

eventually [ɪˈventʃʊəlɪ] *adv* finalmente.

ever [ˈevəʳ] *adv (at any time)* alguma vez; *(in negatives)* nunca; **I don't ~ do that** nunca faço isso; **the best I've ~ seen** o melhor que já vi; **he was ~ so angry** ele estava mesmo zangado; **for ~** *(eternally)* para sempre; **we've been waiting for ~** estamos esperando há muito tempo; **hardly ~** quase nunca; **~ since** *adv* desde então ♦ *prep* desde ♦ *conj* desde que.

evergreen [ˈevəɡriːn] *adj* de folhas persistentes OR perenes ♦ *n* árvore *f* de folhas persistentes OR perenes.

every [ˈevrɪ] *adj* cada; **~ day** cada dia, todos os dias; **~ other day** dia sim, dia não; **one in ~ ten** um em cada dez; **we make ~ effort ...** fazemos o possível ...; **~ so often** de vez em quando.

everybody [ˈevrɪˌbɒdɪ] = **everyone**.

everyday [ˈevrɪdeɪ] *adj* diário(-ria).

everyone [ˈevrɪwʌn] *pron* toda a gente, todos *mpl* (-das *fpl*).

everyplace [ˈevrɪˌpleɪs] *(Am)* = **everywhere**.

everything [ˈevrɪθɪŋ] *pron* tudo.

everywhere [ˈevrɪweəʳ] *adv (be, search)* por todo o lado; *(with verbs of motion)* para todo o lado; **~ you go it's the same** onde quer que se vá é o mesmo.

evict [ɪˈvɪkt] *vt:* **to ~ sb (from)** despejar alguém (de).

evidence [ˈevɪdəns] *n* prova *f*.

evident [ˈevɪdənt] *adj* evidente.

evidently [ˈevɪdəntlɪ] *adv (apparently)* aparentemente; *(obviously)* evidentemente.

evil [ˈiːvl] *adj* mau (má) ♦ *n* o mal.

evolution [ˌiːvəˈluːʃn] *n* evolução *f*.

ewe [juː] *n* ovelha *f*.

ex [eks] *n (inf)* ex *mf*.

exact [ɪɡˈzækt] *adj* exato(-ta); **"~ fare ready please"** aviso em ônibus pedindo que se pague o dinheiro exacto do bilhete, pois não se dá troco.

exactly [ɪɡˈzæktlɪ] *adv* exatamente ♦ *excl* exato!

exaggerate [ɪɡˈzædʒəreɪt] *vt & vi* exagerar.

exaggeration [ɪɡˌzædʒəˈreɪʃn] *n* exagero *m*.

exam [ɪɡˈzæm] *n* exame *m*; **to take** OR **sit an ~** fazer um exame.

examination [ɪɡˌzæmɪˈneɪʃn] *n* exame *m*.

examine [ɪɡˈzæmɪn] *vt* examinar.

examiner [ɪɡˈzæmɪnəʳ] *n* examinador *m* (-ra *f*).

example [ɪɡˈzɑːmpl] *n* exemplo *m*; **for ~** por exemplo.

exasperate [ɪɡˈzæspəreɪt] *vt* exasperar.

excavate [ˈekskəveɪt] *vt* escavar.

exceed [ɪkˈsiːd] *vt* ultrapassar.

exceedingly [ɪkˈsiːdɪŋlɪ] *adv* tremendamente.

excel [ɪkˈsel] *vi:* **to ~ in** OR **at sthg** distinguir-se OR sobressair-se em algo.

excellence [ˈeksələns] *n* excelência *f*, perfeição *f*.

excellent [ˈeksələnt] *adj* excelente.

except [ɪkˈsept] *prep* exceto, a menos que ♦ *conj* exceto; **~ for** exceto; **"~ for access"** "exceto trânsito local"; **"~ for loading"** "exceto cargas e descargas".

excepting [ɪkˈseptɪŋ] *prep & conj* = **except**.

exception [ɪkˈsepʃn] *n* exceção *f*.

exceptional [ɪkˈsepʃnəl] *adj* excecional.

excerpt [ˈeksɔːpt] *n* trecho *m*, excerto *m*.

excess [ɪkˈses, *before nouns* ˈekses] *adj* excessivo(-va), em excesso ♦ *n* excesso *m*.

excess baggage *n* excesso *m* de bagagem.

excess fare *n (Brit)* prolongamento *m*.

excessive [ɪkˈsesɪv] *adj* excessivo(-va).

exchange [ɪksˈtʃeɪndʒ] *n (of telephones)* central *f* telefônica; *(of students)* intercâmbio *m* ♦ *vt* trocar; **to ~ sthg for sthg** trocar algo por algo; **to be on an ~** estar participando de um intercâmbio.

exchange rate *n* taxa *f* de câmbio.

excite [ɪkˈsaɪt] *vt (person)* excitar; *(interest, suspicion)* provocar.

excited [ɪkˈsaɪtɪd] *adj* entusiasmado (-da).

excitement [ɪkˈsaɪtmənt] *n (excited feeling)* entusiasmo *m*; *(exciting thing)* emoção *f*.

exciting [ɪkˈsaɪtɪŋ] *adj* emocionante, excitante.

exclaim [ɪkˈskleɪm] *vt & vi* exclamar.

exclamation mark [ˌekskləˈmeɪʃn-] *n (Brit)* ponto *m* de exclamação.

exclamation point [ˌekskləˈmeɪʃn-] *(Am)* = **exclamation mark**.

exclude [ɪkˈskluːd] *vt* excluir.

excluding [ɪk'sklu:dɪŋ] *prep* excluindo.

exclusive [ɪk'sklu:sɪv] *adj* exclusivo(-va) ◆ *n* exclusivo *m*; ~ **of VAT** IVA não incluído.

excrement ['ekskrɪmənt] *n (fml)* excremento *m*.

excruciating [ɪk'skru:ʃɪeɪtɪŋ] *adj* terrível.

excursion [ɪk'skɜ:ʃn] *n* excursão *f*.

excuse [*n* ɪk'skju:s, *vb* ɪk'skju:z] *n* desculpa *f* ◆ *vt (forgive)* desculpar; *(let off)* dispensar; ~ **me!** *(attracting attention)* desculpe!, faz favor!; *(trying to get past)* com licença!; *(as apology)* desculpe!, perdão!

ex-directory *adj (Brit)* que não figura na lista telefônica.

execute ['eksɪkju:t] *vt* executar.

execution [,eksɪ'kju:ʃn] *n* execução *f*.

executive [ɪg'zekjʊtɪv] *adj (suite, travel)* para executivos ◆ *n (person)* executivo *m (-va f)*.

exempt [ɪg'zempt] *adj*: ~ **(from)** isento(-ta) (de).

exemption [ɪg'zempʃn] *n (from taxes)* isenção *f*; *(from exam)* dispensa *f*.

exercise ['eksəsaɪz] *n* exercício *m* ◆ *vi* exercitar-se, fazer exercício; **to do** ~**s** fazer exercícios.

exercise book *n* caderno *m* (de exercícios).

exert [ɪg'zɜ:t] *vt* exercer.

exertion [ɪg'zɜ:ʃn] *n* esforço *m*.

exhale [eks'heɪl] *vt & vi* exalar.

exhaust [ɪg'zɔ:st] *vt* esgotar ◆ *n*: ~ **(pipe)** cano *m* de descarga *(Br)*, tubo *m* de escape *(Port)*.

exhausted [ɪg'zɔ:stɪd] *adj* exausto (-ta).

exhausting [ɪg'zɔ:stɪŋ] *adj* exaustivo(-va).

exhibit [ɪg'zɪbɪt] *n (in museum, gallery)* objeto *m* exposto ◆ *vt (in exhibition)* exibir.

exhibition [,eksɪ'bɪʃn] *n (of art)* exposição *f*.

exhilarating [ɪg'zɪləreɪtɪŋ] *adj* excitante.

exile ['eksaɪl] *n (condition)* exílio *m* ◆ *vt*: **to** ~ **sb from** exilar alguém de; **in** ~ no exílio.

exist [ɪg'zɪst] *vi* existir.

existence [ɪg'zɪstəns] *n* existência *f*; **to be in** ~ existir.

existing [ɪg'zɪstɪŋ] *adj* existente.

exit ['eksɪt] *n* saída *f* ◆ *vi* sair.

exorbitant [ɪg'zɔ:bɪtənt] *adj* exorbitante.

exotic [ɪg'zɒtɪk] *adj* exótico(-ca).

expand [ɪk'spænd] *vi (in size)* expandir-se; *(in number)* aumentar.

expansion [ɪk'spænʃn] *n (in size)* expansão *f*; *(in number)* aumento *m*.

expect [ɪk'spekt] *vt* esperar; **to** ~ **to do sthg** esperar fazer algo; **to** ~ **sb to do sthg** esperar que alguém faça algo; **to be** ~**ing** *(be pregnant)* estar grávida.

expectant [ɪk'spektənt] *adj (crowd, person)* expectante.

expectant mother *n* futura mãe *f*.

expectation [,ekspek'teɪʃn] *n (hope)* esperança *f*; **it's my** ~ **that ...** creio que ...; **against** OR **contrary to all** ~**s** contra todas as expectativas, ao contrário do que seria de esperar.

expedition [,ekspɪ'dɪʃn] *n* expedição *f*.

expel [ɪk'spel] *vt (from school)* expulsar.

expenditure [ɪk'spendɪtʃə*r*] *n (of money)* despesa *f*; *(of energy, resource)* gasto *m*, consumo *m*.

expense [ɪk'spens] *n* gasto *m*, despesa *f*; **at the** ~ **of** à custa de.

 expenses *npl (of business person)* gastos *mpl*, despesas *fpl*.

expensive [ɪk'spensɪv] *adj* caro(-ra).

experience [ɪk'spɪərɪəns] *n* experiência *f* ◆ *vt* passar por.

experienced [ɪk'spɪərɪənst] *adj* com experiência, experiente.

experiment [ɪk'sperɪmənt] *n* experiência *f* ◆ *vi* experimentar.

expert ['ekspɜ:t] *adj (advice, treatment)* especializado(-da) ◆ *n* perito *m (-ta f)*.

expertise [,ekspɜ:'ti:z] *n* perícia *f*, competência *f*.

expire [ɪk'spaɪə*r*] *vi* caducar.

expiry date [ɪk'spaɪərɪ-] *n* prazo *m* de validade.

explain [ɪk'spleɪn] *vt* explicar.

explanation [,eksplə'neɪʃn] *n* explicação *f*.

explicit [ɪk'splɪsɪt] *adj* explícito(-ta).

explode [ɪk'spləʊd] *vi* explodir.

exploit [ɪk'splɔɪt] *vt* explorar.

exploitation [,eksplɔɪ'teɪʃn] *n* exploração *f*.

exploration [,eksplə'reɪʃn] *n* exploração *f*.

explore [ɪk'splɔ:*r*] *vt* explorar.

explorer [ɪk'splɔ:rə*r*] *n* explorador *m (-ra f)*.

explosion [ɪk'spləʊʒn] *n* explosão *f*.

explosive [ɪkˈspləʊsɪv] *n* explosivo *m*.
export [*n* ˈekspɔːt, *vb* ɪkˈspɔːt] *n* exportação *f* ♦ *vt* exportar.
expose [ɪkˈspəʊz] *vt* expor.
exposed [ɪkˈspəʊzd] *adj* (*place*) desprotegido(-da).
exposure [ɪkˈspəʊʒəʳ] *n* (*photograph*) fotografia *f*; (*to heat, radiation*) exposição *f*; **to die of ~** morrer de frio OR por exposição ao frio.
exposure meter *n* fotômetro *m*.
express [ɪkˈspres] *adj* (*letter, delivery*) urgente; (*train*) rápido(-da) ♦ *n* (*train*) expresso *m* ♦ *vt* exprimir ♦ *adv*: **send it ~** envie-o pelo serviço mais rápido.
expression [ɪkˈspreʃn] *n* expressão *f*.
expressive [ɪkˈspresɪv] *adj* expressivo(-va).
expressly [ɪkˈspreslɪ] *adv* expressamente.
expressway [ɪkˈspresweɪ] *n* (*Am*) auto-estrada *f*.
exquisite [ɪkˈskwɪzɪt] *adj* (*features, manners*) delicado(-da); (*painting, jewellery*) magnífico(-ca); (*taste*) requintado(-da).
extend [ɪkˈstend] *vt* prolongar; (*hand*) estender ♦ *vi* (*stretch*) estender-se.
extension [ɪkˈstenʃn] *n* (*of building*) anexo *m*; (*for phone*) ramal *m* (*Br*), extensão *f* (*Port*); (*for permit*) prolongamento *m*, prorrogação *f*; (*for essay*) prolongamento do prazo de entrega.
extension lead *n* extensão *f*.
extensive [ɪkˈstensɪv] *adj* vasto(-ta).
extensively [ɪkˈstensɪvlɪ] *adv* extensivamente.
extent [ɪkˈstent] *n* (*of damage*) dimensão *f*; (*of knowledge*) grau *m*; **to a certain ~** até certo ponto; **to what ~ ...?** em que medida ...?
exterior [ɪkˈstɪərɪəʳ] *adj* exterior ♦ *n* (*of car, building*) exterior *m*.
exterminate [ɪkˈstɜːmɪneɪt] *vt* exterminar.
external [ɪkˈstɜːnl] *adj* externo(-na).
extinct [ɪkˈstɪŋkt] *adj* extinto(-ta).
extinction [ɪkˈstɪŋkʃn] *n* extinção *f*.
extinguish [ɪkˈstɪŋgwɪʃ] *vt* (*fire, cigarette*) apagar.
extinguisher [ɪkˈstɪŋgwɪʃəʳ] *n* extintor *m*.
extortionate [ɪkˈstɔːʃnət] *adj* exorbitante.
extra [ˈekstrə] *adj* extra (*inv*) ♦ *n* extra *m* ♦ *adv* (*more*) mais, extra; **be ~ care-**

-ful! tenha muito cuidado!; **an ~ special offer** uma oferta extremamente especial; **we'll have to try ~ hard** temos de nos esforçar ainda mais; **~ charge** suplemento *m*; **~ large** XL.
❑ **extras** *npl* (*in price*) extras *mpl*.
extract [*n* ˈekstrækt, *vb* ɪkˈstrækt] *n* (*of yeast, malt etc*) extrato *m*; (*from book, opera*) trecho *m* ♦ *vt* (*tooth*) arrancar.
extractor fan [ɪkˈstræktə-] *n* (*Brit*) exaustor *m*.
extradite [ˈekstrədaɪt] *vt*: **to ~ sb from/to** extraditar alguém de/para.
extraordinary [ɪkˈstrɔːdnrɪ] *adj* extraordinário(-ria).
extravagance [ɪkˈstrævəgəns] *n* extravagância *f*.
extravagant [ɪkˈstrævəgənt] *adj* extravagante.
extreme [ɪkˈstriːm] *adj* extremo(-ma) ♦ *n* extremo *m*.
extremely [ɪkˈstriːmlɪ] *adv* extremamente.
extremist [ɪkˈstriːmɪst] *adj* extremista ♦ *n* extremista *mf*.
extricate [ˈekstrɪkeɪt] *vt*: **to ~ sthg from** retirar algo de; **to ~ o.s. from** livrar-se de.
extrovert [ˈekstrəvɜːt] *n* extrovertido *m* (-da *f*).
exuberance [ɪgˈzjuːbərəns] *n* exuberância *f*.
eye [aɪ] *n* olho *m*; (*of needle*) buraco *m* ♦ *vt* olhar para; **to keep an ~ on** vigiar.
eyeball [ˈaɪbɔːl] *n* globo *m* ocular.
eyebath [ˈaɪbɑːθ] *n* copo *m* (para lavar os olhos).
eyebrow [ˈaɪbraʊ] *n* sobrancelha *f*.
eyebrow pencil *n* lápis *m inv* de sobrancelhas.
eye drops *npl* colírio *m* (*Br*), gotas *fpl* para os olhos (*Port*).
eyeglasses [ˈaɪglɑːsɪz] *npl* (*Am*) óculos *mpl*.
eyelash [ˈaɪlæʃ] *n* pestana *f*.
eyelid [ˈaɪlɪd] *n* pálpebra *f*.
eyeliner [ˈaɪlaɪnəʳ] *n* lápis *m inv* para os olhos.
eye shadow *n* sombra *f* para os olhos.
eyesight [ˈaɪsaɪt] *n* vista *f*.
eyesore [ˈaɪsɔː] *n* monstruosidade *f*.
eyestrain [ˈaɪstreɪn] *n* astenopia *f*, vista *f* cansada.
eye test *n* exame *m* de vista.
eyewitness [ˌaɪˈwɪtnɪs] *n* testemunha *mf* ocular.

F

F (*abbr of Fahrenheit*) F.
fable ['feɪbl] *n* fábula *f*.
fabric ['fæbrɪk] *n (cloth)* tecido *m*.
fabulous ['fæbjuləs] *adj* fabuloso (-osa).
facade [fə'sɑːd] *n* fachada *f*.
face [feɪs] *n* cara *f*, face *f*, rosto *m*; *(of cliff, mountain)* lado *m*; *(of clock, watch)* mostrador *m* ♦ *vt* encarar; **the hotel ~s the harbour** o hotel dá para o porto; **to be ~d with** ver-se perante.
❑ **face up to** *vt fus* fazer face a.
facecloth ['feɪsklɒθ] *n (Brit)* toalhinha *f* de rosto.
face cream *n* creme *m* facial.
face-lift *n* (operação) plástica *f*; **they've given the building a ~** eles reformaram a fachada do edifício.
face powder *n* pó-de-arroz *m*.
face value *n* valor *m* nominal; **to take sthg at ~** levar algo ao pé da letra.
facial ['feɪʃl] *n* limpeza *f* facial OR de pele.
facilitate [fə'sɪlɪteɪt] *vt (fml)* facilitar.
facilities [fə'sɪlɪtiːz] *npl* instalações *fpl*.
facing ['feɪsɪŋ] *adj* oposto(-osta).
facsimile [fæk'sɪmɪlɪ] *n* fac-símile *m*.
fact [fækt] *n* fato *m*; **in ~** na realidade.
factor ['fæktər] *n* fator *m*; **~ ten suntan lotion** bronzeador com fator de proteção dez.
factory ['fæktərɪ] *n* fábrica *f*.
factual ['fæktʃuəl] *adj* fatual.
faculty ['fækltɪ] *n (at university)* faculdade *f*.
fad [fæd] *n (of person)* mania *f* (passageira); *(of society)* moda *f* (passageira).
fade [feɪd] *vi (light, sound)* desaparecer; *(flower)* murchar; *(jeans, wallpaper)* desbotar.
faded ['feɪdɪd] *adj (jeans)* ruço(-ça),

desbotado(-da).
fag [fæg] *n (Brit: inf: cigarette)* cigarro *m*.
Fahrenheit ['færənhaɪt] *adj* Farenheit *(inv)*.
fail [feɪl] *vt (exam)* reprovar ♦ *vi (not succeed)* fracassar; *(in exam)* não passar; *(engine)* falhar; **to ~ to do sthg** *(not do)* não fazer algo.
failing ['feɪlɪŋ] *n* defeito *m* ♦ *prep*: **~ that** senão.
failure ['feɪljər] *n* fracasso *m*; *(unsuccessful person)* fracassado *m* (-da *f*); **~ to comply with the regulations ...** o não cumprimento do regulamento ....
faint [feɪnt] *adj (sound)* fraco(-ca); *(colour)* claro(-ra); *(outline)* vago(-ga); *(dizzy)* tonto(-ta) ♦ *vi* desmaiar; **I haven't the ~est idea** não faço a menor idéia.
fair [feər] *adj (decision, trial, result)* justo(-ta); *(judge, person)* imparcial; *(quite large, good)* considerável; *(scu)* suficiente; *(hair, person)* louro(-ra); *(skin)* claro(-ra); *(weather)* bom (boa) ♦ *n* feira *f*; **~ enough!** está bem!
fairground ['feəgraund] *n* espaço onde se realiza feiras beneficentes ou culturais.
fair-haired [ˌ'heəd] *adj* louro(ra).
fairly ['feəlɪ] *adv (quite)* bastante.
fairness ['feənɪs] *n (of decision, trial, result)* justiça *f*; *(of judge, person)* imparcialidade *f*, equidade *f*.
fairy ['feərɪ] *n* fada *f*.
fairy tale *n* conto *m* de fadas.
faith [feɪθ] *n* fé *f*.
faithful ['feɪθful] *adj* fiel.
faithfully ['feɪθfulɪ] *adv*: **Yours ~** Atenciosamente.
fake [feɪk] *n (false thing)* imitação *f* ♦ *vt (signature, painting)* falsificar.
falcon ['fɔːlkən] *n* falcão *m*.
Falkland Islands ['fɔːklənd-] *npl*:

the ~ as Ilhas Malvinas.
Falklands [ˈfɔːkləndz] = **Falkland Islands**.

fall [fɔːl] (pt **fell**, pp **fallen** [ˈfɔːln]) vi cair; (occur) calhar ◆ n queda f; (Am: autumn) outono m; **to ~ asleep** adormecer; **to ~ ill** adoecer; **to ~ in love** apaixonar-se.
⊔ **falls** npl (waterfall) quedas fpl d'água, cataratas fpl.
⊔ **fall behind** vi (with work, rent) atrasar-se.
⊔ **fall down** vi (lose balance) cair.
⊔ **fall off** vi cair.
⊐ **fall out** vi (argue) zangar-se; **my tooth fell out** meu dente caiu.
⊔ **fall over** vi cair.
⊔ **fall through** vi (plan, deal) falhar.
fallible [ˈfæləbl] adj falível.
fallout [ˈfɔːlaut] n (radiation) poeira f radioativa.
false [fɔːls] adj falso(-sa).
false alarm n alarme m falso.
falsely [ˈfɔːlsli] adv (accuse, imprison) injustamente; (smile, laugh) falsamente.
false teeth npl dentes mpl postiços, dentadura f (postiça).
falsify [ˈfɔːlsɪfaɪ] vt falsificar.
falter [ˈfɔːltər] vi (move unsteadily) vacilar; (become weaker) enfraquecer; (hesitate, lose confidence) hesitar.
fame [feɪm] n fama f.
familiar [fəˈmɪljər] adj (known) familiar; (informal) íntimo(-ma) (demais); **to be ~ with** (know) conhecer, estar familiarizado(-da) com.
familiarity [fəˌmɪlɪˈærətɪ] n familiaridade f.
familiarize [fəˈmɪljəraɪz] vt: **to ~ o.s. with sthg** familiarizar-se com algo; **to ~ sb with sthg** familiarizar alguém com algo.
family [ˈfæmlɪ] n família f ◆ adj (pack) (com) tamanho familiar; (film, holiday) para toda a família.
family doctor n médico m (-ca f) de família.
family planning clinic [-ˈplænɪŋ-] n consultas fpl de planejamento familiar.
family room n (at hotel) quarto m para família; (at pub, airport) sala reservada para famílias com crianças pequenas.
famine [ˈfæmɪn] n fome f.

famished [ˈfæmɪʃt] adj (inf) esfomeado(-da).
famous [ˈfeɪməs] adj famoso(-osa).
fan [fæn] n (held in hand) leque m; (electric) ventoinha f; (enthusiast, supporter) fã mf.
fanatic [fəˈnætɪk] n fanático m (-ca f).
fan belt n correia f do ventilador (Br), correia f de ventoinha (Port).
fancy [ˈfænsɪ] vt (inf) (feel like) ter vontade de; (be attracted to) gostar de ◆ adj (elaborate) complicado(-da); **~ (that)!** quem diria!; **~ going to the cinema?** que tal ir ao cinema?
fancy dress n fantasia f (Br), disfarce m (Port).
fancy-dress party n baile m à fantasia (Br), baile m de máscaras (Port).
fanfare [ˈfænfeər] n fanfarra f.
fang [fæŋ] n dente m.
fan heater n aquecedor m (de ventoinha), termo-ventilador m.
fanlight [ˈfænlaɪt] n (Brit) bandeira f (de porta).
fantasize [ˈfæntəsaɪz] vi fantasiar.
fantastic [fænˈtæstɪk] adj fantástico (-ca).
fantasy [ˈfæntəsɪ] n fantasia f.
far [fuːr] (compar **further** OR **farther**, superl **furthest** OR **farthest**) adv (in distance, time) longe; (in degree) muito ◆ adj (end, side) extremo(-ma); **how ~ did you go?** até onde você foi?; **how ~ is it (to London)?** qual é a distância (até Londres)?; **as ~ as** (place) até; **as ~ as I'm concerned** no que me diz respeito; **as ~ as I know** que eu saiba; **~ better** muito melhor; **by ~** de longe; **so ~** (until now) até agora; **to go too ~** ir longe demais.
faraway [ˈfuːrəweɪ] adj distante.
farce [fuːs] n farsa f.
fare [feər] n (on bus, train etc) bilhete m; (fml: food) comida f ◆ vi sair-se.
Far East n: the ~ o Extremo Oriente.
fare stage n (Brit) = zona f, parada de ônibus a partir da qual o preço do bilhete aumenta.
farewell [feəˈwel] n despedida f ◆ excl adeus!
farm [fuːm] n fazenda f (Br), quinta f (Port).
farmer [ˈfuːmər] n agricultor m (-ra f), fazendeiro m (-ra f) (Br).
farmhand [ˈfuːmhænd] n lavrador m

(-ra *f*), trabalhador *m* (-ra *f*) agrícola.
farmhouse ['fɑːmhaʊs, *pl* -haʊzɪz] *n* casa *f* de fazenda *(Br)*, casa *f* de quinta *(Port)*.
farming ['fɑːmɪŋ] *n* agricultura *f*.
farmland ['fɑːmlænd] *n* terras *fpl* de lavoura, terrenos *mpl* agrícolas.
farmyard ['fɑːmjɑːd] *n* terreno *m* da fazenda *(Br)*, pátio *m* da quinta *(Port)*.
farther ['fɑːðəʳ] *compar* → **far**.
farthest ['fɑːðəst] *superl* → **far**.
fascinate ['fæsɪneɪt] *vt* fascinar.
fascinating ['fæsɪneɪtɪŋ] *adj* fascinante.
fascination [fæsɪ'neɪʃn] *n* fascínio *m*, fascinação *f*.
fascism ['fæʃɪzm] *n* fascismo *m*.
fashion ['fæʃn] *n* moda *f*; *(manner)* maneira *f*; **to be in ~** estar na moda; **to be out of ~** estar fora de moda.
fashionable ['fæʃnəbl] *adj* na moda.
fashion show *n* desfile *m* de moda.
fast [fɑːst] *adj* *(quick)* rápido(-da); *(clock, watch)* adiantado(-da) ◆ *adv* *(quickly)* depressa, rápido; *(securely)* bem seguro(-ra); **to be ~ asleep** estar dormindo profundamente; **a ~ train** um trem rápido.
fasten ['fɑːsn] *vt* *(belt, coat)* apertar; *(two things)* atar.
fastener ['fɑːsnəʳ] *n* fecho *m*.
fast food *n* comida *f* rápida.
fat [fæt] *adj* gordo(-da) ◆ *n* gordura *f*.
fatal ['feɪtl] *adj* *(accident, disease)* fatal.
fate [feɪt] *n* destino *m*; **to tempt ~** tentar o diabo.
father ['fɑːðəʳ] *n* pai *m*.
Father Christmas *n* *(Brit)* Papai *m* Noel *(Br)*, Pai *m* Natal *(Port)*.
father-in-law *n* sogro *m*.
fathom ['fæðəm] *(pl inv OR* **-s***)* *n* braça *f* ◆ *vt*: **to ~ sthg/sb (out)** compreender algo/alguém.
fatten ['fætn] *vt* engordar.
fattening ['fætnɪŋ] *adj* que engorda.
fatty ['fætɪ] *adj* gorduroso(-osa).
faucet ['fɔːsɪt] *n* *(Am)* torneira *f*.
fault [fɔːlt] *n* *(responsibility)* culpa *f*; *(defect)* falha *f*; **it's your ~** a culpa é sua.
faultless ['fɔːltlɪs] *adj* impecável, perfeito(-ta).
faulty ['fɔːltɪ] *adj* defeituoso(-osa).
fauna ['fɔːnə] *n* fauna *f*.
favor ['feɪvəʳ] *(Am)* = **favour**.
favour ['feɪvəʳ] *n* *(Brit)* *(kind act)* favor

m ◆ *vt* *(Brit)* *(prefer)* favorecer; **to be in ~ of** ser a favor de; **to do sb a ~** fazer um favor a alguém.
favourable ['feɪvrəbl] *adj* favorável.
favourite ['feɪvrɪt] *adj* preferido(-da), favorito(-ta) ◆ *n* preferido *m* (-da *f*), favorito *m* (-ta *f*).
favouritism [feɪvrɪtɪzm] *n* favoritismo *m*.
fawn [fɔːn] *adj* bege *(inv)*.
fax [fæks] *n* fax *m* ◆ *vt* *(document)* mandar por fax; *(person)* mandar um fax para.
fax machine *n* fax *m*.
fax modem *n* fax *m* modem.
fear [fɪəʳ] *n* medo *m* ◆ *vt* *(be afraid of)* ter medo de; **for ~ of** por medo de, com receio de.
fearful ['fɪəfʊl] *adj* *(frightened)* receoso(-osa); *(frightening)* terrível.
fearless ['fɪəlɪs] *adj* destemido(-da).
feasible ['fiːzəbl] *adj* viável.
feast [fiːst] *n* banquete *m*.
feat [fiːt] *n* feito *m*.
feather ['feðəʳ] *n* pena *f*.
feature ['fiːtʃəʳ] *n* *(characteristic)* característica *f*; *(of face)* traço *m*; *(in newspaper)* artigo *m* de fundo; *(on radio, TV)* reportagem *f* ◆ *vt* *(subj: film)* ser protagonizado por.
feature film *n* longa-metragem *f*.
Feb. *(abbr of February)* fev.
February ['februərɪ] *n* fevereiro, → **September**.
fed [fed] *pt & pp* → **feed**.
federal ['fedrəl] *adj* federal.
federation [fedə'reɪʃn] *n* federação *f*.
fed up *adj* farto(-ta); **to be ~ with** estar farto de.
fee [fiː] *n* *(for admission)* preço *m*; *(of doctor, solicitor)* honorários *mpl*; *(of university)* anuidade *f (Br)*, propina *f (Port)*.
feeble ['fiːbl] *adj* fraco(-ca).
feed [fiːd] *(pt & pp* **fed***)* *vt* *(person, animal)* alimentar; *(insert)* inserir.
feedback ['fiːdbæk] *n* *(reaction)* reações *fpl*; *(criticism)* comentários *mpl*; *(electrical noise)* feedback *m*.
feeding bottle ['fiːdɪŋ-] *n* *(Brit)* mamadeira *f (Br)*, biberão *m (Port)*.
feel [fiːl] *(pt & pp* **felt***)* *vt* *(touch)* tocar; *(experience)* sentir; *(think)* achar ◆ *vi* *(have emotion)* sentir-se ◆ *n* *(of material)* toque *m*; **I ~ like a cup of tea** eu quero tomar uma xícara de chá; **to ~ up to doing sthg** sentir-se capaz de fazer

algo; **to ~ cold/hot** sentir frio/calor; **my nose ~s cold** meu nariz está frio.

feeler ['fi:lə'] *n (of insect, snail)* antena *m*.

feeling ['fi:lɪŋ] *n (emotion)* sentimento *m*; *(sensation)* sensação *f*; *(belief)* opinião *f*; **to hurt sb's ~s** magoar alguém.

feet [fi:t] *pl* → **foot**.

fell [fel] *pt* → **fall** ♦ *vt (tree)* abater.

fellow ['feləʊ] *n (man)* cara *m (Br)*, tipo *m (Port)* ♦ *adj*: **my ~ students** os meus colegas.

felt [felt] *pt & pp* → **feel** ♦ *n* feltro *m*.

felt-tip pen *n* caneta *f* pilot *(Br)*, caneta *f* de feltro *(Port)*.

female ['fi:meɪl] *adj* fêmea ♦ *n (animal)* fêmea *f*.

feminine ['femɪnɪn] *adj* feminino (-na).

feminist ['femɪnɪst] *n* feminista *mf*.

fence [fens] *n* cerca *f*, vedação *f*.

fencing ['fensɪŋ] *n (SPORT)* esgrima *f*.

fend [fend] *vi*: **to ~ for o.s.** cuidar de si (mesmo OR próprio).

fender ['fendə'] *n (for fireplace)* guarda-fogo *m*; *(Am: on car)* pára-choques *m inv*.

fennel ['fenl] *n* funcho *m*.

ferment [fə'ment] *vi (wine, beer)* fermentar.

fern [fɜ:n] *n* samambaia *f (Br)*, feto *m (Port)*.

ferocious [fə'rəʊʃəs] *adj* feroz.

ferret ['ferɪt] *n* furão *m*.

Ferris wheel ['ferɪs-] *n* roda *f* gigante.

ferry ['feri] *n* ferry *m*, barco *m* de travessia.

fertile ['fɜ:taɪl] *adj* fértil.

fertilizer ['fɜ:tɪlaɪzə'] *n* adubo *m*, fertilizante *m*.

fervent ['fɜ:vənt] *adj* ferveroso(-osa); *(desire)* ardente.

fester ['festə'] *vi (wound, sore)* criar, supurar.

festival ['festəvl] *n (of music, arts etc)* festival *m*; *(holiday)* feriado *m*, dia *m* festivo.

festive ['festɪv] *adj* festivo(-va).

festive season *n*: **the ~** as festas de fim-de-ano *(Br)*, a quadra natalícia *(Port)*.

festivities [fes'tɪvətɪz] *npl* festividades *fpl*.

feta cheese ['fetə-] *n* queijo de origem grega feito com leite de ovelha.

fetch [fetʃ] *vt (go and get)* ir buscar; *(be sold for)* atingir.

fetching ['fetʃɪŋ] *adj*: **you look very ~ in that dress** esse vestido lhe cai muito bem.

fete [feɪt] *n* festa *f (ao ar livre e normalmente de beneficência)*.

fetus ['fi:təs] = **foetus**.

feud [fju:d] *n* feudo *m* ♦ *vi* lutar.

fever ['fi:və'] *n* febre *f*; **to have a ~** ter febre.

feverish ['fi:vərɪʃ] *adj* febril.

few [fju:] *adj* pouco(-ca) ♦ *pron* poucos *mpl* (-cas *fpl*); **the first ~ times** as primeiras vezes; **a ~** *adj* alguns(algumas) ♦ *pron* alguns *mpl* (algumas *fpl*); **quite a ~** bastantes.

fewer ['fju:ə] *adj & pron* menos.

fewest ['fju:əst] *adj* menos.

fiancé [fɪ'ɒnseɪ] *n* noivo *m*.

fiancée [fɪ'ɒnseɪ] *n* noiva *f*.

fiasco [fɪ'æskəʊ] *(pl -s) n* fiasco *m*.

fib [fɪb] *n (inf)* mentira *f*.

fiber ['faɪbə'] *(Am)* = **fibre**.

fibre ['faɪbə'] *n (Brit)* fibra *f*.

fibreglass ['faɪbəglɑ:s] *n* fibra *f* de vidro.

fickle ['fɪkl] *adj* inconstante, volúvel.

fiction ['fɪkʃn] *n* ficção *f*.

fictitious [fɪk'tɪʃəs] *adj* fictício(-cia).

fiddle ['fɪdl] *n (violin)* rabeca *f* ♦ *vi*: **to ~ with sthg** brincar com algo.

fidget ['fɪdʒɪt] *vi* mexer-se; **stop ~ing!** fica quieto!

field [fi:ld] *n* campo *m*.

field glasses *npl* binóculos *mpl*.

field trip *n* viagem *f* de estudos.

fierce [fɪəs] *adj (animal, person)* feroz; *(storm, heat)* violento(-ta).

fifteen [fɪf'ti:n] *num* quinze, → **six**.

fifteenth [fɪf'ti:nθ] *num* décimo quinto (décima quinta), → **sixth**.

fifth [fɪfθ] *num* quinto(-ta), → **sixth**.

fiftieth ['fɪftɪəθ] *num* qüinquagésimo(-ma), → **sixth**.

fifty ['fɪftɪ] *num* cinquenta, → **six**.

fifty-fifty *adj* cinquenta por cento, fifty-fifty *(inv)* ♦ *adv* a meias, fifty-fifty.

fig [fɪg] *n* figo *m*.

fight [faɪt] *(pt & pp* **fought)** *n (physical clash)* briga *f*, luta *f*; *(argument)* discussão *f*; *(struggle)* luta ♦ *vt (physically)* brigar com, lutar com; *(enemy, crime, injustice)* lutar contra, combater ♦ *vi* *(physically)* brigar, lutar; *(in war)* combater; *(quarrel)* discutir; *(struggle)* lutar; **to have a ~ with sb** brigar com alguém.

❏ **fight back** *vi* defender-se.

❏ **fight off** *vt sep* *(attacker)* repelir *(illness)* lutar contra.

fighter ['faɪtə'] *n* *(plane)* caça *m*; *(soldier)* combatente *m*; *(combative person)* lutador *m* (-ra *f*).

fighting ['faɪtɪŋ] *n* luta *f*.

figurative ['fɪgərətɪv] *adj* figurativo(va).

figure ['fɪgə'] *n* *(number, statistic)* número *m*, valor *m*; *(of person)* silhueta *f*, figura *f*; *(diagram)* figura.

❏ **figure out** *vt sep* *(understand)* perceber, compreender.

Fiji ['fiːdʒiː] *n* Fiji *s*.

file [faɪl] *n* *(document holder)* capa *f*; *(information on person, COMPUT)* dossiê *m* *(Br)*, ficheiro *m* *(Port)*; *(tool)* lixa *f* *(Br)*, lima *f* *(Port)* ◆ *vt* *(complaint)* apresentar; *(petition)* fazer; *(nails)* lixar *(Br)*, limar *(Port)*; **in single ~** em fila indiana.

filing cabinet ['faɪlɪŋ-] *n* arquivo *m*.

fill [fɪl] *vt* *(make full)* encher; *(space)* ocupar; *(role)* desempenhar; *(tooth)* obturar *(Br)*, chumbar *(Port)*.

❏ **fill in** *vt sep* *(form)* preencher.

❏ **fill out** *vt sep* = fill in.

❏ **fill up** *vt sep* encher; **~ her up!** *(with petrol)* ateste!

filled roll [fɪld-] *n* sanduíche *m* *(Br)*, sandes *f* inv *(Port)*.

fillet ['fɪlɪt] *n* filé *m*.

fillet steak *n* filé *m* *(Br)*, bife *m* *(Port)*.

filling ['fɪlɪŋ] *n* *(of cake, sandwich)* recheio *m*; *(in tooth)* obturação *f* *(Br)*, chumbo *m* *(Port)* ◆ *adj* que enche.

filling station *n* posto *m* de gasolina *(Br)*, bombas *fpl* de gasolina *(Port)*.

film [fɪlm] *n* *(at cinema)* filme *m*; *(for camera)* filme *m* *(Br)*, rolo *m* *(Port)* ◆ *vt* filmar.

film star *n* estrela *f* de cinema.

Filofax® ['faɪləʊfæks] *n* organizador *m*, agenda *f* *(de folhas soltas)*.

filter ['fɪltə'] *n* filtro *m*.

filter coffee *n* café *m* *(de cafeteira de filtro)*.

filth [fɪlθ] *n* *(dirt)* sujeira *f*, porcaria *f*.

filthy ['fɪlθɪ] *adj* nojento(-ta).

fin [fɪn] *n* barbatana *f*.

final ['faɪnl] *adj* *(last)* último(-ma);

(decision, offer) final ◆ *n* final *f*.

finalist ['faɪnəlɪst] *n* finalista *mf*.

finally ['faɪnəlɪ] *adv* finalmente.

finance [*n* 'faɪnæns, *vb* faɪ'næns] *n* *(money)* financiamento *m*; *(management of money)* finanças *fpl* ◆ *vt* financiar.

❏ **finances** *npl* finanças *fpl*.

financial [fɪ'nænʃl] *adj* financeiro (-ra).

find [faɪnd] *(pt & pp found)* *vt* encontrar; *(find out)* descobrir; *(think)* achar, considerar ◆ *n* descoberta *f*; **to ~ the time to do sthg** arranjar tempo para fazer algo.

❏ **find out** *vt sep* *(fact, truth)* descobrir ◆ *vi*: **to ~ out (about sthg)** *(learn)* ficar sabendo (de algo), descobrir (algo); *(get information)* informar-se (sobre algo).

fine [faɪn] *adj* *(good)* bom (boa); *(thin)* fino(-na); *(wine, food)* excelente ◆ *adv* *(thinly)* finamente; *(well)* bem ◆ *n* multa *f* ◆ *vt* multar; **I'm ~** estou bem; **it's ~** está bem.

fine art *n* belas-artes *fpl*.

finger ['fɪŋgə'] *n* dedo *m*.

fingernail ['fɪŋgəneɪl] *n* unha *f*.

fingertip ['fɪŋgətɪp] *n* ponta *f* do dedo.

finish ['fɪnɪʃ] *n* *(end)* fim *m*, final *m*; *(on furniture)* acabamento *m* ◆ *vt & vi* acabar, terminar; **to ~ doing sthg** acabar de fazer algo.

❏ **finish off** *vt sep* acabar, terminar.

❏ **finish up** *vi* acabar, terminar; **to ~ up doing sthg** acabar por fazer algo.

Finland ['fɪnlənd] *n* Finlândia *f*.

Finn [fɪn] *n* finlandês *m* (-esa *f*).

Finnan haddock ['fɪnən-] *n* *(Scot)* hadoque *m* defumado *(prato típico escocês)*.

Finnish ['fɪnɪʃ] *adj* finlandês(-esa) ◆ *n* *(language)* finlandês *m*.

fir [fɜː'] *n* abeto *m*.

fire ['faɪə'] *n* fogo *m*; *(uncontrolled)* incêndio *m*, fogo; *(made for cooking, heat)* fogueira *f*; *(device)* aquecedor *m* ◆ *vt* *(gun)* disparar; *(from job)* despedir; **on ~** em chamas; **to catch ~** incendiar-se, pegar fogo; **to make a ~** acender uma fogueira.

fire alarm *n* alarme *m* contra incêndios.

fire brigade *n* *(Brit)* corpo *m* de bombeiros.

fire department *(Am)* = fire brigade.

fire engine *n* carro *m* de bombeiros.

fire escape *n* escadas *fpl* de incêndio.

fire exit *n* saída *f* de emergência.

fire extinguisher *n* extintor *m*.

fire hazard *n*: it's a ~ constitui um risco OR perigo de incêndio.

fireman ['faɪəmən] (*pl* -men [-mən]) *n* bombeiro *m*.

fireplace [faɪəpleɪs] *n* lareira *f*.

fire regulations *npl* normas *fpl* de segurança em caso de incêndio.

fire station *n* posto *m* de bombeiros *(Br)*, estação *f* dos bombeiros *(Port)*.

firewood ['faɪəwʊd] *n* lenha *f*.

firework display ['faɪəwɜːk-] *n* queima *f* de fogos-de-artifício.

fireworks ['faɪəwɜːks] *npl (rockets)* fogos-de-artifício *mpl*.

firm [fɜːm] *adj* firme ♦ *n* empresa *f*.

first [fɜːst] *adj* primeiro(-ra) ♦ *adv* primeiro; *(for the first time)* pela primeira vez ♦ *n (event)* estréia *f* ♦ *pron*: the ~ o primeiro (a primeira); I'll do it ~ thing (in the morning) vou fazer isso logo de manhã; ~ (gear) primeira (mudança); for the ~ time pela primeira vez; the ~ of January o dia um de janeiro; at ~ no princípio; ~ of all antes de mais nada.

first aid *n* pronto socorro *m (Br)*, primeiros-socorros *mpl (Port)*.

first-aid kit *n* estojo *m* de pronto socorro *(Br)*, estojo *m* de primeiros-socorros *(Port)*.

first class *n (mail)* = correspondência *f* prioritária *(Br)*, ~ correio-azul *m (Port)*; *(on train, plane, ship)* primeira classe *f*.

first-class *adj (stamp)* = para correio prioritário *(Br)*, = para correio-azul *(Port)*; *(ticket, work)* de primeira classe.

first floor *n (Brit: floor above ground floor)* primeiro andar *m*; *(Am: ground floor)* andar *m* térreo *(Br)*, rés-do-chão *m (Port)*.

firstly ['fɜːstlɪ] *adv* em primeiro lugar.

First World War *n*: the ~ a Primeira Guerra Mundial.

fish [fɪʃ] (*pl inv*) *n* peixe *m* ♦ *vi* pescar.

fish and chips *n* filé de peixe com batatas fritas.

fishcake ['fɪʃkeɪk] *n* croquete *m* de peixe.

fisherman ['fɪʃəmən] (*pl* -men [-mən]) *n* pescador *m*.

fish farm *n* viveiro *m* de peixes.

fish fingers *npl (Brit)* espécie de croquete alongado de peixe congelado.

fishing ['fɪʃɪŋ] *n* pesca *f*; to go ~ ir pescar.

fishing boat *n* barco *m* de pesca.

fishing rod *n* vara *f* de pescar *(Br)*, cana *f* de pesca *(Port)*.

fishmonger's ['fɪʃmʌŋɡəz] *n (shop)* peixaria *f*.

fish sticks *(Am)* = fish fingers.

fish supper *n (Scot)* filé de peixe com batatas fritas.

fist [fɪst] *n* punho *m*.

fit [fɪt] *adj (healthy)* em forma ♦ *vt (be right size for)* servir a; *(a lock, kitchen, bath)* instalar; *(insert)* encaixar ♦ *vi (clothes, shoes)* servir; *(in space)* caber ♦ *n (of clothes, shoes)* tamanho *m*; *(epileptic, of coughing, anger)* ataque *m*; to be ~ for sthg ser adequado para algo; ~ to eat comestível; it doesn't ~ *(jacket, skirt)* não serve; *(object)* não cabe; to get ~ pôr-se em forma; to keep ~ manter-se em forma, manter a forma.
⏋ fit in *vt sep (find time to do)* arranjar tempo para ♦ *vi (belong)* encaixar.

fitness [fɪtnɪs] *n (health)* forma *f* física.

fitted carpet [fɪtəd-] *n* carpete *m (Br)*, alcatifa *f (Port)*.

fitted kitchen [fɪtəd-] *n (Brit)* cozinha *f* com armários embutidos.

fitted sheet [fɪtəd-] *n* lençol *m* capa.

fitting room [fɪtɪŋ-] *n* cabine *f* de provas, vestiário *m*.

five [faɪv] *num* cinco, → six.

fiver ['faɪvəʳ] *n (Brit) (inf) (£5)* cinco libras *fpl*; *(£5 note)* nota *f* de cinco libras.

fix [fɪks] *vt (attach, decide on)* fixar; *(mend)* arranjar; *(drink, food)* arranjar, preparar; *(arrange)* combinar, organizar.
⏋ fix up *vt sep*: to ~ sb up with sthg arranjar algo para alguém.

fixed [fɪkst] *adj* fixo(-xa).

fixture ['fɪkstʃəʳ] *n (SPORT)* encontro *m*; ~s and fittings equipamento *m* doméstico *(armários de cozinha, W.C., luminárias, etc)*.

fizz [fɪz] *vi (drink)* borbulhar.

fizzy ['fɪzɪ] *adj* gasoso(-osa).

flabbergasted [ˈflæbəgɑːstɪd] adj boquiaberto(-ta).

flabby [ˈflæbɪ] adj balofo(-fa), flácido (-da).

flag [flæg] n bandeira f.

flagpole [ˈflægpəʊl] n mastro m.

flagrant [ˈfleɪgrənt] adj flagrante.

flagstone [ˈflægstəʊn] n laje f.

flair [fleəʳ] n (stylishness) estilo m; (talent): **to have a ~ for sthg** ter queda para algo.

flake [fleɪk] n (of snow) floco m ◆ vi desfazer-se.

flamboyant [flæmˈbɔɪənt] adj extravagante.

flame [fleɪm] n chama f.

flamingo [fləˈmɪŋgəʊ] n flamingo m.

flammable [ˈflæməbl] adj inflamável.

flan [flæn] n torta f (Br), tarte f (Port).

flannel [ˈflænl] n (material) flanela f; (Brit: for washing face) luva f de banho. ⏝ **flannels** npl calças fpl de flanela.

flap [flæp] n (of envelope) dobra f; (of tent) porta f; (of pocket) pala f ◆ vt (wings) bater.

flapjack [ˈflæpdʒæk] n (Brit: cake) biscoito ou bolo pequeno feito de flocos de aveia, manteiga e mel ao qual se podem juntar frutos secos, chocolate, etc.

flare [fleəʳ] n (signal) sinal m luminoso.

flared [fleəd] adj (trousers) à boca de sino; (skirt) de roda, evasé.

flash [flæʃ] n (of light) raio m; (for camera) flash m ◆ vi (light) brilhar; **a ~ of lightning** um relâmpago, um clarão; **to ~ one's headlights** fazer sinais com os faróis.

flashback [ˈflæʃbæk] n flashback m.

flashbulb [ˈflæʃbʌlb] n flash m.

flashgun [ˈflæʃgʌn] n disparador m OR botão m do flash.

flashlight [ˈflæʃlaɪt] n lanterna f.

flashy [ˈflæʃɪ] adj (inf) vistoso(-osa), espalhafatoso(-osa).

flask [flɑːsk] n (Thermos) garrafa f térmica (Br), termo m (Port); (hip flask) cantil m.

flat [flæt] adj (level) plano(-na); (battery) descarregado(-da); (drink) choco (choca), que perdeu o gás; (rate, fee) fixo(-xa) ◆ n (Brit: apartment) apartamento m ◆ adv: **to lie ~** estender-se; **a ~ (tyre)** um pneu vazio OR em baixo; **~ out** a toda a velocidade, até não poder mais.

flatly [ˈflætlɪ] adv (absolutely) categoricamente.

flatmate [ˈflætmeɪt] n (Brit) colega mf de apartamento.

flatten [ˈflætn] vt (make flat) alisar. ⏝ **flatten out** vt sep alisar.

flatter [ˈflætəʳ] vt lisonjear, bajular.

flattering [ˈflætərɪŋ] adj (remark, offer) lisonjeiro(-ra); (dress, colour, neckline) favorecedor(-ra).

flattery [ˈflætərɪ] n lisonja f.

flaunt [flɔːnt] vt exibir.

flavor [ˈfleɪvəʳ] (Am) = flavour.

flavour [ˈfleɪvəʳ] n (Brit) sabor m.

flavoured [ˈfleɪvəd] adj aromatizado (-da); **chocolate-~** com sabor de chocolate.

flavouring [ˈfleɪvərɪŋ] n aromatizante m.

flaw [flɔː] n (in plan) falha f; (in glass, china) defeito m.

flea [fliː] n pulga f.

flea market n mercado m das pulgas (Br), feira f da ladra (Port).

flee [fliː] (pt & pp **fled** [fled]) vt fugir de ◆ vi fugir.

fleece [fliːs] n (downy material) velo m, fibra muito macia usada para fazer e forrar casacos de inverno.

fleet [fliːt] n frota f.

Flemish [ˈflemɪʃ] adj flamengo(-ga) ◆ n (language) flamengo m.

flesh [fleʃ] n (of person, animal) carne f; (of fruit, vegetable) polpa f.

flew [fluː] pt → fly.

flex [fleks] n cabo m elétrico.

flexible [ˈfleksəbl] adj flexível.

flick [flɪk] vt (a switch) carregar em; (with finger) dar um piparote em. ⏝ **flick through** vt fus folhear.

flick knife n (Brit) navalha f de ponta em mola.

flies [flaɪz] npl (of trousers) braguilha f, fecho m.

flight [flaɪt] n vôo m; **a ~ (of stairs)** um lance de escadas.

flight attendant n (female) aeromoça f (Br), hospedeira f de bordo (Port); (male) comissário m de bordo.

flight crew n tripulação f (Br), pessoal m de bordo (Port).

flight deck n (of aircraft) cabine f de controle.

flimsy [ˈflɪmzɪ] adj (object) frágil; (clothes) leve.

fling [flɪŋ] (*pt & pp* **flung**) *vt* atirar.

flint [flɪnt] *n* (*of lighter*) pedra *f*.

flip [flɪp] *vt* (*pancake, omelette, record*) virar; **to ~ a coin** tirar cara ou coroa.

❏ **flip on** *vt sep* (*switch*) ligar.

❏ **flip off** *vt sep* (*switch*) desligar.

flip-flop [flɪp-] *n* (*Brit*) sandália *f* japonesa (*Br*), chinelo *m* de dedo (*Port*).

flipper [flɪpə'] *n* barbatana *f*.

flirt [flɜ:t] *vi*: **to ~ (with sb)** flertar (com alguém).

flirtatious [flɜ:'teɪʃəs] *adj* namorador(-ra).

float [fləut] *n* (*for swimming, fishing*) bóia *f*; (*in procession*) carro *m*; (*drink*) bebida servida com uma bola de sorvete ◆ *vi* flutuar.

flock [flɒk] *n* (*of birds*) bando *m*; (*of sheep*) rebanho *m* ◆ *vi* (*people*) afluir.

flood [flʌd] *n* enchente *f*, inundação *f* ◆ *vt* inundar ◆ *vi* transbordar.

flooding [flʌdɪŋ] *n* cheia *f*, inundação *f*.

floodlight [flʌdlaɪt] *n* holofote *m*.

floor [flɔ:'] *n* (*of room*) chão *m*; (*storey*) andar *m*; (*of nightclub*) pista *f*.

floorboard [flɔ:bɔ:d] *n* tábua *f* corrida.

floor show *n* espetáculo *m* de cabaré.

flop [flɒp] *n* (*inf*) fracasso *m*.

floppy [flɒpɪ] *adj* mole.

floppy disk [flɒpɪ-] *n* disquete *f*.

flora [flɔ:rə] *n* flora *f*.

floral [flɔ:rəl] *adj* (*pattern*) de flores.

Florida Keys [flɒrɪdə-] *npl*: **the ~** ilhas situadas ao largo da Flórida.

florist's [flɒrɪsts] *n* (*shop*) florista *f*.

flour [flauə'] *n* farinha *f*.

flourish [flʌrɪʃ] *vi* florescer ◆ *vt* agitar, brandir.

flow [fləu] *n* corrente *f* ◆ *vi* correr.

flower [flauə'] *n* flor *f*.

flowerbed [flauəbed] *n* canteiro *m*.

flowerpot [flauəpɒt] *n* vaso *m*.

flowery [flauərɪ] *adj* florido(-da).

flown [fləun] *pp* → **fly**.

fl oz *abbr* = **fluid ounce**.

flu [flu:] *n* gripe *f*.

fluctuate [flʌktʃueɪt] *vi* flutuar, variar.

fluency [flu:ənsɪ] *n* fluência *f*.

fluent [flu:ənt] *adj*: **to be ~ in Portuguese, to speak ~ Portuguese** falar português fluentemente.

fluff [flʌf] *n* (*on clothes*) pêlo *m*.

fluffy [flʌfɪ] *adj* (*kitten*) peludo(-da); (*fur, jumper*) macio(-cia); (*toy*) de pelúcia.

fluid [flu:ɪd] *n* fluido *m*.

fluid ounce [flu:ɪd-] *n* = 0,03 litros.

fluke [flu:k] *n* (*inf*) acaso *m*.

flume [flu:m] *n* escorrega *m* aquático, rampa *f*.

flung [flʌŋ] *pt & pp* → **fling**.

flunk [flʌŋk] *vt* (*Am: inf: exam*) reprovar em.

fluorescent [fluə'resənt] *adj* fluorescente.

flush [flʌʃ] *vi* (*toilet*) funcionar ◆ *vt*: **to ~ the toilet** dar descarga (*Br*), puxar o autoclismo (*Port*).

flushed [flʌʃt] *adj* (*red-faced*) corado(-da).

flustered [flʌstəd] *adj* agitado(-da).

flute [flu:t] *n* flauta *f*.

fly [flaɪ] (*pt* **flew**, *pp* **flown**) *n* (*insect*) mosca *f*; (*of trousers*) braguilha *f*, fecho *m* ◆ *vt* (*plane, helicopter*) pilotar; (*travel by*) viajar em OR com; (*transport*) enviar por avião ◆ *vi* (*bird, insect, plane*) voar; (*passenger*) viajar de avião; (*pilot a plane*) pilotar; (*flag*) estar hasteado(-da).

fly-drive *n* férias cujo preço inclui a viagem de avião e o aluguel de um carro.

flying [flaɪɪŋ] *n*: **I'm terrified of ~** tenho medo de andar de avião.

flying saucer *n* disco *m* voador.

flying visit *n* visita *f* muito curta, visita de médico.

flyover [flaɪ.əuvə'] *n* (*Brit*) viaduto *m*.

flypaper [flaɪ.peɪpə'] *n* papel *m* mata-moscas.

flysheet [flaɪʃi:t] *n* cobertura exterior de barraca de acampar.

fly spray *n* inseticida *m*.

FM *n* FM *f*.

foal [fəul] *n* potro *m*.

foam [fəum] *n* espuma *f*.

focus [fəukəs] *n* (*of camera*) foco *m* ◆ *vi* (*with camera, binoculars*) focar; **in ~** focado; **out of ~** desfocado.

fodder [fɒdə'] *n* ração *f*, forragem *f*.

foe [fəu] *n* inimigo *m* (-ga *f*).

foetus [fi:təs] *n* feto *m*.

fog [fɒg] *n* nevoeiro *m*, neblina *f*.

fogbound [fɒgbaund] *adj* parado (-da) por causa do nevoeiro.

foggy [fɒgɪ] *adj* (*weather*) de nevoeiro.

foghorn ['fɒghɔːn] *n* sirene *f* de nevoeiro.

fog lamp *n* farol *m* de neblina.

foil [fɔɪl] *n* (*thin metal*) papel *m* OR folha *f* de alumínio.

fold [fəʊld] *n* dobra *f* ♦ *vt* (*paper, material*) dobrar; (*wrap*) envolver; **to ~ one's arms** cruzar os braços.

⏟ **fold up** *vi* (*chair, bed*) dobrar.

folder ['fəʊldə^r] *n* pasta *f*.

folding ['fəʊldɪŋ] *adj* (*chair, table, bicycle*) articulado(-da); (*bed*) de dobrar.

foliage ['fəʊlɪdʒ] *n* folhagem *f*.

folk [fəʊk] *npl* (*people*) gente *f* ♦ *n*: ~ (**music**) música *f* tradicional.

⏟ **folks** *npl* (*inf: relatives*) família *f*.

folklore ['fəʊklɔː^r] *n* folclore *m*.

folk song *n* canção *f* tradicional.

follow ['fɒləʊ] *vt* seguir; (*in order, time*) seguir-se a, vir a seguir de ♦ *vi* (*go behind*) seguir; (*in time*) seguir-se, vir a seguir; (*understand*) entender; **proceed as ~s** ... proceda da seguinte forma ...; **the results are as ~s** ... os resultados são os seguintes ...; **~ed by** seguido de.

⏟ **follow on** *vi* vir a seguir.

follower ['fɒləʊə^r] *n* seguidor *m* (-ra *f*).

following ['fɒləʊɪŋ] *adj* seguinte ♦ *prep* depois de.

follow on call *n* telefonema feito com o dinheiro que sobrou da chamada precedente.

fond [fɒnd] *adj*: **to be ~ of** gostar de.

fondle ['fɒndl] *vt* acariciar.

fondue ['fɒnduː] *n* fondue *m*.

food [fuːd] *n* comida *f*.

food mixer *n* batedeira *f*.

food poisoning [-ˌpɔɪznɪŋ] *n* intoxicação *f* alimentar.

food processor [-ˌprəʊsesə^r] *n* processador *m* de comida.

foodstuffs ['fuːdstʌfs] *npl* gêneros *mpl* alimentícios.

fool [fuːl] *n* (*idiot*) idiota *mf*; (*pudding*) mousse *f* de fruta ♦ *vt* enganar.

foolhardy ['fuːlhɑːdɪ] *adj* imprudente, insensato(-ta).

foolish ['fuːlɪʃ] *adj* tolo(-la).

foolproof ['fuːlpruːf] *adj* (*plan, system*) infalível; (*machine*) fácil de utilizar.

foot [fʊt] (*pl* **feet**) *n* pé *m*; (*of animal*) pata *f*; (*of hill, cliff, stairs*) pé *m*; (*measurement*) pé *m*, = 30,48 cm; **by** OR **on ~** a pé.

footage ['fʊtɪdʒ] *n* sequências *fpl*.

football ['fʊtbɔːl] *n* (*Brit: soccer*) futebol *m*; (*Am: American football*) futebol americano; (*Brit: in soccer*) bola *f* (de futebol); (*Am: in American football*) bola (de futebol americano).

footballer ['fʊtbɔːlə^r] *n* (*Brit*) futebolista *mf*.

football ground *n* (*Brit*) campo *m* de futebol.

football pitch *n* (*Brit*) campo *m* de futebol.

football player *n* jogador *m* (-ra *f*) de futebol.

footbridge ['fʊtbrɪdʒ] *n* passagem *f* aérea para pedestres.

foothills ['fʊthɪlz] *npl* contrafortes *mpl*.

foothold ['fʊthəʊld] *n* ponto *m* de apoio.

footing ['fʊtɪŋ] *n* (*foothold*) equilíbrio *m*; **to lose one's ~** perder o equilíbrio.

footlights ['fʊtlaɪts] *npl* (luzes *fpl* da) ribalta *f*.

footnote ['fʊtnəʊt] *n* nota *f* de rodapé.

footpath ['fʊtpɑːθ, *pl* -pɑːðz] *n* caminho *m*.

footprint ['fʊtprɪnt] *n* pegada *f*.

footstep ['fʊtstep] *n* passo *m*.

footwear ['fʊtweə^r] *n* calçado *m*.

for [fɔː^r] *prep* **1.** (*expressing intention, purpose, reason*) para; **this book is ~ you** este livro é para você; **what did you do that ~?** para quê você fez isso?; **what's it ~?** para quê é?; **to go ~ a walk** ir dar um passeio; **"~ sale"** "vende-se"; **a town famous ~ its wine** uma cidade famosa pelo vinho; **~ this reason** por esta razão.

2. (*during*) durante; **I'm going away ~ a while** vou estar fora durante OR por algum tempo; **I've lived here ~ ten years** vivo aqui há dez anos; **we talked ~ hours** falamos horas e horas.

3. (*by, before*) para; **I'll do it ~ tomorrow** estará pronto (para) amanhã; **be there ~ 8 p.m.** tente estar lá antes das oito da noite.

4. (*on the occasion of*) por; **I got socks ~ Christmas** ganhei meias no Natal, no Natal me deram meias; **~ the first time** pela primeira vez; **what's ~ dinner?** o que há para jantar?; **~ the**

moment no momento.
5. *(on behalf of)* por; **to do sthg ~ sb**
fazer algo para alguém; **to work ~ sb**
trabalhar para alguém.
6. *(with time and space)* para; **there's no
room ~ it** não há espaço para isso; **to
have time ~ sthg** ter tempo para algo.
7. *(expressing distance)*: **road works ~
20 miles** obras na estrada ao longo de
32 km; **we drove ~ miles** guiamos
quilômetros e quilômetros.
8. *(expressing destination)* para; **a ticket
~ Edinburgh** um bilhete para
Edimburgo; **this train is ~ London
only** este trem só pára em Londres.
9. *(expressing price)* por; **I bought it ~
five pounds** comprei-o por cinco
libras.
10. *(expressing meaning)*: **what's the
Portuguese ~ "boy"?** como
é que se diz "boy" em português?
11. *(with regard to)* para; **it's warm ~
November** para novembro está quente; **it's easy ~ you** para você é fácil;
respect ~ human rights respeito pelos
direitos humanos; **I feel sorry ~ them**
sinto pena deles; **it's too far ~ us to
walk** é longe demais para irmos a pé;
it's time ~ dinner está na hora do jantar.
forage ['fɒrɪdʒ] *vi*: **to ~ for sthg** procurar algo.
forbid [fə'bɪd] *(pt* **-bade,** *pp* **-bidden)**
vt proibir; **to ~ sb to do sthg** proibir
alguém de fazer algo.
forbidden [fə'bɪdn] *adj* proibi-
do(-da).
force [fɔːs] *n* força *f* ♦ *vt* forçar; **the
~s** as forças armadas; **to ~ sb to do
sthg** forçar alguém a fazer algo; **to ~
one's way through (sthg)** abrir caminho (por entre algo).
forceps ['fɔːseps] *npl* fórceps *m inv*.
ford [fɔːd] *n* vau *m*.
forearm ['fɔːrɑːm] *n* antebraço *m*.
forecast ['fɔːkɑːst] *n* previsão *f*.
forecourt ['fɔːkɔːt] *n* pátio *m*.
forefinger ['fɔːfɪŋgəʳ] *n* dedo *m* indicador.
forefront ['fɔːfrʌnt] *n*: **in OR at the ~
of sthg** na vanguarda de algo.
foregone conclusion [fɔːgɒn-] *n*:
it's a ~ é mais que certo.
foreground ['fɔːgraʊnd] *n* primeiro
plano *m*.
forehand ['fɔːhænd] *n* direita *f*.

forehead ['fɔːhed] *n* testa *f*.
foreign ['fɒrən] *adj* estrangeiro(-ra);
(visit) ao estrangeiro; *(travel)* para o
estrangeiro.
foreign currency *n* moeda *f*
estrangeira, divisas *fpl*.
foreigner ['fɒrənəʳ] *n* estrangeiro *m*
(-ra *f*).
foreign exchange *n (system)* câmbio *m*; *(money)* divisas *fpl*.
foreign minister *n* ministro *m* (-tra
f) das relações exteriores *(Br)*, secretário *m* (-ria *f*) de Estado dos negócios
estrangeiros *(Port)*.
foreign secretary *n (Brit)* ministro
m (-tra *f*) das relações exteriores *(Br)*,
ministro *m* (-tra *f*) dos negócios
estrangeiros *(Port)*.
foreman ['fɔːmən] *(pl* **-men**
[-mən]) *n* capataz *m*.
forename ['fɔːneɪm] *n (fml)* nome *m*
próprio.
forensic medicine [fə'rensɪk-] *n*
medicina *f* legal.
foresee [fɔː'siː] *(pt* **-saw,** *pp* **-seen)** *vt*
prever.
foreseeable [fɔː'siːəbl] *adj* previsível;
in the ~ future num futuro próximo.
foreseen [fɔː'siːn] *pp* → **foresee**.
forest ['fɒrɪst] *n* floresta *f*.
forestry ['fɒrɪstrɪ] *n* silvicultura *f*.
foretaste ['fɔːteɪst] *n* amostra *f*.
foretell [fɔː'tel] *(pt & pp* **-told)** *vt* predizer, prever.
forever [fə'revəʳ] *adv (eternally)* para
sempre; *(continually)* sempre.
foreword ['fɔːwɜːd] *n* prefácio *m*.
forfeit ['fɔːfɪt] *n* penalização *f* ♦ *vt*
(lose) perder.
forgave [fə'geɪv] *pt* → **forgive**.
forge [fɔːdʒ] *vt (copy)* falsificar, forjar.
forgery ['fɔːdʒərɪ] *n* falsificação *f*.
forget [fə'get] *(pt* **-got,** *pp*
-gotten) *vt* esquecer-se de; *(person,
event)* esquecer ♦ *vi* esquecer-se; **to ~
about sthg** esquecer-se de algo; **to ~
how to do sthg** esquecer-se de como
se faz algo; **to ~ to do sthg** esquecer-
se de fazer algo; **~ it!** esquece!
forgetful [fə'getfʊl] *adj* esquecido
(-da).
forgive [fə'gɪv] *(pt* **-gave,** *pp*
-given) *vt* perdoar.
forgot [fə'gɒt] *pt* → **forget**.
forgotten [fə'gɒtn] *pp* → **forget**.
fork [fɔːk] *n (for eating with)* garfo *m*;

(for gardening) forquilha f; *(of road, path)* bifurcação f.

⌐ **forks** *npl (of bike, motorbike)* garfo m.

forklift truck [ˈfɔːklɪft-] n empilhadora f.

forlorn [fəˈlɔːn] adj *(face, expression, cry)* infeliz; *(hope, attempt)* desesperado(-da).

form [fɔːm] n *(type, shape)* forma f; *(piece of paper)* impresso m, formulário m; *(SCH)* ano m ♦ vt formar ♦ vi formar-se; **to be on/off** ~ estar/não estar em forma; **to** ~ **part of** fazer parte de.

formal [ˈfɔːml] adj formal.

formality [fɔːˈmælɪtɪ] n formalidade f; **it's just a** ~ é só uma formalidade.

format [ˈfɔːmæt] n formato m.

formation [fɔːˈmeɪʃn] n formação f.

former [ˈfɔːmər] adj *(previous)* anterior; *(first)* primeiro(-ra) ♦ pron: **the** ~ o primeiro (a primeira).

formerly [ˈfɔːməlɪ] adv antigamente.

formidable [ˈfɔːmɪdəbl] adj *(frightening)* temível; *(impressive)* tremendo (-da).

formula [ˈfɔːmjʊlə] (pl **-as** OR **-ae** [iː]) n fórmula f.

fort [fɔːt] n forte m.

forthcoming [fɔːθˈkʌmɪŋ] adj *(future)* próximo(-ma), que está para vir.

forthright [ˈfɔːθraɪt] adj *(person)* sem rodeios, direto(-ta); *(manner, opinions)* franco(-ca).

fortieth [ˈfɔːtɪɪθ] num quadragésimo(-ma), → **sixth**.

fortnight [ˈfɔːtnaɪt] n *(Brit)* quinzena f, duas semanas fpl.

fortress [ˈfɔːtrɪs] n fortaleza f.

fortunate [ˈfɔːtʃnət] adj com sorte; **she's** ~ **to have such a good job** ela tem a sorte de ter um emprego tão bom.

fortunately [ˈfɔːtʃnətlɪ] adv felizmente.

fortune [ˈfɔːtʃuːn] n *(money)* fortuna f; *(luck)* sorte f; **it costs a** ~ *(inf)* custa uma fortuna.

fortune teller n cartomante mf.

forty [ˈfɔːtɪ] num quarenta, → **six**.

forward [ˈfɔːwəd] adv para a frente ♦ n avançado m (-da f) ♦ vt *(letter)* remeter; *(goods)* expedir; **to look** ~ **to** estar ansioso por.

forwarding address [ˈfɔː- wədɪŋ-] n novo endereço para onde o correio deve ser remitido.

forwards [ˈfɔːwədz] adv = **forward**.

fossil [ˈfɒsl] n fóssil m.

foster child [ˈfɒstər-] n criança sob os cuidados temporários de uma família adotiva.

foster parents npl família adotiva que cuida de crianças por um tempo limitado.

fought [fɔːt] pt & pp → **fight**.

foul [faʊl] adj *(unpleasant)* nojento(-ta) ♦ n falta f.

found [faʊnd] pt & pp → **find** ♦ vt fundar.

foundation (cream) [faʊnˈdeɪʃn-] n base f.

foundations [faʊnˈdeɪʃnz] npl alicerces mpl, fundações fpl.

founder [ˈfaʊndər] n fundador m (-ra f).

foundry [ˈfaʊndrɪ] n fundição f.

fountain [ˈfaʊntɪn] n repuxo m.

fountain pen n caneta-tinteiro f *(Br)*, caneta f de tinta permanente *(Port)*.

four [fɔːr] num quatro, → **six**.

four-poster (bed) n cama f de colunas.

foursome [ˈfɔːsəm] n grupo m de quatro (pessoas).

four-star (petrol) n gasolina f super.

fourteen [ˌfɔːˈtiːn] num quatorze *(Br)*, catorze, → **six**.

fourteenth [ˌfɔːˈtiːnθ] num décimo quarto (décima quarta), → **sixth**.

fourth [fɔːθ] num quarto(-ta), → sixth.

four-wheel drive n *(car)* veículo m com tração nas quatro rodas.

fowl [faʊl] (pl inv) n ave f *(de capoeira)*.

fox [fɒks] n raposa f.

foyer [ˈfɔɪeɪ] n vestíbulo m, saguão m *(Br)*.

fraction [ˈfrækʃn] n fração f.

fractionally [ˈfrækʃnəlɪ] adv ligeiramente.

fracture [ˈfræktʃər] n fratura f ♦ vt fraturar.

fragile [ˈfrædʒaɪl] adj frágil.

fragment [ˈfrægmənt] n fragmento m.

fragrance [ˈfreɪɡrəns] n fragrância f.

fragrant [ˈfreɪɡrənt] adj perfumado (-da).

frail [freɪl] adj frágil, débil.

frame [freɪm] n *(of window, photo,*

door) moldura f, caixilho m; *(of glasses, tent, bed)* armação f; *(of bicycle)* quadro m ♦ vt *(photo, picture)* emoldurar.

frame of mind n estado m de espírito.

framework ['freɪmwɔ:k] n *(physical structure)* armação f; *(basis)* estrutura f.

France [frɑ:ns] n França f.

frank [fræŋk] adj franco(-ca).

frankfurter ['fræŋkfɜ:tə'] n salsicha f alemã.

frankly ['fræŋklɪ] adv *(to be honest)* francamente; **quite ~, I don't really care** para ser franco, pouco me importa.

frantic ['fræntɪk] adj frenético (-ca).

fraternize ['frætənaɪz] vi *(be on friendly terms)*: **to ~ with sb** fraternizar com alguém.

fraud [frɔ:d] n *(crime)* fraude f, burla f.

frayed [freɪd] adj *(clothing, fabric, rope)* gasto(-ta), puído(-da).

freak [fri:k] adj anormal ♦ n *(inf: fanatic)* fanático m *(-ca f)*.

freckles ['freklz] npl sardas fpl.

free [fri:] adj livre; *(costing nothing)* grátis *(inv)* ♦ vt *(prisoner)* libertar ♦ adv *(without paying)* grátis, de graça; **for ~** grátis, de graça; **~ of charge** grátis; **to be ~ to do sthg** ser livre para fazer algo.

freedom ['fri:dəm] n liberdade f.

freefone ['fri:fəʊn] n *(Brit)* = linha f verde *(Port)*, sistema que permite ao utilizador telefonar sem pagar.

free gift n oferta f.

freehand ['fri:hænd] adj desenhado(-da) à mão *(livre)* ♦ adv à mão *(livre)*.

free house n *(Brit)* pub que não está ligado a nenhuma fábrica de cervejas.

free kick n *(pontapé)* livre m.

freelance ['fri:lɑ:ns] adj free-lance *(inv)*.

freely ['fri:lɪ] adv *(speak)* à vontade; *(move)* livremente; **~ available** fácil de obter.

Freemason ['fri:meɪsn] n franco-maçon m, membro m da franco-maçonaria.

free period n *(SCH)* hora f livre, furo m *(Port)*.

freepost ['fri:pəʊst] n porte m pago.

free-range adj *(chicken)* do campo; **~ eggs** ovos de galinhas criadas livremente.

freestyle ['fri:staɪl] n estilo m livre.

free time n tempo m livre.

freeway ['fri:weɪ] n *(Am)* auto-estrada f.

freeze [fri:z] *(pt froze, pp frozen)* vt congelar ♦ vi gelar ♦ v impers: **it's freezing!** está um gelo!

freezer ['fri:zə'] n *(deep freeze)* frízer m *(Br)*, arca f congeladora *(Port)*; *(part of fridge)* frízer *(Br)*, congelador m *(Port)*.

freezing ['fri:zɪŋ] adj gelado (-da) *(Port)*.

freezing point n: **below ~** abaixo de zero.

freight [freɪt] n *(goods)* mercadorias fpl.

freight train n trem m de mercadorias.

French [frentʃ] adj francês(-esa) ♦ n *(language)* francês m ♦ npl: **the ~** os franceses.

French bean n feijão m verde *(redondo)*.

French bread n ~ bisnaga f *(Br)*, cacete m *(Port)*.

French dressing n *(in UK)* vinagrete m; *(in US)* molho m americano, molho à base de ketchup e maionese.

French fries npl batatas fpl fritas.

Frenchman ['frentʃmən] *(pl -men [-mən])* n francês m.

French stick n *(Brit)* ~ bisnaga f *(Br)*, cacete m *(Port)*.

French toast n rabanada f.

French windows npl portas fpl envidraçadas.

Frenchwoman ['frentʃwʊmən] *(pl -women [-wɪmɪn])* n francesa f.

frenetic [frə'netɪk] adj frenético(-ca).

frenzy ['frenzɪ] n frenesi m.

frequency ['fri:kwənsɪ] n freqüência f.

frequent ['fri:kwənt] adj freqüente.

frequently ['fri:kwəntlɪ] adv freqüentemente.

fresh [freʃ] adj fresco(-ca); *(refreshing)* refrescante; *(water)* doce; *(recent)* recente; *(new)* novo (nova); **to get some ~ air** apanhar ar fresco.

fresh cream n creme m *(Br)*, natas fpl frescas *(Port)*.

freshen ['freʃn] : **freshen up** vi refrescar-se.

fresher ['freʃə'] n *(Brit)* *(inf)* calouro m *(-ra f)*.

freshly ['freʃlɪ] *adv* recentemente.

freshness ['freʃnɪs] *n* frescura *f*; *(of approach, ideas)* originalidade *f*.

fresh orange (juice) *n* suco *m* de laranja *(Br)*, sumo *m* de laranja natural *(Port)*.

freshwater ['freʃ,wɔːtəʳ] *adj* de água doce.

fret [fret] *vi (worry)* preocupar-se.

Fri. *(abbr of Friday)* 6ª, sex.

friar ['fraɪəʳ] *n* frade *m*.

friction ['frɪkʃn] *n* fricção *f*.

Friday ['fraɪdɪ] *n* sexta-feira, → **Saturday.**

fridge [frɪdʒ] *n* geladeira *f (Br)*, frigorífico *m (Port)*.

fridge-freezer *n (Brit)* geladeira *f* (com frízer) *(Br)*, frigorífico *m* (com congelador) *(Port)*.

fried egg [fraɪd-] *n* ovo *m* estrelado OR frito.

fried rice [fraɪd-] *n* arroz *m* frito.

friend [frend] *n* amigo *m* (-ga *f*); **to be ~s with sb** ser amigo de alguém; **to make ~s with sb** tornar-se amigo de alguém.

friendly ['frendlɪ] *adj* amigável; **to be ~ with sb** ser amigo(-ga) de alguém.

friendship ['frendʃɪp] *n* amizade *f*.

fries [fraɪz] = **French fries.**

fright [fraɪt] *n* susto *m*; **to give sb a ~** pregar um susto em alguém.

frighten ['fraɪtn] *vt* assustar.

frightened ['fraɪtnd] *adj* assustado (-da); **to be ~** ter medo; **to be ~ of** ter medo de; **to be ~ (that)** *(worried)* ter medo que.

frightening ['fraɪtnɪŋ] *adj* assustador(-ra).

frightful ['fraɪtfʊl] *adj (very bad, unpleasant)* horrível.

frilly ['frɪlɪ] *adj* de babados *(Br)*, de folhos *(Port)*.

fringe [frɪndʒ] *n* franja *f*.

frisk [frɪsk] *vt* revistar.

fritter ['frɪtəʳ] *n comida, geralmente fruta, passada por um polme e frita.*

frivolous ['frɪvələs] *adj* frívolo (-la).

fro [frəʊ] *adv* → **to.**

frock [frɒk] *n* vestido *m*.

frog [frɒg] *n* rã *f*.

frogman ['frɒgmən] (*pl* **-men** [-mən]) *n* homem-rã *m*.

from [frɒm] *prep* **1.** *(expressing origin, source)* de; **I'm ~ Liverpool** sou de Liverpool; **the train ~ Manchester** o trem de Manchester; **I bought it ~ a supermarket** comprei-o num supermercado.

2. *(expressing removal, deduction)* de; **away ~ home** longe de casa; **to take sthg (away) ~ sb** tirar algo de alguém; **10% will be deducted ~ the total** será deduzido 10% do total .

3. *(expressing distance)* de; **five miles ~ London** a oito quilômetros de Londres; **it's not far ~ here** não é longe daqui.

4. *(expressing position)* de; **~ here you can see the valley** daqui vê-se o vale.

5. *(expressing what thing is made with)* de; **it's made ~ stone** é feito de pedra.

6. *(expressing starting time)* desde; **~ the moment you arrived** desde que chegou; **~ now on** de agora em diante; **~ next year** a partir do próximo ano; **open ~ nine to five** aberto das nove às cinco.

7. *(expressing change)* de; **the price has gone up ~ £1 to £2** o preço subiu de uma libra para duas; **to translate ~ German into English** traduzir do alemão para o inglês.

8. *(expressing range)* de; **tickets are ~ £10** bilhetes a partir de dez libras; **it could take ~ two to six months** pode levar de dois a seis meses.

9. *(as a result of)* de; **I'm tired ~ walking** estou cansado de andar.

10. *(expressing protection)* de; **sheltered ~ the wind** protegido do vento.

11. *(in comparisons)*: **different ~** diferente de.

fromage frais [,frɒmɑːʒ'freɪ] *n tipo de queijo cremoso.*

front [frʌnt] *adj* da frente ◆ *n* (parte da) frente *f*; *(of book)* capa *f*; *(of weather)* frente *f*; *(by the sea)* costa *f*; **in ~** em frente; **in ~ of** em frente de.

front door *n* porta *f* da frente.

frontier [frʌn'tɪəʳ] *n* fronteira *f*.

front page *n* primeira página *f*.

front room *n* sala *f* (de estar).

front seat *n* banco *m* da frente.

front-wheel drive *n (vehicle)* veículo *m* com tração nas rodas dianteiras.

frost [frɒst] *n* geada *f*.

frostbite [ˈfrɒstbaɪt] n ferida f causada pelo frio.

frosted [ˈfrɒstɪd] adj (glass) fosco (-ca).

frosty [ˈfrɒstɪ] adj (morning, weather) de geada.

froth [frɒθ] n espuma f.

frown [fraʊn] n cenho m ♦ vi franzir as sobrancelhas.

froze [frəʊz] pt → **freeze**.

frozen [ˈfrəʊzn] pp → **freeze** ♦ adj gelado(-da); (food) congelado (-da).

fruit [fruːt] n (food) fruta f; (variety of fruit) fruto m; **a piece of ~** uma fruta; **~s of the forest** frutos silvestres.

fruit cake n bolo m inglês.

fruiterer [ˈfruːtərəʳ] n (Brit) fruteiro m (-ra f).

fruitful [ˈfruːtfʊl] adj frutífero(-ra).

fruit juice n suco m de fruta (Br), sumo m de frutas (Port).

fruitless [ˈfruːtlɪs] adj infrutífero(-ra).

fruit machine n (Brit) caça-níqueis m (Br), slot-machine f (Port).

fruit salad n salada f de fruta.

frumpy [ˈfrʌmpɪ] adj (inf) careta (Br), antiquado(-da) (Port).

frustrate [frʌˈstreɪt] vt (person) frustrar; (plan, attempt) gorar.

frustrated [frʌˈstreɪtɪd] adj (person) frustrado(-da); (plan, attempt) gorado (-da), furado(-da).

frustrating [frʌˈstreɪtɪŋ] adj frustrante.

frustration [frʌˈstreɪʃn] n frustração f.

fry [fraɪ] vt fritar.

frying pan [ˈfraɪŋ-] n frigideira f.

ft abbr = **foot, feet**.

fudge [fʌdʒ] n doce m de leite, doce caramelado feito com leite, açúcar e manteiga.

fuel [fjʊəl] n combustível m.

fuel pump n bomba f de gasolina.

fuel tank n tanque m de gasolina.

fugitive [ˈfjuːdʒətɪv] n fugitivo m (-va f).

fulfil [fʊlˈfɪl] vt (Brit) (promise, request, duty) cumprir; (role) desempenhar; (conditions, instructions, need) satisfazer.

fulfill [fʊlˈfɪl] (Am) = **fulfil**.

full [fʊl] adj (filled) cheio (cheia); (name) completo(-ta); (extent, support) total; (maximum) máximo(-ma); (busy) ocupado(-da); (fare) inteiro(-ra); (fla-

vour) rico(-ca) ♦ adv (directly) em cheio; **I'm ~ (up)** estou cheio; **at ~ speed** a toda a velocidade; **~ of** cheio de; **in ~** (pay) na totalidade; (write) por extenso.

full board n pensão f completa.

full-cream milk n leite m integral (Br), leite m gordo (Port).

full-length adj (skirt, dress) comprido(-da) (até aos pés).

full moon n lua f cheia.

full stop n ponto m final.

full-time adj & adv de tempo integral (Br), a tempo inteiro (Port).

full up adj cheio (cheia).

fully [ˈfʊlɪ] adv (completely) completamente.

fully-licensed adj autorizado a vender bebidas alcoólicas.

fumble [ˈfʌmbl] vi: **he ~d in his pockets for his keys** ele apalpou os bolsos à procura das chaves.

fume [fjuːm] vi (with anger) espumar (de raiva).

❏ **fumes** npl (from paint, alcohol) vapores mpl; (from car) gases mpl; (from fire) fumaça f.

fun [fʌn] n divertimento m, diversão f; **it's good ~** é divertido; **for ~** por prazer; **to have ~** divertir-se; **to make ~ of** zombar de.

function [ˈfʌŋkʃn] n função f ♦ vi funcionar.

fund [fʌnd] n fundo m ♦ vt financiar.

❏ **funds** npl fundos mpl.

fundamental [ˌfʌndəˈmentl] adj fundamental.

funding [ˈfʌndɪŋ] n financiamento m.

funeral [ˈfjuːnərəl] n funeral m.

funeral parlour n (agência) funerária f.

funfair [ˈfʌnfeəʳ] n parque m de diversões.

fungus [ˈfʌŋgəs] (pl -gi [-gaɪ]) n fungo m.

funky [ˈfʌŋkɪ] adj (inf: music) funky (inv).

funnel [ˈfʌnl] n (for pouring) funil m; (on ship) chaminé f.

funny [ˈfʌnɪ] adj (amusing) engraçado(-da); (strange) estranho(-nha); **to feel ~ (ill)** não se sentir bem.

fur [fɜːʳ] n (on animal) pêlo m; (garment) pele f.

fur coat n casaco m de peles.

furious [ˈfjʊərɪəs] adj (angry) furioso(-osa).

furnace ['fɜːnɪs] *n* fornalha *f*.
furnish ['fɜːnɪʃ] *vt (house, room)* mobiliar.
furnished ['fɜːnɪʃt] *adj* mobiliado (-da).
furnishings ['fɜːnɪʃɪŋz] *npl* mobiliário *m*.
furniture ['fɜːnɪtʃəʳ] *n* mobília *f*; **a piece of ~** um móvel.
furrow ['fʌrəʊ] *n* rego *m*, sulco *m*.
furry ['fɜːrɪ] *adj (animal)* peludo(-da); *(toy)* de pelúcia; *(material)* com pêlo.
further ['fɜːðəʳ] *compar* → **far** ♦ *adv* mais ♦ *adj (additional)* outro (outra); **until ~ notice** até novo aviso; **it's not much ~** já não falta muito, já não é muito longe.
further education *n (Brit)* educação *f* para adultos.

furthermore [ˌfɜːðəˈmɔːʳ] *adv* além disso, além do mais.
furthest ['fɜːðɪst] *superl* → **far** ♦ *adj (most distant)* mais longe OR distante ♦ *adv (in distance)* mais longe.
fury ['fjʊərɪ] *n* fúria *f*.
fuse [fjuːz] *n (of plug)* fusível *m*; *(on bomb)* detonador *m* ♦ *vi (plug, device)* queimar.
fuse box *n* caixa *f* de fusíveis.
fuss [fʌs] *n (agitation)* agitação *f*; *(complaints)* escândalo *m*.
fussy ['fʌsɪ] *adj (person)* exigente.
futile [*Brit* 'fjuːtaɪl, *Am* 'fuːtl] *adj* inútil.
futon ['fuːtɒn] *n* espécie de sofá-cama japonês.
future ['fjuːtʃəʳ] *n* futuro *m* ♦ *adj* futuro(-ra); **in ~** no futuro, de agora em diante.

G

g (abbr of gram) g.

gable ['geɪbl] n cumeeira f.

gadget ['gædʒɪt] n engenhoca f.

Gaelic ['geɪlɪk] n gaélico m.

gag [gæg] n (inf: joke) piada f.

gain [geɪn] vt ganhar; (subj: clock, watch) adiantar ◆ vi (benefit) lucrar ◆ n ganho m; **to ~ weight** engordar.

gait [geɪt] n andar m.

gal. abbr = gallon.

gala ['gɑːlə] n (celebration) gala f.

galaxy ['gæləksɪ] n galáxia f.

gale [geɪl] n vento m forte, rajada f de vento.

gallant ['gælənt] adj (courageous) corajoso(-osa).

gallery ['gælərɪ] n galeria f.

galley ['gælɪ] n (ship) galera f; (kitchen) cozinha f.

gallon ['gælən] n (in UK) = 4,546 litros, galão m; (in US) = 3,785 litros, galão.

gallop ['gæləp] vi galopar.

gallows ['gæləʊz] (pl inv) n forca f.

galore [gə'lɔːr] adv à farta, em abundância.

gamble ['gæmbl] n aposta f ◆ vi (bet money) apostar, jogar.

gambler ['gæmblər] n jogador m (-ra f).

gambling ['gæmblɪŋ] n jogo m (de azar).

game [geɪm] n jogo m; (of tennis, snooker, chess) partida f; (wild animals, meat) caça f.

❏ games n (SCH) desporto m ◆ npl (sporting event) jogos mpl.

gamekeeper ['geɪm,kiːpər] n guarda-caça mf, couteiro m (-ra f).

game reserve n reserva f de caça, coutada f.

gammon ['gæmən] n presunto cozido, salgado ou fumado.

gang [gæŋ] n (of criminals) gangue f (Br), bando m (Port); (of friends) grupo m, turma f.

gangrene ['gæŋgriːn] n gangrena f.

gangster ['gæŋstər] n bandido m, gangster m.

gangway ['gæŋweɪ] n (for ship) prancha f; (Brit: in bus, aeroplane, theatre) corredor m.

gaol [dʒeɪl] (Brit) = jail.

gap [gæp] n (space) espaço m; (of time) intervalo m; (difference) diferença f.

gape [geɪp] vi (person) ficar de boca aberta.

garage ['gærɑːʒ, 'gærɪdʒ] n (for keeping car) garagem f; (Brit: for petrol) posto m de gasolina; (for repairs) oficina f; (Brit: for selling cars) concessionária f.

garbage ['gɑːbɪdʒ] n (Am: refuse) lixo m.

garbage can n (Am) lata f de lixo.

garbage truck n (Am) caminhão m do lixo.

garbled ['gɑːbld] adj confuso (-sa).

garden ['gɑːdn] n jardim m ◆ vi jardinar.

❏ gardens npl (public park) jardim m público, parque m.

garden centre n centro m de jardinagem.

gardener ['gɑːdnər] n jardineiro m (-ra f).

gardening ['gɑːdnɪŋ] n jardinagem f.

garden peas npl ervilhas fpl.

gargle ['gɑːgl] vi gargarejar.

garish ['geərɪʃ] adj berrante.

garlic ['gɑːlɪk] n alho m.

garlic bread n pão untado com manteiga de alho e aquecido no forno.

garlic butter n manteiga f de alho.

garment [ˈgɑːmənt] *n* peça *f* de roupa.

garnish [ˈgɑːnɪʃ] *n* *(for decoration)* decoração *f*; *(sauce)* molho *m* ◆ *vt* decorar.

garrison [ˈgærɪsn] *n* guarnição *f*.

garter [ˈgɑːtər] *n* liga *f*.

gas [gæs] *n* gás *m*; *(Am: petrol)* gasolina *f*.

gas cooker *n* *(Brit)* fogão *m* a gás.

gas cylinder *n* bujão *m* de gás *(Br)*, botija *f* de gás *(Port)*.

gas fire *n* *(Brit)* aquecedor *m* a gás.

gas gauge *n* *(Am)* indicador *m* do nível de gasolina.

gash [gæʃ] *n* corte *m* (profundo) ◆ *vi* cortar, ferir.

gasket [ˈgæskɪt] *n* junta *f*.

gasman [ˈgæsmæn] *(pl* -men*)* *n* funcionário *m* da companhia de gás.

gas mask *n* máscara *f* antigás.

gasmen [ˈgæsmen] *pl* → **gasman**.

gas meter *n* medidor *m* do gás *(Br)*, contador *m* do gás *(Port)*.

gasoline [ˈgæsəliːn] *n* *(Am)* gasolina *f*.

gasp [gɑːsp] *vi* *(in shock, surprise)* ficar sem fôlego.

gas pedal *n* *(Am)* acelerador *m*.

gas station *n* *(Am)* posto *m* de gasolina *(Br)*; estação *f* de serviço *(Port)*.

gas stove *(Brit)* = **gas cooker**.

gas tank *n* *(Am)* tanque *m* de gasolina.

gastronomy [gæsˈtrɒnəmɪ] *n* gastronomia *f*.

gasworks [ˈgæswɜːks] *(pl inv)* *n* usina *f* de gás *(Br)*, gasômetro *m* *(Br)*, fábrica *f* de gás *(Port)*.

gate [geɪt] *n* *(to garden, field)* portão *m*; *(at airport)* porta *f*.

gâteau [ˈgætəʊ] *(pl* -x [-z]*)* *n* *(Brit)* bolo recheado e coberto com chantilly.

gatecrash [ˈgeɪtkræʃ] *(inf)* *vt* *(inf)* entrar sem ser convidado(-da) em, entrar de penetra em.

gateway [ˈgeɪtweɪ] *n* *(entrance)* entrada *f*.

gather [ˈgæðər] *vt* *(collect)* colher; *(speed)* ganhar; *(understand)* deduzir ◆ *vi* reunir-se.

gathering [ˈgæðərɪŋ] *n* reunião *f*.

gaudy [ˈgɔːdɪ] *adj* berrante.

gauge [geɪdʒ] *n* *(for measuring)* indicador *m*, medidor *m*; *(of railway track)* distância *f* (entre os carris) ◆ *vt* *(calculate)* calcular.

gauze [gɔːz] *n* gaze *f*.

gave [geɪv] *pt* → **give**.

gay [geɪ] *adj* *(homosexual)* homossexual, gay.

gaze [geɪz] *vi*: **to ~ at** olhar (fixamente) para.

gazelle [gəˈzel] *n* gazela *f*.

gazetteer [gæzɪˈtɪər] *n* índice *m* geográfico.

GB *(abbr of Great Britain)* GB.

GCSE *n* *exame realizado no final do nono ano de escolaridade.*

gear [gɪər] *n* *(wheel)* roda *f* de engrenagem; *(speed)* mudança *f*, velocidade *f*; *(equipment)* equipamento *m*; *(belongings)* coisas *fpl*; **in ~** engatado.

gearbox [ˈgɪəbɒks] *n* caixa *f* de mudança *(Br)*, caixa *f* de velocidades *(Port)*.

gear lever *n* alavanca *f* de mudanças.

gear shift *(Am)* = **gear lever**.

gear stick *(Brit)* = **gear lever**.

geese [giːs] *pl* → **goose**.

gel [dʒel] *n* gel *m*.

gelatine [dʒeləˈtiːn] *n* gelatina *f*.

gem [dʒem] *n* pedra *f* preciosa.

Gemini [ˈdʒemɪnaɪ] *n* Gêmeos *m inv*.

gender [ˈdʒendər] *n* gênero *m*.

gene [dʒiːn] *n* gene *m*.

general [ˈdʒenərəl] *adj* geral ◆ *n* general *m*; **in ~** *(as a whole)* em geral; *(usually)* geralmente.

general anaesthetic *n* anestesia *f* geral.

general election *n* eleições *fpl* legislativas.

generalization [dʒenərəlaɪˈzeɪʃn] *n* generalização *f*.

general knowledge *n* cultura *f* geral.

generally [ˈdʒenərəlɪ] *adv* geralmente.

general practitioner [-prækˈtɪʃənər] *n* clínico *m* geral.

general public *n*: **the ~** o público em geral.

general store *n* = mercearia *f*.

generate [ˈdʒenəreɪt] *vt* gerar.

generation [dʒenəˈreɪʃn] *n* geração *f*.

generator [ˈdʒenəreɪtər] *n* gerador *m*.

generosity [dʒenəˈrɒsətɪ] *n* generosidade *f*.

generous [ˈdʒenərəs] *adj* generoso (-osa).

genetic [dʒɪˈnetɪk] adj genético(-ca).
◾ **genetics** n genética f.
Geneva [dʒɪˈniːvə] n Genebra s.
genial [ˈdʒiːnjəl] adj (person) bem-humorado(-da); (remark, smile) amável.
genitals [ˈdʒenɪtlz] npl orgãos mpl genitais.
genius [ˈdʒiːnjəs] n gênio m.
gentle [ˈdʒentl] adj (careful) cuidadoso(-osa); (kind) gentil; (movement, breeze) suave.
gentleman [ˈdʒentlmən] (pl -men [-mən]) n cavalheiro m; "**gentlemen**" (men's toilets) "homens".
gently [ˈdʒentlɪ] adv (carefully) suavemente.
gentry [ˈdʒentrɪ] n pequena nobreza f.
gents [dʒents] n (Brit) banheiro m dos homens.
genuine [ˈdʒenjʊɪn] adj genuíno(-na).
geographical [dʒɪəˈgræfɪkl] adj geográfico(-ca).
geography [dʒɪˈɒgrəfɪ] n geografia f.
geology [dʒɪˈɒlədʒɪ] n geologia f.
geometric(al) [dʒɪəˈmetrɪk(l)] adj geométrico(-ca).
geometry [dʒɪˈɒmətrɪ] n geometria f.
Georgian [ˈdʒɔːdʒən] adj (architecture etc) georgiano(-na) (relativo aos reinados dos reis Jorge I–IV, 1714–1830).
geranium [dʒɪˈreɪnjəm] n gerânio m.
gerbil [ˈdʒɜːbɪl] n gerbilo m, gerbo m.
geriatric [dʒerɪˈætrɪk] adj geriátrico(-ca).
German [ˈdʒɜːmən] adj alemão (-mã) ◆ n (person) alemão m (-mã f); (language) alemão m.
German measles n rubéola f.
Germany [ˈdʒɜːmənɪ] n Alemanha f.
germinate [ˈdʒɜːmɪneɪt] vi germinar.
germs [dʒɜːmz] npl germes mpl.
gesticulate [dʒeˈstɪkjʊleɪt] vi gesticular.
gesture [ˈdʒestʃər] n gesto m.
get [get] (pt & pp got, Am pp gotten) vt 1. (obtain) obter; (buy) comprar; **she got a job** ela arranjou emprego.
2. (receive) receber; **I got a book for Christmas** ganhei um livro no Natal.
3. (means of transport) apanhar; **let's ~**

a **taxi** vamos apanhar um táxi.
4. (fetch) ir buscar; **could you ~ me the manager?** (in shop) podia chamar o gerente?; (on phone) pode me passar o gerente?
5. (illness) apanhar; **I've got a cold** estou resfriado.
6. (cause to become): **to ~ sthg done** mandar fazer algo; **to ~ sthg ready** preparar algo; **can I ~ my car repaired here?** posso mandar consertar o meu carro aqui?
7. (ask, tell): **to ~ sb to do sthg** arranjar alguém para fazer algo.
8. (move): **to ~ sthg out of sthg** tirar algo de algo; **I can't ~ it through the door** não consigo passar com isso na porta.
9. (understand) perceber; **to ~ a joke** sacar uma piada.
10. (time, chance) ter; **we didn't ~ the chance to see everything** não tivemos oportunidade de ver tudo.
11. (idea, feeling) ter; **I ~ a lot of enjoyment from it** me divirto à beça.
12. (phone) atender.
13. (in phrases): **you ~ a lot of rain here in winter** chove muito aqui no inverno, → **have**.
◆ vi 1. (become) ficar; **it's getting late** está a ficando tarde; **to ~ ready** preparar-se; **to ~ lost** perder-se; **~ lost!** não enche o saco!, desapareça!
2. (into particular state, position) meter-se; **how do you ~ to Luton from here?** como é que se vai daqui para Luton?; **to ~ into the car** entrar no carro.
3. (arrive) chegar; **when does the train ~ here?** quando é que o trem chega aqui?
4. (in phrases): **to ~ to do sthg** ter a oportunidade de fazer algo.
◆ aux vb ser; **to ~ delayed** atrasar-se; **to ~ killed** ser morto.
◻ **get back** vi (return) voltar.
◻ **get in** vi (arrive) chegar; (enter) entrar.
◻ **get off** vi (leave) sair.
◻ **get on** vi (enter train, bus) entrar; (in relationship) dar-se, entender-se; (progress): **how are you getting on in your new job?** como você está indo no novo emprego?
◻ **get out** vi (of car, bus, train) sair.
◻ **get through** vi (on phone) conseguir ligação.

❑ **get up** *vi* levantar-se.

getaway ['getəweɪ] *n* fuga *f*.

get-together *n* (*inf*) reunião *f*.

geyser [*Brit* 'giːzəʳ, *Am* 'gaɪzəʳ] *n* (*hot spring*) géiser *m*; (*Brit: water heater*) esquentador *m*.

Ghana ['gɑːnə] *n* Gana *m*.

ghastly ['gɑːstlɪ] *adj* (*inf: very bad*) horrível.

gherkin ['gɜːkɪn] *n* pequeno pepino de conserva.

ghetto ['getəʊ] (*pl* **-s** OR **-es**) *n* gueto *m*.

ghetto blaster ['getəʊ,blɑːstəʳ] *n* (*inf*) rádio-gravador *m* portátil.

ghost [gəʊst] *n* fantasma *m*.

giant ['dʒaɪənt] *adj* gigante ◆ *n* in *stories*) gigante *m* (-ta *f*).

gibberish ['dʒɪbərɪʃ] *n* disparates *mpl*.

gibe [dʒaɪb] *n* chacota *f*, piada *f* (insultuosa).

giblets ['dʒɪblɪts] *npl* miúdos *mpl*.

Gibraltar [dʒɪ'brɔːltəʳ] *n* Gibraltar *s*.

giddy ['gɪdɪ] *adj* (*dizzy*) tonto(-ta).

gift [gɪft] *n* (*present*) presente *m*; (*talent*) dom *m*.

gift certificate (*Am*) = **gift voucher**.

gifted ['gɪftɪd] *adj* dotado(-da).

gift shop *n* loja *f* de presentes.

gift token = **gift voucher**.

gift voucher *n* (*Brit*) vale *m* para presente.

gig [gɪg] *n* (*inf*) concerto *m*.

gigabyte ['gɪgəbaɪt] *n* gigabyte *m*, gigaocteto *m*.

gigantic [dʒaɪ'gæntɪk] *adj* gigantesco(-ca).

giggle ['gɪgl] *vi* dar risadinha.

gill [dʒɪl] *n* (*measurement*) = 0,142 litros.

gills [gɪlz] *npl* (*of fish*) guelras *fpl*.

gilt [gɪlt] *adj* dourado(-da) ◆ *n* dourado *m*.

gimmick ['gɪmɪk] *n* truque *m*, artifício *m*.

gin [dʒɪn] *n* gim *m*; **~ and tonic** gim tônico.

ginger ['dʒɪndʒəʳ] *n* gengibre *m* ◆ *adj* (*colour*) cor-de-cenoura (*inv*).

ginger ale *n* ginger-ale *m*.

ginger beer *n* bebida não alcoólica de gengibre.

gingerbread ['dʒɪndʒəbred] *n* biscoito ou bolacha de gengibre.

ginger-haired [-'heəd] *adj* ruivo (-va).

gipsy ['dʒɪpsɪ] *n* cigano *m* (-na *f*).

giraffe [dʒɪ'rɑːf] *n* girafa *f*.

girder ['gɜːdəʳ] *n* viga *f*.

girdle ['gɜːdl] *n* cinta *f*.

girl [gɜːl] *n* (*child*) menina *f*; (*young woman*) moça *f* (*Br*), rapariga *f* (*Port*); (*daughter*) filha *f*.

girlfriend ['gɜːlfrend] *n* (*of boy, man*) namorada *f*; (*of girl, woman*) amiga *f*.

girl guide *n* (*Brit*) = escoteira *f*.

girl scout (*Am*) = **girl guide**.

giro ['dʒaɪrəʊ] (*pl* **-s**) *n* (*system*) transferência *f* bancária.

girth [gɜːθ] *n* (*of person*) (medida da) cintura *f*.

gist [dʒɪst] *n* ideia *f* geral; **to get the ~ (of sthg)** compreender a idéia geral (de algo).

give [gɪv] (*pt* gave, *pp* given ['gɪvn]) *vt* dar; (*speech, performance*) fazer; **to ~ sb sthg** dar algo a alguém; **to ~ sb a kiss** dar um beijo em alguém; **come on, ~ me a smile!** vamos lá, dê um sorriso!; **to ~ sthg a push** empurrar algo; **~ or take a few minutes** mais minuto menos minuto; **"~ way!"** "perda de prioridade".

❑ **give away** *vt sep* (*get rid of*) dar, desfazer-se de; (*reveal*) revelar.

❑ **give back** *vt sep* devolver.

❑ **give in** *vi* desistir.

❑ **give off** *vt fus* soltar.

❑ **give out** *vt sep* (*distribute*) distribuir.

❑ **give up** *vt sep* (*seat*) ceder ◆ *vi* (*admit defeat*) desistir; **to ~ up smoking** deixar de fumar; **to ~ up chocolate** deixar de comer chocolate.

given name *n* (*Am*) nome *m* próprio OR de batismo.

glacier ['glæsjəʳ] *n* glaciar *m*, geleira *f*.

glad [glæd] *adj* contente; **I'll be ~ to help** será um prazer ajudar.

gladly ['glædlɪ] *adv* (*willingly*) com muito prazer.

glamor ['glæmər] (*Am*) = **glamour**.

glamorous ['glæmərəs] *adj* glamoroso(-osa).

glamour ['glæməʳ] *n* (*Brit*) (*of person*) charme *m*; (*of place*) elegância *f*; (*of job*) prestígio *m*.

glance [glɑːns] *n* olhadela *f* ◆ *vi*: **to ~ (at)** dar uma olhadela (em).

112

gland [glænd] *n* glândula *f*.
glandular fever ['glændjʊlə-] *n* mononucleose *f* infecciosa, febre *f* glandular.
glare [gleə^r] *vi (person)* lançar olhares furiosos; *(sun, light)* brilhar intensamente.
glaring ['gleərɪŋ] *adj (error, weakness)* gritante; *(lights, sun)* ofuscante.
glass [glɑːs] *n (material)* vidro *m*; *(container, glassful)* copo *m* ♦ *adj* de vidro.
❑ **glasses** *npl* óculos *mpl*.
glassware ['glɑːsweə^r] *n* artigos *mpl* de vidro.
glaze [gleɪz] *n (on pottery)* vitrificado *m* ♦ *vt (pottery)* vitrificar.
glazier ['gleɪzjə^r] *n* vidraceiro *m* (-ra *f*).
gleam [gliːm] *n (of gold, candle)* brilho *m*; *(of disapproval, pride)* ponta *f* ♦ *vi (gold, candle)* luzir; *(with pleasure, pride)* brilhar.
gleaming ['gliːmɪŋ] *adj* brilhante.
glee [gliː] *n* contentamento *m*, alegria *f*.
glen [glen] *n (Scot)* vale *m*.
glib [glɪb] *adj (answer, excuse)* fácil; *(person)* com muita lábia.
glide [glaɪd] *vi (fly)* planar.
glider ['glaɪdə^r] *n* planador *m*.
gliding ['glaɪdɪŋ] *n* vôo *m* planado OR sem motor.
glimmer ['glɪmə^r] *n (faint light)* brilho *m* (fraco); *(trace, sign)* pontinha *f*.
glimpse [glɪmps] *n*: **I only caught a ~ of her** só a vi de relance.
glisten ['glɪsn] *vi* brilhar.
glitter ['glɪtə^r] *vi* reluzir.
gloat [gləʊt] *vi*: **to ~ (over sthg)** regozijar-se (com algo).
global ['gləʊbl] *adj (worldwide)* global, mundial.
global warming [-glaʊblˈwɔːmɪŋ] *n* aquecimento *m* da atmosfera.
globe [gləʊb] *n* globo *m*; **the ~ (Earth)** o globo.
gloom [gluːm] *n (darkness)* penumbra *f*; *(unhappiness)* tristeza *f*.
gloomy ['gluːmɪ] *adj (room, day)* sombrio(-bria); *(person)* triste.
glorious ['glɔːrɪəs] *adj (weather, sight)* esplêndido(-da); *(victory, history)* glorioso(-osa).
glory ['glɔːrɪ] *n* glória *f*.
gloss [glɒs] *n (shine)* brilho *m*; **~ (paint)** tinta *f* brilhante.

glossary ['glɒsərɪ] *n* glossário *m*.
glossy ['glɒsɪ] *adj (magazine, photo)* de papel couché.
glove [glʌv] *n* luva *f*.
glove compartment *n* portaluvas *m inv*.
glow [gləʊ] *n* luz *f*, brilho *m* ♦ *vi* luzir, brilhar.
glucose ['gluːkəʊs] *n* glucose *f*.
glue [gluː] *n* cola *f* ♦ *vt* colar.
glum [glʌm] *adj* triste, sorumbático(-ca).
glutton ['glʌtn] *n (greedy person)* glutão *m* (-tona *f*).
gnash [næʃ] *vt*: **to ~ one's teeth** ranger os dentes.
gnat [næt] *n* mosquito *m*.
gnaw [nɔː] *vt* roer.
gnome [nəʊm] *n* anão *m*.
go [gəʊ] *(pt* went, *pp* gone, *pl* goes) *vi*
1. *(move, travel)* ir; **to ~ home** ir para casa; **to ~ to Portugal** ir a Portugal; **to ~ by bus** ir de ônibus; **to ~ for a walk** ir dar um passeio; **to ~ and do sthg** ir fazer algo; **to ~ in** entrar; **to ~ out** sair.
2. *(leave)* ir-se; **it's time for us to ~** é hora de irmos embora; **when does the bus ~?** quando é que o ônibus sai?; **~ away!** vai embora!
3. *(attend)* ir; **to ~ to school** ir para a escola; **which school do you ~ to?** para que escola você vai?
4. *(become)* ficar; **she went pale** empalideceu; **the milk has gone sour** o leite azedou.
5. *(expressing future tense)*: **to be going to do sthg** ir fazer algo.
6. *(function)* funcionar; **the car won't ~** o carro não pega.
7. *(stop working)* ir-se; **the fuse has gone** o fusível queimou.
8. *(time)* passar.
9. *(progress)* correr; **to ~ well** correr bem.
10. *(bell, alarm)* tocar.
11. *(match)* condizer; **to ~ with** condizer com, ficar bem com; **red wine doesn't ~ with fish** vinho tinto não combina com peixe.
12. *(be sold)* ser vendido; **"everything must ~"** "liquidação total".
13. *(fit)* caber.
14. *(lead)* ir; **where does this path ~?** aonde é que este caminho vai dar?
15. *(belong)* ir, ser.

16. *(in phrases)*: **to let ~ of sthg** *(drop)* largar algo; **there are two days to ~** faltam dois dias; **to ~** *(Am: .to take away)* para levar.
♦ *n* **1.** *(turn)* vez *f*; **it's your ~** é a sua vez.
2. *(attempt)* tentativa *f*; **to have a ~ at sthg** experimentar algo; **"50p a ~"** *(for game)* "50 pence cada vez".
⌐ **go ahead** *vi* *(take place)* realizar-se; **~ ahead!** vai em frente!
⊐ **go back** *vi* voltar.
⌐ **go down** *vi* *(decrease)* diminuir; *(sun)* pôr-se; *(tyre)* esvaziar-se.
⊐ **go down with** *vt fus* *(inf: illness)* apanhar.
⌐ **go in** *vi* entrar.
⌐ **go off** *vi* *(alarm, bell)* tocar, soar; *(go bad)* azedar; *(light, heating)* apagar-se.
⌐ **go on** *vi* *(happen)* passar-se; *(light, heating)* acender-se; **to ~ on doing sthg** continuar a fazer algo.
⌐ **go out** *vi* *(leave house)* sair; *(light, fire, cigarette)* apagar-se; *(have relationship)*: **to ~ out with sb** sair com alguém; **to ~ out for a meal** ir comer fora.
⌐ **go over** *vt fus* *(check)* rever.
⌐ **go round** *vi* *(revolve)* rodar; **there isn't enough cake to ~ round** não há bolo que chegue para todos.
⌐ **go through** *vt fus* *(experience)* passar por; *(spend)* gastar; *(search)* revistar.
⊐ **go up** *vi* *(increase)* subir.
⌐ **go without** *vt fus* passar sem.
goad [gəʊd] *vt* espicaçar, incitar.
go-ahead *n* *(permission)* luz *f* verde.
goal [gəʊl] *n* *(posts)* baliza *f*; *(point scored)* gol *m*; *(aim)* objetivo *m*.
goalkeeper [ˈgəʊlˌkiːpəʳ] *n* goleiro *m* (-ra *f*) *(Br)*, guarda-redes *mf inv* *(Port)*.
goalmouth [ˈgəʊlmaʊθ, *pl* -ˌmaʊðz] *n* boca *f* da baliza.
goalpost [ˈgəʊlpəʊst] *n* poste *m* (da baliza).
goat [gəʊt] *n* cabra *f*.
gob [gɒb] *n* *(Brit: inf: mouth)* bico *m*.
gobble [ˈgɒbl] *vt* engolir (sem mastigar).
⌐ **gobble down** *vt sep* engolir (sem mastigar).
⊐ **gobble up** = **gobble down**.
go-between *n* intermediário *m* (-ria *f*).
gobsmacked [ˈgɒbsmækt] *adj* *(Brit: inf)*: **I was ~** fiquei de boca aberta.
go-cart = **go-kart**.

god [gɒd] *n* deus *m*.
⊔ **God** *n* Deus *m*.
godchild [ˈgɒdtʃaɪld] *(pl* -children [-ˌtʃɪldrən]) *n* afilhado *m* (-da *f*).
goddaughter [ˈgɒdˌdɔːtəʳ] *n* afilhada *f*.
goddess [ˈgɒdɪs] *n* deusa *f*.
godfather [ˈgɒdˌfɑːðəʳ] *n* padrinho *m*.
godmother [ˈgɒdˌmʌðəʳ] *n* madrinha *f*.
gods [gɒdz] *npl*: **the ~** *(Brit: inf: in theatre)* o galinheiro.
godsend [ˈgɒdsend] *n*: **to be a ~** cair do céu.
godson [ˈgɒdsʌn] *n* afilhado *m*.
goes [gəʊz] → **go**.
goggles [ˈgɒglz] *npl* óculos *mpl* (protetores).
going [ˈgəʊɪŋ] *adj* *(available)* disponível; **the ~ rate** a tarifa em vigor.
go-kart [-kɑːt] *n* kart *m*.
gold [gəʊld] *n* ouro *m* ♦ *adj* *(bracelet, watch)* de ouro; *(colour)* dourado(-da).
golden [ˈgəʊldən] *adj* *(made of gold)* de ouro; *(gold-coloured)* dourado(-da).
goldfish [ˈgəʊldfɪʃ] *(pl inv)* *n* peixe-dourado *m*.
gold medal *n* medalha *f* de ouro.
gold-plated [-ˈpleɪtɪd] *adj* banhado (-da) a ouro.
golf [gɒlf] *n* golfe *m*.
golf ball *n* bola *f* de golfe.
golf club *n* *(place)* clube *m* de golfe; *(piece of equipment)* taco *m* de golfe.
golf course *n* campo *m* de golfe.
golfer [ˈgɒlfəʳ] *n* jogador *m* (-ra *f*) de golfe.
gone [gɒn] *pp* → **go** ♦ *prep* *(Brit)*: **it's ~ ten** já passa das dez.
gong [gɒŋ] *n* gongo *m*.
good [gʊd] *(compar* **better,** *superl* **best)** *adj* bom (boa); *(well-behaved)* bem comportado(-da) ♦ *n* o bem; **be ~!** porte-se bem!; **to have a ~ time** divertir-se; **to be ~ at sthg** ser bom em algo; **a ~ ten minutes** uns bons dez minutos; **in ~ time** com antecedência; **to make ~ sthg** *(damage)* pagar por algo; *(loss)* compensar algo; **for ~** para sempre; **for the ~ of** para o bem de; **to do sb ~** fazer bem a alguém; **it's no ~** *(there's no point)* não vale a pena; **~ afternoon!** boa tarde!; **~ evening!** boa noite!; **~ morning!** bom

dia!; ~ **night!** boa noite!.
❑ **night!** boa noite!.
goodbye [gʊdˈbaɪ] *excl* adeus!
Good Friday *n* Sexta-feira *f* Santa.
good-humoured *adj* bem-humorado(-da).
good-looking [-ˈlʊkɪŋ] *adj* bonito(-ta).
good-natured [-ˈneɪtʃəd] *adj* amigável.
goodness [ˈgʊdnɪs] *n (kindness)* bondade *f; (nutritive quality)* valor *m* nutritivo ♦ *excl:* **(my) ~!** meu Deus!; **for ~ sake!** por favor!, por amor de Deus!; **thank ~!** graças a Deus!
goods train [gʊdz-] *n* trem *m* de mercadorias.
goodwill [gʊdˈwɪl] *n* boa vontade *f*.
goody [ˈgʊdɪ] *n (inf: in film, book etc)* bom *m* (boa *f*).
❑ **goodies** *npl (inf: desirable things)* coisas *fpl* boas.
goose [guːs] *(pl* geese) *n* ganso *m*.
gooseberry [ˈgʊzbərɪ] *n* groselha *f* branca.
goosebumps [ˈguːsbʌmps] *npl (Am)* = **gooseflesh.**
gooseflesh [ˈguːsfleʃ] *n* pele *f* de galinha, pele *f* arrepiada.
goose pimples *npl (Brit)* = **gooseflesh.**
gorge [gɔːdʒ] *n* garganta *f*, desfiladeiro *m*.
gorgeous [ˈgɔːdʒəs] *adj (day, meal, countryside)* magnífico(-ca); *(inf: goodlooking)* lindo(-da).
gorilla [gəˈrɪlə] *n* gorila *mf*.
gorse [gɔːs] *n* tojo *m* (arnal).
gory [ˈgɔːrɪ] *adj (film)* com muito sangue; *(scene, death)* sangrento(-ta); *(details)* escabroso(-osa).
gosh [gɒʃ] *excl (inf)* caramba!
gospel [ˈgɒspl] *n (doctrine)* evangelho *m*.
❑ **Gospel** *n* Evangelho *m*.
gossip [ˈgɒsɪp] *n (about someone)* mexerico *m*, fofoca *f; (chat)* conversa *f* ♦ *vi (about someone)* fofocar; *(chat)* conversar.
gossip column *n* coluna em jornal ou revista dedicada a mexericos sobre figuras públicas.
got [gɒt] *pt & pp →* get.
gotten [ˈgɒtn] *pp (Am) →* get.
goujons [ˈguːdʒɒnz] *npl* filés *mpl* (de peixe).

goulash [ˈguːlæʃ] *n* gulache *m*, prato húngaro de carne ensopada temperada com colorau ou pimentão-doce.
gourmet [ˈgʊəmeɪ] *n* gastrônomo *m* (-ma *f*) ♦ *adj* gastronômico(-ca).
govern [ˈgʌvən] *vt* governar.
governess [ˈgʌvənɪs] *n* governanta *f*, preceptora *f*.
government [ˈgʌvnmənt] *n* governo *m*.
governor [ˈgʌvənəʳ] *n (of state, colony)* governador *m* (-ra *f*); *(of school, bank, prison)* diretor *m* (-ra *f*).
gown [gaʊn] *n (dress)* vestido *m*.
GP *abbr* = **general practitioner.**
grab [græb] *vt (take hold of)* agarrar.
grace [greɪs] *n (elegance)* graça *f*, elegância *f; (prayer)* ação *f* de graças.
graceful [ˈgreɪsfʊl] *adj* gracioso (-osa).
gracious [ˈgreɪʃəs] *adj (polite)* amável ♦ *excl:* **(good) ~!** santo Deus!
grade [greɪd] *n (quality)* categoria *f; (in exam)* nota *f; (Am: year at school)* ano *m* (de escolaridade).
grade crossing *n (Am)* passagem *f* de nível.
grade school *n (Am)* escola *f* primária.
gradient [ˈgreɪdjənt] *n* inclinação *f*.
gradual [ˈgrædʒʊəl] *adj* gradual.
gradually [ˈgrædʒʊəlɪ] *adv* gradualmente.
graduate [*n* ˈgrædʒʊət, *vb* ˈgrædʒʊeɪt] *n (from university)* licenciado *m* (-da *f*); *(Am: from high school)* pessoa que concluiu o ensino secundário ♦ *vi (from university)* licenciar-se, formar-se; *(Am: from high school)* concluir o ensino secundário.
graduation [grædʒʊˈeɪʃn] *n (ceremony)* entrega *f* dos diplomas.
graffiti [grəˈfiːtɪ] *n* grafite *m*.
grain [greɪn] *n (seed, of sand)* grão *m; (crop)* cereais *mpl; (of salt)* pedra *f*.
gram [græm] *n* grama *m*.
grammar [ˈgræməʳ] *n* gramática *f*.
grammar school *n (in UK)* escola secundária tradicional para alunos dos 11 aos 18 anos, cujo acesso é ditado por um exame.
grammatical [grəˈmætɪkl] *adj (referring to grammar)* gramatical; *(grammatically correct)* (gramaticalmente) correto(-ta).
gramme [græm] = **gram.**

gramophone ['græməfəʊn] *n* gramofone *m*.

gran [græn] *n (Brit) (inf)* avó *f*.

grand [grænd] *adj (impressive)* magnífico(-ca) ◆ *n (inf)* (£1,000) mil libras *fpl*; ($1,000) mil dólares *mpl*.

grandchild ['græntʃaɪld] (*pl* -children [-tʃɪldrən]) *n* neto *m* (-ta *f*).

granddad ['grændæd] *n (inf)* avô *m*.

granddaughter ['græn,dɔːtər] *n* neta *f*.

grandeur ['grændʒər] *n* grandeza *f*, imponência *f*.

grandfather ['grænd,fɑːðər] *n* avô *m*.

grandma ['grænmɑː] *n (inf)* avó *f*.

grandmother ['græn,mʌðər] *n* avó *f*.

grandpa ['grænpɑː] *n (inf)* avô *m*.

grandparents ['græn,peərənts] *npl* avós *mpl*.

grand piano *n* piano *m* de cauda.

grand slam *n (in rugby, football)* pleno *m*.

grandson ['grænsʌn] *n* neto *m*.

grandstand ['grændstænd] *n* tribuna *f*.

granite ['grænɪt] *n* granito *m*.

granny ['grænɪ] *n (inf)* avó *f*.

grant [grɑːnt] *n (for study)* bolsa *f*; *(POL)* subsídio *m* ◆ *vt (fml: give)* conceder; **to take sthg for ~ed** considerar algo como um dado adquirido; **to take sb for ~ed** não dar o devido valor a alguém.

granulated sugar ['grænjʊleɪtɪd-] *n* açúcar *m* cristalizado.

granule ['grænjuːl] *n (of salt, sugar)* pedrinha *f*; *(of coffee)* grânulo *m*.

grape [greɪp] *n* uva *f*.

grapefruit ['greɪpfruːt] *n* toranja *f*.

grapefruit juice *n* suco *m* de toranja *(Br)*, sumo *m* de toranja *(Port)*.

graph [grɑːf] *n* gráfico *m*.

graphic ['græfɪk] *adj (vivid)* minucioso(-osa).

❏ **graphics** *npl (pictures)* gráficos *mpl*.

graph paper *n* papel *m* milimétrico.

grasp [grɑːsp] *vt (grip)* agarrar; *(understand)* perceber.

grass [grɑːs] *n (plant)* grama *f (Br)*, erva *f (Port)*; *(lawn)* relva *f (Port)*; **"keep off the ~"** "não pise na grama".

grasshopper ['grɑːs,hɒpər] *n* gafanhoto *m*.

grate [greɪt] *n* grelha *f*.

grated ['greɪtɪd] *adj* ralado(-da).

grateful ['greɪtfʊl] *adj* agradecido (-da), grato(-ta).

grater ['greɪtər] *n* ralador *m*.

grating ['greɪtɪŋ] *adj* irritante ◆ *n (grille)* gradeamento *m*.

gratitude ['grætɪtjuːd] *n* gratidão *f*.

gratuity [grətjuːɪtɪ] *n (fml)* gratificação *f*.

grave¹ [greɪv] *adj (mistake, news, concern)* grave ◆ *n* sepultura *f*.

grave² [grɑːv] *adj (accent)* grave.

gravel ['grævl] *n* gravilha *f*.

gravestone ['greɪvstəʊn] *n* pedra *f* tumular.

graveyard ['greɪvjɑːd] *n* cemitério *m*.

gravity ['grævɪtɪ] *n* gravidade *f*.

gravy ['greɪvɪ] *n* molho *m* (de carne).

gray [greɪ] *(Am)* = grey.

graze [greɪz] *vt (injure)* esfolar.

grease [griːs] *n* gordura *f*.

greaseproof paper [griːspruːf-] *n (Brit)* papel *m* vegetal.

greasy ['griːsɪ] *adj (clothes, food)* gorduroso(-osa); *(skin, hair)* oleoso(-osa).

great [greɪt] *adj* grande; *(very good)* ótimo(-ma); **(that's) ~!** ótimo!

Great Britain *n* Grã-Bretanha *f*.

Great Dane *n* grande dinamarquês *m (cão)*.

great-grandchild *n* bisneto *m* (-ta *f*).

great-grandfather *n* bisavô *m*.

great-grandmother *n* bisavó *f*.

greatly ['greɪtlɪ] *adv* muito.

greatness ['greɪtnɪs] *n* grandeza *f*, importância *f*.

Greece [griːs] *n* Grécia *f*.

greed [griːd] *n (for food)* gulodice *f*; *(for money)* ganância *f*.

greedy ['griːdɪ] *adj (for food)* guloso(-osa); *(for money)* ganancioso(-osa).

Greek [griːk] *adj* grego(-ga) ◆ *n (person)* grego *m* (-ga *f*); *(language)* grego *m*.

Greek salad *n* salada *f* mista *(com tomate, alface, azeitonas negras e queijo de cabra)*.

green [griːn] *adj* verde ◆ *n (colour)* verde *m*; *(in village)* gramado *m* público; *(on golf course)* green *m*.

❏ **greens** *npl (vegetables)* verduras *fpl*.

green beans *npl* feijão *m* verde.

green belt *n (Brit)* cinturão *m* verde.

green card *n (Brit: for car)* carteira *f*

verde, *seguro necessário para viajar de carro no estrangeiro; (Am: work permit)* autorização *f* de permanência e trabalho.

green channel *n passagem em porto ou aeroporto reservada a passageiros sem artigos a declarar.*

greenery ['gri:nərɪ] *n* verde *m.*

greenfly ['gri:nflaɪ] (*pl inv* OR **-flies**) *n* pulgão *m.*

greengage ['gri:ngeɪdʒ] *n* rainha-cláudia *f.*

greengrocer's ['gri:nɡrəʊsəz] *n (shop) loja onde se vende fruta, legumes e hortaliça.*

greenhouse ['gri:nhaʊs, *pl* -haʊzɪz] *n* estufa *f.*

greenhouse effect *n* efeito *m* estufa.

Greenland ['gri:nlənd] *n* Gronelândia *f.*

green light *n* sinal *m* verde.

green pepper *n* pimentão *m* (verde).

Greens [gri:nz] *npl*: **the ~** os Verdes.

green salad *n* salada *f* verde.

greet [gri:t] *vt (say hello to)* cumprimentar.

greeting ['gri:tɪŋ] *n* cumprimento *m.*

greeting card (*Am*) = **greetings card.**

greetings card *n (Brit)* cartão *m* de felicitações.

grenade [ɡrə'neɪd] *n* granada *f.*

grew [gru:] *pt* → **grow.**

grey [ɡreɪ] *adj* cinzento(-ta); *(hair)* grisalho(-lha) ♦ *n* cinzento *m*; **to go ~** ganhar cabelos brancos.

grey-haired *adj* grisalho(-lha).

greyhound ['ɡreɪhaʊnd] *n* galgo *m.*

grid [ɡrɪd] *n (grating)* gradeamento *m*; *(on map etc)* quadrícula *f.*

grief [ɡri:f] *n* desgosto *m*; **to come to ~** fracassar.

grievance ['ɡri:vns] *n (complaint)* (motivo *m* de) queixa *f.*

grieve [ɡri:v] *vi* estar de luto.

grill [ɡrɪl] *n* grelha *f*; *(part of restaurant)* grill *m* ♦ *vt* grelhar.

grille [ɡrɪl] *n* (AUT) grelha *f* do radiador.

grilled [ɡrɪld] *adj* grelhado(-da).

grim [ɡrɪm] *adj (expression)* severo(-ra); *(place, reality)* sombrio(-bria); *(news)* desagradável.

grimace ['ɡrɪməs] *n* careta *f.*

grime [ɡraɪm] *n* sujeira *f.*

grimy ['ɡraɪmɪ] *adj* sebento(-ta).

grin [ɡrɪn] *n* sorriso *m* (largo) ♦ *vi* sorrir.

grind [ɡraɪnd] (*pt & pp* **ground**) *vt (pepper, coffee)* moer.

grinder ['ɡraɪndə'] *n* moinho *m.*

grip [ɡrɪp] *n (of tyres)* aderência *f*; *(handle)* punho *m*; *(bag)* bolsa *f* de viagem; *(hold)* pega *f* ♦ *vt (hold)* agarrar; **to keep a firm ~ on sthg** *(rope, railings)* agarrar algo com força; **get a ~ on yourself!** controle-se!

gripping ['ɡrɪpɪŋ] *adj* apaixonante.

grisly ['ɡrɪzlɪ] *adj* horripilante, horrendo(-da).

gristle ['ɡrɪsl] *n* nervo *m.*

grit [ɡrɪt] *n (stones)* gravilha *f*; *(sand)* saibro *m*; *(in eye)* cisco *m*, areia *f* ♦ *vt (road, steps)* ensaibrar.

groan [ɡrəʊn] *n* gemido *m* ♦ *vi (in pain)* gemer; *(complain)* resmungar.

groceries ['ɡrəʊsərɪz] *npl* mercearia *f.*

grocer's ['ɡrəʊsəz] *n (shop)* mercearia *f.*

grocery ['ɡrəʊsərɪ] *n (shop)* mercearia *f.*

groggy ['ɡrɒɡɪ] *adj* tonto(-ta), zonzo(-za).

groin [ɡrɔɪn] *n* virilha *f.*

groom [ɡru:m] *n (of horses)* cavalariço *m* (*Br*), moço *m* de estrebaria (*Port*); *(bridegroom)* noivo *m* ♦ *vt (horse, dog)* escovar; *(candidate)* preparar.

groove [ɡru:v] *n* ranhura *f.*

grope [ɡrəʊp] *vi*: **to ~ around for sthg** procurar algo com apalpadelas.

gross [ɡrəʊs] *adj (weight, income)* bruto(-ta).

grossly ['ɡrəʊslɪ] *adv (extremely)* extremamente.

grotesque [ɡrəʊ'tesk] *adj* grotesco(-ca).

grotto ['ɡrɒtəʊ] (*pl* **-s** OR **-es**) *n* gruta *f.*

grotty ['ɡrɒtɪ] *adj (Brit: inf)* mixa (*Br*), rasca (*Port*).

ground [ɡraʊnd] *pt & pp* → **grind** ♦ *n* chão *m*; (SPORT) campo *m* ♦ *adj (coffee)* moído(-da) ♦ *vt*: **to be ~ed** *(plane)* não ter autorização para decolar; *(Am: electrical connection)* estar ligado à terra.

⌐ **grounds** *npl (of building)* área que circunda um prédio; *(of coffee)* borra *f*; *(reason)* razão *f*, motivo *m.*

ground crew *n* pessoal *m* de terra.
ground floor *n* andar *m* térreo *(Br)*, rés-do-chão *m (Port)*.
grounding ['graʊndɪŋ] *n*: ~ **in sthg** conhecimentos *mpl* (básicos) de algo.
groundless ['graʊndlɪs] *adj* infundado(-da).
groundsheet ['graʊndʃiːt] *n* chão *m* OR solo *m* da barraca.
groundwork ['graʊndwɜːk] *n* trabalho *m* preparatório.
group [gruːp] *n* grupo *m*.
groupie ['gruːpɪ] *n (inf)* groupie *mf*, *pessoa que segue o seu grupo ou artista preferido de perto indo a todos os seus concertos.*
grouse [graʊs] *(pl inv) n (bird)* galo silvestre *m*.
grove [grəʊv] *n (group of trees)* mata *f*; **lemon** ~ limoal *m*.
grovel ['grɒvl] *vi (be humble)* humilhar-se.
grow [grəʊ] *(pt grew, pp grown) vi* crescer; *(become)* tornar-se ◆ *vt (plant, crop)* cultivar; *(beard)* deixar crescer.
❑ **grow up** *vi* crescer.
growl [graʊl] *vi (dog)* rosnar.
grown [grəʊn] *pp* → **grow**.
grown-up *adj* adulto(-ta) ◆ *n* adulto *m* (-ta *f*).
growth [grəʊθ] *n (increase)* crescimento *m*; *(MED)* tumor *m*, abcesso *m*.
grub [grʌb] *n (inf: food)* comida *f*.
grubby ['grʌbɪ] *adj (inf)* porco (porca).
grudge [grʌdʒ] *n* ressentimento *m* ◆ *vt*: **to** ~ **sb sthg** invejar algo a alguém; **he seems to have a** ~ **against me** ele parece ter algo contra mim.
grueling ['groəlɪŋ] *(Am)* = **gruelling**.
gruelling ['groəlɪŋ] *adj (Brit)* extenuante.
gruesome ['gruːsəm] *adj* horripilante.
gruff [grʌf] *adj* áspero(-ra).
grumble ['grʌmbl] *vi (complain)* resmungar.
grumpy ['grʌmpɪ] *adj (inf)* resmungão(-gona).
grunt [grʌnt] *vi* grunhir.
guarantee [ˌgærən'tiː] *n* garantia *f* ◆ *vt* garantir.
guaranteed delivery [ˌgærən'tiːd-] *n (Brit)* = correio *m* expresso.
guard [gɑːd] *n (of prisoner etc)* guarda *mf*; *(Brit: on train)* guarda *m*; *(protective*

cover) proteção *f* ◆ *vt (watch over)* guardar; **to be on one's** ~ estar alerta.
guard dog *n* cão *m* de guarda.
guarded ['gɑːdɪd] *adj* cauteloso(-osa), prudente.
guardian ['gɑːdjən] *n (of child)* tutor *m* (-ra *f*); *(protector)* guardião *m* (-diã *f*).
guard's van *n (Brit)* vagão *m* traseiro.
guerilla = **guerrilla**.
Guernsey ['gɜːnzɪ] *n (place)* Guernsey *s*.
guerrilla [gə'rɪlə] *n* guerrilheiro *m* (-ra *f*).
guess [ges] *n* suposição *f* ◆ *vt & vi* adivinhar; **I** ~ **(so)** é provável, imagino que sim.
guesswork ['geswɜːk] *n* conjetura *f*.
guest [gest] *n (in home)* convidado *m* (-da *f*); *(in hotel)* hóspede *mf*.
guesthouse ['gesthaʊs, pl -haʊzɪz] *n* pensão *f*.
guestroom ['gestrʊm] *n* quarto *m* de hóspedes.
guffaw [gʌ'fɔː] *n* gargalhada *f* ◆ *vi* rir às gargalhadas.
guidance ['gaɪdəns] *n* orientação *f*.
guide [gaɪd] *n (for tourists)* guia *mf*; *(guidebook)* guia *m* ◆ *vt* guiar.
❑ **Guide** *n (Brit)* = escoteira *f*.
guidebook ['gaɪdbʊk] *n* guia *m*.
guide dog *n* cão *m* de guia.
guided tour ['gaɪdɪd-] *n* visita *f* com guia.
guidelines ['gaɪdlaɪnz] *npl* diretrizes *fpl*.
guild [gɪld] *n (association)* associação *f*.
guillotine ['gɪlətiːn] *n* guilhotina *f*.
guilt [gɪlt] *n* culpa *f*.
guilty ['gɪltɪ] *adj* culpado(-da).
Guinea-Bissau [ˌgɪnɪbɪ'saʊ] *n* Guiné-Bissau *f*.
guinea pig ['gɪnɪ-] *n* cobaia *f*.
guitar [gɪ'tɑːr] *n (acoustic)* viola *f*; *(electric)* guitarra *f*.
guitarist [gɪ'tɑːrɪst] *n (of acoustic guitar)* tocador *m* (-ra *f*) de viola; *(of electric guitar)* guitarrista *mf*.
gulf [gʌlf] *n (of sea)* golfo *m*.
Gulf War *n*: **the** ~ a Guerra do Golfo.
gull [gʌl] *n* gaivota *f*.
gullet [ˈgʌlɪt] *n* goela *f*.
gullible ['gʌləbl] *adj* ingênuo(-nua).

gully ['gʌlı] n barranco m.
gulp [gʌlp] n (of drink) gole m.
gum [gʌm] n (chewing gum, bubble gum) chiclete m (Br), pastilha f elástica (Port); (adhesive) cola f.
❑ **gums** npl (in mouth) gengivas fpl.
gumboots ['gʌmbuːts] npl (Brit) botas fpl de borracha, galochas fpl.
gun [gʌn] n (pistol) revólver m; (rifle) espingarda f; (cannon) canhão m.
gunfire ['gʌnfaɪəʳ] n tiroteio m.
gunman ['gʌnmən] (pl -men [-mən]) n pessoa f armada.
gunpoint ['gʌnpɔɪnt] n: at ~ sob ameaça de arma.
gunpowder ['gʌnˌpaʊdəʳ] n pólvora f.
gunshot ['gʌnʃɒt] n tiro m.
gurgle ['gɜːgl] vi gorgolejar.
gush [gʌʃ] n jorro m ◆ vi (flow out) jorrar.
gust [gʌst] n rajada f.
gut [gʌt] n (inf: stomach) bucho m.
❑ **guts** npl (inf) (intestines) tripas fpl; (courage) coragem f, peito m.
gutter ['gʌtəʳ] n (beside road) sarjeta f; (of house) calha f (Br), caleira f (Port).

gutter press n imprensa f sensacionalista.
guy [gaɪ] n (inf: man) tipo m.
❑ **guys** npl (Am: inf: people): you ~s vocês.
Guy Fawkes Night [-ˈfɔːks-] n (Brit) 5 de novembro.
guy rope n corda f (de barraca de acampar).
guzzle ['gʌzl] vt (food) devorar; (drink) emborcar.
gym [dʒɪm] n (place) ginásio m; (school lesson) ginástica f.
gymnasium [dʒɪmˈneɪzjəm] (pl -iums OR -ia [-zɪə]) n ginásio m.
gymnast ['dʒɪmnæst] n ginasta mf.
gymnastics [dʒɪmˈnæstɪks] n ginástica f.
gym shoes npl sapatilhas fpl de ginástica.
gymslip ['dʒɪmˌslɪp] n (Brit) veste f escolar (Br), bata f da escola (Port).
gynaecologist [ˌgaɪnəˈkɒlədʒɪst] n ginecologista mf.
gynaecology [ˌgaɪnəˈkɒlədʒɪ] n ginecologia f.
gypsy ['dʒɪpsɪ] = gipsy.

H

H *(abbr of hospital)* H ◆ *abbr* = **hot**.
haberdashery [ˈhæbədæʃərɪ] *n*
(goods) artigos *mpl* de armarinho *(Br)*,
artigos *mpl* de retrosaria *(Port)*; *(shop)*
armarinho *m (Br)*, retrosaria *f (Port)*
habit [ˈhæbɪt] *n* hábito *m*.
habitat [ˈhæbɪtæt] *n* habitat *m*.
habitual [həˈbɪtʃʊəl] *adj (customary)*
habitual; *(offender, smoker, drinker)*
inveterado(-da).
hack [hæk] *vt* cortar, rachar.
hacksaw [ˈhæksɔː] *n* serra *f* para
metal.
had [hæd] *pt & pp* → **have**.
haddock [ˈhædək] *(pl inv)* *n* hadoque
m (Br), eglefim *m (Port)*.
hadn't [ˈhædnt] = **had not**.
haggard [ˈhægəd] *adj (person)* abati-
do(-da).
haggis [ˈhægɪs] *n* bucho de ovelha recheado com aveia, gordura, miudos de
carneiro e especiarias, cozido e servido
com batatas e nabos cozidos, prato tradicional escocês.
haggle [ˈhægl] *vi* regatear.
Hague [heɪg] *n*: **The ~** Haia *s*.
hail [heɪl] *n* granizo *m* ◆ *v impers*: **it's**
~ing está chovendo granizo.
hailstone [ˈheɪlstəʊn] *n* granizo *m*,
pedra *f*
hair [heər] *n (on human head)* cabelo
m; *(on skin)* pêlo *m*; **to have one's ~ cut**
cortar o cabelo; **to wash one's ~** lavar
a cabeça.
hairband [ˈheəbænd] *n* fita *f* para o
cabelo.
hairbrush [ˈheəbrʌʃ] *n* escova *f* (de
cabelo).
hairclip [ˈheəklɪp] *n* grampo *m (Br)*,
gancho *m (Port)*.
haircut [ˈheəkʌt] *n (style)* corte *m* (de
cabelo); **to have a ~** cortar o cabelo.
hairdo [ˈheəduː] *(pl -s)* *n* penteado *m*.

hairdresser [ˈheədresər] *n* cabeleireiro *m (-ra f)*; **~'s** *(salon)* cabeleireiro *m*; **to go to the ~'s** ir ao
cabeleireiro.
hairdryer [ˈheədraɪər] *n* secador *m* de
cabelo.
hair gel *n* gel *m* (para o cabelo).
hairgrip [ˈheəgrɪp] *n (Brit)* grampo *m*
(Br), gancho *m (Port)*.
hairnet [ˈheənet] *n* rede *f* para o cabelo.
hairpin [ˈheəpɪn] *n* grampo *m (Br)*,
gancho *m (Port)*.
hairpin bend *n* curva *f* fechada.
hair-raising [-reɪzɪŋ] *adj* de arrepiar
os cabelos, arrepiante.
hair remover [-rɪˌmuːvər] *n* depilatório *m*.
hair rollers [-rəʊləz] *npl* rolos *mpl*
(para o cabelo).
hair slide *n* grampo *m (Br)*, gancho
m (Port).
hairspray [ˈheəspreɪ] *n* laquê *m (Br)*,
laca *f (Port)*.
hairstyle [ˈheəstaɪl] *n* penteado *m*.
hairy [ˈheərɪ] *adj (person)* cabeludo
(-da); *(chest, legs)* peludo(-da).
Haiti [ˈheɪtɪ] *n* Haiti *m*.
hake [heɪk] *n* pescada *f*.
half [*Brit* hɑːf, *Am* hæf] *(pl* **halves***)* *n*
(50%) metade *f*; *(of match)* parte *f*; *(half*
pint) fino *m (Port)*, = 2,5 cl; *(child's tick-*
et) meia passagem *f (Br)*, meio bilhete
m (Port) ◆ *adj* meio (meia) ◆ *adv* meio;
a day and a ~ um dia e meio; **four and**
a ~ quatro e meio; **an hour and a**
~ uma hora e meia; **~ past seven** sete
e meia; **~ as big as** metade do tamanho de; **~ an hour** meia-hora; **~ a**
dozen meia dúzia; **~ price** a metade
do preço.
half board *n* meia pensão *f*.
half-day *n* meio-dia *m*.

half fare *n* meia passagem *f (Br)*, meio bilhete *m (Port)*.

half-hearted [-'hɑːtɪd] *adj* pouco entusiasta.

half hour *n* meia-hora *f*; **every ~** todas as meias-horas.

half-mast *n (Brit)*: **at ~** a meio mastro, a meia haste.

halfpenny ['heɪpnɪ] *(pl* **-pennies** OR **-pence)** *n* meio pêni *m*.

half portion *n* meia dose *f*.

half-price *adj* a metade do preço.

half term *n (Brit)* semana de férias na metade do trimestre escolar.

half time *n* intervalo *m*.

halfway [hɑːfˈweɪ] *adv (in space)* a meio caminho; *(in time)* a meio.

halibut ['hælɪbət] *(pl inv)* *n* palmeta *f*.

hall [hɔːl] *n (of house)* entrada *f*, hall *m*; *(building, large room)* salão *m*; *(country house)* – mansão *f*.

hallmark ['hɔːlmɑːk] *n (on silver, gold)* marca *f*.

hallo [həˈləʊ] = **hello**.

hall of residence *n* residência *f* universitária.

Halloween [ˌhæləʊˈiːn] *n* noite *f* das bruxas.

hallucinate [həˈluːsɪneɪt] *vi* delirar, estar com alucinações.

hallway ['hɔːlweɪ] *n* corredor *m*.

halo ['heɪləʊ] *(pl* **-es** OR **-s)** *n* halo *m*, auréola *f*.

halt [hɔːlt] *vi* parar ♦ *n*: **to come to a ~** parar.

halve [*Brit* hɑːv, *Am* hæv] *vt (reduce by half)* reduzir à metade; *(divide in two)* dividir ao meio.

halves [*Brit* hɑːvz, *Am* hævz] *pl* → **half**.

ham [hæm] *n* presunto *m*.

hamburger ['hæmbɜːɡəʳ] *n (beefburger)* hambúrguer *m*; *(Am: mince)* carne *f* picada.

hamlet ['hæmlɪt] *n* aldeia *f*, lugarejo *m*.

hammer ['hæməʳ] *n* martelo *m* ♦ *vt (nail)* martelar.

hammock ['hæmək] *n* rede *f*.

hamper ['hæmpəʳ] *n* cesta *f* (de piquenique).

hamster ['hæmstəʳ] *n* hamster *m*.

hamstring ['hæmstrɪŋ] *n* tendão *m* do jarrete.

hand [hænd] *n* mão *f*; *(of clock, watch, dial)* ponteiro *m*; **to give sb a ~** dar uma mão a alguém; **to get out of ~**

fugir ao controle; **by ~** à mão; **in ~** *(time)* disponível; **on the one ~** por um lado; **on the other ~** por outro lado.

❏ **hand in** *vt sep* entregar.

❏ **hand out** *vt sep* distribuir.

❏ **hand over** *vt sep (give)* entregar.

handbag ['hændbæg] *n* bolsa *f*, carteira *f*.

handball ['hændbɔːl] *n* andebol *m*.

handbasin ['hændbeɪsn] *n* pia *f*.

handbook ['hændbʊk] *n* manual *m*.

handbrake ['hændbreɪk] *n* freio *m* de mão *(Br)*, travão *m* de mão *(Port)*.

hand cream *n* creme *m* para as mãos.

handcuffs ['hændkʌfs] *npl* algemas *fpl*.

handful ['hændfʊl] *n (amount)* mãocheia *f*, punhado *m*.

handgun ['hændɡʌn] *n* pistola *f*.

handicap ['hændɪkæp] *n (physical, mental)* deficiência *f*; *(disadvantage)* desvantagem *f*.

handicapped ['hændɪkæpt] *adj* deficiente ♦ *npl*: **the ~** os deficientes.

handicraft ['hændɪkrɑːft] *n* artesanato *m*.

handiwork ['hændɪwɜːk] *n* obra *f*.

handkerchief ['hæŋkətʃɪf] *(pl* **-chiefs** OR **-chieves** [-tʃiːvz]) *n* lenço *m* (de mão).

handle ['hændl] *n (of door, window)* puxador *m*; *(of suitcase)* alça *f*; *(of pan, knife)* cabo *m* ♦ *vt (touch)* pegar em; *(deal with)* lidar com; *(solve)* tratar de; **"~ with care"** "frágil".

handlebars ['hændlbɑːz] *npl* guidom *m (Br)*, guiador *m (Port)*.

hand luggage *n* bagagem *f* de mão.

handmade [ˌhændˈmeɪd] *adj* feito(-ta) à mão.

handout ['hændaʊt] *n (leaflet)* prospecto *m*.

handrail ['hændreɪl] *n* corrimão *m*.

handset ['hændset] *n* fone *m (Br)*, auscultador *m (Port)*; **"please replace the ~"** *mensagem que avisa que o telefone não está bem desligado*.

handshake ['hændʃeɪk] *n* aperto *m* de mão.

handsome ['hænsəm] *adj* bonito(-ta).

handstand ['hændstænd] *n* pino *m*.

handwriting ['hændˌraɪtɪŋ] *n* letra *f*, caligrafia *f*.

handy ['hændɪ] *adj (useful)* prático (-ca); *(good with one's hands)* habilidoso(-osa); *(near)* à mão; **to come in ~** *(inf)* vir mesmo a calhar.

handyman ['hændımæn] *(pl* **-men** [-mɛn])* n* faz-tudo *m*, biscoteiro *m*.

hang [hæŋ] *(pt & pp* **hung)** *vt (on hook, wall etc)* pendurar; *(execute: pt & pp* **hanged)** enforcar ◆ *vi (be suspended)* pender ◆ *n*: **to get the ~ of sthg** pegar o jeito de algo.

◗ **hang about** *vi (Brit: inf)* rondar.

◗ **hang around** *(inf)* = **hang about**.

◗ **hang down** *vi* estar pendurado(-da).

◗ **hang on** *vi (inf: wait)* esperar.

◗ **hang out** *vt sep (washing)* pendurar ◆ *vi (inf: spend time)* passar o tempo.

◗ **hang up** *vi (on phone)* desligar.

hangar ['hæŋəʳ] *n* hangar *m*.

hanger ['hæŋəʳ] *n* cabide *m*.

hang gliding *n* asa-delta *f*.

hangover ['hæŋ,ouvəʳ] *n* ressaca *f*.

hang-up *n (inf)* complexo *m*.

hankie ['hæŋkı] *n (inf)* lenço *m* (de mão).

haphazard [,hæp'hæzəd] *adj* ao acaso; **her work is very ~** o trabalho dela é muito irregular.

happen ['hæpən] *vi* acontecer; **I ~ed to bump into him** encontrei-o por acaso.

happily ['hæpılı] *adv (luckily)* felizmente.

happiness ['hæpınıs] *n* felicidade *f*.

happy ['hæpı] *adj* feliz; **to be ~ about sthg** *(satisfied)* estar satisfeito(-ta) com algo; **to be ~ to do sthg** não se importar de fazer algo; **to be ~ with sthg** estar satisfeito com algo; **Happy Birthday!** Parabéns!, Feliz Aniversário!; **Happy Christmas!** Feliz Natal!; **Happy New Year!** Feliz Ano Novo!

happy-go-lucky *adj* despreocupado(-da).

happy hour *n (inf) período, normalmente ao fim da tarde, em que os bares vendem as bebidas mais barato.*

harass ['hærəs] *vt* assediar, importunar.

harassment ['hærəsmənt] *n* assédio *m*, importúnio *m*.

harbor ['hɑːbəʳ] *(Am)* = **harbour**.

harbour ['hɑːbəʳ] *n (Brit)* porto *m*.

hard [hɑːd] *adj* duro(-ra); *(difficult, strenuous)* difícil; *(forceful)* forte; *(winter, frost)* rigoroso (-osa); *(water)* calcário(-ria), duro(-ra); *(drugs)* pesado(-da)

◆ *adv (work)* muito, arduamente; *(listen)* atentamente; *(hit, rain)* com força; **to try ~** fazer um esforço.

hardback ['hɑːdbæk] *n* livro *m* encadernado.

hardboard ['hɑːdbɔːd] *n* madeira *f* compensada *(Br)*, platex *m (Port)*.

hard-boiled egg [-bɔıld-] *n* ovo *m* cozido.

hard cash *n* dinheiro *m* em espécie, dinheiro *m* vivo.

hard copy *n* cópia *f* impressa.

hard disk *n* disco *m* rígido OR duro.

harden ['hɑːdn] *vt & vi* endurecer.

hard-hearted [-'hɑːtıd] *adj* insensível.

hardly ['hɑːdlı] *adv*: **~ ever** quase nunca; **I ~ know her** mal a conheço; **there's ~ any left** já não há quase nada.

hardness ['hɑːdnıs] *n (solidness)* dureza *f*; *(difficulty)* dificuldade *f*.

hardship ['hɑːdʃıp] *n* dificuldades *fpl*.

hard shoulder *n (Brit)* acostamento *m (Br)*, zona *f* de paragem de urgência.

hard up *adj (inf)* teso(-sa).

hardware ['hɑːdweəʳ] *n (tools, equipment)* ferramenta *f*, *(COMPUT)* hardware *m*.

hardware shop *n* loja *f* de ferragens.

hardware store *n* loja *f* de ferragens.

hardwearing [,hɑːd'weərıŋ] *adj (Brit)* resistente.

hardworking [,hɑːd'wɜːkıŋ] *adj* trabalhador(-ra).

hardy ['hɑːdı] *adj (person, animal)* robusto(-ta); *(plant)* vivaz, resistente.

hare [heəʳ] *n* lebre *f*.

harebrained ['heə,breınd] *adj (inf)* disparatado(-da), desmiolado(-da).

haricot (bean) ['hærıkəʊ-] *n* feijão *m* branco.

harm [hɑːm] *n (injury)* mal *m*; *(damage)* dano *m* ◆ *vt (injure)* magoar; *(reputation, chances)* prejudicar; *(fabric)* danificar.

harmful ['hɑːmfʊl] *adj* prejudicial.

harmless ['hɑːmlıs] *adj* inofensivo(-va).

harmonica [hɑː'mɒnıkə] *n* harmónica *f*.

harmony ['hɑːmənı] *n* harmonia *f*.

harness ['hɑːnıs] *n (for horse)* arreios

mpl; (for child) andadeira *f.*

harp [ha:p] *n* harpa *f.*

harpoon [ha:'pu:n] *n* arpão *m*
◆ *vt* arpear.

harpsichord ['ha:psıkɔ:d] *n* cravo *m.*

harrowing ['hærəʊɪŋ] *adj* horrível,
horroroso(-osa).

harsh [ha:ʃ] *adj (severe)* rigoroso(-osa); *(cruel)* severo(-ra); *(sound, voice)* áspero(-ra).

harvest ['ha:vıst] *n* colheita *f.*

has [*weak form* həz, *strong form* hæz] →
have.

has-been *n (inf)* velha glória *f*, estrela *f* do passado.

hash [hæʃ] *n (meat)* picadinho *m* de
carne; **I made a real ~ of the exam**
(inf) fui extremamente mal no exame.

hash browns [hæʃ-] *npl (Am)* bolinhos fritos de batatas e cebolas picadas.

hasn't ['hæznt] = has not.

hassle ['hæsl] *n (inf)* chatice *f.*

haste [heıst] *n* pressa *f.*

hastily ['heıstılı] *adv* precipitadamente.

hasty ['heıstı] *adj (hurried)* apressado
(-da); *(rash)* precipitado(-da).

hat [hæt] *n* chapéu *m.*

hatch [hætʃ] *n (for serving food)* passa-pratos *m* ◆ *vi (chick)* nascer.

hatchback ['hætʃ,bæk] *n* carro *m* de
três OR cinco portas.

hatchet ['hætʃıt] *n* machado *m.*

hatchway ['hætʃ,weı] *n (on ship)* escotilha *f.*

hate [heıt] *n* ódio *m* ◆ *vt* odiar, detestar; **to ~ doing sthg** detestar fazer
algo.

hateful ['heıtfʊl] *adj* detestável, odioso(-osa).

hatred ['heıtrıd] *n* ódio *m.*

hat trick *n* hat trick *m*, três gols marcados pelo mesmo jogador no mesmo
jogo.

haughty ['hɔ:tı] *adj* altivo(-va).

haul [hɔ:l] *vt* arrastar ◆ *n:* **a long ~** um
longo percurso.

haunch [hɔ:ntʃ] *n (of person)* quadril
m; (of animal) quarto *m* traseiro.

haunt [hɔ:nt] *n* sítio *m* preferido ◆ *vt*
(subj: ghost) assombrar.

haunted ['hɔ:ntıd] *adj (house)* assombrado(-da).

have [hæv] *(pt & pp had) aux vb* **1.** *(to
form perfect tenses):* **I ~ finished** acabei;
~ you been there? – no, I haven't você

já esteve lá? – não; **they hadn't seen it**
não o tinham visto; **we had already
left** nós já tínhamos saído.
2. *(must):* **to ~ (got) to do sthg** ter de
fazer algo; **do you ~ to pay?** é preciso
pagar?
◆ *vt* **1.** *(possess):* **to ~ (got)** ter; **do you
~ OR ~ you got a double room?** você
tem um quarto de casal?; **she has (got)
brown hair** ela tem o cabelo castanho.
2. *(experience)* ter; **to ~ a cold** estar
resfriado; **to ~ a great time** divertir-se
a valer.
3. *(replacing other verbs)* ter; **to ~
breakfast** tomar o café da manhã; **to ~
dinner** jantar; **to ~ lunch** almoçar; **to ~
a bath** tomar banho; **to ~ a drink**
tomar qualquer coisa, tomar um copo;
to ~ a shower tomar um banho; **to ~
a swim** nadar; **to ~ a walk** passear.
4. *(feel)* ter; **I ~ no doubt about it** não
tenho dúvida alguma OR nenhuma
sobre isso.
5. *(cause to be):* **to ~ sthg done** mandar
fazer algo; **to ~ one's hair cut** cortar o
cabelo.
6. *(be treated in a certain way):* **I've had
my wallet stolen** me roubaram a carteira.

haven't ['hævnt] = have not.

haversack ['hævəsæk] *n* mochila *f.*

havoc ['hævək] *n* caos *m.*

Hawaii [hə'waiı] *n* Havaí *m.*

hawk [hɔ:k] *n* falcão *m.*

hawker ['hɔ:kər] *n* vendedor *m* (-ra *f*)
ambulante.

hay [heı] *n* feno *m.*

hay fever *n* febre *f* do feno.

haystack ['heı,stæk] *n* meda *f* de feno.

haywire ['heı,waıər] *adj (inf):* **to go ~**
degringolar *(Br)*, flipar *(Port).*

hazard ['hæzəd] *n* risco *m.*

hazardous ['hæzədəs] *adj* arriscado(-da).

hazard warning lights *npl (Brit)*
pisca-alerta *m (Br)*, luzes *fpl* (avisadoras) de perigo *(Port).*

haze [heız] *n* névoa *f.*

hazel ['heızl] *adj* cor-de-mel *(inv).*

hazelnut ['heızl,nʌt] *n* avelã *f.*

hazy ['heızı] *adj (misty)* nublado(-da).

he [hi:] *pron* ele; **~'s tall** ele é alto.

head [hed] *n* cabeça *f; (of queue)* princípio *m; (of page, letter)* cabeçalho *m;
(of table, bed)* cabeceira *f; (of company,
department)* chefe *m* (-fa *f*); *(head*

teacher) diretor *m* (-ra *f*); *(of beer)* espuma *f* ♦ *vt (list, organization)* encabeçar ♦ vi: **to ~ home** dirigir-se para casa; **£10 a ~** 10 libras por cabeça; **~s or tails?** cara ou coroa?

⌐ **head for** *vt fus (place)* dirigir-se a.

headache ['hɛdeɪk] *n (pain)* dor *f* de cabeça; **I've got a ~** estou com dor de cabeça.

headband ['hɛdbænd] *n* fita *f* de cabelo.

head boy *n (Brit)* representante *m* estudantil.

headdress ['hɛddrɛs] *n* ornamento *m* para a cabeça.

header ['hɛdəʳ] *n (in football)* cabeçada *f.*

headfirst [ˌhɛd'fɜːst] *adv* de cabeça.

head girl *n . (Brit)* representante *f* estudantil.

heading ['hɛdɪŋ] *n* título *m.*

headlamp ['hɛdlæmp] *(Brit)* = **headlight.**

headlight ['hɛdlaɪt] *n* farol *m* (dianteiro).

headline ['hɛdlaɪn] *n (in newspaper)* manchete *f (Br)*, título *m (Port)*; *(on TV, radio)* notícia *f* principal.

headlong ['hɛdlɒŋ] *adv (at great speed)* a toda a velocidade; *(impetuously)* sem pensar; *(dive, fall)* de cabeça.

headmaster [ˌhɛd'mɑːstəʳ] *n* diretor *m* (de escola).

headmistress [ˌhɛd'mɪstrɪs] *n* diretora *f* (de escola).

head of state *n* chefe *m* de estado.

head-on *adj & adv* de frente.

headphones ['hɛdfəʊnz] *npl* fones *mpl* de ouvido *(Br)*, auscultadores *mpl (Port)*.

headquarters [ˌhɛd'kwɔːtəz] *npl (of business)* sede *f*; *(of army)* quartel *m* general; *(of police)* central *f.*

headrest ['hɛdrɛst] *n* apoio-de-cabeça *m.*

headroom ['hɛdrʊm] *n (under bridge)* vão *m* livre.

headscarf ['hɛdskɑːf] *(pl* **-scarves** [-skɑːvz]*) n* lenço *m* de cabeça.

headset ['hɛdsɛt] *n* fones *mpl* de ouvido *(Br)*, auscultadores *mpl* com microfone *(Port)*.

head start *n* vantagem *f*, avanço *m.*

headstrong ['hɛdstrɒŋ] *adj* cabeçudo(-da), teimoso(-osa).

head teacher *n* diretor *m* (-ra *f*) (da escola).

head waiter *n* maître *m (Br)*, chefe *m* de mesa *(Port)*.

heal [hiːl] *vt* curar ♦ *vi* sarar.

healing ['hiːlɪŋ] *n (of a person)* cura *f*; *(of a wound)* cicatrização *f.*

health [hɛlθ] *n* saúde *f*; **to be in good/poor ~** estar bem/mal de saúde; **your (very) good ~!** saúde!

health centre *n* centro *m* de saúde.

health food *n* comida *f* dietética.

health food shop *n* loja *f* de produtos dietéticos.

health insurance *n* seguro *m* de saúde.

health service *n* serviço *m* de saúde.

healthy [hɛlθɪ] *adj* saudável.

heap [hiːp] *n* monte *m*; **~s of** *(inf)* montes de.

hear [hɪəʳ] *(pt & pp* **heard** [hɜːd]*) vt & vi* ouvir; **to ~ about sthg** saber de algo; **to ~ from sb** ter notícias de alguém; **have you heard of him?** você já ouviu falar dele?

hearing ['hɪərɪŋ] *n (sense)* audição *f*; *(at court)* audiência *f*; **to be hard of ~** não ouvir bem.

hearing aid *n* aparelho *m* auditivo.

hearsay ['hɪəseɪ] *n* boato *m.*

hearse [hɜːs] *n* carro *m* fúnebre.

heart [hɑːt] *n* coração *m*; **to know sthg (off) by ~** saber algo de cor; **to lose ~** perder a coragem.

⌐ **hearts** *npl (in cards)* copas *fpl.*

heart attack *n* ataque *m* cardíaco.

heartbeat ['hɑːtbiːt] *n* pulsação *f*, batida *f* cardíaca.

heartbroken ['hɑːtˌbrəʊkn] *adj* desolado(-da), com o coração despedaçado.

heartburn ['hɑːtbɜːn] *n* azia *f.*

heart condition *n*: **to have a ~** ter problemas cardíacos OR de coração.

heartfelt ['hɑːtfɛlt] *adj* sincero(-ra), do fundo do coração.

hearth [hɑːθ] *n* borda *f* da lareira.

heartless ['hɑːtlɪs] *adj (person)* sem coração; *(refusal, decision)* cruel.

heartwarming ['hɑːtˌwɔːmɪŋ] *adj* comovente.

hearty ['hɑːtɪ] *adj (meal)* substancial.

heat [hiːt] *n* calor *m*; *(specific temperature)* temperatura *f.*

⌐ **heat up** *vt sep* aquecer.

heated ['hi:tɪd] *adj (room, swimming pool)* aquecido(-da); *(argument, discussion)* acalorado(-da).

heater ['hi:tər] *n* aquecedor *m*.

heath [hi:θ] *n* charneca *f*.

heathen ['hi:ðn] *adj* pagão(-gã) ◆ *n* pagão *m* (-gã *f*).

heather ['heðər] *n* urze *f*.

heating ['hi:tɪŋ] *n* aquecimento *m*.

heatstroke ['hi:tstrəʊk] *n* insolação *f*.

heat wave *n* onda *f* de calor.

heave [hi:v] *vt (push)* empurrar com força; *(pull)* puxar com força; *(lift)* levantar com força.

Heaven ['hevn] *n* paraíso *m*, céu *m*.

heavily ['hevɪlɪ] *adv* muito.

heavy ['hevɪ] *adj* pesado(-da); *(rain, fighting, traffic)* intenso(-sa); **how ~ is it?** quanto é que (isso) pesa?; **to be a ~ smoker** fumar muito.

heavy cream *n (Am)* creme *m* de leite *(Br)*, natas *fpl* espessas *(Port)*.

heavy goods vehicle *n (Brit)* veículo *m* pesado.

heavy industry *n* indústria *f* pesada.

heavy metal *n* heavy metal *m*.

heavyweight ['hevɪweɪt] *n (SPORT)* peso *m* pesado.

Hebrew ['hi:bru:] *adj* hebraico(-ca) ◆ *n (person)* hebreu *m* (-bréia *f*); *(language)* hebreu *m*, hebraico *m*.

Hebrides ['hebrɪdi:z] *npl*: **the ~** as Hébridas.

heckle ['hekl] *vt* interromper (continuamente).

hectic ['hektɪk] *adj* agitado(-da).

he'd [hi:d] = **he had**.

hedge [hedʒ] *n* cerca *f* viva *(Br)*, sebe *f*.

hedgehog ['hedʒhɒg] *n* ouriço-cacheiro *m*.

heel [hi:l] *n (of person)* calcanhar *m*; *(of shoe)* salto *m*.

hefty ['heftɪ] *adj (person)* robusto(-ta); *(fine)* considerável.

height [haɪt] *n* altura *f*; *(peak period)* ponto *m* alto; **what ~ is it?** quanto é que mede?

heighten ['haɪtn] *vt* aumentar, intensificar ◆ *vi* aumentar, intensificar-se.

heir [eər] *n* herdeiro *m*.

heiress ['eərɪs] *n* herdeira *f*.

heirloom ['eəlu:m] *n* relíquia *f* familiar.

held [held] *pt & pp* → **hold**.

helicopter ['helɪkɒptər] *n* helicóptero *m*.

Hell [hel] *n* o Inferno.

he'll [hi:l] = **he will**.

hellish ['helɪʃ] *adj (inf)* terrível; **the traffic was ~** o trânsito estava um inferno.

hello [hə'ləʊ] *excl (as greeting)* oi! *(Br)*, olá! *(Port)*; *(when answering phone)* alô! *(Br)*, estou! *(Port)*; *(when phoning)* alô? *(Br)*, está? *(Port)*; *(to attract attention)* ei!

helm [helm] *n (of ship)* leme *m*.

helmet ['helmɪt] *n* capacete *m*.

help [help] *n* ajuda *f* ◆ *vt & vi* ajudar ◆ *excl* socorro!; **I can't ~ it** não consigo evitá-lo; **to ~ sb (to) do sthg** ajudar alguém a fazer algo; **to ~ o.s. (to sthg)** servir-se (de algo); **can I ~ you?** *(in shop)* posso ajudá-lo?.

⌐ **help out** *vi* ajudar.

helper ['helpər] *n (assistant)* ajudante *mf*; *(Am: cleaner)* faxineira *f (Br)*, mulher-a-dias *f (Port)*.

helpful ['helpfʊl] *adj (person)* prestativo(-va); *(useful)* útil.

helping ['helpɪŋ] *n* porção *f*; **he had a second ~ of pudding** ele repetiu a sobremesa.

helpless ['helplɪs] *adj* indefeso(-sa).

Helsinki ['helsɪŋkɪ] *n* Helsínque *s*.

hem [hem] *n* bainha *f*.

hemisphere ['hemɪsfɪər] *n* hemisfério *m*.

hemline ['hemlaɪn] *n* bainha *f*.

hemophiliac [hi:mə'fɪlɪæk] *n* hemofílico *m* (-ca *f*).

hemorrhage ['hemərɪdʒ] *n* hemorragia *f*.

hemorrhoids ['hemərɔɪdz] *npl* hemorróidas *fpl*.

hen [hen] *n (chicken)* galinha *f*.

hence [hens] *adv (fml: therefore)* assim; *(from now)*: **ten years ~** daqui a dez anos.

henceforth [hens'fɔ:θ] *adv (fml)* de hoje em diante, doravante.

henna ['henə] *n* hena *f* ◆ *vt* pintar com hena.

henpecked ['henpekt] *adj*: **he's a ~ husband** ele é um pau-mandado da mulher.

hepatitis [hepə'taɪtɪs] *n* hepatite *f*.

her [hɜ:r] *adj* o seu (a sua), dela ◆ *pron*

(direct) a; *(indirect)* lhe; *(after prep)* ela; ~ **books** os livros dela, os seus livros; **I know** ~ eu a conheço; **it's** ~ é ela; **send it to** ~ mande isso para ela; **tell** ~ diz-lhe; **he's worse than** ~ ele é pior do que ela; **Zena brought it with** ~ a Zena trouxe-o consigo OR com ela.

herb [hɜːb] *n* erva *f* aromática.

herbal tea [ˈhɜːbl-] *n* chá *m* de ervas.

herd [hɜːd] *n (of cattle)* manada *f*; *(of sheep)* rebanho *m*.

here [hɪəʳ] *adv* aqui; ~'s **your book** aqui está o seu livro; ~ **you are** aqui tem, aqui está.

hereabout [ˈhɪərəˌbaʊt] *(Am)* = **hereabouts**.

hereabouts [ˈhɪərəˌbaʊts] *adv (Brit)* por aqui.

hereafter [ˌhɪərˈɑːftəʳ] *adv (fml) (from now on)* de hoje em diante; *(in the future)* mais tarde.

hereby [ˌhɪəˈbaɪ] *adv (fml: in letters)* pela presente; **I** ~ **declare this theatre open** declaro aberto este teatro.

hereditary [hɪˈredɪtrɪ] *adj (disease)* hereditário(-ria).

heresy [ˈherəsɪ] *n* heresia *f*.

heritage [ˈherɪtɪdʒ] *n* patrimônio *m*.

heritage centre *n museu ou centro de informação em local de interesse histórico.*

hermit [ˈhɜːmɪt] *n* eremita *mf*.

hernia [ˈhɜːnjə] *n* hérnia *f*.

hero [ˈhɪərəʊ] *(pl -es)* *n* herói *m*.

heroic [hɪˈrəʊɪk] *adj* heróico(-ca).

heroin [ˈherəʊɪn] *n* heroína *f*.

heroine [ˈherəʊɪn] *n* heroína *f*.

heron [ˈherən] *n* garça *f*.

herring [ˈherɪŋ] *n* arenque *m*.

hers [hɜːz] *pron* o seu (a sua), (o/a) dela; **a friend of** ~ um amigo dela OR seu; **those shoes are** ~ estes sapatos são dela OR seus, **these are mine** – **where are** ~? estes são os meus – onde estão os dela?

herself [hɜːˈself] *pron (reflexive)* se; *(after prep)* si própria OR mesma; **she did it** ~ foi ela mesma que o fez; **she hurt** ~ ela machucou-se.

he's [hiːz] = **he is; he has**.

hesitant [ˈhezɪtənt] *adj* hesitante.

hesitate [ˈhezɪteɪt] *vi* hesitar.

hesitation [ˌhezɪˈteɪʃn] *n* hesitação *f*.

heterosexual [ˌhetərəʊˈsekʃʊəl] *adj* heterossexual ◆ *n* heterossexual *mf*.

het up [het-] *adj (inf)* nervoso(-osa).

hexagon [ˈheksəgən] *n* hexágono *m*.

hey [heɪ] *excl (inf)* ei!, é pá! *(Port)*.

heyday [ˈheɪdeɪ] *n* época *f* áurea, auge *m*.

HGV *abbr* = **heavy goods vehicle**.

hi [haɪ] *excl (inf)* oi! *(Br)*, olá! *(Port)*.

hibernate [ˈhaɪbəneɪt] *vi* hibernar.

hiccup [ˈhɪkʌp] *n*: **to have (the)** ~**s** estar com OR ter soluços.

hide [haɪd] *(pt* **hid** [hɪd], *pp* **hidden** [ˈhɪdn])* *vt* esconder; *(truth, feelings)* esconder, ocultar ◆ *vi* esconder-se ◆ *n (of animal)* pele *f*.

hide-and-seek *n* esconde-esconde *m*, escondidas *fpl*.

hideaway [ˈhaɪdəweɪ] *n (inf)* esconde-rijo *m*, refúgio *m*.

hideous [ˈhɪdɪəs] *adj* horrível.

hiding [ˈhaɪdɪŋ] *n*: **in** ~ *(concealment)* escondido(-da); **to give sb a (good)** ~ *(inf: beating)* dar uma surra em alguém.

hiding place *n* esconderijo *m*.

hierarchy [ˈhaɪərɑːkɪ] *n* hierarquia *f*.

hi-fi [ˈhaɪfaɪ] *n* hi-fi *m*, aparelhagem *f* de som.

high [haɪ] *adj* alto(-ta); *(wind)* forte; *(speed, quality)* grande, alto(-ta); *(opinion)* bom (boa); *(position, rank)* elevado(-da); *(sound, voice)* agudo(-da); *(inf: from drugs)* doidão(-dona) *(Br)*, pedrado(-da) *(Port)* ◆ *n (weather front)* zona *f* de alta pressão ◆ *adv* alto; **how** ~ **is it?** quanto é que (isso) mede?; **it's 10 metres** ~ mede 10 metros de altura.

high chair *n* cadeira-de-bebê *f*.

high-class *adj* de grande categoria.

Higher [ˈhaɪəʳ] *n (Scot) exame efetuado na Escócia no fim do ensino secundário.*

higher education *n* ensino *m* superior.

high heels *npl* saltos *mpl* altos.

high jump *n* salto *m* em altura.

Highland Games [ˈhaɪlənd-] *npl jogos tradicionais escoceses.*

Highlands [ˈhaɪləndz] *npl*: **the** ~ *região montanhosa da Escócia.*

highlight [ˈhaɪlaɪt] *n (best part)* ponto *m* alto ◆ *vt (emphasize)* destacar.

❏ **highlights** *npl (of football match etc)* pontos *mpl* altos; *(in hair)* mechas *fpl* *(Br)*, madeixas *fpl* *(Port)*.

highlighter (pen) [ˈhaɪlaɪtəʳ] *n* marcador *m*.

highly [ˈhaɪlɪ] *adv (extremely)* extremamente; *(very well)* muito bem; **to think**

~ **of sb** admirar muito alguém.

highness ['haɪnɪs] *n*: **His/Her/ Your (Royal)** ~ Sua Alteza *f* (Real); **Their (Royal)** ~**es** Suas Altezas (Reais).

high-pitched [-'pɪtʃt] *adj* agudo (-da).

high-rise *adj*: **a** ~ **building** um espigão *(Br)*, uma torre *(Port)*.

high school *n* escola *f* secundária.

high season *n* estação *f* alta.

high-speed train *n* (trem) rápido *m*, trem *m* de grande velocidade.

high street *n (Brit)* rua *f* principal.

high-tech [-'tek] *adj (industry)* de ponta; *(design, method, furniture)* extremamente moderno(-na).

high tide *n* maré-alta *f*.

highway ['haɪweɪ] *n (Am: between towns)* auto-estrada *f*; *(Brit: any main road)* estrada *f*.

Highway Code *n (Brit)* código *m* da estrada.

hijack ['haɪdʒæk] *vt* desviar.

hijacker ['haɪdʒækər] *n* pirata *m* do ar.

hike [haɪk] *n* caminhada *f*, excursão *f* a pé ◆ *vi* caminhar.

hiker ['haɪkər] *n* caminhante *mf*.

hiking ['haɪkɪŋ] *n*: **to go** ~ fazer uma caminhada.

hilarious [hɪ'leərɪəs] *adj* hilariante.

hill [hɪl] *n* colina *f*, monte *m*.

hillside ['hɪlsaɪd] *n* encosta *f*.

hillwalking ['hɪlwɔːkɪŋ] *n* caminhada *f (em montanha)*.

hilly ['hɪlɪ] *adj* montanhoso (-osa).

him [hɪm] *pron (direct)* o; *(indirect)* lhe; *(after prep)* ele; **I know** ~ eu o conheço; **it's** ~ é ele; **send it to** ~ manda isso para ele; **tell** ~ diga-lhe; **she's worse than** ~ ela é pior que ele; **Tony brought it with** ~ o Tony trouxe-o consigo OR com ele.

Himalayas [ˌhɪmə'leɪəz] *npl*: **the** ~ os Himalaias.

himself [hɪm'self] *pron (reflexive)* se; *(after prep)* si próprio OR mesmo; **he did it** ~ foi ele mesmo que o fez; **he hurt** ~ ele machucou-se.

hinder ['hɪndər] *vt* impedir, atrapalhar.

hindrance ['hɪndrəns] *n (obstacle)* obstáculo *m*, impedimento *m*; *(delay)* demora *f*, atraso *m*.

hindsight ['haɪndsaɪt] *n*: **with the**

benefit of ~ em retrospecto *(Br)*, a posteriori *(Port)*.

Hindu ['hɪnduː] *adj* hindu ◆ *n (person)* hindu *mf*.

hinge [hɪndʒ] *n* dobradiça *f*.

hint [hɪnt] *n (indirect suggestion)* alusão *f*; *(piece of advice)* dica *f*, palpite *m*; *(slight amount)* ponta *f* ◆ *vi*: **to** ~ **at sthg** fazer alusão a algo.

hip [hɪp] *n* anca *f*.

hippo [ˌhɪpəʊ] *(pl -s) n (inf)* = **hippopotamus**.

hippopotamus [ˌhɪpə'pɒtəməs] *n* hipopótamo *m*.

hippy ['hɪpɪ] *n* hippy *mf*.

hire ['haɪər] *vt (car, bicycle, television)* alugar; *(person)* contratar; **"for** ~**"** *(boats)* "para alugar"; *(taxi)* "livre".

◗ **hire out** *vt sep (car, bicycle, television)* alugar.

hire car *n (Brit)* carro *m* alugado.

hire purchase *n (Brit)* crediário *m (Br)*, compra *f* a prestações.

his [hɪz] *adj* o seu (a sua), dele ◆ *pron* o seu (a sua), (o/a) dele; ~ **books** os livros dele, os seus livros; **a friend of** ~ um amigo dele OR seu; **these shoes are** ~ estes sapatos são dele OR seus; **these are mine** – **where are** ~? estes são os meus – onde estão os dele?

hiss [hɪs] *n (of snake, gas etc)* silvo *m*; *(of crowd)* assobio *m* ◆ *vi (snake, gas etc)* silvar; *(crowd)* assobiar, vaiar.

historic [hɪ'stɒrɪk] *adj* histórico(-ca).

historical [hɪ'stɒrɪkəl] *adj* histórico(-ca).

history ['hɪstərɪ] *n* história *f*; *(record)* histórico *m*.

hit [hɪt] *(pt & pp* **hit***) vt (strike on purpose)* bater em; *(collide with)* bater contra OR em; *(bang)* bater com; *(a target)* acertar em ◆ *n (record, play, film)* sucesso *m*.

hit-and-run *adj*: ~ **accident** atropelamento *m* com abandono da vítima.

hitch [hɪtʃ] *n (problem)* problema *m* ◆ *vi* pegar carona *(Br)*, pedir boleia *(Port)* ◆ *vt*: **to** ~ **a lift** pegar carona *(Br)*, apanhar boleia *(Port)*.

hitchhike ['hɪtʃhaɪk] *vi* pegar carona *(Br)*, pedir boleia *(Port)*.

hitchhiker ['hɪtʃhaɪkər] *n* pessoa *f* que pega carona *(Br)*, pessoa *f* que viaja à boleia *(Port)*.

hi-tech [ˌhaɪ'tek] = **high-tech**.

hive [haɪv] *n (of bees)* colmeia *f.*
HIV-positive *adj* soropositivo(-va) *(Br),* seropositivo(-va) *(Port).*
hoard [hɔːd] *n (of food)* armazém *m,* reserva *f; (of money)* tesouro *m; (of useless objects)* tralha *f,* monte *m* ♦ *vt (food)* açambarcar; *(money)* amealhar; *(useless objects)* acumular.
hoarding [ˈhɔːdɪŋ] *n (Brit: for adverts)* outdoor *m (Br),* placar *m* publicitário *(Port).*
hoarfrost [ˈhɔːfrɒst] *n* geada *f* (branca).
hoarse [hɔːs] *adj* rouco(-ca).
hoax [həʊks] *n* trote *m (Br),* trapaça *f (Port).*
hob [hɒb] *n parte de cima do fogão.*
hobble [ˈhɒbl] *vi* coxear, mancar.
hobby [ˈhɒbɪ] *n* passatempo *m.*
hobbyhorse [ˈhɒbɪhɔːs] *n (toy)* cavalinho-de-pau *m.*
hobo [ˈhəʊbəʊ] *(pl* **-es** OR **-s)** *n (Am)* vagabundo *m* (-da *f).*
hock [hɒk] *n (wine)* vinho *m* branco alemão.
hockey [ˈhɒkɪ] *n (on grass)* hóquei *m* sobre grama; *(Am: ice hockey)* hóquei sobre gelo.
hoe [həʊ] *n* sacho *m.*
hog [hɒg] *n (Am: pig)* porco; *(inf: greedy person)* alarde *m,* glutão *m* ♦ *vt (inf)* monopolizar.
Hogmanay [ˈhɒgmənei] *n (Scot)* fim *m* de ano, passagem *f* de ano.
hoist [hɔɪst] *vt (load, person)* levantar, içar; *(sail, flag)* içar.
hold [həʊld] *(pt & pp* **held)** *vt* segurar; *(organize)* dar; *(contain)* conter; *(possess)* ter, possuir ♦ *vi (remain unchanged)* manter-se; *(on telephone)* esperar ♦ *n (of ship, aircraft)* porão *m;* **to ~ sb prisoner** manter alguém prisoneiro; **~ the line, please** não desligue, por favor; **to keep a firm ~ of sthg** agarrar algo com força.
❏ **hold back** *vt sep (restrain)* conter; *(keep secret)* reter.
❏ **hold on** *vi (wait, on telephone)* esperar; **to ~ on to sthg** agarrar-se a algo.
❏ **hold out** *vt sep (extend)* estender.
❏ **hold up** *vt sep (delay)* atrasar.
holdall [ˈhəʊldɔːl] *n (Brit)* saco *m* de viagem.
holder [ˈhəʊldəʳ] *n (of passport, licence)* titular *mf; (container)* suporte *m.*
holdup [ˈhəʊldʌp] *n (delay)* atraso *m.*

hole [həʊl] *n* buraco *m.*
holiday [ˈhɒlɪdeɪ] *n (Brit: period of time)* férias *fpl; (day off)* feriado *m* ♦ *vi (Brit)* passar férias; **to be on ~** estar de férias; **to go on ~** ir de férias.
holiday camp *n (Brit)* campo *m* de férias.
holidaymaker [ˈhɒlɪdɪˌmeɪkəʳ] *n (Brit)* turista *mf.*
holiday pay *n (Brit)* férias *fpl* pagas.
holiday resort *n (Brit)* estância *f* de férias.
Holland [ˈhɒlənd] *n* Holanda *f.*
hollow [ˈhɒləʊ] *adj* oco (oca).
holly [ˈhɒlɪ] *n* azevinho *m.*
Hollywood [ˈhɒlɪwʊd] *n* Hollywood *s.*
holocaust [ˈhɒləkɔːst] *n* holocausto *m;* **the Holocaust** o Holocausto.
holy [ˈhəʊlɪ] *adj* sagrado(-da), santo (-ta).
home [həʊm] *n* casa *f, (own country)* país *m* natal; *(for old people)* lar *m* ♦ *adv (in one's home)* em casa; *(to one's home)* para casa ♦ *adj (not foreign)* nacional; *(at one's house)* caseiro(-ra); **at ~** em casa; **make yourself at ~** faça como se estivesse em sua casa; **to go ~** ir para casa; **~ address** endereço *m;* **~ number** número *m* (de telefone) de casa.
home computer *n* computador *m* pessoal.
Home Counties *npl (Brit):* **the ~** *condados situados nos arredores de Londres.*
home economics *n* economia *f* doméstica, *disciplina opcional na escola.*
home help *n (Brit)* auxiliar *m* doméstico (auxiliar *f* doméstica).
homeland [ˈhəʊmlænd] *n (country of birth)* pátria *f,* terra *f* natal.
homeless [ˈhəʊmlɪs] *npl:* **the ~** os sem-abrigo.
homely [ˈhəʊmlɪ] *adj (food)* caseiro (-ra), simples *(inv); (place)* acolhedor(-ra); *(person, features)* sem graça.
homemade [ˌhəʊmˈmeɪd] *adj (food)* caseiro(-ra).
homeopathic [ˌhəʊmɪəʊˈpæθɪk] *adj* homeopático(-ca).
homeopathy [ˌhəʊmɪˈɒpəθɪ] *n* homeopatia *f.*
home page *n (COMPUT)* home page *f.*
Home Secretary *n (Brit)* ≈ Ministro *m* (-tra *f)* do Interior *(Br),* Ministro *m* (-tra *f)* da Administração Interna *(Port).*

homesick [ˈhəʊmsɪk] *adj*: **to be ~** ter saudades de casa.

hometown [ˈhəʊmtaʊn] *n* terra *f* (natal).

homeward [ˈhəʊmwəd] *adj* de regresso a casa.

homewards [ˈhəʊmwədz] *adv*: **to head ~** dirigir-se para casa; **to travel ~** viajar de regresso a casa.

homework [ˈhəʊmwɜːk] *n* dever *m* de casa.

homicide [ˈhɒmɪsaɪd] *n* homicídio *m*.

homosexual [ˌhɒməˈsekʃʊəl] *adj* homossexual ♦ *n* homossexual *mf*.

honest [ˈɒnɪst] *adj* honesto(-ta).

honestly [ˈɒnɪstlɪ] *adv* (*truthfully*) honestamente; (*to express sincerity*) a sério ♦ *excl* francamente!

honesty [ˈɒnɪstɪ] *n* honestidade *f*.

honey [ˈhʌnɪ] *n* mel *m*.

honeycomb [ˈhʌnɪkəʊm] *n* (*of bees*) favo *m* de mel.

honeymoon [ˈhʌnɪmuːn] *n* lua-de-mel *f*.

honeysuckle [ˈhʌnɪˌsʌkl] *n* madressilva *f*.

Hong Kong [ˌhɒŋˈkɒŋ] *n* Hong Kong *s*.

honk [hɒŋk] *vi* (*motorist*) buzinar; (*goose*) grasnar ♦ *vt*: **she ~ed her horn** ela buzinou.

honor [ˈɒnər] (*Am*) = honour.

honorary [*Brit* ˈɒnərərɪ, *Am* ɒnəˈreərɪ] *adj* honorário(-ria); (*degree*) honoris causa.

honour [ˈɒnər] *n* (*Brit*) honra *f*.

honourable [ˈɒnərəbl] *adj* honrado(-da).

hood [hʊd] *n* (*of jacket, coat*) capuz *m*; (*on convertible car*) capota *f*; (*Am: car bonnet*) capô *m*.

hoof [huːf] *n* casco *m*.

hook [hʊk] *n* (*for picture, coat*) gancho *m*; (*for fishing*) anzol *m*; **off the ~** (*telephone*) fora do gancho (*Br*), desligado (*Port*).

hooked [hʊkt] *adj*: **to be ~ (on sthg)** (*inf: addicted*) estar viciado(-da) (em algo).

hooligan [ˈhuːlɪgən] *n* desordeiro *m* (-ra *f*), vândalo *m* (-la *f*).

hoop [huːp] *n* argola *f*.

hoot [huːt] *vi* (*driver*) buzinar.

hooter [ˈhuːtər] *n* (*horn*) buzina *f*.

Hoover® [ˈhuːvər] *n* (*Brit*) aspirador *m*.

hop [hɒp] *vi* pular com um pé só.

hope [həʊp] *n* esperança *f* ♦ *vt* esperar; **to ~ for sthg** esperar algo; **to ~ to do sthg** esperar fazer algo; **I ~ so** espero que sim.

hopeful [ˈhəʊpfʊl] *adj* (*optimistic*) esperançoso(-osa).

hopefully [ˈhəʊpfəlɪ] *adv* (*with luck*) com um pouco de sorte.

hopeless [ˈhəʊplɪs] *adj* (*without any hope*) desesperado(-da); **he is ~!** (*inf*) (ele) é um caso perdido!

hops [hɒps] *npl* lúpulo *m*.

horizon [həˈraɪzn] *n* horizonte *m*.

horizontal [ˌhɒrɪˈzɒntl] *adj* horizontal.

hormone [ˈhɔːməʊn] *n* hormônio *m* (*Br*), hormona *f* (*Port*).

horn [hɔːn] *n* (*of car*) buzina *f*; (*on animal*) corno *m*, chifre *m*.

horoscope [ˈhɒrəskəʊp] *n* horóscopo *m*.

horrendous [hɒˈrendəs] *adj* (*horrific*) horrendo(-da); (*inf: unpleasant*) terrível.

horrible [ˈhɒrəbl] *adj* horrível.

horrid [ˈhɒrɪd] *adj* (*unkind*) antipático(-ca); (*very bad*) horroroso(-osa).

horrific [hɒˈrɪfɪk] *adj* horrendo(-da).

horrify [ˈhɒrɪfaɪ] *vt* horrorizar.

horror [ˈhɒrər] *n* horror *m*.

horror film *n* filme *m* de horror.

hors d'oeuvre [ɔːˈdɜːvr] *n* aperitivo *m*, entrada *f*.

horse [hɔːs] *n* cavalo *m*.

horseback [ˈhɔːsbæk] *n*: **on ~** a cavalo.

horse chestnut *n* castanheiro-da-Índia *m*.

horse-drawn carriage *n* charete *f*.

horseman [ˈhɔːsmən] (*pl* -men [-mən]) *n* cavaleiro *m*.

horsepower [ˈhɔːsˌpaʊər] *n* cavalos *mpl* (vapor).

horse racing *n* corridas *fpl* de cavalos.

horseradish (sauce) [ˈhɔːsrædɪʃ-] *n* molho picante feito de rábano silvestre, tradicionalmente usado para acompanhar rosbife.

horse riding *n* equitação *f*.

horseshoe [ˈhɔːsʃuː] *n* ferradura *f*.

horsewoman [ˈhɔːsˌwʊmən] (*pl* -women [-ˌwɪmɪn]) *n* amazona *f*.

horticulture [ˈhɔːtɪˌkʌltʃər] *n* horticultura *f*.

hose [həʊz] n mangueira f.

hosepipe ['həʊzpaɪp] n mangueira f.

hosiery ['həʊzɪərɪ] n meias fpl e collants.

hospitable [hɒ'spɪtəbl] adj hospitaleiro(-ra).

hospital ['hɒspɪtl] n hospital m; **in ~** no hospital.

hospitality [,hɒspɪ'tælətɪ] n hospitalidade f.

host [həʊst] n (of party, event) anfitrião m; (of show, TV programme) apresentador m (-ra f).

hostage ['hɒstɪdʒ] n refém mf.

hostel ['hɒstl] n (youth hostel) albergue m da juventude (Br), pousada f de juventude (Port).

hostess ['həʊstes] n (on aeroplane) hospedeira f; (of party, event) anfitriã f.

hostile [Brit 'hɒstaɪl, Am 'hɒstl] adj hostil.

hostility [hɒ'stɪlətɪ] n hostilidade f.

hot [hɒt] adj quente; (spicy) picante; **to be ~** (person) ter calor.

hot-air balloon n balão m, aeróstato m.

hot chocolate n chocolate m quente.

hot-cross bun n pequeno pão doce com passas e especiarias que se come na Páscoa.

hot dog n cachorro-quente m.

hotel [həʊ'tel] n hotel m.

hotheaded [,hɒt'hedɪd] adj impulsivo(-va).

hothouse ['hɒthaʊs, pl -haʊzɪz] n (greenhouse) estufa f.

hot line n linha direta em funcionamento 24 horas por dia.

hotplate ['hɒtpleɪt] n placa f (elétrica).

hotpot ['hɒtpɒt] n ensopado de carne cozido no forno e coberto com rodelas de batata.

hot-tempered [-'tempəd] adj exaltado(-da), irascível.

hot-water bottle n saco m de água quente.

hound [haʊnd] n (dog) cão m de caça ◆ vt (persecute) perseguir; **to ~ sb out (of somewhere)** (drive) escorraçar alguém (de algum lugar).

hour ['aʊə'] n hora f; **I've been waiting for ~s** estou esperando há horas.

hourly ['aʊəlɪ] adj por hora ◆ adv (pay, charge) por hora; (depart) de hora em hora.

house [n haʊs, pl 'haʊzɪz, vb haʊz] n casa f; (SCH) divisão dos alunos em grupos para atividades desportivas ◆ vt (person) alojar.

housecoat ['haʊskəʊt] n bata f.

household ['haʊshəʊld] n família f (Br), agregado m familiar (Port).

housekeeper ['haʊs,ki:pə'] n governanta f.

housekeeping ['haʊs,ki:pɪŋ] n manutenção f da casa.

house music n house music f.

House of Commons n Câmara f dos Comuns.

House of Lords n Câmara f dos Lordes.

House of Representatives n Câmara f dos Representantes.

Houses of Parliament npl Parlamento m britânico.

housewife ['haʊswaɪf] (pl -wives) n dona f de casa, doméstica f.

house wine n vinho m da casa.

housewives ['haʊswaɪvz] pl → housewife.

housework ['haʊswɜːk] n afazeres m domésticos.

housing ['haʊzɪŋ] n (houses) alojamento m.

housing estate n (Brit) conjunto m habitacional (Br), urbanização f (Port).

housing project (Am) = housing estate.

hovel ['hɒvl] n barraco m.

hover ['hɒvə'] vi (bird, helicopter) pairar.

hovercraft ['hɒvəkrɑːft] n aerobarco m (Br), hovercraft m.

hoverport ['hɒvəpɔːt] n cais m inv para hovercrafts.

how [haʊ] adv **1.** (asking about way or manner) como; **~ do you get there?** como é que se chega lá?; **~ does it work?** como é que funciona?; **tell me ~ to do it** me diga como fazer isso. **2.** (asking about health, quality) como; **~ are you?** como vai?; **~ are you doing?** como é que você vai?; **~ are things?** como vão as coisas?; **~ do you do?** (greeting) muito prazer; (answer) igualmente; **~ is your room?** como é o seu quarto? **3.** (asking about degree, amount) quanto; **~ far?** a que distância?; **~ long?**

quanto tempo?; ~ **many?** quantos?; ~
much? quanto?; ~ **much is it?** quanto
custa?; ~ **old are you?** quantos anos
você tem?
4. *(in phrases):* ~ **about a drink?** que
tal uma bebida?; ~ **lovely!** que lindo!
however [hau'evə'] *adv* contudo,
todavia; ~ **hard I try** por mais que
tente; ~ **many there are** por muitos
que sejam.
howl [haul] *vi (dog, wind)* uivar; *(person)* gritar.
hp *n (abbr of horsepower)* cv *m*.
HP *abbr* = **hire purchase.**
HQ *n (abbr of headquarters)* QG.
hr *(abbr of hour)* h.
hub [hʌb] *n (of wheel)* cubo *m*.
hub airport *n* aeroporto *m* principal.
hubbub ['hʌbʌb] *n* burburinho *m*.
hubcap ['hʌbkæp] *n* calota *f (Br)*,
tampão *m (Port)*.
huddle ['hʌdl] *vi (crouch, curl up)*
encolher-se; *(crowd together)* juntar-se.
hue [hju:] *n (colour)* tom *m*, matiz *m*.
huff [hʌf] *n*: **in a ~** zangado (-da),
com raiva.
hug [hʌg] *vt* abraçar ◆ *n*: **to give sb a
~** dar um abraço em alguém.
huge [hju:dʒ] *adj* enorme.
hull [hʌl] *n* casco *m*.
hum [hʌm] *vi (bee, machine)* zumbir;
(person) cantarolar.
human ['hju:mən] *adj* humano
(-na) ◆ *n*: ~ **(being)** ser *m* humano.
humane [hju:'mein] *adj* humano(-na).
humanitarian [hju:,mæni'teəriən] *adj*
humanitário(-ria).
humanities [hju:'mænʊtiz] *npl* humanidades *fpl*.
human race *n*: **the** ~ a raça humana.
human rights *npl* direitos *mpl*
humanos.
humble ['hʌmbl] *adj* humilde.
humid ['hju:mid] *adj* úmido (-da).
humidity [hju:'midəti] *n* umidade *f*.
humiliate [hju:'milieit] *vt* humilhar.
humiliating [hju:'milieitiŋ] *adj* humilhante.
humiliation [hju:,mili'eiʃn] *n* humilhação *f*.
hummus ['homəs] *n* puré de grão-de-bico, alho e pasta de gergelim.

humor ['hju:mər] *(Am)* = **humour.**
humorous ['hju:mərəs] *adj (story)*
humorístico(-ca); *(person)* espirituoso
(-osa).
humour ['hju:mər] *n (Brit)* humor *m*.
hump [hʌmp] *n (bump)* elevação *f; (of
camel)* corcova *f (Br)*, bossa *f (Port)*.
humpbacked bridge ['hʌmpbækt-]
n ponte *f* em lomba.
hunch [hʌntʃ] *n* pressentimento *m*.
hunchback ['hʌntʃbæk] *n* corcunda
mf.
hundred ['hʌndrəd] *num* cem; **a ~**
cem; **a ~ and one** cento e um, → **six.**
hundredth ['hʌndrətθ] *num* centésimo(-ma), → **sixth.**
hundredweight ['hʌndrədweit] *n (in
UK)* = 50,8kg; *(in US)* = 45,3kg.
hung [hʌŋ] *pt & pp* → **hang.**
Hungarian [hʌŋ'geəriən] *adj* húngaro(-ra) ◆ *n (person)* húngaro *m* (-ra *f*);
(language) húngaro *m*.
Hungary ['hʌŋgəri] *n* Hungria *f*.
hunger ['hʌŋgə'] *n* fome *f*.
hungry ['hʌŋgri] *adj* esfomeado (-da);
to be ~ estar com OR ter fome.
hunt [hʌnt] *n (Brit: for foxes)* caça *f* à
raposa ◆ *vt & vi* caçar; **to ~ (for sthg)**
(search) procurar (algo).
hunter ['hʌntə'] *n* caçador *m* (-ra *f*).
hunting ['hʌntiŋ] *n (for wild animals)*
caça *f; (Brit: for foxes)* caça à raposa.
hurdle ['hɜ:dl] *n (SPORT)* barreira *f*.
hurl [hɜ:l] *vt* arremessar.
hurray [hu'rei] *excl* hurra!
hurricane ['hʌrikən] *n* furacão *m*.
hurriedly ['hʌridli] *adv* com pressa.
hurry ['hʌri] *vt (person)* apressar ◆ *vi*
apressar-se ◆ *n*: **to be in a ~** estar com
pressa; **to do sthg in a ~** fazer algo
com pressa.
❏ **hurry up** *vi* despachar-se.
hurt [hɜ:t] *(pt & pp* **hurt)** *vt* magoar
◆ *vi* doer; **my arm ~s** meu braço está
doendo; **to ~ o.s.** magoar-se.
husband ['hʌzbənd] *n* marido *m*.
hush [hʌʃ] *n* silêncio *m* ◆ *excl* silêncio!
husky ['hʌski] *adj (voice, laugh)*
rouco(-ca) ◆ *n (dog)* cão *m* esquimó.
hustle ['hʌsl] *n*: ~ **and bustle** bulício
m.
hut [hʌt] *n* cabana *f*.
hutch [hʌtʃ] *n* coelheira *f*.
hyacinth ['haiəsinθ] *n* jacinto *m*.

hydrofoil [ˈhaɪdrəfɔɪl] *n* hidrofólio *m*.
hydrogen [ˈhaɪdrədʒən] *n* hidrogênio *m*.
hyena [haɪˈiːnə] *n* hiena *f*.
hygiene [ˈhaɪdʒiːn] *n* higiene *f*.
hygienic [haɪˈdʒiːnɪk] *adj* higiênico (-ca).
hymn [hɪm] *n* hino *m*.
hypermarket [ˈhaɪpəˌmɑːkɪt] *n* hipermercado *m*.
hyphen [ˈhaɪfn] *n* hífen *m*.
hypnosis [hɪpˈnəʊsɪs] *n* hipnose *f*.
hypnotize [ˈhɪpnətaɪz] *vt* hipnotizar.

hypocrisy [hɪˈpɒkrəsɪ] *n* hipocrisia *f*, cinismo *m*.
hypocrite [ˈhɪpəkrɪt] *n* hipócrita *mf*, cínico *m* (-ca *f*).
hypocritical [ˌhɪpəˈkrɪtɪkl] *adj* hipócrita, cínico(-ca).
hypodermic   needle [ˌhaɪpəˈdɜːmɪk-] *n* agulha *f* hipodérmica.
hypothesis [haɪˈpɒθɪsɪs] (*pl* **-theses** [-θɪsiːz]) *n* hipótese *f*.
hysteria [hɪsˈtɪərɪə] *n* histeria *f*.
hysterical [hɪsˈterɪkl] *adj* histérico (-ca); *(inf: very funny)* hilariante.

I [aɪ] *pron* eu.

ice [aɪs] *n* gelo *m*; *(ice cream)* sorvete *m* *(Br)*, gelado *m* *(Port)*.

iceberg ['aɪsbɜːg] *n* icebergue *m*.

iceberg lettuce *n* alface redonda e crespa.

icebox ['aɪsbɒks] *n* *(Am)* geladeira *f* *(Br)*, frigorífico *m* *(Port)*.

ice-cold *adj* gelado(-da).

ice cream *n* sorvete *m* *(Br)*, gelado *m* *(Port)*.

ice cube *n* cubo *m* de gelo.

ice hockey *n* hóquei *m* sobre o gelo.

Iceland ['aɪslənd] *n* Islândia *f*.

Icelandic [aɪs'lændɪk] *adj* islandês (-esa) ◆ *n* *(language)* islandês *m*.

ice lolly *n* *(Brit)* picolé *m* *(Br)*, gelado *m* *(Port)*.

ice rink *n* rinque *m* (de patinagem).

ice skates *npl* patins *mpl* de lâmina.

ice-skating *n* patinagem *f* sobre o gelo; **to go ~** ir patinar no gelo.

icicle ['aɪsɪkl] *n* sincelo *m*, pingente *m* de gelo.

icing ['aɪsɪŋ] *n* glacé *m*.

icing sugar *n* açúcar *m* em pó.

icy ['aɪsɪ] *adj* gelado(-da); *(road)* com gelo.

I'd [aɪd] = **I would, I had**.

ID *n* *(abbr of identification)* (documentos *mpl* de) identificação *f*.

ID card *n* carteira *f* de identidade *(Br)*, bilhete *m* de identidade, BI *m* *(Port)*.

IDD code *n* indicativo *m* internacional automático.

idea [aɪ'dɪə] *n* ideia *f*; **I've no ~** não faço idéia.

ideal [aɪ'dɪəl] *adj* ideal ◆ *n* ideal *m*.

ideally [aɪ'dɪəlɪ] *adv* *(located, suited)* perfeitamente; *(in an ideal situation)* idealmente.

identical [aɪ'dentɪkl] *adj* idêntico(-ca).

identification [aɪˌdentɪfɪ'keɪʃn] *n* identificação *f*.

identify [aɪ'dentɪfaɪ] *vt* identificar.

identity [aɪ'dentɪtɪ] *n* identidade *f*.

identity card *n* carteira *f* de identidade *(Br)*, bilhete *m* de identidade *(Port)*.

ideology [aɪdɪ'ɒlədʒɪ] *n* ideologia *f*.

idiom ['ɪdɪəm] *n* *(phrase)* expressão *f* idiomática.

idiomatic [ˌɪdɪə'mætɪk] *adj* idiomático(-ca).

idiosyncrasy [ˌɪdɪə'sɪŋkrəsɪ] *n* idiossincrasia *f*.

idiot ['ɪdɪət] *n* idiota *mf*.

idiotic [ˌɪdɪ'ɒtɪk] *adj* idiota.

idle ['aɪdl] *adj* *(lazy)* preguiçoso (-osa); *(not working)* ocioso(-osa) ◆ *vi* *(engine)* estar em ponto morto.

idol ['aɪdl] *n* ídolo *m*.

idolize ['aɪdəlaɪz] *vt* idolatrar.

idyllic [ɪ'dɪlɪk] *adj* idílico(-ca).

i.e. *(abbr of id est)* i.e.

if [ɪf] *conj* se; **~ I were you** no seu lugar; **~ not** *(otherwise)* senão.

igloo ['ɪgluː] *(pl* **-s)** *n* iglu *m*.

ignite [ɪg'naɪt] *vt* inflamar ◆ *vi* inflamar-se.

ignition [ɪg'nɪʃn] *n* *(AUT)* ignição *f*.

ignition key *n* chave *f* de ignição.

ignorance ['ɪgnərəns] *n* ignorância *f*.

ignorant ['ɪgnərənt] *adj* ignorante.

ignore [ɪg'nɔː'] *vt* ignorar.

ill [ɪl] *adj* *(in health)* doente; *(bad)* mau (má).

I'll [aɪl] = **I will, I shall**.

illegal [ɪ'liːgl] *adj* ilegal.

illegible [ɪ'ledʒəbl] *adj* ilegível.

illegitimate [ˌɪlɪ'dʒɪtɪmət] *adj* ilegítimo(-ma).

ill health *n*: **to suffer from ~** não ter saúde.

illicit [ɪˈlɪsɪt] *adj* ilícito(-ta).

illiteracy [ɪˈlɪtərəsɪ] *n* analfabetismo *m*.

illiterate [ɪˈlɪtərət] *adj* analfabeto (-ta).

illness [ˈɪlnɪs] *n* doença *f*.

illogical [ɪˈlɒdʒɪkl] *adj* ilógico(-ca), pouco lógico(-ca).

ill-suited *adj*: **to be ~ to** sthg ser pouco adequado(-da) para algo.

ill-treat *vt* maltratar.

illuminate [ɪˈluːmɪneɪt] *vt* iluminar.

illusion [ɪˈluːʒn] *n (false idea)* ilusão *f*; *(visual)* ilusão ótica.

illustrate [ˈɪləstreɪt] *vt* ilustrar.

illustration [ˌɪləˈstreɪʃn] *n* ilustração *f*.

illustrious [ɪˈlʌstrɪəs] *adj* ilustre.

I'm [aɪm] = **I am**.

image [ˈɪmɪdʒ] *n* imagem *f*.

imaginary [ɪˈmædʒɪnrɪ] *adj* imaginário(-ria).

imagination [ɪˌmædʒɪˈneɪʃn] *n* imaginação *f*.

imaginative [ɪˈmædʒɪnətɪv] *adj* imaginativo(-va).

imagine [ɪˈmædʒɪn] *vt* imaginar; **to ~ (that)** *(suppose)* imaginar que.

imbecile [ˈɪmbɪsiːl] *n* imbecil *mf*.

imitate [ˈɪmɪteɪt] *vt* imitar.

imitation [ˌɪmɪˈteɪʃn] *n* imitação *f* ◆ *adj (fur)* falso(-sa); **~ leather** napa *f*.

immaculate [ɪˈmækjʊlət] *adj* imaculado(-da).

immature [ˌɪməˈtjʊəʳ] *adj* imaturo (-ra).

immediate [ɪˈmiːdjət] *adj (without delay)* imediato(-ta).

immediately [ɪˈmiːdjətlɪ] *adv (at once)* imediatamente ◆ *conj (Brit)* logo que.

immense [ɪˈmens] *adj* imenso (-sa).

immersion heater [ɪˈmɜːʃn-] *n* aquecedor *m* de imersão *(Br)*, esquentador *m* eléctrico *(Port)*.

immigrant [ˈɪmɪgrənt] *n* imigrante *mf*.

immigration [ˌɪmɪˈgreɪʃn] *n* imigração *f*.

imminent [ˈɪmɪnənt] *adj* iminente.

immoral [ɪˈmɒrəl] *adj* imoral.

immortal [ɪˈmɔːtl] *adj* imortal.

immune [ɪˈmjuːn] *adj*: **to be ~ to** *(MED)* estar OR ser imune a.

immunity [ɪˈmjuːnətɪ] *n (MED)* imunidade *f*.

immunize [ˈɪmjuːnaɪz] *vt* imunizar.

impact [ˈɪmpækt] *n* impacto *m*.

impair [ɪmˈpeəʳ] *vt* enfraquecer.

impartial [ɪmˈpɑːʃl] *adj* imparcial.

impassive [ɪmˈpæsɪv] *adj* impassível.

impatience [ɪmˈpeɪʃns] *n* impaciência *f*.

impatient [ɪmˈpeɪʃnt] *adj* impaciente; **to be ~ to do** sthg estar impaciente por fazer algo.

impeccable [ɪmˈpekəbl] *adj (clothes)* impecável; *(behaviour)* excelente; **he has ~ manners** ele é extremamente bem-educado.

impede [ɪmˈpiːd] *vt (person)* impedir; *(progress, negotiations)* dificultar.

impending [ɪmˈpendɪŋ] *adj* iminente.

imperative [ɪmˈperətɪv] *n (GRAMM)* imperativo *m*.

imperfect [ɪmˈpɜːfɪkt] *n (GRAMM)* imperfeito *m*.

impersonate [ɪmˈpɜːsəneɪt] *vt (for amusement)* imitar.

impersonation [ɪmˌpɜːsəˈneɪʃn] *n (for amusement)* imitação *f*; **to do ~s of** sb imitar alguém; **he was charged with ~ of a police officer** ele foi acusado de se fazer passar por um policial.

impertinent [ɪmˈpɜːtɪnənt] *adj* impertinente.

impetuous [ɪmˈpetʃʊəs] *adj* impetuoso(-osa).

impetus [ˈɪmpɪtəs] *n (momentum)* ímpeto *m*; *(stimulus)* impulso *m*.

implement [*n* ˈɪmplɪmənt, *vb* ˈɪmplɪment] *n* ferramenta *f* ◆ *vt* implementar, pôr em prática.

implication [ˌɪmplɪˈkeɪʃn] *n (consequence)* implicação *f*.

implicit [ɪmˈplɪsɪt] *adj* implícito(-ta).

implore [ɪmˈplɔːʳ] *vt*: **to ~ sb to do** sthg implorar a alguém que faça algo.

imply [ɪmˈplaɪ] *vt*: **to ~ (that)** *(suggest)* sugerir, dar a entender que.

impolite [ˌɪmpəˈlaɪt] *adj* indelicado (-da).

import [*n* ˈɪmpɔːt, *vb* ɪmˈpɔːt] *n* importação *f* ◆ *vt* importar.

importance [ɪmˈpɔːtns] *n* importância *f*.

important [ɪmˈpɔːtnt] *adj* importante.

impose [ɪmˈpəʊz] *vt* impor ◆ *vi* impor-

se; **to ~ sthg on** impor algo a.
impossible [ɪmˈpɒsəbl] *adj* impossível.
imposter [ɪmˈpɒstər] *(Am)* = **impostor**.
impostor [ɪmˈpɒstər] *n* impostor *m* (-ra *f*).
impoverished [ɪmˈpɒvərɪʃt] *adj* empobrecido(-da).
impractical [ɪmˈpræktɪkl] *adj* pouco prático(-ca).
impregnable [ɪmˈpregnəbl] *adj* inexpugnável, invencível.
impress [ɪmˈpres] *vt* impressionar.
impression [ɪmˈpreʃn] *n* impressão *f*.
impressive [ɪmˈpresɪv] *adj* impressionante.
imprison [ɪmˈprɪzn] *vt (put in prison)* prender.
improbable [ɪmˈprɒbəbl] *adj* improvável.
improper [ɪmˈprɒpər] *adj (incorrect, rude)* incorreto(-ta); *(illegal)* ilegal.
improve [ɪmˈpruːv] *vt & vi* melhorar.
⌐ **improve on** *vt fus* melhorar.
improvement [ɪmˈpruːvmənt] *n (in weather, health)* melhoria *f*; *(to home)* reforma *f*.
improvise [ˈɪmprəvaɪz] *vi* improvisar.
impudent [ˈɪmpjʊdənt] *adj* insolente.
impulse [ˈɪmpʌls] *n* impulso *m*; **on ~** sem pensar duas vezes.
impulsive [ɪmˈpʌlsɪv] *adj* impulsivo (-va).
impurity [ɪmˈpjʊərətɪ] *n* impureza *f*.
in. *abbr* = **inch**.
in [ɪn] *prep* **1.** *(expressing place, position)* em; **it comes ~ a box** vem numa caixa; **~ the street** na rua; **~ hospital** no hospital; **~ Scotland** na Escócia; **~ Sheffield** em Sheffield; **~ the middle** no meio; **~ the sun/rain** no sol/na chuva; **~ here/there** aqui/ali (dentro); **~ front** à frente.
2. *(participating in)* em; **who's ~ the play?** quem está na peça?
3. *(expressing arrangement)* em; **they come ~ packs of three** vêm em embalagens de três; **~ a row** em fila; **cut it ~ half** corte-o ao meio.
4. *(during)*: **~ April** em abril; **~ the afternoon** à OR de tarde; **~ the morning** de manhã; **ten o'clock ~ the morning** dez (horas) da manhã; **~ 1994** em 1994; **~ summer/winter** no verão/inverno.

5. *(within)* em; *(after)* dentro de, daqui a; **it'll be ready ~ an hour** estará pronto daqui a OR dentro de uma hora; **she did everything ~ ten minutes** ela fez tudo em dez minutos; **they're arriving ~ two weeks** chegam dentro de OR daqui a duas semanas.
6. *(expressing means)*: **~ writing** por escrito; **they were talking ~ English** estavam falando (em) inglês; **write ~ ink** escreva a tinta.
7. *(wearing)* de; **dressed ~ red** vestido de vermelho; **the man ~ the blue suit** o homem com o terno azul.
8. *(expressing state)* em; **to be ~ a hurry** estar com pressa; **to be ~ pain** ter dores; **to cry out ~ pain** gritar de dor OR com dores; **~ ruins** em ruínas; **~ good health** com boa saúde.
9. *(with regard to)* de; **a rise ~ prices** uma subida dos preços; **to be 50 metres ~ length** ter 50 metros de comprimento.
10. *(with numbers)*: **one ~ ten** um em cada dez.
11. *(expressing age)*: **she's ~ her twenties** já entrou na casa dos vinte.
12. *(with colours)*: **it comes ~ green or blue** vem em verde ou azul.
13. *(with superlatives)* de; **the best ~ the world** o melhor do mundo.
♦ *adv* **1.** *(inside)* dentro; **you can go ~ now** pode entrar agora.
2. *(at home, work)*: **she's not ~** (ela) não está; **to stay ~** ficar em casa.
3. *(train, bus, plane)*: **the train's not ~ yet** o trem ainda não chegou.
4. *(tide)*: **the tide is ~** a maré está cheia.
♦ *adj (inf: fashionable)* na moda, in *(inv)*.
inability [ˌɪnəˈbɪlətɪ] *n*: **~ (to do sthg)** incapacidade *f* (para fazer algo).
inaccessible [ˌɪnəkˈsesəbl] *adj* inacessível.
inaccurate [ɪnˈækjʊrət] *adj* incorreto(-ta).
inadequate [ɪnˈædɪkwət] *adj (insufficient)* insuficiente.
inadvertently [ˌɪnədˈvɜːtəntlɪ] *adv* inadvertidamente.
inappropriate [ˌɪnəˈprəʊprɪət] *adj* impróprio(-pria).
inasmuch [ˌɪnəzˈmʌtʃ] : **inasmuch as** *conj (fml)* visto que.
inaudible [ɪnˈɔːdɪbl] *adj* inaudível.

inauguration [ɪˌnɔːgjʊˈreɪʃn] n inauguração f.

incapable [ɪnˈkeɪpəbl] adj: **to be ~ of doing sthg** ser incapaz de fazer algo.

incense [ˈɪnsens] n incenso m.

incentive [ɪnˈsentɪv] n incentivo m.

incessant [ɪnˈsesnt] adj incessante.

inch [ɪntʃ] n = 2,5 cm, polegada f.

incident [ˈɪnsɪdənt] n incidente m.

incidentally [ˌɪnsɪˈdentəlɪ] adv a propósito.

incinerate [ɪnˈsɪnəreɪt] vt incinerar.

incisive [ɪnˈsaɪsɪv] adj incisivo (-va).

incite [ɪnˈsaɪt] vt fomentar; **to ~ sb to do sthg** incitar alguém a fazer algo.

inclination [ˌɪnklɪˈneɪʃn] n (desire) inclinação f; **to have an ~ to do sthg** ter tendência a OR para fazer algo.

incline [ˈɪnklaɪn] n declive m.

inclined [ɪnˈklaɪnd] adj (sloping) inclinado(-da); **to be ~ to do sthg** ter a tendência para fazer algo.

include [ɪnˈkluːd] vt incluir.

included [ɪnˈkluːdɪd] adj incluído (-da); **to be ~ in sthg** estar incluído em algo.

including [ɪnˈkluːdɪŋ] prep incluindo.

inclusive [ɪnˈkluːsɪv] adj: **from the 8th to the 16th ~** do 8ᵘ ao 16ᵘ inclusive; **~ of VAT** IVA incluído.

incoherent [ˌɪnkəʊˈhɪərənt] adj incoerente.

income [ˈɪŋkʌm] n rendimento m.

income support n (Brit) subsídio para pessoas com rendimentos muito baixos ou para desempregados sem direito a auxílio-desemprego.

income tax n imposto m sobre a renda (Br), imposto m sobre o rendimento, IRS m (Port).

incoming [ˈɪnˌkʌmɪŋ] adj (train, plane) de chegada; **"~ calls only"** aviso indicando que aquele telefone apenas serve para receberchamadas.

incompatible [ˌɪnkəmˈpætɪbl] adj incompatível.

incompetent [ɪnˈkɒmpɪtənt] adj incompetente.

incomplete [ˌɪnkəmˈpliːt] adj incompleto(-ta).

incomprehensible [ɪnˌkɒmprɪˈhensəbl] adj incompreensível.

incongruous [ɪnˈkɒŋgrʊəs] adj incongruente.

inconsiderate [ˌɪnkənˈsɪdərət] adj sem consideração; **how ~!** que falta de consideração!

inconsistent [ˌɪnkənˈsɪstənt] adj inconsistente.

inconspicuous [ˌɪnkənˈspɪkjʊəs] adj que não dá nas vistas.

incontinent [ɪnˈkɒntɪnənt] adj incontinente.

inconvenience [ˌɪnkənˈviːnjəns] n inconveniência f, inconveniente m ◆ vt incomodar, perturbar.

inconvenient [ˌɪnkənˈviːnjənt] adj inconveniente.

incorporate [ɪnˈkɔːpəreɪt] vt incorporar.

incorrect [ˌɪnkəˈrekt] adj incorreto (-ta).

increase [n ˈɪnkriːs, vb ɪnˈkriːs] n aumento m ◆ vt & vi aumentar; **an ~ in sthg** um aumento em algo.

increasingly [ɪnˈkriːsɪŋlɪ] adv cada vez mais.

incredible [ɪnˈkredəbl] adj incrível.

incredibly [ɪnˈkredəblɪ] adv incrivelmente.

incredulous [ɪnˈkredjʊləs] adj incrédulo(-la).

incur [ɪnˈkɜːr] vt (expenses) incorrer em; (debts) contrair.

indebted [ɪnˈdetɪd] adj (grateful): **to be ~ to sb** estar em dívida com alguém

indecent [ɪnˈdiːsnt] adj (obscene) indecente.

indecisive [ˌɪndɪˈsaɪsɪv] adj indeciso (-sa).

indeed [ɪnˈdiːd] adv (for emphasis) de fato, realmente; (certainly) certamente.

indefinite [ɪnˈdefɪnɪt] adj (time, number) indeterminado(-da); (answer, opinion) vago(-ga).

indefinitely [ɪnˈdefɪnɪtlɪ] adv (closed, delayed) por tempo indeterminado.

indent [ɪnˈdent] vt (text) recolher.

independence [ˌɪndɪˈpendəns] n independência f.

Independence Day n feriado nacional nos Estados Unidos no dia 4 de julho em que se celebra a independência, obtida em 1776.

independent [ˌɪndɪˈpendənt] adj independente.

independently [ˌɪndɪˈpendəntlɪ] adv independentemente.

independent school n (Brit) colégio m privado.

index ['ɪndeks] *n (of book)* índice *m; (in library)* catálogo *m (Br)*, ficheiro *m (Port)*.

index card *n* ficha *f (de fichário)*.

index finger *n* dedo *m* indicador.

India ['ɪndjə] *n* Índia *f*.

Indian ['ɪndjən] *adj* indiano(-na) ◆ *n* indiano *m (-na f)*; **an ~ restaurant** um restaurante indiano.

Indian Ocean *n* oceano *m* Índico.

indicate ['ɪndɪkeɪt] *vi (AUT)* ligar os indicadores OR o pisca-pisca ◆ *vt* indicar.

indication [,ɪndɪ'keɪʃn] *n (suggestion)* ideia *f; (sign)* indício *m*.

indicator ['ɪndɪkeɪtəʳ] *n (AUT)* pisca-pisca *m*.

indifference [ɪn'dɪfrəns] *n* indiferença *f*.

indifferent [ɪn'dɪfrənt] *adj* indiferente.

indigenous [ɪn'dɪdʒɪnəs] *adj* nativo (-va).

indigestion [,ɪndɪ'dʒestʃn] *n* indigestão *f*.

indignant [ɪn'dɪgnənt] *adj* indignado(-da).

indigo ['ɪndɪgəʊ] *adj* anil *(inv)*, índigo *(inv)*.

indirect [,ɪndɪ'rekt] *adj* indireto(-ta).

indiscreet [,ɪndɪ'skriːt] *adj* indiscreto(-ta).

indispensable [,ɪndɪ'spensəbl] *adj* indispensável.

individual [,ɪndɪ'vɪdʒʊəl] *adj* individual ◆ *n* indivíduo *m*.

individually [,ɪndɪ'vɪdʒʊəlɪ] *adv* individualmente.

Indonesia [,ɪndə'niːzjə] *n* Indonésia *f*.

indoor ['ɪndɔːʳ] *adj (swimming pool)* coberto(-ta); *(sports)* em recinto fechado.

indoors [,ɪn'dɔːz] *adv* lá dentro; **to stay ~** ficar em casa; **to go ~** ir para dentro.

indulge [ɪn'dʌldʒ] *vi*: **to ~ in sthg** permitir-se algo.

indulgent [ɪn'dʌldʒənt] *adj (liberal, kind)* indulgente, complacente.

industrial [ɪn'dʌstrɪəl] *adj (machinery, products)* industrial; *(country, town)* industrializado(-da).

industrial action *n*: **to take ~** entrar em greve.

industrial estate *n (Brit)* parque *m* industrial.

industrialist [ɪn'dʌstrɪəlɪst] *n* industrial *mf*.

industrial relations *npl* relações *fpl* entre o patronato e os trabalhadores.

industrial revolution *n* revolução *f* industrial.

industrious [ɪn'dʌstrɪəs] *adj* trabalhador(-ra).

industry ['ɪndəstrɪ] *n* indústria *f*.

inebriated [ɪ'niːbrɪeɪtɪd] *adj (fml)* ébrio (ébria).

inedible [ɪn'edɪbl] *adj (unpleasant)* intragável; *(unsafe)* não comestível.

inefficient [,ɪnɪ'fɪʃnt] *adj* ineficaz.

ineligible [ɪn'elɪdʒəbl] *adj* não elegível; **to be ~ for sthg** não ter direito a algo.

inept [ɪ'nept] *adj (comment, remark)* despropositado(-da); *(person)* incapaz; **~ at sthg** inábil em algo.

inequality [,ɪnɪ'kwɒlətɪ] *n* desigualdade *f*.

inevitable [ɪn'evɪtəbl] *adj* inevitável.

inevitably [ɪn'evɪtəblɪ] *adv* inevitavelmente.

inexpensive [,ɪnɪk'spensɪv] *adj* barato(-ta).

inexperienced [,ɪnɪk'spɪərɪənst] *adj* inexperiente.

infallible [ɪn'fæləbl] *adj* infalível.

infamous ['ɪnfəməs] *adj* infame.

infant ['ɪnfənt] *n (baby)* bebê *m; (young child)* criança *f (pequena)*.

infantry ['ɪnfəntrɪ] *n* infantaria *f*.

infant school *n (Brit)* primeiros três *anos da escola primária*.

infatuated [ɪn'fætjʊeɪtɪd] *adj*: **to be ~ with** estar apaixonado(-da) por.

infect [ɪn'fekt] *vt (cut, wound)* infectar; **to ~ sb with sthg** contagiar alguém com algo.

infected [ɪn'fektɪd] *adj* infectado (-da).

infection [ɪn'fekʃn] *n* infecção *f*.

infectious [ɪn'fekʃəs] *adj* infeccioso (-osa).

inferior [ɪn'fɪərɪəʳ] *adj* inferior.

infertile [ɪn'fɜːtaɪl] *adj* estéril.

infested [ɪn'festɪd] *adj*: **to be ~ with sthg** estar infestado(-da) com algo.

infiltrate ['ɪnfɪltreɪt] *vt* infiltrar-se em.

infinite ['ɪnfɪnət] *adj* infinito(-ta).

infinitely ['ɪnfɪnətlɪ] *adv* infinitamente.

infinitive [ɪnˈfɪnɪtɪv] n infinitivo m.

infinity [ɪnˈfɪnɪtɪ] n infinidade f.

infirmary [ɪnˈfɜːmərɪ] n hospital m.

inflamed [ɪnˈfleɪmd] adj inflamado (-da).

inflammable [ɪnˈflæməbl] adj inflamável.

inflammation [ˌɪnfləˈmeɪʃn] n inflamação f.

inflatable [ɪnˈfleɪtəbl] adj inflável.

inflate [ɪnˈfleɪt] vt inflar, insuflar.

inflation [ɪnˈfleɪʃn] n (ECON) inflação f.

inflict [ɪnˈflɪkt] vt infligir.

in-flight adj proporcionado(-da) durante o vôo.

influence [ˈɪnfluəns] vt influenciar ◆ n: ~ (on) (effect) influência f (em); **to be a bad/good ~ (on sb)** ser uma má/boa influência (para alguém).

influential [ˌɪnfluˈenʃl] adj influente.

influenza [ˌɪnfluˈenzə] n (fml) gripe f, influenza f.

inform [ɪnˈfɔːm] vt informar.

informal [ɪnˈfɔːml] adj informal.

information [ˌɪnfəˈmeɪʃn] n informação f; **a piece of ~** uma informação.

information desk n informações fpl.

information office n centro m de informações.

information technology n (tecnologia) informática f.

informative [ɪnˈfɔːmətɪv] adj informativo(-va).

infrastructure [ˈɪnfrəˌstrʌktʃəʳ] n infra-estrutura f.

infuriating [ɪnˈfjuərɪeɪtɪŋ] adj extremamente irritante.

ingenious [ɪnˈdʒiːnjəs] adj engenhoso(-osa).

ingot [ˈɪŋgət] n lingote m.

ingredient [ɪnˈgriːdjənt] n ingrediente m.

inhabit [ɪnˈhæbɪt] vt viver em.

inhabitant [ɪnˈhæbɪtənt] n habitante mf.

inhale [ɪnˈheɪl] vi inalar.

inhaler [ɪnˈheɪləʳ] n inalador m.

inherently [ɪnˈhɪərəntlɪ, ɪnˈherəntlɪ] adv inerentemente.

inherit [ɪnˈherɪt] vt herdar.

inheritance [ɪnˈherɪtəns] n herança f.

inhibition [ˌɪnhɪˈbɪʃn] n inibição f.

inhospitable [ˌɪnhɒˈspɪtəbl] adj (climate, area) inóspito(-ta); (unwelcoming) pouco hospitaleiro(-ra).

in-house adj (journal, report) interno(-na); (staff) da casa ◆ adv na fonte.

initial [ɪˈnɪʃl] adj inicial ◆ vt rubricar com as iniciais.

⅃ **initials** npl iniciais fpl.

initially [ɪˈnɪʃəlɪ] adv inicialmente.

initiative [ɪˈnɪʃətɪv] n iniciativa f.

injection [ɪnˈdʒekʃn] n injeção f.

injure [ˈɪndʒəʳ] vt ferir; **to ~ o.s.** ferir-se.

injured [ˈɪndʒəd] adj ferido(-da).

injury [ˈɪndʒərɪ] n ferimento m; (to tendon, muscle, internal organ) lesão f.

injury time n (período de) desconto m.

injustice [ɪnˈdʒʌstɪs] n injustiça f.

ink [ɪŋk] n tinta f.

inland [adj ˈɪnlənd, adv ɪnˈlænd] adj interior ◆ adv para o interior.

Inland Revenue n (Brit) = Receita f Federal (Br), = Direcção f Geral das Contribuições e Impostos (Port).

in-laws npl (inf) (parents-in-law) sogros mpl; (others) parentes mpl afins OR por afinidade.

inlet [ˈɪnlet] n (of lake, sea) braço m; (for fuel, water) entrada f, admissão f.

inmate [ˈɪnmeɪt] n (of prison) preso m (-sa f); (of mental hospital) doente m interno (doente f interna).

inn [ɪn] n estalagem f.

innate [ɪˈneɪt] adj inato(-ta).

inner [ˈɪnəʳ] adj interior.

inner city n centro m urbano.

inner tube n câmara-de-ar f.

innocence [ˈɪnəsəns] n inocência f.

innocent [ˈɪnəsənt] adj inocente.

innocuous [ɪˈnɒkjuəs] adj (harmless) inócuo (-cua), inofensivo(-va).

innovation [ˌɪnəˈveɪʃn] n inovação f.

innovative [ˈɪnəvətɪv] adj inovador (-ra).

inoculate [ɪˈnɒkjuleɪt] vt: **to ~ sb (against sthg)** vacinar alguém (contra algo).

inoculation [ɪˌnɒkjuˈleɪʃn] n inoculação f, vacinação f.

input [ˈɪnput] vt (COMPUT) entrar.

inquire [ɪnˈkwaɪəʳ] = **enquire**.

inquiry [ɪnˈkwaɪərɪ] = **enquiry**.

inquisitive [ɪnˈkwɪzətɪv] adj curioso (-osa), inquiridor(-ra).

insane [ɪn'seɪn] *adj* louco(-ca).
inscription [ɪn'skrɪpʃn] *n (on headstone, plaque)* inscrição *f; (in book)* dedicatória *f*.
insect ['ɪnsekt] *n* inseto *m*.
insecticide [ɪn'sektɪsaɪd] *n* inseticida *m*.
insect repellent *n* repelente *m* de insetos.
insecure [ˌɪnsɪ'kjʊər] *adj (person)* inseguro(-ra); *(hinge, job, wall)* pouco seguro(-ra); *(investment)* arriscado(-da).
insensitive [ɪn'sensətɪv] *adj* insensível.
insert [ɪn'sɜːt] *vt* introduzir.
inside [ɪn'saɪd] *prep* dentro de ♦ *adv (go)* para dentro; *(be, stay)* lá dentro ♦ *adj* interior, interno (-na) ♦ *n*: the ~ *(interior)* o interior; *(AUT: in UK)* a (faixa da) esquerda; *(AUT: in Europe, US)* a (faixa da) direita; ~ out *(clothes)* do lado avesso.
inside lane *n (AUT) (in UK)* faixa *f* da esquerda; *(in Europe, US)* faixa da direita.
inside leg *n* altura *f* de entrepernas.
insight ['ɪnsaɪt] *n (glimpse)* idéia *f*.
insignificant [ˌɪnsɪg'nɪfɪkənt] *adj* insignificante.
insincere [ˌɪnsɪn'sɪər] *adj* falso (-sa).
insinuate [ɪn'sɪnjʊeɪt] *vt* insinuar.
insipid [ɪn'sɪpɪd] *adj* insípido (-da).
insist [ɪn'sɪst] *vi* insistir; to ~ on doing sthg insistir em fazer algo.
insofar [ˌɪnsəʊ'fɑːr] : insofar as *conj* na medida em que.
insole ['ɪnsəʊl] *n* palmilha *f*.
insolent ['ɪnsələnt] *adj* insolente.
insomnia [ɪn'sɒmnɪə] *n* insônia *f*.
inspect [ɪn'spekt] *vt* inspecionar, examinar.
inspection [ɪn'spekʃn] *n* inspeção *f*.
inspector [ɪn'spektər] *n (on bus, train)* fiscal *m; (in police force)* inspetor *m* (-ra *f*).
inspiration [ˌɪnspə'reɪʃn] *n* inspiração *f*.
inspire [ɪn'spaɪər] *vt*: to ~ sb to do sthg inspirar alguém a fazer algo; to ~ sthg in sb inspirar algo a alguém.
instal [ɪn'stɔːl] *(Am)* = install.
install [ɪn'stɔːl] *vt (Brit)* instalar.
installation [ˌɪnstə'leɪʃn] *n* instalação *f*.
installment [ɪn'stɔːlmənt] *(Am)* = instalment.
instalment [ɪn'stɔːlmənt] *n (payment)*

prestação *f; (episode)* episódio *m*.
instamatic (camera) [ˌɪnstə'mætɪk-] *n* máquina *f* de tirar fotografias instantâneas.
instance ['ɪnstəns] *n (example, case)* exemplo *m*; for ~ por exemplo.
instant ['ɪnstənt] *adj* instantâneo (-nea) ♦ *n* instante *m*.
instant coffee *n* café *m* instantâneo OR solúvel.
instantly ['ɪnstəntlɪ] *adv* instantaneamente.
instead [ɪn'sted] *adv* em vez disso; ~ of em vez de.
instep ['ɪnstep] *n* peito *m* do pé.
instinct ['ɪnstɪŋkt] *n* instinto *m*.
instinctive [ɪn'stɪŋktɪv] *adj* instintivo(-va).
institute ['ɪnstɪtjuːt] *n* instituto *m*.
institution [ˌɪnstɪ'tjuːʃn] *n* instituição *f*.
instruct [ɪn'strʌkt] *vt*: to ~ sb to do sthg *(tell, order)* instruir alguém que faça algo; to ~ sb in sthg *(teach)* ensinar algo a alguém.
instructions [ɪn'strʌkʃnz] *npl* instruções *fpl*.
instructor [ɪn'strʌktər] *n* instrutor *m* (-ra *f*).
instrument ['ɪnstrəmənt] *n* instrumento *m*.
insubordinate [ˌɪnsə'bɔːdɪnət] *adj* indisciplinado(-da).
insufficient [ˌɪnsə'fɪʃnt] *adj* insuficiente.
insulate ['ɪnsjʊleɪt] *vt* isolar.
insulating tape ['ɪnsjʊleɪtɪŋ-] *n* fita *f* isolante.
insulation [ˌɪnsjʊ'leɪʃn] *n (material)* isolamento *m*, material *m* isolante.
insulin ['ɪnsjʊlɪn] *n* insulina *f*.
insult [*n* 'ɪnsʌlt, *vb* ɪn'sʌlt] *n* insulto *m* ♦ *vt* insultar.
insurance [ɪn'ʃʊərəns] *n* seguro *m*.
insurance certificate *n* certificado *m* do seguro.
insurance company *n* companhia *f* de seguros.
insurance policy *n* apólice *f* de seguros.
insure [ɪn'ʃʊər] *vt* pôr no seguro.
insured [ɪn'ʃʊəd] *adj*: to be ~ estar segurado(-da), estar no seguro.
intact [ɪn'tækt] *adj* intato(-ta).
integral [ɪntɪgrəl] *adj* essencial; to be ~ to sthg ser essencial para algo.

integrate [ˈɪntɪgreɪt] *vi* integrar-se ♦ *vt* *(include)* integrar; *(combine)* combinar.

integrity [ɪnˈtegrɪtɪ] *n* integridade *f*.

intellect [ˈɪntəlekt] *n* intelecto *m*.

intellectual [ˌɪntəˈlektjʊəl] *adj* intelectual ♦ *n* intelectual *mf*.

intelligence [ɪnˈtelɪdʒəns] *n* inteligência *f*.

intelligent [ɪnˈtelɪdʒənt] *adj* inteligente.

intend [ɪnˈtend] *vt*: **to be ~ed to do sthg** ser suposto fazer algo; **you weren't ~ed to know** não era para você saber; **to ~ to do sthg** ter a intenção de OR tencionar fazer algo.

intense [ɪnˈtens] *adj* intenso(-sa).

intensely [ɪnˈtenslɪ] *adv* *(irritating, boring)* extremamente; *(suffer, dislike)* intensamente.

intensify [ɪnˈtensɪfaɪ] *vt* intensificar ♦ *vi* intensificar-se.

intensity [ɪnˈtensɪtɪ] *n* intensidade *f*.

intensive [ɪnˈtensɪv] *adj* intensivo (-va).

intensive care *n* cuidados *mpl* intensivos

intent [ɪnˈtent] *adj*: **to be ~ on doing sthg** estar decidido(-da) a fazer algo.

intention [ɪnˈtenʃn] *n* intenção *f*.

intentional [ɪnˈtenʃənl] *adj* intencional.

intentionally [ɪnˈtenʃənəlɪ] *adv* intencionalmente.

interact [ˌɪntərˈækt] *vi*: **to ~ (with sb)** *(communicate, cooperate)* comunicar (com alguém); **to ~ (with sthg)** *(react)* interagir (com algo).

intercept [ˌɪntəˈsept] *vt* interceptar.

interchange [ˈɪntətʃeɪndʒ] *n* *(on motorway)* trevo *m* *(Br)*, intersecção *f* *(Port)*.

interchangeable [ˌɪntəˈtʃeɪndʒəbl] *adj* permutável.

Intercity® [ˌɪntəˈsɪtɪ] *n* *(Brit)* = expresso *m* *(Br)*, ~ *(comboio)* intercidades *m* *(Port)*.

intercom [ˈɪntəkɒm] *n* intercomunicador *m*.

intercourse [ˈɪntəkɔːs] *n* *(sexual)* relações *fpl* (sexuais).

interest [ˈɪntrəst] *n* interesse *m*; *(on money)* juros *mpl* ♦ *vt* interessar; **to take an ~ in sthg** interessar-se por algo.

interested [ˈɪntrəstɪd] *adj* interessado(-da); **to be ~ in sthg** estar interessado em algo.

interesting [ˈɪntrəstɪn] *adj* interessante.

interest rate *n* taxa *f* de juro.

interface [ˈɪntəfeɪs] *n* *(COMPUT)* interface *m*.

interfere [ˌɪntəˈfɪəʳ] *vi* *(meddle)* interferir; **to ~ with sthg** *(damage)* interferir em algo.

interference [ˌɪntəˈfɪərəns] *n* *(on TV, radio)* interferência *f*.

interim [ˈɪntərɪm] *adj* provisório(-ria) ♦ *n*: **in the ~** nesse meio tempo, nesse ínterim *(Br)*.

interior [ɪnˈtɪərɪəʳ] *adj* interior ♦ *n* interior *m*.

interlude [ˈɪntəluːd] *n* interlúdio *m*; *(at cinema, theatre)* intervalo *m*.

intermediary [ˌɪntəˈmiːdjərɪ] *n* intermediário *m* (-ria *f*).

intermediate [ˌɪntəˈmiːdjət] *adj* intermédio(-dia).

intermission [ˌɪntəˈmɪʃn] *n* intervalo *m*.

intermittent [ˌɪntəˈmɪtənt] *adj* intermitente.

internal [ɪnˈtɜːnl] *adj* interno (-na)

internal flight *n* voo *m* interno.

Internal Revenue *n* *(Am)*: **the ~** = Receita *f* Federal *(Br)*, = Direcção *f* Geral das Contribuições e Impostos *(Port)*.

international [ˌɪntəˈnæʃənl] *adj* internacional.

international flight *n* vôo *m* internacional.

Internet [ˈɪntənet] *n*: **the ~** a Internet.

interpret [ɪnˈtɜːprɪt] *vi* servir de intérprete.

interpreter [ɪnˈtɜːprɪtəʳ] *n* intérprete *mf*.

interrogate [ɪnˈterəgeɪt] *vt* interrogar.

interrogation [ɪnˌterəˈgeɪʃn] *n* interrogatório *m*.

interrupt [ˌɪntəˈrʌpt] *vt* interromper.

interruption [ˌɪntəˈrʌpʃn] *n* *(comment, question, action)* interrupção *f*; *(disturbance)* interrupções *fpl*.

intersect [ˌɪntəˈsekt] *vi* cruzar-se, intersectar-se ♦ *vt* intersectar.

intersection [ˌɪntəˈsekʃn] *n* *(of roads)* intersecção *f*, cruzamento *m* de nível.

interval [ˈɪntəvl] *n* intervalo *m*.

intervene [ˌɪntəˈviːn] *vi* *(person)* intervir; *(event)* interpor-se.

interview [ˈɪntəvjuː] *n* entrevista *f* ♦ *vt* entrevistar.

interviewer [ˈɪntəvjuːəʳ] n entrevistador m (-ra f).

intestine [ɪnˈtestɪn] n intestino m.

intimate [ˈɪntɪmət] adj íntimo (-ma).

intimidate [ɪnˈtɪmɪdeɪt] vt intimidar.

into [ˈɪntu] prep (inside) dentro de; (against) com; (concerning) acerca de, sobre; **4 ~ 20 goes 5 (times)** 20 dividido por 4 dá 5; **to change ~ sthg** transformar-se em algo; **to get ~ the car** entrar no carro; **to translate ~ Portuguese** traduzir para o português; **to be ~ sthg** (inf: like) gostar de algo.

intolerable [ɪnˈtɒlrəbl] adj intolerável.

intolerant [ɪnˈtɒlərənt] adj intolerante.

intoxicated [ɪnˈtɒksɪkeɪtɪd] adj: **to be ~** (drunk) estar embriagado(-da).

intransitive [ɪnˈtrænzətɪv] adj intransitivo(-va).

in-tray n cesta f de correspondência.

intricate [ˈɪntrɪkət] adj intrincado (-da), complicado(-da).

intriguing [ɪnˈtriːgɪŋ] adj intrigante.

intrinsic [ɪnˈtrɪnsɪk] adj intrínseco(-ca).

introduce [ˌɪntrəˈdjuːs] vt apresentar; **I'd like to ~ you to Fred** gostaria de lhe apresentar ao Fred.

introduction [ˌɪntrəˈdʌkʃn] n (to book, programme) introdução f; (to person) apresentação f.

introductory [ˌɪntrəˈdʌktrɪ] adj (course, chapter) introdutório(-ria); (remarks) inicial.

introvert [ˈɪntrəvɜːt] n introvertido m (-da f).

introverted [ˌɪntrəˈvɜːtɪd] adj introvertido(-da).

intrude [ɪnˈtruːd] vi: **to ~ on sb** incomodar alguém; **to ~ on sthg** intrometer-se em algo.

intruder [ɪnˈtruːdəʳ] n intruso m (-sa f).

intuition [ˌɪntjuːˈɪʃn] n intuição f.

inundate [ˈɪnʌndeɪt] vt (fml: flood) inundar; **to be ~d with sthg** (phone calls, offers etc) receber uma enxurrada de algo.

invade [ɪnˈveɪd] vt invadir.

invalid [adj ɪnˈvælɪd, n ˈɪnvəlɪd] adj (ticket, cheque) não válido(-da) ♦ n inválido m (-da f).

invaluable [ɪnˈvæljuəbl] adj inestimável, valiosíssimo(-ma).

invariably [ɪnˈveərɪəblɪ] adv invariavelmente, sempre.

invasion [ɪnˈveɪʒn] n invasão f.

invent [ɪnˈvent] vt inventar.

invention [ɪnˈvenʃn] n invenção f.

inventive [ɪnˈventɪv] adj inventivo (-va).

inventor [ɪnˈventəʳ] n inventor m (-ra f).

inventory [ˈɪnvəntrɪ] n (list) inventário m; (Am: stock) estoque m.

inverted commas [ɪnˈvɜːtɪd-] npl aspas fpl.

invest [ɪnˈvest] vt investir ♦ vi: **to ~ in sthg** investir em algo.

investigate [ɪnˈvestɪgeɪt] vt investigar.

investigation [ɪnˌvestɪˈgeɪʃn] n investigação f.

investment [ɪnˈvestmənt] n investimento m.

investor [ɪnˈvestəʳ] n investidor m (-ra f).

invincible [ɪnˈvɪnsɪbl] adj invencível.

invisible [ɪnˈvɪzɪbl] adj invisível.

invitation [ˌɪnvɪˈteɪʃn] n convite m.

invite [ɪnˈvaɪt] vt convidar; **to ~ sb to do sthg** (ask) convidar alguém para fazer algo; **to ~ sb round** convidar alguém.

inviting [ɪnˈvaɪtɪŋ] adj convidativo (-va).

invoice [ˈɪnvɔɪs] n fatura f.

involve [ɪnˈvɒlv] vt (entail) envolver; **what does it ~?** o que é que envolve?; **to be ~d in sthg** estar envolvido em algo.

involved [ɪnˈvɒlvd] adj (entailed) envolvido(-da).

involvement [ɪnˈvɒlvmənt] n envolvimento m.

inward [ˈɪnwəd] adj (feelings, satisfaction) íntimo(-ma); (flow, movement) em direção ao interior ♦ adv (Am) = inwards.

inwards [ˈɪnwədz] adv para dentro.

IOU n nota f de dívida, vale m.

IQ n QI m.

IRA n (abbrev of Irish Republican Army) IRA m.

Iran [ɪˈrɑːn] n Irã m.

Iranian [ɪˈreɪnjən] adj iraniano (-na) ♦ n (person) iraniano m (-na f).

Iraq [ɪˈrɑːk] n Iraque m.

Iraqi [ɪˈrɑːkɪ] adj iraquiano(-na) ♦ n (person) iraquiano m (-na f).

Ireland [ˈaɪələnd] n Irlanda f.

iris [ˈaɪərɪs] (pl -es) n (flower) lírio m; (of eye) íris f.

Irish [ˈaɪrɪʃ] *adj* irlandês(-esa) ♦ *n (language)* irlandês *m* ♦ *npl*: **the ~** os irlandeses.

Irish coffee *n* Irish coffee *m*, mistura alcoólica de uísque com café, açúcar e creme.

Irishman [ˈaɪrɪʃmən] (*pl* -men [-mən]) *n* irlandês *m*.

Irish Sea *n*: **the ~** o mar da Irlanda.

Irish stew *n* ensopado de carneiro com batatas e cebolas.

Irishwoman [ˈaɪrɪʃˌwʊmən] (*pl* -women [-ˌwɪmɪn]) *n* irlandesa *f*.

iron [ˈaɪən] *n (metal)* ferro *m*; *(for clothes)* ferro (de engomar OR passar); *(golf club)* ferro, taco *m* de metal ♦ *vt* passar a ferro.

ironic [aɪˈrɒnɪk] *adj* irônico(-ca).

ironing [ˈaɪənɪŋ] *n (clothes to be ironed)* roupa *f* para passar a ferro; **to do the ~** passar (a roupa) a ferro.

ironing board [ˈaɪənɪŋ-] *n* tábua *f* de engomar OR passar (a ferro).

ironmonger's [ˈaɪənˌmʌŋgəz] *n (Brit)* loja *f* de ferragens.

irony [ˈaɪərənɪ] *n* ironia *f*.

irrational [ɪˈræʃənl] *adj* irracional.

irrelevant [ɪˈreləvənt] *adj* irrelevante.

irresistible [ˌɪrɪˈzɪstəbl] *adj* irresistível.

irrespective [ˌɪrɪˈspektɪv] : **irrespective of** *prep* independentemente de.

irresponsible [ˌɪrɪˈspɒnsəbl] *adj* irresponsável.

irrigate [ˈɪrɪgeɪt] *vt* irrigar, regar.

irrigation [ˌɪrɪˈgeɪʃn] *n* irrigação *f*.

irritable [ˈɪrɪtəbl] *adj* irritável.

irritate [ˈɪrɪteɪt] *vt* irritar.

irritating [ˈɪrɪteɪtɪŋ] *adj* irritante.

irritation [ˌɪrɪˈteɪʃn] *n* irritação *f*.

IRS *n (Am)* – Receita *f* Federal *(Br)*, – Direcção *f* Geral das Contribuições e Impostos *(Port)*.

is [ɪz] → **be**.

Islam [ˈɪzlɑːm] *n* islã *m*.

island [ˈaɪlənd] *n (in water)* ilha *f*; *(in road)* abrigo *m (Br)*, placa *f (Port) (que serve de refúgio para os pedestres no meio da rua)*.

islander [ˈaɪləndə^r] *n* ilhéu *m* (ilhoa *f*).

isle [aɪl] *n* ilha *f*.

Isle of Man *n*: **the ~** a ilha de Man.

Isle of Wight [-waɪt] *n*: **the ~** a ilha de Wight.

isn't [ˈɪznt] = **is not**.

isolated [ˈaɪsəleɪtɪd] *adj* isolado (-da).

Israel [ˈɪzreɪəl] *n* Israel *s*.

Israeli [ɪzˈreɪlɪ] *adj* israelita, israelense ♦ *n* israelita *mf*, israelense *mf*

issue [ˈɪʃuː] *n (problem, subject)* questão *f*; *(of newspaper)* edição *f*; *(of magazine)* número *m* ♦ *vt* emitir.

it [ɪt] *pron* **1.** *(referring to specific thing, subject after prep)* ele *m* (ela *f*); *(direct object)* o *m* (a *f*); *(indirect object)* lhe; **a free book came with ~** veio acompanhado de um livro grátis; **give ~ to me** me dê isso; **he gave ~ a kick** ele deu-lhe um pontapé; **~'s big** é grande; **~'s here** está aqui; **she hit ~** (ela) bateu-lhe; **she lost ~** (ela) perdeu-o.
2. *(referring to situation, fact)*: **~'s a difficult question** é uma questão difícil; **I can't remember ~** não me lembro; **tell me about ~** conta-me.
3. *(used impersonally)*: **~'s hot** está calor; **~'s six o'clock** são seis horas; **~'s Sunday** é domingo.
4. *(referring to person)*: **~'s me** sou eu; **who is ~?** quem é?

Italian [ɪˈtæljən] *adj* italiano (-na) ♦ *n (person)* italiano *m* (-na *f*); *(language)* italiano *m*; **an ~ restaurant** um restaurante italiano.

italic [ɪˈtælɪk] *adj* itálico(-ca).

Italy [ˈɪtəlɪ] *n* Itália *f*.

itch [ɪtʃ] *vi (person)* ter coceira *(Br)*, ter comichão *(Port)*; **my arm ~es** estou com coceira no braço.

itchy [ˈɪtʃɪ] *adj*: **it's really ~** está coçando muito.

it'd [ˈɪtəd] = **it would, it had.**

item [ˈaɪtəm] *n (object)* artigo *m*; *(on agenda)* assunto *m*, ponto *m*; **a news ~** uma notícia.

itemized bill [ˈaɪtəmaɪzd-] *n* fatura *f* discriminada.

itinerary [aɪˈtɪnərərɪ] *n* itinerário *m*.

it'll [ɪtl] = **it will.**

its [ɪts] *adj* o seu (a sua), dele (dela); **the cat hurt ~ paw** o gato machucou a pata (dele) OR a (sua) pata.

it's [ɪts] = **it is, it has.**

itself [ɪtˈself] *pron (reflexive)* se; *(after prep)* si mesmo *m* (-ma *f*); **the house ~ is fine** a casa em si é boa.

ITV *n (abbrev of Independent Television)* um dos canais privados da televisão britânica.

I've [aɪv] = **I have.**

ivory [ˈaɪvərɪ] *n* marfim *m*.

ivy [ˈaɪvɪ] *n* hera *f*.

J

jab [dʒæb] n (Brit: inf: injection) injeção f.

jack [dʒæk] n (for car) macaco m; (playing card) valete m.

jacket ['dʒækɪt] n (garment) casaco m, blusão m; (cover) capa f; (of potato) casca f.

jacket potato n batata f assada com casca.

jack-knife vi dar uma guinada, virar na estrada.

jackpot ['dʒækpɒt] n jackpot m.

jacuzzi® [dʒəˈkuːzɪ] n jacuzzi® m.

jade [dʒeɪd] n jade m.

jagged ['dʒægɪd] adj (metal) dentea-do(-da); (outline, tear) irregular.

jail [dʒeɪl] n prisão f.

jailer ['dʒeɪlər] n carcereiro m (-ra f).

jam [dʒæm] n (food) geléia f (Br), compota f, doce m (Port); (of traffic) engarrafamento m; (inf: difficult situation) apuro m ◆ vt (pack tightly) enfiar (até mais não poder) ◆ vi (get stuck) emperrar; **the roads are ~med** as estradas estão congestionadas.

Jamaica [dʒəˈmeɪkə] n Jamaica f.

jam-packed [-ˈpækt] adj (inf): **~ (with)** apinhado(-da) (de).

Jan. [dʒæn] (abbr of January) jan.

janitor ['dʒænɪtər] n (Am & Scot) contínuo m (-nua f).

January ['dʒænjʊərɪ] n janeiro m, → September.

Japan [dʒəˈpæn] n Japão m.

Japanese [ˌdʒæpəˈniːz] adj japonês (-esa) ◆ n (language) japonês m ◆ npl: **the ~** os japoneses.

jar [dʒɑːr] n frasco m.

jargon ['dʒɑːgən] n jargão m.

javelin ['dʒævlɪn] n dardo m (de lançamento).

jaw [dʒɔː] n maxilar m, mandíbula f.

jawbone ['dʒɔːbəʊn] n maxilar m,

mandíbula f; (of animal) queixada f.

jazz [dʒæz] n jazz m.

jealous ['dʒeləs] adj ciumento (-ta).

jealousy ['dʒeləsɪ] n ciúmes mpl.

jeans [dʒiːnz] npl jeans m inv (Br), calças fpl de ganga (Port).

Jeep® [dʒiːp] n jipe m.

jeer [dʒɪər] vt (boo) vaiar; (mock) zombar de ◆ vi: **to ~ at sb** (boo) vaiar alguém; (mock) zombar de alguém.

Jello® ['dʒeləʊ] n (Am) gelatina f.

jelly ['dʒelɪ] n (dessert) gelatina f; (Am: jam) geléia f.

jellyfish ['dʒelɪfɪʃ] (pl inv) n água-viva f.

jeopardize ['dʒepədaɪz] vt pôr em risco.

jerk [dʒɜːk] n (movement) solavanco m; (inf: idiot) idiota mf.

jersey ['dʒɜːzɪ] n (garment) suéter m (Br), camisola f de malha (Port).

Jersey ['dʒɜːzɪ] n Jersey m.

jest [dʒest] n brincadeira f, gracejo m; **in ~** na brincadeira, gracejando.

Jesus (Christ) ['dʒiːzəs-] n Jesus m (Cristo).

jet [dʒet] n jato m; (outlet) cano m de saída.

jet engine n motor m a jato.

jetfoil ['dʒetfɔɪl] n hidrofólio m.

jet lag n jet lag m, cansaço provocado pelas diferenças de fuso horário.

jet-ski n jet-ski m, moto f de água.

jetty ['dʒetɪ] n embarcadouro m.

Jew [dʒuː] n judeu m (-dia f).

jewel ['dʒuːəl] n jóia f.

◡ **jewels** npl (jewellery) jóias fpl.

jeweler's ['dʒuːələz] (Am) = **jeweller's**.

jeweller's ['dʒuːələz] n (Brit) joalheria f, ourivesaria f.

jewellery ['dʒuːəlrɪ] n (Brit) jóias fpl.

jewelry ['dʒuːəlrɪ] (Am) = **jewellery**.

Jewish ['dʒuːɪʃ] *adj* judaico(-ca).

jiffy ['dʒɪfɪ] *n* (*inf*): **in a ~** num instante.

jig [dʒɪg] *n* jiga *f*.

jigsaw (puzzle) ['dʒɪgsɔː-] *n* puzzle *m*.

jilt [dʒɪlt] *vt* deixar, abandonar.

jingle ['dʒɪŋgl] *n* (*of advert*) jingle *m* publicitário.

jinx [dʒɪŋks] *n* mau olhado *m*.

job [dʒɒb] *n* (*regular work*) emprego *m*; (*task, function*) trabalho *m*; **to lose one's ~** perder o emprego.

job centre *n* (*Brit*) centro *m* de emprego.

jockey ['dʒɒkɪ] *n* jóquei *m*.

jog [dʒɒg] *vt* (*bump*) empurrar (*levemente*) ◆ *vi* fazer jogging ◆ *n*: **to go for a ~** fazer jogging.

jogging ['dʒɒgɪŋ] *n* jogging *m*; **to go ~** fazer jogging.

john [dʒɒn] *n* (*Am: inf: toilet*) privada *f*.

join [dʒɔɪn] *vt* (*club, organization*) tornar-se membro de, entrar para; (*fasten together, connect*) ligar, unir; (*come together with*) unir-se a; (*participate in*) juntar-se a; **will you ~ me for dinner?** você me acompanha para jantar?; **to ~ the queue** entrar na fila.

⏄ **join in** *vt fus* juntar-se a, participar em ◆ *vi* participar.

joiner ['dʒɔɪnə'] *n* marceneiro *m* (-ra *f*), carpinteiro *m* (-ra *f*).

joint [dʒɔɪnt] *adj* conjunto(-ta) ◆ *n* (*of body*) articulação *f*; (*Brit: of meat*) corte *m* (de carne); (*in structure*) junta *f*.

jointly ['dʒɔɪntlɪ] *adv* conjuntamente.

joke [dʒəʊk] *n* piada *f*, anedota *f* ◆ *vi* gozar, brincar; **it was only a ~** foi só uma brincadeira.

joker ['dʒəʊkə'] *n* (*playing card*) curinga *m* (*Br*), jóquer *m* (*Port*).

jolly ['dʒɒlɪ] *adj* alegre ◆ *adv* (*Brit: inf: very*) muito.

jolt [dʒəʊlt] *n* solavanco *m*.

Jordan ['dʒɔːdn] *n* Jordânia *f*.

jostle ['dʒɒsl] *vt* empurrar, dar empurrões a ◆ *vi* empurrar, dar empurrões.

jot [dʒɒt] : **jot down** *vt sep* anotar.

journal ['dʒɜːnl] *n* (*professional magazine*) boletim *m*; (*diary*) diário *m*.

journalism ['dʒɜːnəlɪzm] *n* jornalismo *m*.

journalist ['dʒɜːnəlɪst] *n* jornalista *mf*.

journey ['dʒɜːnɪ] *n* viagem *f*.

jovial ['dʒəʊvjəl] *adj* jovial.

joy [dʒɔɪ] *n* (*happiness*) alegria *f*.

joyful ['dʒɔɪfʊl] *adj* alegre.

joypad ['dʒɔɪpæd] *n* joypad *m*.

joyrider ['dʒɔɪraɪdə'] *n* pessoa que rouba um carro para passear e divertir-se e que depois o abandona.

joystick ['dʒɔɪstɪk] *n* (*of video game*) joystick *m*, manípulo *m*.

Jr. (*abbr of Junior*) Jr.

jubilant ['dʒuːbɪlənt] *adj* exultante.

judge [dʒʌdʒ] *n* juiz *m* (juíza *f*) ◆ *vt* julgar.

judg(e)ment ['dʒʌdʒmənt] *n* (*JUR*) julgamento *m*; (*opinion*) parecer *m*; (*capacity to judge*) senso *m*.

judiciary [dʒuːˈdɪʃərɪ] *n*: **the ~** o poder judicial.

judo ['dʒuːdəʊ] *n* judô *m*.

jug [dʒʌg] *n* jarro *m*, jarra *f*.

juggernaut ['dʒʌgənɔːt] *n* (*Brit*) jamanta *f* (*Br*), camião *m*, TIR *m* (*Port*).

juggle ['dʒʌgl] *vi* fazer malabarismos.

juggler ['dʒʌglə'] *n* malabarista *mf*.

juice [dʒuːs] *n* (*from fruit, vegetables*) suco *m* (*Br*), sumo *m* (*Port*); (*from meat*) molho *m*.

juicy ['dʒuːsɪ] *adj* (*food*) suculento(-ta).

jukebox ['dʒuːkbɒks] *n* jukebox *f*, máquina *f* de discos.

Jul. *abbr* = **July**.

July [dʒuːˈlaɪ] *n* julho *m*, → **September**.

jumble ['dʒʌmbl] *n* (*mixture*) miscelânea *f* ◆ *vt*: **to ~ (up)** misturar.

jumble sale *n* (*Brit*) venda de objetos em segunda mão com fins beneficentes.

jumbo ['dʒʌmbəʊ] (*pl* -s) *adj* (*inf: big*) gigante.

jumbo jet *n* jumbo *m*.

jump [dʒʌmp] *n* salto *m* ◆ *vi* (*through air*) saltar; (*with fright*) assustar-se; (*increase*) dar um salto ◆ *vt* (*Am: train, bus*) viajar sem bilhete em; **to ~ the queue** (*Brit*) furar a fila (*Br*), dar o golpe (*Port*).

jumper ['dʒʌmpə'] *n* (*Brit: pullover*) pulôver *m* (*Br*), camisola *f* (de malha) (*Port*); (*Am: dress*) vestido *m* de alças.

jump leads *npl* cabos *mpl* para bateria.

jump-start *vt* fazer arrancar com uma ligação directa.

jumpsuit ['dʒʌmpsuːt] *n* macacão *f*.

jumpy ['dʒʌmpɪ] *adj* nervoso(-osa).
Jun. *abbr* = June.
junction ['dʒʌŋkʃn] *n (road)* cruzamento *m; (railway)* entroncamento *m*.
June [dʒuːn] *n* junho *m*, → **September**.
jungle ['dʒʌŋgl] *n* selva *f*.
junior ['dʒuːnjəʳ] *adj (of lower rank)* subalterno(-na); *(Am: after name)* júnior *(inv)* ◆ *n (younger person)*: **she's my ~** ela é mais nova do que eu.
junior high school *n (Am)* ~ escola *f* secundária *(para alunos entre os 12 e os 15 anos)*.
junior school *n (Brit)* escola *f* primária.
junk [dʒʌŋk] *n (inf: unwanted things)* tralha *f*.
junk food *n (inf)* comida pronta considerada pouco nutritiva ou saudável.
junkie ['dʒʌŋkɪ] *n (inf)* drogado *m* (-da *f*).
junk mail *n* papelada *f (publicitária enviada pelo correio)*.

junk shop *n* loja *f* de objetos usados.
Jupiter ['dʒuːpɪtəʳ] *n* Júpiter *m*.
jurisdiction [,dʒʊərɪs'dɪkʃn] *n* jurisdição *f*.
juror ['dʒʊərəʳ] *n* jurado *m* (-da *f*).
jury ['dʒʊərɪ] *n* júri *m*.
just [dʒʌst] *adv (recently)* agora (mesmo); *(in the next moment)* mesmo; *(exactly)* precisamente; *(only, slightly)* só ◆ *adj* justo(-ta); **I'm ~ coming!** já vou!; **to be ~ about to do sthg** estar prestes fazendo algo; **to have ~ done sthg** acabar de fazer algo; **~ about** *(almost)* praticamente; **~ as good** igualmente bom; **~ as good as** tão bom quanto; **~ over an hour** pouco mais de uma hora; **(only) ~** *(almost not)* quase não, por pouco não; **~ a minute!** só um minuto!
justice ['dʒʌstɪs] *n* justiça *f*.
justify ['dʒʌstɪfaɪ] *vt* justificar.
jut [dʒʌt] : **jut out** *vi* sobressair.
juvenile ['dʒuːvənaɪl] *adj (young)* juvenil; *(childish)* infantil.

K

kaleidoscope [kəˈlaɪdəskəʊp] *n* caleidoscópio *m*.

kangaroo [kæŋɡəˈruː] *n* canguru *m*.

karate [kəˈrɑːtɪ] *n* karatê *m*.

kayak [ˈkaɪæk] *n* kayak *m*, caiaque *m*.

KB (*COMPUT: abbr of kilobyte(s)*) KB *m*.

kebab [kɪˈbæb] *n*: (**doner**) ~ pão árabe cortado servido com carne de carneiro, salada e molho; (**shish**) ~ espeto de carne com tomate, cebola, pimentões, etc.

keel [kiːl] *n* quilha *f*.

keen [kiːn] *adj* (*enthusiastic*) entusiasta; (*eyesight, hearing*) apurado(-da); **to be ~ on** interessar-se por, gostar de; **to be ~ to do sthg** ter muita vontade de fazer algo.

keep [kiːp] (*pt & pp* **kept**) *vt* manter; (*book, change, object loaned*) ficar com; (*store, not tell*) guardar; (*appointment*) não faltar a; (*delay*) atrasar; (*diary*) ter ◆ *vi* (*food*) conservar; (*remain*) manter-se; **to ~ a record of sthg** registrar algo; **to ~ (on) doing sthg** (*do continuously*) continuar fazendo algo; (*do repeatedly*) estar sempre fazendo algo; **to ~ sb from doing sthg** impedir alguém de fazer algo; **~ back!** para trás!; **"~ in lane!"** "mantenha-se na sua faixa"; **"~ left"** "circular pela esquerda"; **"~ off the grass!"** "não pise na grama!"; **"~ out!"** "proibida a entrada"; **"~ your distance!"** "mantenha a distância"; **to ~ clear (of)** manter-se afastado (de).

❑ **keep up** *vt sep* manter ◆ *vi* (*maintain pace, level etc*): **to ~ up with sb** acompanhar alguém; **~ up the good work!** continue com o bom trabalho!

keeper [ˈkiːpəʳ] *n* (*in zoo*) guarda *mf*, zelador *m* (-ra *f*).

keep-fit *n* (*Brit*) ginástica *f*.

keepsake [ˈkiːpseɪk] *n* lembrança *f*.

keg [keɡ] *n* barril *m*.

kennel [ˈkenl] *n* casa *f* de cachorro, canil *m*.

Kenya [ˈkenjə] *n* Quênia *m*.

Kenyan [ˈkenjən] *adj* queniano (-na) ◆ *n* queniano *m* (-na *f*).

kept [kept] *pt & pp* → **keep**.

kerb [kɜːb] *n* (*Brit*) meio-fio *m* (*Br*), borda *f* do passeio (*Port*).

kernel [ˈkɜːnl] *n* (*of nut*) miolo *m*.

kerosene [ˈkerəsiːn] *n* (*Am*) querosene *m*.

ketchup [ˈketʃəp] *n* ketchup *m*, molho *m* de tomate.

kettle [ˈketl] *n* chaleira *f*; **to put the ~ on** pôr a chaleira para ferver.

key [kiː] *n* chave *f*; (*of piano, typewriter*) tecla *f* ◆ *adj* chave (*inv*).

keyboard [ˈkiːbɔːd] *n* (*of typewriter, piano*) teclado *m*; (*musical instrument*) órgão *m*.

keyhole [ˈkiːhəʊl] *n* buraco *m* da fechadura.

keypad [ˈkiːpæd] *n* teclado *m* (numérico).

key ring *n* chaveiro *m* (*Br*), porta-chaves *m inv* (*Port*).

kg (*abbr of kilogram*) kg.

khaki [ˈkɑːkɪ] *adj* cáqui (*inv*) ◆ *n* (*colour*) cáqui *m*.

kick [kɪk] *n* (*of foot*) pontapé *m* ◆ *vt*: **to ~ sb/sthg** dar um pontapé em alguém/algo.

kickoff [ˈkɪkɒf] *n* pontapé *m* inicial.

kid [kɪd] *n* (*inf*) (*child*) garoto *m* (-ta *f*); (*young person*) criança *f* ◆ *vi* (*joke*) gozar, brincar.

kidnap [ˈkɪdnæp] *vt* raptar.

kidnaper [ˈkɪdnæpəʳ] (*Am*) = **kidnapper**.

kidnapper [ˈkɪdnæpəʳ] *n* (*Brit*) raptor *m* (-ra *f*).

kidnapping [ˈkɪdnæpɪŋ] *n* rapto *m*, seqüestro *m*.

kidney [ˈkɪdnɪ] *n* rim *m*.

kidney bean *n* feijão *m* vermelho.

kill [kɪl] *vt* matar; **my feet are ~ing me!** os meus pés estão me matando!
killer ['kɪlɔ'] *n* assassino *m* (-na *f*).
killing ['kɪlɪŋ] *n* (*murder*) assassinato *m*.
killjoy ['kɪldʒɔɪ] *n* desmancha-prazeres *mf inv*).
kiln [kɪln] *n* forno *m*, fornalha *f*.
kilo ['ki:ləʊ] (*pl* -s) *n* quilo *m*.
kilobyte ['kɪləbaɪt] *n* kilobyte *m*.
kilogram ['kɪləgræm] *n* quilograma *m*.
kilohertz ['kɪləhɜ:ts] (*pl inv*) kilohertz *m*.
kilometre ['kɪlə,mi:tə'] *n* quilômetro *m*.
kilowatt ['kɪləwɒt] *n* kilowatt *m*.
kilt [kɪlt] *n* kilt *m*, saia *f* escocesa.
kind [kaɪnd] *adj* amável ◆ *n* tipo *m*; **~ of** (*Am: inf*) um pouco.
kindergarten ['kɪndə,gɑ:tn] *n* jardim-de-infância *m*.
kind-hearted [-'hɑ:tɪd] *adj* bondoso(-osa).
kindly ['kaɪndlɪ] *adv*: **would you ~ ...?** pode fazer o favor de ...?
kindness ['kaɪndnɪs] *n* amabilidade *f*, bondade *f*.
king [kɪŋ] *n* rei *m*.
kingdom ['kɪŋdəm] *n* reino *m*.
kingfisher ['kɪŋ,fɪʃə'] *n* martim-pescador *m*, pica-peixe *m*.
king prawn *n* camarão *m* (gigante) (*Br*), gamba *f* (*Port*).
king-size bed *n* cama *f* de casal (*com 160 cm de largura*).
kinky ['kɪŋkɪ] *adj* (*inf*) bizarro(-a).
kiosk ['ki:ɒsk] *n* (*for newspapers etc*) banca *f* de jornal (*Br*), quiosque *m* (*Port*); (*Brit: phone box*) cabine *f*.
kip [kɪp] *n* (*Brit: inf*) soneca *f* ◆ *vi* (*Brit: inf*) dormir.
kipper ['kɪpə'] *n* arenque *m* defumado.
kiss [kɪs] *n* beijo *m* ◆ *vt* beijar.
kiss of life *n* respiração *f* boca-a-boca.
kit [kɪt] *n* (*set*) estojo *m*; (*clothes*) equipamento *m*; (*for assembly*) kit *m*, modelo *m*.
kit bag *n* saco *m* de viagem.
kitchen ['kɪtʃɪn] *n* cozinha *f*.
kitchen sink *n* pia *f* da cozinha.
kitchen unit *n* módulo *m* de cozinha.

kite [kaɪt] *n* (*toy*) pipa *f* (*Br*), papagaio *m* (de papel) (*Port*).
kitten ['kɪtn] *n* gatinho *m* (-nha *f*).
kitty ['kɪtɪ] *n* (*for regular expenses*) fundo *m* comum.
kiwi fruit ['ki:wi:-] *n* kiwi *m*.
Kleenex® ['kli:neks] *n* Kleenex® *m*, lenço *m* de papel.
km (*abbr of kilometre*) km.
km/h (*abbr of kilometres per hour*) km/h.
knack [næk] *n*: **I've got the ~ (of it)** já peguei o jeito de fazer isso.
knackered ['nækəd] *adj* (*Brit: inf*) estourado(-da).
knapsack ['næpsæk] *n* mochila *f*.
knead [ni:d] *vt* amassar.
knee [ni:] *n* joelho *m*.
kneecap ['ni:kæp] *n* rótula *f*.
kneel [ni:l] (*pt & pp knelt* [nelt]) *vi* (*be on one's knees*) estar ajoelhado(-da) OR de joelhos; (*go down on one's knees*) ajoelhar-se.
knew [nju:] *pt* → **know**.
knickers ['nɪkəz] *npl* (*Brit*) calcinha *f* (*Br*), cuecas *fpl* (de senhora) (*Port*).
knick-knack ['nɪknæk] *n* bugiganga *f*.
knife [naɪf] (*pl* knives) *n* faca *f*.
knight [naɪt] *n* (*in history*) cavaleiro *m*; (*in chess*) cavalo *m*.
knighthood ['naɪthʊd] *n* (*present day title*) título *m* de "Sir".
knit [nɪt] *vt* fazer tricô.
knitted ['nɪtɪd] *adj* tricotado(-da), de malha.
knitting ['nɪtɪŋ] *n* tricô *m* (*Br*), malha *f* (*Port*).
knitting needle *n* agulha *f* de tricô.
knitwear ['nɪtweə'] *n* roupa *f* de tricô.
knives [naɪvz] *pl* → **knife**.
knob [nɒb] *n* (*on door etc*) maçaneta *f*; (*on machine*) botão *m*.
knock [nɒk] *n* (*at door*) pancada *f*, batida *f* ◆ *vt* (*hit*) bater em; (*one's head, elbow*) bater com ◆ *vi* (*at door etc*) bater.
❏ **knock down** *vt sep* (*pedestrian*) atropelar; (*building*) demolir; (*price*) baixar.
❏ **knock out** *vt sep* (*make unconscious*) deixar inconsciente; (*of competition*) eliminar.
❏ **knock over** *vt sep* (*glass, vase*) derrubar; (*pedestrian*) atropelar.

knocker [ˈnɒkəʳ] *n (on door)* batente *m*, aldraba *f*.

knockout [ˈnɒkaʊt] *n (in boxing)* nocaute *m*.

knot [nɒt] *n* nó *m*.

know [nəʊ] *(pt knew, pp known) vt* saber; *(person, place)* conhecer; **to ~ about sthg** saber (acerca) de algo; **to ~ how to do sthg** saber como fazer algo; **to ~ of** saber de; **you'll like him once you get to ~ him** você vai gostar dele quando o conhecer melhor; **to be known as** ser conhecido como; **to let sb ~ sthg** avisar alguém de algo; **you ~** *(for emphasis)* sabe.

know-all *n (Brit)* sabichão *m* (-chona *f*).

know-how *n* know-how *m*, conhecimentos *mpl*.

knowingly [ˈnəʊɪŋlɪ] *adv (look, smile)* com cumplicidade; *(act)* conscientemente.

knowledge [ˈnɒlɪdʒ] *n* saber *m*, conhecimento *m*; **to my ~** que eu saiba.

knowledgeable [ˈnɒlɪdʒəbl] *adj* conhecedor(-ra).

known [nəʊn] *pp →* **know**.

knuckle [ˈnʌkl] *n (of hand)* nó *m* do dedo; *(of pork)* mocotó *m (Br)*, chispe *m (Port)*.

koala (bear) [kəʊˈɑːlə-] *n* (urso) coala *m*.

Koran [kɒˈrɑːn] *n*: **the ~** o Corão.

kosher [ˈkəʊʃəʳ] *adj (meat)* limpo(-pa) (segundo a lei judaica).

kung fu [ˌkʌŋˈfuː] *n* kung-fu *m*.

Kurd [kɜːd] *n* curdo *m* (-da *f*).

Kuwait [kʊˈweɪt] *n (country)* Kuwait *m*.

L

l *(abbr of litre)* l.
L *(abbr of learner, large)* L.
lab [læb] *n (inf)* laboratório *m*.
label ['leɪbl] *n* etiqueta *f*.
labor ['leɪbər] *(Am)* = **labour**.
laboratory [Brit ləˈbɒrətrɪ, Am ˈlæbrətɔːrɪ] *n* laboratório *m*.
labour ['leɪbər] *n (Brit) (work)* trabalho *m*; **in ~** *(MED)* em trabalho de parto.
labourer ['leɪbərər] *n* trabalhador *m* (-ra *f*).
Labour Party *n (Brit)* Partido *m* Trabalhista.
labour-saving *adj* que poupa trabalho.
Labrador ['læbrədɔːr] *n (dog)* cão *m* Labrador.
labyrinth ['læbərɪnθ] *n* labirinto *m*.
lace [leɪs] *n (material)* renda *f*; *(for shoe)* cardaço *m (Br)*, atacador *m (Port)*.
lace-ups *npl* sapatos *mpl* de amarrar.
lack [læk] *n* falta *f* ◆ *vt* carecer de ◆ *vi*: **to be ~ing** faltar; **he ~s confidence** falta-lhe confiança.
lacquer ['lækər] *n* laca *f*.
lad [læd] *n (inf)* garoto *m*.
ladder ['lædər] *n (for climbing)* escada *f*; *(Brit: in tights)* defeito *m*, desfiado *m (Br)*, foguete *m (Port)*.
ladies ['leɪdɪz] *n (Brit) (toilet)* banheiro *m* de senhoras.
ladies room *(Am)* = **ladies**.
ladieswear ['leɪdɪzweər] *n* roupa *f* de senhora.
ladle ['leɪdl] *n* concha *f*.
lady ['leɪdɪ] *n (woman)* senhora *f*; *(woman of high status)* dama *f*.
ladybird ['leɪdɪbɜːd] *n (Brit)* joaninha *f*.
ladybug ['leɪdɪbʌg] *(Am)* = **ladybird**.
lady-in-waiting [-ˈweɪtɪŋ] *n* dama *f* de companhia.

ladylike ['leɪdɪlaɪk] *adj* elegante, distinto(-ta).
lag [læg] *vi* diminuir; **to ~ behind** *(move more slowly)* ficar para trás.
lager ['lɑːgər] *n* cerveja *f* (loura).
lagoon [ləˈguːn] *n* lagoa *f*.
laid [leɪd] *pt & pp* → **lay**.
laid-back *adj (inf)* descontraído(-da).
lain [leɪn] *pp* → **lie**.
lair [leər] *n* toca *f*, covil *m*.
lake [leɪk] *n* lago *m*.
Lake District *n*: **the ~** *região de lagos e montanhas no noroeste de Inglaterra.*
lamb [læm] *n (animal)* cordeiro *m*; *(meat)* carneiro *m*.
lamb chop *n* costeleta *f* de carneiro.
lambswool ['læmzwʊl] *n* lã *m* de carneiro ◆ *adj* de lã de carneiro.
lame [leɪm] *adj* coxo(-xa).
lament [ləˈment] *n* lamento *m* ◆ *vt* lamentar.
laminated ['læmɪneɪtɪd] *adj* laminado(-da).
lamp [læmp] *n* lâmpada *f (Br)*, candeeiro *m (Port)*.
lamppost ['læmppəʊst] *n* poste *m* de iluminação.
lampshade ['læmpʃeɪd] *n* abajur *m (Br)*, quebra-luz *m (Port)*.
lance [lɑːns] *n* lança *f*.
land [lænd] *n* terra *f* ◆ *vi (plane)* aterrar; *(passengers)* desembarcar; *(fall)* cair.
landing ['lændɪŋ] *n (of plane)* aterrissagem *f (Br)*, aterragem *f (Port)*; *(on stairs)* patamar *m*.
landing card *n* cartão *m* de desembarque.
landing gear *n* trem *m* de aterrissagem.
landing strip *n* pista *f* de aterrissagem.

landlady [ˈlændˌleɪdɪ] n (of house) senhoria f; (of pub) dona f.

landlord [ˈlændlɔːd] n (of house) senhorio m; (of pub) dono m.

landmark [ˈlændmɑːk] n (in landscape, city) ponto m de referência.

landowner [ˈlændˌəʊnəʳ] n proprietário m (-ria f) rural.

landscape [ˈlændskeɪp] n paisagem f.

landslide [ˈlændslaɪd] n (of earth, rocks) deslizamento m (Br), desabamento m (Port).

lane [leɪn] n (narrow road) ruela f; (on road, motorway) pista f (Br), faixa f (Port); **"get in ~"** sinal que indica aos motoristas que devem deslocar-se para a pista adequada.

language [ˈlæŋgwɪdʒ] n (of a people, country) língua f; (system of communication, words) linguagem f.

language laboratory n laboratório m de línguas.

languish [ˈlæŋgwɪʃ] vi definhar.

lank [læŋk] adj (hair) escorrido (-da).

lanky [ˈlæŋkɪ] adj magricela.

lantern [ˈlæntən] n lanterna f.

lap [læp] n (of person) colo m; (of race) volta f.

lapel [ləˈpel] n lapela f.

lapse [læps] n lapso m ◆ vi (membership, passport) expirar (Br), caducar (Port).

lap-top (computer) n computador m portátil.

lard [lɑːd] n banha f.

larder [ˈlɑːdəʳ] n despensa f.

large [lɑːdʒ] adj grande.

largely [ˈlɑːdʒlɪ] adv em grande parte.

large-scale adj em grande escala.

lark [lɑːk] n cotovia f.

laryngitis [ˌlærɪnˈdʒaɪtɪs] n laringite f.

lasagne [ləˈzænjə] n lasanha f.

laser [ˈleɪzəʳ] n laser m.

lash [læʃ] n (eyelash) pestana f; (blow with whip) chicotada f ◆ vt (whip) chicotear; (tie) amarrar.

lass [læs] n (inf) garota f.

lasso [læˈsuː] (pl -s) n laço m ◆ vt laçar.

last [lɑːst] adj último(-ma) ◆ adv (most recently) pela última vez; (at the end) em último lugar ◆ vi durar; (be enough) chegar ◆ pron: **the ~ to come** o último a chegar; **the ~ but one** o penúltimo;

the day before ~ anteontem; ~ **year** o ano passado; **the ~ year** o último ano; **at ~** finalmente.

lasting [ˈlɑːstɪŋ] adj duradouro (-ra).

lastly [ˈlɑːstlɪ] adv por último.

last-minute adj de última hora.

last name n sobrenome m (Br), apelido m (Port).

latch [lætʃ] n trinco m; **the door is on the ~** a porta está fechada com o trinco.

late [leɪt] adj (not on time) atrasado (-da); (after usual time) tardio (-dia); (dead) falecido(-da) ◆ adv (after usual time) tarde; (not on time): **the train is two hours ~** o trem está duas horas atrasado; **I had a ~ lunch** almocei tarde; **in the ~ afternoon** no fim da tarde; **in ~ June, ~ in June** no final OR fim de junho.

latecomer [ˈleɪtˌkʌməʳ] n retardatário m (-ria f).

lately [ˈleɪtlɪ] adv ultimamente.

late-night adj (chemist, supermarket) aberto(-ta) até tarde.

later [ˈleɪtəʳ] adj (train) que saia mais tarde ◆ adv: ~ **(on)** mais tarde; **at a ~ date** mais tarde, posteriormente.

latest [ˈleɪtɪst] adj: **the ~ fashion** a última moda; **the ~** (in series, in fashion) o mais recente (a mais recente); **at the ~** o mais tardar.

lathe [leɪð] n torno m.

lather [ˈlɑːðəʳ] n espuma f.

Latin [ˈlætɪn] n (language) latim m.

Latin America n América f Latina.

Latin American adj latino-americano(-na) ◆ n latino-americano m (-na f).

latitude [ˈlætɪtjuːd] n latitude f.

latter [ˈlætəʳ] n: **the ~** este último (esta última).

Latvia [ˈlætvɪə] n Letônia f.

laugh [lɑːf] n riso m ◆ vi rir; **to have a ~** (Brit: inf) divertir-se.

⌐ **laugh at** vt fus (mock) rir-se de.

laughable [ˈlɑːfəbl] adj ridículo (-la).

laughing stock [ˈlɑːfɪŋ-] n alvo m de riso OR gozação.

laughter [ˈlɑːftəʳ] n risos mpl.

launch [lɔːntʃ] vt (boat) lançar ao mar; (new product) lançar.

launderette [ˌlɔːndəˈret] n lavanderia f automática.

laundry [ˈlɔːndrɪ] n (washing) roupa f

suja; *(place)* lavanderia *f*.

lava [ˈlɑːvə] *n* lava *f*.

lavatory [ˈlævətrɪ] *n* privada *f (Br)*, casa *f* de banho *(Port)*.

lavender [ˈlævəndəʳ] *n* alfazema *f*.

lavish [ˈlævɪʃ] *adj (meal, decoration)* suntuoso(-osa).

law [lɔː] *n (JUR: rule)* lei *f; (study)* direito *m*; **the ~** *(JUR: set of rules)* a lei; **to be against the ~** ser contra a lei.

law-abiding [-əˌbaɪdɪŋ] *adj* respeitador(-ra) da lei.

law court *n* tribunal *m*.

lawful [ˈlɔːful] *adj* legal.

lawn [lɔːn] *n* gramado *m (Br)*, relvado *m (Port)*.

lawnmower [ˈlɔːnˌməʊəʳ] *n* máquina *f* de cortar grama.

lawsuit [ˈlɔːsuːt] *n* processo *m*.

lawyer [ˈlɔːjəʳ] *n* advogado *m* (-da *f*).

lax [læks] *adj (person, behaviour, attitude)* negligente; *(standards, morals)* baixo(-xa); *(discipline)* pouco rígido (-da).

laxative [ˈlæksətɪv] *n* laxante *m*.

lay [leɪ] *(pt & pp* **laid)** *pt* → **lie** ◆ *vt (place)* colocar, pôr; *(egg)* pôr; **to ~ the table** pôr a mesa.

❑ **lay off** *vt sep (worker)* despedir.

❑ **lay on** *vt sep* fornecer.

❑ **lay out** *vt sep (display)* dispor.

layabout [ˈleɪəbaʊt] *n (Brit: inf)* vadio *m* (-dia *f*).

lay-by *(pl* **lay-bys)** *n* acostamento *m (Br)*, berma *f (Port)*.

layer [ˈleɪəʳ] *n* camada *f*.

layman [ˈleɪmən] *(pl* **-men** [-mən]) *n* leigo *m* (-ga *f*).

layout [ˈleɪaʊt] *n (of building)* leiaute *m (Br)*, disposição *f (Port)*; *(of streets)* traçado *m*; **"new road ~"** *sinal que indica uma mudança no traçado da estrada ou rua*.

laze [leɪz] *vi*: **I spent the afternoon lazing in the sun** passei a tarde no sol sem fazer nada.

lazy [ˈleɪzɪ] *adj* preguiçoso(-osa).

lb *abbr* = **pound**.

LCD *abbr* = **liquid crystal display**.

lead¹ [liːd] *(pt & pp* **led)** *vt (take)* conduzir, levar; *(team, company)* dirigir; *(race, demonstration)* estar à frente de ◆ *vi (be winning)* estar à frente ◆ *n (for dog)* trela *f; (cable)* cabo *m*, fio *m*; **to ~ sb to do sthg** levar alguém a fazer algo; **to ~ the way** estar à frente; **to ~**

to *(go to)* ir dar em; *(result in)* levar a; **to be in the ~** estar à frente.

lead² [led] *n (metal)* chumbo *m; (for pencil)* grafite *m (Br)*, mina *f (Port)* ◆ *adj* de chumbo.

leaded petrol [ˈledɪd-] *n* gasolina *f* (com chumbo).

leader [ˈliːdəʳ] *n* líder *mf*.

leadership [ˈliːdəʃɪp] *n* liderança *f*.

lead-free [led-] *adj* sem chumbo.

leading [ˈliːdɪŋ] *adj (most important)* principal.

lead singer [liːd-] *n* vocalista *mf*.

leaf [liːf] *(pl* **leaves)** *n (of tree)* folha *f*.

leaflet [ˈliːflɪt] *n* folheto *m*.

league [liːg] *n (SPORT)* campeonato *m; (association)* liga *f*.

leak [liːk] *n (hole)* buraco *m; (of gas, petrol)* vazamento *m (Br)*, fuga *f (Port); (of water)* vazamento *m (Br)*, perda *f (Port); (in roof)* goteira *f* ◆ *vi (roof)* ter goteiras; *(tank)* vazar.

leakage [ˈliːkɪdʒ] *n (of gas, petrol, water)* vazamento *m*.

lean [liːn] *(pt & pp* **leant** OR **-ed)** *adj* magro(-gra) ◆ *vi (bend)* inclinar-se ◆ *vt*: **to ~ sthg against sthg** encostar algo em algo; **to ~ on** apoiar-se em.

❑ **lean forward** *vi* inclinar-se para a frente.

❑ **lean over** *vi* abaixar-se.

leaning [ˈliːnɪŋ] *n*: **~ towards sthg** *(science, arts)* inclinação *f* para algo; **a magazine with Marxist ~s** uma revista com tendências marxistas.

leant [lent] *pt & pp* → **lean**.

leap [liːp] *(pt & pp* **leapt** OR **-ed)** *vi* saltar.

leapfrog [ˈliːpfrɒg] *n* jogo *m* de pular corniça *(Br)*, jogo *m* do eixo *(Port)* ◆ *vt* saltar.

leapt [lept] *pt & pp* → **leap**.

leap year *n* ano *m* bissexto.

learn [lɜːn] *(pt & pp* **learnt** OR **-ed)** *vt (gain knowledge of)* aprender; *(memorize)* decorar; **to ~ (how) to do sthg** aprender a fazer algo; **to ~ about sthg** *(hear about)* ficar sabendo (de) algo; *(study)* estudar algo.

learned [ˈlɜːnɪd] *adj* erudito(-ta).

learner (driver) [ˈlɜːnəʳ-] *n pessoa que está aprendendo a dirigir*.

learning [ˈlɜːnɪŋ] *n* saber *m*, erudição *f*.

learnt [lɜːnt] *pt & pp* → **learn**.

lease [li:s] *n* contrato *m* de arrendamento OR aluguel ♦ *vt* arrendar, alugar; **to ~ sthg from sb** arrendar algo de alguém; **to ~ sthg to sb** arrendar algo a alguém.

leash [li:ʃ] *n* trela *f*.

least [li:st] *adv* & *adj* menos ♦ *pron:* **(the)** ~ o mínimo; **at ~** pelo menos; **I like her the ~** ela é de quem eu gosto menos.

leather [leðə'] *n* couro *m*, cabedal *m* (*Port*), pele *f*.
⊐ **leathers** *npl* (*of motorcyclist*) roupa *f* de couro.

leave [li:v] (*pt* & *pp* left) *vt* deixar; (*house, country*) sair de ♦ *vi* (*person*) irse embora; (*train, bus*) sair, partir ♦ *n* (*time off work*) licença *f*; **to ~ a message** deixar recado, → **left**.
⊐ **leave behind** *vt sep* deixar (para trás).
⊐ **leave out** *vt sep* omitir.

leaves [li:vz] *pl* → **leaf**.

Lebanon [lebanan] *n* Líbano *m*.

lecherous [letʃaras] *adj* (*look, expression*) lascivo(-va); (*person*) devasso(-a).

lecture [lektʃə'] *n* (*at university*) aula *f*; (*at conference*) conferência *f*.

lecturer [lektʃara'] *n* professor *m* universitário (professora *f* universitária).

lecture theatre *n* anfiteatro *m*.

led [led] *pt* & *pp* → **lead¹**.

ledge [ledʒ] *n* (*of window*) peitoril *m*.

leech [li:tʃ] *n* sanguessuga *f*.

leek [li:k] *n* alho-poró *m* (*Br*), alho *m* francês (*Port*).

leer [liə'] *n* olhar *m* lascivo ♦ *vi:* **to ~ at sb** olhar lascivamente para alguém.

leeway [li:wei] *n* (*room to manoeuvre*) margem *f* para manobra.

left [left] *pt* & *pp* → **leave** ♦ *adj* (*not right*) esquerdo(-da) ♦ *adv* (*turn*) à esquerda; (*keep*) pela esquerda ♦ *n* esquerda *f*; **on the ~** à esquerda; **to be ~** sobrar.

left-hand *adj* esquerdo(-da).

left-hand drive *n* veículo *m* com volante do lado esquerdo.

left-handed [-hændid] *adj* (*person*) canhoto(-ota); (*implement*) para canhotos.

left-luggage locker *n* (*Brit*) guarda-volumes *m inv* com chave (*Br*), cacifo *m* (para bagagem) (*Port*).

left-luggage office *n* (*Brit*) depósito *m* de bagagens.

leftover [leftəuvə'] *adj* a mais.
⊐ **leftovers** *npl* restos *mpl*.

left-wing *adj* de esquerda.

leg [leg] *n* perna *f*; **~ of lamb** perna de carneiro.

legacy [legəsi] *n* legado *m*, herança *f*.

legal [li:gl] *adj* legal.

legal aid *n* ajuda financeira estatal para pagamento de um advogado.

legalize [li:gəlaiz] *vt* legalizar.

legal system *n* sistema *m* judiciário.

legal tender *n* moeda *f* corrente.

legend [ledʒənd] *n* lenda *f*.

leggings [legiŋz] *npl* calças *fpl* de malha (justas).

legible [ledʒibl] *adj* legível.

legislation [ledʒisleiʃn] *n* legislação *f*.

legitimate [lidʒitimət] *adj* legítimo (-ma).

legless [leglis] *adj* (*Brit: inf: drunk*): **to be ~** estar bêbado(-da) que nem um gambá.

legroom [legrum] *n* espaço *m* para as pernas.

leg-warmers [-wɔːməz] *npl* caneleiras *fpl*, meias *fpl* sem pé.

leisure [*Brit* leʒə', *Am* li:ʒər] *n* lazer *m*.

leisure centre *n* centro *m* de lazer.

leisurely [*Brit* leʒəli, *Am* li:ʒərli] *adj* despreocupado(-da).

leisure pool *n* parque *m* aquático.

leisure time *n* tempo *m* livre OR de lazer.

lemon [lemən] *n* limão-galego *m* (*Br*), limão *m* (*Port*).

lemonade [leməneid] *n* (*Brit: fizzy drink*) gasosa *f*; (*lemon juice*) limonada *f*.

lemon curd [-kɜːd] *n* (*Brit*) doce *m* de limão (*feito com suco de limão, açúcar, ovos e manteiga*).

lemon juice *n* suco *m* de limão.

lemon meringue pie *n* torta *f* de limão e suspiro.

lemon sole *n* linguado *m*.

lemon tea *n* chá *m* de limão, = carioca *m* de limão (*Port*).

lend [lend] (*pt* & *pp* lent) *vt* emprestar; **to ~ sb sthg** emprestar algo a alguém.

length [leŋθ] *n (in distance)* comprimento *m*; *(in time)* duração *f*.

lengthen ['leŋθən] *vt* aumentar.

lengthways ['leŋθweiz] *adv* ao comprido.

lengthy ['leŋθi] *adj* longo(-ga).

lenient ['li:njənt] *adj* brando (-da).

lens [lenz] *n* lente *f*.

lent [lent] *pt & pp* → **lend**.

Lent [lent] *n* Quaresma *f*.

lentils ['lentlz] *npl* lentilhas *fpl*.

Leo ['li:əʊ] *n* Leão *m*.

leopard ['lepəd] *n* leopardo *m*.

leopard-skin *adj* tipo pele de leopardo.

leotard ['li:ətɑ:d] *n* malha *f* de ginástica.

leper ['lepər] *n* leproso *m* (-osa *f*).

leprosy ['leprəsi] *n* lepra *f*.

lesbian ['lezbiən] *adj* lésbico(-ca) ◆ *n* lésbica *f*.

less [les] *adj, adv & pron* menos; ~ than 20 menos de 20; she earns ~ than him ela ganha menos do que ele.

lessen ['lesn] *vt & vi* diminuir.

lesser ['lesər] *adj* menor; to a ~ extent OR degree em menor grau.

lesson ['lesn] *n (class)* lição *f*.

let [let] *(pt & pp* let) *vt (allow)* deixar; *(rent out)* alugar, arrendar; to ~ sb do sthg deixar alguém fazer algo; to ~ go of sthg largar algo; to ~ sb have sthg dar algo a alguém; to ~ sb know sthg dizer algo a alguém; ~'s go! vamos embora!; "to ~" "para alugar", "aluga-se".

❏ **let in** *vt sep* deixar entrar.

❏ **let off** *vt sep (excuse)* perdoar; can you ~ me off at the station? pode me deixar na estação?.

❏ **let out** *vt sep (allow to go out)* deixar sair.

letdown ['letdaʊn] *n (inf)* decepção *f*.

lethal ['li:θl] *adj* letal, mortal.

lethargic [lə'θɑ:dʒik] *adj* letárgico (-ca).

let's [lets] = **let us**.

letter ['letər] *n (written message)* carta *f*; *(of alphabet)* letra *f*.

letterbox ['letəbɒks] *n (Brit) (in door)* caixa *f* do correio; *(in street)* caixa *f* do correio *(Br)*, marco *m* do correio *(Port)*.

lettuce ['letis] *n* alface *f*.

leuk(a)emia [lu:'ki:miə] *n* leucemia *f*.

level ['levl] *adj (horizontal, flat)* plano (-na) ◆ *n* nível *m*; *(storey)* andar *m*; to be ~ with estar no mesmo nível que.

level crossing *n (Brit)* passagem *f* de nível.

level-headed [-'hedid] *adj* sensato (-ta).

lever *[Brit* 'li:vər, *Am* 'levər] *n* alavanca *f*.

levy ['levi] *vt* lançar; ~ (on sthg) *(financial contribution)* contribuição *f* (para algo); *(tax)* imposto *m* (sobre algo).

lewd [lju:d] *adj (behaviour)* lascivo (-va); *(joke, song)* obsceno(-na).

liability [laiə'biləti] *n (responsibility)* responsabilidade *f*.

liable ['laiəbl] *adj*: to be ~ to do sthg ter tendência a fazer algo; he's ~ to be late é provável que ele chegue tarde; to be ~ for sthg ser responsável por algo.

liaise [li'eiz] *vi*: to ~ with contatar com.

liar ['laiər] *n* mentiroso *m* (-osa *f*).

libel ['laibl] *n* calúnia *f*, difamação *f* ◆ *vt* caluniar, difamar.

liberal ['libərəl] *adj (tolerant)* liberal; *(generous)* generoso(-osa).

Liberal Democrat Party *n* Partido *m* Democrata Liberal.

liberate ['libəreit] *vt* libertar.

liberty ['libəti] *n* liberdade *f*.

Libra ['li:brə] *n* Libra *f (Br)*, Balança *f (Port)*.

librarian [lai'breəriən] *n* bibliotecário *m* (-ria *f*).

library ['laibrəri] *n* biblioteca *f*.

library book *n* livro *m* da biblioteca.

Libya ['libiə] *n* Líbia *f*.

lice [lais] *npl* piolhos *mpl*.

licence ['laisəns] *n (Brit) (official document)* licença *f* ◆ *vt (Am)* = **license**.

license ['laisəns] *vt (Brit)* autorizar ◆ *n (Am)* = **licence**.

licensed ['laisənst] *adj (restaurant, bar)* autorizado(-da) a vender bebidas alcoólicas.

license plate *n (Am)* placa *f (Br)*, matrícula *f (Port)*.

licensing hours ['laisənsiŋ-] *npl (Brit)* horário de abertura dos *pubs*.

lick [lɪk] *vt* lamber.

licorice ['lɪkərɪs] = **liquorice**.

lid [lɪd] *n (cover)* tampa *f.*

lie [laɪ] *(pt* lay, *pp* lain, *cont* lying) *n* mentira *f* ◆ *vi (tell lie: pt & pp* lied) mentir; *(be horizontal)* estar deitado; *(lie down)* deitar-se; *(be situated)* ficar; **to tell ~s** mentir; **to ~ about sthg** mentir sobre algo.

❑ **lie down** *vi* deitar-se.

Liechtenstein ['lɪktənstaɪn] *n* Liechtenstein *m.*

lie-down *n (Brit):* **to have a ~** descansar um pouco, dormir um pouco.

lie-in *n (Brit):* **to have a ~** dormir até (mais) tarde.

lieutenant [*Brit* lefˈtenənt, *Am* luːˈtenənt] *n* tenente *m.*

life [laɪf] *(pl* lives) *n* vida *f.*

life assurance *n* seguro *m* de vida.

life belt *n* bóia *f* (salva-vidas).

lifeboat ['laɪfbəʊt] *n* barco *m* salva-vidas.

lifeguard ['laɪfgɑːd] *n* salva-vidas *mf (Br),* nadador-salvador *m* (nadadora-salvadora *f) (Port).*

life insurance *n* seguro *m* de vida.

life jacket *n* colete *m* salva-vidas.

lifelike ['laɪflaɪk] *adj* realista.

lifelong ['laɪflɒŋ] *adj* vitalício(-cia); *(friendship)* de toda a vida.

life preserver [-prɪˈzɜːvər] *n (Am) (life belt)* bóia *f* (salva-vidas); *(life jacket)* colete *m* salva-vidas.

life raft *n* salva-vidas *m inv.*

lifesaver ['laɪfseɪvər] *n* salva-vidas *mf (Br), (person)* nadador-salvador *m* (nadadora-salvadora *f) (Port).*

life-size *adj* em tamanho natural.

lifespan ['laɪfspæn] *n* tempo *m* de vida.

lifestyle ['laɪfstaɪl] *n* estilo *m* de vida.

lifetime ['laɪftaɪm] *n* vida *f;* **the chance of a ~** uma oportunidade única.

lift [lɪft] *n (Brit: elevator)* elevador *m* ◆ *vt (raise)* levantar ◆ *vi (fog)* levantar; **to give sb a ~** dar uma carona a alguém *(Br),* dar uma boleia a alguém *(Port).*

❑ **lift up** *vt sep* levantar.

lift-off *n* decolagem *f.*

light [laɪt] *(pt & pp* lit OR -ed) *adj* leve; *(not dark)* claro(-ra) ◆ *n* luz *f; (for cigarette)* fogo *m (Br),* lume *m (Port)* ◆ *vt (fire, cigarette)* acender; *(room, stage)* iluminar; **have you got a ~?** você tem fósforo OR isqueiro?; **to set ~ to sthg**

pôr fogo em algo.

❑ **lights** *(traffic lights)* sinais *mpl* de trânsito, semáforos *mpl (Port).*

❑ **light up** *vt sep (house, road)* iluminar ◆ *vi (inf: light a cigarette)* acender um cigarro.

light bulb *n* lâmpada *f.*

lighten ['laɪtn] *vt (room, ceiling)* iluminar; *(hair)* clarear, alourar; *(workload)* aliviar.

lighter ['laɪtər] *n* isqueiro *m.*

light-hearted [-ˈhɑːtɪd] *adj* alegre.

lighthouse ['laɪthaʊs, *pl* -haʊzɪz] *n* farol *m.*

lighting ['laɪtɪŋ] *n* iluminação *f.*

light meter *n* fotômetro *m.*

lightning ['laɪtnɪŋ] *n* relâmpagos *mpl.*

lightweight ['laɪtweɪt] *adj (clothes, object)* leve.

likable ['laɪkəbl] *adj* simpático (-ca).

like [laɪk] *prep* como; *(typical of)* típico de ◆ *vt* gostar de; **~ this/that** assim; **what's it ~?** como é?; **to look ~ sb/sthg** parecer-se com alguém/algo; **would you ~ some more?** quer mais?; **to ~ doing sthg** gostar de fazer algo; **I'd ~ to sit down** gostaria de me sentar; **I'd ~ a drink** gostaria de beber qualquer coisa.

likeable ['laɪkəbl] = **likable**.

likelihood ['laɪklɪhʊd] *n* probabilidade *f.*

likely ['laɪklɪ] *adj* provável.

liken ['laɪkn] *vt:* **to ~ sb/sthg to** comparar alguém/algo a.

likeness ['laɪknɪs] *n* semelhança *f.*

likewise ['laɪkwaɪz] *adv* da mesma maneira; **to do ~** fazer o mesmo.

liking ['laɪkɪŋ] *n* gosto *m;* **to have a ~ for** gostar de; **to be to sb's ~** estar ao gosto de alguém.

lilac ['laɪlək] *adj* lilás *(inv).*

Lilo® ['laɪləʊ] *(pl* -s) *n (Brit)* colchão *m* de ar.

lily ['lɪlɪ] *n* lírio *m.*

lily of the valley *n* lírio-do-vale *m,* lírio-convale *m.*

limb [lɪm] *n* membro *m.*

lime [laɪm] *n (fruit)* limão *m (Br),* lima *f (Port);* **~ (juice)** suco *m* de limão *(Br),* sumo *m* de lima *(Port).*

limelight ['laɪmlaɪt] *n:* **to be in the ~** ser o centro das atenções.

limestone ['laɪmstəʊn] *n* calcário *m.*

limit ['lɪmɪt] *n* limite *m* ◆ *vt* limitar; **the city ~s** os limites da cidade.

limitation [ˌlɪmɪˈteɪʃn] *n* limitação *f*.
limited [ˈlɪmɪtɪd] *adj* limitado (-da).
limousine [ˈlɪməziːn] *n* limusine *f*.
limp [lɪmp] *adj (lettuce)* murcho (-cha); *(body)* flácido(-da); *(fabric)* mole ♦ *vi* mancar.
limpet [ˈlɪmpɪt] *n* lapa *f*.
line [laɪn] *n* linha *f*; *(row)* fila *f*; *(Am: queue)* fila; *(of poem, song)* verso *m*; *(for washing)* varal *m (Br)*, estendal *m (Port)*; *(rope)* corda; *(of business, work)* ramo *m*; *(type of product)* seleção *f* ♦ *vt (coat, drawers)* forrar; **in ~** *(aligned)* alinhado (-da); **it's a bad ~** a linha está péssima; **the ~ is engaged** a linha está ocupada; **to drop sb a ~** *(inf)* mandar uma cartinha para alguém; **to stand in ~** *(Am)* pôr-se na fila.
❏ **line up** *vt sep (arrange)* organizar ♦ *vi* entrar na fila.
lined [laɪnd] *adj (paper)* pautado (-da), de linhas.
linen [ˈlɪnɪn] *n (cloth)* linho *m*; *(sheets)* roupa *f* de cama.
liner [ˈlaɪnər] *n (ship)* transatlântico *m*.
linesman [ˈlaɪnzmən] *(pl* **-men** [-mən]*) n* juiz *m* de linha.
lineup [ˈlaɪnʌp] *n (of players, competitors)* seleção *f*.
linger [ˈlɪŋgər] *vi (smell, taste, smoke)* permanecer; *(person)* atrasar-se.
lingerie [ˈlænʒərɪ] *n* roupa *f* de baixo (de senhora), lingerie *f*.
linguist [ˈlɪŋgwɪst] *n* lingüista *mf*.
linguistics [lɪŋˈgwɪstɪks] *n* lingüística *f*.
lining [ˈlaɪnɪŋ] *n (of coat, jacket)* forro *m*; *(of brake)* lona *f (Br)*, patilha *f (Port)*.
link [lɪŋk] *n (connection)* relação *f* ♦ *vt* ligar; **rail ~** ligação *f* ferroviária; **road ~** ligação rodoviária.
lino [ˈlaɪnəʊ] *n (Brit)* linóleo *m*.
lion [ˈlaɪən] *n* leão *m*.
lioness [ˈlaɪənes] *n* leoa *f*.
lip [lɪp] *n (of person)* lábio *m*.
lip-read *(pt & pp* **lip-read**) *vi* ler os lábios.
lip salve [-sælv] *n* pomada *f* para lábios rachados *(Br)*, batom *m* para o cieiro *(Port)*.
lipstick [ˈlɪpstɪk] *n* batom *m*.
liqueur [lɪˈkjʊər] *n* licor *m*.
liquid [ˈlɪkwɪd] *n* líquido *m*.
liquid crystal display *n* dispositivo *m* cristal líquido.
liquidize [ˈlɪkwɪdaɪz] *vt (Brit)* liquidificar, desfazer.

liquidizer [ˈlɪkwɪdaɪzər] *n (Brit)* liquidificador *m (Br)*, centrifugador *m (Port)*.
liquor [ˈlɪkər] *n (Am)* licor *m*.
liquorice [ˈlɪkərɪs] *n* alcaçuz *m*.
liquor store *n (Am)* loja onde se vendem bebidas alcoólicas para levar.
Lisbon [ˈlɪzbən] *n* Lisboa *s*.
lisp [lɪsp] *n* ceceio *m*.
list [lɪst] *n* lista *f* ♦ *vt* enumerar.
listed building [ˈlɪstɪd-] *n (Brit)* edifício declarado de interesse histórico e artístico.
listen [ˈlɪsn] *vi*: **to ~ (to)** ouvir.
listener [ˈlɪsnər] *n (on radio)* ouvinte *mf*.
lit [lɪt] *pt & pp* → **light**.
liter [ˈliːtər] *(Am)* = **litre**.
literacy [ˈlɪtərəsɪ] *n* alfabetismo *m*.
literal [ˈlɪtərəl] *adj* literal.
literally [ˈlɪtərəlɪ] *adv (actually)* literalmente.
literary [ˈlɪtərərɪ] *adj* literário (-ria).
literate [ˈlɪtərət] *adj (able to read and write)* alfabetizado(-da); *(well-read)* erudito(-ta); **computer-~** versado(-da) em computadores.
literature [ˈlɪtrətʃər] *n* literatura *f*.
lithe [laɪð] *adj* ágil.
Lithuania [ˌlɪθjʊˈeɪnjə] *n* Lituânia *f*.
litre [ˈliːtər] *n (Brit)* litro *m*.
litter [ˈlɪtər] *n (rubbish)* lixo *m*.
litterbin [ˈlɪtəbɪn] *n (Brit)* lata *f* de lixo *(Br)*, caixote *m* do lixo *(Port)*.
little [ˈlɪtl] *adj* pequeno(-na); *(distance, time)* curto(-ta); *(not much)* pouco(-ca); *(sister, brother)* mais novo (nova) ♦ *pron* pouco *m* (-ca *f*) ♦ *adv* pouco; **as ~ as possible** o menos possível; **~ by ~** pouco a pouco; **a ~** *pron & adv* um pouco ♦ *adj* um pouco de.
little finger *n* (dedo) mindinho *m*.
live¹ [lɪv] *vi* viver; *(survive)* sobreviver; **to ~ with sb** viver com alguém.
❏ **live together** *vi* viver juntos.
live² [laɪv] *adj (alive)* vivo(-va); *(programme, performance)* ao vivo; *(wire)* eletrificado(-da) ♦ *adv* ao vivo.
livelihood [ˈlaɪvlɪhʊd] *n* sustento *m*, meio *m* de vida.
lively [ˈlaɪvlɪ] *adj (person)* alegre; *(place, atmosphere)* animado(-da).
liven [ˈlaɪvn] : **liven up** *vt sep* alegrar ♦ *vi (person)* alegrar-se.

liver ['lɪvər] n fígado m.
lives [laɪvz] pl → **life**.
livestock ['laɪvstɒk] n gado m.
livid ['lɪvɪd] adj (inf: angry) lívido (-da).
living ['lɪvɪŋ] adj vivo(-va) ♦ n: **to earn a ~** ganhar a vida; **what do you do for a ~?** o que é que você faz (na vida)?
living conditions npl condições fpl de vida.
living room n sala f de estar.
living standards npl nível m de vida.
lizard ['lɪzəd] n lagarto m.
llama ['lɑːmə] n lhama f.
load [ləʊd] n (thing carried) carga f ♦ vt carregar; **~s of** (inf) toneladas de.
loaf [ləʊf] (pl **loaves**) n: **a ~ (of bread)** um pão de fôrma.
loafers ['ləʊfəz] npl (shoes) sapatos mpl sem cadarços.
loan [ləʊn] n empréstimo m ♦ vt emprestar.
loathe [ləʊð] vt detestar.
loathsome ['ləʊðsəm] adj repugnante.
loaves [ləʊvz] pl → **loaf**.
lob [lɒb] n (in tennis) balão m ♦ vt (throw) atirar ao ar, lançar.
lobby ['lɒbɪ] n (hall) entrada f, hall m.
lobe [ləʊb] n (of ear) lóbulo m.
lobster ['lɒbstər] n lagosta f.
local ['ləʊkl] adj local ♦ n (inf) (local person) habitante mf local; (Brit: pub) = bar m da esquina; (Am: bus) ônibus m (local) (Br), autocarro m (urbano) (Port); (Am: train) trem m (Br), comboio m (Port).
local anaesthetic n anestesia f local.
local authority n (Brit) autarquia f.
local call n chamada f local.
local government n administração f local.
locally ['ləʊkəlɪ] adv (in region) na região; (in neighbourhood) na área.
locate [Brit ləʊ'keɪt, Am 'ləʊkeɪt] vt (find) localizar; **to be ~d** ficar OR estar situado.
location [ləʊ'keɪʃn] n lugar m, localização f.
loch [lɒk, lɒx] n (Scot) lago m.
lock [lɒk] n (on door, drawer) fechadura f; (for bike) cadeado m; (on canal) comporta f ♦ vt fechar com chave ♦ vi (become stuck) ficar preso.
❑ **lock in** vt sep fechar.
❑ **lock out** vt sep: **I've ~ed myself out** deixei a chave por dentro e não posso entrar.
❑ **lock up** vt sep (imprison) prender ♦ vi fechar tudo à chave.
locker ['lɒkər] n compartimento m com chave, cacifo m.
locker room n (Am) vestiário m.
locket ['lɒkɪt] n medalhão m.
locksmith ['lɒksmɪθ] n serralheiro m (-ra f).
locomotive [ləʊkə'məʊtɪv] n locomotiva f.
locum ['ləʊkəm] n (doctor) substituto m (-ta f).
locust ['ləʊkəst] n gafanhoto m (viajante).
lodge [lɒdʒ] n (for skiers) refúgio m; (for hunters) pavilhão m de caça ♦ vi alojar-se.
lodger ['lɒdʒər] n inquilino m (-na f).
lodgings ['lɒdʒɪŋz] npl quarto m alugado (em casa de família).
loft [lɒft] n sótão m.
log [lɒg] n (piece of wood) tora f, lenha f.
logbook ['lɒgbʊk] n (of ship, plane) diário m de bordo; (of car) documentação f (do carro).
logic ['lɒdʒɪk] n lógica f.
logical ['lɒdʒɪkl] adj lógico(-ca).
logo ['ləʊgəʊ] (pl **-s**) n logotipo m.
loin [lɔɪn] n lombo m.
loiter ['lɔɪtər] vi vadiar.
lollipop ['lɒlɪpɒp] n pirulito m (Br), chupa-chupa m (Port).
lollipop lady n (Brit) mulher, que na hora de entrada e saída das aulas, pára o trânsito para as crianças atravessarem em segurança.
lollipop man n (Brit) homem, que na hora de entrada e saída das aulas, pára o trânsito para as crianças atravessarem em segurança.
lolly ['lɒlɪ] n (inf) (lollipop) pirulito m (Br), chupa m (Port); (Brit: ice lolly) picolé m (Br), gelado m (Port).
London ['lʌndən] n Londres s.
Londoner ['lʌndənər] n londrino m (-na f).
lone [ləʊn] adj solitário(-ria).
loneliness ['ləʊnlɪnɪs] n solidão f.
lonely ['ləʊnlɪ] adj (person) só; (place) isolado(-da).

loner [ˈləʊnəʳ] *n* solitário *m* (-ria *f*).
lonesome [ˈləʊnsəm] *adj* (*Am*) (*inf*) (*person*) só; (*place*) solitário(-ria).
long [lɒŋ] *adj* comprido(-da); (*in time*) longo(-ga) ◆ *adv* muito; **it's 2 metres ~** mede 2 metros de comprimento; **it's two hours ~** dura 2 horas; **how ~ is it?** (*in distance*) mede quanto?; (*in time*) dura quanto tempo?; **to take/be ~** demorar muito; **a ~ time** muito tempo; **all day ~** durante todo o dia; **as ~ as** desde que; **for ~** (durante) muito tempo; **no ~er** já não; **so ~!** (*inf*) adeus!
❏ **long for** *vt fus* ansiar por.
long-distance *adj* (*phone call*) inter-rubano(-na).
long drink *n* *mistura de bebida alcoólica com suco ou refrigerante servida num copo alto e estreito*.
long-haul *adj* de longa distância.
longing [ˈlɒŋɪŋ] *adj* ansioso(-osa) ◆ *n* (*desire*) ânsia *f*, desejo *m*; (*nostalgia*) saudade *f*; **to have a ~ for sthg** ansiar por algo.
longitude [ˈlɒndʒɪtjuːd] *n* longitude *f*.
long jump *n* salto *m* em comprimento.
long-life *adj* de longa duração.
longsighted [ˌlɒŋˈsaɪtɪd] *adj* hipermetrope; **to be ~** ter a vista cansada.
long-standing [-ˈstændɪŋ] *adj* de longa data.
long term *n*: **in the ~** a longo prazo.
❏ **long-term** *adj* a longo prazo.
long wave *n* onda *f* longa.
longwearing [ˌlɒŋˈweərɪŋ] *adj* (*Am*) duradouro(-ra).
longwinded [ˌlɒŋˈwɪndɪd] *adj* (*person*) prolixo(-xa); (*speech*) fastidioso(-osa).
loo [luː] (*pl* **-s**) *n* (*Brit*: *inf*) banheiro *m* (*Br*), casa *f* de banho (*Port*).
look [lʊk] *n* (*glance*) olhadela *f*, olhada *f*; (*appearance*) aparência *f*, look *m* ◆ *vi* (*with eyes*) olhar; (*search*) procurar; (*seem*) parecer; **to ~ onto** (*building, room*) ter vista para, dar para; **to have a ~** (*see*) dar uma olhada; (*search*) procurar; (*good*) **~s** beleza *f*; **I'm just ~ing** (*in shop*) estou só olhando; **~ out!** cuidado!
❏ **look after** *vt fus* (*person*) tomar conta de; (*matter, arrangements*) ocupar-se de.
❏ **look at** *vt fus* (*observe*) olhar para; (*examine*) analisar.

❏ **look for** *vt fus* procurar.
❏ **look forward to** *vt fus* esperar (impacientemente).
❏ **look out for** *vt fus* estar atento a.
❏ **look round** *vt fus* (*town, shop*) ver, dar uma volta por ◆ *vi* (*turn head*) virar-se, olhar (para trás).
❏ **look up** *vt sep* (*in dictionary, phone book*) procurar.
lookout [ˈlʊkaʊt] *n* (*search*): **to be on the ~ for sthg** andar à procura de algo.
loom [luːm] *n* tear *m* ◆ *vi* (*rise up*) erguer-se ameaçadoramente; (*date*) aproximar-se; (*threat*) pairar no ar.
❏ **loom up** *vi* surgir.
loony [ˈluːnɪ] *n* (*inf*) doido *m* (-da *f*).
loop [luːp] *n* argola *f*.
loophole [ˈluːphəʊl] *n* lacuna *f*.
loose [luːs] *adj* solto(-ta); (*tooth*) mole (*Br*), a abanar (*Port*); (*sweets*) avulso (-sa); (*clothes*) largo(-ga); **to let sb/sthg ~** soltar alguém/algo.
loose change *n* dinheiro *m* trocado, trocados *mpl*.
loosely [ˈluːslɪ] *adv* (*hold, connect*) sem apertar; (*translated*) livremente; (*associated*) mais ou menos.
loosen [ˈluːsn] *vt* desapertar.
loot [luːt] *n* saque *m* ◆ *vt* saquear, pilhar.
looting [ˈluːtɪŋ] *n* pilhagem *f*.
lop [lɒp] *vt* (*tree*) derramar.
❏ **lop off** *vt sep* cortar.
lop-sided [-ˈsaɪdɪd] *adj* torto (torta).
lord [lɔːd] *n* lorde *m*.
lorry [ˈlɒrɪ] *n* (*Brit*) caminhão *m* (*Br*), camião *m* (*Port*).
lorry driver *n* (*Brit*) caminhoneiro *m* (-ra *f*) (*Br*), camionista *mf* (*Port*).
lose [luːz] (*pt & pp* **lost**) *vt* perder; (*subj: watch, clock*) atrasar ◆ *vi* perder; **to ~ weight** emagrecer.
loser [ˈluːzəʳ] *n* (*in contest*) perdedor *m* (-ra *f*), vencido *m* (-da *f*).
loss [lɒs] *n* (*losing*) perda *f*; (*of business, company*) prejuízo *m*.
lost [lɒst] *pt & pp* → **lose** ◆ *adj* perdido(-da); **to get ~** (*lose way*) perder-se.
lost-and-found office *n* (*Am*) seção *f* de perdidos e achados.
lost property office *n* (*Brit*) seção *f* de perdidos e achados.
lot [lɒt] *n* (*at auction*) lote *m*; (*Am*: *car park*) estacionamento *m*; **you take this ~ and I'll take the rest** leva estes que

eu levo o resto; **a ~** *(large amount)* muito(-ta), muitos(-tas) *(pl)*; *(to a great extent, often)* muito; **a ~ of time** muito tempo; **a ~ of problems** muitos problemas; **the ~** *(everything)* tudo; **~s (of)** muito(-ta), muitos(-tas) *(pl)*.

lotion ['ləʊʃn] *n* loção *f*.

lottery ['lɒtəri] *n* loteria *f*.

loud [laʊd] *adj (voice, music, noise)* alto(-ta); *(colour, clothes)* berrante.

loudhailer [,laʊd'heilər] *n (Brit)* megafone *m*, alto-falante *m*.

loudly ['laʊdlɪ] *adv (shout, talk)* alto; *(dress)* espalhafatosamente.

loudspeaker [,laʊd'spi:kər] *n* alto-falante *m*.

lounge [laʊndʒ] *n (in house)* sala *f* de estar; *(at airport)* sala de espera.

lounge bar *n (Brit)* sala mais confortável e normalmente mais cara num bar, hotel, etc.

lousy ['laʊzɪ] *adj (inf: poor-quality)* péssimo(-ma).

lout [laʊt] *n* bruto *m* (-ta *f*).

lovable ['lʌvəbl] *adj* adorável.

love [lʌv] *n* amor *m*; *(in tennis)* zero *m* ♦ *vt* amar; *(music, food, art etc)* gostar muito de, adorar; **I'd ~ a cup of coffee** um café vinha mesmo a calhar; **to ~ doing sthg** gostar muito de fazer algo; **to be in ~ (with)** estar apaixonado (por); **(with) ~ from** *(in letter)* = beijinhos de.

love affair *n* caso *m* (amoroso).

love life *n* vida *f* amorosa.

lovely ['lʌvlɪ] *adj (very beautiful)* lindo(-da); *(very nice)* muito agradável.

lover ['lʌvər] *n* amante *mf*.

loving ['lʌvɪŋ] *adj* carinhoso(-osa).

low [ləʊ] *adj* baixo(-xa); *(opinion)* fraco(-ca); *(depressed)* para baixo *(Br)*, em baixo *(Port)* ♦ *n (area of low pressure)* depressão *f*, área *f* de baixa pressão; **we're ~ on petrol** estamos quase sem gasolina.

low-alcohol *adj* de baixo teor alcoólico.

low-calorie *adj* de baixas calorias.

low-cut *adj* decotado(-da).

lower ['ləʊər] *adj* inferior ♦ *vt (move downwards)* baixar; *(reduce)* reduzir.

lower sixth *n (Brit)* primeiro de dois anos de preparação para os "A levels".

low-fat *adj* com baixo teor de gordura.

lowly ['ləʊlɪ] *adj* humilde.

low-lying *adj* baixo(-xa).

low tide *n* maré-baixa *f*.

loyal ['lɔɪəl] *adj* leal.

loyalty ['lɔɪəltɪ] *n* lealdade *f*.

lozenge ['lɒzɪndʒ] *n (for throat)* pastilha *f* para a garganta.

LP *n* LP *m*.

L-plate *n (Brit)* placa obrigatória num carro dirigido por alguém que ainda não tirou carteira.

Ltd *(abbr of limited)* Ltda *(Br)*, Lda *(Port)*.

lubricate ['lu:brɪkeɪt] *vt* lubrificar.

lucid ['lu:sɪd] *adj (writing, account)* claro(-ra); *(person)* lúcido(-da).

luck [lʌk] *n* sorte *f*; **bad ~!** pouca sorte!, que azar!; **good ~!** boa sorte!; **with ~** com um pouco de sorte.

luckily ['lʌkɪlɪ] *adv* felizmente, por sorte.

lucky ['lʌkɪ] *adj (person)* sortudo (-da), com sorte; *(event, situation)* feliz; *(number, colour)* de sorte; **to be ~** ter sorte.

lucrative ['lu:krətɪv] *adj* lucrativo (-va).

ludicrous ['lu:dɪkrəs] *adj* ridículo(-la).

lug [lʌg] *vt (inf)* arrastar.

luggage ['lʌgɪdʒ] *n* bagagem *f*.

luggage compartment *n* compartimento *m* para a bagagem.

luggage locker *n* guarda-volumes *m inv* com chave *(Br)*, cacifo *m* (para bagagem) *(Port)*.

luggage rack *n (on train)* porta-bagagem *m*.

lukewarm ['lu:kwɔ:m] *adj* morno (morna).

lull [lʌl] *n (in conversation)* pausa *f*; *(in storm)* calmaria *f*.

lullaby ['lʌləbaɪ] *n* canção *f* de embalar.

lumbago [lʌm'beɪgəʊ] *n* lumbago *m*.

lumber ['lʌmbər] *n (Am: timber)* madeira *f*.

lumberjack ['lʌmbədʒæk] *n* lenhador *m* (-ra *f*).

luminous ['lu:mɪnəs] *adj* luminoso (-osa).

lump [lʌmp] *n (of coal, mud, butter)* pedaço *m*; *(of sugar)* torrão *m*; *(on body)* caroço *m*; *(on head)* galo *m*.

lump sum *n* quantia *f* global.

lumpy ['lʌmpɪ] *adj (sauce)* encaroçado(-da) *(Br)*, grumoso(-osa) *(Port)*; *(mattress)* cheio (cheia) de altos e baixos.

lunatic ['lu:nətɪk] *n (pej)* louco *m* (-ca *f*), maluco *m* (-ca *f*).

lunch [lʌntʃ] *n* almoço *m*; **to have ~** almoçar.

luncheon ['lʌntʃən] *n (fml)* almoço *m*.

luncheon meat *n* tipo de mortadela enlatada.

luncheon voucher *n (Brit)* ticket-refeição *m*.

lunch hour *n* hora *f* de almoço.

lunchtime ['lʌntʃtaɪm] *n* hora *f* de almoço.

lung [lʌŋ] *n* pulmão *m*.

lunge [lʌndʒ] *vi*: **to ~ at** atirar-se a.

lurch [lɜːtʃ] *vi (person)* cambalear.

lure [ljuəʳ] *vt* atrair.

lurid ['ljuərɪd] *adj (clothes, carpet)* garrido(-da); *(story, details)* chocante.

lurk [lɜːk] *vi (person)* estar à espreita *(escondido)*.

luscious ['lʌʃəs] *adj (fruit)* apetitoso (-osa).

lush [lʌʃ] *adj* luxuriante.

lust [lʌst] *n (sexual desire)* luxúria *f*.

Luxembourg ['lʌksəmbɜːg] *n* Luxemburgo *m*.

luxurious [lʌgˈʒuərɪəs] *adj* luxuoso (-osa).

luxury ['lʌkʃərɪ] *adj* de luxo ◆ *n* luxo *m*.

LW *(abbr of long wave)* LW.

Lycra® ['laɪkrə] *n* Lycra® *f* ◆ *adj* de Lycra®.

lying ['laɪɪŋ] *cont* → **lie**.

lynch [lɪntʃ] *vt* linchar.

lyrics ['lɪrɪks] *npl* letra *f (de música)*.

M

m *(abbr of metre)* m ◆ *abbr* = **mile.**
M *(Brit: abbr of motorway)* AE; *(abbr of medium)* M.
MA *abbr* = **Master of Arts.**
mac [mæk] *n (Brit: inf: coat)* impermeável *m*.
macaroni [,mækə'rəʊnɪ] *n* macarrão *m*.
macaroni cheese *n* macarrão *m* com queijo.
mace [meɪs] *n (spice)* macis *m*; *(ornamental rod)* cetro *m*.
machine [mə'ʃiːn] *n* máquina *f*.
machinegun [mə'ʃiːngʌn] *n* metralhadora *f*.
machinery [mə'ʃiːnərɪ] *n* maquinaria *f*.
machine-washable *adj* lavável à máquina.
macho ['mætʃəʊ] *adj (inf) (man)* macho; *(attitude, opinions)* machista.
mackerel ['mækrəl] *(pl inv) n* cavala *f*.
mackintosh ['mækɪntɒʃ] *n (Brit)* impermeável *m*.
mad [mæd] *adj* maluco(-ca); *(angry)* furioso(-osa); *(uncontrolled)* louco(-ca); **to be ~ about** *(inf: like a lot)* ser doido(-da) por; **like ~** como um louco OR doido.
Madagascar [,mædə'gæskə'] *n* Madagáscar *s*.
Madam ['mædəm] *n (form of address)* senhora *f*.
madden ['mædn] *vt* enfurecer.
made [meɪd] *pt & pp* → **make.**
madeira [mə'dɪərə] *n (wine)* vinho *m* da Madeira.
Madeira [mə'dɪərə] *n (island)* Madeira *f*.
made-to-measure *adj* feito (-ta) sob medida.
made-up *adj (face, lips)* maquiado (-da), pintado(-da); *(story, excuse)* inventado(-da).

madly ['mædlɪ] *adv (frantically)* como um louco (uma louca); **~ in love** completamente apaixonado(-da).
madman ['mædmən] *(pl* **madmen** [-mən]) *n* louco *m*.
madness ['mædnɪs] *n (foolishness)* loucura *f*, maluquice *f*.
Madrid [mə'drɪd] *n* Madri *s*.
Mafia ['mæfɪə] *n:* **the ~** a Máfia.
magazine [,mægə'ziːn] *n (journal)* revista *f*.
maggot ['mægət] *n* larva *f*.
magic ['mædʒɪk] *n* magia *f*.
magical ['mædʒɪkl] *adj* mágico(-ca).
magician [mə'dʒɪʃn] *n (conjurer)* mágico *m (-ca f)*.
magistrate ['mædʒɪstreɪt] *n* magistrado *m (-da f)*.
magnet ['mægnɪt] *n* ímã *m*.
magnetic [mæg'netɪk] *adj* magnético(-ca).
magnificent [mæg'nɪfɪsənt] *adj* magnífico(-ca).
magnify ['mægnɪfaɪ] *vt (image)* ampliar.
magnifying glass ['mægnɪfaɪŋ-] *n* lupa *f*.
magpie ['mægpaɪ] *n* pega *f*.
mahogany [mə'hɒgənɪ] *n* mogno *m*.
maid [meɪd] *n* empregada *f*.
maiden name ['meɪdn-] *n* nome *m* de solteira.
mail [meɪl] *n* correio *m* ◆ *vt (Am)* mandar OR enviar pelo correio.
mailbox ['meɪlbɒks] *n (Am) (letterbox)* caixa *f* do correio; *(postbox)* caixa *f* do correio *(Br)*, marco *m* do correio *(Port)*.
mailman ['meɪlmən] *(pl* **-men** [-mən]) *n (Am)* carteiro *m*.
mail order *n* venda *f* por correspondência.
mailshot ['meɪlʃɒt] *n* publicidade *f*

enviada pelo correio.
maim [meɪm] vt mutilar.
main [meɪn] adj principal.
main course n prato m principal.
main deck n convés m principal.
mainland ['meɪnlənd] n: **the ~** o continente.
main line n ferrovia f principal (Br), linha f férrea principal (Port).
mainly ['meɪnlɪ] adv principalmente.
main road n rua f principal.
mains [meɪnz] npl: **the ~** a rede.
mainstream ['meɪnstriːm] adj predominante ◆ n: **the ~** a corrente atual.
main street n (Am) rua f principal.
maintain [meɪn'teɪn] vt manter.
maintenance ['meɪntənəns] n (of car, machine) manutenção f; (money) pensão f alimentícia (Br), alimentos mpl (Port).
maisonette [ˌmeɪzə'net] n (Brit) dúplex m.
maize [meɪz] n milho m.
majestic [mə'dʒestɪk] adj majestoso (-osa).
majesty ['mædʒəstɪ] n majestade f.
◻ Majesty n: **His/Her/Your ~** Sua Majestade.
major ['meɪdʒəʳ] adj (important) importante; (most important) principal ◆ n (MIL) major m ◆ vi (Am): **to ~ in** especializar-se em (na universidade).
majority [mə'dʒɒrətɪ] n maioria f.
major road n estrada f principal.
make [meɪk] (pt & pp made) vt 1. (produce, manufacture) fazer; **to be made of** ser feito de; **to ~ lunch/supper** fazer o almoço/jantar; **made in Japan** fabricado no Japão.
2. (perform, do) fazer; **to ~ a mistake** cometer um erro, enganar-se; **to ~ a phone call** dar um telefonema.
3. (cause to be) tornar; **to ~ sthg better** melhorar algo; **to ~ sb happy** fazer alguém feliz; **to ~ sthg safer** tornar algo mais seguro.
4. (cause to do, force) fazer; **to ~ sb do sthg** obrigar alguém a fazer algo; **it made her laugh** isso a fez rir.
5. (amount to, total) ser; **that ~s £5** são 5 libras.
6. (calculate): **I ~ it seven o'clock** calculo que sejam sete horas; **I ~ it £4** segundo os meus cálculos são 4 libras.

7. (profit, loss) ter.
8. (inf: arrive in time for): **we didn't ~ the 10 o'clock train** não conseguimos apanhar o trem das 10.
9. (friend, enemy) fazer.
10. (have qualities for) dar; **this would ~ a lovely bedroom** isto dava um lindo quarto.
11. (bed) fazer.
12. (in phrases): **to ~ do** contentar-se; **to ~ good** (loss) compensar; (damage) reparar; **to ~ it** (arrive on time) conseguir chegar a tempo; (be able to go) poder ir.
◆ n (of product) marca f.
◻ **make out** vt sep (cheque, receipt) passar; (form) preencher; (see) distinguir; (hear) perceber, entender.
◻ **make up** vt sep (invent) inventar; (comprise) constituir; (difference, extra) cobrir.
◻ **make up for** vt fus compensar.
make-believe n invenção f.
maker ['meɪkəʳ] n (of film, programme) criador m (-ra f); (of product) fabricante mf.
makeshift ['meɪkʃɪft] adj improvisado(-da).
make-up n (cosmetics) maquiagem f.
malaria [mə'leərɪə] n malária f.
Malaysia [mə'leɪzɪə] n Malásia f.
male [meɪl] adj (person) masculino (-na); (animal) macho ◆ n (animal) macho m.
malevolent [mə'levələnt] adj malévolo(-la).
malfunction [mæl'fʌŋkʃn] vi (fml) funcionar mal.
malice ['mælɪs] n rancor m.
malicious [mə'lɪʃəs] adj maldoso (-osa).
malignant [mə'lɪgnənt] adj (disease, tumour) maligno(-gna).
mall [mɔːl] n centro m comercial.
mallet ['mælɪt] n maço m.
malnutrition [ˌmælnjuː'trɪʃn] n subnutrição f.
malt [mɔːlt] n malte m.
Malta ['mɔːltə] n Malta s.
maltreat [ˌmæl'triːt] vt maltratar.
malt whisky n uísque m de malte.
mammal ['mæml] n mamífero m.
mammoth ['mæməθ] adj (effort, task) tremendo(-da); (tower, statue) gigantesco(-ca).

man [mæn] *n* homem *m*; *(mankind)* o Homem ◆ *vt* *(phones, office)*: **manned 24 hours a day** aberto 24 horas (por dia).

manage ['mænɪdʒ] *vt* *(company, business)* gerir; *(suitcase)* poder com; *(job)* conseguir fazer; *(food)* conseguir comer OR acabar ◆ *vi* *(cope)* conseguir; **can you ~ Friday?** sexta-feira está bem para você?; **to ~ to do sthg** conseguir fazer algo.

manageable ['mænɪdʒəbl] *adj* *(task, operation)* viável, possível; *(child)* fácil de controlar; *(rate)* controlável.

management ['mænɪdʒmənt] *n* *(people in charge)* direção *f*, administração *f*; *(control, running)* gestão *f*.

manager ['mænɪdʒər] *n* *(of business, bank, shop)* gerente *mf*; *(of sports team)* = treinador *m*.

manageress [,mænɪdʒə'res] *n* *(of business, bank, shop)* gerente *f*.

managing director ['mænɪdʒɪŋ-] *n* diretor *m* (-ra *f*) geral.

mandarin ['mændərɪn] *n* *(fruit)* tangerina *f*, mandarina *f*.

mane [meɪn] *n* *(of lion)* juba *f*; *(of horse)* crina *f*.

maneuver [mə'nuːvər] *(Am)* = **manoeuvre**.

mangetout [,mɒnʒ'tuː] *n* ervilha *f* de quebrar, ervilha-torta *f*.

mangle ['mæŋgl] *vt* *(crush)* amassar; *(mutilate)* mutilar.

mango ['mæŋgəʊ] *(pl* -s OR -es) *n* manga *f*.

Manhattan [mæn'hætən] *n* Manhattan *s*.

manhole ['mænhəʊl] *n* poço *m* de inspeção.

manhood ['mænhʊd] *n* *(age)* idade *f* adulta.

maniac ['meɪnɪæk] *n* *(inf: wild person)* maníaco *m* (-ca *f*), louco *m* (-ca *f*).

manic ['mænɪk] *adj* maníaco(-ca).

manicure ['mænɪkjʊər] *n* manicure *f*.

manifesto [,mænɪ'festəʊ] *(pl* -s OR -es) *n* manifesto *m*.

manifold ['mænɪfəʊld] *n* *(AUT)* cano *m* de distribuição.

manipulate [mə'nɪpjʊleɪt] *vt* *(person)* manipular; *(machine, controls)* manobrar.

mankind [mæn'kaɪnd] *n* a humanidade.

manly ['mænlɪ] *adj* viril.

man-made *adj* *(lake)* artificial; *(fibre, fabric)* sintético(-ca).

manner ['mænər] *n* *(way)* maneira *f*.
❏ **manners** *npl* maneiras *fpl*.

mannerism ['mænərɪzm] *n* jeito *m*.

manoeuvre [mə'nuːvər] *n* *(Brit)* manobra *f* ◆ *vt* *(Brit)* manobrar.

manor ['mænər] *n* = solar *m*, casa *f* senhorial.

mansion ['mænʃn] *n* mansão *f*.

manslaughter ['mæn,slɔːtər] *n* homicídio *m* involuntário.

mantelpiece ['mæntlpiːs] *n* consolo *m* de lareira *(Br)*, prateleira *f* da lareira *(Port)*.

manual ['mænjʊəl] *adj* manual ◆ *n* manual *m*.

manufacture [,mænjʊ'fæktʃər] *n* fabricação *f*, fabrico *m* ◆ *vt* fabricar.

manufacturer [,mænjʊ'fæktʃərər] *n* fabricante *m*.

manure [mə'njʊər] *n* estrume *m*.

manuscript ['mænjʊskrɪpt] *n* manuscrito *m*.

many ['menɪ] *(compar* **more**, *superl* **most**) *adj* muitos(-tas) ◆ *pron* muitos *mpl* (-tas *fpl*); **as ~ as** tantos(-tas) como; **take as ~ as you like** leve tantos quantos quiser; **twice as ~ as** o dobro de; **how ~?** quantos(-tas)?; **so ~** tantos(-tas); **too ~ people** gente demais.

map [mæp] *n* mapa *m*.

maple ['meɪpl] *n* ácer *m*, bordo *m*.

mar [mɑːr] *vt* prejudicar.

Mar. *abbr* = **March**.

marathon ['mærəθn] *n* maratona *f*.

marble ['mɑːbl] *n* *(stone)* mármore *m*; *(glass ball)* bola *f* de gude *(Br)*, berlinde *m* *(Port)*.

march [mɑːtʃ] *n* *(demonstration)* passeata *f* *(Br)*, manifestação *f* *(Port)* ◆ *vi* *(walk quickly)* marchar.

March [mɑːtʃ] *n* março *m*, → **September**.

marcher ['mɑːtʃər] *n* *(protester)* manifestante *mf*.

mare [meər] *n* égua *f*.

margarine [,mɑːdʒə'riːn] *n* margarina *f*.

marge [mɑːdʒ] *n* *(inf)* margarina *f*.

margin ['mɑːdʒɪn] *n* margem *f*.

marginally ['mɑːdʒɪnəlɪ] *adv* ligeiramente.

marigold ['mærɪgəʊld] *n* malmequer *m*.

marina [mɔ'riːnɔ] *n* marina *f*.

marinated ['mærɪneɪtɪd] *adj* marinado(-da).

marine [mɔ'riːn] *adj (underwater)* marítimo(-ma) ◆ *n (Brit: in the navy)* fuzileiro *m* (-ra *f*) naval; *(Am: in the Marine Corps)* marine *mf*.

marital status ['mærɪtl-] *n* estado *m* civil.

mark [mɑːk] *n* marca *f*; *(SCH)* nota *f* ◆ *vt* marcar; *(correct)* corrigir; **(gas) ~ five** número cinco do termóstato (de forno a gás).

marked [mɑːkt] *adj (noticeable)* sensível.

marker ['mɑːkɔʳ] *n (sign)* marca *f*.

marker pen *n* marcador *m*.

market ['mɑːkɪt] *n* mercado *m*.

market garden *n* horta *f* para fins comerciais *(Br)*, viveiro *m* agrícola *(Port)*.

marketing ['mɑːkɪtɪŋ] *n* marketing *m*.

marketplace ['mɑːkɪtpleɪs] *n* mercado *m*.

marking ['mɑːkɪŋ] *n (of exams, homework)* correção *f*.

⌐ **markings** *npl (on road)* marcas *fpl* rodoviárias.

marksman ['mɑːksmɔn] *(pl* **-men** [-mɔn]*) n* atirador perito *m*.

marmalade ['mɑːmɔleɪd] *n* geléia *f* de laranja *(ou outro citrino)*.

maroon [mɔ'ruːn] *adj* grená.

marooned [mɔ'ruːnd] *adj* isolado(-da), preso(-sa).

marquee [mɑː'kiː] *n* tenda *f* grande.

marriage ['mærɪdʒ] *n* casamento *m*.

married ['mærɪd] *adj* casado(-da); **to get ~** casar-se.

marrow ['mærɔʊ] *n (vegetable)* abóbora *f*.

marry [mærɪ] *vt* casar com ◆ *vi* casar-se, casar.

Mars [mɑːz] *n* Marte *m*.

marsh [mɑːʃ] *n* pântano *m*.

martial arts [mɑːʃl-] *npl* artes *fpl* marciais.

martyr ['mɑːtɔʳ] *n* mártir *mf*.

marvel ['mɑːvl] *n* maravilha *f*; **to ~ at** sthg maravilhar-se com algo.

marvellous ['mɑːvɔlɔs] *adj (Brit)* maravilhoso(-osa).

marvelous ['mɑːvɔlɔs] *(Am)* = **marvellous**.

Marxism ['mɑːksɪzm] *n* marxismo *m*.

Marxist ['mɑːksɪst] *adj* marxista ◆ *n* marxista *mf*.

marzipan ['mɑːzɪpæn] *n* maçapão *m*.

mascara [mæs'kɑːrɔ] *n* rímel® *m*.

masculine ['mæskjʊlɪn] *adj* masculino(-na).

mash [mæʃ] *vt* desfazer.

mashed potatoes [mæʃt-] *npl* purê *m* (de batata).

mask [mɑːsk] *n* máscara *f*.

mason [meɪsn] *n (stonemason)* pedreiro *m*; *(Freemason)* maçon *m*.

masonry ['meɪsnrɪ] *n (stones)* alvenaria *f*.

mass [mæs] *n (large amount)* monte *m*; *(RELIG)* missa *f*; **~es (of)** *(inf: lots)* montes (de).

massacre ['mæsɔkɔʳ] *n* massacre *m*.

massage [*Brit* 'mæsɑːʒ, *Am* mɔ'sɑːʒ] *n* massagem *f* ◆ *vt* massajar.

masseur [mæ'sɔːʳ] *n* massagista *m*.

masseuse [mæ'sɔːz] *n* massagista *f*.

massive ['mæsɪv] *adj* enorme.

mass media *npl*: **the ~** os meios de comunicação de massa.

mast [mɑːst] *n (on boat)* mastro *m*.

master ['mɑːstɔʳ] *n (at school)* professor *m*; *(of servant)* patrão *m*; *(of dog)* dono *m* ◆ *vt (skill, language)* dominar.

Master of Arts *n (titular de um)* mestrado em letras.

Master of Science *n (titular de um)* mestrado em ciências.

masterpiece ['mɑːstɔpiːs] *n* obra-prima *f*.

master's degree *n* mestrado *m*.

mastery ['mɑːstɔrɪ] *n* domínio *m*.

mat [mæt] *n (small rug)* tapete *m*; *(on table)* descanso *m (Br)*, individual *m (Port)*.

match [mætʃ] *n (for lighting)* fósforo *m*; *(game)* jogo *m*, encontro *m* ◆ *vt (in colour, design)* condizer com, combinar com; *(be the same as)* corresponder a; *(be as good as)* equiparar-se a ◆ *vi (in colour, design)* condizer, combinar.

matchbox ['mætʃbɒks] *n* caixa *f* de fósforos.

matching ['mætʃɪŋ] *adj* que combina.

mate [meɪt] *n (inf: friend)* amigo *m* (-ga *f*) ◆ *vi* acasalar, acasalar-se.

material [mɔ'tɪɔrɪɔl] *n* material *m*; *(cloth)* tecido *m*.

⌐ **materials** *npl (equipment)* material *m*.

materialistic [mə,tɪərɪə'lɪstɪk] *adj* materialista.

maternal [mə'tɜ:nl] *adj* maternal.

maternity dress [mə'tɜ:nɪtɪ-] *n* vestido *m* de gestante.

maternity leave [mə'tɜ:nɪtɪ-] *n* licença-maternidade *f (Br)*, licença *f* de parto *(Port)*.

maternity ward [mə'tɜ:nɪtɪ-] *n* enfermaria *f* para parturientes.

math [mæθ] *(Am)* = maths.

mathematical [,mæθə'mætɪkl] *adj* matemático(-ca).

mathematics [,mæθə'mætɪks] *n* matemática *f*.

maths [mæθs] *n (Brit)* matemática *f*.

matinée ['mætɪneɪ] *n* matinê *f*.

matriculation [mə,trɪkjʊ'leɪʃn] *n (at university)* matrícula *f*.

matrix ['meɪtrɪks] *(pl* **-trixes** OR **-trices** [-trɪsi:z]) *n (context, framework)* contexto *m*.

matron ['meɪtrən] *n (Brit) (in hospital)* enfermeira-chefe *f*; *(in school)* enfermeira *f*.

matt [mæt] *adj* fosco(-ca) *(Br)*, mate *(Port)*.

matted ['mætɪd] *adj* eriçado(-da), emaranhado(-da).

matter ['mætər] *n (issue, situation)* assunto *m*; *(physical material)* matéria *f* ◆ *vi* interessar; **it doesn't ~** não tem importância; **no ~ what happens** aconteça o que acontecer; **there's something the ~ with my car** o meu carro está com algum problema; **what's the ~?** qual é o problema?; **as a ~ of course** naturalmente; **as a ~ of fact** aliás, na verdade.

matter-of-fact *adj (person)* terra-a-terra *(inv)*, prático(-ca); *(voice)* calmo (-ma).

mattress ['mætrɪs] *n* colchão *m*.

mature [mə'tjʊər] *adj* maduro(-ra); *(cheese)* curado(-da).

mature student *n (Brit) estudante universitário com mais de 25 anos.*

maul [mɔ:l] *vt* ferir gravemente.

mauve [məʊv] *adj* cor-de-malva *(inv)*.

max. [mæks] *(abbr of maximum)* máx.

maximum ['mæksɪməm] *adj* máximo (-ma) ◆ *n* máximo *m*.

may [meɪ] *aux vb* 1. *(expressing possibility)* poder; **it ~ be done as follows** pode ser feito do seguinte modo; **it ~ rain** pode chover; **they ~ have got lost**

eles talvez tenham se perdido. 2. *(expressing permission)* poder; **~ I smoke?** posso fumar?; **you ~ sit, if you wish** pode sentar-se, se quiser. 3. *(when conceding a point)*: **it ~ be a long walk, but it's worth it** pode ser longe, mas vale a pena o esforço.

May *n* maio *m*, → September.

maybe ['meɪbi:] *adv* talvez.

May Day *n* o Primeiro de Maio.

mayhem ['meɪhem] *n* caos *m inv*.

mayonnaise [,meɪə'neɪz] *n* maionese *f*.

mayor [meər] *n* = Prefeito *m (Br)*, = Presidente *m* da Câmara *(Port)*.

mayoress ['meərɪs] *n* = Prefeita *f (Br)*, = Presidente *f* da Câmara *(Port)*.

maze [meɪz] *n* labirinto *m*.

MB *(abbr of megabyte)* MB *m*.

me [mi:] *pron* me; *(after prep)* mim; **she knows ~** ela me conhece *(Br)*, ela conhece-me *(Port)*; **it's ~** sou eu; **send it to ~** envie ele para mim *(Br)*, envia-mo *(Port)*; **tell ~** diga-me; **he's worse than ~** ele é pior que eu; **it's for ~** é para mim; **with ~** comigo.

meadow ['medəʊ] *n* prado *m*.

meager ['mi:gər] *(Am)* = meagre.

meagre ['mi:gər] *adj (Brit) (amount, pay)* miserável.

meal [mi:l] *n* refeição *f*.

mealtime ['mi:ltaɪm] *n* hora *f* da refeição OR de comer.

mean [mi:n] *(pt & pp* **meant**) *adj (miserly)* sovina; *(unkind)* mau (má) ◆ *vt* querer dizer; *(be a sign of)* ser sinal de; **I ~ it** estou falando a sério; **it ~s a lot to me** é muito importante para mim; **to ~ to do sthg** ter a intenção de fazer algo, tencionar fazer algo; **to be meant to do sthg** dever fazer algo; **it's meant to be good** dizem que é bom.

meaning ['mi:nɪŋ] *n* significado *m*.

meaningful ['mi:nɪŋfʊl] *adj (glance, look)* expressivo(-va); *(relationship, remark)* profundo(-da).

meaningless ['mi:nɪŋlɪs] *adj* sem sentido.

means [mi:nz] *(pl inv) n (method)* meio *m* ◆ *npl (money)* recursos *mpl*; **by all ~!** claro que sim!; **by ~ of** através de.

meant [ment] *pt & pp* → mean.

meantime ['mi:ntaɪm] : **in the meantime** *adv* entretanto.

meanwhile ['mi:nwaɪl] *adv* entretanto, enquanto isso.

measles ['mi:zlz] *n* sarampo *m*.

measly ['mi:zlɪ] *adj (inf)* mísero(-ra).

measure ['meʒəʳ] *vt* medir ♦ *n (step, action)* medida *f*; *(of alcohol)* dose *f*; **the room ~s 10 m²** o quarto mede 10 m².

measurement ['meʒəmənt] *n* medida *f*.

❑ **measurements** *npl (of person)* medidas *fpl*.

meat [mi:t] *n* carne *f*; **red ~** carnes vermelhas *(pl)*; **white ~** carnes brancas *(pl)*.

meatball ['mi:tbɔ:l] *n* almôndega *f*.

meat pie *n (Brit)* empada *f* de carne.

mechanic [mɪ'kænɪk] *n* mecânico *m* (-ca *f*).

mechanical [mɪ'kænɪkl] *adj* mecânico(-ca).

mechanism ['mekənɪzm] *n (of machine, device)* mecanismo *m*.

medal ['medl] *n* medalha *f*.

medallion [mɪ'dæljən] *n* medalhão *m*.

meddle ['medl] *vi*: **to ~ (in sthg)** meter-se (em algo).

media ['mi:djə] *n or npl*: **the ~** os meios de comunicação.

median ['mi:djən] *n (Am: of road)* faixa *f* divisora central.

mediate ['mi:dɪeɪt] *vi* servir de mediador; **to ~ between** servir de mediador entre.

medical ['medɪkl] *adj* médico(-ca) ♦ *n* check-up *m*.

medicated ['medɪkeɪtɪd] *adj* medicinal.

medication [medɪ'keɪʃn] *n* medicamento *m*.

medicine ['medsɪn] *n (substance)* medicamento *m*; *(science)* medicina *f*.

medicine cabinet *n* armário *m* para medicamentos.

medieval [medɪ'i:vl] *adj* medieval.

mediocre [mi:dɪ'əukəʳ] *adj* medíocre.

meditate ['medɪteɪt] *vi* meditar; **to ~ on sthg** meditar sobre algo.

Mediterranean [medɪtə'reɪnjən] *n*: **the ~ (region)** o Mediterrâneo; **the ~ (Sea)** o (mar) Mediterrâneo.

medium ['mi:djəm] *adj* médio(-dia); *(wine)* meio-seco (meia-seca).

medium-dry *adj* meio-seco (meia-seca).

medium-sized [-saɪzd] *adj* de tamanho médio.

medium wave *n* onda *f* média.

medley ['medlɪ] *n (CULIN)* seleção *f*.

meek [mi:k] *adj (person, voice)* dócil;

(behaviour) submisso(-a).

meet [mi:t] *(pt & pp* **met)** *vt (by arrangement)* encontrar-se com; *(members of club, committee)* reunir-se com; *(by chance)* encontrar; *(get to know)* conhecer; *(go to collect)* ir buscar; *(need, requirement)* satisfazer; *(cost, expenses)* cobrir ♦ *vi (by arrangement)* encontrar-se; *(club, committee)* reunir-se; *(by chance)* encontrar-se; *(get to know each other)* conhecer-se; *(intersect)* cruzar-se; **~ me at the bar** encontre-se comigo no bar.

❑ **meet up** *vi* encontrar-se.

❑ **meet with** *vt fus (problems, resistance)* encontrar; *(Am: by arrangement)* encontrar-se com.

meeting ['mi:tɪŋ] *n (for business)* reunião *f*.

meeting point *n* ponto *m* de encontro.

megabyte ['megəbaɪt] *n (COMPUT)* megabyte *m*.

megaphone ['megəfəun] *n* megafone *m*, alto-falante *m*.

melancholy ['melənkəlɪ] *adj* melancólico(-ca).

mellow ['meləu] *adj (sound, colour, wine)* suave; *(person)* descontraído(-da) ♦ *vi* tornar-se mais brando(-da).

melody ['melədɪ] *n* melodia *f*.

melon ['melən] *n* melão *m*.

melt [melt] *vi* derreter.

member ['membəʳ] *n (of party, group)* membro *m*; *(of club)* sócio *m* (-cia *f*).

Member of Congress *n* congressista *mf*, membro *m* do Congresso.

Member of Parliament *n* = deputado *m* (-da *f*).

membership ['membəʃɪp] *n (of party, club)* filiação *f*; **the ~** *(of party)* os membros; *(of club)* os sócios.

membership card *n* carteira *f* de membro OR filiação.

memento [mɪ'mentəu] *(pl* **-s** OR **-es)** *n* lembrança *f*.

memo ['meməu] *(pl* **-s)** *n* memorando *m*.

memoirs ['memwɑ:z] *fpl* memórias *fpl*.

memorandum [memə'rændəm] *(pl* **-da** [-də]) *n* memorando *m*.

memorial [mɪ'mɔ:rɪəl] *n* monumento *m* comemorativo.

memorize ['meməraɪz] *vt* memorizar, decorar.

memory ['mɛmərɪ] *n* memória *f*; *(thing remembered)* lembrança *f*.

men [mɛn] *pl* → **man**.

menace ['mɛnəs] *n (threat, danger)* perigo *m* ♦ *vt (threaten)* ameaçar; *(frighten)* aterrorizar.

menacing ['mɛnəsɪŋ] *adj* ameaçador(-ra).

mend [mɛnd] *vt* arranjar.

meningitis [ˌmɛnɪn'dʒaɪtɪs] *n* meningite *f*.

menopause ['mɛnəpɔ:z] *n* menopausa *f*.

men's room *n (Am)* banheiro *m* dos homens *(Br)*, casa *f* de banho dos homens *(Port)*.

menstruate ['mɛnstrʊeɪt] *vi* menstruar.

menstruation [ˌmɛnstrʊ'eɪʃn] *n* menstruação *f*.

menswear ['mɛnzwɛəʳ] *n* roupa *f* de homem.

mental ['mɛntl] *adj* mental.

mental hospital *n* hospital *m* psiquiátrico.

mentality [mɛn'tælətɪ] *n* mentalidade *f*

mentally handicapped ['mɛntlɪ-] *adj* deficiente mental ♦ *npl*: **the ~** os deficientes mentais.

mentally ill ['mɛntlɪ-] *adj*: **to be ~** ser doente mental.

mention ['mɛnʃn] *vt* mencionar; **don't ~ it!** de nada!, não tem de quê!

menu ['mɛnju:] *n (of food)* cardápio *m (Br)*, ementa *f (Port)*; *(COMPUT)* menu *m*; **children's ~** menu infantil OR para crianças.

meow [mɪ'aʊ] *(Am)* = **miaow**.

merchandise ['mɜ:tʃəndaɪz] *n* mercadoria *f*.

merchant ['mɜ:tʃənt] *n* comerciante *mf*.

merchant marine *(Am)* = **merchant navy**.

merchant navy *n (Brit)* marinha *f* mercante.

merciful ['mɜ:sɪfʊl] *adj (person)* misericordioso(-osa), piedoso(-osa).

merciless ['mɜ:sɪlɪs] *adj (person, enemy, tyrant)* impiedoso(-osa); *(criticism, teasing, attack)* implacável.

mercury ['mɜ:kjʊrɪ] *n* mercúrio *m*.

Mercury ['mɜ:kjʊrɪ] *n (planet)* Mercúrio *m*.

mercy ['mɜ:sɪ] *n* misericórdia *f*.

mere [mɪəʳ] *adj* mero(-ra).

merely ['mɪəlɪ] *adv* apenas.

merge [mɜ:dʒ] *vi (combine)* juntar-se, unir-se; **"merge"** *(Am)* sinal que avisa os motoristas que vão entrar na auto-estrada que devem circular pela faixa da direita.

merger ['mɜ:dʒəʳ] *n* fusão *f*.

meringue [mə'ræŋ] *n* merengue *m*, suspiro *m*.

merit ['mɛrɪt] *n* mérito *m*; *(in exam)* = bom *m*.

mermaid ['mɜ:meɪd] *n* sereia *f*.

merry ['mɛrɪ] *adj* alegre; **Merry Christmas!** Feliz Natal!

merry-go-round *n* carrossel *m*.

mesh [mɛʃ] *n* malha *f* (de rede).

mesmerize ['mɛzməraɪz] *vt*: **to be ~d by** ficar fascinado(-da) com.

mess [mɛs] *n* confusão *f*; **in a ~** *(untidy)* em desordem, de pernas para o ar.

❏ **mess about** *vi (inf) (have fun)* divertir-se; *(behave foolishly)* armar-se em tolo; **to ~ about with sthg** *(interfere)* mexer em algo.

❏ **mess up** *vt sep (inf: ruin, spoil)* estragar.

message ['mɛsɪdʒ] *n* mensagem *f*; **are there any ~s (for me)?** há algum recado (para mim)?

messenger ['mɛsɪndʒəʳ] *n* mensageiro *m* (-ra *f*).

messy ['mɛsɪ] *adj (untidy)* desarrumado(-da).

met [mɛt] *pt & pp* → **meet**.

metal ['mɛtl] *adj* metálico(-ca), de metal ♦ *n* metal *m*.

metallic [mɪ'tælɪk] *adj (sound)* metálico(-ca); *(paint, finish)* metalizado(-da).

metalwork ['mɛtlwɜ:k] *n (craft)* trabalho *m* com metal.

meteor ['mi:tɪəʳ] *n* meteoro *m*.

meteorology [ˌmi:tɪə'rɒlədʒɪ] *n* meteorologia *f*.

meter ['mi:təʳ] *n (device)* contador *m*; *(Am)* = **metre**.

method ['mɛθəd] *n* método *m*.

methodical [mɪ'θɒdɪkl] *adj* metódico(-ca).

Methodist ['mɛθədɪst] *adj* metodista ♦ *n* metodista *mf*.

methylated spirits ['mɛθɪleɪtɪd] *n* álcool *m* metilado OR desnaturado.

meticulous [mɪ'tɪkjʊləs] *adj* meticuloso(-osa).

metre ['miːtər] *n (Brit)* metro *m*.
metric ['mɛtrɪk] *adj* métrico(-ca).
metronome ['mɛtrənəum] *n* metrônomo *m*.
metropolitan [,mɛtrə'pɒlɪtn] *adj* metropolitano(-na).
mews [mjuːz] *(pl inv) n (Brit)* rua, *ou* pátio, ladeada por cavalariças transformadas em casas ou apartamentos de luxo.
Mexican ['mɛksɪkn] *adj* mexicano (-na) ◆ *n* mexicano *m* (-na *f*).
Mexico ['mɛksɪkəu] *n* México *m*.
mg *(abbr of milligram)* mg.
miaow [miːˈau] *n (Brit)* mio *m* ◆ *vi (Brit)* miar.
mice [maɪs] *pl →* mouse.
mickey ['mɪkɪ] *n*: **to take the ~ out of sb** *(Brit: inf)* gozar alguém.
microchip ['maɪkrəutʃɪp] *n* microchip *m*.
microphone ['maɪkrəfəun] *n* microfone *m*.
microscope ['maɪkrəskəup] *n* microscópio *m*.
microwave (oven) ['maɪkrəwɛɪv-] *n* (forno) microondas *m inv*.
midday [,mɪd'deɪ] *n* meio-dia *m*.
middle ['mɪdl] *n* meio ◆ *adj* do meio; **in the ~ of the road** no meio da rua; **in the ~ of April** em meados de abril; **to be in the ~ of doing sthg** estar fazendo algo.
middle-aged *adj* de meia idade.
Middle Ages *npl*: **the ~** a Idade Média.
middle-class *adj* da classe média.
Middle East *n*: **the ~** o Oriente Médio.
middle name *n* segundo nome *m*.
middle school *n (in UK)* escola para crianças dos 8 aos 12 anos.
middleweight ['mɪdlweɪt] *n* peso *m* médio.
midfield [,mɪd'fiːld] *n (in football)* meio-de-campo *m*.
midge [mɪdʒ] *n* mosquito *m*.
midget ['mɪdʒɪt] *n* anão *m* (anã *f*).
midi system ['mɪdɪ-] *n* sistema *m* (de alta fidelidade) midi.
Midlands ['mɪdləndz] *npl*: **the ~** regiões do centro de Inglaterra.
midnight ['mɪdnaɪt] *n* meia-noite *f*.
midst [mɪdst] *n*: **in the ~ of sthg** *(in space)* no meio de algo; **to be in the ~ of doing sthg** estar fazendo algo.

midsummer ['mɪd'sʌmər] *n*: **in ~** em pleno verão.
midway [,mɪd'weɪ] *adv* a meio.
midweek [*adj* 'mɪdwiːk, *adv* mɪd'wiːk] *adj* do meio da semana ◆ *adv* no meio da semana.
midwife ['mɪdwaɪf] *(pl* **-wives** [-waɪvz]) *n* parteira *f*.
midwinter ['mɪd'wɪntər] *n*: **in ~** em pleno inverno.
might [maɪt] *aux vb* **1.** *(expressing possibility)* poder; **I suppose they ~ still come** acho que eles ainda podem vir; **they ~ have been killed** eles podem ter sido assassinados; **I ~ go to Wales** talvez vá a Gales.
2. *(fml: expressing permission)* poder; **~ I have a few words?** podemos conversar?
3. *(when conceding a point)*: **it ~ be expensive, but it's good quality** pode ser caro, mas é bom.
4. *(would)*: **I'd hoped you ~ come too** gostaria que também pudesse vir.
◆ *n (power)* poder *m*; *(physical strength)* força *f*.
mighty ['maɪtɪ] *adj (army, ruler)* poderoso(-osa); *(blow)* tremendo(-da).
migraine ['miːgreɪn, 'maɪgreɪn] *n* enxaqueca *f*.
migrant ['maɪgrənt] *adj (bird, animal)* migratório(-ria).
migrate [*Brit* maɪ'greɪt, *Am* 'maɪgreɪt] *vi* migrar.
mike [maɪk] *n (inf: abbr of microphone)* microfone *m*.
mild [maɪld] *adj (discomfort, pain)* ligeiro(-ra); *(illness)* pequeno(-na); *(weather)* ameno(-na); *(climate)* temperado (-da); *(kind, gentle)* meigo(-ga) ◆ *n (Brit: beer)* cerveja *f* suave.
mildew ['mɪldjuː] *n* míldio *m*.
mildly ['maɪldlɪ] *adv (talk, complain, criticize)* moderadamente; *(interesting, amusing)* mais ou menos.
mile [maɪl] *n* milha *f*; **it's ~s away** é longíssimo.
mileage ['maɪlɪdʒ] *n* distância *f* em milhas, ~ quilometragem *f*.
mileometer [maɪ'lɒmɪtər] *n* contador *m* de milhas, ≈ conta-quilômetros *m inv*.
milestone ['maɪlstəun] *n (marker stone)* marco *m*; *(fig: event)* marco histórico.
military ['mɪlɪtrɪ] *adj* militar.

milk [mɪlk] *n* leite *m* ♦ *vt (cow)* ordenhar, mungir.

milk chocolate *n* chocolate *m* de leite.

milkman ['mɪlkmən] (*pl* **-men** [-mən]) *n* leiteiro *m*.

milk shake *n* milk-shake *m (Br)*, batido *m (Port)*.

milky ['mɪlkɪ] *adj (drink)* com leite.

Milky Way *n*: **the ~** a Via Láctea.

mill [mɪl] *n* moinho *m*; *(factory)* fábrica *f*.

millennium [mɪ'lenɪəm] (*pl* **-nniums** OR **-nnia** [-nɪə]) *n* milênio *m*.

miller ['mɪlə'] *n* moleiro *m* (**-ra** *f*).

milligram ['mɪlɪɡræm] *n* miligrama *m*.

millilitre ['mɪlɪ,liːtə'] *n* mililitro *m*.

millimetre ['mɪlɪ,miːtə'] *n* milímetro *m*.

million ['mɪljən] *n* milhão *m*; **~s of** *(fig)* milhões de.

millionaire [,mɪljə'neə'] *n* milionário *m* (**-ria** *f*).

millstone ['mɪlstəʊn] *n* mó *f*.

mime [maɪm] *vi* fazer mímica.

mimic ['mɪmɪk] (*pt & pp* **-ked**, *cont* **-king**) *n* imitador *m* (**-ra** *f*) ♦ *vt* imitar.

min. [mɪn] *(abbr of minute)* m; *(abbr of minimum)* min.

mince [mɪns] *n (Brit)* carne *f* moída.

mincemeat ['mɪnsmiːt] *n (sweet filling)* mistura de frutos secos e cristalizados usada para rechear tortas e bolos; *(Am: meat)* carne *f* moída.

mince pie *n* pequena torta de Natal, recheada com uma mistura de frutos secos, frutos cristalizados, açúcar e especiarias.

mind [maɪnd] *n* mente *f*; *(memory)* memória *f* ♦ *vi (be bothered)* importar-se ♦ *vt (be careful of)* ter cuidado com; *(look after)* tomar conta de; *(be bothered by)*: **do you ~ the noise?** o barulho está lhe incomodando?; **it slipped my ~** esqueci-me; **state of ~** o estado *m* de espírito; **to my ~** na minha opinião; **to bear sthg in ~** ter algo em conta; **to change one's ~** mudar de idéia; **to have sthg in ~** estar pensando em algo; **to have sthg on one's ~** estar preocupado com algo; **to make one's ~ up** decidir-se; **do you ~ if ...?** importa-se se ...?; **I don't ~** não me importo; **I wouldn't ~ a drink** gostaria de beber qualquer coisa; **"~ the gap!"** aviso aos passageiros para estarem atentos ao espaço entre o cais e o trem; **never ~!** *(don't worry)* não faz mal!, não tem importância!

minder ['maɪndə'] *n (Brit: bodyguard)* guarda-costas *mf inv*.

mindful ['maɪndfʊl] *adj*: **to be ~ of** sthg estar consciente de algo.

mindless ['maɪndlɪs] *adj (violence, crime)* absurdo(-da), sem sentido; *(job, work)* mecânico(-ca), maçante.

mine[1] [maɪn] *pron* o meu (a minha); **a friend of ~** um amigo meu; **those shoes are ~** esses sapatos são meus; **~ are here — where are yours?** os meus estão aqui — onde estão os seus?

mine[2] [maɪn] *n (for coal etc, bomb)* mina *f*.

minefield ['maɪnfiːld] *n* campo *m* de minas.

miner ['maɪnə'] *n* mineiro *m* (**-ra** *f*).

mineral ['mɪnərəl] *n* mineral *m*.

mineral water *n* água *f* mineral.

minestrone [,mɪnɪ'strəʊnɪ] *n* minestrone *m*, sopa de legumes com massa.

mingle ['mɪŋɡl] *vi* misturar-se.

miniature ['mɪnətʃə'] *adj* em miniatura ♦ *n (bottle of alcohol)* miniatura *f*.

minibar ['mɪnɪbɑː'] *n* minibar *m*.

minibus ['mɪnɪbʌs] *n* microônibus *m (Br)*, carrinha *f (Port)*.

minicab ['mɪnɪkæb] *n (Brit)* rádiotaxi *m*.

minimal ['mɪnɪml] *adj* mínimo(-ma).

minimum ['mɪnɪməm] *adj* mínimo (-ma) ♦ *n* mínimo *m*.

mining ['maɪnɪŋ] *n* extração *f* de minério, exploração *f* mineira.

miniskirt ['mɪnɪskɜːt] *n* mini-saia *f*.

minister ['mɪnɪstə'] *n (in government)* ministro *m* (**-tra** *f*); *(in church)* pastor *m*, ministro *m*.

ministry ['mɪnɪstrɪ] *n (of government)* ministério *m*.

mink [mɪŋk] *n (fur)* pele *f* de marta, vison *m*.

minnow ['mɪnəʊ] (*pl inv* OR **-s**) *n* vairão *m*, pequeno peixe de água doce.

minor ['maɪnə'] *adj* pequeno(-na) ♦ *n (fml)* menor *mf* (de idade).

minority [maɪ'nɒrətɪ] *n* minoria *f*.

minor road *n* estrada *f* secundária.

mint [mɪnt] *n (sweet)* bala *f* de hortelã *(Br)*, bombom *m* de mentol *(Port)*; *(plant)* hortelã *f*.

minus ['maɪnəs] *prep (in subtraction)*

menos; **it's ~ 10°C** estão 10°C abaixo de zero.

minuscule [ˈmɪnəskjuːl] *adj* minúsculo(-la).

minute¹ [ˈmɪnɪt] *n* minuto *m*; **any ~** a qualquer momento; **just a ~!** só um minuto!

minute² [maɪˈnjuːt] *adj* diminuto(-ta).

minute steak [ˌmɪnɪt-] *n* bife *m* rápido.

miracle [ˈmɪrəkl] *n* milagre *m*.

miraculous [mɪˈrækjʊləs] *adj* milagroso(-osa).

mirage [mɪˈrɑːʒ] *n* miragem *f*.

mirror [ˈmɪrəʳ] *n* espelho *m*.

misbehave [ˌmɪsbɪˈheɪv] *vi* portar-se mal.

miscalculate [ˌmɪsˈkælkjʊleɪt] *vt* calcular mal, enganar-se em ◆ *vi* enganar-se.

miscarriage [ˌmɪsˈkærɪdʒ] *n* aborto *m* (não intencional).

miscellaneous [ˌmɪsəˈleɪnjəs] *adj* diverso(-sa).

mischief [ˈmɪstʃɪf] *n* (naughty behaviour) travessuras *fpl*; (playfulness) malícia *f*.

mischievous [ˈmɪstʃɪvəs] *adj* (naughty) travesso(-a); (playful) malicioso(-osa).

misconduct [ˌmɪsˈkɒndʌkt] *n* conduta *f* imprópria.

miscount [ˌmɪsˈkaʊnt] *vt* contar mal, enganar-se em ◆ *vi* contar mal, enganar-se.

misdemeanor [ˌmɪsdɪˈmiːnər] (Am) = misdemeanour.

misdemeanour [ˌmɪsdɪˈmiːnəʳ] *n* (Brit: JUR) delito *m* OR crime *m* menor.

miser [ˈmaɪzəʳ] *n* avarento *m* (-ta *f*).

miserable [ˈmɪzrəbl] *adj* miserável; (unhappy) infeliz.

miserly [ˈmaɪzəlɪ] *adj* mesquinho(-nha).

misery [ˈmɪzərɪ] *n* (unhappiness) infelicidade *f*; (poor conditions) miséria *f*.

misfire [ˌmɪsˈfaɪəʳ] *vi* (car) falhar.

misfortune [mɪsˈfɔːtʃuːn] *n* (bad luck) infelicidade *f*.

misgivings [mɪsˈɡɪvɪŋz] *npl* dúvidas *fpl*, receio *m*.

mishap [ˈmɪshæp] *n* incidente *m*.

misinterpret [ˌmɪsɪnˈtɜːprɪt] *vt* interpretar mal.

misjudge [ˌmɪsˈdʒʌdʒ] *vt* (distance, amount) calcular mal; (person, character) julgar mal.

mislay [ˌmɪsˈleɪ] (pt & pp -laid) *vt*: **I've mislaid my keys** não sei onde é que pus as chaves.

mislead [ˌmɪsˈliːd] (pt & pp -led) *vt* enganar.

misleading [ˌmɪsˈliːdɪŋ] *adj* enganador(-ra).

misled [ˌmɪsˈled] pt & pp → mislead.

misplace [ˌmɪsˈpleɪs] *vt*: **I've ~d my keys** não sei onde é que pus as chaves.

misprint [ˈmɪsprɪnt] *n* erro *m* de impressão, gralha *f*.

miss [mɪs] *vt* perder; (not notice) não ver; (fail to hit) falhar; (regret absence of) ter saudades de, sentir falta de; (appointment) faltar a ◆ *vi* falhar.

❑ **miss out** *vt sep* omitir ◆ *vi* perder; **you ~ed out on a great party** você perdeu uma grande festa.

Miss [mɪs] *n* senhorita *f* (Br), Menina *f* (Port).

missile [Brit ˈmɪsaɪl, Am ˈmɪsl] *n* míssil *m*.

missing [ˈmɪsɪŋ] *adj* (lost) perdido(-da); (after accident) desaparecido(-da); **to be ~** (not there) faltar.

missing person *n* desaparecido *m* (-da *f*).

mission [ˈmɪʃn] *n* (assignment) missão *f*.

missionary [ˈmɪʃənrɪ] *n* missionário *m* (-ria *f*).

mist [mɪst] *n* bruma *f*, neblina *f*.

mistake [mɪsˈteɪk] (pt -took, pp -taken) *n* erro *m* ◆ *vt* (misunderstand) entender mal; **by ~** por engano; **to make a ~** enganar-se; **to ~ sb/sthg for** confundir alguém/algo com.

mistaken [mɪsˈteɪkn] *adj* (belief, idea) errado(-da); (person) enganado(-da); **to be ~ about** estar enganado em relação a.

Mister [ˈmɪstəʳ] *n* Senhor *m*.

mistletoe [ˈmɪsltəʊ] *n* visco-branco *m*.

mistook [mɪsˈtʊk] pt → mistake.

mistreat [mɪsˈtriːt] *vt* maltratar.

mistress [ˈmɪstrɪs] *n* (lover) amante *f*; (Brit: teacher) professora *f*.

mistrust [ˌmɪsˈtrʌst] *vt* desconfiar de.

misty [ˈmɪstɪ] *adj* nebuloso(-osa), nublado(-da).

misunderstand [ˌmɪsʌndəˈstænd] (pt & pp -stood) *vt & vi* compreender mal.

misunderstanding [ˌmɪsʌndəˈstændɪŋ] *n* (misinterpretation) mal-

entendido *m*, engano *m*; *(quarrel)*
desentendimento *m*.
misunderstood [,mɪsʌndə'stʊd] *pt &*
pp → **misunderstand**.
misuse [,mɪs'juːs] *n* uso *m* indevido.
miter ['maɪtər] *(Am)* = **mitre**.
mitigate ['mɪtɪgeɪt] *vt* minimizar.
mitre ['maɪtər] *n (Brit: hat)* mitra *f*.
mitten ['mɪtn] *n* luva *f* (com un só
dedo).
mix [mɪks] *vt* misturar ◆ *n (for cake,
sauce)* mistura *f* ◆ *vi*: **I don't like the
people you ~ with** não gosto das pessoas com quem você anda; **to ~ sthg
with sthg** misturar algo com algo.
⊐ **mix up** *vt sep (confuse)* confundir;
(put into disorder) misturar.
mixed [mɪkst] *adj (school)* misto(-ta).
mixed grill *n* grelhado *m* misto.
mixed salad *n* salada *f* mista.
mixed up *adj (confused)* confuso
(-sa); **to be ~ in sthg** *(involved)* estar
envolvido em algo.
mixed vegetables *npl* macedônia *f*
(de legumes).
mixer ['mɪksər] *n (for food)* batedeira *f*;
(drink) bebida não alcoólica que se mistura com bebidas alcoólicas.
mixture ['mɪkstʃər] *n* mistura *f*.
mix-up *n (inf)* engano *m*.
ml *(abbr of millilitre)* ml.
mm *(abbr of millimetre)* mm.
moan [məʊn] *vi (in pain, grief)* gemer;
(inf: complain) resmungar.
moat [məʊt] *n* fosso *m*.
mobile ['məʊbaɪl] *adj* móvel.
mobile phone *n* (telefone *m*) celular *m (Br)*, telemóvel *m (Port)*.
mock [mɒk] *adj* falso(-sa) ◆ *vt* gozar
com ◆ *n (Brit: exam)* exame *m* simula-
do *(que serve de treino)*.
mockery ['mɒkərɪ] *n (scorn)* troça *f*.
mode [məʊd] *n* modo *m*.
model ['mɒdl] *n* modelo *m*; *(fashion
model)* modelo *mf*.
modem ['məʊdem] *n (COMPUT)*
modem *m*.
moderate ['mɒdərət] *adj* moderado
(-da).
moderation [,mɒdə'reɪʃn] *n* moderação *f*; **in ~** com moderação.
modern ['mɒdən] *adj* moderno(-na).
modernized ['mɒdənaɪzd] *adj* mo-
dernizado(-da).
modern languages *npl* línguas *fpl*

modernas OR vivas.
modest ['mɒdɪst] *adj* modesto(-ta).
modesty ['mɒdɪstɪ] *n* modéstia *f*.
modify ['mɒdɪfaɪ] *vt* modificar.
module ['mɒdjuːl] *n* módulo *m*.
mohair ['məʊheər] *n* mohair *m*.
moist [mɔɪst] *adj* úmido(-da).
moisten ['mɔɪsn] *vt* umedecer.
moisture ['mɔɪstʃər] *n* umidade *f*.
moisturizer ['mɔɪstʃəraɪzər] *n* creme
m hidratante.
molar ['məʊlər] *n* molar *m*.
molasses [mə'læsɪz] *n* melaço *m*.
mold [məʊld] *(Am)* = **mould**.
mole [məʊl] *n (animal)* toupeira *f*;
(spot) sinal *m*.
molecule ['mɒlɪkjuːl] *n* molécula *f*.
molest [mə'lest] *vt (child)* abusar
(sexualmente) de; *(woman)* assediar.
mom [mɒm] *n (Am: inf)* mãe *f*.
moment ['məʊmənt] *n* momento *m*;
at the ~ no momento; **for the ~** por
agora.
momentarily [Brit 'məʊməntərɪlɪ, *Am*
,məʊmen'terɪlɪ] *adv (for a short time)*
momentaneamente; *(Am: immediately)*
dentro em pouco, em breve.
momentary ['məʊməntrɪ] *adj* mo-
mentâneo(-nea).
momentous [mə'mentəs] *adj* muito
importante.
Mon. *(abbr of Monday)* 2ª, seg.
Monaco ['mɒnəkəʊ] *n* Mônaco *m*.
monarch ['mɒnək] *n* monarca *m*.
monarchy ['mɒnəkɪ] *n*: **the ~** a
monarquia.
monastery ['mɒnəstrɪ] *n* mosteiro *m*.
Monday ['mʌndɪ] *n* segunda-feira *f*, →
Saturday.
money ['mʌnɪ] *n* dinheiro *m*.
money belt *n* carteira *f* de cintura,
cinto *m* carteira.
moneybox ['mʌnɪbɒks] *n* cofre *m*
(Br), mealheiro *m (Port)*.
money order *n* vale *m*.
mongrel ['mʌŋgrəl] *n* vira-lata *m (Br)*,
rafeiro *m (Port)*.
monitor ['mɒnɪtər] *n (computer screen)*
monitor *m* ◆ *vt (check, observe)* controlar.
monk [mʌŋk] *n* monge *m*.
monkey ['mʌŋkɪ] *(pl* **-s)** *n* macaco *m*.
monkfish ['mʌŋkfɪʃ] *n* tamboril *m*.
monopolize [mə'nɒpəlaɪz] *vt* monopolizar.

monopoly [mə'nɒpəlı] *n (COMM)* monopólio *m*.

monorail ['mɒnəʊreıl] *n* monotrilho *m (Br)*, monocarril *m (Port)*.

monotonous [mə'nɒtənəs] *adj* monótono(-na).

monsoon [mɒn'suːn] *n* monção *f*.

monster ['mɒnstə'] *n* monstro *m*.

monstrous ['mɒnstrəs] *adj* monstruoso(-osa).

month [mʌnθ] *n* mês *m*; **every ~** todos os meses; **in a ~'s time** daqui a um mês.

monthly ['mʌnθlı] *adj* mensal ♦ *adv* mensalmente.

monument ['mɒnjʊmənt] *n* monumento *m*.

monumental [‚mɒnjʊ'mentl] *adj* monumental.

moo [muː] *vi* mugir.

mood [muːd] *n* humor *m*; **to be in a (bad) ~** estar de mau humor; **to be in a good ~** estar de bom humor.

moody ['muːdı] *adj (bad-tempered)* mal-humorado(-da); *(changeable)* temperamental.

moon [muːn] *n* lua *f*.

moonlight ['muːnlaıt] *n* luar *m*. ·

moonlit ['muːnlıt] *adj (night)* de luar; *(landscape)* iluminado(-da) pela lua.

moor [mɔː'] *n* charneca *f* ♦ *vt* atracar.

moose [muːs] *(pl inv) n* alce *m*.

mop [mɒp] *n (for floor)* esfregão *m (Br)*, esfregona *f (Port)* ♦ *vt (floor)* limpar. ◡ **mop up** *vt sep (clean up)* limpar.

mope [məʊp] *vi* andar deprimido(-da).

moped ['məʊped] *n* motocicleta *f*.

moral ['mɒrəl] *adj* moral ♦ *n (lesson)* moral *f*.

morale [mə'rɑːl] *n* moral *m*.

morality [mə'rælıtı] *n* moralidade *f*.

morbid ['mɔːbıd] *adj* mórbido(-da).

more [mɔː'] *adj* 1. *(a larger amount of)* mais; **there are ~ tourists than usual** há mais turistas que o normal.
2. *(additional)* mais; **are there any ~ cakes?** tem mais bolos?; **I'd like two ~ bottles** queria mais duas garrafas; **there's no ~ wine** já não tem mais vinho.
3. *(in phrases):* **~ and more** cada vez mais.
♦ *adv* 1. *(in comparatives)* mais; **it's ~ difficult than before** é mais difícil do que antes; **speak ~ clearly** fala de forma mais clara; **we go there ~ often**

now agora vamos lá mais freqüentemente.
2. *(to a greater degree)* mais; **we ought to go to the cinema ~** devíamos ir mais vezes ao cinema.
3. *(in phrases):* **I don't go there any ~** eu não vou mais lá; **once ~** mais uma vez; **~ or less** mais ou menos; **we'd be ~ than happy to help** teríamos imenso prazer em ajudar.
♦ *pron* 1. *(a larger amount)* mais; **I've got ~ than you** tenho mais que você; **~ than 20 types of pizza** mais de 20 tipos de pizza.
2. *(an additional amount)* mais; **is there any ~?** tem mais?; **there's no ~** não tem mais.

moreover [mɔː'rəʊvə'] *adv (fml)* além disso, além do mais.

morgue [mɔːg] *n* morgue *f*.

morning ['mɔːnıŋ] *n* manhã *f*; **good ~!** bom dia!; **two o'clock in the ~** duas da manhã, duas da madrugada; **in the ~** *(early in the day)* de manhã; *(tomorrow morning)* amanhã de manhã.

morning-after pill *n* pílula *f* do dia seguinte.

morning sickness *n* enjôo *m* matinal.

Moroccan [mə'rɒkən] *adj* marroquino(-na) ♦ *n* marroquino *m* (-na *f*).

Morocco [mə'rɒkəʊ] *n* Marrocos *s*.

moron ['mɔːrɒn] *n (inf: idiot)* estúpido *m* (-da *f*), idiota *mf*.

morose [mə'rəʊs] *adj* taciturno(-na).

Morse (code) [mɔːs-] *n* (código de) Morse *m*.

morsel ['mɔːsl] *n* pedaço *m*.

mortal ['mɔːtl] *adj* mortal ♦ *n* mortal *m*.

mortar ['mɔːtə'] *n (cement mixture)* argamassa *f*; *(gun)* morteiro *m*.

mortgage ['mɔːgıdʒ] *n* hipoteca *f*.

mortified ['mɔːtıfaıd] *adj* mortificado(-da).

mosaic [mə'zeıık] *n* mosaico *m*.

Moscow ['mɒskəʊ] *n* Moscou *m (Br)*, Moscovo *m (Port)*.

Moslem ['mɒzləm] = **Muslim**.

mosque [mɒsk] *n* mesquita *f*.

mosquito [mə'skiːtəʊ] *(pl -es) n* mosquito *m*.

mosquito net *n* mosquiteiro *m*.

moss [mɒs] *n* musgo *m*.

most [məʊst] *adj* 1. *(the majority of)* a maioria de; **~ people agree** a maioria

das pessoas está de acordo.
2. *(the largest amount of)* mais; **I drank (the)** ~ **beer** fui eu que bebi mais cerveja.
♦ *adv* 1. *(in superlatives)* mais; **the** ~ **expensive hotel in town** o hotel mais caro da cidade.
2. *(to the greatest degree)* mais; **I like this one** ~ gosto mais deste.
3. *(fml: very)* muito; **we would be** ~ **grateful** ficaríamos muito gratos.
♦ *pron* 1. *(the majority)* a maioria; ~ **of the villages** a maioria das aldeias; ~ **of the time** a maior parte do tempo.
2. *(the largest amount)* mais; **she earns (the)** ~ ela é a que ganha mais.
3. *(in phrases)*: **at** ~ no máximo; **we want to make the** ~ **of our stay** queremos aproveitar a nossa estada ao máximo.
mostly ['məustlɪ] *adv* principalmente.
MOT *n (Brit: test)* = IPO *f (Port)*, *inspeção anual obrigatória para veículos com mais de três anos.*
motel [məu'tel] *n* motel *m*.
moth [mɒθ] *n* traça *f*.
mothball ['mɒθbɔ:l] *n* bola *f* de naftalina.
mother ['mʌðəʳ] *n* mãe *f*.
mother-in-law *n* sogra *f*.
mother-of-pearl *n* madrepérola *f*.
mother tongue *n* língua *f* materna.
motif [məu'ti:f] *n* motivo *m*.
motion ['məuʃn] *n (movement)* movimento *m* ♦ *vi*: **to** ~ **to sb** fazer sinal a alguém.
motionless ['məuʃənlɪs] *adj* imóvel.
motion picture *n (Am)* filme *m* (cinematográfico).
motivate ['məutɪveɪt] *vt* motivar.
motivated ['məutɪveɪtɪd] *adj* motivado(-da).
motivation [,məutɪ'veɪʃn] *n (sense of purpose)* motivação *f*.
motive ['məutɪv] *n* motivo *m*.
motor ['məutəʳ] *n* motor *m*.
Motorail® ['məutəreɪl] *n* auto-expresso *m*, *trem que transporta carros e passageiros.*
motorbike ['məutəbaɪk] *n* moto *f*.
motorboat ['məutəbəut] *n* barco *m* a motor.
motorcar ['məutəka:ʳ] *n* carro *m*, automóvel *m*.
motorcycle ['məutə,saɪkl] *n* moto *f*.

motorcyclist ['məutə,saɪklɪst] *n* motociclista *mf*.
motoring ['məutərɪŋ] *n* automobilismo *m*.
motorist ['məutərɪst] *n* automobilista *mf*.
motor racing *n* automobilismo *m*.
motor scooter *n* lambreta *f*.
motor vehicle *n* veículo *m* motorizado.
motorway ['məutəweɪ] *n (Brit)* auto-estrada *f*.
mottled ['mɒtld] *adj* sarapintado(-da).
motto ['mɒtəu] *(pl -s) n* lema *m*.
mould [məuld] *n (Brit) (shape)* molde *m*, forma *f*; *(substance)* bolor *m* ♦ *vt (Brit) (shape)* moldar.
moulding ['məuldɪŋ] *n (decoration)* moldura *f*.
mouldy ['məuldɪ] *adj* bolorento(-ta).
mound [maund] *n* monte *m*.
mount [maunt] *n (for photo)* moldura *f*; *(mountain)* monte *m* ♦ *vt (horse)* montar; *(photo)* emoldurar ♦ *vi (increase)* aumentar.
mountain ['mauntɪn] *n* montanha *f*.
mountain bike *n* bicicleta *f* de montanha.
mountaineer [,mauntɪ'nɪəʳ] *n* alpinista *mf*.
mountaineering [,mauntɪ'nɪərɪŋ] *n*: **to go** ~ fazer alpinismo.
mountainous ['mauntɪnəs] *adj* montanhoso(-osa).
Mount Rushmore [-'rʌʃmɔ:ʳ] *n* o monte Rushmore.
mourn [mɔ:n] *vt (person)* chorar; *(thing)* lamentar ♦ *vi* lamentar, **to** ~ **for sb** chorar a morte de alguém.
mourner ['mɔ:nəʳ] *n (related)* parente *mf* do morto; *(unrelated)* amigo *m* (-ga *f*) do morto.
mourning ['mɔ:nɪŋ] *n*: **to be in** ~ estar de luto.
mouse [maus] *(pl mice) n* rato *m*.
moussaka [mu:'sɑ:kə] *n* gratinado de origem grega à base de carne moída e beringela.
mousse [mu:s] *n (food)* mousse *f*; *(for hair)* espuma *f*.
moustache [mə'stɑ:ʃ] *n (Brit)* bigode *m*.
mouth [mauθ] *n* boca *f*; *(of river)* foz *f*.
mouthful ['mauθful] *n (of food)* bocado *m*; *(of drink)* gole *m*.

mouthorgan ['mauθˌɔːgən] *n* gaita-de-boca *f*.

mouthpiece ['mauθpiːs] *n* bocal *m*.

mouthwash ['mauθwɒʃ] *n* desin-fetante *m* para a boca.

mouth-watering [-ˌwɔːtərɪŋ] *adj* de dar água na boca.

movable ['muːvəbl] *adj* móvel.

move [muːv] *n* (change of house) mudança *f*; (movement) movimento *m*; (in games) jogada *f*; (turn to play) vez *f*; (course of action) medida *f* ◆ *vt* (object) mudar; (arm, leg, lips) mexer; (emotionally) comover ◆ *vi* (shift) mover-se; (get out of the way) desviar-se; **to ~ (house)** mudar de casa; **to make a ~ (leave)** ir embora.

❏ **move along** *vi* avançar.

❏ **move in** *vi* (to house) mudar-se para.

❏ **move off** *vi* (train, car) partir.

❏ **move on** *vi* (after stopping) voltar a partir.

❏ **move out** *vi* (from house) mudar-se de.

❏ **move over** *vi* chegar-se para lá/cá.

❏ **move up** *vi* chegar-se para lá/cá.

moveable ['muːvəbl] = **movable**.

movement ['muːvmənt] *n* movimento *m*.

movie ['muːvɪ] *n* filme *m*.

movie camera *n* câmara *f* de filmar.

movie theater *n* (Am) cinema *m*.

moving ['muːvɪŋ] *adj* (emotionally) comovente.

mow [məʊ] *vt*: **to ~ the lawn** cortar a grama.

mower ['məʊər] *n* máquina *f* de cortar grama.

mozzarella [ˌmɒtsəˈrelə] *n* queijo *m* mozzarella.

MP *abbr* = **Member of Parliament**.

mph (abbr of miles per hour) milhas à OR por hora.

Mr ['mɪstər] *abbr* Sr.

Mrs ['mɪsɪz] *abbr* Sra.

Ms [mɪz] *abbr* título que evita que se faça uma distinção entre mulheres casadas e solteiras.

MS *abbr* = **multiple sclerosis**.

MSc *abbr* = **Master of Science**.

much [mʌtʃ] (compar **more**, superl **most**) *adj* muito(-ta); **I haven't got ~ money** não tenho muito dinheiro; **as ~ food as you can eat** o máximo de comida que você conseguir comer; **how ~ time is left?** quanto tempo falta?; **they have so ~ money** eles têm tanto dinheiro; **we have too ~ food** temos comida demais.

◆ *adv* 1. (to a great extent) muito; **he is ~ happier** ele está muito mais feliz; **it's ~ better** é muito melhor; **he's ~ too good** ele é bom demais; **I like it very ~** gosto muitíssimo; **it's not ~ good** (inf) não é muito bom; **thank you very ~** muito obrigado.

2. (often) muitas vezes; **we don't go there ~** não vamos lá muitas vezes.

◆ *pron* muito; **I haven't got ~** não tenho muito; **as ~ as you like** tanto quanto (você) queira; **how ~ is it?** quanto é?; **you've got so ~** você tem tanto; **you've got too ~** você tem demais.

muck [mʌk] *n* (dirt) porcaria *f*.

❏ **muck about** *vi* (Brit: inf: waste time) perder tempo.

❏ **muck up** *vt sep* (Brit: inf) estragar.

mucky ['mʌkɪ] *adj* (inf) porco (porca).

mucus ['mjuːkəs] *n* muco *m*.

mud [mʌd] *n* lama *f*.

muddle ['mʌdl] *n*: **to be in a ~** (confused) estar confuso(-sa); (in a mess) estar em desordem.

muddy ['mʌdɪ] *adj* lamacento(-ta).

mudguard ['mʌdgɑːd] *n* guarda-lamas *m inv*.

muesli ['mjuːzlɪ] *n* muesli *m*.

muff [mʌf] *n* (for hands) regalo *m*; (for ears) protetor *m* para os ouvidos.

muffin ['mʌfɪn] *n* (roll) pãozinho *m*; (cake) bolinho redondo e chato.

muffle ['mʌfl] *vt* (sound) abafar.

muffler ['mʌflər] *n* (Am: silencer) silenciador *m*.

mug [mʌg] *n* (cup) caneca *f* ◆ *vt* assaltar.

mugging ['mʌgɪŋ] *n* assalto *m* (a pessoa).

muggy ['mʌgɪ] *adj* abafado(-da).

mule [mjuːl] *n* mula *f*.

mulled ['mʌld] *adj*: **~ wine** vinho aquecido com especiarias e açúcar.

multicoloured ['mʌltɪˌkʌləd] *adj* multicolor.

multilateral [ˌmʌltɪˈlætərəl] *adj* multilateral.

multinational [ˌmʌltɪˈnæʃənl] *n* multinacional *f*.

multiple ['mʌltɪpl] *adj* múltiplo(-pla).

multiple sclerosis [-sklɪˈrəʊsɪs] *n* esclerose *f* múltipla.

multiplex cinema [ˈmʌltɪpleks-] *n* cinema *m* (com várias salas).

multiplication [ˌmʌltɪplɪˈkeɪʃn] *n* multiplicação *f*.

multiply [ˈmʌltɪplaɪ] *vt* multiplicar ♦ *vi* multiplicar-se.

multistorey (car park) [ˌmʌltɪˈstɔːrɪ-] *n* (parque *m* de) estacionamento *m* com vários andares.

multitude [ˈmʌltɪtjuːd] *n (crowd)* multidão *f*; **a ~ of reasons** inúmeras razões.

mum [mʌm] *n (Brit: inf)* mãe *f*.

mumble [ˈmʌmbl] *vt & vi* balbuciar.

mummy [ˈmʌmɪ] *n (Brit: inf: mother)* mamãe *f*.

mumps [mʌmps] *n* caxumba *f (Br)*, papeira *f (Port)*.

munch [mʌntʃ] *vt* mastigar.

mundane [mʌnˈdeɪn] *adj* desinteressante, trivial.

municipal [mjuːˈnɪsɪpl] *adj* municipal.

mural [ˈmjʊərəl] *n* mural *m*.

murder [ˈmɜːdəʳ] *n* assassínio *m*, assassinato *m* ♦ *vt* assassinar.

murderer [ˈmɜːdərəʳ] *n* assassino *m* (-na *f*).

murky [ˈmɜːkɪ] *adj (place)* sombrio (-bria), lúgubre; *(water)* sujo(-ja), turvo(-va).

murmur [ˈmɜːməʳ] *n* murmúrio *m* ♦ *vt & vi* murmurar.

muscle [ˈmʌsl] *n* músculo *m*.

muscular [ˈmʌskjʊləʳ] *adj (strong)* musculoso(-osa); *(of muscles)* muscular.

museum [mjuːˈziːəm] *n* museu *m*.

mushroom [ˈmʌʃrʊm] *n* cogumelo *m*.

music [ˈmjuːzɪk] *n* música *f*.

musical [ˈmjuːzɪkl] *adj (connected with music)* musical; *(person)* com ouvido para a música ♦ *n* musical *m*.

musical instrument *n* instrumento *m* musical.

music centre *n (machine)* aparelhagem *f* de som.

musician [mjuːˈzɪʃn] *n* músico *m* (-ca *f*).

Muslim [ˈmʊzlɪm] *adj* muçulmano (-na) ♦ *n* muçulmano *m* (-na *f*).

muslin [ˈmʌzlɪn] *n* musselina *f*.

mussels [ˈmʌslz] *npl* mexilhões *mpl*.

must [mʌst] *aux vb (expressing obligation)* ter de; *(expressing certainty)* dever ♦ *n (inf)*: **it's a ~** é de não perder; **I ~ go** tenho de ir; **the room ~ be vacated by ten** o quarto tem de ser desocupado antes das dez; **you ~ have seen it** você deve ter visto; **you ~ see that film** você tem de ver aquele filme; **you ~ be joking!** você deve estar brincando!

mustache [ˈmʌstæʃ] *(Am)* = **moustache**.

mustard [ˈmʌstəd] *n* mostarda *f*.

mustn't [ˈmʌsənt] = **must not**.

must've [ˈmʌstəv] = **must have**.

mute [mjuːt] *adj* mudo(-da) ♦ *n* mudo *m* (-da *f*).

mutilate [ˈmjuːtɪleɪt] *vt* mutilar.

mutiny [ˈmjuːtɪnɪ] *n* motim *m* ♦ *vi* amotinar-se.

mutter [ˈmʌtəʳ] *vt* murmurar.

mutton [ˈmʌtn] *n* carne *f* de carneiro

mutual [ˈmjuːtʃʊəl] *adj* mútuo(-tua).

mutually [ˈmjuːtʃʊəlɪ] *adv* mutuamente.

muzzle [ˈmʌzl] *n (for dog)* focinheira *f (Br)*, açaime *m (Port)*.

MW *abbr* = **medium wave**.

my [maɪ] *adj* meu (minha); **~ books** os meus livros.

myself [maɪˈself] *pron (reflexive)* me; *(after prep)* mim; **I did it ~** eu mesmo o fiz; **I hurt ~** machuquei-me.

mysterious [mɪˈstɪərɪəs] *adj* misterioso(-osa).

mystery [ˈmɪstərɪ] *n* mistério *m*.

mystical [ˈmɪstɪkl] *adj* místico(-ca)

mystified [ˈmɪstɪfaɪd] *adj* confuso (-sa), perplexo(-xa).

myth [mɪθ] *n* mito *m*.

mythical [ˈmɪθɪkl] *adj* mítico (-ca).

mythology [mɪˈθɒlədʒɪ] *n* mitologia *f*.

N

N *(abbr of north)* N.

nab [næb] *vt (inf: arrest)* apanhar; *(inf: claim quickly)* agarrar.

nag [næg] *vt* apoquentar.

nagging [ˈnægɪŋ] *adj (worry, suspicion)* persistente; *(spouse, friend)* chato(-ta).

nail [neɪl] *n (of finger, toe)* unha *f*; *(metal)* prego *m* ♦ *vt (fasten)* pregar.

nailbrush [ˈneɪlbrʌʃ] *n* escova *f* de unhas.

nail file *n* lixa *f* de unhas *(Br)*, lima *f* para as unhas *(Port)*.

nail polish *n* esmalte *m (Br)*, verniz *m* (para as unhas) *(Port)*.

nail scissors *npl* tesoura *f* de unhas.

nail varnish *n* esmalte *m (Br)*, verniz *m* (para as unhas) *(Port)*.

nail varnish remover [-rəˈmuːvəʳ] *n* acetona *f*, removedor *m* de esmalte *(Br)*.

naive [naɪˈiːv] *adj* ingênuo(-nua).

naked [ˈneɪkɪd] *adj (person)* nu (nua).

name [neɪm] *n* nome *m*; *(surname)* sobrenome *m (Br)*, apelido *m (Port)* ♦ *vt (person, place, animal)* chamar; *(date, price)* fixar; **first ~** nome próprio OR de batismo; **last ~** sobrenome *(Br)*, apelido *(Port)*; **what's your ~?** como você se chama?; **my ~ is ...** o meu nome é ....

namely [ˈneɪmlɪ] *adv* isto é, a saber.

namesake [ˈneɪmseɪk] *n* homônimo *m*.

nan bread [næn-] *n* pão indiano grande e achatado com condimentos.

nanny [ˈnænɪ] *n (childminder)* babá *f (Br)*, ama *f (Port)*; *(inf: grandmother)* avó *f*.

nap [næp] *n* soneca *f*; **to have a ~** tirar uma soneca.

nape [neɪp] *n*: **~ (of the neck)** nuca *f*.

napkin [ˈnæpkɪn] *n* guardanapo *m*.

nappy [ˈnæpɪ] *n* fralda *f*.

nappy liner *n* pequena tira descar-

---

tável usada com fraldas de tecido.

narcotic [nɑːˈkɒtɪk] *n* narcótico *m*.

narrative [ˈnærətɪv] *n* narrativa *f*.

narrator [Brit nəˈreɪtəʳ, Am ˈnæreɪtəʳ] *n* narrador *m* (-ra *f*).

narrow [ˈnærəʊ] *adj (road, gap)* estreito(-ta) ♦ *vi* estreitar.

narrowly [ˈnærəʊlɪ] *adv* por pouco, à risca.

narrow-minded [-ˈmaɪndɪd] *adj* tacanho(-nha), de idéias curtas.

nasal [ˈneɪzl] *adj* nasal.

nasty [ˈnɑːstɪ] *adj (person)* mau (má); *(comment)* maldoso(-osa); *(accident, fall)* grave; *(unpleasant)* desgradável.

nation [ˈneɪʃn] *n* nação *f*.

national [ˈnæʃənl] *adj* nacional ♦ *n* natural *mf (de um país)*.

national anthem *n* hino *m* nacional.

National Health Service *n* = Instituto *m* Nacional de Assistência Médica e Previdência Social *(Br)*, = Caixa *f* (de Previdência) *(Port)*.

National Insurance *n (Brit: contributions)* = Previdência *f* Social *(Br)*, = Segurança *f* Social *(Port)*.

nationalist [ˈnæʃnəlɪst] *adj* nacionalista ♦ *n* nacionalista *mf*.

nationality [ˌnæʃəˈnælətɪ] *n* nacionalidade *f*.

national park *n* parque *m* nacional.

national service *n (Brit: MIL)* serviço *m* militar.

National Trust *n (Brit)* organização britânica encarregada da preservação de prédios históricos e locais de interesse.

nationwide [ˈneɪʃənwaɪd] *adj* de âmbito nacional.

native [ˈneɪtɪv] *adj (country)* natal; *(customs, population)* nativo(-va) ♦ *n* natural *mf*; **a ~ speaker of English** um anglófono.

Nativity ['nɔ'tɪvɔtɪ] n: the ~ a Natividade, o Natal.

NATO ['neɪtəʊ] n OTAN f, NATO f.

natural ['nætʃrəl] adj (ability, charm) natural; (swimmer, actor) nato(-ta).

natural gas n gás m natural.

naturally ['nætʃrəlɪ] adv (of course) naturalmente.

natural yoghurt n iogurte m natural.

nature ['neɪtʃə'] n natureza f.

nature reserve n reserva f natural.

naughty ['nɔːtɪ] adj (child) travesso (-a).

nausea ['nɔːzɪə] n enjôo m, náusea f.

nauseating ['nɔːsɪeɪtɪŋ] adj (food, smell) nauseabundo(-da), enjoativo (-va).

naval ['neɪvl] adj naval.

nave [neɪv] n nave f.

navel ['neɪvl] n umbigo m.

navigate ['nævɪgeɪt] vi (in boat) navegar; (in plane) calcular a rota; (in car) fazer de navegador.

navigation [nævɪ'geɪʃn] n (piloting, steering) navegação m.

navy ['neɪvɪ] n (ships) marinha f ◆ adj: ~ (blue) azul-marinho (inv).

Nazi ['nɑːtsɪ] (pl -s) adj nazi ◆ n nazi mf.

NB (abbr of nota bene) N.B.

near [nɪə'] adv perto ◆ adj próximo(-ma) ◆ prep: ~ (to) (edge, object, place) perto de; in the ~ future num futuro próximo, em breve.

nearby [nɪə'baɪ] adv perto ◆ adj próximo(-ma).

nearly ['nɪəlɪ] adv quase.

near side n (for right-hand drive) direita f; (for left-hand drive) esquerda f.

nearsighted [nɪə'saɪtɪd] adj (Am) míope.

neat [niːt] adj (room) arrumado(da); (writing, work) caprichado(-da) (Br), cuidado(-da) (Port); (whisky, vodka etc) puro(-ra).

neatly ['niːtlɪ] adv cuidadosamente.

necessarily [nesə'serɪlɪ, Brit 'nesəsrəlɪ] adv necessariamente; not ~ não necessariamente.

necessary ['nesəsrɪ] adj necessário(-ria); it is ~ to do it é necessário fazê-lo.

necessity [nɪ'sesətɪ] n necessidade f. ⏤ **necessities** npl artigos mpl de primeira necessidade.

neck [nek] n (of person, animal) pescoço m; (of jumper) gola f; (of shirt) colarinho m; (of dress) decote m.

necklace ['neklɪs] n colar m.

neckline ['neklaɪn] n decote m.

necktie ['nektaɪ] n (Am) gravata f.

nectarine ['nektərɪn] n nectarina f.

need [niːd] n necessidade f ◆ vt precisar de, necessitar de; to ~ to do sthg precisar fazer algo.

needle ['niːdl] n agulha f.

needless ['niːdlɪs] adj desnecessário(-ria); ~ to say ... não é preciso dizer que ....

needlework ['niːdlwɜːk] n (SCH) costura f.

needn't ['niːdənt] = need not.

needy ['niːdɪ] adj necessitado(-da)', com necessidades.

negative ['negətɪv] adj negativo(-va) ◆ n (in photography) negativo m; (GRAMM) negativa f.

neglect [nɪ'glekt] vt não prestar atenção a.

negligee ['neglɪʒeɪ] n négligé m.

negligence ['neglɪdʒəns] n negligência f.

negligible ['neglɪdʒəbl] adj insignificante.

negotiate [nɪ'gəʊʃɪeɪt] vt (agreement, deal) negociar; (obstacle, bend) transpor ◆ vi negociar; to ~ with sb for sthg negociar com alguém sobre algo, negociar algo com alguém.

negotiations [nɪgəʊʃɪ'eɪʃnz] npl negociações fpl.

negro ['niːgrəʊ] (pl -es) n negro m (-gra f).

neigh [neɪ] vi relinchar.

neighbor ['neɪbə'] (Am) = neighbour.

neighbour ['neɪbə'] n (Brit) vizinho m (-nha f).

neighbourhood ['neɪbəhʊd] n vizinhança f.

neighbouring ['neɪbərɪŋ] adj vizinho(-nha).

neighbourly ['neɪbəlɪ] adj (deed, relations) de bom vizinho (de boa vizinha); (person) bom vizinho (boa vizinha).

neither ['naɪðə', 'niːðə'] adj: ~ bag is big enough nenhuma das bolsas é suficientemente grande ◆ pron: ~ of us nenhum m (-ma f) de nós ◆ conj: ~ do I nem eu; ~ ... nor nem ... nem.

neon light ['niːɒn-] n luz f de néon.

nephew ['nefjuː] n sobrinho m.

Neptune ['nɛptjuːn] n Netuno m.

nerve [nɜːv] n (in body) nervo m; (courage) ousadia f; **what a ~!** que descaramento!

nerve-racking [-ˌrækɪŋ] adj angustiante.

nervous ['nɜːvəs] adj nervoso(-osa).

nervous breakdown n esgotamento m nervoso.

nest [nest] n ninho m.

net [net] n rede f ◆ adj líquido(-da).

netball ['netbɔːl] n esporte parecido com basquetebol feminino.

Netherlands ['neðələndz] npl: **the ~** os Países Baixos.

netting ['netɪŋ] n (of metal, plastic) rede f; (fabric) tule m.

nettle ['netl] n urtiga f.

network ['netwɜːk] n rede f.

neurotic [ˌnjʊəˈrɒtɪk] adj neurótico(-ca).

neuter ['njuːtər] adj neutro(-tra).

neutral ['njuːtrəl] adj neutro(-tra) ◆ n (AUT): **in ~** em ponto morto.

neutrality [njuːˈtrælətɪ] n neutralidade f.

never ['nevər] adv nunca; **she's ~ late** ela nunca chega tarde; **~ mind!** não faz mal!

never-ending adj interminável.

nevertheless [ˌnevəðəˈles] adv contudo, todavia.

new [njuː] adj novo (nova).

newborn ['njuːbɔːn] adj recém-nascido(-da).

newcomer ['njuːˌkʌmər] n: **~ (to sthg)** recém-chegado m (-da f) (a algo).

newly ['njuːlɪ] adv: **~ married** recém-casado(-da).

newlyweds ['njuːlɪwedz] npl recém-casados mpl.

new potatoes npl batatas fpl tenras.

news [njuːz] n notícias fpl; (on TV) telejornal m; **a piece of ~** uma notícia.

newsagent ['njuːzeɪdʒənt] n (shop) jornaleiro m (Br), quiosque m (Port).

newsflash ['njuːzflæʃ] n flash m informativo, notícia f de última hora.

newsletter ['njuːzˌletər] n boletim m, jornal m.

newspaper ['njuːzˌpeɪpər] n jornal m.

newsreader ['njuːzˌriːdər] n (on TV) apresentador m (-ra f) do telejornal; (on radio) locutor m (-ra f) (que lê o noticiário).

newt [njuːt] n tritão m.

New Year n Ano m Novo.

New Year's Day n dia m de Ano Novo.

New Year's Eve n véspera f de Ano Novo.

New York [-'jɔːk] n: **~ (City)** (a cidade de) Nova Iorque s; **~ (State)** (o estado de) Nova Iorque.

New Zealand [-'ziːlənd] n Nova Zelândia f.

New Zealander [-'ziːləndər] n neo-zelandês m (-esa f).

next [nekst] adj próximo(-ma); (room, house) do lado ◆ adv (afterwards) depois, em seguida; (on next occasion) da próxima vez; **when does the ~ bus leave?** a que horas é o próximo ônibus?; **~ month/year** o mês/ano que vem; **~ to** (by the side of) ao lado de; **the week after ~** daqui a duas semanas.

next door adv ao lado; **the house/people ~** a casa/os vizinhos do lado.

next of kin [-kɪn] n parente m mais próximo (parente f mais próxima).

NHS n (abbr of National Health Service) = INAMPS m (Br), = Caixa f (Port).

nib [nɪb] n aparo m.

nibble ['nɪbl] vt mordiscar.

nice [naɪs] adj (pleasant) agradável; (pretty) bonito(-ta); (kind) amável, simpático(-ca); **to have a ~ time** divertir-se; **~ to see you!** prazer em vê-lo!

nice-looking [-'lʊkɪŋ] adj (person) atraente; (car, room) bonito(-ta).

nicely ['naɪslɪ] adv (dressed, made) bem; (ask) educadamente, delicadamente; (behave, manage) bem; **that will do ~** está perfeito!

nickel ['nɪkl] n (metal) níquel m; (Am: coin) moeda de cinco centavos de um dólar.

nickname ['nɪkneɪm] n apelido m (Br), alcunha f (Port).

nicotine ['nɪkətiːn] n nicotina f.

niece [niːs] n sobrinha f.

Nigeria [naɪˈdʒɪərɪə] n Nigéria f.

Nigerian [naɪˈdʒɪərɪən] adj nigeriano(-na) ◆ n nigeriano m (-na f).

night [naɪt] n noite f; **at ~** à noite; **by**

~ de noite; **last** ~ ontem à noite.

nightcap ['naɪtkæp] *n (drink) bebida, geralmente alcoólica, que se toma antes de ir dormir.*

nightclub ['naɪtklʌb] *n* boate *f (Br)*, clube *m* nocturno *(Port)*.

nightdress ['naɪtdres] *n* camisola *f (Br)*, camisa *f* de noite OR de dormir *(Port)*.

nightfall ['naɪtfɔːl] *n* anoitecer *m*, o cair da noite.

nightgown ['naɪtgaʊn] *n* camisola *f (Br)*, camisa *f* de dormir *(Port)*.

nightie ['naɪtɪ] *n (inf)* camisola *f (Br)*, camisa *f* de dormir *(Port)*.

nightingale ['naɪtɪŋgeɪl] *n* rouxinol *m*.

nightlife ['naɪtlaɪf] *n* vida *f* noturna.

nightly ['naɪtlɪ] *adv* todas as noites.

nightmare ['naɪtmeəʳ] *n* pesadelo *m*.

night safe *n* cofre *m* noturno.

night school *n* aulas *fpl* noturnas.

nightshift ['naɪtʃɪft] *n* turno *m* da noite.

nightshirt ['naɪtʃɜːt] *n* camisa *f* de noite *(para homem)*.

nighttime ['naɪttaɪm] *n* noite *f*; **at** ~ durante a noite, à noite.

nil [nɪl] *n (SPORT)* zero *m*.

Nile [naɪl] *n*: **the** ~ o Nilo.

nimble ['nɪmbl] *adj (agile)* ágil.

nine [naɪn] *num* nove, → **six**.

nineteen [,naɪn'tiːn] *num* dezenove *(Br)*, dezanove *(Port)*; ~ **ninety-seven** mil novecentos e noventa e sete, → **six**.

nineteenth [,naɪn'tiːnθ] *num* décimo nono (décima nona), → **sixth**.

ninetieth ['naɪntɪəθ] *num* nonagésimo(-ma), → **sixth**.

ninety ['naɪntɪ] *num* noventa, → **six**.

ninth [naɪnθ] *num* nono(-na), → **sixth**.

nip [nɪp] *vt (pinch)* beliscar.

nipple ['nɪpl] *n (of breast)* bico *m* do peito, mamilo *m*; *(of bottle)* bico *m (Br)*, tetina *f (Port)*.

nitrogen ['naɪtrədʒən] *n* azoto *m*, nitrogênio *m*.

no [nəʊ] *adv* não ♦ *adj* nenhum(-ma), algum(-ma) ♦ *n* não *m*; **I've got** ~ **money left** não tenho mais um tostão; **it is of** ~ **interest** não tem interesse (nenhum OR algum).

nobility [nə'bɪlətɪ] *n*: **the** ~ a nobreza.

noble ['nəʊbl] *adj* nobre.

nobody ['nəʊbədɪ] *pron* ninguém.

nocturnal [nɒk'tɜːnl] *adj* noturno (-na).

nod [nɒd] *vi (in agreement)* dizer que sim com a cabeça.

noise [nɔɪz] *n* barulho *m*, ruído *m*.

noisy ['nɔɪzɪ] *adj* barulhento(-ta), ruidoso(-osa).

nominate ['nɒmɪneɪt] *vt* nomear.

nonalcoholic [,nɒnælkə'hɒlɪk] *adj* sem álcool.

nonchalant [*Brit* 'nɒnʃələnt, *Am* ,nɒnʃə'lɑːnt] *adj (person, remark)* indiferente; *(gesture)* de indiferença.

nondescript [*Brit* 'nɒndɪskrɪpt, *Am* ,nɒndɪ'skrɪpt] *adj* nada de especial.

none [nʌn] *pron* nenhum *m* (-ma *f*); **there's** ~ **left** não resta nada.

nonetheless [,nʌnðə'les] *adv* todavia, contudo.

nonexistent [,nɒnɪg'zɪstənt] *adj* inexistente.

nonfiction [,nɒn'fɪkʃn] *n* literatura *f* não ficcional.

non-iron *adj* que não necessita de ser passado(-da) a ferro.

nonreturnable [,nɒnrɪ'tɜːnəbl] *adj* sem retorno.

nonsense ['nɒnsəns] *n (stupid words)* disparates *mpl*; *(foolish behaviour)* disparate *m*.

nonsmoker [,nɒn'sməʊkəʳ] *n* não-fumante *mf (Br)*, não-fumador *m* (-ra *f*) *(Port)*.

nonstick [,nɒn'stɪk] *adj* antiaderente.

nonstop [,nɒn'stɒp] *adj (talking, arguing)* constante; *(flight)* direto(-ta) ♦ *adv* sem parar.

noodles ['nuːdlz] *npl* miojo *m (Br)*, macaronete *m (Port)*.

nook [nʊk] *n* recanto *m*; **every** ~ **and cranny** tudo quanto é lugar.

noon [nuːn] *n* meio-dia *m*.

no one = **nobody**.

noose [nuːs] *n (lasso)* nó *m* corrediço OR corredio.

no-place *(Am)* = **nowhere**.

nor [nɔːʳ] *conj* nem; ~ **do I** nem eu, → **neither**.

norm [nɔːm] *n* norma *f*.

normal ['nɔːml] *adj* normal.

normalcy ['nɔːmlsɪ] *(Am)* = **normality**.

normality [nɔː'mælətɪ] *(Brit) n* normalidade *f*.

normally ['nɔːmlɪ] *adv* normalmente.

north [nɔːθ] *n* norte *m* ♦ *adj* norte ♦ *adv (be situated)* a norte; *(fly, walk)* para norte; **in the ~ of England** no norte de Inglaterra.

North Africa *n* a África do Norte, o Norte de África.

North America *n* a América do Norte.

northbound [ˈnɔːθbaʊnd] *adj* em direção ao norte.

northeast [ˌnɔːθˈiːst] *n* nordeste *m*.

northerly [ˈnɔːðəlɪ] *adj (wind)* do norte; **in a ~ direction** em direção ao norte; **the most ~ point** o ponto mais ao norte.

northern [ˈnɔːðən] *adj* do norte.

Northern Ireland *n* Irlanda *f* do Norte.

northernmost [ˈnɔːðənməʊst] *adj* mais ao norte.

North Korea *n* Coréia *f* do Norte.

North Pole *n* Pólo *m* Norte.

North Sea *n* Mar *m* do Norte.

northward [ˈnɔːθwəd] *adj*: **in a ~ direction** em direção ao norte.

northwards [ˈnɔːθwədz] *adv* em direção ao norte, para norte.

northwest [ˌnɔːθˈwest] *n* noroeste *m*.

Norway [ˈnɔːweɪ] *n* Noruega *f*.

Norwegian [nɔːˈwiːdʒən] *adj* norueguês(-esa) ♦ *n (person)* norueguês *m* (-esa *f*); *(language)* norueguês *m*.

nose [nəʊz] *n* nariz *m*; *(of animal)* focinho *m*.

nosebleed [ˈnəʊzbliːd] *n*: **to have a ~** perder sangue pelo nariz.

no smoking area *n* área *f* reservada a não-fumantes.

nostalgia [nɒsˈtældʒə] *n* nostalgia *f*.

nostril [ˈnɒstrəl] *n* narina *f*.

nosy [ˈnəʊzɪ] *adj* bisbilhoteiro(-ra).

not [nɒt] *adv* não; **she's ~ there** ela não está lá; **~ yet** ainda não; **~ at all** *(pleased, interested)* absolutamente nada; *(in reply to thanks)* não tem de quê, de nada.

notable [ˈnəʊtəbl] *adj* notável; **~ for sthg** notável por algo.

notably [ˈnəʊtəblɪ] *adv* especialmente.

note [nəʊt] *n* nota *f*; *(message)* recado *m* ♦ *vt (notice)* notar; *(write down)* anotar; **to take ~s** fazer anotações.

notebook [ˈnəʊtbʊk] *n* caderno *m*, bloco *m* de anotações.

noted [ˈnəʊtɪd] *adj* famoso(-osa).

notepad [ˈnəʊtpæd] *n* bloco *m* de notas.

notepaper [ˈnəʊtpeɪpəʳ] *n* papel *m* de carta.

noteworthy [ˈnəʊtˌwɜːðɪ] *adj* digno (-gna) de nota.

nothing [ˈnʌθɪŋ] *pron* nada; **he did ~** ele não fez nada; **~ new/interesting** nada de novo/interessante; **for ~** *(free)* de graça; *(in vain)* para nada.

notice [ˈnəʊtɪs] *vt* notar ♦ *n* aviso *m*; **to take ~ of** prestar atenção a; **to hand in one's ~** demitir-se, apresentar o seu pedido de demissão.

noticeable [ˈnəʊtɪsəbl] *adj* visível.

notice board *n* quadro *m* de avisos *(Br)*, placar *m* (de anúncios e avisos) *(Port)*.

notify [ˈnəʊtɪfaɪ] *vt*: **to ~ sb of sthg** notificar alguém de algo.

notion [ˈnəʊʃn] *n* noção *f*.

notorious [nəʊˈtɔːrɪəs] *adj* famigerado(-da).

nougat [ˈnuːgɑː] *n* torrone *m*, nugá *m*.

nought [nɔːt] *n* zero *m*; **~s and crosses** *(Brit)* jogo-da-velha *m* *(Br)*, jogo *m* do galo *(Port)*.

noun [naʊn] *n* substantivo *m*.

nourish [ˈnʌrɪʃ] *vt* alimentar.

nourishing [ˈnʌrɪʃɪŋ] *adj* nutritivo (-va).

nourishment [ˈnʌrɪʃmənt] *n* alimento *m*.

Nov. *(abbr of November)* nov.

novel [ˈnɒvl] *n* romance *m* ♦ *adj* original.

novelist [ˈnɒvəlɪst] *n* romancista *mf*.

novelty [ˈnɒvltɪ] *n* novidade *f*; *(cheap object)* bugiganga *f*.

November [nəˈvembəʳ] *n* novembro *m*, → **September**.

novice [ˈnɒvɪs] *n (beginner)* novato *m* (-ta *f*).

now [naʊ] *adv* agora ♦ *conj*: **~ (that)** agora que; **by ~** já; **from ~ on** de agora em diante; **just ~** *(a moment ago)* agora mesmo; *(at the moment)* neste momento; **right ~** *(at the moment)* neste momento; *(immediately)* já, agora mesmo.

nowadays [ˈnaʊədeɪz] *adv* hoje em dia.

nowhere [ˈnəʊweəʳ] *adv* em parte alguma.

nozzle [ˈnɒzl] *n* agulheta *f*.

nuclear ['njuːklɪər] *adj* nuclear.

nuclear bomb *n* bomba *f* atômica.

nuclear disarmament *n* desarmamento *m* nuclear.

nuclear power *n* energia *f* nuclear.

nuclear reactor *n* reator *m* nuclear.

nude [njuːd] *adj* nu (nua).

nudge [nʌdʒ] *vt* cutucar *(Br)*, dar uma cotovelada a *(Port)*.

nuisance ['njuːsns] *n*: **it's a real ~!** é uma chatice!; **he's such a ~!** ele é um chato!

null [nʌl] *adj*: **~ and void** nulo(-la) e sem força legal.

numb [nʌm] *adj (leg, arm)* dormente; *(with shock, fear)* atônito(-ta).

number ['nʌmbər] *n* número *m* ◆ *vt (give number to)* numerar.

numberplate ['nʌmbəpleɪt] *n* chapa *f* (do carro) *(Br)*, matrícula *f* do carro *(Port)*.

numeral ['njuːmərəl] *n* numeral *m*, algarismo *m*.

numerous ['njuːmərəs] *adj* inúmeros(-ras).

nun [nʌn] *n* freira *f*.

nurse [nɜːs] *n* enfermeiro *m* (-ra *f*) ◆ *vt (look after)* tomar conta de.

nursery ['nɜːsərɪ] *n (in house)* quarto *m* de criança; *(for plants)* viveiro *m* para plantas.

nursery rhyme *n* poema *m* OR canção *f* infantil.

nursery (school) *n* escola *f* maternal *(Br)*, infantário *m* (Port).

nursery slope *n (ski)* pista *f* para principiantes.

nursing ['nɜːsɪŋ] *n (profession)* enfermagem *f*.

nursing home *n (for old people)* lar *m* para idosos *(privado)*; *(for childbirth)* maternidade *f (privada)*.

nut [nʌt] *n (to eat)* fruto *m* seco *(noz, avelã, etc)*; *(of metal)* porca *f* (de parafuso).

nutcrackers ['nʌt,krækəz] *npl* quebra-nozes *m inv*.

nutmeg ['nʌtmeg] *n* noz-moscada *f*.

nutritious [njuːtrɪʃəs] *adj* nutritivo(-va).

nutshell [nʌtʃel] *n*: **in a ~** resumindo, em poucas palavras.

nylon ['naɪlɒn] *n* nylon *m* ◆ *adj* de nylon.

o' [ə] *abbr* = **of**.

O *n (zero)* zero *m*.

oak [əʊk] *n* carvalho *m* ♦ *adj* de carvalho.

OAP *abbr* = **old age pensioner**.

oar [ɔ:ʳ] *n* remo *m*.

oasis [əʊˈeɪsɪs] *(pl* **oases** [əʊˈeɪsi:z]*) n* oásis *m inv*.

oatcake [ˈəʊtkeɪk] *n* biscoito *m* de aveia.

oath [əʊθ] *n (promise)* juramento *m*.

oatmeal [ˈəʊtmiːl] *n* flocos *mpl* de aveia.

oats [əʊts] *npl* aveia *f*.

obedience [əˈbiːdjəns] *n* obediência *f*.

obedient [əˈbiːdjənt] *adj* obediente.

obese [əʊˈbiːs] *adj* obeso(-sa).

obey [əˈbeɪ] *vt* obedecer a.

obituary [əˈbɪtjʊərɪ] *n* obituário *m*.

object [*n* ˈɒbdʒɪkt, *vb* əbˈdʒekt] *n (thing)* objeto *m; (purpose)* objetivo *m; (GRAMM)* objeto, complemento *m* ♦ *vi:* **to ~ (to)** opor-se (a).

objection [əbˈdʒekʃn] *n* objeção *f*.

objective [əbˈdʒektɪv] *n* objetivo *m*.

obligation [ˌɒblɪˈɡeɪʃn] *n* obrigação *f*.

obligatory [əˈblɪɡətrɪ] *adj* obrigatório(-ria).

oblige [əˈblaɪdʒ] *vt:* **to ~ sb to do sthg** obrigar alguém a fazer algo.

obliging [əˈblaɪdʒɪŋ] *adj* prestativo (-va).

oblique [əˈbliːk] *adj* oblíquo(-qua).

obliterate [əˈblɪtəreɪt] *vt (destroy)* destruir.

oblivion [əˈblɪvɪən] *n* esquecimento *m*.

oblivious [əˈblɪvɪəs] *adj* inconsciente; **to be ~ to** OR **of sthg** não ter consciência de algo.

oblong [ˈɒblɒŋ] *adj* retangular ♦ *n* retângulo *m*.

obnoxious [əbˈnɒkʃəs] *adj* horroroso(-osa).

oboe [ˈəʊbəʊ] *n* oboé *m*.

obscene [əbˈsiːn] *adj* obsceno(-na).

obscure [əbˈskjʊəʳ] *adj (difficult to understand)* obscuro(-ra); *(not well-known)* desconhecido(-da).

observant [əbˈzɜːvnt] *adj* observador(-ra).

observation [ˌɒbzəˈveɪʃn] *n* observação *f*.

observatory [əbˈzɜːvətrɪ] *n* observatório *m*.

observe [əbˈzɜːv] *vt (watch, see)* observar.

obsessed [əbˈsest] *adj* obcecado(-da).

obsession [əbˈseʃn] *n* obsessão *f*.

obsolete [ˈɒbsəliːt] *adj* obsoleto(-ta).

obstacle [ˈɒbstəkl] *n* obstáculo *m*.

obstetrics [ɒbˈstetrɪks] *n* obstetrícia *f*.

obstinate [ˈɒbstənət] *adj* teimoso (-osa).

obstruct [əbˈstrʌkt] *vt (road, path)* obstruir.

obstruction [əbˈstrʌkʃn] *n (in road, path)* obstrução *f*.

obtain [əbˈteɪn] *vt* obter.

obtainable [əbˈteɪnəbl] *adj* que se pode obter.

obtuse [əbˈtjuːs] *adj (fml: person)* obtuso(-sa), estúpido(-da).

obvious [ˈɒbvɪəs] *adj* óbvio(-via).

obviously [ˈɒbvɪəslɪ] *adv* evidentemente.

occasion [əˈkeɪʒn] *n* ocasião *f*.

occasional [əˈkeɪʒənl] *adj* ocasional, esporádico(-ca).

occasionally [əˈkeɪʒnəlɪ] *adv* de vez em quando.

occult [ɒˈkʌlt] *adj* oculto(-ta).

occupant [ˈɒkjʊpənt] *n (of house)* inquilino *m* (-na *f*), ocupante *mf; (of car, plane)* ocupante.

occupation [ɒkjʊ'peɪʃn] n (job) ocupação f; (pastime) passatempo m.

occupied ['ɒkjʊpaɪd] adj (toilet) ocupado(-da).

occupier ['ɒkjʊpaɪəʳ] n ocupante mf.

occupy ['ɒkjʊpaɪ] vt ocupar.

occur [ə'kɜːʳ] vi ocorrer.

occurrence [ə'kʌrəns] n ocorrência f.

ocean ['əʊʃn] n oceano m; **the ~** (Am: sea) o oceano, o mar.

oceangoing ['əʊʃn,gəʊɪŋ] adj de alto mar.

o'clock [ə'klɒk] adv: **it's one ~** é uma hora; **it's seven ~** são sete horas; **at nine ~** às nove horas.

Oct. (abbr of October) out.

octave ['ɒktɪv] n oitava f.

October [ɒk'təʊbəʳ] n outubro, → September.

octopus ['ɒktəpəs] n polvo m.

odd [ɒd] adj (strange) estranho(-nha); (number) ímpar; (not matching) sem par; (occasional) ocasional; **60 ~ miles** umas 60 milhas; **some ~ bits of paper** alguns pedaços de papel; **~ jobs** biscates mpl.

oddly ['ɒdlɪ] adv (behave, speak, look) de forma estranha; (disappointing, uplifting) estranhamente; **~ enough, I don't care** por muito estranho que pareça, pouco me importa.

odds [ɒdz] npl (in betting) apostas fpl; (chances) probabilidades fpl; **~ and ends** miudezas fpl.

odds-on adj (inf): **the ~ favourite** o grande favorito.

odor ['əʊdəʳ] (Am) = odour.

odour ['əʊdəʳ] n (Brit) odor m.

of [ɒv] prep 1. (belonging to) de; **the colour ~ the car** a cor do carro.

2. (expressing amount) de; **a piece ~ cake** uma fatia de bolo; **a fall ~ 20%** uma queda de 20%; **lots ~ people** muita gente.

3. (containing, made from) de; **a glass ~ beer** um copo de cerveja; **a house ~ stone** uma casa de pedra; **it's made ~ wood** é de madeira.

4. (regarding, relating to, indicating cause) de; **fear ~ spiders** medo de aranhas; **he died ~ cancer** ele morreu de câncer.

5. (referring to time) de; **the summer ~ 1969** o verão de 1969; **the 26th ~ August** o 26 de agosto.

6. (with towns, countries) de; **the city ~**

Glasgow a cidade de Glasgow.

7. (on the part of) de; **that was very kind ~ you** foi muito amável da sua parte.

8. (Am: in telling the time) menos, para; **it's ten ~ four** são dez para as quatro.

off [ɒf] adv 1. (away): **to drive/walk ~** ir-se embora; **to get ~** (from bus, train, etc) descer; **we're ~ to Austria next week** vamos para a Áustria na próxima semana.

2. (expressing removal): **to take sthg ~** tirar algo.

3. (so as to stop working): **to turn sthg ~** (TV, radio, engine) desligar algo; (tap) fechar algo.

4. (expressing distance or time away): **it's a long way ~** (in distance) é muito longe; (in time) ainda falta muito; **it's two months ~** é daqui a dois meses.

5. (not at work) de folga; **I'm taking a week ~** vou tirar uma semana de férias.

♦ prep 1. (away from): **to get ~ sthg** descer de algo; **~ the coast** ao largo da costa; **just ~ the main road** perto da estrada principal.

2. (indicating removal): **take the lid ~ the jar** tire a tampa do frasco; **we'll take £20 ~ the price** descontaremos 20 libras do preço.

3. (absent from): **to be ~ work** não estar trabalhando.

4. (inf: from) a; **I bought it ~ her** eu comprei isso a ela.

5. (inf: no longer liking): **I'm ~ my food** não tenho apetite.

♦ adj 1. (food, drink) estragado(-da).

2. (TV, radio, light) apagado(-da), desligado(-da); (tap) fechado(-da); (engine) desligado(-da).

3. (cancelled) cancelado(-da).

4. (not available): **the soup's ~** não tem mais sopa.

offal ['ɒfl] n fressura f.

off-chance n: **on the ~ you'd be there** no caso de você estar lá.

off colour adj (ill) indisposto(-osta).

off duty adv: **when do you get ~?** a que horas acaba o serviço? ♦ adj que não está de serviço.

offence [ə'fens] n (Brit) (crime) infração f, delito m; (upset) ofensa f.

offend [ə'fend] vt (upset) ofender.

offender [ə'fendəʳ] n infrator m (-ra f), transgressor m (-ra f).

offense [ɔ'fens] *(Am)* = **offence**.

offensive [ə'fensıv] *adj (insulting)* ofensivo(-va).

offer ['nfɔ*] *n* oferta *f* ◆ *vt* oferecer; **on ~** *(available)* à venda; *(reduced)* em oferta; **to ~ to do sthg** oferecer-se para fazer algo; **to ~ sb sthg** oferecer algo a alguém.

off guard *adv*: **to be caught ~** ser apanhado desprevenido (apanhada desprevenida).

offhand [nf'hænd] *adj (person)* brusco(-ca); *(greeting)* frio (fria) ◆ *adv (at this moment)* de repente.

office ['nfıs] *n (room)* escritório *m*.

office block *n* edifício *m* de escritórios.

officer ['nfısə*] *n (MIL)* oficial *mf*; *(policeman)* polícia *mf*.

office worker *n* empregado *m* (-da *f*) de escritório.

official [ə'fıʃl] *adj* oficial ◆ *n* funcionário *m* (-ria *f*).

officially [ə'fıʃəlı] *adv* oficialmente.

off-licence *n (Brit)* loja *f* de bebidas alcoólicas (para levar).

off-line *adj (COMPUT)* off-line, fora de linha.

off-peak *adj (train, ticket)* fora das horas de rush *(Br)*, de horário azul *(Port)*.

off-putting [-putıŋ] *adj (manner)* desconcertante.

off sales *npl (Brit)* venda *f* de bebidas alcoólicas para levar.

off-season *n* época *f* baixa.

offshore ['nfʃɔ:*] *adj (wind)* costeiro(-ra); *(oil production)* no alto mar.

off side *n (for right-hand drive)* esquerda *f*; *(for left-hand drive)* direita *f*.

offspring ['nfsprıŋ] *(pl inv)* *n (fml: of people)* filhos *mpl*; *(fml: of animals)* filhotes *mpl*.

offstage [nf'steıdʒ] *adv (go)* para os bastidores; *(be, wait)* nos bastidores.

off-the-cuff *adj* irrefletido(-da) ◆ *adv* sem pensar.

off-the-peg *adj* pronto(-ta) para vestir.

off-white *adj* branco-sujo *(inv)*.

often ['nfn, 'nftn] *adv* muitas vezes, freqüentemente; **how ~ do the buses run?** qual é a freqüência dos ônibus?; **every so ~** de vez em quando.

oh [əʊ] *excl* oh!

oil [ɔıl] *n* óleo *m*; *(fuel)* petróleo *m*.

oilcan ['ɔılkæn] *n* almotolia *f*.

oilfield ['ɔılfi:ld] *n* campo *m* petrolífero.

oil filter *n* filtro *m* do óleo.

oil painting *n (activity)* pintura *f* a óleo; *(picture)* quadro *m* a óleo.

oil rig *n* plataforma *f* petrolífera.

oilskins ['ɔılskınz] *npl* (capa de) oleado *m*.

oil slick *n* mancha *f* negra *(Br)*, maré *f* negra *(Port)*.

oil tanker *n (ship)* petroleiro *m*; *(lorry)* camião-cisterna *m*.

oil well *n* poço *m* de petróleo.

oily ['ɔılı] *adj (cloth, hands)* oleoso (-osa); *(food)* gordurento(-ta).

ointment ['ɔıntmənt] *n* pomada *f*, ungüento *m*.

OK [,əʊ'keı] *adj (inf)* bom (boa) ◆ *adv (inf)* bem; **is everything ~?** está tudo bem?; **is that ~?** pode ser?, você concorda?; **the film was ~** achei o filme mais ou menos.

okay [,əʊ'keı] = **OK**.

old [əʊld] *adj* velho(-lha); *(former)* antigo(-ga); **how ~ are you?** quantos anos você tem?; **I'm 16 years ~** tenho 16 anos; **to get ~** envelhecer.

old age *n* velhice *f*.

old age pensioner *n* aposentado *m* (-da *f*) *(Br)*, reformado *m* (-da *f*) *(Port)*.

old-fashioned [-'fæʃnd] *adj* antiquado(-da).

old people's home *n* lar *m* para idosos.

O level *n* antigo exame oficial substituído hoje em dia pelo "GCSE".

olive ['nlıv] *n* azeitona *f*.

olive green *adj* verde-azeitona *(inv)*.

olive oil *n* azeite *m*.

Olympic Games [ə'lımpık-] *npl* Jogos *mpl* Olímpicos.

omelette ['nmlıt] *n* omelete *f*; **mushroom ~** omelete de cogumelos.

omen ['əʊmɛn] *n* presságio *m*.

ominous ['nmınəs] *adj (silence, clouds)* ameaçador(-ra); *(event, sign)* de mau agouro.

omission [ə'mıʃn] *n* omissão *f*.

omit [ə'mıt] *vt* omitir.

on [nn] *prep* **1.** *(expressing position, location)* em, sobre; **it's ~ the table** está na mesa, está sobre a mesa; **put it ~ the table** ponha-o na OR sobre a mesa; **~ my right** à minha direita; **~**

the right à direita; **a picture ~ the wall**
um quadro na parede; **the exhaust ~
the car** o cano de descarga do carro;
we stayed ~ a farm ficamos numa
fazenda.
2. *(with forms of transport)*: **~ the plane**
no avião; **to get ~ a bus** subir num
ônibus.
3. *(expressing means, method)* em; **~
foot** a pé; **~ the radio** no rádio; **~ TV**
na televisão; **paid ~ an hourly basis**
pago por hora.
4. *(using)* a; **it runs ~ unleaded petrol**
funciona com gasolina sem chumbo;
to be ~ drugs drogar-se; **to be ~
medication** estar tomando medicamentos.
5. *(about)* sobre; **a book ~ Germany**
um livro sobre a Alemanha.
6. *(expressing time)*: **~ arrival** ao chegar; **~ Tuesday** na terça-feira; **~ 25th
August** no dia 25 de agosto.
7. *(with regard to)* em, sobre; **a tax ~
imports** um imposto sobre as impor-
tações; **the effect ~ Britain** o impacto
na Grã-Bretanha.
8. *(describing activity, state)*: **~ holiday**
de férias; **~ offer** *(reduced)* em promoção; **~ sale** à venda.
9. *(in phrases)*: **do you have any money
~ you?** *(inf)* você tem dinheiro?; **the
drinks are ~ me** as bebidas são por
minha conta.
◆ *adv* **1.** *(in place, covering)*: **to put
one's clothes ~** vestir-se; **to put the lid
~** tapar.
2. *(film, play, programme)*: **the news is
~** está passando no noticiário OR o telejornal; **what's ~ at the cinema?** o que é
que está passando no cinema?
3. *(with transport)*: **to get ~** subir.
4. *(functioning)*: **to turn sthg ~** *(TV,
radio, light)* ligar OR acender algo; *(tap)*
abrir algo; *(engine)* pôr algo para trabalhar.
5. *(taking place)*: **how long is the festival ~?** quanto tempo dura o festival?;
the match is already ~ o jogo já
começou.
6. *(further forward)*: **to drive ~** continuar a dirigir.
7. *(in phrases)*: **I already have something ~ tonight** já tenho planos para
esta noite.
◆ *adj (TV, radio, light)* ligado(-da),
aceso(-sa); *(tap)* aberto(-ta); *(engine)*

funcionando.
once [wʌns] *adv (one time)* uma vez;
(in the past) uma vez, no passado
◆ *conj* quando, assim que; **at ~** *(immediately)* imediatamente; *(at the same
time)* ao mesmo tempo; **for ~** pelo
menos uma vez; **~ more** *(one more
time)* mais uma vez; *(again)* outra vez.
oncoming ['ɒn,kʌmɪŋ] *adj (traffic)* em
sentido contrário.
one [wʌn] *num* um (uma) ◆ *adj (only)*
único(-ca) ◆ *pron (object, person)* um *m*
(uma *f*); *(fml: you)* cada um; **thirty-
one** trinta e um; **~ fifth** um quinto; **the
green ~** o verde; **I want a blue ~** quero
um azul; **that ~** aquele *m* (aquela *f*),
esse *m* (essa *f*); **this ~** este *m* (esta *f*);
which ~? qual?; **the ~ I told you about**
aquele de que lhe falei; **~ of my
friends** um dos meus amigos; **~ day**
um dia.
one-armed bandit *n* slot-machine
f.
one-man band *n (musician)*
homem-orquestra *m*.
one-off *adj (inf)* único(-ca) ◆ *n (inf:
event, person)* caso *m* único; *(product)*
exemplar *m* único.
one-piece (swimsuit) *n* traje *m*
de banho *(Br)*, fato *m* de banho *(Port)*.
oneself [wʌn'self] *pron (reflexive)* se;
(after prep) si próprio OR mesmo (si
própria OR mesma).
one-sided [-'saɪdɪd] *adj (unequal)*
desigual; *(biased)* tendencioso(-osa),
parcial.
one-way *adj (street)* de sentido
único; *(ticket)* de ida.
ongoing ['ɒn,gəʊɪŋ] *adj (project, discus-
sions)* atual, em curso; *(problem)* constante.
onion ['ʌnjən] *n* cebola *f*.
onion bhaji [-'bɑːdʒɪ] *n* bolinho de
cebola picada, farinha e condimentos, frito
e servido como entrada.
onion rings *npl* rodelas de cebolas,
fritas em massa mole.
online ['ɒnlaɪn] *adj & adv (COMPUT)*
online, em linha.
onlooker ['ɒn,lʊkə^r] *n* espectador *m*
(-ra *f*), curioso *m* (-osa *f*).
only ['əʊnlɪ] *adj* único(-ca) ◆ *adv* só;
he's an ~ child ele é filho único; **I ~
want one** só quero um; **we've ~ just
arrived** acabamos de chegar; **there's ~
just enough** só tem a conta certa;

"members ~" "só para membros"; **not ~** não só.

onset ['ɒn.sɛt] *n* início *m*.

onshore ['ɒn.ʃɔːr] *adj* (*wind*) costeiro (-ra); (*oil production*) em terra.

onslaught ['ɒn.slɔːt] *n* investida *f*.

onto ['ɒntuː] *prep* (*with verbs of movement*) para (cima de); **to get ~ sb** (*telephone*) contatar alguém (pelo telefone).

onward ['ɒnwəd] *adv* = **onwards** ◆ *adj*: **the ~ journey** o resto da viagem.

onwards ['ɒnwədz] *adv* (*forwards*) para a frente, para diante; **from now ~** daqui em diante; **from October ~** de outubro em diante.

ooze [uːz] *vt* (*charm, confidence*) respirar ◆ *vi* ressudar; **to ~ from** OR **out of sthg** ressudar de algo.

opal ['əʊpl] *n* opala *f*.

opaque [əʊ'peɪk] *adj* opaco(-ca).

open ['əʊpn] *adj* aberto(-ta); (*honest*) franco(-ca) ◆ *vt* abrir; (*start*) iniciar ◆ *vi* (*door, window, lock*) abrir-se; (*shop, office, bank*) abrir; (*start*) iniciar-se, começar; **are you ~ at the weekend?** está aberto ao fim de semana?; **wide ~** completamente aberto; **in the ~ (air)** ao ar livre.

⌐ **open onto** *vt fus* dar para.

⌐ **open up** *vi* abrir.

open-air *adj* ao ar livre.

opener ['əʊpnər] *n* abridor *m*.

opening ['əʊpnɪŋ] *n* abertura *f*; (*opportunity*) oportunidade *f*.

opening hours *npl* horário *m* de funcionamento.

openly ['əʊpnlɪ] *adv* abertamente.

open-minded [-'maɪndɪd] *adj* aberto(-ta), sem preconceitos.

open-plan *adj* sem divisórias.

open sandwich *n* canapé *m* (*Br*), sandes *f inv* aberta (*Port*).

Open University *n* (*Brit*): **the ~** a Universidade Aberta.

opera ['ɒprə] *n* ópera *f*.

opera house *n* teatro *m* de ópera.

operate ['ɒpəreɪt] *vt* (*machine*) trabalhar com ◆ *vi* (*work*) funcionar; **to ~ on sb** operar alguém.

operating room ['ɒpəreɪtɪŋ-] *n* (*Am*) = **operating theatre**.

operating theatre ['ɒpəreɪtɪŋ-] *n* (*Brit*) sala *f* de operações.

operation [ɒpə'reɪʃn] *n* operação *f*; **to be in ~** (*law, system*) estar em vigor;

to have an ~ ser operado.

operational [ɒpə'reɪʃənl] *adj* operacional.

operator ['ɒpəreɪtər] *n* (*on phone*) telefonista *mf*.

opinion [ə'pɪnjən] *n* opinião *f*; **in my ~** na minha opinião.

opinionated [ə'pɪnjəneɪtɪd] *adj* opinioso(-osa) (*Br*), pirrónico(-ca) (*Port*).

opinion poll *n* pesquisa *f* de opinião pública (*Br*), sondagem *f* de opinião (*Port*).

opponent [ə'pəʊnənt] *n* adversário *m* (-ria *f*).

opportunist [ɒpə'tjuːnɪst] *n* oportunista *mf*.

opportunity [ɒpə'tjuːnətɪ] *n* oportunidade *f*.

oppose [ə'pəʊz] *vt* opor-se a.

opposed [ə'pəʊzd] *adj*: **to be ~ to** opor-se a.

opposing [ə'pəʊzɪŋ] *adj* oposto (-osta).

opposite ['ɒpəzɪt] *adj* oposto(-osta) ◆ *prep* em frente de, frente a ◆ *n*: **the ~ (of)** o oposto (de), o contrário (de); **I live in the house ~** vivo na casa em frente.

opposition [ɒpə'zɪʃn] *n* (*objections*) oposição *f*; (*SPORT*) adversário *m*; **the Opposition** (*POL*) a oposição.

oppress [ə'pres] *vt* oprimir.

opt [ɒpt] *vt*: **to ~ to do sthg** optar por fazer algo.

optical ['ɒptɪkl] *adj* ótico(-ca).

optician's [ɒp'tɪʃnz] *n* (*shop*) oculista *m*.

optimist ['ɒptɪmɪst] *n* otimista *mf*.

optimistic [ɒptɪ'mɪstɪk] *adj* otimista.

optimum ['ɒptɪməm] (*pl* -**mums**, *fml* -**ma** [-mə]) *adj* ideal.

option ['ɒpʃn] *n* opção *f*.

optional ['ɒpʃənl] *adj* facultativo (-va).

or [ɔːr] *conj* ou; (*after negative*) nem; (*otherwise*) senão; **I can't read ~ write** não sei ler nem escrever.

OR *abbr* = **operating room**.

oral ['ɔːrəl] *adj* oral ◆ *n* oral *f*.

orally ['ɔːrəlɪ] *adv* (*in spoken form*) oralmente; (*via the mouth*) por via oral.

orange ['ɒrɪndʒ] *adj* cor-de-laranja (*inv*) ◆ *n* (*fruit*) laranja *f*; (*colour*) cor-de-laranja *m inv*.

orange juice *n* suco *m* de laranja (*Br*), sumo *m* de laranja (*Port*).

orange squash n (Brit) laranjada f (sem gás).

orbit ['ɔːbɪt] n órbita f.

orbital (motorway) ['ɔːbɪtl-] n (Brit) auto-estrada f (em torno de uma grande cidade).

orchard ['ɔːtʃəd] n pomar m.

orchestra ['ɔːkɪstrə] n orquestra f.

orchestral [ɔːˈkestrəl] adj para orquestra, orquestral.

orchid ['ɔːkɪd] n orquídea f.

ordeal [ɔːˈdiːl] n experiência f traumática.

order ['ɔːdəʳ] n ordem f; (in restaurant) pedido m; (COMM) encomenda f ◆ vt (command) mandar; (food, drink) pedir; (taxi) chamar; (COMM) encomendar ◆ vi (in restaurant) pedir; **in ~ to** para; **out of ~** (not working) quebrado(-da) (Br), avariado(-da) (Port); **in working ~** a funcionar; **to ~ sb to do sthg** mandar alguém fazer algo.

order form n folha f de encomenda.

orderly ['ɔːdəlɪ] adj ordenado(-da) ◆ n (in hospital) auxiliar mf.

ordinarily ['ɔːdənrəlɪ, Am ˌɔːrdnˈerəlɪ] adv geralmente.

ordinary ['ɔːdnrɪ] adj comum.

ore [ɔːʳ] n minério m.

oregano [ˌɒrɪˈɡɑːnəʊ] n orégão m.

organ ['ɔːɡən] n órgão m.

organic [ɔːˈɡænɪk] adj orgânico(-ca).

organization [ˌɔːɡənaɪˈzeɪʃn] n organização f.

organize ['ɔːɡənaɪz] vt organizar.

organizer ['ɔːɡənaɪzəʳ] n (person) organizador m (-ra f); (diary) agenda f.

orgasm ['ɔːɡæzm] n orgasmo m.

oriental [ˌɔːrɪˈentl] adj oriental.

orientate ['ɔːrɪenteɪt] vt: **to ~ o.s.** orientar-se.

orienteering [ˌɔːrɪenˈtɪərɪŋ] n orientação f; **to go ~** fazer orientação.

origami [ˌɒrɪˈɡɑːmɪ] n arte japonesa de dobrar papel criando formas de flores, animais, etc.

origin ['ɒrɪdʒɪn] n origem f.

original [əˈrɪdʒənl] adj original.

originally [əˈrɪdʒənəlɪ] adv (formerly) inicialmente.

originate [əˈrɪdʒəneɪt] vi: **to ~ (from)** nascer (de).

Orkney Islands ['ɔːknɪ-] npl: **the ~** as ilhas Órcades.

Orkneys ['ɔːknɪz] = **Orkney Islands**.

ornament ['ɔːnəmənt] n (object) peça f de decoração.

ornamental [ˌɔːnəˈmentl] adj decorativo(-va).

ornate [ɔːˈneɪt] adj ornado(-da).

ornithology [ˌɔːnɪˈθɒlədʒɪ] n ornitologia f.

orphan ['ɔːfn] n órfão m (-fã f).

orphanage ['ɔːfənɪdʒ] n orfanato m.

orthodox ['ɔːθədɒks] adj ortodoxo(-xa).

orthopaedic [ˌɔːθəˈpiːdɪk] adj ortopédico(-ca).

oscillate ['ɒsɪleɪt] vi oscilar.

Oslo ['ɒzləʊ] n Oslo s.

ostensible [ɒˈstensəbl] n aparente.

ostentatious [ˌɒstənˈteɪʃəs] adj pretensioso(-osa).

osteopath ['ɒstɪəpæθ] n osteopata mf.

ostracize ['ɒstrəsaɪz] vt marginalizar; (from party, union) condenar ao ostracismo.

ostrich ['ɒstrɪtʃ] n avestruz f.

other ['ʌðəʳ] adj outro(-tra) ◆ adv: **~ than** exceto; **the ~ (one)** o outro (a outra); **the ~ day** no outro dia; **one after the ~** um depois do outro.

❏ **others** pron pl (additional ones) outros mpl (-tras fpl); **the ~s** (remaining ones) os outros (as outras).

otherwise ['ʌðəwaɪz] adv (or else) senão; (apart from that) de resto; (differently) de outro modo.

otter ['ɒtəʳ] n lontra f.

ouch [aʊtʃ] excl ai!, au!

ought [ɔːt] aux vb dever; **you ~ to have gone** você devia ter ido; **you ~ to see a doctor** você devia ir ao médico; **the car ~ to be ready by Friday** o carro deve estar pronto sexta-feira.

ounce [aʊns] n = 28,35 gr, onça f.

our ['aʊəʳ] adj nosso(-a); **~ books** os nossos livros.

ours ['aʊəz] pron o nosso (a nossa); **a friend of ~** um amigo nosso; **these shoes are ~** estes sapatos são (os) nossos; **~ are here – where are yours?** os nossos estão aqui – onde estão os seus?

ourselves [aʊəˈselvz] pron (reflexive) nos; (after prep) nós mpl mesmos OR próprios (nós fpl mesmas OR próprias); **we did it ~** nós mesmos OR próprios o fizemos; **we hurt ~** nós nos machucamos.

oust [aʊst] *vt (fml)*: **to ~ sb from sthg** obrigar alguém a sair de algo.

out [aʊt] *adj* **1.** *(light, cigarette)* apagado(-da).
2. *(wrong)*: **the bill's £10 ~** há um erro de dez libras na conta.
♦ *adv* **1.** *(outside)* fora; **to get/go ~ (of)** sair (de); **it's cold ~ today** está frio lá fora hoje; **he looked ~** ele olhou para fora.
2. *(not at home, work)* fora; **to be ~** não estar em casa; **to go ~** sair.
3. *(so as to be extinguished)*: **to turn sthg ~** apagar algo; **put your cigarette ~** apague o cigarro.
4. *(expressing removal)*: **to pour sthg ~** despejar algo, jogar algo fora; **to take money ~** *(from cashpoint)* retirar dinheiro; **to take sthg ~ (of)** tirar algo (de).
5. *(outwards)*: **to stick ~** sobressair.
6. *(expressing distribution)*: **to hand sthg ~** distribuir algo.
7. *(in phrases)*: **to get enjoyment ~ of sthg** divertir-se com algo; **stay ~ of the sun** não se exponha ao sol; **made ~ of wood** (feito) de madeira; **five ~ of ten women** cinco em cada dez mulheres; **I'm ~ of cigarettes** não tenho cigarros.

outback [aʊtbæk] *n*: **the ~** o interior australiano.

outboard (motor) [aʊtbɔːd-] *n* motor *m* de borda.

outbreak [aʊtbreɪk] *n (of disease)* surto *m*; *(of violence)* deflagração *f*.

outburst [aʊtbɜːst] *n* explosão *f*.

outcast [aʊtkɑːst] *n* marginalizado *m* (-da *f*), pária *mf*.

outcome [aʊtkʌm] *n* resultado *m*.

outcrop [aʊtkrɒp] *n* afloramento *m*.

outcry [aʊtkraɪ] *n* clamor *m* (de protesto), protesto *m*.

outdated [aʊtdeɪtɪd] *adj* ultrapassado(-da).

outdo [aʊtduː] *(pt* -did, *pp* -done) *vt* ultrapassar, vencer.

outdoor [aʊtdɔːr] *adj (swimming pool, activities)* ao ar livre.

outdoors [aʊtdɔːz] *adv* ao ar livre.

outer [aʊtər] *adj* exterior, externo (-na).

outer space *n* espaço *m* (exterior).

outfit [aʊtfɪt] *n (clothes)* roupa *f*.

outgoing [aʊtgəʊɪŋ] *adj (mail, train)* de saída; *(friendly, sociable)* extrovertido(-da), aberto(-ta).

outgoings *npl (Brit)* gastos *mpl*.

outing [aʊtɪŋ] *n* excursão *f*, saída *f*.

outlaw [aʊtlɔː] *n* foragido *m* (-da *f*)
♦ *vt (make illegal)* proibir.

outlay [aʊtleɪ] *n* despesa *f*, gasto *m*.

outlet [aʊtlet] *n (pipe)* saída *f*; **"no ~"** *(Am)* sinal que indica que a rua não tem saída.

outline [aʊtlaɪn] *n (shape)* contorno *m*; *(description)* linhas *fpl* gerais, esboço *m*.

outlive [aʊtlɪv] *vt (subj: person)* sobreviver a.

outlook [aʊtlʊk] *n (for future)* perspectiva *f*; *(of weather)* previsão *f*; *(attitude)* atitude *f*.

outlying [aʊtlaɪɪŋ] *adj (remote)* remoto(-ta); *(on edge of town)* periférico(-ca).

outnumber [aʊtnʌmbər] *vt* ultrapassar OR exceder em número.

out-of-date *adj (old-fashioned)* antiquado(-da); *(passport, licence)* expirado(-da) *(Br)*, caducado(-da) *(Port)*.

out of doors *adv* ao ar livre.

outpatients' (department) [aʊtpeɪʃnts-] *n* ambulatório *m* *(Br)*, consultas *fpl* externas *(Port)*.

output [aʊtpʊt] *n (of factory)* produção *f*; *(COMPUT: printout)* impressão *f*.

outrage [aʊtreɪdʒ] *n (cruel act)* atrocidade *f*.

outrageous [aʊtreɪdʒəs] *adj (shocking)* escandaloso(-osa).

outright [aʊtraɪt] *adv (tell, deny)* categoricamente; *(own)* completamente, totalmente.

outset [aʊtset] *n*: **from/at the ~** desde o/no início.

outside [*adv* aʊtsaɪd, *adj, prep & n* aʊtsaɪd] *adv* lá fora ♦ *prep* fora de; *(in front of)* em frente de ♦ *adj (exterior)* exterior; *(help, advice)* independente ♦ *n*: **the ~** *(of building, car, container)* o exterior; *(AUT: in UK)* a faixa direita; *(AUT: in Europe, US)* a faixa esquerda; **~ of** *(Am)* *(on the outside of)* fora de; *(apart from)* excepto; **let's go ~** vamos lá para fora; **an ~ line** uma linha externa.

outside lane *n (AUT) (in UK)* faixa *f* direita; *(in Europe, US)* faixa esquerda.

outsider [aʊtsaɪdər] *n (socially)* estranho *m* (-nha *f*); *(in horse race)* cavalo que não estava entre os favoritos.

outsize [aʊtsaɪz] *adj (clothes)* de

tamanho extra grande.

outskirts ['aʊtskɜːts] *npl* arredores *mpl*.

outspoken [aʊt'spəʊkn] *adj* direto (-ta); *(critic)* assumido(-da).

outstanding [,aʊt'stændɪŋ] *adj (remarkable)* notável; *(problem, debt)* pendente.

outstay [aʊt'steɪ] *vt*: **to ~ one's welcome** abusar da hospitalidade de alguém.

outstretched [,aʊt'stretʃt] *adj* estendido(-da).

outstrip [aʊt'strɪp] *vt (do better than)* ganhar de, vencer.

outward ['aʊtwəd] *adj (journey)* de ida; *(external)* exterior.

outwardly ['aʊtwədlɪ] *adv* aparentemente.

outwards ['aʊtwədz] *adv* para fora.

outweigh [aʊt'weɪ] *vt* pesar mais (do) que.

outwit [aʊt'wɪt] *vt* passar a perna em.

oval ['əʊvl] *adj* oval.

ovary ['əʊvərɪ] *n* ovário *m*.

ovation [əʊ'veɪʃn] *n* ovação *f*.

oven ['ʌvn] *n* forno *m*.

oven glove *n* luva *f* de cozinha.

ovenproof ['ʌvnpruːf] *adj* refratário(-ria).

oven-ready *adj* pronto(-ta) para assar (no forno).

over ['əʊvə'] *prep* **1.** *(above)* por cima de; **a bridge ~ the road** uma ponte por cima da estrada.

2. *(across)* por cima de; **with a view ~ the square** com vista sobre a praça; **to step ~ sthg** passar por cima de algo; **it's just ~ the road** é logo do outro lado da rua.

3. *(covering)* sobre; **put a plaster ~ the wound** põe um band-aid na ferida.

4. *(more than)* mais de; **it cost ~ £1,000** custou mais de 1.000 libras.

5. *(during)* em; **~ the past two years** nos últimos dois anos.

6. *(with regard to)* sobre; **an argument ~ the price** uma discussão sobre o preço.

♦ *adv* **1.** *(downwards)*: **to bend ~** abaixar-se; **to fall ~** cair; **to push sthg ~** empurrar algo.

2. *(referring to position, movement)*: **to fly ~ to Canada** ir ao Canadá de avião; **~ here** aqui; **~ there** ali.

3. *(round to other side)*: **to turn sthg ~** virar algo.

4. *(more)*: **children aged 12 and ~** crianças com 12 anos ou mais.

5. *(remaining)*: **to be (left) ~** restar.

6. *(to one's house)*: **to invite sb ~ for dinner** convidar alguém para jantar.

7. *(in phrases)*: **all ~ the world/country** por todo o mundo/país.

♦ *adj (finished)*: **to be ~** acabar, terminar; **it's (all) ~!** acabou-se!

overall [*adv* ,əʊvər'ɔːl, *n* 'əʊvərɔːl] *adv (in general)* no geral ♦ *n (Brit: coat)* bata *f*; *(Am: boiler suit)* macacão *m (Br)*, fatomacaco *m (Port)*; **how much does it cost ~?** quanto custa ao todo?.

⌐ **overalls** *npl (Brit: boiler suit)* macacão *m (Br)*, fato-macaco *m (Port)*; *(Am: dungarees)* jardineiras *fpl*.

overawe [,əʊvər'ɔː] *vt* impressionar.

overbearing [,əʊvə'beərɪŋ] *adj* autoritário(-ria).

overboard ['əʊvəbɔːd] *adv (from ship)* ao mar.

overbooked [,əʊvə'bʊkt] *adj (flight)*: **to be ~** ter mais reservas que lugares.

overcame [,əʊvə'keɪm] *pt → overcome*.

overcast [,əʊvə'kɑːst] *adj* encoberto(-ta).

overcharge [,əʊvə'tʃɑːdʒ] *vt* cobrar demasiado a.

overcoat ['əʊvəkəʊt] *n* sobretudo *m*.

overcome [,əʊvə'kʌm] *(pt -came, pp -come)* *vt (defeat)* vencer.

overcooked [,əʊvə'kʊkt] *adj* cozido (-da) demais OR demasiado.

overcrowded [,əʊvə'kraʊdɪd] *adj* superlotado(-da); *(country)* com excesso populacional.

overcrowding [,əʊvə'kraʊdɪŋ] *n* superlotação *f*; *(of country)* excesso *m* populacional.

overdo [,əʊvə'duː] *(pt -did, pp -done)* *vt (exaggerate)* exagerar em; **to ~ it** exagerar.

overdone [,əʊvə'dʌn] *pp → overdo* ♦ *adj (food)* cozido(-da) demais OR demasiado.

overdose ['əʊvədəʊs] *n* overdose *f*, dose *f* excessiva.

overdraft ['əʊvədrɑːft] *n* saldo *m* negativo.

overdrawn [,əʊvə'drɔːn] *adj*: **to be ~** estar com saldo negativo.

overdue [,əʊvə'djuː] *adj* atrasado(-da).

over easy adj (Am: egg) frito(-ta) dos dois lados.

overestimate [ˌəʊvərˈestɪmeɪt] vt (quantity, bill) exagerar (no cálculo de); (enthusiasm, importance) sobrestimar.

overexposed [ˌəʊvərɪkˈspəʊzd] adj (photograph) demasiado exposto (-osta).

overflow [vb ˌəʊvəˈfləʊ, n ˈəʊvəfləʊ] vi transbordar ♦ n (pipe) cano m de descarga.

overgrown [ˌəʊvəˈɡrəʊn] adj coberto(-ta) de ervas daninhas.

overhaul [ˈəʊvəhɔːl] n (of machine, car) revisão f.

overhead [adj ˈəʊvəhed, adv ˌəʊvəˈhed] adj aéreo(-rea) ♦ adv no alto.

overhead locker n compartimento m superior.

overhead projector n retroprojetor m.

overhear [ˌəʊvəˈhɪər] (pt & pp -heard) vt ouvir (casualmente).

overheat [ˌəʊvəˈhiːt] vi aquecer demais.

overjoyed [ˌəʊvəˈdʒɔɪd] adj: to be ~ (at sthg) estar contentíssimo(-ma) (com algo).

overland [ˈəʊvəlænd] adv por terra.

overlap [ˌəʊvəˈlæp] vi sobrepor-se.

overleaf [ˌəʊvəˈliːf] adv no verso.

overload [ˌəʊvəˈləʊd] vt sobrecarregar.

overlook [vb ˌəʊvəˈlʊk, n ˈəʊvəlʊk] vt (subj: building, room) dar para; (miss) não reparar em ♦ n: (scenic) ~ (Am) miradouro m.

overnight [adv ˌəʊvəˈnaɪt, adj ˈəʊvənaɪt] adv (during the night) durante a noite ♦ adj (train, journey) noturno(-na); why don't you stay ~? por que é que você não fica para dormir?

overnight bag n saco m de viagem.

overpass [ˈəʊvəpɑːs] n viaduto m.

overpower [ˌəʊvəˈpaʊər] vt (in fight) dominar; (fig: overwhelm) tomar conta de.

overpowering [ˌəʊvəˈpaʊərɪŋ] adj intenso(-sa).

overran [ˌəʊvəˈræn] pt → overrun.

overrated [ˌəʊvəˈreɪtɪd] adj: I think the film is totally ~ não acho que o filme seja tão bom como se diz.

override [ˌəʊvəˈraɪd] (pt -rode, pp -ridden) vt (be more important than) prevalecer sobre; (overrule: decision) ir contra.

overrule [ˌəʊvəˈruːl] vt (person) desautorizar; (decision) ir contra; (objection, request) rejeitar, negar.

overrun [ˌəʊvəˈrʌn] (pt -ran, pp -run) vi (last too long) alongar-se, ultrapassar o tempo previsto ♦ vt (occupy) invadir; to be ~ with sthg (fig: covered, filled) ser invadido(-da) por algo.

oversaw [ˌəʊvəˈsɔː] pt → oversee.

overseas [adv ˌəʊvəˈsiːz, adj ˈəʊvəsiːz] adv (go) para o estrangeiro; (live) no estrangeiro ♦ adj estrangeiro(-ra); ~ territories territórios mpl ultramarinos.

oversee [ˌəʊvəˈsiː] (pt -saw, pp -seen) vt supervisionar.

overseer [ˈəʊvəsiːər] n supervisor m (-ra f).

overshadow [ˌəʊvəˈʃædəʊ] vt: to be ~ed by (eclipsed) ser ofuscado(-da) por; (spoiled) ser toldado(-da) por.

overshoot [ˌəʊvəˈʃuːt] (pt & pp -shot) vt passar.

oversight [ˈəʊvəsaɪt] n descuido m.

oversleep [ˌəʊvəˈsliːp] (pt & pp -slept) vi dormir demais, acordar tarde (Port).

overt [ˈəʊvɜːt, əʊˈvɜːt] adj manifesto(-ta), notório(-ria).

overtake [ˌəʊvəˈteɪk] (pt -took, pp -taken) vt & vi ultrapassar; "no overtaking" "proibido ultrapassar".

overthrow [vb ˌəʊvəˈθrəʊ, n ˈəʊvəθrəʊ] (pt -threw, pp -thrown) n (of government) derrube m (Port), derrubada f (Br) ♦ vt (government, president) derrubar.

overtime [ˈəʊvətaɪm] n horas fpl extraordinárias.

overtones [ˈəʊvətəʊnz] npl (of anger, jealousy) ponta f; (political) implicações fpl.

overtook [ˌəʊvəˈtʊk] pt → overtake.

overture [ˈəʊvəˌtjʊər] n (MUS) abertura f.

overturn [ˌəʊvəˈtɜːn] vi (boat) virar; (car) capotar.

overweight [ˌəʊvəˈweɪt] adj gordo (-da).

overwhelm [ˌəʊvəˈwelm] vt: I was ~ed with joy fiquei feliz da vida.

overwhelming [ˌəʊvəˈwelmɪŋ] adj (feeling, quality) tremendo(-da); (victory, defeat, majority) esmagador(-ra).

overwork [ˌəʊvəˈwɜːk] vt (staff, per-

son) sobrecarregar (com trabalho).
owe [əʊ] *vt* dever; **to ~ sb sthg** dever algo a alguém; **owing to** devido a.
owl [aʊl] *n* mocho *m*, coruja *f*.
own [əʊn] *adj* próprio(-pria) ◆ *vt* possuir, ter ◆ *pron*: **my ~** o meu (a minha); **a house of my ~** uma casa só minha; **on my ~** sozinho(-nha); **to get one's ~ back** vingar-se.
❑ **own up** *vi*: **to ~ up (to sthg)** confessar (algo), admitir (algo).
owner [ˈəʊnər] *n* proprietário *m* (-ria *f*), dono *m* (-na *f*).
ownership [ˈəʊnəʃɪp] *n* posse *f*.

ox [ɒks] (*pl* **oxen**) *n* boi *m*.
Oxbridge [ˈɒksbrɪdʒ] *n as Universidades de Oxford e Cambridge*.
oxen [ˈɒksn] *pl* → **ox**.
oxtail soup [ˈɒksteɪl-] *n* sopa *f* de rabo de boi.
oxygen [ˈɒksɪdʒən] *n* oxigênio *m*.
oyster [ˈɔɪstər] *n* ostra *f*.
oz *abbr* = **ounce**.
ozone [ˈəʊzəʊn] *n* ozônio *m*.
ozone-friendly *adj* que não danifica a camada de ozônio.
ozone layer *n* camada *f* de ozônio.

P

p *abbr* = **penny, pence**; *(abbr of page)* pág.

pa [pɑː] *n (inf)* pai *m*.

PA *abbr (Brit)* = **personal assistant, public address system**.

pace [peɪs] *n (speed)* ritmo *m*; *(step)* passo *m*.

pacemaker [ˈpeɪsˌmeɪkəʳ] *n (for heart)* marcapasso *m (Br)*, pacemaker *m (Port)*.

Pacific [pəˈsɪfɪk] *n*: **the ~ (Ocean)** o (Oceano) Pacífico.

pacifier [ˈpæsɪfaɪəʳ] *n (Am: for baby)* chupeta *f*, chucha *f (Port)*.

pacifist [ˈpæsɪfɪst] *n* pacifista *mf*.

pack [pæk] *n (packet)* pacote *m*; *(of cigarettes)* maço *m*; *(Brit: of cards)* baralho *m*; *(rucksack)* mochila *f* ♦ *vt (suitcase, bag)* fazer; *(clothes, camera etc)* colocar na mala; *(to package)* empacotar ♦ *vi (for journey)* fazer as malas; **a ~ of lies** um monte de mentiras; **to ~ sthg into sthg** colocar algo em algo; **to ~ one's bags** fazer as malas.
❏ **pack up** *vi (pack suitcase)* fazer as malas; *(tidy up)* arrumar; *(Brit: inf: machine, car)* parar.

package [ˈpækɪdʒ] *n* pacote *m* ♦ *vt* empacotar.

package deal *n* acordo *m* global, acordo ou oferta cujas condições têm de ser todas respeitadas e aceitas.

package holiday *n* férias *fpl* com tudo incluído.

package tour *n* excursão *f* organizada.

packaging [ˈpækɪdʒɪŋ] *n (material)* embalagem *f*.

packed [pækt] *adj (crowded)* cheio (cheia).

packed lunch *n* almoço *m (que se leva de casa para a escola ou para o trabalho)*.

packet [ˈpækɪt] *n* pacote *m*; **it cost a ~** *(Brit: inf)* custou um dinheirão.

packing [ˈpækɪŋ] *n (material)* embalagem *f*; **to do one's ~** fazer as malas.

pact [pækt] *n* pacto *m*.

pad [pæd] *n (of paper)* bloco *m*; *(of cotton wool)* disco *m*; *(of cloth)* almofada *f*; **elbow ~** cotoveleira *f*; **knee ~** joelheira *f*; **shin ~** caneleira *f*.

padded [ˈpædɪd] *adj (jacket)* acolchoado(-da); *(seat)* almofadado(-da).

padded envelope *n* envelope *m* almofadado.

padding [ˈpædɪŋ] *n (material)* forro *m*.

paddle [ˈpædl] *n (pole)* remo *m (pequeno)* ♦ *vi (wade)* chapinhar, patinhar; *(in canoe)* remar.

paddle boat *n* barco *m* a vapor *(com rodas propulsoras)*.

paddle steamer *n* barco *m* a vapor *(com rodas propulsoras)*.

paddling pool [ˈpædlɪŋ-] *n* piscina *f* para crianças.

paddock [ˈpædək] *n (at racecourse)* paddock *m*, recinto nos hipódromos para onde são levados os cavalos antes das corridas.

paddy field [ˈpædɪ-] *n* arrozal *m*.

padlock [ˈpædlɒk] *n* cadeado *m*.

pagan [ˈpeɪgən] *adj* pagão(-gã) ♦ *n* pagão *m (-gã f)*.

page [peɪdʒ] *n* página *f* ♦ *vt* chamar; **"paging Mr Hill"** "chamando o Sr. Hill".

paid [peɪd] *pt & pp* → **pay** ♦ *adj* pago(-ga).

pain [peɪn] *n* dor *f*; **to be in ~** estar com dores; **he's such a ~!** *(inf)* ele é um saco!
❏ **pains** *npl (trouble)* esforço *m*, trabalho *m*.

pained [peɪnd] *adj* angustiado(-da).

painful [ˈpeɪnfʊl] *adj* doloroso(-osa).

painfully [ˈpeɪnfʊlɪ] *adv (distressingly)*

penosamente; *(for emphasis)* extremamente.

painkiller [ˈpeɪnˌkɪləʳ] *n* analgésico *m*.

painless [ˈpeɪnlɪs] *adj (operation, death)* indolor; *(unproblematic)* fácil.

painstaking [ˈpeɪnzˌteɪkɪŋ] *adj (worker)* meticuloso(-osa); *(attention, detail, care)* extremo(-ma).

paint [peɪnt] *n* tinta *f* ♦ *vt & vi* pintar; **to ~ one's nails** pintar as unhas.

⌐ **paints** *npl (tubes, pots etc)* tintas *fpl*.

paintbrush [ˈpeɪntbrʌʃ] *n (of decorator)* broxa *f*; *(of artist)* pincel.

painter [ˈpeɪntəʳ] *n* pintor *m* (-ra *f*).

painting [ˈpeɪntɪŋ] *n (activity)* pintura *f*; *(picture)* quadro *m*.

paint stripper [-ˈstrɪpəʳ] *n* removedor *m* de tinta.

paintwork [ˈpeɪntwɜːk] *n* pintura *f*.

pair [peəʳ] *n (of two things)* par *m*; **in ~s** aos pares; **a ~ of pliers** um alicate; **a ~ of scissors** uma tesoura; **a ~ of shorts** um calção *(Br)*, uns calções *(Port)*; **a ~ of tights** uma meia-calça *(Br)*, uns collants *(Port)*; **a ~ of trousers** uma calça *(Br)*, um par de calças *(Port)*.

pajamas [pəˈdʒuːməz] *(Am)* = **pyjamas**.

Pakistan [*Brit* ˌpɑːkɪˈstɑːn, *Am* ˌpækɪˈstæn] *n* Paquistão *m*.

Pakistani [*Brit* ˌpɑːkɪˈstɑːnɪ, *Am* ˌpækɪˈstænɪ] *adj* paquistanês(-esa) ♦ *n (person)* paquistanês *m* (-esa *f*).

pakora [pəˈkɔːrə] *npl* especialidade indiana feita com legumes fritos numa massa mole picante, servido como entrada com molhos picantes.

pal [pæl] *n (inf)* amigo *m* (-ga *f*).

palace [ˈpælɪs] *n* palácio *m*.

palatable [ˈpælətəbl] *adj* saboroso(-osa).

palate [ˈpælət] *n* paladar *m*.

pale [peɪl] *adj* pálido(-da).

pale ale *n* cerveja *f (clara e fraca)*.

Palestine [ˈpæləˌstaɪn] *n* Palestina *f*.

Palestinian [ˌpæləˈstɪnɪən] *adj* palestiniano(-na), palestino(-na) ♦ *n (person)* palestiniano *m* (-na *f*), palestino *m* (-na *f*).

palette [ˈpælət] *n* paleta *f*.

palm [pɑːm] *n (of hand)* palma *f*; **~ (tree)** palmeira *f*.

Palm Sunday *n* Domingo *m* de Ramos.

palpitations [ˌpælpɪˈteɪʃnz] *npl* palpitações *fpl*.

paltry [ˈpɔːltrɪ] *adj* mísero(-ra).

pamper [ˈpæmpəʳ] *vt* mimar.

pamphlet [ˈpæmflɪt] *n* folheto *m*.

pan [pæn] *n* panela *f*, tacho *m (Port)*.

pancake [ˈpænkeɪk] *n* panqueca *f*.

Pancake Day *n (Brit)* = terça-feira *f* de Carnaval, Dia *m* de Entrudo *(Port)*.

pancake roll *n* crepe *m* chinês.

panda [ˈpændə] *n* panda *m*.

panda car *n (Brit)* carro *m* da polícia.

pandemonium [ˌpændɪˈməʊnjəm] *n* pandemônio *m*.

pander [ˈpændəʳ] *vi*: **to ~ to sb's every whim** fazer todas as vontades a alguém; **the tabloid press ~s to popular prejudice** a imprensa sensacionalista gosta de alimentar os preconceitos dos seus leitores.

pane [peɪn] *n* vidro *m*, vidraça *f*.

panel [ˈpænl] *n (of wood)* painel *m*; *(group of experts)* equipe *f*; *(on TV, radio)* grupo *m* de convidados.

paneling [ˈpænəlɪŋ] *(Am)* = **panelling**.

panelling [ˈpænəlɪŋ] *n (Brit)* painéis *mpl*.

pang [pæŋ] *n* pontada *f*; **to feel ~s of guilt** ter a consciência pesada.

panic [ˈpænɪk] *(pt & pp* **-ked**, *cont* **-king)** *n* pânico *m* ♦ *vi* entrar em pânico.

panic-stricken [-ˈstrɪkn] *adj* apavorado(-da), tomado(-da) pelo pânico.

panniers [ˈpænɪəz] *npl (for bicycle)* bolsas *fpl* para bicicleta.

panorama [ˌpænəˈrɑːmə] *n* panorama *m*.

panoramic [ˌpænəˈræmɪk] *adj* panorâmico(-ca).

pansy [ˈpænzɪ] *n (flower)* amor-perfeito *m*.

pant [pænt] *vi* arfar, ofegar.

panther [ˈpænθəʳ] *n (pl inv OR* **-s)** *n* pantera *f*.

panties [ˈpæntɪz] *npl (inf)* calcinha *f (Br)*, cuecas *fpl (Port)*.

pantomime [ˈpæntəmaɪm] *n (Brit)* pantomima *f*.

pantry [ˈpæntrɪ] *n* despensa *f*.

pants [pænts] *npl (Brit: underwear)* cueca *f (Br)*, cuecas *fpl (Port)*; *(Am: trousers)* calça *f (Br)*, calças *fpl (Port)*.

panty hose [ˈpæntɪ-] *npl (Am)* meia-calça *f (Br)*, collants *mpl (Port)*.

papa [pəˈpɑː] *n* papá *m*.

papadum [ˈpæpədəm] *n tipo de bola-*

cha, tipicamente indiana, frita, fina e estaladiça.

paper ['peɪpəʳ] *n (material)* papel *m; (newspaper)* jornal *m; (exam)* prova *f; (at university)* exame *m,* frequência *f* ◆ *adj* de papel ◆ *vt* decorar (com papel de parede); **a piece of ~** *(sheet)* uma folha de papel; *(scrap)* um pedaço de papel.

 ◘ **papers** *npl (documents)* papéis *mpl,* documentos *mpl.*

paperback ['peɪpəbæk] *n* livro *m* brochado.

paper bag *n* saco *m* de papel.

paperboy ['peɪpəbɔɪ] *n* rapaz que distribui jornais de casa em casa.

paper clip *n* clipe *m.*

papergirl ['peɪpəgɜːl] *n* moça que distribui jornais de casa em casa.

paper handkerchief *n* lenço *m* de papel.

paper knife *n* corta-papéis *m inv.*

paper shop *n* ~ tabacaria *f,* ~ quiosque *m* de jornais.

paperweight ['peɪpəweɪt] *n* pesa-papéis *m inv.*

paperwork ['peɪpəwɜːk] *n* papelada *f,* burocracia *f*

paprika ['pæprɪkə] *n* colorau *m,* pimentão-doce *m.*

par [pɑːʳ] *n (in golf)* par *m.*

paracetamol [ˌpærəˈsiːtəmɒl] *n* paracetamol *m.*

parachute ['pærəʃuːt] *n* pára-quedas *m.*

parade [pəˈreɪd] *n (procession)* desfile *m; (of shops)* série *f* de pequenas lojas *(na mesma rua).*

paradise ['pærədaɪs] *n (fig)* paraíso *m.*

paradox ['pærədɒks] *n* paradoxo *m.*

paradoxically [ˌpærəˈdɒksɪklɪ] *adv* paradoxalmente.

paraffin ['pærəfɪn] *n* parafina *f.*

paragraph ['pærəgrɑːf] *n* parágrafo *m.*

parallel ['pærəlel] *adj:* ~ **(to)** *(lines)* paralelo(-la) (a).

paralysed ['pærəlaɪzd] *adj (Brit)* paralisado(-da), paralítico(-ca).

paralysis [pəˈrælɪsɪs] *(pl* **-lyses** [-lɪsiːz]*) n* paralisia *f.*

paralyzed ['pærəlaɪzd] *(Am)* = **paralysed.**

paramedic [ˌpærəˈmedɪk] *n* paramédico *m (-ca f).*

paramount ['pærəmaʊnt] *adj* fundamental, vital; **of ~ importance** extre-

mamente importante, vital.

paranoid ['pærənɔɪd] *adj* paranóico(-ca).

parasite ['pærəsaɪt] *n* parasita *m.*

parasol ['pærəsɒl] *n (above table)* guarda-sol *m (Br),* chapéu-de-sol *m (Port); (on beach)* barraca *f* de praia *(Br),* chapéu *m* de praia *(Port); (hand-held)* sombrinha *f.*

parcel ['pɑːsl] *n* embrulho *m.*

parcel post *n* serviço *m* de encomendas postais.

parched [pɑːtʃt] *adj (very dry)* ressecado(-da); **I'm ~** *(inf: very thirsty)* tenho a garganta ressecada, estou morto de sede.

parchment ['pɑːtʃmənt] *n* pergaminho *m.*

pardon ['pɑːdn] *excl:* ~**?** desculpe?, como?; ~ **(me)!** perdão!; **I beg your ~!** *(apologizing)* peço desculpa!; **I beg your ~?** *(asking for repetition)* desculpe?, como?

parent ['peərənt] *n (father)* pai *m; (mother)* mãe *f;* **my ~s** os meus pais.

Paris ['pærɪs] *n* Paris *s.*

parish ['pærɪʃ] *n (of church)* paróquia *f; (village area)* = freguesia *f.*

park [pɑːk] *n* parque *m* ◆ *vt & vi (vehicle)* estacionar.

park and ride *n* sistema que consiste em estacionar o carro nos arredores da cidade e apanhar o ônibus para o centro.

parking ['pɑːkɪŋ] *n* estacionamento *m.*

parking brake *n (Am)* freio *m* de mão *(Br),* travão de mão *(Port).*

parking lot *n (Am)* (parque *m* de) estacionamento *m.*

parking meter *n* parquímetro *m.*

parking space *n* espaço *m* OR lugar *m* para estacionar.

parking ticket *n* multa *f* (por estacionar em lugar proibido).

parliament ['pɑːləmənt] *n* parlamento *m.*

parliamentary [ˌpɑːləˈmentərɪ] *adj* parlamentar.

Parmesan (cheese) [pɑːmɪˈzæn-] *n* (queijo) parmesão *m.*

parody ['pærədɪ] *n* paródia *f* ◆ *vt* parodiar.

parole [pəˈrəʊl] *n* liberdade *f* condicional; **on ~** em liberdade condicional.

parrot ['pærət] *n* papagaio *m.*

parry ['pærɪ] *vt (blow)* esquivar-se de.

parsley ['pɑːslɪ] *n* salsa *f*.

parsnip ['pɑːsnɪp] *n* cherivia *f*, cenoura *f* branca.

parson ['pɑːsn] *n* vigário *m*, pároco *m*.

part [pɑːt] *n* (*portion*) parte *f*; (*of machine, car*) peça *f*; (*in play, film*) papel *m*, parte; (*of serial*) episódio *m*; (*Am: in hair*) risco *m* ♦ *adv* em parte, parcialmente ♦ *vi* (*couple*) separar-se; **in this ~ of Portugal** nesta parte de Portugal; **to form ~ of** fazer parte de; **to play a ~ in** desempenhar um papel em; **to take ~ in** tomar parte em; **for my ~** quanto a mim; **for the most ~** geralmente, em geral; **in these ~s** por aqui, por estas partes.

part exchange *n* troca *f*, *sistema que consiste em comprar algo novo dando como parte do pagamento algo usado*; **in ~** em troca.

partial ['pɑːʃl] *adj* (*not whole*) parcial; **to be ~ to sthg** ter uma certa predileção por algo.

participant [pɑːˈtɪsɪpənt] *n* participante *mf*.

participate [pɑːˈtɪsɪpeɪt] *vi*: **to ~ (in)** participar (em).

participation [pɑːˌtɪsɪˈpeɪʃn] *n* participação *f*.

participle ['pɑːtɪsɪpl] *n* particípio *m*.

particle ['pɑːtɪkl] *n* partícula *f*.

particular [pəˈtɪkjʊləʳ] *adj* especial; (*fussy*) esquisito(-ta); **in ~** em particular; **nothing in ~** nada de especial.

◨ **particulars** *npl* (*details*) pormenores *mpl*, detalhes *mpl*.

particularly [pəˈtɪkjʊləlɪ] *adv* especialmente.

parting ['pɑːtɪŋ] *n* (*Brit: in hair*) repartido *m* (*Br*), risco *m* (*Port*).

partition [pɑːˈtɪʃn] *n* (*wall*) tabique *m*.

partly ['pɑːtlɪ] *adv* em parte.

partner ['pɑːtnəʳ] *n* (*husband, wife*) cônjuge *mf*; (*lover*) companheiro *m* (-ra *f*); (*in game, dance*) parceiro *m* (-ra *f*); (*COMM*) sócio *m* (-cia *f*).

partnership ['pɑːtnəʃɪp] *n* sociedade *f*.

partridge ['pɑːtrɪdʒ] *n* perdiz *f*.

part-time *adj & adv* part-time, em meio expediente.

party ['pɑːtɪ] *n* (*for fun*) festa *f*; (*POL*) partido *m*; (*group of people*) grupo *m*; **to have a ~** dar uma festa.

pass [pɑːs] *vt* passar; (*move past*) passar por; (*law*) aprovar ♦ *vi* passar ♦ *n* (*SPORT, document*) passe *m*; (*in mountain*) desfiladeiro *m*, garganta *f*; (*in exam*) suficiente *m*, médio *m*; **to ~ sb sthg** passar algo a alguém.

◨ **pass by** *vt fus* (*building, window etc*) passar por ♦ *vi* passar.

◨ **pass on** *vt sep* (*message*) transmitir.

◨ **pass out** *vi* (*faint*) desmaiar.

◨ **pass up** *vt sep* (*opportunity*) deixar passar.

passable ['pɑːsəbl] *adj* (*road*) transitável; (*satisfactory*) aceitável, satisfatório(-ria).

passage ['pæsɪdʒ] *n* (*corridor*) passagem *f*, corredor *m*; (*in book*) passagem *f*, trecho *m*; (*sea journey*) travessia *f*.

passageway ['pæsɪdʒweɪ] *n* passagem *f*, corredor *m*.

passbook ['pɑːsbʊk] *n* caderneta *f*.

passenger ['pæsɪndʒəʳ] *n* passageiro *m* (-ra *f*).

passerby [pɑːsəˈbaɪ] *n* transeunte *mf*, passante *mf*.

passing ['pɑːsɪŋ] *adj* (*trend*) passageiro(-ra); (*remark*) de passagem.

◨ **in passing** *adv* por alto, de passagem.

passing place ['pɑːsɪŋ-] *n* (*for cars*) zona *f* para ultrapassagem.

passion ['pæʃn] *n* paixão *f*.

passionate ['pæʃənət] *adj* (*showing strong feeling*) apaixonado(-da); (*sexually*) ardente.

passive ['pæsɪv] *n* passiva *f*.

Passover ['pɑːsˌəʊvəʳ] *n*: **(the) ~** a Páscoa dos judeus.

passport ['pɑːspɔːt] *n* passaporte *m*.

passport control *n* controle *m* de passaportes.

passport photo *n* fotografia *f* para passaporte.

password ['pɑːswɜːd] *n* senha *f*.

past [pɑːst] *adj* passado(-da); (*former*) antigo(-ga) ♦ *prep* (*further than*) depois de; (*in front of*) em frente de ♦ *n* (*former time*) passado *m* ♦ *adv*: **to go ~** passar; **the ~ month** o mês passado; **twenty ~ four** quatro e vinte; **the ~ (tense)** (*GRAMM*) o passado; **in the ~** no passado.

pasta ['pæstə] *n* massa *f*.

paste [peɪst] *n* (*spread*) pasta *f*; (*glue*) cola *f*.

pastel ['pæstl] *n* (*for drawing*) pastel *m*; (*colour*) tom *m* pastel.

pasteurized ['pɑːstʃəraɪzd] *adj* pasteurizado(-da).

pastille ['pæstɪl] *n* pastilha *f*.

pastime ['pɑːstaɪm] *n* passatempo *m*.

past participle *n* particípio *m* passado.

pastrami [pəs'trɑːmɪ] *n* carne de vaca defumada e picante.

pastry ['peɪstrɪ] *n (for pie)* massa *f*; *(cake)* pastel *m*.

pasture ['pɑːstʃəˀ] *n* pasto *m*, pastagem *f*.

pasty ['pæstɪ] *n (Brit)* empada *f*.

pat [pæt] *vt (dog, friend)* dar um tapinha (afetuosa) em.

patch [pætʃ] *n (for clothes)* remendo *m*; *(of colour, damp)* mancha *f*; *(for skin)* esparadrapo *m (Br)*, penso *m (Port)*; *(for eye)* pala *f*, penso; **a bad ~** *(fig)* um mau bocado.

patchwork ['pætʃwɜːk] *n (of fields)* colcha *f* de retalhos.

patchy ['pætʃɪ] *adj (uneven)* irregular; *(incomplete)* incompleto(-ta); *(performance, game)* com altos e baixos.

pâté ['pæteɪ] *n* pasta *f*, paté *m*.

patent [*Brit* 'peɪtənt, *Am* 'pætənt] *n* patente *f*.

patent leather *n* verniz *m (cabedal)*.

paternal [pə'tɜːnl] *adj* paternal.

path [pɑːθ] *n* caminho *m*.

pathetic [pə'θetɪk] *adj (pej: useless)* inútil.

pathological [ˌpæθə'lɒdʒɪkl] *adj* patológico(-ca).

pathway ['pɑːθweɪ] *n* caminho *m*.

patience ['peɪʃns] *n* paciência *f*.

patient ['peɪʃnt] *adj* paciente ◆ *n* doente *mf*, paciente *mf*.

patio ['pætɪəʊ] *(pl -s)* *n* pátio *m*.

patriotic [*Brit* ˌpætrɪ'ɒtɪk, *Am* ˌpeɪtrɪ'ɒtɪk] *adj* patriótico(-ca).

patrol [pə'trəʊl] *vt* patrulhar ◆ *n (group)* patrulha *f*.

patrol car *n* carro *m* de patrulha.

patron ['peɪtrən] *n (fml: customer)* cliente *mf*; **"~s only"** "só para clientes".

patronizing ['pætrənaɪzɪŋ] *adj* condescendente.

patter ['pætəˀ] *n (of raindrops)* tamborilar *m*.

pattern ['pætn] *n (of shapes, colours)* desenho *m*, padrão *m*; *(for sewing)* molde *m*.

patterned ['pætənd] *adj* estampado(-da).

paunch [pɔːntʃ] *n* pança *f*.

pause [pɔːz] *n* pausa *f* ◆ *vi* fazer uma pausa.

pave [peɪv] *vt (with concrete, tarmac)* pavimentar; *(with stones)* calçar; **to ~ the way for** preparar o caminho para.

pavement ['peɪvmənt] *n (Brit: beside road)* calçada *f (Br)*, passeio *m (Port)*; *(Am: roadway)* pavimento *m*, asfalto *m*.

pavilion [pə'vɪljən] *n* pavilhão *m*.

paving ['peɪvɪŋ] *n* calçamento *m*, pavimentação *f*.

paving stone *n* laje *f*.

pavlova [pæv'ləʊvə] *n* bolo feito de camadas de suspiro, creme batido e fruta.

paw [pɔː] *n* pata *f*.

pawn [pɔːn] *vt* empenhar ◆ *n (in chess)* peão *m*.

pawnbroker ['pɔːnˌbrəʊkəˀ] *n* penhorista *mf*.

pawnshop ['pɔːnʃɒp] *n* casa *f* de penhor.

pay [peɪ] *(pt & pp paid)* *vt* pagar; *(person)* pagar a ◆ *vi (give money)* pagar; *(be profitable)* compensar, dar lucro ◆ *n* ordenado *m*, salário *m*; **to ~ sb for sthg** pagar a alguém (por) algo; **to ~ money into an account** depositar dinheiro numa conta; **to ~ attention (to)** prestar atenção (a); **to ~ sb a visit** visitar alguém, fazer uma visita a alguém; **to ~ by credit card** pagar com cartão de crédito.

❏ **pay back** *vt sep (money)* pagar; *(person)* pagar, devolver o dinheiro a.

❏ **pay for** *vt fus (purchase)* pagar (por).

❏ **pay in** *vt sep (cheque, money)* depositar.

❏ **pay out** *vt sep (money)* pagar.

❏ **pay up** *vi* pagar.

payable ['peɪəbl] *adj (bill)* pagável; **~ to** *(cheque)* em nome de, a ordem de.

payday ['peɪdeɪ] *n* dia *f* de pagamento.

payment ['peɪmənt] *n* pagamento *m*.

pay packet *n (Brit: wages)* pagamento *m*.

payphone ['peɪfəʊn] *n* telefone *m* público.

payroll ['peɪrəʊl] *n* folha *f* de pagamentos.

payslip ['peɪslɪp] *n (Brit)* recibo *m* de pagamento, contracheque *m*.

paystub ['peɪstʌb] *(Am)* = **payslip**.

PC *n (abbr of personal computer)* PC *m*; *(Brit: abbr of police constable)* policial *mf*

(Br), = polícia *mf (Port)*.
PE *abbr* = **physical education**.
pea [pi:] *n* ervilha *f*.
peace [pi:s] *n* paz *f*; **to leave sb in ~** deixar alguém em paz; **~ and quiet** paz e sossego.
peaceful ['pi:sful] *adj (place, day, feeling)* calmo(-ma); *(demonstration)* pacífico(-ca).
peacetime ['pi:staim] *n* tempo *m* de paz.
peach [pi:tʃ] *n* pêssego *m*.
peach melba [-'melbə] *n* peach melba *m*, pedaços de pêssego, cobertos com sorvete de baunilha e regados com molho de framboesa.
peacock ['pi:kɒk] *n* pavão *m*.
peak [pi:k] *n (of mountain)* pico *m*; *(of hat)* pala *f*; *(fig: highest point)* auge *m*.
peaked [pi:kt] *adj* com pala.
peak hours *npl* rush *m (Br)*, horas *fpl* de ponta *(Port)*.
peak rate *n* tarifa *f* alta.
peal [pi:l] *n (of bells)* repicar *m*; *(of thunder)* ribombar *m* ♦ *vi (bells)* repicar; **~ of laughter** gargalhadas *fpl*.
peanut ['pi:nʌt] *n* amendoim *m*.
peanut butter *n* manteiga *f* de amendoim.
pear [peər] *n* pêra *f*.
pearl [pɜ:l] *n* pérola *f*.
peasant ['peznt] *n* camponês *m* (-esa *f*).
peat [pi:t] *n* turfa *f*.
pebble ['pebl] *n* seixo *m*.
pecan pie ['pi:kæn-] *n* torta *f* de noz-americana.
peck [pek] *vi (bird)* bicar.
peckish ['pekiʃ] *adj (Brit: inf)*: **I'm feeling ~** bem que eu comeria alguma coisa.
peculiar [pɪ'kju:ljər] *adj (strange)* esquisito(-ta); **to be ~ to** *(exclusive)* ser característico de.
peculiarity [pɪˌkju:lɪ'ærətɪ] *n (special feature)* característica *f*.
pedal ['pedl] *n* pedal *m* ♦ *vi* pedalar.
pedal bin *n* lata *f* de lixo (com pedal).
pedalo ['pedələu] *(pl -s OR -es) n* gaivota *f*.
pedantic [pɪ'dæntɪk] *adj* rigoroso(-osa), picuinhas *(inv)*.
peddle ['pedl] *vt (drugs)* traficar; *(wares)* vender de porta em porta; *(rumour, gossip)* espalhar.

peddler ['pedlər] *(Am)* = **pedlar**.
pedestal ['pedɪstl] *n* pedestal *m*.
pedestrian [pɪ'destrɪən] *n* pedestre *m (Br)*, peão *m (Port)*.
pedestrian crossing *n* passagem *f* para pedestres *(Br)*, passadeira *f* (para peões) *(Port)*.
pedestrianized [pɪ'destrɪənaɪzd] *adj* para pedestre *(Br)*, pedonal *(Port)*.
pedestrian precinct *n (Brit)* zona *f* para pedestre.
pedestrian zone *(Am)* = **pedestrian precinct**.
pedigree ['pedɪgri:] *adj* de raça ♦ *n (of animal)* raça *f*.
pedlar ['pedlər] *n (Brit)* vendedor *m* (-ra *f*) ambulante.
pee [pi:] *vi (inf)* mijar ♦ *n*: **to have a ~** *(inf)* fazer chichi.
peek [pi:k] *vi (inf)* espiar, espreitar ♦ *n (inf)*: **to take** OR **have a ~ at sthg** dar uma espiadela em algo.
peel [pi:l] *n* casca *f* ♦ *vt* descascar ♦ *vi* cair.
peelings ['pi:lɪŋz] *npl* cascas *fpl*.
peep [pi:p] *n*: **to have a ~** dar uma espiadela.
peer [pɪər] *vi* olhar com atenção; **to ~ at** olhar atentamente para.
peeved [pi:vd] *adj (inf)* fulo(-la), zangado(-da).
peevish ['pi:vɪʃ] *adj* rabugento(-ta).
peg [peg] *n (for tent)* estaca *f*; *(hook)* gancho *m*; *(for washing)* pregador *m (Br)*, mola *f* da roupa *(Port)*.
pejorative [pɪ'dʒɒrətɪv] *adj* pejorativo(-va).
pelican ['pelɪkən] *n* pelicano *m*.
pelican crossing *n (Brit)* travessia com sinais acionados manualmente pelos pedestres.
pellet ['pelɪt] *n (of mud, paper)* bolinha *f*; *(for gun)* chumbo *m*.
pelt [pelt] *n (animal skin)* pele *f* ♦ *vi (rain)* chover a cântaros ♦ *vt*: **to ~ sb with sthg** *(eggs, tomatoes)* atirar algo para alguém.
pelvis ['pelvɪs] *n* bacia *f*.
pen [pen] *n (ballpoint pen)* esferográfica *f*; *(fountain pen)* caneta *f* (de tinta permanente); *(for animals)* cerca *f*.
penalty ['penltɪ] *n (fine)* multa *f*; *(in football)* pênalti *m*, grande penalidade *f*.
penance ['penəns] *n* penitência *f*.

pence [pens] *npl* pence *mpl (moeda britânica)*; **it costs 20 ~** custa 20 pence.

penchant [*Brit* pũ∫ũ, *Am* 'pent∫ənt] *n*: **to have a ~ for** ter um fraco por; **to have a ~ for doing sthg** gostar de fazer algo.

pencil ['pensl] *n* lápis *m inv*.

pencil case *n* lapiseira *f (Br)*, porta-lápis *m inv (Port)*.

pencil sharpener *n* apontador *m (Br)*, apara-lápis *m inv (Port)*.

pendant ['pendənt] *n (on necklace)* pingente *m*.

pending ['pendıŋ] *prep (fml)* até.

pendulum ['pendjuləm] *n* pêndulo *m*.

penetrate ['penıtreıt] *vt* penetrar.

penfriend ['penfrend] *n* penfriend *mf*, correspondente *mf*.

penguin ['peŋgwın] *n* pinguim *m*.

penicillin [‚penı'sılın] *n* penicilina *f*.

peninsula [pə'nınsjulə] *n* península *f*.

penis ['pi:nıs] *n* pênis *m inv*.

penknife ['pennaıf] *(pl* **-knives** [-naıvz]*) n* canivete *m*, navalha *f*.

pennant ['penənt] *n* galhardete *m*.

penniless ['penılıs] *adj* sem um tostão.

penny ['penı] *(pl* **pennies**) *n (coin in UK)* péni *m (moeda britânica); (coin in US)* centavo *m (Br)*, cêntimo *m (Port)*.

pen pal *n (inf)* correspondente *mf*.

pension ['pen∫n] *n (for retired people)* aposentadoria *f (Br)*, reforma *f (Port); (for disabled people)* pensão *f*.

pensioner ['pen∫ənər] *n* aposentado *m* (-da *f*) *(Br)*, reformado *m* (-da *f*) *(Port)*.

pensive ['pensıv] *adj* pensativo(-va).

Pentecost ['pentıkɒst] *n* Pentecostes *m*.

penthouse ['penthaus, *pl* -hauzız] *n* cobertura *f*, apartamento de luxo situado no último andar de um edifício.

penultimate [pe'nʌltımət] *adj* penúltimo(-ma).

people ['pi:pl] *npl* pessoas *fpl* ♦ *n (nation)* povo *m*; **the ~** *(citizens)* o povo.

pepper ['pepər] *n (spice)* pimenta *f*; *(vegetable)* pimentão *m (Br)*, pimento *m (Port)*.

peppercorn ['pepəkɔ:n] *n* grão *m* de pimenta.

peppermint ['pepəmınt] *adj* de hortelã-pimenta ♦ *n (sweet)* bala *m* de hortelã-pimenta.

pepper pot *n* pimenteiro *m*.

pepper steak *n* bife *m* au poivre.

Pepsi® ['pepsı] *n* Pepsi® *f*.

per [pɜːr] *prep* por; **~ person/week** por pessoa/semana; **£20 ~ night** 20 libras por noite.

per annum [pər'ænəm] *adv* por ano.

perceive [pə'siːv] *vt* notar.

per cent *adv* por cento.

percentage [pə'sentıdʒ] *n* percentagem *f*.

perception [pə'sep∫n] *n (of colour, sound, time)* percepção *f*; *(insight, understanding)* perspicácia *f*.

perceptive [pə'septıv] *adj* perspicaz.

perch [pɜːt∫] *n (for bird)* poleiro *m*.

percolator ['pɜːkəleıtər] *n* cafeteira *f* de filtro.

percussion [pə'kʌ∫n] *n* percussão *f*.

perennial [pə'renjəl] *adj (problem, feature)* permanente.

perfect [*adj & n* 'pɜːfıkt, *vb* pə'fekt] *adj* perfeito(-ta) ♦ *vt* aperfeiçoar ♦ *n*: **the ~** *(tense)* o perfeito; **the past ~** *(tense)* o pretérito mais-que-perfeito composto.

perfection [pə'fek∫n] *n*: **to do sthg to ~** fazer algo na perfeição.

perfectionist [pə'fek∫ənıst] *n* perfeccionista *mf*.

perfectly ['pɜːfıktlı] *adv (very well)* perfeitamente.

perforate ['pɜːfəreıt] *vt* perfurar.

perforations [‚pɜːfə'reı∫nz] *npl* picotado *m*.

perform [pə'fɔːm] *vt (task, operation)* realizar; *(play)* representar; *(concert)* dar; *(dance, piece of music)* executar ♦ *vi (actor, singer)* atuar.

performance [pə'fɔːməns] *n (of play)* representação *f*; *(of concert)* interpretação *f*; *(of film)* exibição *f*; *(by actor, musician)* atuação *f*; *(of car)* performance *f*.

performer [pə'fɔːmər] *n* artista *mf*.

perfume ['pɜːfjuːm] *n* perfume *m*.

perhaps [pə'hæps] *adv* talvez.

peril ['perıl] *n* perigo *m*.

perimeter [pə'rımıtər] *n* perímetro *m*.

period ['pıərıəd] *n* período *m*; *(Am: full stop)* ponto *m (final)* ♦ *adj (costume, furniture)* da época.

periodic [‚pıərı'ɒdık] *adj* periódico (-ca).

period pains *npl* dores *fpl* menstruais.

peripheral [pə'rıfərəl] *adj (vision, region)* periférico(-ca).

periphery [pə'rıfərı] *n* periferia *f*.

perish ['perıʃ] *vi (die)* morrer; *(decay)* deteriorar-se, estragar-se.

perishable ['perıʃəbl] *adj* perecível.

perk [pɜːk] *n* benefícios extras oferecidos pelo emprego, regalia *f (Port)*.

perm [pɜːm] *n* permanente *f* ♦ *vt*: **to have one's hair ~ed** fazer uma permanente.

permanent ['pɜːmənənt] *adj* permanente.

permanent address *n* endereço *m* fixo.

permanently ['pɜːmənəntlı] *adv* permanentemente.

permeate ['pɜːmıeıt] *vt* infiltrar-se em.

permissible [pə'mısəbl] *adj (fml)* permissível.

permission [pə'mıʃn] *n* permissão *f*.

permissive [pə'mısıv] *adj* permissivo(-va).

permit [*vb* pə'mıt. *n* 'pɜːmıt] *vt* permitir ♦ *n* autorização *f*; **to ~ sb to do sthg** permitir a alguém fazer algo; **"~holders only"** *aviso indicando que no local só pode estacionar quem tiver uma autorização especial.*

pernickety [pə'nıkətı] *adj (inf)* cheio (cheia) de nove horas.

perpendicular [,pɜːpən'dıkjʊlə^r] *adj* perpendicular.

perpetual [pə'petʃʊəl] *adj* perpétuo (-tua).

perplexing [pə'pleksıŋ] *adj* desconcertante.

persecute ['pɜːsıkjuːt] *vt (oppress)* perseguir.

perseverance [,pɜːsı'vıərəns] *n* perseverança *f*.

persevere [,pɜːsı'vıə^r] *vi* perseverar, insistir.

persist [pə'sıst] *vi* persistir; **to ~ in doing sthg** persistir em fazer algo.

persistence [pə'sıstəns] *n* persistência *f*.

persistent [pə'sıstənt] *adj* persistente.

person ['pɜːsn] *(pl* **people**) *n* pessoa *f*; **in ~** em pessoa.

personal ['pɜːsənl] *adj* pessoal; **a ~ friend** um amigo íntimo.

personal assistant *n* assistente *mf* pessoal.

personal belongings *npl* objetos *mpl* pessoais.

personal computer *n* computador *m* pessoal.

personality [,pɜːsə'nælətı] *n* personalidade *f*.

personally ['pɜːsnəlı] *adv* pessoalmente.

personal organizer *n* agenda *f*.

personal property *n* bens *mpl* móveis.

personal stereo *n* Walkman® *m*.

personify [pə'sɒnıfaı] *vt* personificar.

personnel [,pɜːsə'nel] *npl* pessoal *m*.

perspective [pə'spektıv] *n* perspectiva *f*.

Perspex® ['pɜːspeks] *n (Brit)* Perspex® *m*.

perspiration [,pɜːspə'reıʃn] *n* transpiração *f*.

persuade [pə'sweıd] *vt*: **to ~ sb (to do sthg)** persuadir alguém (a fazer algo); **to ~ sb that ...** persuadir alguém de que ....

persuasion [pə'sweıʒn] *n (act of persuading)* persuasão *f*; *(belief)* afinidade *f*.

persuasive [pə'sweısıv] *adj* persuasivo(-va).

pert [pɜːt] *adj (person, reply)* atrevido(-da), descarado(-da).

pertinent ['pɜːtınənt] *adj* pertinente.

perturb [pə'tɜːb] *vt* perturbar.

peruse [pə'ruːz] *vt (read thoroughly)* examinar; *(read quickly)* passar uma vista de olhos por.

perverse [pə'vɜːs] *adj (delight, enjoyment)* perverso(-sa); *(contrary)* difícil.

pervert ['pɜːvɜːt] *n* tarado *m* (-da *f*).

pessimist ['pesımıst] *n* pessimista *mf*.

pessimistic [,pesı'mıstık] *adj* pessimista.

pest [pest] *n (insect, animal)* praga *f*, inseto *m* nocivo; *(inf: person)* peste *f*.

pester ['pestə^r] *vt* importunar.

pesticide ['pestısaıd] *n* pesticida *m*.

pet [pet] *n* animal *m* doméstico; **the teacher's ~** o queridinho do professor.

petal ['petl] *n* pétala *f*.

peter ['piːtə^r] : **peter out** *vi (supplies, interest)* esgotar-se.

pet food *n* comida *f* para animais domésticos.

petition [pı'tıʃn] *n (letter)* petição *f*, abaixo-assinado *m*.

petits pois [ˌpəti'pwa] *npl* ervilhas *fpl*
(pequenas e tenras).
petrified ['petrɪfaɪd] *adj* petrificado
(-da).
petrol ['petrəl] *n (Brit)* gasolina *f.*
petrol bomb *n (Brit)* cocktail *m* OR
coquetel *m* Molotov.
petrol can *n (Brit)* lata *f* de gasolina.
petrol cap *n (Brit)* tampa *f* do tanque de gasolina.
petroleum [pɪ'trəʊljəm] *n* petróleo *m.*
petrol gauge *n (Brit)* indicador *m*
do nível de gasolina.
petrol pump *n (Brit)* bomba *f* de
gasolina.
petrol station *n (Brit)* posto *m* (de
gasolina) *(Br)*, estação *f* de serviço
(Port).
petrol tank *n (Brit)* depósito *m* da
gasolina.
pet shop *n* loja *f* de animais.
petticoat ['petɪkəʊt] *n* combinação *f.*
petty ['petɪ] *adj (pej) (person)* mes-
quinho(-nha); *(rule)* insignificante.
petty cash *n* fundo *m* para pequenas despesas.
petulant ['petjʊlənt] *adj* petulante.
pew [pjuː] *n* banco *m (de igreja)*.
pewter ['pjuːtər] *adj* de peltre.
PG *(abbr of parental guidance) abreviatura que indica que o filme não é aconselhável para menores de doze anos.*
phantom ['fæntəm] *n* fantasma *m,*
espectro *m.*
pharmacist ['fɑːməsɪst] *n* farmacêutico *m* (-ca *f*).
pharmacy ['fɑːməsɪ] *n (shop)* farmácia *f.*
phase [feɪz] *n* fase *f.*
PhD *n (degree)* = doutoramento *m.*
pheasant ['feznt] *n* faisão *m.*
phenomena [fɪ'nɒmɪnə] *pl* → phenomenon.
phenomenal [fɪ'nɒmɪnl] *adj* fenomenal.
phenomenon [fɪ'nɒmɪnən] *(pl
-mena) n* fenômeno *m.*
phial ['faɪəl] *n* ampola *f.*
philanthropist [fɪ'lænθrəpɪst] *n* fi-
lantropo *m* (-pa *f*).
philately [fɪ'lætəlɪ] *n* filatelia *f.*
Philippines ['fɪlɪpiːnz] *npl:* **the ~** as
Filipinas.
philosopher [fɪ'lɒsəfər] *n* filósofo *m*
(-fa *f*).

philosophical [ˌfɪlə'sɒfɪkl] *adj* filosó-
fico(-ca).
philosophy [fɪ'lɒsəfɪ] *n* filosofia *f.*
phlegm [flem] *n (in throat)* fleuma *f
(Br)*, catarro *m.*
phlegmatic [fleg'mætɪk] *adj* fleumáti-
co(-ca).
phobia ['fəʊbjə] *n* fobia *f.*
phone [fəʊn] *n* telefone *m* ♦ *vt (Brit)*
telefonar para, ligar para ♦ *vi (Brit)*
telefonar; **on the ~** *(talking)* no telefone; **we're not on the ~** *(connected)* não
temos telefone.
⏘ **phone up** *vt sep (Brit)* telefonar para,
ligar para ♦ *vi (Brit)* telefonar.
phone book *n* lista *f* telefônica.
phone booth *n* cabine *f* telefônica.
phone box *n (Brit)* cabine *f* telefônica, orelhão *m (Br)*.
phone call *n* chamada *f* telefônica,
telefonema *m.*
phonecard ['fəʊnkɑːd] *n* cartão *m*
telefônico, Credifone® *m (Port)*.
phone number *n* número *m* de
telefone.
phonetics [fə'netɪks] *n* fonética *f.*
photo ['fəʊtəʊ] *(pl -s) n* fotografia *f*;
to take a ~ of tirar uma fotografia de.
photo album *n* álbum *m* de fotografias.
photocopier [ˌfəʊtəʊ'kɒpɪər] *n* foto-
copiadora *f.*
photocopy ['fəʊtəʊˌkɒpɪ] *n* Xerox® *m
inv (Br)*, fotocópia *f* ♦ *vt* xerocar *(Br)*,
fotocopiar.
photograph ['fəʊtəgrɑːf] *n* fotografia
f ♦ *vt* fotografar.
photographer [fə'tɒgrəfər] *n* fotógrafo *m* (-fa *f*).
photography [fə'tɒgrəfɪ] *n* fotografia *f.*
phrasal verb ['freɪzl-] *n* verbo *m*
seguido de preposição.
phrase [freɪz] *n* expressão *f.*
phrasebook ['freɪzbʊk] *n* guia *m* de
conversação.
physical ['fɪzɪkl] *adj* físico(-ca) ♦ *n*
exame *m* médico de aptidão.
physical education *n* educação *f*
física.
physically ['fɪzɪklɪ] *adv* fisicamente.
physically handicapped *adj* deficiente físico(-ca).
physician [fɪ'zɪʃn] *n* médico *m* (-ca *f*).
physicist ['fɪzɪsɪst] *n* físico *m* (-ca *f*).

physics ['fɪzɪks] n física f.
physiotherapy [ˌfɪzɪəʊ'θerəpɪ] n
fisioterapia f.
physique [fɪ'ziːk] n físico m.
pianist ['pɪənɪst] n pianista mf.
piano [pɪ'ænəʊ] (pl -s) n piano m.
pick [pɪk] vt (select) escolher; (fruit,
flowers) apanhar, colher ◆ n (pickaxe)
picareta f; **to ~ a fight** procurar briga;
to ~ one's nose tirar meleca do nariz
(Br), tirar macacos do nariz (Port); **to
take one's ~** escolher à vontade.
❏ **pick on** vt fus implicar com.
❏ **pick out** vt sep (select) escolher; (see)
distinguir.
❏ **pick up** vt sep (lift up) pegar em;
(collect) ir buscar; (language) aprender;
(habit) apanhar; (bargain) conseguir;
(hitchhiker) dar uma carona a (Br), dar
boleia a (Port); (inf: woman, man)
paquerar (Br), engatar (Port) ◆ vi
(improve) recuperar; **to ~ up the phone**
(answer) atender o telefone.
pickaxe ['pɪkæks] n picareta f.
pickle ['pɪkl] n (Brit: food) pickle m;
(Am: pickled cucumber) pepino m de
conserva.
pickled onion ['pɪkld-] n cebola f em
conserva.
pickpocket ['pɪkˌpɒkɪt] n batedor m
(-ra f) de carteiras (Br), carteirista mf
(Port).
pick-up (truck) n camioneta f,
carrinha f (Port).
picnic ['pɪknɪk] n piquenique m.
picnic area n área f para piqueni-
ques.
picture ['pɪktʃəʳ] n (painting, drawing)
quadro m; (photograph) retrato m; (on
TV) imagem f; (film) filme m.
❏ **pictures** npl: **the ~s** (Brit) o cinema.
picture book n livro m ilustrado OR
de figuras.
picture frame n moldura f.
picturesque [ˌpɪktʃə'resk] adj pito-
resco(-ca).
pie [paɪ] n (savoury) empada f; (sweet)
torta f (Br), tarte f (Port).
piece [piːs] n (part, bit) pedaço m,
bocado m; (component, of clothing, of
music) peça f; (in chess) pedra f; **a 20p ~**
uma moeda de 20 pence; **a ~ of advice**
um conselho; **a ~ of furniture** um
móvel; **to fall to ~s** cair aos pedaços;
in one ~ (intact) inteiro, intacto; (unharmed) são e salvo.

piecemeal ['piːsmiːl] adj (fragmentary)
feito(-ta) aos poucos ◆ adv (little by little) aos poucos, por etapas.
pie chart n gráfico m de setores.
pier [pɪəʳ] n cais m.
pierce [pɪəs] vt furar; **to have one's
ears ~d** furar as orelhas.
piercing ['pɪəsɪŋ] adj (sound) estridente.
pig [pɪg] n porco m; (inf: greedy person)
alarde mf.
pigeon ['pɪdʒɪn] n pombo m.
pigeonhole ['pɪdʒɪnhəʊl] n escaninho
m.
piggybank ['pɪgɪbæŋk] n cofre m (Br),
mealheiro m (Port).
pigpen ['pɪgpen] (Am) = pigsty.
pigskin ['pɪgskɪn] adj de pele de
porco.
pigsty ['pɪgstaɪ] n chiqueiro m.
pigtails ['pɪgteɪlz] npl tranças fpl (Br),
puxos mpl (Port).
pike [paɪk] n (fish) lúcio m.
pilau rice ['pɪlaʊ-] n arroz à indiana
com várias cores, condimentado com diferentes especiarias orientais.
pilchard ['pɪltʃəd] n sardinha f grande.
pile [paɪl] n pilha f ◆ vt empilhar; **~s of**
(inf: a lot) montes de.
❏ **pile up** vt sep empilhar ◆ vi (accumulate) acumular-se.
piles [paɪlz] npl (MED) hemorróidas
fpl.
pileup ['paɪlʌp] n choque m em
cadeia.
pilfer ['pɪlfəʳ] vi roubar.
pilgrim ['pɪlgrɪm] n peregrino m (-na
f).
pilgrimage ['pɪlgrɪmɪdʒ] n peregrinação f.
pill [pɪl] n comprimido m; **to be on
the ~** (contraceptive) tomar a pílula.
pillar ['pɪləʳ] n pilar m.
pillar box n (Brit) caixa f do correio
(Br), marco m de correio (Port).
pillion ['pɪljən] n: **to ride ~** viajar no
banco traseiro (de uma motocicleta).
pillow ['pɪləʊ] n (for bed) travesseiro
m, almofada f; (Am: on chair, sofa)
almofada.
pillowcase ['pɪləʊkeɪs] n fronha f,
almofada f.
pilot ['paɪlət] n piloto m.
pilot light n piloto m.

pimp [pimp] *n (inf)* cafetão *m (Br)*, chulo *m (Port)*.

pimple ['pimpl] *n* borbulha *f*.

pin [pin] *n (for sewing)* alfinete *m; (drawing pin)* tachinha *f (Br)*, pionés *m (Port); (safety pin)* alfinete de segurança; *(Am: brooch)* broche *m; (Am: badge)* crachá *m*, pin *m ♦ vt (fasten)* prender; **a two-~ plug** uma tomada *f* elétrica (de dois pinos); **~s and needles** formigueiro *m*.

pinafore ['pinəfɔːʳ] *n (apron)* avental *m (Br)*, bata *f (Port); (Brit: dress)* vestido *m* de alças.

pinball ['pinbɔːl] *n* flippers *mpl*.

pincers ['pinsəz] *npl (tool)* turquês *f*.

pinch [pintʃ] *vt (squeeze)* beliscar; *(Brit: inf: steal)* roubar ♦ *n (of salt)* pitada *f*.

pincushion ['pin,kuʃn] *n* almofada *f* para alfinetes.

pine [pain] *n* pinheiro *m ♦ adj* de pinho.

pineapple ['painæpl] *n* abacaxi *m (Br)*, ananás *m (Port)*.

pinetree ['paintriː] *n* pinheiro *m*.

pink [piŋk] *adj* cor-de-rosa *(inv) ♦ n (colour)* cor-de-rosa *m inv*.

pinkie ['piŋki] *n (Am)* (dedo) mindinho *m*.

pinnacle ['pinəkl] *n* pináculo *m*.

PIN number [pin-] *n* código *m* pessoal, PIN *m*.

pinpoint ['pinpɔint] *vt (difficulty, cause)* determinar; *(position, target, leak)* localizar.

pin-striped [-,straipt] *adj* de listras.

pint [paint] *n (in UK)* = 0,568 l, ~ meio litro *m; (in US)* = 0,473 l, = meio litro; **a ~ (of beer)** *(Brit)* = uma caneca de cerveja.

pioneer [,paiə'niəʳ] *n* pioneiro *m* (-ra *f*) ♦ *vt (new activity)* explorar; *(new invention, scheme)* desenvolver.

pip [pip] *n (of fruit)* caroço *m*, pevide *f (Port)*.

pipe [paip] *n (for smoking)* cachimbo *m; (for gas, water)* cano *m*.

pipe cleaner *n* limpador *m* de cachimbo.

pipeline ['paiplain] *n (for oil)* oleoduto *m; (for gas)* gasoduto *m*.

piper ['paipəʳ] *n (MUS)* gaiteiro *m* (-ra *f*).

pipe tobacco *n* tabaco *m* para cachimbo.

pirate ['pairət] *n* pirata *m*.

pirate radio *n (Brit)* rádio *f* pirata.

Pisces ['paisiːz] *n* Peixes *m inv*.

piss [pis] *vi (vulg)* mijar ♦ *n:* **to have a ~** *(vulg)* mijar, dar uma mijada; **it's ~ing down** *(vulg)* está chovendo canivetes *(Br)*, está chovendo a potes *(Port)*.

pissed [pist] *adj (Brit: vulg: drunk)* bêbado(-da) que nem um gambá; *(Am: vulg: angry)* fulo(-la).

pissed off *adj (vulg):* **to be ~ with** estar de saco cheio de.

pistachio [pi'stɑːʃiəʊ] *(pl -s) n* pistache *m (Br)*, pistácio *m (Port) ♦ adj* de pistácio.

pistol ['pistl] *n* pistola *f*.

piston ['pistən] *n* piston *m*, pistão *m*.

pit [pit] *n (hole, for orchestra)* poço *m; (coalmine)* mina *f; (Am: in fruit)* caroço *m*.

pitch [pitʃ] *n (Brit: SPORT)* campo *m ♦ vt (throw)* atirar; **to ~ a tent** montar uma barraca (de campismo).

pitch-black *adj* escuro(-ra) como breu.

pitcher ['pitʃəʳ] *n (large jug)* jarro *m; (Am: small jug)* jarra *f*.

pitchfork ['pitʃfɔːk] *n* forquilha *f*.

pitfall ['pitfɔːl] *n (difficulty)* armadilha *f; (danger)* perigo *m*.

pith [piθ] *n (of orange)* pele *f* branca.

pitiful ['pitiful] *adj (arousing pity)* lastimoso(-osa); *(arousing contempt)* ridículo(-la).

pitiless ['pitilis] *adj* impiedoso(-osa).

pitta (bread) ['pitə-] *n* pão *m* árabe; *pão chato e oco*.

pittance ['pitəns] *n* miséria *f*.

pitted ['pitid] *adj (olives)* descaroçado(-da), sem caroço.

pity ['piti] *n (compassion)* pena *f;* **to have ~ on sb** ter pena de alguém; **it's a ~ (that) ...** é uma pena que ...; **what a ~!** que pena!

pivot ['pivət] *n* eixo *m*, pivô *m*.

pizza ['piːtsə] *n* pizza *f*.

pizzeria [,piːtsə'riːə] *n* pizzaria *f*.

Pl. *(abbr of Place)* abreviatura do nome de certas ruas na Grã-Bretanha.

placard ['plækɑːd] *n* placar *m*.

placate [plə'keit] *vt* aplacar.

place [pleis] *n* lugar *m; (house, flat)* casa *f; (at table)* lugar, talher *m ♦ vt (put)* colocar; *(an order, bet)* fazer; **in the first ~** em primeiro lugar; **to take ~** ter lugar; **to take sb's ~** substituir

alguém; **all over the ~** por todo o lado;
in ~ of em lugar de.
place mat n descanso m (Br), individual m (Port).
placement ['pleɪsmənt] n (work experience) colocação f temporária, estágio m.
place of birth n local m de nascimento, naturalidade f.
placid ['plæsɪd] adj plácido(-da).
plagiarize ['pleɪdʒəraɪz] vt plagiar.
plague [pleɪg] n peste f.
plaice [pleɪs] (pl inv) n solha f.
plaid [plæd] n tecido de lã escocês.
plain [pleɪn] adj simples (inv); (yoghurt) natural; (clear) claro(-ra); (paper)
liso(-sa); (pej: not attractive) sem atrati-
vos ◆ n planície f.
plain chocolate n chocolate m
preto OR negro.
plain-clothes adj vestido(-da) à
paisana.
plain flour n (Brit) farinha f (sem
fermento).
plainly ['pleɪnlɪ] adv (clearly) claramente.
plaintiff ['pleɪntɪf] n queixoso m (-osa
f), demandante mf.
plait [plæt] n trança f ◆ vt entrançar.
plan [plæn] n (scheme, project) plano m;
(drawing) planta f ◆ vt (organize) planear; **have you any ~s for tonight?**
você tem planos para hoje à noite?;
according to ~ como estava previsto;
to ~ to do sthg, to ~ on doing sthg
pensar em fazer algo.
plane [pleɪn] n (aeroplane) avião m;
(tool) plaina f.
planet ['plænɪt] n planeta m.
plank [plæŋk] n tábua f.
planning ['plænɪŋ] n planejamento m,
planificação f.
planning permission n licença f
para construir OR fazer obras.
plant [plɑːnt] n (living thing) planta f;
(factory) fábrica f; (power, nuclear) central f ◆ vt (seeds, tree) plantar; (land)
cultivar; **"heavy ~ crossing"** aviso que
indica que na área circulam freqüentemente veículos pesados.
plantation [plæn'teɪʃn] n plantação f.
plaque [plɑːk] n placa f.
plaster ['plɑːstər] n (Brit: for cut) esparadrapo m (Br), penso m (Port); (for
walls) estuque m; **in ~** (arm, leg) enges-
sado.

plaster cast n (for broken bones)
gesso m.
plastered ['plɑːstəd] adj (inf: drunk)
bêbado(-da); **to get ~** embebedar-se.
plastic ['plæstɪk] n plástico m ◆ adj de
plástico.
plastic bag n saca f OR saco m de
plástico.
Plasticine® ['plæstɪsiːn] n (Brit) plastilina f (Br), plasticina f (Port).
plastic surgery n cirurgia f plástica.
plate [pleɪt] n (for food) prato m; (of
metal) placa f; **a ~ of glass** um vidro,
uma vidraça.
plateau ['plætəʊ] n planalto m.
plate-glass adj de vidro grosso.
platform ['plætfɔːm] n plataforma f.
platinum ['plætɪnəm] n platina f.
platoon [plə'tuːn] n pelotão m.
platter ['plætər] n (of food) travessa f
(de comida).
plausible ['plɔːzəbl] adj plausível.
play [pleɪ] vt (sport, game) jogar; (instrument, music) tocar; (opponent) jogar
contra; (CD, tape, record) pôr; (role,
character) desempenhar ◆ vi (child)
brincar; (in sport, game) jogar; (musician) tocar ◆ n (in theatre, on TV) peça f;
(button on CD, tape recorder) play m.
❏ **play back** vt sep repetir, colocar de
novo
❏ **play up** vi (machine, car) enguiçar,
estar com problemas.
playboy ['pleɪbɔɪ] n playboy m.
player ['pleɪər] n (of sport, game) jogador m (-ra f); (of musical instrument)
músico m (-ca f), intérprete mf; **guitar
~** guitarrista mf; **piano ~** pianista mf.
playful ['pleɪfʊl] adj brincalhão
(-lhona).
playground ['pleɪgraʊnd] n (in school)
recreio m; (in park etc) parque m infantil.
playgroup ['pleɪgruːp] n tipo de
jardim-de-infância.
playing card ['pleɪɪŋ-] n carta f de
jogar.
playing field ['pleɪɪŋ-] n parque m OR
campo m de jogos.
playmate ['pleɪmeɪt] n companheiro
m (-ra f) de brincadeiras.
playpen ['pleɪpen] n cercado m para
bebês.
playroom ['pleɪrʊm] n sala f para
brincadeiras.

playschool ['pleɪskuːl] = **playgroup**.
plaything ['pleɪθɪŋ] n brinquedo m.
playtime ['pleɪtaɪm] n recreio m.
playwright ['pleɪraɪt] n dramaturgo m (-ga f).
plc (Brit: abbr of public limited company) ~ S.A. (cotada na Bolsa).
plea [pliː] n (appeal) pedido m; (JUR): **to enter a ~ of guilty** declarar-se culpado.
plead [pliːd] vt alegar ♦ vi (JUR) alegar; (beg) pedir, rogar; **to ~ for sthg** pedir algo; **to ~ with sb to do sthg** rogar a alguém que faça algo; **he ~ed not guilty** declarou-se inocente.
pleasant ['plɛznt] adj agradável.
please [pliːz] adv por favor ♦ vt agradar a; **yes ~!** sim, se faz favor!; **whatever you ~** o que quiser.
pleased [pliːzd] adj satisfeito(-ta), contente; **to be ~ with** estar satisfeito com; **to meet you!** prazer em conhecê-lo(-la)!
pleasing ['pliːzɪŋ] adj agradável.
pleasure ['plɛʒər] n prazer m; **with ~** com prazer; **it's a ~!** é um prazer!
pleat [pliːt] n prega f.
pleated ['pliːtɪd] adj com OR de pregas.
pledge [plɛdʒ] n promessa f ♦ vt (promise to provide) prometer.
plentiful ['plɛntɪful] adj abundante.
plenty ['plɛntɪ] pron bastante; **~ of** bastante.
pliers ['plaɪəz] npl alicate m.
plight [plaɪt] n situação f deplorável.
plimsoll ['plɪmsəl] n (Brit) sapatilha f.
plod [plɒd] vi (walk slowly) arrastar-se, caminhar lentamente e com dificuldade.
plonk [plɒŋk] n (Brit: inf: wine) zurrapa f (Br), carrascão m (Port).
plot [plɒt] n (scheme) complot m; (of story, film, play) enredo m; (of land) pedaço m.
plough [plaʊ] n (Brit) charrua f ♦ vt (Brit) lavrar.
ploughman's (lunch) ['plaʊmənz-] n (Brit) prato composto por vários queijos, pão, pickles e salada servido freqüentemente nos pubs.
plow [plaʊ] (Am) = **plough**.
ploy [plɔɪ] n estratagema m.
pluck [plʌk] vt (eyebrows, hair) arrancar, depilar (com pinça); (chicken) depenar.

plug [plʌg] n (with pins) tomada f elétrica, ficha f eléctrica (Port); (socket) tomada f, ficha (Port); (for bath, sink) tampa f, válvula f.
⊐ plug in vt sep ligar (a tomada).
plughole ['plʌghəʊl] n ralo m.
plum [plʌm] n ameixa f.
plumber ['plʌmər] n encanador m (-ra f) (Br), canalizador m (-ra f) (Port).
plumbing ['plʌmɪŋ] n (pipes) canalização f.
plume [pluːm] n pluma f, pena f.
plump [plʌmp] adj roliço(-ça).
plum pudding n pudim natalício com frutos secos e especiarias servido com conhaque que se incendeia antes de servir.
plunder ['plʌndər] n (booty) saque m ♦ vt saquear, pilhar.
plunge [plʌndʒ] vi (fall, dive) mergulhar; (decrease) descer (em flecha).
plunge pool n piscina f pequena.
plunger ['plʌndʒər] n (for unblocking pipe) desentupidor m (de ventosa).
pluperfect (tense) [ˌpluːˈpɜːfɪkt-] n: **the ~** o mais-que-perfeito.
plural ['plʊərəl] n plural m; **in the ~** no plural.
plus [plʌs] prep mais ♦ adj: **30 ~** trinta ou mais.
plush [plʌʃ] adj de luxo.
Pluto ['pluːtəʊ] n Plutão m.
ply [plaɪ] vt (trade) exercer; **to ~ sb with sthg** (food, drinks) não parar de oferecer algo a alguém, encher alguém com algo; (questions) assediar alguém com algo.
plywood ['plaɪwʊd] n compensado m (Br), contraplacado m (Port).
p.m. (abbr of post meridiem): **at 3 ~** às três da tarde, às 15h; **at 10 ~** às dez da noite, às 22h.
PMT n (abbr of premenstrual tension) síndrome f pré-menstrual.
pneumatic drill [njuːˈmætɪk-] n perfuratriz f (Br), broca f pneumática.
pneumonia [njuːˈməʊnjə] n pneumonia f.
poach [pəʊtʃ] vt (game) caçar furtivamente; (fish) pescar furtivamente; (copy) roubar ♦ vi (hunt) caçar (furtivamente); (fish) pescar (furtivamente).
poached egg [pəʊtʃt-] n ovo m pochê (Br), ovo m escalfado (Port).
poached salmon [pəʊtʃt-] n salmão m cozido.

poacher ['pəʊtʃəʳ] *n (hunting)* caçador *m* furtivo (caçadora *f* furtiva); *(fishing)* pescador *m* furtivo (pescadora *f* furtiva).

poaching ['pəʊtʃɪŋ] *n (for game)* caça *f* furtiva; *(for fish)* pesca *f* furtiva.

PO Box *n (abbr of Post Office Box)* caixa *f* postal *(Br)*, apartado *m (Port)*.

pocket ['pɒkɪt] *n* bolso *m* ◆ *adj* de bolso.

pocketbook ['pɒkɪtbʊk] *n (notebook)* bloco *m* de notas *(pequeno)*; *(Am: handbag)* carteira *f*.

pocketknife ['pɒkɪtnaɪf] *(pl -knives* [-naɪvz]*) n* navalha *f*, canivete *m*.

pocket money *n (Brit)* mesada *f (Br)*, semanada *f (Port)*.

podgy ['pɒdʒɪ] *adj (inf)* roliço(-ça), gorducho(-cha).

podiatrist [pə'daɪətrɪst] *n (Am)* pedicuro *m* (-ra *f*), calista *mf*.

podium ['pəʊdɪəm] *n* pódio *m*.

poem ['pəʊɪm] *n* poema *m*.

poet ['pəʊɪt] *n* poeta *m* (-tisa *f*).

poetic [pəʊ'etɪk] *adj* poético(-ca).

poetry ['pəʊɪtrɪ] *n* poesia *f*.

poignant ['pɔɪnjənt] *adj (moment, story)* comovente.

point [pɔɪnt] *n* ponto *m*; *(tip)* ponta *f*; *(most important thing)* razão *f*; *(Brit: electric socket)* tomada *f*, ficha *f (Port)* ◆ *vi*: **to ~ to** apontar para; **five ~ seven** cinco vírgula sete; **what's the ~?** para quê?; **there's no ~** não vale a pena; **to be on the ~ of doing sthg** estar prestes a OR a ponto de fazer algo.

❏ **points** *npl (Brit: on railway)* agulhas *fpl*.

❏ **point out** *vt sep (object, person)* indicar; *(fact, mistake)* apontar.

point-blank *adj (question, range)* à queima-roupa; *(denial, refusal)* categórico(-ca) ◆ *adv (accuse, ask)* sem rodeios; *(shoot)* à queima-roupa; *(deny, refuse)* categoricamente.

pointed ['pɔɪntɪd] *adj (in shape)* pontiagudo(-da).

pointless ['pɔɪntlɪs] *adj* inútil.

point of view *n* ponto *m* de vista.

poised [pɔɪzd] *adj (ready)* pronto(-ta), preparado(-da); **to be ~ for sthg** estar pronto OR preparado para algo; **to be ~ to do sthg** estar pronto OR preparado para fazer algo.

poison ['pɔɪzn] *n* veneno *m* ◆ *vt* envenenar.

poisoning ['pɔɪznɪŋ] *n* envenenamento *m*.

poisonous ['pɔɪznəs] *adj* venenoso(-osa).

poke [pəʊk] *vt (with finger, stick)* cutucar *(Br)*, tocar *(Port)*; *(with elbow)* cutucar *(Br)*, dar cotoveladas em; *(fire)* cutucar *(Br)*, atiçar.

poker ['pəʊkəʳ] *n (card game)* póquer *m*.

poky ['pəʊkɪ] *adj* minúsculo(-la), apertado(-da).

Poland ['pəʊlənd] *n* Polônia *f*.

polar ['pəʊləʳ] *adj* polar.

polar bear *n* urso *m* polar.

Polaroid® ['pəʊlərɔɪd] *n (photograph)* fotografia *f* instantânea; *(camera)* máquina *f* de tirar fotografias instantâneas.

pole [pəʊl] *n (of wood)* poste *m*.

Pole [pəʊl] *n (person)* polonês (-esa *f*) *(Br)*, polaco *m* (-ca *f*) *(Port)*.

pole vault *n* salto *m* com vara.

police [pə'liːs] *npl*: **the ~** a polícia.

police car *n* rádio-patrulha *f (Br)*, carro *m* da polícia.

police constable *n (Brit)* policial *mf (Br)*, polícia *mf (Port)*.

police force *n* forças *fpl* policiais.

policeman [pə'liːsmən] *(pl -men* [-mən]*) n* policial *m (Br)*, polícia *m (Port)*.

police officer *n* policial *mf (Br)*, polícia *mf (Port)*.

police station *n* delegacia *f (Br)*, esquadra *f (Port)*.

policewoman [pə'liːs,wʊmən] *(pl -women* [-,wɪmɪn]*) n* policial *f (Br)*, polícia *f (Port)*.

policy ['pɒləsɪ] *n (approach, attitude)* política *f*; *(for insurance)* apólice *f*.

policy-holder *n* segurado *m* (-da *f*).

polio ['pəʊlɪəʊ] *n* poliomielite *f*, paralisia *f* infantil.

polish ['pɒlɪʃ] *n (for cleaning)* cera *f* ◆ *vt* encerar.

Polish ['pəʊlɪʃ] *adj* polonês(-esa) *(Br)*, polaco(-ca) *(Port)* ◆ *n (language)* polonês *m (Br)*, polaco *m (Port)* ◆ *npl*: **the ~** os poloneses *(Br)*, os polacos *(Port)*.

polished ['pɒlɪʃt] *adj (floor)* encerado(-da); *(metal)* polido(-da); *(speech, performance)* refinado(-da); *(performer)* bom (boa), esmerado(-da).

polite 204

polite [pəˈlaɪt] *adj* educado(-da).
political [pəˈlɪtɪkl] *adj* político(-ca).
politically correct [pəˈlɪtɪklɪ-] *adj* politicamente correto(-ta).
politician [ˌpɒlɪˈtɪʃn] *n* político *m* (-ca *f*).
politics [ˈpɒlətɪks] *n* política *f*.
polka [ˈpɒlkə] *n* polca *f*.
polka dot *n* bolinha *f* (em tecido).
poll [pəʊl] *n* (survey) sondagem *f*; the ~s (election) as eleições.
pollen [ˈpɒlən] *n* pólen *m*.
polling booth [ˈpəʊlɪŋ-] *n* cabine *f* eleitoral.
polling station [ˈpəʊlɪŋ-] *n* mesa *f* OR centro *m* eleitoral.
pollute [pəˈluːt] *vt* poluir.
pollution [pəˈluːʃn] *n* poluição *f*.
polo [ˈpəʊləʊ] (pl -s) *n* pólo *m*.
polo neck *n* (Brit: jumper) gola *f* rulê (Br), camisola *f* de gola alta (Port).
polyester [ˌpɒlɪˈestər] *n* poliéster *m*.
polystyrene [ˌpɒlɪˈstaɪriːn] *n* isopor® *m* (Br), esferovite *m* (Port).
polytechnic [ˌpɒlɪˈteknɪk] *n* escola *f* politécnica.
polythene bag [ˈpɒlɪθiːn-] *n* (Brit) saco *m* OR saca *f* de plástico.
pomegranate [ˈpɒmɪˌɡrænɪt] *n* romã *f*.
pompom [ˈpɒmpɒm] *n* pompom *m*.
pompous [ˈpɒmpəs] *adj* pomposo (-osa).
pond [pɒnd] *n* lago *m*.
ponder [ˈpɒndər] *vt* refletir sobre.
pong [pɒŋ] *n* (Brit: inf) fedor *m*.
pontoon [pɒnˈtuːn] *n* (Brit: card game) vinte-e-um *m*.
pony [ˈpəʊnɪ] *n* pônei *m*.
ponytail [ˈpəʊnɪteɪl] *n* rabo *m* de cavalo.
pony-trekking [-ˌtrekɪŋ] *n* (Brit) excursão *f* em pônei.
poodle [ˈpuːdl] *n* caniche *m*.
pool [puːl] *n* (for swimming) piscina *f*; (of water, blood, milk) poça *f*; (small pond) lago *f*; (game) bilhar *m*.
❑ **pools** *npl* (Brit): the ~s ~ a loteca (Br), a loteria esportiva (Br), o Totobola® (Port).
poor [pɔːr] *adj* (short of money) pobre; (bad) mau (má); (expressing sympathy) coitado(-da), pobre ◆ *npl*: the ~ os pobres.
poorly [ˈpɔːlɪ] *adj* (Brit: ill) adoenta-

do(-da) ◆ *adv* mal.
pop [pɒp] *n* (music) música *f* pop ◆ *vt* (inf: put) meter ◆ *vi* (balloon) rebentar; my ears popped os meus ouvidos deram um estalido.
❑ **pop in** *vi* (Brit): I'll ~ in after work dou um pulo aí depois do trabalho.
pop concert *n* concerto *m* de música pop.
popcorn [ˈpɒpkɔːn] *n* pipoca *f*.
Pope [pəʊp] *n*: the ~ o Papa.
pop group *n* grupo *m* de música pop.
poplar (tree) [ˈpɒplər-] *n* álamo *m*, choupo *m*.
pop music *n* música *f* pop.
popper [ˈpɒpər] *n* (Brit) botão *m* de pressão (Br), mola *f* (Port).
poppy [ˈpɒpɪ] *n* papoula *f*.
Popsicle® [ˈpɒpsɪkl] *n* (Am) picolé *m* (Br), gelado *m* (de fruta) (Port).
pop socks *npl* meias *fpl* até ao joelho, meia-meia *f*.
pop star *n* pop star *f*.
popular [ˈpɒpjʊlər] *adj* (person, place, activity) popular; (opinion, ideas) generalizado(-da).
popularity [ˌpɒpjʊˈlærətɪ] *n* popularidade *f*.
popularize [ˈpɒpjʊləraɪz] *vt* (make popular) popularizar; (simplify) vulgarizar.
populated [ˈpɒpjʊleɪtɪd] *adj* povoado(-da).
population [ˌpɒpjʊˈleɪʃn] *n* população *f*.
porcelain [ˈpɔːsəlɪn] *n* porcelana *f*.
porch [pɔːtʃ] *n* (entrance) átrio *m*; (Am: outside house) terraço *m* (coberto), alpendre *m*.
porcupine [ˈpɔːkjʊpaɪn] *n* porco-espinho *m*.
pore [pɔːr] *n* poro *m*.
❑ **pore over** *vt fus* debruçar-se sobre, estudar atentamente.
pork [pɔːk] *n* carne *f* de porco.
pork chop *n* costeleta *f* de porco.
pork pie *n* empada *f* de carne de porco.
pornographic [ˌpɔːnəˈɡræfɪk] *adj* pornográfico(-ca).
pornography [pɔːˈnɒɡrəfɪ] *n* pornografia *f*.
porous [ˈpɔːrəs] *adj* poroso(-osa).
porridge [ˈpɒrɪdʒ] *n* flocos *mpl* de aveia.

port [pɔːt] n porto m.

portable ['pɔːtəbl] adj portátil.

porter ['pɔːtər] n (at hotel, museum) porteiro m (-ra f); (at station, airport) carregador m (-ra f).

portfolio [pɔːt'fəʊljəʊ] (pl -s) n (case) pasta f; (sample of work) portfolio m.

porthole ['pɔːthəʊl] n vigia f.

portion ['pɔːʃn] n (part) porção f; (of food) dose f.

portly ['pɔːtlɪ] adj corpulento(-ta).

portrait ['pɔːtreɪt] n retrato m.

portray [pɔː'treɪ] vt (in a play, film) representar; (describe, represent) retratar, descrever.

Portugal ['pɔːtʃʊgl] n Portugal s.

Portuguese [pɔːtʃʊ'giːz] adj português(-esa) ♦ n (person) português m (-esa f); (language) português m ♦ npl: the ~ os portugueses.

pose [pəʊz] vt (problem, threat) constituir ♦ vi (for photo) posar.

posh [pɒʃ] adj (inf) fino(-na), chique.

position [pə'zɪʃn] n posição f; "~ closed" "encerrado".

positive ['pɒzətɪv] adj positivo(-va); (certain, sure) seguro(-ra); I'm absolutely ~ tenho a certeza absoluta.

possess [pə'zes] vt possuir.

possession [pə'zeʃn] n (thing owned) bem m.

possessive [pə'zesɪv] adj possessivo(-va).

possibility [pɒsə'bɪlətɪ] n possibilidade f.

possible ['pɒsəbl] adj possível; it's ~ that we may be late é possível que cheguemos atrasados; would it be ~ ...? seria possível ...?; as much as ~ o máximo possível; if ~ se for possível.

possibly ['pɒsəblɪ] adv (perhaps) provavelmente.

post [pəʊst] n correio m; (pole) poste m; (fml: job) lugar m ♦ vt (letter) pôr no correio; (parcel) enviar; by ~ pelo correio.

postage ['pəʊstɪdʒ] n franquia f; ~ and packing custos mpl de envio; ~ paid porte m pago.

postage stamp n (fml) selo m (postal).

postal ['pəʊstl] adj postal.

postal order n vale m postal.

postbox ['pəʊstbɒks] n (Brit) caixa f de coleta (Br), caixa f do correio (Port).

postcard ['pəʊstkɑːd] n (cartão) postal m.

postcode ['pəʊstkəʊd] n (Brit) código m postal.

poster ['pəʊstər] n poster m.

poste restante [pəʊstres'tɑːnt] n (Brit) posta-restante f.

posterior [pɒ'stɪərɪər] n (inf) traseiro m.

post-free adv com porte pago.

postgraduate [pəʊst'grædʒʊət] n pós-graduado m (-da f).

posthumous ['pɒstjʊməs] adj póstumo(-ma).

postman ['pəʊstmən] (pl -men [-mən]) n carteiro m.

postmark ['pəʊstmɑːk] n carimbo m (postal).

postmaster ['pəʊst,mɑːstər] n chefe m dos correios.

postmortem [pəʊst'mɔːtəm] n (autopsy) autópsia f.

post office n (building) estação f de correios; the Post Office ~ a Empresa Nacional dos Correios e Telégrafos (Br), ~ os CTT (Port).

postpone [pəʊst'pəʊn] vt adiar.

postscript ['pəʊsskrɪpt] n (to letter) pós-escrito m.

posture ['pɒstʃər] n postura f.

postwoman ['pəʊst,wʊmən] (pl -women [-,wɪmɪn]) n carteira f (Br), mulher-carteiro f (Port).

pot [pɒt] n (for cooking) panela f; (for jam, paint) frasco m; (for coffee, tea) bule m; (inf: cannabis) maconha f (Br), erva f (Port); a ~ of tea um bule de chá.

potato [pə'teɪtəʊ] (pl -es) n batata f.

potato salad n salada f de batata.

potent ['pəʊtənt] adj (argument, drink) forte.

potential [pə'tenʃl] adj potencial ♦ n potencial m.

potentially [pə'tenʃəlɪ] adv potencialmente.

pothole ['pɒthəʊl] n (in road) buraco m.

potholing ['pɒt,həʊlɪŋ] n (Brit) espeleologia f; to go ~ praticar espeleologia.

potion ['pəʊʃn] n poção f.

pot plant n planta f de interior.

pot scrubber [-'skrʌbər] n esfregão m.

potshot ['pɒtʃɒt] n: to take a ~ (at sthg) disparar (contra algo), atirar (contra algo).

potted ['potɪd] *adj (meat, fish)* de conserva; *(plant)* de vaso, de interior.
potter ['potə^r] *n* oleiro *m* (-ra *f*).
❑ **potter around** *vi (Brit)* ocupar-se de tarefas agradáveis mas sem nenhuma importância.
pottery ['potərɪ] *n (clay objects)* cerâmica *f; (craft)* cerâmica, olaria *f*.
potty ['potɪ] *n* penico *m (para crianças)*.
pouch [paʊtʃ] *n (for money, tobacco)* bolsa *f*.
poultry ['pəʊltrɪ] *n (meat)* carne *f* de aves (domésticas) ♦ *npl (animals)* aves *fpl* domésticas.
pound [paʊnd] *n (unit of money)* libra *f; (unit of weight)* = 453,6 gr, libra ♦ *vi (heart)* palpitar; *(head)* latejar.
pour [pɔː^r] *vt (liquid etc)* jogar; *(drink)* servir ♦ *vi (flow)* correr; **it's ~ing (with rain)** está chovendo canivetes *(Br)*, está a chover a cântaros *(Port)*.
❑ **pour out** *vt sep (drink)* servir.
pouring ['pɔːrɪŋ] *adj (rain)* torrencial.
pout [paʊt] *vi* fazer beicinho.
poverty ['povətɪ] *n* pobreza *f*.
poverty-stricken *adj* empobrecido(-da).
powder ['paʊdə^r] *n* pó *m*.
powdered ['paʊdəd] *adj (milk, sugar)* em pó.
powder room *n* banheiro *m* para senhoras *(Br)*, casa *f* de banho para senhoras *(Port)*.
power ['paʊə^r] *n (control, authority)* poder *m; (ability)* capacidade *f; (strength, force)* força *f; (energy)* energia *f; (electricity)* eletricidade *f* ♦ *vt* alimentar, accionar; **to be in ~** estar no poder.
powerboat ['paʊəbəʊt] *n* barco *m* a motor.
power cut *n* corte *m* de energia.
power failure *n* falha *f* de energia.
powerful ['paʊəful] *adj (having control)* poderoso(-osa); *(machine)* potente.
powerless ['paʊəlɪs] *adj* impotente; **to be ~ to do sthg** não ter poderes para fazer algo, não poder fazer algo.
power point *n (Brit)* tomada *f* elétrica.
power station *n* central *f* elétrica.
power steering *n* direção *f* assistida.
practical ['præktɪkl] *adj* prático(-ca).

practicality [,præktɪ'kælətɪ] *n* aspecto *m* prático.
practical joke *n* partida *f*.
practically ['præktɪklɪ] *adv (almost)* praticamente.
practice ['præktɪs] *n (training, regular activity, custom)* prática *f; (training session)* sessão *f* de treino; *(MUS)* ensaio *m; (of doctor)* consultório *m; (of lawyer)* escritório *m* ♦ *vt (Am)* = **practise**; **out of ~** destreinado(-da).
practise ['præktɪs] *vt (sport, music, technique)* praticar ♦ *vi (train)* praticar; *(doctor, lawyer)* exercer ♦ *n (Am)* = **practice**.
Prague [prɑːg] *n* Praga s.
prairie ['preərɪ] *n* pradaria *f*.
praise [preɪz] *n* elogio *m* ♦ *vt* elogiar.
praiseworthy ['preɪz,wɜːðɪ] *adj* digno(-gna) de louvor.
pram [præm] *n (Brit)* carrinho *m* de bebê.
prance [prɑːns] *vi (person)* pavonearse; *(horse)* dar pinotes.
prank [præŋk] *n* peça *f (Br)*, partida *f (Port)*.
prawn [prɔːn] *n* camarão *m*.
prawn cocktail *n* cocktail *m* de camarão, entrada à base de camarão e maionese com ketchup dispostos sobre uma camada de folhas de alface.
prawn cracker *n* bolacha *f* de camarão, tira-gosto frito chinês de farinha de arroz e camarão, fino e crocante.
pray [preɪ] *vi* rezar; **to ~ for** *(fig)* rezar por; **to ~ for rain** rezar para que chova.
prayer [preə^r] *n* oração *f*.
precarious [prɪ'keərɪəs] *adj* precário (-ria).
precaution [prɪ'kɔːʃn] *n* precaução *f*.
precede [prɪ'siːd] *vt (fml)* preceder.
precedence ['presɪdəns] *n*: **to take ~ over sthg** ter prioridade em relação a OR sobre algo.
precedent ['presɪdənt] *n* precedente *m*.
preceding [prɪ'siːdɪŋ] *adj* precedente.
precinct ['priːsɪŋkt] *n (Brit: for shopping)* zona *f* comercial (pedestre); *(Am: area of town)* circunscrição *f*.
precious ['preʃəs] *adj* precioso(-osa); *(memories, possession)* querido(-da).
precious stone *n* pedra *f* preciosa.
precipice ['presɪpɪs] *n* precipício *m*.
precise [prɪ'saɪs] *adj* preciso(-sa).

precisely [prɪ'saɪslɪ] *adv* precisamente.

precision [prɪ'sɪʒn] *n* precisão *f*.

precocious [prɪ'kəʊʃəs] *adj* precoce.

predator ['predətəʳ] *n (animal)* predador *m*; *(bird)* ave *f* de rapina.

predecessor ['pri:dɪsesəʳ] *n* antecessor *m* (-ra *f*).

predicament [prɪ'dɪkəmənt] *n* situação *f* difícil.

predict [prɪ'dɪkt] *vt* prever.

predictable [prɪ'dɪktəbl] *adj* previsível.

prediction [prɪ'dɪkʃn] *n* previsão *f*.

predominant [prɪ'dɒmɪnənt] *adj* predominante.

predominantly [prɪ'dɒmɪnəntlɪ] *adv* predominantemente.

preempt [,pri:'empt] *vt* adiantar-se a, antecipar-se a.

prefab ['pri:fæb] *n (inf)* pré-fabricado *m*.

preface ['prefɪs] *n* prefácio *m*.

prefect ['pri:fekt] *n (Brit: at school)* prefeito *m* (monitora *f*).

prefer [prɪ'fɜːʳ] *vt*: **to ~ sthg (to)** preferir algo (a); **to ~ to do sthg** preferir fazer algo.

preferable ['prefrəbl] *adj* preferível.

preferably ['prefrəblɪ] *adv* preferivelmente, de preferência.

preference ['prefərəns] *n* preferência *f*.

prefix ['pri:fɪks] *n* prefixo *m*.

pregnancy ['pregnənsɪ] *n* gravidez *f*.

pregnant ['pregnənt] *adj* grávida.

prehistoric [,pri:hɪ'stɒrɪk] *adj* pré-histórico(-ca).

prejudice ['predʒʊdɪs] *n* preconceito *m*.

prejudiced ['predʒʊdɪst] *adj* preconceituoso(-osa).

preliminary [prɪ'lɪmɪnərɪ] *adj* preliminar.

prelude ['prelju:d] *n (event)*: **~ (to sthg)** prelúdio *m* (de algo).

premarital [,pri:'mærɪtl] *adj* pré-matrimonial.

premature ['premətjʊəʳ] *adj* prematuro(-ra).

premeditated [,pri:'medɪteɪtɪd] *adj* premeditado(-da).

premenstrual syndrome [,pri:'menstrʊəl-] *n* síndrome *f* pré-menstrual.

premenstrual tension = premenstrual syndrome.

premier ['premɪəʳ] *adj* melhor ◆ *n* primeiro-ministro *m* (primeira-ministra *f*).

premiere ['premɪeəʳ] *n* estréia *f*.

premises ['premɪsɪz] *npl* instalações *fpl*, local *m*; **on the ~** no estabelecimento.

premium ['pri:mjəm] *n (for insurance)* prêmio *m*.

premium-quality *adj* de primeira (qualidade).

premonition [,premə'nɪʃn] *n* premunição *f*.

preoccupied [,pri:'ɒkjʊpaɪd] *adj* preocupado(-da).

prepacked [,pri:'pækt] *adj* pré-embalado(-da).

prepaid ['pri:peɪd] *adj (envelope)* com porte pago, que não necessita de selo.

preparation [,prepə'reɪʃn] *n (preparing)* preparação *f*.

❏ preparations *npl (arrangements)* preparações *fpl*.

preparatory [prɪ'pærətrɪ] *adj* preparatório(-ria).

preparatory school *n (in UK)* escola particular, de preparação para o ensino secundário, para alunos dos sete aos doze anos; *(in US)* escola secundária particular destinada à preparação para o ensino superior.

prepare [prɪ'peəʳ] *vt* preparar ◆ *vi* preparar-se.

prepared [prɪ'peəd] *adj (ready)* preparado(-da); **to be ~ to do sthg** estar preparado para fazer algo.

preposition [,prepə'zɪʃn] *n* preposição *f*.

preposterous [prɪ'pɒstərəs] *adj* absurdo(-da).

prep school [prep-] = **preparatory school**.

prerequisite [,pri:'rekwɪzɪt] *n* pré-requisito *m*; **to be a ~ of** OR **for sthg** ser um pré-requisito para algo.

preschool [,pri:'sku:l] *adj* pré-escolar ◆ *n (Am)* pré-primário *m*.

prescribe [prɪ'skraɪb] *vt* receitar.

prescription [prɪ'skrɪpʃn] *n* receita *f* (médica).

presence ['prezns] *n* presença *f*; **in sb's ~** na presença de alguém.

present [*adj & n* 'preznt, *vb* prɪ'zent] *adj (in attendance)* presente; *(current)* atual ◆ *n (gift)* presente *m* ◆ *vt (give)* presentear; *(problem, challenge)* representar; *(portray, play, on radio or TV)* apresentar; **the ~** o presente; **the ~ (tense)** *(GRAM)* o presente; **at ~** de momento; **to ~ sb to sb** apresentar alguém a alguém.

presentable [prɪ'zentəbl] *adj* apresentável.

presentation [,prezn'teɪʃn] *n* apresentação *f*.

presenter [prɪ'zentər] *n (of TV, radio programme)* apresentador *m* (-ra *f*).

presently ['prezntlɪ] *adv (soon)* daqui a pouco; *(soon after)* daí a pouco; *(now)* atualmente, neste momento.

preservation [,prezə'veɪʃn] *n (of wildlife, building, food)* conservação *f*; *(of order, peace)* manutenção *f*.

preservative [prɪ'zɜːvətɪv] *n* conservante *m*.

preserve [prɪ'zɜːv] *n (jam)* compota *f* ◆ *vt* conservar; *(order, peace)* manter.

preset [,priː'set] *(pt & pp preset) vt* programar.

president ['prezɪdənt] *n* presidente *mf*.

presidential [,prezɪ'denʃl] *adj* presidencial.

press [pres] *vt (push firmly)* pressionar; *(button, switch)* apertar; *(iron)* passar (a ferro) ◆ *n*: **the ~** a imprensa; **to ~ sb to do sthg** insistir com alguém para que faça algo.

press conference *n* entrevista *f* coletiva (*Br*), conferência *f* de imprensa *(Port)*.

pressed [prest] *adj*: **to be ~ for time/money** estar com falta de tempo/dinheiro, não ter tempo/dinheiro.

pressing ['presɪŋ] *adj (problem, business, need)* urgente, premente; *(appointment)* inadiável.

press-stud *n* botão *m* de pressão (*Br*), mola *f (Port)*.

press-ups *npl* flexões *fpl*.

pressure ['preʃər] *n* pressão *f*.

pressure cooker *n* panela *f* de pressão.

pressure gauge *n* manômetro *m*.

pressure group *n* grupo *m* de pressão.

pressurize ['preʃəraɪz] *vt (Brit: force)*: **to ~ sb to do** OR **into doing sthg** pressionar alguém a fazer algo.

prestige [pre'stiːʒ] *n* prestígio *m*.

prestigious [pre'stɪdʒəs] *adj* prestigioso(-osa).

presumably [prɪ'zjuːməblɪ] *adv* presumivelmente.

presume [prɪ'zjuːm] *vt* presumir.

presumptuous [prɪ'zʌmptʃuəs] *adj* presunçoso(-osa).

pretence [prɪ'tens] *n* fingimento *m*; **to make a ~ of doing sthg** fingir fazer algo.

pretend [prɪ'tend] *vt*: **to ~ to do sthg** fingir fazer algo; **she ~ed she was crying** ela fez de conta que estava chorando.

pretense [prɪ'tens] *(Am)* = **pretence**.

pretension [prɪ'tenʃn] *n* pretensão *f*.

pretentious [prɪ'tenʃəs] *adj* pretencioso(-osa).

pretext ['priːtekst] *n* pretexto *m*; **on** OR **under the ~ of doing sthg** sob o pretexto de fazer algo; **on** OR **under the ~ that** sob o pretexto de que.

pretty ['prɪtɪ] *adj* bonito(-ta) ◆ *adv (inf) (quite)* bastante; *(very)* muito.

prevailing [prɪ'veɪlɪŋ] *adj (belief, opinion, fashion)* dominante, corrente; *(wind)* constante.

prevalent ['prevələnt] *adj* dominante, corrente.

prevent [prɪ'vent] *vt* evitar; **to ~ sb/sthg from doing sthg** impedir alguém/algo de fazer algo.

prevention [prɪ'venʃn] *n* prevenção *f*.

preventive [prɪ'ventɪv] *adj* preventivo(-va).

preview ['priːvjuː] *n (of film)* pré-estréia *f (Br)*, anteestreia *f (Port)*; *(short description)* resumo *m*.

previous ['priːvjəs] *adj* anterior.

previously ['priːvjəslɪ] *adv* anteriormente.

prey [preɪ] *n* presa *f*.

price [praɪs] *n* preço *m* ◆ *vt* fixar o preço de; **to be ~d at** custar.

priceless ['praɪslɪs] *adj (expensive)* de valor incalculável; *(valuable)* valiosíssimo(-ma).

price list *n* lista *f* de preços.

price tag *n* etiqueta *f*, preço *m*.

pricey ['praɪsɪ] *adj (inf)* caro(-ra).

prick [prɪk] *vt* picar.

prickly ['prɪklɪ] *adj (plant, bush)* espinhoso(-osa).

prickly heat *n* brotoeja *f (provocada pelo calor)*.

pride [praɪd] *n* orgulho *m* ♦ *vt*: **to ~ o.s. on sthg** orgulhar-se de algo.

priest [priːst] *n* padre *m*.

priestess [priːstɪs] *n* sacerdotisa *f*.

priesthood [ˈpriːsthʊd] *n*: **the ~** *(position, office)* o sacerdócio; *(priests)* o clero.

prim [prɪm] *adj (proper)* ceremonioso (-osa).

primarily [ˈpraɪmərɪlɪ] *adv* principalmente.

primary [ˈpraɪmərɪ] *adj* primário (-ria).

⊐ **primaries** *npl (Am: POL)* (eleições) primárias *fpl*.

primary school *n* escola *f* primária.

prime [praɪm] *adj (chief)* principal; *(quality, beef, cut)* de primeira.

prime minister *n* primeiro-ministro *m* (primeira-ministra *f*). ·

primer [ˈpraɪmər] *n (paint)* (tinta de) base *f*; *(textbook)* cartilha *f*.

primitive [ˈprɪmɪtɪv] *adj* primitivo (-va).

primrose [ˈprɪmrəʊz] *n* primavera *f*.

prince [prɪns] *n* príncipe *m*.

Prince of Wales *n* Príncipe *m* de Gales.

princess [prɪnˈses] *n* princesa *f*.

principal [ˈprɪnsəpl] *adj* principal ♦ *n (of school)* diretor *m* (-ra *f*); *(of university)* reitor *m* (-ra *f*).

principle [ˈprɪnsəpl] *n* princípio *m*; **in ~** em princípio.

print [prɪnt] *n (words)* letra *f (impressa); (photo)* fotografia *f*; *(of painting)* reprodução *f; (mark)* impressão *f* ♦ *vt (book, newspaper)* imprimir; *(publish)* publicar; *(write)* escrever em letra de imprensa; *(photo)* revelar; **out of ~** esgotado.

⊐ **print out** *vt sep* imprimir.

printed matter [ˈprɪntɪd-] *n* impressos *mpl*.

printer [ˈprɪntər] *n (machine)* impressora *f; (person)* impressor *m* (-ra *f*).

printout [ˈprɪntaʊt] *n* cópia *f* impressa, impressão *f*.

prior [ˈpraɪər] *adj (previous)* prévio (-via); **~ to** *(fml)* antes de.

priority [praɪˈɒrətɪ] *n* prioridade *f*; **to have ~ over** ter prioridade sobre.

prison [ˈprɪzn] *n* prisão *f*.

prisoner [ˈprɪznər] *n* prisioneiro *m* (-ra *f*).

prisoner of war *n* prisioneiro *m* (-ra *f*) de guerra.

prison officer *n* guarda *mf* de prisão.

privacy [ˈprɪvəsɪ] *n* privacidade *f*.

private [ˈpraɪvɪt] *adj* privado(-da); *(class, lesson)* particular; *(quiet)* retirado(-da) ♦ *n (MIL)* soldado *m* raso; **in ~** em particular.

private health care *n* assistência *f* médica privada.

privately [ˈpraɪvɪtlɪ] *adv (meet, speak)* em particular; *(think, believe)* no íntimo; **~ owned** *(company)* pertencente ao setor privado.

private property *n* propriedade *f* privada.

private school *n* escola *f* particular.

privatize [ˈpraɪvɪtaɪz] *vt* privatizar.

privet [ˈprɪvɪt] *n* alfena *f*, alfenheiro *m*, ligustro *m*.

privilege [ˈprɪvɪlɪdʒ] *n* privilégio *m*; **it's a ~!** é uma honra!

prize [praɪz] *n* prêmio *m*.

prize-giving [-ˌgɪvɪŋ] *n* entrega *f* de prêmios.

prizewinner [ˈpraɪzwɪnər] *n* premiado *m* (-da *f*), vencedor *m* (-ra *f*) (do prêmio).

pro [prəʊ] *(pl -s)* *n (inf: professional)* profissional *mf*.

⊐ **pros** *npl*: **~s and cons** os prós e os contras.

probability [ˌprɒbəˈbɪlətɪ] *n* probabilidade *f*.

probable [ˈprɒbəbl] *adj* provável.

probably [ˈprɒbəblɪ] *adv* provavelmente.

probation [prəˈbeɪʃn] *n (of prisoner)* liberdade *f* condicional; *(trial period)* período *m* em experiência; **to be on ~** *(employee)* estar em experiência.

probation officer *n* assistente *mf* social *(responsável por um preso em liberdade condicional)*.

probe [prəʊb] *n (MED: for exploration)* sonda *f* ♦ *vt* sondar.

problem [ˈprɒbləm] *n* problema *m*; **no ~!** *(inf)* não há problema!

procedure [prəˈsiːdʒər] *n* procedimento *m*.

proceed [prəˈsiːd] *vi (fml) (continue)* prosseguir; *(act)* proceder; *(advance)* avançar; **"~ with caution"** "avançar com precaução".

proceeds ['prəʊsiːdz] *npl* receita *f*, dinheiro *m* apurado

process ['prəʊses] *n* processo *m*; **to be in the ~ of doing sthg** estar fazendo algo.

processed cheese ['prəʊsest-] *n (for spreading)* queijo *m* fundido; *(in slices)* queijo fundido em fatias.

procession [prə'seʃn] *n* procissão *f*.

proclaim [prə'kleɪm] *vt* proclamar.

procrastinate [prə'kræstɪneɪt] *vi* procrastinar, adiar.

procure [prə'kjʊəʳ] *vt* arranjar, conseguir.

prod [prɒd] *vt (poke)* empurrar.

prodigal ['prɒdɪɡl] *adj* pródigo(-ga).

prodigy ['prɒdɪdʒɪ] *n* prodígio *m*.

produce [*vb* prə'djuːs, *n* 'prɒdjuːs] *vt* produzir; *(cause)* provocar; *(show)* mostrar ◆ *n* produtos *mpl* agrícolas.

producer [prə'djuːsəʳ] *n* produtor *m* (-ra *f*).

product ['prɒdʌkt] *n* produto *m*.

production [prə'dʌkʃn] *n* produção *f*.

production line *n* linha *f* de produção.

productive [prə'dʌktɪv] *adj* produtivo(-va).

productivity [prɒdʌk'tɪvətɪ] *n* produtividade *f*.

profession [prə'feʃn] *n* profissão *f*.

professional [prə'feʃənl] *adj* profissional ◆ *n* profissional *mf*.

professor [prə'fesəʳ] *n (in UK)* professor *m* catedrático (professora *f* catedrática); *(in US)* professor *m* universitário (professora *f* universitária).

profile ['prəʊfaɪl] *n* perfil *m*.

profit ['prɒfɪt] *n (financial)* lucro *m* ◆ *vi*: **to ~ (from)** tirar proveito (de), lucrar (com).

profitability [prɒfɪtə'bɪlɪtɪ] *n* rentabilidade *f*.

profitable ['prɒfɪtəbl] *adj (financially)* lucrativo(-va), rentável.

profiteroles [prə'fɪtərəʊlz] *npl* profiteroles *mpl*, *bolinhos de massa leve recheados com creme e cobertos de chocolate.*

profound [prə'faʊnd] *adj* profundo (-da).

profusely [prə'fjuːslɪ] *adv (sweat, bleed)* imenso; **to apologize ~** desfazer-se em desculpas.

program ['prəʊɡræm] *n (COMPUT)* pro-

gramá *m*; *(Am)* = **programme** ◆ *vt (COMPUT)* programar.

programme ['prəʊɡræm] *n (Brit)* programa *m*.

programming ['prəʊɡræmɪŋ] *n (COMPUT)* programação *f*.

progress [*n* 'prəʊɡres, *vb* prə'ɡres] *n* progresso *m* ◆ *vi (work, talks, student)* progredir; *(day, meeting)* avançar; **to make ~** *(improve)* progredir, melhorar; *(in journey)* avançar; **in ~** em curso.

progressive [prə'ɡresɪv] *adj (forward-looking)* progressivo(-va).

prohibit [prə'hɪbɪt] *vt* proibir; **"smoking strictly ~ed"** "é proibido fumar".

project ['prɒdʒekt] *n (plan)* projeto *m*; *(at school)* trabalho *m*.

projectile [prɒ'dʒektaɪl] *n* projétil *m*.

projection [prə'dʒekʃn] *n (estimate)* previsão *f*, estimativa *f*; *(protrusion)* saliência *f*.

projector [prə'dʒektəʳ] *n* projetor *m*.

prolific [prə'lɪfɪk] *adj* prolífico(-ca).

prolog ['prəʊlɒɡ] *(Am)* = **prologue**.

prologue ['prəʊlɒɡ] *n* prólogo *m*.

prolong [prə'lɒŋ] *vt* prolongar.

prom [prɒm] *n (Am: dance)* baile *m* de finalistas.

promenade [prɒmə'nɑːd] *n (Brit: by the sea)* passeio *m* (à beira da praia), calçadão *m (Br)*.

prominent ['prɒmɪnənt] *adj* proeminente.

promiscuous [prɒ'mɪskjʊəs] *adj* promíscuo(-cua).

promise ['prɒmɪs] *n* promessa *f* ◆ *vt & vi* prometer; **to show ~** ser prometedor; **to ~ sb sthg** prometer algo a alguém; **to ~ to do sthg** prometer fazer algo; **I ~ (that) I'll come** prometo que vou, prometo ir.

promising ['prɒmɪsɪŋ] *adj* prometedor(-ra).

promote [prə'məʊt] *vt* promover.

promotion [prə'məʊʃn] *n* promoção *f*.

prompt [prɒmpt] *adj (quick)* imediato(-ta) ◆ *adv*: **at six o'clock ~** às seis em ponto.

promptly ['prɒmptlɪ] *adv (reply, react, pay)* imediatamente; *(arrive, leave)* pontualmente.

prone [prəʊn] *adj*: **to be ~ to sthg** ser propenso(-sa) a algo; **to be ~ to do sthg** ter tendência para fazer algo.

prong [prɒŋ] *n (of fork)* dente *m*.

pronoun ['prəʊnaʊn] *n* pronome *m*.
pronounce [prə'naʊns] *vt (word)* pronunciar.
pronunciation [prə,nʌnsɪ'eɪʃn] *n* pronúncia *f*.
proof [pruːf] *n (evidence)* prova *f*; **it's 12% ~** *(alcohol)* tem 12 graus.
prop [prɒp] : **prop up** *vt sep (support)* suster.
propaganda [,prɒpə'gændə] *n* propaganda *f*.
propeller [prə'pelər] *n* hélice *f*.
propelling pencil [prə'pelɪŋ-] *n (Brit)* lapiseira *f (Br)*, porta-minas *m inv (Port)*.
proper ['prɒpər] *adj (suitable)* adequado(-da); *(correct, socially acceptable)* correto(-ta).
properly ['prɒpəlɪ] *adv* corretamente.
proper noun *n* substantivo *m* próprio.
property ['prɒpətɪ] *n* propriedade *f*; *(fml: building)* imóvel *m*, prédio *m*.
prophecy ['prɒfɪsɪ] *n* profecia *f*.
prophesy ['prɒfɪsaɪ] *vt* profetizar.
prophet ['prɒfɪt] *n* profeta *m* (-tisa *f*).
proportion [prə'pɔːʃn] *n (part, amount)* porção *f*, parte *f*; *(ratio, in art)* proporção *f*.
proportional [prə'pɔːʃnl] *adj* proporcional; **to be ~ to sthg** ser proporcional a algo.
proportional representation [-,reprɪzen'teɪʃn] *n* representação *f* proporcional.
proportionate [prə'pɔːʃnət] *adj*: **~ (to)** proporcional (a).
proposal [prə'pəʊzl] *n (suggestion)* proposta *f*.
propose [prə'pəʊz] *vt (suggest)* propor ♦ *vi*: **to ~ to sb** pedir alguém em casamento.
proposition [,prɒpə'zɪʃn] *n (offer)* proposta *f*.
proprietor [prə'praɪətər] *n (fml)* proprietário *m* (-ria *f*).
prose [prəʊz] *n (not poetry)* prosa *f*; *(SCH)* retroversão *f*.
prosecute ['prɒsɪkjuːt] *vt (JUR)* processar, mover uma ação judicial contra ♦ *vi (bring a charge)* instaurar um processo judicial; *(represent in court)* representar o demandante.
prosecutor ['prɒsɪkjuːtər] *n* Promotor *m* Público (Promotora *f* Pública) *(Br)*, Delegado *m* (-da *f*) do

Ministério Público *(Port)*.
prospect ['prɒspekt] *n (possibility)* possibilidade *f*, perspectiva *f*; **I don't relish the ~** não me agrada a perspectiva.
⊐ **prospects** *npl (for the future)* perspectivas *fpl*.
prospective [prə'spektɪv] *adj* potencial.
prospectus [prə'spektəs] *(pl -es)* *n* prospecto *m*.
prosper ['prɒspər] *vi* prosperar.
prosperity [prɒ'sperətɪ] *n* prosperidade *f*.
prosperous ['prɒspərəs] *adj* próspero(-ra).
prostitute ['prɒstɪtjuːt] *n* prostituta *f*.
protagonist [prə'tægənɪst] *n* protagonista *mf*.
protect [prə'tekt] *vt* proteger; **to ~ sb/sthg against** proteger alguém/algo contra; **to ~ sb/sthg from** proteger alguém/algo de.
protection [prə'tekʃn] *n* proteção *f*.
protection factor *n* factor *m* de proteção.
protective [prə'tektɪv] *adj* protetor (-ra).
protein ['prəʊtiːn] *n* proteína *f*.
protest [*n* 'prəʊtest, *vb* prə'test] *n (complaint)* protesto *m*; *(demonstration)* passeata *f (Br)*, protesto, manifestação *f (Port)* ♦ *vt (Am: protest against)* protestar contra ♦ *vi*: **to ~ (against)** protestar (contra).
Protestant ['prɒtɪstənt] *n* protestante *mf*.
protester [prə'testər] *n* manifestante *mf*.
prototype ['prəʊtətaɪp] *n* protótipo *m*.
protractor [prə'træktər] *n* transferidor *m*.
protrude [prə'truːd] *vi* sair.
proud [praʊd] *adj* orgulhoso(-osa); **to be ~ of** ter orgulho em.
prove [pruːv] *(pp -d OR proven* [pruːvn]) *vt (show to be true)* provar; *(turn out to be)* revelar-se.
proverb ['prɒvɜːb] *n* provérbio *m*.
provide [prə'vaɪd] *vt (supply)* fornecer; **to ~ sb with sthg** fornecer algo a alguém.
⊐ **provide for** *vt fus (person)* manter.
provided (that) [prə'vaɪdɪd-] *conj* desde que.

providing (that) [prə'vaıdıŋ-] = provided (that).

province ['prɒvɪns] n província f.

provision [prə'vɪʒn] n (of food, resources) fornecimento m; (in agreement, law) disposição f, cláusula f; (arrangement) precauções fpl; **to make ~ for** (future, eventuality) tomar precauções para.

❏ **provisions** npl (supplies) provisões fpl, mantimentos mpl.

provisional [prə'vɪʒənl] adj provisório(-ria).

provocative [prə'vɒkətɪv] adj provocador(-ra).

provoke [prə'vəʊk] vt provocar.

prow [praʊ] n proa f.

prowess ['praʊɪs] n proeza f.

prowl [praʊl] vi rondar.

proxy ['prɒksɪ] n: **by ~** por OR com procuração.

prudent ['pruːdnt] adj prudente.

prudish ['pruːdɪʃ] adj pudico(-ca).

prune [pruːn] n ameixa f seca ◆ vt (tree, bush) podar.

pry [praɪ] vi: **to ~ (into sthg)** intrometer-se (em algo).

PS (abbr of postscript) PS.

psalm [sɑːm] n salmo m.

pseudonym ['sjuːdənɪm] n pseudônimo m.

psychiatric [ˌsaɪkɪˈætrɪk] adj psiquiátrico(-ca).

psychiatrist [saɪˈkaɪətrɪst] n psiquiatra mf.

psychiatry [saɪˈkaɪətrɪ] n psiquiatria f.

psychic ['saɪkɪk] adj (person) mediúnico(-ca), espírita.

psychoanalysis [ˌsaɪkəʊəˈnæləsɪs] n psicanálise f.

psychoanalyst [ˌsaɪkəʊˈænəlɪst] n psicanalista mf.

psychological [ˌsaɪkəˈlɒdʒɪkl] adj psicológico(-ca).

psychologist [saɪˈkɒlədʒɪst] n psicólogo m (-ga f).

psychology [saɪˈkɒlədʒɪ] n psicologia f.

psychopath ['saɪkəpæθ] n psicopata mf.

psychotherapist [ˌsaɪkəʊˈθerəpɪst] n psicoterapeuta mf.

psychotic [saɪˈkɒtɪk] adj psicopático(-ca).

pt abbr = pint.

PTO (abbr of please turn over) v.s.f.f.

pub [pʌb] n ~ bar m.

puberty ['pjuːbətɪ] n puberdade f.

public ['pʌblɪk] adj público(-ca) ◆ n: **the ~** o público; **in ~** em público.

public-address system n sistema m de difusão pública OR (de reforço) de som.

publican ['pʌblɪkən] n (Brit) pessoa que gere um "pub".

publication [ˌpʌblɪˈkeɪʃn] n publicação f.

public bar n (Brit) parte mais simples e menos confortável de um "pub".

public convenience n (Brit) banheiro m público (Br), casa f de banho pública (Port).

public footpath n (Brit) caminho m público.

public holiday n feriado m (nacional).

public house n (Brit: fml) ~ bar m.

publicity [pʌbˈlɪsɪtɪ] n publicidade f.

publicize [pʌblɪˈsaɪz] vt divulgar, dar a conhecer ao público.

public opinion n opinião f pública.

public relations npl relações fpl públicas. **public school** n (in UK) escola f particular; (in US) escola pública.

public telephone n telefone m público.

public transport n transporte m público OR coletivo.

publish ['pʌblɪʃ] vt publicar.

publisher ['pʌblɪʃər] n (person) editor m (-ra f); (company) editora f.

publishing ['pʌblɪʃɪŋ] n (industry) indústria f editorial.

pub lunch n almoço servido num "pub".

pudding ['pʊdɪŋ] n (sweet dish) pudim m; (Brit: course) sobremesa f.

puddle ['pʌdl] n poça f.

puff [pʌf] vi (breathe heavily) ofegar ◆ n (of air) lufada f, (smoke) baforada f; **to ~ at** tirar baforadas de.

puffin ['pʌfɪn] n papagaio-do-mar m.

puff pastry n massa f folhada.

pull [pʊl] vt & vi puxar ◆ n: **to give sthg a ~** dar um puxão em algo, puxar algo; **to ~ a face** fazer uma careta; **to ~ a muscle** distender um músculo; **"pull"** (on door) "puxe".

❏ **pull apart** vt sep (machine) desmontar; *(book)* desfazer.

❏ **pull down** *vt sep (lower)* baixar; *(demolish)* jogar abaixo, demolir.

❏ **pull in** *vi (train)* dar entrada *(em estação)*; *(car)* estacionar.

❏ **pull out** *vt sep (cork, plug)* tirar; *(tooth)* arrancar ◆ *vi (train)* partir; *(car)* sair; *(withdraw)* retirar-se.

❏ **pull over** *vi (car)* encostar.

❏ **pull up** *vt sep (trousers, sleeve)* arregaçar; *(socks)* puxar ◆ *vi (stop)* parar.

pulley ['pʊlɪ] *(pl* **-s)** *n* roldana *f*.

pull-out *n (Am: beside road)* área *f* de descanso.

pullover ['pʊl,əʊvəʳ] *n* pulôver *m*.

pulp [pʌlp] *n* polpa *f*; *(of wood)* pasta *f* de papel ◆ *adj:* ~ **fiction** literatura *f* de cordel.

pulpit ['pʊlpɪt] *n* púlpito *m*.

pulse [pʌls] *n (MED)* pulso *m*.

puma ['pju:mə] *(pl inv OR* **-s)** *n* puma *m*.

pump [pʌmp] *n* bomba *f*.

❏ **pumps** *npl (sports shoes)* sapatilhas *fpl*, ténis *mpl* (Port).

❏ **pump up** *vt sep* encher.

pumpkin ['pʌmpkɪn] *n* abóbora *f*.

pun [pʌn] *n* trocadilho *m*.

punch [pʌntʃ] *n (blow)* murro *m*, soco *m*; *(drink)* ponche *m* ◆ *vt (hit)* esmurrar, dar um murro OR soco em; *(ticket)* picar, obliterar.

Punch and Judy show [-'dʒu:dɪ-] *n* = show *m* de marionetes OR fantoches.

punch line *n* final *m (de uma anedota ou piada)*.

punch-up *n (Brit: inf)* briga *f*, pancadaria *f*.

punctual ['pʌŋktʃʊəl] *adj* pontual.

punctuation [,pʌŋktʃʊ'eɪʃn] *n* pontuação *f*.

punctuation mark *n* sinal *m* de pontuação.

puncture ['pʌŋktʃəʳ] *n* furo *m* ◆ *vt* furar.

pungent ['pʌndʒənt] *adj (smell)* intenso(-sa), penetrante.

punish ['pʌnɪʃ] *vt:* **to ~ sb (for sthg)** castigar alguém (por algo), pôr alguém de castigo (por algo).

punishing ['pʌnɪʃɪŋ] *adj* penoso (-osa).

punishment ['pʌnɪʃmənt] *n* castigo *m*.

punk [pʌŋk] *n (person)* punk *mf*;

(music) música *f* punk.

punnet ['pʌnɪt] *n (Brit)* cestinho *m*, caixa *f*.

puny ['pju:nɪ] *adj (person, limbs)* magricela; *(effort, attempt)* patético (-ca).

pup [pʌp] *n (young dog)* cachorrinho *m* (Br), cachorro *m* (Port).

pupil ['pju:pl] *n (student)* aluno *m* (-na *f*); *(of eye)* pupila *f*.

puppet ['pʌpɪt] *n* fantoche *m*, marionete *f*.

puppy ['pʌpɪ] *n* cachorrinho *m* (Br), cachorro *m* (Port).

purchase ['pɜ:tʃəs] *vt (fml)* comprar ◆ *n (fml)* compra *f*.

purchaser ['pɜ:tʃəsəʳ] *n* comprador *m* (-ra *f*).

pure [pjʊəʳ] *adj* puro(-ra).

puree ['pjʊəreɪ] *n* purê *m*.

purely ['pjʊəlɪ] *adv (only)* meramente.

purify ['pjʊərɪfaɪ] *vt* purificar.

purity ['pjʊərətɪ] *n* pureza *f*.

purple ['pɜ:pl] *adj* roxo(-xa).

purpose ['pɜ:pəs] *n (reason)* motivo *m*; *(use)* uso *m*: **on ~** de propósito.

purr [pɜ:ʳ] *vi (cat)* ronronar.

purse [pɜ:s] *n* carteira *f*.

purser ['pɜ:səʳ] *n* comissário *m* de bordo.

pursue [pə'sju:] *vt (follow)* perseguir; *(study, inquiry, matter)* continuar com.

pursuer [pə'sju:əʳ] *n* perseguidor *m* (-ra *f*).

pursuit [pə'sju:t] *n (of animal, criminal)* perseguição *f*; *(of happiness, goals)* busca *f*; *(occupation, activity)* atividade *f*; **leisure ~s** passatempos *mpl*.

pus [pʌs] *n* pus *m*.

push [pʊʃ] *vt (shove)* empurrar; *(button, doorbell)* apertar; *(product)* promover ◆ *vi (shove)* empurrar ◆ *n:* **to give sb/sthg a ~** empurrar alguém/algo, dar um empurrão em alguém/algo; **to ~ sb into doing sthg** levar alguém a fazer algo; **"push"** *(on door)* "empurre".

❏ **push in** *vi (in queue)* meter-se na frente.

❏ **push off** *vi (inf: go away)* pirar-se.

push-button telephone *n* telefone *m* de teclas.

pushchair ['pʊʃtʃeəʳ] *n (Brit)* carrinho *m (de bebê)*.

pushed [pʊʃt] *adj (inf):* **to be ~ (for time)** não ter tempo.

pusher ['pʊʃəʳ] *n (drugs seller)* traficante *mf* OR passador *m* (-ra *f*).

push-ups *npl* flexões *fpl*.

pushy ['puʃi] *adj* agressivo(-va), insistente.

puss [pus] = **pussy (cat)**.

pussy (cat) ['pusi-] *n* (*inf*) gatito *m*, bichaninho *m*.

put [put] (*pt & pp* **put**) *vt* pôr; (*express*) exprimir; (*write*) escrever; (*a question*) colocar, fazer; **to ~ sthg at** (*estimate*) avaliar algo em; **to ~ a child to bed** pôr uma criança na cama; **to ~ money into sthg** pôr dinheiro OR investir em algo.

❏ **put aside** *vt sep* (*money*) pôr de lado.

❏ **put away** *vt sep* (*tidy up*) arrumar.

❏ **put back** *vt sep* (*replace*) repor; (*postpone*) adiar; (*clock, watch*) atrasar.

❏ **put down** *vt sep* (*on floor, table*) colocar; (*passenger, deposit*) deixar; (*Brit: animal*) matar, abater.

❏ **put forward** *vt sep* (*clock, watch*) adiantar; (*suggest*) sugerir.

❏ **put in** *vt sep* (*insert*) pôr em; (*install*) instalar.

❏ **put off** *vt sep* (*postpone*) adiar; (*distract*) distrair; (*repel*) dar nojo em; (*passenger*) deixar.

❏ **put on** *vt sep* (*clothes, make-up, CD*) pôr; (*television, light, radio*) acender, ligar; (*play, show*) montar; **to ~ on weight** engordar.

❏ **put out** *vt sep* (*cigarette, fire, light*) apagar; (*publish*) publicar; (*hand, arm, leg*) estender; (*inconvenience*) incomodar; **to ~ one's back out** deslocar uma vértebra.

❏ **put together** *vt sep* juntar.

❏ **put up** *vt sep* (*tent*) montar; (*statue*) erigir, erguer; (*building*) construir; (*umbrella*) abrir; (*a notice, sign*) afixar; (*price, rate*) aumentar, subir; (*provide with accommodation*) alojar ◆ *vi* (*Brit: in hotel*) ficar, hospedar-se.

❏ **put up with** *vt fus* agüentar, suportar.

putt [pʌt] *n* putt *m*, pancada *f* leve ◆ *vi* fazer um putt.

putter ['pʌtəʳ] *n* (*club*) putter *m*.

putting green ['pʌtɪŋ-] *n* green *m*, pequeno campo de golfe.

putty ['pʌti] *n* betume *m*, massa *f* para vidros.

puzzle ['pʌzl] *n* (*game*) quebra-cabeças *m inv*; (*jigsaw*) puzzle *m*; (*mystery*) mistério *m* ◆ *vt* confundir.

puzzling ['pʌzlɪŋ] *adj* intrigante.

pyjamas [pə'dʒuːməz] *npl* (*Brit*) pijama *m*.

pylon ['paɪlən] *n* poste *m* de alta tensão.

pyramid ['pɪrəmɪd] *n* pirâmide *f*.

Pyrenees [,pɪrə'niːz] *npl*: **the ~** os Pirineus.

Pyrex® ['paɪreks] *n* Pirex® *m*.

python ['paɪθn] *n* (*cobra*) piton *f*.

Q

quack [kwæk] *n (noise)* quá-quá *m*; *(inf: doctor)* charlatão *m* (-tona *f*), veterinário *m* (-ria *f*).
quadruple [kwɒ'dru:pl] *vi* quadruplicar ♦ *adj*: sales are ~ last year's figures as vendas aumentaram o quádruplo em relação ao ano passado.
quail [kweɪl] *n* codorna *f (Br)*, codorniz *f (Port)*.
quail's eggs *npl* ovos *mpl* de codorna.
quaint [kweɪnt] *adj* pitoresco(-ca).
quake [kweɪk] *n (inf)* terremoto *m* ♦ *vi* tremer.
qualification [kwɒlɪfɪ'keɪʃn] *n* qualificação *f*.
qualified ['kwɒlɪfaɪd] *adj (trained)* qualificado(-da).
qualify ['kwɒlɪfaɪ] *vi (for competition)* qualificar-se; *(pass exam)* formar-se.
quality ['kwɒlɪtɪ] *n* qualidade *f* ♦ *adj* de qualidade.
quantity ['kwɒntɪtɪ] *n* quantidade *f*.
quarantine ['kwɒrəntiːn] *n* quarentena *f*.
quarrel ['kwɒrəl] *n* discussão *f* ♦ *vi* discutir.
quarrelsome ['kwɒrəlsəm] *adj* conflituoso(-osa); he's in a ~ mood today ele está muito irritadiço hoje.
quarry ['kwɒrɪ] *n (for stone)* pedreira *f*, *(for sand)* areeiro *m*.
quart [kwɔːt] *n (in UK)* = 1,136 l, = litro *m*; *(in US)* = 0,946 l, = litro.
quarter ['kwɔːtəʳ] *n (fraction)* quarto *m*; *(Am: coin)* moeda *f* de 25 centavos; *(4 ounces)* = 0,1134 kg, = cem gramas; *(three months)* trimestre *m*; *(part of town)* bairro *m*; (a) ~ to five *(Brit)* quinze para as cinco; (a) ~ of five *(Am)* quinze para as cinco; (a) ~ past five *(Brit)* cinco e quinze; (a) ~ after five *(Am)* cinco e quinze; (a) ~ of an hour um quarto de hora.

quarterfinal [kwɔːtə'faɪnl] *n* quarta *f* de final.
quarterly ['kwɔːtəlɪ] *adj* trimestral ♦ *adv* trimestralmente ♦ *n* publicação *f* trimestral.
quarterpounder [kwɔːtə'paʊndəʳ] *n* hambúrguer *m* grande.
quartet [kwɔː'tet] *n* quarteto *m*.
quartz [kwɔːts] *adj (watch)* de quartzo.
quartz watch *n* relógio *m* de quartzo.
quay [kiː] *n* cais *m inv*.
quayside ['kiːsaɪd] *n* cais *m inv*.
queasy ['kwiːzɪ] *adj (inf)* enjoado (-da), indisposto(-osta).
queen [kwiːn] *n (in cards)* rainha *f*; dama *f*.
queen mother *n*: the ~ a rainha-mãe.
queer [kwɪəʳ] *adj (strange)* esquisito(-ta); *(inf: ill)* indisposto(-osta) ♦ *n (inf: homosexual)* bicha *f (Br)*, maricas *m inv (Port)*.
quench [kwentʃ] *vt*: to ~ one's thirst matar a sede.
query ['kwɪərɪ] *n* pergunta *f*.
quest [kwest] *n*: ~ (for) busca *f* (de).
question ['kwestʃn] *n* pergunta *f*; *(issue)* questão *f* ♦ *vt (person)* interrogar; it's out of the ~ está fora de questão.
questionable ['kwestʃənəbl] *adj* questionável.
question mark *n* ponto *m* de interrogação.
questionnaire [kwestʃə'neəʳ] *n* questionário *m*.
queue [kjuː] *n (Brit)* fila *f*, bicha *f (Port)* ♦ *vi (Brit)* fazer fila.
⏌ **queue up** *vi (Brit)* fazer fila.
quiche [kiːʃ] *n* quiche *m*.
quick [kwɪk] *adj* rápido(-da) ♦ *adv* rapidamente, depressa.

quicken ['kwɪkn] *vt* apressar, acelerar
♦ *vi* acelerar-se.
quickly ['kwɪklɪ] *adv* rapidamente,
depressa.
quicksand ['kwɪksænd] *n* areia *f*
movediça.
quick-witted [-'wɪtɪd] *adj* vivo(-va).
quid [kwɪd] (*pl inv*) *n* (*Brit: inf*) libra *f*.
quiet ['kwaɪət] *adj* silencioso(-osa);
(calm, peaceful) calmo(-ma); *(voice)*
baixo(-xa) ♦ *n* sossego *m*, calma *f*;
keep ~! está calado!; **to keep ~** *(not
make noise)* estar calado; **please keep ~
about this** por favor não digam nada.
quieten ['kwaɪətn] : **quieten down** *vi*
acalmar-se.
quietly ['kwaɪətlɪ] *adv* silenciosamen-
te; *(calmly)* tranqüilamente.
quilt [kwɪlt] *n* edredom *m*.
quince [kwɪns] *n* marmelo *m*.
quirk [kwɜːk] *n* mania *f*.
quit [kwɪt] (*pt & pp* quit) *vi* (*resign*)
demitir-se; *(give up)* desistir ♦ *vt* (*Am:
school, job*) deixar, abandonar; **to
~ doing sthg** deixar de fazer algo,

desistir de fazer algo.
quite [kwaɪt] *adv* bastante; **it's not ~
big enough** não é suficientemente
grande; **it's not ~ ready** ainda não está
pronto; **you're ~ right** você tem toda a
razão; **~ a lot (of children)** bastantes
(crianças); **~ a lot of money** bastante
dinheiro.
quits [kwɪts] *adj* (*inf*): **we're ~!** estamos
quites!; **give me £10 and we'll call it ~!**
dê-me 10 libras e assunto resolvido!
quiver ['kwɪvəʳ] *n* (*for arrows*) aljava *f*,
carcás *m* ♦ *vi* tremer.
quiz [kwɪz] (*pl* **-zes**) *n* competição *f*
*(que consiste em responder a perguntas de
natureza variada)*.
quizzical ['kwɪzɪkl] *adj* (*look, glance*)
inquiridor(-ra); *(smile)* brincalhão
(-lhona), zombeteiro(-ra).
quota ['kwəʊtə] *n* cota *f*, quota *f*.
quotation [kwəʊ'teɪʃn] *n* (*phrase*)
citação *f*; *(estimate)* orçamento *m*.
quotation marks *npl* aspas *fpl*.
quote [kwəʊt] *vt* (*phrase, writer*) citar;
(price) indicar ♦ *n* (*phrase*) citação *f*;
(estimate) orçamento *m*.

R

rabbi ['ræbaɪ] n rabi m, rabino m.
rabbit ['ræbɪt] n coelho m.
rabbit hutch n coelheira f.
rabies ['reɪbiːz] n raiva f.
RAC n = TCB (Br), ≃ ACP (Port).
race [reɪs] n (competition) corrida f; (ethnic group) raça f ♦ vi (compete) competir; (go fast) correr; (engine) acelerar ♦ vt (compete against) competir com.
race car (Am) = **racing car**.
racecourse ['reɪskɔːs] n hipódromo m.
racehorse ['reɪshɔːs] n cavalo m de corrida.
racetrack ['reɪstræk] n (for horses) hipódromo m.
racial ['reɪʃl] adj racial.
racial discrimination n discriminação f racial.
racing ['reɪsɪŋ] n: (horse) ~ corridas fpl de cavalos.
racing car n carro m de corrida.
racism ['reɪsɪzm] n racismo m.
racist ['reɪsɪst] n racista mf.
rack [ræk] n (for coats) cabide m; (for bottles) garrafeira f; (for plates) escorredor m de louça, (luggage) ~ portabagagens m inv; ~ **of lamb** peito m de carneiro.
racket ['rækɪt] n (for tennis, badminton, squash) raquete f; (noise) barulheira f.
racquet ['rækɪt] n raquete f.
radar ['reɪdɑːʳ] n radar m.
radiant ['reɪdjənt] adj radiante.
radiate ['reɪdɪeɪt] vt irradiar ♦ vi (be emitted) irradiar; (spread from centre) ramificar-se.
radiation [,reɪdɪ'eɪʃn] n radiação f.
radiator ['reɪdɪeɪtəʳ] n radiador m.
radical ['rædɪkl] adj radical.
radically ['rædɪklɪ] adv radicalmente.
radii ['reɪdɪaɪ] pl → **radius**.
radio ['reɪdɪəʊ] (pl -s) n (device) rádio

m; (system) rádio f ♦ vt (person) chamar por rádio; **on the** ~ na rádio.
radioactive [,reɪdɪəʊ'æktɪv] adj radioativo(-va).
radio alarm n rádio-despertador m.
radiology [,reɪdɪ'ɒlədʒɪ] n radiologia f.
radish ['rædɪʃ] n rabanete m.
radius ['reɪdɪəs] (pl **radii**) n raio m.
RAF n (abbr of Royal Air Force) RAF f, força aérea britânica.
raffle ['ræfl] n rifa f.
raft [rɑːft] n (of wood) jangada f; (inflatable) barco m de borracha.
rafter ['rɑːftəʳ] n trave f, barrote m.
rag [ræg] n (old cloth) trapo m.
rag-and-bone man n trapeiro m.
rag doll n boneca f de trapos.
rage [reɪdʒ] n raiva f, fúria f.
ragged ['rægɪd] adj (person, clothes) esfarrapado(-da).
raid [reɪd] n (attack) ataque m; (by police) batida f (Br), rusga f (Port); (robbery) assalto m ♦ vt (subj: police) dar uma batida em; (subj: thieves) assaltar.
rail [reɪl] n (bar) barra f; (for curtain) trilho m (Br), varão m (Port); (on stairs) corrimão m; (for train, tram) trilho m (Br), carril m (Port) ♦ adj ferroviário(-ria); **by** ~ de trem (Br), de comboio (Port).
railcard ['reɪlkɑːd] n (Brit) cartão que permite aos jovens e aposentados obter descontos nas viagens de comboio.
railings ['reɪlɪŋz] npl grades fpl.
railroad ['reɪlrəʊd] (Am) = **railway**.
railway ['reɪlweɪ] n (system) ferrovia f (Br), caminhos-de-ferro mpl (Port); (track) estrada f de ferro (Br), via-férrea f (Port).
railway line n (route) linha f de trem (Br), linha f dos caminhos-de-ferro (Port); (track) estrada f de ferro (Br), via-férrea f (Port).

railway station *n* estação *f* ferroviária *(Br)*, estação *f* dos caminhos-de-ferro *(Port)*.

railway track *n* estrada *f* de ferro *(Br)*, via-férrea *f (Port)*.

rain [reɪn] *n* chuva *f ◆ v impers* chover; **it's ~ing** está chovendo.

rainbow ['reɪnbəʊ] *n* arco-íris *m inv*.

raincoat ['reɪnkəʊt] *n* capa *f* de chuva *(Br)*, gabardina *f (Port)*.

raindrop ['reɪndrɒp] *n* gota *f* OR pingo *m* de chuva.

rainfall ['reɪnfɔːl] *n* precipitação *f*.

rain forest *n* floresta *f* tropical (úmida).

rainy ['reɪnɪ] *adj* chuvoso(-osa).

raise [reɪz] *vt* levantar; *(increase)* aumentar; *(money)* angariar; *(child, animals)* criar *◆ n (Am: pay increase)* aumento *m*.

raisin ['reɪzn] *n* passa *f* (de uva).

rake [reɪk] *n (tool)* ancinho *m*.

rally ['rælɪ] *n (public meeting)* comício *m*; *(motor race)* rali *m*, rally *m*; *(in tennis, badminton, squash)* troca *f* de bolas, rally.

ram [ræm] *n* carneiro *m ◆ vt (bang into)* bater contra.

Ramadan [ˌræməˈdæn] *n* Ramadão *m*.

ramble ['ræmbl] *n* passeio *m*, caminhada *f*.

rambler ['ræmblər] *n* caminhante *mf*.

ramp [ræmp] *n (slope)* rampa *f*; *(Brit: in road)* lombada *f*; *(Am: to freeway)* acesso *m*; **"ramp"** *(Brit)* "lombada".

rampant ['ræmpənt] *adj (inflation)* galopante; *(growth)* desenfreado(-da); **corruption was ~** proliferava a corrupção.

ramparts ['ræmpɑːts] *npl* muralhas *fpl*.

ramshackle ['ræmˌʃækl] *adj* em más condições.

ran [ræn] *pt →* run.

ranch [rɑːntʃ] *n* rancho *m*.

ranch dressing *n (Am)* tempero cremoso e picante para saladas.

rancher ['rɑːntʃər] *n* rancheiro *m* (-ra *f*).

rancid ['rænsɪd] *adj* rançoso(-osa).

random ['rændəm] *adj* ao acaso *◆ n*: **at ~** ao acaso.

randy ['rændɪ] *adj (inf)* e︰ tado(-da).

rang [ræŋ] *pt →* ring.

range [reɪndʒ] *n (of radio, telescope)* alcance *m*; *(of aircraft)* autonomia *f*; *(of prices)* leque *m*; *(of goods, services)* gama *f*, variedade *f*; *(of hills, mountains)* cadeia *f*, cordilheira *f*; *(for shooting)* linha *f* de tiro; *(cooker)* fogão *m ◆ vi*: **to ~ from ... to** oscilar entre ... e; **age ~** faixa *f* etária.

ranger ['reɪndʒər] *n* guarda *mf* florestal.

rank [ræŋk] *n (in armed forces, police)* patente *f ◆ adj (smell)* fétido(-da); *(taste)* horroroso(-osa).

ransack ['rænsæk] *vt (plunder)* pilhar.

ransom ['rænsəm] *n* resgate *m*.

rant [rænt] *vi* arengar.

rap [ræp] *n (music)* rap *m*.

rape [reɪp] *n (crime)* estupro *m ◆ vt* estuprar.

rapeseed ['reɪpsiːd] *n* semente *f* de colza.

rapid ['ræpɪd] *adj* rápido(-da).
⏟ **rapids** *npl* rápidos *mpl*.

rapidly ['ræpɪdlɪ] *adv* rapidamente.

rapist ['reɪpɪst] *n* estuprador *m*.

rapport [ræˈpɔːr] *n* relação *f*; **a ~ with/between** uma relação com/entre.

rapture ['ræptʃər] *n* excitação *f*.

rare [reər] *adj* raro(-ra); *(meat)* malpassado(-da).

rarely ['reəlɪ] *adv* raramente.

rarity ['reərətɪ] *n* raridade *f*.

rascal ['rɑːskl] *n (dishonest person)* patife *mf*.

rash [ræʃ] *n (on skin)* erupção *f* cutânea, brotoeja *f ◆ adj* precipitado(-da).

rasher ['ræʃər] *n* fatia *f (fina de bacon)*.

raspberry ['rɑːzbərɪ] *n* framboesa *f*.

rat [ræt] *n* rato *m*, ratazana *f*.

ratatouille [ˌrætuˈiː] *n* ensopado de cebola, alho, tomate, pimentão, abobrinha e beringela.

rate [reɪt] *n (level)* índice *m*, taxa *f*; *(charge)* tarifa *f*, preço *m*; *(speed)* velocidade *f ◆ vt (consider)* considerar; *(deserve)* merecer; **~ of exchange** taxa de câmbio; **at any ~** *(at least)* pelo menos; *(anyway)* de qualquer modo; **at this ~** desse jeito, nesse passo.

rather ['rɑːðər] *adv (quite)* bastante; **I'd ~ have a beer** prefiro uma cerveja; **I'd ~ not** é melhor não; **would you ~ ...?** você prefere ...?; **~ than** em vez de; **that's ~ a lot** é um pouco demais.

ratify ['rætɪfaɪ] *vt* ratificar.

ratio ['reɪʃɪəʊ] *(pl -s) n* proporção *f*.

ration ['ræʃn] *n* porção *f*.
⏟ **rations** *npl (food)* rações *fpl*.

rational [ˈræʃnl] *adj* racional.
rattle [ˈrætl] *n* (of baby) chocalho *m*
♦ *vi* chocalhar.
rattlesnake [ˈrætlsneɪk] *n* (cobra)
cascavel *f*.
rave [reɪv] *n* (party) rave *f*.
raven [ˈreɪvn] *n* corvo *m*.
ravenous [ˈrævənəs] *adj* (person, animal) faminto(-ta); (appetite) voraz.
ravine [rəˈviːn] *n* ravina *f*.
raving [ˈreɪvɪŋ] *adj* (beauty, success)
tremendo(-da); ~ **mad** doido varrido
(doida varrida).
ravioli [ˌrævɪˈəʊlɪ] *n* ravioli *m*.
ravishing [ˈrævɪʃɪŋ] *adj* (person)
belo(-la).
raw [rɔː] *adj* (uncooked) cru (crua);
(unprocessed) bruto(-ta).
raw material *n* matéria-prima *f*.
ray [reɪ] *n* raio *m*.
rayon [ˈreɪɒn] *n* rayon *m*, seda *f* artificial.
razor [ˈreɪzər] *n* lâmina *f* de barbear.
razor blade *n* lâmina *f* de barbear.
Rd *abbr* = **Road**.
re [riː] *prep* referente a, com respeito
a.
RE *n* (abbr of religious education) = religião *f* e moral.
reach [riːtʃ] *vt* chegar a; (arrive at)
atingir; (contact) contatar ♦ *n*: **out of ~**
fora de alcance; **within ~ of the beach**
próximo da praia.
❏ **reach out** *vi*: **to ~ out (for)** estender
o braço (para).
react [rɪˈækt] *vi* reagir.
reaction [rɪˈækʃn] *n* reação *f*.
reactor [rɪˈæktər] *n* (for nuclear energy)
reator *m*.
read [riːd] (*pt & pp* **read** [red]) *vt* ler;
(subj: sign, note) dizer; (subj: meter,
gauge) marcar ♦ *vi* ler; **I read about it
in the paper** fiquei sabendo pelo jornal.
❏ **read out** *vt sep* ler em voz alta.
readable [ˈriːdəbl] *adj* (book) agradável de ler.
reader [ˈriːdər] *n* (of newspaper, book)
leitor *m* (-ra *f*).
readership [ˈriːdəʃɪp] *n* número *m* de
leitores.
readily [ˈredɪlɪ] *adv* (willingly) de boa
vontade; (easily) facilmente.
reading [ˈriːdɪŋ] *n* leitura *f*.
reading matter *n* leitura *f*.

readjust [ˌriːəˈdʒʌst] *vt* reajustar ♦ *vi*:
to ~ (to sthg) adaptar-se (a algo).
readout [ˈriːdaʊt] *n* (COMPUT) visualização *f*.
ready [ˈredɪ] *adj* (prepared) pronto
(-ta); **to be ~ for sthg** (prepared) estar
preparado para algo; **to be ~ to do
sthg** (willing) estar disposto a fazer
algo; (likely) estar prestes a fazer algo;
to get ~ preparar-se; **to get sthg ~**
preparar algo.
ready cash *n* dinheiro *m* vivo,
numerário *m*.
ready-cooked [-kʊkt] *adj* pré-cozido(-da).
ready-made *adj* (ready to use) (já)
feito(-ta).
ready-to-wear *adj* de pronto para
vestir.
reafforestation [ˌriːəfɒrɪˈsteɪʃn] *n*
reflorestação *f*.
real [rɪəl] *adj* verdadeiro(-ra); (life,
world) real; (leather) genuíno(-na) ♦ *adv*
(Am) mesmo.
real ale *n* (Brit) cerveja feita e armazenada de modo tradicional.
real estate *n* bens *mpl* imóveis.
realism [ˈrɪəlɪzm] *n* realismo *m*.
realistic [rɪəˈlɪstɪk] *adj* realista.
reality [rɪˈælətɪ] *n* realidade *f*; **in ~** na
realidade.
realization [ˌrɪəlaɪˈzeɪʃn] *n* (awareness, recognition) consciência *f*; (of
ambition, goal) realização *f*.
realize [ˈrɪəlaɪz] *vt* (become aware of)
aperceber-se de; (know) saber; (ambition, goal) realizar.
really [ˈrɪəlɪ] *adv* (for emphasis)
mesmo, muito; (in reality) realmente;
was it good? – not ~ foi bom? – nem
por isso; **~?** (expressing surprise) a
sério?
realtor [ˈrɪəltər] *n* (Am) agente *m*
imobiliário (agente *f* imobiliária).
reap [riːp] *vt* colher.
reappear [ˌriːəˈpɪər] *vi* reaparecer.
rear [rɪər] *adj* traseiro(-ra) ♦ *n* (back)
parte *f* de trás, traseira *f*.
rearmost [ˈrɪəməʊst] *adj* último
(-ma).
rearrange [ˌriːəˈreɪndʒ] *vt* (room, furniture) mudar; (meeting) alterar.
rearview mirror [rɪəvjuː-] *n* (espelho) retrovisor *m*.
rear-wheel drive *n* veículo *m* com
tração nas rodas traseiras OR de trás.

reason ['ri:zn] *n* razão *f*, motivo *m*; **for some ~** por alguma razão.
reasonable ['ri:znəbl] *adj* razoável.
reasonably ['ri:znəblɪ] *adv* (quite) razoavelmente.
reasoning ['ri:znɪŋ] *n* raciocínio *m*.
reassess [ˌri:ə'ses] *vt* reexaminar.
reassurance [ˌri:ə'ʃɔ:rəns] *n* (comfort) palavras *fpl* tranqüilizadoras OR de conforto; (promise) garantia *f*.
reassure [ˌri:ə'ʃɔ:ʳ] *vt* tranqüilizar.
reassuring [ˌri:ə'ʃɔ:rɪŋ] *adj* tranqüilizador(-ra).
rebate ['ri:beɪt] *n* devolução *f*, reembolso *m*.
rebel [*n* 'rebl, *vb* rɪ'bel] *n* rebelde *mf* ♦ *vi* revoltar-se.
rebellion [rɪ'beljən] *n* rebelião *f*.
rebellious [rɪ'beljəs] *adj* rebelde.
rebound [rɪ'baʊnd] *vi* (ball) ressaltar (Br), pinchar (Port).
rebuild [ˌri:'bɪld] (pt & pp -built) *vt* reconstruir.
rebuke [rɪ'bju:k] *vt* repreender.
recall [rɪ'kɔ:l] *vt* (remember) recordar-se de, lembrar-se de.
recap ['ri:kæp] *n* (inf) resumo *m*, recapitulação *f* ♦ *vt* & *vi* (inf: summarize) recapitular.
recede [rɪ'si:d] *vi* (person, car) recuar; (hopes, danger) desvanecer-se.
receding [rɪ'si:dɪŋ] *adj*: **~ hairline** entradas *fpl*.
receipt [rɪ'si:t] *n* (for goods, money) recibo *m*; **on ~ of** ao receber, mediante a recepção de.
receive [rɪ'si:v] *vt* receber.
receiver [rɪ'si:vəʳ] *n* (of phone) fone *m* (Br), auscultador *m* (Port).
recent ['ri:snt] *adj* recente.
recently ['ri:sntlɪ] *adv* recentemente.
receptacle [rɪ'septəkl] *n* (fml) recipiente *m*.
reception [rɪ'sepʃn] *n* recepção *f*.
reception desk *n* recepção *f*.
receptionist [rɪ'sepʃənɪst] *n* recepcionista *mf*.
recess ['ri:ses] *n* (in wall) nicho *m*, vão *m*; (Am: SCH) recreio *m*, intervalo *m*.
recession [rɪ'seʃn] *n* recessão *f*.
recharge [ˌri:'tʃɑ:dʒ] *vt* recarregar.
recipe ['resɪpɪ] *n* receita *f*.
recipient [rɪ'sɪpɪənt] *n* (of letter, cheque) destinatário *m* (-ria *f*).

reciprocal [rɪ'sɪprəkl] *adj* recíproco(-ca).
recite [rɪ'saɪt] *vt* (poem) recitar; (list) enumerar.
reckless ['reklɪs] *adj* irresponsável.
reckon ['rekn] *vt* (inf: think): **to ~ (that)** achar que.
◻ **reckon on** *vt fus* contar, esperar.
◻ **reckon with** *vt fus* (expect) contar com.
reclaim [rɪ'kleɪm] *vt* (baggage) recuperar.
reclining seat [rɪ'klaɪnɪŋ-] *n* assento *m* reclinável.
recluse [rɪ'klu:s] *n* solitário *m* (-ria *f*).
recognition [ˌrekəg'nɪʃn] *n* reconhecimento *m*.
recognizable ['rekəgnaɪzəbl] *adj* reconhecível.
recognize ['rekəgnaɪz] *vt* reconhecer.
recollect [ˌrekə'lekt] *vt* recordar-se de.
recollection [ˌrekə'lekʃn] *n* lembrança *f*, recordação *f*; **I have no ~ of what happened** não me lembro de nada do que aconteceu.
recommend [ˌrekə'mend] *vt* recomendar; **to ~ sb to do sthg** recomendar a alguém que faça algo.
recommendation [ˌrekəmen'deɪʃn] *n* recomendação *f*.
reconcile ['rekənsaɪl] *vt* (beliefs, ideas) conciliar; (people) reconciliar; (resign): **to ~ o.s. to sthg** conformar-se com algo; **to ~ sthg with sthg** conciliar algo com algo.
reconnaissance [rɪ'kɒnɪsəns] *n* reconhecimento *m*.
reconsider [ˌri:kən'sɪdəʳ] *vt* reconsiderar.
reconstruct [ˌri:kən'strʌkt] *vt* reconstruir.
record [*n* 'rekɔ:d, *vb* rɪ'kɔ:d] *n* (MUS) disco *m*; (best performance, highest level) recorde *m*; (account) registro *m* ♦ *vt* (keep account of) registrar; (on tape) gravar.
recorded delivery [rɪ'kɔ:dɪd-] *n* (Brit) correio *m* registrado.
recorder [rɪ'kɔ:dəʳ] *n* (tape recorder) gravador *m*; (instrument) flauta *f*, pífaro *m*.
record holder *n* detentor *m* (-ra *f*) do recorde, recordista *mf*.
recording [rɪ'kɔ:dɪŋ] *n* gravação *f*.
record player *n* toca-discos *m inv*

(Br), gira-discos *m inv (Port)*.
record shop *n* loja *f* de discos.
recover [rɪˈkʌvəʳ] *vt & vi* recuperar.
recovery [rɪˈkʌvərɪ] *n* recuperação *f*.
recovery vehicle *n (Brit)* reboque *m*.
recreation [ˌrekrɪˈeɪʃn] *n* distração *f*, divertimento *m*.
recreation ground *n* parque *m* OR campo *m* de jogos.
recriminations [rɪˌkrɪmɪˈneɪʃnz] *npl* recriminações *fpl*.
recruit [rɪˈkruːt] *n* recruta *mf* ♦ *vt* recrutar.
recruitment [rɪˈkruːtmənt] *n* recrutamento *m*.
rectangle [ˈrektæŋgl] *n* retângulo *m*.
rectangular [rekˈtæŋgjʊləʳ] *adj* retangular.
rectify [ˈrektɪfaɪ] *vt* retificar, corrigir.
recuperate [rɪˈkuːpəreɪt] *vi*: **to ~ (from sthg)** recuperar-se (de algo).
recur [rɪˈkɜːʳ] *vi* repetir-se.
recurrence [rɪˈkʌrəns] *n* repetição *f*.
recurrent [rɪˈkʌrənt] *adj* que se repete.
recycle [ˌriːˈsaɪkl] *vt* reciclar.
red [red] *adj (in colour)* vermelho(-lha), encarnado(-da); *(hair)* ruivo(-va) ♦ *n (colour)* vermelho *m*, encarnado *m*; **in the ~** com saldo negativo.
red cabbage *n* couve *f* roxa.
Red Cross *n* Cruz *f* Vermelha.
redcurrant [ˈredkʌrənt] *n* groselha *f*.
redden [redn] *vt* tingir de vermelho ♦ *vi* ficar vermelho(-lha).
redecorate [ˌriːˈdekəreɪt] *vt* redecorar.
red-faced [-ˈfeɪst] *adj* vermelho (-lha).
red-haired [-ˌheəd] *adj* ruivo(-va).
red-handed [-ˈhændɪd] *adj*: **to catch sb ~** apanhar alguém com a boca na botija.
redhead [ˈredhed] *n* ruivo *m* (-va *f*).
red-hot *adj (metal)* incandescente, rubro(-bra).
redial [ˌriːˈdaɪəl] *vi* tornar a discar (o número de telefone).
redid [ˌriːˈdɪd] *pt* → redo.
redirect [ˌriːdɪˈrekt] *vt (letter)* mandar para o novo endereço; *(traffic, plane)* desviar.
rediscover [ˌriːdɪsˈkʌvəʳ] *vt (re-experience)* voltar a descobrir.

red light *n (traffic signal)* sinal *m* vermelho.
redo [ˌriːˈduː] *(pt* -did, *pp* -done) *vt (do again)* tornar a fazer.
red pepper *n* pimentão *m* vermelho.
red tape *n (fig)* burocracia *f*.
reduce [rɪˈdjuːs] *vt (make smaller)* reduzir, diminuir; *(make cheaper)* saldar, reduzir o preço de ♦ *vi (Am: slim)* emagrecer.
reduced price [rɪˈdjuːst-] *n* preço *m* reduzido OR de saldo.
reduction [rɪˈdʌkʃn] *n* redução *f*.
redundancy [rɪˈdʌndənsɪ] *n (Brit: job loss)* demissão *f (Br)*, despedimento *m (Port)*.
redundant [rɪˈdʌndənt] *adj (Brit)*: **to be made ~** ser despedido(-da), perder o emprego.
red wine *n* vinho *m* tinto.
reed [riːd] *n* junco *m*.
reef [riːf] *n* recife *m*.
reek [riːk] *vi*: **to ~ (of)** feder (a).
reel [riːl] *n (of thread)* carro *m*; *(on fishing rod)* molinete *m*, carreto *m*.
refectory [rɪˈfektərɪ] *n* refeitório *m*, cantina *f*.
refer [rɪˈfɜːʳ] : **refer to** *vt fus (speak about)* fazer referência a, referir-se a; *(consult)* consultar.
referee [ˌrefəˈriː] *n (SPORT)* árbitro *m*.
reference [ˈrefrəns] *n* referência *f* ♦ *adj (book)* de consulta; *(library)* para consultas; **with ~ to** com referência a.
reference book *n* livro *m* de consulta.
reference number *n* número *m* de referência.
referendum [ˌrefəˈrendəm] *n* plebiscito *m (Br)*, referendo *m (Port)*.
refill [*n* ˈriːfɪl, *vb* ˌriːˈfɪl] *n (for pen)* recarga *f* ♦ *vt* (voltar a) encher; **would you like a ~?** *(inf: drink)* mais um copo?
refine [rɪˈfaɪn] *vt (oil, sugar)* refinar; *(details, speech)* aperfeiçoar.
refined [rɪˈfaɪnd] *adj (oil, sugar)* refinado(-da); *(person, manners)* requintado(-da); *(process, equipment)* avançado (-da).
refinement [rɪˈfaɪnmənt] *n (improvement)*: **~ (on sthg)** aperfeiçoamento *m* (de algo).
refinery [rɪˈfaɪnərɪ] *n* refinaria *f*.
reflect [rɪˈflekt] *vt & vi* refletir.

reflection [rɪ'flekʃn] *n (image)* reflexo *m*.

reflector [rɪ'flektəʳ] *n* refletor *m*.

reflex ['ri:fleks] *n* reflexo *m*.

reflexive [rɪ'fleksɪv] *adj* reflexo(-xa), reflexivo(-va).

reforestation [ri:,fɒrɪ'steɪʃn] = **reafforestation**.

reform [rɪ'fɔ:m] *n* reforma *f* ◆ *vt* reformar.

refrain [rɪ'freɪn] *n* refrão *m* ◆ *vi*: **to ~ from doing sthg** abster-se de fazer algo.

refresh [rɪ'freʃ] *vt* refrescar.

refreshed [rɪ'freʃt] *adj* repousado(-da).

refresher course [rɪ'freʃəʳ-] *n* curso *m* de reciclagem.

refreshing [rɪ'freʃɪŋ] *adj* refrescante.

refreshments [rɪ'freʃmənts] *npl* lanches *mpl*, comes e bebes.

refrigerator [rɪ'frɪdʒəreɪtəʳ] *n* geladeira *f (Br)*, frigorífico *m (Port)*.

refuel [ri:'fjuəl] *vt* reabastecer ◆ *vi* reabastecer-se.

refuge [refju:dʒ] *n* refúgio *m*; **to seek** OR **take ~** *(hide)* refugiar-se.

refugee [refju'dʒi:] *n* refugiado *m* (-da *f*).

refund [*n* 'ri:fʌnd, *vb* rɪ'fʌnd] *n* reembolso *m* ◆ *vt* reembolsar.

refundable [rɪ'fʌndəbl] *adj* reembolsável.

refurbish [ri:'fɜ:bɪʃ] *vt (building)* restaurar; *(office, shop)* renovar.

refusal [rɪ'fju:zl] *n* recusa *f*.

refuse[1] [rɪ'fju:z] *vt & vi* recusar; **to ~ to do sthg** recusar-se a fazer algo.

refuse[2] ['refju:s] *n (fml)* lixo *m*.

refuse collection ['refju:s-] *n (fml)* coleta *f* do lixo *(Br)*, recolha *f* do lixo *(Port)*.

refute [rɪ'fju:t] *vt (fml)* refutar.

regain [rɪ'geɪn] *vt (recover)* recuperar.

regard [rɪ'gɑ:d] *vt (consider)* considerar ◆ *n*: **with ~ to** a respeito de; **as ~s** no que diz respeito a, quanto a.

❑ **regards** *npl (in greetings)* cumprimentos *mpl*; **give them my ~s** dê-lhes os meus cumprimentos.

regarding [rɪ'gɑ:dɪŋ] *prep* a respeito de, no que diz respeito a.

regardless [rɪ'gɑ:dlɪs] *adv* apesar de tudo; **~ of** independentemente de.

reggae ['regeɪ] *n* reggae *m*.

regime [reɪ'ʒi:m] *n* regime *m*.

regiment ['redʒɪmənt] *n* regimento *m*.

region ['ri:dʒən] *n* região *f*; **in the ~ of** de cerca de, na região de.

regional ['ri:dʒənl] *adj* regional.

register ['redʒɪstəʳ] *n* registro *m* ◆ *vt* registrar ◆ *vi (put one's name down)* inscrever-se; *(at hotel)* preencher o registro.

registered ['redʒɪstəd] *adj (letter, parcel)* registrado(-da).

registration [,redʒɪ'streɪʃn] *n (for course, at conference)* inscrição *f*.

registration (number) *n* placa *f (Br)*, matrícula *f (Port)*.

registry office ['redʒɪstrɪ-] *n* registro *m* civil.

regret [rɪ'gret] *n* arrependimento *m* ◆ *vt* lamentar, arrepender-se de; **to ~ doing sthg** arrepender-se de ter feito algo; **we ~ any inconvenience caused** lamentamos qualquer inconveniência.

regretfully [rɪ'gretfʊlɪ] *adv* com pesar.

regrettable [rɪ'gretəbl] *adj* lamentável.

regular ['regjʊləʳ] *adj* regular; *(normal, in size)* normal ◆ *n (customer)* cliente *mf* habitual, habitué *mf*.

regularly ['regjʊləlɪ] *adv* regularmente.

regulate ['regjʊleɪt] *vt* regular.

regulation [,regjʊ'leɪʃn] *n (rule)* regra *f*.

rehabilitate [ri:ə'bɪlɪteɪt] *vt* reabilitar.

rehearsal [rɪ'hɜ:sl] *n* ensaio *m*.

rehearse [rɪ'hɜ:s] *vt* ensaiar.

reign [reɪn] *n* reino *m* ◆ *vi* reinar.

reimburse [,ri:ɪm'bɜ:s] *vt (fml)* reembolsar.

reindeer ['reɪn,dɪəʳ] *(pl inv)* *n* rena *f*.

reinforce [,ri:ɪn'fɔ:s] *vt* reforçar.

reinforcements [,ri:ɪn'fɔ:smənts] *npl* reforços *mpl*.

reins [reɪnz] *npl (for horse)* rédeas *fpl*; *(for child)* andadeira *f*.

reinstate [,ri:ɪn'steɪt] *vt (employee)* readmitir.

reiterate [ri:'ɪtəreɪt] *vt* reiterar.

reject [rɪ'dʒekt] *vt* rejeitar.

rejection [rɪ'dʒekʃn] *n* rejeição *f*.

rejoice [rɪ'dʒɔɪs] *vi*: **to ~ (at** OR **in sthg)** ficar extremamente contente (com algo).

rejoin [,ri:'dʒɔɪn] *vt (motorway)* retomar, voltar a entrar em.

rejuvenate [rɪ'dʒuːvəneɪt] *vt* rejuvenescer.

rekindle [riː'kɪndl] *vt* avivar.

relapse [rɪ'læps] *n* recaída *f*.

relate [rɪ'leɪt] *vt* (connect) relacionar ♦ *vi*: **to ~ to** (be connected with) estar relacionado(-da) com; (concern) dizer respeito a.

related [rɪ'leɪtɪd] *adj* (of same family) da mesma família, aparentado(-da); (connected) relacionado(-da).

relation [rɪ'leɪʃn] *n* (member of family) parente *mf*; (connection) relação *f*, ligação *f*; **in ~ to** em relação a.
⊐ **relations** *npl* relações *fpl*.

relationship [rɪ'leɪʃnʃɪp] *n* (between countries, people) relações *fpl*; (between lovers) relação *f*; (connection) ligação *f*, relação.

relative ['relətɪv] *adj* relativo(-va) ♦ *n* parente *mf*.

relatively ['relətɪvlɪ] *adv* relativamente.

relax [rɪ'læks] *vi* (person) descontrair-se, relaxar.

relaxation [riːlæk'seɪʃn] *n* (of person) descontração *f*, relaxamento *m*.

relaxed [rɪ'lækst] *adj* descontraído (-da), relaxado(-da).

relaxing [rɪ'læksɪŋ] *adj* relaxante, calmante.

relay ['riːleɪ] *n* (race) corrida *f* de revezamento (Br), corrida *f* de estafetas (Port).

release [rɪ'liːs] *vt* (set free) libertar, soltar; (let go of) largar, soltar; (record, film) lançar; (brake, catch) soltar ♦ *n* (record, film) lançamento *m*.

relegate ['relɪgeɪt] *vt*: **to be ~d** (SPORT) descer de divisão.

relent [rɪ'lent] *vi* (person) ceder; (wind, storm) abrandar.

relentless [rɪ'lentlɪs] *adj* (person) inflexível; (criticism, rain) implacável.

relevant ['reləvənt] *adj* relevante.

reliable [rɪ'laɪəbl] *adj* (person, machine) de confiança, confiável.

reliably [rɪ'laɪəblɪ] *adv* (dependably) sem falhar; **to be ~ informed (that)** ... saber por fontes seguras que ....

reliant [rɪ'laɪənt] *adj*: **~ on** dependente de.

relic ['relɪk] *n* (object) relíquia *f*.

relief [rɪ'liːf] *n* (gladness) alívio *m*; (aid) ajuda *f*.

relief road *n* itinerário alternativo que os motoristas podem usar em caso de congestionamento das vias principais.

relieve [rɪ'liːv] *vt* (pain, headache) aliviar.

relieved [rɪ'liːvd] *adj* aliviado(-da).

religion [rɪ'lɪdʒn] *n* religião *f*.

religious [rɪ'lɪdʒəs] *adj* religioso (-osa).

relinquish [rɪ'lɪŋkwɪʃ] *vt* renunciar a.

relish ['relɪʃ] *n* (sauce) molho *m*.

reluctance [rɪ'lʌktəns] *n* relutância *f*.

reluctant [rɪ'lʌktənt] *adj* relutante.

reluctantly [rɪ'lʌktəntlɪ] *adv* relutantemente.

rely [rɪ'laɪ] : **rely on** *vt fus* (trust) confiar em; (depend on) depender de.

remain [rɪ'meɪn] *vi* (stay) permanecer; (continue to exist) sobrar, restar.
⊐ **remains** *npl* (of meal, body) restos *mpl*; (of ancient buildings etc) ruínas *fpl*.

remainder [rɪ'meɪndər] *n* resto *m*, restante *m*.

remaining [rɪ'meɪnɪŋ] *adj* restante.

remark [rɪ'mɑːk] *n* comentário *m* ♦ *vt* comentar.

remarkable [rɪ'mɑːkəbl] *adj* extraordinário(-ria), incrível.

remarry [riː'mærɪ] *vi* voltar a casar.

remedial [rɪ'miːdjəl] *adj* (class) de apoio (pedagógico); (pupil) que necessita de apoio (pedagógico); (exercise, therapy) de reabilitação; (action) corretivo(-va).

remedy ['remədɪ] *n* remédio *m*.

remember [rɪ'membər] *vt* lembrar-se de ♦ *vi* (recall) lembrar-se; **to ~ doing sth** lembrar-se de ter feito algo; **to ~ to do sth** lembrar-se de fazer algo.

Remembrance Day [rɪ'membrəns-] *n* Dia *m* do Armistício, dia em que na Grã-Bretanha se presta homenagem aos soldados mortos nas grandes guerras.

remind [rɪ'maɪnd] *vt*: **to ~ sb of** (fazer) lembrar a alguém; **to ~ sb to do sth** lembrar alguém de que tem de fazer algo.

reminder [rɪ'maɪndər] *n* (for bill, library book) aviso *m*.

reminisce [remɪ'nɪs] *vi*: **to ~ about sth** relembrar algo.

reminiscent [remɪ'nɪsnt] *adj*: **~ of** (similar to) evocador(-ra) de.

remittance [rɪ'mɪtns] *n* (money) = vale *m* postal.

remnant ['remnənt] *n* resto *m*.

remorse [rɪ'mɔːs] *n* remorsos *mpl*.

remorseful [rɪ'mɔːsful] *adj* cheio (cheia) de remorsos.

remorseless [rɪ'mɔːslɪs] *adj (cruelty, ambition)* sem piedade; *(advance, progress)* implacável.

remote [rɪ'məʊt] *adj* remoto(-ta).

remote control *n (device)* controle *m* remoto OR à distância.

removable [rɪ'muːvəbl] *adj* removível.

removal [rɪ'muːvl] *n* remoção *f*; *(change of house)* mudança *f*.

removal van *n* caminhão *m* de mudanças.

remove [rɪ'muːv] *vt* remover.

remuneration [rɪˌmjuːnə'reɪʃn] *n (fml)* remuneração *f*.

rendezvous ['rɒndɪvuː] *(pl inv* ['rɒndɪvuːz]) *n (meeting)* encontro *m*; *(place)* ponto *m* de encontro.

renegade ['renɪgeɪd] *n* renegado *m* (-da *f*).

renew [rɪ'njuː] *vt* renovar.

renewable [rɪ'njuːəbl] *adj* renovável.

renewal [rɪ'njuːəl] *n (of activity)* ressurgimento *m*; *(of contract, licence, membership)* renovação *f*.

renounce [rɪ'naʊns] *vt* renunciar.

renovate ['renəveɪt] *vt* renovar.

renowned [rɪ'naʊnd] *adj* célebre.

rent [rent] *n* renda *f*, arrendamento *m* ♦ *vt* arrendar.

rental ['rentl] *n* aluguel *m*.

reorganize [ˌriːˈɔːgənaɪz] *vt* reorganizar.

repaid [ˌriːˈpeɪd] *pt & pp* → repay.

repair [rɪ'peəʳ] *vt* reparar ♦ *n*: in good ~ em boas condições.

❏ **repairs** *npl* consertos *mpl*.

repair kit *n* estojo *m* de ferramentas.

repay [ˌriːˈpeɪ] *(pt & pp* **-paid**) *vt (money)* reembolsar; *(favour, kindness)* retribuir.

repayment [ˌriːˈpeɪmənt] *n (money)* reembolso *m*.

repeat [rɪ'piːt] *vt* repetir ♦ *n (on TV, radio)* reposição *f*.

repeatedly [rɪ'piːtɪdlɪ] *adv* repetidamente.

repel [rɪ'pel] *vt* repelir.

repellent [rɪ'pelənt] *adj* repelente.

repent [rɪ'pent] *vi*: to ~ *(of sthg)* arrepender-se (de algo).

repercussions [ˌriːpə'kʌʃnz] *npl*

repercussões *fpl*.

repertoire ['repətwɑːʳ] *n* repertório *m*.

repetition [ˌrepɪ'tɪʃn] *n* repetição *f*.

repetitious [ˌrepɪ'tɪʃəs] *adj* repetitivo(-va).

repetitive [rɪ'petɪtɪv] *adj* repetitivo(-va).

replace [rɪ'pleɪs] *vt (substitute)* substituir; *(faulty goods)* trocar; *(put back)* voltar a pôr no lugar.

replacement [rɪ'pleɪsmənt] *n (substitute)* substituto *m* (-ta *f*).

replay ['riːpleɪ] *n (rematch)* jogo *m* de desempate; *(on TV)* repetição *f*, replay *m*.

replenish [rɪ'plenɪʃ] *vt*: to ~ sthg (with sthg) reabastecer algo (de algo).

replica ['replɪkə] *n* réplica *f*.

reply [rɪ'plaɪ] *n* resposta *f* ♦ *vt & vi* responder.

report [rɪ'pɔːt] *n (account)* relatório *m*; *(in newspaper, on TV, radio)* reportagem *f*; *(Brit: SCH)* boletim *m* (Br), caderneta *f* (Port) *(escolar)* ♦ *vt (announce)* anunciar; *(theft, disappearance)* participar; *(person)* denunciar ♦ *vi (give account)* informar; *(for newspaper, TV, radio)* fazer uma reportagem; to ~ to sb *(go to)* apresentar-se a alguém; to ~ (to sb) on informar (alguém) sobre.

report card *n* boletim *m* (Br), caderneta *f* (Port) *(escolar)*.

reportedly [rɪ'pɔːtɪdlɪ] *adv* segundo se diz, ao que consta.

reporter [rɪ'pɔːtəʳ] *n* repórter *mf*.

represent [ˌreprɪ'zent] *vt* representar.

representative [ˌreprɪ'zentətɪv] *n* representante *mf*.

repress [rɪ'pres] *vt* reprimir.

repression [rɪ'preʃn] *n* repressão *f*.

reprieve [rɪ'priːv] *n (delay)* adiamento *m*.

reprimand ['reprɪmɑːnd] *vt* repreender.

reprisal [rɪ'praɪzl] *n* represália *f*.

reproach [rɪ'prəʊtʃ] *vt* repreender.

reproachful [rɪ'prəʊtʃful] *adj* reprovador(-ra).

reproduce [ˌriːprə'djuːs] *vt* reproduzir ♦ *vi* reproduzir-se.

reproduction [ˌriːprə'dʌkʃn] *n* reprodução *f*.

reptile ['reptaɪl] *n* réptil *m*.

republic [rɪ'pʌblɪk] *n* república *f*.

Republican [rɪ'pʌblɪkən] *n (in US)*

republicano *m* (-na *f*) ◆ *adj (in US)* republicano(-na).

repulsive [rɪ'pʌlsɪv] *adj* repulsivo (-va).

reputable ['rɛpjʊtəbl] *adj* de boa reputação.

reputation [rɛpjʊ'teɪʃn] *n* reputação *f*.

repute [rɪ'pjuːt] *n (reputation)*: **of good/ill ~** de boa/má reputação.

reputed [rɪ'pjuːtɪd] *adj* reputado (-da); **to be ~ to be/do sthg** ter fama de ser/fazer algo.

reputedly [rɪ'pjuːtɪdlɪ] *adv* supostamente.

request [rɪ'kwɛst] *n* pedido *m* ◆ *vt* pedir; **to ~ sb to do sthg** pedir a alguém que faça algo; **available on ~** disponível a pedido do interessado.

request stop *n (Brit)* parada em que o ônibus só pára a pedido dos passageiros.

require [rɪ'kwaɪəʳ] *vt (subj: person)* necessitar de; *(subj: situation)* requerer, exigir; **passengers are ~d to show their tickets** pede-se aos passageiros que mostrem as passagens.

requirement [rɪ'kwaɪəmənt] *n (condition)* requisito *m*; *(need)* necessidade *f*.

rerun [*n* 'riːrʌn, *vb* ,riː'rʌn] *(pt* -ran, *pp* -run) *n (film, programme)* reposição *f*; *(similar situation)* repetição *f* ◆ *vt (film, programme)* repor; *(tape)* voltar a passar.

resat [riː'sæt] *pt & pp* → resit.

rescue ['rɛskjuː] *vt* salvar.

rescuer ['rɛskjuəʳ] *n* salvador *m* (-ra *f*).

research [rɪ'sɜːtʃ] *n* pesquisa *f*, investigação *f*.

researcher [rɪ'sɜːtʃəʳ] *n* pesquisador *m* (-ra *f*) *(Br)*, investigador *m* (-ra *f*) *(Port)*.

resemblance [rɪ'zɛmbləns] *n* parecença *f*.

resemble [rɪ'zɛmbl] *vt* parecer-se com.

resent [rɪ'zɛnt] *vt* ressentir-se com.

resentful [rɪ'zɛntfʊl] *adj* ressentido(-da).

resentment [rɪ'zɛntmənt] *n* ressentimento *m*.

reservation [,rɛzə'veɪʃn] *n* reserva *f*; **to make a ~** fazer uma reserva.

reserve [rɪ'zɜːv] *n (SPORT)* reserva *mf (Br)*, suplente *mf*; *(for wildlife)*

reserva *f* ◆ *vt* reservar.

reserved [rɪ'zɜːvd] *adj* reservado (-da).

reservoir ['rɛzəvwɑːʳ] *n* reservatório *m*, represa *f*.

reset [riː'sɛt] *(pt & pp* reset) *vt (watch)* acertar; *(meter, device)* reajustar.

reshuffle [riː'ʃʌfl] *n (POL.)* reorganização *f*, reforma *f*.

reside [rɪ'zaɪd] *vi (fml)* residir.

residence ['rɛzɪdəns] *n (fml)* residência *f*; **place of ~** *(fml)* (local *m* de) residência.

residence permit *n* autorização *f* de residência.

resident ['rɛzɪdənt] *n (of country)* habitante *mf*; *(of hotel)* hóspede *mf*; *(of area, house)* morador *m* (-ra *f*); **"~s only"** *(for parking)* "reservado para os moradores".

residential [,rɛzɪ'dɛnʃl] *adj* residencial.

residue ['rɛzɪdjuː] *n* resíduo *m*.

resign [rɪ'zaɪn] *vi* demitir-se ◆ *vt*: **to ~ o.s. to sthg** resignar-se com algo, conformar-se com algo.

resignation [,rɛzɪg'neɪʃn] *n (from job)* demissão *f*.

resigned [rɪ'zaɪnd] *adj*: **to be ~ (to sthg)** estar conformado(-da) (com algo).

resilient [rɪ'zɪlɪənt] *adj* forte.

resin ['rɛzɪn] *n* resina *f*.

resist [rɪ'zɪst] *vt* resistir a; **I can't ~ cream cakes** não resisto a bolos com creme; **to ~ doing sthg** resistir a fazer algo.

resistance [rɪ'zɪstəns] *n* resistência *f*.

resit [riː'sɪt] *(pt & pp* -sat) *vt* repetir.

resolute ['rɛzəluːt] *adj* resoluto(-ta).

resolution [,rɛzə'luːʃn] *n* resolução *f*.

resolve [rɪ'zɒlv] *vt (solve)* resolver.

resort [rɪ'zɔːt] *n (for holidays)* estância *f* (de férias); **as a last ~** como último recurso.

❏ **resort to** *vt fus* recorrer a; **to ~ to doing sthg** recorrer a fazer algo.

resounding [rɪ'zaʊndɪŋ] *adj (noise, crash)* sonoro(-ra); *(success, victory)* retumbante.

resource [rɪ'sɔːs] *n* recurso *m*.

resourceful [rɪ'sɔːsfʊl] *adj* desembaraçado(-da), expedito(-ta).

respect [rɪ'spɛkt] *n* respeito *m*; *(aspect)* aspecto *m* ◆ *vt* respeitar; **with**

~ **to** no que respeita a; **in some ~s** em alguns aspectos.

respectable [rɪ'spektəbl] *adj (person, job etc)* respeitável; *(acceptable)* decente.

respectful [rɪ'spektfʊl] *adj* respeitador(-ra).

respective [rɪ'spektɪv] *adj* respectivo(-va).

respectively [rɪ'spektɪvlɪ] *adv* respectivamente.

respite ['respaɪt] *n (pause)* descanso *m; (delay)* prolongamento *m* (de prazo).

resplendent [rɪ'splendənt] *adj* resplandecente.

respond [rɪ'spɒnd] *vi* responder.

response [rɪ'spɒns] *n* resposta *f.*

responsibility [rɪ,spɒnsə'bɪlətɪ] *n* responsabilidade *f.*

responsible [rɪ'spɒnsəbl] *adj* responsável; **to be ~ (for)** *(to blame)* ser responsável (por).

responsive [rɪ'spɒnsɪv] *adj (person)* receptivo(-va); **~ to sthg** receptivo a algo.

rest [rest] *n (relaxation)* descanso *m; (for foot, head, back)* apoio *m ◆ vi (relax)* descansar ◆ *vt:* **to ~ sthg against sthg** encostar algo em algo; **the ~** *(remainder)* o resto; **to have a ~** descansar; **the ladder was ~ing against the wall** a escada estava encostada na parede.

restaurant ['restərɒnt] *n* restaurante *m.*

restaurant car *n (Brit)* vagão-restaurante *m (Br),* carruagem-restaurante *f (Port).*

restful ['restfʊl] *adj* tranqüilo(-la).

rest home *n (for old people)* lar *m,* asilo *m; (for sick people)* casa *f* de repouso.

restless ['restlɪs] *adj (bored, impatient)* impaciente; *(fidgety)* inquieto(-ta).

restore [rɪ'stɔːʳ] *vt (reintroduce)* restabelecer; *(renovate)* restaurar.

restrain [rɪ'streɪn] *vt* conter.

restrained [rɪ'streɪnd] *adj (person)* comedido(-da); *(tone)* moderado(-da).

restraint [rɪ'streɪnt] *n (rule, check)* restrição *f; (control)* restrições *fpl; (moderation)* comedimento *m.*

restrict [rɪ'strɪkt] *vt* restringir.

restricted [rɪ'strɪktɪd] *adj* restrito(-ta).

restriction [rɪ'strɪkʃn] *n* restrição *f.*

restrictive [rɪ'strɪktɪv] *adj* severo(-ra).

rest room *n (Am)* banheiro *m (Br),* casa *f* de banho *(Port).*

result [rɪ'zʌlt] *n* resultado *m ◆ vi:* **to ~ in** resultar em; **as a ~ of** em conseqüência de.

⏊ **results** *npl (of test, exam)* resultados *mpl.*

resume [rɪ'zjuːm] *vt & vi* recomeçar, retomar.

résumé ['rezjuːmeɪ] *n (summary)* resumo *m; (Am: curriculum vitae)* currículo *m.*

resumption [rɪ'zʌmpʃn] *n* recomeço *m.*

resurgence [rɪ'sɜːdʒəns] *n* ressurgimento *m.*

resurrection [rezə'rekʃn] *n (RELIG):* **the ~** a Ressurreição (de Cristo).

resuscitation [rɪ,sʌsɪ'teɪʃn] *n* reanimação *f.*

retail ['riːteɪl] *n* venda *f* a varejo *(Br),* venda *f* a retalho *(Port)* ◆ *vt* vender (a varejo) ◆ *vi:* **to ~ at** vender a.

retailer ['riːteɪləʳ] *n* varejista *mf (Br),* retalhista *mf (Port).*

retail price *n* preço *m* de venda ao público.

retain [rɪ'teɪn] *vt (fml)* reter.

retaliate [rɪ'tælɪeɪt] *vi* retaliar.

retaliation [rɪ,tælɪ'eɪʃn] *n* retaliação *f.*

retch [retʃ] *vi* ter ânsia de vômito *(Br),* sentir vômitos *(Port).*

reticent ['retɪsənt] *adj* reticente.

retina ['retɪnə] *(pl* **-nas** OR **-nae** [-niː]) *n* retina *f.*

retire [rɪ'taɪəʳ] *vi (stop working)* aposentar-se *(Br),* reformar-se *(Port).*

retired [rɪ'taɪəd] *adj* aposentado(-da) *(Br),* reformado(-da) *(Port).*

retirement [rɪ'taɪəmənt] *n* aposentadoria *f (Br),* reforma *f (Port).*

retrain [riː'treɪn] *vt* reciclar.

retreat [rɪ'triːt] *vi* retirar-se ◆ *n (place)* retiro *m.*

retrieval [rɪ'triːvl] *n* recuperação *f.*

retrieve [rɪ'triːv] *vt* recuperar.

retrospect ['retrəspekt] *n:* **in ~** a posteriori.

return [rɪ'tɜːn] *n (arrival back)* regresso *m; (Brit: ticket)* bilhete *m* de ida e volta ◆ *vt* devolver ◆ *vi* voltar, regressar ◆ *adj (Brit: journey)* de volta, de regresso; **by ~ of post** *(Brit)* na volta do correio; **in ~ (for)** em troca (de); **many happy ~s!** que se repita por muitos anos!; **to ~ sthg (to sb)** *(give back)* devolver algo (a alguém).

return flight *n* vôo *m* de volta.

return ticket *n (Brit)* bilhete *m* de ida e volta.

reunite [,ri:ju:'naɪt] *vt* reunir.

rev [rev] *n (inf: of engine)* rotação *f* ◆ *vt (inf):* **to ~ sthg (up)** acelerar algo.

reveal [rɪ'vi:l] *vt* revelar.

revel ['revl] *vi:* **to ~ in sthg** deliciar-se OR deleitar-se com algo.

revelation [,revə'leɪʃn] *n* revelação *f.*

revenge [rɪ'vendʒ] *n* vingança *f.*

revenue ['revənju:] *n* receita *f.*

Reverend ['revərənd] *n* reverendo *m.*

reversal [rɪ'vɜ:sl] *n (of trend, policy, decision)* mudança *f; (of roles, order, position)* inversão *f.*

reverse [rɪ'vɜ:s] *adj* inverso(-sa) ◆ *n (AUT)* marcha *f* à ré *(Br),* marcha *f* atrás *(Port); (of coin)* reverso *m; (of document)* verso *m* ◆ *vt (car)* dar marcha à ré com *(Br),* fazer marcha atrás com *(Port); (decision)* revogar ◆ *vi (car, driver)* dar marcha à ré *(Br),* fazer marcha atrás *(Port);* **in ~ order** na ordem inversa, ao contrário; **the ~** *(opposite)* o contrário; **to ~ the charges** *(Brit)* fazer uma chamada a cobrar no destinatário.

reverse-charge call *n (Brit)* chamada *f* a cobrar.

revert [rɪ'vɜ:t] *vi:* **to ~ to** voltar a.

review [rɪ'vju:] *n (of book, record, film)* crítica *f; (examination)* revisão *f* ◆ *vt (Am: for exam)* rever.

reviewer [rɪ'vju:ər] *n* crítico *m* (-ca *f).*

revise [rɪ'vaɪz] *vt* rever ◆ *vi (Brit)* rever a matéria.

revision [rɪ'vɪʒn] *n (Brit)* revisão *f.*

revitalize [,ri:'vaɪtəlaɪz] *vt* revitalizar.

revival [rɪ'vaɪvl] *n (of person)* reanimação *f; (of economy)* retomada *f; (of custom)* recuperação *f; (of interest)* renovação *f.*

revive [rɪ'vaɪv] *vt (person)* reanimar; *(economy, custom)* recuperar.

revolt [rɪ'vəʊlt] *n* revolta *f.*

revolting [rɪ'vəʊltɪŋ] *adj* repugnante.

revolution [,revə'lu:ʃn] *n* revolução *f.*

revolutionary [,revə'lu:ʃnərɪ] *adj* revolucionário(-ria).

revolve [rɪ'vɒlv] *vi (go round)* girar; **to ~ around** *(be based on)* girar à volta de.

revolver [rɪ'vɒlvər] *n* revólver *m.*

revolving door [rɪ'vɒlvɪŋ-] *n* porta *f* giratória.

revue [rɪ'vju:] *n (teatro m de)* revista *f.*

revulsion [rɪ'vʌlʃn] *n* repugnância *f.*

reward [rɪ'wɔ:d] *n* recompensa *f* ◆ *vt* recompensar.

rewarding [rɪ'wɔ:dɪŋ] *adj* compensador(-ra), gratificante.

rewind [,ri:'waɪnd] *(pt & pp* **-wound)** *vt* rebobinar.

rewire [,ri:'waɪər] *vt* substituir a instalação elétrica de.

rewound [,ri:'waʊnd] *pt & pp →* rewind.

rewrite [,ri:'raɪt] *(pt* **-wrote,** *pp* **-written)** *vt* reescrever.

Reykjavik ['rekjəvɪk] *n* Reikjavik *s.*

rheumatism ['ru:mətɪzm] *n* reumatismo *m.*

Rhine [raɪn] *n:* **the ~** o Reno.

rhinoceros [raɪ'nɒsərəs] *(pl inv* OR **-es)** *n* rinoceronte *m.*

rhododendron [,rəʊdə'dendrən] *n* rododendro *m.*

rhubarb ['ru:bɑ:b] *n* ruibarbo *m.*

rhyme [raɪm] *n (poem)* rima *f* ◆ *vi* rimar.

rhythm ['rɪðm] *n* ritmo *m.*

rib [rɪb] *n* costela *f.*

ribbed [rɪbd] *adj* canelado(-da).

ribbon ['rɪbən] *n* fita *f.*

rice [raɪs] *n* arroz *m.*

rice pudding *n =* arroz-doce *m.*

rich [rɪtʃ] *adj* rico(-ca) ◆ *npl:* **the ~** os ricos; **to be ~ in sthg** ser rico em algo.

richness ['rɪtʃnɪs] *n* riqueza *f.*

rickety ['rɪkətɪ] *adj* pouco firme.

ricotta cheese [rɪ'kɒtə-] *n* ricota *m,* queijo muito semelhante ao requeijão.

rid [rɪd] *vt:* **to get ~ of** ver-se livre de, livrar-se de.

ridden ['rɪdn] *pp →* ride.

riddle ['rɪdl] *n (puzzle)* adivinha *f; (mystery)* enigma *m.*

riddled ['rɪdld] *adj (full):* **to be ~ with sthg** estar cheio(-a) OR crivado(-da) de algo.

ride [raɪd] *(pt* **rode,** *pp* **ridden)** *n (on horse, bike)* passeio *m; (in vehicle)* volta *f* ◆ *vt (horse)* andar a; *(bike)* andar de ◆ *vi (on horse)* andar OR montar a cavalo; *(on bike)* andar de bicicleta; *(in vehicle)* viajar; **to go for a ~** *(in car)* ir dar uma volta (de carro).

rider ['raɪdə'] n (on horse) cavaleiro m (amazona f); (on bike) ciclista mf.

ridge [rɪdʒ] n (of mountain) crista f; (raised surface) rugosidade f.

ridicule ['rɪdɪkjuːl] n ridículo m ◆ vt ridicularizar.

ridiculous [rɪ'dɪkjʊləs] adj ridículo(-la).

riding ['raɪdɪŋ] n equitação f.

riding school n escola f de equitação.

rife [raɪf] adj (widespread) generalizado(-da).

rifle ['raɪfl] n espingarda f.

rift [rɪft] n (quarrel) desentendimento m; ~ between/in desentendimento entre/em.

rig [rɪg] n (oilrig) plataforma f petrolífera ◆ vt falsificar o resultado de.

right [raɪt] adj 1. (correct) certo(-ta); to be ~ (person) ter razão; to be ~ to do sthg fazer bem em fazer algo; have you got the ~ time? você tem a hora certa?; is this the ~ way? é este o caminho certo?; that's ~! é isso mesmo!, exatamente! 2. (fair) certo(-ta); that's not ~! isso não está certo! 3. (on the right) direito(-ta); the ~ side of the road o lado direito da estrada. ◆ n 1. (side): the ~ a direita. 2. (entitlement) direito m; to have the ~ to do sthg ter o direito de fazer algo. ◆ adv 1. (towards the right) à direita; turn ~ at the post office vire à direita junto aos correios. 2. (correctly) bem; am I pronouncing it ~? estou pronunciando isso bem? 3. (for emphasis) mesmo; ~ here aqui mesmo; I'll be ~ back volto já; ~ away imediatamente.

right angle n ângulo m reto.

righteous ['raɪtʃəs] adj (person) justo(-ta), honrado(-da); (anger, indignation) justificado(-da).

rightful ['raɪtful] adj (share, owner) legítimo(-ma); (place) devido(-da).

right-hand adj direito(-ta).

right-hand drive n veículo m com volante à direita.

right-handed [-'hændɪd] adj (person) destro(-tra); (implement) para pessoas destras.

rightly ['raɪtlɪ] adv (correctly) corretamente; (justly) devidamente.

right of way n (AUT) prioridade f;

(path) direito m de passagem.

right-wing adj de direita.

rigid ['rɪdʒɪd] adj rígido(-da).

rigorous ['rɪgərəs] adj rigoroso(-osa).

rim [rɪm] n (of cup) borda f; (of glasses) armação f; (of bicycle wheel) aro m; (of car wheel) aro m (Br), jante f (Port).

rind [raɪnd] n (of fruit, cheese) casca f; (of bacon) couro m (Br), courato m (Port).

ring [rɪŋ] (pt rang, pp rung) n (for finger) anel m; (circle) círculo m; (sound) toque m (de campainha, telefone); (on electric cooker) disco m; (on gas cooker) boca f (Br), bico m (Port); (for boxing) ringue m; (in circus) arena f ◆ vt (Brit) telefonar para, ligar para; (bell) tocar a ◆ vi (Brit: make phone call) telefonar; (doorbell, telephone) tocar; (ears) zumbir; to give sb a ~ (phone call) telefonar para alguém; to ~ the bell (of house, office) tocar a campainha.

❏ **ring back** vt sep (Brit: person) voltar a telefonar a ◆ vi (Brit) voltar a telefonar.

❏ **ring off** vi (Brit) desligar.

❏ **ring up** vt sep (Brit) telefonar para ◆ vi (Brit) telefonar.

ring binder n capa f de argolas, dossier m.

ringing ['rɪŋɪŋ] n (of doorbell, telephone) toque m; (in ears) zumbido m.

ringing tone ['rɪŋɪŋ-] n sinal m de chamada.

ringlet ['rɪŋlɪt] n anel m de cabelo, cacho m.

ring road n (estrada) perimetral f (Br), circunvalação f (Port).

rink [rɪŋk] n rink m, pista f (de patinagem).

rinse [rɪns] vt (clothes, hair) enxaguar, passar uma água (Br); (hands) lavar.

❏ **rinse out** vt sep (clothes) enxaguar, passar uma água (Br); (mouth) bochechar.

riot ['raɪət] n (violent disturbance) distúrbio m.

rioter ['raɪətə'] n desordeiro m (-ra f), manifestante mf.

riot police npl polícia f de choque, forças fpl de intervenção.

rip [rɪp] n rasgão m ◆ vt rasgar ◆ vi rasgar-se.

❏ **rip up** vt sep rasgar em bocadinhos.

ripe [raɪp] adj maduro(-ra).

ripen ['raɪpn] vi amadurecer.

rip-off *n (inf)* roubo *m*.

ripple ['rɪpl] *n* onda *f*.

rise [raɪz] *(pt* **rose**, *pp* **risen** ['rɪzn]) *vi (move upwards)* elevar-se; *(sun, moon)* nascer; *(increase)* subir; *(stand up)* levantar-se ◆ *n* subida *f; (Brit: pay increase)* aumento *m*.

risk [rɪsk] *n* risco *m* ◆ *vt* arriscar; **to take a ~** correr um risco; **at your own ~** por sua conta e risco; **to ~ doing sthg** arriscar-se a fazer algo; **to ~ it** arriscar-se.

risky ['rɪskɪ] *adj* arriscado(-da).

risotto [rɪ'zɒtəʊ] *(pl* **-s**) *n* risoto *m, prato à base de arroz com carne, marisco ou legumes*.

risqué [ri:skeɪ] *adj* picante.

rissole ['rɪsəʊl] *n (Brit)* = croquete *m*.

ritual ['rɪtʃʊəl] *n* ritual *m*.

rival ['raɪvl] *adj* rival ◆ *n* rival *mf*.

rivalry ['raɪvlrɪ] *n* rivalidade *f*.

river ['rɪvər] *n* rio *m*.

river bank *n* margem *f* do rio.

riverbed ['rɪvəbed] *n* leito *m* do rio.

riverside ['rɪvəsaɪd] *n* beira-rio *f*.

rivet ['rɪvɪt] *n* rebite *m*.

Riviera [rɪvɪ'eərə] *n*: **the (French) ~** a Riviera (francesa).

roach [rəʊtʃ] *n (Am: cockroach)* barata *f*.

road [rəʊd] *n* estrada *f;* **by ~** por estrada.

roadblock ['rəʊdblɒk] *n* controle *m* rodoviário.

road book *n* guia *m* das estradas.

road map *n* mapa *m* das estradas.

road safety *n* segurança *f* rodoviária OR na estrada.

roadside ['rəʊdsaɪd] *n*: **the ~** a beira (da estrada).

road sign *n* sinal *m* de trânsito.

road tax *n* imposto *m* de circulação.

roadway ['rəʊdweɪ] *n* rodovia *f*.

road works *npl* obras *fpl* na estrada.

roadworthy ['rəʊd,wɜːðɪ] *adj* em condições de circular.

roam [rəʊm] *vi* vaguear.

roar [rɔːr] *n (of crowd)* gritos *mpl*, brados *mpl; (of aeroplane)* ronco *m; (of lion)* rugido *m* ◆ *vi (crowd)* berrar, bradar; *(lion)* rugir.

roast [rəʊst] *n* assado *m* ◆ *vt* assar ◆ *adj* assado(-da); **~ beef** rosbife *m;* **~ chicken** frango *m* assado; **~ lamb** car-

neiro *m* assado; **~ pork** lombo *m* (de porco assado); **~ potatoes** batatas *fpl* assadas.

rob [rɒb] *vt* assaltar; **to ~ sb of sthg** roubar algo de alguém.

robber ['rɒbər] *n* assaltante *mf*.

robbery ['rɒbərɪ] *n* assalto *m*.

robe [rəʊb] *n (Am: bathrobe)* roupão *m*.

robin ['rɒbɪn] *n* pisco-de-peito-ruivo *m*, pintarroxo *m* (Port).

robot ['rəʊbɒt] *n* robô *m*.

robust [rəʊ'bʌst] *adj (person, health)* robusto(-ta); *(economy, defence, criticism)* forte.

rock [rɒk] *n* rocha *f; (Am: stone)* pedra *f; (music)* rock *m; (Brit: sweet)* pirulito *m* ◆ *vt (baby)* embalar; *(boat)* balançar; **on the ~s** *(drink)* com gelo.

rock and roll *n* rock and roll *m*.

rock climbing *n* escala *f;* **to go ~** ir escalar.

rocket ['rɒkɪt] *n (missile, space rocket)* foguete *m* (Br), foguetão *m* (Port); *(firework)* foguete *m; (salad plant)* rúcola *f*.

rocking chair ['rɒkɪŋ-] *n* cadeira *f* de balanço.

rocking horse *n* cavalo *m* de balanço.

rock 'n' roll [,rɒkən'rəʊl] *n* rock 'n' roll *m*.

rocky ['rɒkɪ] *adj (place)* rochoso(-osa).

rod [rɒd] *n (wooden)* vara *f; (metal)* barra *f; (for fishing)* vara *f* de pescar (Br), cana *f* (Port).

rode [rəʊd] *pt → ride*.

rodent ['rəʊdənt] *n* roedor *m*.

roe [rəʊ] *n* ovas *fpl* de peixe.

rogue [rəʊg] *n (likable rascal)* maroto *m* (-ta *f); (dishonest person)* trapaceiro *m* (-ra *f*).

role [rəʊl] *n* papel *m*.

roll [rəʊl] *n (of bread)* carcaça *f*, pãozinho *m; (of film, paper)* rolo *m* ◆ *vi (ball, rock)* rolar; *(vehicle)* circular; *(ship)* balançar ◆ *vt (ball, rock)* fazer rolar; *(cigarette)* enrolar; *(dice)* lançar.

❏ **roll over** *vi (person, animal)* virar-se; *(car)* capotar.

❏ **roll up** *vt sep (map, carpet)* enrolar; *(sleeves, trousers)* arregaçar.

roller ['rəʊlər] *n (curler)* rolo *m* (de cabelo).

rollerblades ['rəʊləbleɪdz] *npl* patins *mpl* em linha.

rollerblading ['rəʊlə,bleɪdɪŋ] *n*: **to go**

~ ir patinar *(com patins em linha)*.

roller coaster *n* montanha-russa *f*.

roller skates *npl* patins *mpl* de rodas.

roller-skating ['rəʊlə-] *n* patinagem *f* sobre rodas.

rolling pin ['rəʊlɪŋ-] *n* rolo *m* de pastel *(Br)*, rolo *m* da massa *(Port)*.

roll-on *n (deodorant)* roll-on *m*, bastão *m (Br)*.

ROM [rɒm] *(abbr of read only memory) n* ROM *f*.

Roman ['rəʊmən] *adj* romano(-na) ♦ *n* romano *m* (-na *f*).

Roman Catholic *n* católico *m* romano (católica *f* romana).

romance [rəʊ'mæns] *n* romance *m*.

Romania [ruː'meɪnjə] *n* Romênia *f*.

Romanian [ruː'meɪnjən] *adj* romeno(-na) ♦ *n (person)* romeno *m* (-na *f*); *(language)* romeno *m*.

Roman numerals *npl* numeração *f* romana.

romantic [rəʊ'mæntɪk] *adj* romântico(-ca).

Rome [rəʊm] *n* Roma s.

romper suit ['rɒmpə-] *n* macacão *m* (de criança).

roof [ruːf] *n (of building, cave)* telhado *m*; *(of car, caravan, tent)* teto *m*.

roof rack *n* bagageiro *m (Br)*, tejadilho *m (Port)*.

rooftop ['ruːftɒp] *n* telhado *m*.

rook [rʊk] *n (bird)* gralha-calva *f*; *(chess piece)* torre *f*.

rookie ['rʊkɪ] *n (Am: inf)* novato *m* (-ta *f*).

room [ruːm, rʊm] *n (bedroom, in hotel)* quarto *m*; *(in building)* divisão *f*, sala *f*; *(space)* espaço *m*.

roommate ['ruːmmeɪt] *n* colega *mf* de quarto.

room number *n* número *m* do quarto.

room service *n* serviço *m* de quartos.

room temperature *n* temperatura *f* ambiente.

roomy ['ruːmɪ] *adj* espaçoso(-osa).

rooster ['ruːstə'] *n* galo *m*.

root [ruːt] *n* raiz *f*.

rope [rəʊp] *n* corda *f* ♦ *vt* amarrar.

rosary ['rəʊzərɪ] *n* terço *m*, rosário *m*.

rose [rəʊz] *pt* → **rise** ♦ *n (flower)* rosa *f*.

rosé ['rəʊzeɪ] *n (vinho)* rosé *m*.

rose bush *n* roseira *f*.

rosemary ['rəʊzmərɪ] *n* alecrim *m*.

rosette [rəʊ'zet] *n (badge)* emblema *m*.

rostrum ['rɒstrəm] *(pl -trums OR -tra* [-trə]) *n* tribuna *f*.

rosy ['rəʊzɪ] *adj (pink)* rosado(-da); *(promising)* cor-de-rosa *(inv)*.

rot [rɒt] *vi* apodrecer.

rota ['rəʊtə] *n* lista *f* de turnos.

rotate [rəʊ'teɪt] *vi* girar.

rotation [rəʊ'teɪʃn] *n* rotação *f*; **in** ~ rotativamente.

rotten ['rɒtn] *adj (food, wood)* podre; *(inf: not good)* péssimo(-ma); **I feel** ~ *(ill)* sinto-me péssimo.

rouge [ruːʒ] *n* blush *m*.

rough [rʌf] *adj (surface, skin, cloth)* áspero(-ra); *(sea, crossing)* agitado(-da); *(person)* bruto(-ta); *(approximate)* aproximado(-da); *(conditions, wine)* mau (má); *(area, town)* perigoso(-osa) ♦ *n (on golf course)* rough *m*; **a** ~ **guess** um cálculo aproximado; **to have a** ~ **time** passar por um período difícil.

roughen ['rʌfn] *vt* tornar áspero(-ra).

roughly ['rʌflɪ] *adv (approximately)* aproximadamente; *(push, handle)* bruscamente, grosseiramente.

roulade [ruː'luːd] *n* rocambole *m (Br)*, torta *f (Port)*.

roulette [ruː'let] *n* roleta *f*.

round [raʊnd] *adj* redondo(-da).

♦ *n* **1.** *(of drinks)* rodada *f*; **it's my** ~ é a minha rodada.

2. *(of sandwiches)* sanduíche *m (Br)*, sandes *f inv (Port)*; *(of toast)* torrada *f*.

3. *(of competition)* volta *f*.

4. *(in golf)* partida *f*; *(in boxing)* assalto *m*.

5. *(of policeman, postman, milkman)* ronda *f*.

♦ *adv* **1.** *(in a circle)*: **to go** ~ andar em volta; **to spin** ~ girar.

2. *(surrounding)* à volta; **it had a fence all (the way)** ~ tinha uma cerca em toda a volta.

3. *(near)*: ~ **about** em volta.

4. *(to one's house)*: **to ask some friends** ~ convidar uns amigos (para casa); **we went** ~ **to her house** fomos até a casa dela.

5. *(continuously)*: **all year** ~ *(durante)* todo o ano.

♦ *prep* **1.** *(surrounding, circling)* à volta de; **they put a blanket** ~ **him** puseram

um cobertor em volta dele; **we walked
~ the lake** caminhamos em volta do
lago; **to go ~ the corner** virar a esquina.
2. *(visiting)*: **to go ~ a museum** visitar
um museu; **to show sb ~ sthg** mostrar
algo a alguém.
3. *(approximately)* cerca de; **~ (about)
100** cerca de 100; **~ ten o'clock** cerca
das OR por volta das dez horas.
4. *(near)*: **~ here** aqui perto.
5. *(in phrases)*: **it's just ~ the corner**
(nearby) é logo ao virar da esquina; **~
the clock** 24 horas por dia.
⊔ **round off** *vt sep (meal, day, visit)* terminar.

roundabout ['raondəbaot] *n (Brit) (in
road)* cruzamento circular, rotunda *f
(Port)*; *(in playground)* roda *f* (de parque
infantil); *(at fairground)* carrossel *m*.

rounders ['raondəz] *n (Brit) jogo de
bola parecido com o baseball*.

roundly ['raondli] *adv (defeat)* completamente; *(criticize)* sem rodeios;
(deny) redondamente.

round trip *n* viagem *f* de ida e
volta.

roundup ['raondʌp] *n (summary)* resumo *m*.

rouse [raoz] *vt (wake up)* acordar,
despertar; *(excite)* instigar; *(give rise to)*
despertar.

rousing ['raozıŋ] *adj* entusiasmante.

route [ru:t] *n (way)* caminho *m*; *(of
train)* linha *f*; *(of bus)* trajeto *m*; *(of
plane)* rota *f* ♦ *vt (change course of)*
mudar a rota de.

route map *n* (mapa do) trajeto *m*.

routine [ru:'ti:n] *n* rotina *f* ♦ *adj* roti-
neiro(-ra).

row[1] [rao] *n (line)* fila *f* ♦ *vt (boat)*
impelir remando ♦ *vi* remar; **three
times in a ~** três vezes seguidas.

row[2] [rao] *n (argument)* briga *f*, *(inf:
noise)* algazarra *f*; **to have a ~** brigar.

rowboat ['raobaot] *(Am)* = **rowing
boat**.

rowdy ['raodi] *adj* turbulento(-ta).

rowing ['raoıŋ] *n* remo *m*.

rowing boat *n (Brit)* barco *m* a
remos.

royal ['rɔıəl] *adj* real.

Royal Air Force *n*: **the ~** a força
aérea britânica.

royal family *n* família *f* real.

Royal Navy *n*: **the ~** a marinha
britânica.

royalty ['rɔıəltı] *n (royal family)* realeza *f*.

RRP *(abbr of recommended retail price)*
P.V.P.

rub [rʌb] *vt (back, eyes)* esfregar;
(polish) polir ♦ *vi (with hand, cloth)*
esfregar; *(shoes)* friccionar *(Br)*, roçar
(Port).
⊔ **rub in** *vt sep (lotion, oil)* esfregar.
⊔ **rub out** *vt sep* apagar.

rubber ['rʌbər] *adj* de borracha ♦ *n*
borracha *f*; *(Am: inf: condom)* camisinha
f (Br), preservativo *m*.

rubber band *n* elástico *m*.

rubber gloves *npl* luvas *fpl* de
borracha.

rubber plant *n* borracheira *f*.

rubber ring *n* bóia *f*.

rubber stamp *n* carimbo *m* (de
borracha).

rubbish ['rʌbıʃ] *n (refuse)* lixo *m*; *(inf:
worthless thing)* porcaria *f*; *(inf: nonsense)* disparate *m*.

rubbish bin *n (Brit)* lata *f* de lixo
(Br), caixote *m* do lixo *(Port)*.

rubbish dump *n (Brit)* depósito *m*
de lixo *(Br)*, lixeira *f (Port)*.

rubble ['rʌbl] *n* entulho *m*, escombros *mpl*.

ruby ['ru:bı] *n* rubi *m*.

rucksack ['rʌksæk] *n* mochila *f*.

rudder ['rʌdər] *n* leme *m*.

ruddy ['rʌdı] *adj (face, complexion)*
corado(-da).

rude [ru:d] *adj (person)* mal-
educado(-da); *(behaviour, joke, picture)*
grosseiro(-ra).

rudimentary [,ru:dı'mentərı] *adj*
rudimentar.

rueful ['ru:fol] *adj (person, look)* arre-
pendido(-da); *(smile)* de arrependimento.

ruffian [rʌfjən] *n* rufião *m* (-fiona
f).

ruffle ['rʌfl] *vt (hair)* desgrenhar, despentear; *(feathers, fur)* eriçar.

rug [rʌg] *n (for floor)* tapete *m*; *(Brit:
blanket)* manta *f* (de viagem).

rugby ['rʌgbı] *n* rugby *m*, râguebi *m*.

rugged ['rʌgıd] *adj (rocky, uneven)* aci-
dentado(-da); *(sturdy)* resistente.

ruin ['ru:ın] *vt* estragar.
⊔ **ruins** *npl* ruínas *fpl*.

ruined ['ru:ınd] *adj (building)* em ruínas; *(clothes, meal, holiday)* estragado
(-da).

rule [ru:l] *n (law)* regra *f* ♦ *vt (country)* governar; **to be the ~** *(normal)* ser a regra; **against the ~s** contra as regras; **as a ~** geralmente.

⏌ **rule out** *vt sep* excluir.

ruler ['ru:lər] *n (of country)* governante *mf; (for measuring)* régua *f*.

rum [rʌm] *n* rum *m*.

rumble ['rʌmbl] *n (of thunder)* ruído *m; (of stomach)* ronco *m* ♦ *vi (thunder)* trovejar, ribombar; *(stomach)* roncar.

rummage ['rʌmɪdʒ] *vi:* **to ~ through** sthg remexer algo.

rumor ['ru:mər] *(Am)* = **rumour**.

rumour ['ru:mər] *n (Brit)* boato *m*.

rump steak [rʌmp-] *n* alcatra *f*.

rumpus ['rʌmpəs] *n (inf)* chinfrim *m*.

run [rʌn] *(pt* **ran**, *pp* **run)** *vi* **1.** *(on foot)* correr; **we had to ~ for the bus** tivemos de correr para apanhar o ônibus. **2.** *(train, bus)* circular; **the bus ~s every hour** há um ônibus de hora em hora; **the train is running an hour late** o trem vem com uma hora de atraso; **this service doesn't ~ on Sundays** este serviço não se efetua aos domingos. **3.** *(operate)* funcionar; **to ~ on sthg** funcionar a algo; **leave the engine running** deixa o motor a funcionar. **4.** *(tears, liquid, river)* correr; **to leave the tap running** deixar a torneira aberta; **to ~ through** *(river, road)* atravessar; **the path ~s along the coast** o caminho segue ao longo da costa. **5.** *(play)* estar em cartaz OR cena; *(event)* decorrer; **"now running at the Palladium"** "em cartaz OR cena no Palladium". **6.** *(eyes)* chorar; *(nose)* escorrer *(Br)*, pingar *(Port)*. **7.** *(colour, dye, clothes)* desbotar. **8.** *(remain valid)* ser válido; **the offer ~s until July** a oferta é válida até julho.
♦ *vt* **1.** *(on foot)* correr; **to ~ a race** participar de uma corrida. **2.** *(manage, organize)* gerir. **3.** *(car, machine)* manter; **it's cheap to ~** é muito econômico. **4.** *(bus, train)* ter em circulação; **we're running a special bus to the airport** temos em circulação um ônibus especial para o aeroporto. **5.** *(take in car)* levar (de carro); **I'll ~ you home** eu levo você em casa. **6.** *(fill):* **to ~ a bath** encher a banheira.
♦ *n* **1.** *(on foot)* corrida *f;* **to go for a ~** ir dar uma corrida. **2.** *(in car)* passeio *m* de carro; **to go for a ~** ir dar um passeio de carro. **3.** *(of play, show):* **it had a two-year ~** esteve dois anos em cartaz. **4.** *(for skiing)* pista *f*. **5.** *(Am: in tights)* fio *m* puxado *(Br)*, foguete *m* (Port). **6.** *(in phrases):* **in the long ~** a longo prazo.

⏌ **run away** *vi* fugir.

⏌ **run down** *vt sep (run over)* atropelar; *(criticize)* criticar ♦ *vi (clock)* parar; *(battery)* descarregar-se, gastar-se.

⏌ **run into** *vt fus (meet)* encontrar; *(hit)* chocar com, bater em; *(problem, difficulty)* deparar com.

⏌ **run out** *vi (be used up)* esgotar-se.

⏌ **run out of** *vt fus* ficar sem.

⏌ **run over** *vt sep (hit)* atropelar.

runaway ['rʌnəweɪ] *n* fugitivo *m* (-va *f*).

rundown ['rʌndaʊn] *n (report)* breve resumo *m*.

⏌ **run-down** *adj (dilapidated)* delapidado(-da), velho(-lha); *(tired)* cansado(-da).

rung [rʌŋ] *pp* → **ring** ♦ *n (of ladder)* degrau *m*.

runner ['rʌnər] *n (person)* corredor *m* (-ra *f);* *(for door, drawer)* calha *f; (for sledge)* patim *m*.

runner bean *n* vagem *f (Br)*, feijão *m* verde (longo) (Port).

runner-up *(pl* **runners-up)** *n* segundo *m* classificado (segunda *f* classificada).

running ['rʌnɪŋ] *n (SPORT)* corrida *f; (management)* gestão *f* ♦ *adj:* **three days ~** três dias seguidos; **to go ~** ir correr.

running water *n* água *f* corrente.

runny ['rʌnɪ] *adj (sauce)* líquido(-da); *(egg, omelette)* mal-passado(-da); *(nose)* escorrendo *(Br)*, a pingar *(Port); (eye)* lacrimejante.

run-of-the-mill *adj* normal.

runway ['rʌnweɪ] *n* pista *f* (de aterrissagem).

rural ['rʊərəl] *adj* rural.

ruse [ru:z] *n* truque *m*, estratagema *m*.

rush [rʌʃ] *n (hurry)* pressa *f; (of crowd)* onda *f* (de gente), afluência *f* ♦ *vi (move quickly)* ir correndo; *(hurry)* apressar-se
♦ *vt (work)* fazer às pressas; *(food)*

comer às pressas; *(transport quickly)* levar urgentemente; **to be in a ~** estar com OR ter pressa; **there's no ~!** não há pressa!; **don't ~ me!** não me apresse!

rush hour *n* hora *f* do rush *(Br)*, hora *f* de ponta *(Port)*.

rusk [rʌsk] *n* rosca *f* para bebês.

Russia [ˈrʌʃə] *n* Rússia *f*.

Russian [ˈrʌʃn] *adj* russo(-a) ◆ *n (person)* russo *m* (-a *f*); *(language)* russo *m*.

rust [rʌst] *n (corrosion)* ferrugem *f* ◆ *vi* enferrujar.

rustic [ˈrʌstɪk] *adj* rústico(-ca).

rustle [ˈrʌsl] *vi* fazer ruído.

rustproof [ˈrʌstpruːf] *adj* inoxidável.

rusty [ˈrʌstɪ] *adj (metal)* ferrugento (-ta); *(fig: language, person)* enferrujado(-da).

rut [rʌt] *n (furrow)* rodada *f*, marca *f* do pneu; **to be in a ~** estar preso a uma rotina.

ruthless [ˈruːθlɪs] *adj* implacável, sem piedade.

RV *n (Am: abbr of recreational vehicle)* reboque *m (Br)*, roulotte *f (Port)*.

rye [raɪ] *n* centeio *m*.

rye bread *n* pão *m* de centeio.

S

S (abbr of south, small) S.

Sabbath ['sæbəθ] n: **the ~** (for Christians) o domingo; (for Jews) o sábado.

sabotage ['sæbətɑːʒ] n sabotagem f ♦ vt sabotar.

saccharin ['sækərɪn] n sacarina f.

sachet ['sæʃeɪ] n pacote m.

sack [sæk] n (bag) saco m ♦ vt despedir; **to get the ~** ser despedido.

sacred ['seɪkrɪd] adj sagrado(-da).

sacrifice ['sækrɪfaɪs] n (fig) sacrifício m.

sad [sæd] adj triste; (unfortunate) lamentável.

sadden ['sædn] vt entristecer.

saddle ['sædl] n (on horse) sela f; (on bicycle, motorbike) selim m.

saddlebag ['sædlbæg] n (on bicycle, motorbike) bolsa f; (on horse) alforge m.

sadistic [sə'dɪstɪk] adj sádico(-ca).

sadly ['sædlɪ] adv infelizmente.

sadness ['sædnɪs] n tristeza f.

s.a.e. n (Brit: abbr of stamped addressed envelope) envelope selado e sobrescritado.

safari [sə'fɑːrɪ] n safari m.

safari park n reserva f (para animais selvagens).

safe [seɪf] adj seguro(-ra); (out of harm) em segurança ♦ n cofre m; **a ~ place** um local seguro; **(have a) ~ journey!** (faça) boa viagem!; **~ and sound** são e salvo.

safe-deposit box n caixa-forte f, cofre m.

safeguard ['seɪfgɑːd] n salvaguarda f, proteção f ♦ vt: **to ~ sb/sthg (against sthg)** salvaguardar alguém/algo (contra algo), proteger alguém/algo (de algo).

safekeeping [seɪf'kiːpɪŋ] n: **she gave it to me for ~** ela deu-me para eu guardar.

safely ['seɪflɪ] adv em segurança.

safe sex n sexo m sem riscos.

safety ['seɪftɪ] n segurança f.

safety belt n cinto m de segurança.

safety pin n alfinete m de segurança.

saffron ['sæfrən] n açafrão m.

sag [sæg] vi (hang down) pender; (sink) ir abaixo.

sage [seɪdʒ] n (herb) salva f.

Sagittarius [sædʒɪ'teərɪəs] n Sagitário m.

Sahara [sə'hɑːrə] n: **the ~ (Desert)** o (deserto do) Saara.

said [sed] pt & pp → say.

sail [seɪl] n vela f (de barco) ♦ vi velejar, navegar; (depart) zarpar ♦ vt: **to ~ a boat** velejar um barco; **to set ~** zarpar.

sailboat ['seɪlbəʊt] (Am) = **sailing boat**.

sailing ['seɪlɪŋ] n (activity) vela f; (departure) partida f; **to go ~** ir praticar vela.

sailing boat n barco m à vela.

sailing ship n veleiro m.

sailor ['seɪlər] n marinheiro m (-ra f).

saint [seɪnt] n santo m (-ta f).

sake [seɪk] n: **for my/their ~** por mim/eles; **for God's ~!** por amor de Deus!

salad ['sæləd] n salada f.

salad bar n (Brit: area in restaurant) bufê m de saladas; (restaurant) restaurante especializado em saladas.

salad bowl n saladeira f.

salad cream n (Brit) molho parecido com maionese utilizado para temperar saladas.

salad dressing n tempero m (para saladas).

salami [sə'lɑːmɪ] n salame m.

salary ['sælərɪ] *n* salário *m*, ordenado *m*.

sale [seɪl] *n (selling)* venda *f; (at reduced prices)* liquidação *f (Br)*, saldo *m (Port)*; **"for ~"** "vende-se"; **on ~** à venda.

◻ **sales** *npl (COMM)* vendas *fpl*; **the ~s** *(at reduced prices)* as liquidações *(Br)*, os saldos *(Port)*.

sales assistant ['seɪlz-] *n* vendedor *m* (-ra *f)*.

salesclerk ['seɪlzklɜːrk] *(Am)* = **sales assistant.**

salesman ['seɪlzmən] *(pl* **-men** [-mən]) *n (in shop)* vendedor *m; (rep)* representante *m* de vendas.

sales rep(resentative) *n* representante *mf* de vendas.

saleswoman ['seɪlz,wʊmən] *(pl* **-women** [-,wɪmɪn]) *n* vendedora *f*.

saliva [sə'laɪvə] *n* saliva *f*.

salmon ['sæmən] *(pl inv)* *n* salmão *m*.

salmonella [,sælmə'nelə] *n* salmonela *f*.

salon ['sælɒn] *n (hairdresser's)* salão *m* (de cabeleireiro).

saloon [sə'luːn] *n (Brit: car)* sedã *m (Br)*, carrinha *f* (de caixa fechada) *(Port); (Am: bar)* bar *m*; **~ (bar)** = pub *m, (Brit) bar de hotel ou "pub", decorado de forma mais luxuosa, onde se servem bebidas a preços mais altos que nos outros bares.*

salopettes [,sælə'pets] *npl* macacão *m* para esquiar.

salt [sɔːlt, sɒlt] *n* sal *m*.

saltcellar ['sɔːlt,selər] *n (Brit)* saleiro *m*.

salted peanuts ['sɔːltɪd-] *npl* amendoins *mpl* salgados.

salt shaker [-,ʃeɪkər] *(Am)* = **saltcellar.**

saltwater ['sɔːlt,wɔːtər] *adj* de água salgada.

salty ['sɔːltɪ] *adj* salgado(-da).

salute [sə'luːt] *n* continência *f* ◆ *vi* fazer continência.

salvage ['sælvɪdʒ] *n (property rescued)* bens *mpl* OR objetos *mpl* salvos ◆ *vt (rescue)* salvar: **to ~ sthg (from)** salvar algo (de).

same [seɪm] *adj* mesmo(-ma) ◆ *pron*: **the ~** o mesmo (a mesma); **you've got the ~ book as me** você tem o mesmo livro que eu; **they look the ~** parecem iguais; **I'll have the ~ as her** vou tomar

o mesmo que ela; **it's all the ~ to me** para mim tanto faz.

samosa [sə'məʊsə] *n empada picante, de forma triangular, com recheio de carne picada e/ou verduras (especialidade indiana).*

sample ['sɑːmpl] *n* amostra *f* ◆ *vt (food, drink)* provar.

sanctions ['sæŋkʃnz] *npl (POL)* sanções *fpl*.

sanctuary ['sæŋktʃʊərɪ] *n (for birds, animals)* reserva *f* ecológica.

sand [sænd] *n* areia *f* ◆ *vt (wood)* lixar.

◻ **sands** *npl (beach)* areal *m*.

sandal ['sændl] *n* sandália *f*.

sandbox ['sændbɒks] *(Am)* = **sandpit.**

sandcastle ['sænd,kɑːsl] *n* castelo *m* de areia.

sand dune *n* duna *f*.

sandpaper ['sænd,peɪpər] *n* lixa *f*.

sandpit ['sændpɪt] *n (Brit)* caixa de areia para as crianças brincarem.

sandwich ['sænwɪdʒ] *n* sanduíche *m (Br)*, sandes *f inv (Port)*.

sandwich bar *n* local onde se vendem sanduíches e refrescos.

sandy ['sændɪ] *adj (beach)* arenoso(-osa); *(hair)* ruivo(-va).

sane [seɪn] *adj (not mad)* são (sã) (de espírito); *(sensible)* razoável, sensato(-ta).

sang [sæŋ] *pt* → **sing.**

sanitary ['sænɪtrɪ] *adj* sanitário(-ria).

sanitary napkin *(Am)* = **sanitary towel.**

sanitary towel *n (Brit)* toalha *f* higiênica *(Br)*, penso *m* higiénico *(Port)*.

sanity ['sænɪtɪ] *n (saneness)* saúde *f* mental; *(good sense)* sensatez *f*.

sank [sæŋk] *pt* → **sink.**

Santa (Claus) ['sæntə,klɔːz] *n* Papai *m* Noel *(Br)*, Pai *m* Natal *(Port)*.

sap [sæp] *n (of plant)* seiva *f* ◆ *vt (weaken)* absorver, esgotar.

sapling ['sæplɪŋ] *n* árvore *f* jovem.

sapphire ['sæfaɪər] *n* safira *f*.

sarcastic [sɑːˈkæstɪk] *adj* sarcástico (-ca).

sardine [sɑːˈdiːn] *n* sardinha *f*.

sardonic [sɑːˈdɒnɪk] *adj* sardônico (-ca).

SASE *n (Am: abbr of self-addressed stamped envelope)* envelope selado e sobrescritado.

sash [sæʃ] *n* faixa *f*.

sat [sæt] *pt & pp* → **sit**.

Sat. *(abbr of Saturday)* sáb.

Satan ['seɪtn] *n* Satanás *m*.

satchel ['sætʃəl] *n* pasta *f* (da escola).

satellite ['sætəlaɪt] *n (in space)* satélite *m*; *(at airport)* sala *f* de embarque auxiliar.

satellite dish *n* antena *f* parabólica.

satellite TV *n* televisão *f* via satélite.

satin ['sætɪn] *n* cetim *m*.

satire ['sætaɪəʳ] *n* sátira *f*.

satisfaction [,sætɪs'fækʃn] *n* satisfação *f*.

satisfactory [,sætɪs'fæktərɪ] *adj* satisfatório(-ria).

satisfied ['sætɪsfaɪd] *adj* satisfeito (-ta).

satisfy ['sætɪsfaɪ] *vt* satisfazer.

satisfying ['sætɪsfaɪɪŋ] *adj (experience, feeling)* ótimo(-ma).

satsuma [,sæt'suːmə] *n (Brit)* satsuma *f (Port)*, espécie de tangerina.

Saturday ['sætədɪ] *n* sábado *m*; **it's ~** é sábado; **~ morning** sábado de manhã; **on ~** no sábado; **on ~s** aos sábados; **last ~** sábado passado; **this ~** este sábado; **next ~** o próximo sábado; **~ week, a week on ~** de sábado a oito (dias).

sauce [sɔːs] *n* molho *m*.

saucepan ['sɔːspən] *n* panela *f (Br)*, tacho *m (Port)*.

saucer ['sɔːsəʳ] *n* pires *m inv*.

saucy ['sɔːsɪ] *adj (inf)* atrevido(-da).

Saudi Arabia [,saʊdɪə'reɪbjə] *n* Arábia *f* Saudita.

sauna ['sɔːnə] *n* sauna *f*.

saunter ['sɔːntəʳ] *vi* caminhar (despreocupadamente).

sausage ['sɒsɪdʒ] *n* salsicha *f*, lingüiça *f*.

sausage roll *n* = folheado *m* de salsicha *(Br)*, = pastel *m* de carne *(Port)*.

sauté [Brit 'səʊteɪ, Am səʊ'teɪ] *adj* sauté *(Br)*, salteado(-da) *(Port)*.

savage ['sævɪdʒ] *adj* selvagem.

save [seɪv] *vt (rescue)* salvar; *(money, time, space)* poupar; *(reserve)* guardar; *(SPORT)* defender; *(COMPUT)* guardar *(Port)*, salvar *(Br)* ◆ *n* defesa *f*.

❏ **save up** *vi* poupar; **to ~ up (for sthg)** poupar (para comprar algo).

saver ['seɪvəʳ] *n (Brit: ticket)* bilhete de trem que apenas permite ao passageiro viajar fora das horas de rush a preço reduzido.

savings ['seɪvɪŋz] *npl* poupanças *fpl*, economias *fpl*.

savings account *n (Am)* conta *f* poupança.

savings and loan association *n (Am)* caixa *f* de crédito imobiliário.

savings bank *n* caixa *f* econômica.

savior ['seɪvjəʳ] *(Am)* = **saviour**.

saviour ['seɪvjəʳ] *n (Brit)* salvador *m* (-ra *f*).

savory ['seɪvərɪ] *(Am)* = **savoury**.

savoury ['seɪvərɪ] *adj (Brit)* salgado(-da).

saw [sɔː] *(Brit pt -ed, pp sawn, Am pt & pp -ed) pt* → **see** ◆ *n (tool)* serra *f* ◆ *vt* serrar.

sawdust ['sɔːdʌst] *n* serragem *f (Br)*, serradura *f (Port)*.

sawed-off shotgun [sɔːd-] *(Am)* = **sawn-off shotgun**.

sawn [sɔːn] *pp* → **saw**.

sawn-off shotgun *n (Brit)* espingarda *f* de cano serrado.

saxophone ['sæksəfəʊn] *n* saxofone *m*.

say [seɪ] *(pt & pp* **said**) *vt* dizer; *(subj: clock, meter)* marcar ◆ *n*: **I don't have a ~ in the matter** não tenho voto na matéria; **could you ~ that again?** podia repetir o que disse?; **~ we met at nine?** que tal encontrarmo-nos às nove?; **what did you ~?** (o que é) que você disse?

saying ['seɪɪŋ] *n* ditado *m*.

scab [skæb] *n* crosta *f*.

scaffold ['skæfəʊld] *n (frame)* andaime *m*; *(for executions)* cadafalso *m*.

scaffolding ['skæfəldɪŋ] *n* andaimes *mpl*.

scald [skɔːld] *vt* escaldar, queimar.

scale [skeɪl] *n* escala *f*; *(of fish, snake)* escama *f*; *(in kettle)* placa *f*, calcário *m*.

❏ **scales** *npl (for weighing)* balança *f*.

scallion ['skæljən] *n (Am)* cebolinha *f*.

scallop ['skɒləp] *n* vieira *f*.

scalp [skælp] *n* couro *m* cabeludo.

scalpel ['skælpəl] *n* bisturi *m*.

scamper ['skæmpəʳ] *vi* correr.

scampi ['skæmpɪ] *n* camarões *mpl* fritos.

scan [skæn] *vt (consult quickly)* per-

correr, dar uma vista de olhos em ◆ *n*
(MED) exame *m*.
scandal ['skændl] *n* escândalo *m*.
scandalize ['skændəlaız] *vt* escandalizar.
Scandinavia [,skændɪ'neɪvjə] *n*
Escandinávia *f*.
Scandinavian [,skændɪ'neɪvjən] *adj*
escandinavo(-va) ◆ *n* (person) escandinavo *m* (-va *f*).
scant [skænt] *adj* (attention) pouco
(-ca).
scanty ['skæntɪ] *adj* (amount, resources)
escasso(-a); (information) pouco(-ca);
(dress) minúsculo(-la).
scapegoat ['skeɪpgəʊt] *n* bode *m*
expiatório.
scar [skɑːr] *n* cicatriz *f*.
scarce ['skeəs] *adj* escasso(-a).
scarcely ['skeəslɪ] *adv* (hardly) mal; ~
anyone quase ninguém; ~ **ever** quase
nunca.
scare [skeər] *vt* assustar.
scarecrow ['skeəkrəʊ] *n* espantalho
m.
scared ['skeəd] *adj* assustado(-da).
scarf ['skɑːf] (*pl* **scarves**) *n* (woollen)
cachecol *m*; (for women) écharpe *f*.
scarlet ['skɑːlət] *adj* vermelho(-lha),
escarlate.
scarves [skɑːvz] *pl* → **scarf**.
scary ['skeərɪ] *adj* (inf) assustador
(-ra).
scathing ['skeɪðɪŋ] *adj* (glance, criticism) severo(-ra); (reply) mordaz.
scatter ['skætər] *vt* (seeds, papers)
espalhar; (birds) dispersar ◆ *vi*
dispersar-se.
scatterbrain ['skætəbreɪn] *n* (inf)
cabeça *f* de vento (Br), cabeça-no-ar
mf (Port).
scenario [sɪ'nɑːrɪəʊ] (*pl* **-s**) *n* (possible
situation) cenário *m*, panorama *m*; (of
film, play) enredo *m*, roteiro *m* (Br).
scene [siːn] *n* (in play, film, book) cena
f; (of crime, accident) local *m*; (view)
panorama *m*; **the music** ~ o mundo da
música; **to make a** ~ armar um escândalo.
scenery ['siːnərɪ] *n* (countryside) paisagem *f*; (in theatre) cenário *m*.
scenic ['siːnɪk] *adj* pitoresco(-ca).
scent [sent] *n* (smell) fragrância *f*; (of
animal) rasto *m*; (perfume) perfume *m*.
sceptic ['skeptɪk] *n* (Brit) cético *m* (-ca
f).

sceptical ['skeptɪkl] *adj* cético(-ca).
schedule [Brit 'ʃedjuːl, Am 'skedʒʊl] *n*
(of work, things to do) programa *m*,
calendarização *f*; (timetable) horário *m*;
(list) lista *f* ◆ *vt* (plan) programar;
according to ~ de acordo com o previsto; **behind** ~ atrasado; **on** ~ (plane,
train) na hora (prevista).
scheduled flight [Brit 'ʃedjuːld-, Am
'skedʒʊld-] *n* vôo *m* regular, vôo *m* de
linha.
scheme [skiːm] *n* (plan) projeto *m*;
(pej: dishonest plan) esquema *m*.
scheming ['skiːmɪŋ] *adj* cheio (cheia)
de truques.
schizophrenic [,skɪtsə'frenɪk] *adj*
esquizofrênico(-ca) ◆ *n* esquizofrênico
m (-ca *f*).
scholar ['skɒlər] *n* erudito *m* (-ta *f*);
Greek ~ helenista *mf*; **Latin** ~ latinista
mf.
scholarship ['skɒləʃɪp] *n* (award)
bolsa *f* de estudo.
school [skuːl] *n* escola *f*; (university
department) faculdade *f*; (Am: university) universidade *f* ◆ *adj* escolar; **at** ~
na escola.
school age *n* idade *f* escolar.
schoolbag ['skuːlbæg] *n* pasta *f* (da
escola).
schoolbook ['skuːlbʊk] *n* livro *m*
escolar, manual *m* escolar OR didático.
schoolboy ['skuːlbɔɪ] *n* aluno *m*.
school bus *n* ônibus *m* escolar (Br),
autocarro *m* OR carrinha *f* da escola
(Port).
schoolchild ['skuːltʃaɪld] (*pl*
-children [,tʃɪldrən]) *n* aluno *m* (-na *f*).
schooldays ['skuːldeɪz] *npl* tempos
mpl de escola.
schoolgirl ['skuːlgɜːl] *n* aluna *f*.
schooling ['skuːlɪŋ] *n* instrução *f*.
school-leaver [-liːvər] *n* (Brit) jovem
que abandona os estudos após a escolaridade obrigatória.
schoolmaster ['skuːl,mɑːstər] *n* (Brit)
professor *m*.
schoolmistress ['skuːl,mɪstrɪs] *n*
(Brit) professora *f*.
schoolteacher ['skuːl,tiːtʃər] *n* professor *m* (-ra *f*).
school uniform *n* uniforme *m*
escolar.
school year *n* ano *m* letivo.
science ['saɪəns] *n* ciência *f*; (SCH)
ciências *fpl*.

science fiction *n* ficção *f* científica.
scientific [ˌsaɪən'tɪfɪk] *adj* científico (-ca).
scientist ['saɪəntɪst] *n* cientista *mf*.
scintillating ['sɪntɪleɪtɪŋ] *adj* brilhante.
scissors ['sɪzəz] *npl* tesoura *f*; **a pair of ~** uma tesoura.
scold [skəʊld] *vt* ralhar com, repreender.
scone [skɒn] *n* bolo redondo por vezes com passas e que normalmente se come na hora do chá com manteiga e compota.
scoop [skuːp] *n* (for ice cream, flour) colher *f* grande; (of ice cream) bola *f*; (in media) furo *m* jornalístico (Br), exclusivo *m* (Port).
scooter ['skuːtəʳ] *n* (motor vehicle) scooter *f*, lambreta *f*.
scope [skəʊp] *n* (possibility) possibilidade *f*; (range) alcance *m*.
scorch [skɔːtʃ] *vt* chamuscar.
scorching ['skɔːtʃɪŋ] *adj* abrasador(-ra).
score [skɔːʳ] *n* (total, final result) resultado *m*; (in test) ponto *m* (Br), pontuação *f* (Port) ◆ *vt* (SPORT) marcar; (in test) obter ◆ *vi* (SPORT) marcar; **what's the ~?** como é que está (o jogo)?
scoreboard ['skɔːbɔːd] *n* marcador *m*.
scorer ['skɔːrəʳ] *n* marcador *m* (-ra *f*).
scorn [skɔːn] *n* desprezo *m*.
scornful ['skɔːnfʊl] *adj* desdenhoso (-osa); **to be ~ of sthg** desdenhar de algo.
Scorpio ['skɔːpɪəʊ] *n* Escorpião *m*.
scorpion ['skɔːpjən] *n* escorpião *m*.
Scot [skɒt] *n* escocês *m* (-esa *f*).
scotch [skɒtʃ] *n* uísque *m* escocês.
Scotch broth *n* sopa espessa feita com caldo de carne, verduras e cevada.
Scotch tape® *n* (Am) fita *f* durex® (Br), fita-cola *f* (Port).
Scotland ['skɒtlənd] *n* Escócia *f*.
Scotsman ['skɒtsmən] (pl -men [-mən]) *n* escocês *m*.
Scotswoman ['skɒts,wʊmən] (pl -women [-,wɪmɪn]) *n* escocesa *f*.
Scottish ['skɒtɪʃ] *adj* escocês(-esa).
scoundrel ['skaʊndrəl] *n* patife *m*.
scour ['skaʊəʳ] *vt* (clean) esfregar, arear; (search) percorrer.
scout [skaʊt] *n* (boy scout) escoteiro *m*.
scowl [skaʊl] *vi* franzir a testa.

scramble ['skræmbl] *n* (rush) luta *f* ◆ *vi* (climb): **~ up/down a hill** subir/descer um monte (com dificuldade).
scrambled eggs [ˌskræmbld-] *npl* ovos *mpl* mexidos.
scrap [skræp] *n* (of paper, cloth) tira *f*; (old metal) ferro *m* velho, sucata *f*.
scrapbook ['skræpbʊk] *n* álbum *m* de recortes.
scrape [skreɪp] *vt* (rub) raspar; (scratch) arranhar, esfolar.
scraper ['skreɪpəʳ] *n* raspadeira *f*.
scrap paper *n* (Brit) papel *m* de rascunho.
scrapyard ['skræpjuːd] *n* (depósito de) ferro-velho *m*.
scratch [skrætʃ] *n* (cut) arranhão *m*; (mark) risco *m* ◆ *vt* (cut) arranhar; (mark) riscar; (rub) coçar, arranhar; **to be up to ~** ter um nível satisfatório; **to start from ~** começar do nada.
scratch paper (Am) = **scrap paper**.
scrawl [skrɔːl] *n* rabisco *m* ◆ *vt* rabiscar.
scream [skriːm] *n* grito *m* ◆ *vi* gritar.
scree [skriː] *n* depósito de pedras que se desprenderam de uma encosta.
screech [skriːtʃ] *n* (of person, bird) guincho *m*; (of tyres, brakes, car) chio *m*, chiadeira *f* ◆ *vi* (person, bird) guinchar; (tyres, brakes, car) chiar.
screen [skriːn] *n* (of TV) tela *f* (Br), ecrã *m* (Port); (hall in cinema) sala *f* de cinema; (panel) biombo *m* ◆ *vt* (film) exibir; (programme) emitir.
screening ['skriːnɪŋ] *n* (of film) exibição *f*.
screen wash *n* líquido *m* para o pára-brisas.
screw [skruː] *n* parafuso *m* ◆ *vt* (fasten) aparafusar; (twist) enroscar.
screwdriver ['skruː,draɪvəʳ] *n* chave *f* de parafusos OR fendas.
scribble ['skrɪbl] *vi* escrevinhar, rabiscar.
script [skrɪpt] *n* (of play, film) roteiro *m* (Br), guião *m* (Port).
scroll [skrəʊl] *n* rolo *m* de papel/pergaminho.
scrounge [skraʊndʒ] *vt* (inf): **to ~ sthg (off sb)** filar algo (de alguém), cravar algo (a alguém).
scrounger ['skraʊndʒəʳ] *n* (inf) filão *m* (-ona *f*) (Br), crava *mf* (Port).
scrub [skrʌb] *vt* esfregar.
scruff [skrʌf] *n*: **by the ~ of the**

neck pelo cangote.

scruffy [ˈskrʌfɪ] *adj* desmazelado (-da).

scrum(mage) [ˈskrʌm(ɪdʒ)] *n* formação *f*.

scrumpy [ˈskrʌmpɪ] *n* sidra com alto teor alcoólico proveniente do sudoeste da Inglaterra.

scruples [ˈskruːplz] *npl* escrúpulos *mpl*.

scrutinize [ˈskruːtɪnaɪz] *vt* examinar (minuciosamente).

scuba diving [ˈskuːbə-] *n* mergulho *m*.

scuff [skʌf] *vt (furniture, floor)* riscar; *(heels)* gastar.

scuffle [ˈskʌfl] *n* briga *f*.

sculptor [ˈskʌlptər] *n* escultor *m* (-ra *f*).

sculpture [ˈskʌlptʃər] *n* escultura *f*.

scum [skʌm] *n (froth)* espuma *f*; *(inf: pej: worthless people)* escumalha *f*, ralé *f*.

scurry [ˈskʌrɪ] *vi*: **to ~ off/away** escapulir, dar no pé.

scuttle [ˈskʌtl] ♦ *vi (rush)*: **to ~ off/away** sair correndo, dar no pé.

scythe [saɪð] *n* segadeira *f*, gadanha *f*.

sea [siː] *n* mar *m*; **by ~** por mar; **by the ~** à beira-mar.

seabed [ˈsiːbed] *n*: **the ~** o fundo do mar.

seafood [ˈsiːfuːd] *n* marisco *m*.

seafront [ˈsiːfrʌnt] *n* orla *f* marítima.

seagull [ˈsiːɡʌl] *n* gaivota *f*.

seal [siːl] *n (animal)* foca *f*; *(on bottle, container, official mark)* selo *m* ♦ *vt (envelope, container)* selar.

sea level *n* nível *m* do mar.

sea lion *n* leão-marinho *m*.

seam [siːm] *n (in clothes)* costura *f*.

search [sɜːtʃ] *n* procura *f*, busca *f* ♦ *vt* revistar ♦ *vi*: **to ~ for** procurar.

searchlight [ˈsɜːtʃlaɪt] *n* holofote *m*.

seashell [ˈsiːʃel] *n* concha *f*.

seashore [ˈsiːʃɔːr] *n* costa *f* (marítima).

seasick [ˈsiːsɪk] *adj* enjoado(-da).

seaside [ˈsiːsaɪd] *n*: **the ~** a praia.

seaside resort *n* estância *f* balneária.

season [ˈsiːzn] *n (division of year)* estação *f*; *(period)* temporada *f* ♦ *vt (food)* temperar; **in ~** *(fruit, vegetables)* da época; *(holiday)* em época alta; **out**

of ~ *(fruit, vegetables)* fora de época; *(holiday)* em época baixa.

seasonal [ˈsiːzənl] *adj* sazonal.

seasoning [ˈsiːznɪŋ] *n* tempero *m*, condimento *m*.

season ticket *n* passe *m*.

seat [siːt] *n* assento *m*; *(place)* lugar *m* ♦ *vt (subj: building)* ter lugar para; *(subj: vehicle)* levar; **"please wait to be ~ed"** aviso pelo qual se pede aos fregueses que esperem até serem conduzidos a uma mesa vaga.

seat belt *n* cinto *m* de segurança.

seating [ˈsiːtɪŋ] *n (capacity)* lugares *mpl* (sentados).

seaweed [ˈsiːwiːd] *n* alga *f* marinha.

seaworthy [ˈsiːwɜːðɪ] *adj* em condições de navegar.

secluded [sɪˈkluːdɪd] *adj* isolado(-da).

seclusion [sɪˈkluːʒn] *n* isolamento *m*; **to keep sb in ~** manter alguém isolado.

second [ˈsekənd] *n* segundo *m* ♦ *num* segundo *m* (-da *f*); **~ gear** segunda *f* (mudança), → **sixth**.

┛ seconds *npl (goods)* artigos *mpl* de qualidade inferior; *(inf: of food)*: **who wants ~?** quem quer repetir?

secondary school [ˈsekəndrɪ-] *n* escola *f* secundária.

second-class *adj* de segunda classe; *(stamp)* de correio normal.

second-hand *adj* de segunda mão.

secondly [ˈsekəndlɪ] *adv* segundo, em segundo lugar.

second-rate *adj* de segunda (categoria), medíocre.

Second World War *n*: **the ~** a Segunda Guerra Mundial.

secrecy [ˈsiːkrəsɪ] *n* sigilo *m*.

secret [ˈsiːkrɪt] *adj* secreto(-ta) ♦ *n* segredo *m*.

secretary [*Brit* ˈsekrətrɪ, *Am* ˈsekrəterɪ] *n* secretário *m* (-ria *f*).

Secretary of State *n (Am: foreign minister)* Secretário *m* (-ria *f*) de Estado, = Ministro *m* (-tra *f*) dos Negócios Estrangeiros; *(Brit: government minister)* ministro *m* (-tra *f*).

secretive [ˈsiːkrətɪv] *adj (person)* reservado(-da); *(organization)* sigiloso (-osa).

secretly [ˈsiːkrɪtlɪ] *adv (plan, meet)* em segredo; *(hope, think)* no íntimo.

sect [sekt] *n* seita *f*.

section [ˈsekʃn] *n* seção *f*.

sector ['sektə^r] *n* setor *m*.
secure [sɪ'kjuə^r] *adj* seguro(-ra) ◆ *vt*
(fix) fixar; *(fml: obtain)* obter.
security [sɪ'kjuərətɪ] *n* segurança *f*.
security guard *n* segurança *m*,
guarda *m*.
sedate [sɪ'deɪt] *adj* tranqüilo(-la) ◆ *vt*
sedar.
sedative ['sedətɪv] *n* sedativo *m*.
sediment ['sedɪmənt] *n* sedimento *m*.
seduce [sɪ'djuːs] *vt* seduzir.
see [siː] *(pt* saw, *pp* seen) *vt* ver;
(accompany) acompanhar; *(consider)*
considerar ◆ *vi* ver; **I ~** *(understand)*
estou entendendo; **I'll ~ what I can do**
vou ver o que eu posso fazer; **to ~ to**
sthg *(deal with)* tratar de algo; *(repair)*
consertar algo; **~ you!** até mais!; **~ you**
later! até logo!; **~ you soon!** até breve!;
~ p 14 ver pág. 14.
❏ **see off** *vt sep (say goodbye to)*
despedir-se de.
seed [siːd] *n* semente *f*.
seedling ['siːdlɪŋ] *n* planta *f* jovem *(de
sementeira)*.
seedy ['siːdɪ] *adj* sórdido(-da).
seeing (as) ['siːɪŋ-] *conj* visto que.
seek [siːk] *(pt & pp* sought) *vt (fml)*
procurar.
seem [siːm] *vi* parecer ◆ *v impers:* **it ~s**
(that) ... parece que ....
seemingly ['siːmɪŋlɪ] *adv (apparently)*
aparentemente.
seen [siːn] *pp* → **see**.
seep [siːp] *vi (water, gas)* infiltrar-se.
seesaw ['siːsɔː] *n* gangorra *f (Br)*,
baloiço *m (Port)*.
see-through *adj* transparente.
segment ['segmənt] *n (of fruit)* gomo
m.
seize [siːz] *vt (grab)* agarrar; *(drugs,
arms)* confiscar.
❏ **seize up** *vi (engine)* gripar; **my back**
~d up senti um espasmo nas costas.
seldom ['seldəm] *adv* raramente.
select [sɪ'lekt] *vt* selecionar ◆ *adj* sele-
to(-ta).
selection [sɪ'lekʃn] *n* seleção *f*.
selective [sɪ'lektɪv] *adj* seletivo(-va).
self-assured [selfə'ʃuəd] *adj* segu-
ro(-ra) de si.
self-catering [self'keɪtərɪŋ] *adj (flat)*
com cozinha; *(holiday)* em casa alugada.
self-centred [self'sentəd] *adj (per-*

son) egocêntrico(-ca).
self-confident [self-] *adj* segu-
ro(-ra) de si.
self-conscious [self-] *adj* ini-
bido(-da).
self-contained [selfkən'teɪnd] *adj*
(flat) independente *(com cozinha e banheiro)*.
self-control [self-] *n* autodomínio
m.
self-defence [self-] *n* autodefesa *f*.
self-discipline [self-] *n* auto-
disciplina *f*.
self-employed [selfɪm'plɔɪd] *adj* que
trabalha por conta própria, autôno-
mo(-ma).
self-esteem [self-] *n* auto-estima *f*.
self-explanatory [selfɪk'splænətrɪ]
adj claro(-ra).
self-important [self-] *adj* cheio
(cheia) de si.
selfish ['selfɪʃ] *adj* egoísta.
selfishness ['selfɪʃnɪs] *n* egoísmo *m*.
selfless ['selflɪs] *adj* abnegado(-da),
desinteressado(-da).
self-portrait [self-] *n* auto-retrato
m.
self-raising flour [self'reɪzɪŋ-] *n*
(Brit) farinha *f* com fermento.
self-respect [self-] *n* dignidade *f*,
amor-próprio *m*.
self-restraint [self-] *n* autodomínio
m.
self-rising flour [self'raɪzɪŋ-] *(Am)* =
self-raising flour.
self-sacrifice [self-] *n* abnegação *f*.
self-satisfied [self-] *adj (person)*
satisfeito consigo próprio (satisfeita
consigo própria), ufano(-na).
self-service [self-] *adj* self-service
(inv), de auto-serviço.
self-sufficient [self-] *adj:* **~ (in**
sthg) auto-suficiente (no que diz respeito a algo).
self-taught [self-] *adj* autodidata.
sell [sel] *(pt & pp* sold) *vt & vi* vender;
to ~ for vender-se por, ser vendido
por; **to ~ sb sthg** vender algo a
alguém.
sell-by date *n* data *f* limite de
venda.
seller ['selə^r] *n* vendedor *m* (-ra *f)*.
Sellotape® ['seləteɪp] *n (Brit)* fita *f*
durex® *(Br)*, fita-cola *f (Port)*.
semen ['siːmen] *n* sêmen *m*.
semester [sɪ'mestə^r] *n* semestre *m*.

semicircle [ˈsemɪsɜːkl] *n* semicírculo *m*.

semicolon [ˌsemɪˈkəʊlən] *n* ponto *m* e vírgula.

semidetached [ˌsemɪdɪˈtætʃt] *adj* geminado(-da).

semifinal [ˌsemɪˈfaɪnl] *n* semifinal *f*.

seminar [ˈsemɪnɑːʳ] *n* seminário *m*.

semolina [ˌseməˈliːnə] *n* semolina *f*.

senate [ˈsenɪt] *n* (*in US*): **the ~** o Senado.

senator [ˈsenətəʳ] *n* senador *m* (-ra *f*).

send [send] (*pt & pp* sent) *vt* enviar; (*person*) mandar; **to ~ sthg to sb** enviar algo a alguém.

❏ **send back** *vt sep* devolver.

❏ **send off** *vt sep* (*letter, parcel*) enviar; (*SPORT*) expulsar ♦ *vi*: **to ~ off (for sthg)** mandar vir (algo) pelo correio.

sender [ˈsendəʳ] *n* remetente *mf*.

senile [ˈsiːnaɪl] *adj* senil.

senior [ˈsiːnjəʳ] *adj* (*in rank*) superior ♦ *n* (*Brit: SCH*) aluno *m* (-na *f*) (*de escola secundária*); (*Am: SCH*) finalista *mf*.

senior citizen *n* idoso *m* (-osa *f*), pessoa *f* de idade.

sensation [senˈseɪʃn] *n* sensação *f*.

sensational [senˈseɪʃənl] *adj* sensacional.

sensationalist [senˈseɪʃnəlɪst] *adj* sensacionalista.

sense [sens] *n* sentido *m*; (*common sense*) bom-senso *m* ♦ *vt* sentir; **there is no ~ in waiting** não vale a pena esperar; **to make ~** fazer sentido; **~ of direction** sentido de orientação; **~ of humour** senso de humor.

senseless [ˈsenslɪs] *adj* (*stupid*) insensato(-ta), sem sentido; (*unconscious*) inconsciente, sem sentidos.

sensible [ˈsensəbl] *adj* (*person*) sensato(-ta); (*clothes, shoes*) prático(-ca).

sensitive [ˈsensɪtɪv] *adj* sensível; (*easily offended*) susceptível, (*subject, issue*) delicado(-da).

sensual [ˈsensjʊəl] *adj* sensual.

sensuous [ˈsensjʊəs] *adj* sensual.

sent [sent] *pt & pp* → **send**.

sentence [ˈsentəns] *n* (*GRAM*) frase *f*; (*for crime*) sentença *f* ♦ *vt* condenar.

sentimental [ˌsentɪˈmentl] *adj* (*pej*) sentimental.

sentry [ˈsentrɪ] *n* sentinela *f*.

Sep. (*abbr of September*) set.

separate [*adj & n* ˈseprət, *vb* ˈsepəreɪt] *adj* (*different, individual*) diferente, dis-

tinto(-ta); (*not together*) separado(-da) ♦ *vt* separar ♦ *vi* separar-se.

❏ **separates** *npl* (*Brit: clothes*) roupa feminina que pode ser usada em conjunto.

separately [ˈseprətlɪ] *adv* separadamente.

separation [ˌsepəˈreɪʃn] *n* separação *f*.

September [sepˈtembəʳ] *n* setembro *m*; **at the beginning of ~** no início de setembro; **at the end of ~** no fim de setembro; **during ~** em setembro; **every ~** todos os meses de setembro, todos os anos em setembro; **in ~** em setembro; **last ~** setembro último OR passado; **next ~** no próximo mês de setembro; **this ~** setembro que vem; **2 ~ 1997** (*in letters etc*) 2 de setembro de 1997.

septic [ˈseptɪk] *adj* infectado(-da).

septic tank *n* fossa *f* sética.

sequel [ˈsiːkwəl] *n* (*to book, film*) continuação *f*.

sequence [ˈsiːkwəns] *n* (*series*) série *f*; (*order*) ordem *f*.

sequin [ˈsiːkwɪn] *n* lantejoula *f*.

Sorb [sɔːb] = **Serbian**.

Serbia [ˈsɜːbjə] *n* Sérvia *f*.

Serbian [ˈsɜːbjən] *adj* sérvio(-via) ♦ *n* (*person*) sérvio *m* (-via *f*).

serene [sɪˈriːn] *adj* (*calm*) sereno(-na).

sergeant [ˈsɑːdʒənt] *n* (*in police force*) sargento *m* (*Br*), polícia *m* graduado (polícia *f* graduada) (*Port*); (*in army*) sargento *m*.

sergeant major *n* sargento-ajudante *m*.

serial [ˈsɪərɪəl] *n* seriado *m* (*Br*), série *f* (*Port*).

serial number *n* número *m* de série.

series [ˈsɪəriːz] (*pl inv*) *n* série *f*.

serious [ˈsɪərɪəs] *adj* sério(-ria); (*accident, illness*) grave; **are you ~?** você está falando sério?

seriously [ˈsɪərɪəslɪ] *adv* (*really*) de verdade; (*badly*) gravemente.

seriousness [ˈsɪərɪəsnɪs] *n* (*of person, expression, voice*) seriedade *f*; (*of illness, situation, loss*) gravidade *f*.

sermon [ˈsɜːmən] *n* sermão *m*.

serrated [sɪˈreɪtɪd] *adj* dentado(-da); **~ knife** faca *f* de serrilha.

servant [ˈsɜːvənt] *n* criado *m* (-da *f*).

serve [sɜːv] *vt* servir ♦ *vi* (*SPORT*) servir; (*work*) prestar serviço ♦ *n* (*SPORT*) serviço *m*; **the town is ~d by two airports** a cidade tem dois aeroportos; **to ~ as** *(be used for)* servir de; **"~s two"** "para duas pessoas"; **it ~s you right!** bem feito!

service ['sɜːvɪs] *n* serviço *m*; *(at church)* culto *m* (Br), ofício *m* (Port); *(of car)* revisão *f* ♦ *vt* (car) fazer a revisão de; **"out of ~"** "fora de serviço"; **"~ included"** "serviço incluído"; **"~ not included"** "não inclui o serviço"; **can I be of any ~ to you?** *(fml)* em que posso servi-lo?

❏ **services** *npl* (on motorway) posto de gasolina com bares, banheiros etc.; *(of person)* serviços *mpl*.

service area *n* posto de gasolina com bares, banheiros, etc., área *f* de serviço (Port).

service charge *n* serviço *m*.

service department *n* seção *f* de atendimento ao consumidor.

service station *n* posto *m* de gasolina (Br), estação *f* de serviço (Port).

serviette [ˌsɜːvɪ'et] *n* guardanapo *m*.

serving ['sɜːvɪŋ] *n* porção *f*.

serving spoon *n* colher *f* para servir.

sesame seeds ['sɛsəmɪ-] *npl* sementes *fpl* de sésamo.

session ['seʃn] *n* sessão *f*.

set [set] *(pt & pp* set) *adj* **1.** *(fixed)* fixo(-xa); **~ lunch** = almoço *m* a preço fixo (Br), ementa *f* turística (Port).
2. *(text, book)* escolhido(-da).
3. *(situated)* situado(-da).
♦ *n* **1.** *(of stamps, stickers)* coleção *f*; *(for playing chess)* jogo *m*; *(of crockery)* aparelho *m*; *(of tools)* conjunto *m*.
2. *(TV)* aparelho *m*; **a TV ~** uma televisão, um televisor.
3. *(in tennis)* set *m*, partida *f*.
4. *(SCH)* grupo *m*.
5. *(of play)* cenário *m*.
6. *(at hairdresser's)*: **I'd like a shampoo and ~** queria lavar e pentear.
♦ *vt* **1.** *(put)* pôr.
2. *(cause to be)* pôr; **to ~ a machine going** pôr uma máquina em funcionamento.
3. *(clock, alarm, controls)* pôr; **~ the alarm for 7 a.m.** põe o despertador para despertar às sete.
4. *(fix)* fixar.
5. *(the table)* pôr.
6. *(a record)* estabelecer.

7. *(broken bone)* endireitar.
8. *(homework, essay)* marcar.
9. *(play, film, story)*: **to be ~** passar-se.
♦ *vi* **1.** *(sun)* pôr-se.
2. *(glue)* secar; *(jelly)* solidificar.
❏ **set down** *vt sep* (Brit: passengers) deixar.
❏ **set off** *vt sep* (alarm) fazer soar ♦ *vi* partir.
❏ **set out** *vt sep* (arrange) estabelecer ♦ *vi* (on journey) partir.
❏ **set up** *vt sep* (barrier, equipment) montar; *(meeting, interview)* marcar; *(committee)* criar.

setback ['setbæk] *n* contratempo *m*, revés *m*.

set meal *n* menu *m*, ementa *f* (Port).

set menu *n* menu *m* fixo, ementa *f* fixa (Port).

settee [se'tiː] *n* sofá *m*.

setting ['setɪŋ] *n* (on machine) posição *f*; *(surroundings)* cenário *m*.

settle ['setl] *vt* (argument) resolver; *(bill)* pagar, saldar; *(stomach, nerves)* acalmar; *(arrange, decide on)* decidir ♦ *vi* (start to live) estabelecer-se; *(bird, insect)* pousar; *(sediment, dust)* depositar-se.
❏ **settle down** *vi* (calm down) acalmar-se; *(sit comfortably)* instalar-se.
❏ **settle up** *vi* saldar as contas.

settlement ['setlmənt] *n* (agreement) acordo *m*; *(place)* povoado *m*, colônia *f*.

settler ['setlər] *n* colono *m* (-na *f*).

seven ['sevn] *num* sete, → **six**.

seventeen [ˌsevn'tiːn] *num* dezessete (Br), dezassete (Port), → **six**.

seventeenth [ˌsevn'tiːnθ] *num* décimo sétimo (décima sétima), → **sixth**.

seventh ['sevnθ] *num* sétimo(-ma), → **sixth**.

seventieth ['sevntjəθ] *num* septuagésimo(-ma), → **sixth**.

seventy ['sevntɪ] *num* setenta, → **six**.

several ['sevrəl] *adj* vários(-rias) ♦ *pron* vários *mpl* (-rias *fpl*).

severe [sɪ'vɪər] *adj* (damage, illness, problem) grave; *(weather conditions)* rigoroso(-osa); *(criticism, person, punishment)* severo(-ra); *(pain)* intenso(-sa).

severity [sɪ'verətɪ] *n* (of damage, illness, problem) gravidade *f*; *(of weather conditions)* rigor *m*; *(of storm)* violência *f*; *(of criticism, person, punishment)* severidade *f*.

sew [səʊ] (pp **sewn**) vt & vi coser, costurar.

sewage ['suːɪdʒ] n esgotos mpl, águas fpl residuais.

sewer ['suər] n (cano de) esgoto m.

sewing ['səʊɪŋ] n costura f.

sewing machine n máquina f de costura.

sewn [səʊn] pp → sew.

sex [seks] n sexo m; **to have ~ (with)** ter relações sexuais (com).

sexist ['seksɪst] n sexista mf.

sexual ['sekʃʊəl] adj sexual; **~ equality** igualdade f dos sexos.

sexual harassment n assédio m sexual.

sexual intercourse n relações fpl sexuais.

sexy ['seksɪ] adj sexy.

shabby ['ʃæbɪ] adj (clothes, room) em mau estado; (person) esfarrapado (-da).

shack [ʃæk] n barraco m.

shade [ʃeɪd] n (shadow) sombra f; (lampshade) abajur m; (of colour) tom m ◆ vt (protect) proteger.
◡ **shades** npl (inf: sunglasses) óculos mpl escuros.

shadow ['ʃædəʊ] n sombra f.

shady ['ʃeɪdɪ] adj (place) com sombra; (inf: person, deal) duvidoso(-osa).

shaft [ʃɑːft] n (of machine) eixo m; (of lift) poço m.

shaggy ['ʃægɪ] adj (dog) peludo(-da); (rug, carpet) felpudo(-da); (hair, beard) hirsuto(-ta).

shake [ʃeɪk] (pt **shook**, pp **shaken** ['ʃeɪkn]) vt (bottle) agitar; (tree, person) abanar; (rug) sacudir; (shock) abalar ◆ vi tremer; **to ~ hands (with sb)** apertar a mão (a alguém), dar um aperto de mão (em alguém); **to ~ one's head** (saying no) negar com a cabeça.

shaky ['ʃeɪkɪ] adj (chair, table) frágil, trôpego(-ga); (hand, writing, voice) trêmulo(-la); (start) acidentado(-da); (finances) instável; (evidence, argument) pouco sólido(-da); **I'm still a bit ~** ainda não me recuperei.

shall [weak form ʃəl, strong form ʃæl] aux vb 1. (expressing future): **I ~ be ready soon** estarei pronto num instante.
2. (in questions): **~ I buy some wine?** quer que eu compre um vinho?; **~ we listen to the radio?** que tal se ouvisse-

mos rádio?; **where ~ we go?** onde é que vamos?
3. (fml: expressing order): **payment ~ be made within a week** o pagamento deverá ser feito no prazo de uma semana.

shallot [ʃə'lɒt] n cebolinha f, chalota f.

shallow ['ʃæləʊ] adj (pond, water, grave) raso(-sa).

shallow end n (of swimming pool) parte f rasa.

sham [ʃæm] n (piece of deceit) farsa f.

shambles ['ʃæmblz] n confusão f.

shame [ʃeɪm] n vergonha f; **it's a ~** é uma pena; **what a ~!** que pena!

shamefaced [ʃeɪm'feɪst] adj envergonhado(-da).

shameful ['ʃeɪmfʊl] adj vergonhoso(-osa).

shameless ['ʃeɪmlɪs] adj sem vergonha.

shampoo [ʃæm'puː] n (liquid) xampu m (Br), champô m (Port); (wash) lavagem f.

shandy ['ʃændɪ] n cerveja f com soda, panaché m.

shan't [ʃɑːnt] = shall not.

shape [ʃeɪp] n forma f; **to be in good/bad ~** estar em boa/má forma.

shapeless ['ʃeɪplɪs] adj (clothes) sem forma.

shapely ['ʃeɪplɪ] adj bem feito(-ta).

share [ʃeər] n (part) parte f; (in company) ação f ◆ vt partilhar.
◡ **share out** vt sep partilhar.

shareholder ['ʃeəhəʊldər] n acionista mf.

shark [ʃɑːk] n tubarão m.

sharp [ʃɑːp] adj (blade, needle, teeth) afiado(-da); (clear) nítido(-da); (quick, intelligent) perspicaz; (rise, change, bend) brusco(-ca); (painful) agudo(-da); (food, taste) ácido(-da) ◆ adv (exactly) em ponto.

sharpen ['ʃɑːpn] vt (knife) afiar; (pencil) apontar (Br), afiar (Port).

sharpener ['ʃɑːpnər] n (for pencil) apontador m (Br), apara-lápis m inv (Port); (for knife) amolador m.

sharp-eyed [-'aɪd] adj perspicaz.

sharply ['ʃɑːplɪ] adv (stand out, differ) claramente; (change, stop, criticize) bruscamente.

shatter ['ʃætər] vt (break) estilhaçar ◆ vi estilhaçar-se.

shattered ['ʃætəd] adj (Brit: inf: tired) estourado(-da).

shave [ʃeɪv] vt (beard, legs) raspar; (face) barbear ◆ vi barbear-se ◆ n: to have a ~ barbear-se, fazer a barba.

shaver ['ʃeɪvər] n barbeador m, máquina f de barbear.

shaver point n tomada f (para máquina de barbear).

shaving brush ['ʃeɪvɪŋ-] n pincel m para a barba.

shaving cream ['ʃeɪvɪŋ-] n creme m para a barba.

shaving foam ['ʃeɪvɪŋ-] n espuma f para a barba.

shavings ['ʃeɪvɪŋz] npl aparas fpl.

shawl [ʃɔːl] n xale m.

she [ʃiː] pron ela; ~'s tall ela é alta.

sheaf [ʃiːf] (pl sheaves) n (of paper, notes) maço m.

shear [ʃɪər] (pt -ed, pp -ed OR shorn) vt (sheep) tosquiar.

❏ **shears** npl (for gardening) tesoura f de podar OR de jardim.

sheath [ʃiːθ] n (for knife) bainha f.

sheaves [ʃiːvz] pl → sheaf.

shed [ʃed] (pt & pp shed) n galpão m, casinha de madeira em fundo de quintal para guardar ferramentas de jardinagem, etc. ◆ vt (tears, blood) derramar.

she'd [weak form ʃid, strong form ʃiːd] = she had, she would.

sheen [ʃiːn] n brilho m.

sheep [ʃiːp] (pl inv) n ovelha f, carneiro m.

sheepdog ['ʃiːpdɒg] n cão m pastor.

sheepish ['ʃiːpɪʃ] adj embaraçado(-da), envergonhado(-da).

sheepskin ['ʃiːpskɪn] adj de pele de carneiro OR ovelha.

sheer [ʃɪər] adj (pure, utter) puro(-ra); (cliff) escarpado(-da); (stockings) fino (-na).

sheet [ʃiːt] n (for bed) lençol m; (of paper, metal, wood) folha f; a ~ of glass um vidro, uma vidraça.

sheik(h) [ʃeɪk] n xeque m.

shelf [ʃelf] (pl shelves) n prateleira f.

shell [ʃel] n (of egg, nut) casca f; (of oyster, clam, snail) concha f; (of turtle, crab) carapaça f; (bomb) projétil m.

she'll [ʃiːl] = she will, she shall.

shellfish ['ʃelfɪʃ] n (food) marisco m.

shell suit n (Brit) roupa f de jogging (de nylon brilhante).

shelter ['ʃeltər] n abrigo m ◆ vt (protect) abrigar ◆ vi abrigar-se; to take ~ abrigar-se.

sheltered ['ʃeltəd] adj (place) abrigado(-da).

shelve [ʃelv] vt (plan, project) arquivar.

shelves [ʃelvz] pl → shelf.

shepherd ['ʃepəd] n pastor m.

shepherd's pie ['ʃepədz-] n empadão de carne de vaca picada, cebola e especiarias.

sheriff ['ʃerɪf] n (in US) xerife m.

sherry ['ʃerɪ] n xerez m.

she's [ʃiːz] = she is, she has.

Shetland Islands ['ʃetlənd-] npl: the ~ as Ilhas Shetland.

shield [ʃiːld] n (of soldier, policeman) escudo m ◆ vt proteger.

shift [ʃɪft] n (change) mudança f; (period of work) turno m ◆ vt (move) mover ◆ vi (move) mover-se; (change) mudar.

shilling ['ʃɪlɪŋ] n (Brit) xelim m.

shimmer ['ʃɪmər] vi tremeluzir, brilhar com luz trêmula.

shin [ʃɪn] n canela f.

shinbone ['ʃɪnbəʊn] n tíbia f.

shine [ʃaɪn] (pt & pp shone) vi brilhar ◆ vt (shoes) lustrar (Br), puxar o lustro a (Port); (torch) apontar.

shingle ['ʃɪŋgl] n (on beach) seixos mpl, cascalho m.

❏ **shingles** n (MED) zona f.

shiny ['ʃaɪnɪ] adj brilhante.

ship [ʃɪp] n navio m; by ~ de navio.

shipbuilding ['ʃɪpbɪldɪŋ] n construção f naval.

shipment ['ʃɪpmənt] n carregamento m.

shipping ['ʃɪpɪŋ] n (ships) navios mpl.

shipwreck ['ʃɪprek] n (accident) naufrágio m; (wrecked ship) navio m naufragado.

shipyard ['ʃɪpjɑːd] n estaleiro m.

shirk [ʃɜːk] vt fugir de.

shirt [ʃɜːt] n camisa f.

shirtsleeves ['ʃɜːtsliːvz] npl: to be in (one's) ~ estar em mangas de camisa.

shiver ['ʃɪvər] vi tremer.

shoal [ʃəʊl] n cardume m.

shock [ʃɒk] n (surprise) choque m; (force) impacto m ◆ vt chocar; to be in ~ (MED) estar em estado de choque.

shock absorber [-əbˌzɔːbər] n amortecedor m.

shocking ['ʃɒkɪŋ] adj (very bad) chocante.

shoddy ['ʃɒdɪ] adj (work, goods) de segunda.

shoe [ʃuː] n sapato m.

shoebrush ['ʃuːbrʌʃ] n escova f para sapatos.

shoehorn ['ʃuːhɔːn] n calçadeira f.

shoelace ['ʃuːleɪs] n cardaço m (Br), atacador m (Port).

shoe polish n graxa f.

shoe repairer's [-rɪˌpeərəz] n sapateiro m.

shoe shop n sapataria f.

shone [ʃɒn] pt & pp → **shine**.

shook [ʃʊk] pt → **shake**.

shoot [ʃuːt] (pt & pp shot) vt (kill, injure) dar um tiro em; (gun) disparar; (arrow) atirar; (film) filmar ♦ vi (with gun) atirar; (move quickly) passar disparado(-da); (SPORT) rematar ♦ n (of plant) broto m (Br), rebento m (Port).

shooting ['ʃuːtɪŋ] n (killing) assassinato m, morte f (a tiro); (hunting) caça-da f.

shop [ʃɒp] n loja f ♦ vi fazer compras.

shop assistant n (Brit) empregado m (-da f) (de balcão), vendedor m (-ra f).

shopkeeper ['ʃɒpˌkiːpər] n comerciante mf.

shoplifter ['ʃɒpˌlɪftər] n ladrão m (ladra f) de lojas.

shoplifting ['ʃɒpˌlɪftɪŋ] n roubo m em loja.

shopper ['ʃɒpər] n comprador m (-ra f), freguês m (-esa f).

shopping ['ʃɒpɪŋ] n compras fpl; **to do the ~** fazer as compras; **to go ~** ir às compras.

shopping bag n saco m de compras.

shopping basket n cesto m de compras.

shopping centre n centro m comercial, shopping m.

shopping list n lista f de compras.

shopping mall n centro m comercial.

shopsoiled ['ʃɒpsɔɪld] adj (Brit) danificado(-da).

shop steward n delegado m (-da f) sindical.

shop window n vitrine f, montra f (Port).

shopworn ['ʃɒpwɔːn] (Am) = **shopsoiled**.

shore [ʃɔːr] n (of river, lake) margem f; (of sea) costa f; **on ~** em terra.

shorn [ʃɔːn] pp → **shear**.

short [ʃɔːt] adj (not tall) baixo(-xa); (in length, time) curto(-ta) ♦ adv (cut hair) curto ♦ n (Brit: drink) bebida f forte; (film) curta-metragem f; **to be ~ of** sthg (time, money) ter falta de algo; **I'm ~ of breath** estou sem fôlego; **to be ~ for sthg** (be abbreviation of) ser o diminutivo de algo; **in ~** em resumo.

❏ **shorts** npl (short trousers) calções mpl; (Am: underpants) cuecas fpl.

shortage ['ʃɔːtɪdʒ] n falta f, escassez f.

shortbread ['ʃɔːtbred] n biscoito m de manteiga.

short-change vt (in shop, restaurant) dar troco a menos a, roubar no troco de; (fig: treat unfairly) enganar, roubar.

short-circuit vi ter um curto-circuito.

shortcomings ['ʃɔːtˌkʌmɪŋz] npl defeitos mpl.

shortcrust pastry ['ʃɔːtkrʌst-] n massa f areada OR brisée.

short cut n atalho m.

shorten ['ʃɔːtn] vt encurtar.

shortfall ['ʃɔːtfɔːl] n: **a ~ in/of** um déficit em/de.

shorthand ['ʃɔːthænd] n estenografia f.

shorthand typist n (Brit) estenodatilógrafo m (-fa f).

short list n (Brit: for job, prize) lista f de candidatos selecionados.

shortly ['ʃɔːtlɪ] adv (soon) daqui a pouco, em breve; **he arrived ~ before me** ele chegou (um) pouco antes de mim.

shortsighted [ˌʃɔːtˈsaɪtɪd] adj (with poor eyesight) míope, curto(-ta) da vista.

short-sleeved [-ˌsliːvd] adj de manga curta.

short-staffed [-ˈstɑːft] adj: **to be ~** estar com falta de pessoal, ter pessoal a menos.

short-stay car park n parque m de estacionamento de curta duração.

short story n conto m.

short-tempered [-ˈtempəd] adj irritável, com mau gênio.

short-term adj a curto prazo.

short wave n onda f curta.

shot [ʃɒt] pt & pp → **shoot** ♦ n (of gun)

tiro *m; (in football)* remate *m; (in tennis, golf etc)* jogada *f; (photo)* foto *f; (in film)* plano *m; (inf: attempt)* tentativa *f; (drink)* trago *m.*

shotgun [ˈʃɒtgʌn] *n* espingarda *f,* caçadeira *f.*

should [ʃʊd] *aux vb* **1.** *(expressing desirability)* dever; **we ~ leave now** devíamos ir embora agora. **2.** *(asking for advice):* **~ I go too?** você acha que também devo ir? **3.** *(expressing probability)* dever; **she ~ be home soon** ela deve estar chegando a casa. **4.** *(ought to)* dever; **they ~ have won the match** eles é que deviam ter ganho o jogo. **5.** *(fml: in conditionals):* **~ you need anything, call reception** se precisar de algo, ligue para a recepção. **6.** *(fml: expressing wish):* **I ~ like to come with you** gostaria de ir contigo.

shoulder [ˈʃəʊldəʳ] *n (of person)* ombro *m; (of meat)* pá *f; (Am: of road)* acostamento *m (Br),* zona *f* de paragem de urgência *(Port).*

shoulder blade *n* omoplata *f.*

shoulder pad *n* chumaço *m.*

shoulder strap *n* alça *f.*

shouldn't [ʃʊdnt] = **should not.**

should've [ʃʊdəv] = **should have.**

shout [ʃaʊt] *n* grito *m* ◆ *vt & vi* gritar.
⌐ **shout out** *vt sep* gritar.

shouting [ˈʃaʊtɪŋ] *n* gritos *mpl.*

shove [ʃʌv] *vt (push)* empurrar; *(put carelessly)* atirar com.

shovel [ˈʃʌvl] *n* pá *f.*

show [ʃəʊ] *(pp* **-ed** OR **shown)** *n (at theatre, on TV, radio)* espetáculo *m; (exhibition)* exibição *f; (of dogs)* concurso *m* ◆ *vt* mostrar; *(prove, demonstrate)* revelar; *(accompany)* acompanhar; *(film, TV programme)* passar ◆ *vi (be visible)* ver-se; *(film)* passar; **to ~ sthg to sb** mostrar algo a alguém; **to ~ sb how to do sthg** mostrar a alguém como fazer algo.
⌐ **show off** *vi* exibir-se.
⌐ **show up** *vi (come along)* aparecer; *(be visible)* ver-se.

show business *n* mundo *m* do espetáculo, show business *m.*

showdown [ˈʃəʊdaʊn] *n:* **to have a ~ with sb** resolver cara a cara as diferenças com alguém.

shower [ˈʃaʊəʳ] *n (for washing)* chu-

veiro *m; (of rain)* aguaceiro *m* ◆ *vi* tomar banho (de chuveiro); **to have a ~** tomar banho (de chuveiro).

shower cap *n* touca *f* de banho.

shower gel *n* gel *m* de banho.

shower unit *n* chuveiro *m (compartimento).*

showing [ˈʃəʊɪŋ] *n (of film)* sessão *f.*

show jumping *n* competição *f* hípica de salto.

shown [ʃəʊn] *pp* → **show.**

show-off *n (inf)* exibicionista *mf.*

showroom [ˈʃəʊrʊm] *n* salão *m* de exposições.

shrank [ʃræŋk] *pt* → **shrink.**

shrapnel [ˈʃræpnl] *n* estilhaços *mpl,* metralha *f.*

shred [ʃred] *n (small piece)* tira *f* ◆ *vt (CULIN)* cortar em tiras muito finas; *(paper)* cortar em tiras.

shrewd [ʃruːd] *adj (person)* astuto (-ta); *(action, judgment, move)* inteligente.

shriek [ʃriːk] *n* grito *m* ◆ *vi* gritar; **a ~ of laughter** uma gargalhada; **to ~ with laughter** rir às gargalhadas.

shrill [ʃrɪl] *adj* estridente.

shrimp [ʃrɪmp] *n* camarão *m.*

shrine [ʃraɪn] *n* santuário *m.*

shrink [ʃrɪŋk] *(pt* **shrank,** *pp* **shrunk)** *n (inf: psychoanalyst)* psicanalista *mf* ◆ *vi (become smaller)* encolher; *(diminish)* diminuir.

shrivel [ʃrɪvl] *vi:* **to ~ (up)** secar, enrugar.

Shrove Tuesday [ʃrəʊv-] *n* Terça-feira *f* de Carnaval, Dia *m* de Entrudo *(Port).*

shrub [ʃrʌb] *n* arbusto *m.*

shrug [ʃrʌg] *vi* encolher os ombros ◆ *n:* **she gave a ~** ela encolheu os ombros.

shrunk [ʃrʌŋk] *pp* → **shrink.**

shudder [ˈʃʌdəʳ] *vi (person):* **to ~ (with)** estremecer (de).

shuffle [ˈʃʌfl] *vt (cards)* embaralhar ◆ *vi (walk)* andar arrastando os pés.

shut [ʃʌt] *(pt & pp* **shut)** *adj* fechado(-da) ◆ *vt & vi* fechar.
⌐ **shut down** *vt sep* fechar.
⌐ **shut up** *vi (inf: stop talking)* calar-se.

shutter [ˈʃʌtəʳ] *n (on window)* persiana *f; (on camera)* obturador *m.*

shuttle [ˈʃʌtl] *n (plane)* avião *m (que faz vôos curtos regulares); (bus)* serviço *m* regular.

247

shuttlecock [ˈʃʌtlkɒk] *n* peteca *f* (*Br*), volante *m* (*Port*).

shy [ʃaɪ] *adj* tímido(-da).

sibling [ˈsɪblɪŋ] *n* irmão *m* (-mã *f*).

sick [sɪk] *adj* (*ill*) doente; (*nauseous*) mal disposto(-osta); **to be ~** (*vomit*) vomitar; **to feel ~** sentir-se mal disposto; **to be ~ of** (*fed up with*) estar farto de.

sick bag *n* saco posto à disposição dos passageiros em aviões, barcos e ônibus para casos de enjôo.

sickbay [ˈsɪkbeɪ] *n* (*on ship*) enfermaria *f*; (*in school*) gabinete *m* médico.

sickening [ˈsɪknɪŋ] *adj* (*disgusting*) nauseabundo(-da).

sick leave *n* licença *f* por doença (*Br*), baixa *f* (médica) (*Port*).

sickly [ˈsɪklɪ] *adj* (*unhealthy*) adoentado(-da); (*nauseating*) enjoativo(-va).

sickness [ˈsɪknɪs] *n* (*illness*) doença *f*.

sick pay *n* auxílio-doença *m* (*Br*), subsídio *m* de doença (*Port*).

side [saɪd] *n* lado *m*; (*of road, river, pitch*) beira *f*; (*of coin*) cara *f*; (*Brit: TV channel*) canal *m*; (*page of writing*) página *f* ♦ *adj* (*door, pocket*) lateral; **at the ~ of** ao lado de; **on the other ~** no outro lado; **on this ~** neste lado; **~ by ~** lado a lado.

sideboard [ˈsaɪdbɔːd] *n* aparador *m*.

sideboards [ˈsaɪdbɔːdz] *npl* (*Brit*) suíças *fpl*, patilhas *fpl* (*Port*).

sideburns [ˈsaɪdbɜːnz] *npl* suíças *fpl*, patilhas *fpl* (*Port*).

sidecar [ˈsaɪdkɑːʳ] *n* side-car *m*.

side dish *n* acompanhamento *m*, guarnição *f*.

side effect *n* efeito *m* secundário, efeito *m* colateral.

sidelight [ˈsaɪdlaɪt] *n* (*Brit*) luz *f* lateral, farolim *m* (*Port*).

sideline [ˈsaɪdlaɪn] *n* (*SPORT*) linha *f* lateral.

side order *n* acompanhamento *m*, guarnição *f*.

side salad *n* salada *f* (de acompanhamento).

sideshow [ˈsaɪdʃəʊ] *n* barraca *f* (de feira popular ou circo).

side street *n* travessa *f*.

sidewalk [ˈsaɪdwɔːk] *n* (*Am*) passeio *m*.

sideways [ˈsaɪdweɪz] *adv* de lado.

siege [siːdʒ] *n* cerco *m*.

sieve [sɪv] *n* coador *m*; (*for flour*)

peneira *f* ♦ *vt* coar; (*flour*) peneirar.

sift [sɪft] *vt* (*sieve*) peneirar; (*fig: examine carefully*) estudar ♦ *vi*: **to ~ through sth** (*evidence, applications*) estudar algo.

sigh [saɪ] *n* suspiro *m* ♦ *vi* suspirar.

sight [saɪt] *n* vista *f*; **at first ~** à primeira vista; **to catch ~ of** ver, avistar; **in ~** à vista; **to lose ~ of** perder de vista; **to be out of ~** (*hidden*) não estar visível; (*far away*) estar longe da vista.

❑ **sights** *npl* (*of country*) vistas *fpl*; (*of city*) locais *mpl* de interesse.

sightseeing [ˈsaɪtsiːɪŋ] *n*: **to go ~** fazer turismo.

sightseer [ˈsaɪtsiːəʳ] *n* excursionista *mf*, turista *mf*.

sign [saɪn] *n* sinal *m* ♦ *vt & vi* assinar; **there's no ~ of her** dela, nem sinal.

❑ **sign in** *vi* (*at hotel, club*) assinar o registro (*ao chegar*).

signal [ˈsɪgnl] *n* sinal *m* ♦ *vi* fazer sinal.

signature [ˈsɪgnətʃəʳ] *n* assinatura *f*.

significance [sɪgˈnɪfɪkəns] *n* significado *m*.

significant [sɪgˈnɪfɪkənt] *adj* significante.

sign language *n* linguagem *f* gestual.

signpost [ˈsaɪnpəʊst] *n* tabuleta *f*, sinal *m*.

sikh [siːk] *n* sikh *mf*, sique *mf*.

silence [ˈsaɪləns] *n* silêncio *m*.

silencer [ˈsaɪlənsəʳ] *n* (*Brit: AUT*) silencioso *m*.

silent [ˈsaɪlənt] *adj* silencioso(-osa).

silhouette [ˌsɪluːˈet] *n* silhueta *f*.

silicon chip *n* chip *m* de silício.

silk [sɪlk] *n* seda *f*.

silky [ˈsɪlkɪ] *adj* acetinado(-da).

sill [sɪl] *n* bordo *m*.

silly [ˈsɪlɪ] *adj* bobo(-ba), tonto(-ta) (*Port*).

silver [ˈsɪlvəʳ] *n* prata *f*; (*coins*) moedas *fpl* ♦ *adj* de prata.

silver foil *n* folha *f* OR papel *m* de alumínio.

silver-plated [-ˈpleɪtɪd] *adj* banhado(-da) a prata.

silverware [ˈsɪlvəweəʳ] *n* (*objects made of silver*) prata *f*; (*Am: cutlery*) talheres *mpl*, faqueiro *m*.

similar [ˈsɪmɪləʳ] *adj* semelhante; **to be ~ to** ser semelhante a.

similarity [ˌsɪmɪˈlærətɪ] n semelhança f.

similarly [ˈsɪmɪləlɪ] adv igualmente.

simmer [ˈsɪməʳ] vi cozinhar em fogo brando.

simple [ˈsɪmpl] adj simples (inv).

simple-minded adj simplório(-ria).

simplify [ˈsɪmplɪfaɪ] vt simplificar.

simply [ˈsɪmplɪ] adv simplesmente; (easily) facilmente.

simulate [ˈsɪmjʊleɪt] vt simular.

simultaneous [Brit ˌsɪməlˈteɪnjəs, Am ˌsaɪməlˈteɪnjəs] adj simultâneo(-nea).

simultaneously [Brit ˌsɪməlˈteɪnjəslɪ, Am ˌsaɪməlˈteɪnjəslɪ] adv simultaneamente.

sin [sɪn] n pecado m ♦ vi pecar.

since [sɪns] adv desde então ♦ prep desde ♦ conj (in time) desde que; (as) visto que; **ever ~** prep desde ♦ conj desde que.

sincere [sɪnˈsɪəʳ] adj sincero(-ra).

sincerely [sɪnˈsɪəlɪ] adv sinceramente; **Yours ~ ~** Com os melhores cumprimentos.

sincerity [sɪnˈserətɪ] n sinceridade f.

sing [sɪŋ] (pt **sang**, pp **sung**) vt & vi cantar.

singe [sɪndʒ] vt chamuscar.

singer [ˈsɪŋəʳ] n cantor m (-ra f).

singing [ˈsɪŋɪŋ] n canto m.

single [ˈsɪŋgl] adj (just one) único(-ca); (not married) solteiro(-ra) ♦ n (Brit: ticket) bilhete m de ida; (record) single m; **every ~** cada um (uma) de; **every ~ day** todos os dias.

❑ **singles** n (in tennis, badminton, pool) simples f inv (Br), individuais mpl (Port) ♦ adj (bar, club) para solteiros.

single bed n cama f de solteiro.

single cream n (Brit) creme m magro fresco (Br), natas fpl frescas líquidas (Port).

single file n: **in ~** em fila indiana.

single-handed [-ˈhændɪd] adv sozinho(-nha), sem ajuda.

single parent n (mother) mãe f solteira; (father) pai m solteiro.

single room n quarto m de solteiro.

single track road n estrada f de uma só faixa OR via.

singular [ˈsɪŋgjʊləʳ] n singular; **in the ~** no singular.

sinister [ˈsɪnɪstəʳ] adj sinistro(-tra).

sink [sɪŋk] (pt **sank**, pp **sunk**) n (in kitchen) pia f, lava-louça m (Port); (washbasin) pia f ♦ vi (in water, value) afundar-se; (in mud) enterrar-se.

sink unit n pia f (Br), lava-louça m (Port).

sinner [ˈsɪnəʳ] n pecador m (-ra f).

sinuses [ˈsaɪnəsɪz] npl seios mpl nasais.

sip [sɪp] n gole m ♦ vt sorver.

siphon [ˈsaɪfn] n sifão m ♦ vt tirar com sifão.

sir [sɜːʳ] n Senhor; **Dear Sir** Caro Senhor, Exmo. Sr.; **Sir Richard Blair** Sir Richard Blair.

siren [ˈsaɪərən] n sirene f.

sirloin steak [ˌsɜːlɔɪn-] n bife m de lombo de vaca.

sister [ˈsɪstəʳ] n (relative) irmã f; (Brit: nurse) enfermeira f chefe.

sister-in-law n cunhada f.

sit [sɪt] (pt & pp **sat**) vi sentar-se; (be situated) ficar ♦ vt (to place) sentar, colocar; (Brit: exam) fazer; **to be sitting** estar sentado.

❑ **sit down** vi sentar-se; **to be sitting down** estar sentado.

❑ **sit up** vi (after lying down) sentar-se; (stay up late) ficar acordado.

sitcom [ˈsɪtkɒm] n (inf) comédia f de situação.

site [saɪt] n (place) local m; (building site) obra f.

sitting [ˈsɪtɪŋ] n (serving of meal) turno m; (session) sessão f.

sitting room [ˈsɪtɪŋ-] n sala f de estar.

situated [ˈsɪtjʊeɪtɪd] adj: **to be ~** estar OR ficar situado(-da).

situation [ˌsɪtjʊˈeɪʃn] n situação f; **"~s vacant"** "ofertas de emprego".

six [sɪks] num adj seis (inv) ♦ num n seis m inv; **to be ~ (years old)** ter seis anos (de idade); **it's ~ (o'clock)** são seis horas; **a hundred and ~** cento e seis; **~ Hill St** Hill St, n° 6; **it's minus ~ (degrees)** estão seis graus negativos OR abaixo de zero; **~ out of ten** seis em dez.

sixteen [sɪksˈtiːn] num dezesseis (Br), dezasseis (Port), → **six**.

sixteenth [sɪksˈtiːnθ] num décimo sexto (décima sexta), → **sixth**.

sixth [sɪksθ] num adj sexto(-ta) ♦ num pron sexto m (-ta f) ♦ num n (fraction) sexto m ♦ num adv (in race, competition) em sexto (lugar); **the ~ (of September)** o dia seis (de setembro).

sixth form n (Brit) curso secundário de preparação para os "A levels", exames de acesso ao ensino superior.

sixth-form college n (Brit) escola secundária normal ou técnica.

sixtieth ['sɪkstɪəθ] num sexagésimo (-ma), → sixth.

sixty ['sɪkstɪ] num sessenta, → six.

size [saɪz] n (of room, bed, building, country) tamanho m; (of clothes, shoes, hats) número m; **what ~ do you take?** (of clothes) que tamanho OR número você veste?; (of shoes) que número você calça?; **what ~ is this?** que tamanho OR número é?

sizeable ['saɪzəbl] adj considerável.

sizzle ['sɪzl] vi chiar.

skate [skeɪt] n (ice skate, roller skate) patim m; (fish: pl inv) raia f ◆ vi (ice-skate) patinar; (roller-skate) andar de patins.

skateboard ['skeɪtbɔːd] n skate m.

skater ['skeɪtər] n patinador m (-ra f).

skating ['skeɪtɪŋ] n: **to go ~** (ice-skating) ir patinar; (roller-skating) ir andar de patins.

skating rink n rink m OR rinque m de patinagem.

skeleton ['skelɪtn] n (of body) esqueleto m.

skeptic ['skeptɪk] (Am) = sceptic.

sketch [sketʃ] n (drawing) esboço m; (humorous) sketch m ◆ vt (draw) esboçar.

sketchbook ['sketʃbʊk] n caderno m de desenho.

sketchpad ['sketʃpæd] n bloco m de desenho.

skewer ['skjuər] n espeto m (para churrasco).

ski [skiː] (pt & pp **skied**, cont **skiing**) n esqui m, ski m (Port) ◆ vi esquiar.

ski boots npl botas fpl de esquiar.

skid [skɪd] n derrapagem f ◆ vi derrapar.

skier ['skiːər] n esquiador m (-ra f).

skiing ['skiːɪŋ] n esqui m, ski m (Port); **to go ~** ir fazer esqui, ir esquiar; **a ~ holiday** umas férias fazendo esqui.

ski jump n (slope) pista f para saltos de OR com esquis; (event) salto m de OR com esquis.

skilful ['skɪlfʊl] adj (Brit) experiente, hábil.

ski lift n teleférico m, telesqui m.

skill [skɪl] n (ability) habilidade f; (tech-

nique) técnica f.

skilled [skɪld] adj (worker, job) especializado(-da); (driver, chef) experiente, bom (boa).

skilful ['skɪlfʊl] (Am) = skilful.

skimmed milk ['skɪmd-] n leite m desnatado (Br), leite m magro.

skimp [skɪmp] vi: **to ~ on sthg** (on food, material) economizar em algo.

skimpy ['skɪmpɪ] adj (meal) parco(-ca); (skirt, dress) minúsculo(-la); (facts) insuficiente.

skin [skɪn] n pele f; (on milk) nata f.

skin diving n mergulho m (sem macacão ou escafandro, apenas com tubo respiratório).

skin freshener [-.freʃnər] n tônico m (para a pele).

skinny ['skɪnɪ] adj magricela.

skin-tight adj muito justo(-ta).

skip [skɪp] vi (with rope) pular corda (Br), saltar à corda (Port); (jump) saltitar ◆ vt (omit) passar na frente ◆ n (container) container m (grande para desperdícios).

ski pants npl calça f de esquiar.

ski pass n passe m (para esquiar).

ski pole n vara f de esqui.

skipper ['skɪpər] n capitão m (-tã f).

skipping rope ['skɪpɪŋ-] n corda f de pular.

skirmish ['skɜːmɪʃ] n escaramuça f.

skirt [skɜːt] n saia f.

ski slope n pista f de esqui.

ski tow n teleski m.

skittles ['skɪtlz] n (game) boliche m (Br), bowling m (Port).

skive [skaɪv] vi (Brit: inf): **to ~ (off)** faltar.

skull [skʌl] n crânio m.

skunk [skʌŋk] n gambá m (Br), doninha f fedorenta (Port).

sky [skaɪ] n céu m.

skylight ['skaɪlaɪt] n clarabóia f.

skyscraper ['skaɪ,skreɪpər] n arranha-céu m.

slab [slæb] n (of stone, concrete) laje f.

slack [slæk] adj (rope) frouxo(-xa); (careless) negligente; (not busy) calmo (-ma), parado(-da).

slacken ['slækn] vt & vi afrouxar.

slacks [slæks] npl calça f (Br), calças fpl (Port).

slam [slæm] vt bater com ◆ vi bater.

slander ['slɑːndər] n calúnia f.

slang [slæŋ] *n* gíria *f*.
slant [slɑ:nt] *n (slope)* inclinação *f* ♦ *vi* inclinar-se.
slanting ['slɑ:ntɪŋ] *adj* inclinado(-da).
slap [slæp] *n (on face)* bofetada *f*; *(on back)* palmada *f* ♦ *vt (person, face)* esbofetear, dar uma bofetada em; *(back)* dar uma palmada em.
slapstick ['slæpstɪk] *n* palhaçada *f*.
slap-up *adj (Brit: inf)*: **a ~ meal** um banquete.
slash [slæʃ] *vt (cut)* cortar; *(fig: prices)* cortar em ♦ *n (written symbol)* barra *f* (oblíqua).
slate [sleɪt] *n (rock)* ardósia *f*; *(on roof)* telha *f* (de ardósia).
slaughter ['slɔ:tər] *vt* chacinar, massacrar.
slaughterhouse ['slɔ:təhaus, *pl* -hauzɪz] *n* matadouro *m*.
slave [sleɪv] *n* escravo *m* (-va *f*).
slavery ['sleɪvərɪ] *n* escravatura *f*.
sleazy ['sli:zɪ] *adj* de má reputação.
sled [sled] = **sledge**.
sledge [sledʒ] *n* trenó *m*.
sledgehammer ['sledʒ,hæmər] *n* marreta *f*.
sleep [sli:p] *(pt & pp* **slept**) *n (nap)* sono *m* ♦ *vi* dormir ♦ *vt*: **the house ~s six** a casa tem lugar para seis pessoas dormirem; **try to get some ~** vê se você dorme; **I couldn't get to ~** não conseguia adormecer; **to go to ~** adormecer; **did you ~ well?** você dormiu bem?; **to ~ with sb** dormir com alguém.
sleeper ['sli:pər] *n (train)* trem *m* nocturno *(com couchettes ou camas)*; *(sleeping car)* vagão-cama *m (Br)*, carruagem-cama *f (Port)*; *(Brit: on railway track)* dormente *m (Br)*, travessa *f (Port)*; *(Brit: earring)* argola *f*.
sleeping bag ['sli:pɪŋ-] *n* saco *m* de dormir *(Br)*, saco-cama *m (Port)*.
sleeping car ['sli:pɪŋ-] *n* vagão-cama *m (Br)*, carruagem-cama *f (Port)*.
sleeping pill ['sli:pɪŋ-] *n* comprimido *m* para dormir.
sleeping policeman ['sli:pɪŋ-] *n (Brit)* rampa *f*.
sleepless ['sli:plɪs] *adj* sem dormir.
sleepwalk ['sli:pwɔ:k] *vi (be a sleepwalker)* ser sonâmbulo(-la); *(walk in one's sleep)* andar durante o sono.
sleepy ['sli:pɪ] *adj (person)* sonolento(-ta); **I'm ~** estou com sono.

sleet [sli:t] *n* chuva *f* com neve ♦ *v impers*: **it's ~ing** está chovendo neve.
sleeve [sli:v] *n (of garment)* manga *f*; *(of record)* capa *f*.
sleeveless ['sli:vlɪs] *adj* sem mangas.
sleigh [sleɪ] *n* trenó *m*.
slender ['slendər] *adj (person, waist)* esbelto(-ta); *(fingers, neck)* fino(-na); *(resources, means)* escasso(-a); *(hope, chance)* pequeno(-na).
slept [slept] *pt & pp* → **sleep**.
slice [slaɪs] *n* fatia *f* ♦ *vt* cortar.
sliced bread [slaɪst-] *n* pão *m* em fatias.
slick [slɪk] *adj (performance, operation)* bem conseguido(-da); *(pej: salesman)* com muita lábia ♦ *n* mancha *f* negra *(Br)*, maré *f* negra *(Port)*.
slide [slaɪd] *(pt & pp* **slid** [slɪd]) *n (in playground)* escorrega *m*; *(of photograph)* slide *m*, diapositivo *m*; *(Brit: hair slide)* travessão *m*, grampo *m (Br)*, gancho *m (Port)* ♦ *vi (slip)* escorregar.
sliding door [slaɪdɪŋ-] *n* porta *f* deslizante OR corrediça.
slight [slaɪt] *adj (minor)* pequeno(-na); **the ~est** o menor (a menor), o mínimo (a mínima); **not in the ~est** absolutamente nada.
slightly ['slaɪtlɪ] *adv* ligeiramente.
slim [slɪm] *adj (person, waist)* delgado(-da); *(book)* fino(-na) ♦ *vi* emagrecer.
slime [slaɪm] *n (in pond etc)* lodo *m*; *(of snail, slug)* baba *f*.
slimming ['slɪmɪŋ] *n* emagrecimento *m*.
sling [slɪŋ] *(pt & pp* **slung**) *vt (inf: throw)* atirar ♦ *n*: **to have one's arm in a ~** estar com o braço na tipóia *(Br)*, trazer o braço ao peito *(Port)*.
slip [slɪp] *vi (slide)* escorregar ♦ *n (mistake)* deslize *m*; *(of paper)* pedaço *m*; *(half-petticoat)* anágua *f (Br)*, saiote *m (Port)*; *(full-length petticoat)* combinação *f*.
⌐ slip up *vi (make a mistake)* cometer um deslize.
slipped disc [slɪpt-] *n* hérnia *f* discal.
slipper ['slɪpər] *n* chinelo *m* (de quarto); *(winterweight)* pantufa *f*.
slippery ['slɪpərɪ] *adj* escorregadio (-dia).
slip road *n (Brit) (for joining motorway)* acesso *m*; *(for leaving motorway)* saída *f*.

slip-up *n (inf)* deslize *m*.

slit [slɪt] *n* racha *f*.

slob [slɒb] *n (inf) (dirty)* porco *m* (porca *f*); *(lazy)* lambão *m* (-bona *f*).

slogan [ˈsləʊgən] *n* slogan *m*.

slope [sləʊp] *n (incline)* inclinação *f*; *(hill)* encosta *f*; *(for skiing)* pista *f* ♦ *vi (path, hill)* descer; *(floor, roof, shelf)* ser inclinado(-da).

sloping [ˈsləʊpɪŋ] *adj* inclinado(-da).

sloppy [ˈslɒpɪ] *adj (careless)* descuidado(-da).

slot [slɒt] *n* ranhura *f*.

slot machine *n (vending machine)* distribuidora *f* automática; *(for gambling)* slot machine *f*.

Slovakia [sləˈvækɪə] *n* Eslováquia *f*.

slow [sləʊ] *adj* lento(-ta); *(clock, watch)* atrasado(-da)   ♦ *adv* lentamente; "slow" *(sign on road)* ≈ "reduza a velocidade"; **a ~ train** – um trem regional.

❑ **slow down** *vt sep & vi* abrandar, afrouxar.

slowly [ˈsləʊlɪ] *adv* lentamente.

slug [slʌg] *n (animal)* lesma *f*.

sluggish [ˈslʌgɪʃ] *adj (person)* molengão(-gona); *(reaction, business)* lento(-ta).

sluice [sluːs] *n* comporta *f*.

slum [slʌm] *n (building)* barraco *m*, barracão *m*.

❑ **slums** *npl (district)* favela *f (Br)*, bairro *m* de lata *(Port)*.

slumber [ˈslʌmbəʳ] *n* sono *m*.

slung [slʌŋ] *pt & pp → sling*.

slush [slʌʃ] *n* neve *f* meio derretida.

sly [slaɪ] *adj* manhoso(-osa).

smack [smæk] *n (slap)* palmada *f* ♦ *vt* dar uma palmada em.

small [smɔːl] *adj* pequeno(-na).

small ads *npl (Brit)* classificados *mpl*.

small change *n* troco *m*, dinheiro *m* miúdo OR trocado.

small hours *npl* madrugada *f*; **in the ~** de madrugada.

smallpox [ˈsmɔːlpɒks] *n* varíola *f*.

small talk *n* conversa *f* banal.

smarmy [ˈsmɑːmɪ] *adj* bajulador(-ra).

smart [smɑːt] *adj (elegant, posh)* elegante; *(clever)* esperto(-ta).

smart card *n* smart card *m*, cartão com memória electrônica.

smarten [ˈsmɑːtn] : **smarten up** *vt sep (appearance)* melhorar; *(room)* arrumar; **to ~ o.s up** vestir-se melhor.

smash [smæʃ] *n (SPORT)* smash *m*; *(inf: car crash)* desastre *m*, acidente *m* ♦ *vt (plate, window)* partir ♦ *vi (plate, vase etc)* partir-se.

smashing [ˈsmæʃɪŋ] *adj (Brit: inf)* chocante *(Br)*, bestial *(Port)*.

smattering [ˈsmætərɪŋ] *n*: **I have a ~ of Portuguese** só sei umas palavras em português.

smear [smɪəʳ] *n (slander)* calúnia *f* ♦ *vt (smudge)* borrar; *(spread)*: **to ~ sthg onto sthg** espalhar algo em algo; **he ~ed his chest with oil** ele espalhou óleo no peito.

smear test *n* preventivo *m (Br)*, esfregaço *m (Port)*.

smell [smel] *(pt & pp -ed OR smelt)* *n* cheiro *m* ♦ *vt* cheirar ♦ *vi (have odour)* cheirar; *(have bad odour)* cheirar mal; **to ~ of sthg** cheirar a algo.

smelly [ˈsmelɪ] *adj* mal cheiroso(-osa).

smelt [smelt] *pt & pp → smell*.

smile [smaɪl] *n* sorriso *m* ♦ *vi* sorrir.

smirk [smɜːk] *n* sorriso *m* falso.

smock [smɒk] *n* bata *f*.

smog [smɒg] *n* smog *m*, poluição *f*.

smoke [sməʊk] *n (from fire, cigarette)* fumaça *f (Br)*, fumo *m (Port)* ♦ *vt & vi* fumar; **to have a ~** fumar um cigarro.

smoked [sməʊkt] *adj (meat, fish)* defumado(-da); *(cheese)* curado(-da).

smoked salmon *n* salmão *m* defumado.

smoker [ˈsməʊkəʳ] *n (person)* fumante *mf (Br)*, fumador *m* (-ra *f*) *(Port)*.

smoking [ˈsməʊkɪŋ] *n*: "no ~" "proibido fumar".

smoking area *n* área *f* para fumantes.

smoking compartment *n* compartimento *m* para fumantes.

smoky [ˈsməʊkɪ] *adj (room)* enfumaçado(-da).

smolder [ˈsməʊldəʳ] *(Am)* = **smoulder**.

smooth [smuːð] *adj (surface, road)* plano(-na); *(skin)* macio(-cia); *(takeoff, landing, wine)* suave; *(journey, flight)* sem incidentes; *(life)* tranqüilo(-la); *(mixture, liquid)* homogêneo(-nea), cremoso(-osa); *(pej: suave)* meloso (-osa).

❑ **smooth down** *vt sep* alisar.

smother [ˈsmʌðəʳ] *vt (cover)* cobrir.

smoulder [ˈsməʊldəʳ] *vi (Brit) (fire)* arder lentamente (sem chama).

smudge [smʌdʒ] *n* mancha *f*.

smug [smʌg] *adj* satisfeito consigo próprio (satisfeita consigo própria).

smuggle ['smʌgl] *vt* contrabandear; **to ~ in** *(sneak in)* introduzir clandestinamente.

smuggler ['smʌglər] *n* contrabandista *mf*.

snack [snæk] *n* lanche *m*.

snack bar *n* lanchonete *f (Br)*, snack-bar *m (Port)*.

snag [snæg] *n (small problem)* pequeno problema *m*, inconveniente *m* ♦ *vi*: **to ~ (on sthg)** prender-se (em algo).

snail [sneɪl] *n* caracol *m*.

snake [sneɪk] *n* cobra *f*.

snap [snæp] *vt & vi (break)* partir ♦ *n (inf: photo)* foto *f*; *(Brit: card game)* = guerra *f*.

snapshot ['snæpʃɒt] *n* fotografia *f*, foto *f*.

snare [sneər] *n* armadilha *f*.

snarl [snɑːl] *n* rosnadela *f* ♦ *vi (animal)* rosnar.

snatch [snætʃ] *vt (grab)* arrancar à força; *(steal)* roubar.

sneak [sniːk] *(Brit pt & pp* -ed, *Am pt & pp* -ed OR **snuck)** *n (Brit: inf)* queixinhas *mf inv* ♦ *vi*: **to ~ in/out** entrar/sair às escondidas OR sorrateiramente; **to ~ up on sb** surpreender OR assustar alguém.

sneakers ['sniːkəz] *npl (Am)* ténis *mpl*, sapatilhas *fpl*.

sneer [snɪər] *n* riso *m* sarcástico OR de escarninho ♦ *vi (smile unpleasantly)* sorrir desdenhosamente.

sneeze [sniːz] *n* espirro *m* ♦ *vi* espirrar.

sniff [snɪf] *vi (from cold, crying)* fungar ♦ *vt* cheirar.

snigger ['snɪgər] *n* risinho *m* (dissimulado) ♦ *vi* rir furtivamente.

snip [snɪp] *vt* cortar (com tesoura), dar tesouradas em.

sniper ['snaɪpər] *n* franco-atirador *m* (-ra *f*).

snippet ['snɪpɪt] *n*: **I only heard ~s of their conversation** só ouvi trechos da conversa deles.

snivel ['snɪvl] *vi* choramingar.

snob [snɒb] *n* snobe *mf*.

snobbish ['snɒbɪʃ] *adj* snobe, pretencioso(-osa).

snobby ['snɒbɪ] = **snobbish**.

snog [snɒg] *vi (Brit: inf)* beijar-se.

snooker ['snuːkər] *n* sinuca *f (Br)*, snooker *m (Port)*.

snooze [snuːz] *n* soneca *f*.

snore [snɔːr] *vi* roncar, ressonar.

snorkel ['snɔːkl] *n* respirador *m*, tubo *m* respiratório.

snort [snɔːt] *vi* fungar.

snout [snaʊt] *n* focinho *m*.

snow [snəʊ] *n* neve *f* ♦ *v impers*: **it's ~ing** está nevando.

snowball ['snəʊbɔːl] *n* bola *f* de neve.

snowboarding ['snəʊbɔːdɪŋ] *n*: **to go ~** fazer snowboarding.

snowbound ['snəʊbaʊnd] *adj* bloqueado(-da) pela neve.

snowdrift ['snəʊdrɪft] *n* monte *m* de neve *(formado pelo vento)*.

snowdrop ['snəʊdrɒp] *n* campainha-branca *f*.

snowfall ['snəʊfɔːl] *n (fall of snow)* nevada *f (Br)*, nevão *m (Port)*; *(amount)* queda *f* de neve.

snowflake ['snəʊfleɪk] *n* floco *m* de neve.

snowman ['snəʊmæn] *(pl* -men [-men]*)* *n* boneco-de-neve *m*.

snowplough ['snəʊplaʊ] *n* máquina *f* para remoção de neve.

snowshoe ['snəʊʃuː] *n* raquete *f* de neve.

snowstorm ['snəʊstɔːm] *n* tempestade *f* de neve.

snub [snʌb] *n* desfeita *f* ♦ *vt* ignorar.

snuck [snʌk] *pp* → **sneak**.

snug [snʌg] *adj (person)* aconchegado(-da); *(place)* aconchegante.

so [səʊ] *adv* **1.** *(emphasizing degree)* tão; **don't be ~ stupid!** não seja tão idiota!; **it's ~ difficult (that ...)** é tão difícil (que ...); **~ much** tanto(-ta); **~ many** tantos(-tas).
2. *(referring back)*: **I don't think ~** acho que não; **I'm afraid ~** receio que sim; **~ you knew already** então você já sabia; **if ~** nesse caso.
3. *(also)* também; **~ do I** eu também.
4. *(in this way)* deste modo, assim.
5. *(expressing agreement)*: **~ there is** pois há, é verdade.
6. *(in phrases)*: **or ~** mais ou menos; **as ~** para; **~ that** para.
♦ *conj* **1.** *(therefore)* por isso; **I'm away next week ~ I won't be there** não vou estar aqui na semana que vem, por isso não estarei presente.
2. *(summarizing)* então; **~ what have**

you been up to? éntão, o que é que você tem feito?
3. *(in phrases):* **~ what?** *(inf)* e depois?; **~ there!** *(inf)* pronto!, nada a fazer!
soak [səʊk] *vt (leave in water)* pôr de molho; *(make very wet)* ensopar, empapar ♦ *vi:* **to ~ through sthg** ensopar algo.
⊐ **soak up** *vt sep* absorver.
soaked [səʊkt] *adj* encharcado(-da), ensopado(-da).
soaking [ˈsəʊkɪŋ] *adj* encharcado(-da), ensopado(-da).
soap [səʊp] *n* sabonete *m;* *(for clothes)* sabão *m.*
soap opera *n* novela *f (Br)*, telenovela *f.*
soap powder *n* sabão *m* em pó *(Br)*, detergente *m* para a roupa *(Port).*
soar [sɔːʳ] *vi (bird)* pairar, planar; *(balloon, kite)* elevar-se no ar; *(price)* aumentar (repentinamente); *(temperature)* elevar-se (repentinamente); *(unemployment)* crescer a um ritmo acelerado.
sob [sɒb] *n* soluço *m* ♦ *vi* soluçar.
sober [ˈsəʊbəʳ] *adj* sóbrio(-bria).
so-called [-kɔːld] *adj (misleadingly named)* pseudo (pseuda), suposto (-posta); *(widely known as)* assim chamado(-da).
soccer [ˈsɒkəʳ] *n* futebol *m.*
sociable [ˈsəʊʃəbl] *adj* sociável.
social [ˈsəʊʃl] *adj* social.
social club *n* clube *m.*
socialism [ˈsəʊʃəlɪzm] *n* socialismo *m.*
socialist [ˈsəʊʃəlɪst] *adj* socialista ♦ *n* socialista *mf.*
socialize [ˈsəʊʃəlaɪz] *vi:* **to ~ (with sb)** confraternizar (com alguém).
social life *n* vida *f* social.
social security *n* previdência *f* social *(Br)*, segurança *f* social *(Port).*
social services *npl* previdência *f* social *(Br)*, segurança *f* social *(Port).*
social worker *n* assistente *mf* social.
society [səˈsaɪətɪ] *n* sociedade *f.*
sociology [ˌsəʊsɪˈɒlədʒɪ] *n* sociologia *f.*
sock [sɒk] *n* meia *f*, peúga *f (Port).*
socket [ˈsɒkɪt] *n (for plug)* tomada *f*, ficha *f (Port);* *(for light bulb)* casquilho *m.*
soda [ˈsəʊdə] *n (soda water)* água *f* gaseificada OR com gás; *(Am: fizzy*

drink) refrigerante *m.*
soda water *n* água *f* gaseificada OR com gás.
sofa [ˈsəʊfə] *n* sofá *m.*
sofa bed *n* sofá-cama *m.*
Sofia [ˈsəʊfjə] *n* Sófia *s.*
soft [sɒft] *adj (bed, food)* mole; *(skin, fur, fabric)* macio(-cia), suave; *(breeze, sound, tap)* ligeiro(-ra); *(voice)* doce; *(footsteps)* leve.
soft cheese *n* queijo *m* cremoso.
soft drink *n* refrigerante *m.*
soften [ˈsɒfn] *vt (skin, fabric)* amaciar; *(butter)* amolecer; *(blow, impact, effect)* amortecer ♦ *vi (skin, fabric)* ficar mais macio(-cia); *(butter)* amolecer; *(attitude)* tornar-se mais brando(-da).
softly [ˈsɒftlɪ] *adv (touch)* delicadamente; *(move)* sem fazer barulho; *(speak, sing)* em voz baixa.
soft-spoken *adj:* **she's very ~** ela tem uma voz muito doce.
software [ˈsɒftweəʳ] *n* software *m.*
soggy [ˈsɒgɪ] *adj* mole, empapado (-da).
soil [sɔɪl] *n* terra *f.*
soiled [sɔɪld] *adj* sujo(-ja).
solarium [səˈleərɪəm] *n* solário *m*, solarium *m.*
solar panel [ˈsəʊlə-] *n* painel *m* solar.
sold [səʊld] *pt & pp →* sell.
solder [ˈsəʊldəʳ] *n* solda *f* ♦ *vt* soldar.
soldier [ˈsəʊldʒəʳ] *n* soldado *m.*
sold out *adj* esgotado(-da).
sole [səʊl] *adj (only)* adj único(-ca) ♦ *n (of shoe)* sola *f; (of foot)* planta *f; (fish: pl inv)* linguado *m.*
solemn [ˈsɒləm] *adj* solene.
solicitor [səˈlɪsɪtəʳ] *n (Brit)* solicitador *m* (-ra *f*), *advogado que apenas pode atuar nos tribunais de primeira instância.*
solid [ˈsɒlɪd] *adj* sólido(-da); *(chair, wall)* resistente; *(rock, gold, oak)* maciço(-ça).
solidarity [ˌsɒlɪˈdærətɪ] *n* solidariedade *f.*
solitary [ˈsɒlɪtrɪ] *adj* solitário(-ria).
solitude [ˈsɒlɪtjuːd] *n* solidão *f.*
solo [ˈsəʊləʊ] *(pl -s) n* solo *m;* "~ **m/cs**" *(traffic sign) sinal indicando que no local apenas podem estacionar veículos de duas rodas.*
soloist [ˈsəʊləʊɪst] *n* solista *mf.*
soluble [ˈsɒljʊbl] *adj* solúvel.
solution [səˈluːʃn] *n* solução *f.*

solve [sɒlv] vt resolver.
solvent ['sɒlvənt] adj (FIN) dissolvente ◆ n (substance) dissolvente m.
some [sʌm] adj 1. (certain, large amount of) algum (alguma); ~ **meat** alguma carne; ~ **money** algum dinheiro; **I had ~ difficulty getting here** tive algumas dificuldades para chegar aqui. 2. (certain, large number of) alguns (algumas); ~ **sweets** alguns doces; ~ **people** algumas pessoas; **I've known him for ~ years** já o conheço há alguns anos. 3. (not all) alguns (algumas); ~ **jobs are better paid than others** alguns empregos são mais bem pagos que outros. 4. (in imprecise statements) um (uma) ... qualquer; ~ **woman phoned** telefonou uma mulher qualquer.
◆ pron 1. (certain amount) algum m (alguma f), parte f; **can I have ~?** posso ficar com algum OR parte?; ~ **of the money** algum dinheiro, parte do dinheiro. 2. (certain number) alguns mpl (algumas fpl); **can I have ~?** posso ficar com alguns?; ~ **(of them) left early** alguns (deles) foram-se embora cedo.
◆ adv (approximately) aproximadamente; **there were ~ 7,000 people there** havia umas 7000 pessoas.
somebody ['sʌmbədɪ] = **someone**.
someday ['sʌmdeɪ] adv algum dia.
somehow ['sʌmhaʊ] adv (some way or other) de uma maneira ou de outra; (for some reason) por alguma razão; ~ **I don't think he'll come** tenho a impressão de que ele não virá.
someone ['sʌmwʌn] pron alguém.
someplace ['sʌmpleɪs] (Am) = **somewhere**.
somersault ['sʌməsɔːlt] n cambalhota f.
something ['sʌmθɪŋ] pron algo, alguma coisa; **it's really ~** é demais; **or ~** (inf) ou (qualquer) coisa parecida; ~ **like** (approximately) uns (umas), qualquer coisa como.
sometime ['sʌmtaɪm] adv: ~ **in June** em junho.
sometimes ['sʌmtaɪmz] adv às OR por vezes.
someway ['sʌmweɪ] (Am) = **somehow**.
somewhat ['sʌmwɒt] adv um pouco.

somewhere ['sʌmweəʳ] adv (in unspecified place) em algum lugar, em alguma parte; (to specified place) a alguma parte; ~ **around** OR **between** (approximately) aproximadamente.
son [sʌn] n filho m.
song [sɒŋ] n canção f.
son-in-law n genro m.
sonnet ['sɒnɪt] n soneto m.
soon [suːn] adv (in a short time) em breve; (early) cedo; **how ~ can you do it?** para quando é que estará pronto?; **as ~ as** assim que; **as ~ as possible** o mais cedo possível, assim que for possível; ~ **after** pouco depois; **~er or later** mais cedo ou mais tarde.
soot [sʊt] n fuligem f.
soothe [suːð] vt acalmar.
sophisticated [səˈfɪstɪkeɪtɪd] adj sofisticado(-da).
soporific [ˌsɒpəˈrɪfɪk] adj soporífero(-ra).
sopping ['sɒpɪŋ] adj: ~ **(wet)** encharcado(-da), ensopado(-da).
soppy ['sɒpɪ] adj (inf) (book, film) sentimental; (person) piegas (inv).
soprano [səˈprɑːnəʊ] (pl **-nos** OR **-ni** [-niː]) n soprano mf.
sorbet ['sɔːbeɪ] n sorvete m de frutas.
sorcerer ['sɔːsərəʳ] n feiticeiro m.
sordid ['sɔːdɪd] adj sórdido(-da).
sore [sɔːʳ] adj (painful) dolorido(-da); (Am: inf: angry) zangado(-da) ◆ n ferida f; **to have a ~ throat** estar com dor de garganta.
sorrow ['sɒrəʊ] n tristeza f.
sorry ['sɒrɪ] adj: **he isn't even ~** ele nem sequer está arrependido; **I'm ~!** desculpe!; **I'm ~ I'm late** desculpem o atraso; **I'm ~ about the mess** desculpe a confusão; **I'm ~ you didn't get the job** sinto muito que você não tenha conseguido o emprego; **~?** (asking for repetition) perdão?; **to feel ~ for sb** sentir pena de alguém.
sort [sɔːt] n tipo m ◆ vt organizar; ~ **of** (more or less) mais ou menos.
❏ **sort out** vt sep (classify) organizar; (resolve) resolver.
so-so adj (inf) mais ou menos ◆ adv (inf) assim assim.
soufflé ['suːfleɪ] n suflê m (Br), soufflé m (Port).
sought [sɔːt] pt & pp → **seek**.
soul [səʊl] n (spirit) alma f; (soul music) música f soul.

sound [saʊnd] *n* som *m* ◆ *vt (horn, bell)* (fazer) soar ◆ *vi (make a noise)* soar; *(seem to be)* parecer ◆ *adj (in good condition)* sólido(-da); *(health)* sadio(-a); *(heart, mind)* são (sã), bom (boa); **to ~ like** *(make a noise like)* soar como; *(seem to be)* parecer ser.
sound effects *npl* efeitos *mpl* sonoros.
soundly ['saʊndlɪ] *adv (beat)* completamente; *(sleep)* profundamente.
soundproof ['saʊndpru:f] *adj* à prova de som.
soundtrack ['saʊndtræk] *n* trilha *f* sonora *(Br)*, banda *f* sonora *(Port)*.
soup [su:p] *n* sopa *f*.
soup spoon *n* colher *f* de sopa.
sour ['saʊəʳ] *adj (taste)* ácido(-da); *(milk)* azedo(-da); **to go ~** azedar.
source [sɔ:s] *n (supply, origin)* fonte *f*; *(cause)* origem *f*; *(of river)* nascente *f*.
sour cream *n* creme *m* azedo *(Br)*, natas *fpl* azedas *(Port)*.
south [saʊθ] *n* sul *m* ◆ *adj (wind)* sul ◆ *adv (be situated)* ao sul; *(fly, walk)* para o sul; **in the ~ of England** no sul da Inglaterra.
South Africa *n* África *f* do Sul.
South America *n* América *f* do Sul.
southbound ['saʊθbaʊnd] *adj* em direção ao sul.
southeast [ˌsaʊθ'i:st] *n* sudeste *m*.
southerly ['sʌðəlɪ] *adj (wind)* do sul; **in a ~ direction** em direção ao sul, para o sul; **the most ~ point** o ponto mais ao sul.
southern ['sʌðən] *adj* do sul.
South Korea *n* Coréia *f* do Sul.
South Pole *n*: **the ~** o Pólo Sul.
southward ['saʊθwəd] *adj* em direção ao sul, para o sul.
southwards ['saʊθwədz] *adv* em direção ao sul, para o sul
southwest [ˌsaʊθ'west] *n* sudoeste.
souvenir [ˌsu:və'nɪəʳ] *n* lembrança *f*, recordação *f*.
sovereign ['sɒvrɪn] *n (ruler)* soberano *m* (-na *f*).
Soviet Union [ˌsəʊvɪət-] *n*: **the ~** a União Soviética.
sow[1] [səʊ] (*pp* **sown**) *vt (seeds)* semear.
sow[2] [saʊ] *n (pig)* porca *f*.
sown [səʊn] *pp* → **sow**[1].
soya ['sɔɪə] *n* soja *f*.
soya bean *n* semente *f* de soja.
soy sauce [ˌsɔɪ-] *n* molho *m* de soja.
spa [spɑ:] *n* estância *f* hidromineral *(Br)*, termas *fpl (Port)*.
space [speɪs] *n* espaço *m* ◆ *vt* espaçar.
spacecraft ['speɪskrɑ:ft] *n* nave *f* espacial.
spaceman ['speɪsmæn] (*pl* **-men** [-men]) *n (inf)* astronauta *mf*.
spaceship ['speɪsʃɪp] *n* nave *f* espacial.
space shuttle *n* ônibus *m* espacial *(Br)*, vaivém *m* espacial *(Port)*.
spacesuit ['speɪssu:t] *n* macacão *m* espacial *(Br)*, fato *m* espacial *(Port)*.
spacious ['speɪʃəs] *adj* espaçoso (-osa).
spade [speɪd] *n (tool)* pá *f*.
❑ **spades** *npl (in cards)* espadas *fpl*.
spaghetti [spə'getɪ] *n* espaguete *m*.
Spain [speɪn] *n* Espanha *f*.
span [spæn] *pt* → **spin** ◆ *n (length)* distância *f*, palmo *m*; *(of time)* espaço *m* de tempo.
Spaniard ['spænjəd] *n* espanhol *m* (-la *f*).
spaniel ['spænjəl] *n* spaniel *m*, cão *m* de água *(Port)*.
Spanish ['spænɪʃ] *adj* espanhol(-la) ◆ *n (language)* espanhol *m*.
spank [spæŋk] *vt* dar uma palmada em.
spanner ['spænəʳ] *n* chave-inglesa *f*.
spare [speəʳ] *adj (kept in reserve)* a mais; *(not in use)* disponível ◆ *n (spare part)* peça *f* sobressalente; *(spare wheel)* pneu *m* sobressalente ◆ *vt*: **to ~ sb sthg** *(money)* dispensar algo a alguém; **I can't ~ the time** não tenho tempo; **with ten minutes to ~** com dez minutos de antecedência.
spare part *n* peça *f* sobressalente.
spare ribs *npl* costeleta *f* de porco *(Br)*, entrecosto *m (Port)*.
spare room *n* quarto *m* de hóspedes.
spare time *n* tempo *m* livre.
spare wheel *n* pneu *m* sobressalente.
sparing ['speərɪŋ] *adj*: **to be ~ with** OR **of sthg** gastar menos de algo.
sparingly ['speərɪŋlɪ] *adv* com moderação.
spark [spɑ:k] *n (from fire)* fagulha *f*; *(electric)* faísca *f*.
sparkle ['spɑ:kl] *vi (jewel, stars, eyes)* cintilar, brilhar.

256

sparkling ['spuːklɪŋ] *adj (mineral water, soft drink)* gaseificado(-da), com gás.

sparkling wine *n* espumante *m*.

spark plug *n* vela *f*.

sparrow ['spærəʊ] *n* pardal *m*.

sparse [spuːs] *adj* escasso(-a).

spasm ['spæzm] *n (of muscle)* espasmo *m*; *(of coughing, anger)* ataque *m*.

spastic ['spæstɪk] *n (MED)* deficiente *mf* motor.

spat [spæt] *pt & pp* → **spit**.

spawn [spɔːn] *n* ovas *fpl*.

speak [spiːk] *(pt* **spoke,** *pp* **spoken)** *vt (language)* falar; *(say)* dizer ◆ *vi* falar; **who's ~ing?** *(on phone)* quem fala?; **can I ~ to Charlotte? – ~ing!** posso falar com a Charlotte? – é a própria!; **to ~ to sb about sthg** falar com alguém sobre algo.

❏ **speak up** *vi (more loudly)* falar mais alto.

speaker ['spiːkəʳ] *n (person)* orador *m* (-ra *f*); *(loudspeaker)* altofalante *m*; *(of stereo)* altofalante *m (Br)*, coluna *f (Port)*; **a Portuguese ~** um lusófono, uma pessoa que fala português.

spear [spɪəʳ] *n* lança *f*.

spec [spek] *n (Brit: inf)*: **on ~** à sorte.

special ['speʃl] *adj* especial ◆ *n (dish)* prato *m* do dia; **"today's ~"** "prato do dia".

special effects *npl* efeitos *mpl* especiais.

specialist ['speʃəlɪst] *n* especialista *mf*.

speciality [ˌspeʃɪ'ælətɪ] *n* especialidade *f*.

specialize ['speʃəlaɪz] *vi*: **to ~ (in)** especializar-se (em).

specially ['speʃəlɪ] *adv* especialmente.

special offer *n* promoção *f*.

special school *n (Brit)* escola *f* especial *(para alunos com deficiências físicas ou problemas de aprendizagem)*.

specialty ['speʃltɪ] *(Am)* = **speciality**.

species ['spiːʃiːz] *n* espécie *f*.

specific [spə'sɪfɪk] *adj* específico(-ca).

specifically [spə'sɪfɪklɪ] *adv* especificamente.

specifications [ˌspesɪfɪ'keɪʃnz] *npl (of machine, car)* ficha *f* técnica.

specify ['spesɪfaɪ] *vt* especificar.

specimen ['spesɪmən] *n* espécime *m*, espécimen *m*.

speck [spek] *n (of dust, soot)* cisco *m*; *(of blood)* pinta *f*.

specs [speks] *npl (inf)* óculos *mpl*.

spectacle ['spektəkl] *n* espetáculo *m*.

spectacles ['spektəklz] *npl* óculos *mpl*.

spectacular [spek'tækjʊləʳ] *adj* espetacular.

spectator [spek'teɪtəʳ] *n* espectador *m* (-ra *f*).

spectrum ['spektrəm] *n (in physics)* espectro *m*; *(range)* leque *m*.

speculation [ˌspekjʊ'leɪʃn] *n* especulação *f*.

sped [sped] *pt & pp* → **speed**.

speech [spiːtʃ] *n (ability to speak)* fala *f*; *(manner of speaking)* maneira *f* de falar; *(talk)* discurso *m*.

speech impediment [-ɪmˌpedɪmənt] *n* defeito *m* na fala.

speechless ['spiːtʃlɪs] *adj*: **to be ~ (with)** ficar mudo(-da) (de).

speed [spiːd] *(pt & pp* **-ed** OR **sped)** *n* velocidade *f*; *(bicycle gear)* mudança *f* ◆ *vi (move quickly)* ir a grande velocidade; *(drive too fast)* dirigir com excesso de velocidade; **"reduce ~ now"** "reduza a velocidade".

❏ **speed up** *vi* acelerar.

speedboat ['spiːdbəʊt] *n* lancha *f*.

speed camera *n* radar *m (para o controle do excesso de velocidade nas estradas)*.

speeding ['spiːdɪŋ] *n* excesso *m* de velocidade.

speed limit *n* limite *m* de velocidade.

speedometer [spɪ'dɒmɪtəʳ] *n* velocímetro *m*, conta-quilômetros *m inv*.

speedway ['spiːdweɪ] *n (SPORT)* motociclismo *m*, corridas *fpl* de motos; *(Am: road)* auto-estrada *f*.

speedy ['spiːdɪ] *adj* rápido(-da).

spell [spel] *(Brit pt & pp* **-ed** OR **spelt,** *Am pt & pp* **-ed)** *vt (word, name)* soletrar; *(subj: letters)* dar, formar a palavra ◆ *n (period)* período *m*; *(magic)* feitiço *m*.

spelling ['spelɪŋ] *n* ortografia *f*.

spelt [spelt] *pt & pp (Brit)* → **spell**.

spend [spend] *(pt & pp* **spent)** *vt (money)* gastar; *(time)* passar.

spendthrift ['spendθrɪft] *n* esbanjador *m* (-ra *f*), gastador *m* (-ra *f*).

spent [spent] *pt & pp* → **spend** ◆ *adj (fuel, force, patience)* gasto(-ta).

sperm [spɜːm] (*pl inv* OR **-s**) *n* (*cell*) espermatozóide *m*; (*semen*) esperma *m*.

spew [spjuː] *vi* (*flow, spread*): **to ~ (out) from sthg** sair de algo.

sphere [sfɪəʳ] *n* esfera *f*.

spice [spaɪs] *n* especiaria *f* ◆ *vt* condimentar.

spicy ['spaɪsɪ] *adj* picante.

spider ['spaɪdəʳ] *n* aranha *f*.

spider's web *n* teia *f* de aranha.

spike [spaɪk] *n* espigão *m*.

spill [spɪl] (*Brit pt & pp* **-ed** OR **spilt** [spɪlt], *Am pt & pp* **-ed**) *vt* entornar ◆ *vi* entornar-se.

spin [spɪn] (*pt* **span** OR **spun**, *pp* **spun**) *vt* (*wheel, coin, chair*) rodar; (*washing*) centrifugar ◆ *n* (*on ball*) efeito *m*; **to go for a ~** (*inf*) ir dar uma volta.

spinach ['spɪnɪtʃ] *n* espinafre *m*.

spinal column ['spaɪnl-] *n* coluna *f* vertebral.

spinal cord [spaɪnl-] *n* medula *f* espin(h)al.

spin-dryer *n* (*Brit*) centrifugadora *f*.

spine [spaɪn] *n* (*of back*) espinha *f* (dorsal), coluna *f* (vertebral); (*of book*) lombada *f*.

spiral ['spaɪərəl] *n* espiral *f*.

spiral staircase *n* escada *f* em caracol.

spire [spaɪəʳ] *n* pináculo *m*.

spirit ['spɪrɪt] *n* (*soul*) espírito *m*; (*energy*) vigor *m*, energia *f*; (*courage*) coragem *f*; (*mood*) humor *m*.

❏ **spirits** *npl* (*Brit: alcohol*) bebidas *fpl* com teor alcoólico bem alto (*Br*), bebidas *fpl* espirituosas (*Port*).

spirited ['spɪrɪtɪd] *adj* (*debate*) animado(-da); (*action, defence*) energético (-ca); (*performance*) com brio.

spirit level *n* nível *m* de bolha de ar.

spiritual ['spɪrɪtʃʊəl] *adj* espiritual.

spit [spɪt] (*Brit pt & pp* **spat**, *Am pt & pp* **spit**) *vi* (*person*) cuspir; (*fire*) crepitar; (*food*) espirrar ◆ *n* (*saliva*) cuspe *m*; (*for cooking*) espeto *m* ◆ *v impers*: **it's spitting** está chuviscando.

spite [spaɪt] : **in spite of** *prep* apesar de.

spiteful ['spaɪtfʊl] *adj* maldoso(-osa).

spittle ['spɪtl] *n* cuspo *m*, saliva *f*.

splash [splæʃ] *n* (*sound*) chape *m* ◆ *vt* salpicar.

splendid ['splendɪd] *adj* esplêndido(-da).

splint [splɪnt] *n* tala *f*.

splinter ['splɪntəʳ] *n* falha *f*, lasca *f*.

split [splɪt] (*pt & pp* **split**) *n* (*tear*) rasgão *m*; (*crack, in skirt*) racha *f* ◆ *vt* (*wood, stone*) rachar; (*tear*) rasgar; (*bill, profits, work*) dividir ◆ *vi* (*wood, stone*) partir-se; (*tear*) rasgar-se.

❏ **split up** *vi* (*group, couple*) separar-se.

splutter ['splʌtəʳ] *vi* (*person*) balbuciar, gaguejar; (*engine*) engasgar-se.

spoil [spɔɪl] (*pt & pp* **-ed** OR **spoilt**) *vt* (*ruin*) estragar; (*child*) mimar.

spoilsport ['spɔɪlspɔːt] *n* desmancha-prazeres *mf inv*.

spoilt [spɔɪlt] *pt & pp* → **spoil** ◆ *adj* (*food, dinner*) estragado(-da); (*child*) mimado(-da).

spoke [spəʊk] *pt* → **speak** ◆ *n* raio *m*.

spoken ['spəʊkn] *pp* → **speak**.

spokesman ['spəʊksmən] (*pl* **-men** [-mən]) *n* porta-voz *m*.

spokeswoman ['spəʊks,wʊmən] (*pl* **-women** [-wɪmɪn]) *n* porta-voz *f*.

sponge [spʌndʒ] *n* (*for cleaning, washing*) esponja *f*.

sponge bag *n* (*Brit*) estojo *m* de toalete.

sponge cake *n* = pão-de-ló *m*.

sponsor ['spɒnsəʳ] *n* (*of event, TV programme*) patrocinador *m* (-ra *f*).

sponsored walk [spɒnsəd-] *n* caminhada patrocinada com fins benificentes.

sponsorship ['spɒnsəʃɪp] *n* patrocínio *m*.

spontaneous [spɒn'teɪnjəs] *adj* espontâneo(-nea).

spooky ['spuːkɪ] *adj* (*inf*) assustador (-ra).

spool [spuːl] *n* rolo *m*.

spoon [spuːn] *n* colher *f*.

spoonful ['spuːnfʊl] *n* colherada *f*, colher *f*.

sporadic [spə'rædɪk] *adj* esporádico(-ca).

sport [spɔːt] *n* esporte *m* (*Br*), desporto *m* (*Port*).

sporting ['spɔːtɪŋ] *adj* esportivo(-va) (*Br*), desportivo(-va) (*Port*); **to have a ~ chance of doing sthg** ter uma boa chance de fazer algo.

sports car [spɔːts-] *n* carro *m* esporte (*Br*), carro *m* desportivo (*Port*).

sports centre [spɔːts-] *n* centro *m* esportivo (*Br*), pavilhão *m* de desportos (*Port*).

sports jacket [spɔːts-] *n* jaqueta *f* de esporte *(Br)*, casaco *m* de desporto OR desportivo *(Port)*.

sportsman [ˈspɔːtsmən] *(pl* **-men** [-mən]) *n* esportista *m (Br)*, desportista *m (Port)*.

sportsmanship [ˈspɔːtsmənʃɪp] *n* espírito *m* esportivo *(Br)*, desportivismo *m (Port)*.

sports shop [spɔːts-] *n* loja *f* de artigos de esporte *(Br)*, loja *f* de artigos de desporto *(Port)*.

sportswear [ˈspɔːtsweəʳ] *n* roupa *f* de esporte *(Br)*, roupa *f* desportiva *(Port)*.

sportswoman [ˈspɔːtsˌwʊmən] *(pl* **-women** [-ˌwɪmɪn]) *n* esportista *f (Br)*, desportista *f (Port)*.

sporty [ˈspɔːtɪ] *adj (inf: person)* esportivo(-va) *(Br)*, desportivo(-va) *(Port)*.

spot [spɒt] *n (of paint, rain, blood)* gota *f*, pingo *m*; *(on dog, leopard)* mancha *f*; *(on skin)* borbulha *f*; *(place)* lugar *m*, sítio *m (Port)* ♦ *vt* notar, reparar em; **on the ~** *(at once)* imediatamente; *(at the scene)* no local.

spotless [ˈspɒtlɪs] *adj* impecável, imaculado(-da).

spotlight [ˈspɒtlaɪt] *n* projetor *m*.

spotted [ˈspɒtɪd] *adj (material)* de bolas.

spotty [ˈspɒtɪ] *adj* com borbulhas.

spouse [spaʊs] *n (fml)* esposo *m* (-sa *f*).

spout [spaʊt] *n* bico *m*.

sprain [spreɪn] *vt* torcer.

sprang [spræŋ] *pt* → **spring**.

spray [spreɪ] *n (of aerosol, perfume)* spray *m*; *(droplets)* gotas *fpl*; *(of sea)* espuma *f* ♦ *vt (car)* pintar com pistola; *(crops)* pulverizar; *(paint, water etc)* esguichar.

spread [spred] *(pt & pp* **spread**) *vt (butter, jam)* barrar; *(glue, disease, news)* espalhar; *(map, tablecloth, blanket)* estender; *(legs, fingers, arms)* abrir ♦ *vi (disease, fire, news)* espalhar-se; *(stain)* alastrar ♦ *n (food)*: **chocolate ~** pasta *f* de chocolate, Tulicreme® *m*.

❒ **spread out** *vi (disperse)* espalhar-se.

spree [spriː] *n*: **to go on a spending/drinking ~** gastar/beber à valer.

spring [sprɪŋ] *(pt* **sprang**, *pp* **sprung**) *n (season)* primavera *f*; *(coil)* mola *f*; *(in ground)* nascente *f* ♦ *vi (leap)* saltar; **in (the) ~** na primavera.

springboard [ˈsprɪŋbɔːd] *n* prancha *f* (de saltos).

spring-cleaning [-ˈkliːnɪŋ] *n* limpezas *fpl* de primavera.

spring onion *n* cebolinha *f*.

spring roll *n* crepe *m* chinês.

springtime [ˈsprɪŋtaɪm] *n*: **in (the) ~** na primavera.

springy [ˈsprɪŋɪ] *adj (carpet, ground)* mole; *(rubber)* elástico(-ca); *(mattress)* de molas.

sprinkle [ˈsprɪŋkl] *vt*: **to ~ sthg with sugar/flour** polvilhar algo com açúcar/farinha; **to ~ water on sthg** salpicar algo com água.

sprinkler [ˈsprɪŋkləʳ] *n (for fire)* extintor *m* (automático de incêndios); *(for grass)* regador *m* (automático), aspersor *m*.

sprint [sprɪnt] *n (race)* corrida *f* de velocidade ♦ *vi (run fast)* dar uma corrida.

Sprinter® [ˈsprɪntəʳ] *n (Brit: train)* trem *m* interurbano, *trem que serve pequenas distâncias.*

sprout [spraʊt] *n (vegetable)* couve-de-Bruxelas *f*.

spruce [spruːs] *n* espruce *m*.

sprung [sprʌŋ] *pp* → **spring** ♦ *adj (mattress)* de molas.

spud [spʌd] *n (inf)* batata *f*.

spun [spʌn] *pt & pp* → **spin**.

spur [spɜːʳ] *n (for horse rider)* espora *f*; **on the ~ of the moment** sem pensar duas vezes.

spurt [spɜːt] *vi* jorrar.

spy [spaɪ] *n* espião *m* (-pia *f*).

spying [ˈspaɪɪŋ] *n* espionagem *f*.

squabble [ˈskwɒbl] *n* briga *f* ♦ *vi*: **to ~ (about** OR **over sthg)** brigar (por algo).

squad [skwɒd] *n (of police)* brigada *f*; *(group of players)* equipe *f*.

squadron [ˈskwɒdrən] *n (of planes)* esquadrilha *f*; *(of warships)* esquadra *f*; *(of soldiers)* esquadrão *m*.

squall [skwɔːl] *n* tempestade *f*, borrasca *f*.

squalor [ˈskwɒləʳ] *n* sordidez *f*.

squander [ˈskwɒndəʳ] *vt* desperdiçar.

square [skweəʳ] *adj (in shape)* quadrado(-da) ♦ *n (shape)* quadrado *m*; *(in town)* praça *f*; *(of chocolate)* pedaço *m*; *(on chessboard)* casa *f*; **2 ~ metres** 2 metros quadrados; **it's 2 metres ~** tem 2 metros de lado; **we're (all) ~ now**

(not owing money) agora estamos quites.

squarely ['skweəlı] *adv (directly)* exatamente; *(honestly)* francamente.

squash [skwɒʃ] *n (game)* squash *m*;
(Brit: drink) bebida à base de suco de
fruto concentrado e água; *(Am: vegetable)*
abóbora *f* ◆ *vt* esmagar.

squat [skwɒt] *adj* atarracado(-da) ◆ *n*
(building) edifício abandonado e ocupado
clandestinamente ◆ *vi (crouch)* agachar-
se.

squatter ['skwɒtər] *n (Brit)* ocupante
mf ilegal, squatter *mf*.

squawk [skwɔːk] *vi (bird)* gritar.

squeak [skwiːk] *vi* chiar.

squeal [skwiːl] *vi* chiar.

squeamish ['skwiːmıʃ] *adj:* **I'm ~
about the sight of blood** não posso ver
sangue.

squeeze [skwiːz] *vt* espremer.

◻ **squeeze in** *vi* arranjar lugar.

squid [skwɪd] *n* lula *f*.

squint [skwɪnt] *n* estrabismo *m* ◆ *vi*
semicerrar os olhos; **to ~ at** olhar com
os olhos semi-cerrados para.

squirrel [Brit 'skwırəl, Am 'skwɜːrəl] *n*
esquilo *m*.

squirt [skwɜːt] *vi* esguichar.

Sri Lanka [sriːˈlæŋkə] *n* Sri Lanca *m*.

St *(abbr of Street)* R.; *(abbr of Saint)* S.
mf, Sta. *f*.

stab [stæb] *vt (with knife)* apunhalar,
esfaquear.

stable ['steɪbl] *adj* estável ◆ *n* estábulo *m*.

stack [stæk] *n (pile)* pilha *f*; **~s of** *(inf:
lots)* pilhas de.

stadium ['steɪdjəm] *n* estádio *m*.

staff [stɑːf] *n (workers)* pessoal *m*.

stag [stæg] *(pl inv OR -s)* *n* veado *m*
(macho).

stage [steɪdʒ] *n (phase)* fase *f*; *(in theatre)* palco *m*.

stagecoach ['steɪdʒkəʊtʃ] *n* diligên-
cia *f*.

stage fright *n* medo *m* do palco.

stagger ['stægər] *vt (arrange in stages)*
escalonar ◆ *vi* cambalear.

stagnant ['stægnənt] *adj* estagnado
(-da).

stagnate [stægˈneɪt] *vi* estagnar.

staid [steɪd] *adj* conservador(-ra),
antiquado(-da).

stain [steɪn] *n* nódoa *f*, mancha *f* ◆ *vt*
manchar.

stained glass window [steɪnd-] *n*
vitral *m*.

stainless steel ['steɪnlıs-] *n* aço *m*
inoxidável.

stair [steər] *n* degrau *m*.

◻ **stairs** *npl* escadas *fpl*.

staircase ['steəkeɪs] *n* escadaria *f*.

stairway ['steəweɪ] *n* escadaria *f*.

stairwell ['steəwel] *n* vão *m* das escadas.

stake [steɪk] *n (share)* parte *f*; *(in gambling)* aposta *f*; *(post)* estaca *f*; **at ~** em
jogo.

stale [steɪl] *adj (bread)* duro(-ra);
(crisps, biscuits) mole.

stalemate ['steɪlmeɪt] *n (deadlock)*
beco *m* sem saída, impasse *m*; *(in
chess)* empate *m*.

stalk [stɔːk] *n (of flower, plant)* pé *m*,
caule *m*; *(of fruit)* galho *m* (Br), píncaro
m (Port); *(of leaf)* galho (Br), pecíolo *m*
(Port).

stall [stɔːl] *n (at exhibition)* stand *m*; *(in
market, at fair)* barraca *f* ◆ *vi (car, plane,
engine)* morrer (Br), ir abaixo (Port).

◻ **stalls** *npl (Brit: in theatre)* platéia *f*.

stallion ['stæljən] *n* garanhão *m*.

stamina ['stæmınə] *n* resistência *f*.

stammer ['stæmər] *vi* gaguejar.

stamp [stæmp] *n (for letter)* selo *m*; *(in
passport, on document)* carimbo *m* ◆ *vt
(passport, document)* carimbar ◆ *vi:* **to ~
on sthg** esmagar algo com o pé; **to ~
one's foot** bater com o pé no chão.

stamp album *n* álbum *m* de selos.

stamp-collecting [-kəlektıŋ] *n* filatelia *f*.

stampede [stæmˈpiːd] *n* debandada *f*.

stamp machine *n* distribuidor *m*
automático de selos.

stance [stæns] *n (posture)* postura *f*; **~
(on sthg)** *(attitude)* posição *f* (em
relação a algo).

stand [stænd] *(pt & pp* **stood)** *vi (be on
feet)* estar de OR em pé; *(be situated)*
ficar; *(get to one's feet)* levantar-se ◆ *vt
(place)* pôr, colocar; *(bear, withstand)*
agüentar, suportar ◆ *n (in market, at
fair)* barraca *f*; *(at exhibition)* stand *m*;
(for newspapers) banca *f* de jornais (Br),
quiosque *m* (Port); *(for umbrellas)* bengaleiro *m*; *(for coats)* cabide *m*; *(for bike,
motorbike)* descanso *m*; *(at sports stadium)* arquibancada *f* (Br), bancada *f*
(Port); **to ~ sb a drink** pagar uma bebida para alguém; **to be ~ing** estar de OR

em pé; **"no ~ing"** *(Am: AUT)* "zona de estacionamento e parada proibida".

⌐ **stand back** *vi* afastar-se.

⌐ **stand for** *vt fus (mean)* representar; *(tolerate)* tolerar.

⌐ **stand in** *vi*: **to ~ in for sb** substituir alguém.

⌐ **stand out** *vi (be conspicuous)* dar nas vistas; *(be superior)* destacar-se.

⌐ **stand up** *vi (be on feet)* estar de OR em pé; *(get to one's feet)* levantar-se ♦ *vt sep (inf: boyfriend, girlfriend)* deixar plantado(-da).

⌐ **stand up for** *vt fus* defender.

standard ['stændəd] *adj (normal)* normal, padrão *(inv)* ♦ *n (level)* nível *m*; *(point of comparison)* média *f*; *(for product)* norma *f*; **to be up to ~** estar à altura.

⌐ **standards** *npl (principles)* princípios *mpl*.

standard-class *adj (Brit: on train)* de segunda classe.

standard lamp *n (Brit)* abajur *m* de pé *(Br)*, candeeiro *m* de pé *(Port)*.

standard of living *n* padrão *m* de vida *(Br)*, nível *m* de vida.

standby ['stændbaɪ] *adj (ticket)* sem reserva, de última hora.

stand-in *n (replacement)* substituto *m* (-ta *f*); *(stunt person)* dublê *mf (Br)*, duplo *m* (-pla *f*) *(Port)*.

standing order ['stændɪŋ-] *n* transferência *f* bancária.

standing room ['stændɪŋ-] *n (at sports ground, theatre)* lugares *mpl* em pé.

standpoint ['stændpɔɪnt] *n* ponto *m* de vista.

standstill ['stændstɪl] *n*: **to be at a ~** *(traffic)* estar parado(-da), estar imobilizado(-da); **to come to a ~** *(car, train)* parar, imobilizar-se; *(negotiations, work)* cessar.

stank [stæŋk] *pt* → **stink**.

staple ['steɪpl] *n (for paper)* grampo *m* *(Br)*, agrafo *m* *(Port)*.

stapler ['steɪplə'] *n* grampeador *m* *(Br)*, agrafador *m* *(Port)*.

star [stɑː'] *n* estrela *f* ♦ *vt (subj: film, play etc)*: **"starring ..."** "com ...".

⌐ **stars** *npl (horoscope)* horóscopo *m*.

starboard ['stɑːbəd] *adj* de estibordo.

starch [stɑːtʃ] *n (for clothes)* goma *f*; *(in food)* amido *m*.

stare [steə'] *vi*: **to ~ at** fitar, olhar fixamente (para).

starfish ['stɑːfɪʃ] *(pl inv)* *n* estrela-do-mar *f*.

starling ['stɑːlɪŋ] *n* estorninho *m*.

starry ['stɑːrɪ] *adj* estrelado(-da).

Stars and Stripes *n*: **the ~** a bandeira dos Estados Unidos.

start [stɑːt] *n (beginning)* início *m*, começo *m*; *(starting place)* ponto *m* de partida ♦ *vt (begin)* começar; *(car, engine)* ligar; *(business, club)* montar ♦ *vi (begin)* começar; *(car, engine)* pegar; *(begin journey)* sair, partir; **prices ~ at** OR **from £5** preços a partir de 5 libras; **to ~ doing sthg** OR **to do sthg** começar a fazer algo; **to ~ with ...** para começar ....

⌐ **start out** *vi (on journey)* partir; *(be originally)* começar.

⌐ **start up** *vt sep (car, engine)* ligar; *(business, shop)* montar.

starter ['stɑːtə'] *n (Brit: of meal)* entrada *f*; *(of car)* motor *m* de arranque; **for ~s** *(in meal)* como entrada.

starter motor *n* motor *m* de arranque.

starting point ['stɑːtɪŋ-] *n* ponto *m* de partida.

startle ['stɑːtl] *vt* assustar.

startling ['stɑːtlɪŋ] *adj* surpreendente.

starvation [stɑːˈveɪʃn] *n* fome *f*.

starve [stɑːv] *vi (have no food)* passar fome; **I'm starving!** estou esfomeado OR morto de fome!

state [steɪt] *n* estado *m* ♦ *vt (declare)* declarar; *(specify)* especificar, indicar; **the State** o Estado; **the States** os Estados Unidos.

statement ['steɪtmənt] *n (declaration)* declaração *f*; *(from bank)* extrato *m* de conta.

state school *n* escola *f* pública.

statesman ['steɪtsmən] *(pl -men* [-mən]) *n* homem *m* de estado, estadista *m*.

static ['stætɪk] *n (on radio, TV)* interferências *fpl*.

station ['steɪʃn] *n* estação *f*.

stationary ['steɪʃnərɪ] *adj* estacionário(-ria).

stationer's ['steɪʃnəz] *n (shop)* papelaria *f*.

stationery ['steɪʃnərɪ] *n* artigos *mpl* de papelaria.

stationmaster [ˈsteɪʃnˌmɑːstəʳ] *n* chefe *mf* de estação.

station wagon *n (Am)* perua *f (Br)*, carrinha *f (Port)*.

statistics [stəˈtɪstɪks] *npl (figures)* estatísticas *fpl*.

statue [ˈstætʃuː] *n* estátua *f*.

Statue of Liberty *n:* the ~ a Estátua da Liberdade.

stature [ˈstætʃəʳ] *n* estatura *f*.

status [ˈsteɪtəs] *n (legal position)* estado *m; (social position)* status *m (Br)*, estatuto *m (Port); (prestige)* prestígio *m*, status *m*.

statutory [ˈstætjʊtrɪ] *adj* legal.

staunch [stɔːntʃ] *adj* leal ♦ *vt* estancar.

stave [steɪv] *(pt & pp -d* OR **stove**) *n (MUS)* pauta *f*.

❏ **stave off** *vt sep (disaster, defeat)* adiar, protelar; *(hunger)* saciar, aplacar.

stay [steɪ] *n (time spent)* estadia *f* ♦ *vi (remain)* ficar; *(as guest)* ficar (hospedado); *(Scot: reside)* morar, viver; **where are you ~ing?** onde você está hospedado?; **to ~ the night** passar a noite.

❏ **stay away** *vi (not attend)* não ir; *(not go near)* ficar longe.

❏ **stay in** *vi* ficar em casa.

❏ **stay out** *vi (from home)* ficar fora.

❏ **stay up** *vi* ficar acordado.

STD code *n* indicativo *m*.

stead [sted] *n:* **to stand sb in good ~** ser muito útil para alguém.

steadfast [ˈstedfɑːst] *adj (supporter)* leal, fiel; *(resolve)* inabalável; *(gaze)* fixo(-xa).

steadily [ˈstedɪlɪ] *adv (gradually)* gradualmente; *(regularly)* regularmente; *(calmly)* calmamente.

steady [ˈstedɪ] *adj (not shaking, firm)* firme; *(gradual)* gradual; *(stable)* estável; *(job)* fixo(-xa) ♦ *vt (table, ladder)* firmar.

steak [steɪk] *n* bife *m*.

steak and kidney pie *n empada de carne de vaca e rins.*

steakhouse [ˈsteɪkhaʊs, *pl* -haʊzɪz] *n* restaurante especializado em bifes.

steal [stiːl] *(pt* stole, *pp* stolen) *vt* roubar; **to ~ sthg from sb** roubar algo de alguém.

stealthy [ˈstelθɪ] *adj* furtivo(-va).

steam [stiːm] *n* vapor *m* ♦ *vt (food)* cozer no vapor.

steam boat [ˈstiːmbəʊt] *n* barco *m* a vapor.

steam engine *n* máquina *f* a vapor.

steamer [ˈstiːməʳ] *n (ship)* navio *m* a vapor.

steam iron *n* ferro *m* a vapor.

steamroller [ˈstiːmˌrəʊləʳ] *n* cilindro *m*.

steel [stiːl] *n* aço *m* ♦ *adj* de aço.

steep [stiːp] *adj (hill, path)* íngreme; *(increase, drop)* considerável.

steeple [ˈstiːpl] *n* torre *f* da igreja, campanário *m*.

steeplechase [ˈstiːpltʃeɪs] *n* corrida *f* de obstáculos.

steer [stɪəʳ] *vt (car)* dirigir *(Br)*, conduzir *(Port); (boat, plane)* pilotar.

steering [ˈstɪərɪŋ] *n* direção *f*.

steering wheel *n* volante *m*.

stem [stem] *n (of plant)* talo *m*, caule *m; (of glass)* pé *m*.

stench [stentʃ] *n* fedor *m*.

stencil [ˈstensl] *n* stencil *m*.

step [step] *n (stair, rung)* degrau *m; (pace, measure, stage)* passo *m* ♦ *vi:* **to ~ on sthg** pisar em algo; **"mind the ~"** "cuidado com o degrau".

❏ **steps** *npl (stairs)* escadas *fpl*.

❏ **step aside** *vi (move aside)* desviar-se, afastar-se.

❏ **step back** *vi (move back)* recuar, afastar-se.

step aerobics *n* step *m*.

stepbrother [ˈstepˌbrʌðəʳ] *n* meio-irmão *m*.

stepdaughter [ˈstepˌdɔːtəʳ] *n* enteada *f*.

stepfather [ˈstepˌfɑːðəʳ] *n* padrasto *m*.

stepladder [ˈstepˌlædəʳ] *n* escada *f* portátil, escadote *m (Port)*.

stepmother [ˈstepˌmʌðəʳ] *n* madrasta *f*.

stepping-stone [ˈstepɪŋ-] *n (in river)* pedra *f; (fig: way to success)* trampolim *m*.

stepsister [ˈstepˌsɪstəʳ] *n* meia-irmã *f*.

stepson [ˈstepsʌn] *n* enteado *m*.

stereo [ˈsterɪəʊ] *(pl* -s) *adj* estereofônico(-ca) ♦ *n (hi-fi)* aparelhagem *f; (stereo sound)* estereofonia *f*, estéreo *m*.

stereotype [ˈsterɪətaɪp] *n* estereótipo *m*.

sterile [ˈsteraɪl] *adj (germ-free)* esterilizado(-da).

sterilize ['sterəlaız] vt esterilizar.
sterling ['stɜːlıŋ] adj (pound) esterlino(-na) ♦ n libra f esterlina.
sterling silver n prata f de lei.
stern [stɜːn] adj severo(-ra) ♦ n popa f.
steroid ['stıərɔıd] n esteróide m.
stethoscope ['steθəskəʊp] n estetoscópio m.
stew [stjuː] n ensopado m, guisado m.
steward ['stjuəd] n (on plane, ship) comissário m de bordo; (at public event) organizador m.
stewardess ['stjuədıs] n aeromoça f (Br), hospedeira f de bordo (Port).
stewed [stjuːd] adj (fruit) cozido(-da).
stick [stık] (pt & pp stuck) n (of wood) pau m; (for sport) stick m; (of celery) tira f (Br), troço m (Port); (walking stick) bengala f ♦ vt (glue) colar; (push, insert) meter, pôr; (inf: put) meter, pôr ♦ vi (become attached) grudar-se (Br), pegar-se (Port); (jam) encravar.
❏ **stick out** vi sobressair.
❏ **stick to** vt fus (decision, principles, promise) manter-se fiel a.
❏ **stick up** vt sep (poster, notice) afixar ♦ vi: **your hair is ~ing up!** você está com o cabelo todo arrepiado!
❏ **stick up for** vt fus defender.
sticker ['stıkər] n adesivo m (Br), autocolante m (Port).
sticking plaster ['stıkıŋ-] n esparadrapo m (Br), penso m (rápido) (Port).
stick shift n (Am: car) veículo m com mudanças manuais.
stick-up n (inf) assalto m à mão armada.
sticky ['stıkı] adj (substance, hands, sweets) pegajoso(-osa); (label, tape) adesivo(-va), autocolante (Port); (weather) úmido(-da).
stiff [stıf] adj (firm) rijo(-ja); (sheet) teso(-sa); (neck) duro(-ra); (back, person) dolorido(-da); (door, latch, mechanism) emperrado(-da) ♦ adv: **to be bored ~** (inf) estar morrendo de tédio.
stiffen ['stıfn] vi (muscles, person) ficar rígido(-da); (hinge, handle) emperrar; (competition, resolve) endurecer.
stifle ['staıfl] vt (suffocate) sufocar; (suppress) abafar.
stifling ['staıflıŋ] adj (heat) sufocante.
stigma ['stıgmə] n (disgrace) estigma m.
stile [staıl] n conjunto de degraus que

facilita a passagem das pessoas por cima de uma vedação ou vala no campo.
stiletto heels [stı'letəʊ-] npl (shoes) sapatos mpl com saltos finos.
still [stıl] adv ainda ♦ adj (motionless) imóvel; (quiet, calm) calmo(-ma); (not fizzy) sem gás; **we've ~ got 10 minutes** ainda temos 10 minutos; **~ more** ainda mais; **to stand ~** estar quieto.
stillborn ['stılbɔːn] adj nati-morto (nati-morta).
still life (pl -s) n natureza-morta f.
stilted ['stıltıd] adj forçado(-da).
Stilton ['stıltn] n queijo m Stilton, queijo azul inglês com sabor forte e amargo, comido tradicionalmente acompanhado do vinho do Porto.
stilts [stılts] npl pernas fpl de pau (Br), andas fpl (Port).
stimulate ['stımjʊleıt] vt estimular.
stimulating ['stımjʊleıtıŋ] adj (physically) revigorante; (mentally) estimulante.
stimulus ['stımjʊləs] (pl -li [-laı]) n estímulo m.
sting [stıŋ] (pt & pp stung) vt picar ♦ vi (skin, eyes) arder.
stingy ['stındʒı] adj (inf) pão-duro(-ra) (Br), forreta (Port).
stink [stıŋk] (pt stank OR stunk, pp stunk) vi cheirar mal.
stinking ['stıŋkıŋ] adj (inf: headache, cold) horroroso(-osa).
stint [stınt] n (period of time) período m ♦ vi: **to ~ on sthg** poupar em algo.
stipulate ['stıpjʊleıt] vt estipular.
stir [stɜːr] vt (move around, mix) mexer.
stir-fry n prato chinês em que pedaços de legumes e carnes são fritos rapidamente em óleo bem quente ♦ vt fritar rapidamente.
stirrup ['stırəp] n estribo m.
stitch [stıtʃ] n (in sewing, knitting) ponto m; **to have a ~** sentir uma pontada do lado.
❏ **stitches** npl (for wound) pontos mpl.
stoat [stəʊt] n arminho m.
stock [stɒk] n (of shop) estoque m; (FIN) títulos mpl, acções fpl; (CULIN) caldo m ♦ vt (have in stock) ter em estoque; **in ~** em estoque, armazenado; **out of ~** esgotado.
stockbroker ['stɒkbrəʊkər] n corretor m (-ra f) da bolsa.
stock cube n cubo m de caldo.

Stock Exchange *n* bolsa *f* de valores.

stockholder ['stɒk.həʊldə^r] *n (Am)* acionista *mf*.

Stockholm ['stɒkhəʊm] *n* Estocolmo s.

stocking ['stɒkɪŋ] *n* meia *f*.

stock market *n* bolsa *f*, mercado *m* de valores.

stocktaking ['stɒk.teɪkɪŋ] *n* inventário *m*.

stocky ['stɒkɪ] *adj* atarracado(-da).

stodgy ['stɒdʒɪ] *adj (food)* pesado(-da).

stole [stəʊl] *pt* → **steal**.

stolen ['stəʊln] *pp* → **steal**.

stomach ['stʌmək] *n (organ)* estômago *m; (belly)* barriga *f*.

stomachache ['stʌməkeɪk] *n* dor *f* de estômago.

stomach upset [-'ʌpset] *n* indisposição *f* estomacal.

stone [stəʊn] *n (substance)* n pedra *f; (in fruit)* caroço *m; (measurement: pl inv)* = 6,35 kg; *(gem)* pedra preciosa ♦ *adj* de pedra.

stonewashed [stəʊnwɒʃt] *adj* prélavado(-da) com pedras.

stood [stʊd] *pt & pp* → **stand**.

stool [stuːl] *n (for sitting on)* banco *m*, mocho *m* (Port).

stoop [stuːp] *vi (bend over)* abaixar-se; *(hunch shoulders)* corcovar-se.

stop [stɒp] *n* parada *f (Br)*, paragem *f (Port)* ♦ *vt* parar ♦ *vi* parar; *(stay)* ficar; **to ~ sb/sthg from doing sthg** impedir alguém/algo de fazer algo; **to ~ doing sthg** parar de fazer algo; **to put a ~ to sthg** pôr termo OR fim a algo; **"stop"** *(road sign)* "stop"; **"stopping at ..."** *(train, bus)* "com paradas em ...".

⏷ **stop off** *vi* parar.

stopover ['stɒp.əʊvə^r] *n* parada *f (Br)*, paragem *f (Port); (on plane journey)* escala *f*.

stoppage ['stɒpɪdʒ] *n (strike)* greve *f*, paralisação *f; (in sports match)* interrupção *f*.

stopper ['stɒpə^r] *n* tampa *f*.

stopwatch ['stɒpwɒtʃ] *n* cronômetro *m*.

storage ['stɔːrɪdʒ] *n* armazenamento *m*, armazenagem *f*.

storage heater *n (Brit)* termoacumulador *m*, *aquecedor que acumula calor durante a noite para o emitir durante o dia*.

store [stɔː^r] *n (shop)* loja *f; (supply)* estoque *m* ♦ *vt* armazenar.

storehouse ['stɔːhaʊs, *pl* -haʊzɪz] *n* armazém *m*.

storekeeper ['stɔː.kiːpə^r] *n (Am)* comerciante *mf*, dono *m* (-na *f*) de loja.

storeroom ['stɔːrʊm] *n (in shop)* armazém *m; (in house)* dispensa *f*.

storey ['stɔːrɪ] *(pl* -s) *n (Brit)* andar *m*.

stork [stɔːk] *n* cegonha *f*.

storm [stɔːm] *n (bad weather)* tempestade *f*.

stormy ['stɔːmɪ] *adj (weather)* tempestuoso(-osa).

story ['stɔːrɪ] *n (account, tale)* história *f; (news item)* artigo *m; (Am)* = **storey**.

stout [staʊt] *adj (fat)* corpulento(-ta), forte ♦ *n (drink)* cerveja *f* preta.

stove [stəʊv] *pt & pp* → **stave** ♦ *n (for cooking)* fogão *m; (for heating)* estufa *f*.

stow [stəʊ] *vt:* **to ~ sthg (away)** *(luggage)* arrumar algo; *(files)* arquivar algo; *(treasure)* esconder algo.

stowaway ['stəʊəweɪ] *n* passageiro *m* clandestino (passageira *f* clandestina).

straddle ['strædl] *vt (subj: person)* escarranchar-se em.

straggler ['stræglə^r] *n* atrasado *m* (-da *f*).

straight [streɪt] *adj (not curved)* direito(-ta); *(road, line)* reto(-ta); *(hair)* liso(-sa); *(consecutive)* consecutivo(-va); *(drink)* puro(-ra) ♦ *adv (in a straight line)* reto(-ta); *(upright)* direito; *(directly)* diretamente; *(without delay)* imediatamente; **~ ahead** sempre em frente; **~ away** imediatamente, já; **~ in front** mesmo em frente.

straighten [streɪtn] *vt* endireitar; *(room, desk)* arrumar.

⏷ **straighten out** *vt sep (misunderstanding)* esclarecer.

straight face *n:* **to keep a ~** manter-se sério(-ria), conter o riso.

straightforward [streɪt'fɔːwəd] *adj (easy)* simples *(inv)*.

strain [streɪn] *n (force)* força *f; (nervous stress)* stress *m; (tension)* tensão *f; (injury)* distenção *f* ♦ *vt (muscle, eyes)* forçar; *(food, tea)* coar.

strained [streɪnd] *adj (forced)* forçado(-da); *(tense)* tenso(-sa); *(ankle, shoulder)* deslocado(-da); *(muscle)* distendido(-da).

strainer ['streɪnə^r] *n* passador *m*, coador *m*.

strait [streit] *n* estreito *m*.

straitjacket ['streit,dʒækit] *n* camisa-de-força *f*.

straitlaced [,streit'leist] *adj* puritano(-na).

strand [strænd] *n (of cotton, wool)* linha *f*, fio *m*; **a ~ of hair** um cabelo.

stranded ['strændid] *adj (person, car)* preso(-sa); *(boat)* encalhado(-da).

strange [streindʒ] *adj* estranho(-nha).

stranger ['streindʒə*r*] *n (unfamiliar person)* estranho *m* (-nha *f*), desconhecido *m* (-da *f*); *(person from different place)* forasteiro *m* (-ra *f*).

strangle ['stræŋgl] *vt* estrangular.

strap [stræp] *n (of bag)* alça *f*; *(of camera, shoe)* correia *f*; *(of watch)* pulseira *f*.

strapless ['stræplɪs] *adj* sem alças.

strapping ['stræpɪŋ] *adj* bem constituído(-da).

Strasbourg ['stræzbɜːg] *n* Estrasburgo *s*.

strategic [strə'tiːdʒɪk] *adj* estratégico(-ca).

strategy ['strætɪdʒɪ] *n* estratégia *f*.

Stratford-upon-Avon [,strætfədəpɒn'eɪvn] *n* Stratford-Upon-Avon *s*.

straw [strɔː] *n* palha *f*; *(for drinking)* canudo *m (Br)*, palhinha *f (Port)*.

strawberry ['strɔːbərɪ] *n* morango *m*.

stray [streɪ] *adj (animal)* abandonado(-da) ◆ *vi* vaguear.

streak [striːk] *n (stripe, mark)* listra *f*, risca *f*; *(period)* período *m*.

stream [striːm] *n (river)* riacho *m*; *(of traffic, people)* torrente *f*; *(of water, air)* corrente *f*.

streamlined ['striːmlaɪnd] *adj (aerodynamic)* com um perfil aerodinâmico; *(efficient)* eficiente.

street [striːt] *n* rua *f*.

streetcar ['striːtkɑː*r*] *n (Am)* bonde *m (Br)*, eléctrico *m (Port)*.

street light *n* poste *m* de iluminação, candeeiro *m* de rua *(Port)*.

street plan *n* mapa *m* (das ruas).

streetwise ['striːtwaɪz] *adj* esperto (-ta).

strength [streŋθ] *n* força *f*; *(of structure)* solidez *f*; *(strong point)* ponto *m* forte; *(of feeling, wind, smell)* intensidade *f*; *(of drink)* teor *m* alcoólico; *(of drug)* dosagem *f*.

strengthen ['streŋθn] *vt* reforçar.

strenuous ['strenjʊəs] *adj (exercise, activity)* esgotante; *(effort)* vigoroso

(-osa), tremendo(-da).

stress [stres] *n (tension)* stress *m*; *(on word, syllable)* acento *m* tônico ◆ *vt (emphasize)* pôr a tônica em; *(word, syllable)* acentuar.

stressful ['stresfʊl] *adj* desgastante.

stretch [stretʃ] *n (of land, water)* extensão *f*; *(of time)* período *m* ◆ *vt* esticar ◆ *vi (land, sea)* estender-se; *(person, animal)* estirar-se, espreguiçar-se; **to ~ one's legs** *(fig)* esticar as pernas.

⌐ stretch out *vt sep (hand)* estender ◆ *vi (lie down)* estender-se ao comprido, deitar-se.

stretcher ['stretʃə*r*] *n* maca *f*.

strict [strɪkt] *adj* rigoroso(-osa).

strictly ['strɪktlɪ] *adv (absolutely)* estritamente; *(exclusively)* exclusivamente; **~ speaking** a bem dizer.

stride [straɪd] *n* passada *f*.

strident ['straɪdnt] *adj (voice, sound)* estridente.

strife [straɪf] *n* rixas *fpl*, conflitos *mpl*.

strike [straɪk] *(pt & pp* **struck)** *n (of employees)* greve *f* ◆ *vt (fml: hit)* agredir; *(fml: collide with)* colidir OR chocar com; *(a match)* acender ◆ *vi (refuse to work)* fazer greve; *(happen suddenly)* ocorrer; **the clock struck eight** o relógio bateu oito horas.

striker ['straɪkə*r*] *n (person on strike)* grevista *mf*; *(in football)* ponta-de-lança *mf*.

striking ['straɪkɪŋ] *adj (noticeable)* impressionante; *(attractive)* atraente.

string [strɪŋ] *n* cordel *m*, fio *m*; *(of pearls, beads)* colar *m*; *(of musical instrument, tennis racket)* corda *f*; *(series)* série *f*; **a piece of ~** um cordel, um fio.

string bean *n* feijão *m* verde, vagem *f*.

stringed instrument [strɪŋd-] *n* instrumento *m* de cordas.

stringent ['strɪndʒənt] *adj* severo(-ra), austero(-ra).

strip [strɪp] *n (of paper, cloth etc)* tira *f*; *(of land, water)* faixa *f* ◆ *vt (paint)* raspar; *(wallpaper)* arrancar ◆ *vi (undress)* despir-se.

stripe [straɪp] *n* risca *f*, listra *f*.

striped [straɪpt] *adj* de listras.

strip-search *vt* revistar *(mandando tirar a roupa a alguém)*.

strip show *n* espetáculo *m* de striptease.

striptease ['strɪptiːz] *n* striptease *m*.

265 subject

strive [straɪv] (*pt* **strove**, *pp* **striven** ['strɪvn]) *vi*: **to ~ for** sthg lutar por algo; **to ~ to do** sthg esforçar-se por fazer algo.

stroke [strəʊk] *n* (*MED*) trombose *f*; (*in tennis*) batida *f*; (*in golf*) tacada *f*; (*swimming style*) estilo *m* ♦ *vt* fazer festas em; **a ~ of luck** um golpe de sorte.

stroll [strəʊl] *n* passeio *m*.

stroller ['strəʊlər] *n* (*Am: pushchair*) carrinho *m* de bebê.

strong [strɒŋ] *adj* forte; (*structure, bridge, chair*) sólido(-da); (*accent*) forte, acentuado(-da).

strongbox ['strɒŋbɒks] *n* caixa-forte *f*.

stronghold ['strɒŋhəʊld] *n* (*fig: bastion*) bastião *m*.

strongly ['strɒŋlɪ] *adv* (*built*) solidamente; (*advise*) vivamente; (*taste, smell*) intensamente; (*support*) plenamente; **to ~ oppose** sthg opor-se completamente a algo.

strove [strəʊv] *pt* → **strive**.

struck [strʌk] *pt & pp* → **strike**.

structure ['strʌktʃər] *n* (*arrangement, organization*) estrutura *f*; (*building*) construção *f*.

struggle ['strʌgl] *n* (*great effort*) luta *f* ♦ *vi* (*fight*) lutar; (*in order to get free*) debater-se; **to ~ to do** sthg esforçar-se por fazer algo.

stub [stʌb] *n* (*of cigarette*) ponta *f*; (*of cheque, ticket*) talão *m*.

stubble ['stʌbl] *n* (*on face*) barba *f* por fazer.

stubborn ['stʌbən] *adj* (*person*) teimoso(-osa).

stuck [stʌk] *pt & pp* → **stick** ♦ *adj* preso(-sa).

stuck-up *adj* (*inf*) presunçoso(-osa), pedante.

stud [stʌd] *n* (*on boots*) pitão *m*, piton *m*; (*fastener*) botão *m* de pressão (*Br*), mola *f* (*Port*); (*earring*) brinco *m*.

student ['stjuːdnt] *n* estudante *mf*.

student card *n* carteira *f* de estudante.

students' union [ˌstjuːdnts-] *n* (*place*) associação *f* de estudantes.

studio ['stjuːdɪəʊ] (*pl* -s) *n* (*for filming, broadcasting*) estúdio *m*; (*of artist*) atelier *m*.

studio apartment (*Am*) = **studio flat**.

studio flat *n* (*Brit*) conjugado *m* (*Br*), estúdio *m* (*Port*).

studious ['stjuːdjəs] *adj* estudioso (-osa), aplicado(-da).

studiously ['stjuːdjəslɪ] *adv* cuidadosamente.

study ['stʌdɪ] *n* estudo *m*; (*room*) escritório *m* ♦ *vt* (*learn about*) estudar; (*examine*) examinar ♦ *vi* estudar.

stuff [stʌf] *n* (*inf*) (*substance*) coisa *f*; (*things, possessions*) coisas *fpl*, tralha *f* ♦ *vt* (*put roughly*) enfiar; (*fill*) rechear.

stuffed [stʌft] *adj* (*food*) recheado(-da); (*inf: full up*) cheio (cheia); (*dead animal*) embalsamado(-da).

stuffing ['stʌfɪŋ] *n* recheio *m*.

stuffy ['stʌfɪ] *adj* (*room, atmosphere*) abafado(-da).

stumble ['stʌmbl] *vi* (*when walking*) tropeçar.

stumbling block ['stʌmblɪŋ-] *n* entrave *m*, obstáculo *m*.

stump [stʌmp] *n* (*of tree*) toco *m*.

stun [stʌn] *vt* (*shock*) chocar.

stung [stʌŋ] *pt & pp* → **sting**.

stunk [stʌŋk] *pt & pp* → **stink**.

stunning ['stʌnɪŋ] *adj* espantoso(-osa).

stunt [stʌnt] *n* (*for publicity*) golpe *m* OR truque *m* publicitário; (*in film*) cena *f* arriscada.

stunt man *n* dublê *mf* (*Br*), duplo *m* (*Port*).

stupendous [stjuːˈpendəs] *adj* (*inf: wonderful*) estupendo(-da).

stupid ['stjuːpɪd] *adj* estúpido(-da).

stupidity [stjuːˈpɪdətɪ] *n* estupidez *f*.

sturdy ['stɜːdɪ] *adj* robusto(-ta).

stutter ['stʌtər] *vi* gaguejar.

stye [staɪ] *n* terçol *m*, terçolho *m* (*Port*).

style [staɪl] *n* estilo *m*; (*design*) modelo *m* ♦ *vt* (*hair*) pentear.

stylish ['staɪlɪʃ] *adj* elegante.

stylist ['staɪlɪst] *n* (*hairdresser*) cabeleireiro *m* (-ra *f*).

stylus ['staɪləs] (*pl* -es) *n* (*on record player*) agulha *f*.

suave [swɑːv] *adj* polido(-da).

sub [sʌb] *n* (*inf*) (*substitute*) substituto *m* (-ta *f*); (*Brit: subscription*) assinatura *f*; (*Am: filled baguette*) sanduíche *m*.

subconscious [ˌsʌbˈkɒnʃəs] *adj* subconsciente ♦ *n*: **the ~** o subconsciente.

subdued [səbˈdjuːd] *adj* (*person*) abatido(-da); (*lighting, colour*) tênue.

subject [*n* ˈsʌbdʒekt, *vb* səbˈdʒekt] *n* (*topic*) tema *m*; (*at school*) disciplina *f*; (*at university*) cadeira *f*; (*GRAMM*) sujeito *m*; (*fml: of country*) cidadão *m* (-dã *f*)

♦ vt: **to ~ sb to sthg** submeter alguém a algo; **~ to availability** dentro do limite do estoque disponível; **they are ~ to an additional charge** estão sujeitos a um suplemento.

subjective [sɔb'dʒɛktɪv] adj subjetivo(-va).

subjunctive [sɔb'dʒʌŋktɪv] n subjuntivo m (Br), conjuntivo m (Port).

sublet [ˌsʌb'lɛt] (pt & pp sublet) vt subalugar, subarrendar.

sublime [sɔ'blaɪm] adj sublime.

submarine [ˌsʌbmɔ'riːn] n submarino m.

submerge [sɔb'mɜːdʒ] vt submergir.

submit [sɔb'mɪt] vt apresentar ♦ vi submeter-se.

subordinate [sɔ'bɔːdɪnɔt] adj (GRAMM) subordinado(-da).

subscribe [sɔb'skraɪb] vi (to magazine, newspaper) assinar.

subscriber [sɔb'skraɪbɔʳ] n assinante mf.

subscription [sɔb'skrɪpʃn] n assinatura f.

subsequent ['sʌbsɪkwɔnt] adj subseqüente.

subsequently ['sʌbsɪkwɔntlɪ] adv subseqüentemente, posteriormente.

subside [sɔb'saɪd] vi (ground) abater, aluir; (feeling) desaparecer, dissipar-se; (noise) diminuir.

subsidence [sɔb'saɪdns] n (of building) desmoronamento m; (of ground) abaixamento m.

subsidiary [sɔb'sɪdjɔrɪ] adj secundário(-ria) ♦ n: ~ **(company)** subsidiária f, filial f.

subsidize ['sʌbsɪdaɪz] vt subsidiar.

subsidy ['sʌbsɪdɪ] n subsídio m.

substance ['sʌbstɔns] n substância f.

substantial [sɔb'stænʃl] adj substancial.

substantially [sɔb'stænʃɔlɪ] adv substancialmente, consideravelmente; (true) em grande parte; (complete) praticamente.

substitute ['sʌbstɪtjuːt] n (replacement) substituto m (-ta f); (SPORT) suplente mf.

subtitles ['sʌbˌtaɪtlz] npl legendas fpl.

subtle ['sʌtl] adj subtil.

subtlety ['sʌtltɪ] n subtileza f.

subtract [sɔb'trækt] vt subtrair.

subtraction [sɔb'trækʃn] n subtração f.

suburb ['sʌbɜːb] n subúrbio m; **the ~s** os subúrbios.

subway ['sʌbweɪ] n (Brit: for pedestrians) passagem f subterrânea; (Am: underground railway) metrô m.

succeed [sɔk'siːd] vi (be successful) ter êxito OR sucesso ♦ vt (fml: follow) seguir; **to ~ in doing sthg** conseguir fazer algo.

success [sɔk'ses] n êxito m, sucesso m.

successful [sɔk'sesful] adj (plan, person) bem sucedido(-da); (film, book, TV programme) de sucesso.

successive [sɔk'sesɪv] adj sucessivo(-va); **four ~ days** quatro dias seguidos OR consecutivos.

succinct [sɔk'sɪŋkt] adj sucinto(-ta).

succulent ['sʌkjulɔnt] adj suculento(-ta).

succumb [sɔ'kʌm] vi: **to ~ (to sthg)** sucumbir (a algo).

such [sʌtʃ] adj (of stated kind) tal, semelhante; (so great) tamanho(-nha), tal ♦ adv: **~ a lot** tanto; **~ a lot of books** tantos livros; **it's ~ a lovely day** está um dia tão bonito; **she has ~ good luck** ela tem tanta sorte; **~ a thing should never have happened** uma coisa assim nunca deveria ter acontecido; **~ as** tal como.

suck [sʌk] vt (sweet) chupar; (thumb) chupar; (nipple) mamar em.

sudden ['sʌdn] adj repentino(-na); **all of a ~** de repente.

suddenly ['sʌdnlɪ] adv de repente.

suds [sʌdz] npl espuma f (de sabão).

sue [suː] vt processar.

suede [sweɪd] n camurça f.

suet ['suɪt] n sebo m.

suffer ['sʌfɔʳ] vt & vi sofrer; **to ~ from** (illness) sofrer de.

sufferer ['sʌfrɔʳ] n doente mf.

suffering ['sʌfrɪŋ] n sofrimento m.

sufficient [sɔ'fɪʃnt] adj (fml) suficiente.

sufficiently [sɔ'fɪʃntlɪ] adv (fml) bastante, suficientemente.

suffix ['sʌfɪks] n sufixo m.

suffocate ['sʌfɔkeɪt] vi sufocar.

sugar ['ʃugɔʳ] n açúcar m.

sugar beet n beterraba f.

sugarcane ['ʃugɔkeɪn] n cana-de-açúcar f.

sugary ['ʃugɔrɪ] adj (food, drink) açucarado(-da).

suggest [sɔ'dʒest] vt sugerir; **to ~**

doing sthg sugerir fazer algo.
suggestion [sə'dʒestʃn] n sugestão f.
suggestive [sə'dʒestɪv] adj (remark, behaviour) sugestivo(-va); ~ **of sthg** (reminiscent) que sugere algo.
suicide ['soɪsaɪd] n suicídio m; **to commit ~** suicidar-se.
suit [suːt] n (man's clothes) terno m (Br), fato m (Port); (woman's clothes) conjunto m; (in cards) naipe m; (JUR) processo m ◆ vt (subj: clothes, colour, shoes) ficar bem em; (be convenient for) convir a; (be appropriate for) ser apropriado(-da) para.
suitable ['suːtəbl] adj apropriado (-da), conveniente; **to be ~ for** ser apropriado OR conveniente para.
suitcase ['suːtkeɪs] n mala f.
suite [swiːt] n (set of rooms) suíte f; (furniture) conjunto m de mobília.
suited ['suːtɪd] adj: **to be ~ to sthg** (suitable) servir para algo; **I'm not ~ to this humid weather** não me dou bem com este tempo úmido; **they are very well ~** estão bem um para o outro.
sulk [sʌlk] vi amuar.
sulky ['sʌlkɪ] adj amuado(-da).
sullen ['sʌlən] adj taciturno(-na), carrancudo(-da).
sultana [səl'tɑːnə] n (Brit) sultana f.
sultry ['sʌltrɪ] adj (weather, climate) abafado(-da).
sum [sʌm] n soma f.
❑ **sum up** vt sep (summarize) resumir, sumariar.
summarize ['sʌməraɪz] vt resumir.
summary ['sʌmərɪ] n resumo m, sumário m.
summer ['sʌmər] n verão m; **in (the) ~** no verão; **~ holidays** férias fpl de verão.
summer school n cursos mpl de verão.
summertime ['sʌmətaɪm] n verão m.
summit ['sʌmɪt] n (of mountain) topo m, cume m; (meeting) conferência f de cúpula (Br), cimeira f (Port).
summon ['sʌmən] vt (send for) convocar; (JUR) intimar.
sumptuous ['sʌmptʃuəs] adj suntuoso(-osa).
sun [sʌn] n sol m ◆ vt: **to ~ o.s.** apanhar sol; **to catch the ~** bronzear-se; **to sit in the ~** sentar-se no sol; **out of the ~** na sombra.
Sun. (abbr of Sunday) dom.

sunbathe ['sʌnbeɪð] vi apanhar OR tomar banho de sol.
sunbed ['sʌnbed] n aparelho m de raios ultravioletas.
sun block n protetor m solar (com fator de proteção total).
sunburn ['sʌnbɜːn] n queimadura f solar.
sunburnt ['sʌnbɜːnt] adj queimado(-da) (de sol).
sundae ['sʌndeɪ] n sundae m, sorvete regado com molho de fruta ou chocolate, polvilhado com frutos secos (nozes, avelãs, etc) e servido com creme batido.
Sunday ['sʌndɪ] n domingo m, → **Saturday**.
Sunday school n catequese f.
sundial ['sʌndaɪəl] n relógio m de sol.
sundown ['sʌndaʊn] n pôr m do sol.
sundress ['sʌndres] n vestido m de alças.
sundries ['sʌndrɪz] npl (on bill) artigos mpl diversos.
sunflower ['sʌn,flaʊər] n girassol m.
sunflower oil n óleo m de girassol.
sung [sʌŋ] pt → **sing**.
sunglasses ['sʌn,glɑːsɪz] npl óculos mpl de sol, óculos escuros.
sunhat ['sʌnhæt] n chapéu-de-sol m.
sunk [sʌŋk] pp → **sink**.
sunlight ['sʌnlaɪt] n luz f do sol.
sun lounger [-ˌlaʊndʒər] n espreguiçadeira f.
sunny ['sʌnɪ] adj (day, weather) de sol, ensolarado(-da); (room, place) ensolarado(-da).
sunrise ['sʌnraɪz] n nascer m do sol.
sunroof ['sʌnruːf] n teto m solar.
sunset ['sʌnset] n pôr-do-sol m.
sunshade ['sʌnʃeɪd] n sombrinha f.
sunshine ['sʌnʃaɪn] n luz f do sol; **in the ~** ao sol.
sunstroke ['sʌnstrəʊk] n insolação f.
suntan ['sʌntæn] n bronzeado m.
suntan cream n creme m bronzeador, bronzeador m.
suntan lotion n loção f bronzeadora, bronzeador m.
super ['suːpər] adj (wonderful) chocante (Br), formidável ◆ n (petrol) gasolina f super.
superb [suː'pɜːb] adj magnífico(-ca), soberbo(-ba).
superficial [ˌsuːpə'fɪʃl] adj superficial.

superfluous [suːˈpɜːfluəs] *adj* supér-fluo(-flua).

Superglue® [ˈsuːpəgluː] *n* cola *f* ultra-rápida.

superhuman [ˌsuːpəˈhjuːmən] *adj* sobre-humano(-na).

superimpose [ˌsuːpərɪmˈpəuz] *vt*: **to ~ sthg on sthg** sobrepor algo a algo.

superintendent [ˌsuːpərɪnˈtendənt] *n* (*Brit: of police*) = subchefe *m* (-fa *f*).

superior [suːˈpɪərɪəˈ] *adj* superior ◆ *n* superior *mf*.

superlative [suːˈpɜːlətɪv] *adj* superla-tivo(-va) ◆ *n* superlativo *m*.

supermarket [ˈsuːpəˌmɑːkɪt] *n* supermercado *m*.

supernatural [ˌsuːpəˈnætʃrəl] *adj* sobrenatural.

superpower [ˈsuːpəˌpauəˈ] *n* super-potência *f*.

Super Saver® *n* (*Brit*) bilhete de trem com preço reduzido, sob certas condições.

supersede [suːpəˈsiːd] *vt* suplantar.

supersonic [ˌsuːpəˈsɒnɪk] *adj* supersônico(-ca).

superstitious [ˌsuːpəˈstɪʃəs] *adj* supersticioso(-osa).

superstore [ˈsuːpəstɔːˈ] *n* hiper-mercado *m*.

supervise [ˈsuːpəvaɪz] *vt* supervisio-nar.

supervisor [ˈsuːpəvaɪzəˈ] *n* (*of work-ers*) supervisor *m* (-ra *f*), encarregado *m* (-da *f*).

supper [ˈsʌpəˈ] *n* (*main meal*) jantar *m*, ceia *f*; **to have ~** jantar, cear.

supple [ˈsʌpl] *adj* flexível.

supplement [*n* ˈsʌplɪmənt, *vb* ˈsʌplɪment] *n* suplemento *m* ◆ *vt* com-pletar, complementar.

supplementary [ˌsʌplɪˈmentərɪ] *adj* suplementar.

supplier [səˈplaɪəˈ] *n* fornecedor *m* (-ra *f*), abastecedor *m* (-ra *f*).

supply [səˈplaɪ] *n* (*store*) reserva *f*; (*providing*) fornecimento *m* ◆ *vt* forne-cer; **to ~ sb with sthg** fornecer algo a alguém.

⅃ supplies *npl* provisões *fpl*.

support [səˈpɔːt] *n* (*backing, encour-agement*) apoio *m*; (*supporting object*) suporte *m* ◆ *vt* (*cause, campaign, person*) apoiar; (*SPORT*) torcer por (*Br*), ser adepto de (*Port*); (*hold up*) suportar; (*a family*) sustentar.

supporter [səˈpɔːtəˈ] *n* (*SPORT*) torce-dor *m* (-ra *f*) (*Br*), adepto *m* (-ta *f*) (*Port*); (*of cause, political party*) partidá-rio *m* (-ria *f*).

suppose [səˈpəuz] *vt*: **to ~ (that)** supor que ◆ *conj* = **supposing**; **I ~ so** suponho que sim.

supposed [səˈpəuzd] *adj* (*alleged*) suposto(-osta); **it's ~ to be quite good** é supostamente bastante bom; **you were ~ to be here at nine** você era para estar aqui às nove.

supposedly [səˈpəuzɪdlɪ] *adv* supos-tamente.

supposing [səˈpəuzɪŋ] *conj* supondo que.

suppress [səˈpres] *vt* (*uprising, revolt, emotions*) reprimir; (*information, report*) ocultar.

supreme [suˈpriːm] *adj* supremo(-ma).

surcharge [ˈsɜːtʃɑːdʒ] *n* sobretaxa *f*.

sure [ʃuəˈ] *adj* (*certain to happen*) certo(-ta); (*with no doubts*) seguro(-ra) ◆ *adv* (*inf: yes*) claro; **are you ~?** você tem certeza?; **to be ~ of o.s.** ser seguro de si; **to make ~ (that)** ... assegurar-se de que ...; **for ~** com cer-teza.

surely [ˈʃuəlɪ] *adv* com OR de certeza.

surf [sɜːf] *n* surf *m* ◆ *vi* fazer surfe.

surface [ˈsɜːfɪs] *n* superfície *f*; "tem-porary road ~" "asfaltamento tempo-rário" (*Br*), "traçado temporário" (*Port*).

surface area *n* área *f* de superfície.

surface mail *n* correio *m* por via terreste.

surfboard [ˈsɜːfbɔːd] *n* prancha *f* de surfe.

surfing [ˈsɜːfɪŋ] *n* surf *m*; **to go ~** ir fazer surfe.

surge [sɜːdʒ] *n* (*of electricity*) sobre-tensão *f*; (*of interest, support*) onda *f*; (*of sales, applications*) aumento *m* (repenti-no) ◆ *vi* (*people, vehicles*): **~ forward** avançar em massa.

surgeon [ˈsɜːdʒən] *n* cirurgião *m* (-giã *f*).

surgery [ˈsɜːdʒərɪ] *n* (*treatment*) cirur-gia *f*; (*Brit: building*) consultório *m*; (*Brit: period*) horário *m* de atendimen-to, horas *fpl* de consulta.

surgical [ˈsɜːdʒɪkl] *adj* (*instrument, gown*) cirúrgico(-ca).

surgical spirit *n* (*Brit*) álcool *m* etílico.

surly [ˈsɜːlɪ] *adj* mal-humorado(-da).

surmount [sɜːˈmaunt] *vt* vencer, superar.

surname ['sɜːneɪm] n sobrenome m (Br), apelido m (Port).

surpass [sə'pɑːs] vt ultrapassar, exceder.

surplus ['sɜːpləs] n excedente m.

surprise [sə'praɪz] n surpresa f ◆ vt (astonish) surpreender.

surprised [sə'praɪzd] adj surpreso(-sa).

surprising [sə'praɪzɪŋ] adj surpreendente.

surprisingly [sə'praɪzɪŋlɪ] adv: **it was ~ good** foi melhor do que esperávamos; **not ~** como seria de esperar.

surrender [sə'rendər] vi render-se ◆ vt (fml: hand over) entregar.

surreptitious [ˌsʌrəp'tɪʃəs] adj subreptício(-cia).

surround [sə'raʊnd] vt rodear.

surrounding [sə'raʊndɪŋ] adj circundante, à volta.

◘ **surroundings** npl arredores mpl.

surveillance [sɜː'veɪləns] n vigilância f.

survey ['sɜːveɪ] (pl -s) n (investigation) inquérito m; (poll) sondagem f; (of land) levantamento m topográfico; (Brit: of house) inspeção f, vistoria f.

surveyor [sə'veɪər] n (Brit: of houses) inspetor m (-ra f), perito m (-ta f); (of land) agrimensor m (-ra f).

survival [sə'vaɪvl] n sobrevivência f.

survive [sə'vaɪv] vi sobreviver ◆ vt sobreviver a.

survivor [sə'vaɪvər] n sobrevivente mf.

susceptible [sə'septəbl] adj suscetível; **to be ~ to sthg** ser suscetível a algo.

suspect [vb sə'spekt, n & adj 'sʌspekt] vt (mistrust) suspeitar de ◆ n suspeito m (-ta f) ◆ adj suspeito(-ta); **to ~ sb of sthg** suspeitar que alguém tenha feito algo; **to ~ (that)** suspeitar que.

suspend [sə'spend] vt suspender.

suspender belt [sə'spendə-] n cintaliga f (Br), cinto m de ligas (Port).

suspenders [sə'spendəz] npl (Brit: for stockings) cinto m de ligas; (Am: for trousers) suspensórios mpl.

suspense [sə'spens] n suspense m.

suspension [sə'spenʃn] n suspensão f.

suspension bridge n ponte m pênsil.

suspicion [sə'spɪʃn] n (mistrust, idea) suspeita f; (trace) vestígio m.

suspicious [sə'spɪʃəs] adj (behaviour, situation) suspeito(-ta); **to be ~ of** (distrustful) desconfiar OR suspeitar de.

sustain [sə'steɪn] vt (maintain, prolong) manter; (feed) sustentar; (suffer) sofrer; (withstand) agüentar, suportar.

SW abbr = short wave.

swallow ['swɒləʊ] n (bird) andorinha f ◆ vt & vi engolir.

swam [swæm] pt → swim.

swamp [swɒmp] n pântano m.

swan [swɒn] n cisne m.

swap [swɒp] vt (possessions, places) trocar de; (ideas, stories) trocar; **to ~ sthg for sthg** trocar algo por algo.

swarm [swɔːm] n (of bees) enxame m.

swarthy ['swɔːðɪ] adj moreno(-na).

swastika ['swɒstɪkə] n suástica f, cruz f gamada.

swat [swɒt] vt esmagar, matar.

sway [sweɪ] vt (influence) influenciar ◆ vi (swing) balançar, oscilar.

swear [sweər] (pt swore, pp sworn) vi (use rude language) praguejar; (promise) jurar ◆ vt: **to ~ to do sthg** jurar fazer algo.

swearword ['sweəwɜːd] n palavrão m, asneira f.

sweat [swet] n suor m ◆ vi suar.

sweater ['swetər] n suéter m (Br), camisola f (Port).

sweatshirt ['swetʃɜːt] n sweatshirt f, suéter m de algodão (Br), camisola f de algodão (Port).

sweaty ['swetɪ] adj (skin, clothes) suado(-da).

swede [swiːd] n (Brit) nabo m.

Swede [swiːd] n sueco m (-ca f).

Sweden ['swiːdn] n Suécia f.

Swedish ['swiːdɪʃ] adj sueco(-ca) ◆ n (language) sueco m ◆ npl: **the ~** os suecos.

sweep [swiːp] (pt & pp swept) vt (with brush, broom) varrer.

sweet [swiːt] adj doce; (smell) agradável ◆ n (Brit) (candy) bala f (Br), rebuçado m (Port); (dessert) doce m; **how ~ of you!** que gentileza a sua!

sweet-and-sour adj agridoce.

sweet corn n milho m.

sweeten ['swiːtn] vt adoçar.

sweetener ['swiːtnər] n (for drink) adoçante m.

sweetheart ['swiːthɑːt] n (term of endearment) querido m (-da f); (boyfriend or girlfriend) namorado m (-da f).

sweetness ['swiːtnɪs] n doçura f; (of

smell) fragrância *f.*

sweet pea *n* ervilha-de-cheiro *f.*

sweet potato *n* batata-doce *f.*

sweet shop *n (Brit)* confeitaria *f.*

swell [swel] *(pp swollen) vi (ankle, arm etc)* inchar.

swelling ['swelɪŋ] *n* inchaço *m.*

sweltering ['sweltərɪŋ] *adj (weather)* abrasador(-ra); *(person)* encalorado(-da).

swept [swept] *pt & pp →* sweep.

swerve [swɜːv] *vi (vehicle)* dar uma guinada.

swift [swɪft] *adj* rápido(-da) ◆ *n (bird)* andorinhão *m.*

swig [swɪg] *n (inf)* gole *m*, trago *m.*

swim [swɪm] *(pt swam, pp swum) vi (in water)* nadar ◆ *n:* **to go for a ~** ir dar um mergulho.

swimmer ['swɪmə^r] *n* nadador *m* (-ra *f*).

swimming ['swɪmɪŋ] *n* natação *f;* **to go ~** ir nadar.

swimming baths *npl (Brit)* piscina *f* municipal.

swimming cap *n* touca *f* de banho.

swimming costume *n (Brit)* traje *m* de banho *(Br)*, fato *m* de banho *(Port).*

swimming pool *n* piscina *f.*

swimming trunks *npl* calções *mpl* de banho.

swimsuit ['swɪmsuːt] *n* traje *m* de banho *(Br)*, fato *m* de banho *(Port).*

swindle ['swɪndl] *n* fraude *f.*

swine [swaɪn] *(pl inv OR -s) n (inf: person)* canalha *mf.*

swing [swɪŋ] *(pt & pp swung) n (for children)* balanço *m* ◆ *vt (move from side to side)* balançar ◆ *vi (move from side to side)* balançar-se.

swipe [swaɪp] *vt (credit card etc)* passar pela ranhura.

Swiss [swɪs] *adj* suíço(-ça) ◆ *n (person)* suíço *m* (-ça *f*) ◆ *npl:* **the ~** os suíços.

Swiss cheese *n* queijo *m* suíço.

swiss roll *n* rocambole *m* (doce) *(Br)*, torta *f* (doce) *(Port).*

switch [swɪtʃ] *n (for light, power)* interruptor *m; (for TV, radio)* botão *m* ◆ *vt (change)* mudar de; *(exchange)* trocar ◆ *vi* mudar.

⊐ **switch off** *vt sep (light, radio)* apagar, desligar; *(engine)* desligar.

⊐ **switch on** *vt sep (light, radio)* acender, ligar; *(engine)* ligar.

switchboard ['swɪtʃbɔːd] *n* PBX *m.*

Switzerland ['swɪtsələnd] *n* Suíça *f.*

swivel ['swɪvl] *vi* girar.

swollen ['swəʊln] *pp →* swell ◆ *adj (ankle, arm etc)* inchado(-da).

swoop [swuːp] *vi (fly downwards)* descer em vôo picado; *(pounce)* atacar de surpresa.

swop [swɒp] = **swap.**

sword [sɔːd] *n* espada *f.*

swordfish ['sɔːdfɪʃ] *(pl inv) n* peixe-espada *m (Br)*, agulhão *m (Port).*

swore [swɔː^r] *pt →* swear.

sworn [swɔːn] *pp →* swear.

swot [swɒt] *n (Brit: inf: person)* caxias *mf (Br)*, marrão *m* (-ona *f*) *(Port)* ◆ *vi (Brit: inf):* **to ~ for (sthg)** queimar as pestanas (em algo), marrar (para algo) *(Port).*

swum [swʌm] *pp →* swim.

swung [swʌŋ] *pt & pp →* swing.

sycamore ['sɪkəmɔː^r] *n* bordo *m*, plátano-bastardo *m.*

syllable ['sɪləbl] *n* sílaba *f.*

syllabus ['sɪləbəs] *n* programa *m* (de estudos).

symbol ['sɪmbl] *n* símbolo *m.*

symbolize ['sɪmbəlaɪz] *vt* simbolizar.

symmetry ['sɪmɪtrɪ] *n* simetria *f.*

sympathetic [ˌsɪmpə'θetɪk] *adj (understanding)* compreensivo(-va).

sympathize ['sɪmpəθaɪz] *vi:* **to ~ (with)** *(feel sorry)* compadecer-se (de); *(understand)* compreender.

sympathizer ['sɪmpəθaɪzə^r] *n* simpatizante *mf.*

sympathy ['sɪmpəθɪ] *n (understanding)* compreensão *f.*

symphony ['sɪmfənɪ] *n* sinfonia *f.*

symptom ['sɪmptəm] *n* sintoma *m.*

synagogue ['sɪnəgɒg] *n* sinagoga *f.*

syndrome ['sɪndrəʊm] *n* síndrome *f.*

synonym ['sɪnənɪm] *n* sinônimo *m;* **to be a ~ for** OR **of sthg** ser sinônimo de algo.

syntax ['sɪntæks] *n* sintaxe *f.*

synthesizer ['sɪnθəsaɪzə^r] *n* sintetizador *m.*

synthetic [sɪn'θetɪk] *adj* sintético (-ca).

syphon ['saɪfn] = **siphon.**

syringe [sɪ'rɪndʒ] *n* seringa *f.*

syrup ['sɪrəp] *n (for fruit etc)* calda *f.*

system ['sɪstəm] *n* sistema *m; (for gas, heating etc)* instalação *f.*

systematic [ˌsɪstə'mætɪk] *adj* sistemático(-ca).

T

ta [tɑː] *excl (Brit: inf)* obrigado!

tab [tæb] *n (of cloth, paper etc)* etiqueta *f*; *(bill)* conta *f*; **put it on my ~** ponha na minha conta.

table ['teɪbl] *n (piece of furniture)* mesa *f*; *(of figures etc)* quadro *m*.

tablecloth ['teɪblklɒθ] *n* toalha *f* de mesa.

table lamp *n* abajur *m* (de mesa) *(Br)*, candeeiro *m* (de mesa) *(Port)*.

tablemat ['teɪblmæt] *n* descanso *m* para pratos *(Br)*, individual *m (Port)*.

tablespoon ['teɪblspuːn] *n* colher *f* de sopa.

tablet ['tæblɪt] *n (pill)* comprimido *m*; *(of soap)* barra *f*; *(of chocolate)* tablete *f*.

table tennis *n* pingue-pongue *m*, tênis *m* de mesa.

table wine *n* vinho *m* de mesa.

tabloid ['tæblɔɪd] *n* jornal *m* sensacionalista, tablóide *m*.

tacit ['tæsɪt] *adj* tácito(-ta).

taciturn ['tæsɪtɜːn] *adj* taciturno (-na).

tack [tæk] *n (nail)* tacha *f*.

tackle ['tækl] *n (in football, hockey)* ataque *m*; *(in rugby, American football)* placagem *f*; *(for fishing)* apetrechos *mpl* ♦ *vt (in football, hockey)* carregar; *(in rugby, American football)* placar; *(deal with)* enfrentar.

tacky ['tækɪ] *adj (inf: jewellery, design etc)* cafona *(Br)*, piroso(-sa) *(Port)*.

taco ['tækəʊ] *(pl -s) n* taco *m*, espécie de crepe de farinha de milho frito recheado normalmente com carne picada e feijão (especialidade mexicana).

tact [tækt] *n* tato *m*.

tactful ['tæktfʊl] *adj* com muito tato, diplomático(-ca).

tactical ['tæktɪkl] *adj* tático(-ca).

tactics ['tæktɪks] *npl* tática *f*, estratégia *f*.

tactless ['tæktlɪs] *adj* pouco diplomático(-ca).

tadpole ['tædpəʊl] *n* girino *m*.

tag [tæg] *n (label)* etiqueta *f*.

tagliatelle [ˌtæɡljəˈtelɪ] *n* talharins *mpl*.

tail [teɪl] *n* cauda *f*.

⅃ tails *n (of coin)* coroas *fpl* ♦ *npl (formal dress)* fraque *m*.

tailback ['teɪlbæk] *n (Brit)* fila *f* de carros.

tailcoat [ˌteɪlˈkəʊt] *n* fraque *m*.

tailgate ['teɪlɡeɪt] *n (of car)* porta *f* do porta-malas.

tailor ['teɪlər] *n* alfaiate *m*.

tailor-made *adj* feito(-ta) sob medida.

tailwind ['teɪlwɪnd] *n* vento *m* de popa.

tainted ['teɪntɪd] *adj (reputation)* manchado(-da); *(profits, money)* sujo(-ja); *(Am: food)* estragado(-da).

Taiwan [ˌtaɪˈwɔːn] *n* Taiwan *s*, Formosa *f*.

take [teɪk] *(pt took, pp taken) vt* **1.** *(carry, drive, contain)* levar.

2. *(hold, grasp)* segurar.

3. *(do, make)*: **to ~ a bath/shower** tomar um banho/uma ducha; **to ~ an exam** fazer um exame; **to ~ a photo** tirar uma foto.

4. *(require)* requerer; **how long will it ~?** quanto tempo é que vai demorar?

5. *(steal)* tirar.

6. *(train, taxi, plane, bus)* apanhar.

7. *(route, path, road)* seguir por.

8. *(medicine)* tomar.

9. *(size in clothes)* vestir; *(size in shoes)* calçar; **what size do you ~?** *(in clothes)* que tamanho você veste?; *(in shoes)* que número você calça?

10. *(subtract)* tirar, subtrair.

11. *(accept)* aceitar; **do you ~ travel-**

ler's cheques? vocês aceitam cheques de viagem?; **to ~ sb's advice** seguir os conselhos de alguém.

12. *(react to)* reagir a; **to ~ sthg the wrong way** levar algo a mal.

13. *(control, power, attitude)* assumir; **to ~ charge of** assumir a responsabilidade de; **to ~ an interest in sthg** interessar-se por algo.

14. *(tolerate)* agüentar.

15. *(assume):* **I ~ it that ...** presumo que ....

16. *(pulse)* medir; *(temperature)* tirar.

17. *(rent)* alugar.

❑ **take apart** *vt sep* desmontar.

❑ **take away** *vt sep (remove)* levar; *(subtract)* tirar, subtrair.

❑ **take back** *vt sep (thing borrowed)* devolver; *(person)* levar (de volta); *(accept)* aceitar de volta; *(statement)* retirar.

❑ **take down** *vt sep (picture, decorations, curtains)* remover.

❑ **take in** *vt sep (include)* incluir; *(understand)* perceber; *(deceive)* enganar; *(clothes)* apertar.

❑ **take off** *vi (plane)* levantar vôo, decolar ♦ *vt sep (remove)* tirar; **to ~ a day/week off** *(as holiday)* tirar um dia/uma semana de folga.

❑ **take out** *vt sep (from container, pocket)* tirar; *(library book)* pegar *(Br)*, requisitar *(Port)*; *(insurance policy)* fazer; *(loan)* pedir; **to ~ sb out for dinner** convidar alguém para jantar fora.

❑ **take over** *vi* assumir o controle.

❑ **take up** *vt sep (begin)* dedicar-se a; *(use up)* ocupar; *(trousers, skirt, dress)* subir a bainha de.

takeaway [ˈteɪkəˌweɪ] *n (Brit) (shop)* loja *que vende comida para viagem*; *(food)* comida *f* para viagem.

taken [ˈteɪkn] *pp* → take.

takeoff [ˈteɪkɒf] *n (of plane)* decolagem *f.*

takeout [ˈteɪkaʊt] *(Am)* = takeaway.

takeover [ˈteɪkˌəʊvəʳ] *n (of company)* aquisição *f.*

takings [ˈteɪkɪŋz] *npl* receita *f.*

talc [tælk] = talcum powder.

talcum powder [ˈtælkəm-] *n* (pó de) talco *m.*

tale [teɪl] *n (story)* conto *m*; *(account)* história *f.*

talent [ˈtælənt] *n* talento *m.*

talented [ˈtæləntɪd] *adj* talentoso

(-osa); **she's very ~** ela tem muito talento.

talk [tɔːk] *n (conversation)* conversa *f*; *(speech)* conferência *f* ♦ *vi* falar; **to ~ to sb (about sthg)** falar com alguém (sobre algo); **to ~ with sb** falar com alguém.

❑ **talks** *npl* negociações *fpl.*

talkative [ˈtɔːkətɪv] *adj* tagarela.

talk show *n* talk-show *m*, programa *m* de entrevistas.

tall [tɔːl] *adj* alto(-ta); **how ~ are you?** qual é a sua altura?; **I'm six feet ~** meço 1.80 m.

tally [ˈtælɪ] *n* registro *m* ♦ *vi* bater certo.

talon [ˈtælən] *n* garra *f.*

tambourine [ˌtæmbəˈriːn] *n* pandeireta *f.*

tame [teɪm] *adj (animal)* domesticado(-da).

tamper [ˈtæmpəʳ] : **tamper with** *vt fus (machine)* mexer em; *(records, file)* alterar, falsificar; *(lock)* tentar forçar.

tampon [ˈtæmpɒn] *n* tampão *m.*

tan [tæn] *n (suntan)* bronzeado *m* ♦ *vi* bronzear ♦ *adj (colour)* cor-de-mel *(inv).*

tangent [ˈtændʒənt] *n (in geometry)* tangente *f*; **to go off at a ~** divagar.

tangerine [ˌtændʒəˈriːn] *n* tangerina *f.*

tangible [ˈtændʒəbl] *adj* tangível.

tangle [ˈtæŋgl] *n (mass)* emaranhado *m.*

tank [tæŋk] *n* tanque *m.*

tanker [ˈtæŋkəʳ] *n (truck)* caminhão-cisterna *m.*

tanned [tænd] *adj (suntanned)* bronzeado(-da).

Tannoy® [ˈtænɔɪ] *n* (sistema *m* de) altofalantes *mpl.*

tantalizing [ˈtæntəlaɪzɪŋ] *adj* tentador(-ra).

tantrum [ˈtæntrəm] *n*: **to have OR throw a ~** fazer birra.

tap [tæp] *n (for water)* torneira *f* ♦ *vt (hit)* bater (ligeiramente) com.

tap dance *n* sapateado *m.*

tape [teɪp] *n (cassette, video)* fita *f (Br)*, cassete *f*; *(in cassette, strip of material)* fita *f*; *(adhesive material)* fita-cola *f* ♦ *vt (record)* gravar; *(stick)* colar com fita-cola.

tape measure *n* fita *f* métrica.

taper [ˈteɪpəʳ] *vi (corridor)* tornar-se mais estreito(-ta); *(trousers)* afunilar.

tape recorder *n* gravador *m*.
tapestry ['tæpɪstrɪ] *n* tapeçaria *f*.
tap water *n* água *f* da torneira.
tar [tɑːʳ] *n* alcatrão *m*.
target ['tɑːgɪt] *n* alvo *m*.
tariff ['tærɪf] *n* (*price list*) lista *f* de preços; (*Brit: menu*) menu *m*; (*at customs*) tarifa *f*.
tarmac ['tɑːmæk] *n* (*at airport*) pista *f*.
⊔ **Tarmac®** *n* (*on road*) asfalto *m*, macadame *m* betuminoso.
tarnish ['tɑːnɪʃ] *vt* (*make dull*) embaciar; (*fig: damage*) manchar.
tarpaulin [tɑːˈpɔːlɪn] *n* lona *f* alcatroada, oleado *m*.
tart [tɑːt] *n* (*sweet*) tarte *f*.
tartan ['tɑːtn] *n* tartã *m*, tecido de lã com os xadrezes tipicamente escoseses.
tartare sauce [tɑːtə-] *n* molho *m* tártaro, molho usado para acompanhar peixe, feito com maionese, ervas aromáticas, alcaparras e pepino de conserva picado.
task [tɑːsk] *n* tarefa *f*.
tassel ['tæsl] *n* borla *f*.
taste [teɪst] *n* (*flavour*) sabor *m*, gosto *m*; (*discernment, sense*) gosto ♦ *vt* (*sample*) provar; (*detect*) detectar o sabor de ♦ *vi*: **to ~ of sthg** ter gosto de algo; **it ~s bad/good** tem um gosto ruim/bom; **to have a ~ of sthg** (*food, drink*) provar algo; (*fig: experience*) experimentar algo; **bad/good ~** mau/bom gosto.
tasteful ['teɪstful] *adj* com bom gosto.
tasteless ['teɪstlɪs] *adj* (*food*) insípido(-da); (*comment, decoration*) de mau gosto.
tasty ['teɪstɪ] *adj* saboroso(-osa).
tatters ['tætəz] *npl*: **in ~** (*clothes*) em farrapos; (*confidence, reputation*) destruído(-da).
tattoo [tə'tuː] (*pl* -s) *n* (*on skin*) tatuagem *f*; (*military display*) desfile *m* militar.
tatty ['tætɪ] *adj* (*Brit*) (*inf*) (*flat*) caindo aos pedaços; (*clothes*) surrado(-da); (*area*) degradado(-da).
taught [tɔːt] *pt & pp* → **teach**.
taunt [tɔːnt] *vt* gozar de, troçar de ♦ *n* piada *f*, boca *f* (*Port*).
Taurus ['tɔːrəs] *n* Touro *m*.
taut [tɔːt] *adj* (*rope, string*) esticado(-da); (*muscles*) tenso(-sa).
tax [tæks] *n* imposto *m*, taxa *f* ♦ *vt* (*goods*) lançar imposto sobre; (*person*)

cobrar impostos a.
taxable ['tæksəbl] *adj* tributável, sujeito(-ta) a impostos.
tax allowance *n* rendimento *m* mínimo não tributável.
taxation [tæk'seɪʃn] *n* impostos *mpl*.
tax collector *n* cobrador *m* (-ra *f*) de impostos.
tax disc *n* (*Brit*) plaqueta *f* (*Br*), selo *m* automóvel (*Port*).
tax-free *adj* isento(-ta) de imposto, tax-free (*inv*).
taxi ['tæksɪ] *n* táxi *m* ♦ *vi* (*plane*) andar (pela pista).
taxi driver *n* taxista *mf*, motorista *mf* de táxi.
tax inspector *n* fiscal *mf*.
taxi rank *n* (*Brit*) ponto *m* de táxi (*Br*), praça *f* de táxis (*Port*).
taxi stand (*Am*) = **taxi rank**.
taxpayer ['tæks,peɪəʳ] *n* contribuinte *mf*.
tax relief *n* benefício *m* fiscal.
TB *abbr* = **tuberculosis**.
T-bone steak *n* bife *m* com osso (*em forma de T*).
tea [tiː] *n* chá *m*; (*afternoon meal*) lanche *m*; (*evening meal*) jantar *m*.
tea bag *n* saquinho *m* de chá.
tea break *n* (*Brit*) pausa *f* para o chá (*durante as horas de trabalho*).
teacake ['tiːkeɪk] *n* pãozinho doce com passas.
teach [tiːtʃ] (*pt & pp* **taught**) *vt & vi* ensinar; **to ~ sb sthg, to ~ sthg to sb** ensinar algo a alguém; **to ~ sb (how) to do sthg** ensinar alguém a OR como fazer algo.
teacher ['tiːtʃəʳ] *n* professor *m* (-ra *f*).
teaching ['tiːtʃɪŋ] *n* ensino *m*.
tea cloth *n* pano *m* de prato.
tea cosy *n* (*Brit*) abafador *m* (*para o bule do chá*).
tea cozy (*Am*) = **tea cosy**.
teacup ['tiːkʌp] *n* xícara *f* de chá.
team [tiːm] *n* (*SPORT*) time *m* (*Br*), equipa *f* (*Port*); (*group*) equipe *f*.
teammate ['tiːmmeɪt] *n* colega *mf* de equipe.
teamwork ['tiːmwɜːk] *n* trabalho *m* de equipe.
teapot ['tiːpɒt] *n* bule *m*.
tear¹ [teəʳ] (*pt* **tore**, *pp* **torn**) *vt* (*rip*) rasgar ♦ *vi* (*rip*) rasgar-se; (*move quickly*) precipitar-se ♦ *n* (*rip*) rasgão *m*.

⊔ **tear up** *vt sep* rasgar.

tear² [tɪər] *n* lágrima *f*.

teardrop ['tɪədrɒp] *n* lágrima *f*.

tearful ['tɪəful] *adj (person)* em lágrimas, choroso(-osa).

tearoom ['tiːrum] *n* salão *m* de chá.

tease [tiːz] *vt (make fun of)* gozar de.

tea set *n* serviço *m* de chá.

teaspoon ['tiːspuːn] *n* colher *f* de chá.

teaspoonful ['tiːspuːnˌful] *n* colher *f* de chá.

teat [tiːt] *n (of animal)* teta *f*; *(Brit: of bottle)* bico *m (Br)*, tetina *f (Port)*.

teatime ['tiːtaɪm] *n* hora *f* do lanche.

tea towel *n* pano *m* de prato.

technical ['teknɪkl] *adj* técnico(-ca).

technical drawing *n* desenho *m* técnico.

technicality [ˌteknɪ'kælətɪ] *n (detail)* pormenor *m* técnico.

technically ['teknɪklɪ] *adv* tecnicamente.

technician [tek'nɪʃn] *n* técnico *m* (-ca *f*).

technique [tek'niːk] *n* técnica *f*.

technological [ˌteknə'lɒdʒɪkl] *adj* tecnológico(-ca).

technology [tek'nɒlədʒɪ] *n* tecnologia *f*.

teddy (bear) ['tedɪ-] *n* ursinho *m* (de pelúcia).

tedious ['tiːdjəs] *adj* tedioso(-osa).

tee [tiː] *n* tee *m*.

teenager ['tiːnˌeɪdʒər] *n* adolescente *mf*.

teens [tiːnz] *npl* adolescência *f*.

teeth [tiːθ] *pl* → tooth.

teethe [tiːð] *vi*: he's teething os dentes dele estão começando a nascer.

teetotal [tiː'təʊtl] *adj* abstêmio (-mia).

teetotaler [tiː'təʊtlər] *(Am)* = teetotaller.

teetotaller [tiː'təʊtlər] *n (Brit)* abstêmio *m* (-mia *f*).

TEFL [tefl] *(abbr of Teaching (of) English as a Foreign Language) n* ensino do inglês como língua estrangeira.

telecommunications [ˌtelɪkəmjuːnɪ'keɪʃnz] *npl* telecomunicações *fpl*.

telegram ['telɪgræm] *n* telegrama *m*.

telegraph ['telɪgrɑːf] *n* telégrafo *m* ◆ *vt* telegrafar.

telegraph pole *n* poste *m* telegráfico.

telephone ['telɪfəʊn] *n* telefone *m* ◆ *vt* telefonar para ◆ *vi* telefonar; to be on the ~ *(talking)* estar no telefone; *(connected)* ter telefone.

telephone book *n* catálogo *m (Br)*, lista *f* telefônica.

telephone booth *n* cabine *f* telefônica.

telephone box *n* cabine *f* telefônica.

telephone call *n* chamada *f* telefônica, telefonema *m*.

telephone directory *n* catálogo *m (Br)*, lista *f* telefônica.

telephone number *n* número *m* de telefone.

telephonist [tɪ'lefənɪst] *n (Brit)* telefonista *mf*.

telephoto lens [ˌtelɪ'fəʊtəʊ-] *n* teleobjetiva *f*.

telescope ['telɪskəʊp] *n* telescópio *m*.

teletext ['telɪtekst] *n* teletexto *m*.

televise ['telɪvaɪz] *vt* transmitir pela televisão.

television ['telɪˌvɪʒn] *n* televisão *f*; what's on (the) ~ tonight? o que é que tem na televisão hoje à noite?

television set *n* aparelho *m* de televisão, televisor *m*.

telex ['teleks] *n* telex *m*.

tell [tel] *(pt & pp told) vt (inform)* dizer; *(story, joke)* contar; *(truth, lie)* dizer, contar; *(distinguish)* distinguir ◆ *vi*: can you ~? dá para notar?; can you ~ me the time? podia dizer-me as horas?; to ~ sb sthg dizer algo a alguém; to ~ sb about sthg contar algo a alguém; to ~ sb how to do sthg dizer a alguém como fazer algo; to ~ sb to do sthg dizer a alguém para fazer algo; to ~ the difference ver a diferença.

⊔ **tell off** *vt sep* ralhar com, repreender.

teller ['telər] *n (in bank)* caixa *mf*.

telltale ['telteɪl] *n* fofoqueiro *m* (-ra *f*) *(Br)*, queixinhas *mf inv (Port)*.

telly ['telɪ] *n (Brit: inf)* televisão *f*.

temp [temp] *n* empregado *m* temporário (empregada *f* temporária); ◆ *vi* trabalhar como empregado temporário.

temper ['tempər] *n*: to be in a ~ estar de mau humor, estar irritado(-da); to

lose one's ~ perder a paciência, irritar-se.

temperament ['tɛmprəmənt] *n* temperamento *m*.

temperamental [,tɛmprə'mɛntl] *adj* temperamental.

temperate ['tɛmprət] *adj* temperado(-da).

temperature ['tɛmprətʃər] *n* temperatura *f*; **to have a ~** ter febre.

tempestuous [tɛm'pɛstjʊəs] *adj* tempestuoso(-osa).

temple ['tɛmpl] *n (building)* templo *m*; *(of forehead)* têmpora *f*.

temporarily [Brit 'tɛmprərəlɪ, Am ,tɛmpə'rɛrəlɪ] *adv* temporariamente.

temporary ['tɛmpərərɪ] *adj* temporário(-ria).

tempt [tɛmpt] *vt* tentar; **to be ~ed to do sthg** estar OR sentir-se tentado a fazer algo.

temptation [tɛmp'teɪʃn] *n* tentação *f*.

tempting ['tɛmptɪŋ] *adj* tentador(-ra).

ten [tɛn] *num* dez, → **six**.

tenacious [tɪ'neɪʃəs] *adj* tenaz.

tenant ['tɛnənt] *n* inquilino *m* (-na *f*).

tend [tɛnd] *vi*: **to ~ to do sthg** ter tendência para fazer algo.

tendency ['tɛndənsɪ] *n* tendência *f*.

tender ['tɛndər] *adj (affectionate)* meigo(-ga); *(sore)* dolorido(-da); *(meat)* tenro(-ra) ◆ *vt (fml: pay)* pagar.

tendon ['tɛndən] *n* tendão *m*.

tenement ['tɛnəmənt] *n* cortiço *m* (Br), prédio *m* OR bloco *m* de apartamentos (Port) *(normalmente em zonas degradadas e pobres de uma cidade)*.

tennis ['tɛnɪs] *n* tênis *m*.

tennis ball *n* bola *f* de tênis.

tennis court *n* quadra *f* de tênis (Br), campo *m* de ténis (Port).

tennis racket *n* raquete *f* de tênis.

tenor ['tɛnər] *n (singer)* tenor *m*.

tenpin bowling ['tɛnpɪn-] *n (Brit)* boliche *m* (Br), bowling *m*.

tenpins ['tɛnpɪnz] *(Am)* = **tenpin bowling**.

tense [tɛns] *adj* tenso(-sa) ◆ *n* tempo *m*; **the present ~** o presente.

tension ['tɛnʃn] *n* tensão *f*.

tent [tɛnt] *n* barraca *f*, tenda *f*.

tentacle ['tɛntəkl] *n* tentáculo *m*.

tentative ['tɛntətɪv] *adj (unconfident,*

hesitant) hesitante; *(temporary, not final)* provisório(-ria).

tenth [tɛnθ] *num* décimo(-ma), → **sixth**.

tent peg *n* estaca *f*.

tent pole *n* poste *m* de barraca.

tenuous ['tɛnjʊəs] *adj* tênue.

tepid ['tɛpɪd] *adj* tépido(-da), morno (morna).

tequila [tɪ'kiːlə] *n* tequilha *f*.

term [tɜːm] *n (word, expression)* termo *m*; *(at school)* período *m*; *(at university)* = semestre *m*; **in the long ~** a longo prazo; **in the short ~** a curto prazo; **in ~s of** no que diz respeito a; **in business ~s** do ponto de vista comercial.

☐ **terms** *npl (of contract)* termos *mpl*; *(price)* preço *m*.

terminal ['tɜːmɪnl] *adj (illness)* incurável ◆ *n* terminal *m*.

terminate ['tɜːmɪneɪt] *vi (train, bus)* terminar a viagem OR o trajeto.

terminus ['tɜːmɪnəs] *n* estação *f* terminal, terminal *m*.

terrace ['tɛrəs] *n (patio)* terraço *m*; **the ~s** *(at football ground)* a arquibancada (Br), a geral (Port).

terraced house ['tɛrəst-] *n (Brit)* casa que faz parte de uma fileira de casas do mesmo estilo e pegadas.

terrain [tɛ'reɪn] *n* terreno *m*.

terrible ['tɛrəbl] *adj* terrível; **to feel ~** sentir-se péssimo(-ma) OR muito mal.

terribly ['tɛrəblɪ] *adv (extremely)* extremamente, terrivelmente; *(very badly)* imensamente, terrivelmente; **I'm ~ sorry!** sinto muito!

terrier ['tɛrɪər] *n* terrier *m*.

terrific [tə'rɪfɪk] *adj (inf)* incrível.

terrified ['tɛrɪfaɪd] *adj* aterrorizado(-da).

terrifying ['tɛrɪfaɪɪŋ] *adj* aterrorizador(-ra).

territory ['tɛrɪtrɪ] *n* território *m*.

terror ['tɛrər] *n* terror *m*.

terrorism ['tɛrərɪzm] *n* terrorismo *m*.

terrorist ['tɛrərɪst] *n* terrorista *mf*.

terrorize ['tɛrəraɪz] *vt* aterrorizar.

terse [tɜːs] *adj* seco(-ca).

test [tɛst] *n* teste *m*; *(of blood)* análise *f* ◆ *vt (check)* testar; *(give exam to)* avaliar; *(dish, drink)* provar; **driving ~** exame *m* de motorista (Br), exame *m* de condução (Port).

testicles ['tɛstɪklz] *npl* testículos *mpl*.

testify ['tɛstɪfaɪ] *vi (JUR)* testemunhar,

testimony

testimony [*Brit* 'testɪmənɪ, *Am* 'testəməʊnɪ] *n (JUR)* testemunho *m*.

testing ['testɪŋ] *adj* difícil.

test match *n (Brit)* partida *f* internacional.

test tube *n* tubo *m* de ensaio.

test-tube baby *n* bebê *m* de proveta.

tetanus ['tetənəs] *n* tétano *m*.

text [tekst] *n (written material)* texto *m*; *(textbook)* manual *m*.

textbook ['tekstbʊk] *n* manual *m*.

textile ['tekstaɪl] *n* têxtil *m*.

texture ['tekstʃəʳ] *n* textura *f*.

Thai [taɪ] *adj* tailandês(-esa).

Thailand ['taɪlænd] *n* Tailândia *f*.

Thames [temz] *n*: **the ~** o Tâmisa.

than [weak form ðən, strong form ðæn] *conj* que ♦ *prep*: **you're better ~ me** você é melhor (do) que eu; **I'd rather stay in ~ go out** prefiro ficar em casa do que sair; **more ~ ten** mais de dez.

thank [θæŋk] *vt*: **to ~ sb (for sthg)** agradecer a alguém (por) algo.

❑ **thanks** *npl* agradecimentos *mpl* ♦ *excl* obrigado!, obrigada!; **~s to** graças a; **many ~s** muito obrigado OR obrigada.

thankful [θæŋkfʊl] *adj* agradecido (-da); **to be ~ for sthg** estar agradecido por algo.

thankless [θæŋklɪs] *adj* ingrato(-ta).

Thanksgiving [θæŋks,gɪvɪŋ] *n* Dia *m* de Ação de Graças.

thank you *excl* obrigado!, obrigada!; **~ very much!** muito obrigado!; **no ~!** não, obrigado!

that [ðæt, *weak form of pron and conj* ðət] *(pl* **those**) *adj* **1.** *(referring to thing, person mentioned)* esse (essa); **I prefer ~ book** prefiro esse livro.

2. *(referring to thing, person further away)* aquele (aquela); **~ book at the back** aquele livro lá atrás; **I'll have ~ one** quero aquele (ali) OR esse.

♦ *pron* **1.** *(referring to thing, person mentioned)* esse *m* (essa *f*); *(indefinite)* isso; **what's ~?** o que é isso?; **who's ~?** *(on the phone)* quem fala?; *(pointing)* e esse, quem é?; **~'s interesting** que interessante.

2. *(referring to thing, person further away)* aquele *m* (aquela *f*); *(indefinite)* aquilo; **is ~ Lucy?** *(pointing)* aquela é a

Lucy?; **I want those at the back** quero aqueles lá atrás; **what's ~ on the roof?** o que é aquilo no telhado?

3. *(introducing relative clause)* que; **a shop ~ sells antiques** uma loja que vende antiguidades; **the film ~ I saw** o filme que eu vi; **the room ~ I slept in** o quarto onde OR em que dormi.

♦ *adv* assim tão; **it wasn't ~ bad/good** não foi assim tão mau/bom; **it didn't cost ~ much** não custou tanto assim.

♦ *conj* que; **tell him ~ I'm going to be late** diga-lhe que vou chegar atrasado.

thatched [θætʃt] *adj (building)* com telhado de colmo.

that's [ðæts] = **that is.**

thaw [θɔː] *vi (snow, ice)* derreter ♦ *vt (frozen food)* descongelar.

the [weak form ðə, before vowel ðɪ, strong form ðiː] *definite article* **1.** *(gen)* o (a), os (as) *(pl)*; **~ book** o livro; **~ apple** a maçã; **~ girls** as meninas; **~ Wilsons** os Wilson; **to play ~ piano** tocar piano.

2. *(with an adjective to form a noun)* o (a), os (as) *(pl)*; **~ British** os britânicos; **~ young** os jovens; **~ impossible** o impossível.

3. *(in dates)*: **~ twelfth** o dia doze; **~ forties** os anos quarenta.

4. *(in titles)*: **Elizabeth ~ Second** Elizabeth Segunda.

theater [θɪətəʳ] *n (Am) (for plays, drama)* = **theatre**; *(for films)* cinema *m*.

theatre [θɪətəʳ] *n (Brit)* teatro *m*.

theatregoer [θɪətə,gəʊəʳ] *n* freqüentador *m* (-ra *f*) de teatro.

theatrical [θɪˈætrɪkl] *adj* teatral.

theft [θeft] *n* roubo *m*.

their [ðeəʳ] *adj* seu (sua), deles (delas); **~ house** a casa deles, a sua casa.

theirs [ðeəz] *pron* o seu (a sua), o/a deles (o/a delas); **a friend of ~** um amigo deles OR seu; **these books are ~** estes livros são (os) deles OR seus; **these are ours – where are ~?** estes são os nossos – onde estão os deles?

them [weak form ðəm, strong form ðem] *pron (direct object)* os *mpl* (as *fpl*); *(indirect object)* lhes; *(after prep)* eles *mpl* (elas *fpl*); **I know ~** eu os conheço; **it's ~** são eles; **send this to ~** manda-lhes isto; **tell ~** diga-lhes; **he's worse than ~** ele é pior do que eles; **Charlotte and Ricky brought it with ~** a Charlotte e o Ricky trouxeram-no com eles.

theme [θi:m] *n* tema *m*.

theme park *n* parque de diversões baseado num tema específico.

theme tune *n* tema *m* musical.

themselves [ðəm'sɛlvz] *pron (reflexive)* se; *(after prep)* eles *mpl* próprios (elas *fpl* próprias), si *mpl* próprios (si *fpl* próprias); **they did it ~** fizeram-no eles mesmos OR próprios; **they blame ~** eles culpam-se a si próprios; **they hurt ~** eles machucaram-se.

then [ðɛn] *adv (at time in past)* então, naquela altura; *(at time in future)* nessa altura; *(next, afterwards)* depois; *(in that case)* então; **from ~ on** daí em diante; **until ~** até aí.

theoretical [θɪə'rɛtɪkl] *adj* teórico (-ca), teorético(-ca).

theorize [θɪəraɪz] *vi (develop theory):* **to ~ (about sthg)** teorizar (sobre algo).

theory [θɪərɪ] *n* teoria *f*; **in ~** em teoria.

therapist [θerəpɪst] *n* terapeuta *mf*.

therapy [θerəpɪ] *n* terapia *f*.

there [ðeəʳ] *adv (available, existing, present)* lá, ali; *(at, in, to that place)* lá ◆ *pron:* **~ is/are** há; **is Bob ~, please?** *(on phone)* o Bob está?; **I'm going ~ next week** vou lá para a semana; **it's right ~ by the phone** está aí mesmo ao lado do telefone; **over ~** ali; **~'s someone at the door** tem alguém na porta; **~ are several people waiting** várias pessoas estão à espera; **~ you are** *(when giving)* aqui tem.

thereabouts [ðeərə'baʊts] *adv:* **or ~** aproximadamente.

thereafter [ðeərɑ:ftəʳ] *adv (fml)* daí em diante, conseqüentemente.

thereby [ðeəˈbaɪ] *adv (fml)* assim, conseqüentemente.

therefore [ðeəfɔ:ʳ] *adv* portanto, por isso.

there's [ðeəz] = **there is**.

thermal underwear [θɜ:ml-] *n* roupa *f* de baixo térmica.

thermometer [θə'mɒmɪtəʳ] *n* termômetro *m*.

Thermos (flask)® [θɜ:məs-] *n* garrafa *f* térmica.

thermostat [θɜ:məstæt] *n* termostato *m*.

thesaurus [θɪ'sɔ:rəs] *(pl* **-es)** *n* dicionário *m* de sinônimos.

these [ði:z] *pl* → **this**.

thesis [θi:sɪs] *(pl* **theses** [θi:si:z]) *n* tese *f*.

they [ðeɪ] *pron* eles *mpl* (elas *fpl*).

they'd [ðeɪd] = **they had, they would**.

they'll [ðeɪl] = **they shall, they will**.

they're [ðeəʳ] = **they are**.

they've [ðeɪv] = **they have**.

thick [θɪk] *adj (in size)* grosso (grossa); *(fog)* cerrado(-da); *(forest, vegetation)* denso(-sa); *(hair)* abundante; *(liquid, sauce, smoke)* espesso(-a); *(inf: stupid)* estúpido(-da); **it's 1 metre ~** tem 1 metro de espessura.

thicken [θɪkn] *vt (sauce, soup)* engrossar ◆ *vi (mist, fog)* tornar-se mais cerrado, aumentar.

thicket [θɪkɪt] *n* matagal *m*.

thickness [θɪknɪs] *n (of wood, wall, line)* espessura *f*; *(of forest, vegetation)* densidade *f*; *(of hair)* grossura *f*.

thickset [θɪk'sɛt] *adj* atarracado(-da).

thick-skinned [-'skɪnd] *adj* insensível.

thief [θi:f] *(pl* **thieves**) *n* ladrão *m* (ladra *f*).

thieve [θi:v] *vt & vi* furtar.

thieves [θi:vz] *pl* → **thief**.

thigh [θaɪ] *n* coxa *f*.

thimble [θɪmbl] *n* dedal *m*.

thin [θɪn] *adj (in size)* fino(-na); *(not fat)* magro(-gra); *(soup, sauce)* pouco espesso(-a), líquido(-da).

thing [θɪŋ] *n* coisa *f*; **the ~ is** o que se passa é que, acontece que.

◡ **things** *npl (clothes, possessions)* coisas *fpl*; **how are ~s?** *(inf)* como (é que) vão as coisas?

thingummyjig [θɪŋəmɪdʒɪg] *n (inf)* coisa *f*.

think [θɪŋk] *(pt & pp* **thought**) *vt (believe)* achar, pensar; *(have in mind, expect)* pensar ◆ *vi* pensar; **to ~ (that)** achar OR pensar que; **to ~ about** pensar em; **to ~ of** pensar em; *(remember)* lembrar-se de; **to ~ of doing sthg** pensar fazer algo; **I ~ so** acho que sim; **I don't ~ so** acho que não; **do you ~ you could ...?** você acha que podia ...?; **to ~ highly of sb** ter muito boa opinião de alguém.

◻ **think over** *vt sep* refletir sobre.

◻ **think up** *vt sep* imaginar.

third [θɜ:d] *num* terceiro(-ra), → **sixth**.

thirdly [θɜ:dlɪ] *adv* terceiro, em terceiro lugar.

third party insurance *n* seguro *m* contra terceiros.

third-rate *adj* de terceira.

Third World *n*: the ~ o Terceiro Mundo.

thirst [θɜːst] *n* sede *f*.

thirsty [θɜːstɪ] *adj*: **to be ~** ter sede.

thirteen [θɜːˈtiːn] *num* treze, → **six**.

thirteenth [θɜːˈtiːnθ] *num* décimo *m* terceiro (décima *f* terceira), → **sixth**.

thirtieth [θɜːtɪəθ] *num* trigésimo (-ma), → **sixth**.

thirty [θɜːtɪ] *num* trinta, → **six**.

this [ðɪs] (*pl* **these**) *adj* **1.** *(referring to thing, person)* este (esta); **these chocolates are delicious** estes chocolates são deliciosos; ~ **morning/week** esta manhã/semana; **I prefer ~ book** prefiro este livro; **I'll have ~ one** quero este.
2. *(inf: used when telling a story)*: **there was ~ man ...** havia um homem ....
♦ *pron (referring to thing, person)* este *m* (esta *f*); *(indefinite)* isto; ~ **is for you** isto é para ti; **what are these?** o que é isto?, o que é que são estas coisas?; ~ **is David Gregory** *(introducing someone)* este é o David Gregory; *(on telephone)* aqui fala David Gregory.
♦ *adv*: **it was ~ big** era deste tamanho; **I don't remember it being ~ tiring** não me lembro de ser tão cansativo assim.

thistle [θɪsl] *n* cardo *m*.

thorn [θɔːn] *n* espinho *m*.

thorny [θɔːnɪ] *adj* espinhoso(-osa).

thorough [θʌrə] *adj* minucioso (-osa).

thoroughbred [θʌrəbred] *n* purosangue *m inv*.

thoroughfare [θʌrəfeəʳ] *n (fml)* rua *f* principal.

thoroughly [θʌrəlɪ] *adv (completely)* completamente.

those [ðəʊz] *pl* → **that**.

though [ðəʊ] *conj* se bem que ♦ *adv* no entanto; **even ~ it was raining** apesar de estar chovendo.

thought [θɔːt] *pt & pp* → **think** ♦ *n (idea)* ideia *f*; *(thinking)* pensamento *m*; *(careful consideration)* reflexão *f*.
⏌ **thoughts** *npl (opinion)* opinião *f*.

thoughtful [θɔːtfʊl] *adj (quiet and serious)* pensativo(-va); *(considerate)* atencioso(-osa).

thoughtless [θɔːtlɪs] *adj* indelicado(-da).

thousand [θaʊznd] *num* mil; **a** OR **one ~** mil; **~s of** milhares de, → **six**.

thousandth [θaʊzntθ] *num* milésimo(-ma), → **sixth**.

thrash [θræʃ] *vt (inf: defeat heavily)* derrotar.

thread [θred] *n (of cotton etc)* linha *f* ♦ *vt (needle)* enfiar (uma linha em).

threadbare [θredbeəʳ] *adj* surrado (-da), puído(-da).

threat [θret] *n* ameaça *f*.

threaten [θretn] *vt* ameaçar; **to ~ to do sthg** ameaçar fazer algo.

threatening [θretnɪŋ] *adj* ameaçador(-ra).

three [θriː] *num* três, → **six**.

three-D *n*: in ~ em três dimensões.

three-dimensional [-dɪˈmenʃənl] *adj (picture, film, image)* em três dimensões; *(object)* tridimensional.

threefold [θriːfəʊld] *adj* triplo(-pla) ♦ *adv*: **to increase ~** triplicar.

three-piece suite *n* conjunto *m* de um sofá e duas poltronas.

three-ply *adj (wool, rope)* com três fios; *(wood)* com três espessuras.

three-quarters [ˈkwɔːtəz] *n* três quartos *mpl*; ~ **of an hour** três quartos de hora.

threshold [θreʃhəʊld] *n (fml: of door)* limiar *m*, soleira *f*.

threw [θruː] *pt* → **throw**.

thrifty [θrɪftɪ] *adj* poupado(-da).

thrill [θrɪl] *n (sudden feeling)* sensação *f*, arrepio *m*; *(exciting experience)* experiência *f* incrível ♦ *vt* emocionar, fazer vibrar de excitação.

thrilled [θrɪld] *adj* encantado(-da).

thriller [θrɪləʳ] *n* filme *m* de suspense.

thrilling [θrɪlɪŋ] *adj* emocionante, excitante.

thrive [θraɪv] *vi (plant, animal, person)* desenvolver-se; *(business, tourism, place)* prosperar.

thriving [θraɪvɪŋ] *adj (person, community, business)* próspero(-ra); *(plant)* com um bom crescimento.

throat [θrəʊt] *n* garganta *f*.

throb [θrɒb] *vi (head)* latejar; *(noise, engine)* vibrar.

throne [θrəʊn] *n* trono *m*.

throng [θrɒŋ] *n* multidão *f*.

throttle [θrɒtl] *n (of motorbike)* válvula *f* reguladora.

through [θruː] *prep (to other side of, by*

means of) através de; *(because of)* graças a; *(from beginning to end of)* durante; *(throughout)* por todo(-da) ◆ *adv (from beginning to end)* até o fim ◆ *adj*: **I'm ~ (with it)** *(finished)* já acabei; **you're ~** *(on phone)* já tem ligação; **~ traffic** trânsito de passagem; **a ~ train** um trem direto; **"no ~ road"** *(Brit)* "rua sem saída"; **Monday ~ Thursday** *(Am)* de segunda a quinta-feira; **to let sb ~** deixar alguém passar; **to go ~ sthg** atravessar algo.

throughout [θru:'aʊt] *prep (day, morning, year)* ao longo de todo(-da); *(place, country, building)* por todo(-da) ◆ *adv (all the time)* sempre, o tempo todo; *(everywhere)* por todo o lado.

throw [θrəʊ] *(pt* threw, *pp* thrown [θrəʊn]) *vt* atirar; *(javelin, dice)* lançar; *(a switch)* ligar; **to ~ sthg in the bin** jogar algo no lixo *(Br)*, deitar algo para o lixo *(Port)*.

❏ **throw away** *vt sep (get rid of)* jogar fora.

❏ **throw out** *vt sep (get rid of)* jogar fora; *(person)* pôr na rua.

❏ **throw up** *vi (inf: vomit)* vomitar.

throwaway [θrəʊə,weɪ] *adj (product)* descartável; *(bottle)* sem depósito.

throw-in *n (Brit: in football)* lançamento *m* da linha lateral.

thrown [θrəʊn] *pp →* **throw.**

thru [θru:] *(Am)* = **through.**

thrush [θrʌʃ] *n (bird)* tordo *m*.

thrust [θrʌst] *(pt & pp* thrust) *n (of sword)* estocada *f*; *(of knife)* facada *f*; *(of troops)* investida *f* ◆ *vt*: **to ~ sthg into sthg** enfiar algo em algo.

thud [θʌd] *n* barulho *m* seco.

thug [θʌg] *n* marginal *mf*.

thumb [θʌm] *n* polegar *m* ◆ *vt*: **to ~ a lift** pedir carona *(Br)*, pedir boleia *(Port)*.

thumbtack [θʌmtæk] *n (Am)* percevejo *m (Br)*, pionés *m (Port)*.

thump [θʌmp] *n (punch)* soco *m*; *(sound)* barulho *m* seco ◆ *vt* dar um soco em; **he ~ed him** ele deu-lhe um soco.

thunder [θʌndəʳ] *n* trovões *mpl*, trovoada *f*.

thunderbolt [θʌndəbəʊlt] *n* raio *m*.

thunderclap [θʌndəklæp] *n* trovão *m*.

thunderstorm [θʌndəstɔ:m] *n* tem-

pestade *f* (acompanhada de trovoada), temporal *m*.

thundery [θʌndərɪ] *adj* de trovoada.

Thurs. *(abbr of Thursday)* 5ª, quin.

Thursday [θɜ:zdɪ] *n* quinta-feira *f*, → **Saturday.**

thus [ðʌs] *adv (fml) (as a consequence)* conseqüentemente, por conseguinte; *(in this way)* assim.

thwart [θwɔ:t] *vt* gorar.

thyme [taɪm] *n* tomilho *m*.

thyroid [θaɪrɔɪd] *n* tiróide *f*.

tiara [tɪ'ɑːrə] *n* diadema *m*.

Tibet [tɪ'bet] *n* Tibete *m*.

tic [tɪk] *n* tique *m*.

tick [tɪk] *n (written mark)* sinal *m* de visto; *(insect)* carrapato *m (Br)*, carraça *f (Port)* ◆ *vt* marcar OR assinalar (com sinal de visto) ◆ *vi (clock, watch)* fazer tiquetaque.

❏ **tick off** *vt sep (mark off)* marcar OR assinalar (com sinal de visto).

ticket [tɪkɪt] *n (for travel, cinema, match)* bilhete *m*; *(label)* etiqueta *f*; *(for traffic offence)* multa *f*.

ticket collector *n* revisor *m (-ra f)*.

ticket inspector *n* revisor *m (-ra f)*.

ticket machine *n* distribuidor *m* automático de bilhetes.

ticket office *n* bilheteira *f*.

tickle [tɪkl] *vt* fazer cócegas a ◆ *vi* fazer cócegas.

ticklish [tɪklɪʃ] *adj*: **to be ~** ter cócegas.

tick-tack-toe *n (Am)* jogo-da-velha *m (Br)*, jogo *m* de galo *(Port)*.

tidal [taɪdl] *adj (river)* com marés; *(barrier)* contra a maré.

tidbit [tɪdbɪt] *(Am)* = **titbit.**

tiddlywinks [tɪdlɪwɪŋks] *n (game)* jogo *m* de fichas *(Br)*, jogo *m* da pulga *(Port)*.

tide [taɪd] *n (of sea)* maré *f*.

tidy [taɪdɪ] *adj (room, desk, person)* arrumado(-da); *(hair, clothes)* cuidado (-da).

❏ **tidy up** *vt sep* arrumar.

tie [taɪ] *(pt & pp* tied, *cont* tying) *n (around neck)* gravata *f*; *(draw)* empate *m*; *(Am: on railway track)* dormente *m (Br)*, chulipa *f (Port)* ◆ *vt* atar; *(knot)* fazer, dar ◆ *vi (draw)* empatar.

❏ **tie up** *vt sep* atar; *(delay)* atrasar.

tiebreak(er) [taɪbreɪk(əʳ)] *n (in tennis)* tie-break *m*; *(extra question)* pergunta f de desempate.

tiepin ['taɪpɪn] n alfinete m de gravata.

tier [tɪəʳ] n (of seats) fila f, fileira f.

tiff [tɪf] n desentendimento m.

tiger ['taɪgəʳ] n tigre m.

tight [taɪt] adj apertado(-da); (drawer, tap) preso(-sa); (rope, material) esticado(-da); (inf: drunk) bêbado(-da) ♦ adv (hold) com força, bem; **my chest feels ~** estou um pouco congestionado (dos brônquios).

tighten ['taɪtn] vt apertar.

tightfisted [,taɪt'fɪstɪd] adj (inf) sovina.

tightly ['taɪtlɪ] adj (hold, fasten) com força.

tightrope ['taɪtrəʊp] n corda f bamba.

tights [taɪts] npl meia-calça f (Br), collants mpl (Port); **a pair of ~** um par de meias-calças, umas meias-calças.

tile ['taɪl] n (for roof) telha f; (for floor) ladrilho m; (for wall) azulejo m.

tiled [taɪld] adj (roof) de telha; (floor) de ladrilhos; (wall) de azulejos.

till [tɪl] n caixa f registradora ♦ prep & conj até; **I'll wait ~ he arrives** esperarei até ele chegar OR até que ele chegue.

tiller ['tɪləʳ] n barra f do leme.

tilt [tɪlt] vt inclinar ♦ vi inclinar-se.

timber ['tɪmbəʳ] n (wood) madeira f; (of roof) trave f.

time [taɪm] n tempo m; (measured by clock) horas fpl; (moment) altura f; (occasion) vez f ♦ vt (measure) cronometrar; (arrange) prever; **I haven't got (the) ~** não tenho tempo; **it's ~ to go** está na hora de irmos embora; **what's the ~?** que horas são?; **do you have the ~, please?** você tem horas, por favor?; **two ~s** two dois vezes dois; **five ~s as much** cinco vezes mais; **in a month's ~** daqui a um mês; **to have a good ~** divertir-se; **all the ~** sempre, o tempo todo; **every ~** sempre; **from ~ to ~** de vez em quando, de tempos em tempos; **for the ~ being** por enquanto; **in ~** (arrive) a tempo; **in good ~** com tempo; **last ~** a última vez; **most of the ~** a maior parte do tempo; **on ~** na hora; **some of the ~** parte do tempo; **this ~** desta vez; **two at a ~** dois de cada vez.

time difference n diferença f horária.

time lag n intervalo m.

timeless ['taɪmlɪs] adj eterno(-na).

time limit n prazo m, limite m de tempo.

timely ['taɪmlɪ] adj oportuno(-na).

time off n tempo m livre; **to take ~** tirar férias.

time-out n (SPORT) tempo m morto.

timer ['taɪməʳ] n cronômetro m, relógio m.

time scale n período m.

time share n propriedade adquirida por várias pessoas com o direito de utilizá-la por um determinado período a cada ano durante as suas férias.

timetable ['taɪm,teɪbl] n horário m; (of events) programa m.

time zone n fuso m horário.

timid ['tɪmɪd] adj tímido(-da).

timing ['taɪmɪŋ] n: **the ~ of the remark was unfortunate** o comentário foi feito num momento extremamente inoportuno; **the ~ of the election is crucial** a data das eleições é fundamental.

tin [tɪn] n (metal) estanho m; (container) lata f ♦ adj de estanho, de lata.

tin can n lata f.

tinfoil ['tɪnfɔɪl] n papel m OR folha f de alumínio.

tinge [tɪndʒ] n ponta f.

tingle ['tɪŋgl] vi: **my feet are tingling** meus pés estão formigando.

tinker ['tɪŋkəʳ] vi: **to ~ with sthg** mexer em algo.

tinkle ['tɪŋkl] n (Brit: inf: phone call): **to give sb a ~** dar uma ligada para alguém.

tinned food [tɪnd-] n (Brit) comida f enlatada, conservas fpl.

tin opener [-,əʊpnəʳ] n (Brit) abridor m de latas (Br), abre-latas m inv (Port).

tinsel ['tɪnsl] n fios mpl de ouropel (usados para decorar a árvore de Natal).

tint [tɪnt] n (for hair) tinta f (para o cabelo).

tinted glass [,tɪntɪd-] n vidro m colorido OR fumê.

tiny ['taɪnɪ] adj pequenininho(-nha), minúsculo(-la).

tip [tɪp] n (point, end) ponta f; (to waiter, taxi driver etc) gorjeta f; (piece of advice) dica f; (rubbish dump) depósito m de lixo (Br), lixeira f (Port) ♦ vt (waiter, taxi driver etc) dar uma gorjeta a; (tilt) inclinar; (pour) despejar.

◻ **tip over** vt sep entornar ◆ vi entornar-se.

tipped [tɪpt] adj (cigarette) com filtro.

tipsy ['tɪpsɪ] adj (inf) alegre.

tiptoe ['tɪptəʊ] vi andar na ponta dos pés ◆ n: **on ~** na ponta dos pés.

tire ['taɪəʳ] vi cansar-se ◆ n (Am) = **tyre**.

tired ['taɪəd] adj cansado(-da); **to be ~ of** (fed up with) estar farto(-ta) de.

tired out adj exausto(-ta), esgotado(-da).

tireless ['taɪəlɪs] adj incansável.

tiresome ['taɪəsəm] adj cansativo(-va), entediante.

tiring ['taɪərɪŋ] adj cansativo(-va).

tissue ['tɪʃuː] n (handkerchief) lenço m de papel.

tissue paper n papel m de seda.

tit [tɪt] n (vulg: breast) mama f.

titbit ['tɪtbɪt] n (Brit: of food) guloseima f.

titillate ['tɪtɪleɪt] vt excitar, titilar.

title ['taɪtl] n título m.

titter ['tɪtəʳ] vi rir-se baixinho.

T-junction n cruzamento m (em forma de T).

to [unstressed before consonant tə, unstressed before vowel tʊ. stressed tuː] prep
1. (indicating direction) para; **to go ~ Brazil** ir ao Brasil; **to go ~ school** ir para a escola.
2. (indicating position) a; **~ the left/right** à esquerda/direita.
3. (expressing indirect object) a; **to give sthg ~ sb** dar algo a alguém; **give it ~ me** dê-me isso; **to listen ~ the radio** ouvir rádio.
4. (indicating reaction, effect): **~ my surprise** para surpresa minha; **it's ~ your advantage** é em seu benefício.
5. (until) até; **to count ~ ten** contar até dez; **we work from nine ~ five** trabalhamos das nove (até) às cinco.
6. (in stating opinion) para; **~ me, he's lying** para mim, ele está mentindo.
7. (indicating change of state): **to turn ~ sthg** transformar-se em algo; **it could lead ~ trouble** pode vir a dar problemas.
8. (Brit: in expressions of time) para; **it's ten ~ three** são dez para as três; **at quarter ~ seven** às quinze para as sete.
9. (in ratios, rates): **40 miles ~ the gallon** ~ 7 litros por cada 100 quilômetros.

10. (of, for): **the answer ~ the question** a resposta à pergunta; **the key ~ the car** a chave do carro; **a letter ~ my daughter** uma carta para a minha filha.
11. (indicating attitude) (para) com; **to be rude ~ sb** ser grosseiro (para) com alguém.
◆ with infinitive **1.** (forming simple infinitive): **~ walk** andar; **~ laugh** rir.
2. (following another verb): **to begin ~ do sthg** começar a fazer algo; **to try ~ do sthg** tentar fazer algo.
3. (following an adjective): **difficult ~ do** difícil de fazer; **pleased ~ meet you** prazer em conhecê-lo; **ready ~ go** pronto para partir.
4. (indicating purpose) para; **we came here ~ look at the castle** viemos para ver o castelo.

toad [təʊd] n sapo m.

toadstool ['təʊdstuːl] n cogumelo m venenoso.

toast [təʊst] n (bread) torradas fpl; (when drinking) brinde m ◆ vt (bread) torrar; **a piece OR slice of ~** uma torrada.

toasted sandwich ['təʊstɪd-] n sanduíche m quente (Br), tosta f (Port).

toaster ['təʊstəʳ] n torradeira f.

toastie ['təʊstɪ] = **toasted sandwich**.

tobacco [tə'bækəʊ] n tabaco m.

tobacconist's [tə'bækənɪsts] n tabacaria f.

toboggan [tə'bɒgən] n tobogã m.

today [tə'deɪ] n hoje m ◆ adv (on current day) hoje; (these days) hoje em dia.

toddler ['tɒdləʳ] n criança f (que começa a dar os primeiros passos).

toddy ['tɒdɪ] n = ponche m quente.

to-do (pl -s) (inf) confusão f, rebuliço m.

toe [təʊ] n (of person) dedo m do pé.

toe clip n estribo m do pedal.

toenail ['təʊneɪl] n unha f do pé.

toffee ['tɒfɪ] n puxa-puxa m (Br), caramelo m (Port).

toga ['təʊgə] n toga f.

together [tə'geðəʳ] adv juntos(-tas); **~ with** juntamente OR junto com.

toil [tɔɪl] n (fml) labuta f ◆ vi (fml) trabalhar sem descanso, labutar.

toilet ['tɔɪlɪt] n (room) banheiro m (Br), casa f de banho (Port); (bowl) vaso *m* sanitário *(Br)*, sanita *f (Port)*; **to go to the ~** ir ao banheiro; **where's the ~?** onde é o banheiro?

toilet bag *n* estojo *m* de toilette.

toilet paper *n* papel *m* higiênico.

toiletries ['tɔɪlɪtrɪz] *npl* artigos *mpl* de toalete.

toilet roll *n* rolo *m* de papel higiênico.

toilet water *n* água-de-colônia *f*.

token ['tɔʊkn] *n* (metal disc) ficha *f*.

told [tɔʊld] *pt & pp →* **tell**.

tolerable ['tɒlərəbl] *adj* tolerável.

tolerance ['tɒlərəns] *n* tolerância *f*.

tolerant ['tɒlərənt] *adj* tolerante.

tolerate ['tɒləreɪt] *vt* tolerar.

toll [tɔʊl] *n* (for road, bridge) pedágio *m* (Br), portagem *f* (Port).

tollbooth ['tɔʊlbuːθ] *n* pedágio *m* (Br), portagem *f* (Port).

toll-free *adj* (Am) gratuito(-ta).

tomato [Brit tə'mɑːtəʊ, Am tə'meɪtəʊ] (pl -es) *n* tomate *m*.

tomato juice *n* suco *m* de tomate.

tomato ketchup *n* ketchup *m*.

tomato puree *n* concentrado *m* de tomate.

tomato sauce *n* molho *m* de tomate.

tomb [tuːm] *n* túmulo *m*.

tomboy ['tɒmbɔɪ] *n* menina *f* moleque *(Br)*, maria-rapaz *f* (Port).

tombstone ['tuːmstəʊn] *n* lápide *f*, pedra *f* tumular.

tomcat ['tɒmkæt] *n* gato *m* (macho).

tomorrow [tə'mɒrəʊ] *n* amanhã *m* ♦ *adv* amanhã; **the day after ~** depois de amanhã; **~ afternoon** amanhã à tarde; **~ morning** amanhã de manhã; **~ night** amanhã à noite.

ton [tʌn] *n* (in Britain) = 1016 kg; (in U.S.) = 907 kg; (metric tonne) tonelada *f*; **~s of** (inf) toneladas de.

tone [tɔʊn] *n* (of voice, colour) tom *m*; (on phone) sinal *m*.

tongs [tɒŋz] *npl* (for hair) ferro *m* (para enrolar o cabelo); (for sugar) pinça *f*.

tongue [tʌŋ] *n* língua *f*.

tongue-in-cheek *adj* irônico(-ca).

tongue-tied *adj* incapaz de falar (por timidez ou nervos).

tongue-twister *n* trava-língua *m*, expressão *f* difícil de dizer.

tonic ['tɒnɪk] *n* (tonic water) água *f* tônica; (medicine) tônico *m*.

tonic water *n* água *f* tônica.

tonight [tə'naɪt] *n* esta noite *f* ♦ *adv* hoje à noite.

tonne [tʌn] *n* tonelada *f*.

tonsil ['tɒnsl] *n* amígdala *f*.

tonsillitis [ˌtɒnsɪ'laɪtɪs] *n* amigdalite *f*.

too [tuː] *adv* (excessively) demais, demasiado; (also) também; **it's not ~ good** não é lá muito bom; **it's ~ late to go out** é tarde demais OR é demasiado tarde para sair; **~ many** demasiados(-das); **~ much** demasiado(-da).

took [tʊk] *pt →* **take**.

tool [tuːl] *n* ferramenta *f*.

tool box *n* caixa *f* da ferramenta.

tool kit *n* jogo *m* de ferramentas.

tooth [tuːθ] (pl **teeth**) *n* dente *m*.

toothache ['tuːθeɪk] *n* dor *f* de dentes.

toothbrush ['tuːθbrʌʃ] *n* escova *f* de dentes.

toothpaste ['tuːθpeɪst] *n* pasta *f* de dentes.

toothpick ['tuːθpɪk] *n* palito *m* (para os dentes).

top [tɒp] *adj* (highest) de cima; (best, most important) melhor ♦ *n* (highest part) topo *m*, alto *m*; (of table, bed) cabeçeira *f*; (best point) primeiro *m* (-ra *f*); (lid, cap) tampa *f*; (garment) blusa *f* (Br), camisola *f* (Port); (of street, road) final *m* (Br), cimo *m* (Port); **at the ~ (of)** (in highest part) no topo (de); **on ~ of** (on highest part of) em cima de; (of mountain) no topo de; (in addition to) além de; **at ~ speed** a toda velocidade; **~ gear** = quinta *f*.

❑ **top up** *vt sep* (glass, drink) voltar a encher ♦ *vi* (with petrol) completar (Br), atestar (Port).

top floor *n* último andar *m*.

top hat *n* cartola *f*.

topic ['tɒpɪk] *n* tópico *m*.

topical ['tɒpɪkl] *adj* atual.

topless ['tɒplɪs] *adj*: **to go ~** fazer topless.

topmost ['tɒpməʊst] *adj* mais alto(-ta).

topped [tɒpt] *adj*: **~ with sthg** (food) com algo (por cima).

topping ['tɒpɪŋ] *n*: **with a chocolate ~** coberto(-ta) com chocolate; **the ~ of your choice** (on pizza) com os ingredientes que desejar.

topple ['tɒpl] *vt* derrubar ♦ *vi* cair.

top-secret *adj* altamente secreto (-ta).

topspin ['tɒpspɪn] *n* topspin *m*, efeito *m* por cima.

topsy-turvy [ˌtɒpsɪ'tɜːvɪ] *adj* de pernas para o ar.

torch [tɔːtʃ] *n* (*Brit: electric light*) lanterna *f*.

tore [tɔːʳ] *pt* → **tear¹**.

torment [tɔː'ment] *vt* (*annoy*) atormentar.

torn [tɔːn] *pp* → **tear¹** ♦ *adj* (*ripped*) rasgado(-da).

tornado [tɔː'neɪdəʊ] (*pl* **-es** OR **-s**) *n* tornado *m*.

torpedo [tɔː'piːdəʊ] (*pl* **-es**) *n* torpedo *m*.

torrent ['tɒrənt] *n* torrente *f*.

torrential [tɒ'renʃəl] *adj* torrencial.

torrid ['tɒrɪd] *adj* (*hot*) tórrido(-da); (*passionate*) abrasador(-ra).

tortoise ['tɔːtəs] *n* tartaruga *f*.

tortoiseshell ['tɔːtəʃel] *n* tartaruga *f* (*material*).

torture ['tɔːtʃəʳ] *n* tortura ♦ *vt* torturar.

Tory ['tɔːrɪ] *n* conservador *m* (-ra *f*), *membro do partido conservador britânico.*

toss [tɒs] *vt* (*throw*) atirar; (*coin*) atirar ao ar; (*salad, vegetables*) misturar, mexer.

tot [tɒt] *n* (*inf: small child*) pequeno *m* (-na *f*), pequerrucho *m* (-cha *f*) (*Port*); (*of drink*) trago *m*.

total ['təʊtl] *adj* total ♦ *n* total *m*; **in ~** no total.

totalitarian [ˌtəʊtælɪ'teərɪən] *adj* totalitário(-ria).

totally ['təʊtəlɪ] *adv* (*entirely*) totalmente, completamente; **I ~ agree** concordo plenamente.

totter ['tɒtəʳ] *vi* cambalear.

touch [tʌtʃ] *n* (*sense*) tato *m*; (*small amount*) pitada *f*; (*detail*) toque *m*, retoque *m* ♦ *vt* tocar em; (*move emotionally*) tocar ♦ *vi* tocar-se; **to get in ~ (with sb)** entrar em contato (com alguém); **to keep in ~ (with sb)** manter o contato (com alguém).

⌐ **touch down** *vi* (*plane*) aterrissar (*Br*), aterrar (*Port*).

touchdown ['tʌtʃdaʊn] *n* (*of plane*) aterrissagem *f* (*Br*), aterragem *f* (*Port*); (*in American football*) ensaio *m*.

touched [tʌtʃt] *adj* (*grateful*) comovido(-da).

touching ['tʌtʃɪŋ] *adj* (*moving*) comovente.

touchline ['tʌtʃlaɪn] *n* linha *f* de fundo.

touchy ['tʌtʃɪ] *adj* (*person*) suscetível; (*subject, question*) melindroso(-osa).

tough [tʌf] *adj* (*resilient*) forte; (*hard, strong*) resistente; (*meat, terms, policies*) duro(-ra); (*difficult*) difícil.

toughen ['tʌfn] *vt* endurecer.

toupee ['tuːpeɪ] *n* chinó *m*.

tour [tʊəʳ] *n* (*journey*) volta *f*; (*of city, castle etc*) visita *f*; (*of pop group, theatre company*) turnê *f*, digressão *f* ♦ *vt* visitar, viajar por; **on ~** em turnê OR digressão.

tourism ['tʊərɪzm] *n* turismo *m*.

tourist ['tʊərɪst] *n* turista *mf*.

tourist class *n* classe *f* turística.

tourist information office *n* centro *m* de turismo.

tournament ['tɔːnəmənt] *n* torneio *m*.

tour operator *n* agência *f* OR operador *m* de viagens.

tout [taʊt] *n* cambista *mf* (*Br*), revendedor *m* (-ra *f*) de bilhetes (*a um preço mais alto*) (*Port*).

tow [təʊ] *vt* rebocar.

toward [tə'wɔːd] (*Am*) = **towards**.

towards [tə'wɔːdz] *prep* (*Brit*) (*in the direction of*) em direção a; (*facing, to help pay for*) para; (*with regard to*) para com; (*near, around*) perto de.

towaway zone ['təʊəweɪ-] *n* (*Am*) *zona de estacionamento proibido sob pena de reboque.*

towel ['taʊəl] *n* toalha *f*.

toweling ['taʊəlɪŋ] (*Am*) = **towelling**.

towelling ['taʊəlɪŋ] *n* (*Brit*) tecido *m* para toalhas, (pano) turco *m* (*Port*).

towel rail *n* toalheiro *m*.

tower ['taʊəʳ] *n* torre *f*.

tower block *n* (*Brit*) arranha-céu *m*, espigão *m*.

Tower Bridge *n* Tower Bridge *f*, *famosa ponte levadiça londrina.*

towering ['taʊərɪŋ] *adj* muito alto(-ta).

Tower of London *n*: **the ~** a torre de Londres.

town [taʊn] *n* (*small*) vila *f*; (*larger*) cidade *f*; (*town centre*) centro *m* (da cidade).

town centre *n* centro *m* da cidade.

town council *n* ~ câmara *f* municipal.

town hall *n* prefeitura *f (Br)*, câmara *f* municipal *(Port)*.

town planning *n (study)* urbanismo *m*.

towpath ['tɔupɑ:θ] *n* caminho *m* de sirga.

towrope ['tɔurɔup] *n* cabo *m* de reboque.

tow truck *n (Am)* reboque *m*.

toxic ['tɒksɪk] *adj* tóxico(-ca).

toy [tɔɪ] *n* brinquedo *m*.

toy shop *n* loja *f* de brinquedos.

trace [treɪs] *n* indício *m*, vestígio *m* ♦ *vt (find)* localizar.

tracing paper ['treɪsɪŋ-] *n* papel *m* vegetal OR de decalque.

track [træk] *n (path)* caminho *m*; *(of railway)* via *f*; *(SPORT)* pista *f*; *(song)* música *f*.

❏ **track down** *vt sep* localizar.

tracksuit ['træksu:t] *n* roupa *f* de treino OR jogging *(Br)*, fato *m* de treino *(Port)*.

traction ['trækʃn] *n (MED)*: **in ~** sob tração.

tractor ['træktə'] *n* trator *m*.

trade [treɪd] *n (COMM)* comércio *m*; *(job)* ofício *m* ♦ *vt* trocar ♦ *vi* comercializar, negociar.

trade fair *n* feira *f* industrial.

trade-in *n* troca *f*, *sistema que consiste em dar um artigo velho como entrada para comprar um novo*.

trademark ['treɪdmɑ:k] *n* marca *f* (registrada).

trader ['treɪdə'] *n* comerciante *mf*.

tradesman ['treɪdzmən] *(pl -men* [-mən]*) n (deliveryman)* entregador *m*; *(shopkeeper)* comerciante *m*.

trade union *n* sindicato *m*.

trading ['treɪdɪŋ] *n* comércio *m*.

tradition [trə'dɪʃn] *n* tradição *f*.

traditional [trə'dɪʃənl] *adj* tradicional.

traffic ['træfɪk] *(pt & pp -ked, cont -king) n (cars etc)* trânsito *m* ♦ *vi*: **to ~ in** traficar.

traffic circle *n (Am)* rotunda *f*.

traffic island *n* placa *f* (de refúgio para pedestres).

traffic jam *n* engarrafamento *m*.

trafficker ['træfɪkə'] *n* traficante *mf*.

traffic lights *npl* sinais *mpl* de trânsito, semáforos *mpl*.

traffic warden *n (Brit)* guarda *mf*

de trânsito *(Br)*, polícia *mf* de trânsito *(Port)*.

tragedy ['trædʒədɪ] *n* tragédia *f*.

tragic ['trædʒɪk] *adj* trágico(-ca).

trail [treɪl] *n (path)* caminho *m*; *(marks)* rasto *m* ♦ *vi (be losing)* estar perdendo.

trailer ['treɪlə'] *n (for boat, luggage)* atrelado *m*, reboque *m*; *(Am: caravan)* trailer *m (Br)*, caravana *f (Port)*; *(for film, programme)* trailer *m*, excertos *mpl*.

train [treɪn] *n (on railway)* trem *m (Br)*, comboio *m (Port)* ♦ *vt & vi* treinar; **by ~** de trem.

train driver *n* maquinista *mf*.

trained [treɪnd] *adj* qualificado(-da).

trainee [treɪ'ni:] *n* estagiário *m* (-ria *f*).

trainer ['treɪnə'] *n (of athlete etc)* treinador *m* (-ra *f*).

❏ **trainers** *npl (Brit: shoes)* tênis *m inv (Br)*, sapatilhas *fpl (Port)*.

training ['treɪnɪŋ] *n (instruction)* estágio *m*; *(exercises)* treino *m*.

training shoes *npl (Brit)* tênis *m inv (Br)*, sapatilhas *fpl (Port)*.

trait [treɪt] *n* traço *m*.

traitor ['treɪtə'] *n* traidor *m* (-ra *f*).

trajectory [trə'dʒektərɪ] *n* trajetória *f*.

tram [træm] *n (Brit)* bonde *m (Br)*, eléctrico *m (Port)*.

tramp [træmp] *n* vagabundo *m* (-da *f*), mendigo *m* (-ga *f*).

trample ['træmpl] *vt* espezinhar.

trampoline ['træmpəli:n] *n* trampolim *m*.

trance [trɑ:ns] *n* transe *m*.

tranquil ['træŋkwɪl] *adj* tranqüilo (-la), sereno(-na).

tranquilizer ['træŋkwɪlaɪzər] *(Am)* = **tranquillizer**.

tranquillizer ['træŋkwɪlaɪzə'] *n (Brit)* calmante *m*.

transaction [træn'zækʃn] *n* transação *f*.

transatlantic [,trænzət'læntɪk] *adj* transatlântico(-ca).

transcend [træn'send] *vt* transcender.

transcript ['trænskrɪpt] *n* transcrição *f*.

transfer [*n* 'trænsfɜ:', *vb* træns'fɜ:'] *n* transferência *f*; *(picture)* decalcomania *f*; *(Am: ticket)* bilhete que permite fazer transferências durante a viagem ♦ *vt*

transferir ♦ *vi (change bus, plane etc)* efetuar transferências; "**~s**" *(in airport)* "transferências" *(Br)*, "transbordos" *(Port)*.

transfer desk *n* balcão *m* de informação para passageiros em trânsito.

transform [trænsˈfɔːm] *vt* transformar.

transfusion [trænsˈfjuːʒn] *n* transfusão *f.*

transient [ˈtrænzɪənt] *adj* passageiro (-ra).

transistor radio [trænˈzɪstər-] *n* transistor *m.*

transit [ˈtrænsɪt] : **in transit** *adv* durante a viagem.

transitive [ˈtrænzɪtɪv] *adj* transitivo (-va).

transit lounge *n* sala *f* de espera *(para onde vão os passageiros em trânsito).*

transitory [ˈtrænzɪtrɪ] *adj* transitório(-ria).

translate [trænsˈleɪt] *vt* traduzir.

translation [trænsˈleɪʃn] *n* tradução *f.*

translator [trænsˈleɪtər] *n* tradutor *m* (-ra *f*).

transmission [trænzˈmɪʃn] *n* transmissão *f.*

transmit [trænzˈmɪt] *vt* transmitir.

transmitter [trænzˈmɪtər] *n* transmissor *m.*

transparency [trænsˈpærənsɪ] *n (for overhead projector)* transparência *f*, diapositivo *m (Br)*, acetato *m (Port).*

transparent [trænsˈpærənt] *adj* transparente.

transplant [ˈtrænsplɑːnt] *n* transplante *m.*

transport [*n* ˈtrænspɔːt, *vb* trænsˈpɔːt] *n* transporte *m* ♦ *vt* transportar.

transportation [trænspɔːˈteɪʃn] *n (Am)* transporte *m.*

transpose [trænsˈpəʊz] *vt* inverter a ordem de.

trap [træp] *n* armadilha *f* ♦ *vt*: **to be trapped** *(stuck)* estar preso(-sa).

trapdoor [ˌtræpˈdɔːr] *n* alçapão *m.*

trapeze [trəˈpiːz] *n* trapézio *m.*

trash [træʃ] *n (Am)* lixo *m.*

trashcan [ˈtræʃkæn] *n (Am)* lata *f* de lixo *(Br)*, contentor *m* de lixo *(Port).*

trauma [ˈtrɔːmə] *n* trauma *m.*

traumatic [trɔːˈmætɪk] *adj* traumático(-ca).

travel [ˈtrævl] *n* viagem *f* ♦ *vt (distance)* percorrer ♦ *vi* viajar.

travel agency *n* agência *f* de viagens.

travel agent *n* agente *mf* de viagens; **~'s** *(shop)* agência *f* de viagens.

Travelcard [ˈtrævlkɑːd] *n* bilhete normalmente válido por um dia para viajar nos transportes públicos de Londres.

travel centre *n (in railway, bus station)* balcão *m* de informações e venda de bilhetes.

traveler [ˈtrævlər] *(Am)* = **traveller**.

travel insurance *n* seguro *m* de viagem.

traveller [ˈtrævlər] *n (Brit)* viajante *mf.*

traveller's cheque *n* traveller's cheque *m*, cheque *m* de viagem.

travelsick [ˈtrævlsɪk] *adj* enjoado(-da) *(durante uma viagem).*

travesty [ˈtrævəstɪ] *n* paródia *f.*

trawler [ˈtrɔːlər] *n* traineira *f.*

tray [treɪ] *n* bandeja *f*, tabuleiro *m.*

treacherous [ˈtretʃərəs] *adj (person)* traiçoeiro(-ra); *(roads, conditions)* perigoso(-osa).

treachery [ˈtretʃərɪ] *n* traição *f.*

treacle [ˈtriːkl] *n (Brit)* melaço *m.*

tread [tred] *(pt* trod, *pp* trodden) *n (of tyre)* piso *m*, zona *f* de rolagem ♦ *vi*: **to ~ on sthg** pisar em algo.

treason [ˈtriːzn] *n* traição *f.*

treasure [ˈtreʒər] *n* tesouro *m.*

treasurer [ˈtreʒərər] *n* tesoureiro *m* (-ra *f*).

treat [triːt] *vt* tratar ♦ *n (special thing)* presente *m*, **to ~ sb to sthg** oferecer algo a alguém.

treatise [ˈtriːtɪs] *n*: **~ (on sthg)** tratado *m* (sobre algo).

treatment [ˈtriːtmənt] *n* tratamento *m.*

treaty [ˈtriːtɪ] *n* tratado *m.*

treble [ˈtrebl] *adj* triplo(-pla).

tree [triː] *n* árvore *f.*

treetop [ˈtriːtɒp] *n* copa *f* (de árvore).

tree-trunk *n* tronco *m* de árvore.

trek [trek] *n* caminhada *f.*

trellis [ˈtrelɪs] *n* grade *f* de ripas cruzadas.

tremble [ˈtrembl] *vi* tremer.

tremendous [trɪˈmendəs] *adj (very large)* tremendo(-da); *(inf: very good)* espetacular.

tremor ['tremə'] n (small earthquake) sismo m, tremor m de terra.

trench [trentʃ] n (ditch) vala f; (MIL.) trincheira f.

trend [trend] n tendência f.

trendy ['trendı] adj (inf) (person) que segue a moda; (place) muito na moda.

trespass ['trespəs] vi trespassar; "no ~ing" "entrada proibida".

trespasser ['trespəsə'] n intruso m (-sa f); "~s will be prosecuted" "é proibido passar, sob pena de multa".

trestle table n mesa f de cavalete.

trial ['traıəl] n (JUR) julgamento m; (test) prova f; a ~ period um período de experiência.

triangle ['traıæŋgl] n triângulo m.

triangular [traı'æŋgjulə'] adj triangular.

tribe [traıb] n tribo f.

tribunal [traı'bjuːnl] n tribunal m.

tributary ['trıbjotrı] n afluente m.

tribute ['trıbjuːt] n: to be a ~ to (be due to) dever-se a; to pay ~ to render homenagem a.

trick [trık] n truque m ◆ vt enganar; to play a ~ on sb pregar uma peça em alguém.

trickery ['trıkərı] n artifícios mpl.

trickle ['trıkl] vi (liquid) pingar.

tricky ['trıkı] adj difícil.

tricycle ['traısıkl] n triciclo m.

trifle ['traıfl] n (dessert) sobremesa que consiste em bolo ensopado em xerez coberto com fruta, creme de leite, amêndoas e creme batido.

trigger ['trıgə'] n gatilho m.

trim [trım] n (haircut) corte m (de cabelo) ◆ vt (hair) cortar (as pontas de); (beard, hedge) aparar.

trimmings ['trımıŋz] npl (on clothing) enfeites mpl; (CULIN) acompanhamentos mpl.

trinket ['trıŋkıt] n bugiganga f.

trio ['triːəʊ] (pl -s) n trio m.

trip [trıp] n (journey) viagem f; (outing) excursão f ◆ vi tropeçar.

◻ **trip up** vi tropeçar.

tripe [traıp] n (CULIN) dobrada f, tripas fpl.

triple ['trıpl] adj triplo(-pla).

triple jump n: the ~ o triplo salto.

triplets ['trıplıts] npl trigêmeos mpl (-meas fpl).

tripod ['traıpɒd] n tripé m.

trite [traıt] adj batido(-da).

triumph ['traıəmf] n triunfo m.

trivia ['trıvıə] n trivialidades fpl.

trivial ['trıvıəl] adj (pej) trivial.

trod [trɒd] pt → **tread**.

trodden ['trɒdn] pp → **tread**.

trolley ['trɒlı] (pl -s) n (Brit: in supermarket, at airport, for food) carrinho m; (Am: tram) bonde m (Br), trólei m (Port).

trombone [trɒm'bəʊn] n trombone m.

troops [truːps] npl tropas fpl.

trophy ['trəʊfı] n troféu m.

tropical ['trɒpıkl] adj tropical.

tropics ['trɒpıks] npl: the ~ os trópicos.

trot [trɒt] vi (horse) andar a trote, trotar ◆ n: on the ~ (inf) de seguida; three on the ~ três seguidos.

trouble ['trʌbl] n problemas mpl ◆ vt (worry) preocupar; (bother) incomodar; to be in ~ ter problemas; to get into ~ meter-se em problemas; to take the ~ to do sthg dar-se ao trabalho de fazer algo; it's no ~ não custa nada, não é problema nenhum.

troubled ['trʌbld] adj (worried, upset) preocupado(-da); (life, time) difícil; (place) agitado(-da).

troublemaker ['trʌbl,meıkə'] n desordeiro m (-ra f).

troublesome ['trʌblsəm] adj (knee, cold) problemático(-ca); (person, car, job) que só causa problemas.

trough [trɒf] n (for animals) cocho m.

troupe [truːp] n companhia f.

trouser press ['traʊzə'-] n dispositivo para engomar calças.

trousers ['traʊzəz] npl calças fpl; a pair of ~ uma calça (Br), um par de calças (Port).

trout [traʊt] (pl inv) n truta f.

trowel ['traʊəl] n (for gardening) colher f de jardineiro.

truant ['truːənt] n: to play ~ matar aula (Br), fazer gazeta (Port).

truce [truːs] n trégua f.

truck [trʌk] n caminhão m (Br), camião m (Port).

truck driver n camionheiro m (-ra f) (Br), camionista mf (Port).

trucker ['trʌkə'] n (Am) camionheiro m (-ra f) (Br), camionista mf (Port).

truck farm n (Am) viveiro m agrícola.

trudge [trʌdʒ] *vi* arrastar-se, caminhar com dificuldade.

true [tru:] *adj* verdadeiro(-ra); **it's ~ é**
verdade.

truffle ['trʌfl] *n* (sweet) brigadeiro *m*,
trufa *f*; (fungus) trufa *f*.

truly ['tru:lɪ] *adv*: **yours ~ = com os**
melhores cumprimentos, cordialmente.

trumpet ['trʌmpɪt] *n* trompete *m*.

trumps [trʌmps] *npl* trunfo *m*.

truncheon ['trʌntʃən] *n* cassetete *m*,
cacete *m*.

trunk [trʌŋk] *n* (of tree) tronco *m*;
(Am: of car) mala *f* (do carro), porta-
bagagens *m* (Port); (case, box) baú *m*; (of
elephant) tromba *f*.

trunk call *n* (Brit) chamada *f* (telefônica) interurbana.

trunk road *n* (Brit) = estrada *f*
nacional.

trunks [trʌŋks] *npl* (for swimming)
sunga *f* (Br), calções *fpl* (de banho)
(Port).

trust [trʌst] *n* (confidence) confiança *f*
♦ *vt* (believe, have confidence in) confiar
em; (fml: hope): **to ~ (that)** esperar
que.

trusted ['trʌstɪd] *adj* de confiança.

trusting ['trʌstɪŋ] *adj* confiante.

trustworthy ['trʌst,wɜːðɪ] *adj* de
confiança.

truth [tru:θ] *n* (true facts) verdade *f*;
(quality of being true) veracidade *f*.

truthful ['tru:θfʊl] *adj* (statement,
account) verídico(-ca); (person) hones-
to(-ta).

try [traɪ] *n* (attempt) tentativa *f* ♦ *vt*
(attempt) tentar; (experiment with, test,
seek help from) experimentar; (food)
provar; (JUR) processar ♦ *vi* tentar; **to
~ to do sthg** tentar fazer algo.

❏ **try on** *vt sep* (clothes) experimentar.

❏ **try out** *vt sep* (plan, idea) pôr à
prova; (car, machine) testar.

trying ['traɪɪŋ] *adj* difícil.

T-shirt *n* camiseta *f* (Br), T-shirt *f*
(Port).

tub [tʌb] *n* (of margarine etc) pacote *m*,
caixa *f*; (inf: bath) banheira *f*.

tubby ['tʌbɪ] *adj* (inf) gorducho(-cha).

tube [tjuːb] *n* tubo *m*; (Brit: inf: underground) metrô *m*; **by ~** em metrô.

tuberculosis [tjuː,bɜːkjʊˈləʊsɪs] *n*
tuberculose *f*.

tube station *n* (Brit: inf) estação *f*
do metrô.

tubing ['tjuːbɪŋ] *n* tubo *m*.

tubular ['tjuːbjʊlər] *adj* tubular.

tuck [tʌk]: **tuck in** *vt sep* (shirt) enfiar
(dentro das calças); (child, person) acon-
chegar ♦ *vi* (inf): **~ in!** pode comer!

tuck shop *n* (Brit) lojinha *f* de balas
(da escola) (Br), bar *m* (da escola)
(Port).

Tudor ['tjuːdər] *adj* Tudor (inv) (século
XVI).

Tues. (abbr of Tuesday) 3ª, ter.

Tuesday ['tjuːzdɪ] *n* terça-feira *f*, →
Saturday.

tuft [tʌft] *n* tufo *m*.

tug [tʌg] *vt* puxar (com força).

tug-of-war *n* cabo-de-guerra *m* (Br),
jogo *m* da corda (Port), jogo em que cada
uma das equipes puxa o seu lado da
corda para ver quem tem mais força.

tuition [tjuːˈɪʃn] *n* aulas *mpl*; **private
~** aulas *fpl* particulares.

tulip ['tjuːlɪp] *n* tulipa *f*.

tumble ['tʌmbl] *vi* cair.

tumbledown ['tʌmbldaʊn] *adj* caindo aos pedaços.

tumble-dryer ['tʌmbldraɪər] *n*
máquina *f* de secar roupa.

tumbler ['tʌmblər] *n* (glass) copo *m*
de uísque.

tummy ['tʌmɪ] *n* (inf) barriga *f*.

tummy upset *n* (inf) dor *f* de barriga.

tumor ['tuːmər] (Am) = **tumour.**

tumour ['tjuːmər] *n* (Brit) tumor *m*.

tuna (fish) [Brit 'tjuːnə, Am 'tuːnə] *n*
atum *m*.

tuna melt *n* (Am) torrada com atum e
queijo suíço fundido.

tune [tjuːn] *n* melodia *f* ♦ *vt* (radio,
TV) sintonizar; (engine, instrument)
afinar; **in ~** afinado; **out of ~** desafinado.

tuneful ['tjuːnfʊl] *adj* melodioso
(-osa).

tuner ['tjuːnər] *n* (for radio, TV) sinto-
nizador *m*.

tunic ['tjuːnɪk] *n* túnica *f*.

Tunisia [tjuːˈnɪzɪə] *n* Tunísia *f*.

tunnel ['tʌnl] *n* túnel *m*.

turban ['tɜːbən] *n* turbante *m*.

turbine ['tɜːbaɪn] *n* turbina *f*.

turbo ['tɜːbəʊ] (pl -s) *n* (car) turbo
m.

turbulence ['tɜːbjʊləns] *n* turbulência *f*.

turbulent [ˈtɜːbjʊlənt] *adj* agitado (-da).

tureen [təriːn] *n* terrina *f*.

turf [tɜːf] *n* (*grass*) gramado *m* (*Br*), relva *f* (*Port*).

Turk [tɜːk] *n* turco *m* (-ca *f*).

turkey [ˈtɜːkɪ] (*pl* -s) *n* peru *m*.

Turkey *n* Turquia *f*.

Turkish [ˈtɜːkɪʃ] *adj* turco(-ca) ♦ *n* (*language*) turco *m* ♦ *npl*: **the ~** os turcos.

Turkish delight *n* doce gelatinoso coberto de açúcar em pó.

turmoil [ˈtɜːmɔɪl] *n* turbilhão *m*.

turn [tɜːn] *n* (*in road*) cortada *f*; (*of knob, key, switch*) volta *f*; (*go, chance*) vez *f* ♦ *vt* virar; (*become*) tornar-se, ficar; (*cause to become*) pôr, deixar ♦ *vi* (*person*) virar-se; (*car*) virar; (*rotate*) girar; (*milk*) azedar; **it's your ~** é a sua vez; **at the ~ of the century** na virada do século; **to take it in ~s to do sthg** fazer algo revezando; **to ~ into sthg** (*become*) transformar-se em algo; **to ~ left/right** virar à esquerda/direita; **to ~ sthg into sthg** transformar algo em algo; **to ~ sthg inside out** virar algo pelo avesso.

❏ **turn back** *vt sep* (*person*) mandar voltar ♦ *vi* voltar.

❏ **turn down** *vt sep* (*radio, volume, heating*) baixar; (*offer, request*) recusar.

❏ **turn off** *vt sep* (*light, TV, engine*) desligar; (*water, gas, tap*) fechar ♦ *vi* (*leave road*) virar.

❏ **turn on** *vt sep* (*light, TV, engine*) ligar; (*water, gas, tap*) abrir.

❏ **turn out** *vt sep* (*light, fire*) apagar ♦ *vi* (*be in the end*) acabar; (*come, attend*) aparecer; **to ~ out to be sthg** acabar por ser algo.

❏ **turn over** *vi* (*in bed*) virar-se; (*Brit: change channels*) mudar de canal ♦ *vt sep* (*page, card, omelette*) virar.

❏ **turn round** *vt sep* (*car, table etc*) virar ♦ *vi* (*person*) virar-se.

❏ **turn up** *vt sep* (*radio, volume, heating*) aumentar ♦ *vi* (*come, attend*) aparecer.

turning [ˈtɜːnɪŋ] *n* cortada *f*.

turnip [ˈtɜːnɪp] *n* nabo *m*.

turnpike [ˈtɜːnpaɪk] *n* (*Am*) rodovia *f* com pedágio (*Br*), auto-estrada *f* com portagem (*Port*).

turnstile [ˈtɜːnstaɪl] *n* borboleta *f* (*Br*), torniquete *m* (*Port*).

turntable [ˈtɜːnteɪbl] *n* (*on record player*) prato *m*.

turn-up *n* (*Brit: on trousers*) dobra *f*.

turpentine [ˈtɜːpəntaɪn] *n* terebintina *f*, aguarrás *f*.

turps [tɜːps] *n* (*Brit: inf*) terebintina *f*, aguarrás *f*.

turquoise [ˈtɜːkwɔɪz] *adj* turquesa (*inv*).

turret [ˈtʌrɪt] *n* (*on castle*) torinha *f* (*Br*), torreão *m* (*Port*).

turtle [ˈtɜːtl] *n* tartaruga *f*.

turtleneck [ˈtɜːtlnek] *n* camisola *f* de meia gola.

tusk [tʌsk] *n* defesa *f*.

tussle [ˈtʌsl] *n* luta *f*.

tutor [ˈtjuːtər] *n* (*private teacher*) professor *m* (-ra *f*) particular, explicador *m* (-ra *f*).

tutorial [tjuːˈtɔːrɪəl] *n* = seminário *m*.

tuxedo [tʌkˈsiːdəʊ] (*pl* -s) *n* (*Am*) smoking *m*.

TV *n* televisão *f*; **on ~** na televisão.

tweed [twiːd] *n* tweed *m*.

tweezers [ˈtwiːzəz] *npl* pinça *f*.

twelfth [twelfθ] *num* décimo segundo (décima segunda), → **sixth**.

twelve [twelv] *num* doze, → **six**.

twentieth [ˈtwentɪəθ] *num* vigésimo (-ma); **the ~ century** o século vinte, → **sixth**.

twenty [ˈtwentɪ] *num* vinte, → **six**.

twice [twaɪs] *adv* duas vezes; **it's ~ as good** é duas vezes melhor; **~ as much** o dobro.

twiddle [ˈtwɪdl] *vt* dar voltas em, brincar com ♦ *vi*: **to ~ with sthg** brincar com algo.

twig [twɪg] *n* galho *m*.

twilight [ˈtwaɪlaɪt] *n* crepúsculo *m*, lusco-fusco *m*.

twin [twɪn] *n* gêmeo *m* (-mea *f*).

twin beds *npl* camas *fpl* separadas.

twine [twaɪn] *n* barbante *m* (*Br*), cordel *m* (*Port*).

twinge [twɪndʒ] *n* pontinha *f*.

twinkle [ˈtwɪŋkl] *vi* (*star, light*) cintilar; (*eyes*) brilhar.

twin room *n* quarto *m* duplo.

twin town *n* cidade *f* irmanada.

twirl [twɜːl] *vt & vi* girar, rodar.

twist [twɪst] *vt* torcer; (*bottle top, lid, knob*) girar.

twisting [ˈtwɪstɪŋ] *adj* cheio (cheia) de curvas.

twit [twɪt] *n* (*Brit: inf*) idiota *mf*.

twitch [twɪtʃ] *n* tique *m* ♦ *vi (muscle)* contrair-se; *(eye)* palpitar.

two [tuː] *num* dois (duas), → **six**.

two-door *adj* de duas portas.

twofaced [ˌtuːˈfeɪst] *adj* falso(-sa), hipócrita.

twofold [ˈtuːfəʊld] *adj* duplo(-pla) ♦ *adv*: **to increase ~** duplicar.

two-piece *adj* de duas peças.

twosome [ˈtuːsəm] *n (inf)* dupla *f*.

tycoon [taɪˈkuːn] *n* magnata *m*.

tying [ˈtaɪɪŋ] *cont* → **tie**.

type [taɪp] *n (kind)* tipo *m* ♦ *vt & vi* bater à máquina *(Br)*, escrever à máquina *(Port)*.

typewriter [ˈtaɪpˌraɪtəʳ] *n* máquina *f* de escrever.

typhoid [ˈtaɪfɔɪd] *n* febre *f* tifóide.

typhoon [taɪˈfuːn] *n* tufão *m*.

typical [ˈtɪpɪkl] *adj* típico(-ca).

typing [ˈtaɪpɪŋ] *n* datilografia *f*.

typist [ˈtaɪpɪst] *n* datilógrafo *m* (-fa *f*).

tyranny [ˈtɪrəni] *n* tirania *f*.

tyrant [ˈtaɪrənt] *n* tirano *m* (-na *f*).

tyre [ˈtaɪəʳ] *n (Brit)* pneu *m*.

U

U adj (Brit: film) para todos.
U-bend n sifão m.
udder ['ʌdəʳ] n tetas fpl, úbere m.
UFO n (abbr of unidentified flying object) OVNI m.
ugly ['ʌglɪ] adj feio (feia).
UHF n (abbr of ultra-high frequency) UHF f.
UHT adj (abbr of ultra heat treated) UHT.
UK n: the ~ o Reino Unido.
Ukraine [juːˈkreɪn] n: the ~ a Ucrânia.
ulcer ['ʌlsəʳ] n úlcera f.
Ulster ['ʌlstəʳ] n Úlster m.
ulterior [ʌlˈtɪərɪəʳ] adj: ~ motives segundas intenções fpl.
ultimate ['ʌltɪmət] adj (final) final; (best, greatest) máximo(-ma).
ultimately ['ʌltɪmətlɪ] adv no final das contas.
ultimatum [ʌltɪˈmeɪtəm] (pl -tums OR -ta [-tə]) n ultimato m.
ultrasound ['ʌltrəsaʊnd] n ultra-sons mpl; (scan) ecografia f.
ultraviolet [ʌltrəˈvaɪələt] adj ultravioleta.
umbilical cord [ʌmˈbɪlɪkl-] n cordão m umbilical.
umbrella [ʌmˈbrelə] n guarda-chuva m, chapéu-de-chuva m (Port).
umpire ['ʌmpaɪəʳ] n árbitro m.
umpteen [ʌmpˈtiːn] num adj (inf): ~ times não sei quantas vezes, "n" vezes.
umpteenth [ʌmpˈtiːnθ] num adj (inf): for the ~ time pela enésima OR milésima vez.
UN n (abbr of United Nations): the ~ a ONU.
unable [ʌnˈeɪbl] adj: to be ~ to do sthg não ser capaz de fazer algo; I'm afraid I'm ~ to attend sinto muito mas não poderei estar presente.
unacceptable [ʌnəkˈseptəbl] adj inaceitável.
unaccompanied [ʌnəˈkʌmpənɪd] adj (child, luggage) desacompanhado(-da), sozinho(-nha).
unaccustomed [ʌnəˈkʌstəmd] adj: to be ~ to sthg não estar acostumado(-da) a algo.
unadulterated [ʌnəˈdʌltəreɪtɪd] adj (unspoiled) não adulterado(-da).
unanimous [juːˈnænɪməs] adj unânime.
unanimously [juːˈnænɪməslɪ] adv unanimemente.
unappetizing [ʌnˈæpɪtaɪzɪŋ] adj pouco apetitoso(-osa).
unassuming [ʌnəˈsjuːmɪŋ] adj despretensioso(-osa).
unattended [ʌnəˈtendɪd] adj sem vigilância, abandonado(-da).
unattractive [ʌnəˈtræktɪv] adj pouco atraente.
unauthorized [ʌnˈɔːθəraɪzd] adj não autorizado(-da).
unavailable [ʌnəˈveɪləbl] adj não disponível.
unavoidable [ʌnəˈvɔɪdəbl] adj inevitável.
unaware [ʌnəˈweəʳ] adj: to be ~ (that) ignorar que; to be ~ of sthg não ter conhecimento de algo.
unbearable [ʌnˈbeərəbl] adj insuportável.
unbeatable [ʌnˈbiːtəbl] adj imbatível.
unbelievable [ʌnbɪˈliːvəbl] adj inacreditável.
unbias(s)ed [ʌnˈbaɪəst] adj imparcial.
unbutton [ʌnˈbʌtn] vt desabotoar.
uncalled-for [ʌnˈkɔːld-] adj (remark) injusto(-ta); (criticism) injustificado(-da).

uncanny [ʌnˈkænɪ] *adj* estranho(-nha), inquietante.

uncertain [ʌnˈsɜːtn] *adj (not definite)* incerto(-ta); *(not sure)* indeciso(-sa).

uncertainty [ʌnˈsɜːtntɪ] *n* incerteza *f*.

unchanged [ʌnˈtʃeɪndʒd] *adj* na mesma.

unchecked [ʌnˈtʃekt] *adj (growth, expansion)* livre, desenfreado(-da) ◆ *adv (grow, spread)* livremente, desenfreadamente.

uncivilized [ʌnˈsɪvɪlaɪzd] *adj* não civilizado(-da), primitivo(-va).

uncle [ˈʌŋkl] *n* tio *m*.

unclean [ʌnˈkliːn] *adj* sujo(-ja).

unclear [ʌnˈklɪəʳ] *adj* pouco claro (-ra); *(not sure)* pouco seguro(-ra).

uncomfortable [ʌnˈkʌmftəbl] *adj* incómodo(-da); **to feel ~** *(awkward)* sentir-se pouco à vontade.

uncommon [ʌnˈkɒmən] *adj (rare)* invulgar.

unconcerned [ʌnkənˈsɜːnd] *adj* **~ (about)** *(not anxious)* indiferente (a).

unconscious [ʌnˈkɒnʃəs] *adj (after accident)* inconsciente; **to be ~ of** não ter consciência de.

unconventional [ʌnkənˈvenʃənl] *adj* pouco convencional.

unconvinced [ʌnkənˈvɪnst] *adj* cético(-ca); **to remain ~** continuar a não acreditar.

unconvincing [ʌnkənˈvɪnsɪŋ] *adj* pouco convincente.

uncooperative [ʌnkəʊˈɒpərətɪv] *adj* pouco cooperativo(-va).

uncork [ʌnˈkɔːk] *vt* tirar a rolha de.

uncouth [ʌnˈkuːθ] *adj* rude.

uncover [ʌnˈkʌvəʳ] *vt* descobrir.

undecided [ʌndɪˈsaɪdɪd] *adj (person)* indeciso(-sa); *(issue)* por resolver.

undeniable [ʌndɪˈnaɪəbl] *adj* inegável.

under [ˈʌndəʳ] *prep (beneath)* embaixo de *(Br)*, debaixo de *(Port)*; *(less than)* menos de; *(according to)* segundo; *(in classification)* em; **children ~** **ten** crianças com menos de dez anos; **~ the circumstances** nas OR dadas as circunstâncias; **to be ~ pressure** estar sob pressão.

underage [ʌndərˈeɪdʒ] *adj* menor de idade.

undercarriage [ˈʌndəˌkærɪdʒ] *n* trem *m* de aterrissagem.

undercharge [ʌndəˈtʃɑːdʒ] *vt*: **they ~d me by about £2** me cobraram umas duas libras a menos.

underdeveloped [ʌndədɪˈveləpt] *adj* subdesenvolvido(-da).

underdog [ˈʌndədɒg] *n*: **the ~** o mais fraco.

underdone [ʌndəˈdʌn] *adj* mal cozido(-da), cru (crua).

underestimate [ʌndərˈestɪmeɪt] *vt* subestimar.

underexposed [ʌndərɪkˈspəʊzd] *adj (photograph)* com exposição insuficiente.

underfoot [ʌndəˈfʊt] *adv* debaixo dos pés.

undergo [ʌndəˈgəʊ] *(pt* -went, *pp* -gone) *vt (change, difficulties)* sofrer; *(operation)* submeter-se a.

undergraduate [ʌndəˈgrædjʊət] *n* estudante *m* universitário (não licenciado) (estudante *f* universitária (não licenciada)).

underground [ˈʌndəgraʊnd] *adj (below earth's surface)* subterrâneo (-nea); *(secret)* clandestino(-na) ◆ *n (Brit. railway)* metrô *m (Br)*, metropolitano *m (Port)*.

undergrowth [ˈʌndəgrəʊθ] *n* vegetação *f* rasteira, mato *m*.

underhand [ʌndəˈhænd] *adj* escuso (-sa), dúbio(-bia).

underline [ʌndəˈlaɪn] *vt* sublinhar.

undermine [ʌndəˈmaɪn] *vt (weaken)* enfraquecer.

underneath [ʌndəˈniːθ] *prep* embaixo de *(Br)*, debaixo de *(Port)* ◆ *adv* debaixo, embaixo, por baixo ◆ *n* parte *f* inferior OR de baixo.

underpaid [ˈʌndəpeɪd] *adj* mal pago(-ga).

underpants [ˈʌndəpænts] *npl* cueca *f* (de homem).

underpass [ˈʌndəpɑːs] *n* passagem *f* subterrânea.

underrated [ʌndəˈreɪtɪd] *adj (person)* subestimado(-da); **I think it's a much ~ film/book** não acho que tenha sido dado o devido valor ao filme/livro.

undershirt [ˈʌndəʃɜːt] *n (Am)* camiseta *f (Br)*, camisola *f* interior *(Port)*.

underskirt [ˈʌndəskɜːt] *n* anágua *f (Br)*, saiote *m (Port)*.

understand [ʌndəˈstænd] *(pt & pp* -stood) *vt* entender; *(believe)* crer ◆ *vi* entender; **I don't ~** não entendo; **to**

make o.s. understood fazer-se entender.

understandable [ˌʌndəˈstændəbl] *adj* compreensível.

understanding [ˌʌndəˈstændɪŋ] *adj* compreensivo(-va) ♦ *n (agreement)* acordo *m*; *(knowledge)* conhecimento *m*; *(interpretation)* interpretação *f*; *(sympathy)* compreensão *f*.

understatement [ˌʌndəˈsteɪtmənt] *n*: **that's an ~** isso é um eufemismo.

understood [ˌʌndəˈstʊd] *pt & pp* → **understand**.

understudy [ˈʌndəˌstʌdɪ] *n* (ator) substituto *m* ((atriz) substituta *f*).

undertake [ˌʌndəˈteɪk] *(pt* **-took**, *pp* **-taken)** *vt* empreender; **to ~ to do sthg** comprometer-se a fazer algo.

undertaker [ˈʌndəˌteɪkəʳ] *n* agente *m* funerário (agente *f* funerária).

undertaking [ˌʌndəˈteɪkɪŋ] *n (promise)* promessa *f*; *(task)* tarefa *f*.

undertook [ˌʌndəˈtʊk] *pt* → **undertake**.

underwater [ˌʌndəˈwɔːtəʳ] *adj* subaquático(-ca) ♦ *adv* debaixo da água.

underwear [ˈʌndəweəʳ] *n* roupa *f* de baixo *(Br)*, roupa *f* interior *(Port)*.

underwent [ˌʌndəˈwent] *pt* → **undergo**.

undesirable [ˌʌndɪˈzaɪərəbl] *adj* indesejável.

undid [ʌnˈdɪd] *pt* → **undo**.

undies [ˈʌndɪz] *npl (inf)* roupa *f* de baixo *(Br)*, roupa *f* interior *(Port)*.

undisputed [ˌʌndɪˈspjuːtɪd] *adj* indiscutível.

undo [ʌnˈduː] *(pt* **-did**, *pp* **-done)** *vt (coat, shirt)* desabotoar; *(shoelaces, tie)* desamarrar, desapertar; *(parcel)* abrir.

undone [ʌnˈdʌn] *adj (coat, shirt)* desabotoado(-da); *(shoelaces, tie)* desamarrado(-da), desapertado(-da).

undoubtedly [ʌnˈdaʊtɪdlɪ] *adv* sem dúvida (alguma).

undress [ʌnˈdres] *vi* despir-se ♦ *vt* despir.

undressed [ʌnˈdrest] *adj* despido(-da); **to get ~** despir-se.

undue [ʌnˈdjuː] *adj* excessivo(-va).

unearth [ʌnˈɜːθ] *vt* desenterrar.

unease [ʌnˈiːz] *n* mal-estar *m*.

uneasy [ʌnˈiːzɪ] *adj* inquieto(-ta).

uneducated [ʌnˈedjʊkeɪtɪd] *adj* inculto(-ta).

unemployed [ˌʌnɪmˈplɔɪd] *adj* desem-

pregado(-da) ♦ *npl*: **the ~** os desempregados.

unemployment [ˌʌnɪmˈplɔɪmənt] *n* desemprego *m*.

unemployment benefit *n* auxílio-desemprego *m (Br)*, subsídio *m* de desemprego *(Port)*.

unequal [ʌnˈiːkwəl] *adj* desigual.

unerring [ʌnˈɜːrɪŋ] *adj* infalível.

uneven [ʌnˈiːvn] *adj (surface, speed, beat)* irregular; *(share, distribution, competition)* desigual.

uneventful [ˌʌnɪˈventfʊl] *adj* sem incidentes, tranqüilo(-la).

unexpected [ˌʌnɪkˈspektɪd] *adj* inesperado(-da).

unexpectedly [ˌʌnɪkˈspektɪdlɪ] *adv* inesperadamente.

unfailing [ʌnˈfeɪlɪŋ] *adj* constante, inabalável.

unfair [ʌnˈfeəʳ] *adj* injusto(-ta).

unfairly [ʌnˈfeəlɪ] *adv* injustamente.

unfaithful [ʌnˈfeɪθfʊl] *adj* infiel.

unfamiliar [ˌʌnfəˈmɪljəʳ] *adj* desconhecido(-da); **to be ~ with** não estar familiarizado(-da) com.

unfashionable [ʌnˈfæʃnəbl] *adj* fora de moda.

unfasten [ʌnˈfɑːsn] *vt (button)* desabotoar; *(belt, strap)* desapertar; *(knot)* desfazer.

unfavourable [ʌnˈfeɪvrəbl] *adj* desfavorável.

unfinished [ʌnˈfɪnɪʃt] *adj* inacabado(-da).

unfit [ʌnˈfɪt] *adj*: **to be ~** *(not healthy)* não estar em forma; **to be ~ for sthg** *(not suitable)* não ser adequado(-da) para algo.

unfold [ʌnˈfəʊld] *vt (map, sheet)* desdobrar.

unforeseen [ˌʌnfɔːˈsiːn] *adj* imprevisto(-ta).

unforgettable [ˌʌnfəˈgetəbl] *adj* inesquecível.

unforgivable [ˌʌnfəˈgɪvəbl] *adj* imperdoável.

unfortunate [ʌnˈfɔːtʃnət] *adj (unlucky)* infeliz; *(regrettable)* lamentável.

unfortunately [ʌnˈfɔːtʃnətlɪ] *adv* infelizmente.

unfounded [ʌnˈfaʊndɪd] *adj* infundado(-da).

unfriendly [ʌnˈfrendlɪ] *adj* hostil.

unfurnished [ʌnˈfɜːnɪʃt] *adj* sem mobília.

ungainly [ʌnˈgeɪnlɪ] *adj* desajeitado(-da).

ungrateful [ʌnˈgreɪtful] *adj* ingrato(-ta).

unhappy [ʌnˈhæpɪ] *adj (sad)* infeliz; *(not pleased)* descontente; **to be ~ about sthg** não estar feliz OR contente com algo.

unharmed [ʌnˈhɑːmd] *adj* ileso(-sa).

unhealthy [ʌnˈhelθɪ] *adj (person)* doente, pouco saudável; *(food, smoking)* prejudicial para a saúde; *(place)* pouco saudável.

unheard-of [ʌnˈhɜːd-] *adj (unknown, completely absent)* inexistente; *(unprecedented)* sem precedente, inaudito(-ta).

unhelpful [ʌnˈhelpful] *adj (person)* imprestável; *(advice, information)* inútil.

unhurt [ʌnˈhɜːt] *adj* ileso(-sa).

unhygienic [ʌnhaɪˈdʒiːnɪk] *adj* pouco higiênico(-ca).

unification [ˌjuːnɪfɪˈkeɪʃn] *n* unificação *f.*

uniform [ˈjuːnɪfɔːm] *n* uniforme *m.*

unify [ˈjuːnɪfaɪ] *vt* unificar.

unilateral [ˌjuːnɪˈlætərəl] *adj* unilateral.

unimportant [ˌʌnɪmˈpɔːtənt] *adj* sem importância, pouco importante.

uninhabited [ˌʌnɪnˈhæbɪtɪd] *adj* desabitado(-da).

uninjured [ʌnˈɪndʒəd] *adj* ileso(-sa).

unintelligent [ˌʌnɪnˈtelɪdʒənt] *adj* pouco inteligente.

unintentional [ˌʌnɪnˈtenʃənl] *adj* involuntário(-ria).

uninterested [ʌnˈɪntrəstɪd] *adj* desinteressado(-da), pouco interessado(-da).

uninteresting [ʌnˈɪntrəstɪŋ] *adj* sem interesse, pouco interessante.

union [ˈjuːnjən] *n (of workers)* sindicato *m.*

Union Jack *n*: **the ~** a bandeira do *Reino Unido.*

unique [juːˈniːk] *adj* único(-ca); **to be ~ to** ser típico(-ca) de.

unisex [ˈjuːnɪseks] *adj* unisex *inv (Br)*, unissexo *(inv) (Port).*

unison [ˈjuːnɪzn] *n* uníssono *m*; **in ~** em uníssono.

unit [ˈjuːnɪt] *n* unidade *f; (group)* equipe *f.*

unite [juːˈnaɪt] *vt (people)* unir;

(country, party) unificar ◆ *vi* unir-se.

united [juːˈnaɪtɪd] *adj* unido(-da).

United Kingdom *n*: **the ~** o Reino Unido.

United Nations *npl*: **the ~** as Nações Unidas.

United States (of America) *npl*: **the ~** os Estados Unidos (da América).

unity [ˈjuːnətɪ] *n* unidade *f.*

universal [ˌjuːnɪˈvɜːsl] *adj* universal.

universe [ˈjuːnɪvɜːs] *n* universo *m.*

university [ˌjuːnɪˈvɜːsətɪ] *n* universidade *f.*

unjust [ʌnˈdʒʌst] *adj* injusto(-ta).

unkempt [ʌnˈkempt] *adj (person)* desalinhado(-da); *(hair)* despenteado (-da).

unkind [ʌnˈkaɪnd] *adj* cruel.

unknown [ʌnˈnəʊn] *adj* desconhecido(-da).

unlawful [ʌnˈlɔːful] *adj (activity)* ilegal; *(behaviour)* que atenta contra a lei; *(killing)* não justificado(-da).

unleaded (petrol) [ʌnˈledɪd-] *n* gasolina *f* sem chumbo.

unleash [ʌnˈliːʃ] *vt (fury, violence)* desencadear.

unless [ənˈles] *conj* a não ser que.

unlike [ʌnˈlaɪk] *prep (different to)* diferente de; *(in contrast to)* ao contrário de; **it's ~ her to be late** ela não é de chegar atrasada.

unlikely [ʌnˈlaɪklɪ] *adj (not probable)* pouco provável; **she's ~ to agree** é pouco provável que ela concorde.

unlimited [ʌnˈlɪmɪtɪd] *adj* ilimitado(-da); **~ mileage** = quilometragem ilimitada.

unlisted [ʌnˈlɪstɪd] *adj (Am: phone number)* que não consta da lista telefônica.

unload [ʌnˈləʊd] *vt* descarregar.

unlock [ʌnˈlɒk] *vt* abrir (com chave), destrancar.

unlucky [ʌnˈlʌkɪ] *adj (unfortunate)* infeliz; *(bringing bad luck)* que traz má sorte.

unmarried [ʌnˈmærɪd] *adj* solteiro (-ra).

unmistakable [ˌʌnmɪˈsteɪkəbl] *adj* inconfundível.

unnatural [ʌnˈnætʃrəl] *adj (unusual)* invulgar; *(behaviour, person)* pouco natural.

unnecessary [ʌnˈnesəsərɪ] *adj* desnecessário(-ria).

unnerving [ʌnˈnɜːvɪŋ] *adj* desconcertante.

unnoticed [ʌnˈnəʊtɪst] *adj* despercebido(-da).

unobtainable [ʌnəbˈteɪnəbl] *adj* inacessível.

unobtrusive [ʌnəbˈtruːsɪv] *adj* discreto(-ta).

unoccupied [ʌnˈɒkjʊpaɪd] *adj (place, seat)* desocupado(-da).

unofficial [ʌnəˈfɪʃl] *adj* não oficial.

unorthodox [ʌnˈɔːθədɒks] *adj* pouco ortodoxo(-xa).

unpack [ʌnˈpæk] *vt* desfazer ◆ *vi* desfazer as malas.

unpleasant [ʌnˈpleznt] *adj* desagradável.

unplug [ʌnˈplʌg] *vt* desligar (na tomada).

unpopular [ʌnˈpɒpjʊlər] *adj* impopular, pouco popular.

unprecedented [ʌnˈpresɪdəntɪd] *adj* sem precedente.

unpredictable [ʌnprɪˈdɪktəbl] *adj* imprevisível.

unprepared [ʌnprɪˈpeəd] *adj* mal preparado(-da).

unprotected [ʌnprəˈtektɪd] *adj* desprotegido(-da).

unqualified [ʌnˈkwɒlɪfaɪd] *adj (person)* sem qualificação.

unravel [ʌnˈrævl] *vt (knitting, threads)* desmanchar; *(mystery, puzzle)* resolver.

unreal [ʌnˈrɪəl] *adj* irreal.

unrealistic [ʌnrɪəˈlɪstɪk] *adj* pouco realista, irrealista.

unreasonable [ʌnˈriːznəbl] *adj* absurdo(-da), irracional.

unrecognizable [ʌnrekəgˈnaɪzəbl] *adj* irreconhecível.

unrelated [ʌnrɪˈleɪtɪd] *adj*: **to be ~ (to sthg)** não estar relacionado(-da) (com algo).

unrelenting [ʌnrɪˈlentɪŋ] *adj* inexorável, constante.

unreliable [ʌnrɪˈlaɪəbl] *adj* pouco confiável, de pouca confiança.

unrequited [ʌnrɪˈkwaɪtɪd] *adj* não correspondido(-da).

unresolved [ʌnrɪˈzɒlvd] *adj* por resolver.

unrest [ʌnˈrest] *n* agitação *f.*

unroll [ʌnˈrəʊl] *vt* desenrolar.

unruly [ʌnˈruːlɪ] *adj* rebelde.

unsafe [ʌnˈseɪf] *adj (dangerous)* perigoso(-osa); *(in danger)* inseguro (-ra).

unsatisfactory [ʌnsætɪsˈfæktərɪ] *adj* insatisfatório(-ria).

unscathed [ʌnˈskeɪðd] *adj* ileso(-sa).

unscrew [ʌnˈskruː] *vt (lid, top)* desenroscar.

unseemly [ʌnˈsiːmlɪ] *adj* impróprio(-pria).

unselfish [ʌnˈselfɪʃ] *adj* altruísta, desinteressado(-da).

unsettled [ʌnˈsetld] *adj (person)* perturbado(-da); *(weather, region)* instável; *(argument)* por resolver; *(account, bill)* por pagar.

unshaven [ʌnˈʃeɪvn] *adj (face, chin)* por barbear; *(person)* com a barba por fazer.

unsightly [ʌnˈsaɪtlɪ] *adj* feio (feia).

unskilled [ʌnˈskɪld] *adj (worker)* sem qualificação.

unsociable [ʌnˈsəʊʃəbl] *adj* insociável.

unsound [ʌnˈsaʊnd] *adj (building, structure)* inseguro(-ra); *(argument, method)* errôneo(-nea).

unspoiled [ʌnˈspɔɪlt] *adj* intacto(-ta), não destruído(-da).

unstable [ʌnˈsteɪbl] *adj* instável.

unsteady [ʌnˈstedɪ] *adj* instável; *(hand)* trêmulo(-la).

unstuck [ʌnˈstʌk] *adj*: **to come ~** *(label, poster etc)* descolar-se.

unsuccessful [ʌnsəkˈsesfʊl] *adj* mal sucedido(-da).

unsuitable [ʌnˈsuːtəbl] *adj* inadequado(-da).

unsure [ʌnˈʃɔːr] *adj*: **to be ~ (about)** não ter certeza (de).

unsuspecting [ʌnsəˈspektɪŋ] *adj* desprevenido(-da).

unsweetened [ʌnˈswiːtnd] *adj* sem açúcar.

untangle [ʌnˈtæŋgl] *vt* desemaranhar.

untidy [ʌnˈtaɪdɪ] *adj* desarrumado (-da).

untie [ʌnˈtaɪ] *(cont* **untying)** *vt (knot)* desatar; *(person)* desprender.

until [ənˈtɪl] *prep & conj* até; **wait ~ he arrives** espera até ele chegar OR até que ele chegue.

untimely [ʌnˈtaɪmlɪ] *adj (premature)* prematuro(-ra); *(inopportune)* inoportuno(-na).

untold [ʌnˈtəʊld] *adj (incalculable,*

vast) incalculável.

untoward [ˌʌntɔ'wɔːd] *adj (event)* fora do normal; *(behaviour)* impróprio (-pria).

untrue [ʌn'truː] *adj* falso(-sa).

untrustworthy [ˌʌn'trʌstwɜːðɪ] *adj* indigno(-gna) de confiança.

untying [ˌʌn'taɪɪŋ] *cont* → **untie**.

unusual [ʌn'juːʒl] *adj (not common)* invulgar; *(distinctive)* fora do vulgar.

unusually [ʌn'juːʒəlɪ] *adv (more than usual)* excepcionalmente.

unwelcome [ʌn'welkəm] *adj* indesejado(-da).

unwell [ˌʌn'wel] *adj* mal disposto (-osta); **to feel ~** sentir-se mal.

unwieldy [ʌn'wiːldɪ] *adj (object, tool)* difícil de manejar; *(system, method)* pouco eficiente; *(bureaucracy)* pesado(-da).

unwilling [ˌʌn'wɪlɪŋ] *adj*: **to be ~ to do sthg** não estar disposto(-osta) a fazer algo.

unwind [ʌn'waɪnd] *(pt & pp* unwound) *vt* desenrolar ◆ *vi (relax)* relaxar.

unwise [ˌʌn'waɪz] *adj* imprudente.

unworthy [ʌn'wɜːðɪ] *adj (undeserving)*: **to be ~ of** não merecer.

unwound [ˌʌn'waʊnd] *pt & pp* → unwind.

unwrap [ˌʌn'ræp] *vt* desembrulhar.

unzip [ˌʌn'zɪp] *vt* abrir o fecho ecler de.

up [ʌp] *adv* **1.** *(towards higher position, level)* para cima; **to go ~** subir; **prices are going ~** os preços estão subindo; **we walked ~ to the top** subimos até o cume; **to pick sthg ~** apanhar algo.
2. *(in higher position)*: **she's ~ in her bedroom** está lá em cima no seu quarto; **~ there** ali OR lá em cima, **put your hands ~, please!** levantem as mãos, por favor!
3. *(into upright position)*: **to stand ~** pôr-se em OR de pé; **to sit ~** *(from lying position)* sentar-se; *(sit straight)* sentar-se direito.
4. *(northwards)*: **~ in Scotland** na Escócia.
5. *(in phrases)*: **to walk ~ and down** andar de um lado para o outro; **to jump ~ and down** dar pulos; **~ to six weeks** até seis semanas; **~ to ten people** até dez pessoas; **are you ~ to**

travelling? você está em condições de viajar?; **what are you ~ to?** o que você está tramando?; **it's ~ to you** depende de você; **~ until ten o'clock** até às dez horas.
◆ *prep* **1.** *(towards higher position)*: **to walk ~ a hill** subir um monte; **I went ~ the stairs** subi as escadas.
2. *(in higher position)* no topo de; **~ a hill** no topo de um monte; **~ a ladder** no topo de uma escada.
3. *(at end of)*: **they live ~ the road from us** eles vivem no final da nossa rua.
◆ *adj* **1.** *(out of bed)* levantado(-da); **I was ~ at six today** levantei-me às seis hoje.
2. *(at an end)*: **time's ~** acabou-se o tempo.
3. *(rising)*: **the ~ escalator** a escada rolante ascendente.
◆ *n*: **~s and downs** altos e baixos *mpl*.

upbringing ['ʌpbrɪŋɪŋ] *n* educação *f*.

update [ˌʌp'deɪt] *vt* atualizar.

upheaval [ʌp'hiːvl] *n* reviravolta *f*.

upheld [ʌp'held] *pt & pp* → uphold.

uphill [ˌʌp'hɪl] *adv*: **to go ~** subir.

uphold [ʌp'həʊld] *(pt & pp* **-held**) *vt* defender.

upholstery [ʌp'həʊlstərɪ] *n (material)* estofo *m*.

upkeep ['ʌpkiːp] *n* manutenção *f*.

uplifting [ʌp'lɪftɪŋ] *adj* animador(-ra), entusiasmante.

up-market *adj* de alta categoria.

upon [ə'pɒn] *prep (fml: on)* em, sobre; **~ hearing the news …** ao ouvir a notícia ….

upper ['ʌpəʳ] *adj* superior ◆ *n (of shoe)* gáspeas *fpl*.

upper class *n*: **the ~** a alta sociedade.

uppermost [ˌʌpəməʊst] *adj (highest)* mais alto(-ta).

upper sixth *n (Brit: SCH)* segundo e último ano do curso opcional que prepara os alunos de 18 anos para os exames "A level".

upright ['ʌpraɪt] *adj* direito(-ta) ◆ *adv* direito.

uprising ['ʌpˌraɪzɪŋ] *n* revolta *f*, insurreição *f*.

uproar ['ʌprɔːʳ] *n (commotion)* tumulto *m*; *(protest)* indignação *f*.

uproot [ʌp'ruːt] *vt* desenraizar.

upset [ʌp'sɛt] (*pt & pp* upset) *adj*
(*distressed*) transtornado(-da) ♦ *vt*
transtornar; (*knock over*) derrubar; **to
have an ~ stomach** estar indisposto
(-osta).

upshot [ʌpʃɒt] *n* resultado *m*.

upside down [ʌpsaid-] *adj* inverti-
do(-da), ao contrário ♦ *adv* de pernas
para o ar.

upstairs [ʌp'stɛəz] *adj* de cima ♦ *adv*
(*on a higher floor*) lá em cima; **to go ~** ir
lá para cima.

upstart [ʌpstɑːt] *n* pessoa que consegue um cargo de alto nível nem sempre
por mérito e que se mostra extremamente
arrogante.

upstream [ʌp'striːm] *adv* (*sail*) rio
acima; (*swim*) contra a corrente ♦ *adj*:
to be ~ (from sthg) ficar a montante
(de algo).

upsurge [ʌpsɜːdʒ] *n*: **~ of/in sthg**
aumento *m* de/em algo.

uptight [ʌptait] *adj* (*inf: person*) ner-
voso(-osa); **to get ~ about sthg**
enervar-se com algo.

up-to-date *adj* (*modern*) moderno
(-na); (*well-informed*) atualizado(-da).

upturn [ʌptɜːn] *n*: **~ (in sthg)** melhoria *f* (em algo).

upward [ʌpwəd] *adj* (*movement*) para
cima; (*trend*) ascendente.

upwards [ʌpwədz] *adv* para cima; **~
of 100 people** mais de 100 pessoas.

urban [ɜːbən] *adj* urbano(-na).

urban clearway [-'kliəwei] *n* (*Brit*)
rua onde não é permitido parar nem estacionar.

Urdu [ʊədu:] *n* urdu *m*.

urge [ɜːdʒ] *vt*: **to ~ sb to do sthg** incitar alguém a fazer algo.

urgency [ɜːdʒənsi] *n* urgência *f*.

urgent [ɜːdʒənt] *adj* urgente.

urgently [ɜːdʒəntli] *adv* (*immediately*)
urgentemente.

urinal [jʊəˈrainl] *n* (*fml*) urinol *m*.

urinate [jʊərineit] *vi* (*fml*) urinar.

urine [jʊərin] *n* urina *f*.

urn [ɜːn] *n* (*for ashes*) urna *f*; (*for tea,
coffee*) lata *f*.

us [ʌs] *pron* (*direct*) nos; (*indirect, after
prep*) nós; **they know ~** conhecem-
nos; **it's ~** somos nós; **send it to ~**
envia-nos isso; **tell ~** diga-nos; **they're
worse than ~** são piores que nós; **we
brought it with ~** trouxemo-lo connosco.

US *n* (*abbr of United States*): **the ~** os
E.U.A.

USA *n* (*abbr of United States of
America*): **the ~** os E.U.A.

usable [juːzəbl] *adj* utilizável.

use [*n* juːs, *vb* juːz] *n* uso *m* ♦ *vt* usar;
(*run on*) levar; **to be of ~** ser útil; **to
have the ~ of sthg** poder utilizar
algo; **to make ~ of sthg** aproveitar
algo; **"out of ~"** "fora de serviço"; **to
be in ~** estar em funcionamento; **it's
no ~** não vale a pena; **what's the
~?** de que vale?; **to ~ sthg as sthg**
usar algo como algo; **"~ before ..."**
"consumir de preferência antes
de ...".

❏ **use up** *vt sep* gastar.

used [*adj* juːzd, *aux vb* juːst] *adj*
usado(-da) ♦ *aux vb*: **I ~ to live near
here** costumava viver perto daqui; **I ~
to go there every day** costumava ir lá
todos os dias; **to be ~ to sthg** estar
acostumado a algo; **to get ~ to sthg**
acostumar-se a algo.

useful [juːsfʊl] *adj* útil.

useless [juːslis] *adj* inútil; (*inf: very
bad*) péssimo(-ma).

user [juːzər] *n* (*of product, machine*)
utilizador *m* (-ra *f*), usuário *m* (-ria *f*)
(*Br*); (*of public service*) usuário *m* (-ria *f*)
(*Br*), utente *mf* (*Port*).

user-friendly *adj* fácil de usar.

usher [ʌʃər] *n* (*at cinema, theatre*)
lanterninha *m* (*Br*), arrumador *m*
(*Port*).

usherette [ʌʃəˈrɛt] *n* lanterninha *f*
(*Br*), arrumadora *f* (*Port*).

USSR *n*: **the (former) ~** a (antiga)
U.R.S.S.

usual [juːʒəl] *adj* habitual; **as ~** (*in the
normal way*) como de costume; (*as
often happens*) como sempre.

usually [juːʒəli] *adv* normalmente.

usurp [juːzɜːp] *vt* usurpar.

utensil [juːtensl] *n* utensílio *m*.

uterus [juːtərəs] (*pl* -ri [-rai], -ruses)
n útero *m*.

utilize [juːtəlaiz] *vt* (*fml*) utilizar.

utmost [ʌtməʊst] *adj* extremo(-ma)
♦ *n*: **to do one's ~** fazer o possível e o
impossível.

utter [ʌtər] *adj* total ♦ *vt* proferir.

utterly [ʌtəli] *adv* totalmente.

U-turn *n* (*in vehicle*) meia-volta *f*,
reviravolta *f*.

V

vacancy ['veɪkənsɪ] *n* vaga *f*; "vacancies" "vagas"; "no vacancies" "completo".

vacant ['veɪkənt] *adj* (*room, seat*) vago(-ga); "vacant" "livre".

vacate [və'keɪt] *vt* (*fml: room, house*) vagar, desocupar.

vacation [və'keɪʃn] *n* (*Am*) férias *fpl* ◆ *vi* (*Am*) passar férias; **to go on ~** ir de férias.

vacationer [və'keɪʃənər] *n* (*Am*) (*throughout the year*) pessoa *f* de férias; (*in summer*) veranista *mf* (*Br*), veraneante *mf* (*Port*).

vaccinate ['væksɪneɪt] *vt* vacinar.

vaccination [,væksɪ'neɪʃn] *n* vacinação *f*.

vaccine [*Brit* 'væksi:n, *Am* væk'si:n] *n* vacina *f*.

vacuum ['vækjʊəm] *vt* aspirar.

vacuum cleaner *n* aspirador *m* de pó.

vagina [və'dʒaɪnə] (*pl* **-nas** OR **-nae** [-ni:]) *n* vagina *f*.

vagrant ['veɪɡrənt] *n* vagabundo *m* (-da *f*).

vague [veɪɡ] *adj* vago(-ga).

vaguely ['veɪɡlɪ] *adv* vagamente.

vain [veɪn] *adj* (*pej: conceited*) vaidoso (-osa); **in ~** em vão.

Valentine card ['væləntaɪn-] *n* cartão *m* do Dia de São Valentim.

Valentine's Day ['væləntaɪnz-] *n* Dia *m* dos Namorados OR de São Valentim.

valet ['væleɪ, 'vælɪt] *n* (*in hotel*) empregado *m* de hotel (*encarregado do serviço de lavandaria*).

valet service *n* (*in hotel*) serviço *m* de lavandaria; (*for car*) serviço de lavagem de automóveis.

valiant ['væljənt] *adj* valente.

valid ['vælɪd] *adj* (*ticket, passport*) válido(-da).

validate ['vælɪdeɪt] *vt* (*ticket*) validar.

Valium® ['vælɪəm] *n* Valium® *m*.

valley ['vælɪ] (*pl* **-s**) *n* vale *m*.

valuable ['væljʊəbl] *adj* valioso(-osa). ❑ **valuables** *npl* objetos *mpl* de valor.

valuation [,væljʊ'eɪʃn] *n* avaliação *f*.

value ['vælju:] *n* (*financial*) valor *m*; (*usefulness*) sentido *m*; **a ~ pack** um pacote de tamanho econômico; **to be good ~ (for money)** ter um preço módico, estar em conta. ❑ **values** *npl* (*principles*) valores *mpl*.

valued ['vælju:d] *adj* precioso(-osa).

valve [vælv] *n* válvula *f*.

van [væn] *n* caminhonete *f* (*Br*), carrinha *f* (*Port*).

vandal ['vændl] *n* vândalo *m* (-la *f*).

vandalism ['vændəlɪzm] *n* vandalismo *m*.

vandalize ['vændəlaɪz] *vt* destruir, destroçar.

vanilla [və'nɪlə] *n* baunilha *f*.

vanish ['vænɪʃ] *vi* desaparecer.

vanity ['vænɪtɪ] *n* vaidade *f*.

vantagepoint ['vɑ:ntɪdʒ,pɔɪnt] *n* (*for view*) posição *f* estratégica.

vapor ['veɪpər] (*Am*) = **vapour**.

vapour ['veɪpər] *n* (*Brit*) vapor *m*.

variable ['veərɪəbl] *adj* variável.

variation [,veərɪ'eɪʃn] *n* variação *f*.

varicose veins [,værɪkəʊs-] *npl* varizes *fpl*.

varied ['veərɪd] *adj* variado(-da).

variety [və'raɪətɪ] *n* variedade *f*.

variety show *n* espetáculo *m* de variedades.

various ['veərɪəs] *adj* vários(-rias).

varnish ['vɑ:nɪʃ] *n* (*for wood*) verniz *m* ◆ *vt* (*wood*) envernizar.

vary ['veərɪ] *vt & vi* variar; **to ~ from sthg to sthg** variar entre algo e algo; "prices ~" "os preços variam".

vase [Brit vɑːz, Am veɪz] n jarra f.

Vaseline® ['væsəliːn] n vaselina f.

vast [vuːst] adj vasto(-ta).

vat [væt] n tina f (Br), bidon m (Port).

VAT [væt, viːeɪˈtiː] n (abbr of value added tax) ICM/S (Br), I.V.A m (Port).

vault [vɔːlt] n (in bank) caixa-forte f; (ceiling) abóbada f; (in church) cripta f.

VCR n (abbr of video cassette recorder) vídeo m.

VDU n (abbr of visual display unit) monitor m.

veal [viːl] n vitela f.

veer [vɪəʳ] vi (vehicle, road) virar.

veg [vedʒ] abbr = **vegetable**.

vegan ['viːgən] adj vegetalista♦ n vegetalista mf, pessoa vegetariana que não consome carne, peixe ou derivados animais, tais como ovos ou leite.

vegetable ['vedʒtəbl] n vegetal m, legume m.

vegetable oil n óleo m vegetal.

vegetarian [ˌvedʒɪˈteəriən] adj vegetariano(-na) ♦ n vegetariano m (-na f).

vegetation [ˌvedʒɪˈteɪʃn] n vegetação f.

vehement ['viːɪmənt] adj veemente.

vehicle ['viːəkl] n veículo m.

veil [veɪl] n véu m.

vein [veɪn] n veia f.

Velcro® ['velkrəʊ] n Velcro® m.

velocity [vɪˈlɒsətɪ] n velocidade f.

velvet ['velvɪt] n veludo m.

vendetta [venˈdetə] n vendeta f.

vending machine ['vendɪŋ-] n máquina f de venda automática.

vendor ['vendɔːʳ] n vendedor m (-ra f).

veneer [vəˈnɪəʳ] n (of wood) folheado m.

venetian blind [vɪˌniːʃn-] n persiana f (Br), estore m laminado (Port).

vengeance ['vendʒəns] n vingança f; **with a ~** para valer.

venison ['venɪzn] n carne f de veado.

venom ['venəm] n veneno m.

vent [vent] n (for air, smoke etc) saída f de ar, ventilador m.

ventilation [ˌventɪˈleɪʃn] n ventilação f.

ventilator ['ventɪleɪtəʳ] n ventilador m.

venture ['ventʃəʳ] n aventura f ♦ vi (go) aventurar-se.

venue ['venjuː] n local m (de determi-

nado acontecimento esportivo ou cultural).

veranda [vəˈrændə] n terraço m coberto, alpendre m.

verb [vɜːb] n verbo m.

verbal ['vɜːbl] adj verbal.

verdict ['vɜːdɪkt] n (JUR) veredicto m; (opinion) parecer m.

verge [vɜːdʒ] n (of road) acostamento m (Br), berma f (Port); (of lawn, path) beira f; **"soft ~s"** "acostamento mole" (Br), "bermas baixas" (Port).

verify ['verɪfaɪ] vt verificar.

vermin ['vɜːmɪn] n bichos mpl (nocivos ou parasitários).

vermouth ['vɜːməθ] n vermute m.

versa → **vice versa**.

versatile ['vɜːsətaɪl] adj versátil.

verse [vɜːs] n (of song, poem) verso m; (poetry) versos mpl.

versed [vɜːst] adj: **to be well ~ in sthg** ser versado(-da) em algo.

version ['vɜːʃn] n versão f.

versus ['vɜːsəs] prep versus, contra.

vertebra ['vɜːtɪbrə] (pl -bras OR -brae [-briː]) n vértebra f.

vertical ['vɜːtɪkl] adj vertical.

vertigo ['vɜːtɪgəʊ] n vertigens fpl.

very ['verɪ] adv muito ♦ adj: **that's the ~ thing I need** é disso mesmo que eu preciso; **you're the ~ person I wanted to see** era mesmo com você que eu queria falar; **~ much** muito; **not ~** não muito; **my ~ own room** o meu próprio quarto.

vessel ['vesl] n (fml: ship) embarcação f.

vest [vest] n (Brit: underwear) camiseta f (Br), camisola f interior (Port); (Am: waistcoat) colete m.

vet [vet] n (Brit) veterinário m (-ria f).

veteran ['vetrən] n veterano m (-na f).

veterinarian [ˌvetərɪˈneəriən] (Am) = **vet**.

veterinary surgeon ['vetərɪnrɪ-] (Brit: fml) = **vet**.

veto ['viːtəʊ] (pl -es) n veto m ♦ vt vetar.

VHF n (abbr of very high frequency) VHF f.

VHS n (abbr of video home system) VHS m.

via ['vaɪə] prep via.

viable ['vaɪəbl] adj viável.

viaduct ['vaɪədʌkt] n viaduto m.

vibrate [vaɪˈbreɪt] vi vibrar.

vibration [vaɪˈbreɪʃn] n vibração f.

vicar [ˈvɪkəʳ] n vigário m, pároco m.

vicarage [ˈvɪkərɪdʒ] n casa f paroquial.

vice [vaɪs] n (moral fault) vício m; (crime) crime m; (Brit: tool) torno m.

vice-president n vice-presidente m (-ta f).

vice versa [ˌvaɪsɪˈvɜːsə] adv vice-versa.

vicinity [vɪˈsɪnətɪ] n: **in the ~** nas proximidades.

vicious [ˈvɪʃəs] adj (attack, animal) violento(-ta); (comment) cruel.

vicious circle n círculo m vicioso.

victim [ˈvɪktɪm] n vítima f.

victimize [ˈvɪktɪmaɪz] vt tratar injustamente.

Victorian [vɪkˈtɔːrɪən] adj vitoriano(-na) (segunda metade do séc. XIX).

victorious [vɪkˈtɔːrɪəs] adj vitorioso(-osa).

victory [ˈvɪktərɪ] n vitória f.

video [ˈvɪdɪəʊ] (pl -s) n vídeo m; (videotape) cassete f vídeo, videocassete f ♦ vt (using video recorder) gravar; (using camera) filmar; **on ~** em vídeo.

video camera n câmara f de vídeo.

video cassette n videocassete f, cassete f de vídeo.

video game n jogo m de vídeo.

video recorder n videogravador m.

video shop n locadora f de vídeo (Br), clube m de vídeo (Port).

videotape [ˈvɪdɪəʊteɪp] n cassete f vídeo, videocassete f.

vie [vaɪ] (pt & pp vied, cont vying) vi: **to ~ with sb (for sthg)** competir com alguém (por algo).

Vienna [vɪˈenə] n Viena s.

Vietnam [Brit ˌvjetˈnæm, Am ˌvjetˈnɑːm] n Vietnam m.

view [vjuː] n (scene, field of vision) vista f; (opinion) opinião f; (attitude) visão f ♦ vt (look at) ver; **in my ~** na minha opinião; **in ~ of** (considering) tendo em consideração; **to come into ~** aparecer.

viewer [ˈvjuːəʳ] n (of TV) telespectador m (-ra f).

viewfinder [ˈvjuːˌfaɪndəʳ] n visor m.

viewpoint [ˈvjuːpɔɪnt] n (opinion) ponto m de vista; (place) miradouro m.

vigilant [ˈvɪdʒɪlənt] adj (fml) atento(-ta).

vigorous [ˈvɪgərəs] adj vigoroso(-osa).

vile [vaɪl] adj horrível, horroroso (-osa).

villa [ˈvɪlə] n casa f, vivenda f (Port).

village [ˈvɪlɪdʒ] n lugarejo m, aldeia f.

villager [ˈvɪlɪdʒəʳ] n habitante mf da aldeia.

villain [ˈvɪlən] n (of book, film) vilão m (-lã f) da fita; (criminal) criminoso m (-osa f).

vinaigrette [ˌvɪnɪˈgret] n vinagrete m, molho para saladas feito com azeite, vinagre, sal, pimenta e ervas aromáticas.

vindicate [ˈvɪndɪkeɪt] vt justificar.

vindictive [vɪnˈdɪktɪv] adj vingativo(-va).

vine [vaɪn] n (grapevine) videira f; (climbing plant) trepadeira f.

vinegar [ˈvɪnɪgəʳ] n vinagre m.

vineyard [ˈvɪnjəd] n vinha f, vinhedo m.

vintage [ˈvɪntɪdʒ] adj (wine) vintage (inv) ♦ n (year) colheita f, ano m.

vinyl [ˈvaɪnɪl] n vinil m.

viola [vɪˈəʊlə] n (MUS) rabeca f.

violate [ˈvaɪəleɪt] vt (law, human rights) violar.

violence [ˈvaɪələns] n violência f.

violent [ˈvaɪələnt] adj violento(-ta).

violet [ˈvaɪələt] adj roxo(-xa), violeta (inv) ♦ n (flower) violeta f.

violin [ˌvaɪəˈlɪn] n violino m.

violinist [ˌvaɪəˈlɪnɪst] n violinista mf.

VIP n (abbr of very important person) VIP mf.

viper [ˈvaɪpəʳ] n víbora f.

virgin [ˈvɜːdʒɪn] n virgem mf.

Virgo [ˈvɜːgəʊ] (pl -s) n Virgem f.

virile [ˈvɪraɪl] adj viril.

virtually [ˈvɜːtʃʊəlɪ] adv praticamente.

virtual reality [ˈvɜːtʃʊəl-] n realidade f virtual.

virtue [ˈvɜːtjuː] n virtude f; **by ~ of** em virtude de, pelo fato de.

virtuous [ˈvɜːtʃʊəs] adj virtuoso(-osa).

virus [ˈvaɪrəs] n vírus m inv.

visa [ˈviːzə] n visto m.

viscose [ˈvɪskəʊs] n viscose f.

visibility [ˌvɪzɪˈbɪlətɪ] n visibilidade f.

visible ['vɪzəbl] *adj* visível.
visit ['vɪzɪt] *vt* visitar ♦ *n* visita *f*.
visiting hours ['vɪzɪtɪŋ-] *npl* horas *fpl* de visita.
visitor ['vɪzɪtər] *n (to person)* visita *f; (to place)* visitante *mf*.
visitor centre *n (Brit)* estabelecimento que inclui um centro de informação, lojas, cafeteria, etc e que se encontra em locais de interesse turístico.
visitors' book *n* livro *m* de visitantes.
visitor's passport *n (Brit)* passaporte *m* provisório.
visor ['vaɪzər] *n (helmet)* viseira *f; (of hat)* pala *f*.
visual ['vɪʒʊəl] *adj* visual.
vital ['vaɪtl] *adj* vital.
vitamin [*Brit* 'vɪtəmɪn, *Am* 'vaɪtəmɪn] *n* vitamina *f*.
vivacious [vɪ'veɪʃəs] *adj* vivaz, animado(-da).
vivid ['vɪvɪd] *adj* vivo(-va).
VLF *(abbr of very low frequency)* freqüência extremamente baixa.
V-neck *n (design)* decote *m* em bico OR em V.
vocabulary [və'kæbjʊlərɪ] *n* vocabulário *m*.
vocal cords *npl* cordas *fpl* vocais.
vocation [və'keɪʃn] *n* vocação *f*.
vocational [və'keɪʃənl] *adj* profissional.
vociferous [və'sɪfərəs] *adj* vociferante.
vodka ['vɒdkə] *n* vodca *f*.
voice [vɔɪs] *n* voz *f*.
voice mail *n* correio *m* de voz.
void [vɔɪd] *adj (invalid)* nulo(-la).
volcano [vɒl'keɪnəʊ] *(pl -es OR -s) n* vulcão *m*.

volley ['vɒlɪ] *(pl -s) n (in tennis)* vôlei *m* ♦ *vt* bater em *(antes que haja ressalto)*.
volleyball ['vɒlɪbɔːl] *n* voleibol *m*.
volt [vəʊlt] *n* volt *m*.
voltage ['vəʊltɪdʒ] *n* voltagem *f*.
volume ['vɒljuːm] *n* volume *m*.
voluntarily [*Brit* 'vɒləntrɪlɪ, *Am* ˌvɒlən'terəlɪ] *adv* voluntariamente.
voluntary ['vɒləntrɪ] *adj* voluntário (-ria).
volunteer [ˌvɒlən'tɪər] *n* voluntário *m* (-ria *f*) ♦ *vt*: **to ~ to do sthg** oferecer-se para fazer algo.
vomit ['vɒmɪt] *n* vômito *m* ♦ *vi* vomitar.
vote [vəʊt] *n (choice)* voto *m; (process, number of votes)* votação *f* ♦ *vi*: **to ~ (for)** votar (em).
voter ['vəʊtər] *n* eleitor *m* (-ra *f*).
voting ['vəʊtɪŋ] *n* votação *f*.
vouch [vaʊtʃ] : **vouch for** *vt fus (person, child)* responder por; **I can ~ for its accuracy** posso lhe garantir que está correto.
voucher ['vaʊtʃər] *n* vale *m*.
vow [vaʊ] *n* voto *m*, juramento *m* ♦ *vt*: **to ~ (that)** jurar que; **to ~ to do sthg** jurar fazer algo.
vowel ['vaʊəl] *n* vogal *f*.
voyage ['vɔɪdʒ] *n* viagem *f*.
vulgar ['vʌlgər] *adj* ordinário(-ria), vulgar.
vulnerable ['vʌlnərəbl] *adj* vulnerável; **~ to sthg** *(to being hurt)* vulnerável a algo; *(to criticism, influence)* sujeito(-ta) a algo.
vulture ['vʌltʃər] *n* abutre *m*.
vying ['vaɪɪŋ] *cont* → **vie**.

W

W *(abbr of west)* O.
wad [wɒd] *n (of paper, banknotes)* maço *m*; *(of cotton)* bola *f*, novelo *m*.
waddle ['wɒdl] *vi* bambolear-se.
wade [weɪd] *vi* caminhar *(com dificuldade pela água)*.
wading pool ['weɪdɪŋ-] *n (Am)* piscina *f* infantil.
wafer ['weɪfəʳ] *n* bolacha *f (muito fina e leve)*.
waffle ['wɒfl] *n (pancake)* = waffle *m (Br)*, talassa *f (Port)* ◆ *vi (inf)* dizer palha.
wag [wæg] *vt* abanar.
wage [weɪdʒ] *n* ordenado *m*.
❑ **wages** *npl* ordenado *m*.
wage packet *n (pay)* ordenado *m*.
wager ['weɪdʒəʳ] *n* aposta *f*.
wagon ['wægən] *n (vehicle)* carroça *f*; *(Brit: of train)* vagão *m*.
wail [weɪl] *n* lamento *m*, gemido *m* ◆ *vi (person, baby)* chorar.
waist [weɪst] *n* cintura *f*.
waistcoat ['weɪskəʊt] *n* colete *m*.
waistline ['weɪstlaɪn] *n* cintura *f*, cinta *f*.
wait [weɪt] *n* espera *f* ◆ *vi* esperar; **to ~ for sb to do sthg** esperar que alguém faça algo; **I can't ~!** mal posso esperar!
❑ **wait for** *vt fus* esperar por; **I'm ~ing for someone** estou à espera de alguém.
waiter ['weɪtəʳ] *n* garçon *m*, empregado *m* (de mesa) *(Port)*.
waiting list ['weɪtɪŋ-] *n* lista *f* de espera.
waiting room ['weɪtɪŋ-] *n* sala *f* de espera.
waitress ['weɪtrɪs] *n* garçonete *f (Br)*, empregada *f* (de mesa) *(Port)*.
waive [weɪv] *vt (rule)* não aplicar; *(right)* prescindir de.
wake [weɪk] *(pt* **woke**, *pp* **woken)** *vt & vi* acordar.
❑ **wake up** *vt sep & vi* acordar.
Waldorf salad ['wɔːldɔːf-] *n* salada *f* Waldorf, *salada de maçã, nozes e aipo com maionese*.
Wales [weɪlz] *n* País *m* de Gales.
walk [wɔːk] *n (hike)* caminhada *f*; *(stroll)* passeio *m*; *(path)* trilho *m*, caminho *m* ◆ *vi* andar; *(as hobby)* caminhar ◆ *vt (distance)* andar; *(dog)* passear; **to go for a ~** dar um passeio; **it's a short ~** não é muito longe (a pé), fica a dois passos; **to take the dog for a ~** levar o cachorro a passear, passear o cachorro; **"walk"** *(Am) sinal luminoso que indica aos pedestres que podem atravessar*; **"don't ~"** *(Am) sinal luminoso que indica aos pedestres que não podem atravessar*.
❑ **walk away** *vi* ir-se embora.
❑ **walk in** *vi* entrar.
❑ **walk out** *vi (leave angrily)* ir-se embora.
walker ['wɔːkəʳ] *n* caminhante *mf*.
walkie-talkie [ˌwɔːkɪ'tɔːkɪ] *n* walkie-talkie *m*.
walking ['wɔːkɪŋ] *n*: **to go ~** fazer caminhadas.
walking boots ['wɔːkɪŋ-] *npl* botas *fpl* de montanha.
walking stick ['wɔːkɪŋ-] *n* bengala *f*.
Walkman® ['wɔːkmən] *n* walkman® *m*.
wall [wɔːl] *n (of building, room)* parede *f*; *(in garden, countryside, street)* muro *m*.
wallchart ['wɔːltʃɑːt] *n* mapa *m*.
wallet ['wɒlɪt] *n* carteira *f* (de documentos).
wallpaper ['wɔːlˌpeɪpəʳ] *n* papel *m* de parede.
wally ['wɒlɪ] *n (Brit: inf)* palerma *mf*.
walnut ['wɔːlnʌt] *n (nut)* noz *f*.

walrus ['wɔ:lrəs] (*pl inv* OR **-es**) *n* morsa *f*.

waltz [wɔ:ls] *n* valsa *f*.

wand [wɒnd] *n* varinha *f* de condão.

wander ['wɒndər] *vi* vagar, perambular.

want [wɒnt] *vt* (*desire*) querer; (*need*) precisar de; **to ~ to do sthg** querer fazer algo; **to ~ sb to do sthg** querer que alguém faça algo.

wanted ['wɒntɪd] *adj*: **to be ~ (by the police)** ser procurado(-da) (pela polícia).

war [wɔ:r] *n* guerra *f*.

ward [wɔ:d] *n* (*in hospital*) enfermaria *f*.

warden ['wɔ:dn] *n* (*of park*) guarda *mf*; (*of youth hostel*) encarregado *m* (-da *f*).

warder ['wɔ:dər] *n* guarda *mf* (prisional).

wardrobe ['wɔ:drəub] *n* guarda-roupa *m*, armário *m*.

warehouse ['weəhaus, *pl* -hauzɪz] *n* armazém *m*.

warfare ['wɔ:feər] *n* guerra *f*.

warhead ['wɔ:hed] *n* ogiva *f*.

warm [wɔ:m] *adj* quente; (*friendly*) caloroso(-osa) ◆ *vt* aquecer.

❏ **warm up** *vt sep* aquecer ◆ *vi* aquecer; (*do exercises*) fazer exercícios de aquecimento.

war memorial *n* monumento *m* aos mortos na guerra.

warm-hearted [-'hɑ:tɪd] *adj* bondoso(-osa).

warmly ['wɔ:mlɪ] *adv* (*in a friendly way*) calorosamente; **to dress ~** agasalhar-se.

warmth [wɔ:mθ] *n* calor *m*.

warn [wɔ:n] *vt* avisar; **to ~ sb about sthg** avisar alguém de algo; **to ~ sb not to do sthg** avisar alguém para não fazer algo.

warning ['wɔ:nɪŋ] *n* aviso *m*.

warp [wɔ:p] *vt & vi* (*wood*) empenar.

warrant ['wɒrənt] *n* (*JUR*) mandato *m* ◆ *vt* (*fml: justify*) justificar.

warranty ['wɒrəntɪ] *n* (*fml*) garantia *f*.

warrior ['wɒrɪər] *n* guerreiro *m* (-ra *f*).

Warsaw ['wɔ:sɔ:] *n* Varsóvia *s*.

warship ['wɔ:ʃɪp] *n* navio *m* de guerra.

wart [wɔ:t] *n* verruga *f* (*Br*), cravo *m* (*Port*).

wartime ['wɔ:taɪm] *n* tempo *m* de guerra.

wary ['weərɪ] *adj* receoso(-osa); **to be ~ of sthg/of doing sthg** recear algo/fazer algo.

was [wɒz] *pt →* **be**.

wash [wɒʃ] *vt* lavar ◆ *vi* lavar-se ◆ *n*: **to give sthg a ~** dar uma lavada em algo; **to have a ~** lavar-se; **to ~ one's hands** lavar as mãos.

❏ **wash up** *vi* (*Brit: do washing-up*) lavar a louça; (*Am: clean o.s.*) lavar-se.

washable ['wɒʃəbl] *adj* lavável.

washbasin ['wɒʃbeɪsn] *n* pia *f*, lavatório *m* (*Port*).

washbowl ['wɒʃbəul] *n* (*Am*) pia *f*, lavatório *m* (*Port*).

washer ['wɒʃər] *n* (*ring*) bucha *f*, anilha *f*.

washing ['wɒʃɪŋ] *n* (*activity*) lavagem *f*; (*clothes*) roupa *f* suja.

washing line *n* corda *f* de estender a roupa, varal *m* (*Br*), estendal *m* (*Port*).

washing machine *n* máquina *f* de lavar roupa.

washing powder *n* sabão *m* em pó (*Br*), detergente *m* para a roupa (*Port*).

washing-up *n* (*Brit*): **to do the ~** lavar a louça.

washing-up bowl *n* (*Brit*) bacia *f* de lavar louça, lava-louças *m inv* (*Port*).

washing-up liquid *n* (*Brit*) detergente *m* para a louça.

washroom ['wɒʃrum] *n* (*Am*) banheiro *m* (*Br*), casa *f* de banho (*Port*).

wasn't [wɒznt] = **was not**.

wasp [wɒsp] *n* vespa *f*.

waste [weist] *n* (*rubbish*) lixo *m* ◆ *vt* (*money, energy, opportunity*) desperdiçar; (*time*) perder; **a ~ of money** um desperdício de dinheiro; **a ~ of time** um desperdício OR uma perda de tempo.

wastebin ['weistbɪn] *n* lata *f* de lixo (*Br*), caixote *m* do lixo (*Port*).

wasteful ['weistful] *adj* (*person*) esbanjador(-ra); (*activity*) pouco econômico(-ca).

waste ground *n* terreno *m* abandonado, descampado *m*.

wastepaper basket [weist'peipər-] *n* cesta *f* de lixo (*Br*), cesto *m* dos papéis (*Port*).

watch [wɒtʃ] *n* (*wristwatch*) relógio *m* (de pulso) ◆ *vt* (*observe*) ver; (*spy on*) espiar, vigiar; (*be careful with*) ter cuidado com.

❏ **watch out** *vi* (*be careful*) ter cuidado;

to ~ out for (look for) estar atento a.
watchdog ['wɒtʃdɒg] n (dog) cão m de guarda; **a consumer ~** uma organização de defesa do consumidor.
watchmaker ['wɒtʃ,meɪkə'] n relojoeiro m (-ra f).
watchman ['wɒtʃmən] (pl -men [-mən]) n vigia m.
watchstrap ['wɒtʃstræp] n pulseira f de relógio.
water ['wɔːtə'] n água f ◆ vt (plants, garden) regar ◆ vi (eyes) lacrimejar; **to make one's mouth ~** dar água na boca.
water bottle n cantil m.
watercolour ['wɔːtə,kʌlə'] n aquarela f.
watercress ['wɔːtəkres] n agrião m.
waterfall ['wɔːtəfɔːl] n queda f d'água, catarata f.
water heater n aquecedor m (de água) (Br), esquentador m (Port).
watering can ['wɔːtərɪŋ-] n regador m.
water level n nível m de água.
water lily n nenúfar m.
waterlogged ['wɔːtəlɒgd] adj (land) alagado(-da), alagadiço(-ça).
water main n conduta f (principal) da água.
watermark ['wɔːtəmɑːk] n (in paper) marca f de água; (showing water level) marca do nível de água.
watermelon ['wɔːtə,melən] n melancia f.
waterproof ['wɔːtəpruːf] adj à prova de água.
water purification tablets [-pjʊərɪfɪ'keɪʃn-] npl comprimidos mpl para purificar a água.
water skiing n esqui m aquático.
watersports ['wɔːtəspɔːts] npl esportes mpl aquáticos.
water tank n tanque m de água.
watertight ['wɔːtətaɪt] adj à prova d'água.
watery ['wɔːtərɪ] adj (food, drink) aguado(-da).
watt [wɒt] n watt m, vátio m; **a 60-~ bulb** uma lâmpada de 60 watts.
wave [weɪv] n onda f ◆ vt (hand) acenar com; (flag) agitar ◆ vi (move hand) acenar, dizer adeus.
wavelength ['weɪvleŋθ] n comprimento m de onda.
waver ['weɪvə'] vi (person, resolve, con-

fidence) vacilar; (voice) hesitar; (flame, light) oscilar.
wavy ['weɪvɪ] adj ondulado(-da).
wax [wæks] n cera f.
waxworks ['wækswɔːks] (pl inv) n museu m de cera.
way [weɪ] n (manner, means) maneira f, forma f; (route, distance travelled) caminho m; (direction) direção f; **which ~ is the station?** para que lado é a estação?; **the town is out of our ~** a cidade não fica no nosso caminho; **to be in the ~** estar à frente; **to be on the** OR **one's ~** (coming) estar a caminho; **to get out of the ~** sair da frente; **to get under ~** começar; **it's a long ~ to the station** a estação fica muito longe; **to be a long ~ away** ficar muito longe; **to lose one's ~** perder-se, perder o caminho; **on the ~ back** na volta; **on the ~ there** no caminho; **that ~** (like that) daquela maneira, assim; (in that direction) por ali; **this ~** (like this) assim; (in this direction) por aqui; **"give ~"** "dê preferência"; **"~ in"** "entrada"; **"~ out"** "saída"; **no ~!** (inf) nem pensar!
waylay [,weɪ'leɪ] (pt & pp -laid) vt abordar.
wayward ['weɪwəd] adj rebelde.
WC n (abbr of water closet) WC m.
we [wiː] pron nós; **~'re young** (nós) somos jovens.
weak [wiːk] adj fraco(-ca); (not solid) frágil.
weaken ['wiːkn] vt enfraquecer.
weakling ['wiːklɪŋ] n fracote m (-ta f).
weakness ['wiːknɪs] n (weak point) fraqueza f; (fondness) fraco m.
wealth [welθ] n riqueza f.
wealthy ['welθɪ] adj rico(-ca).
wean [wiːn] vt (baby, kitten) desmamar.
weapon ['wepən] n arma f.
weaponry ['wepənrɪ] n armamento m.
wear [weə'] (pt wore, pp worn) vt (clothes, shoes, jewellery) usar ◆ n (clothes) roupa f; **~ and tear** uso m.
⌐ **wear off** vi desaparecer.
⌐ **wear out** vi gastar-se.
weary ['wɪərɪ] adj cansado(-da).
weasel ['wiːzl] n doninha f.
weather ['weðə'] n tempo m; **what's the ~ like?** como está o tempo?; **to be under the ~** (inf) estar um pouco adoentado.

weathercock ['weðəknk] *n* cata-vento *m*.

weather forecast *n* previsão *f* do tempo.

weather forecaster [-ˌfɔːkɑːstəʳ] *n* meteorologista *mf*.

weather report *n* boletim *m* meteorológico.

weather vane [-veɪn] *n* cata-vento *m*.

weave [wiːv] (*pt* **wove**, *pp* **woven**) *vt* tecer.

weaver ['wiːvəʳ] *n* tecelão *m* (tecedeira *f*).

web [web] *n* (*of spider*) teia *f*.

Web site *n* (*COMPUT*) site *m*.

Wed. (*abbr of Wednesday*) 4ª, quar.

we'd [wiːd] = **we had**, **we would**.

wedding ['wedɪŋ] *n* casamento *m*.

wedding anniversary *n* aniversário *m* de casamento.

wedding cake *n* bolo *m* de noiva.

wedding dress *n* vestido *m* de noiva.

wedding ring *n* aliança *f*.

wedge [wedʒ] *n* (*of cake*) fatia *f*; (*of wood etc*) cunha *f*, calço *m*.

Wednesday ['wenzdɪ] *n* quarta-feira *f*, → **Saturday**.

wee [wiː] *adj* (*Scot*) pequeno(-na) ◆ *n* (*inf*) chichi *m*.

weed [wiːd] *n* erva *f* daninha.

weedkiller ['wiːdˌkɪləʳ] *n* herbicida *m*.

weedy ['wiːdɪ] *adj* (*Brit: inf: feeble*) fracote(-ta).

week [wiːk] *n* semana *f*; **a ~ today** daqui a uma semana OR oito dias; **in a ~'s time** daqui a uma semana OR oito dias.

weekday ['wiːkdeɪ] *n* dia *m* útil.

weekend [ˌwiːk'end] *n* fim-de-semana *m*.

weekly ['wiːklɪ] *adj* semanal ◆ *adv* semanalmente ◆ *n* semanário *m*.

weep [wiːp] (*pt & pp* **wept**) *vi* chorar.

weigh [weɪ] *vt* pesar; **how much does it ~?** quanto é que (isso) pesa?

weight [weɪt] *n* peso *m*; **to lose ~** emagrecer; **to put on ~** engordar.

⊐ **weights** *npl* (*for weight training*) pesos *mpl*.

weightlifting ['weɪtˌlɪftɪŋ] *n* halterofilia *f*.

weight training *n* musculação *f*.

weighty ['weɪtɪ] *adj* de peso.

weir [wɪəʳ] *n* represa *f*.

weird [wɪəd] *adj* esquisito(-ta), estranho(-nha).

welcome ['welkəm] *adj* bem-vindo(-da) ◆ *n* boas-vindas *fpl* ◆ *vt* (*greet*) dar as boas-vindas a; (*be grateful for*) agradecer ◆ *excl* bem-vindo!; **you're ~ to use our car** você pode usar o nosso carro à vontade; **to make sb feel ~** fazer alguém sentir-se bem-vindo; **you're ~!** de nada!

weld [weld] *vt* soldar.

welfare ['welfeəʳ] *n* (*happiness, comfort*) bem-estar *m*; (*Am: money*) subsídio *m* da segurança social.

welfare state *n*: **the ~** o estado-previdência.

well [wel] (*compar* **better**, *superl* **best**) *adj* bom (boa) ◆ *adv* bem ◆ *n* poço *m*; **to get ~** melhorar; **to go ~** correr bem; **~ done!** muito bem!; **it may ~ happen** pode muito bem acontecer; **it's ~ worth it** vale bem a pena; **as ~** (*in addition*) também; **as ~ as** (*in addition to*) assim como.

we'll [wiːl] = **we shall**, **we will**.

well-advised *adj*: **you would be ~ to ask her first** seria prudente perguntar-lhe primeiro.

well-behaved [-bɪ'heɪvd] *adj* bem comportado(-da).

wellbeing [ˌwel'biːɪŋ] *n* bem-estar *m*.

well-built *adj* bem constituído(-da), robusto(-ta).

well-done *adj* (*meat*) bem passado(-da).

well-dressed [-'drest] *adj* bem vestido(-da).

wellington (boot) ['welɪŋtən-] *n* bota *f* de borracha, galocha *f*.

well-kept *adj* (*garden*) bem cuidado(-da); (*secret*) bem guardado(-da).

well-known *adj* conhecido(-da).

well-meaning *adj* bem-intencionado(-da).

well-nigh *adv* praticamente.

well-off *adj* (*rich*) rico(-ca).

well-paid *adj* bem pago(-ga), bem remunerado(-da).

well-read [-red] *adj* culto(-ta).

well-timed [-'taɪmd] *adj* oportuno(-na).

well-to-do *adj* rico(-ca), abastado(-da).

well-wisher [-wɪʃəʳ] *n* simpatizante *mf*.

welly ['welɪ] *n* (*Brit: inf*) bota *f* de

borracha, galocha f.

Welsh [welʃ] adj galês(-esa) ◆ n (language) galês m ◆ npl: **the ~** os galeses.

Welshman ['welʃmən] (pl **-men** [-mən]) n galês m.

Welsh rarebit [-'reəbɪt] n torrada com queijo derretido.

Welshwoman ['welʃ,wʊmən] (pl **-women** [-,wɪmɪn]) n galesa f.

went [went] pt → go.

wept [wept] pt & pp → weep.

were [wɜːr] pt → be.

we're [wɪər] = we are.

weren't [wɜːnt] = were not.

west [west] n oeste m ◆ adj ocidental, oeste ◆ adv (be situated) a oeste; (fly, walk) em direção ao oeste, para o oeste; **in the ~ of England** no oeste da Inglaterra.

westbound ['westbaʊnd] adj em direção ao oeste.

West Country n: **the ~** o sudoeste da Inglaterra, especialmente os condados de Somerset, Devon e a Cornualha.

West End n: **the ~** (of London) o West End, famosa área londrina onde se encontram as grandes lojas, cinemas e teatros.

westerly ['westəlɪ] adj (wind) de oeste; **in a ~ direction** em direção ao oeste; **the most ~ point** o ponto mais a oeste.

western ['westən] adj ocidental ◆ n western m, filme m de cow-boys.

West Indian adj antilhano(-na) ◆ n (person) antilhano m (-na f).

West Indies [-'ɪndɪːz] npl Antilhas fpl.

Westminster ['westmɪnstər] n Westminster, bairro do centro de Londres.

Westminster Abbey n abadia f de Westminster.

westward ['westwəd] adj: **in a ~ direction** em direção ao oeste.

westwards ['westwədz] adv em direção ao oeste, para o oeste.

wet [wet] (pt & pp wet OR **-ted**) adj (soaked, damp) molhado(-da); (rainy) chuvoso(-osa) ◆ vt molhar; **to get ~** molhar-se; **"~ paint"** "tinta fresca".

wet suit n traje m de mergulho (Br), fato m de mergulho (Port).

we've [wiːv] = we have.

whack [wæk] n (inf) pancada f ◆ vt (inf) dar uma pancada em.

whale [weɪl] n baleia f.

wharf [wɔːf] (pl **-s** OR **wharves** [wɔːvz]) n cais m inv.

what [wɒt] adj 1. (in questions) que; **~ colour is it?** de que cor é?; **he asked me ~ colour it was** ele perguntou-me de que cor era.
2. (in exclamations) que; **~ a surprise!** mas que surpresa!; **~ a beautiful day!** mas que dia lindo!
◆ pron 1. (in questions) o que; **~ is going on?** o que é que está acontecendo?; **~ is that?** o que é isso?; **~ is that thing called?** como é que se chama aquilo?; **~ is the problem?** qual é o problema?; **she asked me ~ had happened** ela perguntou-me o que é que tinha acontecido; **she asked me ~ I had seen** ela perguntou-me o que é que eu tinha visto.
2. (in questions: after prep) que; **~ are they talking about?** de que é que eles estão falando?; **~ is it for?** para que é isso?; **she asked me ~ I was thinking about** ela perguntou-me em que é que eu estava pensando.
3. (introducing relative clause) o que; **I didn't see ~ happened** não vi o que aconteceu; **you can't have ~ you want** você não pode ter o que quer.
4. (in phrases): **~ for?** para quê?; **~ about going out for a meal?** que tal irmos comer fora?
◆ excl o quê!

whatever [wɒt'evər] pron: **take ~ you want** leve o que quiser; **~ I do, I'll lose** faça o que fizer, perco sempre; **~ that may be** seja lá o que for.

whatsoever [,wɒtsəʊ'evər] adj: **nothing ~** nada; **none ~** nenhum(-ma); **to have no interest ~ in sthg** não ter interesse nenhum em algo.

wheat [wiːt] n trigo m.

wheel [wiːl] n (of car, bicycle etc) roda f; (steering wheel) volante m.

wheelbarrow ['wiːl,bærəʊ] n carrinho m de mão.

wheelchair ['wiːl,tʃeər] n cadeira f de rodas.

wheelclamp ['wiːl,klæmp] n garra f, imobilizador m.

wheezy ['wiːzɪ] adj: **to be ~** respirar com dificuldade.

whelk [welk] n búzio m.

when [wen] adv & conj quando.

whenever [wen'evər] conj sempre que; **~ you like** quando você quiser.

where [weə^r] *adv & conj* onde; **that's ~ you're wrong** aí é que você se engana.

whereabouts [ˈweərəbaʊts] *adv* onde ♦ *npl* paradeiro *m*.

whereas [weərˈæz] *conj* enquanto que.

whereby [weəˈbaɪ] *conj* (*fml*) pelo (pela) qual.

wherever [weərˈevə^r] *conj* onde quer que; **~ that may be** onde quer que isso seja; **~ you like** onde você quiser.

whet [wet] *vt*: **to ~ sb's appetite (for sthg)** abrir o apetite de alguém (para algo).

whether [ˈweðə^r] *conj* (*indicating choice, doubt*) se; **~ you like it or not** queira ou não queira.

which [wɪtʃ] *adj* (*in questions*) qual, que; **~ room do you want?** qual é o quarto que você quer?, que quarto você quer?; **~ one?** qual (deles)?; **she asked me ~ room I wanted** ela perguntou-me qual OR que quarto eu queria.
♦ *pron* **1.** (*in questions*) qual; **~ is the cheapest?** qual é o mais barato?; **~ do you prefer?** qual (é o que) você prefere?; **he asked me ~ was the best** ele perguntou-me qual era o melhor; **he asked me ~ I preferred** ele perguntou-me qual é que eu preferia; **he asked me ~ I was talking about** ele perguntou-me de qual (é que) eu estava falando.
2. (*introducing relative clause: subject*): **take the one ~ is nearer to you** leva o que está mais perto de você; **I can't remember ~ was better** não me lembro de qual era o melhor; **the house ~ is on the corner** a casa da esquina.
3. (*introducing relative clause: object, after prep*): que; **the television ~ I bought** a televisão que eu comprei; **the settee on ~ I'm sitting** o sofá em que estou sentado.
4. (*referring back*) o que; **he's late, ~ annoys me** ele está atrasado, o que me aborrece; **he's always late, ~ I don't like** ele está sempre atrasado, o que eu odeio.

whichever [wɪtʃˈevə^r] *pron* o que (a que) ♦ *adj*: **~ place you like** o lugar que você preferir; **~ way you do it** faça como fizer.

whiff [wɪf] *n* (*smell*) cheirinho *m*.

while [waɪl] *conj* (*during the time that*) enquanto; (*although*) se bem que; (*whereas*) enquanto que ♦ *n*: **a ~** um pouco; **a ~ ago** há algum tempo; **it's been quite a ~ since I last saw him** há muito que não o vejo; **for a ~** durante algum tempo; **in a ~** daqui a pouco.

whilst [waɪlst] *conj* = **while.**

whim [wɪm] *n* capricho *m*.

whimper [ˈwɪmpə^r] *vi* (*dog*) gamir; (*child*) choramingar.

whine [waɪn] *vi* (*make noise*) gemer; (*complain*) queixar-se; (*dog*) ganir.

whinge [wɪndʒ] *vi* (*Brit*): **to ~ (about)** queixar-se (de).

whip [wɪp] *n* chicote *m* ♦ *vt* chicotear.

whipped cream [wɪpt-] *n* creme *m* batido (*Br*), natas *fpl* batidas (*Port*), chantilly *m*.

whip-round *n* (*Brit: inf*): **to have a ~** fazer uma coleta.

whirlpool [ˈwɜːlpuːl] *n* (*Jacuzzi*) Jacuzzi® *m*.

whirlwind [ˈwɜːlwɪnd] *n* remoinho *m* (de vento), furacão *m*.

whirr [wɜː^r] *vi* zumbir.

whisk [wɪsk] *n* (*utensil*) vara *f* de arames, batedor *m* de ovos manual ♦ *vt* (*eggs, cream*) bater.

whiskers [ˈwɪskəz] *npl* (*of person*) suíças *fpl*, patilhas *fpl* (*Port*); (*of animal*) bigodes *mpl*.

whiskey [ˈwɪskɪ] (*pl* -s) *n* uísque *m* (*irlandês ou americano*).

whisky [ˈwɪskɪ] *n* uísque *m* (*escocês*).

whisper [ˈwɪspə^r] *vt & vi* murmurar.

whistle [ˈwɪsl] *n* (*instrument*) apito *m*; (*sound*) assobio *m* ♦ *vi* assobiar.

white [waɪt] *adj* branco(-ca); (*coffee, tea*) com leite ♦ *n* (*colour*) branco *m*; (*of egg*) clara *f*; (*person*) branco *m* (-ca *f*).

white bread *n* pão *m* (branco).

white-hot *adj* incandescente.

White House *n*: **the ~** a Casa Branca.

white lie *n* mentirinha *f*.

whiteness [ˈwaɪtnɪs] *n* brancura *f*.

white sauce *n* molho *m* branco.

white spirit *n* aguarrás *f*, essência *f* de petróleo.

whitewash [ˈwaɪtwɒʃ] *vt* caiar.

white wine *n* vinho *m* branco.

whiting [ˈwaɪtɪŋ] (*pl inv*) *n* faneca *f*.

Whitsun [ˈwɪtsn] *n* Pentecostes *m*.

whizz [wɪz] *n* (*inf*): **to be a ~ at sthg**

ser um gênio em algo ◆ *vi* passar a
grande velocidade.

whizz kid *n* (*inf*) menino-prodígio
m (menina-prodígio *f*).

who [huː] *pron* (*in questions*) quem; (*in
relative clauses*) que.

who'd [huːd] = **who had, who would**.

whoever [huːˈevəʳ] *pron* quem; **~ it is**
quem quer que seja, seja quem for.

whole [həʊl] *adj* inteiro(-ra) ◆ *n*: **the
~ of the journey** a viagem inteira, toda
a viagem; **on the ~** em geral.

wholefoods [ˈhəʊlfuːdz] *npl* produtos *mpl* dietéticos.

whole-hearted *adj* total.

wholemeal bread [ˈhəʊlmiːl-] *n*
(*Brit*) pão *m* integral.

wholesale [ˈhəʊlseɪl] *adv* (*COMM*) por
atacado.

wholesome [ˈhəʊlsəm] *adj* saudável.

wholewheat bread [ˈhəʊlˌwiːt-]
(*Am*) = **wholemeal bread**.

who'll [huːl] = **who will**.

wholly [ˈhəʊlɪ] *adv* totalmente.

whom [huːm] *pron* (*fml: in questions*)
quem; (*in relative clauses: after prep*)
que; **to ~** a quem.

whooping cough [ˈhuːpɪŋ-] *n*
coqueluche *f* (*Br*), tosse *f* convulsa
(*Port*).

whopping [ˈwɒpɪŋ] *adj* (*inf*) tre-
mendo(-da).

whore [hɔːʳ] *n* puta *f*.

who're [ˈhuːəʳ] = **who are**.

whose [huːz] *adj* (*in questions*) de
quem; (*in relative clauses*) cujo(-ja)
◆ *pron* de quem; **~ book is this?** de
quem é este livro?

why [waɪ] *adv* & *conj* porque; **~ not?**
porque não?; **tell me ~** (diz-me) porquê; **I know ~** James isn't here eu sei
porque é que o James não está.

wick [wɪk] *n* (*of candle, lighter*) mecha
f, pavio *m*.

wicked [ˈwɪkɪd] *adj* (*evil*) mau (má);
(*mischievous*) travesso(-a).

wicker [ˈwɪkəʳ] *adj* de vime.

wickerwork [ˈwɪkəwɜːk] *n* trabalho
m em verga OR vime.

wide [waɪd] *adj* largo(-ga); (*range,
variety, gap*) grande ◆ *adv*: **to open
sthg ~** abrir bem algo; **how ~ is the
road?** qual é a largura da estrada?; **it's
12 metres ~** tem 12 metros de largura; **~ open** escancarado, aberto de par
em par.

wide-angle lens *n* (objectiva) grande angular *f*.

wide-awake *adj* completamente
acordado(-da).

widely [ˈwaɪdlɪ] *adv* muito.

widen [ˈwaɪdn] *vt* (*make broader*) alargar ◆ *vi* (*gap, difference*) aumentar.

wide-ranging [-ˈreɪndʒɪŋ] *adj* vasto
(-ta).

widespread [ˈwaɪdspred] *adj* genera-
lizado(-da).

widow [ˈwɪdəʊ] *n* viúva *f*.

widower [ˈwɪdəʊəʳ] *n* viúvo *m*.

width [wɪdθ] *n* largura *f*.

wield [wiːld] *vt* (*weapon*) brandir;
(*power*) exercer.

wife [waɪf] (*pl* **wives**) *n* esposa *f*, mulher *f*.

wig [wɪg] *n* peruca *f*.

wiggle [ˈwɪgl] *vt* (*inf*) mexer; (*tooth*)
balançar.

wild [waɪld] *adj* (*animal, land, area*)
selvagem; (*plant*) silvestre; (*uncontrolled*) descontrolado(-da); (*crazy*)
louco(-ca); **to be ~ about** (*inf*) ser
louco por.

wilderness [ˈwɪldənɪs] *n* (*barren land*)
deserto *m*; (*overgrown land*) selva *f*.

wild flower *n* flor *f* silvestre.

wildlife [ˈwaɪldlaɪf] *n* a fauna e a
flora.

wildly [ˈwaɪldlɪ] *adv* (*applaud, shout*)
como um louco (uma louca); (*guess,
suggest*) ao acaso; (*shoot*) indiscrimina-
damente, em todos os sentidos;
(*funny, different*) extremamente.

will¹ [wɪl] *aux vb* **1.** (*expressing future
tense*): **it ~ be difficult to repair** vai ser
difícil de arranjar; **~ you be here next
Friday?** você vai estar aqui na próxima
sexta?; **I ~ see you next week** vejo-lhe
para a semana; **yes I ~** sim; **no I won't**
não.
2. (*expressing willingness*): **I won't do it**
recuso-me a fazê-lo.
3. (*expressing polite question*): **~ you
have some more tea?** você quer mais
um chá?
4. (*in commands, requests*): **~ you please
be quiet!** pode ficar calado, por favor!;
close that window, ~ you? feche a
janela, faz favor.

will² [wɪl] *n* (*document*) testamento *m*;
against my ~ contra a minha vontade.

willing [ˈwɪlɪŋ] *adj*: **to be ~ to do sthg**
estar disposto(-osta) a fazer algo.

willingly ['wɪlɪŋlɪ] *adv* de boa vontade.

willow ['wɪləʊ] *n* salgueiro *m*.

willpower ['wɪl,paʊəʳ] *n* força *f* de vontade.

wilt [wɪlt] *vi (plant)* murchar.

wily ['waɪlɪ] *adj* astuto(-ta), matreiro (-ra).

wimp [wɪmp] *n (inf)* banana *f (Br)*, medricas *mf inv (Port)*.

win [wɪn] *(pt & pp* **won**) *n* vitória *f ◆ vt* ganhar; *(support, approval)* obter *◆ vi* ganhar.

wince [wɪns] *vi (pull face)* fazer uma careta; **to ~ at sthg** *(memory, thought)* estremecer com algo; **to ~ with sthg** *(pain, embarrassment)* encolher-se com algo.

winch [wɪntʃ] *n* guincho *m*.

wind¹ [wɪnd] *n (air current)* vento *m*; *(in stomach)* gases *mpl*.

wind² [waɪnd] *(pt & pp* **wound**) *vi (road, river)* serpentear *◆ vt*: **to ~ sthg round sthg** enrolar algo à volta de algo.

❑ **wind up** *vt sep (Brit: inf: annoy)* gozar; *(car window)* subir; *(clock, watch)* dar corda em.

windbreak ['wɪndbreɪk] *n* guarda-vento *m*.

windfall ['wɪndfɔːl] *n (unexpected gift)* presente *m* caído do céu.

winding ['waɪndɪŋ] *adj* sinuoso(-osa).

wind instrument [wɪnd-] *n* instrumento *m* de sopro.

windmill ['wɪndmɪl] *n* moinho *m* de vento.

window ['wɪndəʊ] *n* janela *f*; *(of shop)* vitrine *f*.

window box *n* floreira *f* de janela.

window cleaner *n* limpador *m* (-ra *f*) de janelas.

window ledge *n* peitoril *m* da janela.

windowpane ['wɪndəʊ,peɪn] *n* vidro *m*, vidraça *f*.

window seat *n (on plane)* lugar *m* ao lado da janela.

window-shopping *n*: **to go ~** ir ver vitrines.

windowsill ['wɪndəʊsɪl] *n* peitoril *m* da janela.

windpipe ['wɪndpaɪp] *n* traquéia *f*.

windscreen ['wɪndskriːn] *n (Brit)* pára-brisas *m inv*.

windscreen wipers *npl (Brit)* lava-dor *m* de pára-brisas *(Br)*, limpa-pára-brisas *m inv (Port)*.

windshield ['wɪndʃiːld] *n (Am)* pára-brisas *m inv*.

Windsor Castle ['wɪnzə-] *n* o Castelo de Windsor.

windsurfing ['wɪnd,sɜːfɪŋ] *n* windsurfe *m*; **to go ~** fazer windsurfe.

windy ['wɪndɪ] *adj* ventoso(-osa), com muito vento; **it's ~** está ventando muito.

wine [waɪn] *n* vinho *m*.

wine bar *n (Brit)* bar de certa categoria especializado em vinhos, que serve também refeições ligeiras.

wine cellar *n* adega *f*.

wineglass ['waɪnglɑːs] *n* copo *m* de vinho.

wine list *n* lista *f* dos vinhos.

wine tasting [-,teɪstɪŋ] *n* prova *f* de vinhos.

wine waiter *n* garçon *m* que serve o vinho.

wing [wɪŋ] *n* asa *f*; *(Brit: of car)* pára-lamas *m inv*, guarda-lamas *m inv (Port)*; *(of building)* ala *f*.

❑ **wings** *npl*: **the ~s** *(in theatre)* os bastidores.

winger ['wɪŋəʳ] *n (SPORT)* ponta *m*, extremo *m*.

wink [wɪŋk] *vi* piscar o olho.

winner ['wɪnəʳ] *n* vencedor *m* (-ra *f*).

winning ['wɪnɪŋ] *adj (person, team)* vencedor(-ra); *(ticket, number)* premiado(-da).

winter ['wɪntəʳ] *n* inverno *m*; **in (the) ~** no inverno.

winter sports *npl* esportes *mpl* de inverno.

wintertime ['wɪntətaɪm] *n* inverno *m*.

wint(e)ry ['wɪntrɪ] *adj* de inverno, invernal.

wipe [waɪp] *vt* limpar; **to ~ one's hands/feet** limpar as mãos/os pés.

❑ **wipe up** *vt sep & vi* limpar.

wiper ['waɪpəʳ] *n (windscreen wiper)* lavador *m* de pára-brisas *(Br)*, limpa-pára-brisas *m inv (Port)*.

wire ['waɪəʳ] *n* arame *m*; *(electrical wire)* fio *m* (elétrico) *◆ vt (plug)* montar.

wireless ['waɪəlɪs] *n* rádio *m*.

wiring ['waɪərɪŋ] *n* instalação *f* elétrica.

wisdom ['wɪzdəm] *n (of person)* sabedoria *f*.

wisdom tooth *n* dente *m* do siso.
wise [waɪz] *adj* (*person*) · sábio(-bia); (*decision, idea*) sensato(-ta).
wisecrack [ˈwaɪzkræk] *n* piada *f.*
wish [wɪʃ] *n* (*desire*) desejo *m* ♦ *vt*: **I ~ I was younger** quem me dera ser mais novo; **I ~ you'd told me earlier** que pena você não me disse isso antes; **to ~ for sthg** desejar algo; **to ~ to do sthg** (*fml*) desejar fazer algo; **to ~ sb happy birthday** dar os parabéns a alguém; **to ~ sb luck** desejar boa sorte a alguém; **if you ~** (*fml*) se assim o desejar; **best ~es** cumprimentos.
wit [wɪt] *n* (*humour*) espírito *m*; (*intelligence*): **to have the ~ to do sthg** ter a inteligência suficiente para fazer algo. ⊃ **wits** *npl* (*intelligence, mind*): **to have OR keep one's ~s about one** estar alerta OR atento(-ta).
witch [wɪtʃ] *n* bruxa *f.*
with [wɪð] *prep* **1.** (*in company of*) com; **come ~ me/us** vem comigo/conosco; **can I go ~ you?** posso ir com você?; **we stayed ~ friends** ficamos em casa de amigos. **2.** (*in descriptions*) com; **a man ~ a beard** um homem de barba; **a room ~ a bathroom** um quarto com banheiro. **3.** (*indicating means, manner*) com; **I washed it ~ detergent** lavei-o com detergente; **they won ~ ease** ganharam com facilidade. **4.** (*indicating emotion*) de; **to tremble ~ fear** tremer de medo. **5.** (*regarding*) com; **be careful ~ that!** tenha cuidado com isso! **6.** (*indicating opposition*) com; **to argue ~ sb** discutir com alguém. **7.** (*indicating covering, contents*): **to fill sthg ~ sthg** encher algo com OR de algo; **packed ~ people** cheio de gente; **topped ~ cream** coberto com creme.
withdraw [wɪðˈdrɔː] (*pt* **-drew**, *pp* **-drawn**) *vt* (*take out*) retirar; (*money*) levantar ♦ *vi* (*from race, contest*) desistir.
withdrawal [wɪðˈdrɔːəl] *n* (*from bank account*) levantamento *m.*
withdrawal symptoms *npl* síndrome *f* da abstinência.
withdrawn [wɪðˈdrɔːn] *pp* → withdraw.
withdrew [wɪðˈdruː] *pt* → withdraw.
wither [ˈwɪðəʳ] *vi* murchar.
withhold [wɪðˈhəʊld] (*pt & pp* **-held**)

vt (*salary*) reter; (*information*) ocultar.
within [wɪðˈɪn] *prep* (*inside*) dentro de; (*certain distance*) a; (*certain time*) em ♦ *adv* dentro; **~ 10 miles of ...** a 10 milhas de ...; **it arrived ~ a week** chegou em menos de uma semana; **~ the next week** durante a próxima semana.
without [wɪðˈaʊt] *prep* sem; **~ doing sthg** sem fazer algo.
withstand [wɪðˈstænd] (*pt & pp* **-stood**) *vt* resistir a, agüentar.
witness [ˈwɪtnɪs] *n* testemunha *f* ♦ *vt* (*see*) testemunhar.
witticism [ˈwɪtɪsɪzm] *n* dito *m* espirituoso.
witty [ˈwɪtɪ] *adj* espirituoso(-osa).
wives [waɪvz] *pl* → wife.
wizard [ˈwɪzəd] *n* feiticeiro *m*, mago *m.*
wobble [ˈwɒbl] *vi* (*chair, table*) balançar; (*legs, hands*) tremer.
wobbly [ˈwɒblɪ] *adj* (*table, chair*) pouco firme.
woe [wəʊ] *n* mágoa *f.*
wok [wɒk] *n* wok *f, frigideira chinesa grande e com fundo redondo, usada especialmente para cozinhar em fogo alto.*
woke [wəʊk] *pt* → wake.
woken [ˈwəʊkn] *pp* → wake.
wolf [wʊlf] (*pl* **wolves** [wʊlvz]) *n* lobo *m.*
woman [ˈwʊmən] (*pl* **women**) *n* mulher *f.*
womanly [ˈwʊmənlɪ] *adj* feminino (-na).
womb [wuːm] *n* útero *m.*
women [ˈwɪmɪn] *pl* → woman.
won [wʌn] *pt & pp* → win.
wonder [ˈwʌndəʳ] *vi* (*ask o.s.*) perguntar a si mesmo(-ma) ♦ *n* (*amazement*) maravilha *f*; **to ~ if** perguntar a si mesmo se; **I ~ if I could ask you a favour?** podia fazer-me um favor?; **I ~ if they'll come** será que eles vêm?
wonderful [ˈwʌndəfʊl] *adj* maravilhoso(-osa).
wonderfully [ˈwʌndəfʊlɪ] *adv* (*very well*) maravilhosamente; (*for emphasis*) extremamente.
won't [wəʊnt] = will not.
woo [wuː] *vt* cortejar.
wood [wʊd] *n* (*substance*) madeira *f*; (*small forest*) bosque *m*; (*golf club*) taco *m* de madeira.
wooden [ˈwʊdn] *adj* de madeira.
woodland [ˈwʊdlənd] *n* floresta *f.*

woodpecker [ˈwʊdˌpekəʳ] *n* pica-pau *m*.

woodwind [ˈwʊdwɪnd] *n*: the ~ os instrumentos de sopro de madeira.

woodwork [ˈwʊdwɜːk] *n (SCII)* carpintaria *f*.

woodworm [ˈwʊdwɜːm] *n* carcoma *m*, caruncho *m*.

wool [wʊl] *n* lã *f*.

woolen [ˈwʊlən] *(Am)* = **woollen**.

woollen [ˈwʊlən] *adj (Brit)* de lã.

woolly [ˈwʊlɪ] *adj (Brit)* de lã.

wooly [ˈwʊlɪ] *(Am)* = **woolly**.

Worcester sauce [ˈwʊstəʳ-] *n* molho *m* inglês.

word [wɜːd] *n* palavra *f*; **in other ~s** em outras palavras; **to have a ~ with sb** falar com alguém.

wording [ˈwɜːdɪŋ] *n* texto *m*.

word processing [-ˈprəʊsesɪŋ] *n* processamento *m* de texto.

word processor [-ˈprəʊsesəʳ] *n* processador *m* de texto.

wore [wɔːʳ] *pt* → **wear**.

work [wɜːk] *n* trabalho *m*; *(painting, novel etc)* obra *f* ◆ *vi* trabalhar; *(operate, have desired effect)* funcionar; *(take effect)* ter efeito ◆ *vt (machine, controls)* operar; **out of ~** desempregado, sem trabalho; **to be at ~** estar trabalhando; **to be off ~** *(on holiday)* estar de folga; **the ~s** *(inf: everything)* tudo; **how does it ~?** como é que funciona?; **it's not ~ing** não está funcionando.

❑ **work out** *vt sep (price, total)* calcular; *(solution, reason, plan)* descobrir; *(understand)* perceber ◆ *vi (result, be successful)* resultar; *(do exercise)* fazer exercício; **it ~s out at £20 each** *(bill, total)* sai a 20 libras cada.

workable [ˈwɜːkəbl] *adj (plan, idea)* viável; *(system)* passível de funcionar.

workaholic [ˌwɜːkəˈhɒlɪk] *n* viciado *m (-da f)* no trabalho.

workday [ˈwɜːkdeɪ] *n (not weekend)* dia *m* de semana, dia útil.

worked up [ˌwɜːkt-] *adj* exaltado (-da).

worker [ˈwɜːkəʳ] *n* trabalhador *m* (-ra *f*).

workforce [ˈwɜːkfɔːs] *n* mão-de-obra *f*.

working [ˈwɜːkɪŋ] *adj (in operation)* em funcionamento; *(having employment)* que trabalha; *(day, conditions)* de trabalho.

❑ **workings** *npl (of system, machine)* mecanismo *m*.

working class *n*: the ~ a classe trabalhadora.

working hours *npl* horário *m* de trabalho.

working order *n*: **to be in good ~** estar funcionando bem.

workload [ˈwɜːkləʊd] *n* carga *f* OR quantidade *f* de trabalho.

workman [ˈwɜːkmən] *(pl* -men [-mən]) *n* trabalhador *m* (manual), operário *m*.

workmanship [ˈwɜːkmənʃɪp] *n (of person)* arte *f*; *(of object)* trabalho *m*.

workmate [ˈwɜːkmeɪt] *n* colega *mf* de trabalho.

work of art *n* obra *f* de arte.

workout [ˈwɜːkaʊt] *n* sessão *f* de exercícios.

work permit *n* autorização *f* de trabalho.

workplace [ˈwɜːkpleɪs] *n* local *m* de trabalho.

workshop [ˈwɜːkʃɒp] *n (for repairs)* oficina *f*.

work surface *n* bancada *f*.

worktop [ˈwɜːktɒp] *n (Brit)* bancada *f*, aparador *m*.

world [wɜːld] *n* mundo *m* ◆ *adj* mundial; **the best in the ~** o melhor do mundo.

world-class *adj* de primeira categoria.

world-famous *adj* mundialmente famoso(-osa).

worldwide [ˌwɜːldˈwaɪd] *adv* no mundo inteiro.

worm [wɜːm] *n* minhoca *f*.

worn [wɔːn] *pp* → **wear** ◆ *adj (clothes, carpet)* gasto(-ta).

worn-out *adj (clothes, shoes etc)* gasto(-ta); *(tired)* exausto(-ta).

worried [ˈwʌrɪd] *adj* preocupado (-da).

worry [ˈwʌrɪ] *n* preocupação *f* ◆ *vt* preocupar ◆ *vi*: **to ~ (about)** preocupar-se (com).

worrying [ˈwʌrɪŋ] *adj* preocupante.

worse [wɜːs] *adj & adv* pior; **to get ~** piorar; **~ off** em pior situação.

worsen [ˈwɜːsn] *vi* piorar.

worship [ˈwɜːʃɪp] *n (church service)* culto *m* ◆ *vt* adorar.

worst [wɜːst] *adj & adv* pior ◆ *n*: **the ~** o pior (a pior).

311

worth [wɜ:θ] *prep*: **how much is it ~?** quanto é que vale?; **it's ~ £50** vale 50 libras; **it's ~ seeing** vale a pena ver; **it's not ~ it** não vale a pena; **fifty pounds' ~ of traveller's cheques** cheques de viagem no valor de 50 libras.

worthless [ˈwɜ:θlɪs] *adj (jewellery, possessions)* sem valor; *(person, undertaking)* inútil.

worthwhile [ˌwɜ:θˈwaɪl] *adj* que vale a pena.

worthy [ˈwɜ:ðɪ] *adj* merecedor(-ra); **to be ~ of sthg** merecer algo.

would [wʊd] *aux vb* **1.** *(in reported speech)*: **she said she ~ come** ela disse que vinha. **2.** *(indicating condition)*: **what ~ you do?** o que é que você faria?; **what ~ you have done?** o que é que você teria feito?; **I ~ be most grateful** ficaria muito agradecido. **3.** *(indicating willingness)*: **she ~n't go** ela não queria ir embora; **he ~ do anything for her** ele faria qualquer coisa por ela. **4.** *(in polite questions)*: **~ you like a drink?** você quer beber alguma coisa?; **~ you mind closing the window?** importa-se de fechar a janela? **5.** *(indicating inevitability)*: **he ~ say that** não me surpreende que ele tenha dito isso. **6.** *(giving advice)*: **I ~ report him if I were you** eu, no seu lugar, denunciava-o. **7.** *(expressing opinions)*: **I ~ prefer** eu preferia; **I ~ have thought (that)** ... eu pensava que ....

wouldn't [ˈwʊdnt] = **would not.**

would've [ˈwʊdəv] = **would have.**

wound[1] [wu:nd] *n* ferida *f* ◆ *vt* ferir.

wound[2] [waʊnd] *pt & pp* → **wind**[2].

wove [wəʊv] *pt* → **weave.**

woven [ˈwəʊvn] *pp* → **weave.**

wrangle [ˈræŋgl] *n* disputa *f* ◆ *vi* discutir; **to ~ with sb (over sthg)** discutir com alguém (sobre algo).

wrap [ræp] *vt (package)* embrulhar; **to ~ sthg round sthg** enrolar algo em volta de algo.

❏ **wrap up** *vt sep (package)* embrulhar ◆ *vi (dress warmly)* agasalhar-se.

wrapper [ˈræpər] *n (for sweet)* papel *m*.

wrapping [ˈræpɪŋ] *n* invólucro *m*, embrulho *m*.

wrapping paper *n* papel *m* de embrulho.

wrath [rɒθ] *n* ira *f*.

wreak [ri:k] *vt*: **to ~ havoc** causar estragos.

wreath [ri:θ] *n* coroa *f* de flores, grinalda *f*.

wreck [rek] *n (of plane, car)* destroços *mpl*; *(of ship)* restos *mpl* ◆ *vt (destroy)* destruir; *(spoil)* estragar; **to be ~ed** *(ship)* naufragar.

wreckage [ˈrekɪdʒ] *n (of plane, car)* destroços *mpl*; *(of building)* escombros *mpl*.

wren [ren] *n* carriça *f*.

wrench [rentʃ] *n (tool)* chave *f* inglesa.

wrestle [ˈresl] *vi* lutar; **to ~ with sb** lutar com alguém.

wrestler [ˈreslər] *n* lutador *m* (-ra *f*) de luta livre.

wrestling [ˈreslɪŋ] *n* luta *f* livre.

wretch [retʃ] *n* desgraçado *m* (-da *f*).

wretched [ˈretʃɪd] *adj (miserable)* desgraçado(-da); *(very bad)* péssimo (-ma).

wriggle [ˈrɪgl] *vi* mexer-se, contorcer-se; **I ~d free** consegui escapar contorcendo-me.

wring [rɪŋ] *(pt & pp* **wrung)** *vt* torcer.

wringing [ˈrɪŋɪŋ] *adj*: **to be ~ wet** estar encharcado(-da) OR ensopado (-da).

wrinkle [ˈrɪŋkl] *n* ruga *f*.

wrist [rɪst] *n* pulso *m*.

wristwatch [ˈrɪstwɒtʃ] *n* relógio *m* de pulso.

writ [rɪt] *n* mandato *m* judicial.

write [raɪt] *(pt* **wrote,** *pp* **written)** *vt* escrever; *(cheque, prescription)* passar; *(Am: send letter to)* escrever a ◆ *vi* escrever; **to ~ (to sb)** *(Brit)* escrever (para alguém).

❏ **write back** *vi* responder.

❏ **write down** *vt sep* anotar.

❏ **write off** *vt sep (Brit: inf: car)* destruir ◆ *vi*: **to ~ off for sthg** escrever pedindo algo.

❏ **write out** *vt sep (essay)* escrever; *(list)* fazer; *(cheque, receipt)* passar.

write-off *n*: **the car was a ~** o carro ficou completamente destruído.

writer [ˈraɪtər] *n (author)* escritor *m* (-ra *f*).

writhe [raɪð] *vi* contorcer-se, torcer-se.

writing ['raɪtɪŋ] *n (handwriting)* letra *f*; *(written words)* texto *m*; *(activity)* escrita *f*; in ~ por escrito.

writing desk *n* escrivaninha *f*.

writing pad *n* bloco *m* de notas.

writing paper *n* papel *m* de carta.

written ['rɪtn] *pp* → write ◆ *adj* escrito(-ta).

wrong [rɒŋ] *adj* errado(-da) ◆ *adv* mal; what's ~? o que é que está acontecendo?; **something's** ~ with the car o carro está com algum problema; to be in the ~ estar errado; to get sthg ~ enganar-se em algo; to go ~ *(machine)* avariar; "~ way" *(Am) sinal de sentido proibido*.

wrongful [rɒŋful] *adj* injusto(-ta), injustificado(-da).

wrongly ['rɒŋlɪ] *adv* mal.

wrong number *n* número *m* errado; sorry, you've got the ~ desculpe, é engano.

wrote [rəʊt] *pt* → write.

wrought iron [rɔːt] *n* ferro *m* forjado.

wrung [rʌŋ] *pt & pp* → wring.

wry [raɪ] *adj (amused)* irônico(-ca); *(displeased)* descontente.

X

xenophobia [ˌzenəˈfəʊbɪə] *n* xenofobia *f*.

xing *(Am: abbr of crossing)*: **"ped ~"** "travessia para pedestres" *(Br)*, "passagem de peões" *(Port)*.

XL *(abbr of extra-large)* XL.

Xmas [ˈeksməs] *n (inf)* Natal *m*.

X-ray *n (picture)* raio-X *m* ♦ *vt* fazer uma radiografia a; **to have an ~** fazer uma radiografia.

xylophone [ˈzaɪləfəʊn] *n* xilofone *m*.

Y

yacht [jɒt] *n* iate *m*.

yachting [ˈjɒtɪŋ] *n* navegação *f* com iate; **to go ~** ir andar de iate.

yachtsman [ˈjɒtsmən] *(pl* -men [-mən]*) n* dono ou piloto de um iate.

Yank [jæŋk] *n (Brit: inf)* ianque *mf*.

Yankee [ˈjæŋkɪ] *n (Brit: inf)* ianque *mf*.

yap [jæp] *vi (dog)* ladrar, latir.

yard [jɑːd] *n (unit of measurement)* = 91,44 cm, jarda *f*; *(enclosed area)* pátio *m*; *(Am: behind house)* jardim *m*.

yard sale *n (Am)* venda de objectos usados organizada pelo dono no jardim da casa.

yardstick [ˈjɑːdstɪk] *n* critério *m*.

yarn [jɑːn] *n (thread)* linha *f*.

yawn [jɔːn] *vi* bocejar.

yd *abbr* = **yard**.

yeah [jeə] *adv (inf)* sim.

year [jɪəʳ] *n* ano *m*; **next ~** o ano que vem; **this ~** este ano; **I'm 15 ~s old**

tenho 15 anos; **I haven't seen her for ~s** *(inf)* há anos que não a vejo.

yearly [ˈjɪəlɪ] *adj* anualmente.

yearn [jɜːn] *vi*: **to ~ for sthg/to do sthg** ansiar por algo/por fazer algo.

yeast [jiːst] *n* fermento *m*.

yell [jel] *vi* gritar.

yellow [ˈjeləʊ] *adj* amarelo(-la) ♦ *n* amarelo *m*.

yellow lines *npl* linhas *fpl* amarelas.

Yellow Pages® *n*: **the ~** as Páginas Amarelas.

yelp [jelp] *n (dog)* latir; *(person)* gritar.

yeoman of the guard [ˈjəʊmən-] *(pl* **yeomen of the guard** [ˈjəʊmən-]*) n* alabardeiro *m* da guarda real (britânica).

yes [jes] *adv* sim; **to say ~** dizer que sim.

yesterday [ˈjestədɪ] *n* ontem *m* ♦ *adv* ontem; **the day before ~** anteontem; **~ afternoon** ontem à tarde; **~ mor-**

ning ontem de manhã.

yet [jet] *adv* ainda ♦ *conj* contudo; **have they arrived ~?** já chegaram?; **the best one ~** o melhor até agora; **not ~** ainda não; **I've ~ to do it** ainda não o fiz; **~ again** mais uma vez; **~ another delay** mais um atraso.

yew [juː] *n* teixo *m*.

yield [jiːld] *vt* (*profit*) render; (*interest*) ganhar ♦ *vi* (*break, give way*) ceder; **"yield"** (*Am:* AUT) sinal de perda de prioridade.

YMCA *n* = ACM, associação internacional de jovens cristãos que oferece alojamento a um preço acessível.

yob [jɒb] *n* (*Brit: inf*) arruaceiro *m*.

yoga ['jəʊgə] *n* ioga *m* ou *f*.

yoghurt ['jɒgət] *n* iogurte *m*.

yolk [jəʊk] *n* gema *f*.

York Minster [jɔːk'mɪnstəʳ] *n* a catedral de York.

Yorkshire pudding [jɔːkʃə-] *n* pudim *m* de York, *espécie de pudim feito com uma massa semelhante à dos crepes cozido no forno e servido tradicionalmente com rosbife.*

you [juː] *pron* **1.** (*subject: singular*) você, tu; (*subject: singular polite form*) o senhor (a senhora), você (Port); (*subject: plural*) vocês; (*subject: plural polite form*) os senhores (as senhoras); **do ~ speak Portuguese?** (*singular*) você fala português?; (*polite form*) (o senhor) fala português?; **~ Brazilians** vocês brasileiros. **2.** (*direct object: singular*) o (a), te; (*direct object: singular polite form*) o senhor (a senhora); (*direct object: plural*) os (as), vos; (*direct object: plural polite form*) os (as), os senhores (as senhoras); **I saw ~** (*singular*) eu o vi; **can I help ~?** (*polite form: singular*) em que posso ajudá-lo?; (*polite form: plural*) em que posso ajudá-los?; **I'll see ~ later** (*plural*) vejo-os mais tarde. **3.** (*indirect object: singular*) lhe, te; (*indirect object: singular polite form*) lhe; (*indirect object: plural*) lhes, vos; **I would like to ask ~ something** (*polite form: singular*) gostaria de perguntar algo a você; **didn't I tell ~ what happened?** (*polite form: plural*) não lhes contei o que aconteceu? **4.** (*after prep: singular*) você, ti; (*after prep: singular polite form*) o senhor (a senhora), si; (*after prep: plural*) vocês;

(*after prep: plural polite form*) os senhores (as senhoras), vós; **this is for ~** isto é para você/o senhor, etc; **with ~** (*singular*) com você, contigo; (*singular: polite form*) com o senhor (a senhora); (*plural*) com vocês, convosco; (*plural: polite form*) com os senhores (as senhoras). **5.** (*indefinite use: subject*): **the coffee ~ get in Brazil is very strong** o café que se bebe no Brasil é muito forte, **~ never know** nunca se sabe. **6.** (*indefinite use: object*): **exercise is good for ~** exercício faz bem (para a saúde).

you'd [juːd] = **you had, you would**.

you'll [juːl] = **you will**.

young [jʌŋ] *adj* novo (nova) ♦ *npl*: **the ~** os jovens.

younger ['jʌŋgəʳ] *adj* (*brother, sister*) mais novo (nova).

youngest ['jʌŋgəst] *adj* (*brother, sister*) mais novo (nova).

youngster ['jʌŋstəʳ] *n* jovem *mf*.

your [jɔːʳ] *adj* **1.** (*singular subject*) o seu (a sua), o teu (a tua); (*singular subject: polite form*) o/a do senhor (da senhora); (*plural subject*) o vosso (a vossa); (*plural subject: polite form*) o/a dos senhores (das senhoras); **~ dog** o seu/teu/vosso cão, o cão do senhor (da senhora), o cão dos senhores (das senhoras); **~ house** a sua/tua/vossa casa, etc; **~ children** os seus/teus/vossos filhos, etc. **2.** (*indefinite subject*): **it's good for ~ health** é bom para a saúde.

you're [jɔːʳ] = **you are**.

yours [jɔːz] *pron* (*singular subject*) o seu (a sua), o teu (a tua); (*singular subject: polite form*) o/a do senhor (da senhora); (*plural subject*) o vosso (a vossa); (*plural subject: polite form*) o/a dos senhores (das senhoras), **a friend of ~** um amigo seu/teu/vosso/do senhor/da senhora/dos senhores/das senhoras; **these shoes are ~** estes sapatos são (os) seus/teus/vossos, etc; **these are mine – where are yours?** estes são os meus – onde estão os seus/teus/vossos, etc?

yourself [jɔː'self] *pron* **1.** (*reflexive: singular*) se, te; (*reflexive: plural*) se; **did you hurt ~?** (*singular*) você se machucou? **2.** (*after prep: singular*) você mesmo

(-ma), tu mesmo(-ma); *(after prep: plural)* vocês mesmos(-mas); *(after prep: singular polite form)* vós mesmo(-ma); *(after prep: plural polite form)* os senhores mesmos (as senhoras mesmas), vós mesmos(-mas), ; **did you do it ~?** *(singular)* você fez isso sozinho?; *(polite form)* foi o senhor mesmo que o fez?; **did you do it yourselves?** vocês fizeram isso sozinhos?; *(polite form)* foram os senhores mesmos que o fizeram?

youth [ju:θ] *n* juventude *f*; *(young man)* jovem *m*.

youth club *n* clube *m* de jovens.

youthful [ˈju:θful] *adj* juvenil.

youth hostel *n* albergue *m* da juventude *(Br)*, pousada *f* da juventude *(Port)*.

you've [ju:v] = **you have**.

Yugoslav [ˈju:gɔʊˌslɑ:v] = **Yugoslavian**.

Yugoslavia [ˌju:gɔ'slɑ:vɪə] *n* Iugoslávia *f (Br)*, Jugoslávia *f (Port)*.

Yugoslavian [ˌju:gɔʊ'slɑ:vɪən] *adj* iugoslavo(-va) *(Br)*, jugoslavo(-va) *(Port)* ◆ *n* iugoslavo *m* (-va *f*) *(Br)*, jugoslavo *m* (-va *f*) *(Port)*.

yuppie [ˈjʌpɪ] *n* yuppie *mf*.

yuppy = **yuppie**.

YWCA *n* = ACM *f*, *associação internacional de jovens cristãs que oferece alojamento a um preço acessível*.

Z

zany ['zeɪnɪ] *adj (inf)* disparatado (-da).

zap [zæp] *vi (rush)*: **she's always zapping off to new places** ela passa a vida viajando para lugares diferentes.

zeal [ziːl] *n* zelo *m*, fervor *m*.

zealous ['zeləs] *adj* zeloso(-osa), fervoroso(-osa).

zebra [*Brit* 'zebrə, *Am* 'ziːbrə] *n* zebra *f*.

zebra crossing *n (Brit)* faixa *f* (para pedestres) *(Br)*, passadeira *f* (para peões) *(Port)*.

zenith [*Brit* 'zenɪθ, *Am* 'ziːnəθ] *n (fig: highest point)* zênite *m*, auge *m*.

zero ['zɪərəʊ] *n* zero *m*; **five degrees below ~** cinco graus abaixo de zero.

zest [zest] *n (of lemon, orange)* raspa *f*, zesto *m*.

zigzag ['zɪgzæg] *vi* ziguezaguear.

zinc [zɪŋk] *n* zinco *m*.

zip [zɪp] *n (Brit)* fecho ecler *m* ◆ *vt* fechar o fecho ecler de.

⌐ **zip up** *vt sep* fechar o fecho ecler de.

zip code *n (Am)* código *m* postal.

zip fastener *n (Brit)* = **zip**.

zipper ['zɪpəʳ] *n (Am)* fecho ecler *m*.

zit [zɪt] *n (inf)* borbulha *f*.

zodiac ['zəʊdɪæk] *n* zodíaco *m*.

zone [zəʊn] *n* zona *f*.

zoo [zuː] *n (pl -s)* zôo *m*.

zoology [zəʊ'ɒlədʒɪ] *n* zoologia *f*.

zoom [zuːm] *vi (inf: move quickly)*: **to ~ past** passar voando; **to ~ off** sair voando.

zoom lens *n* zoom *m*.

zucchini [zuːˈkiːnɪ] *(pl inv)* *n (Am)* abobrinha *f (Br)*, courgette *f (Port)*.

Achevé d'imprimer par l'Imprimerie
Maury-Eurolivres à Manchecourt
N° de projet 10081639 - 2 - OTB 52°
N° de projet 10096641 - 5 - OTB 49°
Dépôt légal : juin 2002 - N° d'imprimeur : 95175

Imprimé en France - (Printed in France)